Complete Works of Immanuel Kant

Immanuel Kant;

Original Thinkers Institute

Published by

GRAPEVINE INDIA PUBLISHERS PVT LTD

www.grapevineindia.com
Delhi | Mumbai
email: grapevineindiapublishers@gmail.com

Ordering Information:
Quantity sales: Special discounts are available on quantity
purchases by corporations, associations, and others.
For details, reach out to the publisher.

Contents

Critique of Pure Reason

COMPLETE WORKS OF IMMANUEL KANT

First published in 1781 and followed by a revised second edition of 1787, the *Critique of Pure Reason* is now widely regarded as one of the most influential works in the history of philosophy. In the preface to the first edition Kant explains what he means by a critique of pure reason: "I do not mean by this a critique of books and systems, but of the faculty of reason in general, in respect of all knowledge after which it may strive independently of all experience." Dealing with questions concerning the foundations and extent of human knowledge, Kant builds on the work of empiricist philosophers such as John Locke and David Hume, as well as taking into account the theories of rationalist philosophers such as Gottfried Wilhelm Leibniz and Christian Wolff. In the *Critique of Pure Reason* Kant expounds new ideas on the nature of space and time, and claims to solve the problem that Hume posed regarding human knowledge of the relation of cause and effect, assessing the ability of the human mind to engage in metaphysics.

Before Kant, it was generally held that truths of reason must be analytic, meaning that what is stated in the predicate must already be present in the subject (for example, "An intelligent man is intelligent" or "An intelligent man is a man"). In either case, the judgment is analytic, as it is ascertained by analysing the subject. It was thought that all truths of reason, or necessary truths, are of this kind: that in all of them there is a predicate that is only part of the subject of which it is asserted. If this were so, attempting to deny anything that could be known *a priori* (for example, "An intelligent man is not intelligent" or "An intelligent man is not a man") would involve a contradiction. It was therefore thought that the law of contradiction is sufficient to establish all *a priori* knowledge.

David Hume (1711–1776) at first accepted the general view of rationalism about *a priori* knowledge, though upon closer examination of the subject, he discovered that some judgments thought to be analytic, especially those related to cause and effect, were actually synthetic (i.e. no analysis of the subject will reveal the predicate). They thus depend exclusively upon experience and are therefore *a posteriori*. Before Hume, rationalists had held that effect could be deduced from cause; Hume argued that it could not and from this inferred that nothing at all could be known *a priori* in relation to cause and effect. Kant was brought up under the auspices of rationalism and was deeply disturbed by Hume's skepticism. Kant decided to find an answer and spent at least twelve years thinking about the subject. Although *The Critique of Pure Reason* was set down in written form in just four to five months, while Kant was lecturing and teaching, the book is a summation of the development of his philosophy throughout that twelve-year period.

Kant's work was stimulated by his decision to take seriously Hume's skeptical conclusions on such basic principles as cause and effect, which had implications for Kant's grounding in rationalism. In Kant's view, Hume's skepticism rested on the premise that all ideas are presentations of sensory experience. The problem that Hume identified was that basic principles such as causality cannot be derived from sense experience only: experience shows only that one event regularly succeeds another, not that it is caused by it.

In section VI (The General Problem of Pure Reason) of the introduction of the work, Kant explains that Hume stopped short of considering that a synthetic judgment could be made *a priori*. Kant's objective was to find some way to derive cause and effect without relying on empirical knowledge. Kant rejects analytical methods for this, arguing that analytic reasoning cannot tell us anything that is not already self-evident, so his goal was to find a way to demonstrate how the synthetic *a priori* is possible.

To accomplish this, Kant argues that it would be necessary to use synthetic reasoning. However, this poses a new problem — how is it possible to have synthetic knowledge that is not based on empirical observation — that is, how are synthetic a priori truths possible? Kant believes this question is exceedingly important, because he contended that all important metaphysical knowledge is of synthetic *a priori* propositions. If it is impossible to determine which synthetic a priori propositions are true, he argues, then metaphysics as a discipline is impossible. The remainder of the *Critique of Pure Reason* is devoted to examining whether and how knowledge of synthetic *a priori* propositions is possible

The book is arranged around several basic distinctions. After the two Prefaces (the A edition Preface of 1781 and the B edition Preface of 1787) and the Introduction, the book is divided into the *Doctrine of Elements* and the *Doctrine of Method*. The former sets out the *a priori* products of the mind and the correct and incorrect use of these presentations. *The Doctrine of Method* contains four sections. The first section, Discipline of Pure Reason, compares mathematical and logical methods of proof, and the second section, Canon of Pure Reason, distinguishes theoretical from practical reason.

Contents

PREFACE TO THE FIRST EDITION, 1781

Human reason, in one sphere of its cognition, is called upon to consider questions, which it cannot decline, as they are presented by its own nature, but which it cannot answer, as they transcend every faculty of the mind.

It falls into this difficulty without any fault of its own. It begins with principles, which cannot be dispensed with in the field of experience, and the truth and sufficiency of which are, at the same time, insured by experience. With these principles it rises, in obedience to the laws of its own nature, to ever higher and more remote conditions. But it quickly discovers that, in this way, its labours must remain ever incomplete, because new questions never cease to present themselves; and thus it finds itself compelled to have recourse to principles which transcend the region of experience, while they are regarded by common sense without distrust. It thus falls into confusion and contradictions, from which it conjectures the presence of latent errors, which, however, it is unable to discover, because the principles it employs, transcending the limits of experience, cannot be tested by that criterion. The arena of these endless contests is called Metaphysic.

Time was, when she was the queen of all the sciences; and, if we take the will for the deed, she certainly deserves, so far as regards the high importance of her object-matter, this title of honour. Now, it is the fashion of the time to heap contempt and scorn upon her; and the matron mourns, forlorn and forsaken, like Hecuba:

Modo maxima rerum,

Tot generis, natisque potens...

Nunc trahor exul, inops.

— Ovid, Metamorphoses. xiii

At first, her government, under the administration of the dogmatists, was an absolute despotism. But, as the legislative continued to show traces of the ancient barbaric rule, her empire gradually broke up, and intestine wars introduced the reign of anarchy; while the sceptics, like nomadic tribes, who hate a permanent habitation and settled mode of living, attacked from time to time those who had organized themselves into civil communities. But their number was, very happily, small; and thus they could not entirely put a stop to the exertions of those who persisted in raising new edifices, although on no settled or uniform plan. In recent times the hope dawned upon us of seeing those disputes settled, and the legitimacy of her claims established by a kind of physiology of the human understanding — that of the celebrated Locke. But it was found that — although it was affirmed that this so-called queen could not refer her descent to any higher source than that of common experience, a circumstance which necessarily brought suspicion on her claims — as this genealogy was incorrect, she persisted in the advancement of her claims to sovereignty. Thus metaphysics necessarily fell back into the antiquated and rotten constitution of dogmatism, and again became obnoxious to the contempt from which efforts had been made to save it. At present, as all methods, according to the general persuasion, have been tried in vain, there reigns nought but weariness and complete indifferentism — the mother of chaos and night in the scientific world, but at the same time the source of, or at least the prelude to, the re-creation and reinstallation of a science, when it has fallen into confusion, obscurity, and disuse from ill directed effort.

For it is in reality vain to profess indifference in regard to such inquiries, the object of which cannot be indifferent to humanity. Besides, these pretended indifferentists, however much they may try to disguise themselves by the assumption of a popular style and by changes on the language of the schools, unavoidably fall into metaphysical declarations and propositions, which they profess to regard with so much contempt. At the same time, this indifference, which has arisen in the world of science, and which relates to that kind of knowledge which we should wish to see destroyed the last, is a phenomenon that well deserves our attention and reflection. It is plainly not the effect of the levity, but of the matured judgement* of the age, which refuses to be any longer entertained with illusory knowledge, It is, in fact, a call to reason, again to undertake the most laborious of all tasks — that of self-examination, and to establish a tribunal, which may secure it in its well-grounded claims, while it pronounces against all baseless assumptions and pretensions, not in an arbitrary manner, but according to its own eternal and unchangeable laws. This tribunal is nothing less than the critical investigation of pure reason.

[Note: We very often hear complaints of the shallowness of the present age, and of the decay of profound science. But I do not think that those which rest upon a secure foundation, such as mathematics, physical science, etc., in the least deserve this reproach, but that they rather maintain their ancient fame, and in the latter case, indeed, far surpass it. The same would be the case with the other kinds of cognition, if their principles were but firmly established. In the absence of this security, indifference, doubt, and finally, severe criticism are rather signs of a profound habit of thought. Our age is the age of criticism, to which everything must be subjected. The sacredness of religion, and the authority of legislation, are by many regarded as grounds of exemption from the examination of this tribunal. But, if they on they are exempted, they become the subjects of just suspicion, and cannot lay claim to sincere respect, which reason accords only to that which has stood the test of a free and public examination.]

I do not mean by this a criticism of books and systems, but a critical inquiry into the faculty of reason, with reference to the cognitions to which it strives to attain without the aid of experience; in other words, the solution of the question regarding the possibility or impossibility of metaphysics, and the determination of the origin, as well as of the extent and limits of this science. All this must be done on the basis of principles.

This path — the only one now remaining — has been entered upon by me; and I flatter myself that I have, in this way, discovered the cause of — and consequently the mode of removing — all the errors which have hitherto set reason at variance with itself, in the sphere of non-empirical thought. I have not returned an evasive answer to the questions of reason, by alleging the inability and limitation of the faculties of the mind; I have, on the contrary, examined them completely in the light of principles, and, after having discovered the cause of the doubts and contradictions into which reason fell, have solved them to its perfect satisfaction. It is true, these questions have not been solved as dogmatism, in its vain fancies and desires, had expected; for it can only be satisfied by the exercise of magical arts, and of these I have no knowledge. But neither do these come within the compass of our mental powers; and it was the duty of philosophy to destroy the illusions which had their origin in misconceptions, whatever darling hopes and valued expectations may be ruined by its explanations. My chief aim in this work has been thoroughness; and I make bold to say that there is not a single metaphysical problem that does not find its solution, or at least the key to its solution, here. Pure reason is a perfect unity; and therefore, if the principle presented by it prove to be insufficient for the solution of even a single one of those questions to which the very nature of reason gives birth, we must reject it, as we could not be perfectly certain of its sufficiency in the case of the others.

While I say this, I think I see upon the countenance of the reader signs of dissatisfaction mingled with contempt, when he hears declarations which sound so boastful and extravagant; and yet they are beyond comparison more moderate than those advanced by the commonest author of the commonest philosophical programme, in which the dogmatist professes to demonstrate the simple nature of the soul, or the necessity of a primal being. Such a dogmatist promises to extend human knowledge beyond the limits of possible experience; while I humbly confess that this is completely beyond my power. Instead of any such attempt, I confine myself to the examination of reason alone and its pure thought; and I do not need to seek far for the sum-total of its cognition, because it has its seat in my own mind. Besides, common logic presents me with a complete and systematic catalogue of all the simple operations of reason; and it is my task to answer the question how far reason can go, without the material presented and the aid furnished by experience.

So much for the completeness and thoroughness necessary in the execution of the present task. The aims set before us are not arbitrarily proposed, but are imposed upon us by the nature of cognition itself.

The above remarks relate to the matter of our critical inquiry. As regards the form, there are two indispensable conditions, which any one who undertakes so difficult a task as that of a critique of pure reason, is bound to fulfil. These conditions are certitude and clearness.

As regards certitude, I have fully convinced myself that, in this sphere of thought, opinion is perfectly inadmissible, and that everything which bears the least semblance of an hypothesis must be excluded, as of no value in such discussions. For it is a necessary condition of every cognition that is to be established upon a priori grounds that it shall be held to be absolutely necessary; much more is this the case with an attempt to determine all pure a priori cognition, and to furnish the standard — and consequently an example — of all apodeictic (philosophical) certitude. Whether I have succeeded in what I professed to do, it is for the reader to determine; it is the author's business merely to adduce grounds and reasons, without determining what influence these ought to have on the mind of his judges. But, lest anything he may have said may become the innocent cause of doubt in their minds, or tend to weaken the effect which his arguments might otherwise produce — he may be allowed to point out those passages which may occasion mistrust or difficulty, although these do not concern the main purpose of the present work. He does this solely with the view of removing from the mind of the reader any doubts which might affect his judgement of the work as a whole, and in regard to its ultimate aim.

I know no investigations more necessary for a full insight into the nature of the faculty which we call understanding, and at the same time for the determination of the rules and limits of its use, than those undertaken in the second chapter of the "Transcendental Analytic," under the title of "Deduction of the Pure Conceptions of the Understanding"; and they have also cost me by far the greatest labour — labour which, I hope, will not remain uncompensated. The view there taken, which goes somewhat deeply into the subject, has two sides, The one relates to the objects of the pure understanding, and is intended to demonstrate and to render comprehensible the objective validity of its a priori conceptions; and it forms for this reason an essential part of the Critique. The other considers the pure understanding itself, its possibility and its powers of cognition — that is, from a subjective point of view; and, although this exposition is of great importance, it does not belong essentially to the main purpose of the work, because the grand question is what and how much can reason and understanding, apart from experience, cognize, and not, how is the faculty of thought itself possible? As the latter is an inquiry into the cause of a given effect, and has thus in it some semblance of an hypothesis (although, as I shall show on another occasion, this is really not the fact), it would seem that, in the present instance, I had allowed myself to enounce a mere opinion, and that the reader must therefore be at liberty to hold a different opinion. But I beg to remind him that, if my subjective deduction does not produce in his mind the conviction of its certitude at which I aimed, the objective deduction, with which alone the present work is properly concerned, is in every respect satisfactory.

As regards clearness, the reader has a right to demand, in the first place, discursive or logical clearness, that is, on the basis of conceptions, and, secondly, intuitive or aesthetic clearness, by means of intuitions, that is, by examples or other modes of illustration in concreto. I have done what I could for the first kind of intelligibility. This was essential to my purpose; and it thus became the accidental cause of my inability to do complete justice to the second requirement. I have been almost always at a loss, during the progress of this work, how to settle this question. Examples and illustrations always appeared to me necessary, and, in the first sketch of the Critique, naturally fell into their proper places. But I very soon became aware of the magnitude of my task, and the numerous problems with which I should be engaged; and, as I perceived that this critical investigation would, even if delivered in the driest scholastic manner, be far from being brief, I found it unadvisable to enlarge it still more with examples and explanations, which are necessary only from a popular point of view. I was induced to take this course from the consideration also that the present work is not intended for popular use, that those devoted to science do not require such helps, although they are always acceptable, and that they would have materially interfered with my present purpose. Abbe Terrasson remarks with great justice that, if we estimate the size of a work, not from the number of its pages, but from the time which we require to make ourselves master of it, it may be said of many a book that it would be much shorter, if it were not so short. On the other hand, as regards the comprehensibility of a system of speculative cognition, connected under a single principle, we may say with equal justice: many a book would have been much clearer, if it had not been intended to be so very clear. For explanations and examples, and other helps to intelligibility, aid us in the comprehension of parts, but they distract the attention, dissipate the mental power of the reader, and stand in the way of his forming a clear conception of the whole; as he cannot attain soon enough to a survey of the system, and the colouring and embellishments bestowed upon it prevent his observing its articulation or organization — which is the most important consideration with him, when he comes to judge of its unity and stability.

The reader must naturally have a strong inducement to co-operate with the present author, if he has formed the intention of erecting a complete and solid edifice of metaphysical science, according to the plan now laid before him. Metaphysics, as here represented, is the only science which admits of completion — and with little labour, if it is united, in a short time; so that nothing will be left to future generations except the task of illustrating and applying it didactically. For this science is nothing more than the inventory of all that is given us by pure reason, systematically arranged. Nothing can escape our notice; for what reason produces from itself cannot lie concealed, but must be brought to the light by reason itself, so soon as we have discovered the common principle of the ideas we seek. The perfect unity of this kind of cognitions, which are based upon pure conceptions, and uninfluenced by any empirical element, or any peculiar intuition leading to determinate experience, renders this completeness not only practicable, but also necessary.

Tecum habita, et noris quam sit tibi curta supellex.

— Persius. Satirae iv. 52.

Such a system of pure speculative reason I hope to be able to publish under the title of Metaphysic of Nature. The content of this work (which will not be half so long) will be very much richer than that of the present Critique, which has to discover the sources of this cognition and expose the conditions of its possibility, and at the same time to clear and level a fit foundation for the scientific edifice. In the present work, I look for the patient hearing and the impartiality of a judge; in the other, for the good-will and assistance of a co-labourer. For, however complete the list of principles for this system may be in the Critique, the correctness of the system requires that no deduced conceptions should be absent. These cannot be presented a priori, but must be gradually discovered; and, while the synthesis of conceptions has been fully exhausted in the Critique, it is necessary that, in the proposed work, the same should be the case with their analysis. But this will be rather an amusement than a labour.

PREFACE TO THE SECOND EDITION, 1787

Whether the treatment of that portion of our knowledge which lies within the province of pure reason advances with that undeviating certainty which characterizes the progress of science, we shall be at no loss to determine. If we find those who are engaged in metaphysical pursuits, unable to come to an understanding as to the method which they ought to follow; if we find them, after the most elaborate preparations, invariably brought to a stand before the goal is reached, and compelled to retrace their steps and strike into fresh paths, we may then feel quite sure that they are far from having attained to the certainty of scientific progress and may rather be said to be merely groping about in the dark. In these circumstances we shall render an important service to reason if we succeed in simply indicating the path along which it must travel, in order to arrive at any results — even if it should be found necessary to abandon many of those aims which, without reflection, have been proposed for its attainment.

That logic has advanced in this sure course, even from the earliest times, is apparent from the fact that, since Aristotle, it has been unable to advance a step and, thus, to all appearance has reached its completion. For, if some of the moderns have thought to enlarge its domain by introducing psychological discussions on the mental faculties, such as imagination and wit, metaphysical, discussions on the origin of knowledge and the different kinds of certitude, according to the difference of the objects (idealism, scepticism, and so on), or anthropological discussions on prejudices, their causes and remedies: this attempt, on the part of these authors, only shows their ignorance of the peculiar nature of logical science. We do not enlarge but disfigure the sciences when we lose sight of their respective limits and allow them to run into one another. Now logic is enclosed within limits which admit of perfectly clear definition; it is a science which has for its object nothing but the exposition and proof of the formal laws of all thought, whether it be a priori or empirical, whatever be its origin or its object, and whatever the difficulties — natural or accidental — which it encounters in the human mind.

The early success of logic must be attributed exclusively to the narrowness of its field, in which abstraction may, or rather must, be made of all the objects of cognition with their characteristic distinctions, and in which the understanding has only to deal with itself and with its own forms. It is, obviously, a much more difficult task for reason to strike into the sure path of science, where it has to deal not simply with itself, but with objects external to itself. Hence, logic is properly only a propaedeutic — forms, as it were, the vestibule of the sciences; and while it is necessary to enable us to form a correct judgement with regard to the various branches of knowledge, still the acquisition of real, substantive knowledge is to be sought only in the sciences properly so called, that is, in the objective sciences.

Now these sciences, if they can be termed rational at all, must contain elements of a priori cognition, and this cognition may stand in a twofold relation to its object. Either it may have to determine the conception of the object — which must be supplied extraneously, or it may have to establish its reality. The former is theoretical, the latter practical, rational cognition. In both, the pure or a priori element must be treated first, and must be carefully distinguished from that which is supplied from other sources. Any other method can only lead to irremediable confusion.

Mathematics and physics are the two theoretical sciences which have to determine their objects a priori. The former is purely a priori, the latter is partially so, but is also dependent on other sources of cognition.

In the earliest times of which history affords us any record, mathematics had already entered on the sure course of science, among that wonderful nation, the Greeks. Still it is not to be supposed that it was as easy for this science to strike into, or rather to construct for itself, that royal road, as it was for logic, in which reason has only to deal with itself. On the contrary, I believe that it must have remained long — chiefly among the Egyptians — in the stage of blind groping after its true aims and destination, and that it was revolutionized by the happy idea of one man, who struck out and determined for all time the path which this science must follow, and which admits of an indefinite advancement. The history of this intellectual revolution — much more important in its results than the discovery of the passage round the celebrated Cape of Good Hope — and of its author, has not been preserved. But Diogenes Laertius, in naming the supposed discoverer of some of the simplest elements of geometrical demonstration — elements which, according to the ordinary opinion, do not even require to be proved — makes it apparent that the change introduced by the first indication of this new path, must have seemed of the utmost importance to the mathematicians of that age, and it has thus been secured against the chance of oblivion. A new light must have flashed on the mind of the first man (Thales, or whatever may have been his name) who demonstrated the properties of the isosceles triangle. For he found that it was not sufficient to meditate on the figure, as it lay before his eyes, or the conception of it, as it existed in his mind, and thus endeavour to get at the knowledge of its properties, but that it was necessary to produce these properties, as it were, by a positive a priori construction; and that, in order to arrive with certainty at a priori cognition, he must not attribute to the object any other properties than those which necessarily followed from that which he had himself, in accordance with his conception, placed in the object.

A much longer period elapsed before physics entered on the highway of science. For it is only about a century and a half since the wise Bacon gave a new direction to physical studies, or rather — as others were already on the right track — imparted fresh vigour to the pursuit of this new direction. Here, too, as in the case of mathematics, we find evidence of a rapid intellectual revolution. In the remarks which follow I shall confine myself to the empirical side of natural science.

When Galilei experimented with balls of a definite weight on the inclined plane, when Torricelli caused the air to sustain a weight which he had calculated beforehand to be equal to that of a definite column of water, or when Stahl, at a later period, converted metals into lime, and reconverted lime into metal, by the addition and subtraction of certain elements; [Note: I do not here follow with exactness the history of the experimental method, of which, indeed, the first steps are involved in some obscurity.] a light broke upon all natural philosophers. They learned that reason only perceives that which it produces after its own design; that it must not be content to follow, as it were, in the leading-strings of nature, but must proceed in advance with principles of judgement according to unvarying laws, and compel nature to reply its questions. For accidental observations, made according to no preconceived plan, cannot be united under a necessary law. But it is this that reason seeks for and requires. It is only the principles of reason which can give to concordant phenomena the validity of laws, and it is only when experiment is directed by these rational principles that it can have any real utility. Reason must approach nature with the view, indeed, of receiving information from it, not, however, in the character of a pupil, who listens to all that his master chooses to tell him, but in that of a judge, who compels the witnesses to reply to those questions which he himself thinks fit to propose. To this single idea must the revolution be ascribed, by which, after groping in the dark for so many centuries, natural science was at length conducted into the path of certain progress.

We come now to metaphysics, a purely speculative science, which occupies a completely isolated position and is entirely independent of the teachings of experience. It deals with mere conceptions — not, like mathematics, with conceptions applied to intuition — and in it, reason is the pupil of itself alone. It is the oldest of the sciences, and would still survive, even if all the rest were swallowed up in the abyss of an all-destroying barbarism. But it has not yet had the good fortune to attain to the sure scientific method. This will be apparent; if we apply the tests which we proposed at the outset. We find that reason perpetually comes to a stand, when it attempts to gain a priori the perception even of those laws which the most common experience confirms. We find it compelled to retrace its steps in innumerable instances, and to abandon the path on which it had entered, because this does not lead to the desired result. We find, too, that those who are engaged in metaphysical pursuits are far from being able to agree among themselves, but that, on the contrary, this science appears to furnish an arena specially adapted for the display of skill or the exercise of strength in mock-contests — a field in which no combatant ever yet succeeded in gaining an inch of ground, in which, at least, no victory was ever yet crowned with permanent possession.

This leads us to inquire why it is that, in metaphysics, the sure path of science has not hitherto been found. Shall we suppose that it is impossible to discover it? Why then should nature have visited our reason with restless aspirations after it, as if it were one of our weightiest concerns? Nay, more, how little cause should we have to place confidence in our reason, if it abandons us in a matter about which, most of all, we desire to know the truth — and not only so, but even allures us to the pursuit of vain phantoms, only to betray us in the end? Or, if the path has only hitherto been missed, what indications do we possess to guide us in a renewed investigation, and to enable us to hope for greater success than has fallen to the lot of our predecessors?

It appears to me that the examples of mathematics and natural philosophy, which, as we have seen, were brought into their present condition by a sudden revolution, are sufficiently remarkable to fix our attention on the essential circumstances of the change which has proved so advantageous to them, and to induce us to make the experiment of imitating them, so far as the analogy which, as rational sciences, they bear to metaphysics may permit. It has hitherto been assumed that our cognition must conform to the objects; but all attempts to ascertain anything about these objects a priori, by means of conceptions, and thus to extend the range of our knowledge, have been rendered abortive by this assumption. Let us then make the experiment whether we may not be more successful in metaphysics, if we assume that the objects must conform to our cognition. This appears, at all events, to accord better with the possibility of our gaining the end we have in view, that is to say, of arriving at the cognition of objects a priori, of determining something with respect to these objects, before they are given to us. We here propose to do just what Copernicus did in attempting to explain the celestial movements. When he found that he could make no progress by assuming that all the heavenly bodies revolved round the spectator, he reversed the process, and tried the experiment of assuming that the spectator revolved, while the stars remained at rest. We may make the same experiment with regard to the intuition of objects. If the intuition must conform to the nature of the objects, I do not see how we can know anything of them a priori. If, on the other hand, the object conforms to the nature of our faculty of intuition, I can then easily conceive the possibility of such an a priori knowledge. Now as I cannot rest in the mere intuitions, but — if they are to become cognitions — must refer them, as representations, to something, as object, and must determine the latter by means of the former, here again there are two courses open to me. Either, first, I may assume that the conceptions, by which I effect this determination, conform to the object — and in this case I am reduced to the same perplexity as before; or secondly, I may assume that the objects, or, which is the same thing, that experience, in which alone as given objects they are cognized, conform to my conceptions — and then I am at no loss how to proceed. For experience itself is a mode of cognition which requires understanding. Before objects, are given to me, that is, a priori, I must presuppose in myself laws of the understanding which are expressed in conceptions a priori. To these conceptions, then, all the objects of experience must necessarily conform. Now there are objects which reason thinks, and that necessarily, but which cannot be given in experience, or, at least, cannot be given so as reason thinks them. The attempt to think these objects will hereafter furnish an excellent test of the new method of thought which we have adopted, and which is based on the principle that we only cognize in things a priori that which we ourselves place in them.

[Note: This method, accordingly, which we have borrowed from the natural philosopher, consists in seeking for the elements of pure reason in that which admits of confirmation or refutation by experiment. Now the propositions of pure reason, especially when they transcend the limits of possible experience, do not admit of our making any experiment with their objects, as in natural science. Hence, with regard to those conceptions and principles which we assume a priori, our only course ill be to view them from two different sides. We must regard one and the same conception, on the one hand, in relation to experience as an object of the senses and of the understanding, on the other hand, in relation to reason, isolated and transcending the limits of experience, as an object of mere thought. Now if we find that, when we regard things from this double point of view, the result is in harmony with the principle of pure reason, but that, when we regard them from a single point of view, reason is involved in self-contradiction, then the experiment will establish the correctness of this distinction.]

This attempt succeeds as well as we could desire, and promises to metaphysics, in its first part — that is, where it is occupied with conceptions a priori, of which the corresponding objects may be given in experience — the certain course of science. For by this new method we are enabled perfectly to explain the possibility of a priori cognition, and, what is more, to demonstrate satisfactorily the laws which lie a priori at the foundation of nature, as the sum of the objects of experience — neither of which was possible according to the procedure hitherto followed. But from this deduction of the faculty of a priori cognition in the first part of metaphysics, we derive a surprising result, and one which, to all appearance, militates against the great end of metaphysics, as treated in the second part. For we come to the conclusion that our faculty of cognition is unable to transcend the limits of possible experience; and yet this is precisely the most essential object of this science. The estimate of our rational cognition a priori at which we arrive is that it has only to do with phenomena, and that things in themselves, while possessing a real existence, lie beyond its sphere. Here we are enabled to put the justice of this estimate to the test. For that which of necessity impels us to transcend the limits of experience and of all phenomena is the unconditioned, which reason absolutely requires in things as they are in themselves, in order to complete the series of conditions. Now, if it appears that when, on the one hand, we assume that our cognition conforms to its objects as things in themselves, the unconditioned cannot be thought without contradiction, and that when, on the other hand, we assume that our representation of things as they are given to us, does not conform to these things as they are in themselves, but that these objects, as phenomena, conform to our mode of representation, the contradiction disappears: we shall then be convinced of the truth of that which we began by assuming for the sake of experiment; we may look upon it as established that the unconditioned does not lie in things as we know them, or as they are given to us, but in things as they are in themselves, beyond the range of our cognition.

[Note: This experiment of pure reason has a great similarity to that of the chemists, which they term the experiment of reduction, or, more usually, the synthetic process. The analysis of the metaphysician separates pure cognition a priori into two heterogeneous elements, viz., the cognition of things as phenomena, and of things in themselves. Dialectic combines these again into harmony with the necessary rational idea of the unconditioned, and finds that this harmony never results except through the above distinction, which is, therefore, concluded to be just.]

But, after we have thus denied the power of speculative reason to make any progress in the sphere of the supersensible, it still remains for our consideration whether data do not exist in practical cognition which may enable us to determine the transcendent conception of the unconditioned, to rise beyond the limits of all possible experience from a practical point of view, and thus to satisfy the great ends of metaphysics. Speculative reason has thus, at least, made room for such an extension of our knowledge: and, if it must leave this space vacant, still it does not rob us of the liberty to fill it up, if we can, by means of practical data — nay, it even challenges us to make the attempt.

[Note: So the central laws of the movements of the heavenly bodies established the truth of that which Copernicus, first, assumed only as a hypothesis, and, at the same time, brought to light that invisible force (Newtonian attraction) which holds the universe together. The latter would have remained forever undiscovered, if

Copernicus had not ventured on the experiment — contrary to the senses but still just — of looking for the observed movements not in the heavenly bodies, but in the spectator. In this Preface I treat the new metaphysical method as a hypothesis with the view of rendering apparent the first attempts at such a change of method, which are always hypothetical. But in the Critique itself it will be demonstrated, not hypothetically, but apodeictically, from the nature of our representations of space and time, and from the elementary conceptions of the understanding.]

This attempt to introduce a complete revolution in the procedure of metaphysics, after the example of the geometricians and natural philosophers, constitutes the aim of the Critique of Pure Speculative Reason. It is a treatise on the method to be followed, not a system of the science itself. But, at the same time, it marks out and defines both the external boundaries and the internal structure of this science. For pure speculative reason has this peculiarity, that, in choosing the various objects of thought, it is able to define the limits of its own faculties, and even to give a complete enumeration of the possible modes of proposing problems to itself, and thus to sketch out the entire system of metaphysics. For, on the one hand, in cognition a priori, nothing must be attributed to the objects but what the thinking subject derives from itself; and, on the other hand, reason is, in regard to the principles of cognition, a perfectly distinct, independent unity, in which, as in an organized body, every member exists for the sake of the others, and all for the sake of each, so that no principle can be viewed, with safety, in one relationship, unless it is, at the same time, viewed in relation to the total use of pure reason. Hence, too, metaphysics has this singular advantage — an advantage which falls to the lot of no other science which has to do with objects — that, if once it is conducted into the sure path of science, by means of this criticism, it can then take in the whole sphere of its cognitions, and can thus complete its work, and leave it for the use of posterity, as a capital which can never receive fresh accessions. For metaphysics has to deal only with principles and with the limitations of its own employment as determined by these principles. To this perfection it is, therefore, bound, as the fundamental science, to attain, and to it the maxim may justly be applied:

Nil actum reputans, si quid superesset agendum.

But, it will be asked, what kind of a treasure is this that we propose to bequeath to posterity? What is the real value of this system of metaphysics, purified by criticism, and thereby reduced to a permanent condition? A cursory view of the present work will lead to the supposition that its use is merely negative, that it only serves to warn us against venturing, with speculative reason, beyond the limits of experience. This is, in fact, its primary use. But this, at once, assumes a positive value, when we observe that the principles with which speculative reason endeavours to transcend its limits lead inevitably, not to the extension, but to the contraction of the use of reason, inasmuch as they threaten to extend the limits of sensibility, which is their proper sphere, over the entire realm of thought and, thus, to supplant the pure (practical) use of reason. So far, then, as this criticism is occupied in confining speculative reason within its proper bounds, it is only negative; but, inasmuch as it thereby, at the same time, removes an obstacle which impedes and even threatens to destroy the use of practical reason, it possesses a positive and very important value. In order to admit this, we have only to be convinced that there is an absolutely necessary use of pure reason — the moral use — in which it inevitably transcends the limits of sensibility, without the aid of speculation, requiring only to be insured against the effects of a speculation which would involve it in contradiction with itself. To deny the positive advantage of the service which this criticism renders us would be as absurd as to maintain that the system of police is productive of no positive benefit, since its main business is to prevent the violence which citizen has to apprehend from citizen, that so each may pursue his vocation in peace and security. That space and time are only forms of sensible intuition, and hence are only conditions of the existence of things as phenomena; that, moreover, we have no conceptions of the understanding, and, consequently, no elements for the cognition of things, except in so far as a corresponding intuition can be given to these conceptions; that, accordingly, we can have no cognition of an object, as a thing in itself, but only as an object of sensible intuition, that is, as phenomenon — all this is proved in the analytical part of the Critique; and from this the limitation of all possible speculative cognition to the mere objects of experience, follows as a necessary result. At the same time, it must be carefully borne in mind that, while we surrender the power of cognizing, we still reserve the power of thinking objects, as things in themselves.* For, otherwise, we should require to affirm the existence of an appearance, without something that appears — which would be absurd. Now let us suppose, for a moment, that we had not undertaken this criticism and, accordingly, had not drawn the necessary distinction between things as objects of experience and things as they are in themselves. The principle of causality, and, by consequence, the mechanism of nature as determined by causality, would then have absolute validity in relation to all things as efficient causes. I should then be unable to assert, with regard to one and the same being, e.g., the human soul, that its will is free, and yet, at the same time, subject to natural necessity, that is, not free, without falling into a palpable contradiction, for in both propositions I should take the soul in the same signification, as a thing in general, as a thing in itself — as, without previous criticism, I could not but take it. Suppose now, on the other hand, that we have undertaken this criticism, and have learnt that an object may be taken in two senses, first, as a phenomenon, secondly, as a thing in itself; and that, according to the deduction of the conceptions of the understanding, the principle of causality has reference only to things in the first sense. We then see how it does not involve any contradiction to assert, on the one hand, that the will, in the phenomenal sphere — in visible action — is necessarily obedient to the law of nature, and, in so far, not free; and, on the other hand, that, as belonging to a thing in itself, it is not subject to that law, and, accordingly, is free. Now, it is true that I cannot, by means of speculative reason, and still less by empirical observation, cognize my soul as a thing in itself and consequently, cannot cognize liberty as the property of a being to which I ascribe effects in the world of sense. For, to do so, I must cognize this being as existing, and yet not in time, which — since I cannot support my conception by any intuition — is impossible. At the same time, while I cannot cognize, I can quite well think freedom, that is to say, my representation of it involves at least no contradiction, if we bear in mind the critical distinction of the two modes of representation (the sensible and the intellectual) and the consequent limitation of the conceptions of the pure understanding and of the principles which flow from them. Suppose now that morality necessarily presupposed liberty, in the strictest sense, as a property of our will; suppose that reason contained certain practical, original principles a priori, which were absolutely impossible without this presupposition; and suppose, at the same time, that speculative reason had proved that liberty was incapable of being thought at all. It would then follow that the moral presupposition must give way to the speculative affirmation, the opposite of which involves an obvious contradiction, and that liberty and, with it, morality must yield to the mechanism of nature; for the negation of morality involves no contradiction, except on the presupposition of liberty. Now morality does not require the speculative cognition of liberty; it is enough that I can think it, that its conception involves no contradiction, that it does not interfere with the mechanism of nature. But even this requirement we could not satisfy, if we had not learnt the twofold sense in which things may be taken; and it is only in this way that the doctrine of morality and the doctrine of nature are confined within their proper limits. For this result, then, we are indebted to a criticism which warns us of our unavoidable ignorance with regard to things in themselves, and establishes the necessary limitation of our theoretical cognition to mere phenomena.

[Note: In order to cognize an object, I must be able to prove its possibility, either from its reality as attested by experience, or a priori, by means of reason. But I can think what I please, provided only I do not contradict myself; that is, provided my conception is a possible thought, though I may be unable to answer for the existence of a corresponding object in the sum of possibilities. But something more is required before I can attribute to such a conception objective validity, that is real possibility — the other possibility being merely logical. We are not, however, confined to theoretical sources of cognition for the means of satisfying this additional requirement, but may derive them from practical sources.]

The positive value of the critical principles of pure reason in relation to the conception of God and of the simple nature of the soul, admits of a similar exemplification; but on this point I shall not dwell. I cannot even make the assumption — as the practical interests of morality require — of God, freedom, and immortality, if I do not deprive speculative reason of its pretensions to transcendent insight. For to arrive at these, it must make use of principles which, in fact, extend only to the objects of possible experience, and which cannot be applied to objects beyond this sphere without converting them into phenomena, and thus rendering the practical extension of pure reason impossible. I must, therefore, abolish knowledge, to make room for belief. The dogmatism of metaphysics, that is, the presumption that it is possible to advance in metaphysics without previous criticism, is the true source of the unbelief (always dogmatic) which militates against morality.

Thus, while it may be no very difficult task to bequeath a legacy to posterity, in the shape of a system of metaphysics constructed in accordance with the Critique of Pure Reason, still the value of such a bequest is not to be depreciated. It will render an important service to reason, by substituting the certainty of scientific method for that random groping after results without the guidance of principles, which has hitherto characterized the pursuit of metaphysical studies. It will render an important service to the inquiring mind of youth, by leading the student to apply his powers to the cultivation of genuine science, instead of wasting them, as at present, on speculations which can never lead to any result, or on the idle attempt to invent new ideas and opinions. But, above all, it will confer an inestimable benefit on morality and religion, by showing that all the objections urged against them may be silenced for ever by the Socratic method, that is to say, by proving the ignorance of the objector. For, as the world has never been, and, no doubt, never will be without a system of metaphysics of one kind or another, it is the highest and weightiest concern of philosophy to render it powerless for harm, by closing up the sources of error.

This important change in the field of the sciences, this loss of its fancied possessions, to which speculative reason must submit, does not prove in any way detrimental to the general interests of humanity. The advantages which the world has derived from the teachings of pure reason are not at all impaired. The loss falls, in its whole extent, on the monopoly of the schools, but does not in the slightest degree touch the interests of mankind. I appeal to the most obstinate dogmatist, whether the proof of the continued existence of the soul after death, derived from the simplicity of its substance; of the freedom of the will in opposition to the general mechanism of nature, drawn from the subtle but impotent distinction of subjective and objective practical necessity; or of the existence of God, deduced from the conception of an ens realissimum — the contingency of the changeable, and the necessity of a prime mover, has ever been able to pass beyond the limits of the schools, to penetrate the public mind, or to exercise the slightest influence on its convictions. It must be admitted that this has not been the case and that, owing to the unfitness of the common understanding for such subtle speculations, it can never be expected to take place. On the contrary, it is plain that the hope of a future life arises from the feeling, which exists in the breast of every man, that the temporal is inadequate to meet and satisfy the demands of his nature. In like manner, it cannot be doubted that the clear exhibition of duties in opposition to all the claims of inclination, gives rise to the consciousness of freedom, and that the glorious order, beauty, and providential care, everywhere displayed in nature, give rise to the belief in a wise and great Author of the Universe. Such is the genesis of these general convictions of mankind, so far as they depend on rational grounds; and this public property not only remains undisturbed, but is even raised to greater importance, by the doctrine that the schools have no right to arrogate to themselves a more profound insight into a matter of general human concernment than that to which the great mass of men, ever held by us in the highest estimation, can without difficulty attain, and that the schools should, therefore, confine themselves to the elaboration of these universally comprehensible and, from a moral point of view, amply satisfactory proofs. The change, therefore, affects only the arrogant pretensions of the schools, which would gladly retain, in their own exclusive possession, the key to the truths which they impart to the public.

Quod mecum nescit, solus vult scire videri.

At the same time it does not deprive the speculative philosopher of his just title to be the sole depositor of a science which benefits the public without its knowledge — I mean, the Critique of Pure Reason. This can never become popular and, indeed, has no occasion to be so; for finespun arguments in favour of useful truths make just as little impression on the public mind as the equally subtle objections brought against these truths. On the other hand, since both inevitably force themselves on every man who rises to the height of speculation, it becomes the manifest duty of the schools to enter upon a thorough investigation of the rights of speculative reason and, thus, to prevent the scandal which metaphysical controversies are sure, sooner or later, to cause even to the masses. It is only by criticism that metaphysicians (and, as such, theologians too) can be saved from these controversies and from the consequent perversion of their doctrines. Criticism alone can strike a blow at the root of materialism, fatalism, atheism, free-thinking, fanaticism, and superstition, which are universally injurious — as well as of idealism and scepticism, which are dangerous to the schools, but can scarcely pass over to the public. If governments think proper to interfere with the affairs of the learned, it would be more consistent with a wise regard for the interests of science, as well as for those of society, to favour a criticism of this kind, by which alone the labours of reason can be established on a firm basis, than to support the ridiculous despotism of the schools, which raise a loud cry of danger to the public over the destruction of cobwebs, of which the public has never taken any notice, and the loss of which, therefore, it can never feel.

This critical science is not opposed to the dogmatic procedure of reason in pure cognition; for pure cognition must always be dogmatic, that is, must rest on strict demonstration from sure principles a priori — but to dogmatism, that is, to the presumption that it is possible to make any progress with a pure cognition, derived from (philosophical) conceptions, according to the principles which reason has long been in the habit of employing — without first inquiring in what way and by what right reason has come into the possession of these principles. Dogmatism is thus the dogmatic procedure of pure reason without previous criticism of its own powers, and in opposing this procedure, we must not be supposed to lend any countenance to that loquacious shallowness which arrogates to itself the name of popularity, nor yet to scepticism, which makes short work with the whole science of metaphysics. On the contrary, our criticism is the necessary preparation for a thoroughly scientific system of metaphysics which must perform its task entirely a priori, to the complete satisfaction of speculative reason, and must, therefore, be treated, not popularly, but scholastically. In carrying out the plan which the Critique prescribes, that is, in the future system of metaphysics, we must have recourse to the strict method of the celebrated Wolf, the greatest of all dogmatic philosophers. He was the first to point out the necessity of establishing fixed principles, of clearly defining our conceptions, and of subjecting our demonstrations to the most severe scrutiny, instead of rashly jumping at conclusions. The example which he set served to awaken that spirit of profound and thorough investigation which is not yet extinct in Germany. He would have been peculiarly well fitted to give a truly scientific character to metaphysical studies, had it occurred to him to prepare the field by a criticism of the organum, that is, of pure reason itself. That he failed to perceive the necessity of such a procedure must be ascribed to the dogmatic mode of thought which characterized his age, and on this point the philosophers of his time, as well as of all previous times, have nothing to reproach each other with. Those who reject at once the method of Wolf, and of the Critique of Pure Reason, can have no other aim but to shake off the fetters of science, to change labour into sport, certainty into opinion, and philosophy into philodoxy.

In this second edition, I have endeavoured, as far as possible, to remove the difficulties and obscurity which, without fault of mine perhaps, have given rise to many misconceptions even among acute thinkers. In the propositions themselves, and in the demonstrations by which they are supported, as well as in the form and the entire plan of the work, I have found nothing to alter; which must be attributed partly to the long examination to which I had subjected the whole before offering it to the public and partly to the nature of the case. For pure speculative reason is an organic structure in which there is nothing isolated or independent, but every Single part is essential to all the rest; and hence, the slightest imperfection, whether defect or positive error, could not fail to betray itself in use. I venture, further, to hope, that this system will maintain the same unalterable character for the future. I am led to entertain this confidence, not by vanity, but by the evidence which the equality of the result affords, when we proceed, first, from the simplest elements up to the complete whole of pure reason and, and then, backwards from the whole to each part. We find that the attempt to make the slightest alteration, in any part, leads inevitably to contradictions, not merely in this system, but in human reason itself. At the same time, there is still much room for improvement in the exposition of the doctrines contained in this work. In the present edition, I have endeavoured to remove misapprehensions of the aesthetical part, especially with regard to the conception of time; to clear away the obscurity which has been found in the deduction of the conceptions of the understanding; to supply the supposed want of sufficient evidence in the demonstration of the principles of the pure understanding; and, lastly, to obviate the misunderstanding of the paralogisms which immediately precede the rational psychology. Beyond this point — the end of the second main division of the "Transcendental Dialectic" — I have not extended my alterations,* partly from want of time, and partly because I am not aware that any portion of the remainder has given rise to misconceptions among intelligent and impartial critics, whom I do not here mention with that praise which is their due, but who will find that their suggestions have been attended to in the work itself.

[Note: The only addition, properly so called — and that only in the method of proof — which I have made in the present edition, consists of a new refutation of psychological idealism, and a strict demonstration — the only one possible, as I believe — of the objective reality of external intuition. However harmless idealism may be considered — although in reality it is not so — in regard to the essential ends of metaphysics, it must still remain a scandal to philosophy and to the general human reason to be obliged to assume, as an article of mere belief, the existence of things external to ourselves (from which, yet, we derive the whole material of cognition for the internal sense), and not to be able to oppose a satisfactory proof to any one who may call it in question. As there is some obscurity of expression in the demonstration as it stands in the text, I propose to alter the passage in question as follows: "But this permanent cannot be an intuition in me. For all the determining grounds of my existence which can be found in me are representations and, as such, do themselves require a permanent, distinct from them, which may determine my existence in relation to their changes, that is, my existence in time, wherein they change." It may, probably, be urged in opposition to this proof that, after all, I am only conscious immediately of that which is in me, that is, of my representation of external things, and that, consequently, it must always remain uncertain whether anything corresponding to this representation does or does not exist externally to me. But I am conscious, through internal experience, of my existence in time (consequently, also, of the determinability of the former in the latter), and that is more than the simple consciousness of my representation. It is, in fact, the same as the empirical consciousness of my existence, which can only be determined in relation to something, which, while connected with my existence, is external to me. This consciousness of my existence in time is, therefore, identical with the consciousness of a relation to something external to me, and it is, therefore, experience, not fiction, sense, not imagination, which inseparably connects the external with my internal sense. For the external sense is, in itself, the relation of intuition to something real, external to me; and the reality of this something, as opposed to the mere imagination of it, rests solely on its inseparable connection with internal experience as the condition of its possibility. If with the intellectual consciousness of my existence, in the representation: I am, which accompanies all my judgements, and all the operations of my understanding, I could, at the same time, connect a determination of my existence by intellectual intuition, then the consciousness of a relation to something external to me would not be necessary. But the internal intuition in which alone my existence can be determined, though preceded by that purely intellectual consciousness, is itself sensible and attached to the condition of time. Hence this determination of my existence, and consequently my internal experience itself, must depend on something permanent which is not in me, which can be, therefore, only in something external to me, to which I must look upon myself as being related. Thus the reality of the external sense is necessarily connected with that of the internal, in order to the possibility of experience in general; that is, I am just as certainly conscious that there are things external to me related to my sense as I am that I myself exist as determined in time. But in order to ascertain to what given intuitions objects, external me, really correspond, in other words, what intuitions belong to the external sense and not to imagination, I must have recourse, in every particular case, to those rules according to which experience in general (even internal experience) is distinguished from imagination, and which are always based on the proposition that there really is an external experience. We may add the remark that the representation of something permanent in existence, is not the same thing as the permanent representation; for a representation may be very variable and changing — as all our representations, even that of matter, are — and yet refer to something permanent, which must, therefore, be distinct from all my representations and external to me, the existence of which is necessarily included in the determination of my own existence, and with it constitutes one experience — an experience which would not even be possible internally, if it were not also at the same time, in part, external. To the question How? we are no more able to reply, than we are, in general, to think the stationary in time, the coexistence of which with the variable, produces the conception of change.]

In attempting to render the exposition of my views as intelligible as possible, I have been compelled to leave out or abridge various passages which were not essential to the completeness of the work, but which many readers might consider useful in other respects, and might be unwilling to miss. This trifling loss, which could not be avoided without swelling the book beyond due limits, may be supplied, at the pleasure of the reader, by a comparison with the first edition, and will, I hope, be more than compensated for by the greater clearness of the exposition as it now stands.

I have observed, with pleasure and thankfulness, in the pages of various reviews and treatises, that the spirit of profound and thorough investigation is not extinct in Germany, though it may have been overborne and silenced for a time by the fashionable tone of a licence in thinking, which gives itself the airs of genius, and that the difficulties which beset the paths of criticism have not prevented energetic and acute thinkers from making themselves masters of the science of pure reason to which these paths conduct — a science which is not popular, but scholastic in its character, and which alone can hope for a lasting existence or possess an abiding value. To these deserving men, who so happily combine profundity of view with a talent for lucid exposition — a talent which I myself am not conscious of possessing — I leave the task of removing any obscurity which may still adhere to the statement of my doctrines. For, in this case, the danger is not that of being refuted, but of being misunderstood. For my own part, I must henceforward abstain from controversy, although I shall carefully attend to all suggestions, whether from friends or adversaries, which may be of use in the future elaboration of the system of this propaedeutic. As, during these labours, I have advanced pretty far in years this month I reach my sixty-fourth year — it will be necessary for me to economize time, if I am to carry out my plan of elaborating the metaphysics of nature as well as of morals, in confirmation of the correctness of the principles established in this Critique of Pure Reason, both speculative and practical; and I must, therefore, leave the task of clearing up the obscurities of the present work — inevitable, perhaps, at the outset — as well as, the defence of the whole, to those deserving men, who have made my system their own. A philosophical system cannot come forward armed at all points like a mathematical treatise, and hence it may be quite possible to take objection to particular passages, while the organic structure of the system, considered as a unity, has no danger to apprehend. But few possess the ability, and still fewer the inclination, to take a comprehensive view of a new system. By confining the view to particular passages, taking these out of their connection and comparing them with one another, it is easy to pick out apparent contradictions, especially in a work written with any freedom of style. These contradictions place the work in an unfavourable light in the eyes of those who rely on the judgement of others, but are easily reconciled by those who have mastered the idea of the whole. If a theory possesses stability in itself, the action and reaction which seemed at first to threaten its existence serve only, in the course of time, to smooth down any superficial roughness or inequality, and — if men of insight, impartiality, and truly popular gifts, turn their attention to it — to secure to it, in a short time, the requisite elegance also.

Konigsberg, April 1787.

INTRODUCTION

I. Of the difference between Pure and Empirical Knowledge

That all our knowledge begins with experience there can be no doubt. For how is it possible that the faculty of cognition should be awakened into exercise otherwise than by means of objects which affect our senses, and partly of themselves produce representations, partly rouse our powers of understanding into activity, to compare to connect, or to separate these, and so to convert the raw material of our sensuous impressions into a knowledge of objects, which is called experience? In respect of time, therefore, no knowledge of ours is antecedent to experience, but begins with it.

But, though all our knowledge begins with experience, it by no means follows that all arises out of experience. For, on the contrary, it is quite possible that our empirical knowledge is a compound of that which we receive through impressions, and that which the faculty of cognition supplies from itself (sensuous impressions giving merely the occasion), an addition which we cannot distinguish from the original element given by sense, till long practice has made us attentive to, and skilful in separating it. It is, therefore, a question which requires close investigation, and not to be answered at first sight, whether there exists a knowledge altogether independent of experience, and even of all sensuous impressions? Knowledge of this kind is called a priori, in contradistinction to empirical knowledge, which has its sources a posteriori, that is, in experience.

But the expression, "a priori," is not as yet definite enough adequately to indicate the whole meaning of the question above started. For, in speaking of knowledge which has its sources in experience, we are wont to say, that this or that may be known a priori, because we do not derive this knowledge immediately from experience, but from a general rule, which, however, we have itself borrowed from experience. Thus, if a man undermined his house, we say, "he might know a priori that it would have fallen;" that is, he needed not to have waited for the experience that it did actually fall. But still, a priori, he could not know even this much. For, that bodies are heavy, and, consequently, that they fall when their supports are taken away, must have been known to him previously, by means of experience.

By the term "knowledge a priori," therefore, we shall in the sequel understand, not such as is independent of this or that kind of experience, but such as is absolutely so of all experience. Opposed to this is empirical knowledge, or that which is possible only a posteriori, that is, through experience. Knowledge a priori is either pure or impure. Pure knowledge a priori is that with which no empirical element is mixed up. For example, the proposition, "Every change has a cause," is a proposition a priori, but impure, because change is a conception which can only be derived from experience.

II. The Human Intellect, even in an Unphilosophical State, is in Possession of Certain Cognitions "a priori".

The question now is as to a criterion, by which we may securely distinguish a pure from an empirical cognition. Experience no doubt teaches us that this or that object is constituted in such and such a manner, but not that it could not possibly exist otherwise. Now, in the first place, if we have a proposition which contains the idea of necessity in its very conception, it is a if, moreover, it is not derived from any other proposition, unless from one equally involving the idea of necessity, it is absolutely priori. Secondly, an empirical judgement never exhibits strict and absolute, but only assumed and comparative universality (by induction); therefore, the most we can say is — so far as we have hitherto observed, there is no exception to this or that rule. If, on the other hand, a judgement carries with it strict and absolute universality, that is, admits of no possible exception, it is not derived from experience, but is valid absolutely a priori.

Empirical universality is, therefore, only an arbitrary extension of validity, from that which may be predicated of a proposition valid in most cases, to that which is asserted of a proposition which holds good in all; as, for example, in the affirmation, "All bodies are heavy." When, on the contrary, strict universality characterizes a judgement, it necessarily indicates another peculiar source of knowledge, namely, a faculty of cognition a priori. Necessity and strict universality, therefore, are infallible tests for distinguishing pure from empirical knowledge, and are inseparably connected with each other. But as in the use of these criteria the empirical limitation is sometimes more easily detected than the contingency of the judgement, or the unlimited universality which we attach to a judgement is often a more convincing proof than its necessity, it may be advisable to use the criteria separately, each being by itself infallible.

Now, that in the sphere of human cognition we have judgements which are necessary, and in the strictest sense universal, consequently pure a priori, it will be an easy matter to show. If we desire an example from the sciences, we need only take any proposition in mathematics. If we cast our eyes upon the commonest operations of the understanding, the proposition, "Every change must have a cause," will amply serve our purpose. In the latter case, indeed, the conception of a cause so plainly involves the conception of a necessity of connection with an effect, and of a strict universality of the law, that the very notion of a cause would entirely disappear, were we to derive it, like Hume, from a frequent association of what happens with that which precedes; and the habit thence originating of connecting representations — the necessity inherent in the judgement being therefore merely subjective. Besides, without seeking for such examples of principles existing a priori in cognition, we might easily show that such principles are the indispensable basis of the possibility of experience itself, and consequently prove their existence a priori. For whence could our experience itself acquire certainty, if all the rules on which it depends were themselves empirical, and consequently fortuitous? No one, therefore, can admit the validity of the use of such rules as first principles. But, for the present, we may content ourselves with having established the fact, that we do possess and exercise a faculty of pure a priori cognition; and, secondly, with having pointed out the proper tests of such cognition, namely, universality and necessity.

Not only in judgements, however, but even in conceptions, is an a priori origin manifest. For example, if we take away by degrees from our conceptions of a body all that can be referred to mere sensuous experience — colour, hardness or softness, weight, even impenetrability — the body will then vanish; but the space which it occupied still remains, and this it is utterly impossible to annihilate in thought. Again, if we take away, in like manner, from our empirical conception of any object, corporeal or incorporeal, all properties which mere experience has taught us to connect with it, still we cannot think away those through which we cogitate it as substance, or adhering to substance, although our conception of substance is more determined than that of an object. Compelled, therefore, by that necessity with which the conception of substance forces itself upon us, we must confess that it has its seat in our faculty of cognition a priori.

III. Philosophy stands in need of a Science which shall Determine the Possibility, Principles, and Extent of Human Knowledge "a priori"

Of far more importance than all that has been above said, is the consideration that certain of our cognitions rise completely above the sphere of all possible experience, and by means of conceptions, to which there exists in the whole extent of experience no corresponding object, seem to extend the range of our judgements beyond its bounds. And just in this transcendental or supersensible sphere, where experience affords us neither instruction nor guidance, lie the investigations of reason, which, on account of their importance, we consider far preferable to, and as having a far more elevated aim than, all that the understanding can achieve within the sphere of sensuous phenomena. So high a value do we set upon these investigations, that even at the risk of error, we persist in following them out, and permit neither doubt nor disregard nor indifference to restrain us from the pursuit. These unavoidable problems of mere pure reason are God, freedom (of will), and immortality. The science which, with all its preliminaries, has for its especial object the solution of these problems is named metaphysics — a science which is at the very outset dogmatical, that is, it confidently takes upon itself the execution of this task without any previous investigation of the ability or inability of reason for such an undertaking.

Now the safe ground of experience being thus abandoned, it seems nevertheless natural that we should hesitate to erect a building with the cognitions we possess, without knowing whence they come, and on the strength of principles, the origin of which is undiscovered. Instead of thus trying to build without a foundation, it is rather to be expected that we should long ago have put the question, how the understanding can arrive at these a priori cognitions, and what is the extent, validity, and worth which they may possess? We say, "This is natural enough," meaning by the word natural, that which is consistent with a just and reasonable way of thinking; but if we understand by the term, that which usually happens, nothing indeed could be more natural and more comprehensible than that this investigation should be left long unattempted. For one part of our pure knowledge, the science of mathematics, has been long firmly established, and thus leads us to form flattering expectations with regard to others, though these may be of quite a different nature. Besides, when we get beyond the bounds of experience, we are of course safe from opposition in that quarter; and the charm of widening the range of our knowledge is so great that, unless we are brought to a standstill by some evident contradiction, we hurry on undoubtingly in our course. This, however, may be avoided, if we are sufficiently cautious in the construction of our fictions, which are not the less fictions on that account.

Mathematical science affords us a brilliant example, how far, independently of all experience, we may carry our a priori knowledge. It is true that the mathematician occupies himself with objects and cognitions only in so far as they can be represented by means of intuition. But this circumstance is easily overlooked, because the said intuition can itself be given a priori, and therefore is hardly to be distinguished from a mere pure conception. Deceived by such a proof of the power of reason, we can perceive no limits to the extension of our knowledge. The light dove cleaving in free flight the thin air, whose resistance it feels, might imagine that her movements would be far more free and rapid in airless space. Just in the same way did Plato, abandoning the world of sense because of the narrow limits it sets to the understanding, venture upon the wings of ideas beyond it, into the void space of pure intellect. He did not reflect that he made no real progress by all his efforts; for he met with no resistance which might serve him for a support, as it were, whereon to rest, and on which he might apply his powers, in order to let the intellect acquire momentum for its progress. It is, indeed, the common fate of human reason in speculation, to finish the imposing edifice of thought as rapidly as possible, and then for the first time to begin to examine whether the foundation is a solid one or no. Arrived at this point, all sorts of excuses are sought after, in order to console us for its want of stability, or rather, indeed, to enable Us to dispense altogether with so late and dangerous an investigation. But what frees us during the process of building from all apprehension or suspicion, and flatters us into the belief of its solidity, is this. A great part, perhaps the greatest part, of the business of our reason consists in the analysation of the conceptions which we already possess of objects. By this means we gain a multitude of cognitions, which although really nothing more than elucidations or explanations of that which (though in a confused manner) was already thought in our conceptions, are, at least in respect of their form, prized as new introspections; whilst, so far as regards their matter or content, we have really made no addition to our conceptions, but only disinvolved them. But as this process does furnish a real priori knowledge, which has a sure progress and useful results, reason, deceived by this, slips in, without being itself aware of it, assertions of a quite different kind; in which, to given conceptions it adds others, a priori indeed, but entirely foreign to them, without our knowing how it arrives at these, and, indeed, without such a question ever suggesting itself. I shall therefore at once proceed to examine the difference between these two modes of knowledge.

IV. Of the Difference Between Analytical and Synthetical Judgements.

In all judgements wherein the relation of a subject to the predicate is cogitated (I mention affirmative judgements only here; the application to negative will be very easy), this relation is possible in two different ways. Either the predicate B belongs to the subject A, as somewhat which is contained (though covertly) in the conception A; or the predicate B lies completely out of the conception A, although it stands in connection with it. In the first instance, I term the judgement analytical, in the second, synthetical. Analytical judgements (affirmative) are therefore those in which the connection of the predicate with the subject is cogitated through identity; those in which this connection is cogitated without identity, are called synthetical judgements. The former may be called explicative, the latter augmentative judgements; because the former add in the predicate nothing to the conception of the subject, but only analyse it into its constituent conceptions, which were thought already in the subject, although in a confused manner; the latter add to our conceptions of the subject a predicate which was not contained in it, and which no analysis could ever have discovered therein. For example, when I say, "All bodies are extended," this is an analytical judgement. For I need not go beyond the conception of body in order to find extension connected with it, but merely analyse the conception, that is, become conscious of the manifold properties which I think in that conception, in order to discover this predicate in it: it is therefore an analytical judgement. On the other hand, when I say, "All bodies are heavy," the predicate is something totally different from that which I think in the mere conception of a body. By the addition of such a predicate, therefore, it becomes a synthetical judgement.

Judgements of experience, as such, are always synthetical. For it would be absurd to think of grounding an analytical judgement on experience, because in forming such a judgement I need not go out of the sphere of my conceptions, and therefore recourse to the testimony of experience is quite unnecessary. That "bodies are extended" is not an empirical judgement, but a proposition which stands firm a priori. For before addressing myself to experience, I already have in my conception all the requisite conditions for the judgement, and I have only to extract the predicate from the conception, according to the principle of contradiction, and thereby at the same time become conscious of the necessity of the judgement, a necessity which I could never learn from experience. On the other hand, though at first I do not at all include the predicate of weight in my conception of body in general, that conception still indicates an object of experience, a part of the totality of experience, to which I can still add other parts; and this I do when I recognize by observation that bodies are heavy. I can cognize beforehand by analysis the conception of body through the characteristics of extension, impenetrability, shape, etc., all which are cogitated in this conception. But now I extend my knowledge, and looking back on experience from which I had derived this conception of body, I find weight at all times connected with the above characteristics, and therefore I synthetically add to my conceptions this as a predicate, and say, "All bodies are heavy." Thus it is experience upon which rests the possibility of the synthesis of the predicate of weight with the conception of body, because both conceptions, although the one is not contained in the other, still belong to one another (only contingently, however), as parts of a whole, namely, of experience, which is itself a synthesis of intuitions.

But to synthetical judgements a priori, such aid is entirely wanting. If I go out of and beyond the conception A, in order to recognize another B as connected with it, what foundation have I to rest on, whereby to render the synthesis possible? I have here no longer the advantage of looking out in the sphere of experience for what I want. Let us take, for example, the proposition, "Everything that happens has a cause." In the conception of "something that happens," I indeed think an existence which a certain time antecedes, and from this I can derive analytical judgements. But the conception of a cause lies quite out of the above conception, and indicates something entirely different from "that which happens," and is consequently not contained in that conception. How then am I able to assert concerning the general conception— "that which happens" — something entirely different from that conception, and to recognize the conception of cause although not contained in it, yet as belonging to it, and even necessarily? what is here the unknown = X, upon which the understanding rests when it believes it has found, out of the conception A a foreign predicate B, which it nevertheless considers to be connected with it? It cannot be experience, because the principle adduced annexes the two representations, cause and effect, to the representation existence, not only with universality, which experience cannot give, but also with the expression of necessity, therefore completely a priori and from pure conceptions. Upon such synthetical, that is augmentative propositions, depends the whole aim of our speculative knowledge a priori; for although analytical judgements are indeed highly important and necessary, they are so, only to arrive at that clearness of conceptions which is requisite for a sure and extended synthesis, and this alone is a real acquisition.

V. In all Theoretical Sciences of Reason, Synthetical Judgements "a priori" are contained as Principles.

1. Mathematical judgements are always synthetical. Hitherto this fact, though incontestably true and very important in its consequences, seems to have escaped the analysts of the human mind, nay, to be in complete opposition to all their conjectures. For as it was found that mathematical conclusions all proceed according to the principle of contradiction (which the nature of every apodeictic certainty requires), people became persuaded that the fundamental principles of the science also were recognized and admitted in the same way. But the notion is fallacious; for although a synthetical proposition can certainly be discerned by means of the principle of contradiction, this is possible only when another synthetical proposition precedes, from which the latter is deduced, but never of itself.

Before all, be it observed, that proper mathematical propositions are always judgements a priori, and not empirical, because they carry along with them the conception of necessity, which cannot be given by experience. If this be demurred to, it matters not; I will then limit my assertion to pure mathematics, the very conception of which implies that it consists of knowledge altogether non-empirical and a priori.

We might, indeed at first suppose that the proposition $7 + 5 = 12$ is a merely analytical proposition, following (according to the principle of contradiction) from the conception of a sum of seven and five. But if we regard it more narrowly, we find that our conception of the sum of seven and five contains nothing more than the uniting of both sums into one, whereby it cannot at all be cogitated what this single number is which embraces both. The conception of twelve is by no means obtained by merely cogitating the union of seven and five; and we may analyse our conception of such a possible sum as long as we will, still we shall never discover in it the notion of twelve. We must go beyond these conceptions, and have recourse to an intuition which corresponds to one of the two — our five fingers, for example, or like Segner in his Arithmetic five points, and so by degrees, add the units contained in the five given in the intuition, to the conception of seven. For I first take the number 7, and, for the conception of 5 calling in the aid of the fingers of my hand as objects of intuition, I add the units, which I before took together to make up the number 5, gradually now by means of the material image my hand, to the number 7, and by this process, I at length see the number 12 arise. That 7 should be added to 5, I have certainly cogitated in my conception of a sum $= 7 + 5$, but not that this sum was equal to 12. Arithmetical propositions are therefore always synthetical, of which we may become more clearly convinced by trying large numbers. For it will thus become quite evident that, turn and twist our conceptions as we may, it is impossible, without having recourse to intuition, to arrive at the sum total or product by means of the mere analysis of our conceptions. Just as little is any principle of pure geometry analytical. "A straight line between two points is the shortest," is a synthetical proposition. For my conception of straight contains no notion of quantity, but is merely qualitative. The conception of the shortest is therefore fore wholly an addition, and by no analysis can it be extracted from our conception of a straight line. Intuition must therefore here lend its aid, by means of which, and thus only, our synthesis is possible.

Some few principles preposited by geometricians are, indeed, really analytical, and depend on the principle of contradiction. They serve, however, like identical propositions, as links in the chain of method, not as principles — for example, a = a, the whole is equal to itself, or (a+b) — > a, the whole is greater than its part. And yet even these principles themselves, though they derive their validity from pure conceptions, are only admitted in mathematics because they can be presented in intuition. What causes us here commonly to believe that the predicate of such apodeictic judgements is already contained in our conception, and that the judgement is therefore analytical, is merely the equivocal nature of the expression. We must join in thought a certain predicate to a given conception, and this necessity cleaves already to the conception. But the question is, not what we must join in thought to the given conception, but what we really think therein, though only obscurely, and then it becomes manifest that the predicate pertains to these conceptions, necessarily indeed, yet not as thought in the conception itself, but by virtue of an intuition, which must be added to the conception.

2. The science of natural philosophy (physics) contains in itself synthetical judgements a priori, as principles. I shall adduce two propositions. For instance, the proposition, "In all changes of the material world, the quantity of matter remains unchanged"; or, that, "In all communication of motion, action and reaction must always be equal." In both of these, not only is the necessity, and therefore their origin a priori clear, but also that they are synthetical propositions. For in the conception of matter, I do not cogitate its permanency, but merely its presence in space, which it fills. I therefore really go out of and beyond the conception of matter, in order to think on to it something a priori, which I did not think in it. The proposition is therefore not analytical, but synthetical, and nevertheless conceived a priori; and so it is with regard to the other propositions of the pure part of natural philosophy.

3. As to metaphysics, even if we look upon it merely as an attempted science, yet, from the nature of human reason, an indispensable one, we find that it must contain synthetical propositions a priori. It is not merely the duty of metaphysics to dissect, and thereby analytically to illustrate the conceptions which we form a priori of things; but we seek to widen the range of our a priori knowledge. For this purpose, we must avail ourselves of such principles as add something to the original conception — something not identical with, nor contained in it, and by means of synthetical judgements a priori, leave far behind us the limits of experience; for example, in the proposition, "the world must have a beginning," and such like. Thus metaphysics, according to the proper aim of the science, consists merely of synthetical propositions a priori.

VI. The Universal Problem of Pure Reason.

It is extremely advantageous to be able to bring a number of investigations under the formula of a single problem. For in this manner, we not only facilitate our own labour, inasmuch as we define it clearly to ourselves, but also render it more easy for others to decide whether we have done justice to our undertaking. The proper problem of pure reason, then, is contained in the question: "How are synthetical judgements a priori possible?"

That metaphysical science has hitherto remained in so vacillating a state of uncertainty and contradiction, is only to be attributed to the fact that this great problem, and perhaps even the difference between analytical and synthetical judgements, did not sooner suggest itself to philosophers. Upon the solution of this problem, or upon sufficient proof of the impossibility of synthetical knowledge a priori, depends the existence or downfall of the science of metaphysics. Among philosophers, David Hume came the nearest of all to this problem; yet it never acquired in his mind sufficient precision, nor did he regard the question in its universality. On the contrary, he stopped short at the synthetical proposition of the connection of an effect with its cause (principium causalitatis), insisting that such proposition a priori was impossible. According to his conclusions, then, all that we term metaphysical science is a mere delusion, arising from the fancied insight of reason into that which is in truth borrowed from experience, and to which habit has given the appearance of necessity. Against this assertion, destructive to all pure philosophy, he would have been guarded, had he had our problem before his eyes in its universality. For he would then have perceived that, according to his own argument, there likewise could not be any pure mathematical science, which assuredly cannot exist without synthetical propositions a priori — an absurdity from which his good understanding must have saved him.

In the solution of the above problem is at the same time comprehended the possibility of the use of pure reason in the foundation and construction of all sciences which contain theoretical knowledge a priori of objects, that is to say, the answer to the following questions:

How is pure mathematical science possible?

How is pure natural science possible?

Respecting these sciences, as they do certainly exist, it may with propriety be asked, how they are possible? — for that they must be possible is shown by the fact of their really existing.* But as to metaphysics, the miserable progress it has hitherto made, and the fact that of no one system yet brought forward, far as regards its true aim, can it be said that this science really exists, leaves any one at liberty to doubt with reason the very possibility of its existence.

[Note: As to the existence of pure natural science, or physics, perhaps many may still express doubts. But we have only to look at the different propositions which are commonly treated of at the commencement of proper (empirical) physical science — those, for example, relating to the permanence of the same quantity of matter, the vis inertiae, the equality of action and reaction, etc. — to be soon convinced that they form a science of pure physics (physica pura, or rationalis), which well deserves to be separately exposed as a special science, in its whole extent, whether that be great or confined.]

Yet, in a certain sense, this kind of knowledge must unquestionably be looked upon as given; in other words, metaphysics must be considered as really existing, if not as a science, nevertheless as a natural disposition of the human mind (metaphysica naturalis). For human reason, without any instigations imputable to the mere vanity of great knowledge, unceasingly progresses, urged on by its own feeling of need, towards such questions as cannot be answered by any empirical application of reason, or principles derived therefrom; and so there has ever really existed in every man some system of metaphysics. It will always exist, so soon as reason awakes to the exercise of its power of speculation. And now the question arises: "How is metaphysics, as a natural disposition, possible?" In other words, how, from the nature of universal human reason, do those questions arise which pure reason proposes to itself, and which it is impelled by its own feeling of need to answer as well as it can?

But as in all the attempts hitherto made to answer the questions which reason is prompted by its very nature to propose to itself, for example, whether the world had a beginning, or has existed from eternity, it has always met with unavoidable contradictions, we must not rest satisfied with the mere natural disposition of the mind to metaphysics, that is, with the existence of the faculty of pure reason, whence, indeed, some sort of metaphysical system always arises; but it must be possible to arrive at certainty in regard to the question whether we know or do not know the things of which metaphysics treats. We must be able to arrive at a decision on the subjects of its questions, or on the ability or inability of reason to form any judgement respecting them; and therefore either to extend with confidence the bounds of our pure reason, or to set strictly defined and safe limits to its action. This last question, which arises out of the above universal problem, would properly run thus: "How is metaphysics possible as a science?"

Thus, the critique of reason leads at last, naturally and necessarily, to science; and, on the other hand, the dogmatical use of reason without criticism leads to groundless assertions, against which others equally specious can always be set, thus ending unavoidably in scepticism.

Besides, this science cannot be of great and formidable prolixity, because it has not to do with objects of reason, the variety of which is inexhaustible, but merely with Reason herself and her problems; problems which arise out of her own bosom, and are not proposed to her by the nature of outward things, but by her own nature. And when once Reason has previously become able completely to understand her own power in regard to objects which she meets with in experience, it will be easy to determine securely the extent and limits of her attempted application to objects beyond the confines of experience.

We may and must, therefore, regard the attempts hitherto made to establish metaphysical science dogmatically as non-existent. For what of analysis, that is, mere dissection of conceptions, is contained in one or other, is not the aim of, but only a preparation for metaphysics proper, which has for its object the extension, by means of synthesis, of our a priori knowledge. And for this purpose, mere analysis is of course useless, because it only shows what is contained in these conceptions, but not how we arrive, a priori, at them; and this it is her duty to show, in order to be able afterwards to determine their valid use in regard to all objects of experience, to all knowledge in general. But little self-denial, indeed, is needed to give up these pretensions, seeing the undeniable, and in the dogmatic mode of procedure, inevitable contradictions of Reason with herself, have long since ruined the reputation of every system of metaphysics that has appeared up to this time. It will require more firmness to remain undeterred by difficulty from within, and opposition from without, from endeavouring, by a method quite opposed to all those hitherto followed, to further the growth and fruitfulness of a science indispensable to human reason — a science from which every branch it has borne may be cut away, but whose roots remain indestructible.

VII. Idea and Division of a Particular Science, under the Name of a Critique of Pure Reason.

From all that has been said, there results the idea of a particular science, which may be called the Critique of Pure Reason. For reason is the faculty which furnishes us with the principles of knowledge a priori. Hence, pure reason is the faculty which contains the principles of cognizing anything absolutely a priori. An organon of pure reason would be a compendium of those principles according to which alone all pure cognitions a priori can be obtained. The completely extended application of such an organon would afford us a system of pure reason. As this, however, is demanding a great deal, and it is yet doubtful whether any extension of our knowledge be here possible, or, if so, in what cases; we can regard a science of the mere criticism of pure reason, its sources and limits, as the propaedeutic to a system of pure reason. Such a science must not be called a doctrine, but only a critique of pure reason; and its use, in regard to speculation, would be only negative, not to enlarge the bounds of, but to purify, our reason, and to shield it against error — which alone is no little gain. I apply the term transcendental to all knowledge which is not so much occupied with objects as with the mode of our cognition of these objects, so far as this mode of cognition is possible a priori. A system of such conceptions would be called transcendental philosophy. But this, again, is still beyond the bounds of our present essay. For as such a science must contain a complete exposition not only of our synthetical a priori, but of our analytical a priori knowledge, it is of too wide a range for our present purpose, because we do not require to carry our analysis any farther than is necessary to understand, in their full extent, the principles of synthesis a priori, with which alone we have to do. This investigation, which we cannot properly call a doctrine, but only a transcendental critique, because it aims not at the enlargement, but at the correction and guidance, of our knowledge, and is to serve as a touchstone of the worth or worthlessness of all knowledge a priori, is the sole object of our present essay. Such a critique is consequently, as far as possible, a preparation for an organon; and if this new organon should be found to fail, at least for a canon of pure reason, according to which the complete system of the philosophy of pure reason, whether it extend or limit the bounds of that reason, might one day be set forth both analytically and synthetically. For that this is possible, nay, that such a system is not of so great extent as to preclude the hope of its ever being completed, is evident. For we have not here to do with the nature of outward objects, which is infinite, but solely with the mind, which judges of the nature of objects, and, again, with the mind only in respect of its cognition a priori. And the object of our investigations, as it is not to be sought without, but, altogether within, ourselves, cannot remain concealed, and in all probability is limited enough to be completely surveyed and fairly estimated, according to its worth or worthlessness. Still less let the reader here expect a critique of books and systems of pure reason; our present object is exclusively a critique of the faculty of pure reason itself. Only when we make this critique our foundation, do we possess a pure touchstone for estimating the philosophical value of ancient and modern writings on this subject; and without this criterion, the incompetent historian or judge decides upon and corrects the groundless assertions of others with his own, which have themselves just as little foundation.

Transcendental philosophy is the idea of a science, for which the Critique of Pure Reason must sketch the whole plan architectonically, that is, from principles, with a full guarantee for the validity and stability of all the parts which enter into the building. It is the system of all the principles of pure reason. If this Critique itself does not assume the title of transcendental philosophy, it is only because, to be a complete system, it ought to contain a full analysis of all human knowledge a priori. Our critique must, indeed, lay before us a complete enumeration of all the radical conceptions which constitute the said pure knowledge. But from the complete analysis of these conceptions themselves, as also from a complete investigation of those derived from them, it abstains with reason; partly because it would be deviating from the end in view to occupy itself with this analysis, since this process is not attended with the difficulty and insecurity to be found in the synthesis, to which our critique is entirely devoted, and partly because it would be inconsistent with the unity of our plan to burden this essay with the vindication of the completeness of such an analysis and deduction, with which, after all, we have at present nothing to do. This completeness of the analysis of these radical conceptions, as well as of the deduction from the conceptions a priori which may be given by the analysis, we can, however, easily attain, provided only that we are in possession of all these radical conceptions, which are to serve as principles of the synthesis, and that in respect of this main purpose nothing is wanting.

To the Critique of Pure Reason, therefore, belongs all that constitutes transcendental philosophy; and it is the complete idea of transcendental philosophy, but still not the science itself; because it only proceeds so far with the analysis as is necessary to the power of judging completely of our synthetical knowledge a priori.

The principal thing we must attend to, in the division of the parts of a science like this, is that no conceptions must enter it which contain aught empirical; in other words, that the knowledge a priori must be completely pure. Hence, although the highest principles and fundamental conceptions of morality are certainly cognitions a priori, yet they do not belong to transcendental philosophy; because, though they certainly do not lay the conceptions of pain, pleasure, desires, inclinations, etc. (which are all of empirical origin), at the foundation of its precepts, yet still into the conception of duty — as an obstacle to be overcome, or as an incitement which should not be made into a motive — these empirical conceptions must necessarily enter, in the construction of a system of pure morality. Transcendental philosophy is consequently a philosophy of the pure and merely speculative reason. For all that is practical, so far as it contains motives, relates to feelings, and these belong to empirical sources of cognition.

If we wish to divide this science from the universal point of view of a science in general, it ought to comprehend, first, a Doctrine of the Elements, and, secondly, a Doctrine of the Method of pure reason. Each of these main divisions will have its subdivisions, the separate reasons for which we cannot here particularize. Only so much seems necessary, by way of introduction of premonition, that there are two sources of human knowledge (which probably spring from a common, but to us unknown root), namely, sense and understanding. By the former, objects are given to us; by the latter, thought. So far as the faculty of sense may contain representations a priori, which form the conditions under which objects are given, in so far it belongs to transcendental philosophy. The transcendental doctrine of sense must form the first part of our science of elements, because the conditions under which alone the objects of human knowledge are given must precede those under which they are thought.

TRANSCENDENTAL DOCTRINE OF ELEMENTS.

FIRST PART. TRANSCENDENTAL AESTHETIC.

SSI. Introductory.

In whatsoever mode, or by whatsoever means, our knowledge may relate to objects, it is at least quite clear that the only manner in which it immediately relates to them is by means of an intuition. To this as the indispensable groundwork, all thought points. But an intuition can take place only in so far as the object is given to us. This, again, is only possible, to man at least, on condition that the object affect the mind in a certain manner. The capacity for receiving representations (receptivity) through the mode in which we are affected by objects, objects, is called sensibility. By means of sensibility, therefore, objects are given to us, and it alone furnishes us with intuitions; by the understanding they are thought, and from it arise conceptions. But an thought must directly, or indirectly, by means of certain signs, relate ultimately to intuitions; consequently, with us, to sensibility, because in no other way can an object be given to us.

The effect of an object upon the faculty of representation, so far as we are affected by the said object, is sensation. That sort of intuition which relates to an object by means of sensation is called an empirical intuition. The undetermined object of an empirical intuition is called phenomenon. That which in the phenomenon corresponds to the sensation, I term its matter; but that which effects that the content of the phenomenon can be arranged under certain relations, I call its form. But that in which our sensations are merely arranged, and by which they are susceptible of assuming a certain form, cannot be itself sensation. It is, then, the matter of all phenomena that is given to us a posteriori; the form must lie ready a priori for them in the mind, and consequently can be regarded separately from all sensation.

I call all representations pure, in the transcendental meaning of the word, wherein nothing is met with that belongs to sensation. And accordingly we find existing in the mind a priori, the pure form of sensuous intuitions in general, in which all the manifold content of the phenomenal world is arranged and viewed under certain relations. This pure form of sensibility I shall call pure intuition. Thus, if I take away from our representation of a body all that the understanding thinks as belonging to it, as substance, force, divisibility, etc., and also whatever belongs to sensation, as impenetrability, hardness, colour, etc.; yet there is still something left us from this empirical intuition, namely, extension and shape. These belong to pure intuition, which exists a priori in the mind, as a mere form of sensibility, and without any real object of the senses or any sensation.

The science of all the principles of sensibility a priori, I call transcendental aesthetic.* There must, then, be such a science forming the first part of the transcendental doctrine of elements, in contradistinction to that part which contains the principles of pure thought, and which is called transcendental logic.

[Note: The Germans are the only people who at present use this word to indicate what others call the critique of taste. At the foundation of this term lies the disappointed hope, which the eminent analyst, Baumgarten, conceived, of subjecting the criticism of the beautiful to principles of reason, and so of elevating its rules into a science. But his endeavours were vain. For the said rules or criteria are, in respect to their chief sources, merely empirical, consequently never can serve as determinate laws a priori, by which our judgement in matters of taste is to be directed. It is rather our judgement which forms the proper test as to the correctness of the principles. On this account it is advisable to give up the use of the term as designating the critique of taste, and to apply it solely to that doctrine, which is true science — the science of the laws of sensibility — and thus come nearer to the language and the sense of the ancients in their well-known division of the objects of cognition into aiotheta kai noeta, or to share it with speculative philosophy, and employ it partly in a transcendental, partly in a psychological signification.]

In the science of transcendental aesthetic accordingly, we shall first isolate sensibility or the sensuous faculty, by separating from it all that is annexed to its perceptions by the conceptions of understanding, so that nothing be left but empirical intuition. In the next place we shall take away from this intuition all that belongs to sensation, so that nothing may remain but pure intuition, and the mere form of phenomena, which is all that the sensibility can afford a priori. From this investigation it will be found that there are two pure forms of sensuous intuition, as principles of knowledge a priori, namely, space and time. To the consideration of these we shall now proceed.

SECTION I. Of Space.

SS2. Metaphysical Exposition of this Conception.

By means of the external sense (a property of the mind), we represent to ourselves objects as without us, and these all in space. Herein alone are their shape, dimensions, and relations to each other determined or determinable. The internal sense, by means of which the mind contemplates itself or its internal state, gives, indeed, no intuition of the soul as an object; yet there is nevertheless a determinate form, under which alone the contemplation of our internal state is possible, so that all which relates to the inward determinations of the mind is represented in relations of time. Of time we cannot have any external intuition, any more than we can have an internal intuition of space. What then are time and space? Are they real existences? Or, are they merely relations or determinations of things, such, however, as would equally belong to these things in themselves, though they should never become objects of intuition; or, are they such as belong only to the form of intuition, and consequently to the subjective constitution of the mind, without which these predicates of time and space could not be attached to any object? In order to become informed on these points, we shall first give an exposition of the conception of space. By exposition, I mean the clear, though not detailed, representation of that which belongs to a conception; and an exposition is metaphysical when it contains that which represents the conception as given a priori.

1. Space is not a conception which has been derived from outward experiences. For, in order that certain sensations may relate to something without me (that is, to something which occupies a different part of space from that in which I am); in like manner, in order that I may represent them not merely as without, of, and near to each other, but also in separate places, the representation of space must already exist as a foundation. Consequently, the representation of space cannot be borrowed from the relations of external phenomena through experience; but, on the contrary, this external experience is itself only possible through the said antecedent representation.

2. Space then is a necessary representation a priori, which serves for the foundation of all external intuitions. We never can imagine or make a representation to ourselves of the non-existence of space, though we may easily enough think that no objects are found in it. It must, therefore, be considered as the condition of the possibility of phenomena, and by no means as a determination dependent on them, and is a representation a priori, which necessarily supplies the basis for external phenomena.

3. Space is no discursive, or as we say, general conception of the relations of things, but a pure intuition. For, in the first place, we can only represent to ourselves one space, and, when we talk of divers spaces, we mean only parts of one and the same space. Moreover, these parts cannot antecede this one all-embracing space, as the component parts from which the aggregate can be made up, but can be cogitated only as existing in it. Space is essentially one, and multiplicity in it, consequently the general notion of spaces, of this or that space, depends solely upon limitations. Hence it follows that an a priori intuition (which is not empirical) lies at the root of all our conceptions of space. Thus, moreover, the principles of geometry — for example, that "in a triangle, two sides together are greater than the third," are never deduced from

general conceptions of line and triangle, but from intuition, and this a priori, with apodeictic certainty.

4. Space is represented as an infinite given quantity. Now every conception must indeed be considered as a representation which is contained in an infinite multitude of different possible representations, which, therefore, comprises these under itself; but no conception, as such, can be so conceived, as if it contained within itself an infinite multitude of representations. Nevertheless, space is so conceived of, for all parts of space are equally capable of being produced to infinity. Consequently, the original representation of space is an intuition a priori, and not a conception.

SS3. Transcendental Exposition of the Conception of Space.

By a transcendental exposition, I mean the explanation of a conception, as a principle, whence can be discerned the possibility of other synthetical a priori cognitions. For this purpose, it is requisite, firstly, that such cognitions do really flow from the given conception; and, secondly, that the said cognitions are only possible under the presupposition of a given mode of explaining this conception.

Geometry is a science which determines the properties of space synthetically, and yet a priori. What, then, must be our representation of space, in order that such a cognition of it may be possible? It must be originally intuition, for from a mere conception, no propositions can be deduced which go out beyond the conception, and yet this happens in geometry. (Introd. V.) But this intuition must be found in the mind a priori, that is, before any perception of objects, consequently must be pure, not empirical, intuition. For geometrical principles are always apodeictic, that is, united with the consciousness of their necessity, as: "Space has only three dimensions." But propositions of this kind cannot be empirical judgements, nor conclusions from them. (Introd. II.) Now, how can an external intuition anterior to objects themselves, and in which our conception of objects can be determined a priori, exist in the human mind? Obviously not otherwise than in so far as it has its seat in the subject only, as the formal capacity of the subject's being affected by objects, and thereby of obtaining immediate representation, that is, intuition; consequently, only as the form of the external sense in general.

Thus it is only by means of our explanation that the possibility of geometry, as a synthetical science a priori, becomes comprehensible. Every mode of explanation which does not show us this possibility, although in appearance it may be similar to ours, can with the utmost certainty be distinguished from it by these marks.

SS4. Conclusions from the foregoing Conceptions.

(a) Space does not represent any property of objects as things in themselves, nor does it represent them in their relations to each other; in other words, space does not represent to us any determination of objects such as attaches to the objects themselves, and would remain, even though all subjective conditions of the intuition were abstracted. For neither absolute nor relative determinations of objects can be intuited prior to the existence of the things to which they belong, and therefore not a priori.

(b) Space is nothing else than the form of all phenomena of the external sense, that is, the subjective condition of the sensibility, under which alone external intuition is possible. Now, because the receptivity or capacity of the subject to be affected by objects necessarily antecedes all intuitions of these objects, it is easily understood how the form of all phenomena can be given in the mind previous to all actual perceptions, therefore a priori, and how it, as a pure intuition, in which all objects must be determined, can contain principles of the relations of these objects prior to all experience.

It is therefore from the human point of view only that we can speak of space, extended objects, etc. If we depart from the subjective condition, under which alone we can obtain external intuition, or, in other words, by means of which we are affected by objects, the representation of space has no meaning whatsoever. This predicate is only applicable to things in so far as they appear to us, that is, are objects of sensibility. The constant form of this receptivity, which we call sensibility, is a necessary condition of all relations in which objects can be intuited as existing without us, and when abstraction of these objects is made, is a pure intuition, to which we give the name of space. It is clear that we cannot make the special conditions of sensibility into conditions of the possibility of things, but only of the possibility of their existence as far as they are phenomena. And so we may correctly say that space contains all which can appear to us externally, but not all things considered as things in themselves, be they intuited or not, or by whatsoever subject one will. As to the intuitions of other thinking beings, we cannot judge whether they are or are not bound by the same conditions which limit our own intuition, and which for us are universally valid. If we join the limitation of a judgement to the conception of the subject, then the judgement will possess unconditioned validity. For example, the proposition, "All objects are beside each other in space," is valid only under the limitation that these things are taken as objects of our sensuous intuition. But if I join the condition to the conception and say, "All things, as external phenomena, are beside each other in space," then the rule is valid universally, and without any limitation. Our expositions, consequently, teach the reality (i.e., the objective validity) of space in regard of all which can be presented to us externally as object, and at the same time also the ideality of space in regard to objects when they are considered by means of reason as things in themselves, that is, without reference to the constitution of our sensibility. We maintain, therefore, the empirical reality of space in regard to all possible external experience, although we must admit its transcendental ideality; in other words, that it is nothing, so soon as we withdraw the condition upon which the possibility of all experience depends and look upon space as something that belongs to things in themselves.

But, with the exception of space, there is no representation, subjective and referring to something external to us, which could be called objective a priori. For there are no other subjective representations from which we can deduce synthetical propositions a priori, as we can from the intuition of space. (See SS 3.) Therefore, to speak accurately, no ideality whatever belongs to these, although they agree in this respect with the representation of space, that they belong merely to the subjective nature of the mode of sensuous perception; such a mode, for example, as that of sight, of hearing, and of feeling, by means of the sensations of colour, sound, and heat, but which, because they are only sensations and not intuitions, do not of themselves give us the cognition of any object, least of all, an a priori cognition. My purpose, in the above remark, is merely this: to guard any one against illustrating the asserted ideality of space by examples quite insufficient, for example, by colour, taste, etc.; for these must be contemplated not as properties of things, but only as changes in the subject, changes which may be different in different men. For, in such a case, that which is originally a mere phenomenon, a rose, for example, is taken by the empirical understanding for a thing in itself, though to every different eye, in respect of its colour, it may appear different. On the contrary, the transcendental conception of phenomena in space is a critical admonition, that, in general, nothing which is intuited in space is a thing in itself, and that space is not a form which belongs as a property to things; but that objects are quite unknown to us in themselves, and what we call outward objects, are nothing else but mere representations of our sensibility, whose form is space, but whose real correlate, the thing in itself, is not known by means of these representations, nor ever can be, but respecting which, in experience, no inquiry is ever made.

SECTION II. Of Time.

SS5. Metaphysical Exposition of this Conception.

1. Time is not an empirical conception. For neither coexistence nor succession would be perceived by us, if the representation of time did not exist as a foundation a priori. Without this presupposition we could not represent to ourselves that things exist together at one and the same time, or at different times, that is, contemporaneously, or in succession.

2. Time is a necessary representation, lying at the foundation of all our intuitions. With regard to phenomena in general, we cannot think away time from them, and represent them to ourselves as out of and unconnected with time, but we can quite well represent to ourselves time void of phenomena. Time is therefore given a priori. In it alone is all reality of phenomena possible. These may all be annihilated in thought, but time itself, as the universal condition of their possibility, cannot be so annulled.

3. On this necessity a priori is also founded the possibility of apodeictic principles of the relations of time, or axioms of time in general, such as: "Time has only one dimension," "Different times are not coexistent but successive" (as different spaces are not successive but coexistent). These principles cannot be derived from experience, for it would give neither strict universality, nor apodeictic certainty. We should only be able to say, "so common experience teaches us," but not "it must be so." They are valid as rules, through which, in general, experience is possible; and they instruct us respecting experience, and not by means of it.

4. Time is not a discursive, or as it is called, general conception, but a pure form of the sensuous intuition. Different times are merely parts of one and the same time. But the representation which can only be given by a single object is an intuition. Besides, the proposition that different times cannot be coexistent could not be derived from a general conception. For this proposition is synthetical, and therefore cannot spring out of conceptions alone. It is therefore contained immediately in the intuition and representation of tlme.

5. The infinity of time signifies nothing more than that every determined quantity of time is possible only through limitations of one time lying at the foundation. Consequently, the original representation, time, must be given as unlimited. But as the determinate representation of the parts of time and of every quantity of an object can only be obtained by limitation, the complete representation of time must not be furnished by means of conceptions, for these contain only partial representations. Conceptions, on the contrary, must have immediate intuition for their basis.

SS6 Transcendental Exposition of the Conception of Time.

I may here refer to what is said above (SS 5, 3), where, for or sake of brevity, I have placed under the head of metaphysical exposition, that which is properly transcendental. Here I shall add that the conception of change, and with it the conception of motion, as change of place, is possible only through and in the representation of time; that if this representation were not an intuition (internal) a priori, no conception, of whatever kind, could render comprehensible the possibility of change, in other words, of a conjunction of contradictorily opposed predicates in one and the same object, for example, the presence of a thing in a place and the non-presence of the same thing in the same place. It is only in time that it is possible to meet with two contradictorily opposed determinations in one thing, that is, after each other. Thus our conception of time explains the possibility of so much synthetical knowledge a priori, as is exhibited in the general doctrine of motion, which is not a little fruitful.

SS7. Conclusions from the above Conceptions.

(a) Time is not something which subsists of itself, or which inheres in things as an objective determination, and therefore remains, when abstraction is made of the subjective conditions of the intuition of things. For in the former case, it would be something real, yet without presenting to any power of perception any real object. In the latter case, as an order or determination inherent in things themselves, it could not be antecedent to things, as their condition, nor discerned or intuited by means of synthetical propositions a priori. But all this is quite possible when we regard time as merely the subjective condition under which all our intuitions take place. For in that case, this form of the inward intuition can be represented prior to the objects, and consequently a priori.

(b) Time is nothing else than the form of the internal sense, that is, of the intuitions of self and of our internal state. For time cannot be any determination of outward phenomena. It has to do neither with shape nor position; on the contrary, it determines the relation of representations in our internal state. And precisely because this internal intuition presents to us no shape or form, we endeavour to supply this want by analogies, and represent the course of time by a line progressing to infinity, the content of which constitutes a series which is only of one dimension; and we conclude from the properties of this line as to all the properties of time, with this single exception, that the parts of the line are coexistent, whilst those of time are successive. From this it is clear also that the representation of time is itself an intuition, because all its relations can be expressed in an external intuition.

(c) Time is the formal condition a priori of all phenomena whatsoever. Space, as the pure form of external intuition, is limited as a condition a priori to external phenomena alone. On the other hand, because all representations, whether they have or have not external things for their objects, still in themselves, as determinations of the mind, belong to our internal state; and because this internal state is subject to the formal condition of the internal intuition, that is, to time — time is a condition a priori of all phenomena whatsoever — the immediate condition of all internal, and thereby the mediate condition of all external phenomena. If I can say a priori, "All outward phenomena are in space, and determined a priori according to the relations of space," I can also, from the principle of the internal sense, affirm universally, "All phenomena in general, that is, all objects of the senses, are in time and stand necessarily in relations of time."

If we abstract our internal intuition of ourselves and all external intuitions, possible only by virtue of this internal intuition and presented to us by our faculty of representation, and consequently take objects as they are in themselves, then time is nothing. It is only of objective validity in regard to phenomena, because these are things which we regard as objects of our senses. It no longer objective we, make abstraction of the sensuousness of our intuition, in other words, of that mode of representation which is peculiar to us, and speak of things in general. Time is therefore merely a subjective condition of our (human) intuition (which is always sensuous, that is, so far as we are affected by objects), and in itself, independently of the mind or subject, is nothing. Nevertheless, in respect of all phenomena, consequently of all things which come within the sphere of our experience, it is necessarily objective. We cannot say, "All things are in time," because in this conception of things in general, we abstract and make no mention of any sort of intuition of things. But this is the proper condition under which time belongs to our representation of objects. If we add the condition to the conception, and say, "All things, as phenomena, that is, objects of sensuous intuition, are in time," then the proposition has its sound objective validity and universality a priori.

What we have now set forth teaches, therefore, the empirical reality of time; that is, its objective validity in reference to all objects which can ever be presented to our senses. And as our intuition is always sensuous, no object ever can be presented to us in experience, which does not come under the conditions of time. On the other hand, we deny to time all claim to absolute reality; that is, we deny that it, without having regard to the form of our sensuous intuition, absolutely inheres in things as a condition or property. Such properties as belong to objects as things in themselves never can be presented to us through the medium of the senses. Herein consists, therefore, the transcendental ideality of time, according to which, if we abstract the subjective conditions of sensuous intuition, it is nothing, and cannot be reckoned as subsisting or inhering in objects as things in themselves, independently of its relation to our intuition. This ideality, like that of space, is not to be proved or illustrated by fallacious analogies with sensations, for this reason — that in such arguments or illustrations, we make the presupposition that the phenomenon, in which such and such predicates inhere, has objective reality, while in this case we can only find such an objective reality as is itself empirical, that is, regards the object as a mere phenomenon. In reference to this subject, see the remark in Section I (SS 4)

SS8. Elucidation.

Against this theory, which grants empirical reality to time, but denies to it absolute and transcendental reality, I have heard from intelligent men an objection so unanimously urged that I conclude that it must naturally present itself to every reader to whom these considerations are novel. It runs thus: "Changes are real" (this the continual change in our own representations demonstrates, even though the existence of all external phenomena, together with their changes, is denied). Now, changes are only possible in time, and therefore time must be something real. But there is no difficulty in answering this. I grant the whole argument. Time, no doubt, is something real, that is, it is the real form of our internal intuition. It therefore has subjective reality, in reference to our internal experience, that is, I have really the representation of time and of my determinations therein. Time, therefore, is not to be regarded as an object, but as the mode of representation of myself as an object. But if I could intuite myself, or be intuited by another being, without this condition of sensibility, then those very determinations which we now represent to ourselves as changes, would present to us a knowledge in which the representation of time, and consequently of change, would not appear. The empirical reality of time, therefore, remains, as the condition of all our experience. But absolute reality, according to what has been said above, cannot be granted it. Time is nothing but the form of our internal intuition.* If we take away from it the special condition of our sensibility, the conception of time also vanishes; and it inheres not in the objects themselves, but solely in the subject (or mind) which intuites them.

[Note: I can indeed say "my representations follow one another, or are successive"; but this means only that we are conscious of them as in a succession, that is, according to the form of the internal sense. Time, therefore, is not a thing in itself, nor is it any objective determination pertaining to, or inherent in things.]

But the reason why this objection is so unanimously brought against our doctrine of time, and that too by disputants who cannot start any intelligible arguments against the doctrine of the ideality of space, is this — they have no hope of demonstrating apodeictically the absolute reality of space, because the doctrine of idealism is against them, according to which the reality of external objects is not capable of any strict proof. On the other hand, the reality of the object of our internal sense (that is, myself and my internal state) is clear immediately through consciousness. The former — external objects in space — might be a mere delusion, but the latter — the object of my internal perception — is undeniably real. They do not, however, reflect that both, without question of their reality as representations, belong only to the genus phenomenon, which has always two aspects, the one, the object considered as a thing in itself, without regard to the mode of intuiting it, and the nature of which remains for this very reason problematical, the other, the form of our intuition of the object, which must be sought not in the object as a thing in itself, but in the subject to which it appears — which form of intuition nevertheless belongs really and necessarily to the phenomenal object.

Time and space are, therefore, two sources of knowledge, from which, a priori, various synthetical cognitions can be drawn. Of this we find a striking example in the cognitions of space and its relations, which form the foundation of pure mathematics. They are the two pure forms of all intuitions, and thereby make synthetical propositions a priori possible. But these sources of knowledge being merely conditions of our sensibility, do therefore, and as such, strictly determine their own range and purpose, in that they do not and cannot present objects as things in themselves, but are applicable to them solely in so far as they are considered as sensuous phenomena. The sphere of phenomena is the only sphere of their validity, and if we venture out of this, no further objective use can be made of them. For the rest, this formal reality of time and space leaves the validity of our empirical knowledge unshaken; for our certainty in that respect is equally firm, whether these forms necessarily inhere in the things themselves, or only in our intuitions of them. On the other hand, those who maintain the absolute reality of time and space, whether as essentially subsisting, or only inhering, as modifications, in things, must find themselves at utter variance with the principles of experience itself. For, if they decide for the first view, and make space and time into substances, this being the side taken by mathematical natural philosophers, they must admit two self-subsisting nonentities, infinite and eternal, which exist (yet without there being anything real) for the purpose of containing in themselves everything that is real. If they adopt the second view of inherence, which is preferred by some metaphysical natural philosophers, and regard space and time as relations (contiguity in space or succession in time), abstracted from experience, though represented confusedly in this state of separation, they find themselves in that case necessitated to deny the validity of mathematical doctrines a priori in reference to real things (for example, in space) — at all events their apodeictic certainty. For such certainty cannot be found in an a posteriori proposition; and the conceptions a priori of space and time are, according to this opinion, mere creations of the imagination, having their source really in experience, inasmuch as, out of relations abstracted from experience, imagination has made up something which contains, indeed, general statements of these relations, yet of which no application can be made without the restrictions attached thereto by nature. The former of these parties gains this advantage, that they keep the sphere of phenomena free for mathematical science. On the other hand, these very conditions (space and time) embarrass them greatly, when the understanding endeavours to pass the limits of that sphere. The latter has, indeed, this advantage, that the representations of space and time do not come in their way when they wish to judge of objects, not as phenomena, but merely in their relation to the understanding. Devoid, however, of a true and objectively valid a priori intuition, they can neither furnish any basis for the possibility of mathematical cognitions a priori, nor bring the propositions of experience into necessary accordance with those of mathematics. In our theory of the true nature of these two original forms of the sensibility, both difficulties are surmounted.

In conclusion, that transcendental aesthetic cannot contain any more than these two elements — space and time, is sufficiently obvious from the fact that all other conceptions appertaining to sensibility, even that of motion, which unites in itself both elements, presuppose something empirical. Motion, for example, presupposes the perception of something movable. But space considered in itself contains nothing movable, consequently motion must be something which is found in space only through experience — in other words, an empirical datum. In like manner, transcendental aesthetic cannot number the conception of change among its data a priori; for time itself does not change, but only something which is in time. To acquire the conception of change, therefore, the perception of some existing object and of the succession of its determinations, in one word, experience, is necessary.

SS9. General Remarks on Transcendental Aesthetic.

I. In order to prevent any misunderstanding, it will be requisite, in the first place, to recapitulate, as clearly as possible, what our opinion is with respect to the fundamental nature of our sensuous cognition in general. We have intended, then, to say that all our intuition is nothing but the representation of phenomena; that the things which we intuite, are not in themselves the same as our representations of them in intuition, nor are their relations in themselves so constituted as they appear to us; and that if we take away the subject, or even only the subjective constitution of our senses in general, then not only the nature and relations of objects in space and time, but even space and time themselves disappear; and that these, as phenomena, cannot exist in themselves, but only in us. What may be the nature of objects considered as things in themselves and without reference to the receptivity of our sensibility is quite unknown to us. We know nothing more than our mode of perceiving them, which is peculiar to us, and which, though not of necessity pertaining to every animated being, is so to the whole human race. With this alone we have to do. Space and time are the pure forms thereof; sensation the matter. The former alone can we cognize a priori, that is, antecedent to all actual perception; and for this reason such cognition is called pure intuition. The latter is that in our cognition which is called cognition a posteriori, that is, empirical intuition. The former appertain absolutely and necessarily to our sensibility, of whatsoever kind our sensations may be; the latter may be of very diversified character. Supposing that we should carry our empirical intuition even to the very highest degree of clearness, we should not thereby advance one step nearer to a knowledge of the constitution of objects as things in themselves. For we could only, at best, arrive at a complete cognition of our own mode of intuition, that is of our sensibility, and this always under the conditions originally attaching to the subject, namely, the conditions of space and time; while the question: "What are objects considered as things in themselves?" remains unanswerable even after the most thorough examination of the phenomenal world.

To say, then, that all our sensibility is nothing but the confused representation of things containing exclusively that which belongs to them as things in themselves, and this under an accumulation of characteristic marks and partial representations which we cannot distinguish in consciousness, is a falsification of the conception of sensibility and phenomenization, which renders our whole doctrine thereof empty and useless. The difference between a confused and a clear representation is merely logical and has nothing to do with content. No doubt the conception of right, as employed by a sound understanding, contains all that the most subtle investigation could unfold from it, although, in the ordinary practical use of the word, we are not conscious of the manifold representations comprised in the conception. But we cannot for this reason assert that the ordinary conception is a sensuous one, containing a mere phenomenon, for right cannot appear as a phenomenon; but the conception of it lies in the understanding, and represents a property (the moral property) of actions, which belongs to them in themselves. On the other hand, the representation in intuition of a body contains nothing which could belong to an object considered as a thing in itself, but merely the phenomenon or appearance of something, and the mode in which we are affected by that appearance; and this receptivity of our faculty of cognition is called sensibility, and remains toto caelo different from the cognition of an object in itself, even though we should examine the content of the phenomenon to the very bottom.

It must be admitted that the Leibnitz-Wolfian philosophy has assigned an entirely erroneous point of view to all investigations into the nature and origin of our cognitions, inasmuch as it regards the distinction between the sensuous and the intellectual as merely logical, whereas it is plainly transcendental, and concerns not merely the clearness or obscurity, but the content and origin of both. For the faculty of sensibility not only does not present us with an indistinct and confused cognition of objects as things in themselves, but, in fact, gives us no knowledge of these at all. On the contrary, so soon as we abstract in thought our own subjective nature, the object represented, with the properties ascribed to it by sensuous intuition, entirely disappears, because it was only this subjective nature that determined the form of the object as a phenomenon.

In phenomena, we commonly, indeed, distinguish that which essentially belongs to the intuition of them, and is valid for the sensuous faculty of every human being, from that which belongs to the same intuition accidentally, as valid not for the sensuous faculty in general, but for a particular state or organization of this or that sense. Accordingly, we are accustomed to say that the former is a cognition which represents the object itself, whilst the latter presents only a particular appearance or phenomenon thereof. This distinction, however, is only empirical. If we stop here (as is usual), and do not regard the empirical intuition as itself a mere phenomenon (as we ought to do), in which nothing that can appertain to a thing in itself is to be found, our transcendental distinction is lost, and we believe that we cognize objects as things in themselves, although in the whole range of the sensuous world, investigate the nature of its objects as profoundly as we may, we have to do with nothing but phenomena. Thus, we call the rainbow a mere appearance of phenomenon in a sunny shower, and the rain, the reality or thing in itself; and this is right enough, if we understand the latter conception in a merely physical sense, that is, as that which in universal experience, and under whatever conditions of sensuous perception, is known in intuition to be so and so determined, and not otherwise. But if we consider this empirical datum generally, and inquire, without reference to its accordance with all our senses, whether there can be discovered in it aught which represents an object as a thing in itself (the raindrops of course are not such, for they are, as phenomena, empirical objects), the question of the relation of the representation to the object is transcendental; and not only are the raindrops mere phenomena, but even their circular form, nay, the space itself through which they fall, is nothing in itself, but both are mere modifications or fundamental dispositions of our sensuous intuition, whilst the transcendental object remains for us utterly unknown.

The second important concern of our aesthetic is that it does not obtain favour merely as a plausible hypothesis, but possess as undoubted a character of certainty as can be demanded of any theory which is to serve for an organon. In order fully to convince the reader of this certainty, we shall select a case which will serve to make its validity apparent, and also to illustrate what has been said in SS 3.

Suppose, then, that space and time are in themselves objective, and conditions of the — possibility of objects as things in themselves. In the first place, it is evident that both present us, with very many apodeictic and synthetic propositions a priori, but especially space — and for this reason we shall prefer it for investigation at present. As the propositions of geometry are cognized synthetically a priori, and with apodeictic certainty, I inquire: Whence do you obtain propositions of this kind, and on what basis does the understanding rest, in order to arrive at such absolutely necessary and universally valid truths?

There is no other way than through intuitions or conceptions, as such; and these are given either a priori or a posteriori. The latter, namely, empirical conceptions, together with the empirical intuition on which they are founded, cannot afford any synthetical proposition, except such as is itself also empirical, that is, a proposition of experience. But an empirical proposition cannot possess the qualities of necessity and absolute universality, which, nevertheless, are the characteristics of all geometrical propositions. As to the first and only means to arrive at such cognitions, namely, through mere conceptions or intuitions a priori, it is quite clear that from mere conceptions no synthetical cognitions, but only analytical ones, can be obtained. Take, for example, the proposition: "Two straight lines cannot enclose a space, and with these alone no figure is possible," and try to deduce it from the conception of a straight line and the number two; or take the proposition: "It is possible to construct a figure with three straight lines," and endeavour, in like manner, to deduce it from the mere conception of a straight line and the number three. All your endeavours are in vain, and you find yourself forced to have recourse to intuition, as, in fact, geometry always does. You therefore give yourself an object in intuition. But of what kind is this intuition? Is it a pure a priori, or is it an empirical intuition? If the latter, then neither an universally valid, much less an apodeictic proposition can arise from it, for experience never can give us any such proposition. You must, therefore, give yourself an object a priori in intuition, and upon that ground your synthetical proposition. Now if there did not exist within you a faculty of intuition a priori; if this subjective condition were not in respect to its form also the universal condition a priori under which alone the object of this external intuition is itself possible; if the object (that is, the triangle) were something in itself, without relation to you the subject; how could you affirm that that which lies necessarily in your subjective conditions in order to construct a triangle, must also necessarily belong to the triangle in itself? For to your conceptions of three lines, you could not add anything new (that is, the figure); which, therefore, must necessarily be found in the object, because the object is given before your cognition, and not by means of it. If, therefore, space (and time also) were not a mere form of your intuition, which contains conditions a priori, under which alone things can become external objects for you, and without which subjective conditions the objects are in themselves nothing, you could not construct any synthetical proposition whatsoever regarding external objects. It is therefore not merely possible or probable, but indubitably certain, that space and time, as the necessary conditions of all our external and internal experience, are merely subjective conditions of all our intuitions, in relation to which all objects are therefore mere phenomena, and not things in themselves, presented to us in this particular manner. And for this reason, in respect to the form of phenomena, much may be said a priori, whilst of the thing in itself, which may lie at the foundation of these phenomena, it is impossible to say anything.

II. In confirmation of this theory of the ideality of the external as well as internal sense, consequently of all objects of sense, as mere phenomena, we may especially remark that all in our cognition that belongs to intuition contains nothing more than mere relations. (The feelings of pain and pleasure, and the will, which are not cognitions, are excepted.) The relations, to wit, of place in an intuition (extension), change of place (motion), and laws according to which this change is determined (moving forces). That, however, which is present in this or that place, or any operation going on, or result taking place in the things themselves, with the exception of change of place, is not given to us by intuition. Now by means of mere relations, a thing cannot be known in itself; and it may therefore be fairly concluded, that, as through the external sense nothing but mere representations of relations are given us, the said external sense in its representation can contain only the relation of the object to the subject, but not the essential nature of the object as a thing in itself.

The same is the case with the internal intuition, not only because, in the internal intuition, the representation of the external senses constitutes the material with which the mind is occupied; but because time, in which we place, and which itself antecedes the consciousness of, these representations in experience, and which, as the formal condition of the mode according to which objects are placed in the mind, lies at the foundation of them, contains relations of the successive, the coexistent, and of that which always must be coexistent with succession, the permanent. Now that which, as representation, can antecede every exercise of thought (of an object), is intuition; and when it contains nothing but relations, it is the form of the intuition, which, as it presents us with no representation, except in so far as something is placed in the mind, can be nothing else than the mode in which the mind is affected by its own activity, to wit — its presenting to itself representations, consequently the mode in which the mind is affected by itself; that is, it can be nothing but an internal sense in respect to its form. Everything that is represented through the medium of sense is so far phenomenal; consequently, we must either refuse altogether to admit an internal sense, or the subject, which is the object of that sense, could only be represented by it as phenomenon, and not as it would judge of itself, if its intuition were pure spontaneous activity, that is, were intellectual. The difficulty here lies wholly in the question: How can the subject have an internal intuition of itself? But this difficulty is common to every theory. The consciousness of self (apperception) is the simple representation of the "ego"; and if by means of that representation alone, all the manifold representations in the subject were spontaneously given, then our internal intuition would be intellectual. This consciousness in man requires an internal perception of the manifold representations which are previously given in the subject; and the manner in which these representations are given in the mind without spontaneity, must, on account of this difference (the want of spontaneity), be called sensibility. If the faculty of self-consciousness is to apprehend what lies in the mind, it must all act that and can in this way alone produce an intuition of self. But the form of this intuition, which lies in the original constitution of the mind, determines, in the representation of time, the manner in which the manifold representations are to combine themselves in the mind; since the subject intuites itself, not as it would represent itself immediately and spontaneously, but according to the manner in which the mind is internally affected, consequently, as it appears, and not as it is.

III. When we say that the intuition of external objects, and also the self-intuition of the subject, represent both, objects and subject, in space and time, as they affect our senses, that is, as they appear — this is by no means equivalent to asserting that these objects are mere illusory appearances. For when we speak of things as phenomena, the objects, nay, even the properties which we ascribe to them, are looked upon as really given; only that, in so far as this or that property depends upon the mode of intuition of the subject, in the relation of the given object to the subject, the object as phenomenon is to be distinguished from the object as a thing in itself. Thus I do not say that bodies seem or appear to be external to me, or that my soul seems merely to be given in my self-consciousness, although I maintain that the properties of space and time, in conformity to which I set both, as the condition of their existence, abide in my mode of intuition, and not in the objects in themselves. It would be my own fault, if out of that which I should reckon as phenomenon, I made mere illusory appearance.* But this will not happen, because of our principle of the ideality of all sensuous intuitions. On the contrary, if we ascribe objective reality to these forms of representation, it becomes impossible to avoid changing everything into mere appearance. For if we regard space and time as properties, which must be found in objects as things in themselves, as sine quibus non of the possibility of their existence, and reflect on the absurdities in which we then find ourselves involved, inasmuch as we are compelled to admit the existence of two infinite things, which are nevertheless not substances, nor anything really inhering in substances, nay, to admit that they are the necessary conditions of the existence of all things, and moreover, that they must continue to exist, although all existing things were annihilated — we cannot blame the good Berkeley for degrading bodies to mere illusory appearances. Nay, even our own existence, which would in this case depend upon the self-existent reality of such a mere nonentity as time, would necessarily be changed with it into mere appearance — an absurdity which no one has as yet been guilty of.

[Note: The predicates of the phenomenon can be affixed to the object itself in relation to our sensuous faculty; for example, the red colour or the perfume to the rose. But (illusory) appearance never can be attributed as a predicate to an object, for this very reason, that it attributes to this object in itself that which belongs to it only in relation to our sensuous faculty, or to the subject in general, e.g., the two handles which were formerly ascribed to Saturn. That which is never to be found in the object itself, but always in the relation of the object to the subject, and which moreover is inseparable from our representation of the object, we denominate phenomenon. Thus the predicates of space and time are rightly attributed to objects of the senses as such, and in this there is no illusion. On the contrary, if I ascribe redness of the rose as a thing in itself, or to Saturn his handles, or extension to all external objects, considered as things in themselves, without regarding the determinate relation of these objects to the subject, and without limiting my judgement to that relation — then, and then only, arises illusion.]

IV. In natural theology, where we think of an object — God — which never can be an object of intuition to us, and even to himself can never be an object of sensuous intuition, we carefully avoid attributing to his intuition the conditions of space and time — and intuition all his cognition must be, and not thought, which always includes limitation. But with what right can we do this if we make them forms of objects as things in themselves, and such, moreover, as would continue to exist as a priori conditions of the existence of things, even though the things themselves were annihilated? For as conditions of all existence in general, space and time must be conditions of the existence of the Supreme Being also. But if we do not thus make them objective forms of all things, there is no other way left than to make them subjective forms of our mode of intuition — external and internal; which is called sensuous, because it is not primitive, that is, is not such as gives in itself the existence of the object of the intuition (a mode of intuition which, so far as we can judge, can belong only to the Creator), but is dependent on the existence of the object, is possible, therefore, only on condition that the representative faculty of the subject is affected by the object.

It is, moreover, not necessary that we should limit the mode of intuition in space and time to the sensuous faculty of man. It may well be that all finite thinking beings must necessarily in this respect agree with man (though as to this we cannot decide), but sensibility does not on account of this universality cease to be sensibility, for this very reason, that it is a deduced (intuitus derivativus), and not an original (intuitus originarius), consequently not an intellectual intuition, and this intuition, as such, for reasons above mentioned, seems to belong solely to the Supreme Being, but never to a being dependent, quoad its existence, as well as its intuition (which its existence determines and limits relatively to given objects). This latter remark, however, must be taken only as an illustration, and not as any proof of the truth of our aesthetical theory.

SS10. Conclusion of the Transcendental Aesthetic.

We have now completely before us one part of the solution of the grand general problem of transcendental philosophy, namely, the question: "How are synthetical propositions a priori possible?" That is to say, we have shown that we are in possession of pure a priori intuitions, namely, space and time, in which we find, when in a judgement a priori we pass out beyond the given conception, something which is not discoverable in that conception, but is certainly found a priori in the intuition which corresponds to the conception, and can be united synthetically with it. But the judgements which these pure intuitions enable us to make, never reach farther than to objects of the senses, and are valid only for objects of possible experience.

SECOND PART. TRANSCENDENTAL LOGIC.

INTRODUCTION. Idea of a Transcendental Logic.

I. Of Logic in General.

Our knowledge springs from two main sources in the mind, first of which is the faculty or power of receiving representations (receptivity for impressions); the second is the power of cognizing by means of these representations (spontaneity in the production of conceptions). Through the first an object is given to us; through the second, it is, in relation to the representation (which is a mere determination of the mind), thought. Intuition and conceptions constitute, therefore, the elements of all our knowledge, so that neither conceptions without an intuition in some way corresponding to them, nor intuition without conceptions, can afford us a cognition. Both are either pure or empirical. They are empirical, when sensation (which presupposes the actual presence of the object) is contained in them; and pure, when no sensation is mixed with the representation. Sensations we may call the matter of sensuous cognition. Pure intuition consequently contains merely the form under which something is intuited, and pure conception only the form of the thought of an object. Only pure intuitions and pure conceptions are possible a priori; the empirical only a posteriori.

We apply the term sensibility to the receptivity of the mind for impressions, in so far as it is in some way affected; and, on the other hand, we call the faculty of spontaneously producing representations, or the spontaneity of cognition, understanding. Our nature is so constituted that intuition with us never can be other than sensuous, that is, it contains only the mode in which we are affected by objects. On the other hand, the faculty of thinking the object of sensuous intuition is the understanding. Neither of these faculties has a preference over the other. Without the sensuous faculty no object would be given to us, and without the understanding no object would be thought. Thoughts without content are void; intuitions without conceptions, blind. Hence it is as necessary for the mind to make its conceptions sensuous (that is, to join to them the object in intuition), as to make its intuitions intelligible (that is, to bring them under conceptions). Neither of these faculties can exchange its proper function. Understanding cannot intuite, and the sensuous faculty cannot think. In no other way than from the united operation of both, can knowledge arise. But no one ought, on this account, to overlook the difference of the elements contributed by each; we have rather great reason carefully to separate and distinguish them. We therefore distinguish the science of the laws of sensibility, that is, aesthetic, from the science of the laws of the understanding, that is, logic.

Now, logic in its turn may be considered as twofold — namely, as logic of the general, or of the particular use of the understanding. The first contains the absolutely necessary laws of thought, without which no use whatsoever of the understanding is possible, and gives laws therefore to the understanding, without regard to the difference of objects on which it may be employed. The logic of the particular use of the understanding contains the laws of correct thinking upon a particular class of objects. The former may be called elemental logic — the latter, the organon of this or that particular science. The latter is for the most part employed in the schools, as a propaedeutic to the sciences, although, indeed, according to the course of human reason, it is the last thing we arrive at, when the science has been already matured, and needs only the finishing touches towards its correction and completion; for our knowledge of the objects of our attempted science must be tolerably extensive and complete before we can indicate the laws by which a science of these objects can be established.

General logic is again either pure or applied. In the former, we abstract all the empirical conditions under which the understanding is exercised; for example, the influence of the senses, the play of the fantasy or imagination, the laws of the memory, the force of habit, of inclination, etc., consequently also, the sources of prejudice — in a word, we abstract all causes from which particular cognitions arise, because these causes regard the understanding under certain circumstances of its application, and, to the knowledge of them experience is required. Pure general logic has to do, therefore, merely with pure a priori principles, and is a canon of understanding and reason, but only in respect of the formal part of their use, be the content what it may, empirical or transcendental. General logic is called applied, when it is directed to the laws of the use of the understanding, under the subjective empirical conditions which psychology teaches us. It has therefore empirical principles, although, at the same time, it is in so far general, that it applies to the exercise of the understanding, without regard to the difference of objects. On this account, moreover, it is neither a canon of the understanding in general, nor an organon of a particular science, but merely a cathartic of the human understanding.

In general logic, therefore, that part which constitutes pure logic must be carefully distinguished from that which constitutes applied (though still general) logic. The former alone is properly science, although short and dry, as the methodical exposition of an elemental doctrine of the understanding ought to be. In this, therefore, logicians must always bear in mind two rules:

1. As general logic, it makes abstraction of all content of the cognition of the understanding, and of the difference of objects, and has to do with nothing but the mere form of thought.

2. As pure logic, it has no empirical principles, and consequently draws nothing (contrary to the common persuasion) from psychology, which therefore has no influence on the canon of the understanding. It is a demonstrated doctrine, and everything in it must be certain completely a priori.

What I called applied logic (contrary to the common acceptation of this term, according to which it should contain certain exercises for the scholar, for which pure logic gives the rules), is a representation of the understanding, and of the rules of its necessary employment in concreto, that is to say, under the accidental conditions of the subject, which may either hinder or promote this employment, and which are all given only empirically. Thus applied logic treats of attention, its impediments and consequences, of the origin of error, of the state of doubt, hesitation, conviction, etc., and to it is related pure general logic in the same way that pure morality, which contains only the necessary moral laws of a free will, is related to practical ethics, which considers these laws under all the impediments of feelings, inclinations, and passions to which men are more or less subjected, and which never can furnish us with a true and demonstrated science, because it, as well as applied logic, requires empirical and psychological principles.

II. Of Transcendental Logic.

General logic, as we have seen, makes abstraction of all content of cognition, that is, of all relation of cognition to its object, and regards only the logical form in the relation of cognitions to each other, that is, the form of thought in general. But as we have both pure and empirical intuitions (as transcendental aesthetic proves), in like manner a distinction might be drawn between pure and empirical thought (of objects). In this case, there would exist a kind of logic, in which we should not make abstraction of all content of cognition; for or logic which should comprise merely the laws of pure thought (of an object), would of course exclude all those cognitions which were of empirical content. This kind of logic would also examine the origin of our cognitions of objects, so far as that origin cannot be ascribed to the objects themselves; while, on the contrary, general logic has nothing to do with the origin of our cognitions, but contemplates our representations, be they given primitively a priori in ourselves, or be they only of empirical origin, solely according to the laws which the understanding observes in employing them in the process of thought, in relation to each other. Consequently, general logic treats of the form of the understanding only, which can be applied to representations, from whatever source they may have arisen.

And here I shall make a remark, which the reader must bear well in mind in the course of the following considerations, to wit, that not every cognition a priori, but only those through which we cognize that and how certain representations (intuitions or conceptions) are applied or are possible only a priori; that is to say, the a priori possibility of cognition and the a priori use of it are transcendental. Therefore neither is space, nor any a priori geometrical determination of space, a transcendental Representation, but only the knowledge that such a representation is not of empirical origin, and the possibility of its relating to objects of experience, although itself a priori, can be called transcendental. So also, the application of space to objects in general would be transcendental; but if it be limited to objects of sense it is empirical. Thus, the distinction of the transcendental and empirical belongs only to the critique of cognitions, and does not concern the relation of these to their object.

Accordingly, in the expectation that there may perhaps be conceptions which relate a priori to objects, not as pure or sensuous intuitions, but merely as acts of pure thought (which are therefore conceptions, but neither of empirical nor aesthetical origin) — in this expectation, I say, we form to ourselves, by anticipation, the idea of a science of pure understanding and rational cognition, by means of which we may cogitate objects entirely a priori. A science of this kind, which should determine the origin, the extent, and the objective validity of such cognitions, must be called transcendental logic, because it has not, like general logic, to do with the laws of understanding and reason in relation to empirical as well as pure rational cognitions without distinction, but concerns itself with these only in an a priori relation to objects.

III. Of the Division of General Logic into Analytic and Dialectic.

The old question with which people sought to push logicians into a corner, so that they must either have recourse to pitiful sophisms or confess their ignorance, and consequently the vanity of their whole art, is this: "What is truth?" The definition of the word truth, to wit, "the accordance of the cognition with its object," is presupposed in the question; but we desire to be told, in the answer to it, what is the universal and secure criterion of the truth of every cognition.

To know what questions we may reasonably propose is in itself a strong evidence of sagacity and intelligence. For if a question be in itself absurd and unsusceptible of a rational answer, it is attended with the danger — not to mention the shame that falls upon the person who proposes it — of seducing the unguarded listener into making absurd answers, and we are presented with the ridiculous spectacle of one (as the ancients said) "milking the he-goat, and the other holding a sieve."

If truth consists in the accordance of a cognition with its object, this object must be, ipso facto, distinguished from all others; for a cognition is false if it does not accord with the object to which it relates, although it contains something which may be affirmed of other objects. Now an universal criterion of truth would be that which is valid for all cognitions, without distinction of their objects. But it is evident that since, in the case of such a criterion, we make abstraction of all the content of a cognition (that is, of all relation to its object), and truth relates precisely to this content, it must be utterly absurd to ask for a mark of the truth of this content of cognition; and that, accordingly, a sufficient, and at the same time universal, test of truth cannot possibly be found. As we have already termed the content of a cognition its matter, we shall say: "Of the truth of our cognitions in respect of their matter, no universal test can be demanded, because such a demand is self-contradictory."

On the other hand, with regard to our cognition in respect of its mere form (excluding all content), it is equally manifest that logic, in so far as it exhibits the universal and necessary laws of the understanding, must in these very laws present us with criteria of truth. Whatever contradicts these rules is false, because thereby the understanding is made to contradict its own universal laws of thought; that is, to contradict itself. These criteria, however, apply solely to the form of truth, that is, of thought in general, and in so far they are perfectly accurate, yet not sufficient. For although a cognition may be perfectly accurate as to logical form, that is, not self-contradictory, it is notwithstanding quite possible that it may not stand in agreement with its object. Consequently, the merely logical criterion of truth, namely, the accordance of a cognition with the universal and formal laws of understanding and reason, is nothing more than the conditio sine qua non, or negative condition of all truth. Farther than this logic cannot go, and the error which depends not on the form, but on the content of the cognition, it has no test to discover.

General logic, then, resolves the whole formal business of understanding and reason into its elements, and exhibits them as principles of all logical judging of our cognitions. This part of logic may, therefore, be called analytic, and is at least the negative test of truth, because all cognitions must first of an be estimated and tried according to these laws before we proceed to investigate them in respect of their content, in order to discover whether they contain positive truth in regard to their object. Because, however, the mere form of a cognition, accurately as it may accord with logical laws, is insufficient to supply us with material (objective) truth, no one, by means of logic alone, can venture to predicate anything of or decide concerning objects, unless he has obtained, independently of logic, well-grounded information about them, in order afterwards to examine, according to logical laws, into the use and connection, in a cohering whole, of that information, or, what is still better, merely to test it by them. Notwithstanding, there lies so seductive a charm in the possession of a specious art like this — an art which gives to all our cognitions the form of the understanding, although with respect to the content thereof we may be sadly deficient — that general logic, which is merely a canon of judgement, has been employed as an organon for the actual production, or rather for the semblance of production, of objective assertions, and has thus been grossly misapplied. Now general logic, in its assumed character of organon, is called dialectic.

Different as are the significations in which the ancients used this term for a science or an art, we may safely infer, from their actual employment of it, that with them it was nothing else than a logic of illusion — a sophistical art for giving ignorance, nay, even intentional sophistries, the colouring of truth, in which the thoroughness of procedure which logic requires was imitated, and their topic employed to cloak the empty pretensions. Now it may be taken as a safe and useful warning, that general logic, considered as an organon, must always be a logic of illusion, that is, be dialectical, for, as it teaches us nothing whatever respecting the content of our cognitions, but merely the formal conditions of their accordance with the understanding, which do not relate to and are quite indifferent in respect of objects, any attempt to employ it as an instrument (organon) in order to extend and enlarge the range of our knowledge must end in mere prating; any one being able to maintain or oppose, with some appearance of truth, any single assertion whatever.

Such instruction is quite unbecoming the dignity of philosophy. For these reasons we have chosen to denominate this part of logic dialectic, in the sense of a critique of dialectical illusion, and we wish the term to be so understood in this place.

IV. Of the Division of Transcendental Logic into Transcendental Analytic and Dialectic.

In transcendental logic we isolate the understanding (as in transcendental aesthetic the sensibility) and select from our cognition merely that part of thought which has its origin in the understanding alone. The exercise of this pure cognition, however, depends upon this as its condition, that objects to which it may be applied be given to us in intuition, for without intuition the whole of our cognition is without objects, and is therefore quite void. That part of transcendental logic, then, which treats of the elements of pure cognition of the understanding, and of the principles without which no object at all can be thought, is transcendental analytic, and at the same time a logic of truth. For no cognition can contradict it, without losing at the same time all content, that is, losing all reference to an object, and therefore all truth. But because we are very easily seduced into employing these pure cognitions and principles of the understanding by themselves, and that even beyond the boundaries of experience, which yet is the only source whence we can obtain matter (objects) on which those pure conceptions may be employed — understanding runs the risk of making, by means of empty sophisms, a material and objective use of the mere formal principles of the pure understanding, and of passing judgements on objects without distinction — objects which are not given to us, nay, perhaps cannot be given to us in any way. Now, as it ought properly to be only a canon for judging of the empirical use of the understanding, this kind of logic is misused when we seek to employ it as an organon of the universal and unlimited exercise of the understanding, and attempt with the pure understanding alone to judge synthetically, affirm, and determine respecting objects in general. In this case the exercise of the pure understanding becomes dialectical. The second part of our transcendental logic must therefore be a critique of dialectical illusion, and this critique we shall term transcendental dialectic — not meaning it as an art of producing dogmatically such illusion (an art which is unfortunately too current among the practitioners of metaphysical juggling), but as a critique of understanding and reason in regard to their hyperphysical use. This critique will expose the groundless nature of the pretensions of these two faculties, and invalidate their claims to the discovery and enlargement of our cognitions merely by means of transcendental principles, and show that the proper employment of these faculties is to test the judgements made by the pure understanding, and to guard it from sophistical delusion.

FIRST DIVISION. TRANSCENDENTAL ANALYTIC.

SSI.

Transcendental analytic is the dissection of the whole of our a priori knowledge into the elements of the pure cognition of the understanding. In order to effect our purpose, it is necessary: (1) That the conceptions be pure and not empirical; (2) That they belong not to intuition and sensibility, but to thought and understanding; (3) That they be elementary conceptions, and as such, quite different from deduced or compound conceptions; (4) That our table of these elementary conceptions be complete, and fill up the whole sphere of the pure understanding. Now this completeness of a science cannot be accepted with confidence on the guarantee of a mere estimate of its existence in an aggregate formed only by means of repeated experiments and attempts. The completeness which we require is possible only by means of an idea of the totality of the a priori cognition of the understanding, and through the thereby determined division of the conceptions which form the said whole; consequently, only by means of their connection in a system. Pure understanding distinguishes itself not merely from everything empirical, but also completely from all sensibility. It is a unity self-subsistent, self-sufficient, and not to be enlarged by any additions from without. Hence the sum of its cognition constitutes a system to be determined by and comprised under an idea; and the completeness and articulation of this system can at the same time serve as a test of the correctness and genuineness of all the parts of cognition that belong to it. The whole of this part of transcendental logic consists of two books, of which the one contains the conceptions, and the other the principles of pure understanding.

BOOK I. Analytic of Conceptions.

By the term Analytic of Conceptions, I do not understand the analysis of these, or the usual process in philosophical investigations of dissecting the conceptions which present themselves, according to their content, and so making them clear; but I mean the hitherto little attempted dissection of the faculty of understanding itself, in order to investigate the possibility of conceptions a priori, by looking for them in the understanding alone, as their birthplace, and analysing the pure use of this faculty. For this is the proper duty of a transcendental philosophy; what remains is the logical treatment of the conceptions in philosophy in general. We shall therefore follow up the pure conceptions even to their germs and beginnings in the human understanding, in which they lie, until they are developed on occasions presented by experience, and, freed by the same understanding from the empirical conditions attaching to them, are set forth in their unalloyed purity.

CHAPTER I.
Of the Transcendental Clue to the Discovery of all Pure Conceptions of the Understanding.

SS3. Introductory.

When we call into play a faculty of cognition, different conceptions manifest themselves according to the different circumstances, and make known this faculty, and assemble themselves into a more or less extensive collection, according to the time or penetration that has been applied to the consideration of them. Where this process, conducted as it is mechanically, so to speak, will end, cannot be determined with certainty. Besides, the conceptions which we discover in this haphazard manner present themselves by no means in order and systematic unity, but are at last coupled together only according to resemblances to each other, and arranged in series, according to the quantity of their content, from the simpler to the more complex — series which are anything but systematic, though not altogether without a certain kind of method in their construction.

Transcendental philosophy has the advantage, and moreover the duty, of searching for its conceptions according to a principle; because these conceptions spring pure and unmixed out of the understanding as an absolute unity, and therefore must be connected with each other according to one conception or idea. A connection of this kind, however, furnishes us with a ready prepared rule, by which its proper place may be assigned to every pure conception of the understanding, and the completeness of the system of all be determined a priori — both which would otherwise have been dependent on mere choice or chance.

SS4. SECTION 1. Of defined above Use of understanding in General.

The understanding was defined above only negatively, as a non-sensuous faculty of cognition. Now, independently of sensibility, we cannot possibly have any intuition; consequently, the understanding is no faculty of intuition. But besides intuition there is no other mode of cognition, except through conceptions; consequently, the cognition of every, at least of every human, understanding is a cognition through conceptions — not intuitive, but discursive. All intuitions, as sensuous, depend on affections; conceptions, therefore, upon functions. By the word function I understand the unity of the act of arranging diverse representations under one common representation. Conceptions, then, are based on the spontaneity of thought, as sensuous intuitions are on the receptivity of impressions. Now, the understanding cannot make any other use of these conceptions than to judge by means of them. As no representation, except an intuition, relates immediately to its object, a conception never relates immediately to an object, but only to some other representation thereof, be that an intuition or itself a conception. A judgement, therefore, is the mediate cognition of an object, consequently the representation of a representation of it. In every judgement there is a conception which applies to, and is valid for many other conceptions, and which among these comprehends also a given representation, this last being immediately connected with an object. For example, in the judgement— "All bodies are divisible," our conception of divisible applies to various other conceptions; among these, however, it is here particularly applied to the conception of body, and this conception of body relates to certain phenomena which occur to us. These objects, therefore, are mediately represented by the conception of divisibility. All judgements, accordingly, are functions of unity in our representations, inasmuch as, instead of an immediate, a higher representation, which comprises this and various others, is used for our cognition of the object, and thereby many possible cognitions are collected into one. But we can reduce all acts of the understanding to judgements, so that understanding may be represented as the faculty of judging. For it is, according to what has been said above, a faculty of thought. Now thought is cognition by means of conceptions. But conceptions, as predicates of possible judgements, relate to some representation of a yet undetermined object. Thus the conception of body indicates something — for example, metal — which can be cognized by means of that conception. It is therefore a conception, for the reason alone that other representations are contained under it, by means of which it can relate to objects. It is therefore the predicate to a possible judgement; for example: "Every metal is a body." All the functions of the understanding therefore can be discovered, when we can completely exhibit the functions of unity in judgements. And that this may be effected very easily, the following section will show.

SS5. SECTION II. Of the Logical Function of the Understanding in Judgements.

If we abstract all the content of a judgement, and consider only the intellectual form thereof, we find that the function of thought in a judgement can be brought under four heads, of which each contains three momenta. These may be conveniently represented in the following table:

1

Quantity of judgements

Universal

Particular

Singular

2		3
Quality		*Relation*
Affirmative		Categorical
Negative		Hypothetical
Infinite		Disjunctive

4

Modality

Problematical

Assertorical

Apodeictical

As this division appears to differ in some, though not essential points, from the usual technique of logicians, the following observations, for the prevention of otherwise possible misunderstanding, will not be without their use.

1. Logicians say, with justice, that in the use of judgements in syllogisms, singular judgements may be treated like universal ones. For, precisely because a singular judgement has no extent at all, its predicate cannot refer to a part of that which is contained in the conception of the subject and be excluded from the rest. The predicate is valid for the whole conception just as if it were a general conception, and had extent, to the whole of which the predicate applied. On the other hand, let us compare a singular with a general judgement, merely as a cognition, in regard to quantity. The singular judgement relates to the general one, as unity to infinity, and is therefore in itself essentially different. Thus, if we estimate a singular judgement (judicium singulare) not merely according to its intrinsic validity as a judgement, but also as a cognition generally, according to its quantity in comparison with that of other cognitions, it is then entirely different from a general judgement (judicium commune), and in a complete table of the momenta of thought deserves a separate place — though, indeed, this would not be necessary in a logic limited merely to the consideration of the use of judgements in reference to each other.

2. In like manner, in transcendental logic, infinite must be distinguished from affirmative judgements, although in general logic they are rightly enough classed under affirmative. General logic abstracts all content of the predicate (though it be negative), and only considers whether the said predicate be affirmed or denied of the subject. But transcendental logic considers also the worth or content of this logical affirmation — an affirmation by means of a merely negative predicate, and inquires how much the sum total of our cognition gains by this affirmation. For example, if I say of the soul, "It is not mortal" — by this negative judgement I should at least ward off error. Now, by the proposition, "The soul is not mortal," I have, in respect of the logical form, really affirmed, inasmuch as I thereby place the soul in the unlimited sphere of immortal beings. Now, because of the whole sphere of possible existences, the mortal occupies one part, and the immortal the other, neither more nor less is affirmed by the proposition than that the soul is one among the infinite multitude of things which remain over, when I take away the whole mortal part. But by this proceeding we accomplish only this much, that the infinite sphere of all possible existences is in so far limited that the mortal is excluded from it, and the soul is placed in the remaining part of the extent of this sphere. But this part remains, notwithstanding this exception, infinite, and more and more parts may be taken away from the whole sphere, without in the slightest degree thereby augmenting or affirmatively determining our conception of the soul. These judgements, therefore, infinite in respect of their logical extent, are, in respect of the content of their cognition, merely limitative; and are consequently entitled to a place in our transcendental table of all the momenta of thought in judgements, because the function of the understanding exercised by them may perhaps be of importance in the field of its pure a priori cognition.

3. All relations of thought in judgements are those (a) of the predicate to the subject; (b) of the principle to its consequence; (c) of the divided cognition and all the members of the division to each other. In the first of these three classes, we consider only two

conceptions; in the second, two judgements; in the third, several judgements in relation to each other. The hypothetical proposition, "If perfect justice exists, the obstinately wicked are punished," contains properly the relation to each other of two propositions, namely, "Perfect justice exists," and "The obstinately wicked are punished." Whether these propositions are in themselves true is a question not here decided. Nothing is cogitated by means of this judgement except a certain consequence. Finally, the disjunctive judgement contains a relation of two or more propositions to each other — a relation not of consequence, but of logical opposition, in so far as the sphere of the one proposition excludes that of the other. But it contains at the same time a relation of community, in so far as all the propositions taken together fill up the sphere of the cognition. The disjunctive judgement contains, therefore, the relation of the parts of the whole sphere of a cognition, since the sphere of each part is a complemental part of the sphere of the other, each contributing to form the sum total of the divided cognition. Take, for example, the proposition, "The world exists either through blind chance, or through internal necessity, or through an external cause." Each of these propositions embraces a part of the sphere of our possible cognition as to the existence of a world; all of them taken together, the whole sphere. To take the cognition out of one of these spheres, is equivalent to placing it in one of the others; and, on the other hand, to place it in one sphere is equivalent to taking it out of the rest. There is, therefore, in a disjunctive judgement a certain community of cognitions, which consists in this, that they mutually exclude each other, yet thereby determine, as a whole, the true cognition, inasmuch as, taken together, they make up the complete content of a particular given cognition. And this is all that I find necessary, for the sake of what follows, to remark in this place.

4. The modality of judgements is a quite peculiar function, with this distinguishing characteristic, that it contributes nothing to the content of a judgement (for besides quantity, quality, and relation, there is nothing more that constitutes the content of a judgement), but concerns itself only with the value of the copula in relation to thought in general. Problematical judgements are those in which the affirmation or negation is accepted as merely possible (ad libitum). In the assertorical, we regard the proposition as real (true); in the apodeictical, we look on it as necessary.* Thus the two judgements (antecedens et consequens), the relation of which constitutes a hypothetical judgement, likewise those (the members of the division) in whose reciprocity the disjunctive consists, are only problematical. In the example above given the proposition, "There exists perfect justice," is not stated assertorically, but as an ad libitum judgement, which someone may choose to adopt, and the consequence alone is assertorical. Hence such judgements may be obviously false, and yet, taken problematically, be conditions of our cognition of the truth. Thus the proposition, "The world exists only by blind chance," is in the disjunctive judgement of problematical import only: that is to say, one may accept it for the moment, and it helps us (like the indication of the wrong road among all the roads that one can take) to find out the true proposition. The problematical proposition is, therefore, that which expresses only logical possibility (which is not objective); that is, it expresses a free choice to admit the validity of such a proposition — a merely arbitrary reception of it into the understanding. The assertorical speaks of logical reality or truth; as, for example, in a hypothetical syllogism, the antecedens presents itself in a problematical form in

the major, in an assertorical form in the minor, and it shows that the proposition is in harmony with the laws of the understanding. The apodeictical proposition cogitates the assertorical as determined by these very laws of the understanding, consequently as affirming a priori, and in this manner it expresses logical necessity. Now because all is here gradually incorporated with the understanding — inasmuch as in the first place we judge problematically; then accept assertorically our judgement as true; lastly, affirm it as inseparably united with the understanding, that is, as necessary and apodeictical — we may safely reckon these three functions of modality as so many momenta of thought.

[Note: Just as if thought were in the first instance a function of the understanding; in the second, of judgement; in the third, of reason. A remark which will be explained in the sequel.]

SS6. SECTION III. Of the Pure Conceptions of the Understanding, or Categories.

General logic, as has been repeatedly said, makes abstraction of all content of cognition, and expects to receive representations from some other quarter, in order, by means of analysis, to convert them into conceptions. On the contrary, transcendental logic has lying before it the manifold content of a priori sensibility, which transcendental aesthetic presents to it in order to give matter to the pure conceptions of the understanding, without which transcendental logic would have no content, and be therefore utterly void. Now space and time contain an infinite diversity of determinations of pure a priori intuition, but are nevertheless the condition of the mind's receptivity, under which alone it can obtain representations of objects, and which, consequently, must always affect the conception of these objects. But the spontaneity of thought requires that this diversity be examined after a certain manner, received into the mind, and connected, in order afterwards to form a cognition out of it. This Process I call synthesis.

By the word synthesis, in its most general signification, I understand the process of joining different representations to each other and of comprehending their diversity in one cognition. This synthesis is pure when the diversity is not given empirically but a priori (as that in space and time). Our representations must be given previously to any analysis of them; and no conceptions can arise, quoad their content, analytically. But the synthesis of a diversity (be it given a priori or empirically) is the first requisite for the production of a cognition, which in its beginning, indeed, may be crude and confused, and therefore in need of analysis — still, synthesis is that by which alone the elements of our cognitions are collected and united into a certain content, consequently it is the first thing on which we must fix our attention, if we wish to investigate the origin of our knowledge.

Synthesis, generally speaking, is, as we shall afterwards see, the mere operation of the imagination — a blind but indispensable function of the soul, without which we should have no cognition whatever, but of the working of which we are seldom even conscious. But to reduce this synthesis to conceptions is a function of the understanding, by means of which we attain to cognition, in the proper meaning of the term.

Pure synthesis, represented generally, gives us the pure conception of the understanding. But by this pure synthesis, I mean that which rests upon a basis of a priori synthetical unity. Thus, our numeration (and this is more observable in large numbers) is a synthesis according to conceptions, because it takes place according to a common basis of unity (for example, the decade). By means of this conception, therefore, the unity in the synthesis of the manifold becomes necessary.

By means of analysis different representations are brought under one conception — an operation of which general logic treats. On the other hand, the duty of transcendental logic is to reduce to conceptions, not representations, but the pure synthesis of representations. The first thing which must be given to us for the sake of the a priori cognition of all objects, is the diversity of the pure intuition; the synthesis of this diversity by means of the imagination is the second; but this gives, as yet, no cognition. The conceptions which give unity to this pure synthesis, and which consist solely in the representation of this necessary synthetical unity, furnish the third requisite for the cognition of an object, and these conceptions are given by the understanding.

The same function which gives unity to the different representation in a judgement, gives also unity to the mere synthesis of different representations in an intuition; and this unity we call the pure conception of the understanding. Thus, the same understanding, and by the same operations, whereby in conceptions, by means of analytical unity, it produced the logical form of a judgement, introduces, by means of the synthetical unity of the manifold in intuition, a transcendental content into its representations, on which account they are called pure conceptions of the understanding, and they apply a priori to objects, a result not within the power of general logic.

In this manner, there arise exactly so many pure conceptions of the understanding, applying a priori to objects of intuition in general, as there are logical functions in all possible judgements. For there is no other function or faculty existing in the understanding besides those enumerated in that table. These conceptions we shall, with Aristotle, call categories, our purpose being originally identical with his, notwithstanding the great difference in the execution.

This, then, is a catalogue of all the originally pure conceptions of the synthesis which the understanding contains a priori, and these conceptions alone entitle it to be called a pure understanding; inasmuch as only by them it can render the manifold of intuition conceivable, in other words, think an object of intuition. This division is made systematically from a common principle, namely the faculty of judgement (which is just the same as the power of thought), and has not arisen rhapsodically from a search at haphazard after pure conceptions, respecting the full number of which we never could be certain, inasmuch as we employ induction alone in our search, without considering that in this way we can never understand wherefore precisely these conceptions, and none others, abide in the pure understanding. It was a design worthy of an acute thinker like Aristotle, to search for these fundamental conceptions. Destitute, however, of any guiding principle, he picked them up just as they occurred to him, and at first hunted out ten, which he called categories (predicaments). Afterwards be believed that he had discovered five others, which were added under the name of post predicaments. But his catalogue still remained defective. Besides, there are to be found among them some of the modes of pure sensibility (quando, ubi, situs, also prius, simul), and likewise an empirical conception (motus) — which can by no means belong to this genealogical register of the pure understanding. Moreover, there are deduced conceptions (actio, passio) enumerated among the original conceptions, and, of the latter, some are entirely wanting.

With regard to these, it is to be remarked, that the categories, as the true primitive conceptions of the pure understanding, have also their pure deduced conceptions, which, in a complete system of transcendental philosophy, must by no means be passed over; though in a merely critical essay we must be contented with the simple mention of the fact.

Let it be allowed me to call these pure, but deduced conceptions of the understanding, the predicables of the pure understanding, in contradistinction to predicaments. If we are in possession of the original and primitive, the deduced and subsidiary conceptions can easily be added, and the genealogical tree of the understanding completely delineated. As my present aim is not to set forth a complete system, but merely the principles of one, I reserve this task for another time. It may be easily executed by any one who will refer to the ontological manuals, and subordinate to the category of causality, for example, the predicables of force, action, passion; to that of community, those of presence and resistance; to the categories of modality, those of origination, extinction, change; and so with the rest. The categories combined with the modes of pure sensibility, or with one another, afford a great number of deduced a priori conceptions; a complete enumeration of which would be a useful and not unpleasant, but in this place a perfectly dispensable, occupation.

I purposely omit the definitions of the categories in this treatise. I shall analyse these conceptions only so far as is necessary for the doctrine of method, which is to form a part of this critique. In a system of pure reason, definitions of them would be with justice demanded of me, but to give them here would only bide from our view the main aim of our investigation, at the same time raising doubts and objections, the consideration of which, without injustice to our main purpose, may be very well postponed till another opportunity. Meanwhile, it ought to be sufficiently clear, from the little we have already said on this subject, that the formation of a complete vocabulary of pure conceptions, accompanied by all the requisite explanations, is not only a possible, but an easy undertaking. The compartments already exist; it is only necessary to fill them up; and a systematic topic like the present, indicates with perfect precision the proper place to which each conception belongs, while it readily points out any that have not yet been filled up.

SS7.

Our table of the categories suggests considerations of some importance, which may perhaps have significant results in regard to the scientific form of all rational cognitions. For, that this table is useful in the theoretical part of philosophy, nay, indispensable for the sketching of the complete plan of a science, so far as that science rests upon conceptions a priori, and for dividing it mathematically, according to fixed principles, is most manifest from the fact that it contains all the elementary conceptions of the understanding, nay, even the form of a system of these in the understanding itself, and consequently indicates all the momenta, and also the internal arrangement of a projected speculative science, as I have elsewhere shown. [Note: In the Metaphysical Principles of Natural Science.] Here follow some of these observations.

I. This table, which contains four classes of conceptions of the understanding, may, in the first instance, be divided into two classes, the first of which relates to objects of intuition — pure as well as empirical; the second, to the existence of these objects, either in relation to one another, or to the understanding.

The former of these classes of categories I would entitle the mathematical, and the latter the dynamical categories. The former, as we see, has no correlates; these are only to be found in the second class. This difference must have a ground in the nature of the human understanding.

II. The number of the categories in each class is always the same, namely, three — a fact which also demands some consideration, because in all other cases division a priori through conceptions is necessarily dichotomy. It is to be added, that the third category in each triad always arises from the combination of the second with the first.

Thus totality is nothing else but plurality contemplated as unity; limitation is merely reality conjoined with negation; community is the causality of a substance, reciprocally determining, and determined by other substances; and finally, necessity is nothing but existence, which is given through the possibility itself. Let it not be supposed, however, that the third category is merely a deduced, and not a primitive conception of the pure understanding. For the conjunction of the first and second, in order to produce the third conception, requires a particular function of the understanding, which is by no means identical with those which are exercised in the first and second. Thus, the conception of a number (which belongs to the category of totality) is not always possible, where the conceptions of multitude and unity exist (for example, in the representation of the infinite). Or, if I conjoin the conception of a cause with that of a substance, it does not follow that the conception of influence, that is, how one substance can be the cause of something in another substance, will be understood from that. Thus it is evident that a particular act of the understanding is here necessary; and so in the other instances.

III. With respect to one category, namely, that of community, which is found in the third class, it is not so easy as with the others to detect its accordance with the form of the disjunctive judgement which corresponds to it in the table of the logical functions.

In order to assure ourselves of this accordance, we must observe that in every disjunctive judgement, the sphere of the judgement (that is, the complex of all that is contained in it) is represented as a whole divided into parts; and, since one part cannot be contained in the other, they are cogitated as co-ordinated with, not subordinated to each other, so that they do not determine each other unilaterally, as in a linear series, but reciprocally, as in an aggregate — (if one member of the division is posited, all the rest are excluded; and conversely).

Now a like connection is cogitated in a whole of things; for one thing is not subordinated, as effect, to another as cause of its existence, but, on the contrary, is co-ordinated contemporaneously and reciprocally, as a cause in relation to the determination of the others (for example, in a body — the parts of which mutually attract and repel each other). And this is an entirely different kind of connection from that which we find in the mere relation of the cause to the effect (the principle to the consequence), for in such a connection the consequence does not in its turn determine the principle, and therefore does not constitute, with the latter, a whole — just as the Creator does not with the world make up a whole. The process of understanding by which it represents to itself the sphere of a divided conception, is employed also when we think of a thing as divisible; and in the same manner as the members of the division in the former exclude one another, and yet are connected in one sphere, so the understanding represents to itself the parts of the latter, as having — each of them — an existence (as substances), independently of the others, and yet as united in one whole.

SS8.

In the transcendental philosophy of the ancients there exists one more leading division, which contains pure conceptions of the understanding, and which, although not numbered among the categories, ought, according to them, as conceptions a priori, to be valid of objects. But in this case they would augment the number of the categories; which cannot be. These are set forth in the proposition, so renowned among the schoolmen— "Quodlibet ens est UNUM, VERUM, BONUM." Now, though the inferences from this principle were mere tautological propositions, and though it is allowed only by courtesy to retain a place in modern metaphysics, yet a thought which maintained itself for such a length of time, however empty it seems to be, deserves an investigation of its origin, and justifies the conjecture that it must be grounded in some law of the understanding, which, as is often the case, has only been erroneously interpreted. These pretended transcendental predicates are, in fact, nothing but logical requisites and criteria of all cognition of objects, and they employ, as the basis for this cognition, the categories of quantity, namely, unity, plurality, and totality. But these, which must be taken as material conditions, that is, as belonging to the possibility of things themselves, they employed merely in a formal signification, as belonging to the logical requisites of all cognition, and yet most unguardedly changed these criteria of thought into properties of objects, as things in themselves. Now, in every cognition of an object, there is unity of conception, which may be called qualitative unity, so far as by this term we understand only the unity in our connection of the manifold; for example, unity of the theme in a play, an oration, or a story. Secondly, there is truth in respect of the deductions from it. The more true deductions we have from a given conception, the more criteria of its objective reality. This we might call the qualitative plurality of characteristic marks, which belong to a conception as to a common foundation, but are not cogitated as a quantity in it. Thirdly, there is perfection — which consists in this, that the plurality falls back upon the unity of the conception, and accords completely with that conception and with no other. This we may denominate qualitative completeness. Hence it is evident that these logical criteria of the possibility of cognition are merely the three categories of quantity modified and transformed to suit an unauthorized manner of applying them. That is to say, the three categories, in which the unity in the production of the quantum must be homogeneous throughout, are transformed solely with a view to the connection of heterogeneous parts of cognition in one act of consciousness, by means of the quality of the cognition, which is the principle of that connection. Thus the criterion of the possibility of a conception (not of its object) is the definition of it, in which the unity of the conception, the truth of all that may be immediately deduced from it, and finally, the completeness of what has been thus deduced, constitute the requisites for the reproduction of the whole conception. Thus also, the criterion or test of an hypothesis is the intelligibility of the received principle of explanation, or its unity (without help from any subsidiary hypothesis) — the truth of our deductions from it (consistency with each other and with experience) — and lastly, the completeness of the principle of the explanation of these deductions, which refer to neither more nor less than what was admitted in the hypothesis, restoring analytically and a posteriori, what was cogitated synthetically and a priori. By the conceptions, therefore, of unity, truth, and perfection, we have made no addition to the transcendental table of the categories, which is complete without them. We have, on the contrary, merely employed the three categories of quantity, setting aside their application to objects of experience, as general logical laws of the consistency of cognition with itself.

CHAPTER II
Of the Deduction of the Pure Conceptions of the Understanding.

SS9.

SECTION I Of the Principles of a Transcendental Deduction in general.

Teachers of jurisprudence, when speaking of rights and claims, distinguish in a cause the question of right (quid juris) from the question of fact (quid facti), and while they demand proof of both, they give to the proof of the former, which goes to establish right or claim in law, the name of deduction. Now we make use of a great number of empirical conceptions, without opposition from any one; and consider ourselves, even without any attempt at deduction, justified in attaching to them a sense, and a supposititious signification, because we have always experience at hand to demonstrate their objective reality. There exist also, however, usurped conceptions, such as fortune, fate, which circulate with almost universal indulgence, and yet are occasionally challenged by the question, "quid juris?" In such cases, we have great difficulty in discovering any deduction for these terms, inasmuch as we cannot produce any manifest ground of right, either from experience or from reason, on which the claim to employ them can be founded.

Among the many conceptions, which make up the very variegated web of human cognition, some are destined for pure use a priori, independent of all experience; and their title to be so employed always requires a deduction, inasmuch as, to justify such use of them, proofs from experience are not sufficient; but it is necessary to know how these conceptions can apply to objects without being derived from experience. I term, therefore, an examination of the manner in which conceptions can apply a priori to objects, the transcendental deduction of conceptions, and I distinguish it from the empirical deduction, which indicates the mode in which conception is obtained through experience and reflection thereon; consequently, does not concern itself with the right, but only with the fact of our obtaining conceptions in such and such a manner. We have already seen that we are in possession of two perfectly different kinds of conceptions, which nevertheless agree with each other in this, that they both apply to objects completely a priori. These are the conceptions of space and time as forms of sensibility, and the categories as pure conceptions of the understanding. To attempt an empirical deduction of either of these classes would be labour in vain, because the distinguishing characteristic of their nature consists in this, that they apply to their objects, without having borrowed anything from experience towards the representation of them. Consequently, if a deduction of these conceptions is necessary, it must always be transcendental.

Meanwhile, with respect to these conceptions, as with respect to all our cognition, we certainly may discover in experience, if not the principle of their possibility, yet the occasioning causes of their production. It will be found that the impressions of sense give the first occasion for bringing into action the whole faculty of cognition, and for the production of experience, which contains two very dissimilar elements, namely, a matter for cognition, given by the senses, and a certain form for the arrangement of this matter, arising out of the inner fountain of pure intuition and thought; and these, on occasion given by sensuous impressions, are called into exercise and produce conceptions. Such an investigation into the first efforts of our faculty of cognition to mount from particular perceptions to general conceptions is undoubtedly of great utility; and we have to thank the celebrated Locke for having first opened the way for this inquiry. But a deduction of the pure a priori conceptions of course never can be made in this way, seeing that, in regard to their future employment, which must be entirely independent of experience, they must have a far different certificate of birth to show from that of a descent from experience. This attempted physiological derivation, which cannot properly be called deduction, because it relates merely to a quaestio facti, I shall entitle an explanation of the possession of a pure cognition. It is therefore manifest that there can only be a transcendental deduction of these conceptions and by no means an empirical one; also, that all attempts at an empirical deduction, in regard to pure a priori conceptions, are vain, and can only be made by one who does not understand the altogether peculiar nature of these cognitions.

But although it is admitted that the only possible deduction of pure a priori cognition is a transcendental deduction, it is not, for that reason, perfectly manifest that such a deduction is absolutely necessary. We have already traced to their sources the conceptions of space and time, by means of a transcendental deduction, and we have explained and determined their objective validity a priori. Geometry, nevertheless, advances steadily and securely in the province of pure a priori cognitions, without needing to ask from philosophy any certificate as to the pure and legitimate origin of its fundamental conception of space. But the use of the conception in this science extends only to the external world of sense, the pure form of the intuition of which is space; and in this world, therefore, all geometrical cognition, because it is founded upon a priori intuition, possesses immediate evidence, and the objects of this cognition are given a priori (as regards their form) in intuition by and through the cognition itself. With the pure conceptions of understanding, on the contrary, commences the absolute necessity of seeking a transcendental deduction, not only of these conceptions themselves, but likewise of space, because, inasmuch as they make affirmations concerning objects not by means of the predicates of intuition and sensibility, but of pure thought a priori, they apply to objects without any of the conditions of sensibility. Besides, not being founded on experience, they are not presented with any object in a priori intuition upon which, antecedently to experience, they might base their synthesis. Hence results, not only doubt as to the objective validity and proper limits of their use, but that even our conception of space is rendered equivocal; inasmuch as we are very ready with the aid of the categories, to carry the use of this conception beyond the conditions of sensuous intuition — and, for this reason, we have already found a transcendental deduction of it needful. The reader, then, must be quite convinced of the absolute necessity of a transcendental deduction, before taking a single step in the field of pure reason; because otherwise he goes to work blindly, and after he has wondered about in all directions, returns to the state of utter ignorance from which he started. He ought, moreover, clearly to recognize beforehand the unavoidable difficulties in his undertaking, so that he may not afterwards complain of the obscurity in which the subject itself is deeply involved, or become too soon impatient of the obstacles in his path; because we have a choice of only two things — either at once to give up all pretensions to knowledge beyond the limits of possible experience, or to bring this critical investigation to completion.

We have been able, with very little trouble, to make it comprehensible how the conceptions of space and time, although a priori cognitions, must necessarily apply to external objects, and render a synthetical cognition of these possible, independently of all experience. For inasmuch as only by means of such pure form of sensibility an object can appear to us, that is, be an object of empirical intuition, space and time are pure intuitions, which contain a priori the condition of the possibility of objects as phenomena, and an a priori synthesis in these intuitions possesses objective validity.

On the other hand, the categories of the understanding do not represent the conditions under which objects are given to us in intuition; objects can consequently appear to us without necessarily connecting themselves with these, and consequently without any necessity binding on the understanding to contain a priori the conditions of these objects. Thus we find ourselves involved in a difficulty which did not present itself in the sphere of sensibility, that is to say, we cannot discover how the subjective conditions of thought can have objective validity, in other words, can become conditions of the possibility of all cognition of objects; for phenomena may certainly be given to us in intuition without any help from the functions of the understanding. Let us take, for example, the conception of cause, which indicates a peculiar kind of synthesis, namely, that with something, A, something entirely different, B, is connected according to a law. It is not a priori manifest why phenomena should contain anything of this kind (we are of course debarred from appealing for proof to experience, for the objective validity of this conception must be demonstrated a priori), and it hence remains doubtful a priori, whether such a conception be not quite void and without any corresponding object among phenomena. For that objects of sensuous intuition must correspond to the formal conditions of sensibility existing a priori in the mind is quite evident, from the fact that without these they could not be objects for us; but that they must also correspond to the conditions which understanding requires for the synthetical unity of thought is an assertion, the grounds for which are not so easily to be discovered. For phenomena might be so constituted as not to correspond to the conditions of the unity of thought; and all things might lie in such confusion that, for example, nothing could be met with in the sphere of phenomena to suggest a law of synthesis, and so correspond to the conception of cause and effect; so that this conception would be quite void, null, and without significance. Phenomena would nevertheless continue to present objects to our intuition; for mere intuition does not in any respect stand in need of the functions of thought.

If we thought to free ourselves from the labour of these investigations by saying: "Experience is constantly offering us examples of the relation of cause and effect in phenomena, and presents us with abundant opportunity of abstracting the conception of cause, and so at the same time of corroborating the objective validity of this conception"; we should in this case be overlooking the fact, that the conception of cause cannot arise in this way at all; that, on the contrary, it must either have an a priori basis in the understanding, or be rejected as a mere chimera. For this conception demands that something, A, should be of such a nature that something else, B, should follow from it necessarily, and according to an absolutely universal law. We may certainly collect from phenomena a law, according to which this or that usually happens, but the element of necessity is not to be found in it. Hence it is evident that to the synthesis of cause and effect belongs a dignity, which is utterly wanting in any empirical synthesis; for it is no mere mechanical synthesis, by means of addition, but a dynamical one; that is to say, the effect is not to be cogitated as merely annexed to the cause, but as posited by and through the cause, and resulting from it. The strict universality of this law never can be a characteristic of empirical laws, which obtain through induction only a comparative universality, that is, an extended range of practical application. But the pure conceptions of the understanding would entirely lose all their peculiar character, if we treated them merely as the productions of experience.

SS10. Transition to the Transcendental Deduction of the Categories.

There are only two possible ways in which synthetical representation and its objects can coincide with and relate necessarily to each other, and, as it were, meet together. Either the object alone makes the representation possible, or the representation alone makes the object possible. In the former case, the relation between them is only empirical, and an a priori representation is impossible. And this is the case with phenomena, as regards that in them which is referable to mere sensation. In the latter case — although representation alone (for of its causality, by means of the will, we do not here speak) does not produce the object as to its existence, it must nevertheless be a priori determinative in regard to the object, if it is only by means of the representation that we can cognize anything as an object. Now there are only two conditions of the possibility of a cognition of objects; firstly, intuition, by means of which the object, though only as phenomenon, is given; secondly, conception, by means of which the object which corresponds to this intuition is thought. But it is evident from what has been said on aesthetic that the first condition, under which alone objects can be intuited, must in fact exist, as a formal basis for them, a priori in the mind. With this formal condition of sensibility, therefore, all phenomena necessarily correspond, because it is only through it that they can be phenomena at all; that is, can be empirically intuited and given. Now the question is whether there do not exist, a priori in the mind, conceptions of understanding also, as conditions under which alone something, if not intuited, is yet thought as object. If this question be answered in the affirmative, it follows that all empirical cognition of objects is necessarily conformable to such conceptions, since, if they are not presupposed, it is impossible that anything can be an object of experience. Now all experience contains, besides the intuition of the senses through which an object is given, a conception also of an object that is given in intuition. Accordingly, conceptions of objects in general must lie as a priori conditions at the foundation of all empirical cognition; and consequently, the objective validity of the categories, as a priori conceptions, will rest upon this, that experience (as far as regards the form of thought) is possible only by their means. For in that case they apply necessarily and a priori to objects of experience, because only through them can an object of experience be thought.

The whole aim of the transcendental deduction of all a priori conceptions is to show that these conceptions are a priori conditions of the possibility of all experience.

Conceptions which afford us the objective foundation of the possibility of experience are for that very reason necessary. But the analysis of the experiences in which they are met with is not deduction, but only an illustration of them, because from experience they could never derive the attribute of necessity. Without their original applicability and relation to all possible experience, in which all objects of cognition present themselves, the relation of the categories to objects, of whatever nature, would be quite incomprehensible.

The celebrated Locke, for want of due reflection on these points, and because he met with pure conceptions of the understanding in experience, sought also to deduce them from experience, and yet proceeded so inconsequently as to attempt, with their aid, to arrive it cognitions which lie far beyond the limits of all experience. David Hume perceived that, to render this possible, it was necessary that the conceptions should have an a priori origin. But as he could not explain how it was possible that conceptions which are not connected with each other in the understanding must nevertheless be thought as necessarily connected in the object — and it never occurred to him that the understanding itself might, perhaps, by means of these conceptions, be the author of the experience in which its objects were presented to it — he was forced to drive these conceptions from experience, that is, from a subjective necessity arising from repeated association of experiences erroneously considered to be objective — in one word, from habit. But he proceeded with perfect consequence and declared it to be impossible, with such conceptions and the principles arising from them, to overstep the limits of experience. The empirical derivation, however, which both of these philosophers attributed to these conceptions, cannot possibly be reconciled with the fact that we do possess scientific a priori cognitions, namely, those of pure mathematics and general physics.

The former of these two celebrated men opened a wide door to extravagance — (for if reason has once undoubted right on its side, it will not allow itself to be confined to set limits, by vague recommendations of moderation); the latter gave himself up entirely to scepticism — a natural consequence, after having discovered, as he thought, that the faculty of cognition was not trustworthy. We now intend to make a trial whether it be not possible safely to conduct reason between these two rocks, to assign her determinate limits, and yet leave open for her the entire sphere of her legitimate activity.

I shall merely premise an explanation of what the categories are. They are conceptions of an object in general, by means of which its intuition is contemplated as determined in relation to one of the logical functions of judgement. The following will make this plain. The function of the categorical judgement is that of the relation of subject to predicate; for example, in the proposition: "All bodies are divisible." But in regard to the merely logical use of the understanding, it still remains undetermined to which Of these two conceptions belongs the function Of subject and to which that of predicate. For we could also say: "Some divisible is a body." But the category of substance, when the conception of a body is brought under it, determines that; and its empirical intuition in experience must be contemplated always as subject and never as mere predicate. And so with all the other categories.

SS11. SECTION II Transcendental Deduction of the pure Conceptions of the

Understanding.

Of the Possibility of a Conjunction of the manifold representations given by Sense.

The manifold content in our representations can be given in an intuition which is merely sensuous — in other words, is nothing but susceptibility; and the form of this intuition can exist a priori in our faculty of representation, without being anything else but the mode in which the subject is affected. But the conjunction (conjunctio) of a manifold in intuition never can be given us by the senses; it cannot therefore be contained in the pure form of sensuous intuition, for it is a spontaneous act of the faculty of representation. And as we must, to distinguish it from sensibility, entitle this faculty understanding; so all conjunction whether conscious or unconscious, be it of the manifold in intuition, sensuous or non-sensuous, or of several conceptions — is an act of the understanding. To this act we shall give the general appellation of synthesis, thereby to indicate, at the same time, that we cannot represent anything as conjoined in the object without having previously conjoined it ourselves. Of all mental notions, that of conjunction is the only one which cannot be given through objects, but can be originated only by the subject itself, because it is an act of its purely spontaneous activity. The reader will easily enough perceive that the possibility of conjunction must be grounded in the very nature of this act, and that it must be equally valid for all conjunction, and that analysis, which appears to be its contrary, must, nevertheless, always presuppose it; for where the understanding has not previously conjoined, it cannot dissect or analyse, because only as conjoined by it, must that which is to be analysed have been given to our faculty of representation.

But the conception of conjunction includes, besides the conception of the manifold and of the synthesis of it, that of the unity of it also. Conjunction is the representation of the synthetical unity of the manifold.* This idea of unity, therefore, cannot arise out of that of conjunction; much rather does that idea, by combining itself with the representation of the manifold, render the conception of conjunction possible. This unity, which a priori precedes all conceptions of conjunction, is not the category of unity (SS 6); for all the categories are based upon logical functions of judgement, and in these functions we already have conjunction, and consequently unity of given conceptions. It is therefore evident that the category of unity presupposes conjunction. We must therefore look still higher for this unity (as qualitative, SS 8), in that, namely, which contains the ground of the unity of diverse conceptions in judgements, the ground, consequently, of the possibility of the existence of the understanding, even in regard to its logical use.

[Note: Whether the representations are in themselves identical, and consequently whether one can be thought analytically by means of and through the other, is a question which we need not at present consider. Our Consciousness of the one, when we speak of the manifold, is always distinguishable from our consciousness of the other; and it is only respecting the synthesis of this (possible) consciousness that we here treat.]

SS12. Of the Originally Synthetical Unity of Apperception.

The "I think" must accompany all my representations, for otherwise something would be represented in me which could not be thought; in other words, the representation would either be impossible, or at least be, in relation to me, nothing. That representation which can be given previously to all thought is called intuition. All the diversity or manifold content of intuition, has, therefore, a necessary relation to the "I think," in the subject in which this diversity is found. But this representation, "I think," is an act of spontaneity; that is to say, it cannot be regarded as belonging to mere sensibility. I call it pure apperception, in order to distinguish it from empirical; or primitive apperception, because it is self-consciousness which, whilst it gives birth to the representation "I think," must necessarily be capable of accompanying all our representations. It is in all acts of consciousness one and the same, and unaccompanied by it, no representation can exist for me. The unity of this apperception I call the transcendental unity of self-consciousness, in order to indicate the possibility of a priori cognition arising from it. For the manifold representations which are given in an intuition would not all of them be my representations, if they did not all belong to one self-consciousness, that is, as my representations (even although I am not conscious of them as such), they must conform to the condition under which alone they can exist together in a common self-consciousness, because otherwise they would not all without exception belong to me. From this primitive conjunction follow many important results.

For example, this universal identity of the apperception of the manifold given in intuition contains a synthesis of representations and is possible only by means of the consciousness of this synthesis. For the empirical consciousness which accompanies different representations is in itself fragmentary and disunited, and without relation to the identity of the subject. This relation, then, does not exist because I accompany every representation with consciousness, but because I join one representation to another, and am conscious of the synthesis of them. Consequently, only because I can connect a variety of given representations in one consciousness, is it possible that I can represent to myself the identity of consciousness in these representations; in other words, the analytical unity of apperception is possible only under the presupposition of a synthetical unity.* The thought, "These representations given in intuition belong all of them to me," is accordingly just the same as, "I unite them in one self-consciousness, or can at least so unite them"; and although this thought is not itself the consciousness of the synthesis of representations, it presupposes the possibility of it; that is to say, for the reason alone that I can comprehend the variety of my representations in one consciousness, do I call them my representations, for otherwise I must have as many-coloured and various a self as are the representations of which I am conscious. Synthetical unity of the manifold in intuitions, as given a priori, is therefore the foundation of the identity of apperception itself, which antecedes a priori all determinate thought. But the conjunction of representations into a conception is not to be found in objects themselves, nor can it be, as it were, borrowed from them and taken up into the understanding by perception, but it is on the contrary an operation of the understanding itself, which is nothing more than the faculty of conjoining a priori and of bringing the variety of given representations under the unity of apperception. This principle is the highest in all human cognition.

[Note: All general conceptions—as such—depend, for their existence, on the analytical unity of consciousness. For example, when I think of red in general, I thereby think to myself a property which (as a characteristic mark) can be discovered somewhere, or can be united with other representations; consequently, it is only by means of a forethought possible synthetical unity that I can think to myself the analytical. A representation which is cogitated as common to different representations, is regarded as belonging to such as, besides this common representation, contain something different; consequently it must be previously thought in synthetical unity with other although only possible representations, before I can think in it the analytical unity of consciousness which makes it a conceptas communis. And thus the synthetical unity of apperception is the highest point with which we must connect every operation of the understanding, even the whole of logic, and after it our transcendental philosophy; indeed, this faculty is the understanding itself.]

This fundamental principle of the necessary unity of apperception is indeed an identical, and therefore analytical, proposition; but it nevertheless explains the necessity for a synthesis of the manifold given in an intuition, without which the identity of self-consciousness would be incogitable. For the ego, as a simple representation, presents us with no manifold content; only in intuition, which is quite different from the representation ego, can it be given us, and by means of conjunction it is cogitated in one self-consciousness. An understanding, in which all the manifold should be given by means of consciousness itself, would be intuitive; our understanding can only think and must look for its intuition to sense. I am, therefore, conscious of my identical self, in relation to all the variety of representations given to me in an intuition, because I call all of them my representations. In other words, I am conscious myself of a necessary a priori synthesis of my representations, which is called the original synthetical unity of apperception, under which rank all the representations presented to me, but that only by means of a synthesis.

SS13. The Principle of the Synthetical Unity of Apperception is the highest Principle of all exercise of the Understanding.

The supreme principle of the possibility of all intuition in relation to sensibility was, according to our transcendental aesthetic, that all the manifold in intuition be subject to the formal conditions of space and time. The supreme principle of the possibility of it in relation to the understanding is that all the manifold in it be subject to conditions of the originally synthetical unity or apperception.* To the former of these two principles are subject all the various representations of intuition, in so far as they are given to us; to the latter, in so far as they must be capable of conjunction in one consciousness; for without this nothing can be thought or cognized, because the given representations would not have in common the act Of the apperception "I think" and therefore could not be connected in one self-consciousness.

[Note: Space and time, and all portions thereof, are intuitions; consequently are, with a manifold for their content, single representations. (See the Transcendental Aesthetic.) Consequently, they are not pure conceptions, by means of which the same consciousness is found in a great number of representations; but, on the contrary, they are many representations contained in one, the consciousness of which is, so to speak, compounded. The unity of consciousness is nevertheless synthetical and, therefore, primitive. From this peculiar character of consciousness follow many important consequences. (See SS 21.)]

Understanding is, to speak generally, the faculty Of cognitions. These consist in the determined relation of given representation to an object. But an object is that, in the conception of which the manifold in a given intuition is united. Now all union of representations requires unity of consciousness in the synthesis of them. Consequently, it is the unity of consciousness alone that constitutes the possibility of representations relating to an object, and therefore of their objective validity, and of their becoming cognitions, and consequently, the possibility of the existence of the understanding itself.

The first pure cognition of understanding, then, upon which is founded all its other exercise, and which is at the same time perfectly independent of all conditions of mere sensuous intuition, is the principle of the original synthetical unity of apperception. Thus the mere form of external sensuous intuition, namely, space, affords us, per se, no cognition; it merely contributes the manifold in a priori intuition to a possible cognition. But, in order to cognize something in space (for example, a line), I must draw it, and thus produce synthetically a determined conjunction of the given manifold, so that the unity of this act is at the same time the unity of consciousness (in the conception of a line), and by this means alone is an object (a determinate space) cognized. The synthetical unity of consciousness is, therefore, an objective condition of all cognition, which I do not merely require in order to cognize an object, but to which every intuition must necessarily be subject, in order to become an object for me; because in any other way, and without this synthesis, the manifold in intuition could not be united in one consciousness.

This proposition is, as already said, itself analytical, although it constitutes the synthetical unity, the condition of all thought; for it states nothing more than that all my representations in any given intuition must be subject to the condition which alone enables me to connect them, as my representation with the identical self, and so to unite them synthetically in one apperception, by means of the general expression, "I think."

But this principle is not to be regarded as a principle for every possible understanding, but only for the understanding by means of whose pure apperception in the thought I am, no manifold content is given. The understanding or mind which contained the manifold in intuition, in and through the act itself of its own self-consciousness, in other words, an understanding by and in the representation of which the objects of the representation should at the same time exist, would not require a special act of synthesis of the manifold as the condition of the unity of its consciousness, an act of which the human understanding, which thinks only and cannot intuite, has absolute need. But this principle is the first principle of all the operations of our understanding, so that we cannot form the least conception of any other possible understanding, either of one such as should be itself intuition, or possess a sensuous intuition, but with forms different from those of space and time.

SS14. What Objective Unity of Self-consciousness is.

It is by means of the transcendental unity of apperception that all the manifold, given in an intuition is united into a conception of the object. On this account it is called objective, and must be distinguished from the subjective unity of consciousness, which is a determination of the internal sense, by means of which the said manifold in intuition is given empirically to be so united. Whether I can be empirically conscious of the manifold as coexistent or as successive, depends upon circumstances, or empirical conditions. Hence the empirical unity of consciousness by means of association of representations, itself relates to a phenomenal world and is wholly contingent. On the contrary, the pure form of intuition in time, merely as an intuition, which contains a given manifold, is subject to the original unity of consciousness, and that solely by means of the necessary relation of the manifold in intuition to the "I think," consequently by means of the pure synthesis of the understanding, which lies a priori at the foundation of all empirical synthesis. The transcendental unity of apperception is alone objectively valid; the empirical which we do not consider in this essay, and which is merely a unity deduced from the former under given conditions in concreto, possesses only subjective validity. One person connects the notion conveyed in a word with one thing, another with another thing; and the unity of consciousness in that which is empirical, is, in relation to that which is given by experience, not necessarily and universally valid.

SS15. The Logical Form of all Judgements consists in the Objective Unity of Apperception of the Conceptions contained therein.

I could never satisfy myself with the definition which logicians give of a judgement. It is, according to them, the representation of a relation between two conceptions. I shall not dwell here on the faultiness of this definition, in that it suits only for categorical and not for hypothetical or disjunctive judgements, these latter containing a relation not of conceptions but of judgements themselves — a blunder from which many evil results have followed.* It is more important for our present purpose to observe, that this definition does not determine in what the said relation consists.

[Note: The tedious doctrine of the four syllogistic figures concerns only categorical syllogisms; and although it is nothing more than an artifice by surreptitiously introducing immediate conclusions (consequentiae immediatae) among the premises of a pure syllogism, to give ism' give rise to an appearance of more modes of drawing a conclusion than that in the first figure, the artifice would not have had much success, had not its authors succeeded in bringing categorical judgements into exclusive respect, as those to which all others must be referred — a doctrine, however, which, according to SS 5, is utterly false.]

But if I investigate more closely the relation of given cognitions in every judgement, and distinguish it, as belonging to the understanding, from the relation which is produced according to laws of the reproductive imagination (which has only subjective validity), I find that judgement is nothing but the mode of bringing given cognitions under the objective unit of apperception. This is plain from our use of the term of relation is in judgements, in order to distinguish the objective unity of given representations from the subjective unity. For this term indicates the relation of these representations to the original apperception, and also their necessary unity, even although the judgement is empirical, therefore contingent, as in the judgement: "All bodies are heavy." I do not mean by this, that these representations do necessarily belong to each other in empirical intuition, but that by means of the necessary unity of appreciation they belong to each other in the synthesis of intuitions, that is to say, they belong to each other according to principles of the objective determination of all our representations, in so far as cognition can arise from them, these principles being all deduced from the main principle of the transcendental unity of apperception. In this way alone can there arise from this relation a judgement, that is, a relation which has objective validity, and is perfectly distinct from that relation of the very same representations which has only subjective validity — a relation, to wit, which is produced according to laws of association. According to these laws, I could only say: "When I hold in my hand or carry a body, I feel an impression of weight"; but I could not say: "It, the body, is heavy"; for this is tantamount to saying both these representations are conjoined in the object, that is, without distinction as to the condition of the subject, and do not merely stand together in my perception, however frequently the perceptive act may be repeated.

SS16. All Sensuous Intuitions are subject to the Categories, as Conditions under which alone the manifold Content of them can be united in one Consciousness.

The manifold content given in a sensuous intuition comes necessarily under the original synthetical unity of apperception, because thereby alone is the unity of intuition possible (SS 13). But that act of the understanding, by which the manifold content of given representations (whether intuitions or conceptions) is brought under one apperception, is the logical function of judgements (SS 15). All the manifold, therefore, in so far as it is given in one empirical intuition, is determined in relation to one of the logical functions of judgement, by means of which it is brought into union in one consciousness. Now the categories are nothing else than these functions of judgement so far as the manifold in a given intuition is determined in relation to them (SS 9). Consequently, the manifold in a given intuition is necessarily subject to the categories of the understanding.

SS17. Observation.

The manifold in an intuition, which I call mine, is represented by means of the synthesis of the understanding, as belonging to the necessary unity of self-consciousness, and this takes place by means of the category.* The category indicates accordingly that the empirical consciousness of a given manifold in an intuition is subject to a pure self-consciousness a priori, in the same manner as an empirical intuition is subject to a pure sensuous intuition, which is also a priori. In the above proposition, then, lies the beginning of a deduction of the pure conceptions of the understanding. Now, as the categories have their origin in the understanding alone, independently of sensibility, I must in my deduction make abstraction of the mode in which the manifold of an empirical intuition is given, in order to fix my attention exclusively on the unity which is brought by the understanding into the intuition by means of the category. In what follows (SS 22), it will be shown, from the mode in which the empirical intuition is given in the faculty of sensibility, that the unity which belongs to it is no other than that which the category (according to SS 16) imposes on the manifold in a given intuition, and thus, its a priori validity in regard to all objects of sense being established, the purpose of our deduction will be fully attained.

[Note: The proof of this rests on the represented unity of intuition, by means of which an object is given, and which always includes in itself a synthesis of the manifold to be intuited, and also the relation of this latter to unity of apperception.]

But there is one thing in the above demonstration of which I could not make abstraction, namely, that the manifold to be intuited must be given previously to the synthesis of the understanding, and independently of it. How this takes place remains here undetermined. For if I cogitate an understanding which was itself intuitive (as, for example, a divine understanding which should not represent given objects, but by whose representation the objects themselves should be given or produced), the categories would possess no significance in relation to such a faculty of cognition. They are merely rules for an understanding, whose whole power consists in thought, that is, in the act of submitting the synthesis of the manifold which is presented to it in intuition from a very different quarter, to the unity of apperception; a faculty, therefore, which cognizes nothing per se, but only connects and arranges the material of cognition, the intuition, namely, which must be presented to it by means of the object. But to show reasons for this peculiar character of our understandings, that it produces unity of apperception a priori only by means of categories, and a certain kind and number thereof, is as impossible as to explain why we are endowed with precisely so many functions of judgement and no more, or why time and space are the only forms of our intuition.

SS18. In Cognition, its Application to Objects of Experience is the only legitimate use of the Category.

To think an object and to cognize an object are by no means the same thing. In cognition there are two elements: firstly, the conception, whereby an object is cogitated (the category); and, secondly, the intuition, whereby the object is given. For supposing that to the conception a corresponding intuition could not be given, it would still be a thought as regards its form, but without any object, and no cognition of anything would be possible by means of it, inasmuch as, so far as I knew, there existed and could exist nothing to which my thought could be applied. Now all intuition possible to us is sensuous; consequently, our thought of an object by means of a pure conception of the understanding, can become cognition for us only in so far as this conception is applied to objects of the senses. Sensuous intuition is either pure intuition (space and time) or empirical intuition — of that which is immediately represented in space and time by means of sensation as real. Through the determination of pure intuition we obtain a priori cognitions of objects, as in mathematics, but only as regards their form as phenomena; whether there can exist things which must be intuited in this form is not thereby established. All mathematical conceptions, therefore, are not per se cognition, except in so far as we presuppose that there exist things which can only be represented conformably to the form of our pure sensuous intuition. But things in space and time are given only in so far as they are perceptions (representations accompanied with sensation), therefore only by empirical representation. Consequently the pure conceptions of the understanding, even when they are applied to intuitions a priori (as in mathematics), produce cognition only in so far as these (and therefore the conceptions of the understanding by means of them) can be applied to empirical intuitions. Consequently the categories do not, even by means of pure intuition afford us any cognition of things; they can only do so in so far as they can be applied to empirical intuition. That is to say, the categories serve only to render empirical cognition possible. But this is what we call experience. Consequently, in cognition, their application to objects of experience is the only legitimate use of the categories.

SS19.

The foregoing proposition is of the utmost importance, for it determines the limits of the exercise of the pure conceptions of the understanding in regard to objects, just as transcendental aesthetic determined the limits of the exercise of the pure form of our sensuous intuition. Space and time, as conditions of the possibility of the presentation of objects to us, are valid no further than for objects of sense, consequently, only for experience. Beyond these limits they represent to us nothing, for they belong only to sense, and have no reality apart from it. The pure conceptions of the understanding are free from this limitation, and extend to objects of intuition in general, be the intuition like or unlike to ours, provided only it be sensuous, and not intellectual. But this extension of conceptions beyond the range of our intuition is of no advantage; for they are then mere empty conceptions of objects, as to the possibility or impossibility of the existence of which they furnish us with no means of discovery. They are mere forms of thought, without objective reality, because we have no intuition to which the synthetical unity of apperception, which alone the categories contain, could be applied, for the purpose of determining an object. Our sensuous and empirical intuition can alone give them significance and meaning.

If, then, we suppose an object of a non-sensuous intuition to be given we can in that case represent it by all those predicates which are implied in the presupposition that nothing appertaining to sensuous intuition belongs to it; for example, that it is not extended, or in space; that its duration is not time; that in it no change (the effect of the determinations in time) is to be met with, and so on. But it is no proper knowledge if I merely indicate what the intuition of the object is not, without being able to say what is contained in it, for I have not shown the possibility of an object to which my pure conception of understanding could be applicable, because I have not been able to furnish any intuition corresponding to it, but am only able to say that our intuition is not valid for it. But the most important point is this, that to a something of this kind not one category can be found applicable. Take, for example, the conception of substance, that is, something that can exist as subject, but never as mere predicate; in regard to this conception I am quite ignorant whether there can really be anything to correspond to such a determination of thought, if empirical intuition did not afford me the occasion for its application. But of this more in the sequel.

SS20. Of the Application of the Categories to Objects of the Senses in general.

The pure conceptions of the understanding apply to objects of intuition in general, through the understanding alone, whether the intuition be our own or some other, provided only it be sensuous, but are, for this very reason, mere forms of thought, by means of which alone no determined object can be cognized. The synthesis or conjunction of the manifold in these conceptions relates, we have said, only to the unity of apperception, and is for this reason the ground of the possibility of a priori cognition, in so far as this cognition is dependent on the understanding. This synthesis is, therefore, not merely transcendental, but also purely intellectual. But because a certain form of sensuous intuition exists in the mind a priori which rests on the receptivity of the representative faculty (sensibility), the understanding, as a spontaneity, is able to determine the internal sense by means of the diversity of given representations, conformably to the synthetical unity of apperception, and thus to cogitate the synthetical unity of the apperception of the manifold of sensuous intuition a priori, as the condition to which must necessarily be submitted all objects of human intuition. And in this manner the categories as mere forms of thought receive objective reality, that is, application to objects which are given to us in intuition, but that only as phenomena, for it is only of phenomena that we are capable of a priori intuition.

This synthesis of the manifold of sensuous intuition, which is possible and necessary a priori, may be called figurative (synthesis speciosa), in contradistinction to that which is cogitated in the mere category in regard to the manifold of an intuition in general, and is called connection or conjunction of the understanding (synthesis intellectualis). Both are transcendental, not merely because they themselves precede a priori all experience, but also because they form the basis for the possibility of other cognition a priori.

But the figurative synthesis, when it has relation only to the originally synthetical unity of apperception, that is to the transcendental unity cogitated in the categories, must, to be distinguished from the purely intellectual conjunction, be entitled the transcendental synthesis of imagination. Imagination is the faculty of representing an object even without its presence in intuition. Now, as all our intuition is sensuous, imagination, by reason of the subjective condition under which alone it can give a corresponding intuition to the conceptions of the understanding, belongs to sensibility. But in so far as the synthesis of the imagination is an act of spontaneity, which is determinative, and not, like sense, merely determinable, and which is consequently able to determine sense a priori, according to its form, conformably to the unity of apperception, in so far is the imagination a faculty of determining sensibility a priori, and its synthesis of intuitions according to the categories must be the transcendental synthesis of the imagination. It is an operation of the understanding on sensibility, and the first application of the understanding to objects of possible intuition, and at the same time the basis for the exercise of the other functions of that faculty. As figurative, it is distinguished from the merely intellectual synthesis, which is produced by the understanding alone, without the aid of imagination. Now, in so far as imagination is spontaneity, I sometimes call it also the productive imagination, and distinguish it from the reproductive, the synthesis of which is subject entirely to empirical laws, those of association, namely, and which, therefore, contributes nothing to the explanation of the possibility of a priori cognition, and for this reason belongs not to transcendental philosophy, but to psychology.

We have now arrived at the proper place for explaining the paradox which must have struck every one in our exposition of the internal sense (SS 6), namely — how this sense represents us to our own consciousness, only as we appear to ourselves, not as we are in ourselves, because, to wit, we intuite ourselves only as we are inwardly affected. Now this appears to be contradictory, inasmuch as we thus stand in a passive relation to ourselves; and therefore in the systems of psychology, the internal sense is commonly held to be one with the faculty of apperception, while we, on the contrary, carefully distinguish them.

That which determines the internal sense is the understanding, and its original power of conjoining the manifold of intuition, that is, of bringing this under an apperception (upon which rests the possibility of the understanding itself). Now, as the human understanding is not in itself a faculty of intuition, and is unable to exercise such a power, in order to conjoin, as it were, the manifold of its own intuition, the synthesis of understanding is, considered per se, nothing but the unity of action, of which, as such, it is self-conscious, even apart from sensibility, by which, moreover, it is able to determine our internal sense in respect of the manifold which may be presented to it according to the form of sensuous intuition. Thus, under the name of a transcendental synthesis of imagination, the understanding exercises an activity upon the passive subject, whose faculty it is; and so we are right in saying that the internal sense is affected thereby. Apperception and its synthetical unity are by no means one and the same with the internal sense. The former, as the source of all our synthetical conjunction, applies, under the name of the categories, to the manifold of intuition in general, prior to all sensuous intuition of objects. The internal sense, on the contrary, contains merely the form of intuition, but without any synthetical conjunction of the manifold therein, and consequently does not contain any determined intuition, which is possible only through consciousness of the determination of the manifold by the transcendental act of the imagination (synthetical influence of the understanding on the internal sense), which I have named figurative synthesis.

This we can indeed always perceive in ourselves. We cannot cogitate a geometrical line without drawing it in thought, nor a circle without describing it, nor represent the three dimensions of space without drawing three lines from the same point perpendicular to one another. We cannot even cogitate time, unless, in drawing a straight line (which is to serve as the external figurative representation of time), we fix our attention on the act of the synthesis of the manifold, whereby we determine successively the internal sense, and thus attend also to the succession of this determination. Motion as an act of the subject (not as a determination of an object),* consequently the synthesis of the manifold in space, if we make abstraction of space and attend merely to the act by which we determine the internal sense according to its form, is that which produces the conception of succession. The understanding, therefore, does by no means find in the internal sense any such synthesis of the manifold, but produces it, in that it affects this sense. At the same time, how "I who think" is distinct from the "I" which intuites itself (other modes of intuition being cogitable as at least possible), and yet one and the same with this latter as the same subject; how, therefore, I am able to say: "I, as an intelligence and thinking subject, cognize myself as an object thought, so far as I am, moreover, given to myself in intuition — only, like other phenomena, not as I am in myself, and as considered by the understanding, but merely as I appear" — is a question that has in it neither more nor less difficulty than the question— "How can I be an object to myself?" or this— "How I can be an object of my own intuition and internal perceptions?" But that such must be the fact, if we admit that space is merely a pure form of the phenomena of external sense, can be clearly proved by the consideration that we cannot represent time, which is not an object of external intuition, in any other way than under the image of a line, which we draw in thought, a mode of representation without which we could not cognize the unity of its dimension, and also that we are necessitated to take our determination of periods of time, or of points of time, for all our internal perceptions from the changes which we perceive in outward things. It follows that we must arrange the determinations of the internal sense, as phenomena in time, exactly in the same manner as we arrange those of the external senses in space. And consequently, if we grant, respecting this latter, that by means of them we know objects only in so far as we are affected externally, we must also confess, with regard to the internal sense, that by means of it we intuite ourselves only as we are internally affected by ourselves; in other words, as regards internal intuition, we cognize our own subject only as phenomenon, and not as it is in itself.* *

[Note: Motion of an object in space does not belong to a pure science, consequently not to geometry; because, that a thing is movable cannot be known a priori, but only from experience. But motion, considered as the description of a space, is a pure act of the successive synthesis of the manifold in external intuition by means of productive imagination, and belongs not only to geometry, but even to transcendental philosophy.]

[Note: I do not see why so much difficulty should be found in admitting that our internal sense is affected by ourselves. Every act of attention exemplifies it. In such an act the understanding determines the internal sense by the synthetical conjunction which it cogitates, conformably to the internal intuition which corresponds to the manifold in the synthesis of the understanding. How much the mind is usually affected thereby every one will be able to perceive in himself.]

SS21.

On the other hand, in the transcendental synthesis of the manifold content of representations, consequently in the synthetical unity of apperception, I am conscious of myself, not as I appear to myself, nor as I am in myself, but only that "I am." This representation is a thought, not an intuition. Now, as in order to cognize ourselves, in addition to the act of thinking, which subjects the manifold of every possible intuition to the unity of apperception, there is necessary a determinate mode of intuition, whereby this manifold is given; although my own existence is certainly not mere phenomenon (much less mere illusion), the determination of my existence* Can only take place conformably to the form of the internal sense, according to the particular mode in which the manifold which I conjoin is given in internal intuition, and I have therefore no knowledge of myself as I am, but merely as I appear to myself. The consciousness of self is thus very far from a knowledge of self, in which I do not use the categories, whereby I cogitate an object, by means of the conjunction of the manifold in one apperception. In the same way as I require, for the sake of the cognition of an object distinct from myself, not only the thought of an object in general (in the category), but also an intuition by which to determine that general conception, in the same way do I require, in order to the cognition of myself, not only the consciousness of myself or the thought that I think myself, but in addition an intuition of the manifold in myself, by which to determine this thought. It is true that I exist as an intelligence which is conscious only of its faculty of conjunction or synthesis, but subjected in relation to the manifold which this intelligence has to conjoin to a limitative conjunction called the internal sense. My intelligence (that is, I) can render that conjunction or synthesis perceptible only according to the relations of time, which are quite beyond the proper sphere of the conceptions of the understanding and consequently cognize itself in respect to an intuition (which cannot possibly be intellectual, nor given by the understanding), only as it appears to itself, and not as it would cognize itself, if its intuition were intellectual.

[Note: The "I think" expresses the act of determining my own existence. My existence is thus already given by the act of consciousness; but the mode in which I must determine my existence, that is, the mode in which I must place the manifold belonging to my existence, is not thereby given. For this purpose intuition of self is required, and this intuition possesses a form given a priori, namely, time, which is sensuous, and belongs to our receptivity of the determinable. Now, as I do not possess another intuition of self which gives the determining in me (of the spontaneity of which I am conscious), prior to the act of determination, in the same manner as time gives the determinable, it is clear that I am unable to determine my own existence as that of a spontaneous being, but I am only able to represent to myself the spontaneity of my thought, that is, of my determination, and my existence remains ever determinable in a purely sensuous manner, that is to say, like the existence of a phenomenon. But it is because of this spontaneity that I call myself an intelligence.]

SS22. Transcendental Deduction of the universally possible employment in experience of the Pure Conceptions of the Understanding.

In the metaphysical deduction, the a priori origin of categories was proved by their complete accordance with the general logical of thought; in the transcendental deduction was exhibited the possibility of the categories as a priori cognitions of objects of an intuition in general (SS 16 and 17).At present we are about to explain the possibility of cognizing, a priori, by means of the categories, all objects which can possibly be presented to our senses, not, indeed, according to the form of their intuition, but according to the laws of their conjunction or synthesis, and thus, as it were, of prescribing laws to nature and even of rendering nature possible. For if the categories were inadequate to this task, it would not be evident to us why everything that is presented to our senses must be subject to those laws which have an a priori origin in the understanding itself.

I premise that by the term synthesis of apprehension I understand the combination of the manifold in an empirical intuition, whereby perception, that is, empirical consciousness of the intuition (as phenomenon), is possible.

We have a priori forms of the external and internal sensuous intuition in the representations of space and time, and to these must the synthesis of apprehension of the manifold in a phenomenon be always comformable, because the synthesis itself can only take place according to these forms. But space and time are not merely forms of sensuous intuition, but intuitions themselves (which contain a manifold), and therefore contain a priori the determination of the unity of this manifold.* (See the Transcendent Aesthetic.) Therefore is unity of the synthesis of the manifold without or within us, consequently also a conjunction to which all that is to be represented as determined in space or time must correspond, given a priori along with (not in) these intuitions, as the condition of the synthesis of all apprehension of them. But this synthetical unity can be no other than that of the conjunction of the manifold of a given intuition in general, in a primitive act of consciousness, according to the categories, but applied to our sensuous intuition. Consequently all synthesis, whereby alone is even perception possible, is subject to the categories. And, as experience is cognition by means of conjoined perceptions, the categories are conditions of the possibility of experience and are therefore valid a priori for all objects of experience.

[Note: Space represented as an object (as geometry really requires it to be) contains more than the mere form of the intuition; namely, a combination of the manifold given according to the form of sensibility into a representation that can be intuited; so that the form of the intuition gives us merely the manifold, but the formal intuition gives unity of representation. In the aesthetic, I regarded this unity as belonging entirely to sensibility, for the purpose of indicating that it antecedes all conceptions, although it presupposes a synthesis which does not belong to sense, through which alone, however, all our conceptions of space and time are possible. For as by means of this unity alone (the understanding determining the sensibility) space and time are given as intuitions, it follows that the unity of this intuition a priori belongs to space and time, and not to the conception of the understanding (SS 20).]

When, then, for example, I make the empirical intuition of a house by apprehension of the manifold contained therein into a perception, the necessary unity of space and of my external sensuous intuition lies at the foundation of this act, and I, as it were, draw the form of the house conformably to this synthetical unity of the manifold in space. But this very synthetical unity remains, even when I abstract the form of space, and has its seat in the understanding, and is in fact the category of the synthesis of the homogeneous in an intuition; that is to say, the category of quantity, to which the aforesaid synthesis of apprehension, that is, the perception, must be completely conformable.*

[Note: In this manner it is proved, that the synthesis of apprehension, which is empirical, must necessarily be conformable to the synthesis of apperception, which is intellectual, and contained a priori in the category. It is one and the same spontaneity which at one time, under the name of imagination, at another under that of understanding, produces conjunction in the manifold of intuition.]

To take another example, when I perceive the freezing of water, I apprehend two states (fluidity and solidity), which, as such, stand toward each other mutually in a relation of time. But in the time, which I place as an internal intuition, at the foundation of this phenomenon, I represent to myself synthetical unity of the manifold, without which the aforesaid relation could not be given in an intuition as determined (in regard to the succession of time). Now this synthetical unity, as the a priori condition under which I conjoin the manifold of an intuition, is, if I make abstraction of the permanent form of my internal intuition (that is to say, of time), the category of cause, by means of which, when applied to my sensibility, I determine everything that occurs according to relations of time. Consequently apprehension in such an event, and the event itself, as far as regards the possibility of its perception, stands under the conception of the relation of cause and effect: and so in all other cases.

Categories are conceptions which prescribe laws a priori to phenomena, consequently to nature as the complex of all phenomena (natura materialiter spectata). And now the question arises — inasmuch as these categories are not derived from nature, and do not regulate themselves according to her as their model (for in that case they would be empirical) — how it is conceivable that nature must regulate herself according to them, in other words, how the categories can determine a priori the synthesis of the manifold of nature, and yet not derive their origin from her. The following is the solution of this enigma.

It is not in the least more difficult to conceive how the laws of the phenomena of nature must harmonize with the understanding and with its a priori form — that is, its faculty of conjoining the manifold — than it is to understand how the phenomena themselves must correspond with the a priori form of our sensuous intuition. For laws do not exist in the phenomena any more than the phenomena exist as things in themselves. Laws do not exist except by relation to the subject in which the phenomena inhere, in so far as it possesses understanding, just as phenomena have no existence except by relation to the same existing subject in so far as it has senses. To things as things in themselves, conformability to law must necessarily belong independently of an understanding to cognize them. But phenomena are only representations of things which are utterly unknown in respect to what they are in themselves. But as mere representations, they stand under no law of conjunction except that which the conjoining faculty prescribes. Now that which conjoins the manifold of sensuous intuition is imagination, a mental act to which understanding contributes unity of intellectual synthesis, and sensibility, manifoldness of apprehension. Now as all possible perception depends on the synthesis of apprehension, and this empirical synthesis itself on the transcendental, consequently on the categories, it is evident that all possible perceptions, and therefore everything that can attain to empirical consciousness, that is, all phenomena of nature, must, as regards their conjunction, be subject to the categories. And nature (considered merely as nature in general) is dependent on them, as the original ground of her necessary conformability to law (as natura formaliter spectata). But the pure faculty (of the understanding) of prescribing laws a priori to phenomena by means of mere categories, is not competent to enounce other or more laws than those on which a nature in general, as a conformability to law of phenomena of space and time, depends. Particular laws, inasmuch as they concern empirically determined phenomena, cannot be entirely deduced from pure laws, although they all stand under them. Experience must be superadded in order to know these particular laws; but in regard to experience in general, and everything that can be cognized as an object thereof, these a priori laws are our only rule and guide.

SS23. Result of this Deduction of the Conceptions of the Understanding.

We cannot think any object except by means of the categories; we cannot cognize any thought except by means of intuitions corresponding to these conceptions. Now all our intuitions are sensuous, and our cognition, in so far as the object of it is given, is empirical. But empirical cognition is experience; consequently no a priori cognition is possible for us, except of objects of possible experience.*

[Note: Lest my readers should stumble at this assertion, and the conclusions that may be too rashly drawn from it, I must remind them that the categories in the act of thought are by no means limited by the conditions of our sensuous intuition, but have an unbounded sphere of action. It is only the cognition of the object of thought, the determining of the object, which requires intuition. In the absence of intuition, our thought of an object may still have true and useful consequences in regard to the exercise of reason by the subject. But as this exercise of reason is not always directed on the determination of the object, in other words, on cognition thereof, but also on the determination of the subject and its volition, I do not intend to treat of it in this place.]

But this cognition, which is limited to objects of experience, is not for that reason derived entirely, from, experience, but — and this is asserted of the pure intuitions and the pure conceptions of the understanding — there are, unquestionably, elements of cognition, which exist in the mind a priori. Now there are only two ways in which a necessary harmony of experience with the conceptions of its objects can be cogitated. Either experience makes these conceptions possible, or the conceptions make experience possible. The former of these statements will not bold good with respect to the categories (nor in regard to pure sensuous intuition), for they are a priori conceptions, and therefore independent of experience. The assertion of an empirical origin would attribute to them a sort of generatio aequivoca. Consequently, nothing remains but to adopt the second alternative (which presents us with a system, as it were, of the epigenesis of pure reason), namely, that on the part of the understanding the categories do contain the grounds of the possibility of all experience. But with respect to the questions how they make experience possible, and what are the principles of the possibility thereof with which they present us in their application to phenomena, the following section on the transcendental exercise of the faculty of judgement will inform the reader.

It is quite possible that someone may propose a species of preformation-system of pure reason — a middle way between the two — to wit, that the categories are neither innate and first a priori principles of cognition, nor derived from experience, but are merely subjective aptitudes for thought implanted in us contemporaneously with our existence, which were so ordered and disposed by our Creator, that their exercise perfectly harmonizes with the laws of nature which regulate experience. Now, not to mention that with such an hypothesis it is impossible to say at what point we must stop in the employment of predetermined aptitudes, the fact that the categories would in this case entirely lose that character of necessity which is essentially involved in the very conception of them, is a conclusive objection to it. The conception of cause, for example, which expresses the necessity of an effect under a presupposed condition, would be false, if it rested only upon such an arbitrary subjective necessity of uniting certain empirical representations according to such a rule of relation. I could not then say— "The effect is connected with its cause in the object (that is, necessarily)," but only, "I am so constituted that I can think this representation as so connected, and not otherwise." Now this is just what the sceptic wants. For in this case, all our knowledge, depending on the supposed objective validity of our judgement, is nothing but mere illusion; nor would there be wanting people who would deny any such subjective necessity in respect to themselves, though they must feel it. At all events, we could not dispute with any one on that which merely depends on the manner in which his subject is organized.

Short view of the above Deduction.

The foregoing deduction is an exposition of the pure conceptions of the understanding (and with them of all theoretical a priori cognition), as principles of the possibility of experience, but of experience as the determination of all phenomena in space and time in general — of experience, finally, from the principle of the original synthetical unity of apperception, as the form of the understanding in relation to time and space as original forms of sensibility.

I consider the division by paragraphs to be necessary only up to this point, because we had to treat of the elementary conceptions. As we now proceed to the exposition of the employment of these, I shall not designate the chapters in this manner any further.

BOOK II. Analytic of Principles.

General logic is constructed upon a plan which coincides exactly with the division of the higher faculties of cognition. These are, understanding, judgement, and reason. This science, accordingly, treats in its analytic of conceptions, judgements, and conclusions in exact correspondence with the functions and order of those mental powers which we include generally under the generic denomination of understanding.

As this merely formal logic makes abstraction of all content of cognition, whether pure or empirical, and occupies itself with the mere form of thought (discursive cognition), it must contain in its analytic a canon for reason. For the form of reason has its law, which, without taking into consideration the particular nature of the cognition about which it is employed, can be discovered a priori, by the simple analysis of the action of reason into its momenta.

Transcendental logic, limited as it is to a determinate content, that of pure a priori cognitions, to wit, cannot imitate general logic in this division. For it is evident that the transcendental employment of reason is not objectively valid, and therefore does not belong to the logic of truth (that is, to analytic), but as a logic of illusion, occupies a particular department in the scholastic system under the name of transcendental dialectic.

Understanding and judgement accordingly possess in transcendental logic a canon of objectively valid, and therefore true exercise, and are comprehended in the analytical department of that logic. But reason, in her endeavours to arrive by a priori means at some true statement concerning objects and to extend cognition beyond the bounds of possible experience, is altogether dialectic, and her illusory assertions cannot be constructed into a canon such as an analytic ought to contain.

Accordingly, the analytic of principles will be merely a canon for the faculty of judgement, for the instruction of this faculty in its application to phenomena of the pure conceptions of the understanding, which contain the necessary condition for the establishment of a priori laws. On this account, although the subject of the following chapters is the especial principles of understanding, I shall make use of the term Doctrine of the faculty of judgement, in order to define more particularly my present purpose.

INTRODUCTION. Of the Transcendental Faculty of judgement in General.

If understanding in general be defined as the faculty of laws or rules, the faculty of judgement may be termed the faculty of subsumption under these rules; that is, of distinguishing whether this or that does or does not stand under a given rule (casus datae legis). General logic contains no directions or precepts for the faculty of judgement, nor can it contain any such. For as it makes abstraction of all content of cognition, no duty is left for it, except that of exposing analytically the mere form of cognition in conceptions, judgements, and conclusions, and of thereby establishing formal rules for all exercise of the understanding. Now if this logic wished to give some general direction how we should subsume under these rules, that is, how we should distinguish whether this or that did or did not stand under them, this again could not be done otherwise than by means of a rule. But this rule, precisely because it is a rule, requires for itself direction from the faculty of judgement. Thus, it is evident that the understanding is capable of being instructed by rules, but that the judgement is a peculiar talent, which does not, and cannot require tuition, but only exercise. This faculty is therefore the specific quality of the so-called mother wit, the want of which no scholastic discipline can compensate.

For although education may furnish, and, as it were, engraft upon a limited understanding rules borrowed from other minds, yet the power of employing these rules correctly must belong to the pupil himself; and no rule which we can prescribe to him with this purpose is, in the absence or deficiency of this gift of nature, secure from misuse.* A physician therefore, a judge or a statesman, may have in his head many admirable pathological, juridical, or political rules, in a degree that may enable him to be a profound teacher in his particular science, and yet in the application of these rules he may very possibly blunder — either because he is wanting in natural judgement (though not in understanding) and, whilst he can comprehend the general in abstracto, cannot distinguish whether a particular case in concreto ought to rank under the former; or because his faculty of judgement has not been sufficiently exercised by examples and real practice. Indeed, the grand and only use of examples, is to sharpen the judgement. For as regards the correctness and precision of the insight of the understanding, examples are commonly injurious rather than otherwise, because, as casus in terminis they seldom adequately fulfil the conditions of the rule. Besides, they often weaken the power of our understanding to apprehend rules or laws in their universality, independently of particular circumstances of experience; and hence, accustom us to employ them more as formulae than as principles. Examples are thus the go-cart of the judgement, which he who is naturally deficient in that faculty cannot afford to dispense with.

[Note: Deficiency in judgement is properly that which is called stupidity; and for such a failing we know no remedy. A dull or narrow-minded person, to whom nothing is wanting but a proper degree of understanding, may be improved by tuition, even so far as to deserve the epithet of learned. But as such persons frequently labour under a deficiency in the faculty of judgement, it is not uncommon to find men extremely learned who in the application of their science betray a lamentable degree this irremediable want.]

But although general logic cannot give directions to the faculty of judgement, the case is very different as regards transcendental logic, insomuch that it appears to be the especial duty of the latter to secure and direct, by means of determinate rules, the faculty of judgement in the employment of the pure understanding. For, as a doctrine, that is, as an endeavour to enlarge the sphere of the understanding in regard to pure a priori cognitions, philosophy is worse than useless, since from all the attempts hitherto made, little or no ground has been gained. But, as a critique, in order to guard against the mistakes of the faculty of judgement (lapsus judicii) in the employment of the few pure conceptions of the understanding which we possess, although its use is in this case purely negative, philosophy is called upon to apply all its acuteness and penetration.

But transcendental philosophy has this peculiarity, that besides indicating the rule, or rather the general condition for rules, which is given in the pure conception of the understanding, it can, at the same time, indicate a priori the case to which the rule must be applied. The cause of the superiority which, in this respect, transcendental philosophy possesses above all other sciences except mathematics, lies in this: it treats of conceptions which must relate a priori to their objects, whose objective validity consequently cannot be demonstrated a posteriori, and is, at the same time, under the obligation of presenting in general but sufficient tests, the conditions under which objects can be given in harmony with those conceptions; otherwise they would be mere logical forms, without content, and not pure conceptions of the understanding.

Our transcendental doctrine of the faculty of judgement will contain two chapters. The first will treat of the sensuous condition under which alone pure conceptions of the understanding can be employed — that is, of the schematism of the pure understanding. The second will treat of those synthetical judgements which are derived a priori from pure conceptions of the understanding under those conditions, and which lie a priori at the foundation of all other cognitions, that is to say, it will treat of the principles of the pure understanding.

TRANSCENDENTAL DOCTRINE OF THE FACULTY OF JUDGEMENT OR, ANALYTIC OF PRINCIPLES.

CHAPTER I.
Of the Schematism at of the Pure Conceptions of the Understanding.

In all subsumptions of an object under a conception, the representation of the object must be homogeneous with the conception; in other words, the conception must contain that which is represented in the object to be subsumed under it. For this is the meaning of the expression: "An object is contained under a conception." Thus, the empirical conception of a plate is homogeneous with the pure geometrical conception of a circle, inasmuch as the roundness which is cogitated in the former is intuited in the latter.

But pure conceptions of the understanding, when compared with empirical intuitions, or even with sensuous intuitions in general, are quite heterogeneous, and never can be discovered in any intuition. How then is the subsumption of the latter under the former, and consequently the application of the categories to phenomena, possible? — For it is impossible to say, for example: "Causality can be intuited through the senses and is contained in the phenomenon." — This natural and important question forms the real cause of the necessity of a transcendental doctrine of the faculty of judgement, with the purpose, to wit, of showing how pure conceptions of the understanding can be applied to phenomena. In all other sciences, where the conceptions by which the object is thought in the general are not so different and heterogeneous from those which represent the object in concreto — as it is given, it is quite unnecessary to institute any special inquiries concerning the application of the former to the latter.

Now it is quite clear that there must be some third thing, which on the one side is homogeneous with the category, and with the phenomenon on the other, and so makes the application of the former to the latter possible. This mediating representation must be pure (without any empirical content), and yet must on the one side be intellectual, on the other sensuous. Such a representation is the transcendental schema.

The conception of the understanding contains pure synthetical unity of the manifold in general. Time, as the formal condition of the manifold of the internal sense, consequently of the conjunction of all representations, contains a priori a manifold in the pure intuition. Now a transcendental determination of time is so far homogeneous with the category, which constitutes the unity thereof, that it is universal and rests upon a rule a priori. On the other hand, it is so far homogeneous with the phenomenon, inasmuch as time is contained in every empirical representation of the manifold. Thus an application of the category to phenomena becomes possible, by means of the transcendental determination of time, which, as the schema of the conceptions of the understanding, mediates the subsumption of the latter under the former.

After what has been proved in our deduction of the categories, no one, it is to be hoped, can hesitate as to the proper decision of the question, whether the employment of these pure conceptions of the understanding ought to be merely empirical or also transcendental; in other words, whether the categories, as conditions of a possible experience, relate a priori solely to phenomena, or whether, as conditions of the possibility of things in general, their application can be extended to objects as things in themselves. For we have there seen that conceptions are quite impossible, and utterly without signification, unless either to them, or at least to the elements of which they consist, an object be given; and that, consequently, they cannot possibly apply to objects as things in themselves without regard to the question whether and how these may be given to us; and, further, that the only manner in which objects can be given to us is by means of the modification of our sensibility; and, finally, that pure a priori conceptions, in addition to the function of the understanding in the category, must contain a priori formal conditions of sensibility (of the internal sense, namely), which again contain the general condition under which alone the category can be applied to any object. This formal and pure condition of sensibility, to which the conception of the understanding is restricted in its employment, we shall name the schema of the conception of the understanding, and the procedure of the understanding with these schemata we shall call the schematism of the pure understanding.

The schema is, in itself, always a mere product of the imagination. But, as the synthesis of imagination has for its aim no single intuition, but merely unity in the determination of sensibility, the schema is clearly distinguishable from the image. Thus, if I place five points one after another.... this is an image of the number five. On the other hand, if I only think a number in general, which may be either five or a hundred, this thought is rather the representation of a method of representing in an image a sum (e.g., a thousand) in conformity with a conception, than the image itself, an image which I should find some little difficulty in reviewing, and comparing with the conception. Now this representation of a general procedure of the imagination to present its image to a conception, I call the schema of this conception.

In truth, it is not images of objects, but schemata, which lie at the foundation of our pure sensuous conceptions. No image could ever be adequate to our conception of a triangle in general. For the generalness of the conception it never could attain to, as this includes under itself all triangles, whether right-angled, acute-angled, etc., whilst the image would always be limited to a single part of this sphere. The schema of the triangle can exist nowhere else than in thought, and it indicates a rule of the synthesis of the imagination in regard to pure figures in space. Still less is an object of experience, or an image of the object, ever to the empirical conception. On the contrary, the conception always relates immediately to the schema of the imagination, as a rule for the determination of our intuition, in conformity with a certain general conception. The conception of a dog indicates a rule, according to which my imagination can delineate the figure of a four-footed animal in general, without being limited to any particular individual form which experience presents to me, or indeed to any possible image that I can represent to myself in concreto. This schematism of our understanding in regard to phenomena and their mere form, is an art, hidden in the depths of the human soul, whose true modes of action we shall only with difficulty discover and unveil. Thus much only can we say: "The image is a product of the empirical faculty of the productive imagination — the schema of sensuous conceptions (of figures in space, for example) is a product, and, as it were, a monogram of the pure imagination a priori, whereby and according to which images first become possible, which, however, can be connected with the conception only mediately by means of the schema which they indicate, and are in themselves never fully adequate to it." On the other hand, the schema of a pure conception of the understanding is something that cannot be reduced into any image — it is nothing else than the pure synthesis expressed by the category, conformably, to a rule of unity according to conceptions. It is a transcendental product of the imagination, a product which concerns the determination of the internal sense, according to conditions of its form (time) in respect to all representations, in so far as these representations must be conjoined a priori in one conception, conformably to the unity of apperception.

Without entering upon a dry and tedious analysis of the essential requisites of transcendental schemata of the pure conceptions of the understanding, we shall rather proceed at once to give an explanation of them according to the order of the categories, and in connection therewith.

For the external sense the pure image of all quantities (quantorum) is space; the pure image of all objects of sense in general, is time. But the pure schema of quantity (quantitatis) as a conception of the understanding, is number, a representation which comprehends the successive addition of one to one (homogeneous quantities). Thus, number is nothing else than the unity of the synthesis of the manifold in a homogeneous intuition, by means of my generating time itself in my apprehension of the intuition.

Reality, in the pure conception of the understanding, is that which corresponds to a sensation in general; that, consequently, the conception of which indicates a being (in time). Negation is that the conception of which represents a not-being (in time). The opposition of these two consists therefore in the difference of one and the same time, as a time filled or a time empty. Now as time is only the form of intuition, consequently of objects as phenomena, that which in objects corresponds to sensation is the transcendental matter of all objects as things in themselves (Sachheit, reality). Now every sensation has a degree or quantity by which it can fill time, that is to say, the internal sense in respect of the representation of an object, more or less, until it vanishes into nothing (= 0 = negatio). Thus there is a relation and connection between reality and negation, or rather a transition from the former to the latter, which makes every reality representable to us as a quantum; and the schema of a reality as the quantity of something in so far as it fills time, is exactly this continuous and uniform generation of the reality in time, as we descend in time from the sensation which has a certain degree, down to the vanishing thereof, or gradually ascend from negation to the quantity thereof.

The schema of substance is the permanence of the real in time; that is, the representation of it as a substratum of the empirical determination of time; a substratum which therefore remains, whilst all else changes. (Time passes not, but in it passes the existence of the changeable. To time, therefore, which is itself unchangeable and permanent, corresponds that which in the phenomenon is unchangeable in existence, that is, substance, and it is only by it that the succession and coexistence of phenomena can be determined in regard to time.)

The schema of cause and of the causality of a thing is the real which, when posited, is always followed by something else. It consists, therefore, in the succession of the manifold, in so far as that succession is subjected to a rule.

The schema of community (reciprocity of action and reaction), or the reciprocal causality of substances in respect of their accidents, is the coexistence of the determinations of the one with those of the other, according to a general rule.

The schema of possibility is the accordance of the synthesis of different representations with the conditions of time in general (as, for example, opposites cannot exist together at the same time in the same thing, but only after each other), and is therefore the determination of the representation of a thing at any time.

The schema of reality is existence in a determined time.

The schema of necessity is the existence of an object in all time.

It is clear, from all this, that the schema of the category of quantity contains and represents the generation (synthesis) of time itself, in the successive apprehension of an object; the schema of quality the synthesis of sensation with the representation of time, or the filling up of time; the schema of relation the relation of perceptions to each other in all time (that is, according to a rule of the determination of time): and finally, the schema of modality and its categories, time itself, as the correlative of the determination of an object — whether it does belong to time, and how. The schemata, therefore, are nothing but a priori determinations of time according to rules, and these, in regard to all possible objects, following the arrangement of the categories, relate to the series in time, the content in time, the order in time, and finally, to the complex or totality in time.

Hence it is apparent that the schematism of the understanding, by means of the transcendental synthesis of the imagination, amounts to nothing else than the unity of the manifold of intuition in the internal sense, and thus indirectly to the unity of apperception, as a function corresponding to the internal sense (a receptivity). Thus, the schemata of the pure conceptions of the understanding are the true and only conditions whereby our understanding receives an application to objects, and consequently significance. Finally, therefore, the categories are only capable of empirical use, inasmuch as they serve merely to subject phenomena to the universal rules of synthesis, by means of an a priori necessary unity (on account of the necessary union of all consciousness in one original apperception); and so to render them susceptible of a complete connection in one experience. But within this whole of possible experience lie all our cognitions, and in the universal relation to this experience consists transcendental truth, which antecedes all empirical truth, and renders the latter possible.

It is, however, evident at first sight, that although the schemata of sensibility are the sole agents in realizing the categories, they do, nevertheless, also restrict them, that is, they limit the categories by conditions which lie beyond the sphere of understanding — namely, in sensibility. Hence the schema is properly only the phenomenon, or the sensuous conception of an object in harmony with the category. (Numerus est quantitas phaenomenon — sensatio realitas phaenomenon; constans et perdurabile rerum substantia phaenomenon — aeternitas, necessitas, phaenomena, etc.) Now, if we remove a restrictive condition, we thereby amplify, it appears, the formerly limited conception. In this way, the categories in their pure signification, free from all conditions of sensibility, ought to be valid of things as they are, and not, as the schemata represent them, merely as they appear; and consequently the categories must have a significance far more extended, and wholly independent of all schemata. In truth, there does always remain to the pure conceptions of the understanding, after abstracting every sensuous condition, a value and significance, which is, however, merely logical. But in this case, no object is given them, and therefore they have no meaning sufficient to afford us a conception of an object. The notion of substance, for example, if we leave out the sensuous determination of permanence, would mean nothing more than a something which can be cogitated as subject, without the possibility of becoming a predicate to anything else. Of this representation I can make nothing, inasmuch as it does not indicate to me what determinations the thing possesses which must thus be valid as premier subject. Consequently, the categories, without schemata are merely functions of the understanding for the production of conceptions, but do not represent any object. This significance they derive from sensibility, which at the same time realizes the understanding and restricts it.

CHAPTER II.
System of all Principles of the Pure Understanding.

In the foregoing chapter we have merely considered the general conditions under which alone the transcendental faculty of judgement is justified in using the pure conceptions of the understanding for synthetical judgements. Our duty at present is to exhibit in systematic connection those judgements which the understanding really produces a priori. For this purpose, our table of the categories will certainly afford us the natural and safe guidance. For it is precisely the categories whose application to possible experience must constitute all pure a priori cognition of the understanding; and the relation of which to sensibility will, on that very account, present us with a complete and systematic catalogue of all the transcendental principles of the use of the understanding.

Principles a priori are so called, not merely because they contain in themselves the grounds of other judgements, but also because they themselves are not grounded in higher and more general cognitions. This peculiarity, however, does not raise them altogether above the need of a proof. For although there could be found no higher cognition, and therefore no objective proof, and although such a principle rather serves as the foundation for all cognition of the object, this by no means hinders us from drawing a proof from the subjective sources of the possibility of the cognition of an object. Such a proof is necessary, moreover, because without it the principle might be liable to the imputation of being a mere gratuitous assertion.

In the second place, we shall limit our investigations to those principles which relate to the categories. For as to the principles of transcendental aesthetic, according to which space and time are the conditions of the possibility of things as phenomena, as also the restriction of these principles, namely, that they cannot be applied to objects as things in themselves — these, of course, do not fall within the scope of our present inquiry. In like manner, the principles of mathematical science form no part of this system, because they are all drawn from intuition, and not from the pure conception of the understanding. The possibility of these principles, however, will necessarily be considered here, inasmuch as they are synthetical judgements a priori, not indeed for the purpose of proving their accuracy and apodeictic certainty, which is unnecessary, but merely to render conceivable and deduce the possibility of such evident a priori cognitions.

But we shall have also to speak of the principle of analytical judgements, in opposition to synthetical judgements, which is the proper subject of our inquiries, because this very opposition will free the theory of the latter from all ambiguity, and place it clearly before our eyes in its true nature.

SYSTEM OF THE PRINCIPLES OF THE PURE UNDERSTANDING.

SECTION I. Of the Supreme Principle of all Analytical Judgements.

Whatever may be the content of our cognition, and in whatever manner our cognition may be related to its object, the universal, although only negative conditions of all our judgements is that they do not contradict themselves; otherwise these judgements are in themselves (even without respect to the object) nothing. But although there may exist no contradiction in our judgement, it may nevertheless connect conceptions in such a manner that they do not correspond to the object, or without any grounds either a priori or a posteriori for arriving at such a judgement, and thus, without being self-contradictory, a judgement may nevertheless be either false or groundless.

Now, the proposition: "No subject can have a predicate that contradicts it," is called the principle of contradiction, and is a universal but purely negative criterion of all truth. But it belongs to logic alone, because it is valid of cognitions, merely as cognitions and without respect to their content, and declares that the contradiction entirely nullifies them. We can also, however, make a positive use of this principle, that is, not merely to banish falsehood and error (in so far as it rests upon contradiction), but also for the cognition of truth. For if the judgement is analytical, be it affirmative or negative, its truth must always be recognizable by means of the principle of contradiction. For the contrary of that which lies and is cogitated as conception in the cognition of the object will be always properly negatived, but the conception itself must always be affirmed of the object, inasmuch as the contrary thereof would be in contradiction to the object.

We must therefore hold the principle of contradiction to be the universal and fully sufficient Principle of all analytical cognition. But as a sufficient criterion of truth, it has no further utility or authority. For the fact that no cognition can be at variance with this principle without nullifying itself, constitutes this principle the sine qua non, but not the determining ground of the truth of our cognition. As our business at present is properly with the synthetical part of our knowledge only, we shall always be on our guard not to transgress this inviolable principle; but at the same time not to expect from it any direct assistance in the establishment of the truth of any synthetical proposition.

There exists, however, a formula of this celebrated principle — a principle merely formal and entirely without content — which contains a synthesis that has been inadvertently and quite unnecessarily mixed up with it. It is this: "It is impossible for a thing to be and not to be at the same time." Not to mention the superfluousness of the addition of the word impossible to indicate the apodeictic certainty, which ought to be self-evident from the proposition itself, the proposition is affected by the condition of time, and as it were says: "A thing = A, which is something = B, cannot at the same time be non-B." But both, B as well as non-B, may quite well exist in succession. For example, a man who is young cannot at the same time be old; but the same man can very well be at one time young, and at another not young, that is, old. Now the principle of contradiction as a merely logical proposition must not by any means limit its application merely to relations of time, and consequently a formula like the preceding is quite foreign to its true purpose. The misunderstanding arises in this way. We first of all separate a predicate of a thing from the conception of the thing, and afterwards connect with this predicate its opposite, and hence do not establish any contradiction with the subject, but only with its predicate, which has been conjoined with the subject synthetically — a contradiction, moreover, which obtains only when the first and second predicate are affirmed in the same time. If I say: "A man who is ignorant is not learned," the condition "at the same time" must be added, for he who is at one time ignorant, may at another be learned. But if I say: "No ignorant man is a learned man," the proposition is analytical, because the characteristic ignorance is now a constituent part of the conception of the subject; and in this case the negative proposition is evident immediately from the proposition of contradiction, without the necessity of adding the condition "the same time." This is the reason why I have altered the formula of this principle — an alteration which shows very clearly the nature of an analytical proposition.

SECTION II. Of the Supreme Principle of all Synthetical Judgements.

The explanation of the possibility of synthetical judgements is a task with which general logic has nothing to do; indeed she needs not even be acquainted with its name. But in transcendental logic it is the most important matter to be dealt with — indeed the only one, if the question is of the possibility of synthetical judgements a priori, the conditions and extent of their validity. For when this question is fully decided, it can reach its aim with perfect ease, the determination, to wit, of the extent and limits of the pure understanding.

In an analytical judgement I do not go beyond the given conception, in order to arrive at some decision respecting it. If the judgement is affirmative, I predicate of the conception only that which was already cogitated in it; if negative, I merely exclude from the conception its contrary. But in synthetical judgements, I must go beyond the given conception, in order to cogitate, in relation with it, something quite different from that which was cogitated in it, a relation which is consequently never one either of identity or contradiction, and by means of which the truth or error of the judgement cannot be discerned merely from the judgement itself.

Granted, then, that we must go out beyond a given conception, in order to compare it synthetically with another, a third thing is necessary, in which alone the synthesis of two conceptions can originate. Now what is this tertium quid that is to be the medium of all synthetical judgements? It is only a complex in which all our representations are contained, the internal sense to wit, and its form a priori, time.

The synthesis of our representations rests upon the imagination; their synthetical unity (which is requisite to a judgement), upon the unity of apperception. In this, therefore, is to be sought the possibility of synthetical judgements, and as all three contain the sources of a priori representations, the possibility of pure synthetical judgements also; nay, they are necessary upon these grounds, if we are to possess a knowledge of objects, which rests solely upon the synthesis of representations.

If a cognition is to have objective reality, that is, to relate to an object, and possess sense and meaning in respect to it, it is necessary that the object be given in some way or another. Without this, our conceptions are empty, and we may indeed have thought by means of them, but by such thinking we have not, in fact, cognized anything, we have merely played with representation. To give an object, if this expression be understood in the sense of "to present" the object, not mediately but immediately in intuition, means nothing else than to apply the representation of it to experience, be that experience real or only possible. Space and time themselves, pure as these conceptions are from all that is empirical, and certain as it is that they are represented fully a priori in the mind, would be completely without objective validity, and without sense and significance, if their necessary use in the objects of experience were not shown. Nay, the representation of them is a mere schema, that always relates to the reproductive imagination, which calls up the objects of experience, without which they have no meaning. And so it is with all conceptions without distinction.

The possibility of experience is, then, that which gives objective reality to all our a priori cognitions. Now experience depends upon the synthetical unity of phenomena, that is, upon a synthesis according to conceptions of the object of phenomena in general, a synthesis without which experience never could become knowledge, but would be merely a rhapsody of perceptions, never fitting together into any connected text, according to rules of a thoroughly united (possible) consciousness, and therefore never subjected to the transcendental and necessary unity of apperception. Experience has therefore for a foundation, a priori principles of its form, that is to say, general rules of unity in the synthesis of phenomena, the objective reality of which rules, as necessary conditions even of the possibility of experience can which rules, as necessary conditions — even of the possibility of experience — can always be shown in experience. But apart from this relation, a priori synthetical propositions are absolutely impossible, because they have no third term, that is, no pure object, in which the synthetical unity can exhibit the objective reality of its conceptions.

Although, then, respecting space, or the forms which productive imagination describes therein, we do cognize much a priori in synthetical judgements, and are really in no need of experience for this purpose, such knowledge would nevertheless amount to nothing but a busy trifling with a mere chimera, were not space to be considered as the condition of the phenomena which constitute the material of external experience. Hence those pure synthetical judgements do relate, though but mediately, to possible experience, or rather to the possibility of experience, and upon that alone is founded the objective validity of their synthesis.

While then, on the one hand, experience, as empirical synthesis, is the only possible mode of cognition which gives reality to all other synthesis; on the other hand, this latter synthesis, as cognition a priori, possesses truth, that is, accordance with its object, only in so far as it contains nothing more than what is necessary to the synthetical unity of experience.

Accordingly, the supreme principle of all synthetical judgements is: "Every object is subject to the necessary conditions of the synthetical unity of the manifold of intuition in a possible experience."

A priori synthetical judgements are possible when we apply the formal conditions of the a priori intuition, the synthesis of the imagination, and the necessary unity of that synthesis in a transcendental apperception, to a possible cognition of experience, and say: "The conditions of the possibility of experience in general are at the same time conditions of the possibility of the objects of experience, and have, for that reason, objective validity in an a priori synthetical judgement."

SECTION III. Systematic Representation of all Synthetical Principles of the Pure Understanding.

That principles exist at all is to be ascribed solely to the pure understanding, which is not only the faculty of rules in regard to that which happens, but is even the source of principles according to which everything that can be presented to us as an object is necessarily subject to rules, because without such rules we never could attain to cognition of an object. Even the laws of nature, if they are contemplated as principles of the empirical use of the understanding, possess also a characteristic of necessity, and we may therefore at least expect them to be determined upon grounds which are valid a priori and antecedent to all experience. But all laws of nature, without distinction, are subject to higher principles of the understanding, inasmuch as the former are merely applications of the latter to particular cases of experience. These higher principles alone therefore give the conception, which contains the necessary condition, and, as it were, the exponent of a rule; experience, on the other hand, gives the case which comes under the rule.

There is no danger of our mistaking merely empirical principles for principles of the pure understanding, or conversely; for the character of necessity, according to conceptions which distinguish the latter, and the absence of this in every empirical proposition, how extensively valid soever it may be, is a perfect safeguard against confounding them. There are, however, pure principles a priori, which nevertheless I should not ascribe to the pure understanding — for this reason, that they are not derived from pure conceptions, but (although by the mediation of the understanding) from pure intuitions. But understanding is the faculty of conceptions. Such principles mathematical science possesses, but their application to experience, consequently their objective validity, nay the possibility of such a priori synthetical cognitions (the deduction thereof) rests entirely upon the pure understanding.

On this account, I shall not reckon among my principles those of mathematics; though I shall include those upon the possibility and objective validity a priori, of principles of the mathematical science, which, consequently, are to be looked upon as the principle of these, and which proceed from conceptions to intuition, and not from intuition to conceptions.

In the application of the pure conceptions of the understanding to possible experience, the employment of their synthesis is either mathematical or dynamical, for it is directed partly on the intuition alone, partly on the existence of a phenomenon. But the a priori conditions of intuition are in relation to a possible experience absolutely necessary, those of the existence of objects of a possible empirical intuition are in themselves contingent. Hence the principles of the mathematical use of the categories will possess a character of absolute necessity, that is, will be apodeictic; those, on the other hand, of the dynamical use, the character of an a priori necessity indeed, but only under the condition of empirical thought in an experience, therefore only mediately and indirectly. Consequently they will not possess that immediate evidence which is peculiar to the former, although their application to experience does not, for that reason, lose its truth and certitude. But of this point we shall be better able to judge at the conclusion of this system of principles.

The table of the categories is naturally our guide to the table of principles, because these are nothing else than rules for the objective employment of the former. Accordingly, all principles of the pure understanding are:

These appellations I have chosen advisedly, in order that we might not lose sight of the distinctions in respect of the evidence and the employment of these principles. It will, however, soon appear that — a fact which concerns both the evidence of these principles, and the a priori determination of phenomena — according to the categories of quantity and quality (if we attend merely to the form of these), the principles of these categories are distinguishable from those of the two others, in as much as the former are possessed of an intuitive, but the latter of a merely discursive, though in both instances a complete, certitude. I shall therefore call the former mathematical, and the latter dynamical principles.* It must be observed, however, that by these terms I mean just as little in the one case the principles of mathematics as those of general (physical) dynamics in the other. I have here in view merely the principles of the pure understanding, in their application to the internal sense (without distinction of the representations given therein), by means of which the sciences of mathematics and dynamics become possible. Accordingly, I have named these principles rather with reference to their application than their content; and I shall now proceed to consider them in the order in which they stand in the table.

[Note: All combination (conjunctio) is either composition (compositio) or connection (nexus). The former is the synthesis of a manifold, the parts of which do not necessarily belong to each other. For example, the two triangles into which a square is divided by a diagonal, do not necessarily belong to each other, and of this kind is the synthesis of the homogeneous in everything that can be mathematically considered. This synthesis can be divided into those of aggregation and coalition, the former of which is applied to extensive, the latter to intensive quantities. The second sort of combination (nexus) is the synthesis of a manifold, in so far as its parts do belong necessarily to each other; for example, the accident to a substance, or the effect to the cause. Consequently it is a synthesis of that which though heterogeneous, is represented as connected a priori. This combination — not an arbitrary one — I entitle dynamical because it concerns the connection of the existence of the manifold. This, again, may be divided into the physical synthesis, of the phenomena divided among each other, and the metaphysical synthesis, or the connection of phenomena a priori in the faculty of cognition.]

1. AXIOMS OF INTUITION.

The principle of these is: All Intuitions are Extensive Quantities.

PROOF.

All phenomena contain, as regards their form, an intuition in space and time, which lies a priori at the foundation of all without exception. Phenomena, therefore, cannot be apprehended, that is, received into empirical consciousness otherwise than through the synthesis of a manifold, through which the representations of a determinate space or time are generated; that is to say, through the composition of the homogeneous and the consciousness of the synthetical unity of this manifold (homogeneous). Now the consciousness of a homogeneous manifold in intuition, in so far as thereby the representation of an object is rendered possible, is the conception of a quantity (quanti). Consequently, even the perception of an object as phenomenon is possible only through the same synthetical unity of the manifold of the given sensuous intuition, through which the unity of the composition of the homogeneous manifold in the conception of a quantity is cogitated; that is to say, all phenomena are quantities, and extensive quantities, because as intuitions in space or time they must be represented by means of the same synthesis through which space and time themselves are determined.

An extensive quantity I call that wherein the representation of the parts renders possible (and therefore necessarily antecedes) the representation of the whole. I cannot represent to myself any line, however small, without drawing it in thought, that is, without generating from a point all its parts one after another, and in this way alone producing this intuition. Precisely the same is the case with every, even the smallest, portion of time. I cogitate therein only the successive progress from one moment to another, and hence, by means of the different portions of time and the addition of them, a determinate quantity of time is produced. As the pure intuition in all phenomena is either time or space, so is every phenomenon in its character of intuition an extensive quantity, inasmuch as it can only be cognized in our apprehension by successive synthesis (from part to part). All phenomena are, accordingly, to be considered as aggregates, that is, as a collection of previously given parts; which is not the case with every sort of quantities, but only with those which are represented and apprehended by us as extensive.

On this successive synthesis of the productive imagination, in the generation of figures, is founded the mathematics of extension, or geometry, with its axioms, which express the conditions of sensuous intuition a priori, under which alone the schema of a pure conception of external intuition can exist; for example, "be tween two points only one straight line is possible," "two straight lines cannot enclose a space," etc. These are the axioms which properly relate only to quantities (quanta) as such.

But, as regards the quantity of a thing (quantitas), that is to say, the answer to the question: "How large is this or that object?" although, in respect to this question, we have various propositions synthetical and immediately certain (indemonstrabilia); we have, in the proper sense of the term, no axioms. For example, the propositions: "If equals be added to equals, the wholes are equal"; "If equals be taken from equals, the remainders are equal", are analytical, because I am immediately conscious of the identity of the production of the one quantity with the production of the other; whereas axioms must be a priori synthetical propositions. On the other hand, the self-evident propositions as to the relation of numbers, are certainly synthetical but not universal, like those of geometry, and for this reason cannot be called axioms, but numerical formulae. That $7 + 5 = 12$ is not an analytical proposition. For neither in the representation of seven, nor of five, nor of the composition of the two numbers, do I cogitate the number twelve. (Whether I cogitate the number in the addition of both, is not at present the question; for in the case of an analytical proposition, the only point is whether I really cogitate the predicate in the representation of the subject.) But although the proposition is synthetical, it is nevertheless only a singular proposition. In so far as regard is here had merely to the synthesis of the homogeneous (the units), it cannot take place except in one manner, although our use of these numbers is afterwards general. If I say: "A triangle can be constructed with three lines, any two of which taken together are greater than the third," I exercise merely the pure function of the productive imagination, which may draw the lines longer or shorter and construct the angles at its pleasure. On the contrary, the number seven is possible only in one manner, and so is likewise the number twelve, which results from the synthesis of seven and five. Such propositions, then, cannot be termed axioms (for in that case we should have an infinity of these), but numerical formulae.

This transcendental principle of the mathematics of phenomena greatly enlarges our a priori cognition. For it is by this principle alone that pure mathematics is rendered applicable in all its precision to objects of experience, and without it the validity of this application would not be so self-evident; on the contrary, contradictions and confusions have often arisen on this very point. Phenomena are not things in themselves. Empirical intuition is possible only through pure intuition (of space and time); consequently, what geometry affirms of the latter, is indisputably valid of the former. All evasions, such as the statement that objects of sense do not conform to the rules of construction in space (for example, to the rule of the infinite divisibility of lines or angles), must fall to the ground. For, if these objections hold good, we deny to space, and with it to all mathematics, objective validity, and no longer know wherefore, and how far, mathematics can be applied to phenomena. The synthesis of spaces and times as the essential form of all intuition, is that which renders possible the apprehension of a phenomenon, and therefore every external experience, consequently all cognition of the objects of experience; and whatever mathematics in its pure use proves of the former, must necessarily hold good of the latter. All objections are but the chicaneries of an ill-instructed reason, which erroneously thinks to liberate the objects of sense from the formal conditions of our sensibility, and represents these, although mere phenomena, as things in themselves, presented as such to our understanding. But in this case, no a priori synthetical cognition of them could be possible, consequently not through pure conceptions of space and the science which determines these conceptions, that is to say, geometry, would itself be impossible.

2. ANTICIPATIONS OF PERCEPTION.

The principle of these is: In all phenomena the Real, that which is an object of sensation, has Intensive Quantity, that is, has a Degree.

PROOF.

Perception is empirical consciousness, that is to say, a consciousness which contains an element of sensation. Phenomena as objects of perception are not pure, that is, merely formal intuitions, like space and time, for they cannot be perceived in themselves.

[Note: They can be perceived only as phenomena, and some part of them must always belong to the non-ego; whereas pure intuitions are entirely the products of the mind itself, and as such are coguized IN THEMSELVES. — Tr]

They contain, then, over and above the intuition, the materials for an object (through which is represented something existing in space or time), that is to say, they contain the real of sensation, as a representation merely subjective, which gives us merely the consciousness that the subject is affected, and which we refer to some external object. Now, a gradual transition from empirical consciousness to pure consciousness is possible, inasmuch as the real in this consciousness entirely vanishes, and there remains a merely formal consciousness (a priori) of the manifold in time and space;

consequently there is possible a synthesis also of the production of the quantity of a sensation from its commencement, that is, from the pure intuition = 0 onwards up to a certain quantity of the sensation. Now as sensation in itself is not an objective representation, and in it is to be found neither the intuition of space nor of time, it cannot possess any extensive quantity, and yet there does belong to it a quantity (and that by means of its apprehension, in which empirical consciousness can within a certain time rise from nothing = 0 up to its given amount), consequently an intensive quantity. And thus we must ascribe intensive quantity, that is, a degree of influence on sense to all objects of perception, in so far as this perception contains sensation.

All cognition, by means of which I am enabled to cognize and determine a priori what belongs to empirical cognition, may be called an anticipation; and without doubt this is the sense in which Epicurus employed his expression prholepsis. But as there is in phenomena something which is never cognized a priori, which on this account constitutes the proper difference between pure and empirical cognition, that is to say, sensation (as the matter of perception), it follows, that sensation is just that element in cognition which cannot be at all anticipated. On the other hand, we might very well term the pure determinations in space and time, as well in regard to figure as to quantity, anticipations of phenomena, because they represent a priori that which may always be given a posteriori in experience. But suppose that in every sensation, as sensation in general, without any particular sensation being thought of, there existed something which could be cognized a priori, this would deserve to be called anticipation in a special sense — special, because it may seem surprising to forestall experience, in that which concerns the matter of experience, and which we can only derive from itself. Yet such really is the case here.

Apprehension*, by means of sensation alone, fills only one moment, that is, if I do not take into consideration a succession of many sensations. As that in the phenomenon, the apprehension of which is not a successive synthesis advancing from parts to an entire representation, sensation has therefore no extensive quantity; the want of sensation in a moment of time would represent it as empty, consequently = 0. That which in the empirical intuition corresponds to sensation is reality (realitas phaenomenon); that which corresponds to the absence of it, negation = 0. Now every sensation is capable of a diminution, so that it can decrease, and thus gradually disappear. Therefore, between reality in a phenomenon and negation, there exists a continuous concatenation of many possible intermediate sensations, the difference of which from each other is always smaller than that between the given sensation and zero, or complete negation. That is to say, the real in a phenomenon has always a quantity, which however is not discoverable in apprehension, inasmuch as apprehension take place by means of mere sensation in one instant, and not by the successive synthesis of many sensations, and therefore does not progress from parts to the whole. Consequently, it has a quantity, but not an extensive quantity.

[Note: Apprehension is the Kantian word for preception, in the largest sense in which we employ that term. It is the genus which includes under i, as species, perception proper and sensation proper — Tr]

Now that quantity which is apprehended only as unity, and in which plurality can be represented only by approximation to negation = O, I term intensive quantity.

Consequently, reality in a phenomenon has intensive quantity, that is, a degree. If we consider this reality as cause (be it of sensation or of another reality in the phenomenon, for example, a change), we call the degree of reality in its character of cause a momentum, for example, the momentum of weight; and for this reason, that the degree only indicates that quantity the apprehension of which is not successive, but instantaneous. This, however, I touch upon only in passing, for with causality I have at present nothing to do.

Accordingly, every sensation, consequently every reality in phenomena, however small it may be, has a degree, that is, an intensive quantity, which may always be lessened, and between reality and negation there exists a continuous connection of possible realities, and possible smaller perceptions. Every colour — for example, red — has a degree, which, be it ever so small, is never the smallest, and so is it always with heat, the momentum of weight, etc.

This property of quantities, according to which no part of them is the smallest possible (no part simple), is called their continuity. Space and time are quanta continua, because no part of them can be given, without enclosing it within boundaries (points and moments), consequently, this given part is itself a space or a time. Space, therefore, consists only of spaces, and time of times. Points and moments are only boundaries, that is, the mere places or positions of their limitation. But places always presuppose intuitions which are to limit or determine them; and we cannot conceive either space or time composed of constituent parts which are given before space or time. Such quantities may also be called flowing, because synthesis (of the productive imagination) in the production of these quantities is a progression in time, the continuity of which we are accustomed to indicate by the expression flowing.

All phenomena, then, are continuous quantities, in respect both to intuition and mere perception (sensation, and with it reality). In the former case they are extensive quantities; in the latter, intensive. When the synthesis of the manifold of a phenomenon is interrupted, there results merely an aggregate of several phenomena, and not properly a phenomenon as a quantity, which is not produced by the mere continuation of the productive synthesis of a certain kind, but by the repetition of a synthesis always ceasing. For example, if I call thirteen dollars a sum or quantity of money, I employ the term quite correctly, inasmuch as I understand by thirteen dollars the value of a mark in standard silver, which is, to be sure, a continuous quantity, in which no part is the smallest, but every part might constitute a piece of money, which would contain material for still smaller pieces. If, however, by the words thirteen dollars I understand so many coins (be their value in silver what it may), it would be quite erroneous to use the expression a quantity of dollars; on the contrary, I must call them aggregate, that is, a number of coins. And as in every number we must have unity as the foundation, so a phenomenon taken as unity is a quantity, and as such always a continuous quantity (quantum continuum).

Now, seeing all phenomena, whether considered as extensive or intensive, are continuous quantities, the proposition: "All change (transition of a thing from one state into another) is continuous," might be proved here easily, and with mathematical evidence, were it not that the causality of a change lies, entirely beyond the bounds of a transcendental philosophy, and presupposes empirical principles. For of the possibility of a cause which changes the condition of things, that is, which determines them to the contrary to a certain given state, the understanding gives us a priori no knowledge; not merely because it has no insight into the possibility of it (for such insight is absent in several a priori cognitions), but because the notion of change concerns only certain determinations of phenomena, which experience alone can acquaint us with, while their cause lies in the unchangeable. But seeing that we have nothing which we could here employ but the pure fundamental conceptions of all possible experience, among which of course nothing empirical can be admitted, we dare not, without injuring the unity of our system, anticipate general physical science, which is built upon certain fundamental experiences.

Nevertheless, we are in no want of proofs of the great influence which the principle above developed exercises in the anticipation of perceptions, and even in supplying the want of them, so far as to shield us against the false conclusions which otherwise we might rashly draw.

If all reality in perception has a degree, between which and negation there is an endless sequence of ever smaller degrees, and if, nevertheless, every sense must have a determinate degree of receptivity for sensations; no perception, and consequently no experience is possible, which can prove, either immediately or mediately, an entire absence of all reality in a phenomenon; in other words, it is impossible ever to draw from experience a proof of the existence of empty space or of empty time. For in the first place, an entire absence of reality in a sensuous intuition cannot of course be an object of perception; secondly, such absence cannot be deduced from the contemplation of any single phenomenon, and the difference of the degrees in its reality; nor ought it ever to be admitted in explanation of any phenomenon. For if even the complete intuition of a determinate space or time is thoroughly real, that is, if no part thereof is empty, yet because every reality has its degree, which, with the extensive quantity of the phenomenon unchanged, can diminish through endless gradations down to nothing (the void), there must be infinitely graduated degrees, with which space or time is filled, and the intensive quantity in different phenomena may be smaller or greater, although the extensive quantity of the intuition remains equal and unaltered.

We shall give an example of this. Almost all natural philosophers, remarking a great difference in the quantity of the matter of different kinds in bodies with the same volume (partly on account of the momentum of gravity or weight, partly on account of the momentum of resistance to other bodies in motion), conclude unanimously that this volume (extensive quantity of the phenomenon) must be void in all bodies, although in different proportion. But who would suspect that these for the most part mathematical and mechanical inquirers into nature should ground this conclusion solely on a metaphysical hypothesis — a sort of hypothesis which they profess to disparage and avoid? Yet this they do, in assuming that the real in space (I must not here call it impenetrability or weight, because these are empirical conceptions) is always identical, and can only be distinguished according to its extensive quantity, that is, multiplicity. Now to this presupposition, for which they can have no ground in experience, and which consequently is merely metaphysical, I oppose a transcendental demonstration, which it is true will not explain the difference in the filling up of spaces, but which nevertheless completely does away with the supposed necessity of the above-mentioned presupposition that we cannot explain the said difference otherwise than by the hypothesis of empty spaces. This demonstration, moreover, has the merit of setting the understanding at liberty to conceive this distinction in a different manner, if the explanation of the fact requires any such hypothesis. For we perceive that although two equal spaces may be completely filled by matters altogether different, so that in neither of them is there left a single point wherein matter is not present, nevertheless, every reality has its degree (of resistance or of weight), which, without diminution of the extensive quantity, can become less and less ad infinitum, before it passes into nothingness and disappears. Thus an expansion which fills a space — for example, caloric, or any other reality in the phenomenal world — can decrease in its degrees to infinity, yet without leaving the smallest part of the space empty; on the contrary, filling it with those lesser degrees as completely as another phenomenon could with greater. My intention here is by no means to maintain that this is really the case with the difference of matters, in regard to their specific gravity; I wish only to prove, from a principle of the pure understanding, that the nature of our perceptions makes such a mode of explanation possible, and that it is erroneous to regard the real in a phenomenon as equal quoad its degree, and different only quoad its aggregation and extensive quantity, and this, too, on the pretended authority of an a priori principle of the understanding.

Nevertheless, this principle of the anticipation of perception must somewhat startle an inquirer whom initiation into transcendental philosophy has rendered cautious. We must naturally entertain some doubt whether or not the understanding can enounce any such synthetical proposition as that respecting the degree of all reality in phenomena, and consequently the possibility of the internal difference of sensation itself — abstraction being made of its empirical quality. Thus it is a question not unworthy of solution: "How the understanding can pronounce synthetically and a priori respecting phenomena, and thus anticipate these, even in that which is peculiarly and merely empirical, that, namely, which concerns sensation itself?"

The quality of sensation is in all cases merely empirical, and cannot be represented a priori (for example, colours, taste, etc.). But the real — that which corresponds to sensation — in opposition to negation = 0, only represents something the conception of which in itself contains a being (ein seyn), and signifies nothing but the synthesis in an empirical consciousness. That is to say, the empirical consciousness in the internal sense can be raised from 0 to every higher degree, so that the very same extensive quantity of intuition, an illuminated surface, for example, excites as great a sensation as an aggregate of many other surfaces less illuminated. We can therefore make complete abstraction of the extensive quantity of a phenomenon, and represent to ourselves in the mere sensation in a certain momentum, a synthesis of homogeneous ascension from 0 up to the given empirical consciousness, All sensations therefore as such are given only a posteriori, but this property thereof, namely, that they have a degree, can be known a priori. It is worthy of remark, that in respect to quantities in general, we can cognize a priori only a single quality, namely, continuity; but in respect to all quality (the real in phenomena), we cannot cognize a priori anything more than the intensive quantity thereof, namely, that they have a degree. All else is left to experience.

3. ANALOGIES OF EXPERIENCE.

The principle of these is: Experience is possible only through the representation of a necessary connection of Perceptions.

PROOF.

Experience is an empirical cognition; that is to say, a cognition which determines an object by means of perceptions. It is therefore a synthesis of perceptions, a synthesis which is not itself contained in perception, but which contains the synthetical unity of the manifold of perception in a consciousness; and this unity constitutes the essential of our cognition of objects of the senses, that is, of experience (not merely of intuition or sensation). Now in experience our perceptions come together contingently, so that no character of necessity in their connection appears, or can appear from the perceptions themselves, because apprehension is only a placing together of the manifold of empirical intuition, and no representation of a necessity in the connected existence of the phenomena which apprehension brings together, is to be discovered therein. But as experience is a cognition of objects by means of perceptions, it follows that the relation of the existence of the existence of the manifold must be represented in experience not as it is put together in time, but as it is objectively in time. And as time itself cannot be perceived, the determination of the existence of objects in time can only take place by means of their connection in time in general, consequently only by means of a priori connecting conceptions. Now as these conceptions always possess the character of necessity, experience is possible only by means of a representation of the necessary connection of perception.

The three modi of time are permanence, succession, and coexistence. Accordingly, there are three rules of all relations of time in phenomena, according to which the existence of every phenomenon is determined in respect of the unity of all time, and these antecede all experience and render it possible.

The general principle of all three analogies rests on the necessary unity of apperception in relation to all possible empirical consciousness (perception) at every time, consequently, as this unity lies a priori at the foundation of all mental operations, the principle rests on the synthetical unity of all phenomena according to their relation in time. For the original apperception relates to our internal sense (the complex of all representations), and indeed relates a priori to its form, that is to say, the relation of the manifold empirical consciousness in time. Now this manifold must be combined in original apperception according to relations of time — a necessity imposed by the a priori transcendental unity of apperception, to which is subjected all that can belong to my (i.e., my own) cognition, and therefore all that can become an object for me. This synthetical and a priori determined unity in relation of perceptions in time is therefore the rule: "All empirical determinations of time must be subject to rules of the general determination of time"; and the analogies of experience, of which we are now about to treat, must be rules of this nature.

These principles have this peculiarity, that they do not concern phenomena, and the synthesis of the empirical intuition thereof, but merely the existence of phenomena and their relation to each other in regard to this existence. Now the mode in which we apprehend a thing in a phenomenon can be determined a priori in such a manner that the rule of its synthesis can give, that is to say, can produce this a priori intuition in every empirical example. But the existence of phenomena cannot be known a priori, and although we could arrive by this path at a conclusion of the fact of some existence, we could not cognize that existence determinately, that is to say, we should be incapable of anticipating in what respect the empirical intuition of it would be distinguishable from that of others.

The two principles above mentioned, which I called mathematical, in consideration of the fact of their authorizing the application of mathematic phenomena, relate to these phenomena only in regard to their possibility, and instruct us how phenomena, as far as regards their intuition or the real in their perception, can be generated according to the rules of a mathematical synthesis. Consequently, numerical quantities, and with them the determination of a phenomenon as a quantity, can be employed in the one case as well as in the other. Thus, for example, out of 200,000 illuminations by the moon, I might compose and give a priori, that is construct, the degree of our sensations of the sun-light.* We may therefore entitle these two principles constitutive.

[Note: Kant's meaning is: The two principles enunciated under the heads of "Axioms of Intuition," and "Anticipations of Perception," authorize the application to phenomena of determinations of size and number, that is of mathematic. For example, I may compute the light of the sun, and say that its quantity is a certain number of times greater than that of the moon. In the same way, heat is measured by the comparison of its different effects on water, &c., and on mercury in a thermometer. — Tr]

The case is very different with those principles whose province it is to subject the existence of phenomena to rules a priori. For as existence does not admit of being constructed, it is clear that they must only concern the relations of existence and be merely regulative principles. In this case, therefore, neither axioms nor anticipations are to be thought of. Thus, if a perception is given us, in a certain relation of time to other (although undetermined) perceptions, we cannot then say a priori, what and how great (in quantity) the other perception necessarily connected with the former is, but only how it is connected, quoad its existence, in this given modus of time. Analogies in philosophy mean something very different from that which they represent in mathematics. In the latter they are formulae, which enounce the equality of two relations of quantity, and are always constitutive, so that if two terms of the proportion are given, the third is also given, that is, can be constructed by the aid of these formulae. But in philosophy, analogy is not the equality of two quantitative but of two qualitative relations. In this case, from three given terms, I can give a priori and cognize the relation to a fourth member, but not this fourth term itself, although I certainly possess a rule to guide me in the search for this fourth term in experience, and a mark to assist me in discovering it. An analogy of experience is therefore only a rule according to which unity of experience must arise out of perceptions in respect to objects (phenomena) not as a constitutive, but merely as a regulative principle. The same holds good also of the postulates of empirical thought in general, which relate to the synthesis of mere intuition (which concerns the form of phenomena), the synthesis of perception (which concerns the matter of phenomena), and the synthesis of experience (which concerns the relation of these perceptions). For they are only regulative principles, and clearly distinguishable from the mathematical, which are constitutive, not indeed in regard to the certainty which both possess a priori, but in the mode of evidence thereof, consequently also in the manner of demonstration.

But what has been observed of all synthetical propositions, and must be particularly remarked in this place, is this, that these analogies possess significance and validity, not as principles of the transcendental, but only as principles of the empirical use of the understanding, and their truth can therefore be proved only as such, and that consequently the phenomena must not be subjoined directly under the categories, but only under their schemata. For if the objects to which those principles must be applied were things in themselves, it would be quite impossible to cognize aught concerning them synthetically a priori. But they are nothing but phenomena; a complete knowledge of which — a knowledge to which all principles a priori must at last relate — is the only possible experience. It follows that these principles can have nothing else for their aim than the conditions of the empirical cognition in the unity of synthesis of phenomena. But this synthesis is cogitated only in the schema of the pure conception of the understanding, of whose unity, as that of a synthesis in general, the category contains the function unrestricted by any sensuous condition. These principles will therefore authorize us to connect phenomena according to an analogy, with the logical and universal unity of conceptions, and consequently to employ the categories in the principles themselves; but in the application of them to experience, we shall use only their schemata, as the key to their proper application, instead of the categories, or rather the latter as restricting conditions, under the title of "formulae" of the former.

A. FIRST ANALOGY.

Principle of the Permanence of Substance.

In all changes of phenomena, substance is permanent, and the quantum thereof in nature is neither increased nor diminished.

PROOF.

All phenomena exist in time, wherein alone as substratum, that is, as the permanent form of the internal intuition, coexistence and succession can be represented. Consequently time, in which all changes of phenomena must be cogitated, remains and changes not, because it is that in which succession and coexistence can be represented only as determinations thereof. Now, time in itself cannot be an object of perception. It follows that in objects of perception, that is, in phenomena, there must be found a substratum which represents time in general, and in which all change or coexistence can be perceived by means of the relation of phenomena to it. But the substratum of all reality, that is, of all that pertains to the existence of things, is substance; all that pertains to existence can be cogitated only as a determination of substance. Consequently, the permanent, in relation to which alone can all relations of time in phenomena be determined, is substance in the world of phenomena, that is, the real in phenomena, that which, as the substratum of all change, remains ever the same. Accordingly, as this cannot change in existence, its quantity in nature can neither be increased nor diminished.

Our apprehension of the manifold in a phenomenon is always successive, is Consequently always changing. By it alone we could, therefore, never determine whether this manifold, as an object of experience, is coexistent or successive, unless it had for a foundation something fixed and permanent, of the existence of which all succession and coexistence are nothing but so many modes (modi of time). Only in the permanent, then, are relations of time possible (for simultaneity and succession are the only relations in time); that is to say, the permanent is the substratum of our empirical representation of time itself, in which alone all determination of time is possible. Permanence is, in fact, just another expression for time, as the abiding correlate of all existence of phenomena, and of all change, and of all coexistence. For change does not affect time itself, but only the phenomena in time (just as coexistence cannot be regarded as a modus of time itself, seeing that in time no parts are coexistent, but all successive). If we were to attribute succession to time itself, we should be obliged to cogitate another time, in which this succession would be possible. It is only by means of the permanent that existence in different parts of the successive series of time receives a quantity, which we entitle duration. For in mere succession, existence is perpetually vanishing and recommencing, and therefore never has even the least quantity. Without the permanent, then, no relation in time is possible. Now, time in itself is not an object of perception; consequently the permanent in phenomena must be regarded as the substratum of all determination of time, and consequently also as the condition of the possibility of all synthetical unity of perceptions, that is, of experience; and all existence and all change in time can only be regarded as a mode in the existence of that which abides unchangeably. Therefore, in all phenomena, the permanent is the object in itself, that is, the substance (phenomenon); but all that changes or can change belongs only to the mode of the existence of this substance or substances, consequently to its determinations.

I find that in all ages not only the philosopher, but even the common understanding, has preposited this permanence as a substratum of all change in phenomena; indeed, I am compelled to believe that they will always accept this as an indubitable fact. Only the philosopher expresses himself in a more precise and definite manner, when he says: "In all changes in the world, the substance remains, and the accidents alone are changeable." But of this decidedly synthetical proposition, I nowhere meet with even an attempt at proof; nay, it very rarely has the good fortune to stand, as it deserves to do, at the head of the pure and entirely a priori laws of nature. In truth, the statement that substance is permanent, is tautological. For this very permanence is the ground on which we apply the category of substance to the phenomenon; and we should have been obliged to prove that in all phenomena there is something permanent, of the existence of which the changeable is nothing but a determination. But because a proof of this nature cannot be dogmatical, that is, cannot be drawn from conceptions, inasmuch as it concerns a synthetical proposition a priori, and as philosophers never reflected that such propositions are valid only in relation to possible experience, and therefore cannot be proved except by means of a deduction of the possibility of experience, it is no wonder that while it has served as the foundation of all experience (for we feel the need of it in empirical cognition), it has never been supported by proof.

A philosopher was asked: "What is the weight of smoke?" He answered: "Subtract from the weight of the burnt wood the weight of the remaining ashes, and you will have the weight of the smoke." Thus he presumed it to be incontrovertible that even in fire the matter (substance) does not perish, but that only the form of it undergoes a change. In like manner was the saying: "From nothing comes nothing," only another inference from the principle or permanence, or rather of the ever-abiding existence of the true subject in phenomena. For if that in the phenomenon which we call substance is to be the proper substratum of all determination of time, it follows that all existence in past as well as in future time, must be determinable by means of it alone. Hence we are entitled to apply the term substance to a phenomenon, only because we suppose its existence in all time, a notion which the word permanence does not fully express, as it seems rather to be referable to future time. However, the internal necessity perpetually to be, is inseparably connected with the necessity always to have been, and so the expression may stand as it is. "Gigni de nihilo nihil; in nihilum nil posse reverti,"* are two propositions which the ancients never parted, and which people nowadays sometimes mistakenly disjoin, because they imagine that the propositions apply to objects as things in themselves, and that the former might be inimical to the dependence (even in respect of its substance also) of the world upon a supreme cause. But this apprehension is entirely needless, for the question in this case is only of phenomena in the sphere of experience, the unity of which never could be possible, if we admitted the possibility that new things (in respect of their substance) should arise. For in that case, we should lose altogether that which alone can represent the unity of time, to wit, the identity of the substratum, as that through which alone all change possesses complete and thorough unity. This permanence is, however, nothing but the manner in which we represent to ourselves the existence of things in the phenomenal world.

[Note: Persius, Satirae, iii.83-84.]

The determinations of a substance, which are only particular modes of its existence, are called accidents. They are always real, because they concern the existence of substance (negations are only determinations, which express the non-existence of something in the substance). Now, if to this real in the substance we ascribe a particular existence (for example, to motion as an accident of matter), this existence is called inherence, in contradistinction to the existence of substance, which we call subsistence. But hence arise many misconceptions, and it would be a more accurate and just mode of expression to designate the accident only as the mode in which the existence of a substance is positively determined. Meanwhile, by reason of the conditions of the logical exercise of our understanding, it is impossible to avoid separating, as it were, that which in the existence of a substance is subject to change, whilst the substance remains, and regarding it in relation to that which is properly permanent and radical. On this account, this category of substance stands under the title of relation, rather because it is the condition thereof than because it contains in itself any relation.

Now, upon this notion of permanence rests the proper notion of the conception change. Origin and extinction are not changes of that which originates or becomes extinct. Change is but a mode of existence, which follows on another mode of existence of the same object; hence all that changes is permanent, and only the condition thereof changes. Now since this mutation affects only determinations, which can have a beginning or an end, we may say, employing an expression which seems somewhat paradoxical: "Only the permanent (substance) is subject to change; the mutable suffers no change, but rather alternation, that is, when certain determinations cease, others begin."

Change, when, cannot be perceived by us except in substances, and origin or extinction in an absolute sense, that does not concern merely a determination of the permanent, cannot be a possible perception, for it is this very notion of the permanent which renders possible the representation of a transition from one state into another, and from non-being to being, which, consequently, can be empirically cognized only as alternating determinations of that which is permanent. Grant that a thing absolutely begins to be; we must then have a point of time in which it was not. But how and by what can we fix and determine this point of time, unless by that which already exists? For a void time — preceding — is not an object of perception; but if we connect this beginning with objects which existed previously, and which continue to exist till the object in question in question begins to be, then the latter can only be a determination of the former as the permanent. The same holds good of the notion of extinction, for this presupposes the empirical representation of a time, in which a phenomenon no longer exists.

Substances (in the world of phenomena) are the substratum of all determinations of time. The beginning of some, and the ceasing to be of other substances, would utterly do away with the only condition of the empirical unity of time; and in that case phenomena would relate to two different times, in which, side by side, existence would pass; which is absurd. For there is only one time in which all different times must be placed, not as coexistent, but as successive.

Accordingly, permanence is a necessary condition under which alone phenomena, as things or objects, are determinable in a possible experience. But as regards the empirical criterion of this necessary permanence, and with it of the substantiality of phenomena, we shall find sufficient opportunity to speak in the sequel.

B. SECOND ANALOGY.

Principle of the Succession of Time According to the Law of Causality. All changes take place according to the law of the connection of Cause and Effect.

PROOF.

(That all phenomena in the succession of time are only changes, that is, a successive being and non-being of the determinations of substance, which is permanent; consequently that a being of substance itself which follows on the non-being thereof, or a non-being of substance which follows on the being thereof, in other words, that the origin or extinction of substance itself, is impossible — all this has been fully established in treating of the foregoing principle. This principle might have been expressed as follows: "All alteration (succession) of phenomena is merely change"; for the changes of substance are not origin or extinction, because the conception of change presupposes the same subject as existing with two opposite determinations, and consequently as permanent. After this premonition, we shall proceed to the proof.)

I perceive that phenomena succeed one another, that is to say, a state of things exists at one time, the opposite of which existed in a former state. In this case, then, I really connect together two perceptions in time. Now connection is not an operation of mere sense and intuition, but is the product of a synthetical faculty of imagination, which determines the internal sense in respect of a relation of time. But imagination can connect these two states in two ways, so that either the one or the other may antecede in time; for time in itself cannot be an object of perception, and what in an object precedes and what follows cannot be empirically determined in relation to it. I am only conscious, then, that my imagination places one state before and the other after; not that the one state antecedes the other in the object. In other words, the objective relation of the successive phenomena remains quite undetermined by means of mere perception. Now in order that this relation may be cognized as determined, the relation between the two states must be so cogitated that it is thereby determined as necessary, which of them must be placed before and which after, and not conversely. But the conception which carries with it a necessity of synthetical unity, can be none other than a pure conception of the understanding which does not lie in mere perception; and in this case it is the conception of "the relation of cause and effect," the former of which determines the latter in time, as its necessary consequence, and not as something which might possibly antecede (or which might in some cases not be perceived to follow). It follows that it is only because we subject the sequence of phenomena, and consequently all change, to the law of causality, that experience itself, that is, empirical cognition of phenomena, becomes possible; and consequently, that phenomena themselves, as objects of experience, are possible only by virtue of this law.

Our apprehension of the manifold of phenomena is always successive. The representations of parts succeed one another. Whether they succeed one another in the object also, is a second point for reflection, which was not contained in the former. Now we may certainly give the name of object to everything, even to every representation, so far as we are conscious thereof; but what this word may mean in the case of phenomena, not merely in so far as they (as representations) are objects, but only in so far as they indicate an object, is a question requiring deeper consideration. In so far as they, regarded merely as representations, are at the same time objects of consciousness, they are not to be distinguished from apprehension, that is, reception into the synthesis of imagination, and we must therefore say: "The manifold of phenomena is always produced successively in the mind." If phenomena were things in themselves, no man would be able to conjecture from the succession of our representations how this manifold is connected in the object; for we have to do only with our representations. How things may be in themselves, without regard to the representations through which they affect us, is utterly beyond the sphere of our cognition. Now although phenomena are not things in themselves, and are nevertheless the only thing given to us to be cognized, it is my duty to show what sort of connection in time belongs to the manifold in phenomena themselves, while the representation of this manifold in apprehension is always successive. For example, the apprehension of the manifold in the phenomenon of a house which stands before me, is successive. Now comes the question whether the manifold of this house is in itself successive — which no one will be at all willing to grant. But, so soon as I raise my conception of an object to the transcendental signification thereof, I find that the house is not a thing in itself, but only a phenomenon, that is, a representation, the transcendental object of which remains utterly unknown. What then am I to understand by the question: "How can the manifold be connected in the phenomenon itself — not considered as a thing in itself, but merely as a phenomenon?" Here that which lies in my successive apprehension is regarded as representation, whilst the phenomenon which is given me, notwithstanding that it is nothing more than a complex of these representations, is regarded as the object thereof, with which my conception, drawn from the representations of apprehension, must harmonize. It is very soon seen that, as accordance of the cognition with its object constitutes truth, the question now before us can only relate to the formal conditions of empirical truth; and that the phenomenon, in opposition to the representations of apprehension, can only be distinguished therefrom as the object of them, if it is subject to a rule which distinguishes it from every other apprehension, and which renders necessary a mode of connection of the manifold. That in the phenomenon which contains the condition of this necessary rule of apprehension, is the object.

Let us now proceed to our task. That something happens, that is to say, that something or some state exists which before was not, cannot be empirically perceived, unless a phenomenon precedes, which does not contain in itself this state. For a reality which should follow upon a void time, in other words, a beginning, which no state of things precedes, can just as little be apprehended as the void time itself. Every apprehension of an event is therefore a perception which follows upon another perception. But as this is the case with all synthesis of apprehension, as I have shown above in the example of a house, my apprehension of an event is not yet sufficiently distinguished from other apprehensions. But I remark also that if in a phenomenon which contains an occurrence, I call the antecedent state of my perception, A, and the following state, B, the perception B can only follow A in apprehension, and the perception A cannot follow B, but only precede it. For example, I see a ship float down the stream of a river. My perception of its place lower down follows upon my perception of its place higher up the course of the river, and it is impossible that, in the apprehension of this phenomenon, the vessel should be perceived first below and afterwards higher up the stream. Here, therefore, the order in the sequence of perceptions in apprehension is determined; and by this order apprehension is regulated. In the former example, my perceptions in the apprehension of a house might begin at the roof and end at the foundation, or vice versa; or I might apprehend the manifold in this empirical intuition, by going from left to right, and from right to left. Accordingly, in the series of these perceptions, there was no determined order, which necessitated my beginning at a certain point, in order empirically to connect the manifold. But this rule is always to be met with in the perception of that which happens, and it makes the order of the successive perceptions in the apprehension of such a phenomenon necessary.

I must, therefore, in the present case, deduce the subjective sequence of apprehension from the objective sequence of phenomena, for otherwise the former is quite undetermined, and one phenomenon is not distinguishable from another. The former alone proves nothing as to the connection of the manifold in an object, for it is quite arbitrary. The latter must consist in the order of the manifold in a phenomenon, according to which order the apprehension of one thing (that which happens) follows that of another thing (which precedes), in conformity with a rule. In this way alone can I be authorized to say of the phenomenon itself, and not merely of my own apprehension, that a certain order or sequence is to be found therein. That is, in other words, I cannot arrange my apprehension otherwise than in this order.

In conformity with this rule, then, it is necessary that in that which antecedes an event there be found the condition of a rule, according to which in this event follows always and necessarily; but I cannot reverse this and go back from the event, and determine (by apprehension) that which antecedes it. For no phenomenon goes back from the succeeding point of time to the preceding point, although it does certainly relate to a preceding point of time; from a given time, on the other hand, there is always a necessary progression to the determined succeeding time. Therefore, because there certainly is something that follows, I must of necessity connect it with something else, which antecedes, and upon which it follows, in conformity with a rule, that is necessarily, so that the event, as conditioned, affords certain indication of a condition, and this condition determines the event.

Let us suppose that nothing precedes an event, upon which this event must follow in conformity with a rule. All sequence of perception would then exist only in apprehension, that is to say, would be merely subjective, and it could not thereby be objectively determined what thing ought to precede, and what ought to follow in perception. In such a case, we should have nothing but a play of representations, which would possess no application to any object. That is to say, it would not be possible through perception to distinguish one phenomenon from another, as regards relations of time; because the succession in the act of apprehension would always be of the same sort, and therefore there would be nothing in the phenomenon to determine the succession, and to render a certain sequence objectively necessary. And, in this case, I cannot say that two states in a phenomenon follow one upon the other, but only that one apprehension follows upon another. But this is merely subjective, and does not determine an object, and consequently cannot be held to be cognition of an object — not even in the phenomenal world.

Accordingly, when we know in experience that something happens, we always presuppose that something precedes, whereupon it follows in conformity with a rule. For otherwise I could not say of the object that it follows; because the mere succession in my apprehension, if it be not determined by a rule in relation to something preceding, does not authorize succession in the object. Only, therefore, in reference to a rule, according to which phenomena are determined in their sequence, that is, as they happen, by the preceding state, can I make my subjective synthesis (of apprehension) objective, and it is only under this presupposition that even the experience of an event is possible.

No doubt it appears as if this were in thorough contradiction to all the notions which people have hitherto entertained in regard to the procedure of the human understanding. According to these opinions, it is by means of the perception and comparison of similar consequences following upon certain antecedent phenomena that the understanding is led to the discovery of a rule, according to which certain events always follow certain phenomena, and it is only by this process that we attain to the conception of cause. Upon such a basis, it is clear that this conception must be merely empirical, and the rule which it furnishes us with— "Everything that happens must have a cause" — would be just as contingent as experience itself. The universality and necessity of the rule or law would be perfectly spurious attributes of it. Indeed, it could not possess universal validity, inasmuch as it would not in this case be a priori, but founded on deduction. But the same is the case with this law as with other pure a priori representations (e.g., space and time), which we can draw in perfect clearness and completeness from experience, only because we had already placed them therein, and by that means, and by that alone, had rendered experience possible. Indeed, the logical clearness of this representation of a rule, determining the series of events, is possible only when we have made use thereof in experience. Nevertheless, the recognition of this rule, as a condition of the synthetical unity of phenomena in time, was the ground of experience itself and consequently preceded it a priori.

It is now our duty to show by an example that we never, even in experience, attribute to an object the notion of succession or effect (of an event — that is, the happening of something that did not exist before), and distinguish it from the subjective succession of apprehension, unless when a rule lies at the foundation, which compels us to observe this order of perception in preference to any other, and that, indeed, it is this necessity which first renders possible the representation of a succession in the object.

We have representations within us, of which also we can be conscious. But, however widely extended, however accurate and thoroughgoing this consciousness may be, these representations are still nothing more than representations, that is, internal determinations of the mind in this or that relation of time. Now how happens it that to these representations we should set an object, or that, in addition to their subjective reality, as modifications, we should still further attribute to them a certain unknown objective reality? It is clear that objective significancy cannot consist in a relation to another representation (of that which we desire to term object), for in that case the question again arises: "How does this other representation go out of itself, and obtain objective significancy over and above the subjective, which is proper to it, as a determination of a state of mind?" If we try to discover what sort of new property the relation to an object gives to our subjective representations, and what new importance they thereby receive, we shall find that this relation has no other effect than that of rendering necessary the connection of our representations in a certain manner, and of subjecting them to a rule; and that conversely, it is only because a certain order is necessary in the relations of time of our representations, that objective significancy is ascribed to them.

In the synthesis of phenomena, the manifold of our representations is always successive. Now hereby is not represented an object, for by means of this succession, which is common to all apprehension, no one thing is distinguished from another. But so soon as I perceive or assume that in this succession there is a relation to a state antecedent, from which the representation follows in accordance with a rule, so soon do I represent something as an event, or as a thing that happens; in other words, I cognize an object to which I must assign a certain determinate position in time, which cannot be altered, because of the preceding state in the object. When, therefore, I perceive that something happens, there is contained in this representation, in the first place, the fact, that something antecedes; because, it is only in relation to this that the phenomenon obtains its proper relation of time, in other words, exists after an antecedent time, in which it did not exist. But it can receive its determined place in time only by the presupposition that something existed in the foregoing state, upon which it follows inevitably and always, that is, in conformity with a rule. From all this it is evident that, in the first place, I cannot reverse the order of succession, and make that which happens precede that upon which it follows; and that, in the second place, if the antecedent state be posited, a certain determinate event inevitably and necessarily follows. Hence it follows that there exists a certain order in our representations, whereby the present gives a sure indication of some previously existing state, as a correlate, though still undetermined, of the existing event which is given — a correlate which itself relates to the event as its consequence, conditions it, and connects it necessarily with itself in the series of time.

If then it be admitted as a necessary law of sensibility, and consequently a formal condition of all perception, that the preceding necessarily determines the succeeding time (inasmuch as I cannot arrive at the succeeding except through the preceding), it must likewise be an indispensable law of empirical representation of the series of time that the phenomena of the past determine all phenomena in the succeeding time, and that the latter, as events, cannot take place, except in so far as the former determine their existence in time, that is to say, establish it according to a rule. For it is of course only in phenomena that we can empirically cognize this continuity in the connection of times.

For all experience and for the possibility of experience, understanding is indispensable, and the first step which it takes in this sphere is not to render the representation of objects clear, but to render the representation of an object in general, possible. It does this by applying the order of time to phenomena, and their existence. In other words, it assigns to each phenomenon, as a consequence, a place in relation to preceding phenomena, determined a priori in time, without which it could not harmonize with time itself, which determines a place a priori to all its parts. This determination of place cannot be derived from the relation of phenomena to absolute time (for it is not an object of perception); but, on the contrary, phenomena must reciprocally determine the places in time of one another, and render these necessary in the order of time. In other words, whatever follows or happens, must follow in conformity with a universal rule upon that which was contained in the foregoing state. Hence arises a series of phenomena, which, by means of the understanding, produces and renders necessary exactly the same order and continuous connection in the series of our possible perceptions, as is found a priori in the form of internal intuition (time), in which all our perceptions must have place.

That something happens, then, is a perception which belongs to a possible experience, which becomes real only because I look upon the phenomenon as determined in regard to its place in time, consequently as an object, which can always be found by means of a rule in the connected series of my perceptions. But this rule of the determination of a thing according to succession in time is as follows: "In what precedes may be found the condition, under which an event always (that is, necessarily) follows." From all this it is obvious that the principle of cause and effect is the principle of possible experience, that is, of objective cognition of phenomena, in regard to their relations in the succession of time.

The proof of this fundamental proposition rests entirely on the following momenta of argument. To all empirical cognition belongs the synthesis of the manifold by the imagination, a synthesis which is always successive, that is, in which the representations therein always follow one another. But the order of succession in imagination is not determined, and the series of successive representations may be taken retrogressively as well as progressively. But if this synthesis is a synthesis of apprehension (of the manifold of a given phenomenon), then the order is determined in the object, or to speak more accurately, there is therein an order of successive synthesis which determines an object, and according to which something necessarily precedes, and when this is posited, something else necessarily follows. If, then, my perception is to contain the cognition of an event, that is, of something which really happens, it must be an empirical judgement, wherein we think that the succession is determined; that is, it presupposes another phenomenon, upon which this event follows necessarily, or in conformity with a rule. If, on the contrary, when I posited the antecedent, the event did not necessarily follow, I should be obliged to consider it merely as a subjective play of my imagination, and if in this I represented to myself anything as objective, I must look upon it as a mere dream. Thus, the relation of phenomena (as possible perceptions), according to which that which happens is, as to its existence, necessarily determined in time by something which antecedes, in conformity with a rule — in other words, the relation of cause and effect — is the condition of the objective validity of our empirical judgements in regard to the sequence of perceptions, consequently of their empirical truth, and therefore of experience. The principle of the relation of causality in the succession of phenomena is therefore valid for all objects of experience, because it is itself the ground of the possibility of experience.

Here, however, a difficulty arises, which must be resolved. The principle of the connection of causality among phenomena is limited in our formula to the succession thereof, although in practice we find that the principle applies also when the phenomena exist together in the same time, and that cause and effect may be simultaneous. For example, there is heat in a room, which does not exist in the open air. I look about for the cause, and find it to be the fire, Now the fire as the cause is simultaneous with its effect, the heat of the room. In this case, then, there is no succession as regards time, between cause and effect, but they are simultaneous; and still the law holds good. The greater part of operating causes in nature are simultaneous with their effects, and the succession in time of the latter is produced only because the cause cannot achieve the total of its effect in one moment. But at the moment when the effect first arises, it is always simultaneous with the causality of its cause, because, if the cause had but a moment before ceased to be, the effect could not have arisen. Here it must be specially remembered that we must consider the order of time and not the lapse thereof. The relation remains, even though no time has elapsed. The time between the causality of the cause and its immediate effect may entirely vanish, and the cause and effect be thus simultaneous, but the relation of the one to the other remains always determinable according to time. If, for example, I consider a leaden ball, which lies upon a cushion and makes a hollow in it, as a cause, then it is simultaneous with the effect. But I distinguish the two through the relation of time of the dynamical connection of both. For if I lay the ball upon the cushion, then the hollow follows upon the before smooth surface; but supposing the cushion has, from some cause or another, a hollow, there does not thereupon follow a leaden ball.

Thus, the law of succession of time is in all instances the only empirical criterion of effect in relation to the causality of the antecedent cause. The glass is the cause of the rising of the water above its horizontal surface, although the two phenomena are contemporaneous. For, as soon as I draw some water with the glass from a larger vessel, an effect follows thereupon, namely, the change of the horizontal state which the water had in the large vessel into a concave, which it assumes in the glass.

This conception of causality leads us to the conception of action; that of action, to the conception of force; and through it, to the conception of substance. As I do not wish this critical essay, the sole purpose of which is to treat of the sources of our synthetical cognition a priori, to be crowded with analyses which merely explain, but do not enlarge the sphere of our conceptions, I reserve the detailed explanation of the above conceptions for a future system of pure reason. Such an analysis, indeed, executed with great particularity, may already be found in well-known works on this subject. But I cannot at present refrain from making a few remarks on the empirical criterion of a substance, in so far as it seems to be more evident and more easily recognized through the conception of action than through that of the permanence of a phenomenon.

Where action (consequently activity and force) exists, substance also must exist, and in it alone must be sought the seat of that fruitful source of phenomena. Very well. But if we are called upon to explain what we mean by substance, and wish to avoid the vice of reasoning in a circle, the answer is by no means so easy. How shall we conclude immediately from the action to the permanence of that which acts, this being nevertheless an essential and peculiar criterion of substance (phenomenon)? But after what has been said above, the solution of this question becomes easy enough, although by the common mode of procedure — merely analysing our conceptions — it would be quite impossible. The conception of action indicates the relation of the subject of causality to the effect. Now because all effect consists in that which happens, therefore in the changeable, the last subject thereof is the permanent, as the substratum of all that changes, that is, substance. For according to the principle of causality, actions are always the first ground of all change in phenomena and, consequently, cannot be a property of a subject which itself changes, because if this were the case, other actions and another subject would be necessary to determine this change. From all this it results that action alone, as an empirical criterion, is a sufficient proof of the presence of substantiality, without any necessity on my part of endeavouring to discover the permanence of substance by a comparison. Besides, by this mode of induction we could not attain to the completeness which the magnitude and strict universality of the conception requires. For that the primary subject of the causality of all arising and passing away, all origin and extinction, cannot itself (in the sphere of phenomena) arise and pass away, is a sound and safe conclusion, a conclusion which leads us to the conception of empirical necessity and permanence in existence, and consequently to the conception of a substance as phenomenon.

When something happens, the mere fact of the occurrence, without regard to that which occurs, is an object requiring investigation. The transition from the non-being of a state into the existence of it, supposing that this state contains no quality which previously existed in the phenomenon, is a fact of itself demanding inquiry. Such an event, as has been shown in No. A, does not concern substance (for substance does not thus originate), but its condition or state. It is therefore only change, and not origin from nothing. If this origin be regarded as the effect of a foreign cause, it is termed creation, which cannot be admitted as an event among phenomena, because the very possibility of it would annihilate the unity of experience. If, however, I regard all things not as phenomena, but as things in themselves and objects of understanding alone, they, although substances, may be considered as dependent, in respect of their existence, on a foreign cause. But this would require a very different meaning in the words, a meaning which could not apply to phenomena as objects of possible experience.

How a thing can be changed, how it is possible that upon one state existing in one point of time, an opposite state should follow in another point of time — of this we have not the smallest conception a priori. There is requisite for this the knowledge of real powers, which can only be given empirically; for example, knowledge of moving forces, or, in other words, of certain successive phenomena (as movements) which indicate the presence of such forces. But the form of every change, the condition under which alone it can take place as the coming into existence of another state (be the content of the change, that is, the state which is changed, what it may), and consequently the succession of the states themselves can very well be considered a priori, in relation to the law of causality and the conditions of time.*

[Note: It must be remarked that I do not speak of the change of certain relations, but of the change of the state. Thus, when a body moves in a uniform manner, it does not change its state (of motion); but only when all motion increases or decreases.]

When a substance passes from one state, a, into another state, b, the point of time in which the latter exists is different from, and subsequent to that in which the former existed. In like manner, the second state, as reality (in the phenomenon), differs from the first, in which the reality of the second did not exist, as b from zero. That is to say, if the state, b, differs from the state, a, only in respect to quantity, the change is a coming into existence of b -a, which in the former state did not exist, and in relation to which that state is = O.

Now the question arises how a thing passes from one state = a, into another state = b. Between two moments there is always a certain time, and between two states existing in these moments there is always a difference having a certain quantity (for all parts of phenomena are in their turn quantities). Consequently, every transition from one state into another is always effected in a time contained between two moments, of which the first determines the state which leaves, and the second determines the state into the thing passes. The thing leaves, and the second determines the state into which the thing Both moments, then, are limitations of the time of a change, consequently of the intermediate state between both, and as such they belong to the total of the change. Now every change has a cause, which evidences its causality in the whole time during which the charge takes place. The cause, therefore, does not produce the change all at once or in one moment, but in a time, so that, as the time gradually increases from the commencing instant, a, to its completion at b, in like manner also, the quantity of the reality (b - a) is generated through the lesser degrees which are contained between the first and last. All change is therefore possible only through a continuous action of the causality, which, in so far as it is uniform, we call a momentum. The change does not consist of these momenta, but is generated or produced by them as their effect.

Such is the law of the continuity of all change, the ground of which is that neither time itself nor any phenomenon in time consists of parts which are the smallest possible, but that, notwithstanding, the state of a thing passes in the process of a change through all these parts, as elements, to its second state. There is no smallest degree of reality in a phenomenon, just as there is no smallest degree in the quantity of time; and so the new state of reality grows up out of the former state, through all the infinite degrees thereof, the differences of which one from another, taken all together, are less than the difference between o and a.

It is not our business to inquire here into the utility of this principle in the investigation of nature. But how such a proposition, which appears so greatly to extend our knowledge of nature, is possible completely a priori, is indeed a question which deserves investigation, although the first view seems to demonstrate the truth and reality of the principle, and the question, how it is possible, may be considered superfluous. For there are so many groundless pretensions to the enlargement of our knowledge by pure reason that we must take it as a general rule to be mistrustful of all such, and without a thoroughgoing and radical deduction, to believe nothing of the sort even on the clearest dogmatical evidence.

Every addition to our empirical knowledge, and every advance made in the exercise of our perception, is nothing more than an extension of the determination of the internal sense, that is to say, a progression in time, be objects themselves what they may, phenomena, or pure intuitions. This progression in time determines everything, and is itself determined by nothing else. That is to say, the parts of the progression exist only in time, and by means of the synthesis thereof, and are not given antecedently to it. For this reason, every transition in perception to anything which follows upon another in time, is a determination of time by means of the production of this perception. And as this determination of time is, always and in all its parts, a quantity, the perception produced is to be considered as a quantity which proceeds through all its degrees — no one of which is the smallest possible — from zero up to its determined degree. From this we perceive the possibility of cognizing a priori a law of changes — a law, however, which concerns their form merely. We merely anticipate our own apprehension, the formal condition of which, inasmuch as it is itself to be found in the mind antecedently to all given phenomena, must certainly be capable of being cognized a priori.

Thus, as time contains the sensuous condition a priori of the possibility of a continuous progression of that which exists to that which follows it, the understanding, by virtue of the unity of apperception, contains the condition a priori of the possibility of a continuous determination of the position in time of all phenomena, and this by means of the series of causes and effects, the former of which necessitate the sequence of the latter, and thereby render universally and for all time, and by consequence, objectively, valid the empirical cognition of the relations of time.

C. THIRD ANALOGY.

Principle of Coexistence, According to the Law of Reciprocity or Community.

All substances, in so far as they can be perceived in space at the same time, exist in a state of complete reciprocity of action.

PROOF.

Things are coexistent, when in empirical intuition the perception of the one can follow upon the perception of the other, and vice versa — which cannot occur in the succession of phenomena, as we have shown in the explanation of the second principle. Thus I can perceive the moon and then the earth, or conversely, first the earth and then the moon; and for the reason that my perceptions of these objects can reciprocally follow each other, I say, they exist contemporaneously. Now coexistence is the existence of the manifold in the same time. But time itself is not an object of perception; and therefore we cannot conclude from the fact that things are placed in the same time, the other fact, that the perception of these things can follow each other reciprocally. The synthesis of the imagination in apprehension would only present to us each of these perceptions as present in the subject when the other is not present, and contrariwise; but would not show that the objects are coexistent, that is to say, that, if the one exists, the other also exists in the same time, and that this is necessarily so, in order that the perceptions may be capable of following each other reciprocally. It follows that a conception of the understanding or category of the reciprocal sequence of the determinations of phenomena (existing, as they do, apart from each other, and yet contemporaneously), is requisite to justify us in saying that the reciprocal succession of perceptions has its foundation in the object, and to enable us to represent coexistence as objective. But that relation of substances in which the one contains determinations the ground of which is in the other substance, is the relation of influence. And, when this influence is reciprocal, it is the relation of community or reciprocity. Consequently the coexistence of substances in space cannot be cognized in experience otherwise than under the precondition of their reciprocal action. This is therefore the condition of the possibility of things themselves as objects of experience.

Things are coexistent, in so far as they exist in one and the same time. But how can we know that they exist in one and the same time? Only by observing that the order in the synthesis of apprehension of the manifold is arbitrary and a matter of indifference, that is to say, that it can proceed from A, through B, C, D, to E, or contrariwise from E to A. For if they were successive in time (and in the order, let us suppose, which begins with A), it is quite impossible for the apprehension in perception to begin with E and go backwards to A, inasmuch as A belongs to past time and, therefore, cannot be an object of apprehension.

Let us assume that in a number of substances considered as phenomena each is completely isolated, that is, that no one acts upon another. Then I say that the coexistence of these cannot be an object of possible perception and that the existence of one cannot, by any mode of empirical synthesis, lead us to the existence of another. For we imagine them in this case to be separated by a completely void space, and thus perception, which proceeds from the one to the other in time, would indeed determine their existence by means of a following perception, but would be quite unable to distinguish whether the one phenomenon follows objectively upon the first, or is coexistent with it.

Besides the mere fact of existence, then, there must be something by means of which A determines the position of B in time and, conversely, B the position of A; because only under this condition can substances be empirically represented as existing contemporaneously. Now that alone determines the position of another thing in time which is the cause of it or of its determinations. Consequently every substance (inasmuch as it can have succession predicated of it only in respect of its determinations) must contain the causality of certain determinations in another substance, and at the same time the effects of the causality of the other in itself. That is to say, substances must stand (mediately or immediately) in dynamical community with each other, if coexistence is to be cognized in any possible experience. But, in regard to objects of experience, that is absolutely necessary without which the experience of these objects would itself be impossible. Consequently it is absolutely necessary that all substances in the world of phenomena, in so far as they are coexistent, stand in a relation of complete community of reciprocal action to each other.

The word community has in our language [Note: German] two meanings, and contains the two notions conveyed in the Latin communio and commercium. We employ it in this place in the latter sense — that of a dynamical community, without which even the community of place (communio spatii) could not be empirically cognized. In our experiences it is easy to observe that it is only the continuous influences in all parts of space that can conduct our senses from one object to another; that the light which plays between our eyes and the heavenly bodies produces a mediating community between them and us, and thereby evidences their coexistence with us; that we cannot empirically change our position (perceive this change), unless the existence of matter throughout the whole of space rendered possible the perception of the positions we occupy; and that this perception can prove the contemporaneous existence of these places only through their reciprocal influence, and thereby also the coexistence of even the most remote objects — although in this case the proof is only mediate. Without community, every perception (of a phenomenon in space) is separated from every other and isolated, and the chain of empirical representations, that is, of experience, must, with the appearance of a new object, begin entirely de novo, without the least connection with preceding representations, and without standing towards these even in the relation of time. My intention here is by no means to combat the notion of empty space; for it may exist where our perceptions cannot exist, inasmuch as they cannot reach thereto, and where, therefore, no empirical perception of coexistence takes place. But in this case it is not an object of possible experience.

The following remarks may be useful in the way of explanation. In the mind, all phenomena, as contents of a possible experience, must exist in community (communio) of apperception or consciousness, and in so far as it is requisite that objects be represented as coexistent and connected, in so far must they reciprocally determine the position in time of each other and thereby constitute a whole. If this subjective community is to rest upon an objective basis, or to be applied to substances as phenomena, the perception of one substance must render possible the perception of another, and conversely. For otherwise succession, which is always found in perceptions as apprehensions, would be predicated of external objects, and their representation of their coexistence be thus impossible. But this is a reciprocal influence, that is to say, a real community (commercium) of substances, without which therefore the empirical relation of coexistence would be a notion beyond the reach of our minds. By virtue of this commercium, phenomena, in so far as they are apart from, and nevertheless in connection with each other, constitute a compositum reale. Such composita are possible in many different ways. The three dynamical relations then, from which all others spring, are those of inherence, consequence, and composition.

These, then, are the three analogies of experience. They are nothing more than principles of the determination of the existence of phenomena in time, according to the three modi of this determination; to wit, the relation to time itself as a quantity (the quantity of existence, that is, duration), the relation in time as a series or succession, finally, the relation in time as the complex of all existence (simultaneity). This unity of determination in regard to time is thoroughly dynamical; that is to say, time is not considered as that in which experience determines immediately to every existence its position; for this is impossible, inasmuch as absolute time is not an object of perception, by means of which phenomena can be connected with each other. On the contrary, the rule of the understanding, through which alone the existence of phenomena can receive synthetical unity as regards relations of time, determines for every phenomenon its position in time, and consequently a priori, and with validity for all and every time.

By nature, in the empirical sense of the word, we understand the totality of phenomena connected, in respect of their existence, according to necessary rules, that is, laws. There are therefore certain laws (which are moreover a priori) which make nature possible; and all empirical laws can exist only by means of experience, and by virtue of those primitive laws through which experience itself becomes possible. The purpose of the analogies is therefore to represent to us the unity of nature in the connection of all phenomena under certain exponents, the only business of which is to express the relation of time (in so far as it contains all existence in itself) to the unity of apperception, which can exist in synthesis only according to rules. The combined expression of all is this: "All phenomena exist in one nature, and must so exist, inasmuch as without this a priori unity, no unity of experience, and consequently no determination of objects in experience, is possible."

As regards the mode of proof which we have employed in treating of these transcendental laws of nature, and the peculiar character of we must make one remark, which will at the same time be important as a guide in every other attempt to demonstrate the truth of intellectual and likewise synthetical propositions a priori. Had we endeavoured to prove these analogies dogmatically, that is, from conceptions; that is to say, had we employed this method in attempting to show that everything which exists, exists only in that which is permanent — that every thing or event presupposes the existence of something in a preceding state, upon which it follows in conformity with a rule — lastly, that in the manifold, which is coexistent, the states coexist in connection with each other according to a rule, all our labour would have been utterly in vain. For more conceptions of things, analyse them as we may, cannot enable us to conclude from the existence of one object to the existence of another. What other course was left for us to pursue? This only, to demonstrate the possibility of experience as a cognition in which at last all objects must be capable of being presented to us, if the representation of them is to possess any objective reality. Now in this third, this mediating term, the essential form of which consists in the synthetical unity of the apperception of all phenomena, we found a priori conditions of the universal and necessary determination as to time of all existences in the world of phenomena, without which the empirical determination thereof as to time would itself be impossible, and we also discovered rules of synthetical unity a priori, by means of which we could anticipate experience. For want of this method, and from the fancy that it was possible to discover a dogmatical proof of the synthetical propositions which are requisite in the empirical employment of the understanding, has it happened that a proof of the principle of sufficient reason has been so often attempted, and always in vain. The other two analogies nobody has ever thought of, although they have always been silently employed by the mind,* because the guiding thread furnished by the categories was wanting, the guide which alone can enable us to discover every hiatus, both in the system of conceptions and of principles.

[Note: The unity of the universe, in which all phenomena to be connected, is evidently a mere consequence of the admitted principle of the community of all substances which are coexistent. For were substances isolated, they could not as parts constitute a whole, and were their connection (reciprocal action of the manifold) not necessary from the very fact of coexistence, we could not conclude from the fact of the latter as a merely ideal relation to the former as a real one. We have, however, shown in its place that community is the proper ground of the possibility of an empirical cognition of coexistence, and that we may therefore properly reason from the latter to the former as its condition.]

4. THE POSTULATES OF EMPIRICAL THOUGHT.

1. That which agrees with the formal conditions (intuition and conception) of experience, is possible.

2. That which coheres with the material conditions of experience (sensation), is real.

3. That whose coherence with the real is determined according to universal conditions of experience is (exists) necessary.

Explanation.

The categories of modality possess this peculiarity, that they do not in the least determine the object, or enlarge the conception to which they are annexed as predicates, but only express its relation to the faculty of cognition. Though my conception of a thing is in itself complete, I am still entitled to ask whether the object of it is merely possible, or whether it is also real, or, if the latter, whether it is also necessary. But hereby the object itself is not more definitely determined in thought, but the question is only in what relation it, including all its determinations, stands to the understanding and its employment in experience, to the empirical faculty of judgement, and to the reason of its application to experience.

For this very reason, too, the categories of modality are nothing more than explanations of the conceptions of possibility, reality, and necessity, as employed in experience, and at the same time, restrictions of all the categories to empirical use alone, not authorizing the transcendental employment of them. For if they are to have something more than a merely logical significance, and to be something more than a mere analytical expression of the form of thought, and to have a relation to things and their possibility, reality, or necessity, they must concern possible experience and its synthetical unity, in which alone objects of cognition can be given.

The postulate of the possibility of things requires also, that the conception of the things agree with the formal conditions of our experience in general. But this, that is to say, the objective form of experience, contains all the kinds of synthesis which are requisite for the cognition of objects. A conception which contains a synthesis must be regarded as empty and, without reference to an object, if its synthesis does not belong to experience — either as borrowed from it, and in this case it is called an empirical conception, or such as is the ground and a priori condition of experience (its form), and in this case it is a pure conception, a conception which nevertheless belongs to experience, inasmuch as its object can be found in this alone. For where shall we find the criterion or character of the possibility of an object which is cogitated by means of an a priori synthetical conception, if not in the synthesis which constitutes the form of empirical cognition of objects? That in such a conception no contradiction exists is indeed a necessary logical condition, but very far from being sufficient to establish the objective reality of the conception, that is, the possibility of such an object as is thought in the conception. Thus, in the conception of a figure which is contained within two straight lines, there is no contradiction, for the conceptions of two straight lines and of their junction contain no negation of a figure. The impossibility in such a case does not rest upon the conception in itself, but upon the construction of it in space, that is to say, upon the conditions of space and its determinations. But these have themselves objective reality, that is, they apply to possible things, because they contain a priori the form of experience in general.

And now we shall proceed to point out the extensive utility and influence of this postulate of possibility. When I represent to myself a thing that is permanent, so that everything in it which changes belongs merely to its state or condition, from such a conception alone I never can cognize that such a thing is possible. Or, if I represent to myself something which is so constituted that, when it is posited, something else follows always and infallibly, my thought contains no self-contradiction; but whether such a property as causality is to be found in any possible thing, my thought alone affords no means of judging. Finally, I can represent to myself different things (substances) which are so constituted that the state or condition of one causes a change in the state of the other, and reciprocally; but whether such a relation is a property of things cannot be perceived from these conceptions, which contain a merely arbitrary synthesis. Only from the fact, therefore, that these conceptions express a priori the relations of perceptions in every experience, do we know that they possess objective reality, that is, transcendental truth; and that independent of experience, though not independent of all relation to form of an experience in general and its synthetical unity, in which alone objects can be empirically cognized.

But when we fashion to ourselves new conceptions of substances, forces, action, and reaction, from the material presented to us by perception, without following the example of experience in their connection, we create mere chimeras, of the possibility of which we cannot discover any criterion, because we have not taken experience for our instructress, though we have borrowed the conceptions from her. Such fictitious conceptions derive their character of possibility not, like the categories, a priori, as conceptions on which all experience depends, but only, a posteriori, as conceptions given by means of experience itself, and their possibility must either be cognized a posteriori and empirically, or it cannot be cognized at all. A substance which is permanently present in space, yet without filling it (like that tertium quid between matter and the thinking subject which some have tried to introduce into metaphysics), or a peculiar fundamental power of the mind of intuiting the future by anticipation (instead of merely inferring from past and present events), or, finally, a power of the mind to place itself in community of thought with other men, however distant they may be — these are conceptions the possibility of which has no ground to rest upon. For they are not based upon experience and its known laws; and, without experience, they are a merely arbitrary conjunction of thoughts, which, though containing no internal contradiction, has no claim to objective reality, neither, consequently, to the possibility of such an object as is thought in these conceptions. As far as concerns reality, it is self-evident that we cannot cogitate such a possibility in concreto without the aid of experience; because reality is concerned only with sensation, as the matter of experience, and not with the form of thought, with which we can no doubt indulge in shaping fancies.

But I pass by everything which derives its possibility from reality in experience, and I purpose treating here merely of the possibility of things by means of a priori conceptions. I maintain, then, that the possibility of things is not derived from such conceptions per se, but only when considered as formal and objective conditions of an experience in general.

It seems, indeed, as if the possibility of a triangle could be cognized from the conception of it alone (which is certainly independent of experience); for we can certainly give to the conception a corresponding object completely a priori, that is to say, we can construct it. But as a triangle is only the form of an object, it must remain a mere product of the imagination, and the possibility of the existence of an object corresponding to it must remain doubtful, unless we can discover some other ground, unless we know that the figure can be cogitated under the conditions upon which all objects of experience rest. Now, the facts that space is a formal condition a priori of external experience, that the formative synthesis, by which we construct a triangle in imagination, is the very same as that we employ in the apprehension of a phenomenon for the purpose of making an empirical conception of it, are what alone connect the notion of the possibility of such a thing, with the conception of it. In the same manner, the possibility of continuous quantities, indeed of quantities in general, for the conceptions of them are without exception synthetical, is never evident from the conceptions in themselves, but only when they are considered as the formal conditions of the determination of objects in experience. And where, indeed, should we look for objects to correspond to our conceptions, if not in experience, by which alone objects are presented to us? It is, however, true that without antecedent experience we can cognize and characterize the possibility of things, relatively to the formal conditions, under which something is determined in experience as an object, consequently, completely a priori. But still this is possible only in relation to experience and within its limits.

The postulate concerning the cognition of the reality of things requires perception, consequently conscious sensation, not indeed immediately, that is, of the object itself, whose existence is to be cognized, but still that the object have some connection with a real perception, in accordance with the analogies of experience, which exhibit all kinds of real connection in experience.

From the mere conception of a thing it is impossible to conclude its existence. For, let the conception be ever so complete, and containing a statement of all the determinations of the thing, the existence of it has nothing to do with all this, but only with thew question whether such a thing is given, so that the perception of it can in every case precede the conception. For the fact that the conception of it precedes the perception, merely indicates the possibility of its existence; it is perception which presents matter to the conception, that is the sole criterion of reality. Prior to the perception of the thing, however, and therefore comparatively a priori, we are able to cognize its existence, provided it stands in connection with some perceptions according to the principles of the empirical conjunction of these, that is, in conformity with the analogies of perception. For, in this case, the existence of the supposed thing is connected with our perception in a possible experience, and we are able, with the guidance of these analogies, to reason in the series of possible perceptions from a thing which we do really perceive to the thing we do not perceive. Thus, we cognize the existence of a magnetic matter penetrating all bodies from the perception of the attraction of the steel-filings by the magnet, although the constitution of our organs renders an immediate perception of this matter impossible for us. For, according to the laws of sensibility and the connected context of our perceptions, we should in an experience come also on an immediate empirical intuition of this matter, if our senses were more acute — but this obtuseness has no influence upon and cannot alter the form of possible experience in general. Our knowledge of the existence of things reaches as far as our perceptions, and what may be inferred from them according to empirical laws, extend. If we do not set out from experience, or do not proceed according to the laws of the empirical connection of phenomena, our pretensions to discover the existence of a thing which we do not immediately perceive are vain. Idealism, however, brings forward powerful objections to these rules for proving existence mediately. This is, therefore, the proper place for its refutation.

REFUTATION OF IDEALISM.

Idealism — I mean material idealism — is the theory which declares the existence of objects in space without us to be either () doubtful and indemonstrable, or (2) false and impossible. The first is the problematical idealism of Descartes, who admits the undoubted certainty of only one empirical assertion (assertio), to wit, "I am." The second is the dogmatical idealism of Berkeley, who maintains that space, together with all the objects of which it is the inseparable condition, is a thing which is in itself impossible, and that consequently the objects in space are mere products of the imagination. The dogmatical theory of idealism is unavoidable, if we regard space as a property of things in themselves; for in that case it is, with all to which it serves as condition, a nonentity. But the foundation for this kind of idealism we have already destroyed in the transcendental aesthetic. Problematical idealism, which makes no such assertion, but only alleges our incapacity to prove the existence of anything besides ourselves by means of immediate experience, is a theory rational and evidencing a thorough and philosophical mode of thinking, for it observes the rule not to form a decisive judgement before sufficient proof be shown. The desired proof must therefore demonstrate that we have experience of external things, and not mere fancies. For this purpose, we must prove, that our internal and, to Descartes, indubitable experience is itself possible only under the previous assumption of external experience.

THEOREM.

The simple but empirically determined consciousness of my own existence proves the existence of external objects in space.

PROOF

I am conscious of my own existence as determined in time. All determination in regard to time presupposes the existence of something permanent in perception. But this permanent something cannot be something in me, for the very reason that my existence in time is itself determined by this permanent something. It follows that the perception of this permanent existence is possible only through a thing without me and not through the mere representation of a thing without me. Consequently, the determination of my existence in time is possible only through the existence of real things external to me. Now, consciousness in time is necessarily connected with the consciousness of the possibility of this determination in time. Hence it follows that consciousness in time is necessarily connected also with the existence of things without me, inasmuch as the existence of these things is the condition of determination in time. That is to say, the consciousness of my own existence is at the same time an immediate consciousness of the existence of other things without me.

Remark I. The reader will observe, that in the foregoing proof the game which idealism plays is retorted upon itself, and with more justice. It assumed that the only immediate experience is internal and that from this we can only infer the existence of external things. But, as always happens, when we reason from given effects to determined causes, idealism has reasoned with too much haste and uncertainty, for it is quite possible that the cause of our representations may lie in ourselves, and that we ascribe it falsely to external things. But our proof shows that external experience is properly immediate,* that only by virtue of it — not, indeed, the consciousness of our own existence, but certainly the determination of our existence in time, that is, internal experience — is possible. It is true, that the representation "I am," which is the expression of the consciousness which can accompany all my thoughts, is that which immediately includes the existence of a subject. But in this representation we cannot find any knowledge of the subject, and therefore also no empirical knowledge, that is, experience. For experience contains, in addition to the thought of something existing, intuition, and in this case it must be internal intuition, that is, time, in relation to which the subject must be determined. But the existence of external things is absolutely requisite for this purpose, so that it follows that internal experience is itself possible only mediately and through external experience.

[Note: The immediate consciousness of the existence of external things is, in the preceding theorem, not presupposed, but proved, by the possibility of this consciousness understood by us or not. The question as to the possibility of it would stand thus: "Have we an internal sense, but no external sense, and is our belief in external perception a mere delusion?" But it is evident that, in order merely to fancy to ourselves anything as external, that is, to present it to the sense in intuition we must already possess an external sense, and must thereby distinguish immediately the mere receptivity of an external intuition from the spontaneity which characterizes every act of imagination. For merely to imagine also an external sense, would annihilate the faculty of intuition itself which is to be determined by the imagination.]

Remark II. Now with this view all empirical use of our faculty of cognition in the determination of time is in perfect accordance. Its truth is supported by the fact that it is possible to perceive a determination of time only by means of a change in external relations (motion) to the permanent in space (for example, we become aware of the sun's motion by observing the changes of his relation to the objects of this earth). But this is not all. We find that we possess nothing permanent that can correspond and be submitted to the conception of a substance as intuition, except matter. This idea of permanence is not itself derived from external experience, but is an a priori necessary condition of all determination of time, consequently also of the internal sense in reference to our own existence, and that through the existence of external things. In the representation "I," the consciousness of myself is not an intuition, but a merely intellectual representation produced by the spontaneous activity of a thinking subject. It follows, that this "I" has not any predicate of intuition, which, in its character of permanence, could serve as correlate to the determination of time in the internal sense — in the same way as impenetrability is the correlate of matter as an empirical intuition.

Remark III. From the fact that the existence of external things is a necessary condition of the possibility of a determined consciousness of ourselves, it does not follow that every intuitive representation of external things involves the existence of these things, for their representations may very well be the mere products of the imagination (in dreams as well as in madness); though, indeed, these are themselves created by the reproduction of previous external perceptions, which, as has been shown, are possible only through the reality of external objects. The sole aim of our remarks has, however, been to prove that internal experience in general is possible only through external experience in general. Whether this or that supposed experience be purely imaginary must be discovered from its particular determinations and by comparing these with the criteria of all real experience.

Finally, as regards the third postulate, it applies to material necessity in existence, and not to merely formal and logical necessity in the connection of conceptions. Now as we cannot cognize completely a priori the existence of any object of sense, though we can do so comparatively a priori, that is, relatively to some other previously given existence — a cognition, however, which can only be of such an existence as must be contained in the complex of experience, of which the previously given perception is a part — the necessity of existence can never be cognized from conceptions, but always, on the contrary, from its connection with that which is an object of perception. But the only existence cognized, under the condition of other given phenomena, as necessary, is the existence of effects from given causes in conformity with the laws of causality. It is consequently not the necessity of the existence of things (as substances), but the necessity of the state of things that we cognize, and that not immediately, but by means of the existence of other states given in perception, according to empirical laws of causality. Hence it follows that the criterion of necessity is to be found only in the law of possible experience — that everything which happens is determined a priori in the phenomenon by its cause. Thus we cognize only the necessity of effects in nature, the causes of which are given us. Moreover, the criterion of necessity in existence possesses no application beyond the field of possible experience, and even in this it is not valid of the existence of things as substances, because these can never be considered as empirical effects, or as something that happens and has a beginning. Necessity, therefore, regards only the relations of phenomena according to the dynamical law of causality, and the possibility grounded thereon, of reasoning from some given existence (of a cause) a priori to another existence (of an effect). "Everything that happens is hypothetically necessary," is a principle which subjects the changes that take place in the world to a law, that is, to a rule of necessary existence, without which nature herself could not possibly exist. Hence the proposition, "Nothing happens by blind chance (in mundo non datur casus)," is an a priori law of nature. The case is the same with the proposition, "Necessity in nature is not blind," that is, it is conditioned, consequently intelligible necessity (non datur fatum). Both laws subject the play of change to "a nature of things (as phenomena)," or, which is the same thing, to the unity of the understanding, and through the understanding alone can changes belong to an experience, as the synthetical unity of phenomena. Both belong to the class of dynamical principles. The former is properly a consequence of the principle of causality — one of the analogies of experience. The latter belongs to the principles of modality, which to the determination of causality adds the conception of necessity, which is itself, however, subject to a rule of the understanding. The principle of continuity forbids any leap in the series of phenomena regarded as changes (in mundo non datur saltus); and likewise, in the complex of all empirical intuitions in space, any break or hiatus between two phenomena (non datur hiatus) — for we can so express the principle, that experience can admit nothing which proves the existence of a vacuum, or which even admits it as a part of an empirical synthesis. For, as regards a vacuum or void, which we may cogitate as out and beyond the field of possible experience (the world), such a question cannot come before the tribunal of mere understanding, which decides only upon questions that concern the employment of given phenomena for the construction of empirical cognition. It is rather a problem for ideal reason, which passes beyond the sphere of a possible experience and aims at forming a judgement of that which surrounds and circumscribes it, and the proper place for the consideration of it is the transcendental dialectic. These four propositions, "In mundo non datur hiatus, non datur saltus, non datur casus, non datur fatum," as well as all principles of transcendental origin, we could very easily exhibit in their proper order, that is, in conformity with the order of the categories, and assign to each its proper place. But the already practised reader will do this for himself, or discover the clue to such an arrangement. But the combined result of all is simply this, to admit into the empirical synthesis nothing which might cause a break in or be foreign to the understanding and the continuous connection of all phenomena, that is, the unity of the conceptions of the understanding. For in the understanding alone is the unity of experience, in which all perceptions must have their assigned place, possible.

Whether the field of possibility be greater than that of reality, and whether the field of the latter be itself greater than that of necessity, are interesting enough questions, and quite capable of synthetic solution, questions, however, which come under the jurisdiction of reason alone. For they are tantamount to asking whether all things as phenomena do without exception belong to the complex and connected whole of a single experience, of which every given perception is a part which therefore cannot be conjoined with any other phenomena — or, whether my perceptions can belong to more than one possible experience? The understanding gives to experience, according to the subjective and formal conditions, of sensibility as well as of apperception, the rules which alone make this experience possible. Other forms of intuition besides those of space and time, other forms of understanding besides the discursive forms of thought, or of cognition by means of conceptions, we can neither imagine nor make intelligible to ourselves; and even if we could, they would still not belong to experience, which is the only mode of cognition by which objects are presented to us. Whether other perceptions besides those which belong to the total of our possible experience, and consequently whether some other sphere of matter exists, the understanding has no power to decide, its proper occupation being with the synthesis of that which is given. Moreover, the poverty of the usual arguments which go to prove the existence of a vast sphere of possibility, of which all that is real (every object of experience) is but a small part, is very remarkable. "All real is possible"; from this follows naturally, according to the logical laws of conversion, the particular proposition: "Some possible is real." Now this seems to be equivalent to: "Much is possible that is not real." No doubt it does seem as if we ought to consider the sum of the possible to be greater than that of the real, from the fact that something must be added to the former to constitute the latter. But this notion of adding to the possible is absurd. For that which is not in the sum of the possible, and consequently requires to be added to it, is manifestly impossible. In addition to accordance with the formal conditions of experience, the understanding requires a connection with some perception; but that which is connected with this perception is real, even although it is not immediately perceived. But that another series of phenomena, in complete coherence with that which is given in perception, consequently more than one all-embracing experience is possible, is an inference which cannot be concluded from the data given us by experience, and still less without any data at all. That which is possible only under conditions which are themselves merely possible, is not possible in any respect. And yet we can find no more certain ground on which to base the discussion of the question whether the sphere of possibility is wider than that of experience.

I have merely mentioned these questions, that in treating of the conception of the understanding, there might be no omission of anything that, in the common opinion, belongs to them. In reality, however, the notion of absolute possibility (possibility which is valid in every respect) is not a mere conception of the understanding, which can be employed empirically, but belongs to reason alone, which passes the bounds of all empirical use of the understanding. We have, therefore, contented ourselves with a merely critical remark, leaving the subject to be explained in the sequel.

Before concluding this fourth section, and at the same time the system of all principles of the pure understanding, it seems proper to mention the reasons which induced me to term the principles of modality postulates. This expression I do not here use in the sense which some more recent philosophers, contrary to its meaning with mathematicians, to whom the word properly belongs, attach to it — that of a proposition, namely, immediately certain, requiring neither deduction nor proof. For if, in the case of synthetical propositions, however evident they may be, we accord to them without deduction, and merely on the strength of their own pretensions, unqualified belief, all critique of the understanding is entirely lost; and, as there is no want of bold pretensions, which the common belief (though for the philosopher this is no credential) does not reject, the understanding lies exposed to every delusion and conceit, without the power of refusing its assent to those assertions, which, though illegitimate, demand acceptance as veritable axioms. When, therefore, to the conception of a thing an a priori determination is synthetically added, such a proposition must obtain, if not a proof, at least a deduction of the legitimacy of its assertion.

The principles of modality are, however, not objectively synthetical, for the predicates of possibility, reality, and necessity do not in the least augment the conception of that of which they are affirmed, inasmuch as they contribute nothing to the representation of the object. But as they are, nevertheless, always synthetical, they are so merely subjectively. That is to say, they have a reflective power, and apply to the conception of a thing, of which, in other respects, they affirm nothing, the faculty of cognition in which the conception originates and has its seat. So that if the conception merely agree with the formal conditions of experience, its object is called possible; if it is in connection with perception, and determined thereby, the object is real; if it is determined according to conceptions by means of the connection of perceptions, the object is called necessary. The principles of modality therefore predicate of a conception nothing more than the procedure of the faculty of cognition which generated it. Now a postulate in mathematics is a practical proposition which contains nothing but the synthesis by which we present an object to ourselves, and produce the conception of it, for example— "With a given line, to describe a circle upon a plane, from a given point"; and such a proposition does not admit of proof, because the procedure, which it requires, is exactly that by which alone it is possible to generate the conception of such a figure. With the same right, accordingly, can we postulate the principles of modality, because they do not augment* the conception of a thing but merely indicate the manner in which it is connected with the faculty of cognition.

[Note: When I think the reality of a thing, I do really think more than the possibility, but not in the thing; for that can never contain more in reality than was contained in its complete possibility. But while the notion of possibility is merely the notion of a position of thing in relation to the understanding (its empirical use), reality is the conjunction of the thing with perception.]

GENERAL REMARK ON THE SYSTEM OF PRINCIPLES.

It is very remarkable that we cannot perceive the possibility of a thing from the category alone, but must always have an intuition, by which to make evident the objective reality of the pure conception of the understanding. Take, for example, the categories of relation. How (1) a thing can exist only as a subject, and not as a mere determination of other things, that is, can be substance; or how (2), because something exists, some other thing must exist, consequently how a thing can be a cause; or how (3), when several things exist, from the fact that one of these things exists, some consequence to the others follows, and reciprocally, and in this way a community of substances can be possible — are questions whose solution cannot be obtained from mere conceptions. The very same is the case with the other categories; for example, how a thing can be of the same sort with many others, that is, can be a quantity, and so on. So long as we have not intuition we cannot know whether we do really think an object by the categories, and where an object can anywhere be found to cohere with them, and thus the truth is established, that the categories are not in themselves cognitions, but mere forms of thought for the construction of cognitions from given intuitions. For the same reason is it true that from categories alone no synthetical proposition can be made. For example: "In every existence there is substance," that is, something that can exist only as a subject and not as mere predicate; or, "Everything is a quantity" — to construct propositions such as these, we require something to enable us to go out beyond the given conception and connect another with it. For the same reason the attempt to prove a synthetical proposition by means of mere conceptions, for example: "Everything that exists contingently has a cause," has never succeeded. We could never get further than proving that, without this relation to conceptions, we could not conceive the existence of the contingent, that is, could not a priori through the understanding cognize the existence of such a thing; but it does not hence follow that this is also the condition of the possibility of the thing itself that is said to be contingent. If, accordingly; we look back to our proof of the principle of causality, we shall find that we were able to prove it as valid only of objects of possible experience, and, indeed, only as itself the principle of the possibility of experience, Consequently of the cognition of an object given in empirical intuition, and not from mere conceptions. That, however, the proposition: "Everything that is contingent must have a cause," is evident to every one merely from conceptions, is not to be denied. But in this case the conception of the contingent is cogitated as involving not the category of modality (as that the non-existence of which can be conceived) but that of relation (as that which can exist only as the consequence of something else), and so it is really an identical proposition: "That which can exist only as a consequence, has a cause." In fact, when we have to give examples of contingent existence, we always refer to changes, and not merely to the possibility of conceiving the opposite.* But change is an event, which, as such, is possible only through a cause, and considered per se its non-existence is therefore possible, and we become cognizant of its contingency from the fact that it can exist only as the effect of a cause. Hence, if a thing is assumed to be contingent, it is an analytical proposition to say, it has a cause.

[Note: We can easily conceive the non-existence of matter; but the ancients did not thence infer its contingency. But even the alternation of the existence and non-existence of a given state in a thing, in which all change consists, by no means proves the contingency of that state — the ground of proof being the reality of its opposite. For example, a body is in a state of rest after motion, but we cannot infer the contingency of the motion from the fact that the former is the opposite of the latter. For this opposite is merely a logical and not a real opposite to the other. If we wish to demonstrate the contingency of the motion, what we ought to prove is that, instead of the motion which took place in the preceding point of time, it was possible for the body to have been then in rest, not, that it is afterwards in rest; for in this case, both opposites are perfectly consistent with each other.]

But it is still more remarkable that, to understand the possibility of things according to the categories and thus to demonstrate the objective reality of the latter, we require not merely intuitions, but external intuitions. If, for example, we take the pure conceptions of relation, we find that (1) for the purpose of presenting to the conception of substance something permanent in intuition corresponding thereto and thus of demonstrating the objective reality of this conception, we require an intuition (of matter) in space, because space alone is permanent and determines things as such, while time, and with it all that is in the internal sense, is in a state of continual flow; (2) in order to represent change as the intuition corresponding to the conception of causality, we require the representation of motion as change in space; in fact, it is through it alone that changes, the possibility of which no pure understanding can perceive, are capable of being intuited. Change is the connection of determinations contradictorily opposed to each other in the existence of one and the same thing. Now, how it is possible that out of a given state one quite opposite to it in the same thing should follow, reason without an example can not only not conceive, but cannot even make intelligible without intuition; and this intuition is the motion of a point in space; the existence of which in different spaces (as a consequence of opposite determinations) alone makes the intuition of change possible. For, in order to make even internal change cognitable, we require to represent time, as the form of the internal sense, figuratively by a line, and the internal change by the drawing of that line (motion), and consequently are obliged to employ external intuition to be able to represent the successive existence of ourselves in different states. The proper ground of this fact is that all change to be perceived as change presupposes something permanent in intuition, while in the internal sense no permanent intuition is to be found. Lastly, the objective possibility of the category of community cannot be conceived by mere reason, and consequently its objective reality cannot be demonstrated without an intuition, and that external in space. For how can we conceive the possibility of community, that is, when several substances exist, that some effect on the existence of the one follows from the existence of the other, and reciprocally, and therefore that, because something exists in the latter, something else must exist in the former, which could not be understood from its own existence alone? For this is the very essence of community — which is inconceivable as a property of things which are perfectly isolated. Hence, Leibnitz, in attributing to the substances of the world — as cogitated by the understanding alone — a community, required the mediating aid of a divinity; for, from their existence, such a property seemed to him with justice inconceivable. But we can very easily conceive the possibility of community (of substances as phenomena) if we represent them to ourselves as in space, consequently in external intuition. For external intuition contains in itself a priori formal external relations, as the conditions of the possibility of the real relations of action and reaction, and therefore of the possibility of community. With the same ease can it be demonstrated, that the possibility of things as quantities, and consequently the objective reality of the category of quantity, can be grounded only in external intuition, and that by its means alone is the notion of quantity appropriated by the internal sense. But I must avoid prolixity, and leave the task of illustrating this by examples to the reader's own reflection.

The above remarks are of the greatest importance, not only for the confirmation of our previous confutation of idealism, but still more when the subject of self-cognition by mere internal consciousness and the determination of our own nature without the aid of external empirical intuitions is under discussion, for the indication of the grounds of the possibility of such a cognition.

The result of the whole of this part of the analytic of principles is, therefore: "All principles of the pure understanding are nothing more than a priori principles of the possibility of experience, and to experience alone do all a priori synthetical propositions apply and relate"; indeed, their possibility itself rests entirely on this relation.

CHAPTER III
Of the Ground of the Division of all Objects into Phenomena and Noumena.

We have now not only traversed the region of the pure understanding and carefully surveyed every part of it, but we have also measured it, and assigned to everything therein its proper place. But this land is an island, and enclosed by nature herself within unchangeable limits. It is the land of truth (an attractive word), surrounded by a wide and stormy ocean, the region of illusion, where many a fog-bank, many an iceberg, seems to the mariner, on his voyage of discovery, a new country, and, while constantly deluding him with vain hopes, engages him in dangerous adventures, from which he never can desist, and which yet he never can bring to a termination. But before venturing upon this sea, in order to explore it in its whole extent, and to arrive at a certainty whether anything is to be discovered there, it will not be without advantage if we cast our eyes upon the chart of the land that we are about to leave, and to ask ourselves, firstly, whether we cannot rest perfectly contented with what it contains, or whether we must not of necessity be contented with it, if we can find nowhere else a solid foundation to build upon; and, secondly, by what title we possess this land itself, and how we hold it secure against all hostile claims? Although, in the course of our analytic, we have already given sufficient answers to these questions, yet a summary recapitulation of these solutions may be useful in strengthening our conviction, by uniting in one point the momenta of the arguments.

We have seen that everything which the understanding draws from itself, without borrowing from experience, it nevertheless possesses only for the behoof and use of experience. The principles of the pure understanding, whether constitutive a priori (as the mathematical principles), or merely regulative (as the dynamical), contain nothing but the pure schema, as it were, of possible experience. For experience possesses its unity from the synthetical unity which the understanding, originally and from itself, imparts to the synthesis of the imagination in relation to apperception, and in a priori relation to and agreement with which phenomena, as data for a possible cognition, must stand. But although these rules of the understanding are not only a priori true, but the very source of all truth, that is, of the accordance of our cognition with objects, and on this ground, that they contain the basis of the possibility of experience, as the ensemble of all cognition, it seems to us not enough to propound what is true — we desire also to be told what we want to know. If, then, we learn nothing more by this critical examination than what we should have practised in the merely empirical use of the understanding, without any such subtle inquiry, the presumption is that the advantage we reap from it is not worth the labour bestowed upon it. It may certainly be answered that no rash curiosity is more prejudicial to the enlargement of our knowledge than that which must know beforehand the utility of this or that piece of information which we seek, before we have entered on the needful investigations, and before one could form the least conception of its utility, even though it were placed before our eyes. But there is one advantage in such transcendental inquiries which can be made comprehensible to the dullest and most reluctant learner — this, namely, that the understanding which is occupied merely with empirical exercise, and does not reflect on the sources of its own cognition, may exercise its functions very well and very successfully, but is quite unable to do one thing, and that of very great importance, to determine, namely, the bounds that limit its employment, and to know what lies within or without its own sphere. This purpose can be obtained only by such profound investigations as we have instituted. But if it cannot distinguish whether certain questions lie within its horizon or not, it can never be sure either as to its claims or possessions, but must lay its account with many humiliating corrections, when it transgresses, as it unavoidably will, the limits of its own territory, and loses itself in fanciful opinions and blinding illusions.

That the understanding, therefore, cannot make of its a priori principles, or even of its conceptions, other than an empirical use, is a proposition which leads to the most important results. A transcendental use is made of a conception in a fundamental proposition or principle, when it is referred to things in general and considered as things in themselves; an empirical use, when it is referred merely to phenomena, that is, to objects of a possible experience. That the latter use of a conception is the only admissible one is evident from the reasons following. For every conception are requisite, firstly, the logical form of a conception (of thought) general; and, secondly, the possibility of presenting to this an object to which it may apply. Failing this latter, it has no sense, and utterly void of content, although it may contain the logical function for constructing a conception from certain data. Now, object cannot be given to a conception otherwise than by intuition, and, even if a pure intuition antecedent to the object is a priori possible, this pure intuition can itself obtain objective validity only from empirical intuition, of which it is itself but the form. All conceptions, therefore, and with them all principles, however high the degree of their a priori possibility, relate to empirical intuitions, that is, to data towards a possible experience. Without this they possess no objective validity, but are mere play of imagination or of understanding with images or notions. Let us take, for example, the conceptions of mathematics, and first in its pure intuitions. "Space has three dimensions"— "Between two points there can be only one straight line," etc. Although all these principles, and the representation of the object with which this science occupies itself, are generated in the mind entirely a priori, they would nevertheless have no significance if we were not always able to exhibit their significance in and by means of phenomena (empirical objects). Hence it is requisite that an abstract conception be made sensuous, that is, that an object corresponding to it in intuition be forthcoming, otherwise the conception remains, as we say, without sense, that is, without meaning. Mathematics fulfils this requirement by the construction of the figure, which is a phenomenon evident to the senses. The same science finds support and significance in number; this in its turn finds it in the fingers, or in counters, or in lines and points. The conception itself is always produced a priori, together with the synthetical principles or formulas from such conceptions; but the proper employment of them, and their application to objects, can exist nowhere but in experience, the possibility of which, as regards its form, they contain a priori.

That this is also the case with all of the categories and the principles based upon them is evident from the fact that we cannot render intelligible the possibility of an object corresponding to them without having recourse to the conditions of sensibility, consequently, to the form of phenomena, to which, as their only proper objects, their use must therefore be confined, inasmuch as, if this condition is removed, all significance, that is, all relation to an object, disappears, and no example can be found to make it comprehensible what sort of things we ought to think under such conceptions.

The conception of quantity cannot be explained except by saying that it is the determination of a thing whereby it can be cogitated how many times one is placed in it. But this "how many times" is based upon successive repetition, consequently upon time and the synthesis of the homogeneous therein. Reality, in contradistinction to negation, can be explained only by cogitating a time which is either filled therewith or is void. If I leave out the notion of permanence (which is existence in all time), there remains in the conception of substance nothing but the logical notion of subject, a notion of which I endeavour to realize by representing to myself something that can exist only as a subject. But not only am I perfectly ignorant of any conditions under which this logical prerogative can belong to a thing, I can make nothing out of the notion, and draw no inference from it, because no object to which to apply the conception is determined, and we consequently do not know whether it has any meaning at all. In like manner, if I leave out the notion of time, in which something follows upon some other thing in conformity with a rule, I can find nothing in the pure category, except that there is a something of such a sort that from it a conclusion may be drawn as to the existence of some other thing. But in this case it would not only be impossible to distinguish between a cause and an effect, but, as this power to draw conclusions requires conditions of which I am quite ignorant, the conception is not determined as to the mode in which it ought to apply to an object. The so-called principle: "Everything that is contingent has a cause," comes with a gravity and self-assumed authority that seems to require no support from without. But, I ask, what is meant by contingent? The answer is that the non-existence of which is possible. But I should like very well to know by what means this possibility of non-existence is to be cognized, if we do not represent to ourselves a succession in the series of phenomena, and in this succession an existence which follows a non-existence, or conversely, consequently, change. For to say, that the non-existence of a thing is not self-contradictory is a lame appeal to a logical condition, which is no doubt a necessary condition of the existence of the conception, but is far from being sufficient for the real objective possibility of non-existence. I can annihilate in thought every existing substance without self-contradiction, but I cannot infer from this their objective contingency in existence, that is to say, the possibility of their non-existence in itself. As regards the category of community, it may easily be inferred that, as the pure categories of substance and causality are incapable of a definition and explanation sufficient to determine their object without the aid of intuition, the category of reciprocal causality in the relation of substances to each other (commercium) is just as little susceptible thereof. Possibility, existence, and necessity nobody has ever yet been able to explain without being guilty of manifest tautology, when the definition has been drawn entirely from the pure understanding. For the substitution of the logical possibility of the conception — the condition of which is that it be not self-contradictory, for the transcendental possibility of things — the condition of which is that there be an object corresponding to the conception, is a trick which can only deceive the inexperienced.*

[Note: In one word, to none of these conceptions belongs a corresponding object, and consequently their real possibility cannot be demonstrated, if we take away sensuous intuition — the only intuition which we possess — and there then remains nothing but the logical possibility, that is, the fact that the conception or thought is possible — which, however, is not the question; what we want to know being, whether it relates to an object and thus possesses any meaning.]

It follows incontestably, that the pure conceptions of the understanding are incapable of transcendental, and must always be of empirical use alone, and that the principles of the pure understanding relate only to the general conditions of a possible experience, to objects of the senses, and never to things in general, apart from the mode in which we intuite them.

Transcendental analytic has accordingly this important result, to wit, that the understanding is competent' effect nothing a priori, except the anticipation of the form of a possible experience in general, and that, as that which is not phenomenon cannot be an object of experience, it can never overstep the limits of sensibility, within which alone objects are presented to us. Its principles are merely principles of the exposition of phenomena, and the proud name of an ontology, which professes to present synthetical cognitions a priori of things in general in a systematic doctrine, must give place to the modest title of analytic of the pure understanding.

Thought is the act of referring a given intuition to an object. If the mode of this intuition is unknown to us, the object is merely transcendental, and the conception of the understanding is employed only transcendentally, that is, to produce unity in the thought of a manifold in general. Now a pure category, in which all conditions of sensuous intuition — as the only intuition we possess — are abstracted, does not determine an object, but merely expresses the thought of an object in general, according to different modes. Now, to employ a conception, the function of judgement is required, by which an object is subsumed under the conception, consequently the at least formal condition, under which something can be given in intuition. Failing this condition of judgement (schema), subsumption is impossible; for there is in such a case nothing given, which may be subsumed under the conception. The merely transcendental use of the categories is therefore, in fact, no use at all and has no determined, or even, as regards its form, determinable object. Hence it follows that the pure category is incompetent to establish a synthetical a priori principle, and that the principles of the pure understanding are only of empirical and never of transcendental use, and that beyond the sphere of possible experience no synthetical a priori principles are possible.

It may be advisable, therefore, to express ourselves thus. The pure categories, apart from the formal conditions of sensibility, have a merely transcendental meaning, but are nevertheless not of transcendental use, because this is in itself impossible, inasmuch as all the conditions of any employment or use of them (in judgements) are absent, to wit, the formal conditions of the subsumption of an object under these conceptions. As, therefore, in the character of pure categories, they must be employed empirically, and cannot be employed transcendentally, they are of no use at all, when separated from sensibility, that is, they cannot be applied to an object. They are merely the pure form of the employment of the understanding in respect of objects in general and of thought, without its being at the same time possible to think or to determine any object by their means. But there lurks at the foundation of this subject an illusion which it is very difficult to avoid. The categories are not based, as regards their origin, upon sensibility, like the forms of intuition, space, and time; they seem, therefore, to be capable of an application beyond the sphere of sensuous objects. But this is not the case. They are nothing but mere forms of thought, which contain only the logical faculty of uniting a priori in consciousness the manifold given in intuition. Apart, then, from the only intuition possible for us, they have still less meaning than the pure sensuous forms, space and time, for through them an object is at least given, while a mode of connection of the manifold, when the intuition which alone gives the manifold is wanting, has no meaning at all. At the same time, when we designate certain objects as phenomena or sensuous existences, thus distinguishing our mode of intuiting them from their own nature as things in themselves, it is evident that by this very distinction we as it were place the latter, considered in this their own nature, although we do not so intuite them, in opposition to the former, or, on the other hand, we do so place other possible things, which are not objects of our senses, but are cogitated by the understanding alone, and call them intelligible existences (noumena). Now the question arises whether the pure conceptions of our understanding do possess significance in respect of these latter, and may possibly be a mode of cognizing them.

But we are met at the very commencement with an ambiguity, which may easily occasion great misapprehension. The understanding, when it terms an object in a certain relation phenomenon, at the same time forms out of this relation a representation or notion of an object in itself, and hence believes that it can form also conceptions of such objects. Now as the understanding possesses no other fundamental conceptions besides the categories, it takes for granted that an object considered as a thing in itself must be capable of being thought by means of these pure conceptions, and is thereby led to hold the perfectly undetermined conception of an intelligible existence, a something out of the sphere of our sensibility, for a determinate conception of an existence which we can cognize in some way or other by means of the understanding.

If, by the term noumenon, we understand a thing so far as it is not an object of our sensuous intuition, thus making abstraction of our mode of intuiting it, this is a noumenon in the negative sense of the word. But if we understand by it an object of a non-sensuous intuition, we in this case assume a peculiar mode of intuition, an intellectual intuition, to wit, which does not, however, belong to us, of the very possibility of which we have no notion — and this is a noumenon in the positive sense.

The doctrine of sensibility is also the doctrine of noumena in the negative sense, that is, of things which the understanding is obliged to cogitate apart from any relation to our mode of intuition, consequently not as mere phenomena, but as things in themselves. But the understanding at the same time comprehends that it cannot employ its categories for the consideration of things in themselves, because these possess significance only in relation to the unity of intuitions in space and time, and that they are competent to determine this unity by means of general a priori connecting conceptions only on account of the pure ideality of space and time. Where this unity of time is not to be met with, as is the case with noumena, the whole use, indeed the whole meaning of the categories is entirely lost, for even the possibility of things to correspond to the categories is in this case incomprehensible. On this point, I need only refer the reader to what I have said at the commencement of the General Remark appended to the foregoing chapter. Now, the possibility of a thing can never be proved from the fact that the conception of it is not self-contradictory, but only by means of an intuition corresponding to the conception. If, therefore, we wish to apply the categories to objects which cannot be regarded as phenomena, we must have an intuition different from the sensuous, and in this case the objects would be a noumena in the positive sense of the word. Now, as such an intuition, that is, an intellectual intuition, is no part of our faculty of cognition, it is absolutely impossible for the categories to possess any application beyond the limits of experience. It may be true that there are intelligible existences to which our faculty of sensuous intuition has no relation, and cannot be applied, but our conceptions of the understanding, as mere forms of thought for our sensuous intuition, do not extend to these. What, therefore, we call noumenon must be understood by us as such in a negative sense.

If I take away from an empirical intuition all thought (by means of the categories), there remains no cognition of any object; for by means of mere intuition nothing is cogitated, and, from the existence of such or such an affection of sensibility in me, it does not follow that this affection or representation has any relation to an object without me. But if I take away all intuition, there still remains the form of thought, that is, the mode of determining an object for the manifold of a possible intuition. Thus the categories do in some measure really extend further than sensuous intuition, inasmuch as they think objects in general, without regard to the mode (of sensibility) in which these objects are given. But they do not for this reason apply to and determine a wider sphere of objects, because we cannot assume that such can be given, without presupposing the possibility of another than the sensuous mode of intuition, a supposition we are not justified in making.

I call a conception problematical which contains in itself no contradiction, and which is connected with other cognitions as a limitation of given conceptions, but whose objective reality cannot be cognized in any manner. The conception of a noumenon, that is, of a thing which must be cogitated not as an object of sense, but as a thing in itself (solely through the pure understanding), is not self-contradictory, for we are not entitled to maintain that sensibility is the only possible mode of intuition. Nay, further, this conception is necessary to restrain sensuous intuition within the bounds of phenomena, and thus to limit the objective validity of sensuous cognition; for things in themselves, which lie beyond its province, are called noumena for the very purpose of indicating that this cognition does not extend its application to all that the understanding thinks. But, after all, the possibility of such noumena is quite incomprehensible, and beyond the sphere of phenomena, all is for us a mere void; that is to say, we possess an understanding whose province does problematically extend beyond this sphere, but we do not possess an intuition, indeed, not even the conception of a possible intuition, by means of which objects beyond the region of sensibility could be given us, and in reference to which the understanding might be employed assertorically. The conception of a noumenon is therefore merely a limitative conception and therefore only of negative use. But it is not an arbitrary or fictitious notion, but is connected with the limitation of sensibility, without, however, being capable of presenting us with any positive datum beyond this sphere.

The division of objects into phenomena and noumena, and of the world into a mundus sensibilis and intelligibilis is therefore quite inadmissible in a positive sense, although conceptions do certainly admit of such a division; for the class of noumena have no determinate object corresponding to them, and cannot therefore possess objective validity. If we abandon the senses, how can it be made conceivable that the categories (which are the only conceptions that could serve as conceptions for noumena) have any sense or meaning at all, inasmuch as something more than the mere unity of thought, namely, a possible intuition, is requisite for their application to an object? The conception of a noumenon, considered as merely problematical, is, however, not only admissible, but, as a limitative conception of sensibility, absolutely necessary. But, in this case, a noumenon is not a particular intelligible object for our understanding; on the contrary, the kind of understanding to which it could belong is itself a problem, for we cannot form the most distant conception of the possibility of an understanding which should cognize an object, not discursively by means of categories, but intuitively in a non-sensuous intuition. Our understanding attains in this way a sort of negative extension. That is to say, it is not limited by, but rather limits, sensibility, by giving the name of noumena to things, not considered as phenomena, but as things in themselves. But it at the same time prescribes limits to itself, for it confesses itself unable to cognize these by means of the categories, and hence is compelled to cogitate them merely as an unknown something.

I find, however, in the writings of modern authors, an entirely different use of the expressions, mundus sensibilis and intelligibilis, which quite departs from the meaning of the ancients — an acceptation in which, indeed, there is to be found no difficulty, but which at the same time depends on mere verbal quibbling. According to this meaning, some have chosen to call the complex of phenomena, in so far as it is intuited, mundus sensibilis, but in so far as the connection thereof is cogitated according to general laws of thought, mundus intelligibilis. Astronomy, in so far as we mean by the word the mere observation of the starry heaven, may represent the former; a system of astronomy, such as the Copernican or Newtonian, the latter. But such twisting of words is a mere sophistical subterfuge, to avoid a difficult question, by modifying its meaning to suit our own convenience. To be sure, understanding and reason are employed in the cognition of phenomena; but the question is, whether these can be applied when the object is not a phenomenon and in this sense we regard it if it is cogitated as given to the understanding alone, and not to the senses. The question therefore is whether, over and above the empirical use of the understanding, a transcendental use is possible, which applies to the noumenon as an object. This question we have answered in the negative.

When therefore we say, the senses represent objects as they appear, the understanding as they are, the latter statement must not be understood in a transcendental, but only in an empirical signification, that is, as they must be represented in the complete connection of phenomena, and not according to what they may be, apart from their relation to possible experience, consequently not as objects of the pure understanding. For this must ever remain unknown to us. Nay, it is also quite unknown to us whether any such transcendental or extraordinary cognition is possible under any circumstances, at least, whether it is possible by means of our categories. Understanding and sensibility, with us, can determine objects only in conjunction. If we separate them, we have intuitions without conceptions, or conceptions without intuitions; in both cases, representations, which we cannot apply to any determinate object.

If, after all our inquiries and explanations, any one still hesitates to abandon the mere transcendental use of the categories, let him attempt to construct with them a synthetical proposition. It would, of course, be unnecessary for this purpose to construct an analytical proposition, for that does not extend the sphere of the understanding, but, being concerned only about what is cogitated in the conception itself, it leaves it quite undecided whether the conception has any relation to objects, or merely indicates the unity of thought — complete abstraction being made of the modi in which an object may be given: in such a proposition, it is sufficient for the understanding to know what lies in the conception — to what it applies is to it indifferent. The attempt must therefore be made with a synthetical and so-called transcendental principle, for example: "Everything that exists, exists as substance," or, "Everything that is contingent exists as an effect of some other thing, viz., of its cause." Now I ask, whence can the understanding draw these synthetical propositions, when the conceptions contained therein do not relate to possible experience but to things in themselves (noumena)? Where is to be found the third term, which is always requisite PURE site in a synthetical proposition, which may connect in the same proposition conceptions which have no logical (analytical) connection with each other? The proposition never will be demonstrated, nay, more, the possibility of any such pure assertion never can be shown, without making reference to the empirical use of the understanding, and thus, ipso facto, completely renouncing pure and non-sensuous judgement. Thus the conception of pure and merely intelligible objects is completely void of all principles of its application, because we cannot imagine any mode in which they might be given, and the problematical thought which leaves a place open for them serves only, like a void space, to limit the use of empirical principles, without containing at the same time any other object of cognition beyond their sphere.

APPENDIX.

Of the Equivocal Nature or Amphiboly of the Conceptions of Reflection from the Confusion of the Transcendental with the Empirical use of the Understanding.

Reflection (reflexio) is not occupied about objects themselves, for the purpose of directly obtaining conceptions of them, but is that state of the mind in which we set ourselves to discover the subjective conditions under which we obtain conceptions. It is the consciousness of the relation of given representations to the different sources or faculties of cognition, by which alone their relation to each other can be rightly determined. The first question which occurs in considering our representations is to what faculty of cognition do they belong? To the understanding or to the senses? Many judgements are admitted to be true from mere habit or inclination; but, because reflection neither precedes nor follows, it is held to be a judgement that has its origin in the understanding. All judgements do not require examination, that is, investigation into the grounds of their truth. For, when they are immediately certain (for example: "Between two points there can be only one straight line"), no better or less mediate test of their truth can be found than that which they themselves contain and express. But all judgement, nay, all comparisons require reflection, that is, a distinction of the faculty of cognition to which the given conceptions belong. The act whereby I compare my representations with the faculty of cognition which originates them, and whereby I distinguish whether they are compared with each other as belonging to the pure understanding or to sensuous intuition, I term transcendental reflection. Now, the relations in which conceptions can stand to each other are those of identity and difference, agreement and opposition, of the internal and external, finally, of the determinable and the determining (matter and form). The proper determination of these relations rests on the question, to what faculty of cognition they subjectively belong, whether to sensibility or understanding? For, on the manner in which we solve this question depends the manner in which we must cogitate these relations.

Before constructing any objective judgement, we compare the conceptions that are to be placed in the judgement, and observe whether there exists identity (of many representations in one conception), if a general judgement is to be constructed, or difference, if a particular; whether there is agreement when affirmative; and opposition when negative judgements are to be constructed, and so on. For this reason we ought to call these conceptions, conceptions of comparison (conceptus comparationis). But as, when the question is not as to the logical form, but as to the content of conceptions, that is to say, whether the things themselves are identical or different, in agreement or opposition, and so on, the things can have a twofold relation to our faculty of cognition, to wit, a relation either to sensibility or to the understanding, and as on this relation depends their relation to each other, transcendental reflection, that is, the relation of given representations to one or the other faculty of cognition, can alone determine this latter relation. Thus we shall not be able to discover whether the things are identical or different, in agreement or opposition, etc., from the mere conception of the things by means of comparison (comparatio), but only by distinguishing the mode of cognition to which they belong, in other words, by means of transcendental reflection. We may, therefore, with justice say, that logical reflection is mere comparison, for in it no account is taken of the faculty of cognition to which the given conceptions belong, and they are consequently, as far as regards their origin, to be treated as homogeneous; while transcendental reflection (which applies to the objects themselves) contains the ground of the possibility of objective comparison of representations with each other, and is therefore very different from the former, because the faculties of cognition to which they belong are not even the same. Transcendental reflection is a duty which no one can neglect who wishes to establish an a priori judgement upon things. We shall now proceed to fulfil this duty, and thereby throw not a little light on the question as to the determination of the proper business of the understanding.

1. Identity and Difference. When an object is presented to us several times, but always with the same internal determinations (qualitas et quantitas), it, if an object of pure understanding, is always the same, not several things, but only one thing (numerica identitas); but if a phenomenon, we do not concern ourselves with comparing the conception of the thing with the conception of some other, but, although they may be in this respect perfectly the same, the difference of place at the same time is a sufficient ground for asserting the numerical difference of these objects (of sense). Thus, in the case of two drops of water, we may make complete abstraction of all internal difference (quality and quantity), and, the fact that they are intuited at the same time in different places, is sufficient to justify us in holding them to be numerically different. Leibnitz regarded phenomena as things in themselves, consequently as intelligibilia, that is, objects of pure understanding (although, on account of the confused nature of their representations, he gave them the name of phenomena), and in this case his principle of the indiscernible (principium identatis indiscernibilium) is not to be impugned. But, as phenomena are objects of sensibility, and, as the understanding, in respect of them, must be employed empirically and not purely or transcendentally, plurality and numerical difference are given by space itself as the condition of external phenomena. For one part of space, although it may be perfectly similar and equal to another part, is still without it, and for this reason alone is different from the latter, which is added to it in order to make up a greater space. It follows that this must hold good of all things that are in the different parts of space at the same time, however similar and equal one may be to another.

2. Agreement and Opposition. When reality is represented by the pure understanding (realitas noumenon), opposition between realities is incogitable — such a relation, that is, that when these realities are connected in one subject, they annihilate the effects of each other and may be represented in the formula 3 -3 = 0. On the other hand, the real in a phenomenon (realitas phaenomenon) may very well be in mutual opposition, and, when united in the same subject, the one may completely or in part annihilate the effect or consequence of the other; as in the case of two moving forces in the same straight line drawing or impelling a point in opposite directions, or in the case of a pleasure counterbalancing a certain amount of pain.

3. The Internal and External. In an object of the pure understanding, only that is internal which has no relation (as regards its existence) to anything different from itself. On the other hand, the internal determinations of a substantia phaenomenon in space are nothing but relations, and it is itself nothing more than a complex of mere relations. Substance in space we are cognizant of only through forces operative in it,

either drawing others towards itself (attraction), or preventing others from forcing into itself (repulsion and impenetrability). We know no other properties that make up the conception of substance phenomenal in space, and which we term matter. On the other hand, as an object of the pure understanding, every substance must have internal determination and forces. But what other internal attributes of such an object can I think than those which my internal sense presents to me? That, to wit, which in either itself thought, or something analogous to it. Hence Leibnitz, who looked upon things as noumena, after denying them everything like external relation, and therefore also composition or combination, declared that all substances, even the component parts of matter, were simple substances with powers of representation, in one word, monads.

4. Matter and Form. These two conceptions lie at the foundation of all other reflection, so inseparably are they connected with every mode of exercising the understanding. The former denotes the determinable in general, the second its determination, both in a transcendental sense, abstraction being made of every difference in that which is given, and of the mode in which it is determined. Logicians formerly termed the universal, matter, the specific difference of this or that part of the universal, form. In a judgement one may call the given conceptions logical matter (for the judgement), the relation of these to each other (by means of the copula), the form of the judgement. In an object, the composite parts thereof (essentialia) are the matter; the mode in which they are connected in the object, the form. In respect to things in general, unlimited reality was regarded as the matter of all possibility, the limitation thereof (negation) as the form, by which one thing is distinguished from another according to transcendental conceptions. The understanding demands that something be given (at least in the conception), in order to be able to determine it in a certain manner. Hence, in a conception of the pure understanding, the matter precedes the form, and for this reason Leibnitz first assumed the existence of things (monads) and of an internal power of representation in them, in order to found upon this their external relation and the community their state (that is, of their representations). Hence, with him, space and time were possible — the former through the relation of substances, the latter through the connection of their determinations with each other, as causes and effects. And so would it really be, if the pure understanding were capable of an immediate application to objects, and if space and time were determinations of things in themselves. But being merely sensuous intuitions, in which we determine all objects solely as phenomena, the form of intuition (as a subjective property of sensibility) must antecede all matter (sensations), consequently space and time must antecede all phenomena and all data of experience, and rather make experience itself possible. But the intellectual philosopher could not endure that the form should precede the things themselves and determine their possibility; an objection perfectly correct, if we assume that we intuite things as they are, although with confused representation. But as sensuous intuition is a peculiar subjective condition, which is a priori at the foundation of all perception, and the form of which is primitive, the form must be given per se, and so far from matter (or the things themselves which appear) lying at the foundation of experience (as we must conclude, if we judge by mere conceptions), the very possibility of itself presupposes, on the contrary, a given formal intuition (space and time).

REMARK ON THE AMPHIBOLY OF THE CONCEPTIONS OF REFLECTION.

Let me be allowed to term the position which we assign to a conception either in the sensibility or in the pure understanding, the transcendental place. In this manner, the appointment of the position which must be taken by each conception according to the difference in its use, and the directions for determining this place to all conceptions according to rules, would be a transcendental topic, a doctrine which would thoroughly shield us from the surreptitious devices of the pure understanding and the delusions which thence arise, as it would always distinguish to what faculty of cognition each conception properly belonged. Every conception, every title, under which many cognitions rank together, may be called a logical place. Upon this is based the logical topic of Aristotle, of which teachers and rhetoricians could avail themselves, in order, under certain titles of thought, to observe what would best suit the matter they had to treat, and thus enable themselves to quibble and talk with fluency and an appearance of profundity.

Transcendental topic, on the contrary, contains nothing more than the above-mentioned four titles of all comparison and distinction, which differ from categories in this respect, that they do not represent the object according to that which constitutes its conception (quantity, reality), but set forth merely the comparison of representations, which precedes our conceptions of things. But this comparison requires a previous reflection, that is, a determination of the place to which the representations of the things which are compared belong, whether, to wit, they are cogitated by the pure understanding, or given by sensibility.

Conceptions may be logically compared without the trouble of inquiring to what faculty their objects belong, whether as noumena, to the understanding, or as phenomena, to sensibility. If, however, we wish to employ these conceptions in respect of objects, previous transcendental reflection is necessary. Without this reflection I should make a very unsafe use of these conceptions, and construct pretended synthetical propositions which critical reason cannot acknowledge and which are based solely upon a transcendental amphiboly, that is, upon a substitution of an object of pure understanding for a phenomenon.

For want of this doctrine of transcendental topic, and consequently deceived by the amphiboly of the conceptions of reflection, the celebrated Leibnitz constructed an intellectual system of the world, or rather, believed himself competent to cognize the internal nature of things, by comparing all objects merely with the understanding and the abstract formal conceptions of thought. Our table of the conceptions of reflection gives us the unexpected advantage of being able to exhibit the distinctive peculiarities of his system in all its parts, and at the same time of exposing the fundamental principle of this peculiar mode of thought, which rested upon naught but a misconception. He compared all things with each other merely by means of conceptions, and naturally found no other differences than those by which the understanding distinguishes its pure conceptions one from another. The conditions of sensuous intuition, which contain in themselves their own means of distinction, he did not look upon as primitive, because sensibility was to him but a confused mode of representation and not any particular source of representations. A phenomenon was for him the representation of the thing in itself, although distinguished from cognition by the understanding only in respect of the logical form — the former with its usual want of analysis containing, according to him, a certain mixture of collateral representations in its conception of a thing, which it is the duty of the understanding to separate and distinguish. In one word, Leibnitz intellectualized phenomena, just as Locke, in his system of noogony (if I may be allowed to make use of such expressions), sensualized the conceptions of the understanding, that is to say, declared them to be nothing more than empirical or abstract conceptions of reflection. Instead of seeking in the understanding and sensibility two different sources of representations, which, however, can present us with objective judgements of things only in conjunction, each of these great men recognized but one of these faculties, which, in their opinion, applied immediately to things in themselves, the other having no duty but that of confusing or arranging the representations of the former.

Accordingly, the objects of sense were compared by Leibnitz as things in general merely in the understanding.

1st. He compares them in regard to their identity or difference — as judged by the understanding. As, therefore, he considered merely the conceptions of objects, and not their position in intuition, in which alone objects can be given, and left quite out of sight the transcendental locale of these conceptions — whether, that is, their object ought to be classed among phenomena, or among things in themselves, it was to be expected that he should extend the application of the principle of indiscernibles, which is valid solely of conceptions of things in general, to objects of sense (mundus phaenomenon), and that he should believe that he had thereby contributed in no small degree to extend our knowledge of nature. In truth, if I cognize in all its inner determinations a drop of water as a thing in itself, I cannot look upon one drop as different from another, if the conception of the one is completely identical with that of the other. But if it is a phenomenon in space, it has a place not merely in the understanding (among conceptions), but also in sensuous external intuition (in space), and in this case, the physical locale is a matter of indifference in regard to the internal determinations of things, and one place, B, may contain a thing which is perfectly similar and equal to another in a place, A, just as well as if the two things were in every respect different from each other. Difference of place without any other conditions, makes the plurality and distinction of objects as phenomena, not only possible in itself, but even necessary. Consequently, the above so-called law is not a law of nature. It is merely an analytical rule for the comparison of things by means of mere conceptions.

2nd. The principle: "Realities (as simple affirmations) never logically contradict each other," is a proposition perfectly true respecting the relation of conceptions, but, whether as regards nature, or things in themselves (of which we have not the slightest conception), is without any the least meaning. For real opposition, in which A -B is = 0, exists everywhere, an opposition, that is, in which one reality united with another in the same subject annihilates the effects of the other — a fact which is constantly brought before our eyes by the different antagonistic actions and operations in nature, which, nevertheless, as depending on real forces, must be called realitates phaenomena. General mechanics can even present us with the empirical condition of this opposition in an a priori rule, as it directs its attention to the opposition in the direction of forces — a condition of which the transcendental conception of reality can tell us nothing. Although M. Leibnitz did not announce this proposition with precisely the pomp of a new principle, he yet employed it for the establishment of new propositions, and his followers introduced it into their Leibnitzio-Wolfian system of philosophy. According to this principle, for example, all evils are but consequences of the limited nature of created beings, that is, negations, because these are the only opposite of reality. (In the mere conception of a thing in general this is really the case, but not in things as phenomena.) In like manner, the upholders of this system deem it not only possible, but natural also, to connect and unite all reality in one being, because they acknowledge no other sort of opposition than that of contradiction (by which the conception itself of a thing is annihilated), and find themselves unable to conceive an opposition of reciprocal destruction, so to speak, in which one real cause destroys the effect of another, and the conditions of whose representation we meet with only in sensibility.

3rd. The Leibnitzian monadology has really no better foundation than on this philosopher's mode of falsely representing the difference of the internal and external solely in relation to the understanding. Substances, in general, must have something inward, which is therefore free from external relations, consequently from that of composition also. The simple — that which can be represented by a unit — is therefore the foundation of that which is internal in things in themselves. The internal state of substances cannot therefore consist in place, shape, contact, or motion, determinations which are all external relations, and we can ascribe to them no other than that whereby we internally determine our faculty of sense itself, that is to say, the state of representation. Thus, then, were constructed the monads, which were to form the elements of the universe, the active force of which consists in representation, the effects of this force being thus entirely confined to themselves.

For the same reason, his view of the possible community of substances could not represent it but as a predetermined harmony, and by no means as a physical influence. For inasmuch as everything is occupied only internally, that is, with its own representations, the state of the representations of one substance could not stand in active and living connection with that of another, but some third cause operating on all without exception was necessary to make the different states correspond with one another. And this did not happen by means of assistance applied in each particular case (systema assistentiae), but through the unity of the idea of a cause occupied and connected with all substances, in which they necessarily receive, according to the Leibnitzian school, their existence and permanence, consequently also reciprocal correspondence, according to universal laws.

4th. This philosopher's celebrated doctrine of space and time, in which he intellectualized these forms of sensibility, originated in the same delusion of transcendental reflection. If I attempt to represent by the mere understanding, the external relations of things, I can do so only by employing the conception of their reciprocal action, and if I wish to connect one state of the same thing with another state, I must avail myself of the notion of the order of cause and effect. And thus Leibnitz regarded space as a certain order in the community of substances, and time as the dynamical sequence of their states. That which space and time possess proper to themselves and independent of things, he ascribed to a necessary confusion in our conceptions of them, whereby that which is a mere form of dynamical relations is held to be a self-existent intuition, antecedent even to things themselves. Thus space and time were the intelligible form of the connection of things (substances and their states) in themselves. But things were intelligible substances (substantiae noumena). At the same time, he made these conceptions valid of phenomena, because he did not allow to sensibility a peculiar mode of intuition, but sought all, even the empirical representation of objects, in the understanding, and left to sense naught but the despicable task of confusing and disarranging the representations of the former.

But even if we could frame any synthetical proposition concerning things in themselves by means of the pure understanding (which is impossible), it could not apply to phenomena, which do not represent things in themselves. In such a case I should be obliged in transcendental reflection to compare my conceptions only under the conditions of sensibility, and so space and time would not be determinations of things in themselves, but of phenomena. What things may be in themselves, I know not and need not know, because a thing is never presented to me otherwise than as a phenomenon.

I must adopt the same mode of procedure with the other conceptions of reflection. Matter is substantia phaenomenon. That in it which is internal I seek to discover in all parts of space which it occupies, and in all the functions and operations it performs, and which are indeed never anything but phenomena of the external sense. I cannot therefore find anything that is absolutely, but only what is comparatively internal, and which itself consists of external relations. The absolutely internal in matter, and as it should be according to the pure understanding, is a mere chimera, for matter is not an object for the pure understanding. But the transcendental object, which is the foundation of the phenomenon which we call matter, is a mere nescio quid, the nature of which we could not understand, even though someone were found able to tell us. For we can understand nothing that does not bring with it something in intuition corresponding to the expressions employed. If, by the complaint of being unable to perceive the internal nature of things, it is meant that we do not comprehend by the pure understanding what the things which appear to us may be in themselves, it is a silly and unreasonable complaint; for those who talk thus really desire that we should be able to cognize, consequently to intuite, things without senses, and therefore wish that we possessed a faculty of cognition perfectly different from the human faculty, not merely in degree, but even as regards intuition and the mode thereof, so that thus we should not be men, but belong to a class of beings, the possibility of whose existence, much less their nature and constitution, we have no means of cognizing. By observation and analysis of phenomena we penetrate into the interior of nature, and no one can say what progress this knowledge may make in time. But those transcendental questions which pass beyond the limits of nature, we could never answer, even although all nature were laid open to us, because we have not the power of observing our own mind with any other intuition than that of our internal sense. For herein lies the mystery of the origin and source of our faculty of sensibility. Its application to an object, and the transcendental ground of this unity of subjective and objective, lie too deeply concealed for us, who cognize ourselves only through the internal sense, consequently as phenomena, to be able to discover in our existence anything but phenomena, the non-sensuous cause of which we at the same time earnestly desire to penetrate to.

The great utility of this critique of conclusions arrived at by the processes of mere reflection consists in its clear demonstration of the nullity of all conclusions respecting objects which are compared with each other in the understanding alone, while it at the same time confirms what we particularly insisted on, namely, that, although phenomena are not included as things in themselves among the objects of the pure understanding, they are nevertheless the only things by which our cognition can possess objective reality, that is to say, which give us intuitions to correspond with our conceptions.

When we reflect in a purely logical manner, we do nothing more than compare conceptions in our understanding, to discover whether both have the same content, whether they are self-contradictory or not, whether anything is contained in either conception, which of the two is given, and which is merely a mode of thinking that given. But if I apply these conceptions to an object in general (in the transcendental sense), without first determining whether it is an object of sensuous or intellectual intuition, certain limitations present themselves, which forbid us to pass beyond the conceptions and render all empirical use of them impossible. And thus these limitations prove that the representation of an object as a thing in general is not only insufficient, but, without sensuous determination and independently of empirical conditions, self-contradictory; that we must therefore make abstraction of all objects, as in logic, or, admitting them, must think them under conditions of sensuous intuition; that, consequently, the intelligible requires an altogether peculiar intuition, which we do not possess, and in the absence of which it is for us nothing; while, on the other hand phenomena cannot be objects in themselves. For, when I merely think things in general, the difference in their external relations cannot constitute a difference in the things themselves; on the contrary, the former presupposes the latter, and if the conception of one of two things is not internally different from that of the other, I am merely thinking the same thing in different relations. Further, by the addition of one affirmation (reality) to the other, the positive therein is really augmented, and nothing is abstracted or withdrawn from it; hence the real in things cannot be in contradiction with or opposition to itself — and so on.

The true use of the conceptions of reflection in the employment of the understanding has, as we have shown, been so misconceived by Leibnitz, one of the most acute philosophers of either ancient or modern times, that he has been misled into the construction of a baseless system of intellectual cognition, which professes to determine its objects without the intervention of the senses. For this reason, the exposition of the cause of the amphiboly of these conceptions, as the origin of these false principles, is of great utility in determining with certainty the proper limits of the understanding.

It is right to say whatever is affirmed or denied of the whole of a conception can be affirmed or denied of any part of it (dictum de omni et nullo); but it would be absurd so to alter this logical proposition as to say whatever is not contained in a general conception is likewise not contained in the particular conceptions which rank under it; for the latter are particular conceptions, for the very reason that their content is greater than that which is cogitated in the general conception. And yet the whole intellectual system of Leibnitz is based upon this false principle, and with it must necessarily fall to the ground, together with all the ambiguous principles in reference to the employment of the understanding which have thence originated.

Leibnitz's principle of the identity of indiscernibles or indistinguishables is really based on the presupposition that, if in the conception of a thing a certain distinction is not to be found, it is also not to be met with in things themselves; that, consequently, all things are completely identical (numero eadem) which are not distinguishable from each other (as to quality or quantity) in our conceptions of them. But, as in the mere conception of anything abstraction has been made of many necessary conditions of intuition, that of which abstraction has been made is rashly held to be non-existent, and nothing is attributed to the thing but what is contained in its conception.

The conception of a cubic foot of space, however I may think it, is in itself completely identical. But two cubic feet in space are nevertheless distinct from each other from the sole fact of their being in different places (they are numero diversa); and these places are conditions of intuition, wherein the object of this conception is given, and which do not belong to the conception, but to the faculty of sensibility. In like manner, there is in the conception of a thing no contradiction when a negative is not connected with an affirmative; and merely affirmative conceptions cannot, in conjunction, produce any negation. But in sensuous intuition, wherein reality (take for example, motion) is given, we find conditions (opposite directions) — of which abstraction has been made in the conception of motion in general — which render possible a contradiction or opposition (not indeed of a logical kind) — and which from pure positives produce zero = 0. We are therefore not justified in saying that all reality is in perfect agreement and harmony, because no contradiction is discoverable among its conceptions.* According to mere conceptions, that which is internal is the substratum of all relations or external determinations. When, therefore, I abstract all conditions of intuition, and confine myself solely to the conception of a thing in general, I can make abstraction of all external relations, and there must nevertheless remain a conception of that which indicates no relation, but merely internal determinations. Now it seems to follow that in everything (substance) there is something which is absolutely internal and which antecedes all external determinations, inasmuch as it renders them possible; and that therefore this substratum is something which does not contain any external relations and is consequently simple (for corporeal things are never anything but relations, at least of their parts external to each other); and, inasmuch as we know of no other absolutely internal determinations than those of the internal sense, this substratum is not only simple, but also, analogously with our internal sense, determined through representations, that is to say, all things are properly monads, or simple beings endowed with the power of representation. Now all this would be perfectly correct, if the conception of a thing were the only necessary condition of the presentation of objects of external intuition. It is, on the contrary, manifest that a permanent phenomenon in space (impenetrable extension) can contain mere relations, and nothing that is absolutely internal, and yet be the primary substratum of all external perception. By mere conceptions I cannot think anything external, without, at the same time, thinking something internal, for the reason that conceptions of relations presuppose given things, and without these are impossible. But, as an intuition there is something (that is, space, which, with all it contains, consists of purely formal, or, indeed, real relations) which is not found in the mere conception of a thing in general, and this presents to us the substratum which could not be cognized through conceptions alone, I cannot say: because a thing cannot be represented by mere conceptions without something absolutely internal, there is also, in the things themselves which are contained under these conceptions, and in their intuition nothing external to which something absolutely internal does not serve as the foundation. For, when we have made abstraction of all the conditions of intuition, there certainly remains in the mere conception nothing but the internal in general, through which alone the external is possible. But this necessity, which is grounded upon abstraction alone, does not obtain in the case of things themselves, in so far as they are given in intuition with such determinations as express mere relations, without having anything internal as their foundation; for they are not things of a thing of which we can neither for they are not things in themselves, but only phenomena. What we cognize in matter is nothing but relations (what we call its internal determinations are but comparatively internal). But there are some self-subsistent and permanent, through which a determined object is given. That I, when abstraction is made of these relations, have nothing more to think, does not destroy the conception of a thing as phenomenon, nor the conception of an object in abstracto, but it does away with the possibility of an object that is determinable according to mere conceptions, that is, of a noumenon. It is certainly startling to hear that a thing consists solely of relations; but this thing is simply a phenomenon, and cannot be cogitated by means of the mere categories: it does itself consist in the mere relation of something in general to the senses. In the same way, we cannot cogitate relations of things in abstracto, if we commence with conceptions alone, in any other manner than that one is the cause of determinations in the other; for that is itself the conception of the understanding or category of relation. But, as in this case we make abstraction of all intuition, we lose altogether the mode in which the manifold determines to each of its parts its place, that is, the form of sensibility (space); and yet this mode antecedes all empirical causality.

[Note: If any one wishes here to have recourse to the usual subterfuge, and to say, that at least realitates noumena cannot be in opposition to each other, it will be requisite for him to adduce an example of this pure and non-sensuous reality, that it may be understood whether the notion represents something or nothing. But an example cannot be found except in experience, which never presents to us anything more than phenomena; and thus the proposition means nothing more than that the conception which contains only affirmatives does not contain anything negative — a proposition nobody ever doubted.]

If by intelligible objects we understand things which can be thought by means of the pure categories, without the need of the schemata of sensibility, such objects are impossible. For the condition of the objective use of all our conceptions of understanding is the mode of our sensuous intuition, whereby objects are given; and, if we make abstraction of the latter, the former can have no relation to an object. And even if we should suppose a different kind of intuition from our own, still our functions of thought would have no use or signification in respect thereof. But if we understand by the term, objects of a non-sensuous intuition, in respect of which our categories are not valid, and of which we can accordingly have no knowledge (neither intuition nor conception), in this merely negative sense noumena must be admitted. For this is no more than saying that our mode of intuition is not applicable to all things, but only to objects of our senses, that consequently its objective validity is limited, and that room is therefore left for another kind of intuition, and thus also for things that may be objects of it. But in this sense the conception of a noumenon is problematical, that is to say, it is the notion of that it that it is possible, nor that it is impossible, inasmuch as we do not know of any mode of intuition besides the sensuous, or of any other sort of conceptions than the categories — a mode of intuition and a kind of conception neither of which is applicable to a non-sensuous object. We are on this account incompetent to extend the sphere of our objects of thought beyond the conditions of our sensibility, and to assume the existence of objects of pure thought, that is, of noumena, inasmuch as these have no true positive signification. For it must be confessed of the categories that they are not of themselves sufficient for the cognition of things in themselves and, without the data of sensibility, are mere subjective forms of the unity of the understanding. Thought is certainly not a product of the senses, and in so far is not limited by them, but it does not therefore follow that it may be employed purely and without the intervention of sensibility, for it would then be without reference to an object. And we cannot call a noumenon an object of pure thought; for the representation thereof is but the problematical conception of an object for a perfectly different intuition and a perfectly different understanding from ours, both of which are consequently themselves problematical. The conception of a noumenon is therefore not the conception of an object, but merely a problematical conception inseparably connected with the limitation of our sensibility. That is to say, this conception contains the answer to the question: "Are there objects quite unconnected with, and independent of, our intuition?" — a question to which only an indeterminate answer can be given. That answer is: "Inasmuch as sensuous intuition does not apply to all things without distinction, there remains room for other and different objects." The existence of these problematical objects is therefore not absolutely denied, in the absence of a determinate conception of them, but, as no category is valid in respect of them, neither must they be admitted as objects for our understanding.

Understanding accordingly limits sensibility, without at the same time enlarging its own field. While, moreover, it forbids sensibility to apply its forms and modes to things in themselves and restricts it to the sphere of phenomena, it cogitates an object in itself, only, however, as a transcendental object, which is the cause of a phenomenon (consequently not itself a phenomenon), and which cannot be thought either as a quantity or as reality, or as substance (because these conceptions always require sensuous forms in which to determine an object) — an object, therefore, of which we are quite unable to say whether it can be met with in ourselves or out of us, whether it would be annihilated together with sensibility, or, if this were taken away, would continue to exist. If we wish to call this object a noumenon, because the representation of it is non-sensuous, we are at liberty to do so. But as we can apply to it none of the conceptions of our understanding, the representation is for us quite void, and is available only for the indication of the limits of our sensuous intuition, thereby leaving at the same time an empty space, which we are competent to fill by the aid neither of possible experience, nor of the pure understanding.

The critique of the pure understanding, accordingly, does not permit us to create for ourselves a new field of objects beyond those which are presented to us as phenomena, and to stray into intelligible worlds; nay, it does not even allow us to endeavour to form so much as a conception of them. The specious error which leads to this — and which is a perfectly excusable one — lies in the fact that the employment of the understanding, contrary to its proper purpose and destination, is made transcendental, and objects, that is, possible intuitions, are made to regulate themselves according to conceptions, instead of the conceptions arranging themselves according to the intuitions, on which alone their own objective validity rests. Now the reason of this again is that apperception, and with it thought, antecedes all possible determinate arrangement of representations. Accordingly we think something in general and determine it on the one hand sensuously, but, on the other, distinguish the general and in abstracto represented object from this particular mode of intuiting it. In this case there remains a mode of determining the object by mere thought, which is really but a logical form without content, which, however, seems to us to be a mode of the existence of the object in itself (noumenon), without regard to intuition which is limited to our senses.

Before ending this transcendental analytic, we must make an addition, which, although in itself of no particular importance, seems to be necessary to the completeness of the system. The highest conception, with which a transcendental philosophy commonly begins, is the division into possible and impossible. But as all division presupposes a divided conception, a still higher one must exist, and this is the conception of an object in general — problematically understood and without its being decided whether it is something or nothing. As the categories are the only conceptions which apply to objects in general, the distinguishing of an object, whether it is something or nothing, must proceed according to the order and direction of the categories.

1. To the categories of quantity, that is, the conceptions of all, many, and one, the conception which annihilates all, that is, the conception of none, is opposed. And thus the object of a conception, to which no intuition can be found to correspond, is = nothing. That is, it is a conception without an object (ens rationis), like noumena, which cannot be considered possible in the sphere of reality, though they must not therefore be held to be impossible — or like certain new fundamental forces in matter, the existence of which is cogitable without contradiction, though, as examples from experience are not forthcoming, they must not be regarded as possible.

2. Reality is something; negation is nothing, that is, a conception of the absence of an object, as cold, a shadow (nihil privativum).

3. The mere form of intuition, without substance, is in itself no object, but the merely formal condition of an object (as phenomenon), as pure space and pure time. These are certainly something, as forms of intuition, but are not themselves objects which are intuited (ens imaginarium).

4. The object of a conception which is self-contradictory, is nothing, because the conception is nothing — is impossible, as a figure composed of two straight lines (nihil negativum).

The table of this division of the conception of nothing (the corresponding division of the conception of something does not require special description) must therefore be arranged as follows:

We see that the ens rationis is distinguished from the nihil negativum or pure nothing by the consideration that the former must not be reckoned among possibilities, because it is a mere fiction — though not self-contradictory, while the latter is completely opposed to all possibility, inasmuch as the conception annihilates itself. Both, however, are empty conceptions. On the other hand, the nihil privativum and ens imaginarium are empty data for conceptions. If light be not given to the senses, we cannot represent to ourselves darkness, and if extended objects are not perceived, we cannot represent space. Neither the negation, nor the mere form of intuition can, without something real, be an object.

TRANSCENDENTAL LOGIC.

SECOND DIVISION.

TRANSCENDENTAL DIALECTIC.
INTRODUCTION.

I. Of Transcendental Illusory Appearance.

We termed dialectic in general a logic of appearance. This does not signify a doctrine of probability; for probability is truth, only cognized upon insufficient grounds, and though the information it gives us is imperfect, it is not therefore deceitful. Hence it must not be separated from the analytical part of logic. Still less must phenomenon and appearance be held to be identical. For truth or illusory appearance does not reside in the object, in so far as it is intuited, but in the judgement upon the object, in so far as it is thought. It is, therefore, quite correct to say that the senses do not err, not because they always judge correctly, but because they do not judge at all. Hence truth and error, consequently also, illusory appearance as the cause of error, are only to be found in a judgement, that is, in the relation of an object to our understanding. In a cognition which completely harmonizes with the laws of the understanding, no error can exist. In a representation of the senses — as not containing any judgement — there is also no error. But no power of nature can of itself deviate from its own laws. Hence neither the understanding per se (without the influence of another cause), nor the senses per se, would fall into error; the former could not, because, if it acts only according to its own laws, the effect (the judgement) must necessarily accord with these laws. But in accordance with the laws of the understanding consists the formal element in all truth. In the senses there is no judgement — neither a true nor a false one. But, as we have no source of cognition besides these two, it follows that error is caused solely by the unobserved influence of the sensibility upon the understanding. And thus it happens that the subjective grounds of a judgement and are confounded with the objective, and cause them to deviate from their proper determination,* just as a body in motion would always of itself proceed in a straight line, but if another impetus gives to it a different direction, it will then start off into a curvilinear line of motion. To distinguish the peculiar action of the understanding from the power which mingles with it, it is necessary to consider an erroneous judgement as the diagonal between two forces, that determine the judgement in two different directions, which, as it were, form an angle, and to resolve this composite operation into the simple ones of the understanding and the sensibility. In pure a priori judgements this must be done by means of transcendental reflection, whereby, as has been already shown, each representation has its place appointed in the corresponding faculty of cognition, and consequently the influence of the one faculty upon the other is made apparent.

[Note: Sensibility, subjected to the understanding, as the object upon which the understanding employs its functions, is the source of real cognitions. But, in so far as it exercises an influence upon the action of the understanding and determines it to judgement, sensibility is itself the cause of error.]

It is not at present our business to treat of empirical illusory appearance (for example, optical illusion), which occurs in the empirical application of otherwise correct rules of the understanding, and in which the judgement is misled by the influence of imagination. Our purpose is to speak of transcendental illusory appearance, which influences principles — that are not even applied to experience, for in this case we should possess a sure test of their correctness — but which leads us, in disregard of all the warnings of criticism, completely beyond the empirical employment of the categories and deludes us with the chimera of an extension of the sphere of the pure understanding. We shall term those principles the application of which is confined entirely within the limits of possible experience, immanent; those, on the other hand, which transgress these limits, we shall call transcendent principles. But by these latter I do not understand principles of the transcendental use or misuse of the categories, which is in reality a mere fault of the judgement when not under due restraint from criticism, and therefore not paying sufficient attention to the limits of the sphere in which the pure understanding is allowed to exercise its functions; but real principles which exhort us to break down all those barriers, and to lay claim to a perfectly new field of cognition, which recognizes no line of demarcation. Thus transcendental and transcendent are not identical terms. The principles of the pure understanding, which we have already propounded, ought to be of empirical and not of transcendental use, that is, they are not applicable to any object beyond the sphere of experience. A principle which removes these limits, nay, which authorizes us to overstep them, is called transcendent. If our criticism can succeed in exposing the illusion in these pretended principles, those which are limited in their employment to the sphere of experience may be called, in opposition to the others, immanent principles of the pure understanding.

Logical illusion, which consists merely in the imitation of the form of reason (the illusion in sophistical syllogisms), arises entirely from a want of due attention to logical rules. So soon as the attention is awakened to the case before us, this illusion totally disappears. Transcendental illusion, on the contrary, does not cease to exist, even after it has been exposed, and its nothingness clearly perceived by means of transcendental criticism. Take, for example, the illusion in the proposition: "The world must have a beginning in time." The cause of this is as follows. In our reason, subjectively considered as a faculty of human cognition, there exist fundamental rules and maxims of its exercise, which have completely the appearance of objective principles. Now from this cause it happens that the subjective necessity of a certain connection of our conceptions, is regarded as an objective necessity of the determination of things in themselves. This illusion it is impossible to avoid, just as we cannot avoid perceiving that the sea appears to be higher at a distance than it is near the shore, because we see the former by means of higher rays than the latter, or, which is a still stronger case, as even the astronomer cannot prevent himself from seeing the moon larger at its rising than some time afterwards, although he is not deceived by this illusion.

Transcendental dialectic will therefore content itself with exposing the illusory appearance in transcendental judgements, and guarding us against it; but to make it, as in the case of logical illusion, entirely disappear and cease to be illusion is utterly beyond its power. For we have here to do with a natural and unavoidable illusion, which rests upon subjective principles and imposes these upon us as objective, while logical dialectic, in the detection of sophisms, has to do merely with an error in the logical consequence of the propositions, or with an artificially constructed illusion, in imitation of the natural error. There is, therefore, a natural and unavoidable dialectic of pure reason — not that in which the bungler, from want of the requisite knowledge, involves himself, nor that which the sophist devises for the purpose of misleading, but that which is an inseparable adjunct of human reason, and which, even after its illusions have been exposed, does not cease to deceive, and continually to lead reason into momentary errors, which it becomes necessary continually to remove.

II. Of Pure Reason as the Seat of Transcendental Illusory Appearance.

A. OF REASON IN GENERAL.

All our knowledge begins with sense, proceeds thence to understanding, and ends with reason, beyond which nothing higher can be discovered in the human mind for elaborating the matter of intuition and subjecting it to the highest unity of thought. At this stage of our inquiry it is my duty to give an explanation of this, the highest faculty of cognition, and I confess I find myself here in some difficulty. Of reason, as of the understanding, there is a merely formal, that is, logical use, in which it makes abstraction of all content of cognition; but there is also a real use, inasmuch as it contains in itself the source of certain conceptions and principles, which it does not borrow either from the senses or the understanding. The former faculty has been long defined by logicians as the faculty of mediate conclusion in contradistinction to immediate conclusions (consequentiae immediatae); but the nature of the latter, which itself generates conceptions, is not to be understood from this definition. Now as a division of reason into a logical and a transcendental faculty presents itself here, it becomes necessary to seek for a higher conception of this source of cognition which shall comprehend both conceptions. In this we may expect, according to the analogy of the conceptions of the understanding, that the logical conception will give us the key to the transcendental, and that the table of the functions of the former will present us with the clue to the conceptions of reason.

In the former part of our transcendental logic, we defined the understanding to be the faculty of rules; reason may be distinguished from understanding as the faculty of principles.

The term principle is ambiguous, and commonly signifies merely a cognition that may be employed as a principle, although it is not in itself, and as regards its proper origin, entitled to the distinction. Every general proposition, even if derived from experience by the process of induction, may serve as the major in a syllogism; but it is not for that reason a principle. Mathematical axioms (for example, there can be only one straight line between two points) are general a priori cognitions, and are therefore rightly denominated principles, relatively to the cases which can be subsumed under them. But I cannot for this reason say that I cognize this property of a straight line from principles — I cognize it only in pure intuition.

Cognition from principles, then, is that cognition in which I cognize the particular in the general by means of conceptions. Thus every syllogism is a form of the deduction of a cognition from a principle. For the major always gives a conception, through which everything that is subsumed under the condition thereof is cognized according to a principle. Now as every general cognition may serve as the major in a syllogism, and the understanding presents us with such general a priori propositions, they may be termed principles, in respect of their possible use.

But if we consider these principles of the pure understanding in relation to their origin, we shall find them to be anything rather than cognitions from conceptions. For they would not even be possible a priori, if we could not rely on the assistance of pure intuition (in mathematics), or on that of the conditions of a possible experience. That everything that happens has a cause, cannot be concluded from the general conception of that which happens; on the contrary the principle of causality instructs us as to the mode of obtaining from that which happens a determinate empirical conception.

Synthetical cognitions from conceptions the understanding cannot supply, and they alone are entitled to be called principles. At the same time, all general propositions may be termed comparative principles.

It has been a long-cherished wish — that (who knows how late), may one day, be happily accomplished — that the principles of the endless variety of civil laws should be investigated and exposed; for in this way alone can we find the secret of simplifying legislation. But in this case, laws are nothing more than limitations of our freedom upon conditions under which it subsists in perfect harmony with itself; they consequently have for their object that which is completely our own work, and of which we ourselves may be the cause by means of these conceptions. But how objects as things in themselves — how the nature of things is subordinated to principles and is to be determined, according to conceptions, is a question which it seems well nigh impossible to answer. Be this, however, as it may — for on this point our investigation is yet to be made — it is at least manifest from what we have said that cognition from principles is something very different from cognition by means of the understanding, which may indeed precede other cognitions in the form of a principle, but in itself — in so far as it is synthetical — is neither based upon mere thought, nor contains a general proposition drawn from conceptions alone.

The understanding may be a faculty for the production of unity of phenomena by virtue of rules; the reason is a faculty for the production of unity of rules (of the understanding) under principles. Reason, therefore, never applies directly to experience, or to any sensuous object; its object is, on the contrary, the understanding, to the manifold cognition of which it gives a unity a priori by means of conceptions — a unity which may be called rational unity, and which is of a nature very different from that of the unity produced by the understanding.

The above is the general conception of the faculty of reason, in so far as it has been possible to make it comprehensible in the absence of examples. These will be given in the sequel.

B. OF THE LOGICAL USE OF REASON.

A distinction is commonly made between that which is immediately cognized and that which is inferred or concluded. That in a figure which is bounded by three straight lines there are three angles, is an immediate cognition; but that these angles are together equal to two right angles, is an inference or conclusion. Now, as we are constantly employing this mode of thought and have thus become quite accustomed to it, we no longer remark the above distinction, and, as in the case of the so-called deceptions of sense, consider as immediately perceived, what has really been inferred. In every reasoning or syllogism, there is a fundamental proposition, afterwards a second drawn from it, and finally the conclusion, which connects the truth in the first with the truth in the second — and that infallibly. If the judgement concluded is so contained in the first proposition that it can be deduced from it without the meditation of a third notion, the conclusion is called immediate (consequentia immediata); I prefer the term conclusion of the understanding. But if, in addition to the fundamental cognition, a second judgement is necessary for the production of the conclusion, it is called a conclusion of the reason. In the proposition: All men are mortal, are contained the propositions: Some men are mortal, Nothing that is not mortal is a man, and these are therefore immediate conclusions from the first. On the other hand, the proposition: all the learned are mortal, is not contained in the main proposition (for the conception of a learned man does not occur in it), and it can be deduced from the main proposition only by means of a mediating judgement.

In every syllogism I first cogitate a rule (the major) by means of the understanding. In the next place I subsume a cognition under the condition of the rule (and this is the minor) by means of the judgement. And finally I determine my cognition by means of the predicate of the rule (this is the conclusio), consequently, I determine it a priori by means of the reason. The relations, therefore, which the major proposition, as the rule, represents between a cognition and its condition, constitute the different kinds of syllogisms. These are just threefold — analogously with all judgements, in so far as they differ in the mode of expressing the relation of a cognition in the understanding — namely, categorical, hypothetical, and disjunctive.

When as often happens, the conclusion is a judgement which may follow from other given judgements, through which a perfectly different object is cogitated, I endeavour to discover in the understanding whether the assertion in this conclusion does not stand under certain conditions according to a general rule. If I find such a condition, and if the object mentioned in the conclusion can be subsumed under the given condition, then this conclusion follows from a rule which is also valid for other objects of cognition. From this we see that reason endeavours to subject the great variety of the cognitions of the understanding to the smallest possible number of principles (general conditions), and thus to produce in it the highest unity.

C. OF THE PURE USE OF REASON.

Can we isolate reason, and, if so, is it in this case a peculiar source of conceptions and judgements which spring from it alone, and through which it can be applied to objects; or is it merely a subordinate faculty, whose duty it is to give a certain form to given cognitions — a form which is called logical, and through which the cognitions of the understanding are subordinated to each other, and lower rules to higher (those, to wit, whose condition comprises in its sphere the condition of the others), in so far as this can be done by comparison? This is the question which we have at present to answer. Manifold variety of rules and unity of principles is a requirement of reason, for the purpose of bringing the understanding into complete accordance with itself, just as understanding subjects the manifold content of intuition to conceptions, and thereby introduces connection into it. But this principle prescribes no law to objects, and does not contain any ground of the possibility of cognizing or of determining them as such, but is merely a subjective law for the proper arrangement of the content of the understanding. The purpose of this law is, by a comparison of the conceptions of the understanding, to reduce them to the smallest possible number, although, at the same time, it does not justify us in demanding from objects themselves such a uniformity as might contribute to the convenience and the enlargement of the sphere of the understanding, or in expecting that it will itself thus receive from them objective validity. In one word, the question is: "does reason in itself, that is, does pure reason contain a priori synthetical principles and rules, and what are those principles?"

The formal and logical procedure of reason in syllogisms gives us sufficient information in regard to the ground on which the transcendental principle of reason in its pure synthetical cognition will rest.

1. Reason, as observed in the syllogistic process, is not applicable to intuitions, for the purpose of subjecting them to rules — for this is the province of the understanding with its categories — but to conceptions and judgements. If pure reason does apply to objects and the intuition of them, it does so not immediately, but mediately — through the understanding and its judgements, which have a direct relation to the senses and their intuition, for the purpose of determining their objects. The unity of reason is therefore not the unity of a possible experience, but is essentially different from this unity, which is that of the understanding. That everything which happens has a cause, is not a principle cognized and prescribed by reason. This principle makes the unity of experience possible and borrows nothing from reason, which, without a reference to possible experience, could never have produced by means of mere conceptions any such synthetical unity.

2. Reason, in its logical use, endeavours to discover the general condition of its judgement (the conclusion), and a syllogism is itself nothing but a judgement by means of the subsumption of its condition under a general rule (the major). Now as this rule may itself be subjected to the same process of reason, and thus the condition of the condition be sought (by means of a prosyllogism) as long as the process can be continued, it is very manifest that the peculiar principle of reason in its logical use is to find for the conditioned cognition of the understanding the unconditioned whereby the unity of the former is completed.

But this logical maxim cannot be a principle of pure reason, unless we admit that, if the conditioned is given, the whole series of conditions subordinated to one another — a series which is consequently itself unconditioned — is also given, that is, contained in the object and its connection.

But this principle of pure reason is evidently synthetical; for, analytically, the conditioned certainly relates to some condition, but not to the unconditioned. From this principle also there must originate different synthetical propositions, of which the pure understanding is perfectly ignorant, for it has to do only with objects of a possible experience, the cognition and synthesis of which is always conditioned. The unconditioned, if it does really exist, must be especially considered in regard to the determinations which distinguish it from whatever is conditioned, and will thus afford us material for many a priori synthetical propositions.

The principles resulting from this highest principle of pure reason will, however, be transcendent in relation to phenomena, that is to say, it will be impossible to make any adequate empirical use of this principle. It is therefore completely different from all principles of the understanding, the use made of which is entirely immanent, their object and purpose being merely the possibility of experience. Now our duty in the transcendental dialectic is as follows. To discover whether the principle that the series of conditions (in the synthesis of phenomena, or of thought in general) extends to the unconditioned is objectively true, or not; what consequences result therefrom affecting the empirical use of the understanding, or rather whether there exists any such objectively valid proposition of reason, and whether it is not, on the contrary, a merely logical precept which directs us to ascend perpetually to still higher conditions, to approach completeness in the series of them, and thus to introduce into our cognition the highest possible unity of reason. We must ascertain, I say, whether this requirement of reason has not been regarded, by a misunderstanding, as a transcendental principle of pure reason, which postulates a thorough completeness in the series of conditions in objects themselves. We must show, moreover, the misconceptions and illusions that intrude into syllogisms, the major proposition of which pure reason has supplied — a proposition which has perhaps more of the character of a petitio than of a postulatum — and that proceed from experience upwards to its conditions. The solution of these problems is our task in transcendental dialectic, which we are about to expose even at its source, that lies deep in human reason. We shall divide it into two parts, the first of which will treat of the transcendent conceptions of pure reason, the second of transcendent and dialectical syllogisms.

BOOK I. — OF THE CONCEPTIONS OF PURE REASON.

The conceptions of pure reason — we do not here speak of the possibility of them — are not obtained by reflection, but by inference or conclusion. The conceptions of understanding are also cogitated a priori antecedently to experience, and render it possible; but they contain nothing but the unity of reflection upon phenomena, in so far as these must necessarily belong to a possible empirical consciousness. Through them alone are cognition and the determination of an object possible. It is from them, accordingly, that we receive material for reasoning, and antecedently to them we possess no a priori conceptions of objects from which they might be deduced, On the other hand, the sole basis of their objective reality consists in the necessity imposed on them, as containing the intellectual form of all experience, of restricting their application and influence to the sphere of experience.

But the term, conception of reason, or rational conception, itself indicates that it does not confine itself within the limits of experience, because its object-matter is a cognition, of which every empirical cognition is but a part — nay, the whole of possible experience may be itself but a part of it — a cognition to which no actual experience ever fully attains, although it does always pertain to it. The aim of rational conceptions is the comprehension, as that of the conceptions of understanding is the understanding of perceptions. If they contain the unconditioned, they relate to that to which all experience is subordinate, but which is never itself an object of experience — that towards which reason tends in all its conclusions from experience, and by the standard of which it estimates the degree of their empirical use, but which is never itself an element in an empirical synthesis. If, notwithstanding, such conceptions possess objective validity, they may be called conceptus ratiocinati (conceptions legitimately concluded); in cases where they do not, they have been admitted on account of having the appearance of being correctly concluded, and may be called conceptus ratiocinantes (sophistical conceptions). But as this can only be sufficiently demonstrated in that part of our treatise which relates to the dialectical conclusions of reason, we shall omit any consideration of it in this place. As we called the pure conceptions of the understanding categories, we shall also distinguish those of pure reason by a new name and call them transcendental ideas. These terms, however, we must in the first place explain and justify.

SECTION I — Of Ideas in General.

Despite the great wealth of words which European languages possess, the thinker finds himself often at a loss for an expression exactly suited to his conception, for want of which he is unable to make himself intelligible either to others or to himself. To coin new words is a pretension to legislation in language which is seldom successful; and, before recourse is taken to so desperate an expedient, it is advisable to examine the dead and learned languages, with the hope and the probability that we may there meet with some adequate expression of the notion we have in our minds. In this case, even if the original meaning of the word has become somewhat uncertain, from carelessness or want of caution on the part of the authors of it, it is always better to adhere to and confirm its proper meaning — even although it may be doubtful whether it was formerly used in exactly this sense — than to make our labour vain by want of sufficient care to render ourselves intelligible.

For this reason, when it happens that there exists only a single word to express a certain conception, and this word, in its usual acceptation, is thoroughly adequate to the conception, the accurate distinction of which from related conceptions is of great importance, we ought not to employ the expression improvidently, or, for the sake of variety and elegance of style, use it as a synonym for other cognate words. It is our duty, on the contrary, carefully to preserve its peculiar signification, as otherwise it easily happens that when the attention of the reader is no longer particularly attracted to the expression, and it is lost amid the multitude of other words of very different import, the thought which it conveyed, and which it alone conveyed, is lost with it.

Plato employed the expression idea in a way that plainly showed he meant by it something which is never derived from the senses, but which far transcends even the conceptions of the understanding (with which Aristotle occupied himself), inasmuch as in experience nothing perfectly corresponding to them could be found. Ideas are, according to him, archetypes of things themselves, and not merely keys to possible experiences, like the categories. In his view they flow from the highest reason, by which they have been imparted to human reason, which, however, exists no longer in its original state, but is obliged with great labour to recall by reminiscence — which is called philosophy — the old but now sadly obscured ideas. I will not here enter upon any literary investigation of the sense which this sublime philosopher attached to this expression. I shall content myself with remarking that it is nothing unusual, in common conversation as well as in written works, by comparing the thoughts which an author has delivered upon a subject, to understand him better than he understood himself inasmuch as he may not have sufficiently determined his conception, and thus have sometimes spoken, nay even thought, in opposition to his own opinions.

Plato perceived very clearly that our faculty of cognition has the feeling of a much higher vocation than that of merely spelling out phenomena according to synthetical unity, for the purpose of being able to read them as experience, and that our reason naturally raises itself to cognitions far too elevated to admit of the possibility of an object given by experience corresponding to them — cognitions which are nevertheless real, and are not mere phantoms of the brain.

This philosopher found his ideas especially in all that is practical,* that is, which rests upon freedom, which in its turn ranks under cognitions that are the peculiar product of reason. He who would derive from experience the conceptions of virtue, who would make (as many have really done) that, which at best can but serve as an imperfectly illustrative example, a model for or the formation of a perfectly adequate idea on the subject, would in fact transform virtue into a nonentity changeable according to time and circumstance and utterly incapable of being employed as a rule. On the contrary, every one is conscious that, when any one is held up to him as a model of virtue, he compares this so-called model with the true original which he possesses in his own mind and values him according to this standard. But this standard is the idea of virtue, in relation to which all possible objects of experience are indeed serviceable as examples — proofs of the practicability in a certain degree of that which the conception of virtue demands — but certainly not as archetypes. That the actions of man will never be in perfect accordance with all the requirements of the pure ideas of reason, does not prove the thought to be chimerical. For only through this idea are all judgements as to moral merit or demerit possible; it consequently lies at the foundation of every approach to moral perfection, however far removed from it the obstacles in human nature — indeterminable as to degree — may keep us.

[Note: He certainly extended the application of his conception to speculative cognitions also, provided they were given pure and completely a priori, nay, even to mathematics, although this science cannot possess an object otherwhere than in Possible experience.

I cannot follow him in this, and as little can I follow him in his mystical deduction of these ideas, or in his hypostatization of them; although, in truth, the elevated and exaggerated language which he employed in describing them is quite capable of an interpretation more subdued and more in accordance with fact and the nature of things.]

The Platonic Republic has become proverbial as an example — and a striking one — of imaginary perfection, such as can exist only in the brain of the idle thinker; and Brucker ridicules the philosopher for maintaining that a prince can never govern well, unless he is participant in the ideas. But we should do better to follow up this thought and, where this admirable thinker leaves us without assistance, employ new efforts to place it in clearer light, rather than carelessly fling it aside as useless, under the very miserable and pernicious pretext of impracticability. A constitution of the greatest possible human freedom according to laws, by which the liberty of every individual can consist with the liberty of every other (not of the greatest possible happiness, for this follows necessarily from the former), is, to say the least, a necessary idea, which must be placed at the foundation not only of the first plan of the constitution of a state, but of all its laws. And, in this, it not necessary at the outset to take account of the obstacles which lie in our way — obstacles which perhaps do not necessarily arise from the character of human nature, but rather from the previous neglect of true ideas in legislation. For there is nothing more pernicious and more unworthy of a philosopher, than the vulgar appeal to a so-called adverse experience, which indeed would not have existed, if those institutions had been established at the proper time and in accordance with ideas; while, instead of this, conceptions, crude for the very reason that they have been drawn from experience, have marred and frustrated all our better views and intentions. The more legislation and government are in harmony with this idea, the more rare do punishments become and thus it is quite reasonable to maintain, as Plato did, that in a perfect state no punishments at all would be necessary. Now although a perfect state may never exist, the idea is not on that account the less just, which holds up this maximum as the archetype or standard of a constitution, in order to bring legislative government always nearer and nearer to the greatest possible perfection. For at what precise degree human nature must stop in its progress, and how wide must be the chasm which must necessarily exist between the idea and its realization, are problems which no one can or ought to determine — and for this reason, that it is the destination of freedom to overstep all assigned limits between itself and the idea.

But not only in that wherein human reason is a real causal agent and where ideas are operative causes (of actions and their objects), that is to say, in the region of ethics, but also in regard to nature herself, Plato saw clear proofs of an origin from ideas. A plant, and animal, the regular order of nature — probably also the disposition of the whole universe — give manifest evidence that they are possible only by means of and according to ideas; that, indeed, no one creature, under the individual conditions of its existence, perfectly harmonizes with the idea of the most perfect of its kind — just as little as man with the idea of humanity, which nevertheless he bears in his soul as the archetypal standard of his actions; that, notwithstanding, these ideas are in the highest sense individually, unchangeably, and completely determined, and are the original causes of things; and that the totality of connected objects in the universe is alone fully adequate to that idea. Setting aside the exaggerations of expression in the writings of this philosopher, the mental power exhibited in this ascent from the ectypal mode of regarding the physical world to the architectonic connection thereof according to ends, that is, ideas, is an effort which deserves imitation and claims respect. But as regards the principles of ethics, of legislation, and of religion, spheres in which ideas alone render experience possible, although they never attain to full expression therein, he has vindicated for himself a position of peculiar merit, which is not appreciated only because it is judged by the very empirical rules, the validity of which as principles is destroyed by ideas. For as regards nature, experience presents us with rules and is the source of truth, but in relation to ethical laws experience is the parent of illusion, and it is in the highest degree reprehensible to limit or to deduce the laws which dictate what I ought to do, from what is done.

We must, however, omit the consideration of these important subjects, the development of which is in reality the peculiar duty and dignity of philosophy, and confine ourselves for the present to the more humble but not less useful task of preparing a firm foundation for those majestic edifices of moral science. For this foundation has been hitherto insecure from the many subterranean passages which reason in its confident but vain search for treasures has made in all directions. Our present duty is to make ourselves perfectly acquainted with the transcendental use made of pure reason, its principles and ideas, that we may be able properly to determine and value its influence and real worth. But before bringing these introductory remarks to a close, I beg those who really have philosophy at heart — and their number is but small — if they shall find themselves convinced by the considerations following as well as by those above, to exert themselves to preserve to the expression idea its original signification, and to take care that it be not lost among those other expressions by which all sorts of representations are loosely designated — that the interests of science may not thereby suffer. We are in no want of words to denominate adequately every mode of representation, without the necessity of encroaching upon terms which are proper to others. The following is a graduated list of them. The genus is representation in general (representatio). Under it stands representation with consciousness (perceptio). A perception which relates solely to the subject as a modification of its state, is a sensation (sensatio), an objective perception is a cognition (cognitio). A cognition is either an intuition or a conception (intuitus vel conceptus). The former has an immediate relation to the object and is singular and individual; the latter has but a mediate relation, by means of a characteristic mark which may be common to several things. A conception is either empirical or pure. A pure conception, in so far as it has its origin in the understanding alone, and is not the conception of a pure sensuous image, is called notio. A conception formed from notions, which transcends the possibility of experience, is an idea, or a conception of reason. To one who has accustomed himself to these distinctions, it must be quite intolerable to hear the representation of the colour red called an idea. It ought not even to be called a notion or conception of understanding.

SECTION II. Of Transcendental Ideas.

Transcendental analytic showed us how the mere logical form of our cognition can contain the origin of pure conceptions a priori, conceptions which represent objects antecedently to all experience, or rather, indicate the synthetical unity which alone renders possible an empirical cognition of objects. The form of judgements — converted into a conception of the synthesis of intuitions — produced the categories which direct the employment of the understanding in experience. This consideration warrants us to expect that the form of syllogisms, when applied to synthetical unity of intuitions, following the rule of the categories, will contain the origin of particular a priori conceptions, which we may call pure conceptions of reason or transcendental ideas, and which will determine the use of the understanding in the totality of experience according to principles.

The function of reason in arguments consists in the universality of a cognition according to conceptions, and the syllogism itself is a judgement which is determined a priori in the whole extent of its condition. The proposition: "Caius is mortal," is one which may be obtained from experience by the aid of the understanding alone; but my wish is to find a conception which contains the condition under which the predicate of this judgement is given — in this case, the conception of man — and after subsuming under this condition, taken in its whole extent (all men are mortal), I determine according to it the cognition of the object thought, and say: "Caius is mortal."

Hence, in the conclusion of a syllogism we restrict a predicate to a certain object, after having thought it in the major in its whole extent under a certain condition. This complete quantity of the extent in relation to such a condition is called universality (universalitas). To this corresponds totality (universitas) of conditions in the synthesis of intuitions. The transcendental conception of reason is therefore nothing else than the conception of the totality of the conditions of a given conditioned. Now as the unconditioned alone renders possible totality of conditions, and, conversely, the totality of conditions is itself always unconditioned; a pure rational conception in general can be defined and explained by means of the conception of the unconditioned, in so far as it contains a basis for the synthesis of the conditioned.

To the number of modes of relation which the understanding cogitates by means of the categories, the number of pure rational conceptions will correspond. We must therefore seek for, first, an unconditioned of the categorical synthesis in a subject; secondly, of the hypothetical synthesis of the members of a series; thirdly, of the disjunctive synthesis of parts in a system.

There are exactly the same number of modes of syllogisms, each of which proceeds through prosyllogisms to the unconditioned — one to the subject which cannot be employed as predicate, another to the presupposition which supposes nothing higher than itself, and the third to an aggregate of the members of the complete division of a conception. Hence the pure rational conceptions of totality in the synthesis of conditions have a necessary foundation in the nature of human reason — at least as modes of elevating the unity of the understanding to the unconditioned. They may have no valid application, corresponding to their transcendental employment, in concreto, and be thus of no greater utility than to direct the understanding how, while extending them as widely as possible, to maintain its exercise and application in perfect consistence and harmony.

But, while speaking here of the totality of conditions and of the unconditioned as the common title of all conceptions of reason, we again light upon an expression which we find it impossible to dispense with, and which nevertheless, owing to the ambiguity attaching to it from long abuse, we cannot employ with safety. The word absolute is one of the few words which, in its original signification, was perfectly adequate to the conception it was intended to convey — a conception which no other word in the same language exactly suits, and the loss — or, which is the same thing, the incautious and loose employment — of which must be followed by the loss of the conception itself. And, as it is a conception which occupies much of the attention of reason, its loss would be greatly to the detriment of all transcendental philosophy. The word absolute is at present frequently used to denote that something can be predicated of a thing considered in itself and intrinsically. In this sense absolutely possible would signify that which is possible in itself (interne) — which is, in fact, the least that one can predicate of an object. On the other hand, it is sometimes employed to indicate that a thing is valid in all respects — for example, absolute sovereignty. Absolutely possible would in this sense signify that which is possible in all relations and in every respect; and this is the most that can be predicated of the possibility of a thing. Now these significations do in truth frequently coincide. Thus, for example, that which is intrinsically impossible, is also impossible in all relations, that is, absolutely impossible. But in most cases they differ from each other toto caelo, and I can by no means conclude that, because a thing is in itself possible, it is also possible in all relations, and therefore absolutely. Nay, more, I shall in the sequel show that absolute necessity does not by any means depend on internal necessity, and that, therefore, it must not be considered as synonymous with it. Of an opposite which is intrinsically impossible, we may affirm that it is in all respects impossible, and that, consequently, the thing itself, of which this is the opposite, is absolutely necessary; but I cannot reason conversely and say, the opposite of that which is absolutely necessary is intrinsically impossible, that is, that the absolute necessity of things is an internal necessity. For this internal necessity is in certain cases a mere empty word with which the least conception cannot be connected, while the conception of the necessity of a thing in all relations possesses very peculiar determinations. Now as the loss of a conception of great utility in speculative science cannot be a matter of indifference to the philosopher, I trust that the proper determination and careful preservation of the expression on which the conception depends will likewise be not indifferent to him.

In this enlarged signification, then, shall I employ the word absolute, in opposition to that which is valid only in some particular respect; for the latter is restricted by conditions, the former is valid without any restriction whatever.

Now the transcendental conception of reason has for its object nothing else than absolute totality in the synthesis of conditions and does not rest satisfied till it has attained to the absolutely, that is, in all respects and relations, unconditioned. For pure reason leaves to the understanding everything that immediately relates to the object of intuition or rather to their synthesis in imagination. The former restricts itself to the absolute totality in the employment of the conceptions of the understanding and aims at carrying out the synthetical unity which is cogitated in the category, even to the unconditioned. This unity may hence be called the rational unity of phenomena, as the other, which the category expresses, may be termed the unity of the understanding. Reason, therefore, has an immediate relation to the use of the understanding, not indeed in so far as the latter contains the ground of possible experience (for the conception of the absolute totality of conditions is not a conception that can be employed in experience, because no experience is unconditioned), but solely for the purpose of directing it to a certain unity, of which the understanding has no conception, and the aim of which is to collect into an absolute whole all acts of the understanding. Hence the objective employment of the pure conceptions of reason is always transcendent, while that of the pure conceptions of the understanding must, according to their nature, be always immanent, inasmuch as they are limited to possible experience.

I understand by idea a necessary conception of reason, to which no corresponding object can be discovered in the world of sense. Accordingly, the pure conceptions of reason at present under consideration are transcendental ideas. They are conceptions of pure reason, for they regard all empirical cognition as determined by means of an absolute totality of conditions. They are not mere fictions, but natural and necessary products of reason, and have hence a necessary relation to the whole sphere of the exercise of the understanding. And, finally, they are transcendent, and overstep the limits of all experiences, in which, consequently, no object can ever be presented that would be perfectly adequate to a transcendental idea. When we use the word idea, we say, as regards its object (an object of the pure understanding), a great deal, but as regards its subject (that is, in respect of its reality under conditions of experience), exceedingly little, because the idea, as the conception of a maximum, can never be completely and adequately presented in concreto. Now, as in the merely speculative employment of reason the latter is properly the sole aim, and as in this case the approximation to a conception, which is never attained in practice, is the same thing as if the conception were non-existent — it is commonly said of the conception of this kind, "it is only an idea." So we might very well say, "the absolute totality of all phenomena is only an idea," for, as we never can present an adequate representation of it, it remains for us a problem incapable of solution. On the other hand, as in the practical use of the understanding we have only to do with action and practice according to rules, an idea of pure reason can always be given really in concreto, although only partially, nay, it is the indispensable condition of all practical employment of reason. The practice or execution of the idea is always limited and defective, but nevertheless within indeterminable boundaries, consequently always under the influence of the conception of an absolute perfection. And thus the practical idea is always in the highest degree fruitful, and in relation to real actions indispensably necessary. In the idea, pure reason possesses even causality and the power of producing that which its conception contains. Hence we cannot say of wisdom, in a disparaging way, "it is only an idea." For, for the very reason that it is the idea of the necessary unity of all possible aims, it must be for all practical exertions and endeavours the primitive condition and rule — a rule which, if not constitutive, is at least limitative.

Now, although we must say of the transcendental conceptions of reason, "they are only ideas," we must not, on this account, look upon them as superfluous and nugatory. For, although no object can be determined by them, they can be of great utility, unobserved and at the basis of the edifice of the understanding, as the canon for its extended and self-consistent exercise — a canon which, indeed, does not enable it to cognize more in an object than it would cognize by the help of its own conceptions, but which guides it more securely in its cognition. Not to mention that they perhaps render possible a transition from our conceptions of nature and the non-ego to the practical conceptions, and thus produce for even ethical ideas keeping, so to speak, and connection with the speculative cognitions of reason. The explication of all this must be looked for in the sequel.

But setting aside, in conformity with our original purpose, the consideration of the practical ideas, we proceed to contemplate reason in its speculative use alone, nay, in a still more restricted sphere, to wit, in the transcendental use; and here must strike into the same path which we followed in our deduction of the categories. That is to say, we shall consider the logical form of the cognition of reason, that we may see whether reason may not be thereby a source of conceptions which enables us to regard objects in themselves as determined synthetically a priori, in relation to one or other of the functions of reason.

Reason, considered as the faculty of a certain logical form of cognition, is the faculty of conclusion, that is, of mediate judgement — by means of the subsumption of the condition of a possible judgement under the condition of a given judgement. The given judgement is the general rule (major). The subsumption of the condition of another possible judgement under the condition of the rule is the minor. The actual judgement, which enounces the assertion of the rule in the subsumed case, is the conclusion (conclusio). The rule predicates something generally under a certain condition. The condition of the rule is satisfied in some particular case. It follows that what was valid in general under that condition must also be considered as valid in the particular case which satisfies this condition. It is very plain that reason attains to a cognition, by means of acts of the understanding which constitute a series of conditions. When I arrive at the proposition, "All bodies are changeable," by beginning with the more remote cognition (in which the conception of body does not appear, but which nevertheless contains the condition of that conception), "All compound is changeable," by proceeding from this to a less remote cognition, which stands under the condition of the former, "Bodies are compound," and hence to a third, which at length connects for me the remote cognition (changeable) with the one before me, "Consequently, bodies are changeable" — I have arrived at a cognition (conclusion) through a series of conditions (premisses). Now every series, whose exponent (of the categorical or hypothetical judgement) is given, can be continued; consequently the same procedure of reason conducts us to the ratiocinatio polysyllogistica, which is a series of syllogisms, that can be continued either on the side of the conditions (per prosyllogismos) or of the conditioned (per episyllogismos) to an indefinite extent.

But we very soon perceive that the chain or series of prosyllogisms, that is, of deduced cognitions on the side of the grounds or conditions of a given cognition, in other words, the ascending series of syllogisms must have a very different relation to the faculty of reason from that of the descending series, that is, the progressive procedure of reason on the side of the conditioned by means of episyllogisms. For, as in the former case the cognition (conclusio) is given only as conditioned, reason can attain to this cognition only under the presupposition that all the members of the series on the side of the conditions are given (totality in the series of premisses), because only under this supposition is the judgement we may be considering possible a priori; while on the side of the conditioned or the inferences, only an incomplete and becoming, and not a presupposed or given series, consequently only a potential progression, is cogitated. Hence, when a cognition is contemplated as conditioned, reason is compelled to consider the series of conditions in an ascending line as completed and given in their totality. But if the very same condition is considered at the same time as the condition of other cognitions, which together constitute a series of inferences or consequences in a descending line, reason may preserve a perfect indifference, as to how far this progression may extend a parte posteriori, and whether the totality of this series is possible, because it stands in no need of such a series for the purpose of arriving at the conclusion before it, inasmuch as this conclusion is sufficiently guaranteed and determined on grounds a parte priori. It may be the case, that upon the side of the conditions the series of premisses has a first or highest condition, or it may not possess this, and so be a parte priori unlimited; but it must, nevertheless, contain totality of conditions, even admitting that we never could succeed in completely apprehending it; and the whole series must be unconditionally true, if the conditioned, which is considered as an inference resulting from it, is to be held as true. This is a requirement of reason, which announces its cognition as determined a priori and as necessary, either in itself — and in this case it needs no grounds to rest upon — or, if it is deduced, as a member of a series of grounds, which is itself unconditionally true.

SECTION III. System of Transcendental Ideas.

We are not at present engaged with a logical dialectic, which makes complete abstraction of the content of cognition and aims only at unveiling the illusory appearance in the form of syllogisms. Our subject is transcendental dialectic, which must contain, completely a priori, the origin of certain cognitions drawn from pure reason, and the origin of certain deduced conceptions, the object of which cannot be given empirically and which therefore lie beyond the sphere of the faculty of understanding. We have observed, from the natural relation which the transcendental use of our cognition, in syllogisms as well as in judgements, must have to the logical, that there are three kinds of dialectical arguments, corresponding to the three modes of conclusion, by which reason attains to cognitions on principles; and that in all it is the business of reason to ascend from the conditioned synthesis, beyond which the understanding never proceeds, to the unconditioned which the understanding never can reach.

Now the most general relations which can exist in our representations are: 1st, the relation to the subject; 2nd, the relation to objects, either as phenomena, or as objects of thought in general. If we connect this subdivision with the main division, all the relations of our representations, of which we can form either a conception or an idea, are threefold: 1. The relation to the subject; 2. The relation to the manifold of the object as a phenomenon; 3. The relation to all things in general.

Now all pure conceptions have to do in general with the synthetical unity of representations; conceptions of pure reason (transcendental ideas), on the other hand, with the unconditional synthetical unity of all conditions. It follows that all transcendental ideas arrange themselves in three classes, the first of which contains the absolute (unconditioned) unity of the thinking subject, the second the absolute unity of the series of the conditions of a phenomenon, the third the absolute unity of the condition of all objects of thought in general.

The thinking subject is the object-matter of Psychology; the sum total of all phenomena (the world) is the object-matter of Cosmology; and the thing which contains the highest condition of the possibility of all that is cogitable (the being of all beings) is the object-matter of all Theology. Thus pure reason presents us with the idea of a transcendental doctrine of the soul (psychologia rationalis), of a transcendental science of the world (cosmologia rationalis), and finally of a transcendental doctrine of God (theologia transcendentalis). Understanding cannot originate even the outline of any of these sciences, even when connected with the highest logical use of reason, that is, all cogitable syllogisms — for the purpose of proceeding from one object (phenomenon) to all others, even to the utmost limits of the empirical synthesis. They are, on the contrary, pure and genuine products, or problems, of pure reason.

What modi of the pure conceptions of reason these transcendental ideas are will be fully exposed in the following chapter. They follow the guiding thread of the categories. For pure reason never relates immediately to objects, but to the conceptions of these contained in the understanding. In like manner, it will be made manifest in the detailed explanation of these ideas — how reason, merely through the synthetical use of the same function which it employs in a categorical syllogism, necessarily attains to the conception of the absolute unity of the thinking subject — how the logical procedure in hypothetical ideas necessarily produces the idea of the absolutely unconditioned in a series of given conditions, and finally — how the mere form of the disjunctive syllogism involves the highest conception of a being of all beings: a thought which at first sight seems in the highest degree paradoxical.

An objective deduction, such as we were able to present in the case of the categories, is impossible as regards these transcendental ideas. For they have, in truth, no relation to any object, in experience, for the very reason that they are only ideas. But a subjective deduction of them from the nature of our reason is possible, and has been given in the present chapter.

It is easy to perceive that the sole aim of pure reason is the absolute totality of the synthesis on the side of the conditions, and that it does not concern itself with the absolute completeness on the Part of the conditioned. For of the former alone does she stand in need, in order to preposit the whole series of conditions, and thus present them to the understanding a priori. But if we once have a completely (and unconditionally) given condition, there is no further necessity, in proceeding with the series, for a conception of reason; for the understanding takes of itself every step downward, from the condition to the conditioned. Thus the transcendental ideas are available only for ascending in the series of conditions, till we reach the unconditioned, that is, principles. As regards descending to the conditioned, on the other hand, we find that there is a widely extensive logical use which reason makes of the laws of the understanding, but that a transcendental use thereof is impossible; and that when we form an idea of the absolute totality of such a synthesis, for example, of the whole series of all future changes in the world, this idea is a mere ens rationis, an arbitrary fiction of thought, and not a necessary presupposition of reason. For the possibility of the conditioned presupposes the totality of its conditions, but not of its consequences. Consequently, this conception is not a transcendental idea — and it is with these alone that we are at present occupied.

Finally, it is obvious that there exists among the transcendental ideas a certain connection and unity, and that pure reason, by means of them, collects all its cognitions into one system. From the cognition of self to the cognition of the world, and through these to the supreme being, the progression is so natural, that it seems to resemble the logical march of reason from the premisses to the conclusion.* Now whether there lies unobserved at the foundation of these ideas an analogy of the same kind as exists between the logical and transcendental procedure of reason, is another of those questions, the answer to which we must not expect till we arrive at a more advanced stage in our inquiries. In this cursory and preliminary view, we have, meanwhile, reached our aim. For we have dispelled the ambiguity which attached to the transcendental conceptions of reason, from their being commonly mixed up with other conceptions in the systems of philosophers, and not properly distinguished from the conceptions of the understanding; we have exposed their origin and, thereby, at the same time their determinate number, and presented them in a systematic connection, and have thus marked out and enclosed a definite sphere for pure reason.

[Note: The science of Metaphysics has for the proper object of its inquiries only three grand ideas: GOD, FREEDOM, and IMMORTALITY, and it aims at showing, that the second conception, conjoined with the first, must lead to the third, as a necessary conclusion. All the other subjects with which it occupies itself, are merely means for the attainment and realization of these ideas. It does not require these ideas for the construction of a science of nature, but, on the contrary, for the purpose of passing beyond the sphere of nature. A complete insight into and comprehension of them would render Theology, Ethics, and, through the conjunction of both, Religion, solely dependent on the speculative faculty of reason. In a systematic representation of these ideas the above-mentioned arrangement — the synthetical one — would be the most suitable; but in the investigation which must necessarily precede it, the analytical, which reverses this arrangement, would be better adapted to our purpose, as in it we should proceed from that which experience immediately presents to us — psychology, to cosmology, and thence to theology.]

BOOK II. — OF THE DIALECTICAL PROCEDURE OF PURE REASON.

It may be said that the object of a merely transcendental idea is something of which we have no conception, although the idea may be a necessary product of reason according to its original laws. For, in fact, a conception of an object that is adequate to the idea given by reason, is impossible. For such an object must be capable of being presented and intuited in a Possible experience. But we should express our meaning better, and with less risk of being misunderstood, if we said that we can have no knowledge of an object, which perfectly corresponds to an idea, although we may possess a problematical conception thereof.

Now the transcendental (subjective) reality at least of the pure conceptions of reason rests upon the fact that we are led to such ideas by a necessary procedure of reason. There must therefore be syllogisms which contain no empirical premisses, and by means of which we conclude from something that we do know, to something of which we do not even possess a conception, to which we, nevertheless, by an unavoidable illusion, ascribe objective reality. Such arguments are, as regards their result, rather to be termed sophisms than syllogisms, although indeed, as regards their origin, they are very well entitled to the latter name, inasmuch as they are not fictions or accidental products of reason, but are necessitated by its very nature. They are sophisms, not of men, but of pure reason herself, from which the Wisest cannot free himself. After long labour he may be able to guard against the error, but he can never be thoroughly rid of the illusion which continually mocks and misleads him.

Of these dialectical arguments there are three kinds, corresponding to the number of the ideas which their conclusions present. In the argument or syllogism of the first class, I conclude, from the transcendental conception of the subject contains no manifold, the absolute unity of the subject itself, of which I cannot in this manner attain to a conception. This dialectical argument I shall call the transcendental paralogism. The second class of sophistical arguments is occupied with the transcendental conception of the absolute totality of the series of conditions for a given phenomenon, and I conclude, from the fact that I have always a self-contradictory conception of the unconditioned synthetical unity of the series upon one side, the truth of the opposite unity, of which I have nevertheless no conception. The condition of reason in these dialectical arguments, I shall term the antinomy of pure reason. Finally, according to the third kind of sophistical argument, I conclude, from the totality of the conditions of thinking objects in general, in so far as they can be given, the absolute synthetical unity of all conditions of the possibility of things in general; that is, from things which I do not know in their mere transcendental conception, I conclude a being of all beings which I know still less by means of a transcendental conception, and of whose unconditioned necessity I can form no conception whatever. This dialectical argument I shall call the ideal of pure reason.

Transcendental Illusion

CHAPTER I.
Of the Paralogisms of Pure Reason.

The logical paralogism consists in the falsity of an argument in respect of its form, be the content what it may. But a transcendental paralogism has a transcendental foundation, and concludes falsely, while the form is correct and unexceptionable. In this manner the paralogism has its foundation in the nature of human reason, and is the parent of an unavoidable, though not insoluble, mental illusion.

We now come to a conception which was not inserted in the general list of transcendental conceptions, and yet must be reckoned with them, but at the same time without in the least altering, or indicating a deficiency in that table. This is the conception, or, if the term is preferred, the judgement, "I think." But it is readily perceived that this thought is as it were the vehicle of all conceptions in general, and consequently of transcendental conceptions also, and that it is therefore regarded as a transcendental conception, although it can have no peculiar claim to be so ranked, inasmuch as its only use is to indicate that all thought is accompanied by consciousness. At the same time, pure as this conception is from empirical content (impressions of the senses), it enables us to distinguish two different kinds of objects. "I," as thinking, am an object of the internal sense, and am called soul. That which is an object of the external senses is called body. Thus the expression, "I," as a thinking being, designates the object-matter of psychology, which may be called "the rational doctrine of the soul," inasmuch as in this science I desire to know nothing of the soul but what, independently of all experience (which determines me in concreto), may be concluded from this conception "I," in so far as it appears in all thought.

Now, the rational doctrine of the soul is really an undertaking of this kind. For if the smallest empirical element of thought, if any particular perception of my internal state, were to be introduced among the grounds of cognition of this science, it would not be a rational, but an empirical doctrine of the soul. We have thus before us a pretended science, raised upon the single proposition, "I think," whose foundation or want of foundation we may very properly, and agreeably with the nature of a transcendental philosophy, here examine. It ought not to be objected that in this proposition, which expresses the perception of one's self, an internal experience is asserted, and that consequently the rational doctrine of the soul which is founded upon it, is not pure, but partly founded upon an empirical principle. For this internal perception is nothing more than the mere apperception, "I think," which in fact renders all transcendental conceptions possible, in which we say, "I think substance, cause, etc." For internal experience in general and its possibility, or perception in general, and its relation to other perceptions, unless some particular distinction or determination thereof is empirically given, cannot be regarded as empirical cognition, but as cognition of the empirical, and belongs to the investigation of the possibility of every experience, which is certainly transcendental. The smallest object of experience (for example, only pleasure or pain), that should be included in the general representation of self-consciousness, would immediately change the rational into an empirical psychology.

"I think" is therefore the only text of rational psychology, from which it must develop its whole system. It is manifest that this thought, when applied to an object (myself), can contain nothing but transcendental predicates thereof; because the least empirical predicate would destroy the purity of the science and its independence of all experience.

But we shall have to follow here the guidance of the categories — only, as in the present case a thing, "I," as thinking being, is at first given, we shall — not indeed change the order of the categories as it stands in the table — but begin at the category of substance, by which at the a thing in itself is represented and proceeds backwards through the series. The topic of the rational doctrine of the soul, from which everything else it may contain must be deduced, is accordingly as follows:

1

The Soul is SUBSTANCE

2

As regards its quality

it is SIMPLE

3

As regards the different

times in which it exists,

it is numerically identical,

that is UNITY, not Plurality.

4 It is in relation to possible objects in space

[Note: The reader, who may not so easily perceive the psychological sense of these expressions, taken here in their transcendental abstraction, and cannot guess why the latter attribute of the soul belongs to the category of existence, will find the expressions sufficiently explained and justified in the sequel. I have, moreover, to apologize for the Latin terms which have been employed, instead of their German synonyms, contrary to the rules of correct writing. But I judged it better to sacrifice elegance to perspicuity.]

From these elements originate all the conceptions of pure psychology, by combination alone, without the aid of any other principle. This substance, merely as an object of the internal sense, gives the conception of Immateriality; as simple substance, that of Incorruptibility; its identity, as intellectual substance, gives the conception of Personality; all these three together, Spirituality. Its relation to objects in space gives us the conception of connection (commercium) with bodies. Thus it represents thinking substance as the principle of life in matter, that is, as a soul (anima), and as the ground of Animality; and this, limited and determined by the conception of spirituality, gives us that of Immortality.

Now to these conceptions relate four paralogisms of a transcendental psychology, which is falsely held to be a science of pure reason, touching the nature of our thinking being. We can, however, lay at the foundation of this science nothing but the simple and in itself perfectly contentless representation "I" which cannot even be called a conception, but merely a consciousness which accompanies all conceptions. By this "I," or "He," or "It," who or which thinks, nothing more is represented than a transcendental subject of thought = x, which is cognized only by means of the thoughts that are its predicates, and of which, apart from these, we cannot form the least conception. Hence in a perpetual circle, inasmuch as we must always employ it, in order to frame any judgement respecting it. And this inconvenience we find it impossible to rid ourselves of, because consciousness in itself is not so much a representation distinguishing a particular object, as a form of representation in general, in so far as it may be termed cognition; for in and by cognition alone do I think anything.

It must, however, appear extraordinary at first sight that the condition under which I think, and which is consequently a property of my subject, should be held to be likewise valid for every existence which thinks, and that we can presume to base upon a seemingly empirical proposition a judgement which is apodeictic and universal, to wit, that everything which thinks is constituted as the voice of my consciousness declares it to be, that is, as a self-conscious being. The cause of this belief is to be found in the fact that we necessarily attribute to things a priori all the properties which constitute conditions under which alone we can cogitate them. Now I cannot obtain the least representation of a thinking being by means of external experience, but solely through self-consciousness. Such objects are consequently nothing more than the transference of this consciousness of mine to other things which can only thus be represented as thinking beings. The proposition, "I think," is, in the present case, understood in a problematical sense, not in so far as it contains a perception of an existence (like the Cartesian "Cogito, ergo sum"),[Note: "I think, therefore I am."] but in regard to its mere possibility — for the purpose of discovering what properties may be inferred from so simple a proposition and predicated of the subject of it.

If at the foundation of our pure rational cognition of thinking beings there lay more than the mere Cogito — if we could likewise call in aid observations on the play of our thoughts, and the thence derived natural laws of the thinking self, there would arise an empirical psychology which would be a kind of physiology of the internal sense and might possibly be capable of explaining the phenomena of that sense. But it could never be available for discovering those properties which do not belong to possible experience (such as the quality of simplicity), nor could it make any apodeictic enunciation on the nature of thinking beings: it would therefore not be a rational psychology.

Now, as the proposition "I think" (in the problematical sense) contains the form of every judgement in general and is the constant accompaniment of all the categories, it is manifest that conclusions are drawn from it only by a transcendental employment of the understanding. This use of the understanding excludes all empirical elements; and we cannot, as has been shown above, have any favourable conception beforehand of its procedure. We shall therefore follow with a critical eye this proposition through all the predicaments of pure psychology; but we shall, for brevity's sake, allow this examination to proceed in an uninterrupted connection.

Before entering on this task, however, the following general remark may help to quicken our attention to this mode of argument. It is not merely through my thinking that I cognize an object, but only through my determining a given intuition in relation to the unity of consciousness in which all thinking consists. It follows that I cognize myself, not through my being conscious of myself as thinking, but only when I am conscious of the intuition of myself as determined in relation to the function of thought. All the modi of self-consciousness in thought are hence not conceptions of objects (conceptions of the understanding — categories); they are mere logical functions, which do not present to thought an object to be cognized, and cannot therefore present my Self as an object. Not the consciousness of the determining, but only that of the determinable self, that is, of my internal intuition (in so far as the manifold contained in it can be connected conformably with the general condition of the unity of apperception in thought), is the object.

1. In all judgements I am the determining subject of that relation which constitutes a judgement. But that the I which thinks, must be considered as in thought always a subject, and as a thing which cannot be a predicate to thought, is an apodeictic and identical proposition. But this proposition does not signify that I, as an object, am, for myself, a self-subsistent being or substance. This latter statement — an ambitious one — requires to be supported by data which are not to be discovered in thought; and are perhaps (in so far as I consider the thinking self merely as such) not to be discovered in the thinking self at all.

2. That the I or Ego of apperception, and consequently in all thought, is singular or simple, and cannot be resolved into a plurality of subjects, and therefore indicates a logically simple subject — this is self-evident from the very conception of an Ego, and is consequently an analytical proposition. But this is not tantamount to declaring that the thinking Ego is a simple substance — for this would be a synthetical proposition. The conception of substance always relates to intuitions, which with me cannot be other than sensuous, and which consequently lie completely out of the sphere of the understanding and its thought: but to this sphere belongs the affirmation that the Ego is simple in thought. It would indeed be surprising, if the conception of "substance," which in other cases requires so much labour to distinguish from the other elements presented by intuition — so much trouble, too, to discover whether it can be simple (as in the case of the parts of matter) — should be presented immediately to me, as if by revelation, in the poorest mental representation of all.

3. The proposition of the identity of my Self amidst all the manifold representations of which I am conscious, is likewise a proposition lying in the conceptions themselves, and is consequently analytical. But this identity of the subject, of which I am conscious in all its representations, does not relate to or concern the intuition of the subject, by which it is given as an object. This proposition cannot therefore enounce the identity of the person, by which is understood the consciousness of the identity of its own substance as a thinking being in all change and variation of circumstances. To prove this, we should require not a mere analysis of the proposition, but synthetical judgements based upon a given intuition.

4. I distinguish my own existence, as that of a thinking being, from that of other things external to me — among which my body also is reckoned. This is also an analytical proposition, for other things are exactly those which I think as different

or distinguished from myself. But whether this consciousness of myself is possible without things external to me; and whether therefore I can exist merely as a thinking being (without being man) — cannot be known or inferred from this proposition.

Thus we have gained nothing as regards the cognition of myself as object, by the analysis of the consciousness of my Self in thought. The logical exposition of thought in general is mistaken for a metaphysical determination of the object.

Our Critique would be an investigation utterly superfluous, if there existed a possibility of proving a priori, that all thinking beings are in themselves simple substances, as such, therefore, possess the inseparable attribute of personality, and are conscious of their existence apart from and unconnected with matter. For we should thus have taken a step beyond the world of sense, and have penetrated into the sphere of noumena; and in this case the right could not be denied us of extending our knowledge in this sphere, of establishing ourselves, and, under a favouring star, appropriating to ourselves possessions in it. For the proposition: "Every thinking being, as such, is simple substance," is an a priori synthetical proposition; because in the first place it goes beyond the conception which is the subject of it, and adds to the mere notion of a thinking being the mode of its existence, and in the second place annexes a predicate (that of simplicity) to the latter conception — a predicate which it could not have discovered in the sphere of experience. It would follow that a priori synthetical propositions are possible and legitimate, not only, as we have maintained, in relation to objects of possible experience, and as principles of the possibility of this experience itself, but are applicable to things in themselves — an inference which makes an end of the whole of this Critique, and obliges us to fall back on the old mode of metaphysical procedure. But indeed the danger is not so great, if we look a little closer into the question.

There lurks in the procedure of rational Psychology a paralogism, which is represented in the following syllogism:

That which cannot be cogitated otherwise than as subject, does not exist otherwise than as subject, and is therefore substance.

A thinking being, considered merely as such, cannot be cogitated otherwise than as subject.

Therefore it exists also as such, that is, as substance.

In the major we speak of a being that can be cogitated generally and in every relation, consequently as it may be given in intuition. But in the minor we speak of the same being only in so far as it regards itself as subject, relatively to thought and the unity of consciousness, but not in relation to intuition, by which it is presented as an object to thought. Thus the conclusion is here arrived at by a Sophisma figurae dictionis.*

[Note: Thought is taken in the two premisses in two totally different senses. In the major it is considered as relating and applying to objects in general, consequently to objects of intuition also. In the minor, we understand it as relating merely to self-consciousness. In this sense, we do not cogitate an object, but merely the relation to the self-consciousness of the subject, as the form of thought. In the former premiss we speak of things which cannot be cogitated otherwise than as subjects. In the second, we do not speak of things, but of thought (all objects being abstracted), in which the Ego is always the subject of consciousness. Hence the conclusion cannot be, "I cannot exist otherwise than as subject"; but only "I can, in cogitating my existence, employ my Ego only as the subject of the judgement." But this is an identical proposition, and throws no light on the mode of my existence.]

That this famous argument is a mere paralogism, will be plain to any one who will consider the general remark which precedes our exposition of the principles of the pure understanding, and the section on noumena. For it was there proved that the conception of a thing, which can exist per se — only as a subject and never as a predicate, possesses no objective reality; that is to say, we can never know whether there exists any object to correspond to the conception; consequently, the conception is nothing more than a conception, and from it we derive no proper knowledge. If this conception is to indicate by the term substance, an object that can be given, if it is to become a cognition, we must have at the foundation of the cognition a permanent intuition, as the indispensable condition of its objective reality. For through intuition alone can an object be given. But in internal intuition there is nothing permanent, for the Ego is but the consciousness of my thought. If then, we appeal merely to thought, we cannot discover the necessary condition of the application of the conception of substance — that is, of a subject existing per se — to the subject as a thinking being. And thus the conception of the simple nature of substance, which is connected with the objective reality of this conception, is shown to be also invalid, and to be, in fact, nothing more than the logical qualitative unity of self-consciousness in thought; whilst we remain perfectly ignorant whether the subject is composite or not.

Refutation of the Argument of Mendelssohn for the Substantiality or Permanence of the Soul.

This acute philosopher easily perceived the insufficiency of the common argument which attempts to prove that the soul — it being granted that it is a simple being — cannot perish by dissolution or decomposition; he saw it is not impossible for it to cease to be by extinction, or disappearance. He endeavoured to prove in his Phaedo, that the soul cannot be annihilated, by showing that a simple being cannot cease to exist. Inasmuch as, he said, a simple existence cannot diminish, nor gradually lose portions of its being, and thus be by degrees reduced to nothing (for it possesses no parts, and therefore no multiplicity), between the moment in which it is, and the moment in which it is not, no time can be discovered — which is impossible. But this philosopher did not consider that, granting the soul to possess this simple nature, which contains no parts external to each other and consequently no extensive quantity, we cannot refuse to it any less than to any other being, intensive quantity, that is, a degree of reality in regard to all its faculties, nay, to all that constitutes its existence. But this degree of reality can become less and less through an infinite series of smaller degrees. It follows, therefore, that this supposed substance — this thing, the permanence of which is not assured in any other way, may, if not by decomposition, by gradual loss (remissio) of its powers (consequently by elanguescence, if I may employ this expression), be changed into nothing. For consciousness itself has always a degree, which may be lessened.* Consequently the faculty of being conscious may be diminished; and so with all other faculties. The permanence of the soul, therefore, as an object of the internal sense, remains undemonstrated, nay, even indemonstrable. Its permanence in life is evident, per se, inasmuch as the thinking being (as man) is to itself, at the same time, an object of the external senses. But this does not authorize the rational psychologist to affirm, from mere conceptions, its permanence beyond life.*

[Note: Clearness is not, as logicians maintain, the consciousness of a representation. For a certain degree of consciousness, which may not, however, be sufficient for recollection, is to be met with in many dim representations. For without any consciousness at all, we should not be able to recognize any difference in the obscure representations we connect; as we really can do with many conceptions, such as those of right and justice, and those of the musician, who strikes at once several notes in improvising a piece of music. But a representation is clear, in which our consciousness is sufficient for the consciousness of the difference of this representation from others. If we are only conscious that there is a difference, but are not conscious of the difference — that is, what the difference is — the representation must be termed obscure. There is, consequently, an infinite series of degrees of consciousness down to its entire disappearance.]

[Note: There are some who think they have done enough to establish a new possibility in the mode of the existence of souls, when they have shown that there is no contradiction in their hypotheses on this subject. Such are those who affirm the possibility of thought — of which they have no other knowledge than what they derive from its use in connecting empirical intuitions presented in this our human life — after this life has ceased. But it is very easy to embarrass them by the introduction of counter-possibilities, which rest upon quite as good a foundation. Such, for example, is the possibility of the division of a simple substance into several substances; and conversely, of the coalition of several into one simple substance. For, although divisibility presupposes composition, it does not necessarily require a composition of substances, but only of the degrees (of the several faculties) of one and the same substance. Now we can cogitate all the powers and faculties of the soul — even that of consciousness — as diminished by one half, the substance still remaining. In the same way we can represent to ourselves without contradiction, this obliterated half as preserved, not in the soul, but without it; and we can believe that, as in this case every thing that is real in the soul, and has a degree — consequently its entire existence — has been halved, a particular substance would arise out of the soul. For the multiplicity, which has been divided, formerly existed, but not as a multiplicity of substances, but of every reality as the quantum of existence in it; and the unity of substance was merely a mode of existence, which by this division alone has been transformed into a plurality of subsistence. In the same manner several simple substances might coalesce into one, without anything being lost except the plurality of subsistence, inasmuch as the one substance would contain the degree of reality of all the former substances. Perhaps, indeed, the simple substances, which appear under the form of matter, might (not indeed by a mechanical or chemical influence upon each other, but by an unknown influence, of which the former would be but the phenomenal appearance), by means of such a dynamical division of the parent-souls, as intensive quantities, produce other souls, while the former repaired the loss thus sustained with new matter of the same sort. I am far from allowing any value to such chimeras; and the principles of our analytic have clearly proved that no other than an empirical use of the categories — that of substance, for example — is possible. But if the rationalist is bold enough to construct, on the mere authority of the faculty of thought — without any intuition, whereby an object is given — a self-subsistent being, merely because the unity of apperception in thought cannot allow him to believe it a composite being, instead of declaring, as he ought to do, that he is unable to explain the possibility of a thinking nature; what ought to hinder the materialist, with as complete an independence of experience, to employ the principle of the rationalist in a directly opposite manner — still preserving the formal unity required by his opponent?]

If, now, we take the above propositions — as they must be accepted as valid for all thinking beings in the system of rational psychology — in synthetical connection, and proceed, from the category of relation, with the proposition: "All thinking beings are, as such, substances," backwards through the series, till the circle is completed; we come at last to their existence, of which, in this system of rational psychology, substances are held to be conscious, independently of external things; nay, it is asserted that, in relation to the permanence which is a necessary characteristic of substance, they can of themselves determine external things. It follows that idealism — at least problematical idealism, is perfectly unavoidable in this rationalistic system. And, if the existence of outward things is not held to be requisite to the determination of the existence of a substance in time, the existence of these outward things at all, is a gratuitous assumption which remains without the possibility of a proof.

But if we proceed analytically — the "I think" as a proposition containing in itself an existence as given, consequently modality being the principle — and dissect this proposition, in order to ascertain its content, and discover whether and how this Ego determines its existence in time and space without the aid of anything external; the propositions of rationalistic psychology would not begin with the conception of a thinking being, but with a reality, and the properties of a thinking being in general would be deduced from the mode in which this reality is cogitated, after everything empirical had been abstracted; as is shown in the following table:

1

I think,

2

as Subject,

3

as simple Subject,

4

as identical Subject,

in every state of my thought.

Now, inasmuch as it is not determined in this second proposition, whether I can exist and be cogitated only as subject, and not also as a predicate of another being, the conception of a subject is here taken in a merely logical sense; and it remains undetermined, whether substance is to be cogitated under the conception or not. But in the third proposition, the absolute unity of apperception — the simple Ego in the representation to which all connection and separation, which constitute thought, relate, is of itself important; even although it presents us with no information about the constitution or subsistence of the subject. Apperception is something real, and the simplicity of its nature is given in the very fact of its possibility. Now in space there is nothing real that is at the same time simple; for points, which are the only simple things in space, are merely limits, but not constituent parts of space. From this follows the impossibility of a definition on the basis of materialism of the constitution of my Ego as a merely thinking subject. But, because my existence is considered in the first proposition as given, for it does not mean, "Every thinking being exists" (for this would be predicating of them absolute necessity), but only, "I exist thinking"; the proposition is quite empirical, and contains the determinability of my existence merely in relation to my representations in time. But as I require for this purpose something that is permanent, such as is not given in internal intuition; the mode of my existence, whether as substance or as accident, cannot be determined by means of this simple self-consciousness. Thus, if materialism is inadequate to explain the mode in which I exist, spiritualism is likewise as insufficient; and the conclusion is that we are utterly unable to attain to any knowledge of the constitution of the soul, in so far as relates to the possibility of its existence apart from external objects.

And, indeed, how should it be possible, merely by the aid of the unity of consciousness — which we cognize only for the reason that it is indispensable to the possibility of experience — to pass the bounds of experience (our existence in this life); and to extend our cognition to the nature of all thinking beings by means of the empirical — but in relation to every sort of intuition, perfectly undetermined — proposition, "I think"?

There does not then exist any rational psychology as a doctrine furnishing any addition to our knowledge of ourselves. It is nothing more than a discipline, which sets impassable limits to speculative reason in this region of thought, to prevent it, on the one hand, from throwing itself into the arms of a soulless materialism, and, on the other, from losing itself in the mazes of a baseless spiritualism. It teaches us to consider this refusal of our reason to give any satisfactory answer to questions which reach beyond the limits of this our human life, as a hint to abandon fruitless speculation; and to direct, to a practical use, our knowledge of ourselves — which, although applicable only to objects of experience, receives its principles from a higher source, and regulates its procedure as if our destiny reached far beyond the boundaries of experience and life.

From all this it is evident that rational psychology has its origin in a mere misunderstanding. The unity of consciousness, which lies at the basis of the categories, is considered to be an intuition of the subject as an object; and the category of substance is applied to the intuition. But this unity is nothing more than the unity in thought, by which no object is given; to which therefore the category of substance — which always presupposes a given intuition — cannot be applied. Consequently, the subject cannot be cognized. The subject of the categories cannot, therefore, for the very reason that it cogitates these, frame any conception of itself as an object of the categories; for, to cogitate these, it must lay at the foundation its own pure self-consciousness — the very thing that it wishes to explain and describe. In like manner, the subject, in which the representation of time has its basis, cannot determine, for this very reason, its own existence in time. Now, if the latter is impossible, the former, as an attempt to determine itself by means of the categories as a thinking being in general, is no less so.*

[Note: The "I think" is, as has been already stated, an empirical proposition, and contains the proposition, "I exist." But I cannot say,

"Everything, which thinks, exists"; for in this case the property of thought would constitute all beings possessing it, necessary beings.

Hence my existence cannot be considered as an inference from the proposition, "I think," as Descartes maintained — because in this case the major premiss, "Everything, which thinks, exists," must precede — but the two propositions are identical. The proposition, "I think," expresses an undetermined empirical intuition, that perception (proving consequently that sensation, which must belong to sensibility, lies at the foundation of this proposition); but it precedes experience, whose province it is to determine an object of perception by means of the categories in relation to time; and existence in this proposition is not a category, as it does not apply to an undetermined given object, but only to one of which we have a conception, and about which we wish to know whether it does or does not exist, out of, and apart from this conception. An undetermined perception signifies here merely something real that has been given, only, however, to thought in general — but not as a phenomenon, nor as a thing in itself (noumenon), but only as something that really exists, and is designated as such in the proposition, "I think." For it must be remarked that, when I call the proposition, "I think," an empirical proposition, I do not thereby mean that the Ego in the proposition is an empirical representation; on the contrary, it is purely intellectual, because it belongs to thought in general. But without some empirical representation, which presents to the mind material for thought, the mental act, "I think," would not take place; and the empirical is only the condition of the application or employment of the pure intellectual faculty.]

Thus, then, appears the vanity of the hope of establishing a cognition which is to extend its rule beyond the limits of experience — a cognition which is one of the highest interests of humanity; and thus is proved the futility of the attempt of speculative philosophy in this region of thought. But, in this interest of thought, the severity of criticism has rendered to reason a not unimportant service, by the demonstration of the impossibility of making any dogmatical affirmation concerning an object of experience beyond the boundaries of experience. She has thus fortified reason against all affirmations of the contrary. Now, this can be accomplished in only two ways. Either our proposition must be proved apodeictically; or, if this is unsuccessful, the sources of this inability must be sought for, and, if these are discovered to exist in the natural and necessary limitation of our reason, our opponents must submit to the same law of renunciation and refrain from advancing claims to dogmatic assertion.

But the right, say rather the necessity to admit a future life, upon principles of the practical conjoined with the speculative use of reason, has lost nothing by this renunciation; for the merely speculative proof has never had any influence upon the common reason of men. It stands upon the point of a hair, so that even the schools have been able to preserve it from falling only by incessantly discussing it and spinning it like a top; and even in their eyes it has never been able to present any safe foundation for the erection of a theory. The proofs which have been current among men, preserve their value undiminished; nay, rather gain in clearness and unsophisticated power, by the rejection of the dogmatical assumptions of speculative reason. For reason is thus confined within her own peculiar province — the arrangement of ends or aims, which is at the same time the arrangement of nature; and, as a practical faculty, without limiting itself to the latter, it is justified in extending the former, and with it our own existence, beyond the boundaries of experience and life. If we turn our attention to the analogy of the nature of living beings in this world, in the consideration of which reason is obliged to accept as a principle that no organ, no faculty, no appetite is useless, and that nothing is superfluous, nothing disproportionate to its use, nothing unsuited to its end; but that, on the contrary, everything is perfectly conformed to its destination in life — we shall find that man, who alone is the final end and aim of this order, is still the only animal that seems to be excepted from it. For his natural gifts — not merely as regards the talents and motives that may incite him to employ them, but especially the moral law in him — stretch so far beyond all mere earthly utility and advantage, that he feels himself bound to prize the mere consciousness of probity, apart from all advantageous consequences — even the shadowy gift of posthumous fame — above everything; and he is conscious of an inward call to constitute himself, by his conduct in this world — without regard to mere sublunary interests — the citizen of a better. This mighty, irresistible proof — accompanied by an ever-increasing knowledge of the conformability to a purpose in everything we see around us, by the conviction of the boundless immensity of creation, by the consciousness of a certain illimitableness in the possible extension of our knowledge, and by a desire commensurate therewith — remains to humanity, even after the theoretical cognition of ourselves has failed to establish the necessity of an existence after death.

Conclusion of the Solution of the Psychological Paralogism.

The dialectical illusion in rational psychology arises from our confounding an idea of reason (of a pure intelligence) with the conception — in every respect undetermined — of a thinking being in general. I cogitate myself in behalf of a possible experience, at the same time making abstraction of all actual experience; and infer therefrom that I can be conscious of myself apart from experience and its empirical conditions. I consequently confound the possible abstraction of my empirically determined existence with the supposed consciousness of a possible separate existence of my thinking self; and I believe that I cognize what is substantial in myself as a transcendental subject, when I have nothing more in thought than the unity of consciousness, which lies at the basis of all determination of cognition.

The task of explaining the community of the soul with the body does not properly belong to the psychology of which we are here speaking; because it proposes to prove the personality of the soul apart from this communion (after death), and is therefore transcendent in the proper sense of the word, although occupying itself with an object of experience — only in so far, however, as it ceases to be an object of experience. But a sufficient answer may be found to the question in our system. The difficulty which lies in the execution of this task consists, as is well known, in the presupposed heterogeneity of the object of the internal sense (the soul) and the objects of the external senses; inasmuch as the formal condition of the intuition of the one is time, and of that of the other space also. But if we consider that both kinds of objects do not differ internally, but only in so far as the one appears externally to the other — consequently, that what lies at the basis of phenomena, as a thing in itself, may not be heterogeneous; this difficulty disappears. There then remains no other difficulty than is to be found in the question — how a community of substances is possible; a question which lies out of the region of psychology, and which the reader, after what in our analytic has been said of primitive forces and faculties, will easily judge to be also beyond the region of human cognition.

GENERAL REMARK

On the Transition from Rational Psychology to Cosmology.

The proposition, "I think," or, "I exist thinking," is an empirical proposition. But such a proposition must be based on empirical intuition, and the object cogitated as a phenomenon; and thus our theory appears to maintain that the soul, even in thought, is merely a phenomenon; and in this way our consciousness itself, in fact, abuts upon nothing.

Thought, per se, is merely the purely spontaneous logical function which operates to connect the manifold of a possible intuition; and it does not represent the subject of consciousness as a phenomenon — for this reason alone, that it pays no attention to the question whether the mode of intuiting it is sensuous or intellectual. I therefore do not represent myself in thought either as I am, or as I appear to myself; I merely cogitate myself as an object in general, of the mode of intuiting which I make abstraction. When I represent myself as the subject of thought, or as the ground of thought, these modes of representation are not related to the categories of substance or of cause; for these are functions of thought applicable only to our sensuous intuition. The application of these categories to the Ego would, however, be necessary, if I wished to make myself an object of knowledge. But I wish to be conscious of myself only as thinking; in what mode my Self is given in intuition, I do not consider, and it may be that I, who think, am a phenomenon — although not in so far as I am a thinking being; but in the consciousness of myself in mere thought I am a being, though this consciousness does not present to me any property of this being as material for thought.

But the proposition, "I think," in so far as it declares, "I exist thinking," is not the mere representation of a logical function. It determines the subject (which is in this case an object also) in relation to existence; and it cannot be given without the aid of the internal sense, whose intuition presents to us an object, not as a thing in itself, but always as a phenomenon. In this proposition there is therefore something more to be found than the mere spontaneity of thought; there is also the receptivity of intuition, that is, my thought of myself applied to the empirical intuition of myself. Now, in this intuition the thinking self must seek the conditions of the employment of its logical functions as categories of substance, cause, and so forth; not merely for the purpose of distinguishing itself as an object in itself by means of the representation "I," but also for the purpose of determining the mode of its existence, that is, of cognizing itself as noumenon. But this is impossible, for the internal empirical intuition is sensuous, and presents us with nothing but phenomenal data, which do not assist the object of pure consciousness in its attempt to cognize itself as a separate existence, but are useful only as contributions to experience.

But, let it be granted that we could discover, not in experience, but in certain firmly-established a priori laws of the use of pure reason — laws relating to our existence, authority to consider ourselves as legislating a priori in relation to our own existence and as determining this existence; we should, on this supposition, find ourselves possessed of a spontaneity, by which our actual existence would be determinable, without the aid of the conditions of empirical intuition. We should also become aware that in the consciousness of our existence there was an a priori content, which would serve to determine our own existence — an existence only sensuously determinable — relatively, however, to a certain internal faculty in relation to an intelligible world.

But this would not give the least help to the attempts of rational psychology. For this wonderful faculty, which the consciousness of the moral law in me reveals, would present me with a principle of the determination of my own existence which is purely intellectual — but by what predicates? By none other than those which are given in sensuous intuition. Thus I should find myself in the same position in rational psychology which I formerly occupied, that is to say, I should find myself still in need of sensuous intuitions, in order to give significance to my conceptions of substance and cause, by means of which alone I can possess a knowledge of myself: but these intuitions can never raise me above the sphere of experience. I should be justified, however, in applying these conceptions, in regard to their practical use, which is always directed to objects of experience — in conformity with their analogical significance when employed theoretically — to freedom and its subject. At the same time, I should understand by them merely the logical functions of subject and predicate, of principle and consequence, in conformity with which all actions are so determined, that they are capable of being explained along with the laws of nature, conformably to the categories of substance and cause, although they originate from a very different principle. We have made these observations for the purpose of guarding against misunderstanding, to which the doctrine of our intuition of self as a phenomenon is exposed. We shall have occasion to perceive their utility in the sequel.

CHAPTER II.
The Antinomy of Pure Reason.

We showed in the introduction to this part of our work, that all transcendental illusion of pure reason arose from dialectical arguments, the schema of which logic gives us in its three formal species of syllogisms — just as the categories find their logical schema in the four functions of all judgements. The first kind of these sophistical arguments related to the unconditioned unity of the subjective conditions of all representations in general (of the subject or soul), in correspondence with the categorical syllogisms, the major of which, as the principle, enounces the relation of a predicate to a subject. The second kind of dialectical argument will therefore be concerned, following the analogy with hypothetical syllogisms, with the unconditioned unity of the objective conditions in the phenomenon; and, in this way, the theme of the third kind to be treated of in the following chapter will be the unconditioned unity of the objective conditions of the possibility of objects in general.

But it is worthy of remark that the transcendental paralogism produced in the mind only a one-third illusion, in regard to the idea of the subject of our thought; and the conceptions of reason gave no ground to maintain the contrary proposition. The advantage is completely on the side of Pneumatism; although this theory itself passes into naught, in the crucible of pure reason.

Very different is the case when we apply reason to the objective synthesis of phenomena. Here, certainly, reason establishes, with much plausibility, its principle of unconditioned unity; but it very soon falls into such contradictions that it is compelled, in relation to cosmology, to renounce its pretensions.

For here a new phenomenon of human reason meets us — a perfectly natural antithetic, which does not require to be sought for by subtle sophistry, but into which reason of itself unavoidably falls. It is thereby preserved, to be sure, from the slumber of a fancied conviction — which a merely one-sided illusion produces; but it is at the same time compelled, either, on the one hand, to abandon itself to a despairing scepticism, or, on the other, to assume a dogmatical confidence and obstinate persistence in certain assertions, without granting a fair hearing to the other side of the question. Either is the death of a sound philosophy, although the former might perhaps deserve the title of the euthanasia of pure reason.

Before entering this region of discord and confusion, which the conflict of the laws of pure reason (antinomy) produces, we shall present the reader with some considerations, in explanation and justification of the method we intend to follow in our treatment of this subject. I term all transcendental ideas, in so far as they relate to the absolute totality in the synthesis of phenomena, cosmical conceptions; partly on account of this unconditioned totality, on which the conception of the world-whole is based — a conception, which is itself an idea — partly because they relate solely to the synthesis of phenomena — the empirical synthesis; while, on the other hand, the absolute totality in the synthesis of the conditions of all possible things gives rise to an ideal of pure reason, which is quite distinct from the cosmical conception, although it stands in relation with it. Hence, as the paralogisms of pure reason laid the foundation for a dialectical psychology, the antinomy of pure reason will present us with the transcendental principles of a pretended pure (rational) cosmology — not, however, to declare it valid and to appropriate it, but — as the very term of a conflict of reason sufficiently indicates, to present it as an idea which cannot be reconciled with phenomena and experience.

SECTION I. System of Cosmological Ideas.

That We may be able to enumerate with systematic precision these ideas according to a principle, we must remark, in the first place, that it is from the understanding alone that pure and transcendental conceptions take their origin; that the reason does not properly give birth to any conception, but only frees the conception of the understanding from the unavoidable limitation of a possible experience, and thus endeavours to raise it above the empirical, though it must still be in connection with it. This happens from the fact that, for a given conditioned, reason demands absolute totality on the side of the conditions (to which the understanding submits all phenomena), and thus makes of the category a transcendental idea. This it does that it may be able to give absolute completeness to the empirical synthesis, by continuing it to the unconditioned (which is not to be found in experience, but only in the idea). Reason requires this according to the principle: If the conditioned is given the whole of the conditions, and consequently the absolutely unconditioned, is also given, whereby alone the former was possible. First, then, the transcendental ideas are properly nothing but categories elevated to the unconditioned; and they may be arranged in a table according to the titles of the latter. But, secondly, all the categories are not available for this purpose, but only those in which the synthesis constitutes a series — of conditions subordinated to, not co-ordinated with, each other. Absolute totality is required of reason only in so far as concerns the ascending series of the conditions of a conditioned; not, consequently, when the question relates to the descending series of consequences, or to the aggregate of the co-ordinated conditions of these consequences. For, in relation to a given conditioned, conditions are presupposed and considered to be given along with it. On the other hand, as the consequences do not render possible their conditions, but rather presuppose them — in the consideration of the procession of consequences (or in the descent from the given condition to the conditioned), we may be quite unconcerned whether the series ceases or not; and their totality is not a necessary demand of reason.

Thus we cogitate — and necessarily — a given time completely elapsed up to a given moment, although that time is not determinable by us. But as regards time future, which is not the condition of arriving at the present, in order to conceive it; it is quite indifferent whether we consider future time as ceasing at some point, or as prolonging itself to infinity. Take, for example, the series m, n, o, in which n is given as conditioned in relation to m, but at the same time as the condition of o, and let the series proceed upwards from the conditioned n to m (l, k, i, etc.), and also downwards from the condition n to the conditioned o (p, q, r, etc.) — I must presuppose the former series, to be able to consider n as given, and n is according to reason (the totality of conditions) possible only by means of that series. But its possibility does not rest on the following series o, p, q, r, which for this reason cannot be regarded as given, but only as capable of being given (dabilis).

I shall term the synthesis of the series on the side of the conditions — from that nearest to the given phenomenon up to the more remote — regressive; that which proceeds on the side of the conditioned, from the immediate consequence to the more remote, I shall call the progressive synthesis. The former proceeds in antecedentia, the latter in consequentia. The cosmological ideas are therefore occupied with the totality of the regressive synthesis, and proceed in antecedentia, not in consequentia. When the latter takes place, it is an arbitrary and not a necessary problem of pure reason; for we require, for the complete understanding of what is given in a phenomenon, not the consequences which succeed, but the grounds or principles which precede.

In order to construct the table of ideas in correspondence with the table of categories, we take first the two primitive quanta of all our intuitions, time and space. Time is in itself a series (and the formal condition of all series), and hence, in relation to a given present, we must distinguish a priori in it the antecedentia as conditions (time past) from the consequentia (time future). Consequently, the transcendental idea of the absolute totality of the series of the conditions of a given conditioned, relates merely to all past time. According to the idea of reason, the whole past time, as the condition of the given moment, is necessarily cogitated as given. But, as regards space, there exists in it no distinction between progressus and regressus; for it is an aggregate and not a series — its parts existing together at the same time. I can consider a given point of time in relation to past time only as conditioned, because this given moment comes into existence only through the past time rather through the passing of the preceding time. But as the parts of space are not subordinated, but co-ordinated to each other, one part cannot be the condition of the possibility of the other; and space is not in itself, like time, a series. But the synthesis of the manifold parts of space — (the syntheses whereby we apprehend space) — is nevertheless successive; it takes place, therefore, in time, and contains a series. And as in this series of aggregated spaces (for example, the feet in a rood), beginning with a given portion of space, those which continue to be annexed form the condition of the limits of the former — the measurement of a space must also be regarded as a synthesis of the series of the conditions of a given conditioned. It differs, however, in this respect from that of time, that the side of the conditioned is not in itself distinguishable from the side of the condition; and, consequently, regressus and progressus in space seem to be identical. But, inasmuch as one part of space is not given, but only limited, by and through another, we must also consider every limited space as conditioned, in so far as it presupposes some other space as the condition of its limitation, and so on. As regards limitation, therefore, our procedure in space is also a regressus, and the transcendental idea of the absolute totality of the synthesis in a series of conditions applies to space also; and I am entitled to demand the absolute totality of the phenomenal synthesis in space as well as in time. Whether my demand can be satisfied is a question to be answered in the sequel.

Secondly, the real in space — that is, matter — is conditioned. Its internal conditions are its parts, and the parts of parts its remote conditions; so that in this case we find a regressive synthesis, the absolute totality of which is a demand of reason. But this cannot be obtained otherwise than by a complete division of parts, whereby the real in matter becomes either nothing or that which is not matter, that is to say, the simple. Consequently we find here also a series of conditions and a progress to the unconditioned.

Thirdly, as regards the categories of a real relation between phenomena, the category of substance and its accidents is not suitable for the formation of a transcendental idea; that is to say, reason has no ground, in regard to it, to proceed regressively with conditions. For accidents (in so far as they inhere in a substance) are co-ordinated with each other, and do not constitute a series. And, in relation to substance, they are not properly subordinated to it, but are the mode of existence of the substance itself. The conception of the substantial might nevertheless seem to be an idea of the transcendental reason. But, as this signifies nothing more than the conception of an object in general, which subsists in so far as we cogitate in it merely a transcendental subject without any predicates; and as the question here is of an unconditioned in the series of phenomena — it is clear that the substantial can form no member thereof. The same holds good of substances in community, which are mere aggregates and do not form a series. For they are not subordinated to each other as conditions of the possibility of each other; which, however, may be affirmed of spaces, the limits of which are never determined in themselves, but always by some other space. It is, therefore, only in the category of causality that we can find a series of causes to a given effect, and in which we ascend from the latter, as the conditioned, to the former as the conditions, and thus answer the question of reason.

Fourthly, the conceptions of the possible, the actual, and the necessary do not conduct us to any series — excepting only in so far as the contingent in existence must always be regarded as conditioned, and as indicating, according to a law of the understanding, a condition, under which it is necessary to rise to a higher, till in the totality of the series, reason arrives at unconditioned necessity.

There are, accordingly, only four cosmological ideas, corresponding with the four titles of the categories. For we can select only such as necessarily furnish us with a series in the synthesis of the manifold.

1

The absolute Completeness

of the

COMPOSITION

of the given totality of all phenomena.

2

The absolute Completeness

of the

DIVISION

of given totality in a phenomenon.

3

The absolute Completeness

of the

ORIGINATION

of a phenomenon.

4

The absolute Completeness

of the DEPENDENCE of the EXISTENCE

of what is changeable in a phenomenon.

We must here remark, in the first place, that the idea of absolute totality relates to nothing but the exposition of phenomena, and therefore not to the pure conception of a totality of things. Phenomena are here, therefore, regarded as given, and reason requires the absolute completeness of the conditions of their possibility, in so far as these conditions constitute a series — consequently an absolutely (that is, in every respect) complete synthesis, whereby a phenomenon can be explained according to the laws of the understanding.

Secondly, it is properly the unconditioned alone that reason seeks in this serially and regressively conducted synthesis of conditions. It wishes, to speak in another way, to attain to completeness in the series of premises, so as to render it unnecessary to presuppose others. This unconditioned is always contained in the absolute totality of the series, when we endeavour to form a representation of it in thought. But this absolutely complete synthesis is itself but an idea; for it is impossible, at least before hand, to know whether any such synthesis is possible in the case of phenomena. When we represent all existence in thought by means of pure conceptions of the understanding, without any conditions of sensuous intuition, we may say with justice that for a given conditioned the whole series of conditions subordinated to each other is also given; for the former is only given through the latter. But we find in the case of phenomena a particular limitation of the mode in which conditions are given, that is, through the successive synthesis of the manifold of intuition, which must be complete in the regress. Now whether this completeness is sensuously possible, is a problem. But the idea of it lies in the reason — be it possible or impossible to connect with the idea adequate empirical conceptions. Therefore, as in the absolute totality of the regressive synthesis of the manifold in a phenomenon (following the guidance of the categories, which represent it as a series of conditions to a given conditioned) the unconditioned is necessarily contained — it being still left unascertained whether and how this totality exists; reason sets out from the idea of totality, although its proper and final aim is the unconditioned — of the whole series, or of a part thereof.

This unconditioned may be cogitated — either as existing only in the entire series, all the members of which therefore would be without exception conditioned and only the totality absolutely unconditioned — and in this case the regressus is called infinite; or the absolutely unconditioned is only a part of the series, to which the other members are subordinated, but which Is not itself submitted to any other condition.* In the former case the series is a parte priori unlimited (without beginning), that is, infinite, and nevertheless completely given. But the regress in it is never completed, and can only be called potentially infinite. In the second case there exists a first in the series. This first is called, in relation to past time, the beginning of the world; in relation to space, the limit of the world; in relation to the parts of a given limited whole, the simple; in relation to causes, absolute spontaneity (liberty); and in relation to the existence of changeable things, absolute physical necessity.

[Note: The absolute totality of the series of conditions to a given conditioned is always unconditioned; because beyond it there exist no other conditions, on which it might depend. But the absolute totality of such a series is only an idea, or rather a problematical conception, the possibility of which must be investigated — particularly in relation to the mode in which the unconditioned, as the transcendental idea which is the real subject of inquiry, may be contained therein.]

We possess two expressions, world and nature, which are generally interchanged. The first denotes the mathematical total of all phenomena and the totality of their synthesis — in its progress by means of composition, as well as by division. And the world is termed nature,* when it is regarded as a dynamical whole — when our attention is not directed to the aggregation in space and time, for the purpose of cogitating it as a quantity, but to the unity in the existence of phenomena. In this case the condition of that which happens is called a cause; the unconditioned causality of the cause in a phenomenon is termed liberty; the conditioned cause is called in a more limited sense a natural cause. The conditioned in existence is termed contingent, and the unconditioned necessary. The unconditioned necessity of phenomena may be called natural necessity.

[Note: Nature, understood adjective (formaliter), signifies the complex of the determinations of a thing, connected according to an internal principle of causality. On the other hand, we understand by nature, substantive (materialiter), the sum total of phenomena, in so far as they, by virtue of an internal principle of causality, are connected with each other throughout. In the former sense we speak of the nature of liquid matter, of fire, etc., and employ the word only adjective; while, if speaking of the objects of nature, we have in our minds the idea of a subsisting whole.]

The ideas which we are at present engaged in discussing I have called cosmological ideas; partly because by the term world is understood the entire content of all phenomena, and our ideas are directed solely to the unconditioned among phenomena; partly also, because world, in the transcendental sense, signifies the absolute totality of the content of existing things, and we are directing our attention only to the completeness of the synthesis — although, properly, only in regression. In regard to the fact that these ideas are all transcendent, and, although they do not transcend phenomena as regards their mode, but are concerned solely with the world of sense (and not with noumena), nevertheless carry their synthesis to a degree far above all possible experience — it still seems to me that we can, with perfect propriety, designate them cosmical conceptions. As regards the distinction between the mathematically and the dynamically unconditioned which is the aim of the regression of the synthesis, I should call the two former, in a more limited signification, cosmical conceptions, the remaining two transcendent physical conceptions. This distinction does not at present seem to be of particular importance, but we shall afterwards find it to be of some value.

SECTION II. Antithetic of Pure Reason.

Thetic is the term applied to every collection of dogmatical propositions. By antithetic I do not understand dogmatical assertions of the opposite, but the self-contradiction of seemingly dogmatical cognitions (thesis cum antithesis), in none of which we can discover any decided superiority. Antithetic is not, therefore, occupied with one-sided statements, but is engaged in considering the contradictory nature of the general cognitions of reason and its causes. Transcendental antithetic is an investigation into the antinomy of pure reason, its causes and result. If we employ our reason not merely in the application of the principles of the understanding to objects of experience, but venture with it beyond these boundaries, there arise certain sophistical propositions or theorems. These assertions have the following peculiarities: They can find neither confirmation nor confutation in experience; and each is in itself not only self-consistent, but possesses conditions of its necessity in the very nature of reason — only that, unluckily, there exist just as valid and necessary grounds for maintaining the contrary proposition.

The questions which naturally arise in the consideration of this dialectic of pure reason, are therefore: 1st. In what propositions is pure reason unavoidably subject to an antinomy? 2nd. What are the causes of this antinomy? 3rd. Whether and in what way can reason free itself from this self-contradiction?

A dialectical proposition or theorem of pure reason must, according to what has been said, be distinguishable from all sophistical propositions, by the fact that it is not an answer to an arbitrary question, which may be raised at the mere pleasure of any person, but to one which human reason must necessarily encounter in its progress. In the second place, a dialectical proposition, with its opposite, does not carry the appearance of a merely artificial illusion, which disappears as soon as it is investigated, but a natural and unavoidable illusion, which, even when we are no longer deceived by it, continues to mock us and, although rendered harmless, can never be completely removed.

This dialectical doctrine will not relate to the unity of understanding in empirical conceptions, but to the unity of reason in pure ideas. The conditions of this doctrine are — inasmuch as it must, as a synthesis according to rules, be conformable to the understanding, and at the same time as the absolute unity of the synthesis, to the reason — that, if it is adequate to the unity of reason, it is too great for the understanding, if according with the understanding, it is too small for the reason. Hence arises a mutual opposition, which cannot be avoided, do what we will.

These sophistical assertions of dialectic open, as it were, a battle-field, where that side obtains the victory which has been permitted to make the attack, and he is compelled to yield who has been unfortunately obliged to stand on the defensive. And hence, champions of ability, whether on the right or on the wrong side, are certain to carry away the crown of victory, if they only take care to have the right to make the last attack, and are not obliged to sustain another onset from their opponent. We can easily believe that this arena has been often trampled by the feet of combatants, that many victories have been obtained on both sides, but that the last victory, decisive of the affair between the contending parties, was won by him who fought for the right, only if his adversary was forbidden to continue the tourney. As impartial umpires, we must lay aside entirely the consideration whether the combatants are fighting for the right or for the wrong side, for the true or for the false, and allow the combat to be first decided. Perhaps, after they have wearied more than injured each other, they will discover the nothingness of their cause of quarrel and part good friends.

This method of watching, or rather of originating, a conflict of assertions, not for the purpose of finally deciding in favour of either side, but to discover whether the object of the struggle is not a mere illusion, which each strives in vain to reach, but which would be no gain even when reached — this procedure, I say, may be termed the sceptical method. It is thoroughly distinct from scepticism — the principle of a technical and scientific ignorance, which undermines the foundations of all knowledge, in order, if possible, to destroy our belief and confidence therein. For the sceptical method aims at certainty, by endeavouring to discover in a conflict of this kind, conducted honestly and intelligently on both sides, the point of misunderstanding; just as wise legislators derive, from the embarrassment of judges in lawsuits, information in regard to the defective and ill-defined parts of their statutes. The antinomy which reveals itself in the application of laws, is for our limited wisdom the best criterion of legislation. For the attention of reason, which in abstract speculation does not easily become conscious of its errors, is thus roused to the momenta in the determination of its principles.

But this sceptical method is essentially peculiar to transcendental philosophy, and can perhaps be dispensed with in every other field of investigation. In mathematics its use would be absurd; because in it no false assertions can long remain hidden, inasmuch as its demonstrations must always proceed under the guidance of pure intuition, and by means of an always evident synthesis. In experimental philosophy, doubt and delay may be very useful; but no misunderstanding is possible, which cannot be easily removed; and in experience means of solving the difficulty and putting an end to the dissension must at last be found, whether sooner or later. Moral philosophy can always exhibit its principles, with their practical consequences, in concreto — at least in possible experiences, and thus escape the mistakes and ambiguities of abstraction. But transcendental propositions, which lay claim to insight beyond the region of possible experience, cannot, on the one hand, exhibit their abstract synthesis in any a priori intuition, nor, on the other, expose a lurking error by the help of experience. Transcendental reason, therefore, presents us with no other criterion than that of an attempt to reconcile such assertions, and for this purpose to permit a free and unrestrained conflict between them. And this we now proceed to arrange.*

[Note: The antinomies stand in the order of the four transcendental ideas above detailed.]

FIRST CONFLICT OF THE TRANSCENDENTAL IDEAS. THESIS.

The world has a beginning in time, and is also limited in regard to space.

PROOF.

Granted that the world has no beginning in time; up to every given moment of time, an eternity must have elapsed, and therewith passed away an infinite series of successive conditions or states of things in the world. Now the infinity of a series consists in the fact that it never can be completed by means of a successive synthesis. It follows that an infinite series already elapsed is impossible and that, consequently, a beginning of the world is a necessary condition of its existence. And this was the first thing to be proved.

As regards the second, let us take the opposite for granted. In this case, the world must be an infinite given total of coexistent things. Now we cannot cogitate the dimensions of a quantity, which is not given within certain limits of an intuition,* in any other way than by means of the synthesis of its parts, and the total of such a quantity only by means of a completed synthesis, or the repeated addition of unity to itself. Accordingly, to cogitate the world, which fills all spaces, as a whole, the successive synthesis of the parts of an infinite world must be looked upon as completed, that is to say, an infinite time must be regarded as having elapsed in the enumeration of all co-existing things; which is impossible. For this reason an infinite aggregate of actual things cannot be considered as a given whole, consequently, not as a contemporaneously given whole. The world is consequently, as regards extension in space, not infinite, but enclosed in limits. And this was the second thing to be proved.

[Note: We may consider an undetermined quantity as a whole, when it is enclosed within limits, although we cannot construct or ascertain its totality by measurement, that is, by the successive synthesis of its parts. For its limits of themselves determine its completeness as a whole.]

ANTITHESIS.

The world has no beginning, and no limits in space, but is, in relation both to time and space, infinite.

PROOF.

For let it be granted that it has a beginning. A beginning is an existence which is preceded by a time in which the thing does not exist. On the above supposition, it follows that there must have been a time in which the world did not exist, that is, a void time. But in a void time the origination of a thing is impossible; because no part of any such time contains a distinctive condition of being, in preference to that of non-being (whether the supposed thing originate of itself, or by means of some other cause). Consequently, many series of things may have a beginning in the world, but the world itself cannot have a beginning, and is, therefore, in relation to past time, infinite.

As regards the second statement, let us first take the opposite for granted — that the world is finite and limited in space; it follows that it must exist in a void space, which is not limited. We should therefore meet not only with a relation of things in space, but also a relation of things to space. Now, as the world is an absolute whole, out of and beyond which no object of intuition, and consequently no correlate to which can be discovered, this relation of the world to a void space is merely a relation to no object. But such a relation, and consequently the limitation of the world by void space, is nothing. Consequently, the world, as regards space, is not limited, that is, it is infinite in regard to extension.*

[Note: Space is merely the form of external intuition (formal intuition), and not a real object which can be externally perceived. Space, prior to all things which determine it (fill or limit it), or, rather, which present an empirical intuition conformable to it, is, under the title of absolute space, nothing but the mere possibility of external phenomena, in so far as they either exist in themselves, or can annex themselves to given intuitions. Empirical intuition is therefore not a composition of phenomena and space (of perception and empty intuition). The one is not the correlate of the other in a synthesis, but they are vitally connected in the same empirical intuition, as matter and form. If we wish to set one of these two apart from the other — space from phenomena — there arise all sorts of empty determinations of external intuition, which are very far from being possible perceptions. For example, motion or rest of the world in an infinite empty space, or a determination of the mutual relation of both, cannot possibly be perceived, and is therefore merely the predicate of a notional entity.]

OBSERVATIONS ON THE FIRST ANTINOMY. ON THE THESIS.

In bringing forward these conflicting arguments, I have not been on the search for sophisms, for the purpose of availing myself of special pleading, which takes advantage of the carelessness of the opposite party, appeals to a misunderstood statute, and erects its unrighteous claims upon an unfair interpretation. Both proofs originate fairly from the nature of the case, and the advantage presented by the mistakes of the dogmatists of both parties has been completely set aside.

The thesis might also have been unfairly demonstrated, by the introduction of an erroneous conception of the infinity of a given quantity. A quantity is infinite, if a greater than itself cannot possibly exist. The quantity is measured by the number of given units — which are taken as a standard — contained in it. Now no number can be the greatest, because one or more units can always be added. It follows that an infinite given quantity, consequently an infinite world (both as regards time and extension) is impossible. It is, therefore, limited in both respects. In this manner I might have conducted my proof; but the conception given in it does not agree with the true conception of an infinite whole. In this there is no representation of its quantity, it is not said how large it is; consequently its conception is not the conception of a maximum. We cogitate in it merely its relation to an arbitrarily assumed unit, in relation to which it is greater than any number. Now, just as the unit which is taken is greater or smaller, the infinite will be greater or smaller; but the infinity, which consists merely in the relation to this given unit, must remain always the same, although the absolute quantity of the whole is not thereby cognized.

The true (transcendental) conception of infinity is: that the successive synthesis of unity in the measurement of a given quantum can never be completed.* Hence it follows, without possibility of mistake, that an eternity of actual successive states up to a given (the present) moment cannot have elapsed, and that the world must therefore have a beginning.

[Note: The quantum in this sense contains a congeries of given units, which is greater than any number — and this is the mathematical conception of the infinite.]

In regard to the second part of the thesis, the difficulty as to an infinite and yet elapsed series disappears; for the manifold of a world infinite in extension is contemporaneously given. But, in order to cogitate the total of this manifold, as we cannot have the aid of limits constituting by themselves this total in intuition, we are obliged to give some account of our conception, which in this case cannot proceed from the whole to the determined quantity of the parts, but must demonstrate the possibility of a whole by means of a successive synthesis of the parts. But as this synthesis must constitute a series that cannot be completed, it is impossible for us to cogitate prior to it, and consequently not by means of it, a totality. For the conception of totality itself is in the present case the representation of a completed synthesis of the parts; and this completion, and consequently its conception, is impossible.

ON THE ANTITHESIS.

The proof in favour of the infinity of the cosmical succession and the cosmical content is based upon the consideration that, in the opposite case, a void time and a void space must constitute the limits of the world. Now I am not unaware, that there are some ways of escaping this conclusion. It may, for example, be alleged, that a limit to the world, as regards both space and time, is quite possible, without at the same time holding the existence of an absolute time before the beginning of the world, or an absolute space extending beyond the actual world — which is impossible. I am quite well satisfied with the latter part of this opinion of the philosophers of the Leibnitzian school. Space is merely the form of external intuition, but not a real object which can itself be externally intuited; it is not a correlate of phenomena, it is the form of phenomena itself. Space, therefore, cannot be regarded as absolutely and in itself something determinative of the existence of things, because it is not itself an object, but only the form of possible objects. Consequently, things, as phenomena, determine space; that is to say, they render it possible that, of all the possible predicates of space (size and relation), certain may belong to reality. But we cannot affirm the converse, that space, as something self-subsistent, can determine real things in regard to size or shape, for it is in itself not a real thing. Space (filled or void)* may therefore be limited by phenomena, but phenomena cannot be limited by an empty space without them. This is true of time also. All this being granted, it is nevertheless indisputable, that we must assume these two nonentities, void space without and void time before the world, if we assume the existence of cosmical limits, relatively to space or time.

[Note: It is evident that what is meant here is, that empty space, in so far as it is limited by phenomena — space, that is, within the world — does not at least contradict transcendental principles, and may therefore, as regards them, be admitted, although its possibility cannot on that account be affirmed.]

For, as regards the subterfuge adopted by those who endeavour to evade the consequence — that, if the world is limited as to space and time, the infinite void must determine the existence of actual things in regard to their dimensions — it arises solely from the fact that instead of a sensuous world, an intelligible world — of which nothing is known — is cogitated; instead of a real beginning (an existence, which is preceded by a period in which nothing exists), an existence which presupposes no other condition than that of time; and, instead of limits of extension, boundaries of the universe. But the question relates to the mundus phaenomenon, and its quantity; and in this case we cannot make abstraction of the conditions of sensibility, without doing away with the essential reality of this world itself. The world of sense, if it is limited, must necessarily lie in the infinite void. If this, and with it space as the a priori condition of the possibility of phenomena, is left out of view, the whole world of sense disappears. In our problem is this alone considered as given. The mundus intelligibilis is nothing but the general conception of a world, in which abstraction has been made of all conditions of intuition, and in relation to which no synthetical proposition — either affirmative or negative — is possible.

SECOND CONFLICT OF TRANSCENDENTAL IDEAS. THESIS.

Every composite substance in the world consists of simple parts; and there exists nothing that is not either itself simple, or composed of simple parts.

PROOF.

For, grant that composite substances do not consist of simple parts; in this case, if all combination or composition were annihilated in thought, no composite part, and (as, by the supposition, there do not exist simple parts) no simple part would exist. Consequently, no substance; consequently, nothing would exist. Either, then, it is impossible to annihilate composition in thought; or, after such annihilation, there must remain something that subsists without composition, that is, something that is simple. But in the former case the composite could not itself consist of substances, because with substances composition is merely a contingent relation, apart from which they must still exist as self-subsistent beings. Now, as this case contradicts the supposition, the second must contain the truth — that the substantial composite in the world consists of simple parts.

It follows, as an immediate inference, that the things in the world are all, without exception, simple beings — that composition is merely an external condition pertaining to them — and that, although we never can separate and isolate the elementary substances from the state of composition, reason must cogitate these as the primary subjects of all composition, and consequently, as prior thereto — and as simple substances.

ANTITHESIS.

No composite thing in the world consists of simple parts; and there does not exist in the world any simple substance.

PROOF.

Let it be supposed that a composite thing (as substance) consists of simple parts. Inasmuch as all external relation, consequently all composition of substances, is possible only in space; the space, occupied by that which is composite, must consist of the same number of parts as is contained in the composite. But space does not consist of simple parts, but of spaces. Therefore, every part of the composite must occupy a space. But the absolutely primary parts of what is composite are simple. It follows that what is simple occupies a space. Now, as everything real that occupies a space, contains a manifold the parts of which are external to each other, and is consequently composite — and a real composite, not of accidents (for these cannot exist external to each other apart from substance), but of substances — it follows that the simple must be a substantial composite, which is self-contradictory.

The second proposition of the antithesis — that there exists in the world nothing that is simple — is here equivalent to the following: The existence of the absolutely simple cannot be demonstrated from any experience or perception either external or internal; and the absolutely simple is a mere idea, the objective reality of which cannot be demonstrated in any possible experience; it is consequently, in the exposition of phenomena, without application and object. For, let us take for granted that an object may be found in experience for this transcendental idea; the empirical intuition of such an object must then be recognized to contain absolutely no manifold with its parts external to each other, and connected into unity. Now, as we cannot reason from the non-consciousness of such a manifold to the impossibility of its existence in the intuition of an object, and as the proof of this impossibility is necessary for the establishment and proof of absolute simplicity; it follows that this simplicity cannot be inferred from any perception whatever. As, therefore, an absolutely simple object cannot be given in any experience, and the world of sense must be considered as the sum total of all possible experiences: nothing simple exists in the world.

This second proposition in the antithesis has a more extended aim than the first. The first merely banishes the simple from the intuition of the composite; while the second drives it entirely out of nature. Hence we were unable to demonstrate it from the conception of a given object of external intuition (of the composite), but we were obliged to prove it from the relation of a given object to a possible experience in general.

OBSERVATIONS ON THE SECOND ANTINOMY. THESIS.

When I speak of a whole, which necessarily consists of simple parts, I understand thereby only a substantial whole, as the true composite; that is to say, I understand that contingent unity of the manifold which is given as perfectly isolated (at least in thought), placed in reciprocal connection, and thus constituted a unity. Space ought not to be called a compositum but a totum, for its parts are possible in the whole, and not the whole by means of the parts. It might perhaps be called a compositum ideale, but not a compositum reale. But this is of no importance. As space is not a composite of substances (and not even of real accidents), if I abstract all composition therein — nothing, not even a point, remains; for a point is possible only as the limit of a space — consequently of a composite. Space and time, therefore, do not consist of simple parts. That which belongs only to the condition or state of a substance, even although it possesses a quantity (motion or change, for example), likewise does not consist of simple parts. That is to say, a certain degree of change does not originate from the addition of many simple changes. Our inference of the simple from the composite is valid only of self-subsisting things. But the accidents of a state are not self-subsistent. The proof, then, for the necessity of the simple, as the component part of all that is substantial and composite, may prove a failure, and the whole case of this thesis be lost, if we carry the proposition too far, and wish to make it valid of everything that is composite without distinction — as indeed has really now and then happened. Besides, I am here speaking only of the simple, in so far as it is necessarily given in the composite — the latter being capable of solution into the former as its component parts. The proper signification of the word monas (as employed by Leibnitz) ought to relate to the simple, given immediately as simple substance (for example, in consciousness), and not as an element of the composite. As an element, the term atomus would be more appropriate. And as I wish to prove the existence of simple substances, only in relation to, and as the elements of, the composite, I might term the antithesis of the second Antinomy, transcendental Atomistic. But as this word has long been employed to designate a particular theory of corporeal phenomena (moleculae), and thus presupposes a basis of empirical conceptions, I prefer calling it the dialectical principle of Monadology.

ANTITHESIS.

Against the assertion of the infinite subdivisibility of matter whose ground of proof is purely mathematical, objections have been alleged by the Monadists. These objections lay themselves open, at first sight, to suspicion, from the fact that they do not recognize the clearest mathematical proofs as propositions relating to the constitution of space, in so far as it is really the formal condition of the possibility of all matter, but regard them merely as inferences from abstract but arbitrary conceptions, which cannot have any application to real things. Just as if it were possible to imagine another mode of intuition than that given in the primitive intuition of space; and just as if its a priori determinations did not apply to everything, the existence of which is possible, from the fact alone of its filling space. If we listen to them, we shall find ourselves required to cogitate, in addition to the mathematical point, which is simple — not, however, a part, but a mere limit of space — physical points, which are indeed likewise simple, but possess the peculiar property, as parts of space, of filling it merely by their aggregation. I shall not repeat here the common and clear refutations of this absurdity, which are to be found everywhere in numbers: every one knows that it is impossible to undermine the evidence of mathematics by mere discursive conceptions; I shall only remark that, if in this case philosophy endeavours to gain an advantage over mathematics by sophistical artifices, it is because it forgets that the discussion relates solely to Phenomena and their conditions. It is not sufficient to find the conception of the simple for the pure conception of the composite, but we must discover for the intuition of the composite (matter), the intuition of the simple. Now this, according to the laws of sensibility, and consequently in the case of objects of sense, is utterly impossible. In the case of a whole composed of substances, which is cogitated solely by the pure understanding, it may be necessary to be in possession of the simple before composition is possible. But this does not hold good of the Totum substantiale phaenomenon, which, as an empirical intuition in space, possesses the necessary property of containing no simple part, for the very reason that no part of space is simple. Meanwhile, the Monadists have been subtle enough to escape from this difficulty, by presupposing intuition and the dynamical relation of substances as the condition of the possibility of space, instead of regarding space as the condition of the possibility of the objects of external intuition, that is, of bodies. Now we have a conception of bodies only as phenomena, and, as such, they necessarily presuppose space as the condition of all external phenomena. The evasion is therefore in vain; as, indeed, we have sufficiently shown in our Aesthetic. If bodies were things in themselves, the proof of the Monadists would be unexceptionable.

The second dialectical assertion possesses the peculiarity of having opposed to it a dogmatical proposition, which, among all such sophistical statements, is the only one that undertakes to prove in the case of an object of experience, that which is properly a transcendental idea — the absolute simplicity of substance. The proposition is that the object of the internal sense, the thinking Ego, is an absolute simple substance. Without at present entering upon this subject — as it has been considered at length in a former chapter — I shall merely remark that, if something is cogitated merely as an object, without the addition of any synthetical determination of its intuition — as happens in the case of the bare representation, I — it is certain that no manifold and no composition can be perceived in such a representation. As, moreover, the predicates whereby I cogitate this object are merely intuitions of the internal sense, there cannot be discovered in them anything to prove the existence of a manifold whose parts are external to each other, and, consequently, nothing to prove the existence of real composition. Consciousness, therefore, is so constituted that, inasmuch as the thinking subject is at the same time its own object, it cannot divide itself — although it can divide its inhering determinations. For every object in relation to itself is absolute unity. Nevertheless, if the subject is regarded externally, as an object of intuition, it must, in its character of phenomenon, possess the property of composition. And it must always be regarded in this manner, if we wish to know whether there is or is not contained in it a manifold whose parts are external to each other.

THIRD CONFLICT OF THE TRANSCENDENTAL IDEAS. THESIS.

Causality according to the laws of nature, is not the only causality operating to originate the phenomena of the world. A causality of freedom is also necessary to account fully for these phenomena.

PROOF.

Let it be supposed, that there is no other kind of causality than that according to the laws of nature. Consequently, everything that happens presupposes a previous condition, which it follows with absolute certainty, in conformity with a rule. But this previous condition must itself be something that has happened (that has arisen in time, as it did not exist before), for, if it has always been in existence, its consequence or effect would not thus originate for the first time, but would likewise have always existed. The causality, therefore, of a cause, whereby something happens, is itself a thing that has happened. Now this again presupposes, in conformity with the law of nature, a previous condition and its causality, and this another anterior to the former, and so on. If, then, everything happens solely in accordance with the laws of nature, there cannot be any real first beginning of things, but only a subaltern or comparative beginning. There cannot, therefore, be a completeness of series on the side of the causes which originate the one from the other. But the law of nature is that nothing can happen without a sufficient a priori determined cause. The proposition therefore — if all causality is possible only in accordance with the laws of nature — is, when stated in this unlimited and general manner, self-contradictory. It follows that this cannot be the only kind of causality.

From what has been said, it follows that a causality must be admitted, by means of which something happens, without its cause being determined according to necessary laws by some other cause preceding. That is to say, there must exist an absolute spontaneity of cause, which of itself originates a series of phenomena which proceeds according to natural laws — consequently transcendental freedom, without which even in the course of nature the succession of phenomena on the side of causes is never complete.

ANTITHESIS.

There is no such thing as freedom, but everything in the world happens solely according to the laws of nature.

PROOF.

Granted, that there does exist freedom in the transcendental sense, as a peculiar kind of causality, operating to produce events in the world — a faculty, that is to say, of originating a state, and consequently a series of consequences from that state. In this case, not only the series originated by this spontaneity, but the determination of this spontaneity itself to the production of the series, that is to say, the causality itself must have an absolute commencement, such that nothing can precede to determine this action according to unvarying laws. But every beginning of action presupposes in the acting cause a state of inaction; and a dynamically primal beginning of action presupposes a state, which has no connection — as regards causality — with the preceding state of the cause — which does not, that is, in any wise result from it. Transcendental freedom is therefore opposed to the natural law of cause and effect, and such a conjunction of successive states in effective causes is destructive of the possibility of unity in experience and for that reason not to be found in experience — is consequently a mere fiction of thought.

We have, therefore, nothing but nature to which we must look for connection and order in cosmical events. Freedom — independence of the laws of nature — is certainly a deliverance from restraint, but it is also a relinquishing of the guidance of law and rule. For it cannot be alleged that, instead of the laws of nature, laws of freedom may be introduced into the causality of the course of nature. For, if freedom were determined according to laws, it would be no longer freedom, but merely nature. Nature, therefore, and transcendental freedom are distinguishable as conformity to law and lawlessness. The former imposes upon understanding the difficulty of seeking the origin of events ever higher and higher in the series of causes, inasmuch as causality is always conditioned thereby; while it compensates this labour by the guarantee of a unity complete and in conformity with law. The latter, on the contrary, holds out to the understanding the promise of a point of rest in the chain of causes, by conducting it to an unconditioned causality, which professes to have the power of spontaneous origination, but which, in its own utter blindness, deprives it of the guidance of rules, by which alone a completely connected experience is possible.

OBSERVATIONS ON THE THIRD ANTINOMY. ON THE THESIS.

The transcendental idea of freedom is far from constituting the entire content of the psychological conception so termed, which is for the most part empirical. It merely presents us with the conception of spontaneity of action, as the proper ground for imputing freedom to the cause of a certain class of objects. It is, however, the true stumbling-stone to philosophy, which meets with unconquerable difficulties in the way of its admitting this kind of unconditioned causality. That element in the question of the freedom of the will, which has for so long a time placed speculative reason in such perplexity, is properly only transcendental, and concerns the question, whether there must be held to exist a faculty of spontaneous origination of a series of successive things or states. How such a faculty is possible is not a necessary inquiry; for in the case of natural causality itself, we are obliged to content ourselves with the a priori knowledge that such a causality must be presupposed, although we are quite incapable of comprehending how the being of one thing is possible through the being of another, but must for this information look entirely to experience. Now we have demonstrated this necessity of a free first beginning of a series of phenomena, only in so far as it is required for the comprehension of an origin of the world, all following states being regarded as a succession according to laws of nature alone. But, as there has thus been proved the existence of a faculty which can of itself originate a series in time — although we are unable to explain how it can exist — we feel ourselves authorized to admit, even in the midst of the natural course of events, a beginning, as regards causality, of different successions of phenomena, and at the same time to attribute to all substances a faculty of free action. But we ought in this case not to allow ourselves to fall into a common misunderstanding, and to suppose that, because a successive series in the world can only have a comparatively first beginning — another state or condition of things always preceding — an absolutely first beginning of a series in the course of nature is impossible. For we are not speaking here of an absolutely first beginning in relation to time, but as regards causality alone. When, for example, I, completely of my own free will, and independently of the necessarily determinative influence of natural causes, rise from my chair, there commences with this event, including its material consequences in infinitum, an absolutely new series; although, in relation to time, this event is merely the continuation of a preceding series. For this resolution and act of mine do not form part of the succession of effects in nature, and are not mere continuations of it; on the contrary, the determining causes of nature cease to operate in reference to this event, which certainly succeeds the acts of nature, but does not proceed from them. For these reasons, the action of a free agent must be termed, in regard to causality, if not in relation to time, an absolutely primal beginning of a series of phenomena.

The justification of this need of reason to rest upon a free act as the first beginning of the series of natural causes is evident from the fact, that all philosophers of antiquity (with the exception of the Epicurean school) felt themselves obliged, when constructing a theory of the motions of the universe, to accept a prime mover, that is, a freely acting cause, which spontaneously and prior to all other causes evolved this series of states. They always felt the need of going beyond mere nature, for the purpose of making a first beginning comprehensible.

ON THE ANTITHESIS.

The assertor of the all-sufficiency of nature in regard to causality (transcendental Physiocracy), in opposition to the doctrine of freedom, would defend his view of the question somewhat in the following manner. He would say, in answer to the sophistical arguments of the opposite party: If you do not accept a mathematical first, in relation to time, you have no need to seek a dynamical first, in regard to causality. Who compelled you to imagine an absolutely primal condition of the world, and therewith an absolute beginning of the gradually progressing successions of phenomena — and, as some foundation for this fancy of yours, to set bounds to unlimited nature? Inasmuch as the substances in the world have always existed — at least the unity of experience renders such a supposition quite necessary — there is no difficulty in believing also, that the changes in the conditions of these substances have always existed; and, consequently, that a first beginning, mathematical or dynamical, is by no means required. The possibility of such an infinite derivation, without any initial member from which all the others result, is certainly quite incomprehensible. But, if you are rash enough to deny the enigmatical secrets of nature for this reason, you will find yourselves obliged to deny also the existence of many fundamental properties of natural objects (such as fundamental forces), which you can just as little comprehend; and even the possibility of so simple a conception as that of change must present to you insuperable difficulties. For if experience did not teach you that it was real, you never could conceive a priori the possibility of this ceaseless sequence of being and non-being.

But if the existence of a transcendental faculty of freedom is granted — a faculty of originating changes in the world — this faculty must at least exist out of and apart from the world; although it is certainly a bold assumption, that, over and above the complete content of all possible intuitions, there still exists an object which cannot be presented in any possible perception. But, to attribute to substances in the world itself such a faculty, is quite inadmissible; for, in this case; the connection of phenomena reciprocally determining and determined according to general laws, which is termed nature, and along with it the criteria of empirical truth, which enable us to distinguish experience from mere visionary dreaming, would almost entirely disappear. In proximity with such a lawless faculty of freedom, a system of nature is hardly cogitable; for the laws of the latter would be continually subject to the intrusive influences of the former, and the course of phenomena, which would otherwise proceed regularly and uniformly, would become thereby confused and disconnected.

FOURTH CONFLICT OF THE TRANSCENDENTAL IDEAS. THESIS.

There exists either in, or in connection with the world — either as a part of it, or as the cause of it — an absolutely necessary being.

PROOF.

The world of sense, as the sum total of all phenomena, contains a series of changes. For, without such a series, the mental representation of the series of time itself, as the condition of the possibility of the sensuous world, could not be presented to us.* But every change stands under its condition, which precedes it in time and renders it necessary. Now the existence of a given condition presupposes a complete series of conditions up to the absolutely unconditioned, which alone is absolutely necessary. It follows that something that is absolutely necessary must exist, if change exists as its consequence. But this necessary thing itself belongs to the sensuous world. For suppose it to exist out of and apart from it, the series of cosmical changes would receive from it a beginning, and yet this necessary cause would not itself belong to the world of sense. But this is impossible. For, as the beginning of a series in time is determined only by that which precedes it in time, the supreme condition of the beginning of a series of changes must exist in the time in which this series itself did not exist; for a beginning supposes a time preceding, in which the thing that begins to be was not in existence. The causality of the necessary cause of changes, and consequently the cause itself, must for these reasons belong to time — and to phenomena, time being possible only as the form of phenomena. Consequently, it cannot be cogitated as separated from the world of sense — the sum total of all phenomena. There is, therefore, contained in the world, something that is absolutely necessary — whether it be the whole cosmical series itself, or only a part of it.

[Note: Objectively, time, as the formal condition of the possibility of change, precedes all changes; but subjectively, and in consciousness, the representation of time, like every other, is given solely by occasion of perception.]

ANTITHESIS.

An absolutely necessary being does not exist, either in the world, or out of it — as its cause.

PROOF.

Grant that either the world itself is necessary, or that there is contained in it a necessary existence. Two cases are possible. First, there must either be in the series of cosmical changes a beginning, which is unconditionally necessary, and therefore uncaused — which is at variance with the dynamical law of the determination of all phenomena in time; or, secondly, the series itself is without beginning, and, although contingent and conditioned in all its parts, is nevertheless absolutely necessary and unconditioned as a whole — which is self-contradictory. For the existence of an aggregate cannot be necessary, if no single part of it possesses necessary existence.

Grant, on the other band, that an absolutely necessary cause exists out of and apart from the world. This cause, as the highest member in the series of the causes of cosmical changes, must originate or begin* the existence of the latter and their series. In this case it must also begin to act, and its causality would therefore belong to time, and consequently to the sum total of phenomena, that is, to the world. It follows that the cause cannot be out of the world; which is contradictory to the hypothesis. Therefore, neither in the world, nor out of it (but in causal connection with it), does there exist any absolutely necessary being.

[Note: The word begin is taken in two senses. The first is active — the cause being regarded as beginning a series of conditions as its effect (infit). The second is passive — the causality in the cause itself beginning to operate (fit). I reason here from the first to the second.]

OBSERVATIONS ON THE FOURTH ANTINOMY. ON THE THESIS.

To demonstrate the existence of a necessary being, I cannot be permitted in this place to employ any other than the cosmological argument, which ascends from the conditioned in phenomena to the unconditioned in conception — the unconditioned being considered the necessary condition of the absolute totality of the series. The proof, from the mere idea of a supreme being, belongs to another principle of reason and requires separate discussion.

The pure cosmological proof demonstrates the existence of a necessary being, but at the same time leaves it quite unsettled, whether this being is the world itself, or quite distinct from it. To establish the truth of the latter view, principles are requisite, which are not cosmological and do not proceed in the series of phenomena. We should require to introduce into our proof conceptions of contingent beings — regarded merely as objects of the understanding, and also a principle which enables us to connect these, by means of mere conceptions, with a necessary being. But the proper place for all such arguments is a transcendent philosophy, which has unhappily not yet been established.

But, if we begin our proof cosmologically, by laying at the foundation of it the series of phenomena, and the regress in it according to empirical laws of causality, we are not at liberty to break off from this mode of demonstration and to pass over to something which is not itself a member of the series. The condition must be taken in exactly the same signification as the relation of the conditioned to its condition in the series has been taken, for the series must conduct us in an unbroken regress to this supreme condition. But if this relation is sensuous, and belongs to the possible empirical employment of understanding, the supreme condition or cause must close the regressive series according to the laws of sensibility and consequently, must belong to the series of time. It follows that this necessary existence must be regarded as the highest member of the cosmical series.

Certain philosophers have, nevertheless, allowed themselves the liberty of making such a saltus (metabasis eis allo gonos). From the changes in the world they have concluded their empirical contingency, that is, their dependence on empirically-determined causes, and they thus admitted an ascending series of empirical conditions: and in this they are quite right. But as they could not find in this series any primal beginning or any highest member, they passed suddenly from the empirical conception of contingency to the pure category, which presents us with a series — not sensuous, but intellectual — whose completeness does certainly rest upon the existence of an absolutely necessary cause. Nay, more, this intellectual series is not tied to any sensuous conditions; and is therefore free from the condition of time, which requires it spontaneously to begin its causality in time. But such a procedure is perfectly inadmissible, as will be made plain from what follows.

In the pure sense of the categories, that is contingent the contradictory opposite of which is possible. Now we cannot reason from empirical contingency to intellectual. The opposite of that which is changed — the opposite of its state — is actual at another time, and is therefore possible. Consequently, it is not the contradictory opposite of the former state. To be that, it is necessary that, in the same time in which the preceding state existed, its opposite could have existed in its place; but such a cognition is not given us in the mere phenomenon of change. A body that was in motion = A, comes into a state of rest = non-A. Now it cannot be concluded from the fact that a state opposite to the state A follows it, that the contradictory opposite of A is possible; and that A is therefore contingent. To prove this, we should require to know that the state of rest could have existed in the very same time in which the motion took place. Now we know nothing more than that the state of rest was actual in the time that followed the state of motion; consequently, that it was also possible. But motion at one time, and rest at another time, are not contradictorily opposed to each other. It follows from what has been said that the succession of opposite determinations, that is, change, does not demonstrate the fact of contingency as represented in the conceptions of the pure understanding; and that it cannot, therefore, conduct us to the fact of the existence of a necessary being. Change proves merely empirical contingency, that is to say, that the new state could not have existed without a cause, which belongs to the preceding time. This cause — even although it is regarded as absolutely necessary — must be presented to us in time, and must belong to the series of phenomena.

ON THE ANTITHESIS.

The difficulties which meet us, in our attempt to rise through the series of phenomena to the existence of an absolutely necessary supreme cause, must not originate from our inability to establish the truth of our mere conceptions of the necessary existence of a thing. That is to say, our objections not be ontological, but must be directed against the causal connection with a series of phenomena of a condition which is itself unconditioned. In one word, they must be cosmological and relate to empirical laws. We must show that the regress in the series of causes (in the world of sense) cannot conclude with an empirically unconditioned condition, and that the cosmological argument from the contingency of the cosmical state — a contingency alleged to arise from change — does not justify us in accepting a first cause, that is, a prime originator of the cosmical series.

The reader will observe in this antinomy a very remarkable contrast. The very same grounds of proof which established in the thesis the existence of a supreme being, demonstrated in the antithesis — and with equal strictness — the non-existence of such a being. We found, first, that a necessary being exists, because the whole time past contains the series of all conditions, and with it, therefore, the unconditioned (the necessary); secondly, that there does not exist any necessary being, for the same reason, that the whole time past contains the series of all conditions — which are themselves, therefore, in the aggregate, conditioned. The cause of this seeming incongruity is as follows. We attend, in the first argument, solely to the absolute totality of the series of conditions, the one of which determines the other in time, and thus arrive at a necessary unconditioned. In the second, we consider, on the contrary, the contingency of everything that is determined in the series of time — for every event is preceded by a time, in which the condition itself must be determined as conditioned — and thus everything that is unconditioned or absolutely necessary disappears. In both, the mode of proof is quite in accordance with the common procedure of human reason, which often falls into discord with itself, from considering an object from two different points of view. Herr von Mairan regarded the controversy between two celebrated astronomers, which arose from a similar difficulty as to the choice of a proper standpoint, as a phenomenon of sufficient importance to warrant a separate treatise on the subject. The one concluded: the moon revolves on its own axis, because it constantly presents the same side to the earth; the other declared that the moon does not revolve on its own axis, for the same reason. Both conclusions were perfectly correct, according to the point of view from which the motions of the moon were considered.

SECTION III. Of the Interest of Reason in these Self-contradictions.

We have thus completely before us the dialectical procedure of the cosmological ideas. No possible experience can present us with an object adequate to them in extent. Nay, more, reason itself cannot cogitate them as according with the general laws of experience. And yet they are not arbitrary fictions of thought. On the contrary, reason, in its uninterrupted progress in the empirical synthesis, is necessarily conducted to them, when it endeavours to free from all conditions and to comprehend in its unconditioned totality that which can only be determined conditionally in accordance with the laws of experience. These dialectical propositions are so many attempts to solve four natural and unavoidable problems of reason. There are neither more, nor can there be less, than this number, because there are no other series of synthetical hypotheses, limiting a priori the empirical synthesis.

The brilliant claims of reason striving to extend its dominion beyond the limits of experience, have been represented above only in dry formulae, which contain merely the grounds of its pretensions. They have, besides, in conformity with the character of a transcendental philosophy, been freed from every empirical element; although the full splendour of the promises they hold out, and the anticipations they excite, manifests itself only when in connection with empirical cognitions. In the application of them, however, and in the advancing enlargement of the employment of reason, while struggling to rise from the region of experience and to soar to those sublime ideas, philosophy discovers a value and a dignity, which, if it could but make good its assertions, would raise it far above all other departments of human knowledge — professing, as it does, to present a sure foundation for our highest hopes and the ultimate aims of all the exertions of reason. The questions: whether the world has a beginning and a limit to its extension in space; whether there exists anywhere, or perhaps, in my own thinking Self, an indivisible and indestructible unity — or whether nothing but what is divisible and transitory exists; whether I am a free agent, or, like other beings, am bound in the chains of nature and fate; whether, finally, there is a supreme cause of the world, or all our thought and speculation must end with nature and the order of external things — are questions for the solution of which the mathematician would willingly exchange his whole science; for in it there is no satisfaction for the highest aspirations and most ardent desires of humanity. Nay, it may even be said that the true value of mathematics — that pride of human reason — consists in this: that she guides reason to the knowledge of nature — in her greater as well as in her less manifestations — in her beautiful order and regularity — guides her, moreover, to an insight into the wonderful unity of the moving forces in the operations of nature, far beyond the expectations of a philosophy building only on experience; and that she thus encourages philosophy to extend the province of reason beyond all experience, and at the same time provides it with the most excellent materials for supporting its investigations, in so far as their nature admits, by adequate and accordant intuitions.

Unfortunately for speculation — but perhaps fortunately for the practical interests of humanity — reason, in the midst of her highest anticipations, finds herself hemmed in by a press of opposite and contradictory conclusions, from which neither her honour nor her safety will permit her to draw back. Nor can she regard these conflicting trains of reasoning with indifference as mere passages at arms, still less can she command peace; for in the subject of the conflict she has a deep interest. There is no other course left open to her than to reflect with herself upon the origin of this disunion in reason — whether it may not arise from a mere misunderstanding. After such an inquiry, arrogant claims would have to be given up on both sides; but the sovereignty of reason over understanding and sense would be based upon a sure foundation.

We shall at present defer this radical inquiry and, in the meantime, consider for a little what side in the controversy we should most willingly take, if we were obliged to become partisans at all. As, in this case, we leave out of sight altogether the logical criterion of truth, and merely consult our own interest in reference to the question, these considerations, although inadequate to settle the question of right in either party, will enable us to comprehend how those who have taken part in the struggle, adopt the one view rather than the other — no special insight into the subject, however, having influenced their choice. They will, at the same time, explain to us many other things by the way — for example, the fiery zeal on the one side and the cold maintenance of their cause on the other; why the one party has met with the warmest approbations, and the other has always been repulsed by irreconcilable prejudices.

There is one thing, however, that determines the proper point of view, from which alone this preliminary inquiry can be instituted and carried on with the proper completeness — and that is the comparison of the principles from which both sides, thesis and antithesis, proceed. My readers would remark in the propositions of the antithesis a complete uniformity in the mode of thought and a perfect unity of principle. Its principle was that of pure empiricism, not only in the explication of the phenomena in the world, but also in the solution of the transcendental ideas, even of that of the universe itself. The affirmations of the thesis, on the contrary, were based, in addition to the empirical mode of explanation employed in the series of phenomena, on intellectual propositions; and its principles were in so far not simple. I shall term the thesis, in view of its essential characteristic, the dogmatism of pure reason.

On the side of Dogmatism, or of the thesis, therefore, in the determination of the cosmological ideas, we find:

1. A practical interest, which must be very dear to every right-thinking man. That the word has a beginning — that the nature of my thinking self is simple, and therefore indestructible — that I am a free agent, and raised above the compulsion of nature and her laws — and, finally, that the entire order of things, which form the world, is dependent upon a Supreme Being, from whom the whole receives unity and connection — these are so many foundation-stones of morality and religion. The antithesis deprives us of all these supports — or, at least, seems so to deprive us.

2. A speculative interest of reason manifests itself on this side. For, if we take the transcendental ideas and employ them in the manner which the thesis directs, we can exhibit completely a priori the entire chain of conditions, and understand the derivation of the conditioned — beginning from the unconditioned. This the antithesis does not do; and for this reason does not meet with so welcome a reception. For it can give no answer to our question respecting the conditions of its synthesis — except such as must be supplemented by another question, and so on to infinity. According to it, we must rise from a given beginning to one still higher; every part conducts us to a still smaller one; every event is preceded by another event which is its cause; and the conditions of existence rest always upon other and still higher conditions, and find neither end nor basis in some self-subsistent thing as the primal being.

3. This side has also the advantage of popularity; and this constitutes no small part of its claim to favour. The common understanding does not find the least difficulty in the idea of the unconditioned beginning of all synthesis — accustomed, as it is, rather to follow our consequences than to seek for a proper basis for cognition. In the conception of an absolute first, moreover — the possibility of which it does not inquire into — it is highly gratified to find a firmly-established point of departure for its attempts at theory; while in the restless and continuous ascent from the conditioned to the condition, always with one foot in the air, it can find no satisfaction.

On the side of the antithesis, or Empiricism, in the determination of the cosmological ideas:

1. We cannot discover any such practical interest arising from pure principles of reason as morality and religion present. On the contrary, pure empiricism seems to

empty them of all their power and influence. If there does not exist a Supreme Being distinct from the world — if the world is without beginning, consequently without a Creator — if our wills are not free, and the soul is divisible and subject to corruption just like matter — the ideas and principles of morality lose all validity and fall with the transcendental ideas which constituted their theoretical support.

2. But empiricism, in compensation, holds out to reason, in its speculative interests, certain important advantages, far exceeding any that the dogmatist can promise us. For, when employed by the empiricist, understanding is always upon its proper ground of investigation — the field of possible experience, the laws of which it can explore, and thus extend its cognition securely and with clear intelligence without being stopped by limits in any direction. Here can it and ought it to find and present to intuition its proper object — not only in itself, but in all its relations; or, if it employ conceptions, upon this ground it can always present the corresponding images in clear and unmistakable intuitions. It is quite unnecessary for it to renounce the guidance of nature, to attach itself to ideas, the objects of which it cannot know; because, as mere intellectual entities, they cannot be presented in any intuition. On the contrary, it is not even permitted to abandon its proper occupation, under the pretence that it has been brought to a conclusion (for it never can be), and to pass into the region of idealizing reason and transcendent conceptions, which it is not required to observe and explore the laws of nature, but merely to think and to imagine — secure from being contradicted by facts, because they have not been called as witnesses, but passed by, or perhaps subordinated to the so-called higher interests and considerations of pure reason.

Hence the empiricist will never allow himself to accept any epoch of nature for the first — the absolutely primal state; he will not believe that there can be limits to his outlook into her wide domains, nor pass from the objects of nature, which he can satisfactorily explain by means of observation and mathematical thought — which he can determine synthetically in intuition, to those which neither sense nor imagination can ever present in concreto; he will not concede the existence of a faculty in nature, operating independently of the laws of nature — a concession which would introduce uncertainty into the procedure of the understanding, which is guided by necessary laws to the observation of phenomena; nor, finally, will he permit himself to seek a cause beyond nature, inasmuch as we know nothing but it, and from it alone receive an objective basis for all our conceptions and instruction in the unvarying laws of things.

In truth, if the empirical philosopher had no other purpose in the establishment of his antithesis than to check the presumption of a reason which mistakes its true destination, which boasts of its insight and its knowledge, just where all insight and knowledge cease to exist, and regards that which is valid only in relation to a practical interest, as an advancement of the speculative interests of the mind (in order, when it is convenient for itself, to break the thread of our physical investigations, and, under pretence of extending our cognition, connect them with transcendental ideas, by means of which we really know only that we know nothing) — if, I say, the empiricist rested satisfied with this benefit, the principle advanced by him would be a maxim recommending moderation in the pretensions of reason and modesty in its affirmations, and at the same time would direct us to the right mode of extending the province of the understanding, by the help of the only true teacher, experience. In obedience to this advice, intellectual hypotheses and faith would not be called in aid of our practical interests; nor should we introduce them under the pompous titles of science and insight. For speculative cognition cannot find an objective basis any other where than in experience; and, when we overstep its limits our synthesis, which requires ever new cognitions independent of experience, has no substratum of intuition upon which to build.

But if — as often happens — empiricism, in relation to ideas, becomes itself dogmatic and boldly denies that which is above the sphere of its phenomenal cognition, it falls itself into the error of intemperance — an error which is here all the more reprehensible, as thereby the practical interest of reason receives an irreparable injury.

And this constitutes the opposition between Epicureanism* and Platonism.

[Note: It is, however, still a matter of doubt whether Epicurus ever propounded these principles as directions for the objective employment of the understanding. If, indeed, they were nothing more than maxims for the speculative exercise of reason, he gives evidence therein a more genuine philosophic spirit than any of the philosophers of antiquity. That, in the explanation of phenomena, we must proceed as if the field of inquiry had neither limits in space nor commencement in time; that we must be satisfied with the teaching of experience in reference to the material of which the world is posed; that we must not look for any other mode of the origination of events than that which is determined by the unalterable laws of nature; and finally, that we not employ the hypothesis of a cause distinct from the world to account for a phenomenon or for the world itself — are principles for the extension of speculative philosophy, and the discovery of the true sources of the principles of morals, which, however little conformed to in the present day, are undoubtedly correct. At the same time, any one desirous of ignoring, in mere speculation, these dogmatical propositions, need not for that reason be accused of denying them.]

Both Epicurus and Plato assert more in their systems than they know. The former encourages and advances science — although to the prejudice of the practical; the latter presents us with excellent principles for the investigation of the practical, but, in relation to everything regarding which we can attain to speculative cognition, permits reason to append idealistic explanations of natural phenomena, to the great injury of physical investigation.

3. In regard to the third motive for the preliminary choice of a party in this war of assertions, it seems very extraordinary that empiricism should be utterly unpopular. We should be inclined to believe that the common understanding would receive it with pleasure — promising as it does to satisfy it without passing the bounds of experience and its connected order; while transcendental dogmatism obliges it to rise to conceptions which far surpass the intelligence and ability of the most practised thinkers. But in this, in truth, is to be found its real motive. For the common understanding thus finds itself in a situation where not even the most learned can have the advantage of it. If it understands little or nothing about these transcendental conceptions, no one can boast of understanding any more; and although it may not express itself in so scholastically

correct a manner as others, it can busy itself with reasoning and arguments without end, wandering among mere ideas, about which one can always be very eloquent, because we know nothing about them; while, in the observation and investigation of nature, it would be forced to remain dumb and to confess its utter ignorance. Thus indolence and vanity form of themselves strong recommendations of these principles. Besides, although it is a hard thing for a philosopher to assume a principle, of which he can give to himself no reasonable account, and still more to employ conceptions, the objective reality of which cannot be established, nothing is more usual with the common understanding. It wants something which will allow it to go to work with confidence. The difficulty of even comprehending a supposition does not disquiet it, because — not knowing what comprehending means — it never even thinks of the supposition it may be adopting as a principle; and regards as known that with which it has become familiar from constant use. And, at last, all speculative interests disappear before the practical interests which it holds dear; and it fancies that it understands and knows what its necessities and hopes incite it to assume or to believe. Thus the empiricism of transcendentally idealizing reason is robbed of all popularity; and, however prejudicial it may be to the highest practical principles, there is no fear that it will ever pass the limits of the schools, or acquire any favour or influence in society or with the multitude.

Human reason is by nature architectonic. That is to say, it regards all cognitions as parts of a possible system, and hence accepts only such principles as at least do not incapacitate a cognition to which we may have attained from being placed along with others in a general system. But the propositions of the antithesis are of a character which renders the completion of an edifice of cognitions impossible. According to these, beyond one state or epoch of the world there is always to be found one more ancient; in every part always other parts themselves divisible; preceding every event another, the origin of which must itself be sought still higher; and everything in existence is conditioned, and still not dependent on an unconditioned and primal existence. As, therefore, the antithesis will not concede the existence of a first beginning which might be available as a foundation, a complete edifice of cognition, in the presence of such hypothesis, is utterly impossible. Thus the architectonic interest of reason, which requires a unity — not empirical, but a priori and rational — forms a natural recommendation for the assertions of the thesis in our antinomy.

But if any one could free himself entirely from all considerations of interest, and weigh without partiality the assertions of reason, attending only to their content, irrespective of the consequences which follow from them; such a person, on the supposition that he knew no other way out of the confusion than to settle the truth of one or other of the conflicting doctrines, would live in a state of continual hesitation. Today, he would feel convinced that the human will is free; to-morrow, considering the indissoluble chain of nature, he would look on freedom as a mere illusion and declare nature to be all-in-all. But, if he were called to action, the play of the merely speculative reason would disappear like the shapes of a dream, and practical interest would dictate his choice of principles. But, as it well befits a reflective and inquiring being to devote certain periods of time to the examination of its own reason — to divest itself of all partiality, and frankly to communicate its observations for the judgement and opinion of others; so no one can be blamed for, much less prevented from, placing both parties on their trial, with permission to end themselves, free from intimidation, before intimidation, before a sworn jury of equal condition with themselves — the condition of weak and fallible men.

SECTION IV. Of the necessity imposed upon Pure Reason of presenting a Solution of its Transcendental Problems.

To avow an ability to solve all problems and to answer all questions would be a profession certain to convict any philosopher of extravagant boasting and self-conceit, and at once to destroy the confidence that might otherwise have been reposed in him. There are, however, sciences so constituted that every question arising within their sphere must necessarily be capable of receiving an answer from the knowledge already possessed, for the answer must be received from the same sources whence the question arose. In such sciences it is not allowable to excuse ourselves on the plea of necessary and unavoidable ignorance; a solution is absolutely requisite. The rule of right and wrong must help us to the knowledge of what is right or wrong in all possible cases; otherwise, the idea of obligation or duty would be utterly null, for we cannot have any obligation to that which we cannot know. On the other hand, in our investigations of the phenomena of nature, much must remain uncertain, and many questions continue insoluble; because what we know of nature is far from being sufficient to explain all the phenomena that are presented to our observation. Now the question is: Whether there is in transcendental philosophy any question, relating to an object presented to pure reason, which is unanswerable by this reason; and whether we must regard the subject of the question as quite uncertain, so far as our knowledge extends, and must give it a place among those subjects, of which we have just so much conception as is sufficient to enable us to raise a question — faculty or materials failing us, however, when we attempt an answer.

Now I maintain that, among all speculative cognition, the peculiarity of transcendental philosophy is that there is no question, relating to an object presented to pure reason, which is insoluble by this reason; and that the profession of unavoidable ignorance — the problem being alleged to be beyond the reach of our faculties — cannot free us from the obligation to present a complete and satisfactory answer. For the very conception which enables us to raise the question must give us the power of answering it; inasmuch as the object, as in the case of right and wrong, is not to be discovered out of the conception.

But, in transcendental philosophy, it is only the cosmological questions to which we can demand a satisfactory answer in relation to the constitution of their object; and the philosopher is not permitted to avail himself of the pretext of necessary ignorance and impenetrable obscurity. These questions relate solely to the cosmological ideas. For the object must be given in experience, and the question relates to the adequateness of the object to an idea. If the object is transcendental and therefore itself unknown; if the question, for example, is whether the object — the something, the phenomenon of which (internal — in ourselves) is thought — that is to say, the soul, is in itself a simple being; or whether there is a cause of all things, which is absolutely necessary — in such cases we are seeking for our idea an object, of which we may confess that it is unknown to us, though we must not on that account assert that it is impossible.* The cosmological ideas alone posses the peculiarity that we can presuppose the object of them and the empirical synthesis requisite for the conception of that object to be given; and the question, which arises from these ideas, relates merely to the progress of this synthesis, in so far as it must contain absolute totality — which, however, is not empirical, as it cannot be given in any experience. Now, as the question here is solely in regard to a thing as the object of a possible experience and not as a thing in itself, the answer to the transcendental cosmological question need not be sought out of the idea, for the question does not regard an object in itself. The question in relation to a possible experience is not, "What can be given in an experience in concreto" but "what is contained in the idea, to which the empirical synthesis must approximate." The question must therefore be capable of solution from the idea alone. For the idea is a creation of reason itself, which therefore cannot disclaim the obligation to answer or refer us to the unknown object.

[Note: The question, "What is the constitution of a transcendental object?" is unanswerable — we are unable to say what it is; but we can perceive that the question itself is nothing; because it does not relate to any object that can be presented to us. For this reason, we must consider all the questions raised in transcendental psychology as answerable and as really answered; for they relate to the transcendental subject of all internal phenomena, which is not itself phenomenon and consequently not given as an object, in which, moreover, none of the categories — and it is to them that the question is properly directed — find any conditions of its application. Here, therefore, is a case where no answer is the only proper answer. For a question regarding the constitution of a something which cannot be cogitated by any determined predicate, being completely beyond the sphere of objects and experience, is perfectly null and void.]

It is not so extraordinary, as it at first sight appears, that a science should demand and expect satisfactory answers to all the questions that may arise within its own sphere (questiones domesticae), although, up to a certain time, these answers may not have been discovered. There are, in addition to transcendental philosophy, only two pure sciences of reason; the one with a speculative, the other with a practical content — pure mathematics and pure ethics. Has any one ever heard it alleged that, from our complete and necessary ignorance of the conditions, it is uncertain what exact relation the diameter of a circle bears to the circle in rational or irrational numbers? By the former the sum cannot be given exactly, by the latter only approximately; and therefore we decide that the impossibility of a solution of the question is evident. Lambert presented us with a demonstration of this. In the general principles of morals there can be nothing uncertain, for the propositions are either utterly without meaning, or must originate solely in our rational conceptions. On the other hand, there must be in physical science an infinite number of conjectures, which can never become certainties; because the phenomena of nature are not given as objects dependent on our conceptions. The key to the solution of such questions cannot, therefore, be found in our conceptions, or in pure thought, but must lie without us and for that reason is in many cases not to be discovered; and consequently a satisfactory explanation cannot be expected. The questions of transcendental analytic, which relate to the deduction of our pure cognition, are not to be regarded as of the same kind as those mentioned above; for we are not at present treating of the certainty of judgements in relation to the origin of our conceptions, but only of that certainty in relation to objects.

We cannot, therefore, escape the responsibility of at least a critical solution of the questions of reason, by complaints of the limited nature of our faculties, and the seemingly humble confession that it is beyond the power of our reason to decide, whether the world has existed from all eternity or had a beginning — whether it is infinitely extended, or enclosed within certain limits — whether anything in the world is simple, or whether everything must be capable of infinite divisibility — whether freedom can originate phenomena, or whether everything is absolutely dependent on the laws and order of nature — and, finally, whether there exists a being that is completely unconditioned and necessary, or whether the existence of everything is conditioned and consequently dependent on something external to itself, and therefore in its own nature contingent. For all these questions relate to an object, which can be given nowhere else than in thought. This object is the absolutely unconditioned totality of the synthesis of phenomena. If the conceptions in our minds do not assist us to some certain result in regard to these problems, we must not defend ourselves on the plea that the object itself remains hidden from and unknown to us. For no such thing or object can be given — it is not to be found out of the idea in our minds. We must seek the cause of our failure in our idea itself, which is an insoluble problem and in regard to which we obstinately assume that there exists a real object corresponding and adequate to it. A clear explanation of the dialectic which lies in our conception, will very soon enable us to come to a satisfactory decision in regard to such a question.

The pretext that we are unable to arrive at certainty in regard to these problems may be met with this question, which requires at least a plain answer: "From what source do the ideas originate, the solution of which involves you in such difficulties? Are you seeking for an explanation of certain phenomena; and do you expect these ideas to give you the principles or the rules of this explanation?" Let it be granted, that all nature was laid open before you; that nothing was hid from your senses and your consciousness. Still, you could not cognize in concreto the object of your ideas in any experience. For what is demanded is not only this full and complete intuition, but also a complete synthesis and the consciousness of its absolute totality; and this is not possible by means of any empirical cognition. It follows that your question — your idea — is by no means necessary for the explanation of any phenomenon; and the idea cannot have been in any sense given by the object itself. For such an object can never be presented to us, because it cannot be given by any possible experience. Whatever perceptions you may attain to, you are still surrounded by conditions — in space, or in time — and you cannot discover anything unconditioned; nor can you decide whether this unconditioned is to be placed in an absolute beginning of the synthesis, or in an absolute totality of the series without beginning. A whole, in the empirical signification of the term, is always merely comparative. The absolute whole of quantity (the universe), of division, of derivation, of the condition of existence, with the question — whether it is to be produced by finite or infinite synthesis, no possible experience can instruct us concerning. You will not, for example, be able to explain the phenomena of a body in the least degree better, whether you believe it to consist of simple, or of composite parts; for a simple phenomenon — and just as little an infinite series of composition — can never be presented to your perception. Phenomena require and admit of explanation, only in so far as the conditions of that explanation are given in perception; but the sum total of that which is given in phenomena, considered as an absolute whole, is itself a perception — and we cannot therefore seek for explanations of this whole beyond itself, in other perceptions. The explanation of this whole is the proper object of the transcendental problems of pure reason.

Although, therefore, the solution of these problems is unattainable through experience, we must not permit ourselves to say that it is uncertain how the object of our inquiries is constituted. For the object is in our own mind and cannot be discovered in experience; and we have only to take care that our thoughts are consistent with each other, and to avoid falling into the amphiboly of regarding our idea as a representation of an object empirically given, and therefore to be cognized according to the laws of experience. A dogmatical solution is therefore not only unsatisfactory but impossible. The critical solution, which may be a perfectly certain one, does not consider the question objectively, but proceeds by inquiring into the basis of the cognition upon which the question rests.

SECTION V. Sceptical Exposition of the Cosmological Problems presented in the four Transcendental Ideas.

We should be quite willing to desist from the demand of a dogmatical answer to our questions, if we understood beforehand that, be the answer what it may, it would only serve to increase our ignorance, to throw us from one incomprehensibility into another, from one obscurity into another still greater, and perhaps lead us into irreconcilable contradictions. If a dogmatical affirmative or negative answer is demanded, is it at all prudent to set aside the probable grounds of a solution which lie before us and to take into consideration what advantage we shall gain, if the answer is to favour the one side or the other? If it happens that in both cases the answer is mere nonsense, we have in this an irresistible summons to institute a critical investigation of the question, for the purpose of discovering whether it is based on a groundless presupposition and relates to an idea, the falsity of which would be more easily exposed in its application and consequences than in the mere representation of its content. This is the great utility of the sceptical mode of treating the questions addressed by pure reason to itself. By this method we easily rid ourselves of the confusions of dogmatism, and establish in its place a temperate criticism, which, as a genuine cathartic, will successfully remove the presumptuous notions of philosophy and their consequence — the vain pretension to universal science.

If, then, I could understand the nature of a cosmological idea and perceive, before I entered on the discussion of the subject at all, that, whatever side of the question regarding the unconditioned of the regressive synthesis of phenomena it favoured — it must either be too great or too small for every conception of the understanding — I would be able to comprehend how the idea, which relates to an object of experience — an experience which must be adequate to and in accordance with a possible conception of the understanding — must be completely void and without significance, inasmuch as its object is inadequate, consider it as we may. And this is actually the case with all cosmological conceptions, which, for the reason above mentioned, involve reason, so long as it remains attached to them, in an unavoidable antinomy. For suppose:

First, that the world has no beginning — in this case it is too large for our conception;

for this conception, which consists in a successive regress, cannot overtake the whole eternity that has elapsed. Grant that it has a beginning, it is then too small for the conception of the understanding. For, as a beginning presupposes a time preceding, it cannot be unconditioned; and the law of the empirical employment of the understanding imposes the necessity of looking for a higher condition of time; and the world is, therefore, evidently too small for this law.

The same is the case with the double answer to the question regarding the extent, in space, of the world. For, if it is infinite and unlimited, it must be too large for every possible empirical conception. If it is finite and limited, we have a right to ask: "What determines these limits?" Void space is not a self-subsistent correlate of things, and cannot be a final condition — and still less an empirical condition, forming a part of a possible experience. For how can we have any experience or perception of an absolute void? But the absolute totality of the empirical synthesis requires that the unconditioned be an empirical conception. Consequently, a finite world is too small for our conception.

Secondly, if every phenomenon (matter) in space consists of an infinite number of parts, the regress of the division is always too great for our conception; and if the division of space must cease with some member of the division (the simple), it is too small for the idea of the unconditioned. For the member at which we have discontinued our division still admits a regress to many more parts contained in the object.

Thirdly, suppose that every event in the world happens in accordance with the laws of nature; the causality of a cause must itself be an event and necessitates a regress to a still higher cause, and consequently the unceasing prolongation of the series of conditions a parte priori. Operative nature is therefore too large for every conception we can form in the synthesis of cosmical events.

If we admit the existence of spontaneously produced events, that is, of free agency, we are driven, in our search for sufficient reasons, on an unavoidable law of nature and are compelled to appeal to the empirical law of causality, and we find that any such totality of connection in our synthesis is too small for our necessary empirical conception.

Fourthly, if we assume the existence of an absolutely necessary being — whether it be the world or something in the world, or the cause of the world — we must place it in a time at an infinite distance from any given moment; for, otherwise, it must be dependent on some other and higher existence. Such an existence is, in this case, too large for our empirical conception, and unattainable by the continued regress of any synthesis.

But if we believe that everything in the world — be it condition or conditioned — is contingent; every given existence is too small for our conception. For in this case we are compelled to seek for some other existence upon which the former depends.

We have said that in all these cases the cosmological idea is either too great or too small for the empirical regress in a synthesis, and consequently for every possible conception of the understanding. Why did we not express ourselves in a manner exactly the reverse of this and, instead of accusing the cosmological idea of over stepping or of falling short of its true aim, possible experience, say that, in the first case, the empirical conception is always too small for the idea, and in the second too great, and thus attach the blame of these contradictions to the empirical regress? The reason is this. Possible experience can alone give reality to our conceptions; without it a conception is merely an idea, without truth or relation to an object. Hence a possible empirical conception must be the standard by which we are to judge whether an idea is anything more than an idea and fiction of thought, or whether it relates to an object in the world. If we say of a thing that in relation to some other thing it is too large or too small, the former is considered as existing for the sake of the latter, and requiring to be adapted to it. Among the trivial subjects of discussion in the old schools of dialectics was this question: "If a ball cannot pass through a hole, shall we say that the ball is too large or the hole too small?" In this case it is indifferent what expression we employ; for we do not know which exists for the sake of the other. On the other hand, we cannot say: "The man is too long for his coat"; but: "The coat is too short for the man."

We are thus led to the well-founded suspicion that the cosmological ideas, and all the conflicting sophistical assertions connected with them, are based upon a false and fictitious conception of the mode in which the object of these ideas is presented to us; and this suspicion will probably direct us how to expose the illusion that has so long led us astray from the truth.

SECTION VI. Transcendental Idealism as the Key to theSolution of Pure Cosmological Dialectic.

In the transcendental aesthetic we proved that everything intuited in space and time, all objects of a possible experience, are nothing but phenomena, that is, mere representations; and that these, as presented to us — as extended bodies, or as series of changes — have no self-subsistent existence apart from human thought. This doctrine I call Transcendental Idealism.* The realist in the transcendental sense regards these modifications of our sensibility, these mere representations, as things subsisting in themselves.

[Note: I have elsewhere termed this theory formal idealism, to distinguish it from material idealism, which doubts or denies the existence of external things. To avoid ambiguity, it seems advisable in many cases to employ this term instead of that mentioned in the text.]

It would be unjust to accuse us of holding the long-decried theory of empirical idealism, which, while admitting the reality of space, denies, or at least doubts, the existence of bodies extended in it, and thus leaves us without a sufficient criterion of reality and illusion. The supporters of this theory find no difficulty in admitting the reality of the phenomena of the internal sense in time; nay, they go the length of maintaining that this internal experience is of itself a sufficient proof of the real existence of its object as a thing in itself.

Transcendental idealism allows that the objects of external intuition — as intuited in space, and all changes in time — as represented by the internal sense, are real. For, as space is the form of that intuition which we call external, and, without objects in space, no empirical representation could be given us, we can and ought to regard extended bodies in it as real. The case is the same with representations in time. But time and space, with all phenomena therein, are not in themselves things. They are nothing but representations and cannot exist out of and apart from the mind. Nay, the sensuous internal intuition of the mind (as the object of consciousness), the determination of which is represented by the succession of different states in time, is not the real, proper self, as it exists in itself — not the transcendental subject — but only a phenomenon, which is presented to the sensibility of this, to us, unknown being. This internal phenomenon cannot be admitted to be a self-subsisting thing; for its condition is time, and time cannot be the condition of a thing in itself. But the empirical truth of phenomena in space and time is guaranteed beyond the possibility of doubt, and sufficiently distinguished from the illusion of dreams or fancy — although both have a proper and thorough connection in an experience according to empirical laws. The objects of experience then are not things in themselves, but are given only in experience, and have no existence apart from and independently of experience. That there may be inhabitants in the moon, although no one has ever observed them, must certainly be admitted; but this assertion means only, that we may in the possible progress of experience discover them at some future time. For that which stands in connection with a perception according to the laws of the progress of experience is real. They are therefore really existent, if they stand in empirical connection with my actual or real consciousness, although they are not in themselves real, that is, apart from the progress of experience.

There is nothing actually given — we can be conscious of nothing as real, except a perception and the empirical progression from it to other possible perceptions. For phenomena, as mere representations, are real only in perception; and perception is, in fact, nothing but the reality of an empirical representation, that is, a phenomenon. To call a phenomenon a real thing prior to perception means either that we must meet with this phenomenon in the progress of experience, or it means nothing at all. For I can say only of a thing in itself that it exists without relation to the senses and experience. But we are speaking here merely of phenomena in space and time, both of which are determinations of sensibility, and not of things in themselves. It follows that phenomena are not things in themselves, but are mere representations, which if not given in us — in perception — are non-existent.

The faculty of sensuous intuition is properly a receptivity — a capacity of being affected in a certain manner by representations, the relation of which to each other is a pure intuition of space and time — the pure forms of sensibility. These representations, in so far as they are connected and determinable in this relation (in space and time) according to laws of the unity of experience, are called objects. The non-sensuous cause of these representations is completely unknown to us and hence cannot be intuited as an object. For such an object could not be represented either in space or in time; and without these conditions intuition or representation is impossible. We may, at the same time, term the non-sensuous cause of phenomena the transcendental object — but merely as a mental correlate to sensibility, considered as a receptivity. To this transcendental object we may attribute the whole connection and extent of our possible perceptions, and say that it is given and exists in itself prior to all experience. But the phenomena, corresponding to it, are not given as things in themselves, but in experience alone. For they are mere representations, receiving from perceptions alone significance and relation to a real object, under the condition that this or that perception — indicating an object — is in complete connection with all others in accordance with the rules of the unity of experience. Thus we can say: "The things that really existed in past time are given in the transcendental object of experience." But these are to me real objects, only in so far as I can represent to my own mind, that a regressive series of possible perceptions — following the indications of history, or the footsteps of cause and effect — in accordance with empirical laws — that, in one word, the course of the world conducts us to an elapsed series of time as the condition of the present time. This series in past time is represented as real, not in itself, but only in connection with a possible experience. Thus, when I say that certain events occurred in past time, I merely assert the possibility of prolonging the chain of experience, from the present perception, upwards to the conditions that determine it according to time.

If I represent to myself all objects existing in all space and time, I do not thereby place these in space and time prior to all experience; on the contrary, such a representation is nothing more than the notion of a possible experience, in its absolute completeness. In experience alone are those objects, which are nothing but representations, given. But, when I say they existed prior to my experience, this means only that I must begin with the perception present to me and follow the track indicated until I discover them in some part or region of experience. The cause of the empirical condition of this progression — and consequently at what member therein I must stop, and at what point in the regress I am to find this member — is transcendental, and hence necessarily incognizable. But with this we have not to do; our concern is only with the law of progression in experience, in which objects, that is, phenomena, are given. It is a matter of indifference, whether I say, "I may in the progress of experience discover stars, at a hundred times greater distance than the most distant of those now visible," or, "Stars at this distance may be met in space, although no one has, or ever will discover them." For, if they are given as things in themselves, without any relation to possible experience, they are for me non-existent, consequently, are not objects, for they are not contained in the regressive series of experience. But, if these phenomena must be employed in the construction or support of the cosmological idea of an absolute whole, and when we are discussing a question that oversteps the limits of possible experience, the proper distinction of the different theories of the reality of sensuous objects is of great importance, in order to avoid the illusion which must necessarily arise from the misinterpretation of our empirical conceptions.

SECTION VII. Critical Solution of the Cosmological Problem.

The antinomy of pure reason is based upon the following dialectical argument: "If that which is conditioned is given, the whole series of its conditions is also given; but sensuous objects are given as conditioned; consequently..." This syllogism, the major of which seems so natural and evident, introduces as many cosmological ideas as there are different kinds of conditions in the synthesis of phenomena, in so far as these conditions constitute a series. These ideas require absolute totality in the series, and thus place reason in inextricable embarrassment. Before proceeding to expose the fallacy in this dialectical argument, it will be necessary to have a correct understanding of certain conceptions that appear in it.

In the first place, the following proposition is evident, and indubitably certain: "If the conditioned is given, a regress in the series of all its conditions is thereby imperatively required." For the very conception of a conditioned is a conception of something related to a condition, and, if this condition is itself conditioned, to another condition — and so on through all the members of the series. This proposition is, therefore, analytical and has nothing to fear from transcendental criticism. It is a logical postulate of reason: to pursue, as far as possible, the connection of a conception with its conditions.

If, in the second place, both the conditioned and the condition are things in themselves, and if the former is given, not only is the regress to the latter requisite, but the latter is really given with the former. Now, as this is true of all the members of the series, the entire series of conditions, and with them the unconditioned, is at the same time given in the very fact of the conditioned, the existence of which is possible only in and through that series, being given. In this case, the synthesis of the conditioned with its condition, is a synthesis of the understanding merely, which represents things as they are, without regarding whether and how we can cognize them. But if I have to do with phenomena, which, in their character of mere representations, are not given, if I do not attain to a cognition of them (in other words, to themselves, for they are nothing more than empirical cognitions), I am not entitled to say: "If the conditioned is given, all its conditions (as phenomena) are also given." I cannot, therefore, from the fact of a conditioned being given, infer the absolute totality of the series of its conditions. For phenomena are nothing but an empirical synthesis in apprehension or perception, and are therefore given only in it. Now, in speaking of phenomena it does not follow that, if the conditioned is given, the synthesis which constitutes its empirical condition is also thereby given and presupposed; such a synthesis can be established only by an actual regress in the series of conditions. But we are entitled to say in this case that a regress to the conditions of a conditioned, in other words, that a continuous empirical synthesis is enjoined; that, if the conditions are not given, they are at least required; and that we are certain to discover the conditions in this regress.

We can now see that the major, in the above cosmological syllogism, takes the conditioned in the transcendental signification which it has in the pure category, while the minor speaks of it in the empirical signification which it has in the category as applied to phenomena. There is, therefore, a dialectical fallacy in the syllogism — a sophisma figurae dictionis. But this fallacy is not a consciously devised one, but a perfectly natural illusion of the common reason of man. For, when a thing is given as conditioned, we presuppose in the major its conditions and their series, unperceived, as it were, and unseen; because this is nothing more than the logical requirement of complete and satisfactory premises for a given conclusion. In this case, time is altogether left out in the connection of the conditioned with the condition; they are supposed to be given in themselves, and contemporaneously. It is, moreover, just as natural to regard phenomena (in the minor) as things in themselves and as objects presented to the pure understanding, as in the major, in which complete abstraction was made of all conditions of intuition. But it is under these conditions alone that objects are given. Now we overlooked a remarkable distinction between the conceptions. The synthesis of the conditioned with its condition, and the complete series of the latter (in the major) are not limited by time, and do not contain the conception of succession. On the contrary, the empirical synthesis and the series of conditions in the phenomenal world — subsumed in the minor — are necessarily successive and given in time alone. It follows that I cannot presuppose in the minor, as I did in the major, the absolute totality of the synthesis and of the series therein represented; for in the major all the members of the series are given as things in themselves — without any limitations or conditions of time, while in the minor they are possible only in and through a successive regress, which cannot exist, except it be actually carried into execution in the world of phenomena.

After this proof of the viciousness of the argument commonly employed in maintaining cosmological assertions, both parties may now be justly dismissed, as advancing claims without grounds or title. But the process has not been ended by convincing them that one or both were in the wrong and had maintained an assertion which was without valid grounds of proof. Nothing seems to be clearer than that, if one maintains: "The world has a beginning," and another: "The world has no beginning," one of the two must be right. But it is likewise clear that, if the evidence on both sides is equal, it is impossible to discover on what side the truth lies; and the controversy continues, although the parties have been recommended to peace before the tribunal of reason. There remains, then, no other means of settling the question than to convince the parties, who refute each other with such conclusiveness and ability, that they are disputing about nothing, and that a transcendental illusion has been mocking them with visions of reality where there is none. The mode of adjusting a dispute which cannot be decided upon its own merits, we shall now proceed to lay before our readers.

Zeno of Elea, a subtle dialectician, was severely reprimanded by Plato as a sophist, who, merely from the base motive of exhibiting his skill in discussion, maintained and subverted the same proposition by arguments as powerful and convincing on the one side as on the other. He maintained, for example, that God (who was probably nothing more, in his view, than the world) is neither finite nor infinite, neither in motion nor in rest, neither similar nor dissimilar to any other thing. It seemed to those philosophers who criticized his mode of discussion that his purpose was to deny completely both of two self-contradictory propositions — which is absurd. But I cannot believe that there is any justice in this accusation. The first of these propositions I shall presently consider in a more detailed manner. With regard to the others, if by the word of God he understood merely the Universe, his meaning must have been — that it cannot be permanently present in one place — that is, at rest — nor be capable of changing its place — that is, of moving — because all places are in the universe, and the universe itself is, therefore, in no place. Again, if the universe contains in itself everything that exists, it cannot be similar or dissimilar to any other thing, because there is, in fact, no other thing with which it can be compared. If two opposite judgements presuppose a contingent impossible, or arbitrary condition, both — in spite of their opposition (which is, however, not properly or really a contradiction) — fall away; because the condition, which ensured the validity of both, has itself disappeared.

If we say: "Everybody has either a good or a bad smell," we have omitted a third possible judgement — it has no smell at all; and thus both conflicting statements may be false. If we say: "It is either good-smelling or not good-smelling (vel suaveolens vel non-suaveolens)," both judgements are contradictorily opposed; and the contradictory opposite of the former judgement — some bodies are not good-smelling — embraces also those bodies which have no smell at all. In the preceding pair of opposed judgements (per disparata), the contingent condition of the conception of body (smell) attached to both conflicting statements, instead of having been omitted in the latter, which is consequently not the contradictory opposite of the former.

If, accordingly, we say: "The world is either infinite in extension, or it is not infinite (non est infinitus)"; and if the former proposition is false, its contradictory opposite — the world is not infinite — must be true. And thus I should deny the existence of an infinite, without, however affirming the existence of a finite world. But if we construct our proposition thus: "The world is either infinite or finite (non-infinite)," both statements may be false. For, in this case, we consider the world as per se determined in regard to quantity, and while, in the one judgement, we deny its infinite and consequently, perhaps, its independent existence; in the other, we append to the world, regarded as a thing in itself, a certain determination — that of finitude; and the latter may be false as well as the former, if the world is not given as a thing in itself, and thus neither as finite nor as infinite in quantity. This kind of opposition I may be allowed to term dialectical; that of contradictories may be called analytical opposition. Thus then, of two dialectically opposed judgements both may be false, from the fact, that the one is not a mere contradictory of the other, but actually enounces more than is requisite for a full and complete contradiction.

When we regard the two propositions— "The world is infinite in quantity," and, "The world is finite in quantity," as contradictory opposites, we are assuming that the world — the complete series of phenomena — is a thing in itself. For it remains as a permanent quantity, whether I deny the infinite or the finite regress in the series of its phenomena. But if we dismiss this assumption — this transcendental illusion — and deny that it is a thing in itself, the contradictory opposition is metamorphosed into a merely dialectical one; and the world, as not existing in itself — independently of the regressive series of my representations — exists in like manner neither as a whole which is infinite nor as a whole which is finite in itself. The universe exists for me only in the empirical regress of the series of phenomena and not per se. If, then, it is always conditioned, it is never completely or as a whole; and it is, therefore, not an unconditioned whole and does not exist as such, either with an infinite, or with a finite quantity.

What we have here said of the first cosmological idea — that of the absolute totality of quantity in phenomena — applies also to the others. The series of conditions is discoverable only in the regressive synthesis itself, and not in the phenomenon considered as a thing in itself — given prior to all regress. Hence I am compelled to say: "The aggregate of parts in a given phenomenon is in itself neither finite nor infinite; and these parts are given only in the regressive synthesis of decomposition — a synthesis which is never given in absolute completeness, either as finite, or as infinite." The same is the case with the series of subordinated causes, or of the conditioned up to the unconditioned and necessary existence, which can never be regarded as in itself, ind in its totality, either as finite or as infinite; because, as a series of subordinate representations, it subsists only in the dynamical regress and cannot be regarded as existing previously to this regress, or as a self-subsistent series of things.

Thus the antinomy of pure reason in its cosmological ideas disappears. For the above demonstration has established the fact that it is merely the product of a dialectical and illusory opposition, which arises from the application of the idea of absolute totality — admissible only as a condition of things in themselves — to phenomena, which exist only in our representations, and — when constituting a series — in a successive regress. This antinomy of reason may, however, be really profitable to our speculative interests, not in the way of contributing any dogmatical addition, but as presenting to us another material support in our critical investigations. For it furnishes us with an indirect proof of the transcendental ideality of phenomena, if our minds were not completely satisfied with the direct proof set forth in the Trancendental Aesthetic. The proof would proceed in the following dilemma. If the world is a whole existing in itself, it must be either finite or infinite. But it is neither finite nor infinite — as has been shown, on the one side, by the thesis, on the other, by the antithesis. Therefore the world — the content of all phenomena — is not a whole existing in itself. It follows that phenomena are nothing, apart from our representations. And this is what we mean by transcendental ideality.

This remark is of some importance. It enables us to see that the proofs of the fourfold antinomy are not mere sophistries — are not fallacious, but grounded on the nature of reason, and valid — under the supposition that phenomena are things in themselves. The opposition of the judgements which follow makes it evident that a fallacy lay in the initial supposition, and thus helps us to discover the true constitution of objects of sense. This transcendental dialectic does not favour scepticism, although it presents us with a triumphant demonstration of the advantages of the sceptical method, the great utility of which is apparent in the antinomy, where the arguments of reason were allowed to confront each other in undiminished force. And although the result of these conflicts of reason is not what we expected — although we have obtained no positive dogmatical addition to metaphysical science — we have still reaped a great advantage in the correction of our judgements on these subjects of thought.

SECTION VIII. Regulative Principle of Pure Reason in relation to the Cosmological Ideas.

The cosmological principle of totality could not give us any certain knowledge in regard to the maximum in the series of conditions in the world of sense, considered as a thing in itself. The actual regress in the series is the only means of approaching this maximum. This principle of pure reason, therefore, may still be considered as valid — not as an axiom enabling us to cogitate totality in the object as actual, but as a problem for the understanding, which requires it to institute and to continue, in conformity with the idea of totality in the mind, the regress in the series of the conditions of a given conditioned. For in the world of sense, that is, in space and time, every condition which we discover in our investigation of phenomena is itself conditioned; because sensuous objects are not things in themselves (in which case an absolutely unconditioned might be reached in the progress of cognition), but are merely empirical representations the conditions of which must always be found in intuition. The principle of reason is therefore properly a mere rule — prescribing a regress in the series of conditions for given phenomena, and prohibiting any pause or rest on an absolutely unconditioned. It is, therefore, not a principle of the possibility of experience or of the empirical cognition of sensuous objects — consequently not a principle of the understanding; for every experience is confined within certain proper limits determined by the given intuition. Still less is it a constitutive principle of reason authorizing us to extend our conception of the sensuous world beyond all possible experience. It is merely a principle for the enlargement and extension of experience as far as is possible for human faculties. It forbids us to consider any empirical limits as absolute. It is, hence, a principle of reason, which, as a rule, dictates how we ought to proceed in our empirical regress, but is unable to anticipate or indicate prior to the empirical regress what is given in the object itself. I have termed it for this reason a regulative principle of reason; while the principle of the absolute totality of the series of conditions, as existing in itself and given in the object, is a constitutive cosmological principle. This distinction will at once demonstrate the falsehood of the constitutive principle, and prevent us from attributing (by a transcendental subreptio) objective reality to an idea, which is valid only as a rule.

In order to understand the proper meaning of this rule of pure reason, we must notice first that it cannot tell us what the object is, but only how the empirical regress is to be proceeded with in order to attain to the complete conception of the object. If it gave us any information in respect to the former statement, it would be a constitutive principle — a principle impossible from the nature of pure reason. It will not therefore enable us to establish any such conclusions as: "The series of conditions for a given conditioned is in itself finite," or, "It is infinite." For, in this case, we should be cogitating in the mere idea of absolute totality, an object which is not and cannot be given in experience; inasmuch as we should be attributing a reality objective and independent of the empirical synthesis, to a series of phenomena. This idea of reason cannot then be regarded as valid — except as a rule for the regressive synthesis in the series of conditions, according to which we must proceed from the conditioned, through all intermediate and subordinate conditions, up to the unconditioned; although this goal is unattained and unattainable. For the absolutely unconditioned cannot be discovered in the sphere of experience.

We now proceed to determine clearly our notion of a synthesis which can never be complete. There are two terms commonly employed for this purpose. These terms are regarded as expressions of different and distinguishable notions, although the ground of the distinction has never been clearly exposed. The term employed by the mathematicians is progressus in infinitum. The philosophers prefer the expression progressus in indefinitum. Without detaining the reader with an examination of the reasons for such a distinction, or with remarks on the right or wrong use of the terms, I shall endeavour clearly to determine these conceptions, so far as is necessary for the purpose in this Critique.

We may, with propriety, say of a straight line, that it may be produced to infinity. In this case the distinction between a progressus in infinitum and a progressus in indefinitum is a mere piece of subtlety. For, although when we say, "Produce a straight line," it is more correct to say in indefinitum than in infinitum; because the former means, "Produce it as far as you please," the second, "You must not cease to produce it"; the expression in infinitum is, when we are speaking of the power to do it, perfectly correct, for we can always make it longer if we please — on to infinity.

And this remark holds good in all cases, when we speak of a progressus, that is, an advancement from the condition to the conditioned; this possible advancement always proceeds to infinity. We may proceed from a given pair in the descending line of generation from father to son, and cogitate a never-ending line of descendants from it. For in such a case reason does not demand absolute totality in the series, because it does not presuppose it as a condition and as given (datum), but merely as conditioned, and as capable of being given (dabile).

Very different is the case with the problem: "How far the regress, which ascends from the given conditioned to the conditions, must extend"; whether I can say: "It is a regress in infinitum," or only "in indefinitum"; and whether, for example, setting out from the human beings at present alive in the world, I may ascend in the series of their ancestors, in infinitum — mr whether all that can be said is, that so far as I have proceeded, I have discovered no empirical ground for considering the series limited, so that I am justified, and indeed, compelled to search for ancestors still further back, although I am not obliged by the idea of reason to presuppose them.

My answer to this question is: "If the series is given in empirical intuition as a whole, the regress in the series of its internal conditions proceeds in infinitum; but, if only one member of the series is given, from which the regress is to proceed to absolute totality, the regress is possible only in indefinitum." For example, the division of a portion of matter given within certain limits — of a body, that is — proceeds in infinitum. For, as the condition of this whole is its part, and the condition of the part a part of the part, and so on, and as in this regress of decomposition an unconditioned indivisible member of the series of conditions is not to be found; there are no reasons or grounds in experience for stopping in the division, but, on the contrary, the more remote members of the division are actually and empirically given prior to this division. That is to say, the division proceeds to infinity. On the other hand, the series of ancestors of any given human being is not given, in its absolute totality, in any experience, and yet the regress proceeds from every genealogical member of this series to one still higher, and does not meet with any empirical limit presenting an absolutely unconditioned member of the series. But as the members of such a series are not contained in the empirical intuition of the whole, prior to the regress, this regress does not proceed to infinity, but only in indefinitum, that is, we are called upon to discover other and higher members, which are themselves always conditioned.

In neither case — the regressus in infinitum, nor the regressus in indefinitum, is the series of conditions to be considered as actually infinite in the object itself. This might be true of things in themselves, but it cannot be asserted of phenomena, which, as conditions of each other, are only given in the empirical regress itself. Hence, the question no longer is, "What is the quantity of this series of conditions in itself — is it finite or infinite?" for it is nothing in itself; but, "How is the empirical regress to be commenced, and how far ought we to proceed with it?" And here a signal distinction in the application of this rule becomes apparent. If the whole is given empirically, it is possible to recede in the series of its internal conditions to infinity. But if the whole is not given, and can only be given by and through the empirical regress, I can only say: "It is possible to infinity, to proceed to still higher conditions in the series." In the first case, I am justified in asserting that more members are empirically given in the object than I attain to in the regress (of decomposition). In the second case, I am justified only in saying, that I can always proceed further in the regress, because no member of the series is given as absolutely conditioned, and thus a higher member is possible, and an inquiry with regard to it is necessary. In the one case it is necessary to find other members of the series, in the other it is necessary to inquire for others, inasmuch as experience presents no absolute limitation of the regress. For, either you do not possess a perception which absolutely limits your empirical regress, and in this case the regress cannot be regarded as complete; or, you do possess such a limitative perception, in which case it is not a part of your series (for that which limits must be distinct from that which is limited by it), and it is incumbent you to continue your regress up to this condition, and so on.

These remarks will be placed in their proper light by their application in the following section.

SECTION IX. Of the Empirical Use of the Regulative Principle of Reason with regard to the Cosmological Ideas.

We have shown that no transcendental use can be made either of the conceptions of reason or of understanding. We have shown, likewise, that the demand of absolute totality in the series of conditions in the world of sense arises from a transcendental employment of reason, resting on the opinion that phenomena are to be regarded as things in themselves. It follows that we are not required to answer the question respecting the absolute quantity of a series — whether it is in itself limited or unlimited. We are only called upon to determine how far we must proceed in the empirical regress from condition to condition, in order to discover, in conformity with the rule of reason, a full and correct answer to the questions proposed by reason itself.

This principle of reason is hence valid only as a rule for the extension of a possible experience — its invalidity as a principle constitutive of phenomena in themselves having been sufficiently demonstrated. And thus, too, the antinomial conflict of reason with itself is completely put an end to; inasmuch as we have not only presented a critical solution of the fallacy lurking in the opposite statements of reason, but have shown the true meaning of the ideas which gave rise to these statements. The dialectical principle of reason has, therefore, been changed into a doctrinal principle. But in fact, if this principle, in the subjective signification which we have shown to be its only true sense, may be guaranteed as a principle of the unceasing extension of the employment of our understanding, its influence and value are just as great as if it were an axiom for the a priori determination of objects. For such an axiom could not exert a stronger influence on the extension and rectification of our knowledge, otherwise than by procuring for the principles of the understanding the most widely expanded employment in the field of experience.

I. Solution of the Cosmological Idea of the Totality of the Composition of Phenomena in the Universe.

Here, as well as in the case of the other cosmological problems, the ground of the regulative principle of reason is the proposition that in our empirical regress no experience of an absolute limit, and consequently no experience of a condition, which is itself absolutely unconditioned, is discoverable. And the truth of this proposition itself rests upon the consideration that such an experience must represent to us phenomena as limited by nothing or the mere void, on which our continued regress by means of perception must abut — which is impossible.

Now this proposition, which declares that every condition attained in the empirical regress must itself be considered empirically conditioned, contains the rule in terminis, which requires me, to whatever extent I may have proceeded in the ascending series, always to look for some higher member in the series — whether this member is to become known to me through experience, or not.

Nothing further is necessary, then, for the solution of the first cosmological problem, than to decide, whether, in the regress to the unconditioned quantity of the universe (as regards space and time), this never limited ascent ought to be called a regressus in infinitum or indefinitum.

The general representation which we form in our minds of the series of all past states or conditions of the world, or of all the things which at present exist in it, is itself nothing more than a possible empirical regress, which is cogitated — although in an undetermined manner — in the mind, and which gives rise to the conception of a series of conditions for a given object.* Now I have a conception of the universe, but not an intuition — that is, not an intuition of it as a whole. Thus I cannot infer the magnitude of the regress from the quantity or magnitude of the world, and determine the former by means of the latter; on the contrary, I must first of all form a conception of the quantity or magnitude of the world from the magnitude of the empirical regress. But of this regress I know nothing more than that I ought to proceed from every given member of the series of conditions to one still higher. But the quantity of the universe is not thereby determined, and we cannot affirm that this regress proceeds in infinitum. Such an affirmation would anticipate the members of the series which have not yet been reached, and represent the number of them as beyond the grasp of any empirical synthesis; it would consequently determine the cosmical quantity prior to the regress (although only in a negative manner) — which is impossible. For the world is not given in its totality in any intuition: consequently, its quantity cannot be given prior to the regress. It follows that we are unable to make any declaration respecting the cosmical quantity in itself — not even that the regress in it is a regress in infinitum; we must only endeavour to attain to a conception of the quantity of the universe, in conformity with the rule which determines the empirical regress in it. But this rule merely requires us never to admit an absolute limit to our series — how far soever we may have proceeded in it, but always, on the contrary, to subordinate every phenomenon to some other as its condition, and consequently to proceed to this higher phenomenon. Such a regress is, therefore, the regressus in indefinitum, which, as not determining a quantity in the object, is clearly distinguishable from the regressus in infinitum.

[Note: The cosmical series can neither be greater nor smaller than the possible empirical regress, upon which its conception is based. And as this regress cannot be a determinate infinite regress, still less a determinate finite (absolutely limited), it is evident that we cannot regard the world as either finite or infinite, because the regress, which gives us the representation of the world, is neither finite nor infinite.]

It follows from what we have said that we are not justified in declaring the world to be infinite in space, or as regards past time. For this conception of an infinite given quantity is empirical; but we cannot apply the conception of an infinite quantity to the world as an object of the senses. I cannot say, "The regress from a given perception to everything limited either in space or time, proceeds in infinitum," for this presupposes an infinite cosmical quantity; neither can I say, "It is finite," for an absolute limit is likewise impossible in experience. It follows that I am not entitled to make any assertion at all respecting the whole object of experience — the world of sense; I must limit my declarations to the rule according to which experience or empirical knowledge is to be attained.

To the question, therefore, respecting the cosmical quantity, the first and negative answer is: "The world has no beginning in time, and no absolute limit in space."

For, in the contrary case, it would be limited by a void time on the one hand, and by a void space on the other. Now, since the world, as a phenomenon, cannot be thus limited in itself for a phenomenon is not a thing in itself; it must be possible for us to have a perception of this limitation by a void time and a void space. But such a perception — such an experience is impossible; because it has no content. Consequently, an absolute cosmical limit is empirically, and therefore absolutely, impossible.*

[Note: The reader will remark that the proof presented above is very different from the dogmatical demonstration given in the antithesis of the first antinomy. In that demonstration, it was taken for granted that the world is a thing in itself — given in its totality prior to all regress, and a determined position in space and time was denied to it — if it was not considered as occupying all time and all space. Hence our conclusion differed from that given above; for we inferred in the antithesis the actual infinity of the world.]

From this follows the affirmative answer: "The regress in the series of phenomena — as a determination of the cosmical quantity, proceeds in indefinitum." This is equivalent to saying: "The world of sense has no absolute quantity, but the empirical regress (through which alone the world of sense is presented to us on the side of its conditions) rests upon a rule, which requires it to proceed from every member of the series, as conditioned, to one still more remote (whether through personal experience, or by means of history, or the chain of cause and effect), and not to cease at any point in this extension of the possible empirical employment of the understanding." And this is the proper and only use which reason can make of its principles.

The above rule does not prescribe an unceasing regress in one kind of phenomena. It does not, for example, forbid us, in our ascent from an individual human being through the line of his ancestors, to expect that we shall discover at some point of the regress a primeval pair, or to admit, in the series of heavenly bodies, a sun at the farthest possible distance from some centre. All that it demands is a perpetual progress from phenomena to phenomena, even although an actual perception is not presented by them (as in the case of our perceptions being so weak as that we are unable to become conscious of them), since they, nevertheless, belong to possible experience.

Every beginning is in time, and all limits to extension are in space. But space and time are in the world of sense. Consequently phenomena in the world are conditionally limited, but the world itself is not limited, either conditionally or unconditionally.

For this reason, and because neither the world nor the cosmical series of conditions to a given conditioned can be completely given, our conception of the cosmical quantity is given only in and through the regress and not prior to it — in a collective intuition. But the regress itself is really nothing more than the determining of the cosmical quantity, and cannot therefore give us any determined conception of it — still less a conception of a quantity which is, in relation to a certain standard, infinite. The regress does not, therefore, proceed to infinity (an infinity given), but only to an indefinite extent, for or the of presenting to us a quantity — realized only in and through the regress itself.

II. Solution of the Cosmological Idea of the Totality of the Division of a Whole given in Intuition.

When I divide a whole which is given in intuition, I proceed from a conditioned to its conditions. The division of the parts of the whole (subdivisio or decompositio) is a regress in the series of these conditions. The absolute totality of this series would be actually attained and given to the mind, if the regress could arrive at simple parts. But if all the parts in a continuous decomposition are themselves divisible, the division, that is to say, the regress, proceeds from the conditioned to its conditions in infinitum; because the conditions (the parts) are themselves contained in the conditioned, and, as the latter is given in a limited intuition, the former are all given along with it. This regress cannot, therefore, be called a regressus in indefinitum, as happened in the case of the preceding cosmological idea, the regress in which proceeded from the conditioned to the conditions not given contemporaneously and along with it, but discoverable only through the empirical regress. We are not, however, entitled to affirm of a whole of this kind, which is divisible in infinitum, that it consists of an infinite number of parts. For, although all the parts are contained in the intuition of the whole, the whole division is not contained therein. The division is contained only in the progressing decomposition — in the regress itself, which is the condition of the possibility and actuality of the series. Now, as this regress is infinite, all the members (parts) to which it attains must be contained in the given whole as an aggregate. But the complete series of division is not contained therein. For this series, being infinite in succession and always incomplete, cannot represent an infinite number of members, and still less a composition of these members into a whole.

To apply this remark to space. Every limited part of space presented to intuition is a whole, the parts of which are always spaces — to whatever extent subdivided. Every limited space is hence divisible to infinity.

Let us again apply the remark to an external phenomenon enclosed in limits, that is, a body. The divisibility of a body rests upon the divisibility of space, which is the condition of the possibility of the body as an extended whole. A body is consequently divisible to infinity, though it does not, for that reason, consist of an infinite number of parts.

It certainly seems that, as a body must be cogitated as substance in space, the law of divisibility would not be applicable to it as substance. For we may and ought to grant, in the case of space, that division or decomposition, to any extent, never can utterly annihilate composition (that is to say, the smallest part of space must still consist of spaces); otherwise space would entirely cease to exist — which is impossible. But, the assertion on the other band that when all composition in matter is annihilated in thought, nothing remains, does not seem to harmonize with the conception of substance, which must be properly the subject of all composition and must remain, even after the conjunction of its attributes in space — which constituted a body — is annihilated in thought. But this is not the case with substance in the phenomenal world, which is not a thing in itself cogitated by the pure category. Phenomenal substance is not an absolute subject; it is merely a permanent sensuous image, and nothing more than an intuition, in which the unconditioned is not to be found.

But, although this rule of progress to infinity is legitimate and applicable to the subdivision of a phenomenon, as a mere occupation or filling of space, it is not applicable to a whole consisting of a number of distinct parts and constituting a quantum discretum — that is to say, an organized body. It cannot be admitted that every part in an organized whole is itself organized, and that, in analysing it to infinity, we must always meet with organized parts; although we may allow that the parts of the matter which we decompose in infinitum, may be organized. For the infinity of the division of a phenomenon in space rests altogether on the fact that the divisibility of a phenomenon is given only in and through this infinity, that is, an undetermined number of parts is given, while the parts themselves are given and determined only in and through the subdivision; in a word, the infinity of the division necessarily presupposes that the whole is not already divided in se. Hence our division determines a number of parts in the whole — a number which extends just as far as the actual regress in the division; while, on the other hand, the very notion of a body organized to infinity represents the whole as already and in itself divided. We expect, therefore, to find in it a determinate, but at the same time, infinite, number of parts — which is self-contradictory. For we should thus have a whole containing a series of members which could not be completed in any regress — which is infinite, and at the same time complete in an organized composite. Infinite divisibility is applicable only to a quantum continuum, and is based entirely on the infinite divisibility of space, But in a quantum discretum the multitude of parts or units is always determined, and hence always equal to some number. To what extent a body may be organized, experience alone can inform us; and although, so far as our experience of this or that body has extended, we may not have discovered any inorganic part, such parts must exist in possible experience. But how far the transcendental division of a phenomenon must extend, we cannot know from experience — it is a question which experience cannot answer; it is answered only by the principle of reason which forbids us to consider the empirical regress, in the analysis of extended body, as ever absolutely complete.

Concluding Remark on the Solution of the Transcendental Mathematical Ideas — and Introductory to the Solution of the Dynamical Ideas.

We presented the antinomy of pure reason in a tabular form, and we endeavoured to show the ground of this self-contradiction on the part of reason, and the only means of bringing it to a conclusion — namely, by declaring both contradictory statements to be false. We represented in these antinomies the conditions of phenomena as belonging to the conditioned according to relations of space and time — which is the usual supposition of the common understanding. In this respect, all dialectical representations of totality, in the series of conditions to a given conditioned, were perfectly homogeneous. The condition was always a member of the series along with the conditioned, and thus the homogeneity of the whole series was assured. In this case the regress could never be cogitated as complete; or, if this was the case, a member really conditioned was falsely regarded as a primal member, consequently as unconditioned. In such an antinomy, therefore, we did not consider the object, that is, the conditioned, but the series of conditions belonging to the object, and the magnitude of that series. And thus arose the difficulty — a difficulty not to be settled by any decision regarding the claims of the two parties, but simply by cutting the knot — by declaring the series proposed by reason to be either too long or too short for the understanding, which could in neither case make its conceptions adequate with the ideas.

But we have overlooked, up to this point, an essential difference existing between the conceptions of the understanding which reason endeavours to raise to the rank of ideas — two of these indicating a mathematical, and two a dynamical synthesis of phenomena. Hitherto, it was necessary to signalize this distinction; for, just as in our general representation of all transcendental ideas, we considered them under phenomenal conditions, so, in the two mathematical ideas, our discussion is concerned solely with an object in the world of phenomena. But as we are now about to proceed to the consideration of the dynamical conceptions of the understanding, and their adequateness with ideas, we must not lose sight of this distinction. We shall find that it opens up to us an entirely new view of the conflict in which reason is involved. For, while in the first two antinomies, both parties were dismissed, on the ground of having advanced statements based upon false hypothesis; in the present case the hope appears of discovering a hypothesis which may be consistent with the demands of reason, and, the judge completing the statement of the grounds of claim, which both parties had left in an unsatisfactory state, the question may be settled on its own merits, not by dismissing the claimants, but by a comparison of the arguments on both sides. If we consider merely their extension, and whether they are adequate with ideas, the series of conditions may be regarded as all homogeneous. But the conception of the understanding which lies at the basis of these ideas, contains either a synthesis of the homogeneous (presupposed in every quantity — in its composition as well as in its division) or of the heterogeneous, which is the case in the dynamical synthesis of cause and effect, as well as of the necessary and the contingent.

Thus it happens that in the mathematical series of phenomena no other than a sensuous condition is admissible — a condition which is itself a member of the series; while the dynamical series of sensuous conditions admits a heterogeneous condition, which is not a member of the series, but, as purely intelligible, lies out of and beyond it. And thus reason is satisfied, and an unconditioned placed at the head of the series of phenomena, without introducing confusion into or discontinuing it, contrary to the principles of the understanding.

Now, from the fact that the dynamical ideas admit a condition of phenomena which does not form a part of the series of phenomena, arises a result which we should not have expected from an antinomy. In former cases, the result was that both contradictory dialectical statements were declared to be false. In the present case, we find the conditioned in the dynamical series connected with an empirically unconditioned, but non-sensuous condition; and thus satisfaction is done to the understanding on the one hand and to the reason on the other.* While, moreover, the dialectical arguments for unconditioned totality in mere phenomena fall to the ground, both propositions of reason may be shown to be true in their proper signification. This could not happen in the case of the cosmological ideas which demanded a mathematically unconditioned unity; for no condition could be placed at the head of the series of phenomena, except one which was itself a phenomenon and consequently a member of the series.

[Note: For the understanding cannot admit among phenomena a condition which is itself empirically unconditioned. But if it is possible to cogitate an intelligible condition — one which is not a member of the series of phenomena — for a conditioned phenomenon, without breaking the series of empirical conditions, such a condition may be admissible as empirically unconditioned, and the empirical regress continue regular, unceasing, and intact.]

III. Solution of the Cosmological Idea of the Totality of the Deduction of Cosmical Events from their Causes.

There are only two modes of causality cogitable — the causality of nature or of freedom. The first is the conjunction of a particular state with another preceding it in the world of sense, the former following the latter by virtue of a law. Now, as the causality of phenomena is subject to conditions of time, and the preceding state, if it had always existed, could not have produced an effect which would make its first appearance at a particular time, the causality of a cause must itself be an effect — must itself have begun to be, and therefore, according to the principle of the understanding, itself requires a cause.

We must understand, on the contrary, by the term freedom, in the cosmological sense, a faculty of the spontaneous origination of a state; the causality of which, therefore, is not subordinated to another cause determining it in time. Freedom is in this sense a pure transcendental idea, which, in the first place, contains no empirical element; the object of which, in the second place, cannot be given or determined in any experience, because it is a universal law of the very possibility of experience, that everything which happens must have a cause, that consequently the causality of a cause, being itself something that has happened, must also have a cause. In this view of the case, the whole field of experience, how far soever it may extend, contains nothing that is not subject to the laws of nature. But, as we cannot by this means attain to an absolute totality of conditions in reference to the series of causes and effects, reason creates the idea of a spontaneity, which can begin to act of itself, and without any external cause determining it to action, according to the natural law of causality.

It is especially remarkable that the practical conception of freedom is based upon the transcendental idea, and that the question of the possibility of the former is difficult only as it involves the consideration of the truth of the latter. Freedom, in the practical sense, is the independence of the will of coercion by sensuous impulses. A will is sensuous, in so far as it is pathologically affected (by sensuous impulses); it is termed animal (arbitrium brutum), when it is pathologically necessitated. The human will is certainly an arbitrium sensitivum, not brutum, but liberum; because sensuousness does not necessitate its action, a faculty existing in man of self-determination, independently of all sensuous coercion.

It is plain that, if all causality in the world of sense were natural — and natural only — every event would be determined by another according to necessary laws, and that, consequently, phenomena, in so far as they determine the will, must necessitate every action as a natural effect from themselves; and thus all practical freedom would fall to the ground with the transcendental idea. For the latter presupposes that although a certain thing has not happened, it ought to have happened, and that, consequently, its phenomenal cause was not so powerful and determinative as to exclude the causality of our will — a causality capable of producing effects independently of and even in opposition to the power of natural causes, and capable, consequently, of spontaneously originating a series of events.

Here, too, we find it to be the case, as we generally found in the self-contradictions and perplexities of a reason which strives to pass the bounds of possible experience, that the problem is properly not physiological, but transcendental. The question of the possibility of freedom does indeed concern psychology; but, as it rests upon dialectical arguments of pure reason, its solution must engage the attention of transcendental philosophy. Before attempting this solution, a task which transcendental philosophy cannot decline, it will be advisable to make a remark with regard to its procedure in the settlement of the question.

If phenomena were things in themselves, and time and space forms of the existence of things, condition and conditioned would always be members of the same series; and thus would arise in the present case the antinomy common to all transcendental ideas — that their series is either too great or too small for the understanding. The dynamical ideas, which we are about to discuss in this and the following section, possess the peculiarity of relating to an object, not considered as a quantity, but as an existence; and thus, in the discussion of the present question, we may make abstraction of the quantity of the series of conditions, and consider merely the dynamical relation of the condition to the conditioned. The question, then, suggests itself, whether freedom is possible; and, if it is, whether it can consist with the universality of the natural law of causality; and, consequently, whether we enounce a proper disjunctive proposition when we say: "Every effect must have its origin either in nature or in freedom," or whether both cannot exist together in the same event in different relations. The principle of an unbroken connection between all events in the phenomenal world, in accordance with the unchangeable laws of nature, is a well-established principle of transcendental analytic which admits of no exception. The question, therefore, is: "Whether an effect, determined according to the laws of nature, can at the same time be produced by a free agent, or whether freedom and nature mutually exclude each other?" And here, the common but fallacious hypothesis of the absolute reality of phenomena manifests its injurious influence in embarrassing the procedure of reason. For if phenomena are things in themselves, freedom is impossible. In this case, nature is the complete and all-sufficient cause of every event; and condition and conditioned, cause and effect are contained in the same series, and necessitated by the same law. If, on the contrary, phenomena are held to be, as they are in fact, nothing more than mere representations, connected with each other in accordance with empirical laws, they must have a ground which is not phenomenal. But the causality of such an intelligible cause is not determined or determinable by phenomena; although its effects, as phenomena, must be determined by other phenomenal existences. This cause and its causality exist therefore out of and apart from the series of phenomena; while its effects do exist and are discoverable in the series of empirical conditions. Such an effect may therefore be considered to be free in relation to its intelligible cause, and necessary in relation to the phenomena from which it is a necessary consequence — a distinction which, stated in this perfectly general and abstract manner, must appear in the highest degree subtle and obscure. The sequel will explain. It is sufficient, at present, to remark that, as the complete and unbroken connection of phenomena is an unalterable law of nature, freedom is impossible — on the supposition that phenomena are absolutely real. Hence those philosophers who adhere to the common opinion on this subject can never succeed in reconciling the ideas of nature and freedom.

Possibility of Freedom in Harmony with the Universal Law of Natural Necessity.

That element in a sensuous object which is not itself sensuous, I may be allowed to term intelligible. If, accordingly, an object which must be regarded as a sensuous phenomenon possesses a faculty which is not an object of sensuous intuition, but by means of which it is capable of being the cause of phenomena, the causality of an object or existence of this kind may be regarded from two different points of view. It may be considered to be intelligible, as regards its action — the action of a thing which is a thing in itself, and sensuous, as regards its effects — the effects of a phenomenon belonging to the sensuous world. We should accordingly, have to form both an empirical and an intellectual conception of the causality of such a faculty or power — both, however, having reference to the same effect. This twofold manner of cogitating a power residing in a sensuous object does not run counter to any of the conceptions which we ought to form of the world of phenomena or of a possible experience. Phenomena — not being things in themselves — must have a transcendental object as a foundation, which determines them as mere representations; and there seems to be no reason why we should not ascribe to this transcendental object, in addition to the property of self-phenomenization, a causality whose effects are to be met with in the world of phenomena, although it is not itself a phenomenon. But every effective cause must possess a character, that is to say, a law of its causality, without which it would cease to be a cause. In the above case, then, every sensuous object would possess an empirical character, which guaranteed that its actions, as phenomena, stand in complete and harmonious connection, conformably to unvarying natural laws, with all other phenomena, and can be deduced from these, as conditions, and that they do thus, in connection with these, constitute a series in the order of nature. This sensuous object must, in the second place, possess an intelligible character, which guarantees it to be the cause of those actions, as phenomena, although it is not itself a phenomenon nor subordinate to the conditions of the world of sense. The former may be termed the character of the thing as a phenomenon, the latter the character of the thing as a thing in itself.

Now this active subject would, in its character of intelligible subject, be subordinate to no conditions of time, for time is only a condition of phenomena, and not of things in themselves. No action would begin or cease to be in this subject; it would consequently be free from the law of all determination of time — the law of change, namely, that everything which happens must have a cause in the phenomena of a preceding state. In one word, the causality of the subject, in so far as it is intelligible, would not form part of the series of empirical conditions which determine and necessitate an event in the world of sense. Again, this intelligible character of a thing cannot be immediately cognized, because we can perceive nothing but phenomena, but it must be capable of being cogitated in harmony with the empirical character; for we always find ourselves compelled to place, in thought, a transcendental object at the basis of phenomena although we can never know what this object is in itself.

In virtue of its empirical character, this subject would at the same time be subordinate to all the empirical laws of causality, and, as a phenomenon and member of the sensuous world, its effects would have to be accounted for by a reference to preceding phenomena. Eternal phenomena must be capable of influencing it; and its actions, in accordance with natural laws, must explain to us how its empirical character, that is, the law of its causality, is to be cognized in and by means of experience. In a word, all requisites for a complete and necessary determination of these actions must be presented to us by experience.

In virtue of its intelligible character, on the other hand (although we possess only a general conception of this character), the subject must be regarded as free from all sensuous influences, and from all phenomenal determination. Moreover, as nothing happens in this subject — for it is a noumenon, and there does not consequently exist in it any change, demanding the dynamical determination of time, and for the same reason no connection with phenomena as causes — this active existence must in its actions be free from and independent of natural necessity, for or necessity exists only in the world of phenomena. It would be quite correct to say that it originates or begins its effects in the world of sense from itself, although the action productive of these effects does not begin in itself. We should not be in this case affirming that these sensuous effects began to exist of themselves, because they are always determined by prior empirical conditions — by virtue of the empirical character, which is the phenomenon of the intelligible character — and are possible only as constituting a continuation of the series of natural causes. And thus nature and freedom, each in the complete and absolute signification of these terms, can exist, without contradiction or disagreement, in the same action.

Exposition of the Cosmological Idea of Freedom in Harmony with the Universal Law of Natural Necessity.

I have thought it advisable to lay before the reader at first merely a sketch of the solution of this transcendental problem, in order to enable him to form with greater ease a clear conception of the course which reason must adopt in the solution. I shall now proceed to exhibit the several momenta of this solution, and to consider them in their order.

The natural law that everything which happens must have a cause, that the causality of this cause, that is, the action of the cause (which cannot always have existed, but must be itself an event, for it precedes in time some effect which it has originated), must have itself a phenomenal cause, by which it is determined and, and, consequently, all events are empirically determined in an order of nature — this law, I say, which lies at the foundation of the possibility of experience, and of a connected system of phenomena or nature is a law of the understanding, from which no departure, and to which no exception, can be admitted. For to except even a single phenomenon from its operation is to exclude it from the sphere of possible experience and thus to admit it to be a mere fiction of thought or phantom of the brain.

Thus we are obliged to acknowledge the existence of a chain of causes, in which, however, absolute totality cannot be found. But we need not detain ourselves with this question, for it has already been sufficiently answered in our discussion of the antinomies into which reason falls, when it attempts to reach the unconditioned in the series of phenomena. If we permit ourselves to be deceived by the illusion of transcendental idealism, we shall find that neither nature nor freedom exists. Now the question is: "Whether, admitting the existence of natural necessity in the world of phenomena, it is possible to consider an effect as at the same time an effect of nature and an effect of freedom — or, whether these two modes of causality are contradictory and incompatible?"

No phenomenal cause can absolutely and of itself begin a series. Every action, in so far as it is productive of an event, is itself an event or occurrence, and presupposes another preceding state, in which its cause existed. Thus everything that happens is but a continuation of a series, and an absolute beginning is impossible in the sensuous world. The actions of natural causes are, accordingly, themselves effects, and presuppose causes preceding them in time. A primal action which forms an absolute beginning, is beyond the causal power of phenomena.

Now, is it absolutely necessary that, granting that all effects are phenomena, the causality of the cause of these effects must also be a phenomenon and belong to the empirical world? Is it not rather possible that, although every effect in the phenomenal world must be connected with an empirical cause, according to the universal law of nature, this empirical causality may be itself the effect of a non-empirical and intelligible causality — its connection with natural causes remaining nevertheless intact? Such a causality would be considered, in reference to phenomena, as the primal action of a cause, which is in so far, therefore, not phenomenal, but, by reason of this faculty or power, intelligible; although it must, at the same time, as a link in the chain of nature, be regarded as belonging to the sensuous world.

A belief in the reciprocal causality of phenomena is necessary, if we are required to look for and to present the natural conditions of natural events, that is to say, their causes. This being admitted as unexceptionably valid, the requirements of the understanding, which recognizes nothing but nature in the region of phenomena, are satisfied, and our physical explanations of physical phenomena may proceed in their regular course, without hindrance and without opposition. But it is no stumbling-block in the way, even assuming the idea to be a pure fiction, to admit that there are some natural causes in the possession of a faculty which is not empirical, but intelligible, inasmuch as it is not determined to action by empirical conditions, but purely and solely upon grounds brought forward by the understanding — this action being still, when the cause is phenomenized, in perfect accordance with the laws of empirical causality. Thus the acting subject, as a causal phenomenon, would continue to preserve a complete connection with nature and natural conditions; and the phenomenon only of the subject (with all its phenomenal causality) would contain certain conditions, which, if we ascend from the empirical to the transcendental object, must necessarily be regarded as intelligible. For, if we attend, in our inquiries with regard to causes in the world of phenomena, to the directions of nature alone, we need not trouble ourselves about the relation in which the transcendental subject, which is completely unknown to us, stands to these phenomena and their connection in nature. The intelligible ground of phenomena in this subject does not concern empirical questions. It has to do only with pure thought; and, although the effects of this thought and action of the pure understanding are discoverable in phenomena, these phenomena must nevertheless be capable of a full and complete explanation, upon purely physical grounds and in accordance with natural laws. And in this case we attend solely to their empirical and omit all consideration of their intelligible character (which is the transcendental cause of the former) as completely unknown, except in so far as it is exhibited by the latter as its empirical symbol. Now let us apply this to experience. Man is a phenomenon of the sensuous world and, at the same time, therefore, a natural cause, the causality of which must be regulated by empirical laws. As such, he must possess an empirical character, like all other natural phenomena. We remark this empirical character in his actions, which reveal the presence of certain powers and faculties. If we consider inanimate or merely animal nature, we can discover no reason for ascribing to ourselves any other than a faculty which is determined in a purely sensuous manner. But man, to whom nature reveals herself only through sense, cognizes himself not only by his senses, but also through pure apperception; and this in actions and internal determinations, which he cannot regard as sensuous impressions. He is thus to himself, on the one hand, a phenomenon, but on the other hand, in respect of certain faculties, a purely intelligible object — intelligible, because its action cannot be ascribed to sensuous receptivity. These faculties are understanding and reason. The latter, especially, is in a peculiar manner distinct from all empirically-conditioned faculties, for it employs ideas alone in the consideration of its objects, and by means of these determines the understanding, which then proceeds to make an empirical use of its own conceptions, which, like the ideas of reason, are pure and non-empirical.

That reason possesses the faculty of causality, or that at least we are compelled so to represent it, is evident from the imperatives, which in the sphere of the practical we impose on many of our executive powers. The words I ought express a species of necessity, and imply a connection with grounds which nature does not and cannot present to the mind of man. Understanding knows nothing in nature but that which is, or has been, or will be. It would be absurd to say that anything in nature ought to be other than it is in the relations of time in which it stands; indeed, the ought, when we consider merely the course of nature, has neither application nor meaning. The question, "What ought to happen in the sphere of nature?" is just as absurd as the question, "What ought to be the properties of a circle?" All that we are entitled to ask is, "What takes place in nature?" or, in the latter case, "What are the properties of a circle?"

But the idea of an ought or of duty indicates a possible action, the ground of which is a pure conception; while the ground of a merely natural action is, on the contrary, always a phenomenon. This action must certainly be possible under physical conditions, if it is prescribed by the moral imperative ought; but these physical or natural conditions do not concern the determination of the will itself, they relate to its effects alone, and the consequences of the effect in the world of phenomena. Whatever number of motives nature may present to my will, whatever sensuous impulses — the moral ought it is beyond their power to produce. They may produce a volition, which, so far from being necessary, is always conditioned — a volition to which the ought enunciated by reason, sets an aim and a standard, gives permission or prohibition. Be the object what it may, purely sensuous — as pleasure, or presented by pure reason — as good, reason will not yield to grounds which have an empirical origin. Reason will not follow the order of things presented by experience, but, with perfect spontaneity, rearranges them according to ideas, with which it compels empirical conditions to agree. It declares, in the name of these ideas, certain actions to be necessary which nevertheless have not taken place and which perhaps never will take place; and yet presupposes that it possesses the faculty of causality in relation to these actions. For, in the absence of this supposition, it could not expect its ideas to produce certain effects in the world of experience.

Now, let us stop here and admit it to be at least possible that reason does stand in a really causal relation to phenomena. In this case it must — pure reason as it is — exhibit an empirical character. For every cause supposes a rule, according to which certain phenomena follow as effects from the cause, and every rule requires uniformity in these effects; and this is the proper ground of the conception of a cause — as a faculty or power. Now this conception (of a cause) may be termed the empirical character of reason; and this character is a permanent one, while the effects produced appear, in conformity with the various conditions which accompany and partly limit them, in various forms.

Thus the volition of every man has an empirical character, which is nothing more than the causality of his reason, in so far as its effects in the phenomenal world manifest the presence of a rule, according to which we are enabled to examine, in their several kinds and degrees, the actions of this causality and the rational grounds for these actions, and in this way to decide upon the subjective principles of the volition. Now we learn what this empirical character is only from phenomenal effects, and from the rule of these which is presented by experience; and for this reason all the actions of man in the world of phenomena are determined by his empirical character, and the co-operative causes of nature. If, then, we could investigate all the phenomena of human volition to their lowest foundation in the mind, there would be no action which we could not anticipate with certainty, and recognize to be absolutely necessary from its preceding conditions. So far as relates to this empirical character, therefore, there can be no freedom; and it is only in the light of this character that we can consider the human will, when we confine ourselves to simple observation and, as is the case in anthropology, institute a physiological investigation of the motive causes of human actions.

But when we consider the same actions in relation to reason — not for the purpose of explaining their origin, that is, in relation to speculative reason, but to practical reason, as the producing cause of these actions — we shall discover a rule and an order very different from those of nature and experience. For the declaration of this mental faculty may be that what has and could not but take place in the course of nature, ought not to have taken place. Sometimes, too, we discover, or believe that we discover, that the ideas of reason did actually stand in a causal relation to certain actions of man; and that these actions have taken place because they were determined, not by empirical causes, but by the act of the will upon grounds of reason.

Now, granting that reason stands in a causal relation to phenomena; can an action of reason be called free, when we know that, sensuously, in its empirical character, it is completely determined and absolutely necessary? But this empirical character is itself determined by the intelligible character. The latter we cannot cognize; we can only indicate it by means of phenomena, which enable us to have an immediate cognition only of the empirical character.* An action, then, in so far as it is to be ascribed to an intelligible cause, does not result from it in accordance with empirical laws. That is to say, not the conditions of pure reason, but only their effects in the internal sense, precede the act. Pure reason, as a purely intelligible faculty, is not subject to the conditions of time. The causality of reason in its intelligible character does not begin to be; it does not make its appearance at a certain time, for the purpose of producing an effect. If this were not the case, the causality of reason would be subservient to the natural law of phenomena, which determines them according to time, and as a series of causes and effects in time; it would consequently cease to be freedom and become a part of nature. We are therefore justified in saying: "If reason stands in a causal relation to phenomena, it is a faculty which originates the sensuous condition of an empirical series of effects." For the condition, which resides in the reason, is non-sensuous, and therefore cannot be originated, or begin to be. And thus we find — what we could not discover in any empirical series — a condition of a successive series of events itself empirically unconditioned. For, in the present case, the condition stands out of and beyond the series of phenomena — it is intelligible, and it consequently cannot be subjected to any sensuous condition, or to any time-determination by a preceding cause.

[Note: The real morality of actions — their merit or demerit, and even that of our own conduct, is completely unknown to us. Our estimates can relate only to their empirical character. How much is the result of the action of free will, how much is to be ascribed to nature and to blameless error, or to a happy constitution of temperament (merito fortunae), no one can discover, nor, for this reason, determine with perfect justice.]

But, in another respect, the same cause belongs also to the series of phenomena. Man is himself a phenomenon. His will has an empirical character, which is the empirical cause of all his actions. There is no condition — determining man and his volition in conformity with this character — which does not itself form part of the series of effects in nature, and is subject to their law — the law according to which an empirically undetermined cause of an event in time cannot exist. For this reason no given action can have an absolute and spontaneous origination, all actions being phenomena, and belonging to the world of experience. But it cannot be said of reason, that the state in which it determines the will is always preceded by some other state determining it. For reason is not a phenomenon, and therefore not subject to sensuous conditions;

and, consequently, even in relation to its causality, the sequence or conditions of time do not influence reason, nor can the dynamical law of nature, which determines the sequence of time according to certain rules, be applied to it.

Reason is consequently the permanent condition of all actions of the human will. Each of these is determined in the empirical character of the man, even before it has taken place. The intelligible character, of which the former is but the sensuous schema, knows no before or after; and every action, irrespective of the time-relation in which it stands with other phenomena, is the immediate effect of the intelligible character of pure reason, which, consequently, enjoys freedom of action, and is not dynamically determined either by internal or external preceding conditions. This freedom must not be described, in a merely negative manner, as independence of empirical conditions, for in this case the faculty of reason would cease to be a cause of phenomena; but it must be regarded, positively, as a faculty which can spontaneously originate a series of events. At the same time, it must not be supposed that any beginning can take place in reason; on the contrary, reason, as the unconditioned condition of all action of the will, admits of no time-conditions, although its effect does really begin in a series of phenomena — a beginning which is not, however, absolutely primal.

I shall illustrate this regulative principle of reason by an example, from its employment in the world of experience; proved it cannot be by any amount of experience, or by any number of facts, for such arguments cannot establish the truth of transcendental propositions. Let us take a voluntary action — for example, a falsehood — by means of which a man has introduced a certain degree of confusion into the social life of humanity, which is judged according to the motives from which it originated, and the blame of which and of the evil consequences arising from it, is imputed to the offender. We at first proceed to examine the empirical character of the offence, and for this purpose we endeavour to penetrate to the sources of that character, such as a defective education, bad company, a shameless and wicked disposition, frivolity, and want of reflection — not forgetting also the occasioning causes which prevailed at the moment of the transgression. In this the procedure is exactly the same as that pursued in the investigation of the series of causes which determine a given physical effect. Now, although we believe the action to have been determined by all these circumstances, we do not the less blame the offender. We do not blame him for his unhappy disposition, nor for the circumstances which influenced him, nay, not even for his former course of life; for we presuppose that all these considerations may be set aside, that the series of preceding conditions may be regarded as having never existed, and that the action may be considered as completely unconditioned in relation to any state preceding, just as if the agent commenced with it an entirely new series of effects. Our blame of the offender is grounded upon a law of reason, which requires us to regard this faculty as a cause, which could have and ought to have otherwise determined the behaviour of the culprit, independently of all empirical conditions. This causality of reason we do not regard as a co-operating agency, but as complete in itself. It matters not whether the sensuous impulses favoured or opposed the action of this causality, the offence is estimated according to its intelligible character — the offender is decidedly worthy of blame, the moment he utters a falsehood. It follows that we regard reason, in spite of the empirical conditions of the act, as completely free, and therefore, therefore, as in the present case, culpable.

The above judgement is complete evidence that we are accustomed to think that reason is not affected by sensuous conditions, that in it no change takes place — although its phenomena, in other words, the mode in which it appears in its effects, are subject to change — that in it no preceding state determines the following, and, consequently, that it does not form a member of the series of sensuous conditions which necessitate phenomena according to natural laws. Reason is present and the same in all human actions and at all times; but it does not itself exist in time, and therefore does not enter upon any state in which it did not formerly exist. It is, relatively to new states or conditions, determining, but not determinable. Hence we cannot ask: "Why did not reason determine itself in a different manner?" The question ought to be thus stated: "Why did not reason employ its power of causality to determine certain phenomena in a different manner?" But this is a question which admits of no answer. For a different intelligible character would have exhibited a different empirical character; and, when we say that, in spite of the course which his whole former life has taken, the offender could have refrained from uttering the falsehood, this means merely that the act was subject to the power and authority — permissive or prohibitive — of reason. Now, reason is not subject in its causality to any conditions of phenomena or of time; and a difference in time may produce a difference in the relation of phenomena to each other — for these are not things and therefore not causes in themselves — but it cannot produce any difference in the relation in which the action stands to the faculty of reason.

Thus, then, in our investigation into free actions and the causal power which produced them, we arrive at an intelligible cause, beyond which, however, we cannot go; although we can recognize that it is free, that is, independent of all sensuous conditions, and that, in this way, it may be the sensuously unconditioned condition of phenomena. But for what reason the intelligible character generates such and such phenomena and exhibits such and such an empirical character under certain circumstances, it is beyond the power of our reason to decide. The question is as much above the power and the sphere of reason as the following would be: "Why does the transcendental object of our external sensuous intuition allow of no other form than that of intuition in space?" But the problem, which we were called upon to solve, does not require us to entertain any such questions. The problem was merely this — whether freedom and natural necessity can exist without opposition in the same action. To this question we have given a sufficient answer; for we have shown that, as the former stands in a relation to a different kind of condition from those of the latter, the law of the one does not affect the law of the other and that, consequently, both can exist together in independence of and without interference with each other.

The reader must be careful to remark that my intention in the above remarks has not been to prove the actual existence of freedom, as a faculty in which resides the cause of certain sensuous phenomena. For, not to mention that such an argument would not have a transcendental character, nor have been limited to the discussion of pure conceptions — all attempts at inferring from experience what cannot be cogitated in accordance with its laws, must ever be unsuccessful. Nay, more, I have not even aimed at demonstrating the possibility of freedom; for this too would have been a vain endeavour, inasmuch as it is beyond the power of the mind to cognize the possibility of a reality or of a causal power by the aid of mere a priori conceptions. Freedom has been considered in the foregoing remarks only as a transcendental idea, by means of which reason aims at originating a series of conditions in the world of phenomena with the help of that which is sensuously unconditioned, involving itself, however, in an antinomy with the laws which itself prescribes for the conduct of the understanding. That this antinomy is based upon a mere illusion, and that nature and freedom are at least not opposed — this was the only thing in our power to prove, and the question which it was our task to solve.

IV. Solution of the Cosmological Idea of the Totality of the Dependence of Phenomenal Existences.

In the preceding remarks, we considered the changes in the world of sense as constituting a dynamical series, in which each member is subordinated to another — as its cause. Our present purpose is to avail ourselves of this series of states or conditions as a guide to an existence which may be the highest condition of all changeable phenomena, that is, to a necessary being. Our endeavour to reach, not the unconditioned causality, but the unconditioned existence, of substance. The series before us is therefore a series of conceptions, and not of intuitions (in which the one intuition is the condition of the other).

But it is evident that, as all phenomena are subject to change and conditioned in their existence, the series of dependent existences cannot embrace an unconditioned member, the existence of which would be absolutely necessary. It follows that, if phenomena were things in themselves, and — as an immediate consequence from this supposition — condition and conditioned belonged to the same series of phenomena, the existence of a necessary being, as the condition of the existence of sensuous phenomena, would be perfectly impossible.

An important distinction, however, exists between the dynamical and the mathematical regress. The latter is engaged solely with the combination of parts into a whole, or with the division of a whole into its parts; and therefore are the conditions of its series parts of the series, and to be consequently regarded as homogeneous, and for this reason, as consisting, without exception, of phenomena. If the former regress, on the contrary, the aim of which is not to establish the possibility of an unconditioned whole consisting of given parts, or of an unconditioned part of a given whole, but to demonstrate the possibility of the deduction of a certain state from its cause, or of the contingent existence of substance from that which exists necessarily, it is not requisite that the condition should form part of an empirical series along with the conditioned.

In the case of the apparent antinomy with which we are at present dealing, there exists a way of escape from the difficulty; for it is not impossible that both of the contradictory statements may be true in different relations. All sensuous phenomena may be contingent, and consequently possess only an empirically conditioned existence, and yet there may also exist a non-empirical condition of the whole series, or, in other words, a necessary being. For this necessary being, as an intelligible condition, would not form a member — not even the highest member — of the series; the whole world of sense would be left in its empirically determined existence uninterfered with and uninfluenced. This would also form a ground of distinction between the modes of solution employed for the third and fourth antinomies. For,

while in the consideration of freedom in the former antinomy, the thing itself —
the cause (substantia phaenomenon) — was regarded as belonging to the series of
conditions, and only its causality to the intelligible world — we are obliged in the
present case to cogitate this necessary being as purely intelligible and as existing
entirely apart from the world of sense (as an ens extramundanum); for otherwise it
would be subject to the phenomenal law of contingency and dependence.

In relation to the present problem, therefore, the regulative principle of reason is that
everything in the sensuous world possesses an empirically conditioned existence —
that no property of the sensuous world possesses unconditioned necessity — that we
are bound to expect, and, so far as is possible, to seek for the empirical condition of
every member in the series of conditions — and that there is no sufficient reason to
justify us in deducing any existence from a condition which lies out of and beyond
the empirical series, or in regarding any existence as independent and self-subsistent;
although this should not prevent us from recognizing the possibility of the whole
series being based upon a being which is intelligible, and for this reason free from all
empirical conditions.

But it has been far from my intention, in these remarks, to prove the existence of
this unconditioned and necessary being, or even to evidence the possibility of a
purely intelligible condition of the existence or all sensuous phenomena. As bounds
were set to reason, to prevent it from leaving the guiding thread of empirical
conditions and losing itself in transcendent theories which are incapable of concrete
presentation; so it was my purpose, on the other band, to set bounds to the law of
the purely empirical understanding, and to protest against any attempts on its part at
deciding on the possibility of things, or declaring the existence of the intelligible to
be impossible, merely on the ground that it is not available for the explanation and
exposition of phenomena. It has been shown, at the same time, that the contingency
of all the phenomena of nature and their empirical conditions is quite consistent with
the arbitrary hypothesis of a necessary, although purely intelligible condition, that
no real contradiction exists between them and that, consequently, both may be true.
The existence of such an absolutely necessary being may be impossible; but this can
never be demonstrated from the universal contingency and dependence of sensuous
phenomena, nor from the principle which forbids us to discontinue the series at some
member of it, or to seek for its cause in some sphere of existence beyond the world of
nature. Reason goes its way in the empirical world, and follows, too, its peculiar path
in the sphere of the transcendental.

The sensuous world contains nothing but phenomena, which are mere representations,
and always sensuously conditioned; things in themselves are not, and cannot be,
objects to us. It is not to be wondered at, therefore, that we are not justified in leaping
from some member of an empirical series beyond the world of sense, as if empirical
representations were things in themselves, existing apart from their transcendental
ground in the human mind, and the cause of whose existence may be sought out of the
empirical series. This would certainly be the case with contingent things; but it cannot
be with mere representations of things, the contingency of which is itself merely a
phenomenon and can relate to no other regress than that which determines phenomena,
that is, the empirical. But to cogitate an intelligible ground of phenomena, as free,

moreover, from the contingency of the latter, conflicts neither with the unlimited nature of the empirical regress, nor with the complete contingency of phenomena. And the demonstration of this was the only thing necessary for the solution of this apparent antinomy. For if the condition of every conditioned — as regards its existence — is sensuous, and for this reason a part of the same series, it must be itself conditioned, as was shown in the antithesis of the fourth antinomy. The embarrassments into which a reason, which postulates the unconditioned, necessarily falls, must, therefore, continue to exist; or the unconditioned must be placed in the sphere of the intelligible. In this way, its necessity does not require, nor does it even permit, the presence of an empirical condition: and it is, consequently, unconditionally necessary.

The empirical employment of reason is not affected by the assumption of a purely intelligible being; it continues its operations on the principle of the contingency of all phenomena, proceeding from empirical conditions to still higher and higher conditions, themselves empirical. Just as little does this regulative principle exclude the assumption of an intelligible cause, when the question regards merely the pure employment of reason — in relation to ends or aims. For, in this case, an intelligible cause signifies merely the transcendental and to us unknown ground of the possibility of sensuous phenomena, and its existence, necessary and independent of all sensuous conditions, is not inconsistent with the contingency of phenomena, or with the unlimited possibility of regress which exists in the series of empirical conditions.

Concluding Remarks on the Antinomy of Pure Reason.

So long as the object of our rational conceptions is the totality of conditions in the world of phenomena, and the satisfaction, from this source, of the requirements of reason, so long are our ideas transcendental and cosmological. But when we set the unconditioned — which is the aim of all our inquiries — in a sphere which lies out of the world of sense and possible experience, our ideas become transcendent. They are then not merely serviceable towards the completion of the exercise of reason (which remains an idea, never executed, but always to be pursued); they detach themselves completely from experience and construct for themselves objects, the material of which has not been presented by experience, and the objective reality of which is not based upon the completion of the empirical series, but upon pure a priori conceptions. The intelligible object of these transcendent ideas may be conceded, as a transcendental object. But we cannot cogitate it as a thing determinable by certain distinct predicates relating to its internal nature, for it has no connection with empirical conceptions; nor are we justified in affirming the existence of any such object. It is, consequently, a mere product of the mind alone. Of all the cosmological ideas, however, it is that occasioning the fourth antinomy which compels us to venture upon this step. For the existence of phenomena, always conditioned and never self-subsistent, requires us to look for an object different from phenomena — an intelligible object, with which all contingency must cease. But, as we have allowed ourselves to assume the existence of a self-subsistent reality out of the field of experience, and are therefore obliged to regard phenomena as merely a contingent mode of representing intelligible objects employed by beings which are themselves intelligences — no other course remains for us than to follow analogy and employ the same mode in forming some conception of intelligible things, of which we have not the least knowledge, which nature taught us to use in the formation of empirical conceptions. Experience made us acquainted with the contingent. But we are at present engaged in the discussion of things which are not objects of experience; and must, therefore, deduce our knowledge of them from that which is necessary absolutely and in itself, that is, from pure conceptions. Hence the first step which we take out of the world of sense obliges us to begin our system of new cognition with the investigation of a necessary being, and to deduce from our conceptions of it all our conceptions of intelligible things. This we propose to attempt in the following chapter.

CHAPTER III.
The Ideal of Pure Reason.

SECTION I. Of the Ideal in General.

We have seen that pure conceptions do not present objects to the mind, except under sensuous conditions; because the conditions of objective reality do not exist in these conceptions, which contain, in fact, nothing but the mere form of thought. They may, however, when applied to phenomena, be presented in concreto; for it is phenomena that present to them the materials for the formation of empirical conceptions, which are nothing more than concrete forms of the conceptions of the understanding. But ideas are still further removed from objective reality than categories; for no phenomenon can ever present them to the human mind in concreto. They contain a certain perfection, attainable by no possible empirical cognition; and they give to reason a systematic unity, to which the unity of experience attempts to approximate, but can never completely attain.

But still further removed than the idea from objective reality is the Ideal, by which term I understand the idea, not in concreto, but in individuo — as an individual thing, determinable or determined by the idea alone. The idea of humanity in its complete perfection supposes not only the advancement of all the powers and faculties, which constitute our conception of human nature, to a complete attainment of their final aims, but also everything which is requisite for the complete determination of the idea; for of all contradictory predicates, only one can conform with the idea of the perfect man. What I have termed an ideal was in Plato's philosophy an idea of the divine mind — an individual object present to its pure intuition, the most perfect of every kind of possible beings, and the archetype of all phenomenal existences.

Without rising to these speculative heights, we are bound to confess that human reason contains not only ideas, but ideals, which possess, not, like those of Plato, creative, but certainly practical power — as regulative principles, and form the basis of the perfectibility of certain actions. Moral conceptions are not perfectly pure conceptions of reason, because an empirical element — of pleasure or pain — lies at the foundation of them. In relation, however, to the principle, whereby reason sets bounds to a freedom which is in itself without law, and consequently when we attend merely to their form, they may be considered as pure conceptions of reason. Virtue and wisdom in their perfect purity are ideas. But the wise man of the Stoics is an ideal, that is to say, a human being existing only in thought and in complete conformity with the idea of wisdom. As the idea provides a rule, so the ideal serves as an archetype for the perfect and complete determination of the copy. Thus the conduct of this wise and divine man serves us as a standard of action, with which we may compare and judge ourselves, which may help us to reform ourselves, although the perfection it demands can never be attained by us. Although we cannot concede objective reality to these ideals, they are not to be considered as chimeras; on the contrary, they provide reason with a standard, which enables it to estimate, by comparison, the degree of incompleteness in the objects presented to it. But to aim at realizing the ideal in an example in the world of experience — to describe, for instance, the character of the perfectly wise man in a romance — is impracticable. Nay more, there is something absurd in the attempt; and the result must be little edifying, as the natural limitations, which are continually breaking in upon the perfection and completeness of the idea, destroy the illusion in the story and throw an air of suspicion even on what is good in the idea, which hence appears fictitious and unreal.

Such is the constitution of the ideal of reason, which is always based upon determinate conceptions, and serves as a rule and a model for limitation or of criticism. Very different is the nature of the ideals of the imagination. Of these it is impossible to present an intelligible conception; they are a kind of monogram, drawn according to no determinate rule, and forming rather a vague picture — the production of many diverse experiences — than a determinate image. Such are the ideals which painters and physiognomists profess to have in their minds, and which can serve neither as a model for production nor as a standard for appreciation. They may be termed, though improperly, sensuous ideals, as they are declared to be models of certain possible empirical intuitions. They cannot, however, furnish rules or standards for explanation or examination.

In its ideals, reason aims at complete and perfect determination according to a priori rules; and hence it cogitates an object, which must be completely determinable in conformity with principles, although all empirical conditions are absent, and the conception of the object is on this account transcendent.

SECTION II. Of the Transcendental Ideal (Prototypon Trancendentale).

Every conception is, in relation to that which is not contained in it, undetermined and subject to the principle of determinability. This principle is that, of every two contradictorily opposed predicates, only one can belong to a conception. It is a purely logical principle, itself based upon the principle of contradiction; inasmuch as it makes complete abstraction of the content and attends merely to the logical form of the cognition.

But again, everything, as regards its possibility, is also subject to the principle of complete determination, according to which one of all the possible contradictory predicates of things must belong to it. This principle is not based merely upon that of contradiction; for, in addition to the relation between two contradictory predicates, it regards everything as standing in a relation to the sum of possibilities, as the sum total of all predicates of things, and, while presupposing this sum as an a priori condition, presents to the mind everything as receiving the possibility of its individual existence from the relation it bears to, and the share it possesses in, the aforesaid sum of possibilities.* The principle of complete determination relates the content and not to the logical form. It is the principle of the synthesis of all the predicates which are required to constitute the complete conception of a thing, and not a mere principle analytical representation, which enounces that one of two contradictory predicates must belong to a conception. It contains, moreover, a transcendental presupposition — that, namely, of the material for all possibility, which must contain a priori the data for this or that particular possibility.

[Note: Thus this principle declares everything to possess a relation to a common correlate — the sum-total of possibility, which, if discovered to exist in the idea of one individual thing, would establish the affinity of all possible things, from the identity of the ground of their complete determination. The determinability of every conception is subordinate to the universality (Allgemeinheit, universalitas) of the principle of excluded middle; the determination of a thing to the totality (Allheit, universitas) of all possible predicates.]

The proposition, everything which exists is completely determined, means not only that one of every pair of given contradictory attributes, but that one of all possible attributes, is always predicable of the thing; in it the predicates are not merely compared logically with each other, but the thing itself is transcendentally compared with the sum-total of all possible predicates. The proposition is equivalent to saying: "To attain to a complete knowledge of a thing, it is necessary to possess a knowledge of everything that is possible, and to determine it thereby in a positive or negative manner." The conception of complete determination is consequently a conception which cannot be presented in its totality in concreto, and is therefore based upon an idea, which has its seat in the reason — the faculty which prescribes to the understanding the laws of its harmonious and perfect exercise.

Now, although this idea of the sum-total of all possibility, in so far as it forms the condition of the complete determination of everything, is itself undetermined in relation to the predicates which may constitute this sum-total, and we cogitate in it merely the sum-total of all possible predicates — we nevertheless find, upon closer examination, that this idea, as a primitive conception of the mind, excludes a large number of predicates — those deduced and those irreconcilable with others, and that it is evolved as a conception completely determined a priori. Thus it becomes the conception of an individual object, which is completely determined by and through the mere idea, and must consequently be termed an ideal of pure reason.

When we consider all possible predicates, not merely logically, but transcendentally, that is to say, with reference to the content which may be cogitated as existing in them a priori, we shall find that some indicate a being, others merely a non-being. The logical negation expressed in the word not does not properly belong to a conception, but only to the relation of one conception to another in a judgement, and is consequently quite insufficient to present to the mind the content of a conception. The expression not mortal does not indicate that a non-being is cogitated in the object; it does not concern the content at all. A transcendental negation, on the contrary, indicates non-being in itself, and is opposed to transcendental affirmation, the conception of which of itself expresses a being. Hence this affirmation indicates a reality, because in and through it objects are considered to be something — to be things; while the opposite negation, on the other band, indicates a mere want, or privation, or absence, and, where such negations alone are attached to a representation, the non-existence of anything corresponding to the representation.

Now a negation cannot be cogitated as determined, without cogitating at the same time the opposite affirmation. The man born blind has not the least notion of darkness, because he has none of light; the vagabond knows nothing of poverty, because he has never known what it is to be in comfort;* the ignorant man has no conception of his ignorance, because he has no conception of knowledge. All conceptions of negatives are accordingly derived or deduced conceptions; and realities contain the data, and, so to speak, the material or transcendental content of the possibility and complete determination of all things.

[Note: The investigations and calculations of astronomers have taught us much that is wonderful; but the most important lesson we have received from them is the discovery of the abyss of our ignorance in relation to the universe — an ignorance the magnitude of which reason, without the information thus derived, could never have conceived. This discovery of our deficiencies must produce a great change in the determination of the aims of human reason.]

If, therefore, a transcendental substratum lies at the foundation of the complete determination of things — a substratum which is to form the fund from which all possible predicates of things are to be supplied, this substratum cannot be anything else than the idea of a sum-total of reality (omnitudo realitatis). In this view, negations are nothing but limitations — a term which could not, with propriety, be applied to them, if the unlimited (the all) did not form the true basis of our conception.

This conception of a sum-total of reality is the conception of a thing in itself, regarded as completely determined; and the conception of an ens realissimum is the conception of an individual being, inasmuch as it is determined by that predicate of all possible contradictory predicates, which indicates and belongs to being. It is, therefore, a transcendental ideal which forms the basis of the complete determination of everything that exists, and is the highest material condition of its possibility — a condition on which must rest the cogitation of all objects with respect to their content. Nay, more, this ideal is the only proper ideal of which the human mind is capable; because in this case alone a general conception of a thing is completely determined by and through itself, and cognized as the representation of an individuum.

The logical determination of a conception is based upon a disjunctive syllogism, the major of which contains the logical division of the extent of a general conception, the minor limits this extent to a certain part, while the conclusion determines the conception by this part. The general conception of a reality cannot be divided a priori, because, without the aid of experience, we cannot know any determinate kinds of reality, standing under the former as the genus. The transcendental principle of the complete determination of all things is therefore merely the representation of the sum-total of all reality; it is not a conception which is the genus of all predicates under itself, but one which comprehends them all within itself. The complete determination of a thing is consequently based upon the limitation of this total of reality, so much being predicated of the thing, while all that remains over is excluded — a procedure which is in exact agreement with that of the disjunctive syllogism and the determination of the objects in the conclusion by one of the members of the division. It follows that reason, in laying the transcendental ideal at the foundation of its determination of all possible things, takes a course in exact analogy with that which it pursues in disjunctive syllogisms — a proposition which formed the basis of the systematic division of all transcendental ideas, according to which they are produced in complete parallelism with the three modes of syllogistic reasoning employed by the human mind.

It is self-evident that reason, in cogitating the necessary complete determination of things, does not presuppose the existence of a being corresponding to its ideal, but merely the idea of the ideal — for the purpose of deducing from the unconditional totality of complete determination, The ideal is therefore the prototype of all things, which, as defective copies (ectypa), receive from it the material of their possibility, and approximate to it more or less, though it is impossible that they can ever attain to its perfection.

The possibility of things must therefore be regarded as derived — except that of the thing which contains in itself all reality, which must be considered to be primitive and original. For all negations — and they are the only predicates by means of which all other things can be distinguished from the ens realissimum — are mere limitations of a greater and a higher — nay, the highest reality; and they consequently presuppose this reality, and are, as regards their content, derived from it. The manifold nature of things is only an infinitely various mode of limiting the conception of the highest reality, which is their common substratum; just as all figures are possible only as different modes of limiting infinite space. The object of the ideal of reason — an object existing only in reason itself — is also termed the primal being (ens originarium); as having no existence superior to him, the supreme being (ens summum); and as being the condition of all other beings, which rank under it, the being of all beings (ens entium). But none of these terms indicate the objective relation of an actually existing object to other things, but merely that of an idea to conceptions; and all our investigations into this subject still leave us in perfect uncertainty with regard to the existence of this being.

A primal being cannot be said to consist of many other beings with an existence which is derivative, for the latter presuppose the former, and therefore cannot be constitutive parts of it. It follows that the ideal of the primal being must be cogitated as simple.

The deduction of the possibility of all other things from this primal being cannot, strictly speaking, be considered as a limitation, or as a kind of division of its reality; for this would be regarding the primal being as a mere aggregate — which has been shown to be impossible, although it was so represented in our first rough sketch. The highest reality must be regarded rather as the ground than as the sum-total of the possibility of all things, and the manifold nature of things be based, not upon the limitation of the primal being itself, but upon the complete series of effects which flow from it. And thus all our powers of sense, as well as all phenomenal reality, phenomenal reality, may be with propriety regarded as belonging to this series of effects, while they could not have formed parts of the idea, considered as an aggregate. Pursuing this track, and hypostatizing this idea, we shall find ourselves authorized to determine our notion of the Supreme Being by means of the mere conception of a highest reality, as one, simple, all-sufficient, eternal, and so on — in one word, to determine it in its unconditioned completeness by the aid of every possible predicate. The conception of such a being is the conception of God in its transcendental sense, and thus the ideal of pure reason is the object-matter of a transcendental theology.

But, by such an employment of the transcendental idea, we should be over stepping the limits of its validity and purpose. For reason placed it, as the conception of all reality, at the basis of the complete determination of things, without requiring that this conception be regarded as the conception of an objective existence. Such an existence would be purely fictitious, and the hypostatizing of the content of the idea into an ideal, as an individual being, is a step perfectly unauthorized. Nay, more, we are not even called upon to assume the possibility of such an hypothesis, as none of the deductions drawn from such an ideal would affect the complete determination of things in general — for the sake of which alone is the idea necessary.

It is not sufficient to circumscribe the procedure and the dialectic of reason; we must also endeavour to discover the sources of this dialectic, that we may have it in our power to give a rational explanation of this illusion, as a phenomenon of the human mind. For the ideal, of which we are at present speaking, is based, not upon an arbitrary, but upon a natural, idea. The question hence arises: How happens it that reason regards the possibility of all things as deduced from a single possibility, that, to wit, of the highest reality, and presupposes this as existing in an individual and primal being?

The answer is ready; it is at once presented by the procedure of transcendental analytic. The possibility of sensuous objects is a relation of these objects to thought, in which something (the empirical form) may be cogitated a priori; while that which constitutes the matter — the reality of the phenomenon (that element which corresponds to sensation) — must be given from without, as otherwise it could not even be cogitated by, nor could its possibility be presentable to the mind. Now, a sensuous object is completely determined, when it has been compared with all phenomenal predicates, and represented by means of these either positively or negatively. But, as that which constitutes the thing itself — the real in a phenomenon, must be given, and that, in which the real of all phenomena is given, is experience, one, sole, and all-embracing — the material of the possibility of all sensuous objects must be presupposed as given in a whole, and it is upon the limitation of this whole that the possibility of all empirical objects, their distinction from each other and their complete determination, are based. Now, no other objects are presented to us besides sensuous objects, and these can be given only in connection with a possible experience; it follows that a thing is not an object to us, unless it presupposes the whole or sum-total of empirical reality as the condition of its possibility. Now, a natural illusion leads us to consider this principle, which is valid only of sensuous objects, as valid with regard to things in general. And thus we are induced to hold the empirical principle of our conceptions of the possibility of things, as phenomena, by leaving out this limitative condition, to be a transcendental principle of the possibility of things in general.

We proceed afterwards to hypostatize this idea of the sum-total of all reality, by changing the distributive unity of the empirical exercise of the understanding into the collective unity of an empirical whole — a dialectical illusion, and by cogitating this whole or sum of experience as an individual thing, containing in itself all empirical reality. This individual thing or being is then, by means of the above-mentioned transcendental subreption, substituted for our notion of a thing which stands at the head of the possibility of all things, the real conditions of whose complete determination it presents.*

[Note: This ideal of the ens realissimum — although merely a mental representation — is first objectivized, that is, has an objective existence attributed to it, then hypostatized, and finally, by the natural progress of reason to the completion of unity, personified, as we shall show presently. For the regulative unity of experience is not based upon phenomena themselves, but upon the connection of the variety of phenomena by the understanding in a consciousness, and thus the unity of the supreme reality and the complete determinability of all things, seem to reside in a supreme understanding, and, consequently, in a conscious intelligence.]

SECTION III. Of the Arguments employed by Speculative Reason in Proof of the Existence of a Supreme Being.

Notwithstanding the pressing necessity which reason feels, to form some presupposition that shall serve the understanding as a proper basis for the complete determination of its conceptions, the idealistic and factitious nature of such a presupposition is too evident to allow reason for a moment to persuade itself into a belief of the objective existence of a mere creation of its own thought. But there are other considerations which compel reason to seek out some resting place in the regress from the conditioned to the unconditioned, which is not given as an actual existence from the mere conception of it, although it alone can give completeness to the series of conditions. And this is the natural course of every human reason, even of the most uneducated, although the path at first entered it does not always continue to follow. It does not begin from conceptions, but from common experience, and requires a basis in actual existence. But this basis is insecure, unless it rests upon the immovable rock of the absolutely necessary. And this foundation is itself unworthy of trust, if it leave under and above it empty space, if it do not fill all, and leave no room for a why or a wherefore, if it be not, in one word, infinite in its reality.

If we admit the existence of some one thing, whatever it may be, we must also admit that there is something which exists necessarily. For what is contingent exists only under the condition of some other thing, which is its cause; and from this we must go on to conclude the existence of a cause which is not contingent, and which consequently exists necessarily and unconditionally. Such is the argument by which reason justifies its advances towards a primal being.

Now reason looks round for the conception of a being that may be admitted, without inconsistency, to be worthy of the attribute of absolute necessity, not for the purpose of inferring a priori, from the conception of such a being, its objective existence (for if reason allowed itself to take this course, it would not require a basis in given and actual existence, but merely the support of pure conceptions), but for the purpose of discovering, among all our conceptions of possible things, that conception which possesses no element inconsistent with the idea of absolute necessity. For that there must be some absolutely necessary existence, it regards as a truth already established. Now, if it can remove every existence incapable of supporting the attribute of absolute necessity, excepting one — this must be the absolutely necessary being, whether its necessity is comprehensible by us, that is, deducible from the conception of it alone, or not.

Now that, the conception of which contains a therefore to every wherefore, which is not defective in any respect whatever, which is all-sufficient as a condition, seems to be the being of which we can justly predicate absolute necessity — for this reason, that, possessing the conditions of all that is possible, it does not and cannot itself require any condition. And thus it satisfies, in one respect at least, the requirements of the conception of absolute necessity. In this view, it is superior to all other conceptions, which, as deficient and incomplete, do not possess the characteristic of independence of all higher conditions. It is true that we cannot infer from this that what does not contain in itself the supreme and complete condition — the condition of all other things — must possess only a conditioned existence; but as little can we assert the contrary, for this supposed being does not possess the only characteristic which can enable reason to cognize by means of an a priori conception the unconditioned and necessary nature of its existence.

The conception of an ens realissimum is that which best agrees with the conception of an unconditioned and necessary being. The former conception does not satisfy all the requirements of the latter; but we have no choice, we are obliged to adhere to it, for we find that we cannot do without the existence of a necessary being; and even although we admit it, we find it out of our power to discover in the whole sphere of possibility any being that can advance well-grounded claims to such a distinction.

The following is, therefore, the natural course of human reason. It begins by persuading itself of the existence of some necessary being. In this being it recognizes the characteristics of unconditioned existence. It then seeks the conception of that which is independent of all conditions, and finds it in that which is itself the sufficient condition of all other things — in other words, in that which contains all reality. But the unlimited all is an absolute unity, and is conceived by the mind as a being one and supreme; and thus reason concludes that the Supreme Being, as the primal basis of all things, possesses an existence which is absolutely necessary.

This conception must be regarded as in some degree satisfactory, if we admit the existence of a necessary being, and consider that there exists a necessity for a definite and final answer to these questions. In such a case, we cannot make a better choice, or rather we have no choice at all, but feel ourselves obliged to declare in favour of the absolute unity of complete reality, as the highest source of the possibility of things. But if there exists no motive for coming to a definite conclusion, and we may leave the question unanswered till we have fully weighed both sides — in other words, when we are merely called upon to decide how much we happen to know about the question, and how much we merely flatter ourselves that we know — the above conclusion does not appear to be so great advantage, but, on the contrary, seems defective in the grounds upon which it is supported.

For, admitting the truth of all that has been said, that, namely, the inference from a given existence (my own, for example) to the existence of an unconditioned and necessary being is valid and unassailable; that, in the second place, we must consider a being which contains all reality, and consequently all the conditions of other things, to be absolutely unconditioned; and admitting too, that we have thus discovered the conception of a thing to which may be attributed, without inconsistency, absolute necessity — it does not follow from all this that the conception of a limited being, in which the supreme reality does not reside, is therefore incompatible with the idea of absolute necessity. For, although I do not discover the element of the unconditioned in the conception of such a being — an element which is manifestly existent in the sum-total of all conditions — I am not entitled to conclude that its existence is therefore conditioned; just as I am not entitled to affirm, in a hypothetical syllogism, that where a certain condition does not exist (in the present, completeness, as far as pure conceptions are concerned), the conditioned does not exist either. On the contrary, we are free to consider all limited beings as likewise unconditionally necessary, although we are unable to infer this from the general conception which we have of them. Thus conducted, this argument is incapable of giving us the least notion of the properties of a necessary being, and must be in every respect without result.

This argument continues, however, to possess a weight and an authority, which, in spite of its objective insufficiency, it has never been divested of. For, granting that certain responsibilities lie upon us, which, as based on the ideas of reason, deserve to be respected and submitted to, although they are incapable of a real or practical application to our nature, or, in other words, would be responsibilities without motives, except upon the supposition of a Supreme Being to give effect and influence to the practical laws: in such a case we should be bound to obey our conceptions, which, although objectively insufficient, do, according to the standard of reason, preponderate over and are superior to any claims that may be advanced from any other quarter. The equilibrium of doubt would in this case be destroyed by a practical addition; indeed, Reason would be compelled to condemn herself, if she refused to comply with the demands of the judgement, no superior to which we know — however defective her understanding of the grounds of these demands might be.

This argument, although in fact transcendental, inasmuch as it rests upon the intrinsic insufficiency of the contingent, is so simple and natural, that the commonest understanding can appreciate its value. We see things around us change, arise, and pass away; they, or their condition, must therefore have a cause. The same demand must again be made of the cause itself — as a datum of experience. Now it is natural that we should place the highest causality just where we place supreme causality, in that being, which contains the conditions of all possible effects, and the conception of which is so simple as that of an all-embracing reality. This highest cause, then, we regard as absolutely necessary, because we find it absolutely necessary to rise to it, and do not discover any reason for proceeding beyond it. Thus, among all nations, through the darkest polytheism glimmer some faint sparks of monotheism, to which these idolaters have been led, not from reflection and profound thought, but by the study and natural progress of the common understanding.

There are only three modes of proving the existence of a Deity, on the grounds of speculative reason.

All the paths conducting to this end begin either from determinate experience and the peculiar constitution of the world of sense, and rise, according to the laws of causality, from it to the highest cause existing apart from the world — or from a purely indeterminate experience, that is, some empirical existence — or abstraction is made of all experience, and the existence of a supreme cause is concluded from a priori conceptions alone. The first is the physico-theological argument, the second the cosmological, the third the ontological. More there are not, and more there cannot be.

I shall show it is as unsuccessful on the one path — the empirical — as on the other — the transcendental, and that it stretches its wings in vain, to soar beyond the world of sense by the mere might of speculative thought. As regards the order in which we must discuss those arguments, it will be exactly the reverse of that in which reason, in the progress of its development, attains to them — the order in which they are placed above. For it will be made manifest to the reader that, although experience presents the occasion and the starting-point, it is the transcendental idea of reason which guides it in its pilgrimage and is the goal of all its struggles. I shall therefore begin with an examination of the transcendental argument, and afterwards inquire what additional strength has accrued to this mode of proof from the addition of the empirical element.

SECTION IV. Of the Impossibility of an Ontological Proof of the Existence of God.

It is evident from what has been said that the conception of an absolutely necessary being is a mere idea, the objective reality of which is far from being established by the mere fact that it is a need of reason. On the contrary, this idea serves merely to indicate a certain unattainable perfection, and rather limits the operations than, by the presentation of new objects, extends the sphere of the understanding. But a strange anomaly meets us at the very threshold; for the inference from a given existence in general to an absolutely necessary existence seems to be correct and unavoidable, while the conditions of the understanding refuse to aid us in forming any conception of such a being.

Philosophers have always talked of an absolutely necessary being, and have nevertheless declined to take the trouble of conceiving whether — and how — a being of this nature is even cogitable, not to mention that its existence is actually demonstrable. A verbal definition of the conception is certainly easy enough: it is something the non-existence of which is impossible. But does this definition throw any light upon the conditions which render it impossible to cogitate the non-existence of a thing — conditions which we wish to ascertain, that we may discover whether we think anything in the conception of such a being or not? For the mere fact that I throw away, by means of the word unconditioned, all the conditions which the understanding habitually requires in order to regard anything as necessary, is very far from making clear whether by means of the conception of the unconditionally necessary I think of something, or really of nothing at all.

Nay, more, this chance-conception, now become so current, many have endeavoured to explain by examples which seemed to render any inquiries regarding its intelligibility quite needless. Every geometrical proposition — a triangle has three angles — it was said, is absolutely necessary; and thus people talked of an object which lay out of the sphere of our understanding as if it were perfectly plain what the conception of such a being meant.

All the examples adduced have been drawn, without exception, from judgements, and not from things. But the unconditioned necessity of a judgement does not form the absolute necessity of a thing. On the contrary, the absolute necessity of a judgement is only a conditioned necessity of a thing, or of the predicate in a judgement. The proposition above-mentioned does not enounce that three angles necessarily exist, but, upon condition that a triangle exists, three angles must necessarily exist — in it. And thus this logical necessity has been the source of the greatest delusions. Having formed an a priori conception of a thing, the content of which was made to embrace existence, we believed ourselves safe in concluding that, because existence belongs necessarily to the object of the conception (that is, under the condition of my positing this thing as given), the existence of the thing is also posited necessarily, and that it is therefore absolutely necessary — merely because its existence has been cogitated in the conception.

If, in an identical judgement, I annihilate the predicate in thought, and retain the subject, a contradiction is the result; and hence I say, the former belongs necessarily to the latter. But if I suppress both subject and predicate in thought, no contradiction arises; for there is nothing at all, and therefore no means of forming a contradiction. To suppose the existence of a triangle and not that of its three angles, is self-contradictory; but to suppose the non-existence of both triangle and angles is perfectly admissible. And so is it with the conception of an absolutely necessary being. Annihilate its existence in thought, and you annihilate the thing itself with all its predicates; how then can there be any room for contradiction? Externally, there is nothing to give rise to a contradiction, for a thing cannot be necessary externally; nor internally, for, by the annihilation or suppression of the thing itself, its internal properties are also annihilated. God is omnipotent — that is a necessary judgement. His omnipotence cannot be denied, if the existence of a Deity is posited — the existence, that is, of an infinite being, the two conceptions being identical. But when you say, God does not exist, neither omnipotence nor any other predicate is affirmed; they must all disappear with the subject, and in this judgement there cannot exist the least self-contradiction.

You have thus seen that when the predicate of a judgement is annihilated in thought along with the subject, no internal contradiction can arise, be the predicate what it may. There is no possibility of evading the conclusion — you find yourselves compelled to declare: There are certain subjects which cannot be annihilated in thought. But this is nothing more than saying: There exist subjects which are absolutely necessary — the very hypothesis which you are called upon to establish. For I find myself unable to form the slightest conception of a thing which when annihilated in thought with all its predicates, leaves behind a contradiction; and contradiction is the only criterion of impossibility in the sphere of pure a priori conceptions.

Against these general considerations, the justice of which no one can dispute, one argument is adduced, which is regarded as furnishing a satisfactory demonstration from the fact. It is affirmed that there is one and only one conception, in which the non-being or annihilation of the object is self-contradictory, and this is the conception of an ens realissimum. It possesses, you say, all reality, and you feel yourselves justified in admitting the possibility of such a being. (This I am willing to grant for the present, although the existence of a conception which is not self-contradictory is far from being sufficient to prove the possibility of an object.)* Now the notion of all reality embraces in it that of existence; the notion of existence lies, therefore, in the conception of this possible thing. If this thing is annihilated in thought, the internal possibility of the thing is also annihilated, which is self-contradictory.

[Note: A conception is always possible, if it is not self-contradictory. This is the logical criterion of possibility, distinguishing the object of such a conception from the nihil negativum. But it may be, notwithstanding, an empty conception, unless the objective reality of this synthesis, but which it is generated, is demonstrated; and a proof of this kind must be based upon principles of possible experience, and not upon the principle of analysis or contradiction. This remark may be serviceable as a warning against concluding, from the possibility of a conception — which is logical — the possibility of a thing — which is real.]

I answer: It is absurd to introduce — under whatever term disguised — into the conception of a thing, which is to be cogitated solely in reference to its possibility, the conception of its existence. If this is admitted, you will have apparently gained the day, but in reality have enounced nothing but a mere tautology. I ask, is the proposition, this or that thing (which I am admitting to be possible) exists, an analytical or a synthetical proposition? If the former, there is no addition made to the subject of your thought by the affirmation of its existence; but then the conception in your minds is identical with the thing itself, or you have supposed the existence of a thing to be possible, and then inferred its existence from its internal possibility — which is but a miserable tautology. The word reality in the conception of the thing, and the word existence in the conception of the predicate, will not help you out of the difficulty. For, supposing you were to term all positing of a thing reality, you have thereby posited the thing with all its predicates in the conception of the subject and assumed its actual existence, and this you merely repeat in the predicate. But if you confess, as every reasonable person must, that every existential proposition is synthetical, how can it be maintained that the predicate of existence cannot be denied without contradiction? — a property which is the characteristic of analytical propositions, alone.

I should have a reasonable hope of putting an end for ever to this sophistical mode of argumentation, by a strict definition of the conception of existence, did not my own experience teach me that the illusion arising from our confounding a logical with a real predicate (a predicate which aids in the determination of a thing) resists almost all the endeavours of explanation and illustration. A logical predicate may be what you please, even the subject may be predicated of itself; for logic pays no regard to the content of a judgement. But the determination of a conception is a predicate, which adds to and enlarges the conception. It must not, therefore, be contained in the conception.

Being is evidently not a real predicate, that is, a conception of something which is added to the conception of some other thing. It is merely the positing of a thing, or of certain determinations in it. Logically, it is merely the copula of a judgement. The proposition, God is omnipotent, contains two conceptions, which have a certain object or content; the word is, is no additional predicate — it merely indicates the relation of the predicate to the subject. Now, if I take the subject (God) with all its predicates (omnipotence being one), and say: God is, or, There is a God, I add no new predicate to the conception of God, I merely posit or affirm the existence of the subject with all its predicates — I posit the object in relation to my conception. The content of both is the same; and there is no addition made to the conception, which expresses merely the possibility of the object, by my cogitating the object — in the expression, it is — as absolutely given or existing. Thus the real contains no more than the possible. A hundred real dollars contain no more than a hundred possible dollars. For, as the latter indicate the conception, and the former the object, on the supposition that the content of the former was greater than that of the latter, my conception would not be an expression of the whole object, and would consequently be an inadequate conception of it. But in reckoning my wealth there may be said to be more in a hundred real dollars than in a hundred possible dollars — that is, in the mere conception of them. For the real object — the dollars — is not analytically contained in my conception, but forms a synthetical addition to my conception (which is merely a determination of my mental state), although this objective reality — this existence — apart from my conceptions, does not in the least degree increase the aforesaid hundred dollars.

By whatever and by whatever number of predicates — even to the complete determination of it — I may cogitate a thing, I do not in the least augment the object of my conception by the addition of the statement: This thing exists. Otherwise, not exactly the same, but something more than what was cogitated in my conception, would exist, and I could not affirm that the exact object of my conception had real existence. If I cogitate a thing as containing all modes of reality except one, the mode of reality which is absent is not added to the conception of the thing by the affirmation that the thing exists; on the contrary, the thing exists — if it exist at all — with the same defect as that cogitated in its conception; otherwise not that which was cogitated, but something different, exists. Now, if I cogitate a being as the highest reality, without defect or imperfection, the question still remains — whether this being exists or not? For, although no element is wanting in the possible real content of my conception, there is a defect in its relation to my mental state, that is, I am ignorant whether the cognition of the object indicated by the conception is possible a posteriori. And here the cause of the present difficulty becomes apparent. If the question regarded an object of sense merely, it would be impossible for me to confound the conception with the existence of a thing. For the conception merely enables me to cogitate an object as according with the general conditions of experience; while the existence of the object permits me to cogitate it as contained in the sphere of actual experience. At the same time, this connection with the world of experience does not in the least augment the conception, although a possible perception has been added to the experience of the mind. But if we cogitate existence by the pure category alone, it is not to be wondered at, that we should find ourselves unable to present any criterion sufficient to distinguish it from mere possibility.

Whatever be the content of our conception of an object, it is necessary to go beyond it, if we wish to predicate existence of the object. In the case of sensuous objects, this is attained by their connection according to empirical laws with some one of my perceptions; but there is no means of cognizing the existence of objects of pure thought, because it must be cognized completely a priori. But all our knowledge of existence (be it immediately by perception, or by inferences connecting some object with a perception) belongs entirely to the sphere of experience — which is in perfect unity with itself; and although an existence out of this sphere cannot be absolutely declared to be impossible, it is a hypothesis the truth of which we have no means of ascertaining.

The notion of a Supreme Being is in many respects a highly useful idea; but for the very reason that it is an idea, it is incapable of enlarging our cognition with regard to the existence of things. It is not even sufficient to instruct us as to the possibility of a being which we do not know to exist. The analytical criterion of possibility, which consists in the absence of contradiction in propositions, cannot be denied it. But the connection of real properties in a thing is a synthesis of the possibility of which an a priori judgement cannot be formed, because these realities are not presented to us specifically; and even if this were to happen, a judgement would still be impossible, because the criterion of the possibility of synthetical cognitions must be sought for in the world of experience, to which the object of an idea cannot belong. And thus the celebrated Leibnitz has utterly failed in his attempt to establish upon a priori grounds the possibility of this sublime ideal being.

The celebrated ontological or Cartesian argument for the existence of a Supreme Being is therefore insufficient; and we may as well hope to increase our stock of knowledge by the aid of mere ideas, as the merchant to augment his wealth by the addition of noughts to his cash account.

SECTION V. Of the Impossibility of a Cosmological Proof of the Existence of God.

It was by no means a natural course of proceeding, but, on the contrary, an invention entirely due to the subtlety of the schools, to attempt to draw from a mere idea a proof of the existence of an object corresponding to it. Such a course would never have been pursued, were it not for that need of reason which requires it to suppose the existence of a necessary being as a basis for the empirical regress, and that, as this necessity must be unconditioned and a priori, reason is bound to discover a conception which shall satisfy, if possible, this requirement, and enable us to attain to the a priori cognition of such a being. This conception was thought to be found in the idea of an ens realissimum, and thus this idea was employed for the attainment of a better defined knowledge of a necessary being, of the existence of which we were convinced, or persuaded, on other grounds. Thus reason was seduced from her natural courage; and, instead of concluding with the conception of an ens realissimum, an attempt was made to begin with it, for the purpose of inferring from it that idea of a necessary existence which it was in fact called in to complete. Thus arose that unfortunate ontological argument, which neither satisfies the healthy common sense of humanity, nor sustains the scientific examination of the philosopher.

The cosmological proof, which we are about to examine, retains the connection between absolute necessity and the highest reality; but, instead of reasoning from this highest reality to a necessary existence, like the preceding argument, it concludes from the given unconditioned necessity of some being its unlimited reality. The track it pursues, whether rational or sophistical, is at least natural, and not only goes far to persuade the common understanding, but shows itself deserving of respect from the speculative intellect; while it contains, at the same time, the outlines of all the arguments employed in natural theology — arguments which always have been, and still will be, in use and authority. These, however adorned, and hid under whatever embellishments of rhetoric and sentiment, are at bottom identical with the arguments we are at present to discuss. This proof, termed by Leibnitz the argumentum a contingentia mundi, I shall now lay before the reader, and subject to a strict examination.

It is framed in the following manner: If something exists, an absolutely necessary being must likewise exist. Now I, at least, exist. Consequently, there exists an absolutely necessary being. The minor contains an experience, the major reasons from a general experience to the existence of a necessary being.* Thus this argument really begins at experience, and is not completely a priori, or ontological. The object of all possible experience being the world, it is called the cosmological proof. It contains no reference to any peculiar property of sensuous objects, by which this world of sense might be distinguished from other possible worlds; and in this respect it differs from the physico-theological proof, which is based upon the consideration of the peculiar constitution of our sensuous world.

[Note: This inference is too well known to require more detailed discussion. It is based upon the spurious transcendental law of causality, that everything which is contingent has a cause, which, if itself contingent, must also have a cause; and so on, till the series of subordinated causes must end with an absolutely necessary cause, without which it would not possess completeness.]

The proof proceeds thus: A necessary being can be determined only in one way, that is, it can be determined by only one of all possible opposed predicates; consequently, it must be completely determined in and by its conception. But there is only a single conception of a thing possible, which completely determines the thing a priori: that is, the conception of the ens realissimum. It follows that the conception of the ens realissimum is the only conception by and in which we can cogitate a necessary being. Consequently, a Supreme Being necessarily exists.

In this cosmological argument are assembled so many sophistical propositions that speculative reason seems to have exerted in it all her dialectical skill to produce a transcendental illusion of the most extreme character. We shall postpone an investigation of this argument for the present, and confine ourselves to exposing the stratagem by which it imposes upon us an old argument in a new dress, and appeals to the agreement of two witnesses, the one with the credentials of pure reason, and the other with those of empiricism; while, in fact, it is only the former who has changed his dress and voice, for the purpose of passing himself off for an additional witness. That it may possess a secure foundation, it bases its conclusions upon experience, and thus appears to be completely distinct from the ontological argument, which places its confidence entirely in pure a priori conceptions. But this experience merely aids reason in making one step — to the existence of a necessary being. What the properties of this being are cannot be learned from experience; and therefore reason abandons it altogether, and pursues its inquiries in the sphere of pure conception, for the purpose of discovering what the properties of an absolutely necessary being ought to be, that is, what among all possible things contain the conditions (requisita) of absolute necessity. Reason believes that it has discovered these requisites in the conception of an ens realissimum — and in it alone, and hence concludes: The ens realissimum is an absolutely necessary being. But it is evident that reason has here presupposed that the conception of an ens realissimum is perfectly adequate to the conception of a being of absolute necessity, that is, that we may infer the existence of the latter from that of the former — a proposition which formed the basis of the ontological argument, and which is now employed in the support of the cosmological argument, contrary to the wish and professions of its inventors. For the existence of an absolutely necessary being is given in conceptions alone. But if I say: "The conception of the ens realissimum is a conception of this kind, and in fact the only conception which is adequate to our idea of a necessary being," I am obliged to admit, that the latter may be inferred from the former. Thus it is properly the ontological argument which figures in the cosmological, and constitutes the whole strength of the latter; while the spurious basis of experience has been of no further use than to conduct us to the conception of absolute necessity, being utterly insufficient to demonstrate the presence of this attribute in any determinate existence or thing. For when we propose to ourselves an aim of this character, we must abandon the sphere of experience, and rise to that of pure conceptions, which we examine with the purpose of discovering whether any one contains the conditions of the possibility of an absolutely necessary being. But if the possibility of such a being is thus demonstrated, its existence is also proved; for we may then assert that, of all possible beings there is one which possesses the attribute of necessity — in other words, this being possesses an absolutely necessary existence.

All illusions in an argument are more easily detected when they are presented in the formal manner employed by the schools, which we now proceed to do.

If the proposition: "Every absolutely necessary being is likewise an ens realissimum," is correct (and it is this which constitutes the nervus probandi of the cosmological argument), it must, like all affirmative judgements, be capable of conversion — the conversio per accidens, at least. It follows, then, that some entia realissima are absolutely necessary beings. But no ens realissimum is in any respect different from another, and what is valid of some is valid of all. In this present case, therefore, I may employ simple conversion, and say: "Every ens realissimum is a necessary being." But as this proposition is determined a priori by the conceptions contained in it, the mere conception of an ens realissimum must possess the additional attribute of absolute necessity. But this is exactly what was maintained in the ontological argument, and not recognized by the cosmological, although it formed the real ground of its disguised and illusory reasoning.

Thus the second mode employed by speculative reason of demonstrating the existence of a Supreme Being, is not only, like the first, illusory and inadequate, but possesses the additional blemish of an ignoratio elenchi — professing to conduct us by a new road to the desired goal, but bringing us back, after a short circuit, to the old path which we had deserted at its call.

I mentioned above that this cosmological argument contains a perfect nest of dialectical assumptions, which transcendental criticism does not find it difficult to expose and to dissipate. I shall merely enumerate these, leaving it to the reader, who must by this time be well practised in such matters, to investigate the fallacies residing therein.

The following fallacies, for example, are discoverable in this mode of proof: 1. The transcendental principle: "Everything that is contingent must have a cause" — a principle without significance, except in the sensuous world. For the purely intellectual conception of the contingent cannot produce any synthetical proposition, like that of causality, which is itself without significance or distinguishing characteristic except in the phenomenal world. But in the present case it is employed to help us beyond the limits of its sphere. 2. "From the impossibility of an infinite ascending series of causes in the world of sense a first cause is inferred"; a conclusion which the principles of the employment of reason do not justify even in the sphere of experience, and still less when an attempt is made to pass the limits of this sphere. 3. Reason allows itself to be satisfied upon insufficient grounds, with regard to the completion of this series. It removes all conditions (without which, however, no conception of Necessity can take place); and, as after this it is beyond our power to form any other conceptions, it accepts this as a completion of the conception it wishes to form of the series. 4. The logical possibility of a conception of the total of reality (the criterion of this possibility being the absence of contradiction) is confounded with the transcendental, which requires a principle of the practicability of such a synthesis — a principle which again refers us to the world of experience. And so on.

The aim of the cosmological argument is to avoid the necessity of proving the existence of a necessary being priori from mere conceptions — a proof which must be ontological, and of which we feel ourselves quite incapable. With this purpose, we reason from an actual existence — an experience in general, to an absolutely necessary condition of that existence. It is in this case unnecessary to demonstrate its possibility. For after having proved that it exists, the question regarding its possibility is superfluous. Now, when we wish to define more strictly the nature of this necessary being, we do not look out for some being the conception of which would enable us to comprehend the necessity of its being — for if we could do this, an empirical presupposition would be unnecessary; no, we try to discover merely the negative condition (conditio sine qua non), without which a being would not be absolutely necessary. Now this would be perfectly admissible in every sort of reasoning, from a consequence to its principle; but in the present case it unfortunately happens that the condition of absolute necessity can be discovered in but a single being, the conception of which must consequently contain all that is requisite for demonstrating the presence of absolute necessity, and thus entitle me to infer this absolute necessity a priori. That is, it must be possible to reason conversely, and say: The thing, to which the conception of the highest reality belongs, is absolutely necessary. But if I cannot reason thus — and I cannot, unless I believe in the sufficiency of the ontological argument — I find insurmountable obstacles in my new path, and am really no farther than the point from which I set out. The conception of a Supreme Being satisfies all questions a priori regarding the internal determinations of a thing, and is for this reason an ideal without equal or parallel, the general conception of it indicating it as at the same time an ens individuum among all possible things. But the conception does not satisfy the question regarding its existence — which was the purpose of all our inquiries; and, although the existence of a necessary being were admitted, we should find it impossible to answer the question: What of all things in the world must be regarded as such?

It is certainly allowable to admit the existence of an all-sufficient being — a cause of all possible effects — for the purpose of enabling reason to introduce unity into its mode and grounds of explanation with regard to phenomena. But to assert that such a being necessarily exists, is no longer the modest enunciation of an admissible hypothesis, but the boldest declaration of an apodeictic certainty; for the cognition of that which is absolutely necessary must itself possess that character.

The aim of the transcendental ideal formed by the mind is either to discover a conception which shall harmonize with the idea of absolute necessity, or a conception which shall contain that idea. If the one is possible, so is the other; for reason recognizes that alone as absolutely necessary which is necessary from its conception. But both attempts are equally beyond our power — we find it impossible to satisfy the understanding upon this point, and as impossible to induce it to remain at rest in relation to this incapacity.

Unconditioned necessity, which, as the ultimate support and stay of all existing things, is an indispensable requirement of the mind, is an abyss on the verge of which human reason trembles in dismay. Even the idea of eternity, terrible and sublime as it is, as depicted by Haller, does not produce upon the mental vision such a feeling of awe and terror; for, although it measures the duration of things, it does not support them. We cannot bear, nor can we rid ourselves of the thought that a being, which we regard as the greatest of all possible existences, should say to himself: I am from eternity to eternity; beside me there is nothing, except that which exists by my will; whence then am I? Here all sinks away from under us; and the greatest, as the smallest, perfection, hovers without stay or footing in presence of the speculative reason, which finds it as easy to part with the one as with the other.

Many physical powers, which evidence their existence by their effects, are perfectly inscrutable in their nature; they elude all our powers of observation. The transcendental object which forms the basis of phenomena, and, in connection with it, the reason why our sensibility possesses this rather than that particular kind of conditions, are and must ever remain hidden from our mental vision; the fact is there, the reason of the fact we cannot see. But an ideal of pure reason cannot be termed mysterious or inscrutable, because the only credential of its reality is the need of it felt by reason, for the purpose of giving completeness to the world of synthetical unity. An ideal is not even given as a cogitable object, and therefore cannot be inscrutable; on the contrary, it must, as a mere idea, be based on the constitution of reason itself, and on this account must be capable of explanation and solution. For the very essence of reason consists in its ability to give an account, of all our conceptions, opinions, and assertions — upon objective, or, when they happen to be illusory and fallacious, upon subjective grounds.

Detection and Explanation of the Dialectical Illusion in all Transcendental Arguments for the Existence of a Necessary Being.

Both of the above arguments are transcendental; in other words, they do not proceed upon empirical principles. For, although the cosmological argument professed to lay a basis of experience for its edifice of reasoning, it did not ground its procedure upon the peculiar constitution of experience, but upon pure principles of reason — in relation to an existence given by empirical consciousness; utterly abandoning its guidance, however, for the purpose of supporting its assertions entirely upon pure conceptions. Now what is the cause, in these transcendental arguments, of the dialectical, but natural, illusion, which connects the conceptions of necessity and supreme reality, and hypostatizes that which cannot be anything but an idea? What is the cause of this unavoidable step on the part of reason, of admitting that some one among all existing things must be necessary, while it falls back from the assertion of the existence of such a being as from an abyss? And how does reason proceed to explain this anomaly

to itself, and from the wavering condition of a timid and reluctant approbation —
always again withdrawn — arrive at a calm and settled insight into its cause?

It is something very remarkable that, on the supposition that something exists, I cannot
avoid the inference that something exists necessarily. Upon this perfectly natural —
but not on that account reliable — inference does the cosmological argument rest.
But, let me form any conception whatever of a thing, I find that I cannot cogitate the
existence of the thing as absolutely necessary, and that nothing prevents me — be
the thing or being what it may — from cogitating its non-existence. I may thus be
obliged to admit that all existing things have a necessary basis, while I cannot cogitate
any single or individual thing as necessary. In other words, I can never complete
the regress through the conditions of existence, without admitting the existence of a
necessary being; but, on the other hand, I cannot make a commencement from this
being.

If I must cogitate something as existing necessarily as the basis of existing things,
and yet am not permitted to cogitate any individual thing as in itself necessary, the
inevitable inference is that necessity and contingency are not properties of things
themselves — otherwise an internal contradiction would result; that consequently
neither of these principles are objective, but merely subjective principles of reason —
the one requiring us to seek for a necessary ground for everything that exists, that is,
to be satisfied with no other explanation than that which is complete a priori, the other
forbidding us ever to hope for the attainment of this completeness, that is, to regard
no member of the empirical world as unconditioned. In this mode of viewing them,
both principles, in their purely heuristic and regulative character, and as concerning
merely the formal interest of reason, are quite consistent with each other. The one
says: "You must philosophize upon nature," as if there existed a necessary primal
basis of all existing things, solely for the purpose of introducing systematic unity
into your knowledge, by pursuing an idea of this character — a foundation which is
arbitrarily admitted to be ultimate; while the other warns you to consider no individual
determination, concerning the existence of things, as such an ultimate foundation, that
is, as absolutely necessary, but to keep the way always open for further progress in
the deduction, and to treat every determination as determined by some other. But if
all that we perceive must be regarded as conditionally necessary, it is impossible that
anything which is empirically given should be absolutely necessary.

It follows from this that you must accept the absolutely necessary as out of and beyond
the world, inasmuch as it is useful only as a principle of the highest possible unity
in experience, and you cannot discover any such necessary existence in the would,
the second rule requiring you to regard all empirical causes of unity as themselves
deduced.

The philosophers of antiquity regarded all the forms of nature as contingent; while
matter was considered by them, in accordance with the judgement of the common
reason of mankind, as primal and necessary. But if they had regarded matter, not
relatively — as the substratum of phenomena, but absolutely and in itself — as
an independent existence, this idea of absolute necessity would have immediately
disappeared. For there is nothing absolutely connecting reason with such an existence;
on the contrary, it can annihilate it in thought, always and without self-contradiction.

But in thought alone lay the idea of absolute necessity. A regulative principle must, therefore, have been at the foundation of this opinion. In fact, extension and impenetrability — which together constitute our conception of matter — form the supreme empirical principle of the unity of phenomena, and this principle, in so far as it is empirically unconditioned, possesses the property of a regulative principle. But, as every determination of matter which constitutes what is real in it — and consequently impenetrability — is an effect, which must have a cause, and is for this reason always derived, the notion of matter cannot harmonize with the idea of a necessary being, in its character of the principle of all derived unity. For every one of its real properties, being derived, must be only conditionally necessary, and can therefore be annihilated in thought; and thus the whole existence of matter can be so annihilated or suppressed. If this were not the case, we should have found in the world of phenomena the highest ground or condition of unity — which is impossible, according to the second regulative principle. It follows that matter, and, in general, all that forms part of the world of sense, cannot be a necessary primal being, nor even a principle of empirical unity, but that this being or principle must have its place assigned without the world. And, in this way, we can proceed in perfect confidence to deduce the phenomena of the world and their existence from other phenomena, just as if there existed no necessary being; and we can at the same time, strive without ceasing towards the attainment of completeness for our deduction, just as if such a being — the supreme condition of all existences — were presupposed by the mind.

These remarks will have made it evident to the reader that the ideal of the Supreme Being, far from being an enouncement of the existence of a being in itself necessary, is nothing more than a regulative principle of reason, requiring us to regard all connection existing between phenomena as if it had its origin from an all-sufficient necessary cause, and basing upon this the rule of a systematic and necessary unity in the explanation of phenomena. We cannot, at the same time, avoid regarding, by a transcendental subreptio, this formal principle as constitutive, and hypostatizing this unity. Precisely similar is the case with our notion of space. Space is the primal condition of all forms, which are properly just so many different limitations of it; and thus, although it is merely a principle of sensibility, we cannot help regarding it as an absolutely necessary and self-subsistent thing — as an object given a priori in itself. In the same way, it is quite natural that, as the systematic unity of nature cannot be established as a principle for the empirical employment of reason, unless it is based upon the idea of an ens realissimum, as the supreme cause, we should regard this idea as a real object, and this object, in its character of supreme condition, as absolutely necessary, and that in this way a regulative should be transformed into a constitutive principle. This interchange becomes evident when I regard this supreme being, which, relatively to the world, was absolutely (unconditionally) necessary, as a thing per se. In this case, I find it impossible to represent this necessity in or by any conception, and it exists merely in my own mind, as the formal condition of thought, but not as a material and hypostatic condition of existence.

SECTION VI. Of the Impossibility of a Physico-Theological Proof.

If, then, neither a pure conception nor the general experience of an existing being can provide a sufficient basis for the proof of the existence of the Deity, we can make the attempt by the only other mode — that of grounding our argument upon a determinate experience of the phenomena of the present world, their constitution and disposition, and discover whether we can thus attain to a sound conviction of the existence of a Supreme Being. This argument we shall term the physico-theological argument. If it is shown to be insufficient, speculative reason cannot present us with any satisfactory proof of the existence of a being corresponding to our transcendental idea.

It is evident from the remarks that have been made in the preceding sections, that an answer to this question will be far from being difficult or unconvincing. For how can any experience be adequate with an idea? The very essence of an idea consists in the fact that no experience can ever be discovered congruent or adequate with it. The transcendental idea of a necessary and all-sufficient being is so immeasurably great, so high above all that is empirical, which is always conditioned, that we hope in vain to find materials in the sphere of experience sufficiently ample for our conception, and in vain seek the unconditioned among things that are conditioned, while examples, nay, even guidance is denied us by the laws of empirical synthesis.

If the Supreme Being forms a link in the chain of empirical conditions, it must be a member of the empirical series, and, like the lower members which it precedes, have its origin in some higher member of the series. If, on the other hand, we disengage it from the chain, and cogitate it as an intelligible being, apart from the series of natural causes — how shall reason bridge the abyss that separates the latter from the former? All laws respecting the regress from effects to causes, all synthetical additions to our knowledge relate solely to possible experience and the objects of the sensuous world, and, apart from them, are without significance.

The world around us opens before our view so magnificent a spectacle of order, variety, beauty, and conformity to ends, that whether we pursue our observations into the infinity of space in the one direction, or into its illimitable divisions in the other, whether we regard the world in its greatest or its least manifestations — even after we have attained to the highest summit of knowledge which our weak minds can reach, we find that language in the presence of wonders so inconceivable has lost its force, and number its power to reckon, nay, even thought fails to conceive adequately, and our conception of the whole dissolves into an astonishment without power of expression — all the more eloquent that it is dumb. Everywhere around us we observe a chain of causes and effects, of means and ends, of death and birth; and, as nothing has entered of itself into the condition in which we find it, we are constantly referred to some other thing, which itself suggests the same inquiry regarding its cause, and thus the universe must sink into the abyss of nothingness, unless we admit that, besides this infinite chain of contingencies, there exists something that is primal and self-subsistent — something which, as the cause of this phenomenal world, secures its continuance and preservation.

This highest cause — what magnitude shall we attribute to it? Of the content of the world we are ignorant; still less can we estimate its magnitude by comparison with the sphere of the possible. But this supreme cause being a necessity of the human mind, what is there to prevent us from attributing to it such a degree of perfection as to place it above the sphere of all that is possible? This we can easily do, although only by the aid of the faint outline of an abstract conception, by representing this being to ourselves as containing in itself, as an individual substance, all possible perfection — a conception which satisfies that requirement of reason which demands parsimony in principles, which is free from self-contradiction, which even contributes to the extension of the employment of reason in experience, by means of the guidance afforded by this idea to order and system, and which in no respect conflicts with any law of experience.

This argument always deserves to be mentioned with respect. It is the oldest, the clearest, and that most in conformity with the common reason of humanity. It animates the study of nature, as it itself derives its existence and draws ever new strength from that source. It introduces aims and ends into a sphere in which our observation could not of itself have discovered them, and extends our knowledge of nature, by directing our attention to a unity, the principle of which lies beyond nature. This knowledge of nature again reacts upon this idea — its cause; and thus our belief in a divine author of the universe rises to the power of an irresistible conviction.

For these reasons it would be utterly hopeless to attempt to rob this argument of the authority it has always enjoyed. The mind, unceasingly elevated by these considerations, which, although empirical, are so remarkably powerful, and continually adding to their force, will not suffer itself to be depressed by the doubts suggested by subtle speculation; it tears itself out of this state of uncertainty, the moment it casts a look upon the wondrous forms of nature and the majesty of the universe, and rises from height to height, from condition to condition, till it has elevated itself to the supreme and unconditioned author of all.

But although we have nothing to object to the reasonableness and utility of this procedure, but have rather to commend and encourage it, we cannot approve of the claims which this argument advances to demonstrative certainty and to a reception upon its own merits, apart from favour or support by other arguments. Nor can it injure the cause of morality to endeavour to lower the tone of the arrogant sophist, and to teach him that modesty and moderation which are the properties of a belief that brings calm and content into the mind, without prescribing to it an unworthy subjection. I maintain, then, that the physico-theological argument is insufficient of itself to prove the existence of a Supreme Being, that it must entrust this to the ontological argument — to which it serves merely as an introduction, and that, consequently, this argument contains the only possible ground of proof (possessed by speculative reason) for the existence of this being.

The chief momenta in the physico-theological argument are as follow: 1. We observe in the world manifest signs of an arrangement full of purpose, executed with great wisdom, and argument in whole of a content indescribably various, and of an extent without limits. 2. This arrangement of means and ends is entirely foreign to the things existing in the world — it belongs to them merely as a contingent attribute; in other words, the nature of different things could not of itself, whatever means were employed, harmoniously tend towards certain purposes, were they not chosen and directed for these purposes by a rational and disposing principle, in accordance with certain fundamental ideas. 3. There exists, therefore, a sublime and wise cause (or several), which is not merely a blind, all-powerful nature, producing the beings and events which fill the world in unconscious fecundity, but a free and intelligent cause of the world. 4. The unity of this cause may be inferred from the unity of the reciprocal relation existing between the parts of the world, as portions of an artistic edifice — an inference which all our observation favours, and all principles of analogy support.

In the above argument, it is inferred from the analogy of certain products of nature with those of human art, when it compels Nature to bend herself to its purposes, as in the case of a house, a ship, or a watch, that the same kind of causality — namely, understanding and will — resides in nature. It is also declared that the internal possibility of this freely-acting nature (which is the source of all art, and perhaps also of human reason) is derivable from another and superhuman art — a conclusion which would perhaps be found incapable of standing the test of subtle transcendental criticism. But to neither of these opinions shall we at present object. We shall only remark that it must be confessed that, if we are to discuss the subject of cause at all, we cannot proceed more securely than with the guidance of the analogy subsisting between nature and such products of design — these being the only products whose causes and modes of organization are completely known to us. Reason would be unable to satisfy her own requirements, if she passed from a causality which she does know, to obscure and indemonstrable principles of explanation which she does not know.

According to the physico-theological argument, the connection and harmony existing in the world evidence the contingency of the form merely, but not of the matter, that is, of the substance of the world. To establish the truth of the latter opinion, it would be necessary to prove that all things would be in themselves incapable of this harmony and order, unless they were, even as regards their substance, the product of a supreme wisdom. But this would require very different grounds of proof from those presented by the analogy with human art. This proof can at most, therefore, demonstrate the existence of an architect of the world, whose efforts are limited by the capabilities of the material with which he works, but not of a creator of the world, to whom all things are subject. Thus this argument is utterly insufficient for the task before us — a demonstration of the existence of an all-sufficient being. If we wish to prove the contingency of matter, we must have recourse to a transcendental argument, which the physico-theological was constructed expressly to avoid.

We infer, from the order and design visible in the universe, as a disposition of a thoroughly contingent character, the existence of a cause proportionate thereto. The conception of this cause must contain certain determinate qualities, and it must therefore be regarded as the conception of a being which possesses all power, wisdom, and so on, in one word, all perfection — the conception, that is, of an all-sufficient being. For the predicates of very great, astonishing, or immeasurable power and excellence, give us no determinate conception of the thing, nor do they inform us what the thing may be in itself. They merely indicate the relation existing between the magnitude of the object and the observer, who compares it with himself and with his own power of comprehension, and are mere expressions of praise and reverence, by which the object is either magnified, or the observing subject depreciated in relation to the object. Where we have to do with the magnitude (of the perfection) of a thing, we can discover no determinate conception, except that which comprehends all possible perfection or completeness, and it is only the total (omnitudo) of reality which is completely determined in and through its conception alone.

Now it cannot be expected that any one will be bold enough to declare that he has a perfect insight into the relation which the magnitude of the world he contemplates bears (in its extent as well as in its content) to omnipotence, into that of the order and design in the world to the highest wisdom, and that of the unity of the world to the absolute unity of a Supreme Being. Physico-theology is therefore incapable of presenting a determinate conception of a supreme cause of the world, and is therefore insufficient as a principle of theology — a theology which is itself to be the basis of religion.

The attainment of absolute totality is completely impossible on the path of empiricism. And yet this is the path pursued in the physico-theological argument. What means shall we employ to bridge the abyss?

After elevating ourselves to admiration of the magnitude of the power, wisdom, and other attributes of the author of the world, and finding we can advance no further, we leave the argument on empirical grounds, and proceed to infer the contingency of the world from the order and conformity to aims that are observable in it. From this contingency we infer, by the help of transcendental conceptions alone, the existence of something absolutely necessary; and, still advancing, proceed from the conception of the absolute necessity of the first cause to the completely determined or determining conception thereof — the conception of an all-embracing reality. Thus the physico-theological, failing in its undertaking, recurs in its embarrassment to the cosmological argument; and, as this is merely the ontological argument in disguise, it executes its design solely by the aid of pure reason, although it at first professed to have no connection with this faculty and to base its entire procedure upon experience alone.

The physico-theologians have therefore no reason to regard with such contempt the transcendental mode of argument, and to look down upon it, with the conceit of clear-sighted observers of nature, as the brain-cobweb of obscure speculatists. For, if they reflect upon and examine their own arguments, they will find that, after following for some time the path of nature and experience, and discovering themselves no nearer their object, they suddenly leave this path and pass into the region of pure possibility, where they hope to reach upon the wings of ideas what had eluded all their empirical investigations. Gaining, as they think, a firm footing after this immense leap, they extend their determinate conception — into the possession of which they have come, they know not how — over the whole sphere of creation, and explain their ideal, which is entirely a product of pure reason, by illustrations drawn from experience — though in a degree miserably unworthy of the grandeur of the object, while they refuse to acknowledge that they have arrived at this cognition or hypothesis by a very different road from that of experience.

Thus the physico-theological is based upon the cosmological, and this upon the ontological proof of the existence of a Supreme Being; and as besides these three there is no other path open to speculative reason, the ontological proof, on the ground of pure conceptions of reason, is the only possible one, if any proof of a proposition so far transcending the empirical exercise of the understanding is possible at all.

SECTION VII. Critique of all Theology based upon Speculative Principles of Reason.

If by the term theology I understand the cognition of a primal being, that cognition is based either upon reason alone (theologia rationalis) or upon revelation (theologia revelata). The former cogitates its object either by means of pure transcendental conceptions, as an ens originarium, realissimum, ens entium, and is termed transcendental theology; or, by means of a conception derived from the nature of our own mind, as a supreme intelligence, and must then be entitled natural theology. The person who believes in a transcendental theology alone, is termed a deist; he who acknowledges the possibility of a natural theology also, a theist. The former admits that we can cognize by pure reason alone the existence of a Supreme Being, but at the same time maintains that our conception of this being is purely transcendental, and that all we can say of it is that it possesses all reality, without being able to define it more closely. The second asserts that reason is capable of presenting us, from the analogy with nature, with a more definite conception of this being, and that its operations, as the cause of all things, are the results of intelligence and free will. The former regards the Supreme Being as the cause of the world — whether by the necessity of his nature, or as a free agent, is left undetermined; the latter considers this being as the author of the world.

Transcendental theology aims either at inferring the existence of a Supreme Being from a general experience, without any closer reference to the world to which this experience belongs, and in this case it is called cosmotheology; or it endeavours to cognize the existence of such a being, through mere conceptions, without the aid of experience, and is then termed ontotheology.

Natural theology infers the attributes and the existence of an author of the world, from the constitution of, the order and unity observable in, the world, in which two modes of causality must be admitted to exist — those of nature and freedom. Thus it rises from this world to a supreme intelligence, either as the principle of all natural, or of all moral order and perfection. In the former case it is termed physico-theology, in the latter, ethical or moral-theology.*

[Note: Not theological ethics; for this science contains ethical laws, which presuppose the existence of a Supreme Governor of the world; while moral-theology, on the contrary, is the expression of a conviction of the existence of a Supreme Being, founded upon ethical laws.]

As we are wont to understand by the term God not merely an eternal nature, the operations of which are insensate and blind, but a Supreme Being, who is the free and intelligent author of all things, and as it is this latter view alone that can be of interest to humanity, we might, in strict rigour, deny to the deist any belief in God at all, and regard him merely as a maintainer of the existence of a primal being or thing — the supreme cause of all other things. But, as no one ought to be blamed, merely because he does not feel himself justified in maintaining a certain opinion, as if he altogether denied its truth and asserted the opposite, it is more correct — as it is less harsh — to say, the deist believes in a God, the theist in a living God (summa intelligentia). We shall now proceed to investigate the sources of all these attempts of reason to establish the existence of a Supreme Being.

It may be sufficient in this place to define theoretical knowledge or cognition as knowledge of that which is, and practical knowledge as knowledge of that which ought to be. In this view, the theoretical employment of reason is that by which I cognize a priori (as necessary) that something is, while the practical is that by which I cognize a priori what ought to happen. Now, if it is an indubitably certain, though at the same time an entirely conditioned truth, that something is, or ought to happen, either a certain determinate condition of this truth is absolutely necessary, or such a condition may be arbitrarily presupposed. In the former case the condition is postulated (per thesin), in the latter supposed (per hypothesin). There are certain practical laws — those of morality — which are absolutely necessary. Now, if these laws necessarily presuppose the existence of some being, as the condition of the possibility of their obligatory power, this being must be postulated, because the conditioned, from which we reason to this determinate condition, is itself cognized a priori as absolutely necessary. We shall at some future time show that the moral laws not merely presuppose the existence of a Supreme Being, but also, as themselves absolutely necessary in a different relation, demand or postulate it — although only from a practical point of view. The discussion of this argument we postpone for the present.

When the question relates merely to that which is, not to that which ought to be, the conditioned which is presented in experience is always cogitated as contingent. For this reason its condition cannot be regarded as absolutely necessary, but merely as relatively necessary, or rather as needful; the condition is in itself and a priori a mere arbitrary presupposition in aid of the cognition, by reason, of the conditioned. If, then, we are to possess a theoretical cognition of the absolute necessity of a thing, we cannot attain to this cognition otherwise than a priori by means of conceptions; while it is impossible in this way to cognize the existence of a cause which bears any relation to an existence given in experience.

Theoretical cognition is speculative when it relates to an object or certain conceptions of an object which is not given and cannot be discovered by means of experience. It is opposed to the cognition of nature, which concerns only those objects or predicates which can be presented in a possible experience.
The principle that everything which happens (the empirically contingent) must have a cause, is a principle of the cognition of nature, but not of speculative cognition. For, if we change it into an abstract principle, and deprive it of its reference to experience and the empirical, we shall find that it cannot with justice be regarded any longer as a synthetical proposition, and that it is impossible to discover any mode of transition from that which exists to something entirely different — termed cause. Nay, more, the conception of a cause likewise that of the contingent — loses, in this speculative mode of employing it, all significance, for its objective reality and meaning are comprehensible from experience alone.

When from the existence of the universe and the things in it the existence of a cause of the universe is inferred, reason is proceeding not in the natural, but in the speculative method. For the principle of the former enounces, not that things themselves or substances, but only that which happens or their states — as empirically contingent, have a cause: the assertion that the existence of substance itself is contingent is not justified by experience, it is the assertion of a reason employing its principles in a speculative manner. If, again, I infer from the form of the universe, from the way in which all things are connected and act and react upon each other, the existence of a cause entirely distinct from the universe — this would again be a judgement of purely speculative reason; because the object in this case — the cause — can never be an object of possible experience. In both these cases the principle of causality, which is valid only in the field of experience — useless and even meaningless beyond this region, would be diverted from its proper destination.

Now I maintain that all attempts of reason to establish a theology by the aid of speculation alone are fruitless, that the principles of reason as applied to nature do not conduct us to any theological truths, and, consequently, that a rational theology can have no existence, unless it is founded upon the laws of morality. For all synthetical principles of the understanding are valid only as immanent in experience; while the cognition of a Supreme Being necessitates their being employed transcendentally, and of this the understanding is quite incapable. If the empirical law of causality is to conduct us to a Supreme Being, this being must belong to the chain of empirical objects — in which case it would be, like all phenomena, itself conditioned. If the possibility of passing the limits of experience be admitted, by means of the dynamical law of the relation of an effect to its cause, what kind of conception shall we obtain by this procedure? Certainly not the conception of a Supreme Being, because experience never presents us with the greatest of all possible effects, and it is only an effect of this character that could witness to the existence of a corresponding cause. If, for the purpose of fully satisfying the requirements of Reason, we recognize her right to assert the existence of a perfect and absolutely necessary being, this can be admitted only from favour, and cannot be regarded as the result or irresistible demonstration. The physico-theological proof may add weight to others — if other proofs there are — by connecting speculation with experience; but in itself it rather prepares the mind for theological cognition, and gives it a right and natural direction, than establishes a sure foundation for theology.

It is now perfectly evident that transcendental questions admit only of transcendental answers — those presented a priori by pure conceptions without the least empirical admixture. But the question in the present case is evidently synthetical — it aims at the extension of our cognition beyond the bounds of experience — it requires an assurance respecting the existence of a being corresponding with the idea in our minds, to which no experience can ever be adequate. Now it has been abundantly proved that all a priori synthetical cognition is possible only as the expression of the formal conditions of a possible experience; and that the validity of all principles depends upon their immanence in the field of experience, that is, their relation to objects of empirical cognition or phenomena. Thus all transcendental procedure in reference to speculative theology is without result.

If any one prefers doubting the conclusiveness of the proofs of our analytic to losing the persuasion of the validity of these old and time honoured arguments, he at least cannot decline answering the question — how he can pass the limits of all possible experience by the help of mere ideas. If he talks of new arguments, or of improvements upon old arguments, I request him to spare me. There is certainly no great choice in this sphere of discussion, as all speculative arguments must at last look for support to the ontological, and I have, therefore, very little to fear from the argumentative fecundity of the dogmatical defenders of a non-sensuous reason. Without looking upon myself as a remarkably combative person, I shall not decline the challenge to detect the fallacy and destroy the pretensions of every attempt of speculative theology. And yet the hope of better fortune never deserts those who are accustomed to the dogmatical mode of procedure. I shall, therefore, restrict myself to the simple and equitable demand that such reasoners will demonstrate, from the nature of the human mind as well as from that of the other sources of knowledge, how we are to proceed to extend our cognition completely a priori, and to carry it to that point where experience abandons us, and no means exist of guaranteeing the objective reality of our conceptions. In whatever way the understanding may have attained to a conception, the existence of the object of the conception cannot be discovered in it by analysis, because the cognition of the existence of the object depends upon the object's being posited and given in itself apart from the conception. But it is utterly impossible to go beyond our conception, without the aid of experience — which presents to the mind nothing but phenomena, or to attain by the help of mere conceptions to a conviction of the existence of new kinds of objects or supernatural beings.

But although pure speculative reason is far from sufficient to demonstrate the existence of a Supreme Being, it is of the highest utility in correcting our conception of this being — on the supposition that we can attain to the cognition of it by some other means — in making it consistent with itself and with all other conceptions of intelligible objects, clearing it from all that is incompatible with the conception of an ens summun, and eliminating from it all limitations or admixtures of empirical elements.

Transcendental theology is still therefore, notwithstanding its objective insufficiency, of importance in a negative respect; it is useful as a test of the procedure of reason when engaged with pure ideas, no other than a transcendental standard being in this case admissible. For if, from a practical point of view, the hypothesis of a Supreme and All-sufficient Being is to maintain its validity without opposition, it must be of the highest importance to define this conception in a correct and rigorous manner — as the transcendental conception of a necessary being, to eliminate all phenomenal elements (anthropomorphism in its most extended signification), and at the same time to overflow all contradictory assertions — be they atheistic, deistic, or anthropomorphic. This is of course very easy; as the same arguments which demonstrated the inability of human reason to affirm the existence of a Supreme Being must be alike sufficient to prove the invalidity of its denial. For it is impossible to gain from the pure speculation of reason demonstration that there exists no Supreme Being, as the ground of all that exists, or that this being possesses none of those properties which we regard as analogical with the dynamical qualities of a thinking being, or that, as the anthropomorphists would have us believe, it is subject to all the limitations which sensibility imposes upon those intelligences which exist in the world of experience.

A Supreme Being is, therefore, for the speculative reason, a mere ideal, though a faultless one — a conception which perfects and crowns the system of human cognition, but the objective reality of which can neither be proved nor disproved by pure reason. If this defect is ever supplied by a moral theology, the problematic transcendental theology which has preceded, will have been at least serviceable as demonstrating the mental necessity existing for the conception, by the complete determination of it which it has furnished, and the ceaseless testing of the conclusions of a reason often deceived by sense, and not always in harmony with its own ideas. The attributes of necessity, infinitude, unity, existence apart from the world (and not as a world soul), eternity (free from conditions of time), omnipresence (free from conditions of space), omnipotence, and others, are pure transcendental predicates; and thus the accurate conception of a Supreme Being, which every theology requires, is furnished by transcendental theology alone.

APPENDIX. Of the Regulative Employment of the Ideas of Pure Reason.

The result of all the dialectical attempts of pure reason not only confirms the truth of what we have already proved in our Transcendental Analytic, namely, that all inferences which would lead us beyond the limits of experience are fallacious and groundless, but it at the same time teaches us this important lesson, that human reason has a natural inclination to overstep these limits, and that transcendental ideas are as much the natural property of the reason as categories are of the understanding. There exists this difference, however, that while the categories never mislead us, outward objects being always in perfect harmony therewith, ideas are the parents of irresistible illusions, the severest and most subtle criticism being required to save us from the fallacies which they induce.

Whatever is grounded in the nature of our powers will be found to be in harmony with the final purpose and proper employment of these powers, when once we have discovered their true direction and aim. We are entitled to suppose, therefore, that there exists a mode of employing transcendental ideas which is proper and immanent; although, when we mistake their meaning, and regard them as conceptions of actual things, their mode of application is transcendent and delusive. For it is not the idea itself, but only the employment of the idea in relation to possible experience, that is transcendent or immanent. An idea is employed transcendently, when it is applied to an object falsely believed to be adequate with and to correspond to it; imminently, when it is applied solely to the employment of the understanding in the sphere of experience. Thus all errors of subreptio — of misapplication, are to be ascribed to defects of judgement, and not to understanding or reason.

Reason never has an immediate relation to an object; it relates immediately to the understanding alone. It is only through the understanding that it can be employed in the field of experience. It does not form conceptions of objects, it merely arranges them and gives to them that unity which they are capable of possessing when the sphere of their application has been extended as widely as possible. Reason avails itself of the conception of the understanding for the sole purpose of producing totality in the different series. This totality the understanding does not concern itself with; its only occupation is the connection of experiences, by which series of conditions in accordance with conceptions are established. The object of reason is, therefore, the understanding and its proper destination. As the latter brings unity into the diversity of objects by means of its conceptions, so the former brings unity into the diversity of conceptions by means of ideas; as it sets the final aim of a collective unity to the operations of the understanding, which without this occupies itself with a distributive unity alone.

I accordingly maintain that transcendental ideas can never be employed as constitutive ideas, that they cannot be conceptions of objects, and that, when thus considered, they assume a fallacious and dialectical character. But, on the other hand, they are capable of an admirable and indispensably necessary application to objects — as regulative ideas, directing the understanding to a certain aim, the guiding lines towards which all its laws follow, and in which they all meet in one point. This point — though a mere idea (focus imaginarius), that is, not a point from which the conceptions of the understanding do really proceed, for it lies beyond the sphere of possible experience — serves, notwithstanding, to give to these conceptions the greatest possible unity combined with the greatest possible extension. Hence arises the natural illusion which induces us to believe that these lines proceed from an object which lies out of the sphere of empirical cognition, just as objects reflected in a mirror appear to be behind it. But this illusion — which we may hinder from imposing upon us — is necessary and unavoidable, if we desire to see, not only those objects which lie before us, but those which are at a great distance behind us; that is to say, when, in the present case, we direct the aims of the understanding, beyond every given experience, towards an extension as great as can possibly be attained.

If we review our cognitions in their entire extent, we shall find that the peculiar business of reason is to arrange them into a system, that is to say, to give them connection according to a principle. This unity presupposes an idea — the idea of the form of a whole (of cognition), preceding the determinate cognition of the parts, and containing the conditions which determine a priori to every part its place and relation to the other parts of the whole system. This idea, accordingly, demands complete unity in the cognition of the understanding — not the unity of a contingent aggregate, but that of a system connected according to necessary laws. It cannot be affirmed with propriety that this idea is a conception of an object; it is merely a conception of the complete unity of the conceptions of objects, in so far as this unity is available to the understanding as a rule. Such conceptions of reason are not derived from nature; on the contrary, we employ them for the interrogation and investigation of nature, and regard our cognition as defective so long as it is not adequate to them. We admit that such a thing as pure earth, pure water, or pure air, is not to be discovered. And yet we require these conceptions (which have their origin in the reason, so far as regards their absolute purity and completeness) for the purpose of determining the share which each of these natural causes has in every phenomenon. Thus the different kinds of matter are all referred to earths, as mere weight; to salts and inflammable bodies, as pure force; and finally, to water and air, as the vehicula of the former, or the machines employed by them in their operations — for the purpose of explaining the chemical action and reaction of bodies in accordance with the idea of a mechanism. For, although not actually so expressed, the influence of such ideas of reason is very observable in the procedure of natural philosophers.

If reason is the faculty of deducing the particular from the general, and if the general be certain in se and given, it is only necessary that the judgement should subsume the particular under the general, the particular being thus necessarily determined. I shall term this the demonstrative or apodeictic employment of reason. If, however, the general is admitted as problematical only, and is a mere idea, the particular case is certain, but the universality of the rule which applies to this particular case remains a problem. Several particular cases, the certainty of which is beyond doubt, are then taken and examined, for the purpose of discovering whether the rule is applicable to them; and if it appears that all the particular cases which can be collected follow from the rule, its universality is inferred, and at the same time, all the causes which have not, or cannot be presented to our observation, are concluded to be of the same character with those which we have observed. This I shall term the hypothetical employment of the reason.

The hypothetical exercise of reason by the aid of ideas employed as problematical conceptions is properly not constitutive. That is to say, if we consider the subject strictly, the truth of the rule, which has been employed as an hypothesis, does not follow from the use that is made of it by reason. For how can we know all the possible cases that may arise? some of which may, however, prove exceptions to the universality of the rule. This employment of reason is merely regulative, and its sole aim is the introduction of unity into the aggregate of our particular cognitions, and thereby the approximating of the rule to universality.

The object of the hypothetical employment of reason is therefore the systematic unity of cognitions; and this unity is the criterion of the truth of a rule. On the other hand, this systematic unity — as a mere idea — is in fact merely a unity projected, not to be regarded as given, but only in the light of a problem — a problem which serves, however, as a principle for the various and particular exercise of the understanding in experience, directs it with regard to those cases which are not presented to our observation, and introduces harmony and consistency into all its operations.

All that we can be certain of from the above considerations is that this systematic unity is a logical principle, whose aim is to assist the understanding, where it cannot of itself attain to rules, by means of ideas, to bring all these various rules under one principle, and thus to ensure the most complete consistency and connection that can be attained. But the assertion that objects and the understanding by which they are cognized are so constituted as to be determined to systematic unity, that this may be postulated a priori, without any reference to the interest of reason, and that we are justified in declaring all possible cognitions — empirical and others — to possess systematic unity, and to be subject to general principles from which, notwithstanding their various character, they are all derivable such an assertion can be founded only upon a transcendental principle of reason, which would render this systematic unity not subjectively and logically — in its character of a method, but objectively necessary.

We shall illustrate this by an example. The conceptions of the understanding make us acquainted, among many other kinds of unity, with that of the causality of a substance, which is termed power. The different phenomenal manifestations of the same substance appear at first view to be so very dissimilar that we are inclined to assume the existence of just as many different powers as there are different effects — as, in the case of the human mind, we have feeling, consciousness, imagination, memory, wit, analysis, pleasure, desire and so on. Now we are required by a logical maxim to reduce these differences to as small a number as possible, by comparing them and discovering the hidden identity which exists. We must inquire, for example, whether or not imagination (connected with consciousness), memory, wit, and analysis are not merely different forms of understanding and reason. The idea of a fundamental power, the existence of which no effort of logic can assure us of, is the problem to be solved, for the systematic representation of the existing variety of powers. The logical principle of reason requires us to produce as great a unity as is possible in the system of our cognitions; and the more the phenomena of this and the other power are found to be identical, the more probable does it become, that they are nothing but different manifestations of one and the same power, which may be called, relatively speaking, a fundamental power. And so with other cases.

These relatively fundamental powers must again be compared with each other, to discover, if possible, the one radical and absolutely fundamental power of which they are but the manifestations. But this unity is purely hypothetical. It is not maintained, that this unity does really exist, but that we must, in the interest of reason, that is, for the establishment of principles for the various rules presented by experience, try to discover and introduce it, so far as is practicable, into the sphere of our cognitions.

But the transcendental employment of the understanding would lead us to believe that this idea of a fundamental power is not problematical, but that it possesses objective reality, and thus the systematic unity of the various powers or forces in a substance is demanded by the understanding and erected into an apodeictic or necessary principle. For, without having attempted to discover the unity of the various powers existing in nature, nay, even after all our attempts have failed, we notwithstanding presuppose that it does exist, and may be, sooner or later, discovered. And this reason does, not only, as in the case above adduced, with regard to the unity of substance, but where many substances, although all to a certain extent homogeneous, are discoverable, as in the case of matter in general. Here also does reason presuppose the existence of the systematic unity of various powers — inasmuch as particular laws of nature are subordinate to general laws; and parsimony in principles is not merely an economical principle of reason, but an essential law of nature.

We cannot understand, in fact, how a logical principle of unity can of right exist, unless we presuppose a transcendental principle, by which such a systematic unit — as a property of objects themselves — is regarded as necessary a priori. For with what right can reason, in its logical exercise, require us to regard the variety of forces which nature displays, as in effect a disguised unity, and to deduce them from one fundamental force or power, when she is free to admit that it is just as possible that all forces should be different in kind, and that a systematic unity is not conformable to the design of nature? In this view of the case, reason would be proceeding in direct opposition to her own destination, by setting as an aim an idea which entirely conflicts with the procedure and arrangement of nature. Neither can we assert that reason has previously inferred this unity from the contingent nature of phenomena. For the law of reason which requires us to seek for this unity is a necessary law, inasmuch as without it we should not possess a faculty of reason, nor without reason a consistent and self-accordant mode of employing the understanding, nor, in the absence of this, any proper and sufficient criterion of empirical truth. In relation to this criterion, therefore, we must suppose the idea of the systematic unity of nature to possess objective validity and necessity.

We find this transcendental presupposition lurking in different forms in the principles of philosophers, although they have neither recognized it nor confessed to themselves its presence. That the diversities of individual things do not exclude identity of species, that the various species must be considered as merely different determinations of a few genera, and these again as divisions of still higher races, and so on — that, accordingly, a certain systematic unity of all possible empirical conceptions, in so far as they can be deduced from higher and more general conceptions, must be sought for, is a scholastic maxim or logical principle, without which reason could not be employed by us. For we can infer the particular from the general, only in so far as general properties of things constitute the foundation upon which the particular rest.

That the same unity exists in nature is presupposed by philosophers in the well-known scholastic maxim, which forbids us unnecessarily to augment the number of entities or principles (entia praeter necessitatem non esse multiplicanda). This maxim asserts that nature herself assists in the establishment of this unity of reason, and that the seemingly infinite diversity of phenomena should not deter us from the expectation of discovering beneath this diversity a unity of fundamental properties, of which the aforesaid variety is but a more or less determined form. This unity, although a mere idea, thinkers have found it necessary rather to moderate the desire than to encourage it. It was considered a great step when chemists were able to reduce all salts to two main genera — acids and alkalis; and they regard this difference as itself a mere variety, or different manifestation of one and the same fundamental material. The different kinds of earths (stones and even metals) chemists have endeavoured to reduce to three, and afterwards to two; but still, not content with this advance, they cannot but think that behind these diversities there lurks but one genus — nay, that even salts and earths have a common principle. It might be conjectured that this is merely an economical plan of reason, for the purpose of sparing itself trouble, and an attempt of a purely hypothetical character, which, when successful, gives an appearance of probability to the principle of explanation employed by the reason. But a selfish purpose of this kind is easily to be distinguished from the idea, according to which every one presupposes that this unity is in accordance with the laws of nature, and that reason does not in this case request, but requires, although we are quite unable to determine the proper limits of this unity.

If the diversity existing in phenomena — a diversity not of form (for in this they may be similar) but of content — were so great that the subtlest human reason could never by comparison discover in them the least similarity (which is not impossible), in this case the logical law of genera would be without foundation, the conception of a genus, nay, all general conceptions would be impossible, and the faculty of the understanding, the exercise of which is restricted to the world of conceptions, could not exist. The logical principle of genera, accordingly, if it is to be applied to nature (by which I mean objects presented to our senses), presupposes a transcendental principle. In accordance with this principle, homogeneity is necessarily presupposed in the variety of phenomena (although we are unable to determine a priori the degree of this homogeneity), because without it no empirical conceptions, and consequently no experience, would be possible.

The logical principle of genera, which demands identity in phenomena, is balanced by another principle — that of species, which requires variety and diversity in things, notwithstanding their accordance in the same genus, and directs the understanding to attend to the one no less than to the other. This principle (of the faculty of distinction) acts as a check upon the reason and reason exhibits in this respect a double and conflicting interest — on the one hand, the interest in the extent (the interest of generality) in relation to genera; on the other, that of the content (the interest of individuality) in relation to the variety of species. In the former case, the understanding cogitates more under its conceptions, in the latter it cogitates more in them. This distinction manifests itself likewise in the habits of thought peculiar to natural philosophers, some of whom — the remarkably speculative heads — may be said to be hostile to heterogeneity in phenomena, and have their eyes always fixed on the unity of genera, while others — with a strong empirical tendency — aim unceasingly at the analysis of phenomena, and almost destroy in us the hope of ever being able to estimate the character of these according to general principles.

The latter mode of thought is evidently based upon a logical principle, the aim of which is the systematic completeness of all cognitions. This principle authorizes me, beginning at the genus, to descend to the various and diverse contained under it; and in this way extension, as in the former case unity, is assured to the system. For if we merely examine the sphere of the conception which indicates a genus, we cannot discover how far it is possible to proceed in the division of that sphere; just as it is impossible, from the consideration of the space occupied by matter, to determine how far we can proceed in the division of it. Hence every genus must contain different species, and these again different subspecies; and as each of the latter must itself contain a sphere (must be of a certain extent, as a conceptus communis), reason demands that no species or sub-species is to be considered as the lowest possible. For a species or sub-species, being always a conception, which contains only what is common to a number of different things, does not completely determine any individual thing, or relate immediately to it, and must consequently contain other conceptions, that is, other sub-species under it. This law of specification may be thus expressed: entium varietates non temere sunt minuendae.

But it is easy to see that this logical law would likewise be without sense or application, were it not based upon a transcendental law of specification, which certainly does not require that the differences existing phenomena should be infinite in number, for the logical principle, which merely maintains the indeterminateness of the logical sphere of a conception, in relation to its possible division, does not authorize this statement; while it does impose upon the understanding the duty of searching for subspecies to every species, and minor differences in every difference. For, were there no lower conceptions, neither could there be any higher. Now the understanding cognizes only by means of conceptions; consequently, how far soever it may proceed in division, never by mere intuition, but always by lower and lower conceptions. The cognition of phenomena in their complete determination (which is possible only by means of the understanding) requires an unceasingly continued specification of conceptions, and a progression to ever smaller differences, of which abstraction bad been made in the conception of the species, and still more in that of the genus.

This law of specification cannot be deduced from experience; it can never present us with a principle of so universal an application. Empirical specification very soon stops in its distinction of diversities, and requires the guidance of the transcendental law, as a principle of the reason — a law which imposes on us the necessity of never ceasing in our search for differences, even although these may not present themselves to the senses. That absorbent earths are of different kinds could only be discovered by obeying the anticipatory law of reason, which imposes upon the understanding the task of discovering the differences existing between these earths, and supposes that nature is richer in substances than our senses would indicate. The faculty of the understanding belongs to us just as much under the presupposition of differences in the objects of nature, as under the condition that these objects are homogeneous, because we could not possess conceptions, nor make any use of our understanding, were not the phenomena included under these conceptions in some respects dissimilar, as well as similar, in their character.

Reason thus prepares the sphere of the understanding for the operations of this faculty: 1. By the principle of the homogeneity of the diverse in higher genera; 2. By the principle of the variety of the homogeneous in lower species; and, to complete the systematic unity, it adds, 3. A law of the affinity of all conceptions which prescribes a continuous transition from one species to every other by the gradual increase of diversity. We may term these the principles of the homogeneity, the specification, and the continuity of forms. The latter results from the union of the two former, inasmuch as we regard the systematic connection as complete in thought, in the ascent to higher genera, as well as in the descent to lower species. For all diversities must be related to each other, as they all spring from one highest genus, descending through the different gradations of a more and more extended determination.

We may illustrate the systematic unity produced by the three logical principles in the following manner. Every conception may be regarded as a point, which, as the standpoint of a spectator, has a certain horizon, which may be said to enclose a number of things that may be viewed, so to speak, from that centre. Within this horizon there must be an infinite number of other points, each of which has its own horizon, smaller and more circumscribed; in other words, every species contains sub-species, according to the principle of specification, and the logical horizon consists of smaller horizons (subspecies), but not of points (individuals), which possess no extent. But different horizons or genera, which include under them so many conceptions, may have one common horizon, from which, as from a mid-point, they may be surveyed; and we may proceed thus, till we arrive at the highest genus, or universal and true horizon, which is determined by the highest conception, and which contains under itself all differences and varieties, as genera, species, and subspecies.

To this highest standpoint I am conducted by the law of homogeneity, as to all lower and more variously-determined conceptions by the law of specification. Now as in this way there exists no void in the whole extent of all possible conceptions, and as out of the sphere of these the mind can discover nothing, there arises from the presupposition of the universal horizon above mentioned, and its complete division, the principle: Non datur vacuum formarum. This principle asserts that there are not different primitive and highest genera, which stand isolated, so to speak, from each other, but all the various genera are mere divisions and limitations of one highest and universal genus; and hence follows immediately the principle: Datur continuum formarum. This principle indicates that all differences of species limit each other, and do not admit of transition from one to another by a saltus, but only through smaller degrees of the difference between the one species and the other. In one word, there are no species or sub-species which (in the view of reason) are the nearest possible to each other; intermediate species or sub-species being always possible, the difference of which from each of the former is always smaller than the difference existing between these.

The first law, therefore, directs us to avoid the notion that there exist different primal genera, and enounces the fact of perfect homogeneity; the second imposes a check upon this tendency to unity and prescribes the distinction of sub-species, before proceeding to apply our general conceptions to individuals. The third unites both the former, by enouncing the fact of homogeneity as existing even in the most various diversity, by means of the gradual transition from one species to another. Thus it indicates a relationship between the different branches or species, in so far as they all spring from the same stem.

But this logical law of the continuum specierum (formarum logicarum) presupposes a transcendental principle (lex continui in natura), without which the understanding might be led into error, by following the guidance of the former, and thus perhaps pursuing a path contrary to that prescribed by nature. This law must, consequently, be based upon pure transcendental, and not upon empirical, considerations. For, in the latter case, it would come later than the system; whereas it is really itself the parent of all that is systematic in our cognition of nature. These principles are not mere hypotheses employed for the purpose of experimenting upon nature; although when any such connection is discovered, it forms a solid ground for regarding the hypothetical unity as valid in the sphere of nature — and thus they are in this respect not without their use. But we go farther, and maintain that it is manifest that these principles of parsimony in fundamental causes, variety in effects, and affinity in phenomena, are in accordance both with reason and nature, and that they are not mere methods or plans devised for the purpose of assisting us in our observation of the external world.

But it is plain that this continuity of forms is a mere idea, to which no adequate object can be discovered in experience. And this for two reasons. First, because the species in nature are really divided, and hence form quanta discreta; and, if the gradual progression through their affinity were continuous, the intermediate members lying between two given species must be infinite in number, which is impossible. Secondly, because we cannot make any determinate empirical use of this law, inasmuch as it does not present us with any criterion of affinity which could aid us in determining how far we ought to pursue the graduation of differences: it merely contains a general indication that it is our duty to seek for and, if possible, to discover them.

When we arrange these principles of systematic unity in the order conformable to their employment in experience, they will stand thus: Variety, Affinity, Unity, each of them, as ideas, being taken in the highest degree of their completeness. Reason presupposes the existence of cognitions of the understanding, which have a direct relation to experience, and aims at the ideal unity of these cognitions — a unity which far transcends all experience or empirical notions. The affinity of the diverse, notwithstanding the differences existing between its parts, has a relation to things, but a still closer one to the mere properties and powers of things. For example, imperfect experience may represent the orbits of the planets as circular. But we discover variations from this course, and we proceed to suppose that the planets revolve in a path which, if not a circle, is of a character very similar to it. That is to say, the movements of those planets which do not form a circle will approximate more or less to the properties of a circle, and probably form an ellipse. The paths of comets exhibit still greater variations, for, so far as our observation extends, they do not return upon their own course in a circle or ellipse. But we proceed to the conjecture that comets describe a parabola, a figure which is closely allied to the ellipse. In fact, a parabola is merely an ellipse, with its longer axis produced to an indefinite extent. Thus these principles conduct us to a unity in the genera of the forms of these orbits, and, proceeding farther, to a unity as regards the cause of the motions of the heavenly bodies — that is, gravitation. But we go on extending our conquests over nature, and endeavour to explain all seeming deviations from these rules, and even make additions to our system which no experience can ever substantiate — for example, the theory, in affinity with that of ellipses, of hyperbolic paths of comets, pursuing which, these bodies leave our solar system and, passing from sun to sun, unite the most distant parts of the infinite universe, which is held together by the same moving power.

The most remarkable circumstance connected with these principles is that they seem to be transcendental, and, although only containing ideas for the guidance of the empirical exercise of reason, and although this empirical employment stands to these ideas in an asymptotic relation alone (to use a mathematical term), that is, continually approximate, without ever being able to attain to them, they possess, notwithstanding, as a priori synthetical propositions, objective though undetermined validity, and are available as rules for possible experience. In the elaboration of our experience, they may also be employed with great advantage, as heuristic [Note: From the Greek, eurhioko.] principles. A transcendental deduction of them cannot be made; such a deduction being always impossible in the case of ideas, as has been already shown.

We distinguished, in the Transcendental Analytic, the dynamical principles of the understanding, which are regulative principles of intuition, from the mathematical, which are constitutive principles of intuition. These dynamical laws are, however, constitutive in relation to experience, inasmuch as they render the conceptions without which experience could not exist possible a priori. But the principles of pure reason cannot be constitutive even in regard to empirical conceptions, because no sensuous schema corresponding to them can be discovered, and they cannot therefore have an object in concreto. Now, if I grant that they cannot be employed in the sphere of experience, as constitutive principles, how shall I secure for them employment and objective validity as regulative principles, and in what way can they be so employed?

The understanding is the object of reason, as sensibility is the object of the understanding. The production of systematic unity in all the empirical operations of the understanding is the proper occupation of reason; just as it is the business of the understanding to connect the various content of phenomena by means of conceptions, and subject them to empirical laws. But the operations of the understanding are, without the schemata of sensibility, undetermined; and, in the same manner, the unity of reason is perfectly undetermined as regards the conditions under which, and the extent to which, the understanding ought to carry the systematic connection of its conceptions. But, although it is impossible to discover in intuition a schema for the complete systematic unity of all the conceptions of the understanding, there must be some analogon of this schema. This analogon is the idea of the maximum of the division and the connection of our cognition in one principle. For we may have a determinate notion of a maximum and an absolutely perfect, all the restrictive conditions which are connected with an indeterminate and various content having been abstracted. Thus the idea of reason is analogous with a sensuous schema, with this difference, that the application of the categories to the schema of reason does not present a cognition of any object (as is the case with the application of the categories to sensuous schemata), but merely provides us with a rule or principle for the systematic unity of the exercise of the understanding. Now, as every principle which imposes upon the exercise of the understanding a priori compliance with the rule of systematic unity also relates, although only in an indirect manner, to an object of experience, the principles of pure reason will also possess objective reality and validity in relation to experience. But they will not aim at determining our knowledge in regard to any empirical object; they will merely indicate the procedure, following which the empirical and determinate exercise of the understanding may be in complete harmony and connection with itself — a result which is produced by its being brought into harmony with the principle of systematic unity, so far as that is possible, and deduced from it.

I term all subjective principles, which are not derived from observation of the constitution of an object, but from the interest which Reason has in producing a certain completeness in her cognition of that object, maxims of reason. Thus there are maxims of speculative reason, which are based solely upon its speculative interest, although they appear to be objective principles.

When principles which are really regulative are regarded as constitutive, and employed as objective principles, contradictions must arise; but if they are considered as mere maxims, there is no room for contradictions of any kind, as they then merely indicate the different interests of reason, which occasion differences in the mode of thought. In effect, Reason has only one single interest, and the seeming contradiction existing between her maxims merely indicates a difference in, and a reciprocal limitation of, the methods by which this interest is satisfied.

This reasoner has at heart the interest of diversity — in accordance with the principle of specification; another, the interest of unity — in accordance with the principle of aggregation. Each believes that his judgement rests upon a thorough insight into the subject he is examining, and yet it has been influenced solely by a greater or less degree of adherence to some one of the two principles, neither of which are objective, but originate solely from the interest of reason, and on this account to be termed maxims rather than principles. When I observe intelligent men disputing about the distinctive characteristics of men, animals, or plants, and even of minerals, those on the one side assuming the existence of certain national characteristics, certain well-defined and hereditary distinctions of family, race, and so on, while the other side maintain that nature has endowed all races of men with the same faculties and dispositions, and that all differences are but the result of external and accidental circumstances — I have only to consider for a moment the real nature of the subject of discussion, to arrive at the conclusion that it is a subject far too deep for us to judge of, and that there is little probability of either party being able to speak from a perfect insight into and understanding of the nature of the subject itself. Both have, in reality, been struggling for the twofold interest of reason; the one maintaining the one interest, the other the other. But this difference between the maxims of diversity and unity may easily be reconciled and adjusted; although, so long as they are regarded as objective principles, they must occasion not only contradictions and polemic, but place hinderances in the way of the advancement of truth, until some means is discovered of reconciling these conflicting interests, and bringing reason into union and harmony with itself.

The same is the case with the so-called law discovered by Leibnitz, and supported with remarkable ability by Bonnet — the law of the continuous gradation of created beings, which is nothing more than an inference from the principle of affinity; for observation and study of the order of nature could never present it to the mind as an objective truth. The steps of this ladder, as they appear in experience, are too far apart from each other, and the so-called petty differences between different kinds of animals are in nature commonly so wide separations that no confidence can be placed in such views (particularly when we reflect on the great variety of things, and the ease with which we can discover resemblances), and no faith in the laws which are said to express the aims and purposes of nature. On the other hand, the method of investigating the order of nature in the light of this principle, and the maxim which requires us to regard this order — it being still undetermined how far it extends — as really existing in nature, is beyond doubt a legitimate and excellent principle of reason — a principle which extends farther than any experience or observation of ours and which, without giving us any positive knowledge of anything in the region of experience, guides us to the goal of systematic unity.

Of the Ultimate End of the Natural Dialectic of Human Reason.

The ideas of pure reason cannot be, of themselves and in their own nature, dialectical; it is from their misemployment alone that fallacies and illusions arise. For they originate in the nature of reason itself, and it is impossible that this supreme tribunal for all the rights and claims of speculation should be itself undeserving of confidence and promotive of error. It is to be expected, therefore, that these ideas have a genuine and legitimate aim. It is true, the mob of sophists raise against reason the cry of inconsistency and contradiction, and affect to despise the government of that faculty, because they cannot understand its constitution, while it is to its beneficial influences alone that they owe the position and the intelligence which enable them to criticize and to blame its procedure.

We cannot employ an a priori conception with certainty, until we have made a transcendental deduction therefore. The ideas of pure reason do not admit of the same kind of deduction as the categories. But if they are to possess the least objective validity, and to represent anything but mere creations of thought (entia rationis ratiocinantis), a deduction of them must be possible. This deduction will complete the critical task imposed upon pure reason; and it is to this part Of our labours that we now proceed.

There is a great difference between a thing's being presented to the mind as an object in an absolute sense, or merely as an ideal object. In the former case I employ my conceptions to determine the object; in the latter case nothing is present to the mind but a mere schema, which does not relate directly to an object, not even in a hypothetical sense, but which is useful only for the purpose of representing other objects to the mind, in a mediate and indirect manner, by means of their relation to the idea in the intellect. Thus I say the conception of a supreme intelligence is a mere idea; that is to say, its objective reality does not consist in the fact that it has an immediate relation to an object (for in this sense we have no means of establishing its objective validity), it is merely a schema constructed according to the necessary conditions of the unity of reason — the schema of a thing in general, which is useful towards the production of the highest degree of systematic unity in the empirical exercise of reason, in which we deduce this or that object of experience from the imaginary object of this idea, as the ground or cause of the said object of experience. In this way, the idea is properly a heuristic, and not an ostensive, conception; it does not give us any information respecting the constitution of an object, it merely indicates how, under the guidance of the idea, we ought to investigate the constitution and the relations of objects in the world of experience. Now, if it can be shown that the three kinds of transcendental ideas (psychological, cosmological, and theological), although not relating directly to any object nor determining it, do nevertheless, on the supposition of the existence of an ideal object, produce systematic unity in the laws of the empirical employment of the reason, and extend our empirical cognition, without ever being inconsistent or in opposition with it — it must be a necessary maxim of reason to regulate its procedure according to these ideas. And this forms the transcendental deduction of all speculative ideas, not as constitutive principles of the extension of our cognition beyond the limits of our experience, but as regulative principles of the systematic unity of empirical cognition, which is by the aid of these ideas arranged and emended within its own proper limits, to an extent unattainable by the operation of the principles of the understanding alone.

I shall make this plainer. Guided by the principles involved in these ideas, we must, in the first place, so connect all the phenomena, actions, and feelings of the mind, as if it were a simple substance, which, endowed with personal identity, possesses a permanent existence (in this life at least), while its states, among which those of the body are to be included as external conditions, are in continual change. Secondly, in cosmology, we must investigate the conditions of all natural phenomena, internal as well as external, as if they belonged to a chain infinite and without any prime or supreme member, while we do not, on this account, deny the existence of intelligible grounds of these phenomena, although we never employ them to explain phenomena, for the simple reason that they are not objects of our cognition. Thirdly, in the sphere of theology, we must regard the whole system of possible experience as forming an absolute, but dependent and sensuously-conditioned unity, and at the same time as based upon a sole, supreme, and all-sufficient ground existing apart from the world itself — a ground which is a self-subsistent, primeval and creative reason, in relation to which we so employ our reason in the field of experience, as if all objects drew their origin from that archetype of all reason. In other words, we ought not to deduce the internal phenomena of the mind from a simple thinking substance, but deduce them from each other under the guidance of the regulative idea of a simple being; we ought not to deduce the phenomena, order, and unity of the universe from a supreme intelligence, but merely draw from this idea of a supremely wise cause the rules which must guide reason in its connection of causes and effects.

Now there is nothing to hinder us from admitting these ideas to possess an objective and hyperbolic existence, except the cosmological ideas, which lead reason into an antinomy: the psychological and theological ideas are not antinomial. They contain no contradiction; and how, then, can any one dispute their objective reality, since he who denies it knows as little about their possibility as we who affirm? And yet, when we wish to admit the existence of a thing, it is not sufficient to convince ourselves that there is no positive obstacle in the way; for it cannot be allowable to regard mere creations of thought, which transcend, though they do not contradict, all our conceptions, as real and determinate objects, solely upon the authority of a speculative reason striving to compass its own aims. They cannot, therefore, be admitted to be real in themselves; they can only possess a comparative reality — that of a schema of the regulative principle of the systematic unity of all cognition. They are to be regarded not as actual things, but as in some measure analogous to them. We abstract from the object of the idea all the conditions which limit the exercise of our understanding, but which, on the other hand, are the sole conditions of our possessing a determinate conception of any given thing. And thus we cogitate a something, of the real nature of which we have not the least conception, but which we represent to ourselves as standing in a relation to the whole system of phenomena, analogous to that in which phenomena stand to each other.

By admitting these ideal beings, we do not really extend our cognitions beyond the objects of possible experience; we extend merely the empirical unity of our experience, by the aid of systematic unity, the schema of which is furnished by the idea, which is therefore valid — not as a constitutive, but as a regulative principle. For although we posit a thing corresponding to the idea — a something, an actual existence — we do not on that account aim at the extension of our cognition by means of transcendent conceptions. This existence is purely ideal, and not objective; it is the mere expression of the systematic unity which is to be the guide of reason in the field of experience. There are no attempts made at deciding what the ground of this unity may be, or what the real nature of this imaginary being.

Thus the transcendental and only determinate conception of God, which is presented to us by speculative reason, is in the strictest sense deistic. In other words, reason does not assure us of the objective validity of the conception; it merely gives us the idea of something, on which the supreme and necessary unity of all experience is based. This something we cannot, following the analogy of a real substance, cogitate otherwise than as the cause of all things operating in accordance with rational laws, if we regard it as an individual object; although we should rest contented with the idea alone as a regulative principle of reason, and make no attempt at completing the sum of the conditions imposed by thought. This attempt is, indeed, inconsistent with the grand aim of complete systematic unity in the sphere of cognition — a unity to which no bounds are set by reason.

Hence it happens that, admitting a divine being, I can have no conception of the internal possibility of its perfection, or of the necessity of its existence. The only advantage of this admission is that it enables me to answer all other questions relating to the contingent, and to give reason the most complete satisfaction as regards the unity which it aims at attaining in the world of experience. But I cannot satisfy reason with regard to this hypothesis itself; and this proves that it is not its intelligence and insight into the subject, but its speculative interest alone which induces it to proceed from a point lying far beyond the sphere of our cognition, for the purpose of being able to consider all objects as parts of a systematic whole.

Here a distinction presents itself, in regard to the way in which we may cogitate a presupposition — a distinction which is somewhat subtle, but of great importance in transcendental philosophy. I may have sufficient grounds to admit something, or the existence of something, in a relative point of view (suppositio relativa), without being justified in admitting it in an absolute sense (suppositio absoluta). This distinction is undoubtedly requisite, in the case of a regulative principle, the necessity of which we recognize, though we are ignorant of the source and cause of that necessity, and which we assume to be based upon some ultimate ground, for the purpose of being able to cogitate the universality of the principle in a more determinate way. For example, I cogitate the existence of a being corresponding to a pure transcendental idea. But I cannot admit that this being exists absolutely and in itself, because all of the conceptions by which I can cogitate an object in a determinate manner fall short of assuring me of its existence; nay, the conditions of the objective validity of my conceptions are excluded by the idea — by the very fact of its being an idea. The conceptions of reality, substance, causality, nay, even that of necessity in existence, have no significance out of the sphere of empirical cognition, and cannot, beyond that sphere, determine any object. They may, accordingly, be employed to explain the possibility of things in the world of sense, but they are utterly inadequate to explain the possibility of the universe itself considered as a whole; because in this case the ground of explanation must lie out of and beyond the world, and cannot, therefore, be an object of possible experience. Now, I may admit the existence of an incomprehensible being of this nature — the object of a mere idea, relatively to the world of sense; although I have no ground to admit its existence absolutely and in itself. For if an idea (that of a systematic and complete unity, of which I shall presently speak more particularly) lies at the foundation of the most extended empirical employment of reason, and if this idea cannot be adequately represented in concreto, although it is indispensably necessary for the approximation of empirical unity to the highest possible degree — I am not only authorized, but compelled, to realize this idea, that is, to posit a real object corresponding thereto. But I cannot profess to know this object; it is to me merely a something, to which, as the ground of systematic unity in cognition, I attribute such properties as are analogous to the conceptions employed by the understanding in the sphere of experience. Following the analogy of the notions of reality, substance, causality, and necessity, I cogitate a being, which possesses all these attributes in the highest degree; and, as this idea is the offspring of my reason alone, I cogitate this being as self-subsistent reason, and as the cause of the universe operating by means of ideas of the greatest possible harmony and unity. Thus I abstract all conditions that would limit my idea, solely for the purpose of rendering systematic unity possible in the world of empirical diversity, and thus securing the widest possible extension for the exercise of reason in that sphere. This I am enabled to do, by regarding all connections and relations in the world of sense, as if they were the dispositions of a supreme reason, of which our reason is but a faint image. I then proceed to cogitate this Supreme Being by conceptions which have, properly, no meaning or application, except in the world of sense. But as I am authorized to employ the transcendental hypothesis of such a being in a relative respect alone, that is, as the substratum of the greatest possible unity in experience — I may attribute to a being which I regard as distinct from the world, such properties as belong solely to the sphere of sense and experience. For I do not desire, and am not justified in desiring, to cognize this object of my idea, as it exists in itself; for I possess no conceptions sufficient for or task, those of reality, substance, causality, nay, even that of necessity in existence, losing all significance, and becoming merely the signs of conceptions, without content and without applicability, when I attempt to carry them beyond the limits of the world of sense. I cogitate merely the relation of a perfectly unknown being to the greatest possible systematic unity of experience, solely for the purpose of employing it as the schema of the regulative principle which directs reason in its empirical exercise.

It is evident, at the first view, that we cannot presuppose the reality of this transcendental object, by means of the conceptions of reality, substance, causality, and so on, because these conceptions cannot be applied to anything that is distinct from the world of sense. Thus the supposition of a Supreme Being or cause is purely relative; it is cogitated only in behalf of the systematic unity of experience; such a being is but a something, of whose existence in itself we have not the least conception. Thus, too, it becomes sufficiently manifest why we required the idea of a necessary being in relation to objects given by sense, although we can never have the least conception of this being, or of its absolute necessity.

And now we can clearly perceive the result of our transcendental dialectic, and the proper aim of the ideas of pure reason — which become dialectical solely from misunderstanding and inconsiderateness. Pure reason is, in fact, occupied with itself, and not with any object. Objects are not presented to it to be embraced in the unity of an empirical conception; it is only the cognitions of the understanding that are presented to it, for the purpose of receiving the unity of a rational conception, that is, of being connected according to a principle. The unity of reason is the unity of system; and this systematic unity is not an objective principle, extending its dominion over objects, but a subjective maxim, extending its authority over the empirical cognition of objects. The systematic connection which reason gives to the empirical employment of the understanding not only advances the extension of that employment, but ensures its correctness, and thus the principle of a systematic unity of this nature is also objective, although only in an indefinite respect (principium vagum). It is not, however, a constitutive principle, determining an object to which it directly relates; it is merely a regulative principle or maxim, advancing and strengthening the empirical exercise of reason, by the opening up of new paths of which the understanding is ignorant, while it never conflicts with the laws of its exercise in the sphere of experience.

But reason cannot cogitate this systematic unity, without at the same time cogitating an object of the idea — an object that cannot be presented in any experience, which contains no concrete example of a complete systematic unity. This being (ens rationis ratiocinatae) is therefore a mere idea and is not assumed to be a thing which is real absolutely and in itself. On the contrary, it forms merely the problematical foundation of the connection which the mind introduces among the phenomena of the sensuous world. We look upon this connection, in the light of the above-mentioned idea, as if it drew its origin from the supposed being which corresponds to the idea. And yet all we aim at is the possession of this idea as a secure foundation for the systematic unity of experience — a unity indispensable to reason, advantageous to the understanding, and promotive of the interests of empirical cognition.

We mistake the true meaning of this idea when we regard it as an enouncement, or even as a hypothetical declaration of the existence of a real thing, which we are to regard as the origin or ground of a systematic constitution of the universe. On the contrary, it is left completely undetermined what the nature or properties of this so-called ground may be. The idea is merely to be adopted as a point of view, from which this unity, so essential to reason and so beneficial to the understanding, may be regarded as radiating. In one word, this transcendental thing is merely the schema of a regulative principle, by means of which Reason, so far as in her lies, extends the dominion of systematic unity over the whole sphere of experience.

The first object of an idea of this kind is the ego, considered merely as a thinking nature or soul. If I wish to investigate the properties of a thinking being, I must interrogate experience. But I find that I can apply none of the categories to this object, the schema of these categories, which is the condition of their application, being given only in sensuous intuition. But I cannot thus attain to the cognition of a systematic unity of all the phenomena of the internal sense. Instead, therefore, of an empirical conception of what the soul really is, reason takes the conception of the empirical unity of all thought, and, by cogitating this unity as unconditioned and primitive, constructs the rational conception or idea of a simple substance which is in itself unchangeable, possessing personal identity, and in connection with other real things external to it; in one word, it constructs the idea of a simple self-subsistent intelligence. But the real aim of reason in this procedure is the attainment of principles of systematic unity for the explanation of the phenomena of the soul. That is, reason desires to be able to represent all the determinations of the internal sense as existing in one subject, all powers as deduced from one fundamental power, all changes as mere varieties in the condition of a being which is permanent and always the same, and all phenomena in space as entirely different in their nature from the procedure of thought. Essential simplicity (with the other attributes predicated of the ego) is regarded as the mere schema of this regulative principle; it is not assumed that it is the actual ground of the properties of the soul. For these properties may rest upon quite different grounds, of which we are completely ignorant; just as the above predicates could not give us any knowledge of the soul as it is in itself, even if we regarded them as valid in respect of it, inasmuch as they constitute a mere idea, which cannot be represented in concreto. Nothing but good can result from a psychological idea of this kind, if we only take proper care not to consider it as more than an idea; that is, if we regard it as valid merely in relation to the employment of reason, in the sphere of the phenomena of the soul. Under the guidance of this idea, or principle, no empirical laws of corporeal phenomena are called in to explain that which is a phenomenon of the internal sense alone; no windy hypotheses of the generation, annihilation, and palingenesis of souls are admitted. Thus the consideration of this object of the internal sense is kept pure, and unmixed with heterogeneous elements; while the investigation of reason aims at reducing all the grounds of explanation employed in this sphere of knowledge to a single principle. All this is best effected, nay, cannot be effected otherwise than by means of such a schema, which requires us to regard this ideal thing as an actual existence. The psychological idea is, therefore, meaningless and inapplicable, except as the schema of a regulative conception. For, if I ask whether the soul is not really of a spiritual nature — it is a question which has no meaning. From such a conception has been abstracted, not merely all corporeal nature, but all nature, that is, all the predicates of a possible experience; and consequently, all the conditions which enable us to cogitate an object to this conception have disappeared. But, if these conditions are absent, it is evident that the conception is meaningless.

The second regulative idea of speculative reason is the conception of the universe. For nature is properly the only object presented to us, in regard to which reason requires regulative principles. Nature is twofold — thinking and corporeal nature. To cogitate the latter in regard to its internal possibility, that is, to determine the application of the categories to it, no idea is required — no representation which transcends experience. In this sphere, therefore, an idea is impossible, sensuous intuition being our only guide; while, in the sphere of psychology, we require the fundamental idea (I), which contains a priori a certain form of thought namely, the unity of the ego. Pure reason has, therefore, nothing left but nature in general, and the completeness of conditions in nature in accordance with some principle. The absolute totality of the series of these conditions is an idea, which can never be fully realized in the empirical exercise of reason, while it is serviceable as a rule for the procedure of reason in relation to that totality. It requires us, in the explanation of given phenomena (in the regress or ascent in the series), to proceed as if the series were infinite in itself, that is, were prolonged in indefinitum; while on the other hand, where reason is regarded as itself the determining cause (in the region of freedom), we are required to proceed as if we had not before us an object of sense, but of the pure understanding. In this latter case, the conditions do not exist in the series of phenomena, but may be placed quite out of and beyond it, and the series of conditions may be regarded as if it had an absolute beginning from an intelligible cause. All this proves that the cosmological ideas are nothing but regulative principles, and not constitutive; and that their aim is not to realize an actual totality in such series. The full discussion of this subject will be found in its proper place in the chapter on the antinomy of pure reason.

The third idea of pure reason, containing the hypothesis of a being which is valid merely as a relative hypothesis, is that of the one and all-sufficient cause of all cosmological series, in other words, the idea of God. We have not the slightest ground absolutely to admit the existence of an object corresponding to this idea; for what can empower or authorize us to affirm the existence of a being of the highest perfection — a being whose existence is absolutely necessary — merely because we possess the conception of such a being? The answer is: It is the existence of the world which renders this hypothesis necessary. But this answer makes it perfectly evident that the idea of this being, like all other speculative ideas, is essentially nothing more than a demand upon reason that it shall regulate the connection which it and its subordinate faculties introduce into the phenomena of the world by principles of systematic unity and, consequently, that it shall regard all phenomena as originating from one all-embracing being, as the supreme and all-sufficient cause. From this it is plain that the only aim of reason in this procedure is the establishment of its own formal rule for the extension of its dominion in the world of experience; that it does not aim at an extension of its cognition beyond the limits of experience; and that, consequently, this idea does not contain any constitutive principle.

The highest formal unity, which is based upon ideas alone, is the unity of all things

— a unity in accordance with an aim or purpose; and the speculative interest of reason renders it necessary to regard all order in the world as if it originated from the intention and design of a supreme reason. This principle unfolds to the view of reason in the sphere of experience new and enlarged prospects, and invites it to connect the phenomena of the world according to teleological laws, and in this way to attain to the highest possible degree of systematic unity. The hypothesis of a supreme intelligence, as the sole cause of the universe — an intelligence which has for us no more than an ideal existence — is accordingly always of the greatest service to reason. Thus, if we presuppose, in relation to the figure of the earth (which is round, but somewhat flattened at the poles),* or that of mountains or seas, wise designs on the part of an author of the universe, we cannot fail to make, by the light of this supposition, a great number of interesting discoveries. If we keep to this hypothesis, as a principle which is purely regulative, even error cannot be very detrimental. For, in this case, error can have no more serious consequences than that, where we expected to discover a teleological connection (nexus finalis), only a mechanical or physical connection appears. In such a case, we merely fail to find the additional form of unity we expected, but we do not lose the rational unity which the mind requires in its procedure in experience. But even a miscarriage of this sort cannot affect the law in its general and teleological relations. For although we may convict an anatomist of an error, when he connects the limb of some animal with a certain purpose, it is quite impossible to prove in a single case that any arrangement of nature, be it what it may, is entirely without aim or design. And thus medical physiology, by the aid of a principle presented to it by pure reason, extends its very limited empirical knowledge of the purposes of the different parts of an organized body so far that it may be asserted with the utmost confidence, and with the approbation of all reflecting men, that every organ or bodily part of an animal has its use and answers a certain design. Now, this is a supposition which, if regarded as of a constitutive character, goes much farther than any experience or observation of ours can justify. Hence it is evident that it is nothing more than a regulative principle of reason, which aims at the highest degree of systematic unity, by the aid of the idea of a causality according to design in a supreme cause — a cause which it regards as the highest intelligence.

[Note: The advantages which a circular form, in the case of the earth, has over every other, are well known. But few are aware that the slight flattening at the poles, which gives it the figure of a spheroid, is the only cause which prevents the elevations of continents or even of mountains, perhaps thrown up by some internal convulsion, from continually altering the position of the axis of the earth — and that to some considerable degree in a short time. The great protuberance of the earth under the Equator serves to overbalance the impetus of all other masses of earth, and thus to preserve the axis of the earth, so far as we can observe, in its present position. And yet this wise arrangement has been unthinkingly explained from the equilibrium of the formerly fluid mass.]

If, however, we neglect this restriction of the idea to a purely regulative influence, reason is betrayed into numerous errors. For it has then left the ground of experience, in which alone are to be found the criteria of truth, and has ventured into the region of the incomprehensible and unsearchable, on the heights of which it loses its power and collectedness, because it has completely severed its connection with experience.

The first error which arises from our employing the idea of a Supreme Being as a constitutive (in repugnance to the very nature of an idea), and not as a regulative principle, is the error of inactive reason (ignava ratio).* We may so term every principle which requires us to regard our investigations of nature as absolutely complete, and allows reason to cease its inquiries, as if it had fully executed its task. Thus the psychological idea of the ego, when employed as a constitutive principle for the explanation of the phenomena of the soul, and for the extension of our knowledge regarding this subject beyond the limits of experience — even to the condition of the soul after death — is convenient enough for the purposes of pure reason, but detrimental and even ruinous to its interests in the sphere of nature and experience. The dogmatizing spiritualist explains the unchanging unity of our personality through all changes of condition from the unity of a thinking substance, the interest which we take in things and events that can happen only after our death, from a consciousness of the immaterial nature of our thinking subject, and so on. Thus he dispenses with all empirical investigations into the cause of these internal phenomena, and with all possible explanations of them upon purely natural grounds; while, at the dictation of a transcendent reason, he passes by the immanent sources of cognition in experience, greatly to his own ease and convenience, but to the sacrifice of all, genuine insight and intelligence. These prejudicial consequences become still more evident, in the case of the dogmatical treatment of our idea of a Supreme Intelligence, and the theological system of nature (physico-theology) which is falsely based upon it. For, in this case, the aims which we observe in nature, and often those which we merely fancy to exist, make the investigation of causes a very easy task, by directing us to refer such and such phenomena immediately to the unsearchable will and counsel of the Supreme Wisdom, while we ought to investigate their causes in the general laws of the mechanism of matter. We are thus recommended to consider the labour of reason as ended, when we have merely dispensed with its employment, which is guided surely and safely only by the order of nature and the series of changes in the world — which are arranged according to immanent and general laws. This error may be avoided, if we do not merely consider from the view-point of final aims certain parts of nature, such as the division and structure of a continent, the constitution and direction of certain mountain-chains, or even the organization existing in the vegetable and animal kingdoms, but look upon this systematic unity of nature in a perfectly general way, in relation to the idea of a Supreme Intelligence. If we pursue this advice, we lay as a foundation for all investigation the conformity to aims of all phenomena of nature in accordance with universal laws, for which no particular arrangement of nature is exempt, but only cognized by us with more or less difficulty; and we possess a regulative principle of the systematic unity of a teleological connection, which we do not attempt to anticipate or predetermine. All that we do, and ought to do, is to follow out the physico-mechanical connection in nature according to general laws, with the hope of discovering, sooner or later, the teleological connection also. Thus, and thus only, can the principle of final unity aid in the extension of the employment of reason in the sphere of experience, without being in any case detrimental to its interests.

[Note: This was the term applied by the old dialecticians to a sophistical argument, which ran thus: If it is your fate to die of this disease, you will die, whether you employ a physician or not. Cicero says that this mode of reasoning has received this appellation, because, if followed, it puts an end to the employment of reason in the affairs of life. For a similar reason, I have applied this designation to the sophistical argument of pure reason.]

The second error which arises from the misconception of the principle of systematic unity is that of perverted reason (perversa ratio, usteron roteron rationis). The idea of systematic unity is available as a regulative principle in the connection of phenomena according to general natural laws; and, how far soever we have to travel upon the path of experience to discover some fact or event, this idea requires us to believe that we have approached all the more nearly to the completion of its use in the sphere of nature, although that completion can never be attained. But this error reverses the procedure of reason. We begin by hypostatizing the principle of systematic unity, and by giving an anthropomorphic determination to the conception of a Supreme Intelligence, and then proceed forcibly to impose aims upon nature. Thus not only does teleology, which ought to aid in the completion of unity in accordance with general laws, operate to the destruction of its influence, but it hinders reason from attaining its proper aim, that is, the proof, upon natural grounds, of the existence of a supreme intelligent cause. For, if we cannot presuppose supreme finality in nature a priori, that is, as essentially belonging to nature, how can we be directed to endeavour to discover this unity and, rising gradually through its different degrees, to approach the supreme perfection of an author of all — a perfection which is absolutely necessary, and therefore cognizable a priori? The regulative principle directs us to presuppose systematic unity absolutely and, consequently, as following from the essential nature of things — but only as a unity of nature, not merely cognized empirically, but presupposed a priori, although only in an indeterminate manner. But if I insist on basing nature upon the foundation of a supreme ordaining Being, the unity of nature is in effect lost. For, in this case, it is quite foreign and unessential to the nature of things, and cannot be cognized from the general laws of nature. And thus arises a vicious circular argument, what ought to have been proved having been presupposed.

To take the regulative principle of systematic unity in nature for a constitutive principle, and to hypostatize and make a cause out of that which is properly the ideal ground of the consistent and harmonious exercise of reason, involves reason in inextricable embarrassments. The investigation of nature pursues its own path under the guidance of the chain of natural causes, in accordance with the general laws of nature, and ever follows the light of the idea of an author of the universe — not for the purpose of deducing the finality, which it constantly pursues, from this Supreme Being, but to attain to the cognition of his existence from the finality which it seeks in the existence of the phenomena of nature, and, if possible, in that of all things to cognize this being, consequently, as absolutely necessary. Whether this latter purpose succeed or not, the idea is and must always be a true one, and its employment, when merely regulative, must always be accompanied by truthful and beneficial results.

Complete unity, in conformity with aims, constitutes absolute perfection. But if we do not find this unity in the nature of the things which go to constitute the world of experience, that is, of objective cognition, consequently in the universal and necessary laws of nature, how can we infer from this unity the idea of the supreme and absolutely necessary perfection of a primal being, which is the origin of all causality? The greatest systematic unity, and consequently teleological unity, constitutes the very foundation of the possibility of the most extended employment of human reason. The idea of unity is therefore essentially and indissolubly connected with the nature of our reason. This idea is a legislative one; and hence it is very natural that we should assume the existence of a legislative reason corresponding to it, from which the systematic unity of nature — the object of the operations of reason — must be derived.

In the course of our discussion of the antinomies, we stated that it is always possible to answer all the questions which pure reason may raise; and that the plea of the limited nature of our cognition, which is unavoidable and proper in many questions regarding natural phenomena, cannot in this case be admitted, because the questions raised do not relate to the nature of things, but are necessarily originated by the nature of reason itself, and relate to its own internal constitution. We can now establish this assertion, which at first sight appeared so rash, in relation to the two questions in which reason takes the greatest interest, and thus complete our discussion of the dialectic of pure reason.

If, then, the question is asked, in relation to transcendental theology,* first, whether there is anything distinct from the world, which contains the ground of cosmical order and connection according to general laws? The answer is: Certainly. For the world is a sum of phenomena; there must, therefore, be some transcendental basis of these phenomena, that is, a basis cogitable by the pure understanding alone. If, secondly, the question is asked whether this being is substance, whether it is of the greatest reality, whether it is necessary, and so forth? I answer that this question is utterly without meaning. For all the categories which aid me in forming a conception of an object cannot be employed except in the world of sense, and are without meaning when not applied to objects of actual or possible experience. Out of this sphere, they are not properly conceptions, but the mere marks or indices of conceptions, which we may admit, although they cannot, without the help of experience, help us to understand any subject or thing. If, thirdly, the question is whether we may not cogitate this being, which is distinct from the world, in analogy with the objects of experience? The answer is: Undoubtedly, but only as an ideal, and not as a real object. That is, we must cogitate it only as an unknown substratum of the systematic unity, order, and finality of the world — a unity which reason must employ as the regulative principle of its investigation of nature. Nay, more, we may admit into the idea certain anthropomorphic elements, which are promotive of the interests of this regulative principle. For it is no more than an idea, which does not relate directly to a being distinct from the world, but to the regulative principle of the systematic unity of the world, by means, however, of a schema of this unity — the schema of a Supreme Intelligence, who is the wisely-designing author of the universe. What this basis of cosmical unity may be in itself, we know not — we cannot discover from the idea; we merely know how we ought to employ the idea of this unity, in relation to the systematic operation of reason in the sphere of experience.

[Note: After what has been said of the psychological idea of the ego and its proper employment as a regulative principle of the operations of reason, I need not enter into details regarding the transcendental illusion by which the systematic unity of all the various phenomena of the internal sense is hypostatized. The procedure is in this case very similar to that which has been discussed in our remarks on the theological ideal.]

But, it will be asked again, can we on these grounds, admit the existence of a wise and omnipotent author of the world? Without doubt; and not only so, but we must assume the existence of such a being. But do we thus extend the limits of our knowledge beyond the field of possible experience? By no means. For we have merely presupposed a something, of which we have no conception, which we do not know as it is in itself; but, in relation to the systematic disposition of the universe, which we must presuppose in all our observation of nature, we have cogitated this unknown being in analogy with an intelligent existence (an empirical conception), that is to say, we have endowed it with those attributes, which, judging from the nature of our own reason, may contain the ground of such a systematic unity. This idea is therefore valid only relatively to the employment in experience of our reason. But if we attribute to it absolute and objective validity, we overlook the fact that it is merely an ideal being that we cogitate; and, by setting out from a basis which is not determinable by considerations drawn from experience, we place ourselves in a position which incapacitates us from applying this principle to the empirical employment of reason.

But, it will be asked further, can I make any use of this conception and hypothesis in my investigations into the world and nature? Yes, for this very purpose was the idea established by reason as a fundamental basis. But may I regard certain arrangements, which seemed to have been made in conformity with some fixed aim, as the arrangements of design, and look upon them as proceeding from the divine will, with the intervention, however, of certain other particular arrangements disposed to that end? Yes, you may do so; but at the same time you must regard it as indifferent, whether it is asserted that divine wisdom has disposed all things in conformity with his highest aims, or that the idea of supreme wisdom is a regulative principle in the investigation of nature, and at the same time a principle of the systematic unity of nature according to general laws, even in those cases where we are unable to discover that unity. In other words, it must be perfectly indifferent to you whether you say, when you have discovered this unity: God has wisely willed it so; or: Nature has wisely arranged this. For it was nothing but the systematic unity, which reason requires as a basis for the investigation of nature, that justified you in accepting the idea of a supreme intelligence as a schema for a regulative principle; and, the farther you advance in the discovery of design and finality, the more certain the validity of your idea. But, as the whole aim of this regulative principle was the discovery of a necessary and systematic unity in nature, we have, in so far as we attain this, to attribute our success to the idea of a Supreme Being; while, at the same time, we cannot, without involving ourselves in contradictions, overlook the general laws of nature, as it was in reference to them alone that this idea was employed. We cannot, I say, overlook the general laws of nature, and regard this conformity to aims observable in nature as contingent or hyperphysical in its origin; inasmuch as there is no ground which can justify us in the admission of a being with such properties distinct from and above nature. All that we are authorized to assert is that this idea may be employed as a principle, and that the properties of the being which is assumed to correspond to it may be regarded as systematically connected in analogy with the causal determination of phenomena.

For the same reasons we are justified in introducing into the idea of the supreme cause other anthropomorphic elements (for without these we could not predicate anything of it); we may regard it as allowable to cogitate this cause as a being with understanding, the feelings of pleasure and displeasure, and faculties of desire and will corresponding to these. At the same time, we may attribute to this being infinite perfection — a perfection which necessarily transcends that which our knowledge of the order and design in the world authorize us to predicate of it. For the regulative law of systematic unity requires us to study nature on the supposition that systematic and final unity in infinitum is everywhere discoverable, even in the highest diversity. For, although we may discover little of this cosmical perfection, it belongs to the legislative prerogative of reason to require us always to seek for and to expect it; while it must always be beneficial to institute all inquiries into nature in accordance with this principle. But it is evident that, by this idea of a supreme author of all, which I place as the foundation of all inquiries into nature, I do not mean to assert the existence of such a being, or that I have any knowledge of its existence; and, consequently, I do not really deduce anything from the existence of this being, but merely from its idea, that is to say, from the nature of things in this world, in accordance with this idea. A certain dim consciousness of the true use of this idea seems to have dictated to the philosophers of all times the moderate language used by them regarding the cause of the world. We find them employing the expressions wisdom and care of nature, and divine wisdom, as synonymous — nay, in purely speculative discussions, preferring the former, because it does not carry the appearance of greater pretensions than such as we are entitled to make, and at the same time directs reason to its proper field of action — nature and her phenomena.

Thus, pure reason, which at first seemed to promise us nothing less than the extension of our cognition beyond the limits of experience, is found, when thoroughly examined, to contain nothing but regulative principles, the virtue and function of which is to introduce into our cognition a higher degree of unity than the understanding could of itself. These principles, by placing the goal of all our struggles at so great a distance, realize for us the most thorough connection between the different parts of our cognition, and the highest degree of systematic unity. But, on the other hand, if misunderstood and employed as constitutive principles of transcendent cognition, they become the parents of illusions and contradictions, while pretending to introduce us to new regions of knowledge.

Thus all human cognition begins with intuitions, proceeds from thence to conceptions, and ends with ideas. Although it possesses, in relation to all three elements, a priori sources of cognition, which seemed to transcend the limits of all experience, a thoroughgoing criticism demonstrates that speculative reason can never, by the aid of these elements, pass the bounds of possible experience, and that the proper destination of this highest faculty of cognition is to employ all methods, and all the principles of these methods, for the purpose of penetrating into the innermost secrets of nature, by the aid of the principles of unity (among all kinds of which teleological unity is the highest), while it ought not to attempt to soar above the sphere of experience, beyond which there lies nought for us but the void inane. The critical examination, in our Transcendental Analytic, of all the propositions which professed to extend cognition beyond the sphere of experience, completely demonstrated that they can only conduct us to a possible experience. If we were not distrustful even of the clearest abstract theorems, if we were not allured by specious and inviting prospects to escape from the constraining power of their evidence, we might spare ourselves the laborious examination of all the dialectical arguments which a transcendent reason adduces in support of its pretensions; for we should know with the most complete certainty that, however honest such professions might be, they are null and valueless, because they relate to a kind of knowledge to which no man can by any possibility attain. But, as there is no end to discussion, if we cannot discover the true cause of the illusions by which even the wisest are deceived, and as the analysis of all our transcendent cognition into its elements is of itself of no slight value as a psychological study, while it is a duty incumbent on every philosopher — it was found necessary to investigate the dialectical procedure of reason in its primary sources. And as the inferences of which this dialectic is the parent are not only deceitful, but naturally possess a profound interest for humanity, it was advisable at the same time, to give a full account of the momenta of this dialectical procedure, and to deposit it in the archives of human reason, as a warning to all future metaphysicians to avoid these causes of speculative error.

II. TRANSCENDENTAL DOCTRINE OF METHOD.

If we regard the sum of the cognition of pure speculative reason as an edifice, the idea of which, at least, exists in the human mind, it may be said that we have in the Transcendental Doctrine of Elements examined the materials and determined to what edifice these belong, and what its height and stability. We have found, indeed, that, although we had purposed to build for ourselves a tower which should reach to Heaven, the supply of materials sufficed merely for a habitation, which was spacious enough for all terrestrial purposes, and high enough to enable us to survey the level plain of experience, but that the bold undertaking designed necessarily failed for want of materials — not to mention the confusion of tongues, which gave rise to endless disputes among the labourers on the plan of the edifice, and at last scattered them over all the world, each to erect a separate building for himself, according to his own plans and his own inclinations. Our present task relates not to the materials, but to the plan of an edifice; and, as we have had sufficient warning not to venture blindly upon a design which may be found to transcend our natural powers, while, at the same time, we cannot give up the intention of erecting a secure abode for the mind, we must proportion our design to the material which is presented to us, and which is, at the same time, sufficient for all our wants.

I understand, then, by the transcendental doctrine of method, the determination of the formal conditions of a complete system of pure reason. We shall accordingly have to treat of the discipline, the canon, the architectonic, and, finally, the history of pure reason. This part of our Critique will accomplish, from the transcendental point of view, what has been usually attempted, but miserably executed, under the name of practical logic. It has been badly executed, I say, because general logic, not being limited to any particular kind of cognition (not even to the pure cognition of the understanding) nor to any particular objects, it cannot, without borrowing from other sciences, do more than present merely the titles or signs of possible methods and the technical expressions, which are employed in the systematic parts of all sciences; and thus the pupil is made acquainted with names, the meaning and application of which he is to learn only at some future time.

CHAPTER I.
The Discipline of Pure Reason.

Negative judgements — those which are so not merely as regards their logical form, but in respect of their content — are not commonly held in especial respect. They are, on the contrary, regarded as jealous enemies of our insatiable desire for knowledge; and it almost requires an apology to induce us to tolerate, much less to prize and to respect them.

All propositions, indeed, may be logically expressed in a negative form; but, in relation to the content of our cognition, the peculiar province of negative judgements is solely to prevent error. For this reason, too, negative propositions, which are framed for the purpose of correcting false cognitions where error is absolutely impossible, are undoubtedly true, but inane and senseless; that is, they are in reality purposeless and, for this reason, often very ridiculous. Such is the proposition of the schoolman that Alexander could not have subdued any countries without an army.

But where the limits of our possible cognition are very much contracted, the attraction to new fields of knowledge great, the illusions to which the mind is subject of the most deceptive character, and the evil consequences of error of no inconsiderable magnitude — the negative element in knowledge, which is useful only to guard us against error, is of far more importance than much of that positive instruction which makes additions to the sum of our knowledge. The restraint which is employed to repress, and finally to extirpate the constant inclination to depart from certain rules, is termed discipline. It is distinguished from culture, which aims at the formation of a certain degree of skill, without attempting to repress or to destroy any other mental power, already existing. In the cultivation of a talent, which has given evidence of an impulse towards self-development, discipline takes a negative,* culture and doctrine a positive, part.

[Note: I am well aware that, in the language of the schools, the term discipline is usually employed as synonymous with instruction.

But there are so many cases in which it is necessary to distinguish the notion of the former, as a course of corrective training, from that of the latter, as the communication of knowledge, and the nature of things itself demands the appropriation of the most suitable expressions for this distinction, that it is my desire that the former terms should never be employed in any other than a negative signification.]

That natural dispositions and talents (such as imagination and wit), which ask a free and unlimited development, require in many respects the corrective influence of discipline, every one will readily grant. But it may well appear strange that reason, whose proper duty it is to prescribe rules of discipline to all the other powers of the mind, should itself require this corrective. It has, in fact, hitherto escaped this humiliation, only because, in presence of its magnificent pretensions and high position, no one could readily suspect it to be capable of substituting fancies for conceptions, and words for things.

Reason, when employed in the field of experience, does not stand in need of criticism, because its principles are subjected to the continual test of empirical observations. Nor is criticism requisite in the sphere of mathematics, where the conceptions of reason must always be presented in concreto in pure intuition, and baseless or arbitrary assertions are discovered without difficulty. But where reason is not held in a plain track by the influence of empirical or of pure intuition, that is, when it is employed in the transcendental sphere of pure conceptions, it stands in great need of discipline, to restrain its propensity to overstep the limits of possible experience and to keep it from wandering into error. In fact, the utility of the philosophy of pure reason is entirely of this negative character. Particular errors may be corrected by particular animadversions, and the causes of these errors may be eradicated by criticism. But where we find, as in the case of pure reason, a complete system of illusions and fallacies, closely connected with each other and depending upon grand general principles, there seems to be required a peculiar and negative code of mental legislation, which, under the denomination of a discipline, and founded upon the nature of reason and the objects of its exercise, shall constitute a system of thorough examination and testing, which no fallacy will be able to withstand or escape from, under whatever disguise or concealment it may lurk.

But the reader must remark that, in this the second division of our transcendental Critique the discipline of pure reason is not directed to the content, but to the method of the cognition of pure reason. The former task has been completed in the doctrine of elements. But there is so much similarity in the mode of employing the faculty of reason, whatever be the object to which it is applied, while, at the same time, its employment in the transcendental sphere is so essentially different in kind from every other, that, without the warning negative influence of a discipline specially directed to that end, the errors are unavoidable which spring from the unskillful employment of the methods which are originated by reason but which are out of place in this sphere.

SECTION I. The Discipline of Pure Reason in the Sphere of Dogmatism.

The science of mathematics presents the most brilliant example of the extension of the sphere of pure reason without the aid of experience. Examples are always contagious; and they exert an especial influence on the same faculty, which naturally flatters itself that it will have the same good fortune in other case as fell to its lot in one fortunate instance. Hence pure reason hopes to be able to extend its empire in the transcendental sphere with equal success and security, especially when it applies the same method which was attended with such brilliant results in the science of mathematics. It is, therefore, of the highest importance for us to know whether the method of arriving at demonstrative certainty, which is termed mathematical, be identical with that by which we endeavour to attain the same degree of certainty in philosophy, and which is termed in that science dogmatical.

Philosophical cognition is the cognition of reason by means of conceptions; mathematical cognition is cognition by means of the construction of conceptions. The construction of a conception is the presentation a priori of the intuition which corresponds to the conception. For this purpose a non-empirical intuition is requisite, which, as an intuition, is an individual object; while, as the construction of a conception (a general representation), it must be seen to be universally valid for all the possible intuitions which rank under that conception. Thus I construct a triangle, by the presentation of the object which corresponds to this conception, either by mere imagination, in pure intuition, or upon paper, in empirical intuition, in both cases completely a priori, without borrowing the type of that figure from any experience. The individual figure drawn upon paper is empirical; but it serves, notwithstanding, to indicate the conception, even in its universality, because in this empirical intuition we keep our eye merely on the act of the construction of the conception, and pay no attention to the various modes of determining it, for example, its size, the length of its sides, the size of its angles, these not in the least affecting the essential character of the conception.

Philosophical cognition, accordingly, regards the particular only in the general; mathematical the general in the particular, nay, in the individual. This is done, however, entirely a priori and by means of pure reason, so that, as this individual figure is determined under certain universal conditions of construction, the object of the conception, to which this individual figure corresponds as its schema, must be cogitated as universally determined.

The essential difference of these two modes of cognition consists, therefore, in this formal quality; it does not regard the difference of the matter or objects of both. Those thinkers who aim at distinguishing philosophy from mathematics by asserting that the former has to do with quality merely, and the latter with quantity, have mistaken the effect for the cause. The reason why mathematical cognition can relate only to quantity is to be found in its form alone. For it is the conception of quantities only that is capable of being constructed, that is, presented a priori in intuition; while qualities cannot be given in any other than an empirical intuition. Hence the cognition of qualities by reason is possible only through conceptions. No one can find an intuition which shall correspond to the conception of reality, except in experience; it cannot be presented to the mind a priori and antecedently to the empirical consciousness of a reality. We can form an intuition, by means of the mere conception of it, of a cone, without the aid of experience; but the colour of the cone we cannot know except from experience. I cannot present an intuition of a cause, except in an example which experience offers to me. Besides, philosophy, as well as mathematics, treats of quantities; as, for example, of totality, infinity, and so on. Mathematics, too, treats of the difference of lines and surfaces — as spaces of different quality, of the continuity of extension — as a quality thereof. But, although in such cases they have a common object, the mode in which reason considers that object is very different in philosophy from what it is in mathematics. The former confines itself to the general conceptions; the latter can do nothing with a mere conception, it hastens to intuition. In this intuition it regards the conception in concreto, not empirically, but in an a priori intuition, which it has constructed; and in which, all the results which follow from the general conditions of the construction of the conception are in all cases valid for the object of the constructed conception.

Suppose that the conception of a triangle is given to a philosopher and that he is required to discover, by the philosophical method, what relation the sum of its angles bears to a right angle. He has nothing before him but the conception of a figure enclosed within three right lines, and, consequently, with the same number of angles. He may analyse the conception of a right line, of an angle, or of the number three as long as he pleases, but he will not discover any properties not contained in these conceptions. But, if this question is proposed to a geometrician, he at once begins by constructing a triangle. He knows that two right angles are equal to the sum of all the contiguous angles which proceed from one point in a straight line; and he goes on to produce one side of his triangle, thus forming two adjacent angles which are together equal to two right angles. He then divides the exterior of these angles, by drawing a line parallel with the opposite side of the triangle, and immediately perceives that he has thus got an exterior adjacent angle which is equal to the interior. Proceeding in this way, through a chain of inferences, and always on the ground of intuition, he arrives at a clear and universally valid solution of the question.

But mathematics does not confine itself to the construction of quantities (quanta), as in the case of geometry; it occupies itself with pure quantity also (quantitas), as in the case of algebra, where complete abstraction is made of the properties of the object indicated by the conception of quantity. In algebra, a certain method of notation by signs is adopted, and these indicate the different possible constructions of quantities, the extraction of roots, and so on. After having thus denoted the general conception of quantities, according to their different relations, the different operations by which quantity or number is increased or diminished are presented in intuition in accordance with general rules. Thus, when one quantity is to be divided by another, the signs which denote both are placed in the form peculiar to the operation of division; and thus algebra, by means of a symbolical construction of quantity, just as geometry, with its ostensive or geometrical construction (a construction of the objects themselves), arrives at results which discursive cognition cannot hope to reach by the aid of mere conceptions.

Now, what is the cause of this difference in the fortune of the philosopher and the mathematician, the former of whom follows the path of conceptions, while the latter pursues that of intuitions, which he represents, a priori, in correspondence with his conceptions? The cause is evident from what has been already demonstrated in the introduction to this Critique. We do not, in the present case, want to discover analytical propositions, which may be produced merely by analysing our conceptions — for in this the philosopher would have the advantage over his rival; we aim at the discovery of synthetical propositions — such synthetical propositions, moreover, as can be cognized a priori. I must not confine myself to that which I actually cogitate in my conception of a triangle, for this is nothing more than the mere definition; I must try to go beyond that, and to arrive at properties which are not contained in, although they belong to, the conception. Now, this is impossible, unless I determine the object present to my mind according to the conditions, either of empirical, or of pure, intuition. In the former case, I should have an empirical proposition (arrived at by actual measurement of the angles of the triangle), which would possess neither universality nor necessity; but that would be of no value. In the latter, I proceed by geometrical construction, by means of which I collect, in a pure intuition, just as I would in an empirical intuition, all the various properties which belong to the schema of a triangle in general, and consequently to its conception, and thus construct synthetical propositions which possess the attribute of universality.

It would be vain to philosophize upon the triangle, that is, to reflect on it discursively;

I should get no further than the definition with which I had been obliged to set out. There are certainly transcendental synthetical propositions which are framed by means of pure conceptions, and which form the peculiar distinction of philosophy; but these do not relate to any particular thing, but to a thing in general, and enounce the conditions under which the perception of it may become a part of possible experience. But the science of mathematics has nothing to do with such questions, nor with the question of existence in any fashion; it is concerned merely with the properties of objects in themselves, only in so far as these are connected with the conception of the objects.

In the above example, we merely attempted to show the great difference which exists between the discursive employment of reason in the sphere of conceptions, and its intuitive exercise by means of the construction of conceptions. The question naturally arises: What is the cause which necessitates this twofold exercise of reason, and how are we to discover whether it is the philosophical or the mathematical method which reason is pursuing in an argument?

All our knowledge relates, finally, to possible intuitions, for it is these alone that present objects to the mind. An a priori or non-empirical conception contains either a pure intuition — and in this case it can be constructed; or it contains nothing but the synthesis of possible intuitions, which are not given a priori. In this latter case, it may help us to form synthetical a priori judgements, but only in the discursive method, by conceptions, not in the intuitive, by means of the construction of conceptions.

The only a priori intuition is that of the pure form of phenomena — space and time. A conception of space and time as quanta may be presented a priori in intuition, that is, constructed, either alone with their quality (figure), or as pure quantity (the mere synthesis of the homogeneous), by means of number. But the matter of phenomena, by which things are given in space and time, can be presented only in perception, a posteriori. The only conception which represents a priori this empirical content of phenomena is the conception of a thing in general; and the a priori synthetical cognition of this conception can give us nothing more than the rule for the synthesis of that which may be contained in the corresponding a posteriori perception; it is utterly inadequate to present an a priori intuition of the real object, which must necessarily be empirical.

Synthetical propositions, which relate to things in general, an a priori intuition of which is impossible, are transcendental. For this reason transcendental propositions cannot be framed by means of the construction of conceptions; they are a priori, and based entirely on conceptions themselves. They contain merely the rule, by which we are to seek in the world of perception or experience the synthetical unity of that which cannot be intuited a priori. But they are incompetent to present any of the conceptions which appear in them in an a priori intuition; these can be given only a posteriori, in experience, which, however, is itself possible only through these synthetical principles.

If we are to form a synthetical judgement regarding a conception, we must go beyond it, to the intuition in which it is given. If we keep to what is contained in the conception, the judgement is merely analytical — it is merely an explanation of what we have cogitated in the conception. But I can pass from the conception to the pure or empirical intuition which corresponds to it. I can proceed to examine my conception in concreto, and to cognize, either a priori or a posterio, what I find in the object of the conception. The former — a priori cognition — is rational-mathematical cognition by means of the construction of the conception; the latter — a posteriori cognition — is purely empirical cognition, which does not possess the attributes of necessity and universality. Thus I may analyse the conception I have of gold; but I gain no new information from this analysis, I merely enumerate the different properties which I had connected with the notion indicated by the word. My knowledge has gained in logical clearness and arrangement, but no addition has been made to it. But if I take the matter which is indicated by this name, and submit it to the examination of my senses, I am enabled to form several synthetical — although still empirical — propositions. The mathematical conception of a triangle I should construct, that is, present a priori in intuition, and in this way attain to rational-synthetical cognition. But when the transcendental conception of reality, or substance, or power is presented to my mind, I find that it does not relate to or indicate either an empirical or pure intuition, but that it indicates merely the synthesis of empirical intuitions, which cannot of course be given a priori. The synthesis in such a conception cannot proceed a priori — without the aid of experience — to the intuition which corresponds to the conception; and, for this reason, none of these conceptions can produce a determinative synthetical proposition, they can never present more than a principle of the synthesis* of possible empirical intuitions. A transcendental proposition is, therefore, a synthetical cognition of reason by means of pure conceptions and the discursive method, and it renders possible all synthetical unity in empirical cognition, though it cannot present us with any intuition a priori.

[Note: In the case of the conception of cause, I do really go beyond the empirical conception of an event — but not to the intuition which presents this conception in concreto, but only to the time-conditions, which may be found in experience to correspond to the conception. My procedure is, therefore, strictly according to conceptions; I cannot in a case of this kind employ the construction of conceptions, because the conception is merely a rule for the synthesis of perceptions, which are not pure intuitions, and which, therefore, cannot be given a priori.]

There is thus a twofold exercise of reason. Both modes have the properties of universality and an a priori origin in common, but are, in their procedure, of widely different character. The reason of this is that in the world of phenomena, in which alone objects are presented to our minds, there are two main elements — the form of intuition (space and time), which can be cognized and determined completely a priori, and the matter or content — that which is presented in space and time, and which, consequently, contains a something — an existence corresponding to our powers of sensation. As regards the latter, which can never be given in a determinate mode except by experience, there are no a priori notions which relate to it, except the undetermined conceptions of the synthesis of possible sensations, in so far as these belong (in a possible experience) to the unity of consciousness. As regards the former, we can determine our conceptions a priori in intuition, inasmuch as we are ourselves the creators of the objects of the conceptions in space and time — these objects being regarded simply as quanta. In the one case, reason proceeds according to conceptions and can do nothing more than subject phenomena to these — which can only be determined empirically, that is, a posteriori — in conformity, however, with those conceptions as the rules of all empirical synthesis. In the other case, reason proceeds by the construction of conceptions; and, as these conceptions relate to an a priori intuition, they may be given and determined in pure intuition a priori, and without the aid of empirical data. The examination and consideration of everything that exists in space or time — whether it is a quantum or not, in how far the particular something (which fills space or time) is a primary substratum, or a mere determination of some other existence, whether it relates to anything else — either as cause or effect, whether its existence is isolated or in reciprocal connection with and dependence upon others, the possibility of this existence, its reality and necessity or opposites — all these form part of the cognition of reason on the ground of conceptions, and this cognition is termed philosophical. But to determine a priori an intuition in space (its figure), to divide time into periods, or merely to cognize the quantity of an intuition in space and time, and to determine it by number — all this is an operation of reason by means of the construction of conceptions, and is called mathematical.

The success which attends the efforts of reason in the sphere of mathematics naturally fosters the expectation that the same good fortune will be its lot, if it applies the mathematical method in other regions of mental endeavour besides that of quantities. Its success is thus great, because it can support all its conceptions by a priori intuitions and, in this way, make itself a master, as it were, over nature; while pure philosophy, with its a priori discursive conceptions, bungles about in the world of nature, and cannot accredit or show any a priori evidence of the reality of these conceptions. Masters in the science of mathematics are confident of the success of this method; indeed, it is a common persuasion that it is capable of being applied to any subject of human thought. They have hardly ever reflected or philosophized on their favourite science — a task of great difficulty; and the specific difference between the two modes of employing the faculty of reason has never entered their thoughts. Rules current in the field of common experience, and which common sense stamps everywhere with its approval, are regarded by them as axiomatic. From what source the conceptions of space and time, with which (as the only primitive quanta) they have to deal, enter their minds, is a question which they do not trouble themselves to answer; and they think it just as unnecessary to examine into the origin of the pure conceptions of the understanding and the extent of their validity. All they have to do with them is to employ them. In all this they are perfectly right, if they do not overstep the limits of the sphere of nature. But they pass, unconsciously, from the world of sense to the insecure ground of pure transcendental conceptions (instabilis tellus, innabilis unda), where they can neither stand nor swim, and where the tracks of their footsteps are obliterated by time; while the march of mathematics is pursued on a broad and magnificent highway, which the latest posterity shall frequent without fear of danger or impediment.

As we have taken upon us the task of determining, clearly and certainly, the limits of pure reason in the sphere of transcendentalism, and as the efforts of reason in this direction are persisted in, even after the plainest and most expressive warnings, hope still beckoning us past the limits of experience into the splendours of the intellectual world — it becomes necessary to cut away the last anchor of this fallacious and fantastic hope. We shall, accordingly, show that the mathematical method is unattended in the sphere of philosophy by the least advantage — except, perhaps, that it more plainly exhibits its own inadequacy — that geometry and philosophy are two quite different things, although they go band in hand in hand in the field of natural science, and, consequently, that the procedure of the one can never be imitated by the other.

The evidence of mathematics rests upon definitions, axioms, and demonstrations. I shall be satisfied with showing that none of these forms can be employed or imitated in philosophy in the sense in which they are understood by mathematicians; and that the geometrician, if he employs his method in philosophy, will succeed only in building card-castles, while the employment of the philosophical method in mathematics can result in nothing but mere verbiage. The essential business of philosophy, indeed, is to mark out the limits of the science; and even the mathematician, unless his talent is naturally circumscribed and limited to this particular department of knowledge, cannot turn a deaf ear to the warnings of philosophy, or set himself above its direction.

I. Of Definitions. A definition is, as the term itself indicates, the representation, upon primary grounds, of the complete conception of a thing within its own limits.* Accordingly, an empirical conception cannot be defined, it can only be explained. For, as there are in such a conception only a certain number of marks or signs, which denote a certain class of sensuous objects, we can never be sure that we do not cogitate under the word which indicates the same object, at one time a greater, at another a smaller number of signs. Thus, one person may cogitate in his conception of gold, in addition to its properties of weight, colour, malleability, that of resisting rust, while another person may be ignorant of this quality. We employ certain signs only so long as we require them for the sake of distinction; new observations abstract some and add new ones, so that an empirical conception never remains within permanent limits. It is, in fact, useless to define a conception of this kind. If, for example, we are speaking of water and its properties, we do not stop at what we actually think by the word water, but proceed to observation and experiment; and the word, with the few signs attached to it, is more properly a designation than a conception of the thing. A definition in this case would evidently be nothing more than a determination of the word. In the second place, no a priori conception, such as those of substance, cause, right, fitness, and so on, can be defined. For I can never be sure, that the clear representation of a given conception (which is given in a confused state) has been fully developed, until I know that the representation is adequate with its object. But, inasmuch as the conception, as it is presented to the mind, may contain a number of obscure representations, which we do not observe in our analysis, although we employ them in our application of the conception, I can never be sure that my analysis is complete, while examples may make this probable, although they can never demonstrate the fact. Instead of the word definition, I should rather employ the term exposition — a more modest expression, which the critic may accept without surrendering his doubts as to the completeness of the analysis of any such conception. As, therefore, neither empirical nor a priori conceptions are capable of definition, we have to see whether the only other kind of conceptions — arbitrary conceptions — can be subjected to this mental operation. Such a conception can always be defined; for I must know thoroughly what I wished to cogitate in it, as it was I who created it, and it was not given to my mind either by the nature of my understanding or by experience. At the same time, I cannot say that, by such a definition, I have defined a real object. If the conception is based upon empirical conditions, if, for example, I have a conception of a clock for a ship, this arbitrary conception does not assure me of the existence or even of the possibility of the object. My definition of such a conception would with more propriety be termed a declaration of a project than a definition of an object. There are no other conceptions which can bear definition, except those which contain an arbitrary synthesis, which can be constructed a priori. Consequently, the science of mathematics alone possesses definitions. For the object here thought is presented a priori in intuition; and thus it can never contain more or less than the conception, because the conception of the object has been given by the definition — and primarily, that is, without deriving the definition from any other source. Philosophical definitions are, therefore, merely expositions of given conceptions, while mathematical definitions are constructions of conceptions originally formed by the mind itself; the former are produced by analysis, the completeness of which is never demonstratively certain, the latter by a synthesis. In a mathematical definition the conception is formed, in a philosophical definition it is only explained. From this it follows:

[Note: The definition must describe the conception completely that is, omit none of the marks or signs of which it composed; within its own limits, that is, it must be precise, and enumerate no more signs than belong to the conception; and on primary grounds, that is to say, the limitations of the bounds of the conception must not be deduced from other conceptions, as in this case a proof would be necessary, and the so-called definition would be incapable of taking its place at the bead of all the judgements we have to form regarding an object.]

(a) That we must not imitate, in philosophy, the mathematical usage of commencing with definitions — except by way of hypothesis or experiment. For, as all so-called philosophical definitions are merely analyses of given conceptions, these conceptions, although only in a confused form, must precede the analysis; and the incomplete exposition must precede the complete, so that we may be able to draw certain inferences from the characteristics which an incomplete analysis has enabled us to discover, before we attain to the complete exposition or definition of the conception. In one word, a full and clear definition ought, in philosophy, rather to form the conclusion than the commencement of our labours.* In mathematics, on the contrary, we cannot have a conception prior to the definition; it is the definition which gives us the conception, and it must for this reason form the commencement of every chain of mathematical reasoning.

[Note: Philosophy abounds in faulty definitions, especially such as contain some of the elements requisite to form a complete definition.

If a conception could not be employed in reasoning before it had been defined, it would fare ill with all philosophical thought. But, as incompletely defined conceptions may always be employed without detriment to truth, so far as our analysis of the elements contained in them proceeds, imperfect definitions, that is, propositions which are properly not definitions, but merely approximations thereto, may be used with great advantage. In mathematics, definition belongs ad esse, in philosophy ad melius esse. It is a difficult task to construct a proper definition. Jurists are still without a complete definition of the idea of right.]

(b) Mathematical definitions cannot be erroneous. For the conception is given only in and through the definition, and thus it contains only what has been cogitated in the definition. But although a definition cannot be incorrect, as regards its content, an error may sometimes, although seldom, creep into the form. This error consists in a want of precision. Thus the common definition of a circle — that it is a curved line, every point in which is equally distant from another point called the centre — is faulty, from the fact that the determination indicated by the word curved is superfluous. For there ought to be a particular theorem, which may be easily proved from the definition, to the effect that every line, which has all its points at equal distances from another point, must be a curved line — that is, that not even the smallest part of it can be straight. Analytical definitions, on the other hand, may be erroneous in many respects, either by the introduction of signs which do not actually exist in the conception, or by wanting in that completeness which forms the essential of a definition. In the latter case, the definition is necessarily defective, because we can never be fully certain of the completeness of our analysis. For these reasons, the method of definition employed in mathematics cannot be imitated in philosophy.

2. Of Axioms. These, in so far as they are immediately certain, are a priori synthetical principles. Now, one conception cannot be connected synthetically and yet immediately with another; because, if we wish to proceed out of and beyond a conception, a third mediating cognition is necessary. And, as philosophy is a cognition of reason by the aid of conceptions alone, there is to be found in it no principle which deserves to be called an axiom. Mathematics, on the other hand, may possess axioms, because it can always connect the predicates of an object a priori, and without any mediating term, by means of the construction of conceptions in intuition. Such is the case with the proposition: Three points can always lie in a plane. On the other hand, no synthetical principle which is based upon conceptions, can ever be immediately certain (for example, the proposition: Everything that happens has a cause), because I require a mediating term to connect the two conceptions of event and cause — namely, the condition of time-determination in an experience, and I cannot cognize any such principle immediately and from conceptions alone. Discursive principles are, accordingly, very different from intuitive principles or axioms. The former always require deduction, which in the case of the latter may be altogether dispensed with. Axioms are, for this reason, always self-evident, while philosophical principles, whatever may be the degree of certainty they possess, cannot lay any claim to such a distinction. No synthetical proposition of pure transcendental reason can be so evident, as is often rashly enough declared, as the statement, twice two are four. It is true that in the Analytic I introduced into the list of principles of the pure understanding, certain axioms of intuition; but the principle there discussed was not itself an axiom, but served merely to present the principle of the possibility of axioms in general, while it was really nothing more than a principle based upon conceptions. For it is one part of the duty of transcendental philosophy to establish the possibility of mathematics itself. Philosophy possesses, then, no axioms, and has no right to impose its a priori principles upon thought, until it has established their authority and validity by a thoroughgoing deduction.

3. Of Demonstrations. Only an apodeictic proof, based upon intuition, can be termed a demonstration. Experience teaches us what is, but it cannot convince us that it might not have been otherwise. Hence a proof upon empirical grounds cannot

be apodeictic. A priori conceptions, in discursive cognition, can never produce intuitive certainty or evidence, however certain the judgement they present may be. Mathematics alone, therefore, contains demonstrations, because it does not deduce its cognition from conceptions, but from the construction of conceptions, that is, from intuition, which can be given a priori in accordance with conceptions. The method of algebra, in equations, from which the correct answer is deduced by reduction, is a kind of construction — not geometrical, but by symbols — in which all conceptions, especially those of the relations of quantities, are represented in intuition by signs; and thus the conclusions in that science are secured from errors by the fact that every proof is submitted to ocular evidence. Philosophical cognition does not possess this advantage, it being required to consider the general always in abstracto (by means of conceptions), while mathematics can always consider it in concreto (in an individual intuition), and at the same time by means of a priori representation, whereby all errors are rendered manifest to the senses. The former — discursive proofs — ought to be termed acroamatic proofs, rather than demonstrations, as only words are employed in them, while demonstrations proper, as the term itself indicates, always require a reference to the intuition of the object.

It follows from all these considerations that it is not consonant with the nature of philosophy, especially in the sphere of pure reason, to employ the dogmatical method, and to adorn itself with the titles and insignia of mathematical science. It does not belong to that order, and can only hope for a fraternal union with that science. Its attempts at mathematical evidence are vain pretensions, which can only keep it back from its true aim, which is to detect the illusory procedure of reason when transgressing its proper limits, and by fully explaining and analysing our conceptions, to conduct us from the dim regions of speculation to the clear region of modest self-knowledge. Reason must not, therefore, in its transcendental endeavours, look forward with such confidence, as if the path it is pursuing led straight to its aim, nor reckon with such security upon its premisses, as to consider it unnecessary to take a step back, or to keep a strict watch for errors, which, overlooked in the principles, may be detected in the arguments themselves — in which case it may be requisite either to determine these principles with greater strictness, or to change them entirely.

I divide all apodeictic propositions, whether demonstrable or immediately certain, into dogmata and mathemata. A direct synthetical proposition, based on conceptions, is a dogma; a proposition of the same kind, based on the construction of conceptions, is a mathema. Analytical judgements do not teach us any more about an object than what was contained in the conception we had of it; because they do not extend our cognition beyond our conception of an object, they merely elucidate the conception. They cannot therefore be with propriety termed dogmas. Of the two kinds of a priori synthetical propositions above mentioned, only those which are employed in philosophy can, according to the general mode of speech, bear this name; those of arithmetic or geometry would not be rightly so denominated. Thus the customary mode of speaking confirms the explanation given above, and the conclusion arrived at, that only those judgements which are based upon conceptions, not on the construction of conceptions, can be termed dogmatical.

Thus, pure reason, in the sphere of speculation, does not contain a single direct synthetical judgement based upon conceptions. By means of ideas, it is, as we have shown, incapable of producing synthetical judgements, which are objectively valid; by means of the conceptions of the understanding, it establishes certain indubitable principles, not, however, directly on the basis of conceptions, but only indirectly by means of the relation of these conceptions to something of a purely contingent nature, namely, possible experience. When experience is presupposed, these principles are apodeictically certain, but in themselves, and directly, they cannot even be cognized a priori. Thus the given conceptions of cause and event will not be sufficient for the demonstration of the proposition: Every event has a cause. For this reason, it is not a dogma; although from another point of view, that of experience, it is capable of being proved to demonstration. The proper term for such a proposition is principle, and not theorem (although it does require to be proved), because it possesses the remarkable peculiarity of being the condition of the possibility of its own ground of proof, that is, experience, and of forming a necessary presupposition in all empirical observation.

If then, in the speculative sphere of pure reason, no dogmata are to be found; all dogmatical methods, whether borrowed from mathematics, or invented by philosophical thinkers, are alike inappropriate and inefficient. They only serve to conceal errors and fallacies, and to deceive philosophy, whose duty it is to see that reason pursues a safe and straight path. A philosophical method may, however, be systematical. For our reason is, subjectively considered, itself a system, and, in the sphere of mere conceptions, a system of investigation according to principles of unity, the material being supplied by experience alone. But this is not the proper place for discussing the peculiar method of transcendental philosophy, as our present task is simply to examine whether our faculties are capable of erecting an edifice on the basis of pure reason, and how far they may proceed with the materials at their command.

SECTION II. The Discipline of Pure Reason in Polemics.

Reason must be subject, in all its operations, to criticism, which must always be permitted to exercise its functions without restraint; otherwise its interests are imperilled and its influence obnoxious to suspicion. There is nothing, however useful, however sacred it may be, that can claim exemption from the searching examination of this supreme tribunal, which has no respect of persons. The very existence of reason depends upon this freedom; for the voice of reason is not that of a dictatorial and despotic power, it is rather like the vote of the citizens of a free state, every member of which must have the privilege of giving free expression to his doubts, and possess even the right of veto.

But while reason can never decline to submit itself to the tribunal of criticism, it has not always cause to dread the judgement of this court. Pure reason, however, when engaged in the sphere of dogmatism, is not so thoroughly conscious of a strict observance of its highest laws, as to appear before a higher judicial reason with perfect confidence. On the contrary, it must renounce its magnificent dogmatical pretensions in philosophy.

Very different is the case when it has to defend itself, not before a judge, but against an equal. If dogmatical assertions are advanced on the negative side, in opposition to those made by reason on the positive side, its justification kat authrhopon is complete, although the proof of its propositions is kat aletheian unsatisfactory.

By the polemic of pure reason I mean the defence of its propositions made by reason, in opposition to the dogmatical counter-propositions advanced by other parties. The question here is not whether its own statements may not also be false; it merely regards the fact that reason proves that the opposite cannot be established with demonstrative certainty, nor even asserted with a higher degree of probability. Reason does not hold her possessions upon sufferance; for, although she cannot show a perfectly satisfactory title to them, no one can prove that she is not the rightful possessor.

It is a melancholy reflection that reason, in its highest exercise, falls into an antithetic; and that the supreme tribunal for the settlement of differences should not be at union with itself. It is true that we had to discuss the question of an apparent antithetic, but we found that it was based upon a misconception. In conformity with the common prejudice, phenomena were regarded as things in themselves, and thus an absolute completeness in their synthesis was required in the one mode or in the other (it was shown to be impossible in both); a demand entirely out of place in regard to phenomena. There was, then, no real self-contradiction of reason in the propositions: The series of phenomena given in themselves has an absolutely first beginning; and: This series is absolutely and in itself without beginning. The two propositions are perfectly consistent with each other, because phenomena as phenomena are in themselves nothing, and consequently the hypothesis that they are things in themselves must lead to self-contradictory inferences.

But there are cases in which a similar misunderstanding cannot be provided against, and the dispute must remain unsettled. Take, for example, the theistic proposition: There is a Supreme Being; and on the other hand, the atheistic counter-statement: There exists no Supreme Being; or, in psychology: Everything that thinks possesses the attribute of absolute and permanent unity, which is utterly different from the transitory unity of material phenomena; and the counter-proposition: The soul is not an immaterial unity, and its nature is transitory, like that of phenomena. The objects of these questions contain no heterogeneous or contradictory elements, for they relate to things in themselves, and not to phenomena. There would arise, indeed, a real contradiction, if reason came forward with a statement on the negative side of these questions alone. As regards the criticism to which the grounds of proof on the affirmative side must be subjected, it may be freely admitted, without necessitating the surrender of the affirmative propositions, which have, at least, the interest of reason in their favour — an advantage which the opposite party cannot lay claim to.

I cannot agree with the opinion of several admirable thinkers — Sulzer among the rest — that, in spite of the weakness of the arguments hitherto in use, we may hope, one day, to see sufficient demonstrations of the two cardinal propositions of pure reason — the existence of a Supreme Being, and the immortality of the soul. I am certain, on the contrary, that this will never be the case. For on what ground can reason base such synthetical propositions, which do not relate to the objects of experience and their internal possibility? But it is also demonstratively certain that no one will ever be able to maintain the contrary with the least show of probability. For, as he can attempt such a proof solely upon the basis of pure reason, he is bound to prove that a Supreme Being, and a thinking subject in the character of a pure intelligence, are impossible.

But where will he find the knowledge which can enable him to enounce synthetical judgements in regard to things which transcend the region of experience? We may, therefore, rest assured that the opposite never will be demonstrated. We need not, then, have recourse to scholastic arguments; we may always admit the truth of those propositions which are consistent with the speculative interests of reason in the sphere of experience, and form, moreover, the only means of uniting the speculative with the practical interest. Our opponent, who must not be considered here as a critic solely, we can be ready to meet with a non liquet which cannot fail to disconcert him; while we cannot deny his right to a similar retort, as we have on our side the advantage of the support of the subjective maxim of reason, and can therefore look upon all his sophistical arguments with calm indifference.

From this point of view, there is properly no antithetic of pure reason. For the only arena for such a struggle would be upon the field of pure theology and psychology; but on this ground there can appear no combatant whom we need to fear. Ridicule and boasting can be his only weapons; and these may be laughed at, as mere child's play. This consideration restores to Reason her courage; for what source of confidence could be found, if she, whose vocation it is to destroy error, were at variance with herself and without any reasonable hope of ever reaching a state of permanent repose?

Everything in nature is good for some purpose. Even poisons are serviceable; they destroy the evil effects of other poisons generated in our system, and must always find a place in every complete pharmacopoeia. The objections raised against the fallacies and sophistries of speculative reason, are objections given by the nature of this reason itself, and must therefore have a destination and purpose which can only be for the good of humanity. For what purpose has Providence raised many objects, in which we have the deepest interest, so far above us, that we vainly try to cognize them with certainty, and our powers of mental vision are rather excited than satisfied by the glimpses we may chance to seize? It is very doubtful whether it is for our benefit to advance bold affirmations regarding subjects involved in such obscurity; perhaps it would even be detrimental to our best interests. But it is undoubtedly always beneficial to leave the investigating, as well as the critical reason, in perfect freedom, and permit it to take charge of its own interests, which are advanced as much by its limitation, as by its extension of its views, and which always suffer by the interference of foreign powers forcing it, against its natural tendencies, to bend to certain preconceived designs.

Allow your opponent to say what he thinks reasonable, and combat him only with the weapons of reason. Have no anxiety for the practical interests of humanity — these are never imperilled in a purely speculative dispute. Such a dispute serves merely to disclose the antinomy of reason, which, as it has its source in the nature of reason, ought to be thoroughly investigated. Reason is benefited by the examination of a subject on both sides, and its judgements are corrected by being limited. It is not the matter that may give occasion to dispute, but the manner. For it is perfectly permissible to employ, in the presence of reason, the language of a firmly rooted faith, even after we have been obliged to renounce all pretensions to knowledge.

If we were to ask the dispassionate David Hume — a philosopher endowed, in a degree that few are, with a well-balanced judgement: What motive induced you to spend so much labour and thought in undermining the consoling and beneficial persuasion that reason is capable of assuring us of the existence, and presenting us with a determinate conception of a Supreme Being? — his answer would be: Nothing but the desire of teaching reason to know its own powers better, and, at the same time, a dislike of the procedure by which that faculty was compelled to support foregone conclusions, and prevented from confessing the internal weaknesses which it cannot but feel when it enters upon a rigid self-examination. If, on the other hand, we were to ask Priestley — a philosopher who had no taste for transcendental speculation, but was entirely devoted to the principles of empiricism — what his motives were for overturning those two main pillars of religion — the doctrines of the freedom of the will and the immortality of the soul (in his view the hope of a future life is but the expectation of the miracle of resurrection) — this philosopher, himself a zealous and pious teacher of religion, could give no other answer than this: I acted in the interest of reason, which always suffers, when certain objects are explained and judged by a reference to other supposed laws than those of material nature — the only laws which we know in a determinate manner. It would be unfair to decry the latter philosopher, who endeavoured to harmonize his paradoxical opinions with the interests of religion, and to undervalue an honest and reflecting man, because he finds himself at a loss the moment he has left the field of natural science. The same grace must be accorded to Hume, a man not less well-disposed, and quite as blameless in his moral character, and who pushed his abstract speculations to an extreme length, because, as he rightly believed, the object of them lies entirely beyond the bounds of natural science, and within the sphere of pure ideas.

What is to be done to provide against the danger which seems in the present case to menace the best interests of humanity? The course to be pursued in reference to this subject is a perfectly plain and natural one. Let each thinker pursue his own path; if he shows talent, if he gives evidence of profound thought, in one word, if he shows that he possesses the power of reasoning — reason is always the gainer. If you have recourse to other means, if you attempt to coerce reason, if you raise the cry of treason to humanity, if you excite the feelings of the crowd, which can neither understand nor sympathize with such subtle speculations — you will only make yourselves ridiculous. For the question does not concern the advantage or disadvantage which we are expected to reap from such inquiries; the question is merely how far reason can advance in the field of speculation, apart from all kinds of interest, and whether we may depend upon the exertions of speculative reason, or must renounce all reliance on it. Instead of joining the combatants, it is your part to be a tranquil spectator of the struggle — a laborious struggle for the parties engaged, but attended, in its progress as well as in its result, with the most advantageous consequences for the interests of thought and knowledge. It is absurd to expect to be enlightened by Reason, and at the same time to prescribe to her what side of the question she must adopt. Moreover, reason is sufficiently held in check by its own power, the limits imposed on it by its own nature are sufficient; it is unnecessary for you to place over it additional guards, as if its power were dangerous to the constitution of the intellectual state. In the dialectic of reason there is no victory gained which need in the least disturb your tranquility.

The strife of dialectic is a necessity of reason, and we cannot but wish that it had been conducted long ere this with that perfect freedom which ought to be its essential condition. In this case, we should have had at an earlier period a matured and profound criticism, which must have put an end to all dialectical disputes, by exposing the illusions and prejudices in which they originated.

There is in human nature an unworthy propensity — a propensity which, like everything that springs from nature, must in its final purpose be conducive to the good of humanity — to conceal our real sentiments, and to give expression only to certain received opinions, which are regarded as at once safe and promotive of the common good. It is true, this tendency, not only to conceal our real sentiments, but to profess those which may gain us favour in the eyes of society, has not only civilized, but, in a certain measure, moralized us; as no one can break through the outward covering of respectability, honour, and morality, and thus the seemingly-good examples which we which we see around us form an excellent school for moral improvement, so long as our belief in their genuineness remains unshaken. But this disposition to represent ourselves as better than we are, and to utter opinions which are not our own, can be nothing more than a kind of provisionary arrangement of nature to lead us from the rudeness of an uncivilized state, and to teach us how to assume at least the appearance and manner of the good we see. But when true principles have been developed, and have obtained a sure foundation in our habit of thought, this conventionalism must be attacked with earnest vigour, otherwise it corrupts the heart, and checks the growth of good dispositions with the mischievous weed of air appearances.

I am sorry to remark the same tendency to misrepresentation and hypocrisy in the sphere of speculative discussion, where there is less temptation to restrain the free expression of thought. For what can be more prejudicial to the interests of intelligence than to falsify our real sentiments, to conceal the doubts which we feel in regard to our statements, or to maintain the validity of grounds of proof which we well know to be insufficient? So long as mere personal vanity is the source of these unworthy artifices — and this is generally the case in speculative discussions, which are mostly destitute of practical interest, and are incapable of complete demonstration — the vanity of the opposite party exaggerates as much on the other side; and thus the result is the same, although it is not brought about so soon as if the dispute had been conducted in a sincere and upright spirit. But where the mass entertains the notion that the aim of certain subtle speculators is nothing less than to shake the very foundations of public welfare and morality — it seems not only prudent, but even praise worthy, to maintain the good cause by illusory arguments, rather than to give to our supposed opponents the advantage of lowering our declarations to the moderate tone of a merely practical conviction, and of compelling us to confess our inability to attain to apodeictic certainty in speculative subjects. But we ought to reflect that there is nothing, in the world more fatal to the maintenance of a good cause than deceit, misrepresentation, and falsehood. That the strictest laws of honesty should be observed in the discussion of a purely speculative subject is the least requirement that can be made. If we could reckon with security even upon so little, the conflict of speculative reason regarding the important questions of God, immortality, and freedom, would have been either decided long ago, or would very soon be brought to a conclusion. But, in general, the uprightness of the defence stands in an inverse ratio to the goodness of the cause; and perhaps more honesty and fairness are shown by those who deny than by those who uphold these doctrines.

I shall persuade myself, then, that I have readers who do not wish to see a righteous cause defended by unfair arguments. Such will now recognize the fact that, according to the principles of this Critique, if we consider not what is, but what ought to be the case, there can be really no polemic of pure reason. For how can two persons dispute about a thing, the reality of which neither can present in actual or even in possible experience? Each adopts the plan of meditating on his idea for the purpose of drawing from the idea, if he can, what is more than the idea, that is, the reality of the object which it indicates. How shall they settle the dispute, since neither is able to make his assertions directly comprehensible and certain, but must restrict himself to attacking and confuting those of his opponent? All statements enounced by pure reason transcend the conditions of possible experience, beyond the sphere of which we can discover no criterion of truth, while they are at the same time framed in accordance with the laws of the understanding, which are applicable only to experience; and thus it is the fate of all such speculative discussions that while the one party attacks the weaker side of his opponent, he infallibly lays open his own weaknesses.

The critique of pure reason may be regarded as the highest tribunal for all speculative disputes; for it is not involved in these disputes, which have an immediate relation to certain objects and not to the laws of the mind, but is instituted for the purpose of determining the rights and limits of reason.

Without the control of criticism, reason is, as it were, in a state of nature, and can only establish its claims and assertions by war. Criticism, on the contrary, deciding all questions according to the fundamental laws of its own institution, secures to us the peace of law and order, and enables us to discuss all differences in the more tranquil manner of a legal process. In the former case, disputes are ended by victory, which both sides may claim and which is followed by a hollow armistice; in the latter, by a sentence, which, as it strikes at the root of all speculative differences, ensures to all concerned a lasting peace. The endless disputes of a dogmatizing reason compel us to look for some mode of arriving at a settled decision by a critical investigation of reason itself; just as Hobbes maintains that the state of nature is a state of injustice and violence, and that we must leave it and submit ourselves to the constraint of law, which indeed limits individual freedom, but only that it may consist with the freedom of others and with the common good of all.

This freedom will, among other things, permit of our openly stating the difficulties and doubts which we are ourselves unable to solve, without being decried on that account as turbulent and dangerous citizens. This privilege forms part of the native rights of human reason, which recognizes no other judge than the universal reason of humanity; and as this reason is the source of all progress and improvement, such a privilege is to be held sacred and inviolable. It is unwise, moreover, to denounce as dangerous any bold assertions against, or rash attacks upon, an opinion which is held by the largest and most moral class of the community; for that would be giving them an importance which they do not deserve. When I hear that the freedom of the will, the hope of a future life, and the existence of God have been overthrown by the arguments of some able writer, I feel a strong desire to read his book; for I expect that he will add to my knowledge and impart greater clearness and distinctness to my views by the argumentative power shown in his writings. But I am perfectly certain, even before I have opened the book, that he has not succeeded in a single point, not because I believe I am in possession of irrefutable demonstrations of these important propositions, but because this transcendental critique, which has disclosed to me the power and the limits of pure reason, has fully convinced me that, as it is insufficient to establish the affirmative, it is as powerless, and even more so, to assure us of the truth of the negative answer to these questions. From what source does this free-thinker derive his knowledge that there is, for example, no Supreme Being? This proposition lies out of the field of possible experience, and, therefore, beyond the limits of human cognition. But I would not read at, all the answer which the dogmatical maintainer of the good cause makes to his opponent, because I know well beforehand, that he will merely attack the fallacious grounds of his adversary, without being able to establish his own assertions. Besides, a new illusory argument, in the construction of which talent and acuteness are shown, is suggestive of new ideas and new trains of reasoning, and in this respect the old and everyday sophistries are quite useless. Again, the dogmatical opponent of religion gives employment to criticism, and enables us to test and correct its principles, while there is no occasion for anxiety in regard to the influence and results of his reasoning.

But, it will be said, must we not warn the youth entrusted to academical care against such writings, must we not preserve them from the knowledge of these dangerous assertions, until their judgement is ripened, or rather until the doctrines which we wish to inculcate are so firmly rooted in their minds as to withstand all attempts at instilling the contrary dogmas, from whatever quarter they may come?

If we are to confine ourselves to the dogmatical procedure in the sphere of pure reason, and find ourselves unable to settle such disputes otherwise than by becoming a party in them, and setting counter-assertions against the statements advanced by our opponents, there is certainly no plan more advisable for the moment, but, at the same time, none more absurd and inefficient for the future, than this retaining of the youthful mind under guardianship for a time, and thus preserving it — for so long at least — from seduction into error. But when, at a later period, either curiosity, or the prevalent fashion of thought places such writings in their hands, will the so-called convictions of their youth stand firm? The young thinker, who has in his armoury none but dogmatical weapons with which to resist the attacks of his opponent, and who cannot detect the latent dialectic which lies in his own opinions as well as in those of the opposite party, sees the advance of illusory arguments and grounds of proof which have the advantage of novelty, against as illusory grounds of proof destitute of this advantage, and which, perhaps, excite the suspicion that the natural credulity of his youth has been abused by his instructors. He thinks he can find no better means of showing that he has out grown the discipline of his minority than by despising those well-meant warnings, and, knowing no system of thought but that of dogmatism, he drinks deep draughts of the poison that is to sap the principles in which his early years were trained.

Exactly the opposite of the system here recommended ought to be pursued in academical instruction. This can only be effected, however, by a thorough training in the critical investigation of pure reason. For, in order to bring the principles of this critique into exercise as soon as possible, and to demonstrate their perfect even in the presence of the highest degree of dialectical illusion, the student ought to examine the assertions made on both sides of speculative questions step by step, and to test them by these principles. It cannot be a difficult task for him to show the fallacies inherent in these propositions, and thus he begins early to feel his own power of securing himself against the influence of such sophistical arguments, which must finally lose, for him, all their illusory power. And, although the same blows which overturn the edifice of his opponent are as fatal to his own speculative structures, if such he has wished to rear; he need not feel any sorrow in regard to this seeming misfortune, as he has now before him a fair prospect into the practical region in which he may reasonably hope to find a more secure foundation for a rational system.

There is, accordingly, no proper polemic in the sphere of pure reason. Both parties beat the air and fight with their own shadows, as they pass beyond the limits of nature, and can find no tangible point of attack — no firm footing for their dogmatical conflict. Fight as vigorously as they may, the shadows which they hew down, immediately start up again, like the heroes in Walhalla, and renew the bloodless and unceasing contest.

But neither can we admit that there is any proper sceptical employment of pure reason, such as might be based upon the principle of neutrality in all speculative disputes. To excite reason against itself, to place weapons in the hands of the party on the one side as well as in those of the other, and to remain an undisturbed and sarcastic spectator of the fierce struggle that ensues, seems, from the dogmatical point of view, to be a part fitting only a malevolent disposition. But, when the sophist evidences an invincible obstinacy and blindness, and a pride which no criticism can moderate, there is no other practicable course than to oppose to this pride and obstinacy similar feelings and pretensions on the other side, equally well or ill founded, so that reason, staggered by the reflections thus forced upon it, finds it necessary to moderate its confidence in such pretensions and to listen to the advice of criticism. But we cannot stop at these doubts, much less regard the conviction of our ignorance, not only as a cure for the conceit natural to dogmatism, but as the settlement of the disputes in which reason is involved with itself. On the contrary, scepticism is merely a means of awakening reason from its dogmatic dreams and exciting it to a more careful investigation into its own powers and pretensions. But, as scepticism appears to be the shortest road to a permanent peace in the domain of philosophy, and as it is the track pursued by the many who aim at giving a philosophical colouring to their contemptuous dislike of all inquiries of this kind, I think it necessary to present to my readers this mode of thought in its true light.

Scepticism not a Permanent State for Human Reason.

The consciousness of ignorance — unless this ignorance is recognized to be absolutely necessary ought, instead of forming the conclusion of my inquiries, to be the strongest motive to the pursuit of them. All ignorance is either ignorance of things or of the limits of knowledge. If my ignorance is accidental and not necessary, it must incite me, in the first case, to a dogmatical inquiry regarding the objects of which I am ignorant; in the second, to a critical investigation into the bounds of all possible knowledge. But that my ignorance is absolutely necessary and unavoidable, and that it consequently absolves from the duty of all further investigation, is a fact which cannot be made out upon empirical grounds — from observation — but upon critical grounds alone, that is, by a thoroughgoing investigation into the primary sources of cognition. It follows that the determination of the bounds of reason can be made only on a priori grounds; while the empirical limitation of reason, which is merely an indeterminate cognition of an ignorance that can never be completely removed, can take place only a posteriori. In other words, our empirical knowledge is limited by that which yet remains for us to know. The former cognition of our ignorance, which is possible only on a rational basis, is a science; the latter is merely a perception, and we cannot say how far the inferences drawn from it may extend. If I regard the earth, as it really appears to my senses, as a flat surface, I am ignorant how far this surface extends. But experience teaches me that, how far soever I go, I always see before me a space in which I can proceed farther; and thus I know the limits — merely visual — of my actual knowledge of the earth, although I am ignorant of the limits of the earth itself. But if I have got so far as to know that the earth is a sphere, and that its surface is spherical, I can cognize a priori and determine upon principles, from my knowledge of a small part of this surface — say to the extent of a degree — the diameter and circumference of the earth; and although I am ignorant of the objects which this surface contains, I have a perfect knowledge of its limits and extent.

The sum of all the possible objects of our cognition seems to us to be a level surface, with an apparent horizon — that which forms the limit of its extent, and which has been termed by us the idea of unconditioned totality. To reach this limit by empirical means is impossible, and all attempts to determine it a priori according to a principle, are alike in vain. But all the questions raised by pure reason relate to that which lies beyond this horizon, or, at least, in its boundary line.

The celebrated David Hume was one of those geographers of human reason who believe that they have given a sufficient answer to all such questions by declaring them to lie beyond the horizon of our knowledge — a horizon which, however, Hume was unable to determine. His attention especially was directed to the principle of causality; and he remarked with perfect justice that the truth of this principle, and even the objective validity of the conception of a cause, was not commonly based upon clear insight, that is, upon a priori cognition. Hence he concluded that this law does not derive its authority from its universality and necessity, but merely from its general applicability in the course of experience, and a kind of subjective necessity thence arising, which he termed habit. From the inability of reason to establish this principle as a necessary law for the acquisition of all experience, he inferred the nullity of all the attempts of reason to pass the region of the empirical.

This procedure of subjecting the facta of reason to examination, and, if necessary, to disapproval, may be termed the censura of reason. This censura must inevitably lead us to doubts regarding all transcendent employment of principles. But this is only the second step in our inquiry. The first step in regard to the subjects of pure reason, and which marks the infancy of that faculty, is that of dogmatism. The second, which we have just mentioned, is that of scepticism, and it gives evidence that our judgement has been improved by experience. But a third step is necessary — indicative of the maturity and manhood of the judgement, which now lays a firm foundation upon universal and necessary principles. This is the period of criticism, in which we do not examine the facta of reason, but reason itself, in the whole extent of its powers, and in regard to its capability of a priori cognition; and thus we determine not merely the empirical and ever-shifting bounds of our knowledge, but its necessary and eternal limits. We demonstrate from indubitable principles, not merely our ignorance in respect to this or that subject, but in regard to all possible questions of a certain class. Thus scepticism is a resting place for reason, in which it may reflect on its dogmatical wanderings and gain some knowledge of the region in which it happens to be, that it may pursue its way with greater certainty; but it cannot be its permanent dwelling-place. It must take up its abode only in the region of complete certitude, whether this relates to the cognition of objects themselves, or to the limits which bound all our cognition.

Reason is not to be considered as an indefinitely extended plane, of the bounds of which we have only a general knowledge; it ought rather to be compared to a sphere, the radius of which may be found from the curvature of its surface — that is, the nature of a priori synthetical propositions — and, consequently, its circumference and extent. Beyond the sphere of experience there are no objects which it can cognize; nay, even questions regarding such supposititious objects relate only to the subjective principles of a complete determination of the relations which exist between the understanding-conceptions which lie within this sphere.

We are actually in possession of a priori synthetical cognitions, as is proved by the existence of the principles of the understanding, which anticipate experience. If any one cannot comprehend the possibility of these principles, he may have some reason to doubt whether they are really a priori; but he cannot on this account declare them to be impossible, and affirm the nullity of the steps which reason may have taken under their guidance. He can only say: If we perceived their origin and their authenticity, we should be able to determine the extent and limits of reason; but, till we can do this, all propositions regarding the latter are mere random assertions. In this view, the doubt respecting all dogmatical philosophy, which proceeds without the guidance of criticism, is well grounded; but we cannot therefore deny to reason the ability to construct a sound philosophy, when the way has been prepared by a thorough critical investigation. All the conceptions produced, and all the questions raised, by pure reason, do not lie in the sphere of experience, but in that of reason itself, and hence they must be solved, and shown to be either valid or inadmissible, by that faculty. We have no right to decline the solution of such problems, on the ground that the solution can be discovered only from the nature of things, and under pretence of the limitation of human faculties, for reason is the sole creator of all these ideas, and is therefore bound either to establish their validity or to expose their illusory nature.

The polemic of scepticism is properly directed against the dogmatist, who erects a system of philosophy without having examined the fundamental objective principles on which it is based, for the purpose of evidencing the futility of his designs, and thus bringing him to a knowledge of his own powers. But, in itself, scepticism does not give us any certain information in regard to the bounds of our knowledge. All unsuccessful dogmatical attempts of reason are facia, which it is always useful to submit to the censure of the sceptic. But this cannot help us to any decision regarding the expectations which reason cherishes of better success in future endeavours; the investigations of scepticism cannot, therefore, settle the dispute regarding the rights and powers of human reason.

Hume is perhaps the ablest and most ingenious of all sceptical philosophers, and his writings have, undoubtedly, exerted the most powerful influence in awakening reason to a thorough investigation into its own powers. It will, therefore, well repay our labours to consider for a little the course of reasoning which he followed and the errors into which he strayed, although setting out on the path of truth and certitude.

Hume was probably aware, although he never clearly developed the notion, that we proceed in judgements of a certain class beyond our conception if the object. I have termed this kind of judgement synthetical. As regard the manner in which I pass beyond my conception by the aid of experience, no doubts can be entertained. Experience is itself a synthesis of perceptions; and it employs perceptions to increment the conception, which I obtain by means of another perception. But we feel persuaded that we are able to proceed beyond a conception, and to extend our cognition a priori. We attempt this in two ways — either, through the pure understanding, in relation to that which may become an object of experience, or, through pure reason, in relation to such properties of things, or of the existence of things, as can never be presented in any experience. This sceptical philosopher did not distinguish these two kinds of judgements, as he ought to have done, but regarded this augmentation of conceptions, and, if we may so express ourselves, the spontaneous generation of understanding and reason, independently of the impregnation of experience, as altogether impossible. The so-called a priori principles of these faculties he consequently held to be invalid and imaginary, and regarded them as nothing but subjective habits of thought originating in experience, and therefore purely empirical and contingent rules, to which we attribute a spurious necessity and universality. In support of this strange assertion, he referred us to the generally acknowledged principle of the relation between cause and effect. No faculty of the mind can conduct us from the conception of a thing to the existence of something else; and hence he believed he could infer that, without experience, we possess no source from which we can augment a conception, and no ground sufficient to justify us in framing a judgement that is to extend our cognition a priori. That the light of the sun, which shines upon a piece of wax, at the same time melts it, while it hardens clay, no power of the understanding could infer from the conceptions which we previously possessed of these substances; much less is there any a priori law that could conduct us to such a conclusion, which experience alone can certify. On the other hand, we have seen in our discussion of transcendental logic, that, although we can never proceed immediately beyond the content of the conception which is given us, we can always cognize completely a priori — in relation, however, to a third term, namely, possible experience — the law of its connection with other things. For example, if I observe that a piece of wax melts, I can cognize a priori that there must have been something (the sun's heat) preceding, which this law; although, without the aid of experience, I could not cognize a priori and in a determinate manner either the cause from the effect, or the effect from the cause. Hume was, therefore, wrong in inferring, from the contingency of the determination according to law, the contingency of the law itself; and the passing beyond the conception of a thing to possible experience (which is an a priori proceeding, constituting the objective reality of the conception), he confounded with our synthesis of objects in actual experience, which is always, of course, empirical. Thus, too, he regarded the principle of affinity, which has its seat in the understanding and indicates a necessary connection, as a mere rule of association, lying in the imitative faculty of imagination, which can present only contingent, and not objective connections.

The sceptical errors of this remarkably acute thinker arose principally from a defect, which was common to him with the dogmatists, namely, that he had never made a systematic review of all the different kinds of a priori synthesis performed by the understanding. Had he done so, he would have found, to take one example among many, that the principle of permanence was of this character, and that it, as well as the principle of causality, anticipates experience. In this way he might have been able to describe the determinate limits of the a priori operations of understanding and reason. But he merely declared the understanding to be limited, instead of showing what its limits were; he created a general mistrust in the power of our faculties, without giving us any determinate knowledge of the bounds of our necessary and unavoidable ignorance; he examined and condemned some of the principles of the understanding, without investigating all its powers with the completeness necessary to criticism. He denies, with truth, certain powers to the understanding, but he goes further, and declares it to be utterly inadequate to the a priori extension of knowledge, although he has not fully examined all the powers which reside in the faculty; and thus the fate which always overtakes scepticism meets him too. That is to say, his own declarations are doubted, for his objections were based upon facta, which are contingent, and not upon principles, which can alone demonstrate the necessary invalidity of all dogmatical assertions.

As Hume makes no distinction between the well-grounded claims of the understanding and the dialectical pretensions of reason, against which, however, his attacks are mainly directed, reason does not feel itself shut out from all attempts at the extension of a priori cognition, and hence it refuses, in spite of a few checks in this or that quarter, to relinquish such efforts. For one naturally arms oneself to resist an attack, and becomes more obstinate in the resolve to establish the claims he has advanced. But a complete review of the powers of reason, and the conviction thence arising that we are in possession of a limited field of action, while we must admit the vanity of higher claims, puts an end to all doubt and dispute, and induces reason to rest satisfied with the undisturbed possession of its limited domain.

To the uncritical dogmatist, who has not surveyed the sphere of his understanding, nor determined, in accordance with principles, the limits of possible cognition, who, consequently, is ignorant of his own powers, and believes he will discover them by the attempts he makes in the field of cognition, these attacks of scepticism are not only dangerous, but destructive. For if there is one proposition in his chain of reasoning which be he cannot prove, or the fallacy in which he cannot evolve in accordance with a principle, suspicion falls on all his statements, however plausible they may appear.

And thus scepticism, the bane of dogmatical philosophy, conducts us to a sound investigation into the understanding and the reason. When we are thus far advanced, we need fear no further attacks; for the limits of our domain are clearly marked out, and we can make no claims nor become involved in any disputes regarding the region that lies beyond these limits. Thus the sceptical procedure in philosophy does not present any solution of the problems of reason, but it forms an excellent exercise for its powers, awakening its circumspection, and indicating the means whereby it may most fully establish its claims to its legitimate possessions.

SECTION III. The Discipline of Pure Reason in Hypothesis.

This critique of reason has now taught us that all its efforts to extend the bounds of knowledge, by means of pure speculation, are utterly fruitless. So much the wider field, it may appear, lies open to hypothesis; as, where we cannot know with certainty, we are at liberty to make guesses and to form suppositions.

Imagination may be allowed, under the strict surveillance of reason, to invent suppositions; but, these must be based on something that is perfectly certain — and that is the possibility of the object. If we are well assured upon this point, it is allowable to have recourse to supposition in regard to the reality of the object; but this supposition must, unless it is utterly groundless, be connected, as its ground of explanation, with that which is really given and absolutely certain. Such a supposition is termed a hypothesis.

It is beyond our power to form the least conception a priori of the possibility of dynamical connection in phenomena; and the category of the pure understanding will not enable us to excogitate any such connection, but merely helps us to understand it, when we meet with it in experience. For this reason we cannot, in accordance with the categories, imagine or invent any object or any property of an object not given, or that may not be given in experience, and employ it in a hypothesis; otherwise, we should be basing our chain of reasoning upon mere chimerical fancies, and not upon conceptions of things. Thus, we have no right to assume the existence of new powers, not existing in nature — for example, an understanding with a non-sensuous intuition, a force of attraction without contact, or some new kind of substances occupying space, and yet without the property of impenetrability — and, consequently, we cannot assume that there is any other kind of community among substances than that observable in experience, any kind of presence than that in space, or any kind of duration than that in time. In one word, the conditions of possible experience are for reason the only conditions of the possibility of things; reason cannot venture to form, independently of these conditions, any conceptions of things, because such conceptions, although not self-contradictory, are without object and without application.

The conceptions of reason are, as we have already shown, mere ideas, and do not relate to any object in any kind of experience. At the same time, they do not indicate imaginary or possible objects. They are purely problematical in their nature and, as aids to the heuristic exercise of the faculties, form the basis of the regulative principles for the systematic employment of the understanding in the field of experience. If we leave this ground of experience, they become mere fictions of thought, the possibility of which is quite indemonstrable; and they cannot, consequently, be employed as hypotheses in the explanation of real phenomena. It is quite admissible to cogitate the soul as simple, for the purpose of enabling ourselves to employ the idea of a perfect and necessary unity of all the faculties of the mind as the principle of all our inquiries into its internal phenomena, although we cannot cognize this unity in concreto. But to assume that the soul is a simple substance (a transcendental conception) would be enouncing a proposition which is not only indemonstrable — as many physical hypotheses are — but a proposition which is purely arbitrary, and in the highest degree rash. The simple is never presented in experience; and, if by substance is here meant the permanent object of sensuous intuition, the possibility of a simple phenomenon is perfectly inconceivable. Reason affords no good grounds for admitting the existence of intelligible beings, or of intelligible properties of sensuous things, although — as we have no conception either of their possibility or of their impossibility — it will always be out of our power to affirm dogmatically that they do not exist. In the explanation of given phenomena, no other things and no other grounds of explanation can be employed than those which stand in connection with the given phenomena according to the known laws of experience. A transcendental hypothesis, in which a mere idea of reason is employed to explain the phenomena of nature, would not give us any better insight into a phenomenon, as we should be trying to explain what we do not sufficiently understand from known empirical principles, by what we do not understand at all. The principles of such a hypothesis might conduce to the satisfaction of reason, but it would not assist the understanding in its application to objects. Order and conformity to aims in the sphere of nature must be themselves explained upon natural grounds and according to natural laws; and the wildest hypotheses, if they are only physical, are here more admissible than a hyperphysical hypothesis, such as that of a divine author. For such a hypothesis would introduce the principle of ignava ratio, which requires us to give up the search for causes that might be discovered in the course of experience and to rest satisfied with a mere idea. As regards the absolute totality of the grounds of explanation in the series of these causes, this can be no hindrance to the understanding in the case of phenomena; because, as they are to us nothing more than phenomena, we have no right to look for anything like completeness in the synthesis of the series of their conditions.

Transcendental hypotheses are therefore inadmissible; and we cannot use the liberty of employing, in the absence of physical, hyperphysical grounds of explanation. And this for two reasons; first, because such hypothesis do not advance reason, but rather stop it in its progress; secondly, because this licence would render fruitless all its exertions in its own proper sphere, which is that of experience. For, when the explanation of natural phenomena happens to be difficult, we have constantly at hand a transcendental ground of explanation, which lifts us above the necessity of investigating nature; and our inquiries are brought to a close, not because we have obtained all the requisite knowledge, but because we abut upon a principle which is incomprehensible and which, indeed, is so far back in the track of thought as to contain the conception of the absolutely primal being.

The next requisite for the admissibility of a hypothesis is its sufficiency. That is, it must determine a priori the consequences which are given in experience and which are supposed to follow from the hypothesis itself. If we require to employ auxiliary hypotheses, the suspicion naturally arises that they are mere fictions; because the necessity for each of them requires the same justification as in the case of the original hypothesis, and thus their testimony is invalid. If we suppose the existence of an infinitely perfect cause, we possess sufficient grounds for the explanation of the conformity to aims, the order and the greatness which we observe in the universe; but we find ourselves obliged, when we observe the evil in the world and the exceptions to these laws, to employ new hypothesis in support of the original one. We employ the idea of the simple nature of the human soul as the foundation of all the theories we may form of its phenomena; but when we meet with difficulties in our way, when we observe in the soul phenomena similar to the changes which take place in matter, we require to call in new auxiliary hypotheses. These may, indeed, not be false, but we do not know them to be true, because the only witness to their certitude is the hypothesis which they themselves have been called in to explain.

We are not discussing the above-mentioned assertions regarding the immaterial unity of the soul and the existence of a Supreme Being as dogmata, which certain philosophers profess to demonstrate a priori, but purely as hypotheses. In the former case, the dogmatist must take care that his arguments possess the apodeictic certainty of a demonstration. For the assertion that the reality of such ideas is probable is as absurd as a proof of the probability of a proposition in geometry. Pure abstract reason, apart from all experience, can either cognize nothing at all; and hence the judgements it enounces are never mere opinions, they are either apodeictic certainties, or declarations that nothing can be known on the subject. Opinions and probable judgements on the nature of things can only be employed to explain given phenomena, or they may relate to the effect, in accordance with empirical laws, of an actually existing cause. In other words, we must restrict the sphere of opinion to the world of experience and nature. Beyond this region opinion is mere invention; unless we are groping about for the truth on a path not yet fully known, and have some hopes of stumbling upon it by chance.

But, although hypotheses are inadmissible in answers to the questions of pure speculative reason, they may be employed in the defence of these answers. That is to say, hypotheses are admissible in polemic, but not in the sphere of dogmatism. By the defence of statements of this character, I do not mean an attempt at discovering new grounds for their support, but merely the refutation of the arguments of opponents. All a priori synthetical propositions possess the peculiarity that, although the philosopher who maintains the reality of the ideas contained in the proposition is not in possession of sufficient knowledge to establish the certainty of his statements, his opponent is as little able to prove the truth of the opposite. This equality of fortune does not allow the one party to be superior to the other in the sphere of speculative cognition; and it is this sphere, accordingly, that is the proper arena of these endless speculative conflicts. But we shall afterwards show that, in relation to its practical exercise, Reason has the right of admitting what, in the field of pure speculation, she would not be justified in supposing, except upon perfectly sufficient grounds; because all such suppositions destroy the necessary completeness of speculation — a condition which the practical reason, however, does not consider to be requisite. In this sphere, therefore, Reason is mistress of a possession, her title to which she does not require to prove — which, in fact, she could not do. The burden of proof accordingly rests upon the opponent. But as he has just as little knowledge regarding the subject discussed, and is as little able to prove the non-existence of the object of an idea, as the philosopher on the other side is to demonstrate its reality, it is evident that there is an advantage on the side of the philosopher who maintains his proposition as a practically necessary supposition (melior est conditio possidentis). For he is at liberty to employ, in self-defence, the same weapons as his opponent makes use of in attacking him; that is, he has a right to use hypotheses not for the purpose of supporting the arguments in favour of his own propositions, but to show that his opponent knows no more than himself regarding the subject under 'discussion and cannot boast of any speculative advantage.

Hypotheses are, therefore, admissible in the sphere of pure reason only as weapons for self-defence, and not as supports to dogmatical assertions. But the opposing party we must always seek for in ourselves. For speculative reason is, in the sphere of transcendentalism, dialectical in its own nature. The difficulties and objections we have to fear lie in ourselves. They are like old but never superannuated claims; and we must seek them out, and settle them once and for ever, if we are to expect a permanent peace. External tranquility is hollow and unreal. The root of these contradictions, which lies in the nature of human reason, must be destroyed; and this can only be done by giving it, in the first instance, freedom to grow, nay, by nourishing it, that it may send out shoots, and thus betray its own existence. It is our duty, therefore, to try to discover new objections, to put weapons in the bands of our opponent, and to grant him the most favourable position in the arena that he can wish. We have nothing to fear from these concessions; on the contrary, we may rather hope that we shall thus make ourselves master of a possession which no one will ever venture to dispute.

The thinker requires, to be fully equipped, the hypotheses of pure reason, which, although but leaden weapons (for they have not been steeled in the armoury of experience), are as useful as any that can be employed by his opponents. If, accordingly, we have assumed, from a non-speculative point of view, the immaterial nature of the soul, and are met by the objection that experience seems to prove that the growth and decay of our mental faculties are mere modifications of the sensuous organism — we can weaken the force of this objection by the assumption that the body is nothing but the fundamental phenomenon, to which, as a necessary condition, all sensibility, and consequently all thought, relates in the present state of our existence; and that the separation of soul and body forms the conclusion of the sensuous exercise of our power of cognition and the beginning of the intellectual. The body would, in this view of the question, be regarded, not as the cause of thought, but merely as its restrictive condition, as promotive of the sensuous and animal, but as a hindrance to the pure and spiritual life; and the dependence of the animal life on the constitution of the body, would not prove that the whole life of man was also dependent on the state of the organism. We might go still farther, and discover new objections, or carry out to their extreme consequences those which have already been adduced.

Generation, in the human race as well as among the irrational animals, depends on so many accidents — of occasion, of proper sustenance, of the laws enacted by the government of a country of vice even, that it is difficult to believe in the eternal existence of a being whose life has begun under circumstances so mean and trivial, and so entirely dependent upon our own control. As regards the continuance of the existence of the whole race, we need have no difficulties, for accident in single cases is subject to general laws; but, in the case of each individual, it would seem as if we could hardly expect so wonderful an effect from causes so insignificant. But, in answer to these objections, we may adduce the transcendental hypothesis that all life is properly intelligible, and not subject to changes of time, and that it neither began in birth, nor will end in death. We may assume that this life is nothing more than a sensuous representation of pure spiritual life; that the whole world of sense is but an image, hovering before the faculty of cognition which we exercise in this sphere, and with no more objective reality than a dream; and that if we could intuite ourselves and other things as they really are, we should see ourselves in a world of spiritual natures, our connection with which did not begin at our birth and will not cease with the destruction of the body. And so on.

We cannot be said to know what has been above asserted, nor do we seriously maintain the truth of these assertions; and the notions therein indicated are not even ideas of reason, they are purely fictitious conceptions. But this hypothetical procedure is in perfect conformity with the laws of reason. Our opponent mistakes the absence of empirical conditions for a proof of the complete impossibility of all that we have asserted; and we have to show him that he has not exhausted the whole sphere of possibility and that he can as little compass that sphere by the laws of experience and nature, as we can lay a secure foundation for the operations of reason beyond the region of experience. Such hypothetical defences against the pretensions of an opponent must not be regarded as declarations of opinion. The philosopher abandons them, so soon as the opposite party renounces its dogmatical conceit. To maintain a simply negative position in relation to propositions which rest on an insecure foundation, well befits the moderation of a true philosopher; but to uphold the objections urged against an opponent as proofs of the opposite statement is a proceeding just as unwarrantable and arrogant as it is to attack the position of a philosopher who advances affirmative propositions regarding such a subject.

It is evident, therefore, that hypotheses, in the speculative sphere, are valid, not as independent propositions, but only relatively to opposite transcendent assumptions. For, to make the principles of possible experience conditions of the possibility of things in general is just as transcendent a procedure as to maintain the objective reality of ideas which can be applied to no objects except such as lie without the limits of possible experience. The judgements enounced by pure reason must be necessary, or they must not be enounced at all. Reason cannot trouble herself with opinions. But the hypotheses we have been discussing are merely problematical judgements, which can neither be confuted nor proved; while, therefore, they are not personal opinions, they are indispensable as answers to objections which are liable to be raised. But we must take care to confine them to this function, and guard against any assumption on their part of absolute validity, a proceeding which would involve reason in inextricable difficulties and contradictions.

SECTION IV. The Discipline of Pure Reason in Relation to Proofs.

It is a peculiarity, which distinguishes the proofs of transcendental synthetical propositions from those of all other a priori synthetical cognitions, that reason, in the case of the former, does not apply its conceptions directly to an object, but is first obliged to prove, a priori, the objective validity of these conceptions and the possibility of their syntheses. This is not merely a prudential rule, it is essential to the very possibility of the proof of a transcendental proposition. If I am required to pass, a priori, beyond the conception of an object, I find that it is utterly impossible without the guidance of something which is not contained in the conception. In mathematics, it is a priori intuition that guides my synthesis; and, in this case, all our conclusions may be drawn immediately from pure intuition. In transcendental cognition, so long as we are dealing only with conceptions of the understanding, we are guided by possible experience. That is to say, a proof in the sphere of transcendental cognition does not show that the given conception (that of an event, for example) leads directly to another conception (that of a cause) — for this would be a saltus which nothing can justify; but it shows that experience itself, and consequently the object of experience, is impossible without the connection indicated by these conceptions. It follows that such a proof must demonstrate the possibility of arriving, synthetically and a priori, at a certain knowledge of things, which was not contained in our conceptions of these things. Unless we pay particular attention to this requirement, our proofs, instead of pursuing the straight path indicated by reason, follow the tortuous road of mere subjective association. The illusory conviction, which rests upon subjective causes of association, and which is considered as resulting from the perception of a real and objective natural affinity, is always open to doubt and suspicion. For this reason, all the attempts which have been made to prove the principle of sufficient reason, have, according to the universal admission of philosophers, been quite unsuccessful; and, before the appearance of transcendental criticism, it was considered better, as this principle could not be abandoned, to appeal boldly to the common sense of mankind (a proceeding which always proves that the problem, which reason ought to solve, is one in which philosophers find great difficulties), rather than attempt to discover new dogmatical proofs.

But, if the proposition to be proved is a proposition of pure reason, and if I aim at passing beyond my empirical conceptions by the aid of mere ideas, it is necessary that the proof should first show that such a step in synthesis is possible (which it is not), before it proceeds to prove the truth of the proposition itself. The so-called proof of the simple nature of the soul from the unity of apperception, is a very plausible one. But it contains no answer to the objection, that, as the notion of absolute simplicity is not a conception which is directly applicable to a perception, but is an idea which must be inferred — if at all — from observation, it is by no means evident how the mere fact of consciousness, which is contained in all thought, although in so far a simple representation, can conduct me to the consciousness and cognition of a thing which is purely a thinking substance. When I represent to my mind the power of my body as in motion, my body in this thought is so far absolute unity, and my representation of it is a simple one; and hence I can indicate this representation by the motion of a point, because I have made abstraction of the size or volume of the body. But I cannot hence infer that, given merely the moving power of a body, the body may be cogitated as simple substance, merely because the representation in my mind takes no account of its content in space, and is consequently simple. The simple, in abstraction, is very different from the objectively simple; and hence the Ego, which is simple in the first sense, may, in the second sense, as indicating the soul itself, be a very complex conception, with a very various content. Thus it is evident that in all such arguments there lurks a paralogism. We guess (for without some such surmise our suspicion would not be excited in reference to a proof of this character) at the presence of the paralogism, by keeping ever before us a criterion of the possibility of those synthetical propositions which aim at proving more than experience can teach us. This criterion is obtained from the observation that such proofs do not lead us directly from the subject of the proposition to be proved to the required predicate, but find it necessary to presuppose the possibility of extending our cognition a priori by means of ideas. We must, accordingly, always use the greatest caution; we require, before attempting any proof, to consider how it is possible to extend the sphere of cognition by the operations of pure reason, and from what source we are to derive knowledge, which is not obtained from the analysis of conceptions, nor relates, by anticipation, to possible experience. We shall thus spare ourselves much severe and fruitless labour, by not expecting from reason what is beyond its power, or rather by subjecting it to discipline, and teaching it to moderate its vehement desires for the extension of the sphere of cognition.

The first rule for our guidance is, therefore, not to attempt a transcendental proof, before we have considered from what source we are to derive the principles upon which the proof is to be based, and what right we have to expect that our conclusions from these principles will be veracious. If they are principles of the understanding, it is vain to expect that we should attain by their means to ideas of pure reason; for these principles are valid only in regard to objects of possible experience. If they are principles of pure reason, our labour is alike in vain. For the principles of reason, if employed as objective, are without exception dialectical and possess no validity or truth, except as regulative principles of the systematic employment of reason in experience. But when such delusive proof are presented to us, it is our duty to meet them with the non liquet of a matured judgement; and, although we are unable to expose the particular sophism upon which the proof is based, we have a right to demand a deduction of the principles employed in it; and, if these principles have their origin in pure reason alone, such a deduction is absolutely impossible. And thus it is unnecessary that we should trouble ourselves with the exposure and confutation of every sophistical illusion; we may, at once, bring all dialectic, which is inexhaustible in the production of fallacies, before the bar of critical reason, which tests the principles upon which all dialectical procedure is based. The second peculiarity of transcendental proof is that a transcendental proposition cannot rest upon more than a single proof. If I am drawing conclusions, not from conceptions, but from intuition corresponding to a conception, be it pure intuition, as in mathematics, or empirical, as in natural science, the intuition which forms the basis of my inferences presents me with materials for many synthetical propositions, which I can connect in various modes, while, as it is allowable to proceed from different points in the intention, I can arrive by different paths at the same proposition.

But every transcendental proposition sets out from a conception, and posits the synthetical condition of the possibility of an object according to this conception. There must, therefore, be but one ground of proof, because it is the conception alone which determines the object; and thus the proof cannot contain anything more than the determination of the object according to the conception. In our Transcendental Analytic, for example, we inferred the principle: Every event has a cause, from the only condition of the objective possibility of our conception of an event. This is that an event cannot be determined in time, and consequently cannot form a part of experience, unless it stands under this dynamical law. This is the only possible ground of proof; for our conception of an event possesses objective validity, that is, is a true conception, only because the law of causality determines an object to which it can refer. Other arguments in support of this principle have been attempted —

such as that from the contingent nature of a phenomenon; but when this argument is considered, we can discover no criterion of contingency, except the fact of an event — of something happening, that is to say, the existence which is preceded by the non-existence of an object, and thus we fall back on the very thing to be proved. If the proposition: "Every thinking being is simple," is to be proved, we keep to the conception of the ego, which is simple, and to which all thought has a relation. The same is the case with the transcendental proof of the existence of a Deity, which is based solely upon the harmony and reciprocal fitness of the conceptions of an ens realissimum and a necessary being, and cannot be attempted in any other manner.

This caution serves to simplify very much the criticism of all propositions of reason. When reason employs conceptions alone, only one proof of its thesis is possible, if any. When, therefore, the dogmatist advances with ten arguments in favour of a proposition, we may be sure that not one of them is conclusive. For if he possessed one which proved the proposition he brings forward to demonstration — as must always be the case with the propositions of pure reason — what need is there for any more? His intention can only be similar to that of the advocate who had different arguments for different judges; this availing himself of the weakness of those who examine his arguments, who, without going into any profound investigation, adopt the view of the case which seems most probable at first sight and decide according to it.

The third rule for the guidance of pure reason in the conduct of a proof is that all transcendental proofs must never be apagogic or indirect, but always ostensive or direct. The direct or ostensive proof not only establishes the truth of the proposition to be proved, but exposes the grounds of its truth; the apagogic, on the other hand, may assure us of the truth of the proposition, but it cannot enable us to comprehend the grounds of its possibility. The latter is, accordingly, rather an auxiliary to an argument, than a strictly philosophical and rational mode of procedure. In one respect, however, they have an advantage over direct proofs, from the fact that the mode of arguing by contradiction, which they employ, renders our understanding of the question more clear, and approximates the proof to the certainty of an intuitional demonstration.

The true reason why indirect proofs are employed in different sciences is this. When the grounds upon which we seek to base a cognition are too various or too profound, we try whether or not we may not discover the truth of our cognition from its consequences. The modus ponens of reasoning from the truth of its inferences to the truth of a proposition would be admissible if all the inferences that can be drawn from it are known to be true; for in this case there can be only one possible ground for these inferences, and that is the true one. But this is a quite impracticable procedure, as it surpasses all our powers to discover all the possible inferences that can be drawn from a proposition. But this mode of reasoning is employed, under favour, when we wish to prove the truth of an hypothesis; in which case we admit the truth of the conclusion — which is supported by analogy — that, if all the inferences we have drawn and examined agree with the proposition assumed, all other possible inferences will also agree with it. But, in this way, an hypothesis can never be established as a demonstrated truth. The modus tollens of reasoning from known inferences to the unknown proposition, is not only a rigorous, but a very easy mode of proof. For, if it can be shown that but one inference from a proposition is false, then the proposition must itself be false. Instead, then, of examining, in an ostensive argument, the whole series of the grounds on which the truth of a proposition rests, we need only take the opposite of this proposition, and if one inference from it be false, then must the opposite be itself false; and, consequently, the proposition which we wished to prove must be true.

The apagogic method of proof is admissible only in those sciences where it is impossible to mistake a subjective representation for an objective cognition. Where this is possible, it is plain that the opposite of a given proposition may contradict merely the subjective conditions of thought, and not the objective cognition; or it may happen that both propositions contradict each other only under a subjective condition, which is incorrectly considered to be objective, and, as the condition is itself false, both propositions may be false, and it will, consequently, be impossible to conclude the truth of the one from the falseness of the other.

In mathematics such subreptions are impossible; and it is in this science, accordingly, that the indirect mode of proof has its true place. In the science of nature, where all assertion is based upon empirical intuition, such subreptions may be guarded against by the repeated comparison of observations; but this mode of proof is of little value in this sphere of knowledge. But the transcendental efforts of pure reason are all made in the sphere of the subjective, which is the real medium of all dialectical illusion; and thus reason endeavours, in its premisses, to impose upon us subjective representations for objective cognitions. In the transcendental sphere of pure reason, then, and in the case of synthetical propositions, it is inadmissible to support a statement by disproving the counter-statement. For only two cases are possible; either, the counter-statement is nothing but the enouncement of the inconsistency of the opposite opinion with the subjective conditions of reason, which does not affect the real case (for example, we cannot comprehend the unconditioned necessity of the existence of a being, and hence every speculative proof of the existence of such a being must be opposed on subjective grounds, while the possibility of this being in itself cannot with justice be denied); or, both propositions, being dialectical in their nature, are based upon an impossible conception. In this latter case the rule applies: non entis nulla sunt predicata; that is to say, what we affirm and what we deny, respecting such an object, are equally untrue, and the apagogic mode of arriving at the truth is in this case impossible. If, for example, we presuppose that the world of sense is given in itself in its totality, it is false, either that it is infinite, or that it is finite and limited in space. Both are false, because the hypothesis is false. For the notion of phenomena (as mere representations) which are given in themselves (as objects) is self-contradictory; and the infinitude of this imaginary whole would, indeed, be unconditioned, but would be inconsistent (as everything in the phenomenal world is conditioned) with the unconditioned determination and finitude of quantities which is presupposed in our conception.

The apagogic mode of proof is the true source of those illusions which have always had so strong an attraction for the admirers of dogmatical philosophy. It may be compared to a champion who maintains the honour and claims of the party he has adopted by offering battle to all who doubt the validity of these claims and the purity of that honour; while nothing can be proved in this way, except the respective strength of the combatants, and the advantage, in this respect, is always on the side of the attacking party. Spectators, observing that each party is alternately conqueror and conquered, are led to regard the subject of dispute as beyond the power of man to decide upon. But such an opinion cannot be justified; and it is sufficient to apply to these reasoners the remark:

Non defensoribus istis

Tempus eget.

Each must try to establish his assertions by a transcendental deduction of the grounds of proof employed in his argument, and thus enable us to see in what way the claims of reason may be supported. If an opponent bases his assertions upon subjective grounds, he may be refuted with ease; not, however to the advantage of the dogmatist, who likewise depends upon subjective sources of cognition and is in like manner driven into a corner by his opponent. But, if parties employ the direct method of procedure, they will soon discover the difficulty, nay, the impossibility of proving their assertions, and will be forced to appeal to prescription and precedence; or they will, by the help of criticism, discover with ease the dogmatical illusions by which they had been mocked, and compel reason to renounce its exaggerated pretensions to speculative insight and to confine itself within the limits of its proper sphere — that of practical principles.

CHAPTER II.
The Canon of Pure Reason.

It is a humiliating consideration for human reason that it is incompetent to discover truth by means of pure speculation, but, on the contrary, stands in need of discipline to check its deviations from the straight path and to expose the illusions which it originates. But, on the other hand, this consideration ought to elevate and to give it confidence, for this discipline is exercised by itself alone, and it is subject to the censure of no other power. The bounds, moreover, which it is forced to set to its speculative exercise, form likewise a check upon the fallacious pretensions of opponents; and thus what remains of its possessions, after these exaggerated claims have been disallowed, is secure from attack or usurpation. The greatest, and perhaps the only, use of all philosophy of pure reason is, accordingly, of a purely negative character. It is not an organon for the extension, but a discipline for the determination, of the limits of its exercise; and without laying claim to the discovery of new truth, it has the modest merit of guarding against error.

At the same time, there must be some source of positive cognitions which belong to the domain of pure reason and which become the causes of error only from our mistaking their true character, while they form the goal towards which reason continually strives. How else can we account for the inextinguishable desire in the human mind to find a firm footing in some region beyond the limits of the world of experience? It hopes to attain to the possession of a knowledge in which it has the deepest interest. It enters upon the path of pure speculation; but in vain. We have some reason, however, to expect that, in the only other way that lies open to it — the path of practical reason — it may meet with better success.

I understand by a canon a list of the a priori principles of the proper employment of certain faculties of cognition. Thus general logic, in its analytical department, is a formal canon for the faculties of understanding and reason. In the same way, Transcendental Analytic was seen to be a canon of the pure understanding; for it alone is competent to enounce true a priori synthetical cognitions. But, when no proper employment of a faculty of cognition is possible, no canon can exist. But the synthetical cognition of pure speculative reason is, as has been shown, completely impossible. There cannot, therefore, exist any canon for the speculative exercise of this faculty — for its speculative exercise is entirely dialectical; and, consequently, transcendental logic, in this respect, is merely a discipline, and not a canon. If, then, there is any proper mode of employing the faculty of pure reason — in which case there must be a canon for this faculty — this canon will relate, not to the speculative, but to the practical use of reason. This canon we now proceed to investigate.

SECTION I. Of the Ultimate End of the Pure Use of Reason.

There exists in the faculty of reason a natural desire to venture beyond the field of experience, to attempt to reach the utmost bounds of all cognition by the help of ideas alone, and not to rest satisfied until it has fulfilled its course and raised the sum of its cognitions into a self-subsistent systematic whole. Is the motive for this endeavour to be found in its speculative, or in its practical interests alone?

Setting aside, at present, the results of the labours of pure reason in its speculative exercise, I shall merely inquire regarding the problems the solution of which forms its ultimate aim, whether reached or not, and in relation to which all other aims are but partial and intermediate. These highest aims must, from the nature of reason, possess complete unity; otherwise the highest interest of humanity could not be successfully promoted.

The transcendental speculation of reason relates to three things: the freedom of the will, the immortality of the soul, and the existence of God. The speculative interest which reason has in those questions is very small; and, for its sake alone, we should not undertake the labour of transcendental investigation — a labour full of toil and ceaseless struggle. We should be loth to undertake this labour, because the discoveries we might make would not be of the smallest use in the sphere of concrete or physical investigation. We may find out that the will is free, but this knowledge only relates to the intelligible cause of our volition. As regards the phenomena or expressions of this will, that is, our actions, we are bound, in obedience to an inviolable maxim, without which reason cannot be employed in the sphere of experience, to explain these in the same way as we explain all the other phenomena of nature, that is to say, according to its unchangeable laws. We may have discovered the spirituality and immortality of the soul, but we cannot employ this knowledge to explain the phenomena of this life, nor the peculiar nature of the future, because our conception of an incorporeal nature is purely negative and does not add anything to our knowledge, and the only inferences to be drawn from it are purely fictitious. If, again, we prove the existence of a supreme intelligence, we should be able from it to make the conformity to aims existing in the arrangement of the world comprehensible; but we should not be justified in deducing from it any particular arrangement or disposition, or inferring any where it is not perceived. For it is a necessary rule of the speculative use of reason that we must not overlook natural causes, or refuse to listen to the teaching of experience, for the sake of deducing what we know and perceive from something that transcends all our knowledge. In one word, these three propositions are, for the speculative reason, always transcendent, and cannot be employed as immanent principles in relation to the objects of experience; they are, consequently, of no use to us in this sphere, being but the valueless results of the severe but unprofitable efforts of reason.

If, then, the actual cognition of these three cardinal propositions is perfectly useless, while Reason uses her utmost endeavours to induce us to admit them, it is plain that their real value and importance relate to our practical, and not to our speculative interest.

I term all that is possible through free will, practical. But if the conditions of the exercise of free volition are empirical, reason can have only a regulative, and not a constitutive, influence upon it, and is serviceable merely for the introduction of unity into its empirical laws. In the moral philosophy of prudence, for example, the sole business of reason is to bring about a union of all the ends, which are aimed at by our inclinations, into one ultimate end — that of happiness — and to show the agreement which should exist among the means of attaining that end. In this sphere, accordingly, reason cannot present to us any other than pragmatical laws of free action, for our guidance towards the aims set up by the senses, and is incompetent to give us laws which are pure and determined completely a priori. On the other hand, pure practical laws, the ends of which have been given by reason entirely a priori, and which are not empirically conditioned, but are, on the contrary, absolutely imperative in their nature, would be products of pure reason. Such are the moral laws; and these alone belong to the sphere of the practical exercise of reason, and admit of a canon.

All the powers of reason, in the sphere of what may be termed pure philosophy, are, in fact, directed to the three above-mentioned problems alone. These again have a still higher end — the answer to the question, what we ought to do, if the will is free, if there is a God and a future world. Now, as this problem relates to our in reference to the highest aim of humanity, it is evident that the ultimate intention of nature, in the constitution of our reason, has been directed to the moral alone.

We must take care, however, in turning our attention to an object which is foreign* to the sphere of transcendental philosophy, not to injure the unity of our system by digressions, nor, on the other hand, to fail in clearness, by saying too little on the new subject of discussion. I hope to avoid both extremes, by keeping as close as possible to the transcendental, and excluding all psychological, that is, empirical, elements.

[Note: All practical conceptions relate to objects of pleasure and pain, and consequently — in an indirect manner, at least — to objects of feeling. But as feeling is not a faculty of representation, but lies out of the sphere of our powers of cognition, the elements of our judgements, in so far as they relate to pleasure or pain, that is, the elements of our practical judgements, do not belong to transcendental philosophy, which has to do with pure a priori cognitions alone.]

I have to remark, in the first place, that at present I treat of the conception of freedom in the practical sense only, and set aside the corresponding transcendental conception, which cannot be employed as a ground of explanation in the phenomenal world, but is itself a problem for pure reason. A will is purely animal (arbitrium brutum) when it is determined by sensuous impulses or instincts only, that is, when it is determined in a pathological manner. A will, which can be determined independently of sensuous impulses, consequently by motives presented by reason alone, is called a free will (arbitrium liberum); and everything which is connected with this free will, either as principle or consequence, is termed practical. The existence of practical freedom can be proved from experience alone. For the human will is not determined by that alone which immediately affects the senses; on the contrary, we have the power, by calling up the notion of what is useful or hurtful in a more distant relation, of overcoming the immediate impressions on our sensuous faculty of desire. But these considerations of what is desirable in relation to our whole state, that is, is in the end good and useful, are based entirely upon reason. This faculty, accordingly, enounces laws, which are imperative or objective laws of freedom and which tell us what ought to take place, thus distinguishing themselves from the laws of nature, which relate to that which does take place. The laws of freedom or of free will are hence termed practical laws.

Whether reason is not itself, in the actual delivery of these laws, determined in its turn by other influences, and whether the action which, in relation to sensuous impulses, we call free, may not, in relation to higher and more remote operative causes, really form a part of nature — these are questions which do not here concern us. They are purely speculative questions; and all we have to do, in the practical sphere, is to inquire into the rule of conduct which reason has to present. Experience demonstrates to us the existence of practical freedom as one of the causes which exist in nature, that is, it shows the causal power of reason in the determination of the will. The idea of transcendental freedom, on the contrary, requires that reason — in relation to its causal power of commencing a series of phenomena — should be independent of all sensuous determining causes; and thus it seems to be in opposition to the law of nature and to all possible experience. It therefore remains a problem for the human mind. But this problem does not concern reason in its practical use; and we have, therefore, in a canon of pure reason, to do with only two questions, which relate to the practical interest of pure reason: Is there a God? and, Is there a future life? The question of transcendental freedom is purely speculative, and we may therefore set it entirely aside when we come to treat of practical reason. Besides, we have already discussed this subject in the antinomy of pure reason.

SECTION II. Of the Ideal of the Summum Bonum as a Determining Ground of the Ultimate End of Pure Reason.

Reason conducted us, in its speculative use, through the field of experience and, as it can never find complete satisfaction in that sphere, from thence to speculative ideas — which, however, in the end brought us back again to experience, and thus fulfilled the purpose of reason, in a manner which, though useful, was not at all in accordance with our expectations. It now remains for us to consider whether pure reason can be employed in a practical sphere, and whether it will here conduct us to those ideas which attain the highest ends of pure reason, as we have just stated them. We shall thus ascertain whether, from the point of view of its practical interest, reason may not be able to supply us with that which, on the speculative side, it wholly denies us.

The whole interest of reason, speculative as well as practical, is centred in the three following questions:

1. WHAT CAN I KNOW?

2. WHAT OUGHT I TO DO?

3. WHAT MAY I HOPE?

The first question is purely speculative. We have, as I flatter myself, exhausted all the replies of which it is susceptible, and have at last found the reply with which reason must content itself, and with which it ought to be content, so long as it pays no regard to the practical. But from the two great ends to the attainment of which all these efforts of pure reason were in fact directed, we remain just as far removed as if we had consulted our ease and declined the task at the outset. So far, then, as knowledge is concerned, thus much, at least, is established, that, in regard to those two problems, it lies beyond our reach.

The second question is purely practical. As such it may indeed fall within the province of pure reason, but still it is not transcendental, but moral, and consequently cannot in itself form the subject of our criticism.

The third question: If I act as I ought to do, what may I then hope? — is at once practical and theoretical. The practical forms a clue to the answer of the theoretical, and — in its highest form — speculative question. For all hoping has happiness for its object and stands in precisely the same relation to the practical and the law of morality as knowing to the theoretical cognition of things and the law of nature. The former arrives finally at the conclusion that something is (which determines the ultimate end), because something ought to take place; the latter, that something is (which operates as the highest cause), because something does take place.

Happiness is the satisfaction of all our desires; extensive, in regard to their multiplicity; intensive, in regard to their degree; and protensive, in regard to their duration. The practical law based on the motive of happiness I term a pragmatical law (or prudential rule); but that law, assuming such to exist, which has no other motive than the worthiness of being happy, I term a moral or ethical law. The first tells us what we have to do, if we wish to become possessed of happiness; the second dictates how we ought to act, in order to deserve happiness. The first is based upon empirical principles; for it is only by experience that I can learn either what inclinations exist which desire satisfaction, or what are the natural means of satisfying them. The second takes no account of our desires or the means of satisfying them, and regards only the freedom of a rational being, and the necessary conditions under which alone this freedom can harmonize with the distribution of happiness according to principles. This second law may therefore rest upon mere ideas of pure reason, and may be cognized a priori.

I assume that there are pure moral laws which determine, entirely a priori (without regard to empirical motives, that is, to happiness), the conduct of a rational being, or in other words, to use which it makes of its freedom, and that these laws are absolutely imperative (not merely hypothetically, on the supposition of other empirical ends), and therefore in all respects necessary. I am warranted in assuming this, not only by the arguments of the most enlightened moralists, but by the moral judgement of every man who will make the attempt to form a distinct conception of such a law.

Pure reason, then, contains, not indeed in its speculative, but in its practical, or, more strictly, its moral use, principles of the possibility of experience, of such actions, namely, as, in accordance with ethical precepts, might be met with in the history of man. For since reason commands that such actions should take place, it must be possible for them to take place; and hence a particular kind of systematic unity — the moral — must be possible. We have found, it is true, that the systematic unity of nature could not be established according to speculative principles of reason, because, while reason possesses a causal power in relation to freedom, it has none in relation to the whole sphere of nature; and, while moral principles of reason can produce free actions, they cannot produce natural laws. It is, then, in its practical, but especially in its moral use, that the principles of pure reason possess objective reality.

I call the world a moral world, in so far as it may be in accordance with all the ethical laws — which, by virtue of the freedom of reasonable beings, it can be, and according to the necessary laws of morality it ought to be. But this world must be conceived only as an intelligible world, inasmuch as abstraction is therein made of all conditions (ends), and even of all impediments to morality (the weakness or pravity of human nature). So far, then, it is a mere idea — though still a practical idea — which may have, and ought to have, an influence on the world of sense, so as to bring it as far as possible into conformity with itself. The idea of a moral world has, therefore, objective reality, not as referring to an object of intelligible intuition — for of such an object we can form no conception whatever — but to the world of sense — conceived, however, as an object of pure reason in its practical use — and to a corpus mysticum of rational beings in it, in so far as the liberum arbitrium of the individual is placed, under and by virtue of moral laws, in complete systematic unity both with itself and with the freedom of all others.

That is the answer to the first of the two questions of pure reason which relate to its practical interest: Do that which will render thee worthy of happiness. The second question is this: If I conduct myself so as not to be unworthy of happiness, may I hope thereby to obtain happiness? In order to arrive at the solution of this question, we must inquire whether the principles of pure reason, which prescribe a priori the law, necessarily also connect this hope with it.

I say, then, that just as the moral principles are necessary according to reason in its practical use, so it is equally necessary according to reason in its theoretical use to assume that every one has ground to hope for happiness in the measure in which he has made himself worthy of it in his conduct, and that therefore the system of morality is inseparably (though only in the idea of pure reason) connected with that of happiness.

Now in an intelligible, that is, in the moral world, in the conception of which we make abstraction of all the impediments to morality (sensuous desires), such a system of happiness, connected with and proportioned to morality, may be conceived as necessary, because freedom of volition — partly incited, and partly restrained by moral laws — would be itself the cause of general happiness; and thus rational beings, under the guidance of such principles, would be themselves the authors both of their own enduring welfare and that of others. But such a system of self-rewarding morality is only an idea, the carrying out of which depends upon the condition that every one acts as he ought; in other words, that all actions of reasonable beings be such as they would be if they sprung from a Supreme Will, comprehending in, or under, itself all particular wills. But since the moral law is binding on each individual in the use of his freedom of volition, even if others should not act in conformity with this law, neither the nature of things, nor the causality of actions and their relation to morality, determine how the consequences of these actions will be related to happiness; and the necessary connection of the hope of happiness with the unceasing endeavour to become worthy of happiness, cannot be cognized by reason, if we take nature alone for our guide. This connection can be hoped for only on the assumption that the cause of nature is a supreme reason, which governs according to moral laws.

I term the idea of an intelligence in which the morally most perfect will, united with supreme blessedness, is the cause of all happiness in the world, so far as happiness stands in strict relation to morality (as the worthiness of being happy), the ideal of the supreme Good. It is only, then, in the ideal of the supreme original good, that pure reason can find the ground of the practically necessary connection of both elements of the highest derivative good, and accordingly of an intelligible, that is, moral world. Now since we are necessitated by reason to conceive ourselves as belonging to such a world, while the senses present to us nothing but a world of phenomena, we must assume the former as a consequence of our conduct in the world of sense (since the world of sense gives us no hint of it), and therefore as future in relation to us. Thus God and a future life are two hypotheses which, according to the principles of pure reason, are inseparable from the obligation which this reason imposes upon us.

Morality per se constitutes a system. But we can form no system of happiness, except in so far as it is dispensed in strict proportion to morality. But this is only possible in the intelligible world, under a wise author and ruler. Such a ruler, together with life in such a world, which we must look upon as future, reason finds itself compelled to assume; or it must regard the moral laws as idle dreams, since the necessary consequence which this same reason connects with them must, without this hypothesis, fall to the ground. Hence also the moral laws are universally regarded as commands, which they could not be did they not connect a priori adequate consequences with their dictates, and thus carry with them promises and threats. But this, again, they could not do, did they not reside in a necessary being, as the Supreme Good, which alone can render such a teleological unity possible.

Leibnitz termed the world, when viewed in relation to the rational beings which it contains, and the moral relations in which they stand to each other, under the government of the Supreme Good, the kingdom of Grace, and distinguished it from the kingdom of Nature, in which these rational beings live, under moral laws, indeed, but expect no other consequences from their actions than such as follow according to the course of nature in the world of sense. To view ourselves, therefore, as in the kingdom of grace, in which all happiness awaits us, except in so far as we ourselves limit our participation in it by actions which render us unworthy of happiness, is a practically necessary idea of reason.

Practical laws, in so far as they are subjective grounds of actions, that is, subjective principles, are termed maxims. The judgements of moral according to in its purity and ultimate results are framed according ideas; the observance of its laws, according to according to maxims.

The whole course of our life must be subject to moral maxims; but this is impossible, unless with the moral law, which is a mere idea, reason connects an efficient cause which ordains to all conduct which is in conformity with the moral law an issue either in this or in another life, which is in exact conformity with our highest aims. Thus, without a God and without a world, invisible to us now, but hoped for, the glorious ideas of morality are, indeed, objects of approbation and of admiration, but cannot be the springs of purpose and action. For they do not satisfy all the aims which are natural to every rational being, and which are determined a priori by pure reason itself, and necessary.

Happiness alone is, in the view of reason, far from being the complete good. Reason does not approve of it (however much inclination may desire it), except as united with desert. On the other hand, morality alone, and with it, mere desert, is likewise far from being the complete good. To make it complete, he who conducts himself in a manner not unworthy of happiness, must be able to hope for the possession of happiness. Even reason, unbiased by private ends, or interested considerations, cannot judge otherwise, if it puts itself in the place of a being whose business it is to dispense all happiness to others. For in the practical idea both points are essentially combined, though in such a way that participation in happiness is rendered possible by the moral disposition, as its condition, and not conversely, the moral disposition by the prospect of happiness. For a disposition which should require the prospect of happiness as its necessary condition would not be moral, and hence also would not be worthy of complete happiness — a happiness which, in the view of reason, recognizes no limitation but such as arises from our own immoral conduct.

Happiness, therefore, in exact proportion with the morality of rational beings (whereby they are made worthy of happiness), constitutes alone the supreme good of a world into which we absolutely must transport ourselves according to the commands of pure but practical reason. This world is, it is true, only an intelligible world; for of such a systematic unity of ends as it requires, the world of sense gives us no hint. Its reality can be based on nothing else but the hypothesis of a supreme original good. In it independent reason, equipped with all the sufficiency of a supreme cause, founds, maintains, and fulfils the universal order of things, with the most perfect teleological harmony, however much this order may be hidden from us in the world of sense.

This moral theology has the peculiar advantage, in contrast with speculative theology, of leading inevitably to the conception of a sole, perfect, and rational First Cause, whereof speculative theology does not give us any indication on objective grounds, far less any convincing evidence. For we find neither in transcendental nor in natural theology, however far reason may lead us in these, any ground to warrant us in assuming the existence of one only Being, which stands at the head of all natural causes, and on which these are entirely dependent. On the other band, if we take our stand on moral unity as a necessary law of the universe, and from this point of view consider what is necessary to give this law adequate efficiency and, for us, obligatory force, we must come to the conclusion that there is one only supreme will, which comprehends all these laws in itself. For how, under different wills, should we find complete unity of ends? This will must be omnipotent, that all nature and its relation to morality in the world may be subject to it; omniscient, that it may have knowledge of the most secret feelings and their moral worth; omnipresent, that it may be at hand to supply every necessity to which the highest weal of the world may give rise; eternal, that this harmony of nature and liberty may never fail; and so on.

But this systematic unity of ends in this world of intelligences — which, as mere nature, is only a world of sense, but, as a system of freedom of volition, may be termed an intelligible, that is, moral world (regnum gratiae) — leads inevitably also to the teleological unity of all things which constitute this great whole, according to universal natural laws — just as the unity of the former is according to universal and necessary moral laws — and unites the practical with the speculative reason. The world must be represented as having originated from an idea, if it is to harmonize with that use of reason without which we cannot even consider ourselves as worthy of reason — namely, the moral use, which rests entirely on the idea of the supreme good. Hence the investigation of nature receives a teleological direction, and becomes, in its widest extension, physico-theology. But this, taking its rise in moral order as a unity founded on the essence of freedom, and not accidentally instituted by external commands, establishes the teleological view of nature on grounds which must be inseparably connected with the internal possibility of things. This gives rise to a transcendental theology, which takes the ideal of the highest ontological perfection as a principle of systematic unity; and this principle connects all things according to universal and necessary natural laws, because all things have their origin in the absolute necessity of the one only Primal Being.

What use can we make of our understanding, even in respect of experience, if we do not propose ends to ourselves? But the highest ends are those of morality, and it is only pure reason that can give us the knowledge of these. Though supplied with these, and putting ourselves under their guidance, we can make no teleological use of the knowledge of nature, as regards cognition, unless nature itself has established teleological unity. For without this unity we should not even possess reason, because we should have no school for reason, and no cultivation through objects which afford the materials for its conceptions. But teleological unity is a necessary unity, and founded on the essence of the individual will itself. Hence this will, which is the condition of the application of this unity in concreto, must be so likewise. In this way the transcendental enlargement of our rational cognition would be, not the cause, but merely the effect of the practical teleology which pure reason imposes upon us.

Hence, also, we find in the history of human reason that, before the moral conceptions were sufficiently purified and determined, and before men had attained to a perception of the systematic unity of ends according to these conceptions and from necessary principles, the knowledge of nature, and even a considerable amount of intellectual culture in many other sciences, could produce only rude and vague conceptions of the Deity, sometimes even admitting of an astonishing indifference with regard to this question altogether. But the more enlarged treatment of moral ideas, which was rendered necessary by the extreme pure moral law of our religion, awakened the interest, and thereby quickened the perceptions of reason in relation to this object. In this way, and without the help either of an extended acquaintance with nature, or of a reliable transcendental insight (for these have been wanting in all ages), a conception of the Divine Being was arrived at, which we now bold to be the correct one, not because speculative reason convinces us of its correctness, but because it accords with the moral principles of reason. Thus it is to pure reason, but only in its practical use, that we must ascribe the merit of having connected with our highest interest a cognition, of which mere speculation was able only to form a conjecture, but the validity of which it was unable to establish — and of having thereby rendered it, not indeed a demonstrated dogma, but a hypothesis absolutely necessary to the essential ends of reason.

But if practical reason has reached this elevation, and has attained to the conception of a sole Primal Being as the supreme good, it must not, therefore, imagine that it has transcended the empirical conditions of its application, and risen to the immediate cognition of new objects; it must not presume to start from the conception which it has gained, and to deduce from it the moral laws themselves. For it was these very laws, the internal practical necessity of which led us to the hypothesis of an independent cause, or of a wise ruler of the universe, who should give them effect. Hence we are not entitled to regard them as accidental and derived from the mere will of the ruler, especially as we have no conception of such a will, except as formed in accordance with these laws. So far, then, as practical reason has the right to conduct us, we shall not look upon actions as binding on us, because they are the commands of God, but we shall regard them as divine commands, because we are internally bound by them. We shall study freedom under the teleological unity which accords with principles of reason; we shall look upon ourselves as acting in conformity with the divine will only in so far as we hold sacred the moral law which reason teaches us from the nature of actions themselves, and we shall believe that we can obey that will only by promoting the weal of the universe in ourselves and in others. Moral theology is, therefore, only of immanent use. It teaches us to fulfil our destiny here in the world, by placing ourselves in harmony with the general system of ends, and warns us against the fanaticism, nay, the crime of depriving reason of its legislative authority in the moral conduct of life, for the purpose of directly connecting this authority with the idea of the Supreme Being. For this would be, not an immanent, but a transcendent use of moral theology, and, like the transcendent use of mere speculation, would inevitably pervert and frustrate the ultimate ends of reason.

SECTION III. Of Opinion, Knowledge, and Belief.

The holding of a thing to be true is a phenomenon in our understanding which may rest on objective grounds, but requires, also, subjective causes in the mind of the person judging. If a judgement is valid for every rational being, then its ground is objectively sufficient, and it is termed a conviction. If, on the other hand, it has its ground in the particular character of the subject, it is termed a persuasion.

Persuasion is a mere illusion, the ground of the judgement, which lies solely in the subject, being regarded as objective. Hence a judgement of this kind has only private validity — is only valid for the individual who judges, and the holding of a thing to be true in this way cannot be communicated. But truth depends upon agreement with the object, and consequently the judgements of all understandings, if true, must be in agreement with each other (consentientia uni tertio consentiunt inter se). Conviction may, therefore, be distinguished, from an external point of view, from persuasion, by the possibility of communicating it and by showing its validity for the reason of every man; for in this case the presumption, at least, arises that the agreement of all judgements with each other, in spite of the different characters of individuals, rests upon the common ground of the agreement of each with the object, and thus the correctness of the judgement is established.

Persuasion, accordingly, cannot be subjectively distinguished from conviction, that is, so long as the subject views its judgement simply as a phenomenon of its own mind. But if we inquire whether the grounds of our judgement, which are valid for us, produce the same effect on the reason of others as on our own, we have then the means, though only subjective means, not, indeed, of producing conviction, but of detecting the merely private validity of the judgement; in other words, of discovering that there is in it the element of mere persuasion.

If we can, in addition to this, develop the subjective causes of the judgement, which we have taken for its objective grounds, and thus explain the deceptive judgement as a phenomenon in our mind, apart altogether from the objective character of the object, we can then expose the illusion and need be no longer deceived by it, although, if its subjective cause lies in our nature, we cannot hope altogether to escape its influence.

I can only maintain, that is, affirm as necessarily valid for every one, that which produces conviction. Persuasion I may keep for myself, if it is agreeable to me; but I cannot, and ought not, to attempt to impose it as binding upon others.

Holding for true, or the subjective validity of a judgement in relation to conviction (which is, at the same time, objectively valid), has the three following degrees: opinion, belief, and knowledge. Opinion is a consciously insufficient judgement, subjectively as well as objectively. Belief is subjectively sufficient, but is recognized as being objectively insufficient. Knowledge is both subjectively and objectively sufficient. Subjective sufficiency is termed conviction (for myself); objective sufficiency is termed certainty (for all). I need not dwell longer on the explanation of such simple conceptions.

I must never venture to be of opinion, without knowing something, at least, by which my judgement, in itself merely problematical, is brought into connection with the truth — which connection, although not perfect, is still something more than an arbitrary fiction. Moreover, the law of such a connection must be certain. For if, in relation to this law, I have nothing more than opinion, my judgement is but a play of the imagination, without the least relation to truth. In the judgements of pure reason, opinion has no place. For, as they do not rest on empirical grounds and as the sphere of pure reason is that of necessary truth and a priori cognition, the principle of connection in it requires universality and necessity, and consequently perfect certainty — otherwise we should have no guide to the truth at all. Hence it is absurd to have an opinion in pure mathematics; we must know, or abstain from forming a judgement altogether. The case is the same with the maxims of morality. For we must not hazard an action on the mere opinion that it is allowed, but we must know it to be so. In the transcendental sphere of reason, on the other hand, the term opinion is too weak, while the word knowledge is too strong. From the merely speculative point of view, therefore, we cannot form a judgement at all. For the subjective grounds of a judgement, such as produce belief, cannot be admitted in speculative inquiries, inasmuch as they cannot stand without empirical support and are incapable of being communicated to others in equal measure.

But it is only from the practical point of view that a theoretically insufficient judgement can be termed belief. Now the practical reference is either to skill or to morality; to the former, when the end proposed is arbitrary and accidental, to the latter, when it is absolutely necessary.

If we propose to ourselves any end whatever, the conditions of its attainment are hypothetically necessary. The necessity is subjectively, but still only comparatively, sufficient, if I am acquainted with no other conditions under which the end can be attained. On the other hand, it is sufficient, absolutely and for every one, if I know for certain that no one can be acquainted with any other conditions under which the attainment of the proposed end would be possible. In the former case my supposition — my judgement with regard to certain conditions — is a merely accidental belief; in the latter it is a necessary belief. The physician must pursue some course in the case of a patient who is in danger, but is ignorant of the nature of the disease. He observes the symptoms, and concludes, according to the best of his judgement, that it is a case of phthisis. His belief is, even in his own judgement, only contingent: another man might, perhaps come nearer the truth. Such a belief, contingent indeed, but still forming the ground of the actual use of means for the attainment of certain ends, I term Pragmatical belief.

The usual test, whether that which any one maintains is merely his persuasion, or his subjective conviction at least, that is, his firm belief, is a bet. It frequently happens that a man delivers his opinions with so much boldness and assurance, that he appears to be under no apprehension as to the possibility of his being in error. The offer of a bet startles him, and makes him pause. Sometimes it turns out that his persuasion may be valued at a ducat, but not at ten. For he does not hesitate, perhaps, to venture a ducat, but if it is proposed to stake ten, he immediately becomes aware of the possibility of his being mistaken — a possibility which has hitherto escaped his observation. If we imagine to ourselves that we have to stake the happiness of our whole life on the truth of any proposition, our judgement drops its air of triumph, we take the alarm, and discover the actual strength of our belief. Thus pragmatical belief has degrees, varying in proportion to the interests at stake.

Now, in cases where we cannot enter upon any course of action in reference to some object, and where, accordingly, our judgement is purely theoretical, we can still represent to ourselves, in thought, the possibility of a course of action, for which we suppose that we have sufficient grounds, if any means existed of ascertaining the truth of the matter. Thus we find in purely theoretical judgements an analogon of practical judgements, to which the word belief may properly be applied, and which we may term doctrinal belief. I should not hesitate to stake my all on the truth of the proposition — if there were any possibility of bringing it to the test of experience — that, at least, some one of the planets, which we see, is inhabited. Hence I say that I have not merely the opinion, but the strong belief, on the correctness of which I would stake even many of the advantages of life, that there are inhabitants in other worlds.

Now we must admit that the doctrine of the existence of God belongs to doctrinal belief. For, although in respect to the theoretical cognition of the universe I do not require to form any theory which necessarily involves this idea, as the condition of my explanation of the phenomena which the universe presents, but, on the contrary, am rather bound so to use my reason as if everything were mere nature, still teleological unity is so important a condition of the application of my reason to nature, that it is impossible for me to ignore it — especially since, in addition to these considerations, abundant examples of it are supplied by experience. But the sole condition, so far as my knowledge extends, under which this unity can be my guide in the investigation of nature, is the assumption that a supreme intelligence has ordered all things according to the wisest ends. Consequently, the hypothesis of a wise author of the universe is necessary for my guidance in the investigation of nature — is the condition under which alone I can fulfil an end which is contingent indeed, but by no means unimportant. Moreover, since the result of my attempts so frequently confirms the utility of this assumption, and since nothing decisive can be adduced against it, it follows that it would be saying far too little to term my judgement, in this case, a mere opinion, and that, even in this theoretical connection, I may assert that I firmly believe in God. Still, if we use words strictly, this must not be called a practical, but a doctrinal belief, which the theology of nature (physico-theology) must also produce in my mind. In the wisdom of a Supreme Being, and in the shortness of life, so inadequate to the development of the glorious powers of human nature, we may find equally sufficient grounds for a doctrinal belief in the future life of the human soul.

The expression of belief is, in such cases, an expression of modesty from the objective point of view, but, at the same time, of firm confidence, from the subjective. If I should venture to term this merely theoretical judgement even so much as a hypothesis which I am entitled to assume; a more complete conception, with regard to another world and to the cause of the world, might then be justly required of me than I am, in reality, able to give. For, if I assume anything, even as a mere hypothesis, I must, at least, know so much of the properties of such a being as will enable me, not to form the conception, but to imagine the existence of it. But the word belief refers only to the guidance which an idea gives me, and to its subjective influence on the conduct of my reason, which forces me to hold it fast, though I may not be in a position to give a speculative account of it.

But mere doctrinal belief is, to some extent, wanting in stability. We often quit our hold of it, in consequence of the difficulties which occur in speculation, though in the end we inevitably return to it again.

It is quite otherwise with moral belief. For in this sphere action is absolutely necessary, that is, I must act in obedience to the moral law in all points. The end is here incontrovertibly established, and there is only one condition possible, according to the best of my perception, under which this end can harmonize with all other ends, and so have practical validity — namely, the existence of a God and of a future world. I know also, to a certainty, that no one can be acquainted with any other conditions which conduct to the same unity of ends under the moral law. But since the moral precept is, at the same time, my maxim (as reason requires that it should be), I am irresistibly constrained to believe in the existence of God and in a future life; and I am sure that nothing can make me waver in this belief, since I should thereby overthrow my moral maxims, the renunciation of which would render me hateful in my own eyes.

Thus, while all the ambitious attempts of reason to penetrate beyond the limits of experience end in disappointment, there is still enough left to satisfy us in a practical point of view. No one, it is true, will be able to boast that he knows that there is a God and a future life; for, if he knows this, he is just the man whom I have long wished to find. All knowledge, regarding an object of mere reason, can be communicated; and I should thus be enabled to hope that my own knowledge would receive this wonderful extension, through the instrumentality of his instruction. No, my conviction is not logical, but moral certainty; and since it rests on subjective grounds (of the moral sentiment), I must not even say: It is morally certain that there is a God, etc., but: I am morally certain, that is, my belief in God and in another world is so interwoven with my moral nature that I am under as little apprehension of having the former torn from me as of losing the latter.

The only point in this argument that may appear open to suspicion is that this rational belief presupposes the existence of moral sentiments. If we give up this assumption, and take a man who is entirely indifferent with regard to moral laws, the question which reason proposes, becomes then merely a problem for speculation and may, indeed, be supported by strong grounds from analogy, but not by such as will compel the most obstinate scepticism to give way.* But in these questions no man is free from all interest. For though the want of good sentiments may place him beyond the influence of moral interests, still even in this case enough may be left to make him fear the existence of God and a future life. For he cannot pretend to any certainty of the non-existence of God and of a future life, unless — since it could only be proved by mere reason, and therefore apodeictically — he is prepared to establish the impossibility of both, which certainly no reasonable man would undertake to do. This would be a negative belief, which could not, indeed, produce morality and good sentiments, but still could produce an analogon of these, by operating as a powerful restraint on the outbreak of evil dispositions.

[Note: The human mind (as, I believe, every rational being must of necessity do) takes a natural interest in morality, although this interest is not undivided, and may not be practically in preponderance.

If you strengthen and increase it, you will find the reason become docile, more enlightened, and more capable of uniting the speculative interest with the practical. But if you do not take care at the outset, or at least midway, to make men good, you will never force them into an honest belief.]

But, it will be said, is this all that pure reason can effect, in opening up prospects beyond the limits of experience? Nothing more than two articles of belief? Common sense could have done as much as this, without taking the philosophers to counsel in the matter!

I shall not here eulogize philosophy for the benefits which the laborious efforts of its criticism have conferred on human reason — even granting that its merit should turn out in the end to be only negative — for on this point something more will be said in the next section. But, I ask, do you require that that knowledge which concerns all men, should transcend the common understanding, and should only be revealed to you by philosophers? The very circumstance which has called forth your censure, is the best confirmation of the correctness of our previous assertions, since it discloses, what could not have been foreseen, that Nature is not chargeable with any partial distribution of her gifts in those matters which concern all men without distinction and that, in respect to the essential ends of human nature, we cannot advance further with the help of the highest philosophy, than under the guidance which nature has vouchsafed to the meanest understanding.

CHAPTER III.
The Architectonic of Pure Reason.

By the term architectonic I mean the art of constructing a system. Without systematic unity, our knowledge cannot become science; it will be an aggregate, and not a system. Thus architectonic is the doctrine of the scientific in cognition, and therefore necessarily forms part of our methodology.

Reason cannot permit our knowledge to remain in an unconnected and rhapsodistic state, but requires that the sum of our cognitions should constitute a system. It is thus alone that they can advance the ends of reason. By a system I mean the unity of various cognitions under one idea. This idea is the conception — given by reason — of the form of a whole, in so far as the conception determines a priori not only the limits of its content, but the place which each of its parts is to occupy. The scientific idea contains, therefore, the end and the form of the whole which is in accordance with that end. The unity of the end, to which all the parts of the system relate, and through which all have a relation to each other, communicates unity to the whole system, so that the absence of any part can be immediately detected from our knowledge of the rest; and it determines a priori the limits of the system, thus excluding all contingent or arbitrary additions. The whole is thus an organism (articulatio), and not an aggregate (coacervatio); it may grow from within (per intussusceptionem), but it cannot increase by external additions (per appositionem). It is, thus, like an animal body, the growth of which does not add any limb, but, without changing their proportions, makes each in its sphere stronger and more active.

We require, for the execution of the idea of a system, a schema, that is, a content and an arrangement of parts determined a priori by the principle which the aim of the system prescribes. A schema which is not projected in accordance with an idea, that is, from the standpoint of the highest aim of reason, but merely empirically, in accordance with accidental aims and purposes (the number of which cannot be predetermined), can give us nothing more than technical unity. But the schema which is originated from an idea (in which case reason presents us with aims a priori, and does not look for them to experience), forms the basis of architectonical unity. A science, in the proper acceptation of that term, cannot be formed technically, that is, from observation of the similarity existing between different objects, and the purely contingent use we make of our knowledge in concreto with reference to all kinds of arbitrary external aims; its constitution must be framed on architectonical principles, that is, its parts must be shown to possess an essential affinity, and be capable of being deduced from one supreme and internal aim or end, which forms the condition of the possibility of the scientific whole. The schema of a science must give a priori the plan of it (monogramma), and the division of the whole into parts, in conformity with the idea of the science; and it must also distinguish this whole from all others, according to certain understood principles.

No one will attempt to construct a science, unless he have some idea to rest on as a proper basis. But, in the elaboration of the science, he finds that the schema, nay, even the definition which he at first gave of the science, rarely corresponds with his idea;

for this idea lies, like a germ, in our reason, its parts undeveloped and hid even from microscopical observation. For this reason, we ought to explain and define sciences, not according to the description which the originator gives of them, but according to the idea which we find based in reason itself, and which is suggested by the natural unity of the parts of the science already accumulated. For it will of ten be found that the originator of a science and even his latest successors remain attached to an erroneous idea, which they cannot render clear to themselves, and that they thus fail in determining the true content, the articulation or systematic unity, and the limits of their science.

It is unfortunate that, only after having occupied ourselves for a long time in the collection of materials, under the guidance of an idea which lies undeveloped in the mind, but not according to any definite plan of arrangement — nay, only after we have spent much time and labour in the technical disposition of our materials, does it become possible to view the idea of a science in a clear light, and to project, according to architectonical principles, a plan of the whole, in accordance with the aims of reason. Systems seem, like certain worms, to be formed by a kind of generatio aequivoca — by the mere confluence of conceptions, and to gain completeness only with the progress of time. But the schema or germ of all lies in reason; and thus is not only every system organized according to its own idea, but all are united into one grand system of human knowledge, of which they form members. For this reason, it is possible to frame an architectonic of all human cognition, the formation of which, at the present time, considering the immense materials collected or to be found in the ruins of old systems, would not indeed be very difficult. Our purpose at present is merely to sketch the plan of the architectonic of all cognition given by pure reason; and we begin from the point where the main root of human knowledge divides into two, one of which is reason. By reason I understand here the whole higher faculty of cognition, the rational being placed in contradistinction to the empirical.

If I make complete abstraction of the content of cognition, objectively considered, all cognition is, from a subjective point of view, either historical or rational. Historical cognition is cognitio ex datis, rational, cognitio ex principiis. Whatever may be the original source of a cognition, it is, in relation to the person who possesses it, merely historical, if he knows only what has been given him from another quarter, whether that knowledge was communicated by direct experience or by instruction. Thus the Person who has learned a system of philosophy — say the Wolfian — although he has a perfect knowledge of all the principles, definitions, and arguments in that philosophy, as well as of the divisions that have been made of the system, possesses really no more than an historical knowledge of the Wolfian system; he knows only what has been told him, his judgements are only those which he has received from his teachers. Dispute the validity of a definition, and he is completely at a loss to find another. He has formed his mind on another's; but the imitative faculty is not the productive. His knowledge has not been drawn from reason; and although, objectively considered, it is rational knowledge, subjectively, it is merely historical. He has learned this or that philosophy and is merely a plaster cast of a living man. Rational cognitions which are objective, that is, which have their source in reason, can be so termed from a subjective point of view, only when they have been drawn by the individual himself from the sources of reason, that is, from principles; and it is in this way alone that criticism, or even the rejection of what has been already learned, can spring up in the mind.

All rational cognition is, again, based either on conceptions, or on the construction of conceptions. The former is termed philosophical, the latter mathematical. I have already shown the essential difference of these two methods of cognition in the first chapter. A cognition may be objectively philosophical and subjectively historical — as is the case with the majority of scholars and those who cannot look beyond the limits of their system, and who remain in a state of pupilage all their lives. But it is remarkable that mathematical knowledge, when committed to memory, is valid, from the subjective point of view, as rational knowledge also, and that the same distinction cannot be drawn here as in the case of philosophical cognition. The reason is that the only way of arriving at this knowledge is through the essential principles of reason, and thus it is always certain and indisputable; because reason is employed in concreto — but at the same time a priori — that is, in pure and, therefore, infallible intuition; and thus all causes of illusion and error are excluded. Of all the a priori sciences of reason, therefore, mathematics alone can be learned. Philosophy — unless it be in an historical manner — cannot be learned; we can at most learn to philosophize.

Philosophy is the system of all philosophical cognition. We must use this term in an objective sense, if we understand by it the archetype of all attempts at philosophizing, and the standard by which all subjective philosophies are to be judged. In this sense, philosophy is merely the idea of a possible science, which does not exist in concreto, but to which we endeavour in various ways to approximate, until we have discovered the right path to pursue — a path overgrown by the errors and illusions of sense — and the image we have hitherto tried in vain to shape has become a perfect copy of the great prototype. Until that time, we cannot learn philosophy — it does not exist; if it does, where is it, who possesses it, and how shall we know it? We can only learn to philosophize; in other words, we can only exercise our powers of reasoning in accordance with general principles, retaining at the same time, the right of investigating the sources of these principles, of testing, and even of rejecting them.

Until then, our conception of philosophy is only a scholastic conception — a conception, that is, of a system of cognition which we are trying to elaborate into a science; all that we at present know being the systematic unity of this cognition, and consequently the logical completeness of the cognition for the desired end. But there is also a cosmical conception (conceptus cosmicus) of philosophy, which has always formed the true basis of this term, especially when philosophy was personified and presented to us in the ideal of a philosopher. In this view philosophy is the science of the relation of all cognition to the ultimate and essential aims of human reason (teleologia rationis humanae), and the philosopher is not merely an artist — who occupies himself with conceptions — but a lawgiver, legislating for human reason. In this sense of the word, it would be in the highest degree arrogant to assume the title of philosopher, and to pretend that we had reached the perfection of the prototype which lies in the idea alone.

The mathematician, the natural philosopher, and the logician — how far soever the first may have advanced in rational, and the two latter in philosophical knowledge — are merely artists, engaged in the arrangement and formation of conceptions; they cannot be termed philosophers. Above them all, there is the ideal teacher, who employs them as instruments for the advancement of the essential aims of human reason. Him alone can we call philosopher; but he nowhere exists. But the idea of his legislative power resides in the mind of every man, and it alone teaches us what kind of systematic unity philosophy demands in view of the ultimate aims of reason. This idea is, therefore, a cosmical conception.*

[Note: By a cosmical conception, I mean one in which all men necessarily take an interest; the aim of a science must accordingly be determined according to scholastic conceptions, if it is regarded merely as a means to certain arbitrarily proposed ends.]

In view of the complete systematic unity of reason, there can only be one ultimate end of all the operations of the mind. To this all other aims are subordinate, and nothing more than means for its attainment. This ultimate end is the destination of man, and the philosophy which relates to it is termed moral philosophy. The superior position occupied by moral philosophy, above all other spheres for the operations of reason, sufficiently indicates the reason why the ancients always included the idea — and in an especial manner — of moralist in that of philosopher. Even at the present day, we call a man who appears to have the power of self-government, even although his knowledge may be very limited, by the name of philosopher.

The legislation of human reason, or philosophy, has two objects — nature and freedom — and thus contains not only the laws of nature, but also those of ethics, at first in two separate systems, which, finally, merge into one grand philosophical system of cognition. The philosophy of nature relates to that which is, that of ethics to that which ought to be.

But all philosophy is either cognition on the basis of pure reason, or the cognition of reason on the basis of empirical principles. The former is termed pure, the latter empirical philosophy.

The philosophy of pure reason is either propaedeutic, that is, an inquiry into the powers of reason in regard to pure a priori cognition, and is termed critical philosophy; or it is, secondly, the system of pure reason — a science containing the systematic presentation of the whole body of philosophical knowledge, true as well as illusory, given by pure reason — and is called metaphysic. This name may, however, be also given to the whole system of pure philosophy, critical philosophy included, and may designate the investigation into the sources or possibility of a priori cognition, as well as the presentation of the a priori cognitions which form a system of pure philosophy — excluding, at the same time, all empirical and mathematical elements.

Metaphysic is divided into that of the speculative and that of the practical use of pure reason, and is, accordingly, either the metaphysic of nature, or the metaphysic of ethics. The former contains all the pure rational principles — based upon conceptions alone (and thus excluding mathematics) — of all theoretical cognition; the latter, the principles which determine and necessitate a priori all action. Now moral philosophy alone contains a code of laws — for the regulation of our actions — which are deduced from principles entirely a priori. Hence the metaphysic of ethics is the only pure moral philosophy, as it is not based upon anthropological or other empirical considerations. The metaphysic of speculative reason is what is commonly called metaphysic in the more limited sense. But as pure moral philosophy properly forms a part of this system of cognition, we must allow it to retain the name of metaphysic, although it is not requisite that we should insist on so terming it in our present discussion.

It is of the highest importance to separate those cognitions which differ from others both in kind and in origin, and to take great care that they are not confounded with those with which they are generally found connected. What the chemist does in the analysis of substances, what the mathematician in pure mathematics, is, in a still higher degree, the duty of the philosopher, that the value of each different kind of cognition, and the part it takes in the operations of the mind, may be clearly defined. Human reason has never wanted a metaphysic of some kind, since it attained the power of thought, or rather of reflection; but it has never been able to keep this sphere of thought and cognition pure from all admixture of foreign elements. The idea of a science of this kind is as old as speculation itself; and what mind does not speculate — either in the scholastic or in the popular fashion? At the same time, it must be admitted that even thinkers by profession have been unable clearly to explain the distinction between the two elements of our cognition — the one completely a priori, the other a posteriori; and hence the proper definition of a peculiar kind of cognition, and with it the just idea of a science which has so long and so deeply engaged the attention of the human mind, has never been established. When it was said: "Metaphysic is the science of the first principles of human cognition," this definition did not signalize a peculiarity in kind, but only a difference in degree; these first principles were thus declared to be more general than others, but no criterion of distinction from empirical principles was given. Of these some are more general, and therefore higher, than others; and — as we cannot distinguish what is completely a priori from that which is known to be a posteriori — where shall we draw the line which is to separate the higher and so-called first principles, from the lower and subordinate principles of cognition? What would be said if we were asked to be satisfied with a division of the epochs of the world into the earlier centuries and those following them? "Does the fifth, or the tenth century belong to the earlier centuries?" it would be asked. In the same way I ask: Does the conception of extension belong to metaphysics? You answer, "Yes." Well, that of body too? "Yes." And that of a fluid body? You stop, you are unprepared to admit this; for if you do, everything will belong to metaphysics. From this it is evident that the mere degree of subordination — of the particular to the general — cannot determine the limits of a science; and that, in the present case, we must expect to find a difference in the conceptions of metaphysics both in kind and in origin. The fundamental idea of metaphysics was obscured on another side by the fact that this kind of a priori cognition showed a certain similarity in character with the science of mathematics. Both have the property in common of possessing an a priori origin; but, in the one, our knowledge is based upon conceptions, in the other, on the construction of conceptions. Thus a decided dissimilarity between philosophical and mathematical cognition comes out — a dissimilarity which was always felt, but which could not be made distinct for want of an insight into the criteria of the difference. And thus it happened that, as philosophers themselves failed in the proper development of the idea of their science, the elaboration of the science could not proceed with a definite aim, or under trustworthy guidance. Thus, too, philosophers, ignorant of the path they ought to pursue and always disputing with each other regarding the discoveries which each asserted he had made, brought their science into disrepute with the rest of the world, and finally, even among themselves.

All pure a priori cognition forms, therefore, in view of the peculiar faculty which originates it, a peculiar and distinct unity; and metaphysic is the term applied to the philosophy which attempts to represent that cognition in this systematic unity. The speculative part of metaphysic, which has especially appropriated this appellation — that which we have called the metaphysic of nature — and which considers everything, as it is (not as it ought to be), by means of a priori conceptions, is divided in the following manner.

Metaphysic, in the more limited acceptation of the term, consists of two parts — transcendental philosophy and the physiology of pure reason. The former presents the system of all the conceptions and principles belonging to the understanding and the reason, and which relate to objects in general, but not to any particular given objects (Ontologia); the latter has nature for its subject-matter, that is, the sum of given objects — whether given to the senses, or, if we will, to some other kind of intuition — and is accordingly physiology, although only rationalis. But the use of the faculty of reason in this rational mode of regarding nature is either physical or hyperphysical, or, more properly speaking, immanent or transcendent. The former relates to nature, in so far as our knowledge regarding it may be applied in experience (in concreto); the latter to that connection of the objects of experience, which transcends all experience. Transcendent physiology has, again, an internal and an external connection with its object, both, however, transcending possible experience; the former is the physiology of nature as a whole, or transcendental cognition of the world, the latter of the connection of the whole of nature with a being above nature, or transcendental cognition of God.

Immanent physiology, on the contrary, considers nature as the sum of all sensuous objects, consequently, as it is presented to us — but still according to a priori conditions, for it is under these alone that nature can be presented to our minds at all. The objects of immanent physiology are of two kinds: 1. Those of the external senses, or corporeal nature; 2. The object of the internal sense, the soul, or, in accordance with our fundamental conceptions of it, thinking nature. The metaphysics of corporeal nature is called physics; but, as it must contain only the principles of an a priori cognition of nature, we must term it rational physics. The metaphysics of thinking nature is called psychology, and for the same reason is to be regarded as merely the rational cognition of the soul.

Thus the whole system of metaphysics consists of four principal parts: 1. Ontology; 2. Rational Physiology; 3. Rational cosmology; and 4. Rational theology. The second part — that of the rational doctrine of nature — may be subdivided into two, physica rationalis* and psychologia rationalis.

[Note: It must not be supposed that I mean by this appellation what is generally called physica general is, and which is rather mathematics than a philosophy of nature. For the metaphysic of nature is completely different from mathematics, nor is it so rich in results, although it is of great importance as a critical test of the application of pure understanding — cognition to nature. For want of its guidance, even mathematicians, adopting certain common notions — which are, in fact, metaphysical — have unconsciously crowded their theories of nature with hypotheses, the fallacy of which becomes evident upon the application of the principles of this metaphysic, without detriment, however, to the employment of mathematics in this sphere of cognition.]

The fundamental idea of a philosophy of pure reason of necessity dictates this division; it is, therefore, architectonical — in accordance with the highest aims of reason, and not merely technical, or according to certain accidentally-observed similarities existing between the different parts of the whole science. For this reason, also, is the division immutable and of legislative authority. But the reader may observe in it a few points to which he ought to demur, and which may weaken his conviction of its truth and legitimacy.

In the first place, how can I desire an a priori cognition or metaphysic of objects, in so far as they are given a posteriori? and how is it possible to cognize the nature of things according to a priori principles, and to attain to a rational physiology? The answer is this. We take from experience nothing more than is requisite to present us with an object (in general) of the external or of the internal sense; in the former case, by the mere conception of matter (impenetrable and inanimate extension), in the latter, by the conception of a thinking being — given in the internal empirical representation, I think. As to the rest, we must not employ in our metaphysic of these objects any empirical principles (which add to the content of our conceptions by means of experience), for the purpose of forming by their help any judgements respecting these objects.

Secondly, what place shall we assign to empirical psychology, which has always been considered a part of metaphysics, and from which in our time such important philosophical results have been expected, after the hope of constructing an a priori system of knowledge had been abandoned? I answer: It must be placed by the side of empirical physics or physics proper; that is, must be regarded as forming a part of applied philosophy, the a priori principles of which are contained in pure philosophy, which is therefore connected, although it must not be confounded, with psychology. Empirical psychology must therefore be banished from the sphere of metaphysics, and is indeed excluded by the very idea of that science. In conformity, however, with scholastic usage, we must permit it to occupy a place in metaphysics — but only as an appendix to it. We adopt this course from motives of economy; as psychology is not as yet full enough to occupy our attention as an independent study, while it is, at the same time, of too great importance to be entirely excluded or placed where it has still less affinity than it has with the subject of metaphysics. It is a stranger who has been long a guest; and we make it welcome to stay, until it can take up a more suitable abode in a complete system of anthropology — the pendant to empirical physics.

The above is the general idea of metaphysics, which, as more was expected from it than could be looked for with justice, and as these pleasant expectations were unfortunately never realized, fell into general disrepute. Our Critique must have fully convinced the reader that, although metaphysics cannot form the foundation of religion, it must always be one of its most important bulwarks, and that human reason, which naturally pursues a dialectical course, cannot do without this science, which checks its tendencies towards dialectic and, by elevating reason to a scientific and clear self-knowledge, prevents the ravages which a lawless speculative reason would infallibly commit in the sphere of morals as well as in that of religion. We may be sure, therefore, whatever contempt may be thrown upon metaphysics by those who judge a science not by its own nature, but according to the accidental effects it may have produced, that it can never be completely abandoned, that we must always return to it as to a beloved one who has been for a time estranged, because the questions with which it is engaged relate to the highest aims of humanity, and reason must always labour either to attain to settled views in regard to these, or to destroy those which others have already established.

Metaphysic, therefore — that of nature, as well as that of ethics, but in an especial manner the criticism which forms the propaedeutic to all the operations of reason — forms properly that department of knowledge which may be termed, in the truest sense of the word, philosophy. The path which it pursues is that of science, which, when it has once been discovered, is never lost, and never misleads. Mathematics, natural science, the common experience of men, have a high value as means, for the most part, to accidental ends — but at last also, to those which are necessary and essential to the existence of humanity. But to guide them to this high goal, they require the aid of rational cognition on the basis of pure conceptions, which, be it termed as it may, is properly nothing but metaphysics.

For the same reason, metaphysics forms likewise the completion of the culture of human reason. In this respect, it is indispensable, setting aside altogether the influence which it exerts as a science. For its subject-matter is the elements and highest maxims of reason, which form the basis of the possibility of some sciences and of the use of all. That, as a purely speculative science, it is more useful in preventing error than in the extension of knowledge, does not detract from its value; on the contrary, the supreme office of censor which it occupies assures to it the highest authority and importance. This office it administers for the purpose of securing order, harmony, and well-being to science, and of directing its noble and fruitful labours to the highest possible aim — the happiness of all mankind.

CHAPTER IV.
The History of Pure Reason.

This title is placed here merely for the purpose of designating a division of the system of pure reason of which I do not intend to treat at present. I shall content myself with casting a cursory glance, from a purely transcendental point of view — that of the nature of pure reason — on the labours of philosophers up to the present time. They have aimed at erecting an edifice of philosophy; but to my eye this edifice appears to be in a very ruinous condition.

It is very remarkable, although naturally it could not have been otherwise, that, in the infancy of philosophy, the study of the nature of God and the constitution of a future world formed the commencement, rather than the conclusion, as we should have it, of the speculative efforts of the human mind. However rude the religious conceptions generated by the remains of the old manners and customs of a less cultivated time, the intelligent classes were not thereby prevented from devoting themselves to free inquiry into the existence and nature of God; and they easily saw that there could be no surer way of pleasing the invisible ruler of the world, and of attaining to happiness in another world at least, than a good and honest course of life in this. Thus theology and morals formed the two chief motives, or rather the points of attraction in all abstract inquiries. But it was the former that especially occupied the attention of speculative reason, and which afterwards became so celebrated under the name of metaphysics.

I shall not at present indicate the periods of time at which the greatest changes in metaphysics took place, but shall merely give a hasty sketch of the different ideas which occasioned the most important revolutions in this sphere of thought. There are three different ends in relation to which these revolutions have taken place.

1. In relation to the object of the cognition of reason, philosophers may be divided into sensualists and intellectualists. Epicurus may be regarded as the head of the former, Plato of the latter. The distinction here signalized, subtle as it is, dates from the earliest times, and was long maintained. The former asserted that reality resides in sensuous objects alone, and that everything else is merely imaginary; the latter, that the senses are the parents of illusion and that truth is to be found in the understanding alone. The former did not deny to the conceptions of the understanding a certain kind of reality; but with them it was merely logical, with the others it was mystical. The former admitted intellectual conceptions, but declared that sensuous objects alone possessed real existence. The latter maintained that all real objects were intelligible, and believed that the pure understanding possessed a faculty of intuition apart from sense, which, in their opinion, served only to confuse the ideas of the understanding.

2. In relation to the origin of the pure cognitions of reason, we find one school maintaining that they are derived entirely from experience, and another that they have their origin in reason alone. Aristotle may be regarded as the bead of the empiricists, and Plato of the noologists. Locke, the follower of Aristotle in modern times, and Leibnitz of Plato (although he cannot be said to have imitated him in his mysticism), have not been able to bring this question to a settled conclusion. The procedure of Epicurus in his sensual system, in which he always restricted his conclusions to the

sphere of experience, was much more consequent than that of Aristotle and Locke. The latter especially, after having derived all the conceptions and principles of the mind from experience, goes so far, in the employment of these conceptions and principles, as to maintain that we can prove the existence of God and the existence of God and the immortality of them objects lying beyond the soul — both of them of possible experience — with the same force of demonstration as any mathematical proposition.

3. In relation to method. Method is procedure according to principles. We may divide the methods at present employed in the field of inquiry into the naturalistic and the scientific. The naturalist of pure reason lays it down as his principle that common reason, without the aid of science — which he calls sound reason, or common sense — can give a more satisfactory answer to the most important questions of metaphysics than speculation is able to do. He must maintain, therefore, that we can determine the content and circumference of the moon more certainly by the naked eye, than by the aid of mathematical reasoning. But this system is mere misology reduced to principles; and, what is the most absurd thing in this doctrine, the neglect of all scientific means is paraded as a peculiar method of extending our cognition. As regards those who are naturalists because they know no better, they are certainly not to be blamed. They follow common sense, without parading their ignorance as a method which is to teach us the wonderful secret, how we are to find the truth which lies at the bottom of the well of Democritus.

Quod sapio satis est mihi, non ego curo Esse quod

Arcesilas aerumnosique Solones. PERSIUS

— Satirae, iii. 78-79.

is their motto, under which they may lead a pleasant and praiseworthy life, without troubling themselves with science or troubling science with them.

As regards those who wish to pursue a scientific method, they have now the choice of following either the dogmatical or the sceptical, while they are bound never to desert the systematic mode of procedure. When I mention, in relation to the former, the celebrated Wolf, and as regards the latter, David Hume, I may leave, in accordance with my present intention, all others unnamed. The critical path alone is still open. If my reader has been kind and patient enough to accompany me on this hitherto untravelled route, he can now judge whether, if he and others will contribute their exertions towards making this narrow footpath a high road of thought, that which many centuries have failed to accomplish may not be executed before the close of the present — namely, to bring Reason to perfect contentment in regard to that which has always, but without permanent results, occupied her powers and engaged her ardent desire for knowledge.

An Answer to The Question: "What Is Enlightenment?"

Enlightenment is man's release from his self-incurred tutelage. Tutelage is man's inability to make use of his understanding without direction from another. Self-incurred is this tutelage when its cause lies not in lack of reason but in lack of resolution and courage to use it without direction from another. *Sapere aude!* "Have courage to use your own reason!" - that is the motto of enlightenment.

Laziness and cowardice are the reasons why so great a portion of mankind, after nature has long since discharged them from external direction (naturaliter maiorennes), nevertheless remains under lifelong tutelage, and why it is so easy for others to set themselves up as their guardians. It is so easy not to be of age. If I have a book which understands for me, a pastor who has a conscience for me, a physician who decides my diet, and so forth, I need not trouble myself. I need not think, if I can only pay - others will easily undertake the irksome work for me.

That the step to competence is held to be very dangerous by the far greater portion of mankind (and by the entire fair sex) - quite apart from its being arduous is seen to by those guardians who have so kindly assumed superintendence over them. After the guardians have first made their domestic cattle dumb and have made sure that these placid creatures will not dare take a single step without the harness of the cart to which they are tethered, the guardians then show them the danger which threatens if they try to go alone. Actually, however, this danger is not so great, for by falling a few times they would finally learn to walk alone. But an example of this failure makes them timid and ordinarily frightens them away from all further trials.

For any single individual to work himself out of the life under tutelage which has become almost his nature is very difficult. He has come to be fond of his state, and he is for the present really incapable of making use of his reason, for no one has ever let him try it out. Statutes and formulas, those mechanical tools of the rational employment or rather misemployment of his natural gifts, are the fetters of an everlasting tutelage. Whoever throws them off makes only an uncertain leap over the narrowest ditch because he is not accustomed to that kind of free motion. Therefore, there are few who have succeeded by their own exercise of mind both in freeing themselves from incompetence and in achieving a steady pace.

But that the public should enlighten itself is more possible; indeed, if only freedom is granted enlightenment is almost sure to follow. For there will always be some independent thinkers, even among the established guardians of the great masses, who, after throwing off the yoke of tutelage from their own shoulders, will disseminate the spirit of the rational appreciation of both their own worth and every man's vocation for thinking for himself. But be it noted that the public, which has first been brought under this yoke by their guardians, forces the guardians themselves to remain bound when it is incited to do so by some of the guardians who are themselves capable of some enlightenment - so harmful is it to implant prejudices, for they later take vengeance on their cultivators or on their descendants. Thus the public can only slowly attain enlightenment. Perhaps a fall of personal despotism or of avaricious or tyrannical oppression may be accomplished by revolution, but never a true reform in ways of thinking. Farther, new prejudices will serve as well as old ones to harness the great unthinking masses.

For this enlightenment, however, nothing is required but freedom, and indeed the most harmless among all the things to which this term can properly be applied. It is the freedom to make public use of one's reason at every point. But I hear on all sides,

"Do not argue!" The Officer says: "Do not argue but drill!" The tax collector: "Do not argue but pay!" The cleric: "Do not argue but believe!" Only one prince in the world says, "Argue as much as you will, and about what you will, but obey!" Everywhere there is restriction on freedom.

Which restriction is an obstacle to enlightenment, and which is not an obstacle but a promoter of it? I answer: The public use of one's reason must always be free, and it alone can bring about enlightenment among men. The private use of reason, on the other hand, may often be very narrowly restricted without particularly hindering the progress of enlightenment. By the public use of one's reason I understand the use which a person makes of it as a scholar before the reading public. Private use I call that which one may make of it in a particular civil post or office which is entrusted to him. Many affairs which are conducted in the interest of the community require a certain mechanism through which some members of the community must passively conduct themselves with an artificial unanimity, so that the government may direct them to public ends, or at least prevent them from destroying those ends. Here argument is certainly not allowed - one must obey. But so far as a part of the mechanism regards himself at the same time as a member of the whole community or of a society of world citizens, and thus in the role of a scholar who addresses the public (in the proper sense of the word) through his writings, he certainly can argue without hurting the affairs for which he is in part responsible as a passive member. Thus it would be ruinous for an officer in service to debate about the suitability or utility of a command given to him by his superior; he must obey. But the right to make remarks on errors in the military service and to lay them before the public for judgment cannot equitably be refused him as a scholar. The citizen cannot refuse to pay the taxes imposed on him; indeed, an impudent complaint at those levied on him can be punished as a scandal (as it could occasion general refractoriness). But the same person nevertheless does not act contrary to his duty as a citizen, when, as a scholar, he publicly expresses his thoughts on the inappropriateness or even the injustices of these levies, Similarly a clergyman is obligated to make his sermon to his pupils in catechism and his congregation conform to the symbol of the church which he serves, for he has been accepted on this condition. But as a scholar he has complete freedom, even the calling, to communicate to the public all his carefully tested and well meaning thoughts on that which is erroneous in the symbol and to make suggestions for the better organization of the religious body and church. In doing this there is nothing that could be laid as a burden on his conscience. For what he teaches as a consequence of his office as a representative of the church, this he considers something about which he has not freedom to teach according to his own lights; it is something which he is appointed to propound at the dictation of and in the name of another. He will say, "Our church teaches this or that; those are the proofs which it adduces." He thus extracts all practical uses for his congregation from statutes to which he himself would not subscribe with full conviction but to the enunciation of which he can very well pledge himself because it is not impossible that truth lies hidden in them, and, in any case, there is at least nothing in them contradictory to inner religion. For if he believed he had found such in them, he could not conscientiously discharge the duties of his office; he would have to give it up. The use, therefore, which an appointed teacher makes of his reason before his congregation is merely private, because this congregation is only a domestic one (even if it be a large gathering); with respect to it, as a priest, he is not free, nor can he be free, because he carries out the orders of another. But as a scholar, whose writings speak to his public, the world, the clergyman in the public use of his reason enjoys an unlimited freedom to use his own reason to speak in his own person. That the guardian of the people (in spiritual things) should themselves be incompetent is an absurdity which amounts to the eternalization of absurdities.

But would not a society of clergymen, perhaps a church conference or a venerable classis (as they call themselves among the Dutch), be justified in obligating itself by oath to a certain unchangeable symbol in order to enjoy an unceasing guardianship over each of its numbers and thereby over the people as a whole, and even to make it eternal? I answer that this is altogether impossible. Such contract, made to shut off all further enlightenment from the human race, is absolutely null and void even if confirmed by the supreme power, by parliaments, and by the most ceremonious of peace treaties. An age cannot bind itself and ordain to put the succeeding one into such a condition that it cannot extend its (at best very occasional) knowledge, purify itself of errors, and progress in general enlightenment. That would be a crime against human nature, the proper destination of which lies precisely in this progress and the descendants would be fully justified in rejecting those decrees as having been made in an unwarranted and malicious manner.

The touchstone of everything that can be concluded as a law for a people lies in the question whether the people could have imposed such a law on itself. Now such religious compact might be possible for a short and definitely limited time, as it were, in expectation of a better. One might let every citizen, and especially the clergyman, in the role of scholar, make his comments freely and publicly, i.e. through writing, on the erroneous aspects of the present institution. The newly introduced order might last until insight into the nature of these things had become so general and widely approved that through uniting their voices (even if not unanimously) they could bring a proposal to the throne to take those congregations under protection which had united into a changed religious organization according to their better ideas, without, however hindering others who wish to remain in the order. But to unite in a permanent religious institution which is not to be subject to doubt before the public even in the lifetime of one man, and thereby to make a period of time fruitless in the progress of mankind toward improvement, thus working to the disadvantage of posterity - that is absolutely forbidden. For himself (and only for a short time) a man may postpone enlightenment in what he ought to know, but to renounce it for posterity is to injure and trample on the rights of mankind. And what a people may not decree for itself can even less be decreed for them by a monarch, for his lawgiving authority rests on his uniting the general public will in his own. If he only sees to it that all true or alleged improvement stands together with civil order, he can leave it to his subjects to do what they find necessary for their spiritual welfare. This is not his concern, though it is incumbent on him to prevent one of them from violently hindering another in determining and promoting this welfare to the best of his ability. To meddle in these matters lowers his own majesty, since by the writings in which his own subjects seek to present their views he may evaluate his own governance. He can do this when, with deepest understanding, he lays upon himself the reproach, Caesar non est supra grammaticos. Far more does he injure his own majesty when he degrades his supreme power by supporting the ecclesiastical despotism of some tyrants in his state over his other subjects.

If we are asked, "Do we now live in an enlightened age?" the answer is, "No," but we do live in an age of enlightenment. As things now stand, much is lacking which prevents men from being, or easily becoming, capable of correctly using their own reason in religious matters with assurance and free from outside direction. But on the other hand, we have clear indications that the field has now been opened wherein men may freely deal with these things and that the obstacles to general enlightenment or the release from self-imposed tutelage are gradually being reduced. In this respect, this is the age of enlightenment, or the century of Frederick.

A prince who does not find it unworthy of himself to say that he holds it to be his duty to prescribe nothing to men in religious matters but to give them complete freedom while renouncing the haughty name of tolerance, is himself enlightened and deserves to be esteemed by the grateful world and posterity as the first, at least from the side of government, who divested the human race of its tutelage and left each man free to make use of his reason in matters of conscience. Under him venerable ecclesiastics are allowed, in the role of scholar, and without infringing on their official duties, freely to submit for public testing their judgments and views which here and there diverge from the established symbol. And an even greater freedom is enjoyed by those who are restricted by no official duties. This spirit of freedom spreads beyond this land, even to those in which it must struggle with external obstacles erected by a government which misunderstands its own interest. For an example gives evidence to such a government that in freedom there is not the least cause for concern about public peace and the stability of the community. Men work themselves gradually out of barbarity if only intentional artifices are not made to hold them in it.

I have placed the main point of enlightenment - the escape of men from their self-incurred tutelage - chiefly in matters of religion because our rulers have no interest in playing guardian with respect to the arts and sciences and also because religious incompetence is not only the most harmful but also the most degrading of all. But the manner of thinking of the head of a state who favors religious enlightenment goes further, and he sees that there is no danger to his lawgiving in allowing his subjects to make public use of their reason and to publish their thoughts on a better formulation of his legislation and even their open-minded criticisms of the laws already made. Of this we have a shining example wherein no monarch is superior to him we honor.

But only one who is himself enlightened, is not afraid of shadows, and has a numerous and well-disciplined army to assure public peace, can say: "Argue as much as you will, and about what you will, only obey!" A republic could not dare say such a thing. Here is shown a strange and unexpected trend in human affairs in which almost everything, looked at in the large, is paradoxical. A greater degree of civil freedom appears advantageous to the freedom of mind of the people, and yet it places inescapable limitations upon it. A lower degree of civil freedom, on the contrary, provides the mind with room for each man to extend himself to his full capacity. As nature has uncovered from under this hard shell the seed for which she most tenderly cares - the propensity and vocation to free thinking - this gradually works back upon the character of the people, who thereby gradually become capable of managing freedom; finally, it affects the principles of government, which finds it to its advantage to treat men, who are now more than machines, in accordance with their dignity.

The Moral Law:
Groundwork of the Metaphysics of Morals

Contents

Commentary and Analysis of the Argument

Preface

Pages i–iii—The Different Branches of Philosophy

The three main branches of philosophy are logic, physics, and ethics. Of these *logic* is formal: it abstracts from all differences in the objects (or matter) about which we think and considers only the necessary laws (or forms) of thinking as such. Since it borrows nothing from our sensuous experience of objects, it must be regarded as a wholly non-empirical or *a priori* science. *Physics* deals with the laws of nature, and ethics with the laws of free moral action. These two philosophical sciences deal therefore with objects of thought which are sharply distinguished from one another.

Unlike logic, both physics and ethics must have an *empirical* part (one based on sensuous experience) as well as a non-empirical or *a priori* part (one not so based); for physical laws must apply to nature as an object of experience, and ethical laws must apply to human wills as affected by desires and instincts which can be known only by experience.

A philosopher of today would have to argue that these sciences have an *a priori* part rather than that they have an empirical part; and indeed many philosophers would deny the first possibility altogether. Nevertheless, if we take physics in a wide sense as the philosophy of nature, it appears to proceed in accordance with certain principles which are more than mere generalisations based on such data as are given to our senses. The task of formulating and, if possible, justifying these principles Kant regards as the *a priori* or pure part of physics (or as *a metaphysic of nature*). Among these principles he includes, for example, the principle that every event must have a cause, and this can never be proved (though it may be confirmed) by experience. He holds that it states a condition without which experience of nature, and so physical science itself, would be impossible.

It should be obvious that from experience of what men in fact do we are unable to prove what they ought to do; for we must admit that they often do what they ought not to do—provided we allow that there is such a thing as a moral 'ought' or a moral duty. Hence if there are moral principles in accordance with which men ought to act, knowledge of these principles must be *a priori* knowledge: it cannot be based on sensuous experience. The *a priori* or pure part of ethics is concerned with the *formulation* and *justification* of moral principles—with such terms as 'ought', 'duty', 'good' and 'evil', 'right' and 'wrong'. This *a priori* part of ethics may be called *a metaphysic of morals* (though at other times 'justification'—as opposed to 'formulation'—is reserved by Kant for *a critique of practical reason*). For detailed knowledge of particular human duties we require experience of human nature (and indeed of many other things). This belongs to the empirical part of ethics and is called by Kant '*practical anthropology*', though his use of the term is not altogether clear.

Kant's doctrine of *a priori* knowledge rests mainly on the assumption that mind—or reason, as he calls it—functions actively in accordance with principles which it can know and understand. He holds that such rational principles can be manifested, not only in thinking as such (which is studied in logic), but also in scientific knowledge and in moral action. We can separate out these rational principles, and we can understand how they are necessary for any rational being so far as he seeks to think rationally about the world and to act rationally in the world. If we believe that reason has no activity and no principles of its own and that mind is merely a bundle of sensations and desires, there can be for us no *a priori* knowledge; but we are hardly entitled to assert this without considering the arguments on the other side.

Pages iii–ix—The Need for Pure Ethics

If the distinction between *a priori* and empirical ethics is sound, it is desirable to treat each part separately. The result of mixing them up is bound to be intellectual confusion, but it is also likely to lead to moral degeneration. If actions are to be morally good, they must be done for the sake of duty, and only the *a priori* or pure part of ethics can show us what the nature of duty is. By mixing up the different parts of ethics we may easily begin to confuse duty with self-interest, and this is bound to have disastrous effects in practice.

Pages ix–xi—The Philosophy of Willing as Such

The *a priori* part of ethics is not to be confused with a philosophy of willing *as such*, since it deals, not with all willing, but with a particular *kind* of willing—namely, with willing that is morally good.

Pages xi–xiii—The Aim of the *Groundwork*

The aim of the *Groundwork* is not to give us a complete exposition of the *a priori* part of ethics—that is, a complete metaphysic of morals. Its aim is rather to lay the *foundations* for such a metaphysic of morals, and so to separate out the really difficult part. Even as regards these foundations the *Groundwork* does not pretend to be complete: we require a full 'critique of practical reason' for this purpose. The need for such a critique of reason is, however, less pressing in practical matters than in theoretical, since ordinary human reason is a far safer guide in morals than it is in speculation; and Kant is anxious to avoid the complications of a full critique.

The essential point in all this is that the *Groundwork* has the limited, and yet all-important, aim of establishing the *supreme principle of morality*. It excludes all questions concerned with the *application* of this principle (although it occasionally gives illustrations of the way in which such applications may be made). Hence we should not expect from this book any detailed account of the application of moral principles, nor should we blame Kant for failing to supply it—still less should we invent theories of what he must have thought on this subject. If we want to know how he applied his supreme principle, we must read his neglected *Metaphysic of Morals*. In the *Groundwork* itself the only question to be considered is whether Kant has succeeded or failed in establishing the supreme principle of morality.

Page xiv—The Method of the *Groundwork*

Kant's method is to start with the provisional assumption that our ordinary moral judgements may legitimately claim to be true. He then asks what are the *conditions* which must hold if these claims are to be justified. This is what he calls an *analytic* (or regressive) argument, and by it he hopes to discover a series of conditions till he comes to the ultimate condition of all moral judgements—the supreme principle of morality. He attempts to do this in Chapters 1 and 2. In Chapter 3 his method is different. There he starts with the insight of reason into its own activity and attempts to derive from this the supreme principle of morality. This is what he calls a *synthetic* (or progressive) argument. If it were successful, we could reverse the direction of the argument in the first two chapters: beginning with the insight of reason into the principle of its own activity we could pass to the supreme principle of morality and from this to the ordinary moral judgements with which we started. In this way we should be able to justify our provisional assumption that ordinary moral judgements may legitimately claim to be true.

Chapter 1 attempts to lead us by an analytic argument from ordinary moral judgement to a philosophical statement of the first principle of morality. Chapter 2, after dismissing the confusions of a 'popular' philosophy which works with examples and mixes the empirical with the *a priori*, proceeds (still by an analytic argument) to *formulate* the first principle of morality in different ways: it belongs to a metaphysic of morals. Chapter 3 attempts (in a synthetic argument) to *justify* the first principle of morality by deriving it from its source in pure practical reason: it belongs to a critique of pure practical reason.

1
The Approach to Moral Philosophy

Pages 1–3—The Good Will

The only thing that is good without qualification or restriction is a good will. That is to say, a good will alone is good *in all circumstances* and in that sense is an absolute or unconditioned good. We may also describe it as the only thing that is good *in itself,* good independently of its relation to other things.

This does not mean that a good will is the only good. On the contrary, there are plenty of things which are good in many respects. These, however, are not good in all circumstances, and they may all be thoroughly bad when they are used by a bad will. They are therefore only conditioned goods—that is, good under certain conditions, not good absolutely or in themselves.

Pages 3–4—The Good Will and its Results

The goodness of a good will is not derived from the goodness of the results which it produces. The conditioned goodness of its product cannot be the source of the unconditioned goodness which belongs to a good will alone. Besides, a good will continues to have its own unique goodness even where, by some misfortune, it is unable to produce the results at which it aims.

There is nothing in this to suggest that for Kant a good will does not aim at producing results. He holds, on the contrary, that a good will, and indeed any kind of will, must aim at producing results.

Pages 4–8—The Function of Reason

Ordinary moral consciousness supports the view that a good will alone is an unconditioned good. Indeed, this is the presupposition (or condition) of all our ordinary moral judgements. Nevertheless the claim may seem to be fantastic, and we must seek further corroboration by considering the function of reason in action.

In order to do this we have to presuppose that in organic life every organ has a purpose or function to which it is well adapted. This applies also to mental life; and in human beings reason is, as it were, the organ which controls action, just as instinct is the organ which controls action in animals. If the function of reason in action were merely to attain happiness, this is a purpose for which instinct would have been a very much better guide. Hence if we assume that reason, like other organs, must be well adapted to its purpose, its purpose cannot be merely to produce a will which is good as a means to happiness, but rather to produce a will which is good in itself.

Such a purposive (or teleological) view of nature is not readily accepted today. We need only note that Kant does hold this belief (though by no means in a simple form) and that it is very much more fundamental to his ethics than is commonly supposed. In particular we should note that reason in action has for him two main functions, the first of which has to be subordinated to the second. The first function is to secure the individual's own happiness (a conditioned good), while the second is to manifest a will good in itself (an unconditioned good).

Page 8—The Good Will and Duty

Under human conditions, where we have to struggle against unruly impulses and desires, a good will is manifested in acting *for the sake of duty*. Hence if we are to understand human goodness, we must examine the concept of duty. Human goodness is most conspicuous in struggling against the obstacles placed in its way by unruly impulses, but it must not be thought that goodness as such consists in overcoming obstacles. On the contrary, a perfectly good will would have no obstacles to overcome, and the concept of duty (which involves the overcoming of obstacles) would not apply to such a perfect will.

Pages 8–13—The Motive of Duty

A human action is morally good, not because it is done from immediate inclination—still less because it is done from self-interest—but because it is done for the sake of duty. This is Kant's first proposition about duty, though he does not state it in this general form.

An action—even if it accords with duty and is in that sense right—is not commonly regarded as morally good if it is done solely out of self-interest. We may, however, be inclined to attribute moral goodness to right actions done solely from some immediate inclination—for example, from a direct impulse of sympathy or generosity. In order to test this we must *isolate* our motives: we must consider first an action done solely out of inclination and *not* out of duty, and then an action done solely out of duty and *not* out of inclination. If we do this, then, we shall find—to take the case most favourable to immediate inclination—that an action done solely out of natural sympathy may be right and praiseworthy, but that nevertheless it has no distinctively moral worth. The same kind of action done solely out of duty does have distinctively moral worth. The goodness shown in helping others is all the more conspicuous if a man does this for the sake of duty at a time when he is fully occupied with his own troubles and when he is not impelled to do so by his natural inclinations.

Kant's doctrine would be absurd if it meant that the presence of a natural inclination to good actions (or even of a feeling of satisfaction in doing them) detracted from their moral worth. The ambiguity of his language lends some colour to this interpretation, which is almost universally accepted. Thus he says that a man shows moral worth if he does good, not from inclination, but from duty. But we must remember that he is here contrasting two motives taken in *isolation* in order to find out which of them is the source of moral worth. He would have avoided the ambiguity if he had said that a man shows moral worth, not in doing good from inclination, but in doing it for the sake of duty. It is the motive of duty, not the motive of inclination, that gives moral worth to an action.

Whether these two kinds of motive can be present in the same moral action and whether one can support the other is a question which is not even raised in this passage nor is it discussed at all in the *Groundwork*. Kant's assumption on this subject is that if an action is to be morally good, the motive of duty, while it may be present *at the same time* as other motives, must by itself be sufficient to determine the action. Furthermore, he never wavers in the belief that generous inclinations are a help in doing good actions, that for this reason it is a duty to cultivate them, and that without them a great moral adornment would be absent from the world.

It should also be observed that, so far from decrying happiness, Kant holds that we have at least an indirect duty to seek our own happiness.

Pages 13–14—The Formal Principle of Duty

Kant's second proposition is this: *An action done from duty has its moral worth, not from the results it attains or seeks to attain, but from a formal principle or maxim—the principle of doing one's duty whatever that may be.*

This re-states the first proposition in a more technical way. We have already seen that a good will cannot derive its unconditioned goodness from the conditioned goodness of the *results* at which it aims, and this is true also of the morally good actions in which a good will acting for the sake of duty is manifested. What we have to do now is to state our doctrine in terms of what Kant calls ' maxims'.

A maxim is a principle upon which we act. It is a purely personal principle—not a copy-book maxim—and it may be good or it may be bad. Kant calls it a 'subjective' principle, meaning by this a principle on which a rational agent (or subject of action) *does* act—a principle manifested in actions which are in fact performed. An 'objective' principle, on the other hand, is one on which every rational agent *would necessarily* act if reason had full control over his actions, and therefore one on which he *ought* to act if he is so irrational as to be tempted to act otherwise. Only when we act on objective principles do they become *also* subjective, but they continue to be objective whether we act on them or not.

We need not formulate in words the maxim of our action, but if we know what we are doing and will our action as an action of a particular *kind*, then our action has a maxim or subjective principle. A maxim is thus always some sort of *general* principle under which we will a particular action. Thus if I decide to commit suicide in order to avoid unhappiness, I may be said to act on the principle or maxim 'I will kill myself *whenever* life offers more pain than pleasure'.

All such maxims are *material* maxims: they generalise a particular action with its particular motive and its intended result. Since the moral goodness of an action cannot be derived from its intended results, it manifestly cannot be derived from a material maxim of this kind.

The maxim which gives moral worth to actions is the maxim or principle of doing one's duty whatever one's duty may be. Such a maxim is empty of any particular matter: it is not a maxim of satisfying particular desires or attaining particular results. In Kant's language it is a *formal* maxim. To act for the sake of duty is to act on a formal maxim 'irrespective of all objects of the faculty of desire'. A good man adopts or rejects the material maxim of any proposed action according as it harmonises or conflicts with the controlling and formal maxim of doing his duty for its own sake. Only such 'dutiful' actions can be morally good.

Pages 14–17—Reverence for the Law

A third proposition is alleged to follow from the first two. It is this: *Duty is the necessity to act out of reverence for the law.*

This proposition cannot be derived from the first two unless we can read into them a good deal more than has been explicitly stated: both 'reverence' and 'the law' appear to be terms which we have not met in the premises. Furthermore the proposition itself is not altogether clear. Perhaps it would be better to say that to act on the maxim of doing one's duty for its own sake is to act out of reverence for the law.

It is not altogether easy to follow Kant's argument. He appears to hold that if the maxim of a morally good action is a *formal* maxim (not a material maxim of satisfying one's desires), it must be a maxim of acting reasonably—that is, of acting on a law valid for all rational beings as such independently of their particular desires. Because of our human frailty such a law must appear to us as a law of duty, a law which commands or compels obedience. Such a law, considered as *imposed* upon us, must excite a feeling analogous to fear. Considered, on the other hand, as self-imposed (since it is imposed by our own rational nature), it must excite a feeling analogous to inclination or attraction. This complex feeling is *reverence* (or respect)—a unique feeling which is due, not to any stimulus of the senses, but to the thought that my will is subordinated to such a universal law independently of any influence of sense. So far as the motive of a good action is to be found in feeling, we must say that a morally good action is one which is done out of reverence for the law, and that this is what gives it its unique and unconditioned value.

Pages 17–20—The Categorical Imperative

It may seem to be a very strange kind of law which the good man is supposed to reverence and obey. It is a law which does not depend on our desire for particular consequences and does not in itself even prescribe any particular actions: all it imposes on us is law-abidingness for its own sake—'the conformity of actions to universal law as such'. To many this conception must seem empty, if not revolting, and we have certainly passed from ordinary moral judgements to the very highest pitch of philosophical abstraction—to the *form* common to all genuine morality, whatever its matter may be. Yet is not Kant merely saying the minimum that can and must be said about morality? A man is morally good, not as seeking to satisfy his own desires or to attain his own happiness (though he may do both these things), but as seeking to obey a law valid for *all* men and to follow an objective standard not determined by his own desires.

Because of the obstacles due to our impulses and desires, this law appears to us as a law that we *ought* to obey for its own sake, and so as what Kant calls a categorical imperative. We are here given the first statement of the categorical imperative (though in a negative form): 'I ought never to act except in such a way *that I can also will that my maxim should become a universal law*'. This is the first formulation of the supreme principle of morality—the ultimate condition of all particular moral laws and all ordinary moral judgements. From this all moral laws must be '*derived*'—in the sense that it is 'original', while they are 'derivative' or dependent. Yet, as the formula itself shows, there is no question of *deducing* particular moral laws from the empty form of law as such. On the contrary, what we have to do is to examine the *material* maxims of our contemplated actions and to accept or reject them according as they can or cannot be willed as universal laws—that is, as laws valid for all men, and not as special privileges of our own.

From the example Kant gives in applying this method to the contemplated action of telling a lie it is obvious that he believed the application of his principle to be easier than it in fact is. Nevertheless he has stated the supreme condition of moral actions, and his sharp distinction between moral action and merely prudential or impulsive action is fundamentally sound.

Pages 20–22—Ordinary Practical Reason

The ordinary good man does not formulate this moral principle in abstraction, but he does use this principle in making particular moral judgements. Indeed in practical affairs (though not in speculation) ordinary human reason is almost a better guide than philosophy. Might it not then be advisable to leave moral questions to the ordinary man and to regard moral philosophy as the occupation (or the game) of the philosophical specialist?

Pages 22–24—The Need for Philosophy

The ordinary man needs philosophy because the claims of pleasure tempt him to become a self-deceiver and to argue sophistically against what appear to be the harsh demands of morality. This gives rise to what Kant calls a natural *dialectic*—a tendency to indulge in plausible arguments which contradict one another, and in this way to undermine the claims of duty. This may be disastrous to morality in practice, so disastrous that in the end ordinary human reason is impelled to seek for some solution of its difficulties. This solution is to be found only in philosophy, and in particular in a critique of practical reason, which will trace our moral principle to its source in reason itself.

2
Outline of a Metaphysic of Morals

Pages 25–30—The Use of Examples

Although we have extracted the supreme principle of morality from ordinary moral judgements, this does not mean that we have arrived at it by generalising from examples of morally good actions given to us in experience. Such an empirical method would be characteristic of a 'popular' philosophy, which depends on examples and illustrations. In actual fact we can never be sure that there are any examples of 'dutiful' actions (actions whose determining motive is that of duty). What we are discussing is not what men in fact do, but what they ought to do.

Even if we had experience of dutiful actions, this would not be enough for our purposes. What we have to show is that there is a moral law valid for all rational beings as such and for all men in virtue of their rationality—a law which rational beings as such ought to follow if they are tempted to do otherwise. This could never be established by any experience of actual human behaviour.

Furthermore, examples of morally good action can never be a substitute for moral principles nor can they supply a ground on which moral principles can be based. It is only if we already possess moral principles that we can judge an action to be an example of moral goodness.

Morality is not a matter of blind imitation, and the most that examples can do is to encourage us to do our duty: they can show that right action is possible, and they can bring it more vividly before our minds.

Pages 30–34—Popular Philosophy

Popular philosophy, instead of separating sharply the *a priori* and empirical parts of ethics, offers us a disgusting hotch-potch in which *a priori* and empirical elements are hopelessly intermingled. Moral principles are confused with principles of self-interest, and this has the effect of weakening the claims of morality in a misguided effort to strengthen them.

Pages 34–36—Review of Conclusions

Moral principles must be grasped entirely *a priori*. To mix them up with empirical considerations of self-interest and the like is not merely a confusion of thought but an obstacle in the way of moral progress. Hence before we attempt to apply moral principles we must endeavour to formulate them precisely in a pure metaphysic of morals from which empirical considerations are excluded.

Pages 36–39—Imperatives in General

We must now try to explain what is meant by words like 'good' and 'ought', and in particular what is meant by an 'imperative'. There are different kinds of imperative, but we have to deal first with imperatives *in general* (or what is common to all kinds of imperative): we are not concerned merely with the moral imperative (though we may have this particularly in mind). This is a source of difficulty on a first reading, especially as the word 'good' has different senses when used in connection with different kinds of imperative.

We begin with the conception of a rational agent. A rational agent is one who has the power to act in accordance with his idea of laws—that is, to act in accordance with *principles*. This is what we mean when we say that he has a will. 'Practical reason' is another term for such a will.

We have already seen that the actions of rational agents have a *subjective* principle or maxim, and that in beings who are only imperfectly rational such subjective principles must be distinguished from *objective* principles—that is, from principles on which a rational agent would necessarily act if reason had full control over passion. So far as an agent acts on objective principles, his will and his actions may be described as *in some sense* 'good'.

Imperfectly rational beings like men do not always act on objective principles: they may do so or they may not. This is expressed more technically by saying that for men actions which are objectively necessary are subjectively contingent.

To imperfectly rational beings objective principles seem almost to *constrain* or (in Kant's technical language) to *necessitate* the will—that is, they seem to be imposed upon the will from without instead of being its *necessary* manifestation (as they would be in the case of a wholly rational agent). There is in this respect a sharp difference between being *necessary*, and being *necessitating*, for a rational will.

Where an objective principle is conceived as *necessitating* (and not merely as necessary), it may be described as a *command*. The formula of such a command may be called an *imperative* (though Kant does not in practice distinguish sharply between a command and an imperative).

All imperatives (not merely moral ones) are expressed by the words '*I ought*'. 'I ought' may be said to express from the side of the subject the relation of *necessitation* which holds between a principle recognised as objective and an imperfectly rational will. When I say that 'I ought' to do something, I mean that I recognise an action of this kind to be imposed or necessitated by an objective principle valid for any rational agent as such.

Since imperatives are objective principles considered as necessitating, and since action in accordance with objective principles is good action (in some sense), all imperatives command us to do *good* actions (not merely—as some philosophers hold—actions that are obligatory or right).

A perfectly rational and wholly good agent would *necessarily* act on the same objective principles which for us are imperatives, and so would manifest a kind of goodness just as we do when we obey these imperatives. But for him such objective principles would not be imperatives: they would be necessary but not necessitating, and the will which followed them could be described as a 'holy' will. Where we say 'I ought', an agent of this kind would say 'I will'. He would have no duties nor would he feel reverence for the moral law (but something more akin to love).

In an important footnote Kant explains, if somewhat obscurely, what he means by such terms as 'inclination' and 'interest', and he distinguishes between 'pathological' (or sensuous) interest and 'practical' (or moral) interest. For this *see* the analysis of pages 121–123.

Pages 39–44—Classification of Imperatives

There are three different kinds of imperatives. Since imperatives are objective principles considered as necessitating, there must equally be three corresponding kinds of objective principle and three corresponding kinds (or senses) of 'good'.

Some objective principles are *conditioned* by a will for some end—that is to say, they would necessarily be followed by a fully rational agent *if* he willed the end. These principles give rise to *hypothetical* imperatives, which have the general form '*If* I will this end, I ought to do such and such'. They bid us do actions which are *good as means* to an end that we already will (or might will).

When the end is merely one that we might will, the imperatives are *problematic* or *technical*. They may be called imperatives of skill, and the actions they enjoin are good in the sense of being '*skilful*' or '*useful*'.

Where the end is one that every rational agent wills by his very nature, the imperatives are *assertoric* or *pragmatic*. The end which every rational agent wills by his very nature is his own happiness, and the actions enjoined by a pragmatic imperative are good in the sense of being '*prudent*'.

Some objective principles are *unconditioned*: they would necessarily be followed by a fully rational agent but are not based on the previous willing of some further end. These principles give rise to *categorical* imperatives, which have the general form 'I ought to do such and such' (without any 'if' as a prior condition). They may also be called 'apodeictic'—that is, necessary in the sense of being unconditioned and absolute. These are the unconditioned imperatives of morality, and the actions they enjoin are *morally good*—good in themselves and not merely good as a means to some further end.

The different kinds of imperative exercise a different kind of *necessitation*. This difference may be marked by describing them as rules of skill, *counsels* of prudence, *commands* (or *laws*) of morality. Only commands or laws are absolutely binding.

Pages 44–50—How are Imperatives Possible?

We have now to consider how these imperatives are 'possible'—that is, how they can be *justified*. To justify them is to show that the principles on which they bid us act are *objective* in the sense of being valid for any rational being as such. Kant always assumes that a principle on which a fully rational agent as such would *necessarily* act is also one on which an imperfectly rational agent *ought* to act if he is tempted to do otherwise.

In order to understand the argument we must grasp the distinction between analytic and synthetic propositions.

In an *analytic* proposition the predicate is contained in the subject-concept and can be derived by analysis of the subject-concept. Thus 'Every *effect* must have a cause' is an analytic proposition; for it is impossible to conceive an effect without conceiving it as having a cause. Hence in order to justify an analytic proposition we do not need to go beyond the concept of the subject. In a *synthetic* proposition the predicate is *not* contained in the subject-concept and cannot be derived by analysis of the subject-concept. Thus 'Every *event* must have a cause' is a synthetic proposition; for it is possible to conceive an event without conceiving that it has a cause. In order to justify any synthetic proposition we have to go beyond the concept of the subject and discover some 'third term' which will entitle us to attribute the predicate to the subject.

Any fully rational agent who wills an end necessarily wills the means to the end. This is an analytic proposition; for to will (and not merely to wish) an end is to will the action which is a means to this end. Hence any rational agent who wills an end *ought* to will the means to this end if he is irrational enough to be tempted to do otherwise. There is thus no difficulty in justifying *imperatives of skill.*

It should be noted that in finding out what are in fact the means to our ends we make use of synthetic propositions: we have to discover what causes will produce certain desired effects, and it is impossible to discover the cause of any effect by a mere analysis of the concept of the effect by itself. These synthetic propositions, however, are theoretical only: when we know what cause will produce the desired effect, the principle determining our will as rational beings is the analytic proposition that any fully rational agent who wills an end necessarily wills the known means to that end.

When we come to consider *imperatives of prudence*, we meet a special difficulty. Although happiness is an end which we all in fact seek, our concept of it is unfortunately vague and indeterminate: we do not know clearly what our end is. At times Kant himself speaks as if the pursuit of happiness were merely a search for the means to the maximum possible amount of pleasant feeling throughout the whole course of life. At other times he recognises that it involves the choice and harmonising of ends as well as of the means to them. Apart from these difficulties, however, imperatives of prudence are justified in the same way as imperatives of skill. They rest on the analytic proposition that any fully rational agent who wills an end must necessarily will the known means to that end.

This kind of justification is not possible in the case of *moral or categorical imperatives*; for when I recognise a moral duty by saying 'I ought to do such and such', this does not rest on the presupposition that some further end is already willed. To justify a categorical imperative we have to show that a fully rational agent would necessarily act in a certain way—not if he happens to want something else, but simply and solely as a rational agent. A predicate of this kind, however, is not contained in the concept 'rational agent' and cannot be derived by analysis of this concept. The proposition is not analytic but synthetic, and yet it is an assertion of what a rational agent as such would *necessarily* do. Such an assertion can never be justified by experience of examples nor, as we have seen, can we be sure that we have any such experience. The proposition is not merely synthetic, but also *a priori*, and the difficulty of justifying such a proposition is likely to be very great. This task must be postponed till later.

Pages 51–52—The Formula of Universal Law

Our first problem is to *formulate* the categorical imperative—that is, to state what it commands or enjoins. This topic is pursued ostensibly for its own sake, and we are given a succession of formulae; but in all this the analytic argument to the supreme principle of morality (the principle of autonomy) is still being carried on; and we shall find later that it is the principle of autonomy which enables us to connect morality with the Idea of freedom as expounded in the final chapter.

A categorical imperative, as we have already seen, merely bids us act in accordance with universal law as such—that is, it bids us act on a principle valid for all rational beings as such, and not merely on one that is valid *if* we happen to want some further end. Hence it bids us accept or reject the *material* maxim of a contemplated action according as it can or cannot be willed also as a universal law. We may express this in the formula '*Act only on that maxim through which you can at the same time will that it should become a universal law*'.

There is thus only one categorical imperative. We may also more loosely describe as categorical imperatives the various particular moral laws in which the one general categorical imperative is applied—as, for example, the law 'Thou shalt not kill'. Such laws are all 'derived' from the one categorical imperative as their principle. In the *Groundwork* Kant appears to think that they can be derived from this formula by itself, but in the *Critique of Practical Reason* he holds that for this purpose we require to make use of the formula which immediately follows.

Page 52—The Formula of the Law of Nature

'*Act as if the maxim of your action were to become through your will* a universal law of nature.'

This formula, though subordinate to the previous one, is entirely distinct from it: it refers to a law of nature, not of freedom, and it is the formula which Kant himself uses in his illustrations. He gives no explanation of why he does so beyond saying— on page 81—that there is an *analogy* between the universal law of morality and the universal law of nature. The subject is a highly technical one and is expounded further in the *Critique of Practical Reason*, but for this I must refer to my book, *The Categorical Imperative*, especially pages 157–164.

A law of nature is primarily a law of cause and effect. Nevertheless, when Kant asks us to consider our maxims *as if* they were laws of nature, he treats them as purposive (or teleological) laws. He is already supposing that nature—or at least human nature—is teleological or is what he later calls a kingdom of nature and not a mere mechanism.

In spite of these difficulties and complications Kant's doctrine is simple. He holds that a man is morally good, not so far as he acts from passion or self-interest, but so far as he acts on an impersonal principle valid for others as well as for himself. This is the *essence* of morality; but if we wish to *test* the maxim of a proposed action we must ask whether, if universally adopted, it would further a systematic harmony of purposes in the individual and in the human race. Only if it would do this can we say that it is fit to be willed as a universal moral law.

The *application* of such a test is manifestly impossible without empirical knowledge of human nature, and Kant takes this for granted in his illustrations.

Pages 52–57—Illustrations

Duties may be divided into duties towards self and duties towards others, and again into perfect and imperfect duties. This gives us four main *types* of duty, and Kant gives us one illustration of each type in order to show that his formula can be applied to all four.

A perfect duty is one which admits of no exception in the interests of inclination. Under this heading the examples given are the ban on suicide and on making a false promise in order to receive a loan. We are not entitled to commit suicide because we have a strong inclination to do so, nor are we entitled to pay our debt to one man and not to another because we happen to like him better. In the case of imperfect duties the position is different: we are bound only to adopt the *maxim* of developing our talents and of helping others, and we are to some extent entitled to decide arbitrarily *which* talents we will develop and *which* persons we will help. There is here a certain 'latitude' or 'playroom' for mere inclination.

In the case of duties towards self Kant assumes that our various capacities have a natural function or purpose in life. It is a perfect duty *not* to thwart such purposes; and it is also a positive, but imperfect, duty to further such purposes.

In the case of duties towards others we have a perfect duty *not* to thwart the realisation of a possible systematic harmony of purposes among men; and we have a positive, but imperfect, duty to further the realisation of such a systematic harmony.

The qualifications to be attached to such principles are necessarily omitted in such a book as the *Groundwork*.

Pages 57–59—The Canon of Moral Judgement

The general canon of moral judgement is that we should be able to *will* that the maxim of our action should become a universal law (of *freedom*). When we consider our maxims as possible (teleological) laws of *nature*, we find that some of them cannot even be *conceived* as such laws: for example, a law that self-love (which considered as falling under a law of nature becomes something like a feeling—or instinct—of self-preservation) should both further and destroy life is inconceivable. In such a case the maxim is opposed to perfect or strict duty. Other maxims, though not inconceivable as possible (teleological) laws of nature, yet cannot be consistently *willed* as such laws: there would be inconsistency or inconsequence in willing, for example, that men should possess talents, and yet should never use them. Maxims of this kind are opposed to imperfect duty.

Whatever may be thought of the details of Kant's argument—and the argument against suicide is particularly weak—we have to ask ourselves whether a teleological view of human nature is not necessary to ethics, just as some sort of teleological view of the human body is necessary to medicine. It should also be observed that on Kant's view moral questions are not merely questions of what we can *think* but of what we can *will*, and that bad action involves, not a theoretical contradiction, but an opposition (or antagonism) of inclination to a rational will supposed to be in some sense actually present in ourselves.

Pages 59–63—The Need for Pure Ethics

Kant re-emphasises his previous contentions on this subject.

Pages 63–67—The Formula of the End in Itself

Act in such a way that you always treat humanity, whether in your own person or in the person of any other, never simply as a means, but always at the same time as an end.

This formula brings in a second aspect of all action; for all rational action, besides having a principle, must also set before itself an end. Ends—like principles—may be merely *subjective*: they may be arbitrarily adopted by an individual. Subjective or relative ends which a particular agent seeks to produce are, as we have seen, the ground only of *hypothetical* imperatives, and their value is relative and conditioned. If there were also *objective* ends given to us by reason, ends which in all circumstances a fully rational agent would necessarily pursue, these would have an absolute and unconditioned value. They would also be ends which an imperfectly rational agent *ought* to pursue if he were irrational enough to be tempted to do otherwise.

Such ends could not be mere products of our actions, for—as we have seen all along—no mere product of our action can have an unconditioned and absolute value. They must be already existent ends; and their mere existence would impose on us the duty of pursuing them (so far as this was in our power). That is to say, they would be the *ground* of a *categorical* imperative in somewhat the same way as merely subjective ends are the ground of hypothetical imperatives. Such ends may be described as ends in themselves—not merely as ends relative to particular rational agents.

Only rational agents or *persons* can be ends in themselves. As they alone can have an unconditioned and absolute value, it is wrong to use them simply as means to an end whose value is only relative. Without such ends in themselves there would be no unconditioned good, no supreme principle of action, and so—for human beings—no categorical imperative. Thus, like our first formula, the Formula of the End in Itself follows from the very essence of the categorical imperative—provided we remember that all action must have an end as well as a principle.

Kant adds that every rational agent necessarily conceives his own existence in this way on grounds valid for every rational agent as such. The justification for this depends, however, on his account of the Idea of freedom, which is reserved till later.

The new formula, like the first one, must give rise to particular categorical imperatives when applied to the special nature of man.

Pages 67–68—Illustrations

The same set of examples brings out even more clearly the teleological presuppositions necessary for any *test* by which the categorical imperative can be applied. We have a perfect duty not to use ourselves or others *merely* as a means to the satisfaction of our inclinations. We have an imperfect, but *positive*, duty to further the ends of nature in ourselves and in others—that is, to seek our own perfection and the happiness of others.

As Kant himself indicates in one passage, we are concerned only with very general *types* of duty. It would be quite unfair to complain that he does not deal with all the qualifications that might be necessary in dealing with special problems.

Pages 69–71—The Formula of Autonomy

So act that your will can regard itself at the same time as making universal law through its maxim.

This formula may seem at first sight to be a mere repetition of the Formula of Universal Law. It has, however, the advantage of making explicit the doctrine that the categorical imperative bids us, not merely to follow universal law, but to follow a universal law which we ourselves make as rational agents and one which we ourselves particularise through our maxims. This is for Kant the most important formulation of the supreme principle of morality, since it leads straight to the Idea of freedom. We are subject to the moral law only because it is the necessary expression of our own nature as rational agents.

The Formula of Autonomy—though the argument is obscurely stated—is derived from combining the Formula of Universal Law and the Formula of the End in Itself. We have not only seen that we are bound to obey the law in virtue of its universality (its objective validity for all rational agents); we have also seen that rational agents as subjects are the *ground* of this categorical imperative. If this is so, the law which we are bound to obey must be the product of our own will (so far as we are rational agents)—that is to say, it rests on 'the Idea of the will of every rational being as a will which makes universal law'.

Kant puts his point more simply later—page 83—when he says of a rational being 'it is precisely the fitness of his maxims to make universal law that marks him out as an end in himself'. If a rational agent is truly an end in himself, he must be the author of the laws which he is bound to obey, and it is this which gives him his supreme value.

Pages 71–74—The Exclusion of Interest

A categorical imperative excludes interest: it says simply 'I ought to do this', and it does *not* say 'I ought to do this if I happen to want that'. This was implicit in our previous formulae from the mere fact that they were formulae of an imperative recognised to be categorical. It is now made explicit in the Formula of Autonomy. A will may be subject to laws because of some interest (as we have seen in hypothetical imperatives). A will which is not subject to law because of any interest can be subject only to laws which it itself makes. Only if we conceive the will as making its own laws can we understand how an imperative can exclude interest and so be categorical. The supreme merit of the Formula of Autonomy is this: by the express statement that a rational will makes the laws which it is bound to obey the essential character of the categorical imperative is for the first time made fully explicit. Hence the Formula of Autonomy follows directly from the character of the categorical imperative itself.

All philosophies which seek to explain moral obligation by any kind of interest make a categorical imperative inconceivable and deny morality altogether. They may all be said to propound a doctrine of *heteronomy*—that is, they portray the will as bound only by a law which has its origin in some object or end *other* than the will itself. Theories of this kind can give rise only to hypothetical, and so non-moral, imperatives.

Pages 74–77—The Formula of the Kingdom of Ends

So act as if you were through your maxims a law-making member of a kingdom of ends.

This formula springs directly from the Formula of Autonomy. So far as rational agents are all subject to universal laws which they themselves make, they constitute a kingdom—that is, a State or commonwealth. So far as these laws bid them treat each other as ends in themselves, the kingdom so constituted is a kingdom of ends. These ends cover, not only persons as ends in themselves, but also the personal ends which each of these may set before himself in accordance with universal law. The concept of the kingdom of ends is connected with the Idea of an intelligible world in the final chapter.

We must distinguish between the *members* of such a kingdom (all finite rational agents) and its supreme *head* (an infinite rational agent). As law-making members of such a kingdom rational agents have what is called 'dignity'—that is, an intrinsic, unconditioned, incomparable worth or worthiness.

Pages 77–79—The Dignity of Virtue

A thing has a *price* if any substitute or equivalent can be found for it. It has *dignity* or worthiness if it admits of no equivalent.

Morality or virtue—and humanity so far as it is capable of morality—alone has dignity. In this respect it cannot be compared with things that have economic value (a market price) or even with things that have an aesthetic value (a fancy price). The incomparable worth of a good man springs from his being a law-making member in a kingdom of ends.

Pages 79–81—Review of the Formulae

In the final review three formulae only are mentioned: (1) the Formula of the Law of Nature, (2) the Formula of the End in Itself, and (3) the Formula of the Kingdom of Ends. The first formula is said to be concerned with the form of a moral maxim—that is, with its universality; the second with its matter—that is, with its ends; while the third combines both form and matter. In addition, however, the Formula of Universal Law is mentioned as the strict test to apply (presumably because it is concerned primarily with the motive of moral action). The purpose of the others is to bring the Idea of duty closer to intuition (or imagination).

A new version is given for the Formula of the Kingdom of Ends. '*All maxims as proceeding from our own making of laws ought to harmonise with a possible kingdom of ends as a kingdom of nature.*' The kingdom of nature has not been mentioned before, and it seems to stand to the kingdom of ends in the same sort of relation as the universal law of nature stands to the universal law of freedom. Kant makes it perfectly clear that when he regards nature as offering an analogy for morality, nature is considered to be teleological.

The Formula of Autonomy is here amalgamated with the Formula of the Kingdom of Ends.

Pages 81–87—Review of the Whole Argument

The final review summarises the whole argument from beginning to end—from the concept of a good will to the concept of the dignity of virtue and the dignity of man as capable of virtue. The transitions from one formula to another are simplified and in some ways improved. The most notable addition is, however, the account given of the kingdom of nature. The kingdom of ends can be realised only if *all* men obey the categorical imperative, but even this would not be enough: unless nature itself also *co-operates* with our moral strivings, this ideal can never be attained. We cannot be confident of co-operation either from other men or from nature, but in spite of this the imperative which bids us act as law-making members of a kingdom remains categorical. We ought to pursue this ideal whether or not we can expect to secure results, and this disinterested pursuit of the moral ideal is at once the source of man's dignity and the standard by which he must be judged.

Pages 87–88—Autonomy of the Will

We have shown by an analytic argument that the principle of the autonomy of the will (and consequently also a categorical imperative enjoining action in accordance with such autonomy) is a necessary condition of the validity of moral judgements. If, however, we wish to establish the validity of the principle of autonomy, we must pass beyond our judgements about moral actions to a critique of pure practical reason.

Pages 88–89—Heteronomy of the Will

Any moral philosophy which rejects the principle of autonomy has to fall back on a principle of heteronomy: it must make the law governing human action depend, not on the will itself, but on objects other than the will. Such a view can give rise only to hypothetical and so non-moral imperatives.

Pages 89–90—Classification of Heteronomous Principles

Heteronomous principles are either *empirical* or *rational*. When they are empirical, their principle is always the pursuit of *happiness*, although some of them may be based on natural feelings of pleasure and pain, while others may be based on a supposed moral feeling or moral sense. When they are rational, their principle is always the pursuit of *perfection*, either a perfection to be attained by our own will or one supposed to be already existent in the will of God which imposes certain tasks upon our will.

Pages 90–91—Empirical Principles of Heteronomy

Since all empirical principles are based on sense and so lack universality, they are quite unfitted to serve as a basis for moral law. The principle of seeking one's own happiness is, however, the most objectionable. We have a right (and even an indirect duty) to seek our own happiness so far as this is compatible with moral law; but to be happy is one thing and to be good is another; and to confuse the two is to abolish the specific distinction between virtue and vice.

The doctrine of moral sense has at least the merit of finding a direct satisfaction in virtue and not merely satisfaction in its alleged pleasant results. Kant always recognises the reality of moral feeling, but he insists that it is a consequence of our recognition of the law: it cannot itself provide any uniform standard for ourselves and still less can it legislate for others. The doctrine of moral sense must in the last resort be classed with doctrines which regard pleasure or happiness as the only good, since it too finds the good in the satisfaction of a particular kind of feeling.

Pages 91–93—Rational Principles of Heteronomy

The rational principle of perfection as an end to be attained by us is the best of the proposed heteronomous principles of morality since it at least appeals to reason for a decision. So far, however, as it merely bids us aim at the maximum reality appropriate to us, it is utterly vague; and if it includes moral perfection, it is obviously circular. Kant himself holds that the moral law bids us cultivate our natural perfection (the exercise of our talents) and our moral perfection (the doing of duty for duty's sake). His objections are directed against the view that we should obey the moral law for the sake of realising our own perfection.

The theological principle that to be moral is to obey the perfect will of God must be utterly rejected. If we suppose that God is good, this can only be because we already know what moral goodness is, and our theory is a vicious circle. If, on the other hand, we exclude goodness from our concept of God's will and conceive Him merely as all-powerful, we base morality on fear of an arbitrary, but irresistible, will. A moral system of this kind is in direct opposition to morality. Although morality on Kant's view must lead to religion, it cannot be derived from religion.

Pages 93–95—The Failure of Heteronomy

All these doctrines suppose that moral law has to be derived, not from the will itself, but from some object of the will. In being thus heteronomous they can give us no moral or categorical imperative and must consider morally good action to be good, not in itself, but merely as a means to an anticipated result. They thus destroy all *immediate* interest in moral action, and they place man under a law of nature rather than under a law of freedom.

Pages 95–96—The Position of the Argument

All Kant claims to have done is to have shown by an analytic argument that the principle of autonomy is the necessary condition of all our moral judgements. If there is such a thing as morality, and if our moral judgements are not merely chimerical, then the principle of autonomy must be accepted. Many thinkers might take this as sufficient proof of the principle, but Kant does not regard such an argument as a proof. He has not even asserted the truth of the principle, still less pretended to prove it.

The principle of autonomy and the corresponding categorical imperative are synthetic *a priori* propositions: they assert that a rational agent—if he had full control over passion—would necessarily act only on maxims by which he can regard himself as making universal law, and that he ought so to act if he is irrational enough to be tempted to act otherwise. Such a proposition requires a synthetic use of pure practical reason, and on this we cannot venture without a critique of this power of reason itself.

3
Outline of a Critique of Practical Reason

Pages 97–99—Freedom and Autonomy

When we consider *will* (or practical reason), we may define it as a kind of causality (a power of causal action) belonging to living beings so far as they are rational. To describe such a will as *free* would be to say that it can act causally *without* being caused to do so by something other than itself. Non-rational beings can act causally only so far as they are caused to do so by something other than themselves, and this is what is meant by natural *necessity* as opposed to freedom: if one billiard ball causes another to move, it does so only because it has itself been caused to move by something else.

So far our description of freedom is negative. But a lawless free will would be self-contradictory, and we must make our description positive by saying that a free will would act under laws, but that these laws could not be imposed on it by something other than itself; for, if they were, they would merely be laws of natural necessity. If the laws of freedom cannot be other-imposed (if we may use such an expression), they must be self-imposed. That is to say, freedom would be identical with autonomy; and since autonomy is the principle of morality, a free will would be a will under moral laws.

If then we could presuppose freedom, autonomy, and therefore morality, would follow by mere analysis of the concept of freedom. Nevertheless, as we have seen, the principle of autonomy is a synthetic *a priori* proposition and so can be justified only by bringing in a third term to connect the subject and the predicate of the proposition. The positive concept of freedom furnishes, or directs us to, this third term; but we require further preparation if we are to show what this third term is and to deduce freedom from the concept of pure practical reason.

Pages 99–100—Freedom as a Necessary Presupposition

If morality is to be derived from freedom, and if—as we have maintained—morality must be valid for all rational beings as such, it looks as if we have got to prove that the will of a rational being as such is necessarily free. This can never be proved by any experience of merely human action, nor indeed can it be proved at all from the point of view of philosophical theory. For purposes of action, however, it would be enough if we could show that a rational being can act only under the *presupposition* of freedom; for if this were so, the moral laws bound up with freedom would be valid for him just as much as if he were *known* to be free.

Reason as such must necessarily function under the presupposition that it is free both negatively and positively: it must presuppose that it is not determined by outside influences and that it is the source of its own principles. If a rational subject supposed his judgements to be determined, not by rational principles, but by external impulsion, he could not regard these judgements as his own. This must be equally true of practical reason: a rational agent must regard himself as capable of acting on his own rational principles and only so can he regard his will as his own. That is to say, from a practical point of view every rational agent must presuppose his will to be free. Freedom is a necessary presupposition of all action as well as of all thinking.

Pages 101–105—Moral Interest and the Vicious Circle

We have argued that in action rational beings must presuppose their own freedom and that from this presupposition there necessarily follows the principle of autonomy and consequently the corresponding categorical imperative. In this way we have at least formulated the principle of morality more precisely than has been done before. But why should I simply as a rational being subject myself, and so also other rational beings, to this principle? Why should I attach such supreme value to moral action and feel in this a personal worth in comparison with which pleasure is to count as nothing? Why should I take an interest in moral excellence for its own sake? Have we really given a convincing answer to these difficult questions?

It is no doubt true that we do in fact take an interest in moral excellence, but this interest arises only because we assume that the moral law is binding. We do not as yet see how the moral law can be binding. It may seem that we have fallen into a vicious circle: we have argued that we must suppose ourselves to be free because we are under moral laws and have then argued that we must be under moral laws because we have supposed ourselves to be free. To do this is very far from giving us any justification of the moral law.

Pages 105–110—The Two Standpoints

In order to escape from such a vicious circle we must ask ourselves whether we have not two different standpoints (or points of view) from which we may regard our actions. Do we have one standpoint when we conceive ourselves as acting freely and another when we contemplate our actions as observed events?

This doctrine of the two standpoints is an essential part of Kant's Critical Philosophy, which has hitherto been kept in the background. In dealing with it he has to face a difficulty: he cannot assume the elaborate arguments of the *Critique of Pure Reason* to be familiar to his readers nor can he attempt to repeat these elaborate arguments in a short treatise on ethics. He consequently falls back on some rather elementary considerations which, taken by themselves, cannot be very convincing.

All the ideas that are given to our senses come to us without any volition of our own. We assume that these ideas come to us from objects, but by means of ideas so given we can know objects only as they affect ourselves: what these objects are in themselves we do not know. This gives rise to a distinction between things as they appear to us and things as they are in themselves—or again between *appearances* and *things in themselves*. Only appearances can be known by us; but behind appearances we must assume things in themselves, although these things can never be known as they are in themselves, but only as they affect us. This gives us a rough distinction—it is only rough—between a *sensible* world (a world given to sense or at least through sense) and an *intelligible* world (one which we can conceive but never know, since all human knowledge requires a combination of sensing and conceiving).

This distinction applies also to man's knowledge of himself. By inner sense (or introspection) he can know himself only as he appears, but behind this appearance he must assume that there is an Ego as it is in itself. So far as he is known by inner sense, and indeed so far as he is capable of receiving sensations passively, man must regard himself as belonging to the sensible world. So far, however, as he may be capable of pure activity apart from sense, he must regard himself as belonging to the intelligible world. The intelligible world is here described as an 'intellectual' world—a world which is intelligible because it is intelligent—although it is added that of this world we can know nothing further.

Now man actually finds in himself a pure activity apart from sense. He finds in himself a power of reason. Here, it should be noted, Kant appeals first, as he did before, to theoretical reason, although he now takes reason in his own special Critical sense. We have a spontaneous power of 'understanding' which (no doubt along with other factors) produces from itself such concepts (or *categories*) as that of cause and effect and uses these concepts to bring the ideas of sense under rules. Thus in spite of its genuine spontaneity understanding is still bound up with sense, and apart from sense it would think nothing at all. 'Reason', on the other hand, is a power of *Ideas*—that is, it produces concepts (of the unconditioned) which go beyond sense altogether and can have no examples given to sense. Unlike understanding, reason shows a pure spontaneity which is entirely independent of sense.

In virtue of this spontaneity man must conceive himself as belonging, *qua* intelligence, to the intelligible world and as subject to laws which have their ground in reason alone. So far as he is sensuous and is known to himself by means of inner sense he must regard himself as belonging to the sensible world and as subject to the laws of nature. These are the two standpoints from which a finite rational being must view himself.

This doctrine applies equally to pure practical reason. Since from one standpoint man, as a finite rational being, must conceive himself as belonging to the intelligible world, he must conceive his will as free from determination by sensuous causes and as obedient to laws having their ground in reason alone. To say this is to say that he can never conceive the causal action of his own will except under the Idea of freedom. Thus he must, as a rational being, act only on the presupposition of freedom, and from this there follows, as we have seen, the principle of autonomy and the categorical imperative.

The suspicion of a vicious cricle is now removed. From the standpoint of a rational agent who conceives himself as free and as a member of the intelligible world, man must recognise the principle of autonomy. When he thinks of himself as a member of both the intelligible and the sensible world, he must recognise the principle of autonomy as a categorical imperative.

In all this Kant does not make it wholly clear whether his inference is from membership of the intelligible world to freedom or *vice versa*. It might well be suggested that we conceive ourselves as free in action and so as members of the intelligible world only because we already recognise the principle of autonomy and the categorical imperative; and indeed this appears to be Kant's own view in the *Critique of Practical Reason*. Nevertheless, his comparison between pure theoretical reason and pure practical reason is of very great interest; and we must remember that just as pure theoretical reason conceives Ideas of the unconditioned, so pure practical reason seeks in action to realise the Idea of an unconditioned law.

Pages 110–112—How is a Categorical Imperative Possible?

As a finite rational agent man must regard himself from two standpoints—first as a member of the intelligible world, and secondly as a member of the sensible world. If I were solely a member of the intelligible world, all my actions would necessarily accord with the principle of autonomy; if I were solely a part of the sensible world, they would necessarily be entirely subject to the law of nature. At this point unfortunately we come to an argument which may be new but is certainly confused in expression and hard to interpret. *The intelligible world contains the ground of the sensible world and also of its laws.* From this premise (which itself demands considerable expansion) Kant appears to infer that the law governing my will as a member of the intelligible world *ought* to govern my will in spite of the fact that I am also (from another point of view) a member of the sensible world.

This looks like a metaphysical argument from the superior reality of the intelligible world and so of the rational will, but such an interpretation seems to be immediately repudiated by Kant. The categorical 'I ought', we are told, is a synthetic *a priori* proposition; and the third term which connects this 'ought' with the will of an imperfectly rational agent like myself is the *Idea* of the same will, viewed, however, as a pure will belonging to the intelligible world. This *Idea* is apparently the third term to which freedom was said to direct us at the end of the first section of the present chapter: it may indeed be described as a more precise Idea of freedom—that is, of a free will. Its function is said to be roughly similar to that played by the categories in the synthetic *a priori* propositions which are necessary for our experience of nature.

This doctrine is confirmed by an appeal to our ordinary moral consciousness as present even in a bad man. The moral 'I ought' is really an 'I will' for man regarded as a member of the intelligible world. It is conceived as an 'I ought' only because he considers himself to be also a member of the sensible world—and so subject to the hindrances of sensuous desires.

Pages 113–115—The Antinomy of Freedom and Necessity

Kant's argument obviously raises the problem of freedom and necessity. This problem constitutes what Kant calls an 'antinomy'—that is to say, we are faced with mutually conflicting propositions each of which appears to be the necessary conclusion of an irrefutable argument.

The concept of freedom is an Idea of reason without which there could be no moral judgements, just as the concept of natural necessity (or of cause and effect) is a category of the understanding without which there could be no knowledge of nature. Yet the two concepts are apparently incompatible with each other. According to the first concept our actions must be free; and according to the second concept our actions (as events in the known world of nature) must be governed by the laws of cause and effect. Reason has to show that there is no genuine contradiction between the two concepts or else to abandon freedom in favour of natural necessity, which has at least the advantage of being confirmed in experience.

Pages 115–118—The Two Standpoints

It would be impossible to resolve the contradiction if we conceived of ourselves as free and as determined in the same sense and in the same relationship. We have to show that the contradiction arises from conceiving ourselves in two different senses and relationships and that from this double standpoint these two characteristics not only can, but must, be combined in the same subject. This task is incumbent on speculative philosophy if practical (or moral) philosophy is to be freed from damaging external attacks.

The two standpoints in question are those we have already encountered. Man must—from different points of view—consider himself both as a member of the intelligible world and as a part of the sensible world. Once this is grasped the contradiction disappears. Man can, and indeed must, consider himself to be free as a member of the intelligible world and determined as a part of the sensible world; nor is there any contradiction in supposing that as an *appearance* in the sensible world he is subject to laws which do not apply to him as a *thing in itself*. Thus man does not consider himself responsible for his desires and inclinations, but he does consider himself responsible for indulging them to the detriment of the moral law.

In this passage Kant speaks as if we *know* the intelligible world to be governed by reason. This unguarded statement he immediately proceeds to qualify.

Pages 118–120—There is No Knowledge of the Intelligible World

In thus *conceiving* the intelligible world and so *thinking itself into* the intelligible world practical reason does not overstep its limits: it would do this only if it claimed to *know* the intelligible world and so to *intuit itself* into the intelligible world (since all human knowledge requires sensuous intuition as well as concepts). Our thought of the intelligible world is negative—that is to say, it is only the thought of a world which is *not* known through sense. It enables us, however, not only to conceive the will as negatively free (free from determination by sensuous causes), but also to conceive it as positively free (free to act on its own principle of autonomy). Without this concept of the intelligible world we should have to regard our will as completely determined by sensuous causes, and consequently this concept (or point of view) is necessary if we are to regard our will as rational and so far as free. Admittedly when we think ourselves into the intelligible world our thought carries with it the Idea of an order and a law different from that of the world of sense: it becomes necessary for us to conceive the intelligible world as the totality of rational beings considered as things in themselves. Nevertheless this is not a claim to knowledge of the intelligible world: it is merely a claim to conceive it as compatible with the formal condition of morality— the principle of autonomy.

Pages 120–121—There is No Explanation of Freedom

Reason would overstep all its limits if it pretended to explain how freedom is possible or, in other words, to explain how pure reason can be practical.

The only things we can explain are objects of experience, and to explain them is to bring them under the laws of nature (the laws of cause and effect). Freedom, however, is merely an Idea: it does not supply us with examples which can be known by experience and can be brought under the law of cause and effect. We obviously cannot explain a free action by pointing out its cause, and this means that we cannot explain it at all. All we can do is to *defend* freedom against the attacks of those who claim to know that freedom is impossible. Those who do this very properly apply the laws of nature to man considered as an appearance; but they continue to regard him as an appearance when they are asked to conceive him, *qua* intelligence, as also a thing in himself. To insist on considering man only from one point of view is admittedly to exclude the possibility of regarding him as both free and determined; but the seeming contradiction would fall away if they were willing to reflect that things in themselves must lie behind appearances as their ground and that the laws governing things in themselves need not be the same as the laws governing their appearances.

Pages 121–123—There is No Explanation of Moral Interest

To say that we cannot explain how freedom is possible is also to say that we cannot explain how it is possible to take an interest in the moral law.

An interest arises only through a combination of feeling and reason. A sensuous impulse becomes an interest only when it is conceived by reason, and consequently interests are found only in finite rational agents who are also sensuous. Interests may be regarded as the motives of human action, but we must remember that there are two kinds of interest. When the interest is based on the feeling and desire aroused by some object of experience, we may be said to have a mediate (or pathological) interest in the action appropriate to attain the object. When the interest is aroused by the Idea of the moral law, we may be said to take an immediate (or practical) interest in the action willed in accordance with this Idea.

The basis of the interest we take in moral action is what is called 'moral feeling'. This feeling is the result of recognising the binding character of the moral law and not—as is often held—the gauge of our moral judgements.

This means that pure reason by its Idea of the moral law must be the cause of a moral feeling which can be regarded as the sensuous motive of moral action. We have here a special kind of causality—the causality of a mere Idea—and it is always impossible to know *a priori* what cause will produce what effect. In order to determine the cause of any effect we must have recourse to experience; but experience can discover the relation of cause and effect only between two objects of experience; and in this case the cause is not an object of experience, but is, on the contrary, a mere Idea which can have no object in experience. Hence it is impossible to explain moral interest—that is, to explain why we should take an interest in the universality of our maxim as a law. This doctrine, it may be added, does not appear to be self-consistent, and a different view is taken in the *Critique of Practical Reason*.

The really important point is that the moral law is not valid merely because it interests us. On the contrary, it interests us because we recognise it to be valid.

Kant concludes by saying that the moral law is valid because it springs from our own will as intelligence and so from our proper self; '*but what belongs to mere appearance is necessarily subordinated by reason to the character of the thing in itself*'.

This looks like a metaphysical argument for morality, one based on the superior reality of the intelligible world and so of the rational will. This type of argument seemed to be suggested also (although immediately repudiated) in the section '*How is a categorical imperative possible?*' In the main, however, Kant's metaphysics rests on his ethics rather than *vice versa*.

Pages 124–126—General View of the Argument

We must now turn back to our main question 'How is a categorical imperative possible?' We have answered this question so far as we have shown that it is possible only on the presupposition of freedom and that this presupposition is one which is necessary for rational agents as such. From this presupposition there follows the principle of autonomy and so of the categorical imperative; and this is sufficient for purposes of action—sufficient to convince us of the validity of the categorical imperative as a principle of action. We have also shown that it is not only possible to presuppose freedom without contradicting the necessity which must prevail in the world of nature but that it is also objectively necessary for a rational agent conscious of possessing reason and a will to make this presupposition the condition of all his actions. We cannot, however, explain how freedom is possible, how pure reason by itself can be practical, or how we can take a moral interest in the mere validity of our maxims as universal laws.

We can explain things only by showing them to be the effects of some cause, and this kind of explanation is here excluded. Kant is careful to insist that it is impossible to use the intelligible world as the basis for the required explanation. He is so often charged with doing precisely this that his statement here is worthy of very close attention. I have a necessary Idea of the intelligible world, but it is only an Idea: I can have no knowledge of this world since I have, and can have, no *acquaintance* with such a world (by means of intuition). My Idea of it signifies only a world *not* accessible to our senses—a 'something more' beyond the world of sense: if we could not conceive this 'something more', we should have to say that all action is determined by sensuous motives. Even of the *pure reason* which conceives the Idea or Ideal of the intelligible world (and which also conceives itself as a member of such a world) we have still only an *Idea*: we have only a concept of its form (the principle of autonomy) and a corresponding concept of it as causing actions solely in virtue of its form. Here all sensuous motives are removed, and a mere Idea would itself have to be the motive of moral action. To make this intelligible *a priori* is altogether beyond our powers.

Pages 126–127—The Extreme Limit of Moral Enquiry

With this Idea of an intelligible world as a something more and other than the sensible world we come to the extreme limit of all moral enquiry. To fix this limit is, however, of the utmost practical importance. Unless we see that the world of sense is not the whole of reality, reason will never be kept from trying to discover empirical interests as a basis for morality—a proceeding fatal to morality itself. And unless we see that we can have no knowledge of the 'something more' beyond the world of sense, reason will never be kept from fluttering about impotently in a space which for it is empty— the space of transcendent concepts known to it as 'the intelligible world'—and so from getting lost among mere phantoms of the brain. Empirical and mystical theories of morality can alike be got rid of only when we have determined the limit of moral enquiry.

Yet although all *knowledge* ends when we come to the limit of the sensible world, the Idea of the intelligible world as a whole of all intelligences may serve the purpose of a rational *belief*; and it may arouse a lively interest in the moral law by means of the splendid ideal of a universal kingdom of ends.

Pages 127–128—Concluding Note

In his final note Kant gives some indication of the character of 'reason' in his own technical sense. Reason cannot be satisfied with the merely contingent and always seeks for knowledge of the necessary. But it can grasp the necessary only by finding its condition. Unless the condition is itself necessary reason must still be unsatisfied, so it must seek the condition of the condition and so on *ad infinitum*. Thus it is bound to conceive the Idea of the *totality* of conditions—a totality which, if it is a totality, can have no further conditions and so must be *unconditionally necessary* if there is to be anything necessary at all. Such an Idea of the unconditionally necessary cannot, however, give us knowledge since it has no corresponding sensible object.

We have seen that pure practical reason must similarly conceive a law of action which is unconditionally necessary and is therefore a categorical imperative (for imperfectly rational agents). If we can comprehend a necessity only by discovering its condition, an unconditioned necessity must be incomprehensible. Hence Kant concludes—with an unnecessary appearance of paradox—that the unconditioned necessity of the categorical imperative must be incomprehensible, but that we can comprehend its incomprehensibility.

The practical point of all this is that it is absurd to ask why we should do our duty (or obey the categorical imperative) and to expect as an answer that we should do so because of *something else*—some interest or satisfaction of our own in this world or the next. If such an answer could be given, it would mean that no imperatives were categorical and that duty is a mere illusion.

Groundwork of the Metaphysic of Morals

Preface

[The Different Branches of Philosophy]

Ancient Greek philosophy was divided into three sciences: *physics, ethics*, and *logic*. This division fits the nature of the subject perfectly, and there is no need to improve on it—except perhaps by adding the principle on which it is based. By so doing we may be able on the one hand to guarantee its completeness and on the other to determine correctly its necessary subdivisions.

All rational knowledge is either *material* and concerned with some object, or *formal* and concerned solely with the form of understanding and reason themselves—with the universal rules of thinking as such without regard to differences in its objects. Formal philosophy is called *logic*; while material philosophy, ii which has to do with determinate objects and with the laws to which they are subject, is in turn divided into two, since the laws in question are laws either of *nature* or of *freedom*. The science of the first is called *physics*, that of the second *ethics*. The former is also called natural philosophy, the latter moral philosophy.

Logic can have no empirical part[1]—that is, no part in which the universal and necessary laws of thinking are based on grounds taken from experience. Otherwise it would not be logic—that is, it would not be a canon for understanding and reason, valid for all thinking and capable of demonstration. As against this, both natural and moral philosophy can each have an empirical part, since the former has to formulate its laws for nature as an object of experience, and the latter for the will of man so far as affected by nature—the first set of laws being those in accordance with which everything happens, the second being those in accordance with which everything ought to happen, although they also take into account the conditions under which what ought to happen very often does not happen.

All philosophy so far as it rests on the basis of experience can be called *empirical* philosophy. If it sets forth its doctrines as depending entirely on *a priori* principles, it can be called *pure* philosophy. The latter when wholly formal is called *logic*; but if it is confined to determinate objects of the understanding, it is then called *metaphysics*.

In this way there arises the Idea of a two-fold metaphysic—*a metaphysic of nature* and *a metaphysic of morals*. Thus physics will have its empirical part, but it will also have a rational one; and likewise ethics—although here the empirical part might be called specifically *practical anthropology*, while the rational part might properly be called *morals*.

[The Need for Pure Ethics]

All industries, arts, and crafts have gained by the division of labour—that is to say, one man no longer does everything, but each confines himself to a particular task, differing markedly from others in its technique, so that he may be able to perform it with the highest perfection and with greater ease. Where tasks are not so distinguished and divided, where every man is a jack of all trades, there industry is still sunk in utter barbarism. In itself it might well be a subject not unworthy of examination, if we asked whether pure philosophy in all its parts does not demand its own special craftsman. Would it not be better for the whole of this learned industry if those accustomed to purvey, in accordance with the public taste, a mixture of the empirical and the rational in various proportions unknown even to themselves—the self-styled 'creative thinkers' as opposed to the 'hair-splitters' who attend to the purely rational part—were to be warned against carrying on at once two jobs very different in their technique, each perhaps requiring a special talent and the combination of both in one person producing mere bunglers? Here, however, I confine myself to asking whether the nature of science does not always require that the empirical part should be scrupulously separated from the rational one, and that (empirical) physics proper should be prefaced by a metaphysic of nature, while practical anthropology should be prefaced by a metaphysic of morals—each metaphysic having to be scrupulously cleansed of everything empirical if we are to know how much pure reason can accomplish in both cases and from what sources it can by itself draw its own *a priori* teaching. I leave it an open question whether the latter business[2] is to be conducted by all moralists (whose name is legion) or only by those who feel a vocation for the subject.

Since my aim here is directed strictly to moral philosophy, I limit my proposed question to this point only—Do we not think it a matter of the utmost necessity to work out for once a pure moral philosophy completely cleansed of everything that can only be empirical and appropriate to anthropology?[3] That there must be such a philosophy is already obvious from the common Idea[4] of duty and from the laws of morality. Every one must admit that a law has to carry with it absolute necessity if it is to be valid morally—valid, that is, as a ground of obligation; that the command 'Thou shalt not lie' could not hold merely for men, other rational beings having no obligation to abide by it—and similarly with all other genuine moral laws; that here consequently the ground of obligation must be looked for, not in the nature of man nor in the circumstances of the world in which he is placed, but solely *a priori* in the concepts of pure reason; and that every other precept based on principles of mere experience—and even a precept that may in a certain sense be considered universal, so far as it rests in its slightest part, perhaps only in its motive, on empirical grounds[5]— can indeed be called a practical rule, but never a moral law.

Thus in practical knowledge as a whole, not only are moral laws, together with their principles, essentially different from all the rest in which there is some empirical element, but the whole of moral philosophy is based on the part of it that is pure. When applied to man it does not borrow in the slightest from acquaintance with him (in anthropology), but gives him laws *a priori* as a rational being.[6] These laws admittedly require in addition a power of judgement sharpened by experience, partly in order to distinguish the cases to which they apply, partly to procure for them admittance to the will of man and influence over practice; for man, affected as he is by so many inclinations,[7] is capable of the Idea of a pure practical reason, but he has not so easily the power to realise the Idea *in concreto* in his conduct of life.

A metaphysic of morals is thus indispensably necessary, not merely in order to investigate, from motives of speculation, the source of practical principles which are present *a priori* in our reason, but because morals themselves remain exposed to corruption of all sorts as long as this guiding thread is lacking, this ultimate norm for correct moral judgement. For if any action is to be morally good, it is not enough that it should *conform* to the moral law—it must also be done *for the sake of the moral law*: where this is not so, the conformity is only too contingent and precarious, since the non-moral ground at work will now and then produce actions which accord with the law, but very often actions which transgress it. Now the moral law in its purity and genuineness (and in the field of action it is precisely this that matters most) is to be looked for nowhere else than in a pure philosophy. Hence pure philosophy (that is, metaphysics[8]) must come first, and without it there can be no moral philosophy at all. Indeed a philosophy which mixes up these pure principles with empirical ones does not deserve the name of philosophy (since philosophy is distinguished from ordinary rational knowledge precisely because it sets forth in a separate science what the latter apprehends only as confused with other things). Still less does it deserve the name of moral philosophy, since by this very confusion it undermines even the purity of morals themselves and acts against its own proper purpose.

[The Philosophy of Willing as Such]

It must not be imagined that in the propaedeutics prefixed to his moral philosophy by the celebrated *Wolff*—that is, in the '*Universal Practical Philosophy*',[9] as he called it—we already have what is here demanded and consequently do not need to break entirely new ground. Precisely because it was supposed to be a universal practical philosophy, it has taken into consideration, not a special kind of will—not such a will as is completely determined by *a priori* principles apart from any empirical motives and so can be called a pure will—but willing as such, together with all activities and conditions belonging to it in this general sense. Because of this it differs from a metaphysic of morals in the same way as general logic differs from transcendental philosophy, the first of which sets forth the activities and rules of thinking *as such*, while the second expounds the special activities and rules of *pure* thinking—that is, of the thinking whereby objects are known completely *a priori*;[10] for a metaphysic of morals has to investigate the Idea and principles of a possible *pure* will, and not the activities and conditions of human willing as such, which are drawn for the most part from psychology. The fact that in this 'universal practical philosophy' there is also talk (though quite unjustifiably) about moral laws and duty is no objection to what I say. For the authors of this science remain true to their Idea of it on this point as well: they do not distinguish motives which, as such, are conceived completely *a priori* by reason alone and are genuinely moral, from empirical motives which understanding raises to general concepts by the mere comparison of experiences. On the contrary, without taking into account differences in their origin they consider motives only as regards their relative strength or weakness (looking upon all of them as homogeneous) and construct on this basis their concept of *obligation*. This concept is anything but moral; but its character is only such as is to be expected from a philosophy which never decides, as regards the *source* of all practical concepts, whether they arise only *a posteriori* or *arise a priori* as well.

[The Aim of the *Groundwork*]

Intending, as I do, to publish some day a metaphysic of morals, I issue this *Groundwork* in advance. For such a metaphysic there is strictly no other foundation than a critique of *pure practical reason*, just as for metaphysics[11] there is no other foundation than the critique of pure speculative reason which I have already published. Yet, on the one hand, there is not the same extreme necessity for the former critique as for the latter, since human reason can, in matters of morality, be easily brought to a high degree of accuracy and precision even in the most ordinary intelligence, whereas in its theoretical, but pure, activity it is, on the contrary, out and out dialectical;[12] and, on the other hand, a critique of practical reason, if it is to be complete, requires, on my view, that we should be able at the same time to show the unity of practical and theoretical reason in a common principle, since in the end there can only be one and the same reason, which must be differentiated solely in its application. Here, however, I found myself as yet unable to bring my work to such completeness without introducing considerations of quite another sort and so confusing the reader. This is why, instead of calling it a '*Critique of Pure Practical Reason*', I have adopted the title '*Groundwork of the Metaphysic of Morals*'.

But, in the third place, since a metaphysic of morals, in spite of its horrifying title, can be in a high degree popular and suited to the ordinary intelligence, I think it useful to issue separately this preparatory work on its foundations so that later I need not insert the subtleties inevitable in these matters into doctrines more easy to understand.

The sole aim of the present *Groundwork* is to seek out and establish *the supreme principle of morality*. This by itself is a business which by its very purpose constitutes a whole and has to be separated off from every other enquiry. The application of the principle to the whole system would no doubt throw much light on my answers to this central question, so important and yet hitherto so far from being satisfactorily discussed; and the adequacy it manifests throughout would afford it strong confirmation. All the same, I had to forego this advantage, which in any case would be more flattering to myself than helpful to others, since the convenience of a principle in use and its seeming adequacy afford no completely safe proof of its correctness. They rather awaken a certain bias against examining and weighing it in all strictness for itself without any regard to its consequences.

[The Method of the *Groundwork*]

The method I have adopted in this book is, I believe, one which will work best if we proceed analytically from common knowledge to the formulation of its supreme principle and then back again synthetically from an examination of this principle and its origins to the common knowledge in which we find its application. Hence the division turns out to be as follows:

Chapter 1: Passage from ordinary rational knowledge of morality to philosophical.

Chapter 2: Passage from popular moral philosophy to a metaphysic of morals.

Chapter 3: Final step from a metaphysic of morals to a critique of pure practical reason.

1

Passage from Ordinary Rational Knowledge of Morality to Philosophical

[The Good Will]

It is impossible to conceive anything at all in the world, or even out of it, which can be taken as good without qualification, except a *good will*. Intelligence, wit, judgement, and any other *talents* of the mind we may care to name, or courage, resolution, and constancy of purpose, as qualities of *temperament*, are without doubt good and desirable in many respects; but they can also be extremely bad and hurtful when the will is not good which has to make use of these gifts of nature, and which for this reason has the term '*character*' applied to its peculiar quality. It is exactly the same with *gifts of fortune*. Power, wealth, honour, even health and that complete well-being and contentment with one's state which goes by the name of '*happiness*', produce boldness, and as a consequence often over-boldness as well, unless a good will is present by which their influence on the mind—and so too the whole principle of action—may be corrected and adjusted to universal ends; not to mention that a rational and impartial spectator can never feel approval in contemplating the uninterrupted prosperity of a being graced by no touch of a pure and good will, and that consequently a good will seems to constitute the indispensable condition of our very worthiness to be happy.

Some qualities are even helpful to this good will itself and can make its task very much easier.[1] They have none the less no inner unconditioned worth, but rather presuppose a good will which sets a limit to the esteem in which they are rightly held[2] and does not permit us to regard them as absolutely good. Moderation in affections and passions,[3] self-control, and sober reflexion are not only good in many respects: they may even seem to constitute part of the *inner* worth of a person. Yet they are far from being properly described as good without qualification (however unconditionally they have been commended by the ancients). For without the principles of a good will they may become exceedingly bad; and the very coolness of a scoundrel makes him, not merely more dangerous, but also immediately more abominable in our eyes than we should have taken him to be without it.

[The Good Will and its Results]

A good will is not good because of what it effects or accomplishes—because of its fitness for attaining some proposed end: it is good through its willing alone—that is, good in itself. Considered in itself it is to be esteemed beyond comparison as far higher than anything it could ever bring about merely in order to favour some inclination or, if you like, the sum total of inclinations. Even if, by some special disfavour of destiny or by the niggardly endowment of step-motherly nature, this will is entirely lacking in power to carry out its intentions; if by its utmost effort it still accomplishes nothing, and only good will is left (not, admittedly, as a mere wish, but as the straining of every means so far as they are in our control); even then it would still shine like a jewel for its own sake as something which has its full value in itself. Its usefulness or fruitfulness can neither add to, nor subtract from, this value. Its usefulness would be merely, as it were, the setting which enables us to handle it better in our ordinary dealings or to attract the attention of those not yet sufficiently expert, but not to commend it to experts or to determine its value.

[The Function of Reason]

Yet in this Idea of the absolute value of a mere will, all useful results being left out of account in its assessment, there is something so strange that, in spite of all the agreement it receives even from ordinary reason, there must arise the suspicion that perhaps its secret basis is merely some high-flown fantasticality, and that we may have misunderstood the purpose of nature in attaching reason to our will as its governor. We will therefore submit our Idea to an examination from this point of view.

In the natural constitution of an organic being—that is, of one contrived for the purpose of life—let us take it as a principle that in it no organ is to be found for any end unless it is also the most appropriate to that end and the best fitted for it. Suppose now that for a being possessed of reason and a will the real purpose of nature were his *preservation*, his *welfare*, or in a word his *happiness*. In that case nature would have hit on a very bad arrangement by choosing reason in the creature to carry out this purpose. For all the actions he has to perform with this end in view, and the whole rule of his behaviour, would have been mapped out for him far more accurately by instinct; and the end in question could have been maintained far more surely by instinct than it ever can be by reason. If reason should have been imparted to this favoured creature as well, it would have had to serve him only for contemplating the happy disposition of his nature, for admiring it, for enjoying it, and for being grateful to its beneficent Cause—not for subjecting his power of appetition to such feeble and defective guidance or for meddling incompetently with the purposes of nature. In a word, nature would have prevented reason from striking out into a *practical use* and from presuming, with its feeble vision, to think out for itself a plan for happiness and for the means to its attainment. Nature would herself have taken over the choice, not only of ends, but also of means, and would with wise precaution have entrusted both to instinct alone.

In actual fact too we find that the more a cultivated reason concerns itself with the aim of enjoying life and happiness, the farther does man get away from true contentment. This is why there arises in many, and that too in those who have made most trial of this use of reason, if they are only candid enough to admit it, a certain degree of *misology*—that is, a hatred of reason;[4] for when they balance all the advantage they draw, I will not say from thinking out all the arts of ordinary indulgence, but even from science (which in the last resort seems to them to be also an indulgence of the mind), they discover that they have in fact only brought more trouble on their heads than they have gained in the way of happiness. On this account they come to envy, rather than to despise, the more common run of men, who are closer to the guidance of mere natural instinct, and who do not allow their reason to have much influence on their conduct. So far we must admit that the judgement of those who seek to moderate—and even to reduce below zero—the conceited glorification of such advantages as reason is supposed to provide in the way of happiness and contentment with life is in no way soured or ungrateful to the goodness with which the world is governed. These judgements rather have as their hidden ground the Idea of another and much more worthy purpose of existence, for which, and not for happiness, reason is quite properly designed, and to which, therefore, as a supreme condition the private purposes of man must for the most part be subordinated.

For since reason is not sufficiently serviceable for guiding the will safely as regards its objects and the satisfaction of all 7 our needs (which it in part even multiplies)—a purpose for which an implanted natural instinct would have led us much more surely; and since none the less reason has been imparted to us as a practical power—that is, as one which is to have influence on the *will*; its true function must be to produce a *will* which is *good*, not as a *means* to some further end, but *in itself*; and for this function reason was absolutely necessary in a world where nature, in distributing her aptitudes, has everywhere else gone to work in a purposive manner. Such a will need not on this account be the sole and complete good,[5] but it must be the highest good and the condition of all the rest, even of all our demands for happiness. In that case we can easily reconcile with the wisdom of nature our observation that the cultivation of reason which is required for the first and unconditioned purpose may in many ways, at least in this life, restrict the attainment of the second purpose—namely, happiness— which is always conditioned; and indeed that it can even reduce happiness to less than zero without nature proceeding contrary to its purpose; for reason, which recognises as its highest practical function the establishment of a good will, in attaining this end is capable only of its own peculiar kind of contentment[6]—contentment in fulfilling a purpose which in turn is determined by reason alone, even if this fulfilment should often involve interference with the purposes of inclination.

[The Good Will and Duty]

We have now to elucidate the concept of a will estimable in itself and good apart from any further end. This concept, which is already present in a sound natural understanding and requires not so much to be taught as merely to be clarified, always holds the highest place in estimating the total worth of our actions and constitutes the condition of all the rest. We will therefore take up the concept of *duty*, which includes that of a good will, exposed, however, to certain subjective limitations and obstacles. These, so far from hiding a good will or disguising it, rather bring it out by contrast and make it shine forth more brightly.[7]

[The Motive of Duty]

I will here pass over all actions already recognised as contrary to duty, however useful they may be with a view to this or that end; for about these the question does not even arise whether they could have been done *for the sake of duty* inasmuch as they are directly opposed to it. I will also set aside actions which in fact accord with duty, yet for which men have *no immediate inclination*, but perform them because impelled to do so by some other inclination. For there it is easy to decide whether the action which accords with duty has been done *from duty* or from some purpose of self-interest. This distinction is far more difficult to perceive when the action accords with duty and the subject has in addition an *immediate* inclination to the action. For example,[8] it certainly accords with duty that a grocer should not overcharge his inexperienced customer; and where there is much competition a sensible shopkeeper refrains from so doing and keeps to a fixed and general price for everybody so that a child can buy from him just as well as anyone else. Thus people are served *honestly*; but this is not nearly enough to justify us in believing that the shopkeeper has acted in this way from duty or from principles of fair dealing; his interest required him to do so. We cannot assume him to have in addition an immediate inclination towards his customers, leading him, as it were out of love, to give no man preference over another in the matter of price. Thus the action was done neither from duty nor from immediate inclination, but solely from purposes of self-interest.

On the other hand, to preserve one's life is a duty, and besides this every one has also an immediate inclination to do so. But on account of this the often anxious precautions taken by the greater part of mankind for this purpose have no inner worth, and the maxim[9] of their action is without moral content. They do protect their lives *in conformity with duty*, but not *from the motive* of duty. When on the contrary, disappointments and hopeless misery have quite taken away the taste for life; when a wretched man, strong in soul and more angered at his fate than fainthearted or cast down, longs for death and still preserves his life without loving it—not from inclination or fear but from duty; then indeed his maxim has a moral content.

To help others where one can is a duty, and besides this there are many spirits of so sympathetic a temper that, without any further motive of vanity or self-interest, they find an inner pleasure in spreading happiness around them and can take delight in the contentment of others as their own work. Yet I maintain that in such a case an action of this kind, however right and however amiable it may be, has still no genuinely moral worth. It stands on the same footing as other inclinations[10]—for example, the inclination for honour, which if fortunate enough to hit on something beneficial and right and consequently honourable, deserves praise and encouragement, but not esteem; for its maxim lacks moral content, namely, the performance of such actions, not from inclination, but *from duty*. Suppose then that the mind of this friend of man were overclouded by sorrows of his own which extinguished all sympathy with the fate of others, but that he still had power to help those in distress, though no longer stirred by the need of others because sufficiently occupied with his own; and suppose that, when no longer moved by any inclination, he tears himself out of this deadly insensibility and does the action without any inclination for the sake of duty alone; then for the first time his action has its genuine moral worth. Still further: if nature had implanted little sympathy in this or that man's heart; if (being in other respects an honest fellow) he were cold in temperament and indifferent to the sufferings of others—perhaps because, being endowed with the special gift of patience and robust endurance in his own sufferings, he assumed the like in others or even demanded it; if such a man (who would in truth not be the worst product of nature) were not exactly fashioned by her to be a philanthropist, would he not still find in himself a source from which he might draw a worth far higher than any that a good-natured temperament can have? Assuredly he would. It is precisely in this that the worth of character begins to show—a moral worth and beyond all comparison the highest—namely, that he does good, not from inclination, but from duty.

To assure one's own happiness is a duty (at least indirectly); for discontent with one's state, in a press of cares and amidst unsatisfied wants, might easily become a great *temptation to the transgression of duty*. But here also, apart from regard to duty, all men have already of themselves the strongest and deepest inclination towards happiness, because precisely in this Idea of happiness all inclinations are combined into a sum total.[11] The prescription for happiness is, however, often so constituted as greatly to interfere with some inclinations, and yet men cannot form under the name of 'happiness' any determinate and assured conception of the satisfaction of all inclinations as a sum. Hence it is not to be wondered at that a single inclination which is determinate as to what it promises and as to the time of its satisfaction may outweigh a wavering Idea; and that a man, for example, a sufferer from gout, may choose to enjoy what he fancies and put up with what he can—on the ground that on balance he has here at least not killed the enjoyment of the present moment because of some possibly groundless expectations of the good fortune supposed to attach to soundness of health. But in this case also, when the universal inclination towards happiness has failed to determine his will, when good health, at least for him, has not entered into his calculations as so necessary, what remains over, here as in other cases, is a law—the law of furthering his happiness, not from inclination, but from duty; and in this for the first time his conduct has a real moral worth.

It is doubtless in this sense that we should understand too the passages from Scripture in which we are commanded to love our neighbour and even our enemy. For love out of inclination cannot be commanded; but kindness done from duty—although no inclination impels us, and even although natural and unconquerable disinclination stands in our way—is *practical*, and not *pathological*, love, residing in the will and not in the propensions of feeling, in principles of action and not of melting compassion; and it is this practical love alone which can be an object of command.

[The Formal Principle of Duty]

Our second proposition[12] is this: An action done from duty has its moral worth, *not in the purpose* to be attained by it, but in the maxim according with which it is decided upon; it depends therefore, not on the realisation of the object of the action, but solely on the *principle* of *volition* in accordance with which, irrespective of all objects of the faculty of desire,[13] the action has been performed. That the purposes we may have in our actions, and also their effects considered as ends and motives of the will, can give to actions no unconditioned and moral worth is clear from what has gone before. Where then can this worth be found if we are not to find it in the will's relation to the effect hoped for from the action? It can be found nowhere but *in the principle of the will*, irrespective of the ends which can be brought about by such an action; for between its *a priori* principle, which is formal, and its *a posteriori* motive, which is material, the will stands, so to speak, at a parting of the ways; and since it must be determined by some principle, it will have to be determined by the formal principle or volition when an action is done from duty, where, as we have seen, every material principle is taken away from it.

[Reverence for the Law]

Our third proposition, as an inference from the two preceding, I would express thus: *Duty is the necessity to act out of reverence for the law.* For an object as the effect of my proposed action I can have an *inclination*, but *never reverence*, precisely because it is merely the effect, and not the activity, of a will. Similarly for inclination as such, whether my own or that of another, I cannot have reverence: I can at most in the first case approve, and in the second case sometimes even love—that is, regard it as favourable to my own advantage. Only something which is conjoined with my will solely as a ground and never as an effect—something which does not serve my inclination, but outweighs it or at least leaves it entirely out of account in my choice—and therefore only bare law for its own sake, can be an object of reverence and therewith a command. Now an action done from duty has to set aside altogether the influence of inclination, and along with inclination every object of the will; so there is nothing left able to determine the will except objectively the *law* and subjectively *pure reverence* for this practical law, and therefore the maxim[14] of obeying this law even to the detriment of all my inclinations.

Thus the moral worth of an action does not depend on the result expected from it, and so too does not depend on any principle of action that needs to borrow its motive from this expected result. For all these results (agreeable states and even the promotion of happiness in others) could have been brought about by other causes as well, and consequently their production did not require the will of a rational being, in which, however, the highest and unconditioned good can alone be found. Therefore nothing but the *idea of the law* in itself, *which admittedly is present only in a rational being*—so far as it, and not an expected result, is the ground determining the will—can constitute that pre-eminent good which we call moral, a good which is already present in the person acting on this idea and has not to be awaited merely from the result.[15]

[The Categorical Imperative]

But what kind of law can this be the thought of which, even without regard to the results expected from it, has to determine the will if this is to be called good absolutely and without qualification? Since I have robbed the will of every inducement that might arise for it as a consequence of obeying any particular law, nothing is left but the conformity of actions to universal law as such, and this alone must serve the will as its principle. That is to say, I ought never to act except in such a way *that I can also will that my maxim should become a universal law*. Here bare conformity to universal law as such (without having as its base any law prescribing particular actions) is what serves the will as its principle, and must so serve it if duty is not to be everywhere an empty delusion and a chimerical concept. The ordinary reason of mankind also agrees with this completely in its practical judgements and always has the aforesaid principle before its eyes.

Take this question, for example. May I not, when I am hard pressed, make a promise with the intention of not keeping it? Here I readily distinguish the two senses which the question can have—Is it prudent, or is it right, to make a false promise? The first no doubt can often be the case. I do indeed see that it is not enough for me to extricate myself from present embarrassment by this subterfuge: I have to consider whether from this lie there may not subsequently accrue to me much greater inconvenience than that from which I now escape, and also—since, with all my supposed *astuteness*, to foresee the consequences is not so easy that I can be sure there is no chance, once confidence in me is lost, of this proving far more disadvantageous than all the ills I now think to avoid—whether it may not be a *more prudent* action to proceed here on a general maxim and make it my habit not to give a promise except with the intention of keeping it. Yet it becomes clear to me at once that such a maxim is always founded solely on fear of consequences. To tell the truth for the sake of duty is something entirely different from doing so out of concern for inconvenient results; for in the first case the concept of the action already contains in itself a law for me, while in the second case I have first of all to look around elsewhere in order to see what effects may be bound up with it for me. When I deviate from the principle of duty, this is quite certainly bad; but if I desert my prudential maxim, this can often be greatly to my advantage, though it is admittedly safer to stick to it. Suppose I seek, however, to learn in the quickest way and yet unerringly how to solve the problem 'Does a lying promise accord with duty?' I have then to ask myself 'Should I really be content that my maxim (the maxim of getting out of a difficulty by a false promise) should hold as a universal law (one valid both for myself and others)? And could I really say to myself that every one may make a false promise if he finds himself in a difficulty from which he can extricate himself in no other way?' I then become aware at once that I can indeed will to lie, but I can by no means will a universal law of lying; for by such a law there could properly be no promises at all, since it would be futile to profess a will for future action to others who would not believe my profession or who, if they did so over-hastily, would pay me back in like coin;[16] and consequently my maxim, as soon as it was made a universal law, would be bound to annul itself.

Thus I need no far-reaching ingenuity to find out what I have to do in order to possess a good will. Inexperienced in the course of world affairs and incapable of being prepared for all the chances that happen in it, I ask myself only 'Can you also will that your maxim should become a universal law?' Where you cannot, it is to be rejected, and that not because of a prospective loss to you or even to others, but because it cannot fit as a principle into a possible enactment of universal law. For such an enactment reason compels my immediate reverence, into whose grounds (which the philosopher may investigate) I have as yet no *insight*,[17] although I do at least understand this much: reverence is the assessment of a worth which far outweighs all the worth of what is commended by inclination, and the necessity for me to act out of *pure* reverence for the practical law is what constitutes duty, to which every other motive must give way because it is the condition of a will good *in itself*, whose value is above all else.

[Ordinary Practical Reason]

In studying the moral knowledge of ordinary human reason we have now arrived at its first principle. This principle it admittedly does not conceive thus abstractly in its universal form; but it does always have it actually before its eyes and does use it as a norm of judgement. It would be easy to show here how human reason, with this compass in hand, is well able to distinguish, in all cases that present themselves, what is good or evil, right or wrong—provided that, without the least attempt to teach it anything new, we merely make reason attend, as Socrates did, to its own principle; and how in consequence there is no need of science or philosophy for knowing what man has to do in order to be honest and good, and indeed to be wise and virtuous. It might even be surmised in advance that acquaintance with what every man is obliged to do, and so also to know, will be the affair of every man, even the most ordinary. Yet we cannot observe without admiration the great advantage which the power of practical judgement has over that of theoretical in the minds of ordinary men. In theoretical judgements, when ordinary reason ventures to depart from the laws of experience and the perceptions of sense, it falls into sheer unintelligibility and selfcontradiction, or at least into a chaos of uncertainty, obscurity, and vacillation. On the practical side, however, the power of judgement first begins to show what advantages it has in itself when the ordinary mind excludes all sensuous motives from its practical laws. Then ordinary intelligence becomes even subtle—it may be in juggling with conscience or with other claims as to what is to be called right, or in trying to determine honestly for its own instruction the value of various actions; and, what is most important, it can in the latter case have as good hope of hitting the mark as any that a philosopher can promise himself. Indeed it is almost surer in this than even a philosopher, because he can have no principle different from that of ordinary intelligence, but may easily confuse his judgement with a mass of alien and irrelevant considerations and cause it to swerve from the straight path. Might it not then be more advisable in moral questions to abide by the judgement of ordinary reason and, at the most, to bring in philosophy only in order to set forth the system of morals more fully and intelligibly and to present its rules in a form more convenient for use (though still more so for disputation)—but not in order to lead ordinary human intelligence away from its happy simplicity in respect of action and to set it by means of philosophy on a new path of enquiry and instruction?

[The Need for Philosophy]

Innocence is a splendid thing, only it has the misfortune not to keep very well and to be easily misled. On this account even wisdom—which in itself consists more in doing and not doing than in knowing—does require science as well, not in order to learn from it, but in order to win acceptance and durability for its own prescriptions. Man feels in himself a powerful counterweight to all the commands of duty presented to him by reason as so worthy of esteem—the counterweight of his needs and inclinations, whose total satisfaction he grasps under the name of 'happiness'. But reason, without promising anything to inclination, enjoins its commands relentlessly, and therefore, so to speak, with disregard and neglect of these turbulent and seemingly equitable claims (which refuse to be suppressed by any command). From this there arises a *natural dialectic*—that is, a disposition to quibble with these strict laws of duty, to throw doubt on their validity or at least on their purity and strictness, and to make them, where possible, more adapted to our wishes and inclinations; that is, to pervert their very foundations and destroy their whole dignity—a result which in the end even ordinary human reason is unable to approve.

In this way the *common reason of mankind* is impelled, not by any need for speculation (which never assails it so long as it is content to be mere sound reason), but on practical grounds themselves, to leave its own sphere and take a step into the field of *practical philosophy*. It there seeks to acquire information and precise instruction about the source of its own principle, and about the correct function of this principle in comparison with maxims based on need and inclination, in order that it may escape from the embarrassment of antagonistic claims and may avoid the risk of losing all genuine moral principles because of the ambiguity into which it easily falls. Thus ordinary reason, when cultivated in its practical use, gives rise insensibly to a *dialectic* which constrains it to seek help in philosophy, just as happens in its theoretical use; and consequently in the first case as little as in the second will it anywhere else than in a full critique of our reason be able to find peace.

* A *maxim* is the subjective principle of a volition: an objective principle (that is, one which would also serve subjectively as a practical principle for all rational beings if reason had full control over the faculty of desire) is a practical *law*.

* It might be urged against me that I have merely tried, under cover of the word '*reverence*', to take refuge in an obscure feeling instead of giving a clearly articulated answer to the question by means of a concept of reason. Yet although reverence is a feeling, it is not a feeling *received* through outside influence, but one *self-produced* by a rational concept, and therefore specifically distinct from feelings of the first kind, all of which can be reduced to inclination or fear. What I recognise immediately as law for me, I recognise with reverence, which means merely consciousness of the *subordination* of my will to a law without the mediation of external influences on my senses. Immediate determination of the will by the law and consciousness of this determination is called '*reverence*', so that reverence is regarded as the *effect* of the law on the subject and not as the *cause* of the law. Reverence is properly awareness of a value which demolishes my self-love. Hence there is something which is regarded neither as an object of inclination nor as an object of fear, though it has at the same time analogy with both. The *object* of reverence is the *law* alone—that law which we impose *on ourselves* but yet as necessary in itself. Considered as a law, we are subject to it without any consultation of self-love; considered as self-imposed it is a consequence of our will. In the first respect it[1] is analogous to fear, in the second to inclination. All reverence for a person is properly only reverence for the law (of honesty and so on) of which that person gives us an example. Because we regard the developments of our talents as a duty,[1] we see too in a man of talent a sort of *example of the law* (the law of becoming like him by practice), and this is what constitutes our reverence for him. All moral *interest*, so-called, consists solely in *reverence* for the law.

2

Passage from Popular Moral Philosophy to a Metaphysic of Morals

[The Use of Examples]

If so far we have drawn our concept of duty from the ordinary use of our practical reason, it must by no means be inferred that we have treated it as a concept of experience. On the contrary, when we pay attention to our experience of human conduct, we meet frequent and—as we ourselves admit—justified complaints that we can adduce no certain examples of the spirit which acts out of pure duty, and that, although much may be done *in accordance with* the commands of *duty*, it remains doubtful whether it really is done *for the sake of duty* and so has a moral value. Hence at all times there have been philosophers who have absolutely denied the presence of this spirit in human actions and have ascribed everything to a more or less refined self-love. Yet they have not cast doubt on the rightness of the concept of morality. They have spoken rather with deep regret of the frailty and impurity of human nature, which is on their view noble enough to take as its rule an Idea so worthy of reverence, but at the same time too weak to follow it: the reason which should serve it for making laws it uses only to look after the interest of inclinations, whether singly or—at the best—in their greatest mutual compatibility.

In actual fact it is absolutely impossible for experience to establish with complete certainty a single case in which the maxim of an action in other respects right has rested solely on moral grounds and on the thought of one's duty. It is indeed at times the case that after the keenest self-examination we find nothing that without the moral motive of duty could have been strong enough to move us to this or that good action and to so great a sacrifice; but we cannot infer from this with certainty that it is not some secret impulse of self-love which has actually, under the mere show of the Idea of duty, been the cause genuinely determining our will. We are pleased to flatter ourselves with the false claim to a nobler motive, but in fact we can never, even by the most strenuous self-examination, get to the bottom of our secret impulsions; for when moral value is in question, we are concerned, not with the actions which we see, but with their inner principles, which we cannot see.

Furthermore, to those who deride all morality as the mere phantom of a human imagination which gets above itself out of vanity we can do no service more pleasing than to admit that the concepts of duty must be drawn solely from experience (just as out of slackness we willingly persuade ourselves that this is so in the case of all other concepts); for by so doing we prepare for them an assured triumph. Out of love for humanity I am willing to allow that most of our actions may accord with duty; but if we look more closely at our scheming and striving, we everywhere come across the dear self, which is always turning up; and it is on this that the purpose of our actions is based—not on the strict command of duty, which would often require self-denial. One need not be exactly a foe to virtue, but merely a dispassionate observer declining to take the liveliest wish for goodness straight away as its realisation, in order at certain moments (particularly with advancing years and with a power of judgement at once made shrewder by experience and also more keen in observation) to become doubtful whether any genuine virtue is actually to be encountered in the world. And then nothing can protect us against a complete falling away from our Ideas of duty, or can preserve in the soul a grounded reverence for its law, except the clear conviction that even if there never have been actions springing from such pure sources, the question at issue here is not whether this or that has happened; that, on the contrary, reason by itself and independently of all appearances commands what ought to happen; that consequently actions of which the world has perhaps hitherto given no example— actions whose practicability might well be doubted by those who rest everything on experience—are nevertheless commanded unrelentingly by reason; and that, for instance, although up to now there may have existed no loyal friend, pure loyalty in friendship can be no less required from every man, inasmuch as this duty, prior to all experience, is contained as duty in general[1] in the Idea of a reason which determines the will by *a priori* grounds.

It may be added that unless we wish to deny to the concept of morality all truth and all relation to a possible object, we cannot dispute that its law is of such widespread significance as to hold, not merely for men, but for all *rational beings as such*—not merely subject to contingent conditions and exceptions, but *with absolute necessity*.[2] It is therefore clear that no experience can give us occasion to infer even the possibility of such apodeictic laws. For by what right can we make what is perhaps valid only under the contingent conditions of humanity into an object of unlimited reverence as a universal precept for every rational nature? And how could laws for determining *our* will be taken as laws for determining the will of a rational being as such—and only because of this for determining ours—if these laws were merely empirical and did not have their source completely *a priori* in pure, but practical, reason?

What is more, we cannot do morality a worse service than by seeking to derive it from examples. Every example of it presented to me must first be judged by moral principles in order to decide if it is fit to serve as an original example—that is, as a model: it can in no way supply the prime source for the concept of morality. Even the Holy One of the gospel must first be compared with our ideal of moral perfection before we can recognise him to be such. He also says of himself: 'Why callest thou me (whom thou seest) good? There is none good (the archetype of the good) but one, that is, God (whom thou seest not)'. But where do we get the concept of God as the highest good? Solely from the *Idea* of moral perfection,[3] which reason traces *a priori* and conjoins inseparably with the concept of a free will. Imitation has no place in morality, and examples serve us only for encouragement—that is, they set beyond doubt the practicability of what the law commands; they make perceptible what the practical law expresses more generally; but they can never entitle us to set aside their true original, which resides in reason, and to model ourselves upon examples.

[Popular Philosophy]

If there can be no genuine supreme principle of morality which is not grounded on pure reason alone independently of all experience, it should be unnecessary, I think, even to raise the question whether it is a good thing to set forth in general (*in abstracto*) these concepts which hold *a priori*, together with their corresponding principles, so far as our knowledge is to be distinguished from ordinary knowledge and described as philosophical. Yet in our days it may well be necessary to do so. For if we took a vote on which is to be preferred, pure rational knowledge detached from everything empirical—that is to say, a metaphysic of morals—or popular practical philosophy, we can guess at once on which side the preponderance would fall.

It is certainly most praiseworthy to come down to the level of popular thought when we have previously risen to the principles of pure reason and are fully satisfied of our success. This could be described as first *grounding* moral philosophy on metaphysics[4] and subsequently winning *acceptance* for it by giving it a popular character after it has been established. But it is utterly senseless to aim at popularity in our first enquiry, upon which the whole correctness of our principles depends. It is not merely that such a procedure can never lay claim to the extremely rare merit of a truly *philosophical popularity*, since we require no skill to make ourselves intelligible to the multitude once we renounce all profundity of thought: what it turns out is a disgusting hotch-potch of second-hand observations and semi-rational principles on which the empty-headed regale themselves, because this is something that can be used in the chit-chat of daily life. Men of insight, on the other hand, feel confused by it and avert their eyes with a dissatisfaction which, however, they are unable to cure. Yet philosophers, who can perfectly well see through this deception, get little hearing when they summon us for a time from this would-be popularity in order that they may win the right to be genuinely popular only after definite insight has been attained.

We need only look at the attempts to deal with morality in this favoured style. What we shall encounter in an amazing medley is at one time the particular character of human nature (but along with this also the Idea of a rational nature as such), at another perfection, at another happiness; here moral feeling and there the fear of God; something of this and also something of that. But it never occurs to these writers to ask whether the principles of morality are to be sought at all in our acquaintance with human nature (which we can get only from experience); nor does it occur to them that if this is not so—if these principles are to be found completely *a priori* and free from empirical elements in the concepts of pure reason and absolutely nowhere else even to the slightest extent—they had better adopt the plan of separating off this enquiry altogether as pure practical philosophy or (if one may use a name so much decried) as a metaphysic* of morals; of bringing this to full completeness entirely by itself; and of bidding the public which demands popularity to await in hope the outcome of this undertaking.

Nevertheless such a completely isolated metaphysic of morals, mixed with no anthropology, no theology, no physics or hyper-physics, still less with occult qualities (which might be called hypophysical), is not only an indispensable substratum of all theoretical and precisely defined knowledge of duties, but is at the same time a desideratum of the utmost importance for the actual execution of moral precepts. Unmixed with the alien element of added empirical inducements, the pure thought of duty, and in general of the moral law, has by way of reason alone (which first learns from this that by itself it is able to be practical as well as theoretical) an influence on the human heart so much more powerful than all the further impulsions** capable of being called up from the field of experience that in the consciousness of its own dignity[5] reason despises these impulsions and is able gradually to become their master. In place of this, a mixed moral philosophy, compounded of impulsions from feeling and inclination and at the same time of rational concepts, must make the mind waver between motives which can be brought under no single principle and which can guide us only by mere accident to the good, but very often also to the evil.

[Review of Conclusions]

From these considerations the following conclusions emerge. All moral concepts have their seat and origin in reason completely *a priori*, and indeed in the most ordinary human reason just as much as in the most highly speculative: they cannot be abstracted from any empirical, and therefore merely contingent, knowledge. In this purity of their origin is to be found their very worthiness to serve as supreme practical principles, and everything empirical added to them is just so much taken away from their genuine influence and from the absolute value of the corresponding actions.[6] It is not only a requirement of the utmost necessity in respect of theory, where our concern is solely with speculation, but is also of the utmost practical importance, to draw these concepts and laws from pure reason, to set them forth pure and unmixed, and indeed to determine the extent of this whole practical, but pure, rational knowledge— that is, to determine the whole power of pure practical reason. We ought never— as speculative philosophy[7] does allow and even at times finds necessary—to make principles depend on the special nature of human reason. Since moral laws have to hold for every rational being as such, we ought rather to derive our principles from the general concept of a rational being as such,[8] and on this basis to expound the whole of ethics—which requires anthropology for its *application* to man—at first independently as pure philosophy, that is, entirely as metaphysics[9] (which we can very well do in this wholly abstract kind of knowledge). We know well that without possessing such a metaphysics it is a futile endeavour, I will not say to determine accurately for speculative judgement the moral element of duty in all that accords with duty—but that it is impossible, even in ordinary and practical usage, particularly in that of moral instruction, to base morals on their genuine principles and so to bring about pure moral dispositions and engraft them on men's minds for the highest good of the world.

In this task of ours we have to progress by natural stages, not merely from ordinary moral judgement (which is here worthy of great respect) to philosophical judgement, as we have already done,[10] but from popular philosophy, which goes no further than it can get by fumbling about with the aid of examples, to metaphysics. (This no longer lets itself be held back by anything empirical, and indeed—since it must survey the complete totality[11] of this kind of knowledge—goes right to Ideas, where examples themselves fail.) For this purpose we must follow— and must portray in detail—the power of practical reason from the general rules determining it right up to the point where there springs from it the concept of duty.[12]

[Imperatives in General]

Everything in nature works in accordance with laws. Only a rational being has the power to act *in accordance with his idea* of laws—that is, in accordance with principles—and only so has he a *will*. Since *reason* is required in order to derive actions from laws,[13] the will is nothing but practical reason. If reason infallibly determines the will, then in a being of this kind the actions which are recognised to be objectively necessary are also subjectively necessary—that is to say, the will is then a power to choose *only that* which reason independently of inclination recognises to be practically necessary, that is, to be good. But if reason solely by itself is not sufficient to determine the will; if the will is exposed also to subjective conditions (certain impulsions) which do not always harmonise with the objective ones; if, in a word, the will is not in *itself* completely in accord with reason (as actually happens in the case of men); then actions which are recognised to be objectively necessary are subjectively contingent and the determining of such a will in accordance with objective laws is *necessitation*. That is to say, the relation of objective laws to a will not good through and through is conceived as one in which the will of a rational being, although it is determined[14] by principles of reason, does not necessarily follow these principles in virtue of its own nature.

The conception of an objective principle so far as this principle is necessitating for a will is called a command (of reason), and the formula of this command is called an *Imperative*.

All imperatives are expressed by an '*ought*' (*Sollen*). By this they mark the relation of an objective law of reason to a will which is not necessarily determined by this law in virtue of its subjective constitution (the relation of necessitation). They say that something would be good to do or to leave undone; only they say it to a will which does not always do a thing because it has been informed that this is a good thing to do. The practically *good* is that which determines the will by concepts of reason, and therefore not by subjective causes, but objectively—that is, on grounds valid for every rational being as such. It is distinguished from the *pleasant* as that which influences the will, not as a principle of reason valid for every one, but solely through the medium of sensation by purely subjective causes valid only for the senses of this person or that.*

A perfectly good will would thus stand quite as much under objective laws (laws of the good), but it could not on this account be conceived as *necessitated* to act in conformity with law, since of itself, in accordance with its subjective constitution, it can be determined only by the concept of the good. Hence for the *divine* will, and in general for a *holy* will, there are no imperatives: '*I ought*' is here out of place, because '*I will*' is already of itself necessarily in harmony with the law. Imperatives are in consequence only formulae for expressing the relation of objective laws of willing to the subjective imperfection of the will of this or that rational being—for example, of the human will.

[Classification of Imperatives]

All *imperatives* command either *hypothetically* or *categorically*. Hypothetical imperatives declare a possible action to be practically necessary as a means to the attainment of something else that one wills (or that one may will). A categorical imperative would be one which represented an action as objectively necessary in itself apart from its relation to a further end.

Every practical law represents a possible action as good and therefore as necessary for a subject whose actions are determined by reason. Hence all imperatives are formulae for determining an action which is necessary in accordance with the principle of a will in some sense good. If the action would be good solely as a means *to something else*, the imperative is *hypothetical*; if the action is represented as good *in itself* and therefore as necessary, in virtue of its[15] principle, for a will which of itself accords with reason, then the imperative is *categorical*.

An imperative therefore tells me which of my possible actions would be good; and it formulates a practical rule for a will that does not perform an action straight away because the action is good—whether because the subject does not always know that it is good or because, even if he did know this, he might still act on maxims contrary to the objective principles of practical reason.

A hypothetical imperative thus says only that an action is good for some purpose or other, either *possible* or *actual*. In the first case it is a *problematic* practical principle; in the second case an *assertoric* practical principle. A categorical imperative, which declares an action to be objectively necessary in itself without reference to some purpose—that is, even without any further end—ranks as an *apodeictic* practical principle.

Everything that is possible only through the efforts of some rational being can be conceived as a possible purpose of some will; and consequently there are in fact innumerable principles of action so far as action is thought necessary in order to achieve some possible purpose which can be effected by it. All sciences have a practical part consisting of problems which suppose that some end is possible for us and of imperatives which tell us how it is to be attained. Hence the latter can in general be called imperatives of *skill*. Here there is absolutely no question about the rationality or goodness of the end, but only about what must be done to attain it. A prescription required by a doctor in order to cure his man completely and one required by a poisoner in order to make sure of killing him are of equal value so far as each serves to effect its purpose perfectly. Since in early youth we do not know what ends may present themselves to us in the course of life, parents seek above all to make their children learn things *of many kinds*; they provide carefully for *skill* in the use of means to all sorts of *arbitrary* ends, of none of which can they be certain that it could not[16] in the future become an actual purpose of their ward, while it is always *possible* that he might adopt it. Their care in this matter is so great that they commonly neglect on this account to form and correct the judgement of their children about the worth of the things which they might possibly adopt as ends.

There is, however, *one* end that can be presupposed as actual in all rational beings (so far as they are dependent beings to whom imperatives apply); and thus there is one purpose which they not only *can* have, but which we can assume with certainty that they all do have by a natural necessity—the purpose, namely, of *happiness*. A hypothetical imperative which affirms the practical necessity of an action as a means to the furtherance of happiness is *assertoric*. We may represent it, not simply as necessary to an uncertain, merely possible purpose, but as necessary to a purpose which we can presuppose *a priori* and with certainty to be present in every man because it belongs to his very being. Now skill in the choice of means to one's own greatest well-being can be called *prudence** in the narrowest sense.[17] Thus an imperative concerned with the choice of means to one's own happiness—that is, a precept of prudence—still remains *hypothetical*: an action is commanded, not absolutely, but only as a means to a further purpose.

Finally, there is an imperative which, without being based on, and conditioned by, any further purpose to be attained by a certain line of conduct, enjoins this conduct immediately. This imperative is *categorical*. It is concerned, not with the matter of the action and its presumed results, but with its form and with the principle from which it follows; and what is essentially good in the action consists in the mental disposition, let the consequences be what they may. This imperative may be called the imperative of *morality*.

Willing in accordance with these three kinds of principle is also sharply distinguished by a *dissimilarity* in the necessitation of the will. To make this dissimilarity obvious we should, I think, name these kinds of principle most appropriately in their order if we said there were either *rules* of skill or *counsels* of prudence or *commands* (*laws*) of morality. For only *law* carries with it the concept of an *unconditioned*, and yet objective and so universally valid, *necessity*; and commands are laws which must be obeyed— that is, must be followed even against inclination. *Counsel* does indeed involve necessity, but necessity valid only under a subjective and contingent condition— namely, if this or that man counts this or that as belonging to his happiness. As against this, a categorical imperative is limited by no condition and can quite precisely be called a command, as being absolutely, although practically,[18] necessary. We could also call imperatives of the first kind technical (concerned with art); of the second kind *pragmatic** (concerned with well-being); of the third kind *moral* (concerned with free conduct as such[19]—that is, with morals).

[How are Imperatives Possible?]

The question now arises 'How are all these imperatives possible?' This question does not ask how we can conceive the execution of an action commanded by the imperative, but merely how we can conceive the necessitation of the will expressed by the imperative in setting us a task.[20] How an imperative of skill is possible requires no special discussion. Who wills the end, wills (so far as reason has decisive influence on his actions) also the means which are indispensably necessary and in his power. So far as willing is concerned, this proposition is analytic: for in my willing of an object as an effect there is already conceived[21] the causality of myself as an acting cause—that is, the use of means; and from the concept of willing an end the imperative merely extracts the concept of actions necessary to this end. (Synthetic propositions are required in order to determine the means to a proposed end, but these are concerned, not with the reason for performing the act of will, but with the cause which produces the object.) That in order to divide a line into two equal parts on a sure principle I must from its ends describe two intersecting arcs—this is admittedly taught by mathematics only in synthetic propositions; but when I know that the aforesaid effect can be produced only by such an action, the proposition 'If I fully will the effect, I also will the action required for it' is analytic; for it is one and the same thing to conceive something as an effect possible in a certain way through me and to conceive myself as acting in the same way with respect to it.

If it were only as easy to find a determinate concept of happiness, the imperatives of prudence would agree entirely with those of skill and would be equally analytic. For here as there it could alike be said 'Who wills the end, wills also (necessarily, if he accords with reason) the sole means which are in his power'. Unfortunately, however, the concept of happiness is so indeterminate a concept that although every man wants to attain happiness, he can never say definitely and in unison with himself what it really is that he wants and wills. The reason for this is that all the elements which belong to the concept of happiness are without exception empirical—that is, they must be borrowed from experience; but that none the less there is required for the Idea of happiness an absolute whole, a maximum of well-being in my present, and in every future, state. Now it is impossible for the most intelligent, and at the same time most powerful, but nevertheless finite, being to form here a determinate concept of what he really wills. Is it riches that he wants? How much anxiety, envy, and pestering might he not bring in this way on his own head! Is it knowledge and insight? This might perhaps merely give him an eye so sharp that it would make evils at present hidden from him and yet unavoidable seem all the more frightful, or would add a load of still further needs to the desires which already give him trouble enough. Is it long life? Who will guarantee that it would not be a long misery? Is it at least health? How often has infirmity of body kept a man from excesses into which perfect health would have let him fall!—and so on. In short, he has no principle by which he is able to decide with complete certainty what will make him truly happy, since for this he would require omniscience. Thus we cannot act on determinate principles in order to be happy, but only on empirical counsels, for example, of diet, frugality, politeness, reserve, and so on—things which experience shows contribute most to well-being on the average. From this it follows that imperatives of prudence, speaking strictly, do not command at all—that is, cannot exhibit actions objectively as practically *necessary*; that they are rather to be taken as recommendations (*consilia*), than as commands (*praecepta*), of reason; that the problem of determining certainly and universally what action will promote the happiness of a rational being is completely insoluble; and consequently that in regard to this there is no imperative possible which in the strictest sense could command us to do what will make us happy, since happiness is an Ideal, not of reason, but of imagination—an Ideal resting merely on empirical grounds, of which it is vain to expect that they should determine an action by which we could attain the totality of a series of consequences which is in fact infinite. Nevertheless, if we assume that the means to happiness could be discovered with certainty, this imperative of prudence would be an analytic practical proposition; for it differs from the imperative of skill only in this— that in the latter the end is merely possible, while in the former the end is given. In spite of this difference, since both command solely the means to something assumed to be willed as an end, the imperative which commands him who wills the end to will the means is in both cases analytic. Thus there is likewise no difficulty in regard to the possibility of an imperative of prudence.

Beyond all doubt, the question 'How is the imperative of *morality* possible?' is the only one in need of a solution; for it is in no way hypothetical, and consequently we cannot base the objective necessity which it affirms on any presupposition, as we can with hypothetical imperatives. Only we must never forget here that it is impossible to settle *by an example*, and so empirically, whether there is any imperative of this kind at all: we must rather suspect that all imperatives which seem to be categorical may none the less be covertly hypothetical. Take, for example, the saying 'Thou shalt make no false promises'. Let us assume that the necessity for this abstention is no mere device for the avoidance of some further evil—as it might be said 'You ought not to make a lying promise lest, when this comes to light, you destroy your credit'. Let us hold, on the contrary, that an action of this kind must be considered as bad in itself, and that the imperative of prohibition is therefore categorical. Even so, we cannot with any certainty show by an example that the will is determined here solely by the law without any further motive, although it may appear to be so; for it is always possible that fear of disgrace, perhaps also hidden dread of other risks, may unconsciously influence the will. Who can prove by experience that a cause is not present? Experience shows only that it is not perceived. In such a case, however, the so-called moral imperative, which as such appears to be categorical and unconditioned, would in fact be only a pragmatic prescription calling attention to our advantage and merely bidding us take this into account.

We shall thus have to investigate the possibility of a *categorical* imperative entirely *a priori*, since here we do not enjoy the advantage of having its reality given in experience and so of being obliged merely to explain, and not to establish, its possibility.[22] So much, however, can be seen provisionally—that the categorical imperative alone purports to be a practical *law*, while all the rest may be called *principles* of the will but not laws; for an action necessary merely in order to achieve an arbitrary purpose can be considered as in itself contingent, and we can always escape from the precept if we abandon the purpose; whereas an unconditioned command does not leave it open to the will to do the opposite at its discretion and therefore alone carries with it that necessity which we demand from a law.

In the second place, with this categorical imperative or law of morality the reason for our difficulty (in comprehending its possibility) is a very serious one. We have here a synthetic *a priori* practical proposition;* and since in theoretical knowledge there is so much difficulty in comprehending the possibility of propositions of this kind, it may readily be gathered that in practical knowledge the difficulty will be no less.

[The Formula of Universal Law]

In this task we wish first to enquire whether perhaps the mere concept of a categorical imperative may not also provide us with the formula containing the only proposition that can be a categorical imperative; for even when we know the purport of such an absolute command, the question of its possibility will still require a special and troublesome effort, which we postpone to the final chapter.

When I conceive a *hypothetical* imperative in general, I do not know beforehand what it will contain—until its condition is given. But if I conceive a *categorical* imperative, I know at once what it contains. For since besides the law this imperative contains only the necessity that our maxim* should conform[23] to this law, while the law, as we have seen, contains no condition to limit it, there remains nothing over to which the maxim has to conform except the universality of a law as such; and it is this conformity alone that the imperative properly asserts to be necessary.

There is therefore only a single categorical imperative and it is this: '*Act only on that maxim through*[24] *which you can at the same time will that it should become a universal law.'*

Now if all imperatives of duty can be derived from this one imperative as their principle, then even although we leave it unsettled whether what we call duty may not be an empty concept, we shall still be able to show at least what we understand by it and what the concept means.

[The Formula of the Law of Nature]

Since the universality of the law governing the production of effects constitutes what is properly called *nature* in its most general sense (nature as regards its form)[25]— that is, the existence of things so far as determined by universal laws—the universal imperative of duty may also run as follows: '*Act as if the maxim of your action were to become through your will a universal law of nature.'*

[Illustrations]

We will now enumerate a few duties, following their customary division into duties towards self and duties towards others and into perfect and imperfect duties.*

1. A man feels sick of life as the result of a series of misfortunes that has mounted to the point of despair, but he is still so far in possession of his reason as to ask himself whether taking his own life may not be contrary to his duty to himself. He now applies the test 'Can the maxim of my action really become a universal law of nature?' His maxim is 'From self-love I make it my principle to shorten my life if its continuance threatens more evil than it promises pleasure'. The only further question to ask is whether this principle of self-love can become a universal law of nature. It is then seen at once that a system of nature by whose law the very same feeling whose function (*Bestimmung*) is to stimulate the furtherance of life should actually destroy life would contradict itself and consequently could not subsist as a system of nature.[26] Hence this maxim cannot possibly hold as a universal law of nature and is therefore entirely opposed to the supreme principle of all duty.

2. Another finds himself driven to borrowing money because of need. He well knows that he will not be able to pay it back; but he sees too that he will get no loan unless he gives a firm promise to pay it back within a fixed time. He is inclined to make such a promise; but he has still enough conscience to ask 'Is it not unlawful and contrary to duty to get out of difficulties in this way?' Supposing, however, he did resolve to do so, the maxim of his action would run thus: 'Whenever I believe myself short of money, I will borrow money and promise to pay it back, though I know that this will never be done.' Now this principle of self-love or personal advantage is perhaps quite compatible with my own entire future welfare; only there remains the question 'Is it right?' I therefore transform the demand of self-love into a universal law and frame my question thus: 'How would things stand if my maxim became a universal law?' I then see straight away that this maxim can never rank as a universal law of nature and be self-consistent, but must necessarily contradict itself. For the universality of a law that every one believing himself to be in need can make any promise he pleases with the intention not to keep it would make promising, and the very purpose of promising, itself impossible, since no one would believe he was being promised anything, but would laugh at utterances of this kind as empty shams.

3. A third finds in himself a talent whose cultivation would make him a useful man for all sorts of purposes. But he sees himself in comfortable circumstances, and he prefers to give himself up to pleasure rather than to bother about increasing and improving his fortunate natural aptitudes. Yet he asks himself further 'Does my maxim of neglecting my natural gifts, besides agreeing in itself with my tendency to indulgence, agree also with what is called duty?' He then sees that a system of nature could indeed always subsist under such a universal law, although (like the South Sea Islanders) every man should let his talents rust and should be bent on devoting his life solely to idleness, indulgence, procreation, and, in a word, to enjoyment. Only he cannot possibly *will* that this should become a universal law of nature or should be implanted in us as such a law by a natural instinct. For as a rational being he necessarily wills that all his powers should be developed, since they serve him, and are given him, for all sorts of possible ends.

4. Yet a *fourth* is himself flourishing, but he sees others who have to struggle with great hardships (and whom he could easily help); and he thinks 'What does it matter to me? Let every one be as happy as Heaven wills or as he can make himself; I won't deprive him of anything; I won't even envy him; only I have no wish to contribute anything to his well-being or to his support in distress!' Now admittedly if such an attitude were a universal law of nature, mankind could get on perfectly well—better no doubt than if everybody prates about sympathy and goodwill, and even takes pains, on occasion, to practise them, but on the other hand cheats where he can, traffics in human rights, or violates them in other ways. But although it is possible that a universal law of nature could subsist in harmony with this maxim, yet it is impossible to *will* that such a principle should hold everywhere as a law of nature. For a will which decided in this way would be in conflict with itself, since many a situation might arise in which the man needed love and sympathy from others,[27] and in which, by such a law of nature sprung from his own will, he would rob himself of all hope of the help he wants for himself.

[The Canon of Moral Judgement]

These are some of the many actual duties—or at least of what we take to be such— whose derivation from the single principle cited above leaps to the eye. We must *be able* to will that a maxim of our action should become a universal law—this is the general canon for all moral judgement of action. Some actions are so constituted that their maxim cannot even be *conceived* as a universal law of nature without contradiction, let alone be *willed* as what *ought* to become one. In the case of others we do not find this inner impossibility, but it is still impossible to *will* that their maxim should be raised to the universality of a law of nature, because such a will would contradict itself. It is easily seen that the first kind of action is opposed to strict or narrow (rigorous) duty, the second only to wider (meritorious) duty;[28] and thus that by these examples all duties—so far as the type of obligation is concerned (not the object of dutiful action)[29] —are fully set out in their dependence on our single principle.

If we now attend to ourselves whenever we transgress a duty, we find that we in fact do not will that our maxim should become a universal law—since this is impossible for us—but rather that its opposite should remain a law universally: we only take the liberty of making an *exception* to it for ourselves (or even just for this once) to the advantage of our inclinations. Consequently if we weighed it all up from one and the same point of view—that of reason—we should find a contradiction in our own will, the contradiction that a certain principle should be objectively necessary as a universal law and yet subjectively should not hold universally but should admit of exceptions. Since, however, we first consider our action from the point of view of a will wholly in accord with reason, and then consider precisely the same action from the point of view of a will affected by inclination, there is here actually no contradiction, but rather an opposition of inclination to the precept of reason (*antagonismus*), whereby the universality of the principle (*universalitas*) is turned into a mere generality (*generalitas*) so that the practical principle of reason may meet our maxim half-way. This procedure, though in our own impartial judgement it cannot be justified, proves none the less that we in fact recognise the validity of the categorical imperative and (with all respect for it) merely permit ourselves a few exceptions which are, as we pretend, inconsiderable and apparently forced upon us.

We have thus at least shown this much—that if duty is a concept which is to have meaning and real legislative authority for our actions, this can be expressed only in categorical imperatives and by no means in hypothetical ones. At the same time—and this is already a great deal—we have set forth distinctly, and determinately for every type of application, the content of the categorical imperative, which must contain the principle of all duty (if there is to be such a thing at all). But we are still not so far advanced as to prove *a priori* that there actually is an imperative of this kind—that there is a practical law which by itself commands absolutely and without any further motives, and that the following of this law is duty.

[The Need for Pure Ethics]

For the purpose of achieving this proof it is of the utmost importance to take warning that we should not dream for a moment of trying to derive the reality of this principle from *the special characteristics of human nature*. For duty has to be a practical, unconditioned necessity of action; it must therefore hold for all rational beings (to whom alone an imperative can apply at all), and *only because of this* can it also be a law for all human wills. Whatever, on the other hand, is derived from the special predisposition of humanity, from certain feelings and propensities, and even, if this were possible, from some special bent peculiar to human reason and not holding necessarily for the will of every rational being—all this can indeed supply a personal maxim, but not a law: it can give us a subjective principle—one on which we have a propensity and inclination to act—but not an objective one on which we should be *directed* to act although our every propensity, inclination, and natural bent were opposed to it; so much so that the sublimity and inner worth of the command is the more manifest[30] in a duty, the fewer are the subjective causes for obeying it and the more those against—without, however, on this account weakening in the slightest the necessitation exercised by the law or detracting anything from its validity.

It is here that philosophy is seen in actual fact to be placed in a precarious position, which is supposed to be firm although neither in heaven nor on earth is there anything from which it depends or on which it is based. It is here that she has to show her purity as the authoress of her own laws—not as the mouthpiece of laws whispered to her by some implanted sense or by who knows what tutelary nature, all of which laws together, though they may always be better than nothing, can never furnish us with principles dictated by reason. These principles must have an origin entirely and completely *a priori* and must at the same time derive from this their sovereign authority—that they expect nothing from the inclinations of man, but everything from the supremacy of the law and from the reverence due to it, or in default of this condemn man to self-contempt and inward abhorrence.

Hence everything that is empirical is, as a contribution to the principle of morality,[31] not only wholly unsuitable for the purpose, but is even highly injurious to the purity of morals; for in morals the proper worth of an absolutely good will, a worth elevated above all price, lies precisely in this—that the principle of action is free from all influence by contingent grounds, the only kind that experience can supply. Against the slack, or indeed ignoble, attitude which seeks for the moral principle among empirical motives and laws we cannot give a warning too strongly or too often; for human reason in its weariness is fain to rest upon this pillow and in a dream of sweet illusions (which lead it to embrace a cloud in mistake for Juno)[32] to foist into the place of morality some misbegotten mongrel patched up from limbs of very varied ancestry and looking like anything you please, only not like virtue, to him who has once beheld her in her true shape.*

Our question therefore is this: 'Is it a necessary law *for all rational beings* always to judge their actions by reference to those maxims of which they can themselves will that they should serve as universal laws?' If there is such a law, it must already be connected (entirely *a priori*) with the concept of the will of a rational being as such.[33] But in order to discover this connexion we must, however much we may bristle, take a step beyond it— that is, into metaphysics, although into a region of it different from that of speculative philosophy, namely, the metaphysic of morals.[34] In practical philosophy we are not concerned with accepting reasons for what *happens*, but with accepting laws of what *ought to happen* even if it never does happen—that is, objective practical laws. And here we have no need to set up an enquiry as to the reasons why anything pleases or displeases; how the pleasure of mere sensation differs from taste, and whether the latter differs from a universal approval by reason;[35] whereon feelings of pleasure and displeasure are based; how from these feelings there arise desires and inclinations; and how from these in turn, with the co-operation of reason, there arise maxims. All this belongs to empirical psychology, which would constitute the second part of the doctrine of nature, if we take this doctrine to be the *philosophy of nature* so far as grounded on *empirical laws*.[36] Here, however, we are discussing objective practical laws, and consequently the relation of a will to itself as determined solely by reason. Everything related to the empirical then falls away of itself; for if *reason entirely by itself* determines conduct (and it is the possibility of this which we now wish to investigate), it must necessarily do so *a priori*.

[The Formula of the End in Itself]

The will is conceived as a power of determining oneself to action *in accordance with the idea of certain laws*. And such a power can be found only in rational beings. Now what serves the will as a subjective[37] ground of its self-determination is an *end*; and this, if it is given by reason alone, must be equally valid for all rational beings. What, on the other hand, contains merely the ground of the possibility of an action whose effect is an end is called a *means*.[38] The subjective ground of a desire is an *impulsion* (*Triebfeder*); the objective ground of a volition is a *motive* (*Bewegungsgrund*). Hence the difference between subjective ends, which are based on impulsions, and objective ends, which depend on motives valid for every rational being. Practical principles are *formal* if they abstract from all subjective ends; they are *material*, on the other hand, if they are based on such ends and consequently on certain impulsions.[39] Ends that a rational being adopts arbitrarily as *effects* of his action (material ends) are in every case only relative; for it is solely their relation to special characteristics in the subject's power of appetition which gives them their value. Hence this value can provide no universal principles, no principles valid and necessary for all rational beings and also for every volition[40]—that is, no practical laws. Consequently all these relative ends can be the ground only of hypothetical imperatives.

Suppose, however, there were something *whose existence* has *in itself* an absolute value, something which as *an end in itself* could be a ground of determinate laws; then in it, and in it alone, would there be the ground of a possible categorical imperative— that is, of a practical law.

Now I say that man, and in general every rational being, *exists* as an end in himself, *not merely as a means* for arbitrary use by this or that will: he must in all his actions, whether they are directed to himself or to other rational beings, always be viewed *at the same time as an end*. All the objects of inclination have only a conditioned value; for if there were not these inclinations and the needs grounded on them,[41] their object would be valueless. Inclinations themselves, as sources of needs, are so far from having an absolute value to make them desirable for their own sake that it must rather be the universal wish of every rational being to be wholly free from them.[42] Thus the value of all objects that can *be* produced by our actions is always conditioned. Beings whose existence depends, not on our will, but on nature, have none the less, if they are non-rational beings, only a relative value as means and are consequently called *things*. Rational beings, on the other hand, are called *persons* because their nature already marks them out as ends in themselves—that is, as something which ought not to be used merely as a means—and consequently imposes to that extent a limit on all arbitrary treatment of them (and is an object of reverence). Persons, therefore, are not merely subjective ends whose existence as an object of our actions has a value *for us*: they are *objective ends*—that is, things whose existence is in itself an end, and indeed an end such that in its place we can put no other end to which they should serve *simply* as means; for unless this is so, nothing at all of *absolute* value would be found anywhere. But if all value were conditioned—that is, contingent—then no supreme principle could be found for reason at all.

If then there is to be a supreme practical principle and—so far as the human will is concerned—a categorical imperative,[43] it must be such that from the idea of something which is necessarily an end for every one because it is an *end in itself* it forms an *objective* principle of the will and consequently can serve as a practical law. The ground of this principle is: *Rational nature exists as an end in itself*. This is the way in which a man necessarily conceives his own existence: it is therefore so far a *subjective* principle of human actions. But it is also the way in which every other rational being conceives his existence on the same rational ground which is valid also for me;* hence it is at the same time an *objective* principle, from which, as a supreme practical ground, it must be possible to derive all laws for the will. The practical imperative will therefore be as follows: *Act in such a way that you always treat humanity,*[44] *whether in your own person or in the person of any other, never simply*[45] *as a means, but always at the same time as an end.* We will now consider whether this can be carried out in practice.

[Illustrations]

Let us keep to our previous examples.

First, as regards the concept of necessary duty to oneself, the man who contemplates suicide will ask 'Can my action be compatible with the Idea of humanity *as an end in itself?*' If he does away with himself in order to escape from a painful situation, he is making use of a person merely *as a means* to maintain a tolerable state of affairs till the end of his life. But man is not a thing—not something to be used *merely* as a means: he must always in all his actions be regarded as an end in himself. Hence I cannot dispose of man in my person by maiming, spoiling, or killing. (A more precise determination of this principle in order to avoid all misunderstanding—for example, about having limbs amputated to save myself or about exposing my life to danger in order to preserve it, and so on—I must here forgo: this question belongs to morals proper.)

Secondly, so far as necessary or strict duty to others is concerned, the man who has a mind to make a false promise to others will see at once that he is intending to make use of another man *merely as a means* to an end he does not share. For the man whom I seek to use for my own purposes by such a promise cannot possibly agree with my way of behaving to him, and so cannot himself share the end of the action. This incompatibility with the principle of duty to others leaps to the eye more obviously when we bring in examples of attempts on the freedom and property of others. For then it is manifest that a violator of the rights of man intends to use the person of others merely as a means without taking into consideration that, as rational beings, they ought always at the same time to be rated as ends—that is, only as beings who must themselves be able to share in the end of the very same action.*

Thirdly, in regard to contingent (meritorious) duty to oneself, it is not enough that an action should refrain from conflicting with humanity in our own person as an end in itself: it must also *harmonise with this end*. Now there are in humanity capacities for greater perfection which form part of nature's purpose for humanity in our person.[46] To neglect these can admittedly be compatible with the *maintenance* of humanity as an end in itself, but not with the *promotion* of this end.

Fourthly, as regards meritorious duties to others, the natural end which all men seek is their own happiness. Now humanity could no doubt subsist if everybody contributed nothing to the happiness of others but at the same time refrained from deliberately impairing their happiness. This is, however, merely to agree negatively and not positively with *humanity as an end in itself* unless every one endeavours also, so far as in him lies, to further the ends of others. For the ends of a subject who is an end in himself must, if this conception is to have its *full* effect in me, be also, as far as possible, *my* ends.

[The Formula of Autonomy]

This principle of humanity, and in general of every rational agent, *as an end in itself* (a principle which is the supreme limiting condition of every man's freedom of action) is not borrowed from experience; firstly, because it is universal, applying as it does to all rational beings as such, and no experience is adequate to determine universality; secondly, because in it humanity is conceived, not as an end of man (subjectively)— that is, as an object which, as a matter of fact, happens to be made an end— but as an objective end—one which, be our ends what they may, must, as a law, constitute the supreme limiting condition of all subjective ends and so must spring from pure reason. That is to say, the ground for every enactment of practical law lies *objectively in the rule* and in the form of universality which (according to our first principle) makes the rule capable of being a law (and indeed a law of nature); *subjectively*, however, it lies in the *end*; but (according to our second principle) the subject of all ends is to be found in every rational being as an end in himself. From this there now follows our third practical principle for the will—as the supreme condition of the will's conformity with universal practical reason—namely, the Idea *of the will of every rational being as a will which makes universal law.*

By this principle all maxims are repudiated which cannot accord with the will's own enactment of universal law. The will is therefore not merely subject to the law, but is so subject that it must be considered as also *making the law* for itself and precisely on this account as first of all subject to the law (of which it can regard itself as the author).

[The Exclusion of Interest]

Imperatives as formulated above—namely, the imperative enjoining conformity of actions to universal law on the analogy of a *natural order* and that enjoining the universal *supremacy* of rational beings in themselves *as ends*—did, by the mere fact that they were represented as categorical, exclude from their sovereign authority every admixture of interest as a motive. They were, however, merely *assumed* to be categorical because we were bound to make this assumption if we wished to explain the concept of duty. That there were practical propositions which commanded categorically could not itself be proved, any more than it can be proved in this chapter generally; but one thing could have been done—namely, to show that in willing for the sake of duty renunciation of all interest,[47] as the specific mark distinguishing a categorical from a hypothetical imperative, was expressed in the very imperative itself by means of some determination inherent in it. This is what is done in the present third formulation of the principle—namely, in the Idea of the will of every rational being as *a will which makes universal law.*

Once we conceive a will of this kind, it becomes clear that while a will *which is subject to law* may be bound to this law by some interest, nevertheless a will which is itself a supreme lawgiver cannot possibly as such depend on any interest; for a will which is dependent in this way would itself require yet a further law in order to restrict the interest of self-love to the condition that this interest should itself be valid as a universal law.[48]

Thus the *principle* that every human will is *a will which by all its maxims enacts universal law**—provided only that it were right in other ways—would be *well suited* to be a categorical imperative in this respect: that precisely because of the Idea of making universal law it is *based on no interest* and consequently can alone among all possible imperatives be *unconditioned*. Or better still—to convert the proposition—if there is a categorical imperative (that is, a law for the will of every rational being), it can command us only to act always on the maxim of such a will in us as can at the same time look upon itself as making universal law; for only then is the practical principle and the imperative which we obey unconditioned, since it is wholly impossible for it to be based on any interest.

We need not now wonder, when we look back upon all the previous efforts that have been made to discover the principle of morality, why they have one and all been bound to fail. Their authors saw man as tied to laws by his duty, but it never occurred to them that he is subject only to *laws which are made by himself* and yet are *universal*, and that he is bound only to act in conformity with a will which is his own but has as nature's purpose for it[49] the function of making universal law. For when they thought of man merely as subject to a law (whatever it might be), the law had to carry with it some interest in order to attract or compel, because it did not spring as a law from *his own* will: in order to conform with the law his will had to be necessitated by *something else* to act in a certain way. This absolutely inevitable conclusion meant that all the labour spent in trying to find a supreme principle of duty was lost beyond recall; for what they discovered was never duty, but only the necessity of acting from a certain interest. This interest might be one's own or another's; but on such a view the imperative was bound to be always a conditioned one and could not possibly serve as a moral law. I will therefore call my principle the principle of the *Autonomy* of the will in contrast with all others, which I consequently class under *Heteronomy*.

[The Formula of the Kingdom of Ends]

The concept of every rational being as one who must regard himself as making universal law by all the maxims of his will, and must seek to judge himself and his actions from this point of view, leads to a closely connected and very fruitful concept—namely, that of *a kingdom of ends*.

I understand by a '*kingdom*' a systematic union of different rational beings under common laws. Now since laws determine ends as regards their universal validity, we shall be able—if we abstract from the personal differences between rational beings, and also from all the content of their private ends—to conceive a whole of all ends in systematic conjunction (a whole both of rational beings as ends in themselves and also of the personal ends[50] which each may set before himself); that is, we shall be able to conceive a kingdom of ends which is possible in accordance with the above principles.

For rational beings all stand under the *law* that each of them should treat himself and all others, *never merely as a means*, but always *at the same time as an end in himself.* But by so doing there arises a systematic union of rational beings under common objective laws—that is, a kingdom. Since these laws are directed precisely to the relation of such beings to one another as ends and means, this kingdom can be called a kingdom of ends (which is admittedly only an Ideal).

A rational being belongs to the kingdom of ends as a *member*, when, although he makes its universal laws, he is also himself subject to these laws. He belongs to it as its *head*, when as the maker of laws he is himself subject to the will of no other.[51]

A rational being must always regard himself as making laws in a kingdom of ends which is possible through freedom of the will—whether it be as member or as head. The position of the latter he can maintain, not in virtue of the maxim of his will alone, but only if he is a completely independent being, without needs and with an unlimited power adequate to his will.

Thus morality consists in the relation of all action to the making of laws whereby alone a kingdom of ends is possible. This making of laws must be found in every rational being himself and must be able to spring from his will. The principle of his will is therefore never to perform an action except on a maxim such as can also be a universal law, and consequently such *that the will can regard itself as at the same time making universal law by means of its maxim.* Where maxims are not already by their very nature in harmony with this objective principle of rational beings as makers of universal law, the necessity of acting on this principle is practical necessitation—that is, *duty.* Duty does not apply to the head in a kingdom of ends, but it does apply to every member and to all members in equal measure.

The practical necessity of acting on this principle—that is, duty—is in no way based on feelings, impulses, and inclinations, but only on the relation of rational beings to one another, a relation in which the will of a rational being must always be regarded as *making universal law*, because otherwise he could not be conceived as *an end in himself.* Reason thus related every maxim of the will, considered as making universal law, to every other will and also to every action towards oneself: it does so, not because of any further motive or future advantage, but from the Idea of the *dignity* of a rational being who obeys no law other than that which he at the same time enacts himself.

[The Dignity of Virtue]

In the kingdom of ends everything has either a *price* or a *dignity.* If it has a price, something else can be put in its place as an *equivalent*; if it is exalted above all price and so admits of no equivalent, then it has a dignity.

What is relative to universal human inclinations and needs has a *market price*; what, even without presupposing a need, accords with a certain taste—that is, with satisfaction in the mere purposeless play of our mental powers[52] —has a *fancy price* (*Affektionspreis*); but that which constitutes the sole condition under which anything can be an end in itself has not merely a relative value—that is, a price—but has an intrinsic value—that is, *dignity.*

Now morality is the only condition under which a rational being can be an end in himself; for only through this is it possible to be a law-making member in a kingdom of ends. Therefore morality, and humanity so far as it is capable of morality, is the only thing which has dignity. Skill and diligence in work have a market price; wit, lively imagination, and humour have a fancy price; but fidelity to promises and kindness based on principle (not on instinct) have an intrinsic worth. In default of these, nature and art alike contain nothing to put in their place;[53] for their worth consists, not in the effects which result from them, not in the advantage or profit they produce, but in the attitudes of mind—that is, in the maxims of the will— which are ready in this way to manifest themselves in action even if they are not favoured by success. Such actions too need no recommendation from any subjective disposition or taste in order to meet with immediate favour and approval; they need no immediate propensity or feeling for themselves; they exhibit the will which performs them as an object of immediate reverence; nor is anything other than reason required to *impose* them upon the will, not to *coax* them from the will—which last would anyhow be a contradiction in the case of duties. This assessment reveals as dignity the value of such a mental attitude and puts it infinitely above all price, with which it cannot be brought into reckoning or comparison without, as it were, a profanation of its sanctity.

What is it then that entitles a morally good attitude of mind—or virtue—to make claims so high? It is nothing less than the *share* which it affords to a rational being *in the making of universal law*, and which therefore fits him to be a member in a possible kingdom of ends. For this he was already marked out in virtue of his own proper nature as an end in himself and consequently as a maker of laws in the kingdom of ends—as free in respect of all laws of nature, obeying only those laws which he makes himself and in virtue of which his maxims can have their part in the making of universal law (to which he at the same time subjects himself). For nothing can have a value other than that determined for it by the law. But the law-making which determines all value must for this reason have a dignity—that is, an unconditioned and incomparable worth—for the appreciation of which, as necessarily given by a rational being, the word '*reverence*' is the only becoming expression. *Autonomy* is therefore the ground of the dignity of human nature and of every rational nature.

[Review of the Formulae]

The aforesaid three ways of representing the principle of morality are at bottom merely so many formulations of precisely the same law, one of them by itself containing a combination of the other two. There is nevertheless a difference between them, which, however, is subjectively rather than objectively practical: that is to say, its purpose is to bring an Idea of reason nearer to intuition (in accordance with a certain analogy) and so nearer to feeling. All maxims have, in short,

1. a *form*, which consists in their universality; and in this respect the formula of the moral imperative is expressed thus: 'Maxims must be chosen as if they had to hold as universal laws of nature' ;

2. a *matter*—that is, an end; and in this respect the formula says: 'A rational being, as by his very nature an end and consequently an end in himself, must serve for every maxim as a condition limiting all merely relative and arbitrary ends';

3. a *complete determination*[54] of all maxims by the following formula, namely: 'All maxims as proceeding from our own making of law ought to harmonise with a possible kingdom of ends as a kingdom of nature.'* This progression may be said to take place through the categories of the *unity* of the form of will (its universality); of the *multiplicity* of its matter (its objects—that is, its ends); and of the *totality* or completeness of its system of ends.[55] It is, however, better if in moral *judgement* we proceed always in accordance with the strict method and take as our basis the universal formula of the categorical imperative: '*Act on the maxim which can at the*

same time be made a universal law'. If, however, we wish also to secure acceptance for the moral law, it is very useful to bring one and the same action under the above-mentioned three concepts and so, as far as we can, to bring the universal formula[56] nearer to intuition.

[Review of the Whole Argument]

We can now end at the point from which we started out at the beginning—namely, the concept of an unconditionally good will. The *will is absolutely good* if it cannot be evil—that is, if its maxim, when made into a universal law, can never be in conflict with itself. This principle is therefore also its supreme law: 'Act always on that maxim whose universality as a law you can at the same time will'. This is the one principle on which a will can never be in conflict with itself, and such an imperative is categorical. Because the validity of the will as a universal law for possible actions is analogous to the universal interconnexion of existent things in accordance with universal laws—which constitutes the formal aspect of nature as such[57]—we can also express the categorical imperative as follows: '*Act on that maxim which can at the same time have for its object[58] itself as a universal law of nature*'. In this way we provide the formula for an absolutely good will.

Rational nature separates itself out from all other things by the fact that it sets itself an end. An end would thus be the matter of every good will. But in the Idea of a will which is absolutely good—good without any qualifying condition (namely, that it should attain this or that end)—there must be complete abstraction from every end that has to be *produced* (as something which would make every will only relatively good). Hence the end must here be conceived, not as an end to be produced, *but as a self-existent* end. It must therefore be conceived only negatively[59]—that is, as an end against which we should never act, and consequently as one which in all our willing we must never rate *merely* as a means, but always at the same time as an end. Now this end can be nothing other than the subject of all possible ends himself, because this subject is also the subject of a will that may be absolutely good; for such a will cannot without contradiction be subordinated to any other object. The principle 'So act in relation to every rational being (both to yourself and to others) that he may at the same time count in your maxim as an end in himself' is thus at bottom the same as the principle 'Act on a maxim which at the same time contains in itself its own universal validity for every rational being'. For to say that in using means to every end I ought to restrict my maxim by the condition that it should also be universally valid as a law for every subject is just the same as to say this—that a subject of ends, namely, a rational being himself, must be made the ground for all maxims of action, never *merely* as a means, but as a supreme condition restricting the use of every means—that is, always also as an end.

Now from this it unquestionably follows that every rational being, as an end in himself, must be able to regard himself as also the maker of universal law in respect of any law whatever to which he may be subjected; for it is precisely the fitness of his maxims to make universal law that marks him out as an end in himself. It follows equally that this dignity (or prerogative) of his above all the mere things of nature carries with it the necessity of always choosing his maxims from the point of view of himself—and also of every other rational being—as a maker of law (and this is why they are called persons). It is in this way that a world of rational beings (*mundus intelligibilis*) is possible as a kingdom of ends—possible, that is, through the making of their own laws by all persons as its members. Accordingly every rational being must so act as if he were through his maxims always a law-making member in the universal kingdom of ends. The formal principle of such maxims is 'So act as if your maxims had to serve at the same time as a universal law (for all rational beings)'. Thus a kingdom of ends is possible only on the analogy of a kingdom of nature; yet the kingdom of ends is possible only through maxims—that is, self-imposed rules— while nature is possible only through laws concerned with causes whose action is necessitated from without. In spite of this difference, we give to nature as a whole, even although it is regarded as a machine, the name of a 'kingdom of nature' so far as—and for the reason that—it stands in a relation to rational beings as its ends.[60] Now a kingdom of ends would actually come into existence through maxims which the categorical imperative prescribes as a rule for all rational beings, *if these maxims were universally followed.* Yet even if a rational being were himself to follow such a maxim strictly, he cannot count on everybody else being faithful to it on this ground, nor can he be confident that the kingdom of nature and its purposive order will work in harmony with him, as a fitting member, towards a kingdom of ends made possible by himself—or, in other words, that it will favour his expectation of happiness.[61] But in spite of this the law 'Act on the maxims of a member who makes universal laws for a merely possible kingdom of ends' remains in full force, since its command is categorical. And precisely here we encounter the paradox that without any further end or advantage to be attained the mere dignity of humanity, that is, of rational nature in man—and consequently that reverence for a mere Idea—should function as an inflexible precept for the will; and that it is just this freedom from dependence on interested motives which constitutes the sublimity of a maxim and the worthiness of every rational subject to be a law-making member in the kingdom of ends; for otherwise he would have to be regarded as subject only to the law of nature—the law of his own needs. Even if it were thought that both the kingdom of nature and the kingdom of ends were united under one head and that thus the latter kingdom ceased to be a mere Idea and achieved genuine reality, the Idea would indeed gain by this the addition of a strong motive, but never any increase in its intrinsic worth; for, even if this were so, it would still be necessary to conceive the unique and absolute law-giver himself as judging the worth of rational beings solely by the disinterested behaviour they prescribed to themselves in virtue of this Idea alone. The essence of things does not vary with their external relations; and where there is something which, without regard to such relations, constitutes by itself the absolute worth of man, it is by this that man must also be judged by everyone whatsoever—even by the Supreme Being. Thus *morality* lies in the relation of actions to the autonomy of the will— that is, to a possible making of universal laws by means of its maxims. An action which is compatible with the autonomy of the will is *permitted*; one which does not harmonise with it is *forbidden*. A will whose maxims necessarily accord with the laws of autonomy is a *holy*, or absolutely good, will. The dependence of a will not absolutely good on the principle of autonomy (that is, moral necessitation) is *obligation*. Obligation can thus have no reference to a holy being. The objective necessity to act from obligation is called *duty*.

From what was said a little time ago we can now easily explain how it comes about that, although in the concept of duty we think of subjection to the law, yet we also at the same time attribute to the person who fulfils all his duties a certain sublimity and *dignity*. For it is not in so far as he is *subject* to the law that he has sublimity, but rather in so far as, in regard to this very same law, he is at the same time its *author* and is subordinated to it only on this ground. We have also shown above[62] how neither fear nor inclination, but solely reverence for the law, is the motive which can give an action moral worth. Our own will, provided it were to act only under the condition of being able to make universal law by means of its maxims—this ideal will which can be ours is the proper object of reverence; and the dignity of man consists precisely in his capacity to make universal law, although only on condition of being himself also subject to the law he makes.

Autonomy of the Will as the Supreme Principle of Morality

Autonomy of the will is the property the will has of being a law to itself (independently of every property belonging to the object of volition). Hence the principle of autonomy is 'Never to choose except in such a way that in the same volition the maxims of your choice are also present as universal law'. That this practical rule is an imperative— that is, that the will of every rational being is necessarily bound to the rule as a condition—cannot be proved by mere analysis of the concepts contained in it, since it is a synthetic proposition. For proof we should have to go beyond knowledge of objects and pass to a critique of the subject—that is, of pure practical reason—since this synthetic proposition, as commanding apodeictically, must be capable of being known entirely *a priori*. This task does not belong to the present chapter. None the less by mere analysis of the concepts of morality we can quite well show that the above principle of autonomy is the sole principle of ethics. For analysis finds that the principle of morality must be a categorical imperative, and that this in turn commands nothing more nor less than precisely this autonomy.

Heteronomy of the Will as the Source of All Spurious Principles of Morality

If the will seeks the law that is to determine it *anywhere else* than in the fitness of its maxims for its own making of universal law—if therefore in going beyond itself it seeks this law in the character of any of its objects—the result is always *heteronomy*. In that case the will does not give itself the law, but the object does so in virtue of its relation to the will. This relation, whether based on inclination or on rational ideas, can give rise only to hypothetical imperatives: 'I ought to do something *because I will something else*'. As against this, the moral, and therefore categorical, imperative, says: 'I ought to will thus or thus, although I have not willed something else'. For example, the first says: 'I ought not to lie if I want to maintain my reputation'; while the second says: 'I ought not to lie even if so doing were to bring me not the slightest disgrace.' The second imperative must therefore abstract from all objects to this extent—they should be without any *influence*[63] at all on the will so that practical reason (the will) may not merely administer an alien interest but may simply manifest its own sovereign authority as the supreme maker of law. Thus, for example, the reason[64] why I ought to promote the happiness of others is not because the realisation of their happiness is of consequence to myself (whether on account of immediate inclination or on account of some satisfaction gained indirectly through reason), but solely because a maxim which excludes this cannot also be present in one and the same volition as a universal law.

Classification of All Possible Principles of Morality Based on the Assumption of Heteronomy as their Fundamental Concept

Here, as everywhere else, human reason in its pure use—so long as it lacks a critique—pursues every possible wrong way before it succeeds in finding the only right one.

All the principles that can be adopted from this point of view are either *empirical* or *rational*. The first kind, drawn from the principle of *happiness*, are based either on natural, or on moral, feeling. The *second* kind, drawn from the principle of *perfection*, are based either on the rational concept of perfection as a possible effect of our will or else on the concept of a self-existent perfection (God's will) as a determining cause of our will.

[Empirical Principles of Heteronomy]

Empirical principles are always unfitted to serve as a ground for moral laws. The universality with which these laws should hold for all rational beings without exception—the unconditioned practical necessity which they thus impose—falls away if their basis is taken from the *special constitution of human nature* or from the accidental circumstances in which it is placed. The principle of *personal happiness* is, however, the most objectionable, not merely because it is false and because its pretence that well-being always adjusts itself to well-doing is contradicted by experience; nor merely because it contributes nothing whatever towards establishing morality, since making a man happy is quite different from making him good and making him prudent or astute in seeking his advantage quite different from making him virtuous; but because it bases morality on sensuous motives which rather undermine it and totally destroy its sublimity, inasmuch as the motives of virtue are put in the same class as those of vice and we are instructed only to become better at calculation, the specific difference between virtue and vice being completely wiped out. On the other hand, moral feeling, this alleged special sense* (however shallow be the appeal to it when men who are unable to *think* hope to help themselves out by *feeling*, even when the question is solely one of universal law, and however little feelings, differing as they naturally do from one another by an infinity of degrees, can supply a uniform measure of good and evil— let alone that one man by his feeling can make no valid judgements at all for others)—moral feeling still remains closer to morality and to its dignity in this respect: it does virtue the honour of ascribing to her *immediately* the approval and esteem in which she is held, and does not, as it were, tell her to her face that we are attached to her, not for her beauty, but only for our own advantage.

[Rational Principles of Heteronomy]

Among the *rational* bases of morality—those springing from reason—the ontological concept of *perfection*[65] (however empty, however indefinite it is, and consequently useless for discovering in the boundless field of possible reality the maximum reality appropriate to us; and however much, in trying to distinguish specifically between the reality here in question and every other, it shows an inevitable tendency to go round in a circle and is unable to avoid covertly presupposing the morality it has to explain) — this concept none the less is better than the theological concept which derives morality from a divine and supremely perfect will;[66] not merely because we cannot intuit God's perfection and can only derive it from our own concepts, among which that of morality is the most eminent; but because, if we do not do this (and to do so would be to give a crudely circular explanation), the concept of God's will still remaining to us—one drawn from such characteristics as lust for glory and domination and bound up with frightful ideas of power and vengefulness—would inevitably form the basis for a moral system which would be in direct opposition to morality.

Yet if I had to choose between the concept of moral sense and that of perfection in general[67] (both of which at least do not undermine morality, though they are totally incompetent to support it as its foundation), I should decide for the latter; for this, since it at least withdraws the settlement of this question from sensibility and brings it before the court of pure reason, even although it there gets no decision, does still preserve unfalsified for more precise determination the indeterminate Idea (of a will good in itself).

[The Failure of Heteronomy]

For the rest I believe I may be excused from a lengthy refutation of all these systems. This is so easy and is presumably so well understood even by those whose office requires them to declare themselves for one or other of these theories (since their audience will not lightly put up with a suspension of judgement) that to spend time on it would be merely superfluous labour. But what is of more interest to us here is to know that these principles never lay down anything but heteronomy as the first basis of morality and must in consequence necessarily fail in their object.

Wherever an object of the will has to be put down as the basis for prescribing a rule to determine the will, there the rule is heteronomy; the imperative is conditioned, as follows: '*If*, or *because*, you will this object, you ought to act thus or thus'; consequently it can never give a moral—that is, a categorical— command. However the object determines the will—whether by means of inclination, as in the principle of personal happiness, or by means of reason directed to objects of our possible volitions generally, as in the principle of perfection—the will never determines itself *immediately* by the thought of an action, but only by the impulsion which the anticipated effect of the action exercises on the will: '*I ought to do something because I will something else.*' And the basis for this must be yet a further law in me as a subject, whereby I necessarily will this 'something else'—which law in turn requires an imperative to impose limits on this maxim.[68] The impulsion supposed to be exercised on the will of the subject, in accordance with his natural constitution, by the idea of a result to be attained by his own powers belongs to the nature of the subject—whether to his sensibility (his inclinations and taste) or to his understanding and reason, whose operation on an object is accompanied by satisfaction in virtue of the special equipment of their nature—and consequently, speaking strictly, it is nature which would make the law. This law, as a law of nature, not only must be known and proved by experience and therefore is in itself contingent and consequently unfitted to serve as an apodeictic rule of action such as a moral rule must be, but it is *always merely heteronomy of the will*: the will does not give itself the law, but an alien impulsion does so through the medium of the subject's own nature as tuned for its reception.

[The Position of the Argument]

An absolutely good will, whose principle must be a categorical imperative, will therefore, being undetermined in respect of all objects, contain only the *form* of *willing*, and that as autonomy. In other words, the fitness of the maxim of every good will to make itself a universal law is itself the sole law which the will of every rational being spontaneously imposes on itself without basing it on any impulsion or interest.

How such a synthetic a priori *proposition is possible* and why it is necessary—this is a problem whose solution lies no longer within the bounds of a metaphysic of morals; nor have we here asserted the truth of this proposition, much less pretended to have a proof of it in our power. We have merely shown by developing the concept of morality generally in vogue that autonomy of the will is unavoidably bound up with it or rather is its very basis. Any one therefore who takes morality to be something, and not merely a chimerical Idea without truth, must at the same time admit the principle we have put forward. This chapter, consequently, like the first, has been merely analytic. In order to prove that morality is no mere phantom of the brain—a conclusion which follows if the categorical imperative, and with it the autonomy of the will, is true and is absolutely necessary as an *a priori* principle—we require a *possible synthetic use of pure practical reason.*[69] On such a use we cannot venture without prefacing it by a *critique* of this power of reason itself—a critique whose main features, so far as is sufficient for our purpose, we must outline in our final chapter.

* We can, if we like, distinguish pure moral philosophy (metaphysics) from applied (applied, that is, to human nature)—just as pure mathematics is distinguished from applied mathematics and pure logic from applied logic. By this terminology we are at once reminded that moral principles are not grounded on the peculiarities of human nature, but must be established *a priori* by themselves; and yet that from such principles it must be possible to derive practical rules for human nature as well, just as it is for every kind of rational nature.

** I have a letter from the late distinguished Professor Sulzer,[70] in which he asks me what it is that makes moral instruction so ineffective, however convincing it may be in the eyes of reason. Because of my efforts to make it complete, my answer came too late. Yet it is just this: the teachers themselves do not make their concepts pure, but— since they try to do too well by hunting everywhere for inducements to be moral— they spoil their medicine altogether by their very attempt to make it really powerful. For the most ordinary observation shows that when a righteous act is represented as being done with a steadfast mind in complete disregard of any advantage in this or in another world, and even under the greatest temptations of affliction or allurement, it leaves far behind it any similar action affected even in the slightest degree by an alien impulsion and casts it into the shade: it uplifts the soul and rouses a wish that we too could act in this way. Even children of moderate age feel this impression, and duties should never be presented to them in any other way.

* The dependence of the power of appetition on sensation is called an inclination, and thus an inclination always indicates a *need*. The dependence of a contingently determinable will on principles of reason is called an *interest*. Hence an interest is found only where there is a dependent will which in itself is not always in accord

with reason: to a divine will we cannot ascribe any interest. But even the human will can *take an interest* in something without therefore *acting from interest*. The first expression signifies *practical* interest in the action; the second *pathological* interest in the object of the action. The first indicates only dependence of the will on principles of reason by itself; the second its dependence on principles of reason at the service of inclination— that is to say, where reason merely supplies a practical rule for meeting the need of inclination.[71] In the first case what interests me is the action; in the second case what interests me is the object of the action (so far as this object is pleasant to me). We have seen in Chapter 1 that in an action done for the sake of duty we must have regard, not to interest in the object, but to interest in the action itself and in its rational principle (namely, the law).

* The word 'prudence' (*Klugheit*) is used in a double sense: in one sense it can have the name of 'worldly wisdom' (*Weltklugheit*); in a second sense that of 'personal wisdom' (*Privatklugheit*). The first is the skill of a man in influencing others in order to use them for his own ends. The second is sagacity in combining all these ends to his own lasting advantage.[72] The latter is properly that to which the value of the former can itself be traced; and of him who is prudent in the first sense, but not in the second, we might better say that he is clever and astute, but on the whole imprudent.

* It seems to me that the proper meaning of the word '*pragmatic* can be defined most accurately in this way. For those *Sanctions* are called Pragmatic which, properly speaking, do not spring as necessary laws from the Natural Right of States, but from *forethought* in regard to the general welfare.[73] A *history* is written pragmatically when it teaches *prudence*—that is, when it instructs the world of today how to provide for its own advantage better than, or at least as well as, the world of other times.

* Without presupposing a condition taken from some inclination I connect an action with the will *a priori* and therefore necessarily (although only objectively so—that is, only subject to the Idea of a reason having full power over all subjective impulses to action). Here we have a practical proposition in which the willing of any action is not derived analytically from some other willing already presupposed[74] (for we do not possess any such perfect will[75]), but is on the contrary connected immediately[76] with the concept of the will of a rational being as something which is not contained in this concept.

* A *maxim* is a subjective principle of action and must be distinguished from an *objective principle*—namely, a practical law. The former contains a practical rule determined by reason in accordance with the conditions of the subject (often his ignorance or again his inclinations): it is thus a principle on which the subject *acts*. A law, on the other hand, is an objective principle valid for every rational being; and it is a principle on which he *ought to act*—that is, an imperative.[77]

* It should be noted that I reserve my division of duties entirely for a future *Metaphysic of Morals* and that my present division is therefore put forward as arbitrary (merely for the purpose of arranging my examples). Further, I understand here by a perfect duty one which allows no exception in the interest of inclination,[78] and so I recognise among *perfect* duties, not only outer ones, but also inner.[79] This is contrary to the accepted usage of the schools, but I do not intend to justify it here, since for my

purpose it is all one whether this point is conceded or not.

* To behold virtue in her proper shape is nothing other than to show morality stripped of all admixture with the sensuous and of all the spurious adornments of reward or self-love. How much she then casts into the shade all else that appears attractive to the inclinations can be readily perceived by every man if he will exert his reason in the slightest—provided he has not entirely ruined it for all abstractions.

* This proposition I put forward here as a postulate. The grounds for it will be found in the final chapter.[80]

* Let no one think that here the trivial '*quod tibi non vis fieri, etc.*'[81] can serve as a standard or principle. For it is merely derivative from our principle, although subject to various qualifications: it cannot be a universal law[82] since it contains the ground neither of duties to oneself nor of duties of kindness to others (for many a man would readily agree that others should not help him if only he could be dispensed from affording help to them), nor finally of strict duties towards others; for on this basis the criminal would be able to dispute with the judges who punish him, and so on.

* I may be excused from bringing forward examples to illustrate this principle, since those which were first used as illustrations of the categorical imperative and its formula can all serve this purpose here.

* Teleology views nature as a kingdom of ends; ethics views a possible kingdom of ends as a kingdom of nature. In the first case the kingdom of ends is a theoretical Idea used to explain what exists. In the second case it is a practical Idea used to bring into existence what does not exist but can be made actual by our conduct—and indeed to bring it into existence in conformity with this Idea.

* I class the principle of moral feeling with that of happiness because every empirical principle promises a contribution to our well-being merely from the satisfaction afforded by something—whether this satisfaction is given immediately and without any consideration of advantage or is given in respect of such advantage. Similarly we must with *Hutcheson*[83] class the principle of sympathy for the happiness of others along with the principle of moral sense as adopted by him.

3

Passage from a Metaphysic of Morals to a Critique of Pure Practical Reason

The Concept of Freedom is the Key to Explain Autonomy of the Will

Will is a kind of causality belonging to living beings so far as they are rational. *Freedom* would then be the property this causality has of being able to work independently of *determination* by alien causes; just as *natural necessity* is a property characterising the causality of all non-rational beings—the property of being determined to activity by the influence of alien causes.

The above definition of freedom is *negative* and consequently unfruitful as a way of grasping its essence; but there springs from it a *positive* concept, which, as positive, is richer and more fruitful. The concept of causality carries with it that of *laws* (*Gesetze*) in accordance with which, because of something we call a cause, something else— namely, its effect—must be posited (*gesetzt*). Hence freedom of will, although it is not the property of conforming to laws of nature, is not for this reason lawless: it must rather be a causality conforming to immutable laws, though of a special kind; for otherwise a free will would be self-contradictory. Natural necessity, as we have seen, is a heteronomy of efficient causes; for every effect is possible only in conformity with the law that something else determines the efficient cause to causal action. What else then can freedom of will be but autonomy—that is, the property which will has of being a law to itself? The proposition 'Will is in all its actions a law to itself' expresses, however, only the principle of acting on no maxim other than the one which can have for its object[1] itself as at the same time a universal law. This is precisely the formula of the categorical imperative and the principle of morality. Thus a free will and a will under moral laws are one and the same.[2]

Consequently if freedom of the will is presupposed, morality, together with its principle, follows by mere analysis of the concept of freedom. Nevertheless the principle of morality is still a synthetic proposition, namely: 'An absolutely good will is one whose maxim can always have as its content itself considered as a universal law'; for we cannot discover this characteristic of its maxim by analysing the concept of an absolutely good will. Such synthetic propositions are possible only because two cognitions[3] are bound to one another by their connexion with a third term in which both of them are to be found. The *positive* concept of freedom furnishes this third term, which cannot, as in the case of physical causes, be the nature of the sensible world (in the concept of which there come together the concepts of something as cause and of *something else* as effect in their relation to one another). What this third term is to which freedom directs us and of which we have an Idea *a priori*, we are not yet in a position to show here straight away,[4] nor can we as yet make intelligible the deduction of the concept of freedom from pure practical reason and so the possibility of a categorical imperative: we require some further preparation.

Freedom must be Presupposed as a Property of the Will of All Rational Beings

It is not enough to ascribe freedom to our will, on whatever ground, unless we have sufficient reason for attributing the same freedom to all rational beings as well. For since morality is a law for us only as *rational beings*, it must be equally valid for all rational beings; and since it must be derived solely from the property of freedom, we have got to prove that freedom too is a property of the will of all rational beings. It is not enough to demonstrate freedom from certain alleged experiences of human nature (though to do this is in any case absolutely impossible and freedom can be demonstrated only *a priori*):[5] we must prove that it belongs universally to the activity of rational beings endowed with a will. Now I assert that every being who cannot act except *under the Idea of freedom* is by this alone—from a practical point of view— really free; that is to say, for him all the laws inseparably bound up with freedom are valid just as much as if his will could be pronounced free in itself on grounds valid for theoretical philosophy.* And I maintain that to every rational being possessed of a will we must also lend the Idea of freedom as the only one under which he can act. For in such a being we conceive a reason which is practical—that is, which exercises causality in regard to its objects. But we cannot possibly conceive of a reason as being consciously directed from outside in regard to its judgements;[6] for in that case the subject would attribute the determination of his power of judgement, not to his reason, but to an impulsion. Reason must look upon itself as the author of its own principles independently of alien influences. Therefore as practical reason,[7] or as the will of a rational being, it must be regarded by itself as free; that is, the will of a rational being can be a will of his own only under the Idea of freedom, and such a will must therefore—from a practical point of view—be attributed to all rational beings.

The Interest Attached to the Ideas of Morality

[Moral Interest and the Vicious Circle]

We have at last traced the determinate concept of morality back to the Idea of freedom, but we have been quite unable to demonstrate freedom as something actual in ourselves and in human nature: we saw merely that we must presuppose it if we wish to conceive a being as rational and as endowed with consciousness of his causality in regard to actions—that is, as endowed with a will. Thus we find that on precisely the same ground we must attribute to every being endowed with reason and a will this property of determining himself to action under the Idea of his own freedom.[8]

From the presupposition of this Idea there springs, as we further saw, consciousness of a law of action, the law that subjective principles of action—that is, maxims—must always be adopted in such a way that they can also hold as principles objectively—that is, universally—and can therefore serve for our own enactment of universal law. But why should I subject myself to this principle simply as a rational being and in so doing also subject to it every other being endowed with reason? I am willing to admit that no interest *impels* me to do so since this would not produce a categorical imperative; but all the same I must necessarily *take* an interest in it and understand how this happens; for this 'I ought' is properly an 'I will' which holds necessarily for every rational being provided that reason in him is practical without any hindrance. For beings who, like us, are affected also by sensibility—that is, by motives of a different kind—and who do not always act as reason by itself would act, this necessity is expressed as an 'I ought' and the subjective necessity is distinct from the objective one.[9]

It looks as if, in our Idea of freedom, we have in fact merely taken the moral law for granted—that is, the very principle of the autonomy of the will—and have been unable to give an independent proof of its reality and objective necessity. In that case we should still have made a quite considerable gain inasmuch as we should at least have formulated the genuine principle more precisely than has been done before. As regards its validity, however, and the practical necessity of subjecting ourselves to it we should have got no further. Why must the validity of our maxim as a universal law be a condition limiting our action? On what do we base the worth we attach to this way of acting—worth supposed to be so great that there cannot be any interest which is higher? And how does it come about that in this alone man believes himself to feel his own personal worth, in comparison with which that of a pleasurable or painful state is to count as nothing? To these questions we should have been unable to give any sufficient answer.

We do indeed find ourselves able to take an interest in a personal characteristic which carries with it no interest in mere states,[10] but only makes us fit to have a share in such states in the event of their being distributed by reason. That is to say, the mere fact of deserving happiness can by itself interest us even without the motive of getting a share in this happiness. Such a judgement, however, is in fact merely the result of the importance we have already assumed to belong to moral laws (when we detach ourselves from every empirical interest by our Idea of freedom). But on this basis we can as yet have no insight into the principle that we ought to detach ourselves from such interest—that is, that we ought to regard ourselves as free in our actions and yet to hold ourselves bound by certain laws in order to find solely in our own person a worth which can compensate us for the loss of everything that makes our state valuable. We do not see how this is possible nor consequently *how the moral law can be binding*.

In this, we must frankly admit, there is shown a kind of circle, from which, as it seems, there is no way of escape. In the order of efficient causes we take ourselves to be free so that we may conceive ourselves to be under moral laws in the order of ends; and we then proceed to think of ourselves as subject to moral laws on the ground that we have described our will as free. Freedom and the will's enactment of its own laws are indeed both autonomy—and therefore are reciprocal concepts[11]—but precisely for this reason one of them cannot be used to explain the other or to furnish its ground. It can at most be used for logical purposes in order to bring seemingly different ideas of the same object under a single concept (just as different fractions of equal value can be reduced to their simplest expression).

[The Two Standpoints]

One shift, however, still remains open to us. We can enquire whether we do not take one standpoint when by means of freedom we conceive ourselves as causes acting *a priori*, and another standpoint when we contemplate ourselves with reference to our actions as effects which we see before our eyes.

One observation is possible without any need for subtle reflexion and, we may assume, can be made by the most ordinary intelligence—no doubt in its own fashion through some obscure discrimination of the power of judgement known to it as 'feeling'. The observation is this—that all ideas coming to us apart from our own volition (as do those of the senses) enable us to know objects only as they affect ourselves: what they may be in themselves remains unknown. Consequently, ideas of this kind, even with the greatest effort of attention and clarification brought to bear by understanding, serve only for knowledge of *appearances*, never of *things in themselves*. Once this distinction is made (it may be merely by noting the difference between ideas given to us from without, we ourselves being passive, and those which we produce entirely from ourselves, and so manifest our own activity), it follows of itself that behind appearances we must admit and assume something else which is not appearance—namely, things in themselves—although, since we can never be acquainted with these, but only with the way in which they affect us, we must resign ourselves to the fact that we can never get any nearer to them and can never know what they are in themselves. This must yield us a distinction, however rough, between the *sensible world* and the *intelligible world*, the first of which can vary a great deal according to differences of sensibility in sundry observers, while the second, which is its ground, always remains the same. Even as regards himself—so far as man is acquainted with himself by inner sensation[12]—he cannot claim to know what he is in himself. For since he does not, so to say, make himself, and since he acquires his concept of self not *a priori* but empirically, it is natural that even about himself he should get information through sense—that is, through inner sense—and consequently only through the mere appearance of his own nature and through the way in which his consciousness is affected. Yet beyond this character of himself as a subject[13] made up, as it is, of mere appearances he must suppose there to be something else which is its ground—namely, his Ego as this may be constituted in itself; and thus as regards mere perception and the capacity for receiving sensations[14] he must count himself as belonging to the *sensible world*, but as regards whatever there may be in him of pure activity (whatever comes into consciousness, not through affection of the senses, but immediately)[15] he must count himself as belonging to the *intellectual world*, of which, however, he knows nothing further.

A conclusion of this kind must be reached by a thinking man about everything that may be presented to him. It is presumably to be found even in the most ordinary intelligence, which, as is well known, is always very much disposed to look behind the objects of the senses for something further that is invisible and is spontaneously active; but it goes on to spoil this by immediately sensifying this invisible something in its turn—that is to say, it wants to make it an object of intuition, and so by this procedure it does not become in any degree wiser.

Now man actually finds in himself a power which distinguishes him from all other things—and even from himself so far as he is affected by objects. This power is *reason*.[16] As pure spontaneity reason is elevated even above *understanding* in the following respect. Understanding—although it too is spontaneous activity and is not, like sense, confined to ideas which arise only when we are affected by things (and therefore are passive)—understanding cannot produce by its own activity any concepts other than those whose sole service is *to bring sensuous ideas under rules* and so to unite them in one consciousness: without this employment of sensibility it would think nothing at all. Reason, on the other hand—in what are called 'Ideas'— shows a spontaneity so pure that it goes far beyond anything sensibility can offer: it manifests its highest function in distinguishing the sensible and intelligible worlds from one another and so in marking out limits for understanding itself.[17]

Because of this a rational being must regard himself *qua intelligence* (and accordingly not on the side of his lower faculties) as belonging to the intelligible world, not to the sensible one. He has therefore two points of view from which he can regard himself and from which he can know laws governing the employment of his powers and consequently governing all his actions. He can consider himself *first*—so far as he belongs to the sensible world—to be under laws of nature (heteronomy); and *secondly*—so far as he belongs to the intelligible world—to be under laws which, being independent of nature, are not empirical but have their ground in reason alone.

As a rational being, and consequently as belonging to the intelligible world, man can never conceive the causality of his own will except under the Idea of freedom; for to be independent of determination by causes in the sensible world (and this is what reason must always attribute to itself) is to be free. To the Idea of freedom there is inseparably attached the concept of *autonomy*, and to this in turn the universal principle of morality—a principle which in Idea[18] forms the ground for all the actions of *rational* beings, just as the law of nature does for all appearances.

The suspicion which we raised above is now removed—namely, that there might be a hidden circle in our inference from freedom to autonomy and from autonomy to the moral law; that in effect we had perhaps assumed the Idea of freedom only because of the moral law in order subsequently to infer the moral law in its turn from freedom; and that consequently we had been able to assign no ground at all for the moral law, but had merely assumed it by begging a principle which well-meaning souls will gladly concede us, but which we could never put forward as a demonstrable proposition. We see now that when we think of ourselves as free, we transfer ourselves into the intelligible world as members and recognise the autonomy of the will together with its consequence—morality; whereas when we think of ourselves as under obligation, we look upon ourselves as belonging to the sensible world and yet to the, intelligible world at the same time.

How is a Categorical Imperative Possible?

A rational being counts himself, *qua* intelligence, as belonging to the intelligible world, and solely *qua* efficient cause belonging to the intelligible world does he give to his causality the name of '*will*'. On the other side, however, he is conscious of himself as also a part of the sensible world, where his actions are encountered as mere appearances of this causality. Yet the possibility of these actions cannot be made intelligible by means of such causality, since with this we have no direct acquaintance; and instead these actions, as belonging to the sensible world, have to be understood as determined by other appearances—namely, by desires and inclinations. Hence, if I were solely a member of the intelligible world, all my actions would be in perfect conformity with the principle of the autonomy of a pure will; if I were solely a part of the sensible world, they would have to be taken as in complete conformity with the law of nature governing desires and inclinations—that is, with the heteronomy of nature. (In the first case they would be grounded on the supreme principle of morality; in the second case on that of happiness.) *But the intelligible world contains the ground of the sensible world and therefore also of its laws*; and so in respect of my will, for which (as belonging entirely to the intelligible world) it gives laws immediately,[19] it must also be conceived as containing such a ground.[20] Hence, in spite of regarding myself from one point of view as a being that belongs to the sensible world, I shall have to recognise that, *qua* intelligence, I am subject to the law of the intelligible world—that is, to the reason which contains this law in the Idea of freedom, and so to the autonomy of the will—and therefore I must look on the laws of the intelligible world as imperatives for me and on the actions which conform to this principle as duties.

And in this way categorical imperatives are possible because the Idea of freedom makes me a member of an intelligible world. This being so, if I were solely a member of the intelligible world, all my actions *would* invariably accord with the autonomy of the will; but because I intuit myself at the same time as a member of the sensible world, they *ought* so to accord. This *categorical* 'ought' presents us with a synthetic *a priori* proposition, since to my will as affected by sensuous desires there is added the Idea of the same will,[21] viewed, however, as a pure will belonging to the intelligible world and active on its own account—a will which contains the supreme condition of the former will, so far as reason is concerned. This is roughly like the way in which concepts of the understanding, which by themselves signify nothing but the form of law in general, are added to intuitions of the sensible world and so make synthetic *a priori* propositions possible on which all our knowledge of nature is based.

The practical use of ordinary human reason confirms the rightness of this deduction. There is no one, not even the most hardened scoundrel—provided only he is accustomed to use reason in other ways—who, when presented with examples of honesty in purpose, of faithfulness to good maxims, of sympathy, and of kindness towards all (even when these are bound up with great sacrifices of advantage and comfort), does not wish that he too might be a man of like spirit. He is unable to realise such an aim in his own person—though only on account of his desires and impulses; but yet at the same time he wishes to be free from these inclinations, which are a burden to himself. By such a wish he shows that having a will free from sensuous impulses he transfers himself in thought into an order of things quite different from that of his desires in the field of sensibility; for from the fulfilment of this wish he can expect no gratification of his sensuous desires and consequently no state which would satisfy any of his actual or even conceivable inclinations (since by such an expectation the very Idea which elicited the wish would be deprived of its superiority); all he can expect is a greater inner worth of his own person. This better person he believes himself to be when he transfers himself to the standpoint of a member of the intelligible world. He is involuntarily constrained to do so by the Idea of freedom—that is, of not being dependent on *determination* by causes in the sensible world; and from this standpoint he is conscious of possessing a good will which, on his own admission, constitutes the law for the bad will belonging to him as a member of the sensible world—a law of whose authority he is aware even in transgressing it. The moral 'I ought' is thus an 'I will' for man as a member of the intelligible world; and it is conceived by him as an 'I ought' only in so far as he considers himself at the same time to be a member of the sensible world.

The Extreme Limit of Practical Philosophy

[The Antinomy of Freedom and Necessity]

All men think of themselves as having a free will. From this arise all judgements that actions are such as *ought to have been done*, although they *have not been done*. This freedom is no concept of experience, nor can it be such, since it continues to hold although experience shows the opposite of those requirements which are regarded as necessary[22] under the presupposition of freedom. On the other hand, it is just as necessary that everything which takes place should be infallibly determined in accordance with the laws of nature; and this necessity of nature is likewise no concept of experience, precisely because it carries with it the concept of necessity and so of *a priori* knowledge. The concept of nature is, however, confirmed by experience and must inevitably be presupposed if experience—that is, coherent knowledge of sensible objects in accordance with universal laws—is to be possible. Hence, while freedom is only an *Idea* of reason whose objective reality is in itself questionable, nature is a *concept of the understanding*, which proves, and must necessarily prove, its reality in examples from experience.

From this there arises a dialectic[23] of reason, since the freedom attributed to the will seems incompatible with the necessity of nature; and although at this parting of the ways reason finds the road of natural necessity much more beaten and serviceable than that of freedom for *purposes of speculation*, yet for *purposes of action* the footpath of freedom is the only one on which we can make use of reason in our conduct. Hence to argue freedom away is as impossible for the most abstruse philosophy as it is for the most ordinary human reason. Reason must therefore suppose that no genuine contradiction is to be found between the freedom and the natural necessity ascribed to the very same human actions; for it can abandon the concept of nature as little as it can abandon that of freedom.

All the same we must at least get rid of this seeming contradiction in a convincing fashion—although we shall never be able to comprehend how freedom is possible. For if the thought of freedom is self-contradictory or incompatible with nature—a concept which is equally necessary—freedom would have to be completely abandoned in favour of natural necessity.

[The Two Standpoints]

From this contradiction it would be impossible to escape if the subject who believes himself free were to conceive himself *in the same sense*, or *in precisely the same relationship*, when he calls himself free as when he holds himself subject to the law of nature in respect of the same action. Hence speculative philosophy has the unavoidable task of showing at least this—that its illusion about the contradiction rests on our conceiving man in one sense and relationship when we call him free and in another when we consider him, as a part of nature, to be subject to nature's laws; and that both characteristics not merely *can* get on perfectly well together but must be conceived as *necessarily combined* in the same subject; for otherwise we could not explain why we should trouble reason with an Idea which—even if it can *without contradiction* be combined with a different and adequately verified concept—does yet involve us in a business which puts reason to sore straits in its theoretical use. This duty is incumbent on speculative philosophy solely in order that it may clear a path for practical philosophy. Thus it is not left to the discretion of philosophers whether they will remove the seeming contradiction or leave it untouched; for in the latter case the theory on this topic becomes *bonum vacans*,[24] of which the fatalist can justifiably take possession and can chase all morality out of its supposed property, which it has no title to hold.

Nevertheless at this point we cannot yet say that the boundary of practical philosophy begins. For practical philosophy has no part in the settlement of this controversy: it merely requires speculative reason to bring to an end the dissension in which it is entangled on theoretical questions so that practical reason may have peace and security from external attacks capable of bringing into dispute the territory it seeks to cultivate.

The lawful title to freedom of will claimed even by ordinary human reason is grounded on a consciousness—and an accepted presupposition—that reason is independent of purely subjective determination by causes which collectively make up all that belongs to sensation and comes under the general name of sensibility. In thus regarding himself as intelligence man puts himself into another order of things, and into relation with determining causes of quite another sort, when he conceives himself as intelligence endowed with a will and consequently with causality, than he does when he perceives himself as a phenomenon in the sensible world (which he actually is as well) and subjects his causality to external determination in accordance with laws of nature. He then becomes aware at once that both of these can, and indeed must, take place at the same time; for there is not the slightest contradiction in holding that *a thing as an appearance* (as belonging to the sensible world) is subject to certain laws of which it is independent *as a thing* or being *in itself*. That he must represent and conceive himself in this double way rests, as regards the first side, on consciousness of himself as an object affected through the senses; as concerns the second side, on consciousness of himself as intelligence—that is, as independent of sensuous impressions in his use of reason (and so as belonging to the intelligible world).

Hence it comes about that man claims for himself a will which does not impute to itself anything appertaining merely to his desires and inclinations; and, on the other hand, that he conceives as possible through its agency, and indeed as necessary, actions which can be done only by disregarding all desires and incitements of sense. The causality of such actions lies in man as intelligence and in the laws of such effects and actions as accord with the principles of an intelligible world. Of that world he knows[25] no more than this—that in it reason alone, and indeed pure reason independent of sensibility, is the source of law; and also that since he is there his proper self only as intelligence (while as a human being he is merely an appearance of himself), these laws apply to him immediately[26] and categorically. It follows that incitements from desires and impulses (and therefore from the whole sensible world of nature) cannot impair the laws which govern his will as intelligence. Indeed he does not answer for the former nor impute them to his proper self—that is, to his will; but he does impute to himself the indulgence which he would show them if he admitted their influence on his maxims to the detriment of the rational laws governing his will.

[There is No Knowledge of the Intelligible World]

By *thinking* itself into the intelligible world practical reason does not overstep its limits in the least: it would do so only if it sought to *intuit or feel itself* into that world. The thought in question is a merely negative one with respect to the sensible world: it gives reason no laws for determining the will and is positive only in this one point, that it combines freedom as a negative characteristic with a (positive) power as well— and indeed with a causality of reason called by us 'a will'—a power so to act that the principle of our actions may accord with the essential character of a rational cause, that is, with the condition that the maxim of these actions should have the validity of a universal law. If practical reason were also to import an *object of the will*—that is, a motive of action—from the intelligible world, it would overstep its limits and pretend to an acquaintance with something of which it has no knowledge. The concept of the intelligible world is thus only *a point of view*[27] which reason finds itself constrained to adopt outside appearances *in order to conceive itself as practical*. To conceive itself thus would not be possible if the influences of sensibility were able to determine man; but it is none the less necessary so far as we are not to deny him consciousness of himself as intelligence and consequently as a rational cause which is active by means of reason—that is, which is free in its operation. This thought admittedly carries with it the Idea of an order and a legislation different from that of the mechanism of nature appropriate to the world of sense. It makes necessary the concept of an intelligible world (that is, of the totality of rational beings as things in themselves); but it makes not the slightest pretension to do more than conceive such a world with respect to its *formal* condition—to conceive it, that is, as conforming to the condition that the maxim of the will should have the universality of a law, and so as conforming to the autonomy of the will, which alone is compatible with freedom. In contrast with this all laws determined by reference to an object give us heteronomy, which can be found only in laws of nature and can apply only to the world of sense.

[There is No Explanation of Freedom]

Reason would overstep all its limits if it took upon itself to *explain how* pure reason can be practical. This would be identical, with the task of explaining *how freedom is possible*.

We are unable to explain anything unless we can bring it under laws which can have an object given in some possible experience. Freedom, however, is a mere Idea: its objective validity can in no way be exhibited by reference to laws of nature and consequently cannot be exhibited in any possible experience. Thus the Idea of freedom can never admit of full comprehension, or indeed of insight,[28] since it can never by any analogy have an example falling under it. It holds only as a necessary presupposition of reason in a being who believes himself to be conscious of a will— that is, of a power distinct from mere appetition (a power, namely, of determining himself to act as intelligence and consequently to act in accordance with laws of reason independently of natural instincts). But where determination by laws of nature comes to an end, all *explanation* comes to an end as well. Nothing is left but *defence*— that is, to repel the objections of those who profess to have seen more deeply into the essence of things and on this ground audaciously declare freedom to be impossible. We can only show them that their pretended discovery of a contradiction in it consists in nothing but this: in order to make the law of nature apply to human actions they have necessarily had to consider man as an appearance; and now that they are asked to conceive him, *qua* intelligence, as a thing in himself as well, they continue to look upon him as an appearance in this respect also. In that case, admittedly, to exempt man's causality (that is, his will) from all the natural laws of the sensible world would, in one and the same subject, give rise to a contradiction. The contradiction would fall away if they were willing to reflect and to admit, as is reasonable, that things in themselves (although hidden) must lie behind appearances as their ground, and that we cannot require the laws of their operations to be identical with those that govern their appearances.

[There is No Explanation of Moral Interest]

The subjective impossibility of *explaining* freedom of will is the same as the impossibility of finding out and making comprehensible what *interest** man can take in moral laws; and yet he does in fact take such an interest. The basis of this in ourselves we call 'moral feeling'. Some people have mistakenly given out this feeling to be the gauge of our moral judgements: it should be regarded rather as the *subjective* effect exercised on our will by the law and having its objective ground in reason alone.

If we are to will actions for which reason by itself prescribes an 'ought' to a rational, yet sensuously affected, being, it is admittedly necessary that reason should have a power of *infusing a feeling of pleasure* or satisfaction in the fulfilment of duty,[29] and consequently that it should possess a kind of causality by which it can determine sensibility in accordance with rational principles. It is, however, wholly impossible to comprehend—that is, to make intelligible *a priori*—how a mere thought containing nothing sensible in itself can bring about a sensation of pleasure or displeasure; for there is here a special kind of causality, and—as with all causality—we are totally unable to determine its character *a priori*: on this we must consult experience alone. The latter cannot provide us with a relation of cause and effect except between two objects of experience—whereas here pure reason by means of mere Ideas (which furnish absolutely no objects for experience) has to be the cause of an effect admittedly found in experience. Hence for us men it is wholly impossible to explain how and why the *universality of a maxim as a law*—and therefore morality—should interest us. This much only is certain: the law is not valid for us *because it interests us* (for this is heteronomy and makes practical reason depend on sensibility—that is to say, on an underlying feeling—in which case practical reason could never give us moral law); the law interests us because it is valid for us as men in virtue of having sprung from our will as intelligence and so from our proper self; *but what belongs to mere appearance is necessarily subordinated by reason to the character of the thing in itself.*

[General Review of the Argument]

Thus the question 'How is a categorical imperative possible?' can be answered so far as we can supply the sole presupposition under which it is possible—namely, the Idea of freedom—and also so far as we can have insight into the necessity of this presupposition. This is sufficient for the *practical use* of reason—that is, for conviction of the *validity of this imperative*, and so too of the moral law. But how this presupposition itself is possible is never open to the insight of any human reason. Yet, on the presupposition that the will of an intelligence is free, there follows necessarily its *autonomy* as the formal condition under which alone it can be determined. It is not only perfectly *possible* (as speculative philosophy can show) to presuppose such freedom of the will (without contradicting the principle that natural necessity governs the connexion of appearances in the sensible world); it is also *necessary*, without any further condition, for a rational being conscious of exercising causality by means of reason and so of having a will (which is distinct from desires) to make such freedom in practice—that is, in Idea—underlie all his voluntary actions as their condition.[30] But *how* pure reason can be practical in itself without further motives drawn from some other source; that is, how the bare *principle of the universal validity of all its maxims as laws* (which would admittedly be the form of a pure practical reason) can by itself—without any matter (or object) of the will in which we could take some antecedent interest—supply a motive and create an interest which could be called purely *moral*; or, in other words, *how pure reason can be practical*—all human reason is totally incapable of explaining this, and all the effort and labour to seek such an explanation is wasted.

It is precisely the same as if I sought to fathom how freedom itself is possible as the causality of a will. There I abandon a philosophical basis[31] of explanation, and I have no other. I could, no doubt, proceed to flutter about in the intelligible world, which still remains left to me—the world of intelligences; but although I have an *Idea* of it, which has its own good grounds, yet I have not the slightest *acquaintance* with such a world, nor can I ever attain such acquaintance by all the efforts of my natural power of reason. My Idea signifies only a 'something' that remains over when I have excluded from the grounds determining my will everything that belongs to the world of sense: its sole purpose is to restrict the principle that all motives come from the field of sensibility, by setting bounds to this field and by showing that it does not comprise all in all within itself, but that there is still more beyond it; yet with this 'more' I have no further acquaintance. Of the pure reason which conceives this Ideal, after I have set aside all matter—that is, all knowledge of objects—there remains nothing over for me except its form—namely, the practical law that maxims should be universally valid— and the corresponding conception of reason, in its relation to a purely intelligible world, as a possible efficient cause, that is, a cause determining the will. Here all sensuous motives must entirely fail; this Idea of an intelligible world would itself have to be the motive or to be that wherein reason originally took an interest. To make this comprehensible is, however, precisely the problem that we are unable to solve.

[The Extreme Limit of Moral Enquiry]

Here then is the extreme limit of all moral enquiry. To determine this limit is, however, of great importance in this respect: by so doing reason may be kept, on the one hand, from searching around in the sensible world—greatly to the detriment of morality—for the supreme motive and for some interest, comprehensible indeed, but empirical; and it may be kept, on the other hand, from flapping its wings impotently, without leaving the spot, in a space that for it is empty—the space of transcendent concepts known as 'the intelligible world'—and so from getting lost among mere phantoms of the brain. For the rest, the Idea of a purely intelligible world, as a whole of all intelligences to which we ourselves belong as rational beings (although from another point of view we are members of the sensible world as well), remains always a serviceable and permitted Idea for the purposes of a rational belief, though all knowledge ends at its boundary: it serves to produce in us a lively interest in the moral law by means of the splendid ideal of a universal kingdom of *ends in themselves* (rational beings), to which we can belong as members only if we are scrupulous to live in accordance with maxims of freedom as if they were laws of nature.

Perpetual Peace

This 1795 essay provides a peace program to be implemented by governments. The "Preliminary Articles" describe the steps that should be taken immediately, or with all deliberate speed:

"No secret treaty of peace shall be held valid in which there is tacitly reserved matter for a future war"

"No independent states, large or small, shall come under the dominion of another state by inheritance, exchange, purchase, or donation"

"Standing armies shall in time be totally abolished"

"National debts shall not be contracted with a view to the external friction of states"

"No state shall by force interfere with the constitution or government of another state"

"No state shall, during war, permit such acts of hostility which would make mutual confidence in the subsequent peace impossible: such are the employment of assassins (percussores), poisoners (venefici), breach of capitulation, and incitement to treason (perduellio) in the opposing state"

Three Definitive Articles would provide not merely a cessation of hostilities, but a foundation on which to build a peace.

"The civil constitution of all states to be republican"

"The law of nations shall be founded on a federation of free states"

"The law of world citizenship shall be limited to conditions of universal hospitality"

Kant claims that republics will be at peace not only with each other, but are more pacific than other forms of government in general. The general idea that popular and responsible governments would be more inclined to promote peace and commerce became one current in the stream of European thought and political practice. It was one element of the American policy of George Canning and the foreign policy of Lord Palmerston. It was also represented in the liberal internationalism of Woodrow Wilson, George Creel and H. G. Wells. Kant's recommendations were clearly represented in the 1940's in the United Nations.

CONTENTS

"For I dipt into the future, far as human eye could see,

Saw the Vision of the world, and all the wonder that would be;

Saw the heavens fill with commerce, argosies of magic sails,

Pilots of the purple twilight, dropping down with costly bales;

Heard the heavens fill with shouting, and there rain'd a ghastly dew

From the nations' airy navies grappling in the central blue;

Far along the world-wide whisper of the south-wind rushing warm,

With the standards of the peoples plunging thro' the thunder-storm;

Till the war-drum throbb'd no longer, and the battle-flags were furl'd

In the Parliament of man, the Federation of the world.

There the common sense of most shall hold a fretful realm in awe,

And the kindly earth shall slumber, lapt in universal law."

Tennyson: Locksley Hall.

PREFACE

This translation of Kant's essay on *Perpetual Peace* was undertaken by Miss Mary Campbell Smith at the suggestion of the late Professor Ritchie of St. Andrews, who had promised to write for it a preface, indicating the value of Kant's work in relation to recent discussions regarding the possibility of "making wars to cease." In view of the general interest which these discussions have aroused and of the vague thinking and aspiration which have too often characterised them, it seemed to Professor Ritchie that a translation of this wise and sagacious essay would be both opportune and valuable.[1]* His untimely death has prevented the fulfilment of his promise, and I have been asked, in his stead, to introduce the translator's work.

This is, I think, the only complete translation into English of Kant's essay, including all the notes as well as the text, and the translator has added a full historical Introduction, along with numerous notes of her own, so as (in Professor Ritchie's words) "to meet the needs (1) of the student of Politicalp. vi Science who wishes to understand the relation of Kant's theories to those of Grotius, Hobbes, Locke, Rousseau etc., and (2) of the general reader who wishes to understand the significance of Kant's proposals in connection with the ideals of Peace Congresses, and with the development of International Law from the end of the Middle Ages to the Hague Conference."

Although it is more than 100 years since Kant's essay was written, its substantial value is practically unimpaired. Anyone who is acquainted with the general character of the mind of Kant will expect to find in him sound common-sense, clear recognition of the essential facts of the case and a remarkable power of analytically exhibiting the conditions on which the facts necessarily depend. These characteristics are manifest in the essay on *Perpetual Peace*. Kant is not pessimist enough to believe that a perpetual peace is an unrealisable dream or a consummation devoutly to be feared, nor is he optimist enough to fancy that it is an ideal which could easily be realised if men would but turn their hearts to one another. For Kant perpetual peace is an ideal, not merely as a speculative Utopian idea, with which in fancy we may play, but as a moral principle, which ought to be, and therefore can be, realised. Yet he makes it perfectly clear that we cannot hope to approach the realisationp. vii of it unless we honestly face political facts and get a firm grasp of the indispensable conditions of a lasting peace. To strive after the ideal in contempt or in ignorance of these conditions is a labour that must inevitably be either fruitless or destructive of its own ends. Thus Kant demonstrates the hopelessness of any attempt to secure perpetual peace between independent nations. Such nations may make treaties; but these are binding only for so long as it is not to the interest of either party to denounce them. To enforce them is impossible while the nations remain independent. "There is," as Professor Ritchie put it (*Studies in Political and Social Ethics,*), "only one way in which war between independent nations can be prevented; and that is by the nations ceasing to be independent." But this does not necessarily mean the establishment of a despotism, whether autocratic or democratic. On the other hand, Kant maintains that just as peace between individuals within a state can only be permanently secured by the institution of a "republican" (that is to say, a representative) government, so the only real guarantee of a permanent peace between nations is the establishment of a federation of free "republican" states.

Such a federation he regards as practically possible. "For if Fortune ordains that a powerful and enlightened people should form a republicp. viii — which by its very nature is inclined to perpetual peace — this would serve as a centre of federal union for other states wishing to join, and thus secure conditions of freedom among the states in accordance with the idea of the law of nations. Gradually, through different unions of this kind, the federation would extend further and further."

Readers who are acquainted with the general philosophy of Kant will find many traces of its influence in the essay on *Perpetual Peace*. Those who have no knowledge of his philosophy may find some of his forms of statement rather difficult to understand, and it may therefore not be out of place for me to indicate very briefly the meaning of some terms which he frequently uses, especially in the Supplements and Appendices. Thus at the beginning of the First Supplement, Kant draws a distinction between the mechanical and the teleological view of things, between "nature" and "Providence", which depends upon his main philosophical position. According to Kant, pure reason has two aspects, theoretical and practical. As concerning knowledge, strictly so called, the *a priori* principles of reason (*e.g.* substance and attribute, cause and effect etc.) are valid only within the realm of possible sense-experience. Such ideas, for instance, cannot be extended to God, since He is not a possible object of sense-experience. They are limitedp. ix to the world of phenomena. This world of phenomena ("nature" or the world of sense-experience) is a purely mechanical system. But in order to understand fully the phenomenal world, the pure theoretical reason must postulate certain ideas (the ideas of the soul, the world and God), the objects of which transcend sense-experience. These ideas are not theoretically valid, but their validity is practically established by the pure practical reason, which does not yield speculative truth, but prescribes its principles "dogmatically" in the form of imperatives to the will. The will is itself practical reason, and thus it imposes its imperatives upon itself. The fundamental imperative of the practical reason is stated by Kant in Appendix I. :— "Act so that thou canst will that thy maxim should be a universal law, be the end of thy action what it will." If the end of perpetual peace is a duty, it must be necessarily deduced from this general law. And Kant does regard it as a duty. "We must desire perpetual peace not only as a material good, but also as a state of things resulting from our recognition of the precepts of duty" (*loc. cit.*). This is further expressed in the maxim :— "Seek ye first the kingdom of pure practical reason and its righteousness, and the object of your endeavour, the blessing of perpetual peace, will be added unto you." The distinction between thep. x moral politician and the political moralist, which is developed in Appendix I., is an application of the general distinction between duty and expediency, which is a prominent feature of the Kantian ethics. Methods of expediency, omitting all reference to the pure practical reason, can only bring about re-arrangements of circumstances in the mechanical course of nature. They can never guarantee the attainment of their end: they can never make it more than a speculative ideal, which may or may not be practicable. But if the end can be shown to be a duty, we have, from Kant's point of view, the only reasonable ground for a conviction that it is realisable. We cannot, indeed, theoretically *know* that it is realisable. "Reason is not sufficiently enlightened to survey the series of predetermining causes which would make it possible for us to predict with certainty the good or bad results of human action, as they follow from the mechanical laws of nature; although we may hope that things will turn out as we should desire" . On the other hand, since the idea of perpetual peace is a moral ideal, an "idea of duty", we are entitled to believe that it is practicable. "Nature guarantees the coming of perpetual peace, through the natural course of human propensities; not indeed with sufficient certainty to enable us to prophesy the future of this ideal theoretically, but yet clearlyp. xi enough for practical purposes" . One might extend this discussion indefinitely; but what has been said may suffice for general guidance.

The "wise and sagacious" thought of Kant is not expressed in a simple style, and the translation has consequently been a very difficult piece of work. But the translator has shown great skill in manipulating the involutions, parentheses and prodigious sentences of the original. In this she has had the valuable help of Mr. David Morrison, M.A., who revised the whole translation with the greatest care and to whom she owes the solution of a number of difficulties. Her work will have its fitting reward if it succeeds in familiarising the English-speaking student of politics with a political essay of enduring value, written by one of the master thinkers of modern times.

R. LATTA.

University of Glasgow, *May 1903.*

TRANSLATOR'S INTRODUCTION

This is an age of unions. Not merely in the economic sphere, in the working world of unworthy ends and few ideals do we find great practical organizations; but law, medicine, science, art, trade, commerce, politics and political economy — we might add philanthropy — standing institutions, mighty forces in our social and intellectual life, all have helped to swell the number of our nineteenth century Conferences and Congresses. It is an age of Peace Movements and Peace Societies, of peace-loving monarchs and peace-seeking diplomats. This is not to say that we are preparing for the millennium. Men are working together, there is a newborn solidarity of interest, but rivalries between nation and nation, the bitternesses and hatreds inseparable from competition are not less keen; prejudice and misunderstanding not less frequent; subordinate conflicting interests are not fewer, are perhaps, in view of changing political conditions and an ever-growing international commerce, multiplying with every year. The talisman is, perhaps, self-interest, but, none the less, the spirit of union is there; it is impossible to ignore a clearly marked tendency towards international federation, towards political peace. This slow movement was not born with Peace Societies; its consummation lies perhaps far off in the ages to come. History at best moves slowly. But something of its past progress we shall do well to know. No political idea seems to have so great a future before it as this idea of a federation of the world. It is bound to realise itself some day; let us consider what are the chances that this day come quickly, what that it be long delayed. What obstacles lie in the way, and how may they be removed? What historical grounds have we for hoping that they may ever be removed? What, in a word, is the origin and history of the idea of a perpetual peace between nations, and what would be the advantage, what is the prospect of realising it?

The international relations of states find their expression, we are told, in war and peace. What has been the part played by these great counteracting forces in the history of nations? What has it been in prehistoric times, in the life of man in what is called the "state of nature"? "It is no easy enterprise," says Rousseau, in more than usually careful language, "to disentangle that which is original from that which is artificial in the actual state of man, and to make ourselves well acquainted with a state which no longer exists, which perhaps never has existed and which probably never will exist in the future." (Preface to the *Discourse on the Causes of Inequality*, 1753, publ. 1754.) This is a difficulty which Rousseau surmounts only too easily. A knowledge of history, a scientific spirit may fail him: an imagination ever ready to pour forth detail never does. Man lived, says he, "without industry, without speech, without habitation, without war, without connection of any kind, without any need of his fellows or without any desire to harm them ... sufficing to himself."[2*] (*Discourse on the Sciences and Arts*, 1750.) Nothing, we are now certain, is less probable. We cannot paint the life of man at this stage of his development with any definiteness, but the conclusion is forced upon us that our race had no golden age,[3*] no peaceful beginning, that this early state was indeed, as Hobbes held, a state of war, of incessant war between individuals, families and, finally, tribes.

The Early Conditions of Society.

For the barbarian, war is the rule; peace the exception. His gods, like those of Greece, are warlike gods; his spirit, at death, flees to some Valhalla. For him life is one long battle; his arms go with him even to the grave. Food and the means of existence he seeks through plunder and violence. Here right is with might; the battle is to the strong. Nature has given all an equal claim to all things, but not everyone can have them. This state of fearful insecurity is bound to come to an end. "Government," says Locke, (*On Civil Government*, Chap. VIII., § 105) "is hardly to be avoided amongst men that live together."[4*] A constant dread of attack and a growing consciousness of the necessity of presenting a united front against it result in the choice of some leader — the head of a family perhaps — who acts, it may be, only as captain of the hosts, as did Joshua in Israel, or who may discharge the simple duties of a primitive governor or king.[5*] Peace within is found to be strength without. The civil state is established, so that "if there needs must be war, it may not yet be against all men, nor yet without some helps." (Hobbes: *On Liberty*, Chap. I., § 13.) This foundation of the state is the first establishment in history of a peace institution. It changes the character of warfare, it gives it method and system; but it does not bring peace in its train. We have now, indeed, no longer a wholesale war of all against all, a constant irregular raid and plunder of one individual by another; but we have the systematic, deliberate war of community against community, of nation against nation.[6*]

War in Classical Times.

In early times, there were no friendly neighbouring nations: beyond the boundaries of every nation's territory, lay the land of a deadly foe. This was the way of thinking, even of so highly cultured a people as the Greeks, who believed that a law of nature had made every outsider, every barbarian their inferior and their enemy.[7*] Their treaties of peace, at the time of the Persian War, were frankly of the kind denounced by Kant, mere armistices concluded for the purpose of renewing their fighting strength. The ancient world is a world of perpetual war in which defeat meant annihilation. In the East no right was recognised in the enemy; and even in Greece and Rome the fate of the unarmed was death or slavery.[8*] The barbaric or non-Grecian states had, according to Plato and Aristotle, no claim upon humanity, no rights in fact of any kind. Among the Romans things were little better. According to Mr. T. J. Lawrence — see his *Principles of International Law*, III., §§ 21, 22 — they were worse. For Rome stood alone in the world: she was bound by ties of kinship to no other state. She was, in other words, free from a sense of obligation to other races. War, according to Roman ideas, was made by the gods, apart altogether from the quarrels of rulers or races. To disobey the sacred command, expressed in signs and auguries would have been to hold in disrespect the law and religion of the land. When, in the hour of victory, the Romans refrained from pressing their rights against the conquered — rights recognised by all Roman jurists — it was from no spirit of leniency, but in the pursuit of a prudent and far-sighted policy, aiming at the growth of Roman supremacy and the establishment of a world-embracing empire, shutting out all war as it blotted out natural boundaries, reducing all rights to the one right of imperial citizenship. There was no real *jus belli*, even here in the cradle of international law; the only limits to the fury of war were of a religious character.

The treatment of a defeated enemy among the Jews rested upon a similar religious foundation. In the East, we find a special cruelty in the conduct of war. The wars of the Jews and Assyrians were wars of extermination. The whole of the *Old Testament*, it has been said, resounds with the clash of arms.[9] "An eye for an eye, a tooth for a tooth!" was the command of Jehovah to his chosen people. Vengeance was bound up in their very idea of the Creator. The Jews, unlike the followers of Mahomet, attempted, and were commanded to attempt no violent conversion[10]; they were then too weak a nation; but they fought, and fought with success against the heathen of neighbouring lands, the Lord of Hosts leading them forth to battle. The God of Israel stood to his chosen people in a unique and peculiarly logical relation. He had made a covenant with them; and, in return for their obedience and allegiance, cared for their interests and advanced their national prosperity. The blood of this elect people could not be suffered to intermix with that of idolaters. Canaan must be cleared of the heathen, on the coming of the children of Israel to their promised land; and mercy to the conquered enemy, even to women, children or animals was held by the Hebrew prophets to be treachery to Jehovah. (*Sam.* XV.; *Josh.* VI. 21.)

Hence the attitude of the Jews to neighbouring nations[11] was still more hostile than that of the Greeks. The cause of this difference is bound up with the transition from polytheism to monotheism. The most devout worshipper of the national gods of ancient times could endure to see other gods than his worshipped in the next town or by a neighbouring nation. There was no reason why all should not exist side by side. Religious conflicts in polytheistic countries, when they arose, were due not to the rivalry of conflicting faiths, but to an occasional attempt to put one god above the others in importance. There could be no interest here in the propagation of belief through the sword. But, under the Jews, these relations were entirely altered. Jehovah, their Creator, became the one invisible God. Such an one can suffer no others near him; their existence is a continual insult to him. Monotheism is, in its very nature, a religion of intolerance. Its spirit among the Jews was warlike: it commanded the subjugation of other nations, but its instrument was rather extermination than conversion.

The Attitude of Christianity and the Early Church to War.

From the standpoint of the peace of nations, we may say that the Christian faith, compared with other prominent monotheistic religious systems, occupies an intermediate position between two extremes — the fanaticism of Islam, and to a less extent of Judaism, and the relatively passive attitude of the Buddhist who thought himself bound to propagate his religion, but held himself justified only in the employment of peaceful means. Christianity, on the other hand, contains no warlike principles: it can in no sense be called a religion of the sword, but circumstances gave the history of the Church, after the first few centuries of its existence, a character which cannot be called peace-loving.

This apparent contradiction between the spirit of the new religion and its practical attitude to war has led to some difference of opinion as to the actual teaching of Christ. The *New Testament* seems, at a superficial glance, to furnish support as readily to the champions of war as to its denouncers. The Messiah is the Prince of Peace (*Is.* IX. 6, 7; *Heb.* VI.), and here lies the way of righteousness (*Rom.* III. 19): but Christ came not to bring peace, but a sword (*Matth.* X. 34). Such statements may be given the meaning which we wish them to bear — the quoting of Scripture is ever an unsatisfactory form of evidence; but there is no direct statement in the *New Testament* in favour of war, no saying of Christ which, fairly interpreted, could be understood too regard this proof of human imperfection as less condemnable than any other.[12*] When men shall be without sin, nation shall rise up against nation no more. But man the individual can attain peace only when he has overcome the world, when, in the struggle with his lower self, he has come forth victorious. This is the spiritual sword which Christ brought into the world — strife, not with the unbeliever, but with the lower self: meekness and the spirit of the Word of God are the weapons with which man must fight for the Faith.

An elect people there was no longer: Israel had rejected its Messiah. Instead there was a complete brotherhood of all men, the bond and the free, as children of one God. The aim of the Church was a world-empire, bound together by a universal religion. In this sense, as sowing the first seeds of a universal peace, we may speak of Christianity as a re-establishment of peace among mankind.

The later attitude of Christians to war, however, by no means corresponds to the earliest tenets of the Church. Without doubt, certain sects, from the beginning of our era and through the ages up to the present time, held, like the Mennonites and Quakers in our day, that the divine command, "Love your enemies," could not be reconciled with the profession of a soldier. The early Christians were reproached under the Roman Emperors, before the time of Constantine, with avoiding the citizen's duty of military service.[13*] "To those enemies of our faith," wrote Origen (*Contra Celsum,* VIII., Ch. LXXIII., Anti-Nicene Christian Library), "who require us to bear arms for the commonwealth, and to slay men, we can reply: 'Do not those who are priests at certain shrines, and those who attend on certain gods, as you account them, keep their hands free from blood, that they may with hands unstained and free from human blood offer the appointed sacrifices to your gods; and even when war is upon you, you never enlist the priests in the army. If that, then, is a laudable custom, how much more so, that while others are engaged in battle, these too should engage as the priests and ministers of God, keeping their hands pure, and wrestling in prayers to God on behalf of those who are fighting in a righteous cause, and for the king who reigns righteously, that whatever is opposed to those who act righteously may be destroyed!' ... And we do take our part in public affairs, when along with righteous prayers we join self-denying exercises and meditations, which teach us to despise pleasures, and not to be led away by them. And none fight better for the king than we do. We do not indeed fight under him, although he require it; but we fight on his behalf, forming a special army — an army of piety — by offering our prayers to God." The Fathers of the Church, Justin Martyr, Clement of Alexandria, Tertullian, Ambrose and the rest gave the same testimony against war. The pagan rites connected with the taking of the military oath had no doubt some influence in determining the feeling of the pious with regard to this life of bloodshed; but the reasons lay deeper. "Shall it be held lawful," asked Tertullian, (*De Corona,*) "to make an occupation of the sword, when the Lord proclaims that he who uses the sword shall perish by the sword? And shall the son of peace take part in the battle when it does not become him even to sue at law? And shall he apply the chain, and the prison, and the torture, and the punishment, who is not the avenger even of his own wrongs?"

The doctrine of the Church developed early in the opposite direction. It was its fighting spirit and not a love of peace that made Christianity a state religion under Constantine. Nor was Augustine the first of the Church Fathers to regard military service as permissible. To come to a later time, this change of attitude has been ascribed partly to the rise of Mahometan power and the wave of fanaticism which broke over Europe. To destroy these unbelievers with fire and sword was regarded as a deed of piety pleasing to God. Hence the wars of the Crusades against the infidel were holy wars, and appear as a new element in the history of civilisation. The nations of ancient times had known only civil and foreign war.[14] They had rebelled at home, and they had fought mainly for material interests abroad. In the Middle Ages there were, besides, religious wars and, with the rise of Feudalism, private war:[15] among all the powers of the Dark Ages and for centuries later, none was more aggressive than the Catholic Church, nor a more active and untiring defender of its rights and claims, spiritual or temporal. It was in some respects a more warlike institution than the states of Greece and Rome. It struggled through centuries with the Emperor:[16] it pronounced its ban against disobedient states and disloyal cities: it pursued with its vengeance each heretical or rebellious prince: unmindful of its early traditions about peace, it showed in every crisis a fiercely military spirit.[17]

For more than a thousand years the Church counted fighting clergy[18] among its most active supporters. This strange anomaly was, it must be said, at first rather suffered in deference to public opinion than encouraged by ecclesiastical canons and councils, but it gave rise to great discontent at the time of the Reformation.[19] The whole question of the lawfulness of military service for Christians was then raised again. "If there be anything in the affairs of mortals," wrote Erasmus at this time (*Opera*, II., *Prov.*, 951 C) "which it becomes us deliberately to attack, which we ought indeed to shun by every possible means, to avert and to abolish, it is certainly war, than which there is nothing more wicked, more mischievous or more widely destructive in its effects, nothing harder to be rid of, or more horrible and, in a word, more unworthy of a man, not to say of a Christian."[20] The mediæval Church indeed succeeded, by the establishment of such institutions as the Truce of God, in setting some limits to the fury of the soldier: but its endeavours (and it made several to promote peace)[21] were only to a trifling extent successful. Perhaps custom and public opinion in feudal Europe were too strong, perhaps the Church showed a certain apathy in denouncing the evils of a military society: no doubt the theoretical tenets of its doctrine did less to hinder war than its own strongly military tendency, its lust for power and the force of its example did to encourage it.

Hence, in spite of Christianity and its early vision of a brotherhood of men, the history of the Middle Ages came nearer to a realization of the idea of perpetual war than was possible in ancient times. The tendency of the growth of Roman supremacy was to diminish the number of wars, along with the number of possible causes of racial friction. It united many nations in one great whole, and gave them, to a certain extent, a common culture and common interests; even, when this seemed prudent, a common right of citizenship. The fewer the number of boundaries, the less the likelihood of war. The establishment of great empires is of necessity a force, and a great and permanent force working on the side of peace. With the fall of Rome this guarantee was removed.

The Development of the New Science of International Law.

Out of the ruins of the old feudal system arose the modern state as a free independent unity. Private war between individuals or classes of society was now branded as a breach of the peace: it became the exclusive right of kings to appeal to force. War, wrote Gentilis[22*] towards the end of sixteenth century, is the just or unjust conflict between states. Peace was now regarded as the normal condition of society. As a result of these great developments in which the name "state" acquired new meaning, jurisprudence freed itself from the trammelling conditions of mediæval Scholasticism. Men began to consider the problem of the rightfulness or wrongfulness of war, to question even the possibility of a war on rightful grounds. Out of theses new ideas — partly too as one of the fruits of the Reformation,[23*] — arose the first consciously formulated principles of the science of international law, whose fuller, but not yet complete, development belongs to modern times.

From the beginning of history every age, every people has something to show here, be it only a rudimentary sense of justice in their dealings with one another. We may instance the Amphictyonic League in Greece which, while it had a merely Hellenic basis and was mainly a religious survival, shows the germ of some attempt at arbitration between Greek states. Among the Romans we have the *jus feciale*[24*] and the *jus gentium*, as distinguished from the civil law of Rome, and certain military regulations about the taking of booty in war. Ambassadors were held inviolate in both countries; the formal declaration of war was never omitted. Many Roman writers held the necessity of a just cause for war. But nowhere do these considerations form the subject matter of a special science.

In the Middle Ages the development of these ideas received little encouragement. All laws are silent in the time of war,[25*] and this was a period of war, both bloody and constant. There was no time to think of the right or wrong of anything. Moreover, the Church emphasised the lack of rights in unbelievers, and gave her blessing on their annihilation.[26*] The whole Christian world was filled with the idea of a spiritual universal monarchy. Not such as that in the minds of Greek and Jew and Roman who had been able to picture international peace only under the form of a great national and exclusive empire. In this great Christian state there were to be no distinctions between nations; its sphere was bounded by the universe. But, here, there was no room or recognition for independent national states with equal and personal rights. This recognition, opposed by the Roman Church, is the real basis of international law. The Reformation was the means by which the personality of the peoples, the unity and independence of the state were first openly admitted. On this foundation, mainly at first in Protestant countries, the new science developed rapidly. Like the civil state and the Christian religion, international law may be called a peace institution.

Grotius, Puffendorf and Vattel.

In the beginning of the seventeenth century, Grotius laid the foundations of a code of universal law (*De Jure Belli et Pacis*, 1625) independent of differences of religion, in the hope that its recognition might simplify the intercourse between the newly formed nations. The primary object of this great work, written during the misery and horrors of the Thirty Years' war, was expressly to draw attention to these evils and suggest some methods by which the severity of warfare might be mitigated. Grotius originally meant to explain only one chapter of the law of nations:[27*] his book was to be called *De Jure Belli*, but there is scarcely any subject of international law which he leaves untouched. He obtained, moreover, a general recognition for the doctrine of the Law of Nature which exerted so strong an influence upon succeeding centuries; indeed, between these two sciences, as between international law and ethics, he draws no very sharp line of demarcation, although, on the whole, in spite of an unscientific, scholastic use of quotation from authorities, his treatment of the new field is clear and comprehensive. Grotius made the attempt to set up an ethical principle of right, in the stead of such doctrines of self-interest as had been held by many of the ancient writers. There was a law, he held, established in each state purely with a view to the interests of that state, but, besides this, there was another higher law in the interest of the whole society of nations. Its origin was divine; the reason of man commanded his obedience. This was what we call international law.[28*]

Grotius distinctly holds, like Kant and Rousseau, and unlike Hobbes, that the state can never be regarded as a unity or institution separable from the people; the terms *civitas, communitas, coetus, populus*, he uses indiscriminately. But these nations, these independent units of society cannot live together side by side just as they like; they must recognise one another as members of a European society of states.[29*] Law, he said, stands above force even in war, "which may only be begun to pursue the right;" and the beginning and manner of conduct of war rests on fixed laws and can be justified only in certain cases. War is not to be done away with: Grotius accepts it as fact,[30*] (as Hobbes did later) as the natural method for settling the disputes which were bound constantly to arise between so many independent and sovereign nations. A terrible scourge it must ever remain, but as the only available form of legal procedure, it is sanctioned by the practice of states and not less by the law of nature and of nations. Grotius did not advance beyond this position. Every violation of the law of nations can be settled but in one way — by war, the force of the stronger.

The necessary distinction between law and ethics was drawn by Puffendorf,[31*] a successor of Grotius who gave an outwardly systematic form to the doctrine of the great jurist, without adding to it either strength or completeness. His views, when they were not based upon the system of Grotius, were strongly influenced by the speculation of Hobbes, his chronological predecessor, to whom we shall have later occasion to refer. In the works of Vattel,[32*] who was, next to Rousseau, the most celebrated of Swiss publicists, we find the theory of the customs and practice in war widely developed, and the necessity for humanising its methods and limiting its destructive effects upon neutral countries strongly emphasised. Grotius and Puffendorf, while they recommend acts of mercy, hold that there is legally no right which requires that a conquered enemy shall be spared. This is a matter of humanity alone. It is to the praise of Vattel that he did much to popularise among the highest and most powerful classes of society, ideas of humanity in warfare, and of the rights and obligations of nations. He is, moreover, the first to make a clear separation between this science and the Law of Nature. What, he asks, is international law as distinguished from the Law of Nature? What are the powers of a state and the duties of nations to one another? What are the causes of quarrel among nations, and what the means by which they can be settled without any sacrifice of dignity?

They are, in the first place, a friendly conciliatory attitude; and secondly, such means of settlement as mediation, arbitration and Peace Congresses. These are the refuges of a peace-loving nation, in cases where vital interests are not at stake. "Nature gives us no right to use force, except where mild and conciliatory measures are useless." (*Law of Nations*, II. Ch. xviii. § 331.) "Every power owes it in this matter to the happiness of human society to show itself ready for every means of reconciliation, in cases where the interests at stake are neither vital nor important." (*ibid.* § 332.) At the same time, it is never advisable that a nation should forgive an insult which it has not the power to resent.

The Dream of a Perpetual Peace.

But side by side with this development and gradual popularisation of the new science of International Law, ideas of a less practical, but not less fruitful kind had been steadily making their way and obtaining a strong hold upon the popular mind. The Decree of Eternal Pacification of 1495 had abolished private war, one of the heavy curses of the Middle Ages. Why should it not be extended to banish warfare between states as well? Gradually one proposal after another was made to attain this end, or, at least, to smooth the way for its future realisation. The first of these in point of time is to be found in a somewhat bare, vague form in Sully's *Memoirs*,[33*] said to have been published in 1634. Half a century later the Quaker William Penn suggested an international tribunal of arbitration in the interests of peace.[34*] But it was by the French Abbé St. Pierre that the problem of perpetual peace was fairly introduced into political literature: and this, in an age of cabinet and dynastic wars, while the dreary cost of the war of the Spanish succession was yet unpaid. St. Pierre was the first who really clearly realised and endeavoured to prove that the establishment of a permanent state of peace is not only in the interest of the weaker, but is required by the European society of nations and by the reason of man. From the beginning of the history of humanity, poets and prophets had cherished the "sweet dream" of a peaceful civilisation: it is in the form of a practical project that this idea is new.

The ancient world actually represented a state of what was almost perpetual war. This was the reality which confronted man, his inevitable doom, it seemed, as it had been pronounced to the fallen sinners of Eden. Peace was something which man had enjoyed once, but forfeited. The myth- and poetry-loving Greeks, and, later, the poets of Rome delighted to paint a state of eternal peace, not as something to whose coming they could look forward in the future, but as a golden age of purity whose records lay buried in the past, a paradise which had been, but which was no more. Voices, more scientific, were raised even in Greece in attempts, such as Aristotle's, to show that the evolution of man had been not a course of degeneration from perfection, but of continual progress upwards from barbarism to civilisation and culture. But the change in popular thinking on this matter was due less to the arguments of philosophy than to a practical experience of the causes which operate in the interests of peace. The foundation of a universal empire under Alexander the Great gave temporary rest to nations heretofore incessantly at war. Here was a proof that the Divine Will had not decreed that man was to work out his punishment under unchanging conditions of perpetual warfare. This idea of a universal empire became the Greek ideal of a perpetual peace. Such an empire was, in the language of the Stoics, a world-state in which all men had rights of citizenship, in which all other nations were absorbed.

Parallel to this ideal among the Greeks, we find the hope in Israel of a Messiah whose coming was to bring peace, not only to the Jewish race, but to all the nations of the earth. This idea stands out in the sharpest contrast to the early nationalism of the Hebrew people, who regarded every stranger as an idolater and an enemy. The prophecies of Judaism, combined with the cosmopolitan ideas of Greece, were the source of the idea, which is expressed in the teaching of Christ, of a spiritual world-empire, an empire held together solely by the tie of a common religion.

This hope of peace did not actually die during the first thousand years of our era, nor even under the morally stagnating influences of the Middle Ages. When feudalism and private war were abolished in Europe, it wakened to a new life. Not merely in the mouths of poets and religious enthusiasts was the cry raised against war, but by scholars like Thomas More and Erasmus, jurists like Gentilis and Grotius, men high in the state and in the eyes of Europe like Henry IV. of France and the Duc de Sully or the Abbé de St. Pierre whose *Projet de Paix Perpétuelle* (1713)[35*] obtained immediate popularity and wide-spread fame. The first half of the eighteenth century was already prepared to receive and mature a plan of this kind.

Henry IV. and St. Pierre.

The *Grand Dessein* of Henry IV. is supposed to have been formed by that monarch and reproduced in Sully's *Memoirs*, written in 1634 and discovered nearly a century later by St. Pierre. The story goes that the Abbé found the book buried in an old garden. It has been shewn, however, that there is little likelihood that this project actually originated with the king, who probably corresponded fairly well to Voltaire's picture of him as war hero of the *Henriade*. The plan was more likely conceived by Sully, and ascribed to the popular king for the sake of the better hearing and greater influence it might in this way be likely to have, and also because, thereby, it might be less likely to create offence in political circles. St. Pierre himself may or may not have been acquainted with the facts.

The so-called *Grand Dessein* of Henry IV. was, shortly, as follows.[36*] It proposed to divide Europe between fifteen Powers,[37*] in such a manner that the balance of power should be established and preserved. These were to form a Christian republic on the basis of the freedom and equality of its members, the armed forces of the federation being supported by fixed contribution. A general council, consisting of representatives from the fifteen states, was to make all laws necessary for cementing the union thus formed and for maintaining the order once established. It would also be the business of this senate to "deliberate on questions that might arise, to occupy themselves with discussing different interests, to settle quarrels amicably, to throw light upon and arrange all the civil, political and religious affairs of Europe, whether internal or foreign." (*Mémoires*, vol. VI., *seq.*)

This scheme of the king or his minister was expanded with great thoroughness and clear-sightedness by the Abbé St. Pierre: none of the many later plans for a perpetual peace has been so perfect in details. He proposes that there should be a permanent and perpetual union between, if possible, all Christian sovereigns — of whom he suggests nineteen, excluding the Czar— "to preserve unbroken peace in Europe," and that a permanent Congress or senate should be formed by deputies of the federated states. The union should protect weak sovereigns, minors during a regency, and so on, and should banish civil as well as international war — it should "render prompt and adequate assistance to rulers and chief magistrates against seditious persons and rebels." All warfare henceforth is to be waged between the troops of the federation — each nation contributing an equal number — and the enemies of European security, whether outsiders or rebellious members of the union. Otherwise, where it is possible, all disputes occurring within the union are to be settled by the arbitration of the senate, and the combined military force of the federation is to be applied to drive the Turks out of Europe. There is to be a rational rearrangement of boundaries, but after this no change is to be permitted in the map of Europe. The union should bind itself to tolerate the different forms of faith.

The objections to St. Pierre's scheme are, many of them, obvious. He himself produces sixty-two arguments likely to be raised against his plan, and he examines these in turn with acuteness and eloquence. But there are other criticisms which he was less likely to be able to forestall. Of the nineteen states he names as a basis of the federation, some have disappeared and the governments of others have completely changed. Indeed St. Pierre's scheme did not look far beyond the present. But it has besides a too strongly political character.[38*] From this point of view, the Abbé's plan amounts practically to a European coalition against the Ottoman Empire. Moreover, we notice with a smile that the French statesman and patriot is not lost in the cosmopolitan political reformer. "The kingdom of Spain shall not go out of the House of Bourbon!"[39*] France is to enjoy more than the privileges of honour; she is to reap distinct material and political advantages from the union. Humanity is to be a brotherhood, but, in the federation of nations, France is to stand first.[40*] We see that these "rêves d'un homme de bien," as Cardinal Dubois called them, are not without their practical element. But the great mistake of St. Pierre is this: he actually thought that his plan could be put into execution in the near future, that an ideal of this kind was realisable at once.[41*] "I, myself, form'd it," he says in the preface, "in full expectation to see it one Day executed." As Hobbes, says, "there can be nothing so absurd, but may be found in the books of philosophers."[42*] St. Pierre was not content to make his influence felt on the statesmen of his time and prepare the way for the abolition of all arbitrary forms of government. This was the flaw which drew down upon the good Abbé Voltaire's sneering epigram[43*] and the irony of Leibniz.[44*] Here, above all, in this unpractical enthusiasm his scheme differs from that of Kant.

Rousseau's Criticism of St. Pierre.

Rousseau took St. Pierre's project[45*] much more seriously than either Leibniz or Voltaire. But sovereigns, he thought, are deaf to the voice of justice; the absolutism of princely power would never allow a king to submit to a tribunal of nations. Moreover war was, according to Rousseau's experience, a matter not between nations, but between princes and cabinets. It was one of the ordinary pleasures of royal existence and one not likely to be voluntarily given up.[46*] We know that history has not supported Rousseau's contention. Dynastic wars are now no more. The Great Powers have shown themselves able to impose their own conditions, where the welfare and security of Europe have seemed to demand it. Such a development seemed impossible enough in the eighteenth century. In the military organisation of the nations of Europe and in the necessity of making their internal development subordinate to the care for their external security, Rousseau saw the cause of all the defects in their administration.[47*] The formation of unions on the model of the Swiss Confederation or the German *Bund* would, he thought, be in the interest of all rulers. But great obstacles seemed to him to lie in the way of the realisation of such a project as that of St. Pierre. "Without doubt," says Rousseau in conclusion, "the proposal of a perpetual peace is at present an absurd one.... It can only be put into effect by methods which are violent in themselves and dangerous to humanity. One cannot conceive of the possibility of a federative union being established, except by a revolution. And, that granted, who among us would venture to say whether this European federation is to be desired or to be feared? It would work, perhaps, more harm in a moment than it would prevent in the course of centuries." (*Jugement sur la Paix Perpétuelle.*)

The Position of Hobbes.

The most profound and searching analysis of this problem comes from Immanuel Kant, whose indebtedness in the sphere of politics to Hobbes, Locke, Montesquieu and Rousseau it is difficult to overestimate. Kant's doctrine of the sovereignty of the people comes to him from Locke through Rousseau. His explanation of the origin of society is practically that of Hobbes. The direct influence on politics of this philosopher, apart from his share in moulding the Kantian theory of the state, is one we cannot afford to neglect. His was a great influence on the new science just thrown on the world by Grotius, and his the first clear and systematic statement we have of the nature of society and the establishment of the state. The natural state of man, says Hobbes, is a state of war,[48*] a *bellum omnium contra omnes*, where all struggle for honour and for preferment and the prizes to which every individual is by natural right equally entitled, but which can of necessity fall only to the few, the foremost in the race. Men hate and fear the society of their kind, but through this desire to excel are forced to seek it: only where there are many can there be a first. This state of things, this apparent sociability which is brought about by and coupled with the least sociable of instincts, becomes unendurable. "It is necessary to peace," writes Hobbes (*On Dominion*, Ch. VI. 3) "that a man be so far forth protected against the violence of others, that he may live securely; that is, that he may have no just cause to fear others, so long as he doth them no injury. Indeed, to make men altogether safe from mutual harms, so as they cannot be hurt or injuriously killed, is impossible; and, therefore, comes not within deliberation." But to protect them so far as is possible the state is formed. Hobbes has no great faith in human contracts or promises. Man's nature is malicious and untrustworthy. A coercive power is necessary to guarantee this long-desired security within the community. "We must therefore," he adds, "provide for our security, not by compacts, but by punishments; and there is then sufficient provision made, when there are so great punishments appointed for every injury, as apparently it prove a greater evil to have done it, than not to have done it. For all men, by a necessity of nature, choose that which to them appears to be the less evil." (*Op. cit.*, Ch. VI. 4.)

These precautions secure that relative peace within the state which is one of the conditions of the safety of the people. But it is, besides, the duty of a sovereign to guarantee an adequate protection to his subjects against foreign enemies. A state of defence as complete and perfect as possible is not only a national duty, but an absolute necessity. The following statement of the relation of the state to other states shows how closely Hobbes has been followed by Kant. "There are two things necessary," says Hobbes, (*On Dominion*, Ch. XIII. 7) "for the people's defence; to be warned and to be forearmed. *For the state of commonwealths considered in themselves, is natural, that is to say, hostile.*[49] Neither, if they cease from fighting, is it therefore to be called peace; but rather a breathing time, in which one enemy observing the motion and countenance of the other, values his security not according to pacts, but the forces and counsels of his adversary."

Hobbes is a practical philosopher: no man was less a dreamer, a follower after ideals than he. He is, moreover, a pessimist, and his doctrine of the state is a political absolutism,[50] the form of government which above all has been, and is, favourable to war. He would no doubt have ridiculed the idea of a perpetual peace between nations, had such a project as that of St. Pierre — a practical project, counting upon a realisation in the near future — been brought before him. He might not even have accepted it in the very much modified form which Kant adopts, that of an ideal — an unattainable ideal — towards which humanity could not do better than work. He expected the worst possible from man the individual. *Homo homini lupus.* The strictest absolutism, amounting almost to despotism, was required to keep the vicious propensities of the human animal in check. States he looked upon as units of the same kind, members also of a society. They had, and openly exhibited, the same faults as individual men. They too might be driven with a strong enough coercive force behind them, but not without it; and such a coercive force as this did not exist in a society of nations. Federation and federal troops are terms which represent ideas of comparatively recent origin. Without something of this kind, any enduring peace was not to be counted upon. International relations were and must remain at least potentially warlike in character. Under no circumstances could ideal conditions be possible either between the members of a state or between the states themselves. Human nature could form no satisfactory basis for a counsel of perfection.

Hence Hobbes never thought of questioning the necessity of war. It was in his eyes the natural condition of European society; but certain rules were necessary both for its conduct and, where this was compatible with a nation's dignity and prosperity, for its prevention. He held that international law was only a part of the Law of Nature, and that this Law of Nature laid certain obligations upon nations and their kings. Mediation must be employed between disputants as much as possible, the person of the mediators of peace being held inviolate; an umpire ought to be chosen to decide a controversy, to whose judgment the parties in dispute agree to submit themselves; such an arbiter must be impartial. These are all what Hobbes calls precepts of the Law of Nature. And he appeals to the Scriptures in confirmation of his assertion that peace is the way of righteousness and that the laws of nature of which these are a few are also laws of the heavenly kingdom. But peace is like the straight path of Christian endeavour, difficult to find and difficult to keep. We must seek after it where it may be found; but, having done this and sought in vain, we have no alternative but to fall back upon war. Reason requires "that every man ought to endeavour peace," (*Lev.* I. Ch. XIV.) "as far as he has hope of obtaining it; and when he cannot obtain it, that he may seek, and use, all helps, and advantages of war."[51*] This, says Hobbes elsewhere, (*On Liberty*, Ch. I. 15) is the dictate of right reason, the first and fundamental law of nature.

Kant's Idea of a Perpetual Peace.

With regard to the problems of international law, Kant is of course a hundred and fifty years ahead of Hobbes. But he starts from the same point: his theory of the beginning of society is practically identical with that of the older philosopher. Men are by nature imperfect creatures, unsociable and untrustworthy, cursed by a love of glory, of possession, and of power, passions which make happiness something for ever unattainable by them. Hobbes is content to leave them here with their imperfections, and let a strong government help them out as it may. But not so Kant. He looks beyond man the individual, developing slowly by stages scarcely measurable, progressing at one moment, and the next, as it seems, falling behind: he looks beyond the individual, struggling and never attaining, to the race. Here Kant is no pessimist. The capacities implanted in man by nature are not all for evil: they are, he says, "destined to unfold themselves completely in the course of time, and in accordance with the end to which they are adapted." (*Idea of a Universal History from a Cosmopolitan Point of View*, 1784. Pro.) This end of humanity is the evolution of man from the stage of mere self-satisfied animalism to a high state of civilisation. Through his own reason man is to attain a perfect culture, intellectual and moral. In this long period of struggle, the potential faculties which nature or Providence has bestowed upon him reach their full development. The process in which this evolution takes place is what we call history.

To man nature has given none of the perfect animal equipments for self-preservation and self-defence which she has bestowed on others of her creatures. But she has given to him reason and freedom of will, and has determined that through these faculties and without the aid of instinct he shall win for himself a complete development of his capacities and natural endowments. It is, says Kant, no happy life that nature has marked out for man. He is filled with desires which he can never satisfy. His life is one of endeavour and not of attainment: not even the consciousness of the well-fought battle is his, for the struggle is more or less an unconscious one, the end unseen. Only in the race, and not in the individual, can the natural capacities of the human species reach full development. Reason, says Kant, (Pro, *op. cit.*) "does not itself work by instinct, but requires experiments, exercise and instruction in order to advance gradually from one stage of insight to another. Hence each individual man would necessarily have to live an enormous length of time, in order to learn by himself how to make a complete use of all his natural endowments. Or, if nature should have given him but a short lease of life, as is actually the case, reason would then require an almost interminable series of generations, the one handing down its enlightenment to the other, in order that the seeds she has sown in our species may be brought at last to a stage of development which is in perfect accordance with her design." Man the individual shall travel towards the land of promise and fight for its possession, but not he, nor his children, nor his children's children shall inherit the land. "Only the latest comers can have the good fortune of inhabiting the dwelling which the long series of their predecessors have toiled — though," adds Kant, "without any conscious intent — to build up without even the possibility of participating in the happiness which they were preparing." (Proposition 3.)

The means which nature employs to bring about this development of all the capacities implanted in men is their mutual antagonism in society — what Kant calls the "unsocial sociableness of men, that is to say, their inclination to enter into society, an inclination which yet is bound up at every point with a resistance which threatens continually to break up the society so formed." (Proposition 4.) Man hates society, and yet there alone he can develop his capacities; he cannot live there peaceably, and yet cannot live without it. It is the resistance which others offer to his inclinations and will — which he, on his part, shows likewise to the desires of others — that awakens all the latent powers of his nature and the determination to conquer his natural propensity to indolence and love of material comfort and to struggle for the first place among his fellow-creatures, to satisfy, in outstripping them, his love of glory and possession and power. "Without those, in themselves by no means lovely, qualities which set man in social opposition to man, so that each finds his selfish claims resisted by the selfishness of all the others, men would have lived on in an Arcadian shepherd life, in perfect harmony, contentment, and mutual love; but all their talents would forever have remained hidden and undeveloped. Thus, kindly as the sheep they tended, they would scarcely have given to their existence a greater value than that of their cattle. And the place among the ends of creation which was left for the development of rational beings would not have been filled. Thanks be to nature for the unsociableness, for the spiteful competition of vanity, for the insatiate desires of gain and power! Without these, all the excellent natural capacities of humanity would have slumbered undeveloped. Man's will is for harmony; but nature knows better what is good for his species: her will is for dissension. He would like a life of comfort and satisfaction, but nature wills that he should be dragged out of idleness and inactive content and plunged into labour and trouble, in order that he may be made to seek in his own prudence for the means of again delivering himself from them. The natural impulses which prompt this effort, — the causes of unsociableness and mutual conflict, out of which so many evils spring, — are also in turn the spurs which drive him to the development of his powers. Thus, they really betray the providence of a wise Creator, and not the interference of some evil spirit which has meddled with the world which God has nobly planned, and enviously overturned its order." (Proposition 4: Caird's translation in *The Critical Philosophy of Kant*, Vol. II., p, 551.)

The problem now arises, How shall men live together, each free to work out his own development, without at the same time interfering with a like liberty on the part of his neighbour? The solution of this problem is the state. Here the liberty of each member is guaranteed and its limits strictly defined. A perfectly just civil constitution, administered according to the principles of right, would be that under which the greatest possible amount of liberty was left to each citizen within these limits. This is the ideal of Kant, and here lies the greatest practical problem which has presented itself to humanity. An ideal of this kind is difficult of realisation. But nature imposes no such duty upon us. "Out of such crooked material as man is made," says Kant, "nothing can be hammered quite straight." (Proposition 6.) We must make our constitution as good as we can and, with that, rest content.

The direct cause of this transition from a state of nature and conditions of unlimited freedom to civil society with its coercive and restraining forces is found in the evils of that state of nature as they are painted by Hobbes. A wild lawless freedom becomes impossible for man: he is compelled to seek the protection of a civil society. He lives in uncertainty and insecurity: his liberty is so far worthless that he cannot peacefully enjoy it. For this peace he voluntarily yields up some part of his independence. The establishment of the state is in the interest of his development to a higher civilisation. It is more — the guarantee of his existence and self-preservation. This is the sense, says Professor Paulsen, in which Kant like Hobbes regards the state as "resting on a contract,"[52*] that is to say, on the free will of all.[53*] *Volenti non fit injuria*. Only, adds Paulsen, we must remember that this contract is not a historical fact, as it seemed to some writers of the eighteenth century, but an "idea of reason": we are speaking here not of the history of the establishment of the state, but of the reason of its existence. (Paulsen's *Kant*, .)[54*]

In this civil union, self-sought, yet sought reluctantly, man is able to turn his most unlovable qualities to a profitable use. They bind this society together. They are the instrument by which he wins for himself self-culture. It is here with men, says Kant, as it is with the trees in a forest: "just because each one strives to deprive the other of air and sun, they compel each other to seek both above, and thus they grow beautiful and straight. Whereas those that, in freedom and isolation from one another, shoot out their branches at will, grow stunted and crooked and awry." (Proposition 5, *op. cit.*) Culture, art, and all that is best in the social order are the fruits of that self-loving unsociableness in man.

The problem of the establishment of a perfect civil constitution cannot be solved, says this treatise (*Idea for a Universal History*), until the external relations of states are regulated in accordance with principles of right. For, even if the ideal internal constitution were attained, what end would it serve in the evolution of humanity, if commonwealths themselves were to remain like individuals in a state of nature, each existing in uncontrolled freedom, a law unto himself? This condition of things again cannot be permanent. Nature uses the same means as before to bring about a state of law and order. War, present or near at hand, the strain of constant preparation for a possible future campaign or the heavy burden of debt and devastation left by the last, — these are the evils which must drive states to leave a lawless, savage state of nature, hostile to man's inward development, and seek in union the end of nature, peace. All wars are the attempts nature makes to bring about new political relations between nations, relations which, in their very nature, cannot be, and are not desired to be, permanent. These combinations will go on succeeding each other, until at last a federation of all powers is formed for the establishment of perpetual peace. This is the end of humanity, demanded by reason. Justice will reign, not only in the state, but in the whole human race when perpetual peace exists between the nations of the world.

This is the point of view of the *Idea for a Universal History*. But equally, we may say, law and justice will reign between nations, when a legally and morally perfect constitution adorns the state. External perpetual peace presupposes internal peace — peace civil, social, economic, religious. Now, when men are perfect — and what would this be but perfection — how can there be war? Cardinal Fleury's only objection — no light one — to St. Pierre's project was that, as even the most peace-loving could not avoid war, all men must first be men of noble character. This seems to be what is required in the treatise on *Perpetual Peace*. Kant demands, to a certain extent, the moral regeneration of man. There must be perfect honesty in international dealings, good faith in the interpretation and fulfilment of treaties and so on (Art. 1)[55*]: and again, every state must have a republican constitution — a term by which Kant understands a constitution as nearly as possible in accordance with the spirit of right. (Art. 1.)[56*] This is to say that we have to start with our reformation at home, look first to the culture and education and morals of our citizens, then to our foreign relations. This is a question of self-interest as well as of ethics. On the civil and religious liberty of a state depends its commercial success. Kant saw the day coming, when industrial superiority was to be identified with political pre-eminence. The state which does not look to the enlightenment and liberty of its subjects must fail in the race. But the advantages of a high state of civilisation are not all negative. The more highly developed the individuals who form a state, the more highly developed is its consciousness of its obligations to other nations. In the ignorance and barbarism of races lies the great obstacle to a reign of law among states. Uncivilised states cannot be conceived as members of a federation of Europe. First, the perfect civil constitution according to right: then the federation of these law-abiding Powers. This is the path which reason marks out. The treatise on *Perpetual Peace* seems to be in this respect more practical than the *Idea for a Universal History*. But it matters little which way we take it. The point of view is the same in both cases: the end remains the development of man towards good, the order of his steps in this direction is indifferent.

The Political and Social Conditions of Kant's Time.

The history of the human race, viewed as a whole, Kant regards as the realisation of a hidden plan of nature to bring about a political constitution internally and externally perfect — the only condition under which the faculties of man can be fully developed. Does experience support this theory? Kant thought that, to a certain degree, it did. This conviction was not, however, a fruit of his experience of citizenship in Prussia, an absolute dynastic state, a military monarchy waging perpetual dynastic wars of the kind he most hotly condemned. Kant had no feeling of love to Prussia,[57*] and little of a citizen's patriotic pride, or even interest, in its political achievements. This was partly because of his sympathy with republican doctrines: partly due to his love of justice and peculiar hatred of war,[58*] a hatred based, no doubt, not less on principle than on a close personal experience of the wretchedness it brings with it. It was not the political and social conditions in which he lived which fostered Kant's love of liberty and gave him inspiration, unless in the sense in which the mind reacts upon surrounding influences. Looking beyond Prussia to America, in whose struggle for independence he took a keen interest, and looking to France where the old dynastic monarchy had been succeeded by a republican state, Kant seemed to see the signs of a coming democratisation of the old monarchical society of Europe. In this growing influence on the state of the mass of the people who had everything to lose in war and little to gain by victory, he saw the guarantee of a future perpetual peace. Other forces too were at work to bring about this consummation. There was a growing consciousness that war, this costly means of settling a dispute, is not even a satisfactory method of settlement. Hazardous and destructive in its effect, it is also uncertain in its results. Victory is not always gain; it no longer signifies a land to be plundered, a people to be sold to slavery. It brings fresh responsibilities to a nation, at a time when it is not always strong enough to bear them. But, above all, Kant saw, even at the end of the eighteenth century, the nations of Europe so closely bound together by commercial interests that a war — and especially a maritime war where the scene of conflict cannot be to the same extent localised as on land — between any two of them could not but seriously affect the prosperity of the others.[59*] He clearly realised that the spirit of commerce was the strongest force in the service of the maintenance of peace, and that in it lay a guarantee of future union.

This scheme of a federation of the nations of the world, in accordance with principles which would put an end to war between them, was one whose interest for Kant seemed to increase during the last twenty years of his life.[60*] It was according to him an idea of reason, and, in his first essay on the subject — that of 1784 — we see the place this ideal of a perpetual peace held in the Kantian system of philosophy. Its realisation is the realisation of the highest good — the ethical and political *summum bonum*, for here the aims of morals and politics coincide: only in a perfect development of his faculties in culture and in morals can man at last find true happiness. History is working towards the consummation of this end. A moral obligation lies on man to strive to establish conditions which bring its realisation nearer. It is the duty of statesmen to form a federative union as it was formerly the duty of individuals to enter the state. The moral law points the way here as clearly as in the sphere of pure ethics:— "Thou can'st, therefore thou ought'st."

Let us be under no misapprehension as to Kant's attitude to the problem of perpetual peace. It is an ideal. He states plainly that he so regards it[61*] and that as such it is unattainable. But this is the essence of all ideals: they have not the less value in shaping the life and character of men and nations on that account. They are not ends to be realised but ideas according to which we must live, regulative principles. We cannot, says Kant, shape our life better than in acting as if such ideas of reason have objective validity and there be an immortal life in which man shall live according to the laws of reason, in peace with his neighbour and in freedom from the trammels of sense.

Hence we are concerned here, not with an end, but with the means by which we might best set about attaining it, if it were attainable. This is the subject matter of the *Treatise on Perpetual Peace* (1795), a less eloquent and less purely philosophical essay than that of 1784, but throughout more systematic and practical. We have to do, not with the favourite dream of philanthropists like St. Pierre and Rousseau, but with a statement of the conditions on the fulfilment of which the transition to a reign of peace and law depends.

The Conditions of the Realisation of the Kantian Ideal.

These means are of two kinds. In the first place, what evils must we set about removing? What are the negative conditions? And, secondly, what are the general positive conditions which will make the realisation of this idea possible and guarantee the permanence of an international peace once attained? These negative and positive conditions Kant calls Preliminary and Definitive Articles respectively, the whole essay being carefully thrown into the form of a treaty. The Preliminary Articles of a treaty for perpetual peace are based on the principle that anything that hinders or threatens the peaceful co-existence of nations must be abolished. These conditions have been classified by Kuno Fischer. Kant, he points out,[62*] examines the principles of right governing the different sets of circumstances in which nations find themselves — namely, (*a*) while they are actually at war; (*b*) when the time comes to conclude a treaty of peace; (*c*) when they are living in a state of peace. The six Preliminary Articles fall naturally into these groups. War must not be conducted in such a manner as to increase national hatred and embitter a future peace. (Art. 6.)[63*] The treaty which brings hostilities to an end must be concluded in an honest desire for peace. (Art. 1.)[64*] Again a nation, when in a state of peace, must do nothing to threaten the political independence of another nation or endanger its existence, thereby giving the strongest of all motives for a fresh war. A nation may commit this injury in two ways: (1) indirectly, by causing danger to others through the growth of its standing army (Art. 3)[65*] — always a menace to the state of peace — or by any unusual war preparations: and (2) through too great a supremacy of another kind, by amassing money, the most powerful of all weapons in warfare. The National Debt (Art. 4)[66*] is another standing danger to the peaceful co-existence of nations. But, besides, we have the danger of actual attack. There is no right of intervention between nations. (Art. 5.)[67*] Nor can states be inherited or conquered (Art. 2),[68*] or in any way treated in a manner subversive of their independence and sovereignty as individuals. For a similar reason, armed troops cannot be hired and sold as things.

These then are the negative conditions of peace.[69*] There are, besides, three positive conditions:

(*a*) The intercourse of nations is to be confined to a right of hospitality. (Art. 3.)[70*] There is nothing new to us in this assertion of a right of way. The right to free means of international communication has in the last hundred years become a commonplace of law. And the change has been brought about, as Kant anticipated, not through an abstract respect for the idea of right, but through the pressure of purely commercial interests. Since Kant's time the nations of Europe have all been more or less transformed from agricultural to commercial states whose interests run mainly in the same direction, whose existence and development depend necessarily upon "conditions of universal hospitality." Commerce depends upon this freedom of international intercourse, and on commerce mainly depends our hope of peace.

(*b*) The first Definitive Article[71*] requires that the constitution of every state should be republican. What Kant understands by this term is that, in the state, law should rule above force and that its constitution should be a representative one, guaranteeing public justice and based on the freedom and equality of its members and their mutual dependence on a common legislature. Kant's demand is independent of the *form* of the government. A constitutional monarchy like that of Prussia in the time of Frederick the Great, who regarded himself as the first servant of the state and ruled with the wisdom and forethought which the nation would have had the right to demand from such an one — such a monarchy is not in contradiction to the idea of a true republic. That the state should have a constitution in accordance with the principles of right is the essential point.[72*] To make this possible, the law-giving power must lie with the representatives of the people: there must be a complete separation, such as Locke and Rousseau demand, between the legislature and executive. Otherwise we have despotism. Hence, while Kant admitted absolutism under certain conditions, he rejected democracy where, in his opinion, the mass of the people was despot.

An internal constitution, firmly established on the principles of right, would not only serve to kill the seeds of national hatred and diminish the likelihood of foreign war. It would do more: it would destroy sources of revolution and discontent within the state. Kant, like many writers on this subject, does not directly allude to civil war[73*] and the means by which it may be prevented or abolished. Actually to achieve this would be impossible: it is beyond the power of either arbitration or disarmament. But in a representative government and the liberty of a people lie the greatest safeguards against internal discontent. Civil peace and international peace must to a certain extent go hand in hand.

We come now to the central idea of the treatise: (c) the law of nations must be based upon a federation of free states. (Art. 2.)[74*] This must be regarded as the end to which mankind is advancing. The problem here is not out of many nations to make one. This would be perhaps the surest way to attain peace, but it is scarcely practicable, and, in certain forms, it is undesirable. Kant is inclined to approve of the separation of nations by language and religion, by historical and social tradition and physical boundaries: nature seems to condemn the idea of a universal monarchy.[75*] The only footing on which a thorough-going, indubitable system of international law is in practice possible is that of the society of nations: not the world-republic[76*] the Greeks dreamt of, but a federation of states. Such a union in the interests of perpetual peace between nations would be the "highest political good." The relation of the federated states to one another and to the whole would be fixed by cosmopolitan law: the link of self-interest which would bind them would again be the spirit of commerce.

This scheme of a perpetual peace had not escaped ridicule in the eighteenth century: the name of Kant protected it henceforth. The facts of history, even more conclusively than the voices of philosophers, soldiers and princes, show how great has been the progress of this idea in recent years. But it has not gained its present hold upon the popular mind without great and lasting opposition. Indeed we have here what must still be regarded as a controversial question. There have been, and are still, men who regard perpetual peace as a state of things as undesirable as it is unattainable. For such persons, war is a necessity of our civilisation: it is impossible that it should ever cease to exist. All that we can do, and there is no harm, nor any contradiction in the attempt, is to make wars shorter, fewer and more humane: the whole question, beyond this, is without practical significance. Others, on the other hand, — and these perhaps more thoughtful — regard war as hostile to culture, an evil of the worst kind, although a necessary evil. In peace, for them, lies the true ideal of humanity, although in any perfect form this cannot be realised in the near future. The extreme forms of these views are to be sought in what has been called in Germany "the philosophy of the barracks" which comes forward with a glorification of war for its own sake, and in the attitude of modern Peace Societies which denounce all war wholesale, without respect of causes or conditions.

Hegel, Schiller and Moltke.

Hegel, the greatest of the champions of war, would have nothing to do with Kant's federation of nations formed in the interests of peace. The welfare of a state, he held, is its own highest law; and he refused to admit that this welfare was to be sought in an international peace. Hegel lived in an age when all power and order seemed to lie with the sword. Something of the charm of Napoleonism seems to hang over him. He does not go the length of writers like Joseph de Maistre, who see in war the finger of God or an arrangement for the survival of the fittest — a theory, as far as regards individuals, quite in contradiction with the real facts, which show that it is precisely the physically unfit whom war, as a method of extermination, cannot reach. But, like Schiller and Moltke, Hegel sees in war an educative instrument, developing virtues in a nation which could not be fully developed otherwise, (much as pain and suffering bring patience and resignation and other such qualities into play in the individual), and drawing the nation together, making each citizen conscious of his citizenship, as no other influence can. War, he holds, leaves a nation always stronger than it was before; it buries causes of inner dissension, and consolidates the internal power of the state.[77*] No other trial can, in the same way, show what is the real strength and weakness of a nation, what it *is*, not merely materially, but physically, intellectually and morally.

With this last statement most people will be inclined to agree. There is only a part of the truth in Napoleon's dictum that "God is on the side of the biggest battalions"; or in the old saying that war requires three necessaries — in the first place, money; in the second place, money; and in the third, money. Money is a great deal: it is a necessity; but what we call national back-bone and character is more. So far we are with Hegel. But he goes further. In peace, says he, mankind would grow effeminate and degenerate in luxury. This opinion was expressed in forcible language in his own time by Schiller,[78*] and in more recent years by Count Moltke. "Perpetual peace," says a letter of the great general,[79*] "is a dream and not a beautiful dream either: war is part of the divine order of the world. During war are developed the noblest virtues which belong to man — courage and self-denial, fidelity to duty and the spirit of self-sacrifice: the soldier is called upon to risk his life. Without war the world would sink in materialism."[80*] "Want and misery, disease, suffering and war," he says elsewhere, "are all given elements in the Divine order of the universe." Moltke's eulogy of war, however, is somewhat modified by his additional statement that "the greatest kindness in war lies in its being quickly ended." (Letter to Bluntschli, 11th Dec., 1880.)[81*] The great forces which we recognise as factors in the moral regeneration of mankind are always slow of action as they are sure. War, if too quickly over, could not have the great moral influence which has been attributed to it. The explanation may be that it is not all that it naturally appears to a great and successful general. Hegel, Moltke, Trendelenburg, Treitschke[82*] and the others — not Schiller[83*] who was able to sing the blessings of peace as eloquently as of war — were apt to forget that war is as efficient a school for forming vices as virtues; and that, moreover, those virtues which military life is said to cultivate — courage, self-sacrifice and the rest — can be at least as perfectly developed in other trials. There are in human life dangers every day bravely met and overcome which are not less terrible than those which face the soldier, in whom patriotism may be less a sentiment than a duty, and whose cowardice must be dearly paid.

War under Altered Conditions.

The Peace Societies of our century, untiring supporters of a point of view diametrically opposite to that of Hegel, owe their existence in the first place to new ideas on the subject of the relative advantages and disadvantages of war, which again were partly due to changes in the character of war itself, partly to a new theory that the warfare of the future should be a war of free competition for industrial interests, or, in Herbert Spencer's language, that the warlike type of mankind should make room for an industrial type. This theory, amounting in the minds of some thinkers to a fervid conviction, and itself, in a sense, the source of what has been contemptuously styled our British "shopkeeper's policy" in Europe, was based on something more solid than mere enthusiasm. The years of peace which followed the downfall of Napoleon had brought immense increase in material wealth to countries like France and Britain. Something of the glamour had fallen away from the sword of the great Emperor. The illusive excitement of a desire for conquest had died: the glory of war had faded with it, but the burden still remained: its cost was still there, something to be calmly reckoned up and not soon to be forgotten. Europe was seen to be actually moving towards ruin. "We shall have to get rid of war in all civilised countries," said Louis Philippe in 1843. "Soon no nation will be able to afford it." War was not only becoming more costly. New conditions had altered it in other directions. With the development of technical science and its application to the perfecting of methods and instruments of destruction every new war was found to be bloodier than the last; and the day seemed to be in sight, when this very development would make war (with instruments of extermination) impossible altogether. The romance and picturesqueness with which it was invested in the days of hand-to-hand combat was gone. But, above all, war was now waged for questions fewer and more important than in the time of Kant. Napoleon's successful appeal to the masses had suggested to Prussia the idea of consciously nationalising the army. Our modern national wars exact a sacrifice, necessarily much more heavy, much more reluctantly made than those of the past which were fought with mercenary troops. Such wars have not only greater dignity: they are more earnest, and their issue, as in a sense the issue of conflict between higher and lower types of civilisation, is speedier and more decisive.

In the hundred years since Kant's death, much that he prophesied has come to pass, although sometimes by different paths than he anticipated. The strides made in recent years by commerce and the growing power of the people in every state have had much of the influence which he foretold. There is a greater reluctance to wage war.[84*] But, unfortunately, as Professor Paulsen points out, the progress of democracy and the nationalisation of war have not worked merely in the direction of progress towards peace. War has now become popular for the first time. "The progress of democracy in states," he says, (*Kant*, [85*]) "has not only not done away with war, but has very greatly changed the feeling of people towards it. With the universal military service, introduced by the Revolution, war has become the people's affair and popular, as it could not be in the case of dynastic wars carried on with mercenary troops." In the people the love of peace is strong, but so too is the love of a fight, the love of victory.

It is in the contemplation of facts and conflicting tendencies like these that Peace Societies[86*] have been formed. The peace party is, we may say, an eclectic body: it embraces many different sections of political opinion. There are those who hold, for instance, that peace is to be established on a basis of communism of property.

There are others who insist on the establishment throughout Europe of a republican form of government, or again, on a redistribution of European territory in which Alsace-Lorraine is restored to France — changes of which at least the last two would be difficult to carry out, unless through international warfare. But these are not the fundamental general principles of peace workers. The members of this party agree in rejecting the principle of intervention, in demanding a complete or partial disarmament of the nations of Europe, and in requiring that all disputes between nations — and they admit the prospects of dispute — should be settled by means of arbitration. In how far are these principles useful or practicable?

The Value of Arbitration.

There is a strong feeling in favour of arbitration on the part of all classes of society. It is cheaper under all circumstances than war. It is a judgment at once more certain and more complete, excluding as far as possible the element of chance, leaving irritation perhaps behind it, but none of the lasting bitterness which is the legacy of every war. Arbitration has an important place in all peace projects except that of Kant, whose federal union would naturally fulfil the function of a tribunal of arbitration. St. Pierre, Jeremy Bentham,[87] Bluntschli[88] the German publicist, Professor Lorimer[89] and others among political writers,[90] and among rulers, Louis Napoleon and the Emperor Alexander I. of Russia, have all made proposals more or less ineffectual for the peaceful settlement of international disputes. A number of cases have already been decided by this means. But let us examine the questions which have been at issue. Of a hundred and thirty matters of dispute settled by arbitration since 1815 (cf. *International Tribunals*, published by the Peace Society, 1899) it will be seen that all, with the exception of one or two trifling cases of doubt as to the succession to certain titles or principalities, can be classified roughly under two heads — disputes as to the determination of boundaries or the possession of certain territory, and questions of claims for compensation and indemnities due either to individuals or states, arising from the seizure of fleets or merchant vessels, the insult or injury to private persons and so on — briefly, questions of money or of territory. These may fairly be said to be trifling causes, not touching national honour or great political questions. That they should have been settled in this way, however, shows a great advance. Smaller causes than these have made some of the bloodiest wars in history. That arbitration should have been the means of preventing even one war which would otherwise have been waged is a strong reason why we should fully examine its claims. "Quand l'institution d'une haute cour," writes Laveleye, (*Des causes actuelles de guerre en Europe et de l'arbitrage*) "n'éviterait qu'une guerre sur vingt, il vaudrait encore la peine de l'établir." But history shows us that there is no single instance of a supreme conflict having been settled otherwise than by war. Arbitration is a method admirably adapted to certain cases: to those we have named, where it has been successfully applied, to the interpretation of contracts, to offences against the Law of Nations — some writers say to trivial questions of honour — in all cases where the use of armed force would be impossible, as, for instance, in any quarrel in which neutralised countries[91] like Belgium or Luxembourg should take a principal part, or in a difference between two nations, such as (to take an extreme case) the United States and Switzerland, which could not easily engage in actual combat. These cases, which we cannot too carefully examine, show that what is here essential is that it should be possible to formulate a juridical statement of the conflicting claims. In Germany the *Bundestag* had only power to decide questions of law. Other disputes were left to be fought out. Questions on which the existence and vital honour of a state depend — any question which nearly concerns the disputants — cannot be reduced to any cut and dry legal formula of right and wrong. We may pass over the consideration that in some cases (as in the Franco-Prussian War) the delay caused by seeking mediation of any kind would deprive a nation of the advantage its state of military preparation deserved. And we may neglect the problem of finding an impartial judge on some questions of dispute, although its solution might be a matter of extreme difficulty, so closely are the interests of modern nations bound up in one another. How could the Eastern Question, for example, be settled by arbitration? It is impossible that such a means should be sufficient for every case. Arbitration in other words may prevent war, but can never be a substitute for war. We cannot wonder that this is so. So numerous and conflicting are the interests of states, so various are the grades of civilisation to which they have attained and the directions along which they are developing, that differences of the most vital kind are bound to occur and these can never be settled by any peaceful means at present known to Europe. This is above all true where the self-preservation[92*] or independence of a people are concerned. Here the "good-will" of the nations who disagree would necessarily be wanting: there could be no question of the arbitration of an outsider.

But, indeed, looking away from questions so vital and on which there can be little difference of opinion, we are apt to forget, when we allow ourselves to talk extravagantly of the future of arbitration, that every nation thinks, or at least pretends to think, that it is in the right in every dispute in which it appears (cf. Kant: *Perpetual Peace*, .): and, as a matter of history, there has never been a conflict between civilised states in which an appeal to this "right" on the part of each has not been made. We talk glibly of the right and wrong of this question or of that, of the justice of this war, the iniquity of that. But what do these terms really mean? *Do* we know, in spite of the labour which has been spent on this question by the older publicists, which are the causes that justify a war? Is it not true that the same war might be just in one set of circumstances and unjust in another? Practically all writers on this subject, exclusive of those who apply the biblical doctrine of non-resistance, agree in admitting that a nation is justified in defending its own existence or independence, that this is even a moral duty as it is a fundamental right of a state. Many, especially the older writers, make the confident assertion that all wars of defence are just. But will this serve as a standard? Gibbon tells us somewhere, that Livy asserts that the Romans conquered the world in self-defence. The distinction between wars of aggression and defence is one very difficult to draw. The cause of a nation which waits to be actually attacked is often lost: the critical moment in its defence may be past. The essence of a state's defensive power may lie in a readiness to strike the first blow, or its whole interests may be bound up in the necessity of fighting the matter out in its enemy's country, rather than at home. It is not in the strictly military interpretation of the term "defensive", but in its wider ethical and political sense that we can speak of wars of defence as just. But, indeed, we cannot judge these questions abstractly. Where a war is necessary, it matters very little whether it is just or not. Only the judgment of history can finally decide; and generally it seems at the time that both parties have something of right on their side, something perhaps too of wrong.[93*]

A consideration of difficulties like these brings us to a realisation of the fact that the chances are small that a nation, in the heat of a dispute, will admit the likelihood of its being in the wrong. To refuse to admit this is generally tantamount to a refusal to submit the difficulty to arbitration. And neither international law, nor the moral force of public opinion can induce a state to act contrary to what it believes to be its own interest. Moreover, as international law now stands, it is not a duty to have recourse to arbitration. This was made quite clear in the proceedings of the Peace Conference at the Hague in 1899.[94*] It was strongly recommended that arbitration should be sought wherever it was possible, but, at the same time definitely stated, that this course could in no case be compulsory. In this respect things have not advanced beyond the position of the Paris Congress of 1856.[95*] The wars waged in Europe subsequent to that date, have all been begun without previous attempt at mediation.

But the work of the peace party regarding the humaner methods of settlement is not to be neglected. The popular feeling which they have been partly the means of stimulating has no doubt done something to influence the action of statesmen towards extreme caution in the treatment of questions likely to arouse national passions and prejudices. Arbitration has undoubtedly made headway in recent years. Britain and America, the two nations whose names naturally suggest themselves to us as future centres of federative union, both countries whose industrial interests are numerous and complicated, have most readily, as they have most frequently, settled disputes in this practical manner. It has shown itself to be a policy as economical as it is business-like. Its value, in its proper place, cannot be overrated by any Peace Congress or by any peace pamphlet; but we have endeavoured to make it clear that this sphere is but a limited one. The "good-will" may not be there when it ought perhaps to appear: it will certainly not be there when any vital interest is at stake. But, even if this were not so and arbitration were the natural sequence of every dispute, no coercive force exists to enforce the decree of the court. The moral restraint of public opinion is here a poor substitute. Treaties, it is often said, are in the same position; but treaties have been broken, and will no doubt be broken again. We are moved to the conclusion that a thoroughly logical peace programme cannot stop short of the principle of federation. Federal troops are necessary to carry out the decrees of a tribunal of arbitration, if that court is not to run a risk of being held feeble and ineffectual. Except on some such basis, arbitration, as a substitute for war, stands on but a weak footing.

Disarmament.

The efforts of the Peace Society are directed with even less hope of complete success against another evil of our time, the crushing burden of modern armaments. We have peace at this moment, but at a daily increasing cost. The Peace Society is rightly concerned in pressing this point. It is not enough to keep off actual war: there is a limit to the price we can afford to pay even for peace. Probably no principle has cost Europe so much in the last century as that handed down from Rome:— "Si vis pacem, para bellum." It is now a hundred and fifty years since Montesquieu[96*] protested against this "new distemper" which was spreading itself over Europe; but never, in time of peace, has complaint been so loud or so general as now: and this, not only against the universal burden of taxation which weighs upon all nations alike, but, in continental countries, against the waste of productive force due to compulsory military service, a discontent which seems to strike at the very foundations of society. Vattel relates that in early times a treaty of peace generally stipulated that both parties should afterwards disarm. And there is no doubt that Kant was right in regarding standing armies as a danger to peace, not only as openly expressing the rivalry and distrust between nation and nation which Hobbes regards as the basis of international relations, but also as putting a power into the hand of a nation which it may some day have the temptation to abuse. A war-loving, overbearing spirit in a people thrives none the worse for a consciousness that its army or navy can hold its own with any other in Europe. Were it not the case that the essence of armed peace is that a high state of efficiency should be general, the danger to peace would be very great indeed. No doubt it is due to this fact that France has kept quietly to her side of the Rhine during the last thirty years. The annexation of Alsace-Lorraine was an immediate stimulus to the increase of armaments; but otherwise, just because of this greater efficiency and the slightly stronger military position of Germany, it has been an influence on the side of peace.

The Czar's Rescript of 1898 gave a new stimulus to an interest in this question which the subsequent conference at the Hague was unable fully to satisfy. We are compelled to consider carefully how a process of simultaneous disarmament can actually be carried out, and what results might be anticipated from this step, with a view not only to the present but the future. Can this be done in accordance with the principles of justice? Organisations like a great navy or a highly disciplined army have been built up, in the course of centuries, at great cost and at much sacrifice to the nation. They are the fruit of years of wise government and a high record of national industry. Are such visible tokens of the culture and character and worth of a people to be swept away and Britain, France, Germany, Italy, Spain, Turkey to stand on the same level? And, even if no such ethical considerations should arise, on what method are we to proceed? The standard as well as the nature of armament depends in every state on its geographical conditions and its historical position. An ocean-bound empire like Britain is comparatively immune from the danger of invasion: her army can be safely despatched to the colonies, her fleet protects her at home, her position is one of natural defence. But Germany and Austria find themselves in exactly opposite circumstances, with the hard necessity imposed upon them of guarding their frontiers on every side. The safety of a nation like Germany is in the hands of its army: its military strength lies in an almost perfect mastery of the science of attack.

The Peace Society has hitherto made no attempt to face the difficulties inseparable from any attempt to apply a uniform method of treatment to peculiarities and conditions so conflicting and various as these. Those who have been more conscientious have not been very successful in solving them. Indeed, so constantly is military technique changing that it is difficult to prophesy wherein will lie, a few years hence, the essence of a state's defensive power or what part the modern navy will play in this defence. No careful thinker would suggest, in the face of dangers threatening from the East,[97] a complete disarmament. The simplest of many suggestions made — but this on the basis of universal conscription — seems to be that the number of years or months of compulsory military service should be reduced to some fixed period. But this does not touch the difficulty of colonial empires[98] like Britain which might to a certain extent disarm, like their neighbours, in Europe, but would be compelled to keep an army for the defence of their colonies elsewhere. It is, in the meantime, inevitable that Europe should keep up a high standard of armament — this is, (and even if we had European federation, would remain) an absolute necessity as a protection against the yellow races, and in Europe itself there are at present elements hostile to the cause of peace. Alsace-Lorraine, Polish Prussia, Russian Poland and Finland are still, to a considerable degree, sources of discontent and dissatisfaction. But in Russia itself lies the great obstacle to a future European peace or European federation: we can scarcely picture Russia as a reliable member of such a union. That Russia should disarm is scarcely feasible, in view of its own interest: it has always to face the danger of rebellion in Poland and anarchy at home. But that Europe should disarm, before Russia has attained a higher civilisation, a consciousness of its great future as a north-eastern, inter-oceanic empire, and a government more favourable to the diffusion of liberty, is still less practicable.[99*] We have here to fall back upon federation again. It is not impossible that, in the course of time, this problem may be solved and that the contribution to the federal troops of a European union may be regulated upon some equitable basis the form of which we cannot now well prophesy.

European federation would likewise meet all difficulties where a risk might be likely to occur of one nation intervening to protect another. As we have said (above, , *note*) nations are now-a-days slow to intervene in the interests of humanity: they are in general constrained to do so only by strong motives of self-interest, and when these are not at hand they are said to refrain from respect for another's right of independent action. Actually a state which is actuated by less selfish impulses is apt to lose considerably more than it gains, and the feeling of the people expresses itself strongly against any quixotic or sentimental policy. It is not impossible that the Powers may have yet to intervene to protect Turkey against Russia. Such a step might well be dictated purely by a proper care for the security of Europe; but wars of this kind seem not likely to play an important part in the near future.

We have said that the causes of difference which may be expected to disturb the peace of Europe are now fewer. A modern sovereign no longer spends his leisure time in the excitement of slaying or seeing slain. He could not, if he would. His honour and his vanity are protected by other means: they play no longer an important part in the affairs of nations. The causes of war can no more be either trifling or personal. Some crises there are, which are ever likely to be fatal to peace. There present themselves, in the lives of nations, ideal ends for which everything must be sacrificed: there are rights which must at all cost be defended. The question of civil war we may neglect: liberty and wise government are the only medicine for social discontent, and much may be hoped from that in the future. But now, looking beyond the state to the great family of civilised nations, we may say that the one certain cause of war between them or of rebellion within a future federated union will be a menace to the sovereign rights, the independence and existence of any member of that federation. Other causes of quarrel offer a more hopeful prospect. Some questions have been seen to be specially fitted for the legal procedure of a tribunal of arbitration, others to be such as a federal court would quickly settle. The preservation of the balance of power which Frederick the Great regarded as the talisman of peace in Europe — a judgment surely not borne out by experience — is happily one of the causes of war which are of the past. Wars of colonisation, such as would be an attempt on the part of Russia to conquer India, seem scarcely likely to recur except between higher and lower races. The cost is now-a-days too great. Political wars, wars for national union and unity, of which there were so many during the past century, seem at present not to be near at hand; and the integration of European nations — what may be called the great mission of war — is, for the moment, practically complete; for it is highly improbable that either Alsace-Lorraine or Poland — still less Finland — will be the cause of a war of this kind.

Our hope lies in a federated Europe. Its troops would serve to preserve law and order in the country from which they were drawn and to protect its colonies abroad; but their higher function would be to keep peace in Europe, to protect the weaker members of the Federation and to enforce the decision of the majority, either, if necessary, by actual war, or by the mere threatening demonstrations of fleets, such as have before proved effectual.

We have carefully considered what has been attempted by peace workers, and we have now to take note that all the results of the last fifty years are not to be attributed to their conscientious but often ill-directed labour. The diminution of the causes of war is to be traced less to the efforts of the Peace Society, (except indirectly, in so far as they have influenced the minds of the masses) than to the increasing power of the people themselves. The various classes of society are opposed to violent methods of settlement, not in the main from a conviction as to the wrongfulness of war or from any fanatical enthusiasm for a brotherhood of nations, but from self-interest. War is death to the industrial interests of a nation. It is vain to talk, in the language of past centuries, of trade between civilised countries being advanced and markets opened up or enlarged by this means.[100*] Kings give up the dream of military glory and accept instead the certainty of peaceful labour and industrial progress, and all this (for we may believe that to some monarchs it is much) from no enthusiastic appreciation of the efforts of Peace Societies, from no careful examination of the New Testament nor inspired interpretation of its teaching. It is self-interest, the prosperity of the country — patriotism, if you will — that seems better than war.

What may be expected from Federation.

Federation and federation alone can help out the programme of the Peace Society. It cannot be pretended that it will do everything. To state the worst at once, it will not prevent war. Even the federations of the states of Germany and America, bound together by ties of blood and language and, in the latter case, of sentiment, were not strong enough within to keep out dissension and disunion.[101*] Wars would not cease, but they would become much less frequent. "Why is there no longer war between England and Scotland? Why did Prussian and Hanoverian fight side by side in 1870, though they had fought against each other only four years before?... If we wish to know how war is to cease, we should ask ourselves how it *has* ceased" (Professor D. G. Ritchie, *op. cit.*,). Wars between different grades of civilisation are bound to exist as long as civilisation itself exists. The history of culture and of progress has been more or less a history of war. A calm acceptance of this position may mean to certain short-sighted, enthusiastic theorists an impossible sacrifice of the ideal; but, the sacrifice once made, we stand on a better footing with regard to at least one class of arguments against a federation of the world. Such a union will lead, it is said, to an equality in culture, a sameness of interests fatal to progress; all struggle and conflict will be cast out of the state itself; national characteristics and individuality will be obliterated; the lamb and the wolf will lie down together: stagnation will result, intellectual progress will be at an end, politics will be no more, history will stand still. This is a sweeping assertion, an alarming prophecy. But a little thought will assure us that there is small cause for apprehension. There can be no such standstill, no millennium in human affairs. A gradual smoothing down of sharply accentuated national characteristics there might be: this is a result which a freer, more friendly intercourse between nations would be very likely to produce. But conflicting interests, keen rivalry in their pursuit, difference of culture and natural aptitude, and all or much of the individuality which language and literature, historical and religious traditions, even climatic and physical conditions produce are bound to survive until the coming of some more overwhelming and far-spreading revolution than this. It would not be well if it were otherwise, if those "unconscious and invisible peculiarities" in which Fichte sees the hand of God and the guarantee of a nation's future dignity, virtue and merit should be swept away. (*Reden an die deutsche Nation*,[102*] 1807.) Nor is stagnation to be feared. "Strife," said the old philosopher, "is the father of all things." There can be no lasting peace in the processes of nature and existence. It has been in the constant rivalry between classes within themselves, and in the struggle for existence with other races that great nations have reached the highwater mark of their development. A perpetual peace in international relations we may — nay, surely will — one day have, but eternity will not see the end to the feverish unrest within the state and the jealous competition and distrust between individuals, groups and classes of society. Here there must ever be perpetual war.

It was only of this political peace between civilised nations that Kant thought.[103*] In this form it is bound to come. The federation of Europe will follow the federation of Germany and of Italy, not only because it offers a solution of many problems which have long taxed Europe, but because great men and careful thinkers believe in it.[104*] It may not come quickly, but such men can afford to wait. "If I were legislator," cried Jean Jacques Rousseau, "I should not say what ought to be done, but I would do it." This is the attitude of the unthinking, unpractical enthusiast. The wish is not enough: the will is not enough. The mills of God must take their own time: no hope or faith of ours, no struggle or labour even can hurry them.

It is a misfortune that the Peace Society has identified itself with so narrow and uncritical an attitude towards war, and that the copious eloquence of its members is not based upon a consideration of the practical difficulties of the case. This well-meaning, hard working and enthusiastic body would like to do what is impossible by an impossible method. The end which it sets for itself is an unattainable one. But this need not be so. To make unjustifiable aggression difficult, to banish unworthy pretexts for making war might be a high enough ideal for any enthusiasm and offer scope wide enough for the labours of any society. But the Peace Society has not contented itself with this great work. Through its over-estimation of the value of peace,[105*] its cause has been injured and much of its influence has been weakened or lost. Our age is one which sets a high value upon human life; and to this change of thinking may be traced our modern reform in the methods of war and all that has been done for the alleviation of suffering by the great Conventions of recent years. For the eyes of most people war is merely a hideous spectacle of bloodshed and deliberate destruction of life: this is its obvious side. But it is possible to exaggerate this confessedly great evil. Peace has its sacrifices as well as war: the progress of humanity requires that the individual should often be put aside for the sake of lasting advantage to the whole. An opposite view can only be reckoned individualistic, perhaps materialistic. "The reverence for human life," says Martineau, (*Studies of Christianity*, p, 354) "is carried to an immoral idolatry, when it is held more sacred than justice and right, and when the spectacle of blood becomes more horrible than the sight of desolating tyrannies and triumphant hypocrisies.... We have, therefore, no more doubt that a war may be right, than that a policeman may be a security for justice, and we object to a fortress as little as to a handcuff."

The Peace Society are not of this opinion: they greatly doubt that a war may be right, and they rarely fail to take their doubts to the tribunal of Scripture. Their efforts are well meant, this piety may be genuine enough; but a text is rarely a proof of anything, and in any case serves one man in as good stead as another. We remember that "the devil can cite Scripture for his purpose." This unscientific method of proof or persuasion has ever been widely popular. It is a serious examination of the question that we want, a more careful study of its actual history and of the possibilities of human nature; less vague, exaggerated language about what ought to be done, and a realisation of what has been actually achieved; above all, a clear perception of what may fairly be asked from the future.

It used to be said — is perhaps asserted still by the war-lovers — that there was no path to civilisation which had not been beaten by the force of arms, no height to which the sword had not led the way. The inspiration of war was upon the great arts of civilisation: its hand was upon the greatest of the sciences. These obligations extended even to commerce. War not only created new branches of industry, it opened new markets and enlarged the old. These are great claims, according to which war might be called the moving principle of history. If we keep our eyes fixed upon the history of the past, they seem not only plausible: they are in a great sense true. Progress did tread at the heels of the great Alexander's army: the advance of European culture stands in the closest connection with the Crusades. But was this happy compensation for a miserable state of affairs not due to the peculiarly unsocial conditions of early times and the absence of every facility for the interchange of ideas or material advantages? It is inconceivable that now-a-days[106] any aid to the development of thought in Europe should come from war. The old adage, in more than a literal sense, has but too often been proved true:— "Inter arma, Musae silent." Peace is for us the real promoter of culture.

We have to endeavour to take an intermediate course between uncritical praise and wholesale condemnation, between extravagant expectation and unjustifiable pessimism. War used to be the rule: it is now an overwhelming and terrible exception — an interruption to the peaceful prosperous course of things, inflicting unlimited suffering and temporary or lasting loss. Its evils are on the surface, apparent to the most unthinking observer. The day may yet dawn, when Europeans will have learned to regard the force of arms as an instrument for the civilisation of savage or half-savage races, and war within their continent as civil war, necessary and justifiable sometimes perhaps, but still a blot upon their civilisation and brotherhood as men.

Such a suggestion rings strangely. But the great changes, which the roll of centuries has marked, once came upon the world not less unexpectedly. How far off must the idea of a civil peace have seemed to small towns and states of Europe in the fifteenth century! How strange, only a century ago, would the idea of applying steam power or electrical force have seemed to ourselves! Let us not despair. War has played a great part in the history of the world: it has been ever the great architect of nations, the true mother of cities. It has justified itself to-day in the union of kindred peoples, the making of great empires. It may be that one decisive war may yet be required to unite Europe. May Europe survive that struggle and go forward fearlessly to her great future! A peaceful future that may not be. It must never be forgotten that war is sometimes a moral duty, that it is ever the natural sequence of human passion and human prejudice. An unbroken peace we cannot and do not expect; but it is this that we must work for. As Kant says, we must keep it before us as an ideal.

TRANSLATION
"PERPETUAL PEACE"

We need not try to decide whether this satirical inscription, (once found on a Dutch innkeeper's sign-board above the picture of a churchyard) is aimed at mankind in general, or at the rulers of states in particular, unwearying in their love of war, or perhaps only at the philosophers who cherish the sweet dream of perpetual peace. The author of the present sketch would make one stipulation, however. The practical politician stands upon a definite footing with the theorist: with great self-complacency he looks down upon him as a mere pedant whose empty ideas can threaten no danger to the state (starting as it does from principles derived from experience), and who may always be permitted to knock down his eleven skittles at once without a worldly-wise statesman needing to disturb himself. Hence, in the event of a quarrel arising between the two, the practical statesman must always act consistently, and not scent danger to the state behind opinions ventured by the theoretical politician at random and publicly expressed. With which saving clause (*clausula salvatoria*) the author will herewith consider himself duly and expressly protected against all malicious misinterpretation.

FIRST SECTION

CONTAINING THE PRELIMINARY ARTICLES OF PERPETUAL PEACE BETWEEN STATES

1.— "No treaty of peace shall be regarded as valid, if made with the secret reservation of material for a future war."

For then it would be a mere truce, a mere suspension of hostilities, not peace. A peace signifies the end of all hostilities and to attach to it the epithet "eternal" is not only a verbal pleonasm, but matter of suspicion. The causes of a future war existing, although perhaps not yet known to the high contracting parties themselves, are entirely annihilated by the conclusion of peace, however acutely they may be ferreted out of documents in the public archives. There may be a mental reservation of old claims to be thought out at a future time, which are, none of them, mentioned at this stage, because both parties are too much exhausted to continue the war, while the evil intention remains of using the first favourable opportunity for further hostilities. Diplomacy of this kind only Jesuitical casuistry can justify: it is beneath the dignity of a ruler, just as acquiescence in such processes of reasoning is beneath the dignity of his minister, if one judges the facts as they really are.[109*]

If, however, according to present enlightened ideas of political wisdom, the true glory of a state lies in the uninterrupted development of its power by every possible means, this judgment must certainly strike one as scholastic and pedantic.

2.— "No state having an independent existence — whether it be great or small — shall be acquired by another through inheritance, exchange, purchase or donation."[110*]

For a state is not a property (*patrimonium*), as may be the ground on which its people are settled. It is a society of human beings over whom no one but itself has the right to rule and to dispose. Like the trunk of a tree, it has its own roots, and to graft it on to another state is to do away with its existence as a moral person, and to make of it a thing. Hence it is in contradiction to the idea of the original contract without which no right over a people is thinkable.[111*] Everyone knows to what danger the bias in favour of these modes of acquisition has brought Europe (in other parts of the world it has never been known). The custom of marriage between states, as if they were individuals, has survived even up to the most recent times,[112*] and is regarded partly as a new kind of industry by which ascendency may be acquired through family alliances, without any expenditure of strength; partly as a device for territorial expansion. Moreover, the hiring out of the troops of one state to another to fight against an enemy not at war with their native country is to be reckoned in this connection; for the subjects are in this way used and abused at will as personal property.

3.— "Standing armies (*miles perpetuus*) shall be abolished in course of time."

For they are always threatening other states with war by appearing to be in constant readiness to fight. They incite the various states to outrival one another in the number of their soldiers, and to this number no limit can be set. Now, since owing to the sums devoted to this purpose, peace at last becomes even more oppressive than a short war, these standing armies are themselves the cause of wars of aggression, undertaken in order to get rid of this burden. To which we must add that the practice of hiring men to kill or to be killed seems to imply a use of them as mere machines and instruments in the hand of another (namely, the state) which cannot easily be reconciled with the right of humanity in our own person.[113*] The matter stands quite differently in the case of voluntary periodical military exercise on the part of citizens of the state, who thereby seek to secure themselves and their country against attack from without.

The accumulation of treasure in a state would in the same way be regarded by other states as a menace of war, and might compel them to anticipate this by striking the first blow. For of the three forces, the power of arms, the power of alliance and the power of money, the last might well become the most reliable instrument of war, did not the difficulty of ascertaining the amount stand in the way.

4.— "No national debts shall be contracted in connection with the external affairs of the state."

This source of help is above suspicion, where assistance is sought outside or within the state, on behalf of the economic administration of the country (for instance, the improvement of the roads, the settlement and support of new colonies, the establishment of granaries to provide against seasons of scarcity, and so on). But, as a common weapon used by the Powers against one another, a credit system under which debts go on indefinitely increasing and are yet always assured against immediate claims (because all the creditors do not put in their claim at once) is a dangerous money power. This ingenious invention of a commercial people in the present century is, in other words, a treasure for the carrying on of war which may exceed the treasures of all the other states taken together, and can only be exhausted by a threatening deficiency in the taxes — an event, however, which will long be kept off by the very briskness of commerce resulting from the reaction of this system on industry and trade. The ease, then, with which war may be waged, coupled with the inclination of rulers towards it — an inclination which seems to be implanted in human nature — is a great obstacle in the way of perpetual peace. The prohibition of this system must be laid down as a preliminary article of perpetual peace, all the more necessarily because the final inevitable bankruptcy of the state in question must involve in the loss many who are innocent; and this would be a public injury to these states. Therefore other nations are at least justified in uniting themselves against such an one and its pretensions.

5.— "No state shall violently interfere with the constitution and administration of another."

For what can justify it in so doing? The scandal which is here presented to the subjects of another state? The erring state can much more serve as a warning by exemplifying the great evils which a nation draws down on itself through its own lawlessness. Moreover, the bad example which one free person gives another, (as *scandalum acceptum*) does no injury to the latter. In this connection, it is true, we cannot count the case of a state which has become split up through internal corruption into two parts, each of them representing by itself an individual state which lays claim to the whole. Here the yielding of assistance to one faction could not be reckoned as interference on the part of a foreign state with the constitution of another, for here anarchy prevails. So long, however, as the inner strife has not yet reached this stage the interference of other powers would be a violation of the rights of an independent nation which is only struggling with internal disease.[114*] It would therefore itself cause a scandal, and make the autonomy of all states insecure.

6.— "No state at war with another shall countenance such modes of hostility as would make mutual confidence impossible in a subsequent state of peace: such are the employment of assassins (*percussores*) or of poisoners (*venefici*), breaches of capitulation, the instigating and making use of treachery (*perduellio*) in the hostile state."

These are dishonourable stratagems. For some kind of confidence in the disposition of the enemy must exist even in the midst of war, as otherwise peace could not be concluded, and the hostilities would pass into a war of extermination (*bellum internecinum*). War, however, is only our wretched expedient of asserting a right by force, an expedient adopted in the state of nature, where no court of justice exists which could settle the matter in dispute. In circumstances like these, neither of the two parties can be called an unjust enemy, because this form of speech presupposes a legal decision: the issue of the conflict — just as in the case of the so-called judgments of God — decides on which side right is. Between states, however, no punitive war (*bellum punitivum*) is thinkable, because between them a relation of superior and inferior does not exist. Whence it follows that a war of extermination, where the process of annihilation would strike both parties at once and all right as well, would bring about perpetual peace only in the great graveyard of the human race. Such a war then, and therefore also the use of all means which lead to it, must be absolutely forbidden. That the methods just mentioned do inevitably lead to this result is obvious from the fact that these infernal arts, already vile in themselves, on coming into use, are not long confined to the sphere of war. Take, for example, the use of spies (*uti exploratoribus*). Here only the dishonesty of others is made use of; but vices such as these, when once encouraged, cannot in the nature of things be stamped out and would be carried over into the state of peace, where their presence would be utterly destructive to the purpose of that state.

Although the laws stated are, objectively regarded, (*i.e.* in so far as they affect the action of rulers) purely prohibitive laws (*leges prohibitivæ*), some of them (*leges strictæ*) are strictly valid without regard to circumstances and urgently require to be enforced. Such are Nos. 1, 5, 6. Others, again, (like Nos. 2, 3, 4) although not indeed exceptions to the maxims of law, yet in respect of the practical application of these maxims allow subjectively of a certain latitude to suit particular circumstances. The enforcement of these *leges latæ* may be legitimately put off, so long as we do not lose sight of the ends at which they aim. This purpose of reform does not permit of the deferment of an act of restitution (as, for example, the restoration to certain states of freedom of which they have been deprived in the manner described in article 2) to an infinitely distant date — as Augustus used to say, to the "Greek Kalends", a day that will never come. This would be to sanction non-restitution. Delay is permitted only with the intention that restitution should not be made too precipitately and so defeat the purpose we have in view. For the prohibition refers here only to the *mode of acquisition* which is to be no longer valid, and not to the *fact of possession* which, although indeed it has not the necessary title of right, yet at the time of so-called acquisition was held legal by all states, in accordance with the public opinion of the time. [115*]

SECOND SECTION

CONTAINING THE DEFINITIVE ARTICLES OF A PERPETUAL PEACE BETWEEN STATES

A state of peace among men who live side by side is not the natural state (*status naturalis*), which is rather to be described as a state of war:[116*] that is to say, although there is not perhaps always actual open hostility, yet there is a constant threatening that an outbreak may occur. Thus the state of peace must be *established*.[117*] For the mere cessation of hostilities is no guarantee of continued peaceful relations, and unless this guarantee is given by every individual to his neighbour — which can only be done in a state of society regulated by law — one man is at liberty to challenge another and treat him as an enemy.[118*]

FIRST DEFINITIVE ARTICLE OF PERPETUAL PEACE

I.— "The civil constitution of each state shall be republican."

The only constitution which has its origin in the idea of the original contract, upon which the lawful legislation of every nation must be based, is the republican.[119*] It is a constitution, in the first place, founded in accordance with the principle of the freedom of the members of society as human beings: secondly, in accordance with the principle of the dependence of all, as subjects, on a common legislation: and, thirdly, in accordance with the law of the equality of the members as citizens. It is then, looking at the question of right, the only constitution whose fundamental principles lie at the basis of every form of civil constitution. And the only question for us now is, whether it is also the one constitution which can lead to perpetual peace.

Now the republican constitution apart from the soundness of its origin, since it arose from the pure source of the concept of right, has also the prospect of attaining the desired result, namely, perpetual peace. And the reason is this. If, as must be so under this constitution, the consent of the subjects is required to determine whether there shall be war or not, nothing is more natural than that they should weigh the matter well, before undertaking such a bad business. For in decreeing war, they would of necessity be resolving to bring down the miseries of war upon their country. This implies: they must fight themselves; they must hand over the costs of the war out of their own property; they must do their poor best to make good the devastation which it leaves behind; and finally, as a crowning ill, they have to accept a burden of debt which will embitter even peace itself, and which they can never pay off on account of the new wars which are always impending. On the other hand, in a government where the subject is not a citizen holding a vote, (*i.e.* in a constitution which is not republican), the plunging into war is the least serious thing in the world. For the ruler is not a citizen, but the owner of the state, and does not lose a whit by the war, while he goes on enjoying the delights of his table or sport, or of his pleasure palaces and gala days. He can therefore decide on war for the most trifling reasons, as if it were a kind of pleasure party.[120*] Any justification of it that is necessary for the sake of decency he can leave without concern to the diplomatic corps who are always only too ready with their services.

* * *

The following remarks must be made in order that we may not fall into the common error of confusing the republican with the democratic constitution. The forms of the state (*civitas*)[121*] may be classified according to either of two principles of division: — the difference of the persons who hold the supreme authority in the state, and the manner in which the people are governed by their ruler whoever he may be. The first is properly called the form of sovereignty (*forma imperii*), and there can be only three constitutions differing in this respect: where, namely, the supreme authority belongs to only one, to several individuals working together, or to the whole people constituting the civil society. Thus we have autocracy or the sovereignty of a monarch, aristocracy or the sovereignty of the nobility, and democracy or the sovereignty of the people. The second principle of division is the form of government (*forma regiminis*), and refers to the way in which the state makes use of its supreme power: for the manner of government is based on the constitution, itself the act of that universal will which transforms a multitude into a nation. In this respect the form of government is either republican or despotic. Republicanism is the political principle of severing the executive power of the government from the legislature. Despotism is that principle in pursuance of which the state arbitrarily puts into effect laws which it has itself made: consequently it is the administration of the public will, but this is identical with the private will of the ruler. Of these three forms of a state, democracy, in the proper sense of the word, is of necessity despotism, because it establishes an executive power, since all decree regarding — and, if need be, against — any individual who dissents from them. Therefore the "whole people", so-called, who carry their measure are really not all, but only a majority: so that here the universal will is in contradiction with itself and with the principle of freedom.

Every form of government in fact which is not representative is really no true constitution at all, because a law-giver may no more be, in one and the same person, the administrator of his own will, than the universal major premise of a syllogism may be, at the same time, the subsumption under itself of the particulars contained in the minor premise. And, although the other two constitutions, autocracy and aristocracy, are always defective in so far as they leave the way open for such a form of government, yet there is at least always a possibility in these cases, that they may take the form of a government in accordance with the spirit of a representative system. Thus Frederick the Great used at least to *say* that he was "merely the highest servant of the state."[122*] The democratic constitution, on the other hand, makes this impossible, because under such a government every one wishes to be master. We may therefore say that the smaller the staff of the executive — that is to say, the number of rulers — and the more real, on the other hand, their representation of the people, so much the more is the government of the state in accordance with a possible republicanism; and it may hope by gradual reforms to raise itself to that standard. For this reason, it is more difficult under an aristocracy than under a monarchy — while under a democracy it is impossible except by a violent revolution — to attain to this, the one perfectly lawful constitution. The kind of government,[123*] however, is of infinitely more importance to the people than the kind of constitution, although the greater or less aptitude of a people for this ideal greatly depends upon such external form. The form of government, however, if it is to be in accordance with the idea of right, must embody the representative system in which alone a republican form of administration is possible and without which it is despotic and violent, be the constitution what it may. None of the ancient so-called republics were aware of this, and they necessarily slipped into absolute despotism which, of all despotisms, is most endurable under the sovereignty of one individual.

SECOND DEFINITIVE ARTICLE OF PERPETUAL PEACE

II.— "The law of nations shall be founded on a federation of free states."

Nations, as states, may be judged like individuals who, living in the natural state of society — that is to say, uncontrolled by external law — injure one another through their very proximity.[124*] Every state, for the sake of its own security, may — and ought to — demand that its neighbour should submit itself to conditions, similar to those of the civil society where the right of every individual is guaranteed. This would give rise to a federation of nations which, however, would not have to be a State of nations.[125*] That would involve a contradiction. For the term "state" implies the relation of one who rules to those who obey — that is to say, of law-giver to the subject people: and many nations in one state would constitute only one nation, which contradicts our hypothesis, since here we have to consider the right of one nation against another, in so far as they are so many separate states and are not to be fused into one.

The attachment of savages to their lawless liberty, the fact that they would rather be at hopeless variance with one another than submit themselves to a legal authority constituted by themselves, that they therefore prefer their senseless freedom to a reason-governed liberty, is regarded by us with profound contempt as barbarism and uncivilisation and the brutal degradation of humanity. So one would think that civilised races, each formed into a state by itself, must come out of such an abandoned condition as soon as they possibly can. On the contrary, however, every state thinks rather that its majesty (the "majesty" of a people is an absurd expression) lies just in the very fact that it is subject to no external legal authority; and the glory of the ruler consists in this, that, without his requiring to expose himself to danger, thousands stand at his command ready to let themselves be sacrificed for a matter of no concern to them.[126*] The difference between the savages of Europe and those of America lies chiefly in this, that, while many tribes of the latter have been entirely devoured by their enemies, Europeans know a better way of using the vanquished than by eating them; and they prefer to increase through them the number of their subjects, and so the number of instruments at their command for still more widely spread war.

The depravity of human nature[127*] shows itself without disguise in the unrestrained relations of nations to each other, while in the law-governed civil state much of this is hidden by the check of government. This being so, it is astonishing that the word "right" has not yet been entirely banished from the politics of war as pedantic, and that no state has yet ventured to publicly advocate this point of view. For Hugo Grotius, Puffendorf, Vattel and others — Job's comforters, all of them — are always quoted in good faith to justify an attack, although their codes, whether couched in philosophical or diplomatic terms, have not — nor can have — the slightest legal force, because states, as such, are under no common external authority; and there is no instance of a state having ever been moved by argument to desist from its purpose, even when this was backed up by the testimony of such great men. This homage which every state renders — in words at least — to the idea of right, proves that, although it may be slumbering, there is, notwithstanding, to be found in man a still higher natural moral capacity by the aid of which he will in time gain the mastery over the evil principle in his nature, the existence of which he is unable to deny. And he hopes the same of others; for otherwise the word "right" would never be uttered by states who wish to wage war, unless to deride it like the Gallic Prince who declared:— "The privilege which nature gives the strong is that the weak must obey them."[128*]

The method by which states prosecute their rights can never be by process of law — as it is where there is an external tribunal — but only by war. Through this means, however, and its favourable issue, victory, the question of right is never decided. A treaty of peace makes, it may be, an end to the war of the moment, but not to the conditions of war which at any time may afford a new pretext for opening hostilities; and this we cannot exactly condemn as unjust, because under these conditions everyone is his own judge. Notwithstanding, not quite the same rule applies to states according to the law of nations as holds good of individuals in a lawless condition according to the law of nature, namely, "that they ought to advance out of this condition." This is so, because, as states, they have already within themselves a legal constitution, and have therefore advanced beyond the stage at which others, in accordance with their ideas of right, can force them to come under a wider legal constitution. Meanwhile, however, reason, from her throne of the supreme law-giving moral power, absolutely condemns war[129*] as a morally lawful proceeding, and makes a state of peace, on the other hand, an immediate duty. Without a compact between the nations, however, this state of peace cannot be established or assured. Hence there must be an alliance of a particular kind which we may call a covenant of peace (*foedus pacificum*), which would differ from a treaty of peace (*pactum pacis*) in this respect, that the latter merely puts an end to one war, while the former would seek to put an end to war for ever. This alliance does not aim at the gain of any power whatsoever of the state, but merely at the preservation and security of the freedom of the state for itself and of other allied states at the same time.[130*] The latter do not, however, require, for this reason, to submit themselves like individuals in the state of nature to public laws and coercion. The practicability or objective reality of this idea of federation which is to extend gradually over all states and so lead to perpetual peace can be shewn. For, if Fortune ordains that a powerful and enlightened people should form a republic, — which by its very nature is inclined to perpetual peace — this would serve as a centre of federal union for other states wishing to join, and thus secure conditions of freedom among the states in accordance with the idea of the law of nations. Gradually, through different unions of this kind, the federation would extend further and further.

It is quite comprehensible that a people should say:— "There shall be no war among us, for we shall form ourselves into a state, that is to say, constitute for ourselves a supreme legislative, administrative and judicial power which will settle our disputes peaceably." But if this state says:— "There shall be no war between me and other states, although I recognise no supreme law-giving power which will secure me my rights and whose rights I will guarantee;" then it is not at all clear upon what grounds I could base my confidence in my right, unless it were the substitute for that compact on which civil society is based — namely, free federation which reason must necessarily connect with the idea of the law of nations, if indeed any meaning is to be left in that concept at all.

There is no intelligible meaning in the idea of the law of nations as giving a right to make war; for that must be a right to decide what is just, not in accordance with universal, external laws limiting the freedom of each individual, but by means of one-sided maxims applied by force. We must then understand by this that men of such ways of thinking are quite justly served, when they destroy one another, and thus find perpetual peace in the wide grave which covers all the abominations of acts of violence as well as the authors of such deeds. For states, in their relation to one another, there can be, according to reason, no other way of advancing from that lawless condition which unceasing war implies, than by giving up their savage lawless freedom, just as individual men have done, and yielding to the coercion of public laws. Thus they can form a State of nations (*civitas gentium*), one, too, which will be ever increasing and would finally embrace all the peoples of the earth. States, however, in accordance with their understanding of the law of nations, by no means desire this, and therefore reject *in hypothesi* what is correct *in thesi*. Hence, instead of the positive idea of a world-republic, if all is not to be lost, only the negative substitute for it, a federation averting war, maintaining its ground and ever extending over the world may stop the current of this tendency to war and shrinking from the control of law. But even then there will be a constant danger that this propensity may break out.[131*] "Furor impius intus — fremit horridus ore cruento." (Virgil.)[132*]

THIRD DEFINITIVE ARTICLE OF PERPETUAL PEACE

III.— "The rights of men, as citizens of the world, shall be limited to the conditions of universal hospitality."

We are speaking here, as in the previous articles, not of philanthropy, but of right; and in this sphere hospitality signifies the claim of a stranger entering foreign territory to be treated by its owner without hostility. The latter may send him away again, if this can be done without causing his death; but, so long as he conducts himself peaceably, he must not be treated as an enemy. It is not a right to be treated as a guest to which the stranger can lay claim — a special friendly compact on his behalf would be required to make him for a given time an actual inmate — but he has a right of visitation. This right[133*] to present themselves to society belongs to all mankind in virtue of our common right of possession on the surface of the earth on which, as it is a globe, we cannot be infinitely scattered, and must in the end reconcile ourselves to existence side by side: at the same time, originally no one individual had more right than another to live in any one particular spot. Uninhabitable portions of the surface, ocean and desert, split up the human community, but in such a way that ships and camels— "the ship of the desert" — make it possible for men to come into touch with one another across these unappropriated regions and to take advantage of our common claim to the face of the earth with a view to a possible intercommunication. The inhospitality of the inhabitants of certain sea coasts — as, for example, the coast of Barbary — in plundering ships in neighbouring seas or making slaves of shipwrecked mariners; or the behaviour of the Arab Bedouins in the deserts, who think that proximity to nomadic tribes constitutes a right to rob, is thus contrary to the law of nature. This right to hospitality, however — that is to say, the privilege of strangers arriving on foreign soil — does not amount to more than what is implied in a permission to make an attempt at intercourse with the original inhabitants. In this way far distant territories may enter into peaceful relations with one another. These relations may at last come under the public control of law, and thus the human race may be brought nearer the realisation of a cosmopolitan constitution.

Let us look now, for the sake of comparison, at the inhospitable behaviour of the civilised nations, especially the commercial states of our continent. The injustice which they exhibit on visiting foreign lands and races — this being equivalent in their eyes to conquest — is such as to fill us with horror. America, the negro countries, the Spice Islands, the Cape etc. were, on being discovered, looked upon as countries which belonged to nobody; for the native inhabitants were reckoned as nothing. In Hindustan, under the pretext of intending to establish merely commercial depots, the Europeans introduced foreign troops; and, as a result, the different states of Hindustan were stirred up to far-spreading wars. Oppression of the natives followed, famine, insurrection, perfidy and all the rest of the litany of evils which can afflict mankind.

China[134*] and Japan (Nipon) which had made an attempt at receiving guests of this kind, have now taken a prudent step. Only to a single European people, the Dutch, has China given the right of access to her shores (but not of entrance into the country), while Japan has granted both these concessions; but at the same time they exclude the Dutch who enter, as if they were prisoners, from social intercourse with the inhabitants. The worst, or from the standpoint of ethical judgment the best, of all this is that no satisfaction is derived from all this violence, that all these trading companies stand on the verge of ruin, that the Sugar Islands, that seat of the most horrible and deliberate slavery, yield no real profit, but only have their use indirectly and for no very praiseworthy object — namely, that of furnishing men to be trained as sailors for the men-of-war and thereby contributing to the carrying on of war in Europe. And this has been done by nations who make a great ado about their piety, and who, while they are quite ready to commit injustice, would like, in their orthodoxy, to be considered among the elect.

The intercourse, more or less close, which has been everywhere steadily increasing between the nations of the earth, has now extended so enormously that a violation of right in one part of the world is felt all over it. Hence the idea of a cosmopolitan right is no fantastical, high-flown notion of right, but a complement of the unwritten code of law — constitutional as well as international law — necessary for the public rights of mankind in general and thus for the realisation of perpetual peace. For only by endeavouring to fulfil the conditions laid down by this cosmopolitan law can we flatter ourselves that we are gradually approaching that ideal.

FIRST SUPPLEMENT
CONCERNING THE GUARANTEE OF PERPETUAL PEACE

This guarantee is given by no less a power than the great artist nature (*natura dædala rerum*) in whose mechanical course is clearly exhibited a predetermined design to make harmony spring from human discord, even against the will of man. Now this design, although called Fate when looked upon as the compelling force of a cause, the laws of whose operation are unknown to us, is, when considered as the purpose manifested in the course of nature, called Providence,[135*] as the deep-lying wisdom of a Higher Cause, directing itself towards the ultimate practical end of the human race and predetermining the course of things with a view to its realisation. This Providence we do not, it is true, perceive in the cunning contrivances *Kunstanstalten* of nature; nor can we even conclude from the fact of their existence that it is there; but, as in every relation between the form of things and their final cause, we can, and must, supply the thought of a Higher Wisdom, in order that we may be able to form an idea of the possible existence of these products after the analogy of human works of art *Kunsthandlungen*.[136*] The representation to ourselves of the relation and agreement of these formations of nature to the moral purpose for which they were made and which reason directly prescribes to us, is an Idea, it is true, which is in theory superfluous; but in practice it is dogmatic, and its objective reality is well established.[137*] Thus we see, for example, with regard to the ideal *Pflichtbegriff* of perpetual peace, that it is our duty to make use of the mechanism of nature for the realisation of that end. Moreover, in a case like this where we are interested merely in the theory and not in the religious question, the use of the word "nature" is more appropriate than that of "providence", in view of the limitations of human reason, which, in considering the relation of effects to their causes, must keep within the limits of possible experience. And the term "nature" is also less presumptuous than the other. To speak of a Providence knowable by us would be boldly to put on the wings of Icarus in order to draw near to the mystery of its unfathomable purpose.

Before we determine the surety given by nature more exactly, we must first look at what ultimately makes this guarantee of peace necessary — the circumstances in which nature has carefully placed the actors in her great theatre. In the next place, we shall proceed to consider the manner in which she gives this surety.

The provisions she has made are as follow: (1) she has taken care that men *can* live in all parts of the world; (2) she has scattered them by means of war in all directions, even into the most inhospitable regions, so that these too might be populated; (3) by this very means she has forced them to enter into relations more or less controlled by law. It is surely wonderful that, on the cold wastes round the Arctic Ocean, there is always to be found moss for the reindeer to scrape out from under the snow, the reindeer itself either serving as food or to draw the sledge of the Ostiak or Samoyedes. And salt deserts which would otherwise be left unutilised have the camel, which seems as if created for travelling in such lands. This evidence of design in things, however, is still more clear when we come to know that, besides the fur-clad animals of the shores of the Arctic Ocean, there are seals, walruses and whales whose flesh furnishes food and whose oil fire for the dwellers in these regions. But the providential care of nature excites our wonder above all, when we hear of the driftwood which is carried — whence no one knows — to these treeless shores: for without the aid of this material the natives could neither construct their craft, nor weapons, nor huts for shelter. Here too they have so much to do, making war against wild animals, that they live at peace with one another. But what drove them originally into these regions was probably nothing but war.

Of animals, used by us as instruments of war, the horse was the first which man learned to tame and domesticate during the period of the peopling of the earth; the elephant belongs to the later period of the luxury of states already established. In the same way, the art of cultivating certain grasses called cereals — no longer known to us in their original form — and also the multiplication and improvement, by transplanting and grafting, of the original kinds of fruit — in Europe, probably only two species, the crab-apple and wild pear — could only originate under the conditions accompanying established states where the rights of property are assured. That is to say it would be after man, hitherto existing in lawless liberty, had advanced beyond the occupations of a hunter,[138*] a fisherman or a shepherd to the life of a tiller of the soil, when salt and iron were discovered, — to become, perhaps, the first articles of commerce between different peoples, — and were sought far and near. In this way the peoples would be at first brought into peaceful relation with one another, and so come to an understanding and the enjoyment of friendly intercourse, even with their most distant neighbours.

Now while nature provided that men could live on all parts of the earth, she also at the same time despotically willed that they *should* live everywhere on it, although against their own inclination and even although this imperative did not presuppose an idea of duty which would compel obedience to nature with the force of a moral law. But, to attain this end, she has chosen war. So we see certain peoples, widely separated, whose common descent is made evident by affinity in their languages. Thus, for instance, we find the Samoyedes on the Arctic Ocean, and again a people speaking a similar language on the Altai Mts., 200 miles *Meilen*[139*] off, between whom has pressed in a mounted tribe, warlike in character and of Mongolian origin, which has driven one branch of the race far from the other, into the most inhospitable regions where their own inclination would certainly not have carried them.[140*] In the same way, through the intrusion of the Gothic and Sarmatian tribes, the Finns in the most northerly regions of Europe, whom we call Laplanders, have been separated by as great a distance from the Hungarians, with whose language their own is allied. And what but war can have brought the Esquimos to the north of America, a race quite distinct from those of that country and probably European adventurers of prehistoric times? And war too, nature's method of populating the earth, must have driven the Pescherais[141*] in South America as far as Patagonia. War itself, however, is in need of no special stimulating cause, but seems engrafted in human nature, and is even regarded as something noble in itself to which man is inspired by the love of glory apart from motives of self-interest. Hence, among the savages of America as well as those of Europe in the age of chivalry, martial courage is looked upon as of great value itself, not merely when a war is going on, as is reasonable enough, but in order that there should be war: and thus war is often entered upon merely to exhibit this quality. So that an intrinsic dignity is held to attach to war in itself, and even philosophers eulogise it as an ennobling, refining influence on humanity, unmindful of the Greek proverb, "War is evil, in so far as it makes more bad people than it takes away."

So much, then, of what nature does for her own ends with regard to the human race as members of the animal world. Now comes the question which touches the essential points in this design of a perpetual peace:— "What does nature do in this respect with reference to the end which man's own reason sets before him as a duty? and consequently what does she do to further the realisation of his moral purpose? How does she guarantee that what man, by the laws of freedom, ought to do and yet fails to do, he will do, without any infringement of his freedom by the compulsion of nature and that, moreover, this shall be done in accordance with the three forms of public right — constitutional or political law, international law and cosmopolitan law?" When I say of nature that she *wills* that this or that should take place, I do not mean that she imposes upon us the duty to do it — for only the free, unrestrained, practical reason can do that — but that she does it herself, whether we will or not. "*Fata volentem ducunt, nolentem trahunt.*"

1. Even if a people were not compelled through internal discord to submit to the restraint of public laws, war would bring this about, working from without. For, according to the contrivance of nature which we have mentioned, every people finds another tribe in its neighbourhood, pressing upon it in such a manner that it is compelled to form itself internally into a state to be able to defend itself as a power should. Now the republican constitution is the only one which is perfectly adapted to the rights of man, but it is also the most difficult to establish and still more to maintain. So generally is this recognised that people often say the members of a republican state would require to be angels,[142*] because men, with their self-seeking propensities, are not fit for a constitution of so sublime a form. But now nature comes to the aid of the universal, reason-derived will which, much as we honour it, is in practice powerless. And this she does, by means of these very self-seeking propensities, so that it only depends — and so much lies within the power of man — on a good organisation of the state for their forces to be so pitted against one another, that the one may check the destructive activity of the other or neutralise its effect. And hence, from the standpoint of reason, the result will be the same as if both forces did not exist, and each individual is compelled to be, if not a morally good man, yet at least a good citizen. The problem of the formation of the state, hard as it may sound, is not insoluble, even for a race of devils, granted that they have intelligence. It may be put thus:— "Given a multitude of rational beings who, in a body, require general laws for their own preservation, but each of whom, as an individual, is secretly inclined to exempt himself from this restraint: how are we to order their affairs and how establish for them a constitution such that, although their private dispositions may be really antagonistic, they may yet so act as a check upon one another, that, in their public relations, the effect is the same as if they had no such evil sentiments." Such a problem must be capable of solution. For it deals, not with the moral reformation of mankind, but only with the mechanism of nature; and the problem is to learn how this mechanism of nature can be applied to men, in order so to regulate the antagonism of conflicting interests in a people that they may even compel one another to submit to compulsory laws and thus

necessarily bring about the state of peace in which laws have force. We can see, in states actually existing, although very imperfectly organised, that, in externals, they already approximate very nearly to what the Idea of right prescribes, although the principle of morality is certainly not the cause. A good political constitution, however, is not to be expected as a result of progress in morality; but rather, conversely, the good moral condition of a nation is to be looked for, as one of the first fruits of such a constitution. Hence the mechanism of nature, working through the self-seeking propensities of man (which of course counteract one another in their external effects), may be used by reason as a means of making way for the realisation of her own purpose, the empire of right, and, as far as is in the power of the state, to promote and secure in this way internal as well as external peace. We may say, then, that it is the irresistible will of nature that right shall at last get the supremacy. What one here fails to do will be accomplished in the long run, although perhaps with much inconvenience to us. As Bouterwek says, "If you bend the reed too much it breaks: he who would do too much does nothing."

2. The idea of international law presupposes the separate existence of a number of neighbouring and independent states; and, although such a condition of things is in itself already a state of war, (if a federative union of these nations does not prevent the outbreak of hostilities) yet, according to the Idea of reason, this is better than that all the states should be merged into one under a power which has gained the ascendency over its neighbours and gradually become a universal monarchy.[143*] For the wider the sphere of their jurisdiction, the more laws lose in force; and soulless despotism, when it has choked the seeds of good, at last sinks into anarchy. Nevertheless it is the desire of every state, or of its ruler, to attain to a permanent condition of peace in this very way; that is to say, by subjecting the whole world as far as possible to its sway. But nature wills it otherwise. She employs two means to separate nations, and prevent them from intermixing: namely, the differences of language and of religion.[144*] These differences bring with them a tendency to mutual hatred, and furnish pretexts for waging war. But, none the less, with the growth of culture and the gradual advance of men to greater unanimity of principle, they lead to concord in a state of peace which, unlike the despotism we have spoken of, (the churchyard of freedom) does not arise from the weakening of all forces, but is brought into being and secured through the equilibrium of these forces in their most active rivalry.

3. As nature wisely separates nations which the will of each state, sanctioned even by the principles of international law, would gladly unite under its own sway by stratagem or force; in the same way, on the other hand, she unites nations whom the principle of a cosmopolitan right would not have secured against violence and war. And this union she brings about through an appeal to their mutual interests. The commercial spirit cannot co-exist with war, and sooner or later it takes possession of every nation. For, of all the forces which lie at the command of a state, the power of money is probably the most reliable. Hence states find themselves compelled — not, it is true, exactly from motives of morality — to further the noble end of peace and to avert war, by means of mediation, wherever it threatens to break out, just as if they had made a permanent league for this purpose. For great alliances with a view to war can, from the nature of things, only very rarely occur, and still more seldom succeed.

In this way nature guarantees the coming of perpetual peace, through the natural course of human propensities: not indeed with sufficient certainty to enable us to prophesy the future of this ideal theoretically, but yet clearly enough for practical purposes. And thus this guarantee of nature makes it a duty that we should labour for this end, an end which is no mere chimera.

SECOND SUPPLEMENT

A SECRET ARTICLE FOR PERPETUAL PEACE

A secret article in negotiations concerning public right is, when looked at objectively or with regard to the meaning of the term, a contradiction. When we view it, however, from the subjective standpoint, with regard to the character and condition of the person who dictates it, we see that it might quite well involve some private consideration, so that he would regard it as hazardous to his dignity to acknowledge such an article as originating from him.

The only article of this kind is contained in the following proposition:— "The opinions of philosophers, with regard to the conditions of the possibility of a public peace, shall be taken into consideration by states armed for war."

It seems, however, to be derogatory to the dignity of the legislative authority of a state — to which we must of course attribute all wisdom — to ask advice from subjects (among whom stand philosophers) about the rules of its behaviour to other states. At the same time, it is very advisable that this should be done. Hence the state will silently invite suggestion for this purpose, while at the same time keeping the fact secret. This amounts to saying that the state will allow philosophers to discuss freely and publicly the universal principles governing the conduct of war and establishment of peace; for they will do this of their own accord, if no prohibition is laid upon them.[145*] The arrangement between states, on this point, does not require that a special agreement should be made, merely for this purpose; for it is already involved in the obligation imposed by the universal reason of man which gives the moral law. We would not be understood to say that the state must give a preference to the principles of the philosopher, rather than to the opinions of the jurist, the representative of state authority; but only that he should be heard. The latter, who has chosen for a symbol the scales of right and the sword of justice,[146*] generally uses that sword not merely to keep off all outside influences from the scales; for, when one pan of the balance will not go down, he throws his sword into it; and then *Væ victis*! The jurist, not being a moral philosopher, is under the greatest temptation to do this, because it is his business only to apply existing laws and not to investigate whether these are not themselves in need of improvement; and this actually lower function of his profession he looks upon as the nobler, because it is linked to power (as is the case also in both the other faculties, theology and medicine). Philosophy occupies a very low position compared with this combined power. So that it is said, for example, that she is the handmaid of theology; and the same has been said of her position with regard to law and medicine. It is not quite clear, however, "whether she bears the torch before these gracious ladies, or carries the train."

That kings should philosophise, or philosophers become kings, is not to be expected. But neither is it to be desired; for the possession of power is inevitably fatal to the free exercise of reason. But it is absolutely indispensable, for their enlightenment as to the full significance of their vocations, that both kings and sovereign nations, which rule themselves in accordance with laws of equality, should not allow the class of philosophers to disappear, nor forbid the expression of their opinions, but should allow them to speak openly. And since this class of men, by their very nature, are incapable of instigating rebellion or forming unions for purposes of political agitation, they should not be suspected of propagandism.

APPENDIX I

ON THE DISAGREEMENT BETWEEN MORALS AND POLITICS WITH REFERENCE TO PERPETUAL PEACE

In an objective sense, morals is a practical science, as the sum of laws exacting unconditional obedience, in accordance with which we *ought* to act. Now, once we have admitted the authority of this idea of duty, it is evidently inconsistent that we should think of saying that we *cannot* act thus. For, in this case, the idea of duty falls to the ground of itself; *"ultra posse nemo obligatur."* Hence there can be no quarrel between politics, as the practical science of right, and morals, which is also a science of right, but theoretical. That is, theory cannot come into conflict with practice. For, in that case, we would need to understand under the term "ethics" or "morals" a universal doctrine of expediency, or, in other words, a theory of precepts which may guide us in choosing the best means for attaining ends calculated for our advantage. This is to deny that a science of morals exists.

Politics says, "Be wise as serpents"; morals adds the limiting condition, "and guileless as doves." If these precepts cannot stand together in one command, then there is a real quarrel between politics and morals.[147]* But if they can be completely brought into accord, then the idea of any antagonism between them is absurd, and the question of how best to make a compromise between the two points of view ceases to be even raised. Although the saying, "Honesty is the best policy," expresses a theory which, alas, is often contradicted in practice, yet the likewise theoretical maxim, "Honesty is better than any policy," is exalted high above every possible objection, is indeed the necessary condition of all politics.

The Terminus of morals does not yield to Jupiter, the Terminus of force; for the latter remains beneath the sway of Fate. In other words, reason is not sufficiently enlightened to survey the series of predetermining causes which would make it possible for us to predict with certainty the good or bad results of human action, as they follow from the mechanical laws of nature; although we may hope that things will turn out as we should desire. But what we have to do, in order to remain in the path of duty guided by the rules of wisdom, reason makes everywhere perfectly clear, and does this for the purpose of furthering her ultimate ends.

The practical man, however, for whom morals is mere theory, even while admitting that what ought to be can be, bases his dreary verdict against our well-meant hopes really on this: he pretends that he can foresee from his observation of human nature, that men will never be willing to do what is required in order to bring about the wished-for results leading to perpetual peace. It is true that the will of all individual men to live under a legal constitution according to the principles of liberty — that is to say, the distributive unity of the wills of all — is not sufficient to attain this end. We must have the collective unity of their united will: all as a body must determine these new conditions. The solution of this difficult problem is required in order that civil society should be a whole. To all this diversity of individual wills there must come a uniting cause, in order to produce a common will which no distributive will is able to give. Hence, in the practical realisation of that idea, no other beginning of a law-governed society can be counted upon than one that is brought about by force: upon this force, too, public law afterwards rests. This state of things certainly prepares us to meet considerable deviation in actual experience from the theoretical idea of perpetual peace, since we cannot take into account the moral character and disposition of a law-giver in this connection, or expect that, after he has united a wild multitude into one people, he will leave it to them to bring about a legal constitution by their common will.

It amounts to this. Any ruler who has once got the power in his hands will not let the people dictate laws for him. A state which enjoys an independence of the control of external law will not submit to the judgment of the tribunals of other states, when it has to consider how to obtain its rights against them. And even a continent, when it feels its superiority to another, whether this be in its way or not, will not fail to take advantage of an opportunity offered of strengthening its power by the spoliation or even conquest of this territory. Hence all theoretical schemes, connected with constitutional, international or cosmopolitan law, crumble away into empty impracticable ideals. While, on the other hand, a practical science, based on the empirical principles of human nature, which does not disdain to model its maxims on an observation of actual life, can alone hope to find a sure foundation on which to build up a system of national policy.

Now certainly, if there is neither freedom nor a moral law founded upon it, and every actual or possible event happens in the mere mechanical course of nature, then politics, as the art of making use of this physical necessity in things for the government of men, is the whole of practical wisdom and the idea of right is an empty concept. If, on the other hand, we find that this idea of right is necessarily to be conjoined with politics and even to be raised to the position of a limiting condition of that science, then the possibility of reconciling them must be admitted. I can thus imagine a moral politician, that is to say, one who understands the principles of statesmanship to be such as do not conflict with morals; but I cannot conceive of a political moralist who fashions for himself such a system of ethics as may serve the interest of statesmen.

The moral politician will always act upon the following principle:— "If certain defects which could not have been avoided are found in the political constitution or foreign relations of a state, it is a duty for all, especially for the rulers of the state, to apply their whole energy to correcting them as soon as possible, and to bringing the constitution and political relations on these points into conformity with the Law of Nature, as it is held up as a model before us in the idea of reason; and this they should do even at a sacrifice of their own interest." Now it is contrary to all politics — which is, in this particular, in agreement with morals — to dissever any of the links binding citizens together in the state or nations in cosmopolitan union, before a better constitution is there to take the place of what has been thus destroyed. And hence it would be absurd indeed to demand that every imperfection in political matters must be violently altered on the spot. But, at the same time, it may be required of a ruler at least that he should earnestly keep the maxim in mind which points to the necessity of such a change; so that he may go on constantly approaching the end to be realised, namely, the best possible constitution according to the laws of right. Even although it is still under despotic rule, in accordance with its constitution as then existing, a state may govern itself on republican lines, until the people gradually become capable of being influenced by the mere idea of the authority of law, just as if it had physical power. And they become accordingly capable of self-legislation, their faculty for which is founded on original right. But if, through the violence of revolution, the product of a bad government, a constitution more in accord with the spirit of law were attained even by unlawful means, it should no longer be held justifiable to bring the people back to the old constitution, although, while the revolution was going on, every one who took part in it by use of force or stratagem, may have been justly punished as a rebel. As regards the external relations of nations, a state cannot be asked to give up its constitution, even although that be a despotism (which is, at the same time, the strongest constitution where foreign enemies are concerned), so long as it runs the risk of being immediately swallowed up by other states. Hence, when such a proposal is made, the state whose constitution is in question must at least be allowed to defer acting upon it until a more convenient time.[148*]

It is always possible that moralists who rule despotically, and are at a loss in practical matters, will come into collision with the rules of political wisdom in many ways, by adopting measures without sufficient deliberation which show themselves afterwards to have been overestimated. When they thus offend against nature, experience must gradually lead them into a better track. But, instead of this being the case, politicians who are fond of moralising do all they can to make moral improvement impossible and to perpetuate violations of law, by extenuating political principles which are antagonistic to the idea of right, on the pretext that human nature is not capable of good, in the sense of the ideal which reason prescribes.

These politicians, instead of adopting an open, straightforward way of doing things (as they boast), mix themselves up in intrigue. They get at the authorities in power and say what will please them; their sole bent is to sacrifice the nation, or even, if they can, the whole world, with the one end in view that their own private interest may be forwarded. This is the manner of regular jurists (I mean the journeyman lawyer not the legislator), when they aspire to politics. For, as it is not their business to reason too nicely over legislation, but only to enforce the laws of the country, every legal constitution in its existing form and, when this is changed by the proper authorities, the one which takes its place, will always seem to them the best possible. And the consequence is that everything is purely mechanical. But this adroitness in suiting themselves to any circumstances may lead them to the delusion that they are also capable of giving an opinion about the principles of political constitutions in general, in so far as they conform to ideas of right, and are therefore not empirical, but *a priori*. And they may therefore brag about their knowledge of men, — which indeed one expects to find, since they have to deal with so many — without really knowing the nature of man and what can be made of it, to gain which knowledge a higher standpoint of anthropological observation than theirs is required. Filled with ideas of this kind, if they trespass outside their own sphere on the boundaries of political and international law, looked upon as ideals which reason holds before us, they can do so only in the spirit of chicanery. For they will follow their usual method of making everything conform mechanically to compulsory laws despotically made and enforced, even here, where the ideas of reason recognise the validity of a legal compulsory force, only when it is in accordance with the principles of freedom through which a permanently valid constitution becomes first of all possible. The would-be practical man, leaving out of account this idea of reason, thinks that he can solve this problem empirically by looking to the way in which those constitutions which have best survived the test of time were established, even although the spirit of these may have been generally contrary to the idea of right. The principles which he makes use of here, although indeed he does not make them public, amount pretty much to the following sophistical maxims.

1. Fac et excusa. Seize the most favourable opportunity for arbitrary usurpation — either of the authority of the state over its own people or over a neighbouring people; the justification of the act and extenuation of the use of force will come much more easily and gracefully, when the deed is done, than if one has to think out convincing reasons for taking this step and first hear through all the objections which can be made against it. This is especially true in the first case mentioned, where the supreme power in the state also controls the legislature which we must obey without any reasoning about it. Besides, this show of audacity in a statesman even lends him a certain semblance of inward conviction of the justice of his action; and once he has got so far the god of success (*bonus eventus*) is his best advocate.

2. Si fecisti, nega. As for any crime you have committed, such as has, for instance, brought your people to despair and thence to insurrection, deny that it has happened owing to any fault of yours. Say rather that it is all caused by the insubordination of your subjects, or, in the case of your having usurped a neighbouring state, that human nature is to blame; for, if a man is not ready to use force and steal a march upon his neighbour, he may certainly count on the latter forestalling him and taking him prisoner.

3. Divide et impera. That is to say, if there are certain privileged persons, holding authority among the people, who have merely chosen you for their sovereign as *primus inter pares*, bring about a quarrel among them, and make mischief between them and the people. Now back up the people with a dazzling promise of greater freedom; everything will now depend unconditionally on your will. Or again, if there is a difficulty with foreign states, then to stir up dissension among them is a pretty sure means of subjecting first one and then the other to your sway, under the pretext of aiding the weaker.

It is true that now-a-days no body is taken in by these political maxims, for they are all familiar to everyone. Moreover, there is no need of being ashamed of them, as if their injustice were too patent. For the great Powers never feel shame before the judgment of the common herd, but only before one another; so that as far as this matter goes, it is not the revelation of these guiding principles of policy that can make rulers ashamed, but only the unsuccessful use of them. For as to the morality of these maxims, politicians are all agreed. Hence there is always left political prestige on which they can safely count; and this means the glory of increasing their power by any means that offer.[149*]

* * *

In all these twistings and turnings of an immoral doctrine of expediency which aims at substituting a state of peace for the warlike conditions in which men are placed by nature, so much at least is clear; — that men cannot get away from the idea of right in their private any more than in their public relations; and that they do not dare (this is indeed most strikingly seen in the concept of an international law) to base politics merely on the manipulations of expediency and therefore to refuse all obedience to the idea of a public right. On the contrary, they pay all fitting honour to the idea of right in itself, even although they should, at the same time, devise a hundred subterfuges and excuses to avoid it in practice, and should regard force, backed up by cunning, as having the authority which comes from being the source and unifying principle of all right. It will be well to put an end to this sophistry, if not to the injustice it extenuates, and to bring the false advocates of the mighty of the earth to confess that it is not right but might in whose interest they speak, and that it is the worship of might from which they take their cue, as if in this matter they had a right to command. In order to do this, we must first expose the delusion by which they deceive themselves and others; then discover the ultimate principle from which their plans for a perpetual peace proceed; and thence show that all the evil which stands in the way of the realisation of that ideal springs from the fact that the political moralist begins where the moral politician rightly ends and that, by subordinating principles to an end or putting the cart before the horse, he defeats his intention of bringing politics into harmony with morals.

In order to make practical philosophy consistent with itself, we must first decide the following question: — In dealing with the problems of practical reason must we begin from its material principle — the end as the object of free choice — or from its formal principle which is based merely on freedom in its external relation? — from which comes the following law:— "Act so that thou canst will that thy maxim should be a universal law, be the end of thy action what it will."[150*]

Without doubt, the latter determining principle of action must stand first; for, as a principle of right, it carries unconditional necessity with it, whereas the former is obligatory only if we assume the empirical conditions of the end set before us, — that is to say, that it is an end capable of being practically realised. And if this end — as, for example, the end of perpetual peace — should be also a duty, this same duty must necessarily have been deduced from the formal principle governing the maxims which guide external action. Now the first principle is the principle of the political moralist; the problems of constitutional, international and cosmopolitan law are mere technical problems (*problema technicum*). The second or formal principle, on the other hand, as the principle of the moral politician who regards it as a moral problem (*problema morale*), differs widely from the other principle in its methods of bringing about perpetual peace, which we desire not only as a material good, but also as a state of things resulting from our recognition of the precepts of duty.[151*]

To solve the first problem — that, namely, of political expediency — much knowledge of nature is required, that her mechanical laws may be employed for the end in view. And yet the result of all knowledge of this kind is uncertain, as far as perpetual peace is concerned. This we find to be so, whichever of the three departments of public law we take. It is uncertain whether a people could be better kept in obedience and at the same time prosperity by severity or by baits held out to their vanity; whether they would be better governed under the sovereignty of a single individual or by the authority of several acting together; whether the combined authority might be better secured merely, say, by an official nobility or by the power of the people within the state; and, finally, whether such conditions could be long maintained. There are examples to the contrary in history in the case of all forms of government, with the exception of the only true republican constitution, the idea of which can occur only to a moral politician. Still more uncertain is a law of nations, ostensibly established upon statutes devised by ministers; for this amounts in fact to mere empty words, and rests on treaties which, in the very act of ratification, contain a secret reservation of the right to violate them. On the other hand, the solution of the second problem — the problem of political wisdom — forces itself, we may say, upon us; it is quite obvious to every one, and puts all crooked dealings to shame; it leads, too, straight to the desired end, while at the same time, discretion warns us not to drag in the conditions of perpetual peace by force, but to take time and approach this ideal gradually as favourable circumstances permit.

This may be expressed in the following maxim:— "Seek ye first the kingdom of pure practical reason and its righteousness, and the object of your endeavour, the blessing of perpetual peace, will be added unto you." For the science of morals generally has this peculiarity, — and it has it also with regard to the moral principles of public law, and therefore with regard to a science of politics knowable *a priori*, — that the less it makes a man's conduct depend on the end he has set before him, his purposed material or moral gain, so much the more, nevertheless, does it conform in general to this end. The reason for this is that it is just the universal will, given *a priori*, which exists in a people or in the relation of different peoples to one another, that alone determines what is lawful among men. This union of individual wills, however, if we proceed consistently in practice, in observance of the mechanical laws of nature, may be at the same time the cause of bringing about the result intended and practically realizing the idea of right. Hence it is, for example, a principle of moral politics that a people should unite into a state according to the only valid concepts of right, the ideas of freedom and equality; and this principle is not based on expediency, but upon duty. Political moralists, however, do not deserve a hearing, much and sophistically as they may reason about the existence, in a multitude of men forming a society, of certain natural tendencies which would weaken those principles and defeat their intention. They may endeavour to prove their assertion by giving instances of badly organised constitutions, chosen both from ancient and modern times, (as, for example, democracies without a representative system); but such arguments are to be treated with contempt, all the more, because a pernicious theory of this kind may perhaps even bring about the evil which it prophesies. For, in accordance with such reasoning, man is thrown into a class with all other living machines which only require the consciousness that they are not free creatures to make them in their own judgment the most miserable of all beings.

Fiat justitia, pereat mundus. This saying has become proverbial, and although it savours a little of boastfulness, is also true. We may translate it thus:— "Let justice rule on earth, although all the rogues in the world should go to the bottom." It is a good, honest principle of right cutting off all the crooked ways made by knavery or violence. It must not, however, be misunderstood as allowing anyone to exercise his own rights with the utmost severity, a course in contradiction to our moral duty; but we must take it to signify an obligation, binding upon rulers, to refrain from refusing to yield anyone his rights or from curtailing them, out of personal feeling or sympathy for others. For this end, in particular, we require, firstly, that a state should have an internal political constitution, established according to the pure principles of right; secondly, that a union should be formed between this state and neighbouring or distant nations for a legal settlement of their differences, after the analogy of the universal state. This proposition means nothing more than this: — Political maxims must not start from the idea of a prosperity and happiness which are to be expected from observance of such precepts in every state; that is, not from the end which each nation makes the object of its will as the highest empirical principle of political wisdom; but they must set out from the pure concept of the duty of right, from the *"ought"* whose principle is given *a priori* through pure reason. This is the law, whatever the material consequences may be. The world will certainly not perish by any means, because the number of wicked people in it is becoming fewer. The morally bad has one peculiarity, inseparable from its nature; — in its purposes, especially in relation to other evil influences, it is in contradiction with itself, and counteracts its own natural effect, and thus makes room for the moral principle of good, although advance in this direction may be slow.

Hence objectively, in theory, there is no quarrel between morals and politics. But subjectively, in the self-seeking tendencies of men (which we cannot actually call their morality, as we would a course of action based on maxims of reason,) this disagreement in principle exists and may always survive; for it serves as a whetstone to virtue. According to the principle, *Tu ne cede malis, sed contra audentior ito*, the true courage of virtue in the present case lies not so much in facing the evils and self-sacrifices which must be met here as in firmly confronting the evil principle in our own nature and conquering its wiles. For this is a principle far more dangerous, false, treacherous and sophistical which puts forward the weakness in human nature as a justification for every transgression.

In fact the political moralist may say that a ruler and people, or nation and nation do *one another* no wrong, when they enter on a war with violence or cunning, although they do wrong, generally speaking, in refusing to respect the idea of right which alone could establish peace for all time. For, as both are equally wrongly disposed to one another, each transgressing the duty he owes to his neighbour, they are both quite rightly served, when they are thus destroyed in war. This mutual destruction stops short at the point of extermination, so that there are always enough of the race left to keep this game going on through all the ages, and a far-off posterity may take warning by them. The Providence that orders the course of the world is hereby justified. For the moral principle in mankind never becomes extinguished, and human reason, fitted for the practical realisation of ideas of right according to that principle, grows continually in fitness for that purpose with the ever advancing march of culture; while at the same time, it must be said, the guilt of transgression increases as well. But it seems that, by no theodicy or vindication of the justice of God, can we justify Creation in putting such a race of corrupt creatures into the world at all, if, that is, we assume that the human race neither will nor can ever be in a happier condition than it is now. This standpoint, however, is too high a one for us to judge from, or to theorise, with the limited concepts we have at our command, about the wisdom of that supreme Power which is unknowable by us. We are inevitably driven to such despairing conclusions as these, if we do not admit that the pure principles of right have objective reality — that is to say, are capable of being practically realised — and consequently that action must be taken on the part of the people of a state and, further, by states in relation to one another, whatever arguments empirical politics may bring forward against this course. Politics in the real sense cannot take a step forward without first paying homage to the principles of morals. And, although politics, *per se*, is a difficult art,[152] in its union with morals no art is required; for in the case of a conflict arising between the two sciences, the moralist can cut asunder the knot which politics is unable to untie. Right must be held sacred by man, however great the cost and sacrifice to the ruling power. Here is no half-and-half course. We cannot devise a happy medium between right and expediency, a right pragmatically conditioned. But all politics must bend the knee to the principle of right, and may, in that way, hope to reach, although slowly perhaps, a level whence it may shine upon men for all time.

APPENDIX II

CONCERNING THE HARMONY OF POLITICS WITH MORALS ACCORDING TO THE TRANSCENDENTAL IDEA OF PUBLIC RIGHT

If I look at public right from the point of view of most professors of law, and abstract from its *matter* or its empirical elements, varying according to the circumstances given in our experience of individuals in a state or of states among themselves, then there remains the *form* of publicity. The possibility of this publicity, every legal title implies. For without it there could be no justice, which can only be thought as before the eyes of men; and, without justice, there would be no right, for, from justice only, right can come.

This characteristic of publicity must belong to every legal title. Hence, as, in any particular case that occurs, there is no difficulty in deciding whether this essential attribute is present or not, (whether, that is, it is reconcilable with the principles of the agent or not), it furnishes an easily applied criterion which is to be found *a priori* in the reason, so that in the particular case we can at once recognise the falsity or illegality of a proposed claim (*praetensio juris*), as it were by an experiment of pure reason.

Having thus, as it were, abstracted from all the empirical elements contained in the concept of a political and international law, such as, for instance, the evil tendency in human nature which makes compulsion necessary, we may give the following proposition as the *transcendental formula* of public right:— "All actions relating to the rights of other men are wrong, if the maxims from which they follow are inconsistent with publicity."

This principle must be regarded not merely as ethical, as belonging to the doctrine of virtue, but also as juridical, referring to the rights of men. For there is something wrong in a maxim of conduct which I cannot divulge without at once defeating my purpose, a maxim which must therefore be kept secret, if it is to succeed, and which I could not publicly acknowledge without infallibly stirring up the opposition of everyone. This necessary and universal resistance with which everyone meets me, a resistance therefore evident *a priori*, can be due to no other cause than the injustice with which such a maxim threatens everyone. Further, this testing principle is merely negative; that is, it serves only as a means by which we may know when an action is unjust to others. Like axioms, it has a certainty incapable of demonstration; it is besides easy of application as appears from the following examples of public right.

1. — Constitutional Law. Let us take in the first place the public law of the state (*jus civitatis*), particularly in its application to matters within the state. Here a question arises which many think difficult to answer, but which the transcendental principle of publicity solves quite readily:— "Is revolution a legitimate means for a people to adopt, for the purpose of throwing off the oppressive yoke of a so-called tyrant (*non*

titulo, sed exercitio talis)?" The rights of a nation are violated in a government of this kind, and no wrong is done to the tyrant in dethroning him. Of this there is no doubt. None the less, it is in the highest degree wrong of the subjects to prosecute their rights in this way; and they would be just as little justified in complaining, if they happened to be defeated in their attempt and had to endure the severest punishment in consequence.

A great many reasons for and against both sides of this question may be given, if we seek to settle it by a dogmatic deduction of the principles of right. But the transcendental principle of the publicity of public right can spare itself this diffuse argumentation. For, according to that principle, the people would ask themselves, before the civil contract was made, whether they could venture to publish maxims, proposing insurrection when a favourable opportunity should present itself. It is quite clear that if, when a constitution is established, it were made a condition that force may be exercised against the sovereign under certain circumstances, the people would be obliged to claim a lawful authority higher than his. But in that case, the so-called sovereign would be no longer sovereign: or, if both powers, that of the sovereign and that of the people, were made a condition of the constitution of the state, then its establishment (which was the aim of the people) would be impossible. The wrongfulness of revolution is quite obvious from the fact that openly to acknowledge maxims which justify this step would make attainment of the end at which they aim impossible. We are obliged to keep them secret. But this secrecy would not be necessary on the part of the head of the state. He may say quite plainly that the ringleaders of every rebellion will be punished by death, even although they may hold that it was he who first transgressed the fundamental law. For, if a ruler is conscious of possessing irresistible sovereign power (and this must be assumed in every civil constitution, because a sovereign who has not power to protect any individual member of the nation against his neighbour has also not the right to exercise authority over him), then he need have no fear that making known the maxims which guide him will cause the defeat of his plans. And it is quite consistent with this view to hold that, if the people are successful in their insurrection, the sovereign must return to the rank of a subject, and refrain from inciting rebellion with a view to regaining his lost sovereignty. At the same time he need have no fear of being called to account for his former administration.[153*]

2. — International Law. There can be no question of an international law, except on the assumption of some kind of a law-governed state of things, the external condition under which any right can belong to man. For the very idea of international law, as public right, implies the publication of a universal will determining the rights and property of each individual nation; and this *status juridicus* must spring out of a contract of some sort which may not, like the contract to which the state owes its origin, be founded upon compulsory laws, but may be, at the most, the agreement of a permanent free association such as the federation of the different states, to which we have alluded above. For, without the control of law to some extent, to serve as an active bond of union among different merely natural or moral individuals, — that is to say, in a state of nature, — there can only be private law. And here we find a disagreement between morals, regarded as the science of right, and politics. The criterion, obtained by observing the effect of publicity on maxims, is just as easily

applied, but only when we understand that this agreement binds the contracting states solely with the object that peace may be preserved among them, and between them and other states; in no sense with a view to the acquisition of new territory or power. The following instances of antinomy occur between politics and morals, which are given here with the solution in each case.

a. "When either of these states has promised something to another, (as, for instance, assistance, or a relinquishment of certain territory, or subsidies and such like), the question may arise whether, in a case where the safety of the state thus bound depends on its evading the fulfilment of this promise, it can do so by maintaining a right to be regarded as a double person: — firstly, as sovereign and accountable to no one in the state of which that sovereign power is head; and, secondly, merely as the highest official in the service of that state, who is obliged to answer to the state for every action. And the result of this is that the state is acquitted in its second capacity of any obligation to which it has committed itself in the first." But, if a nation or its sovereign proclaimed these maxims, the natural consequence would be that every other would flee from it, or unite with other states to oppose such pretensions. And this is a proof that politics, with all its cunning, defeats its own ends, if the test of making principles of action public, which we have indicated, be applied. Hence the maxim we have quoted must be wrong.

b. "If a state which has increased its power to a formidable extent (*potentia tremenda*) excites anxiety in its neighbours, is it right to assume that, since it has the means, it will also have the will to oppress others; and does that give less powerful states a right to unite and attack the greater nation without any definite cause of offence?" A state which would here answer openly in the affirmative would only bring the evil about more surely and speedily. For the greater power would forestall those smaller nations, and their union would be but a weak reed of defence against a state which knew how to apply the maxim, *divide et impera.* This maxim of political expediency then, when openly acknowledged, necessarily defeats the end at which it aims, and is therefore wrong.

c. "If a smaller state by its geographical position breaks up the territory of a greater, so as to prevent a unity necessary to the preservation of that state, is the latter not justified in subjugating its less powerful neighbour and uniting the territory in question with its own?" We can easily see that the greater state dare not publish such a maxim beforehand; for either all smaller states would without loss of time unite against it, or other powers would contend for this booty. Hence the impracticability of such a maxim becomes evident under the light of publicity. And this is a sign that it is wrong, and that in a very great degree; for, although the victim of an act of injustice may be of small account, that does not prevent the injustice done from being very great.

3. — Cosmopolitan Law. We may pass over this department of right in silence, for, owing to its analogy with international law, its maxims are easily specified and estimated.

* * *

In this principle of the incompatibility of the maxims of international law with their publicity, we have a good indication of the non-agreement between politics and morals, regarded as a science of right. Now we require to know under what conditions these maxims do agree with the law of nations. For we cannot conclude that the converse holds, and that all maxims which can bear publicity are therefore just. For anyone who has a decided supremacy has no need to make any secret about his maxims. The condition of a law of nations being possible at all is that, in the first place, there should be a law-governed state of things. If this is not so, there can be no public right, and all right which we can think of outside the law-governed state, — that is to say, in the state of nature, — is mere private right. Now we have seen above that something of the nature of a federation between nations, for the sole purpose of doing away with war, is the only rightful condition of things reconcilable with their individual freedom. Hence the agreement of politics and morals is only possible in a federative union, a union which is necessarily given *a priori*, according to the principles of right. And the lawful basis of all politics can only be the establishment of this union in its widest possible extent. Apart from this end, all political sophistry is folly and veiled injustice. Now this sham politics has a casuistry, not to be excelled in the best Jesuit school. It has its mental reservation (*reservatio mentalis*): as in the drawing up of a public treaty in such terms as we can, if we will, interpret when occasion serves to our advantage; for example, the distinction between the *status quo* in fact (*de fait*) and in right (*de droit*). Secondly, it has its probabilism; when it pretends to discover evil intentions in another, or makes, the probability of their possible future ascendency a lawful reason for bringing about the destruction of other peaceful states. Finally, it has its philosophical sin (*peccatum philosophicum, peccatillum, baggatelle*) which is that of holding it a trifle easily pardoned that a smaller state should be swallowed up, if this be to the gain of a nation much more powerful; for such an increase in power is supposed to tend to the greater prosperity of the whole world.[154*]

Duplicity gives politics the advantage of using one branch or the other of morals, just as suits its own ends. The love of our fellowmen is a duty: so too is respect for their rights. But the former is only conditional: the latter, on the other hand, an unconditional, absolutely imperative duty; and anyone who would give himself up to the sweet consciousness of well-doing must be first perfectly assured that he has not transgressed its commands. Politics has no difficulty in agreeing with morals in the first sense of the term, as ethics, to secure that men should give to superiors their rights. But when it comes to morals, in its second aspect, as the science of right before which politics must bow the knee, the politician finds it prudent to have nothing to do with compacts and rather to deny all reality to morals in this sense, and reduce all duty to mere benevolence. Philosophy could easily frustrate the artifices of a politics like this, which shuns the light of criticism, by publishing its maxims, if only statesmen would have the courage to grant philosophers the right to ventilate their opinions.

With this end in view, I propose another principle of public right, which is at once transcendental and affirmative. Its formula would be as follows:— "All maxims which require publicity, in order that they may not fail to attain their end, are in agreement both with right and politics."

For, if these maxims can only attain the end at which they aim by being published, they must be in harmony with the universal end of mankind, which is happiness; and to be in sympathy with this (to make the people contented with their lot) is the real business of politics. Now, if this end should be attainable only by publicity, or in other words, through the removal of all distrust of the maxims of politics, these must be in harmony with the right of the people; for a union of the ends of all is only possible in a harmony with this right.

I must postpone the further development and discussion of this principle till another opportunity. That it is a transcendental formula is quite evident from the fact that all the empirical conditions of a doctrine of happiness, or the *matter* of law, are absent, and that it has regard only to the *form* of universal conformity to law.

* * *

If it is our duty to realise a state of public right, if at the same time there are good grounds for hope that this ideal may be realised, although only by an approximation advancing *ad infinitum*, then perpetual peace, following hitherto falsely so-called conclusions of peace, which have been in reality mere cessations of hostilities, is no mere empty idea. But rather we have here a problem which gradually works out its own solution and, as the periods in which a given advance takes place towards the realisation of the ideal of perpetual peace will, we hope, become with the passing of time shorter and shorter, we must approach ever nearer to this goal

Dreams of a Spirit-Seer

Contents

TRANSLATOR'S NOTE

The difficulties which Kant's style presents to the translator into English need not be dwelt upon with those who are familiar with his works. My main endeavour has been to produce a readable translation. I have, therefore, laid stress on the faithful and lucid representation of the author's thought, while the preservation of the periodic constructions of the original was of secondary interest. I am, however, conscious that I have not in all places succeeded in sailing with even keel between the extremes of strictly literal translation and paraphrase.

Emanuel F. Goerwitz.

Cambridge, Mass., U.S.A.,

July, 1899.

THE EDITOR'S PREFACE.

Kant's "Dreams of a Spirit-Seer, illustrated by those of Metaphysics," was published in the year 1766. His mental attitude at the time has been well described by his latest biographer and critic, M. Kronenberg: *Kant; Sein Leben, and Seine Lehre: München: Beck:* 1897. 8vo. VII., 312. The writer says in regard to the alleged scepticism of Kant about the year 1764: "All around the metaphysicians were still directing their telescopes to the farthest ends of the universe: Kant, on the contrary, having long returned from this high-strung flight, was making himself comfortably at home on earth." (.) Of the "Dreams of a Spirit-Seer" he says: —

"Between the visions of Swedenborg and those of the metaphysicians of his time, Kant drew a surprising parallel. Swedenborg believed himself to be as familiarly acquainted with the beyond as with his own house. Was not the case the same with the philosophers? Kant believed himself to be in a position to explain these delusions, the one by the other, and so to get rid of both.

"So entirely did Kant look down upon Swedenborg and his contemporaries the metaphysicians that he merely played with them, handling them now with serious irony, now with sly humour, sometimes pouring upon them his gallish scorn and dealing them the sharpest blows of his cynical wit. Such a tone is only assumed by one who sees his subject far beneath him. So did Kant hold himself in regard to the metaphysicians, to general philosophical knowledge, yea even to knowledge itself as a whole." (p, 163).

This judgment may be compared with Kuno Fischer: *Geschichte der neu. Phil., Bd. III., :* 2nd Ed., 1869, for remarkable agreements.

That the "Dreams of a Spirit-Seer" was a humorous critique aimed chiefly at the philosophers of his day, using Swedenborg as a convenient because non-combative and comparatively unknown mark for his blows, is now generally conceded. But the century and a half that have elapsed since that time have brought Swedenborg out of his obscurity into light, and his real relation to Kant and the latter's great indebtedness to him is now first seriously arousing the attention of the students of German philosophy. See especially the notices by Professor Vaihinger, of the University of Halle, in his *Commentar zur Kritik d. R. V.*, Vol. II., p, 345, 431, 512, 513, Stuttgart, 1893; and in *Kant Studien*, Vol. I: II., on Kant and Swedenborg: also Heinze's "Observations on Kant's Lectures on Metaphysics" in *Abhandlungen der Sächsischen Gesellschaft der Wissenschaften*. Leipzig, 1894: P. von Linds *Kants Mystische Weltanschauung, ein Wahn der Modernen Mystik;* Munich 1892: Du Prel's Essay on *Kant's Mystical View of the World*, in his edition of Kant's *Lectures on Psychology*, Leipzig, 1809; and *Der Angebliche Mysticismus Kants:* Robert Hoar, Brugg, 1895.

In these investigations it comes to light that not only did Kant find in Swedenborg a system of spiritual philosophy so parallel to that of the philosophers in reasonableness that the validity of the one could be measured by that of the other, but that the very system finally followed by Kant himself when he came, later in life, as a lecturer in the University on Psychology and Metaphysics, to enter upon the domain of these inquiries, was largely identical with that of the "Dreams" he had once affected to be amused at. The fair and rational vision of a *mundus intelligibilis* avowedly erected on the testimony of Swedenborg, in Chapter II. of the First Part of the treatise here published, he amuses himself with tearing down by the negative criticism of Chapter III., little forseeing that in four years' time, for his inaugural dissertation of 1770, he would be choosing no other theme than that of the same vision he had thus destroyed that namely of a *mundus intelligibilis et mundus sensibilis*,and that all through his subsequent teaching and writing, including the *Critique* and the *Religion i. d. Gr.*, he would be finding the basis of his positive idealism only in those principles of the *Arcana* he had once affected to despise. Will not this circumstance account for the instruction given by Kant to his editor Tieftrunk (see Kant's Werke: Edition Hartenstein: Bd. VIII., 812). "I assent with pleasure to your proposal for collecting and editing my minor writings. Only I wish you would not include writings earlier than 1770. In this case a German translation of my Inaugural Dissertation *De Mundi Sensibilis atque Intelligibilis Forma et Principiis* might form the beginning." Thus omitting the "Dreams."

In view of these investigations the importance of the *Traüme* as a potent factor in Kant's development is so manifest as to make a longer delay in its translation into English inexcusable.

At the same time the growing appreciation among students of the profound philosophic principles which underlie the teachings of Swedenborg make the occasion of this publication an opportune one for placing side by side with the leading affirmations made by Kant in the Dissertation and his University Lectures, a citation of those passages in Swedenborg by which they were evidently suggested or with which they stand in interesting relation.

In this way the "Seer," however it may fare with the "Metaphysicians" in Kant's hands, will at least be allowed to speak for himself, and the reader may form his judgments at first hand. To the student of modern philosophical development it will not be time lost to witness here, where it has been least suspected, the first decided and controlling influence of Swedenborg's spiritual philosophy upon modern idealistic thought.

To aid the reader in arriving at a truer understanding and appreciation of these "Dreams" and of their import in Kant's entire system I have translated and brought together the recent utterances of German and other philosophers on the subject of Swedenborg's real influence upon Kant, as shown especially in the latter's *Lectures on Psychology* and *Lectures on Metaphysics*.

FRANK SEWALL.

Washington, D.C., U.S.A., December, 1899.

INTRODUCTION.

RECENT GERMAN DISCUSSION OF THE RELATION OF KANT TO SWEDENBORG.

INCLUDING NOTES FROM

Professor VAIHINGER, Commentar zu Kants Kritik der Reinen Vernunft: *Vol. II.*

The *Kant-Studien*, edited by Professor VAIHINGER at the University of Halle:

The Archiv für Geschichte der Philosophie. *Berlin: 1895.*

Professor Heinze of Leipzig in Abhandlungen der Sächsischen Gesellschaft der Wissenschaften, *Leipzig, 1894.*

P. von Lind: Kants Mystische Weltanschauung: *Munich: 1892.*

Carl du Prel: Kants Vorlesungen über Psychologie: *1889.*

A PREFACE

which promises very little for the discussion.

The land of shadows is the paradise of dreamers. Here they find an unlimited country where they may build their houses *ad libitum*. Hypochondriac vapours, nursery tales, and monastic miracles, provide them with ample building material. Their ground plans are sketched by the philosophers, who keep on changing or rejecting them, as is their wont. Holy Rome alone possesses in this land profitable provinces; the two crowns of the invisible kingdom support the third, which is the frail diadem of earthly sovereignty; and the keys which open the gates of the other world open at the same time, sympathetically, the money chests of the present. Such jurisdiction of the spirit world, when policy furnishes the proofs for its claims, is far above all feeble objections of the learned, and its use, or abuse, is already too venerable to feel the need of being exposed to their depraved scrutiny. But the common tales which are so strongly believed by some, while disputed by others, who have as little foundation for their opinion, why do they still float about for no visible reason, and yet unrefuted, and creep even into systems of doctrine, although they do not have in their favour that most convincing of proofs, the proof derived from utility (*argumentum ab utili*)? What philosopher has not at one time or another cut the queerest figure imaginable, between the affirmations of a reasonable and firmly convinced eye-witness, and the inner resistance of insurmountable doubt? Shall he wholly deny the truth of all the apparitions they tell about? What reasons can he quote to disprove them?

Shall he, on the other hand, admit even one of these stories? How important would be such an avowal, and what astonishing consequences we should see before us, if we could suppose even one such occurence to be proved? A third way out, perhaps, is possible, namely, not to trouble one's self with such impertinent or idle questions, and to hold on to the *useful*. But because this plan is reasonable, therefore profound scholars have at all times, by a majority of votes, rejected it!

Since it is just as much a silly prejudice to believe without reason *nothing* of the many things that are told with an appearance of truth, as to believe without examination *everything* that common report says, the author of this book has been led away partly by the latter prejudice, in trying to escape the former. He confesses, with a certain humiliation, that he has been naive enough to trace the truth of some of the stories of the kind mentioned. He found — as usual where it is not our business to search — he found nothing. This is indeed by itself a sufficient reason for writing a book; but add to this what has many a time wrung books from modest authors, the impetuous appeals from known and unknown friends. Moreover, he had bought a big work, and, what is worse, had read it, and this labour was not to be thrown away. Thence originated the present treatise, which, we flatter ourselves, will fully satisfy the reader; for the main part he will not understand, another part he will not believe, and the rest he will laugh at.

PART FIRST, WHICH IS DOGMATIC.

CHAPTER FIRST.
A COMPLICATED METAPHYSICAL KNOT WHICH CAN BE UNTIED OR CUT ACCORDING TO CHOICE.

If we put all together, that the school-boy rehearses, that the crowd relates, and that the philosopher demonstrates about spirits, this would seem to constitute no small part of our knowledge. Nevertheless, I dare assert that all these smatterers could be placed in a most awkward embarrassment, if it should occur to somebody to insist upon the question, just what kind of a thing that is about which these people think they understand so much. The methodical talk of learned institutions is often simply an agreement to beg a question which is difficult to solve, by the variable meaning of words. For we seldom hear at academies the comfortable and ofttimes reasonable "I do not know." Certain newer philosophers, as they like to be called, overcome this question easily. A spirit, they say, is a being possessed of reason. Then it is no miracle to see spirits; for he who sees men, sees beings possessing reason. But, they continue, this being in man, possessing reason, is only a part of man, and this part, the animating part, is a spirit. Very well then. Before you prove that only a spiritual being can have reason, take care that first of all I understand what kind of conception I must have of a spiritual being. Self-deception in this matter, while large enough to be seen with eyes half-open, is moreover of very evident origin. For, later on and in old age, we are sure to know nothing of that which was very well known to us at an early date, as children, and the man of thoroughness finally becomes at best a sophist in regard to his youthful delusions.

Thus I do not know if there are spirits, yea, what is more, I do not even know what the word "spirit" signifies. But, as I have often used it myself, and have heard others using it, something must be understood by it, be this something mere fancy or reality. To evolve this hidden meaning, I will compare my badly understood conception of it with sundry cases of application, and, by observing with which it conforms, and to which it is opposed, I hope to unfold its hidden sense.

Take, for example, the space of a cubic foot, and suppose something filling this space, i.e., resisting the intrusion of any other thing. Then nobody would call the substance occupying that space "spiritual." It evidently would be called material, because it is expanded, impenetrable, and, like everything corporeal, subject to divisibility and to the laws of impact. Thus far we are still on the smooth track of other philosophers. But imagine a simple being, and impart to it at the same time reason. Would that, then, comprise the meaning of "spirit?" To discover this, I will leave to the aforesaid simple being reason as an inner quality, and will consider that being only in its external relations. And now I ask, if I want to place this simple substance in that space of one cubic foot, which is full of matter, would a single element have to make room for it, so that the spirit might enter? You think yes? Very well, then this supposed space would have to lose a second elementary particle — were it to take in a second spirit, and thus, if you keep on, a cubic foot of space would be filled with spirits whose mass exists just as well by impenetrability, as if it was full of matter, and, just like the latter, must be subject to the laws of impact. But substances of this kind, although they might contain the power of reason, would not differ at all from the elements of matter of which also we know only the powers which they exert externally by their very existence, and do not at all know what might belong to their interior qualities. Thus it is beyond doubt that simple substances of that kind, of which masses could be accumulated, would not be called spiritual beings. You will, therefore, be able to retain the conception of a spirit only if you imagine beings who can be present even in a space filled with matter, thus beings who do not possess the quality of impenetrability, and who never form a solid whole, no matter how many you unite. Simple beings of this kind would be called immaterial beings, and, if they have reason, spirits. But simple substances which, if combined, result in an *expanded and impenetrable whole*, would be called material units, and their whole, matter. Either the name of a spirit is a mere word without any meaning, or, its significance is of the nature described.

From the explanation of what a spirit consists in, it is a long step indeed to the proposition that such natures are real, yea, even possible. We find in the works of philosophers many good and reliable proofs that everything which thinks must be simple; and that every substance which thinks according to reason, must be a unit of nature; and that the undivisible Ego could not be divided among many connected things which make up a whole. My soul, therefore, must be a simple substance. But this proof leaves still undecided, whether the soul be of the nature of such things as, united in space, form an expanded and impenetrable whole; whether, therefore, it be material, or whether it be immaterial, and, consequently, a spirit; and, what is more, whether such beings as are called spirits, are possible.

At this point I cannot but recommend caution against rash conclusions which enter most easily into the deepest and obscurest questions. For that which belongs to the common conceptions of experience is commonly regarded as if the reason why it existed was also comprehended. But of that which differs from experience, and cannot be made comprehensible by any experience, not even by analogy, we of course can form no conception, and, therefore, are apt to reject it immediately as impossible. All matter offers resistance in the space in which it is present, and on that account is called impenetrable. That this is so, experience teaches us, and the abstraction of this experience produces in us the general conception of matter. But this resistance which something makes in the space in which it is present, is in that manner indeed *recognized*, but not yet *conceived*. For this resistance, as everything that counteracts an action, is true force, and, as its direction is opposed to the prolonged lines of *approach*, it is a force of *repulsion* which must be attributed to matter and, therefore, to its elements. Every reasonable man will readily concede that here human intelligence has reached its limit. For while, by experience alone, we can perceive that things of this world which we call "material" possess such a force, we can never conceive of the reason why they exist.2 Now, if I suppose other substances being present in space with other forces than that *propelling* force which has for its consequence impenetrability, then, of course, I cannot think in the concrete of their activity, because it has no analogy with my conceptions from experience. And if, in addition, I take away from those substances the quality to *fill* the space in which they are present, I miss a conception which makes thinkable the things which come within the range of my senses; thence, necessarily, they must become in a way unthinkable. But this cannot be said to be a recognized impossibility, for the very reason that the *possibility of the existence of its opposite remains also unintelligible*, although its reality comes within the range of my senses.

The possibility of the existence of immaterial beings can, therefore, be supposed without fear of its being disproved, but also without hope of proving it by reason. Such spiritual natures would be present in space in such a manner that it would still be penetrable for corporeal beings. For by their presence they *operate* in space, but do not *fill* it, i.e., they cause no resistance, which is the basis of solidity.3 If such a simple spiritual substance be supposed, — notwithstanding its indivisibility, — it can be said that the space where it is immediately present is not a point, but itself a space. For, calling in the aid of analogy, even the simple elements of the body must occupy there a space which is a proportionate part of its whole extension, inasmuch as points are not parts but limits of space. Thus space is filled by means of an active force — repulsion. But the fact that it is being filled is apparent only by a greater activity of its components. The way, therefore, in which it is being filled — by accumulating individual elements — does not at all conflict with its simple nature, although the possibility of this cannot be pointed out more clearly, for this can never be done with first causes and effects. In the same way I shall meet with at least no demonstrable impossibility, although the thing itself remains incomprehensible, if I state that a spiritual substance, although it is simple, still can occupy a space, i.e., can immediately be active in it without *filling* it, which means without offering resistance to material substances in it.4 Such an immaterial substance also could not be said to possess expansion, any more than the units of matter. For only that which, existing separate and for itself alone, occupies a space, possesses extent; but the substances which are elements of matter occupy space only by the exterior effect which they have upon others. But for themselves alone, where no other things can be thought of as being in connection with them, and as they contain in themselves nothing which could exist separately, they contain no space. This applies to corporeal elements. The same would apply also to spiritual natures. The limits of extent are determined by the figure of a thing. Consequently, we cannot think of the figures of spiritual natures. These are reasons for the supposed possibility of the existence of immaterial beings in the universe, but they can be comprehended with difficulty. He who is in possession of means which can lead more easily to this intelligence, should not deny instruction to one eager to learn, before whose eyes, in the progress of research, Alps often rise where others see before them a level and comfortable footpath on which they walk forward, or think they do so.

Suppose now that it had been proved that the soul of man is a spirit (although it may be seen from the preceding that this, as yet, has *not* been proved), then the next question which might be raised is — Where is the place of this human soul in the corporeal world? I would answer, that body the changes of which are *my* changes, is *my* body, and its place is, at the same time, my place. If the question be continued, where then is your (your soul's) place in that *body?* then I might suspect that there is a catch in the question. For it is easily observed that it presupposes something which is not known by experience, but rests, perhaps, in imaginary conclusions, namely, that my thinking Ego is in a place which differs from the places of other parts of that body which belongs to me. Nobody, however, is conscious of occupying a separate place in his body, but only of that place which he occupies as man in regard to the world around him. I would, therefore, keep to common experience, and would say, provisionally, where I sense, there I *am*.5 I am just as immediately in the tips of my fingers, as in my head. It is myself who suffers in the heel and whose heart beats in affection. I feel the most painful impression when my corn torments me, not in a cerebral nerve, but at the end of my toes. No experience teaches me to believe some parts of my sensation to be removed from myself, to shut up my Ego into a microscopically small place in my brain from whence it may move the levers of my body-machine, and cause me to be thereby affected. Thus I should demand a strong proof to make inconsistent what the schoolmasters say: *my soul is as a whole in my whole body, and wholly in each part.* Common sense often perceives a truth before comprehending the reasons with which to prove or explain it. I should not be entirely disconcerted by the objection, that thus I am believing that the soul possesses extension and is diffused through the whole body, just as it is pictured for children in the "orbis pictus." For I would remove this obstacle by saying: the fact that the soul is present in the whole body goes only to prove the extent of its sphere of exterior activity, but not a multiplicity of its inner parts and thus no extension or figure, for these exist only in a being which occupies a space set apart for itself, i.e., if the being contains parts which exist outside of each other. Finally, I should either claim to know this little of the spiritual quality of my soul, or, if that should not be conceded, I should be satisfied that I know nothing about it.

If one would insist upon showing how incomprehensible, or, what amounts to the same for the most people, how impossible these thoughts are, I would admit even that; and then I would sit down at the feet of the wise to hear them talk as follows: The soul of man has its seat in the brain, and its abode there is indescribably small; there it exercises its sensitive faculty, as the spider in the centre of its web. The nerves of the brain push or shake it, and cause thereby that not this immediate impression, but the one which is made upon quite remote parts of the body, is represented as an object which is present outside of the brain. From this seat it moves the ropes and levers of the whole machinery, causing arbitrary movements at will. Such propositions can be proved only very superficially or not at all, and as the nature of the soul is, indeed, not well enough known, they can be just as weakly combatted. And so I do not care to join in that kind of learned dispute, in which both parties usually have most to say about that of which they know nothing. But I will follow only the conclusions to which a doctrine of this nature must lead me. In the first instance, according to the propositions so much recommended to me, my soul does not differ from any element of matter in the way in which it is present in space. Further, the power of reasoning is an internal quality which I could not perceive anyhow, although it might be found in all these elements. From these considerations no valid reason can be brought forward, why my soul should not be one of the substances of which matter consists, nor why its peculiar manifestations should not originate in the place which it occupies in such an ingenious machine as the human body, where the combination of nerves favours the inner faculty of thinking and of will-power. In that case, however, there would remain no peculiar characteristic of the soul by which it could be surely recognized and distinguished from crude elementary matter, and the jocose suggestion of Leibnitz would not be laughable any more, that in our coffee we swallow, perhaps, atoms which are to become human souls. But in such a case would not this thinking Ego be subjected to the common fate of material natures, and, as it was drawn out of the chaos of all elements to vivify an animal machine, why should it not, after this casual combination has ceased, return in future to its origin? It is at times necessary to frighten the thinker who is on the wrong path, by the consequences, so that he may pay more attention to the principles by which he has been led off as in a dream.

I confess that I am very much inclined to assert the existence of immaterial natures in the world, and to put my soul itself into that class of beings. But then, how mysterious does the communion of soul and body become?8 But, at the same time, how natural that it is incomprehensible, inasmuch as our conceptions of external actions are derived from those of matter, and are always connected with the conditions of impact and pressure, which do not exist in this case. For how could an immaterial being be such an obstruction so that matter in its motion could collide with it, a spirit; and how could corporeal things act upon an unknown being which does not oppose them with impenetrability, and which does not hinder them in any way from being at the same time present in the space in which it is itself? It seems that a spiritual essence is inmostly present in matter, and that it does not act upon those forces which determine the mutual relations of elements, but upon the inner principle of their state. For every substance, even a simple element of matter, must have an inner activity as the reason for its external efficiency, although I cannot specify in what it consists. 9

But what is the necessity which causes a spirit and a body to form a unit; and, again, what is the cause which breaks up this unit in case of certain disturbances? These are questions which, among various others, are above my intelligence.10 And although I have as a rule hardly the daring to measure my power of reasoning with the secrets of nature, I should, nevertheless, have sufficient confidence not to be afraid, in such a case, of putting any opponent to the test, if it were my nature to be inclined to fight, nor of attempting to refute him by contrary reasons, which with scholars means nothing else but the art of convincing another that he does not know.

SECOND CHAPTER.

A FRAGMENT OF SECRET PHILOSOPHY AIMING TO ESTABLISH COMMUNION WITH THE SPIRIT-WORLD.

Gross reason which cleaves to the bodily senses has, I trust, by this time become so accustomed to higher and abstract conceptions that now it can see spiritual figures, devoid of corporeal clothing, in that dusk in which the faint light of metaphysics renders visible the kingdom of shadows. We will venture therefore upon the dangerous road, since we have endured such laborious preparation for it.

Ibant sub nocte per umbras

Perque domos Ditis vacuas et inania regna.

Virgil.

The characteristics of the dead matter which fills the universe are stability and inertia; it further possesses solidity, expansion, and form, and its manifestations, resulting from all these three causes, admit of *physical* explanations, which, at the same time, are mathematical, and, collectively, are called mechanical. But let us direct our attention to the kind of beings which contain the cause of *life* in the universe — those which therefore neither add to the mass and extent of lifeless matter, nor are influenced by it according to the laws of contact and collision, but which rather, by inner activity, move themselves and dead matter as well — and we shall find ourselves convinced, if not with the distinctness of demonstration, still with the presentiment of well applied reason, that immaterial beings exist. Their peculiar laws of operation we may call "spiritual," or, in so far as bodies are the medium of their operation in the material world, "organic." As these immaterial beings are self-active principles, consequently, substances and natures existing by themselves, the conclusion which suggests itself first is, that, immediately united with each other, they might form, perhaps, a great whole which might be called the immaterial world (mundus intelligibilis). For what reason could render the assertion probable that such beings of similar nature could communicate only by means of other beings (corporeal) of dissimilar nature? This latter supposition would really be much more mysterious than the first.

This *immaterial world*, therefore, can be regarded as a whole existing by itself, and its parts, as being in mutual conjunction and intercourse without the instrumentality of anything corporeal. The relation by means of things corporeal is consequently to be regarded as accidental; it can belong only to a few; yea, where we meet with it, it does not hinder even those very immaterial beings, while acting upon one another through matter, from standing also in their special universal relationship, so that at any time they may exercise upon one another mutual influences by virtue of the laws of their immaterial existence. Their relation by means of matter is thus accidental, and is due to a special divine institution, while their direct relation is natural and insoluble.11

By combining in this way all principles of life in the whole of nature, as so many 'incorporeal substances, communicating with each other, partly also united with matter, we conceive of the immaterial world as a great whole, an immeasurable but unknown gradation of beings and active natures by which alone the dead matter of the corporeal world is endued with life. But to which members of nature life is extended, and which those degrees of it are which are next to utter lifelessness, can, perhaps, never be made out with certainty.12 Hylozoism imputes life to everything; materialism, carefully considered, kills everything. Maupertuis attributed to the organic particles of the nutriment of all animals the lowest degree of life, other philosophers see in them nothing else but dead masses which serve only to augment the lever-apparatus of animal machines.13 The undoubted characteristic of life in that which appeals to our external senses is, I may say, the free movement which shows that it is arbitrary, but the conclusion is not certain that, wherever this characteristic is not found, there is no degree of life.14 Boerhave says somewhere: The animal is a plant which has its roots in the stomach (inside). Another might, perhaps, play without censure with these conceptions by saying: The plant is an animal which has its stomach in the root (outside). The plants, therefore, may lack the organs of arbitrary movement, and thus the external characteristics of life. These are necessary to the animals, because a being which has the instruments of nourishment inside must be able to move about according to its needs; but a being where these are outside and planted in the nourishing element, is already sufficiently maintained by external forces. Such a being contains indeed a principle of inner life in the fact of vegetation, yet it does not need an organic apparatus for external free activity. I do not propose to use any of these considerations as evidence, for, aside from the fact that I could say very little in favour of such conjectures, they have the ridicule of fashion against them, as being dusty antiquated fancies. The ancients, namely, thought that they could assume three kinds of life, the vegetable, the animal, and the reasonable. In uniting in man the three immaterial principles of those kinds of life, they very likely erred; but so far as they distributed the three principles among the three kinds of growing beings which propagate their kind, they indeed said something undemonstrable, but not, on that account, unreasonable, especially not in the judgment of one who considers the close relation of the polyps and other zoophytes with the plants, or who takes into account the special life belonging to the separated parts of some animals, irritability — that quality of the fibres of an animal body and of some plants, so well demonstrated, and, at the same time, so inexplicable. But, after all, the appeal to immaterial principles is a subterfuge of bad philosophy. Explanations of that kind should be avoided as much as possible, so that those causes of the world's phenomena which rest on the laws of motion of matter alone, and which solely and alone are capable of being conceived, may be recognized in their full extent.15 Nevertheless, I am convinced that Stahl, who likes to explain animal processes organically, is often nearer to the truth than Hofmann, Boerhave, and others, who leave immaterial forces out of their plan and keep to mechanical reasons. Yet these follow thereby a more philosophical method, which sometimes perhaps fails, but oftener proves right, and which alone can be applied to advantage in science. For the influence of beings of incorporeal nature can only be said to exist, but it can never be shown how it proceeds, nor how far its efficiency extends.16

The immaterial then would primarily comprise all created intelligences. Some of these are combined with matter, thus forming a person, and some not. It further comprises the sensating subjects in all kinds of animals, and finally all the principles of life wherever in nature they may be found, although such life may not make itself evident by the external characteristics of arbitrary movement. All these immaterial natures, I say, whether they exercise their influences in the corporeal world or not, and all the rational beings who are, accidentally, in an animal state, here on earth or on other terrestrial bodies, while they may be vivifying gross matter now or in future, or may have done so in the past, nevertheless form, according to these conceptions, a communion in conformity with their nature.17 And this communion would not rest upon the conditions by which the relations of bodies are limited, but distance in space and time,18 which forms in the visible world the great cleft severing all communion, would disappear. We should, therefore, have to regard the human soul as being conjoined in its present life with two worlds at the same time, of which it clearly perceives only the material world, in so far as it is conjoined with a body, and thus forms a personal unit.19 But as a member of the spiritual world it receives and gives out the pure influences of immaterial natures, so that, as soon as the accidental conjunction has ceased, only that communion remains which at all times it has with spiritual natures. 20

It begins to be a real trouble for me, always to use the cautious language of reason. Why should I, too, not be allowed to talk in academical style? This exempts the writer as well as the reader from thinking, which, after all, sooner or later must lead only to annoying indecision. Thus "it is as good as demonstrated," or, to be explicit, "it could easily be proved," or still better, "it will be proved" I don't know where or when, that the human soul also in this life forms an indissoluble communion with all immaterial natures of the spirit-world, that, alternately, it acts upon and receives impressions from that world of which nevertheless it is not conscious while it is still man and as long as everything is in proper condition.23 On the other hand it is probable that the spiritual natures on their side can have no immediate conscious sensation of the corporeal world,24 because they are not conjoined with any part of matter which could make them aware of their place in the material world-whole, nor have they elaborate organs for entering into the mutual relations of beings of spacial extent. But they can, probably, flow into the souls of men as into beings of their own nature, and it is likely that they are actually at all times in mutual intercourse with them, yet, in such a way that those conceptions which the soul entertains as a being dependent on the corporeal world cannot be communicated to the other purely spiritual beings; nor can .the conceptions of these latter, being conceptions of immaterial things, be transferred into the consciousness of men, at least not as long as these conceptions preserve their peculiar quality, for the components of the two sets of ideas are of different kind.

It would be beautiful if such a systematic constitution of the spirit-world, as we conceive it, could be determined, or only with some probability supposed, not merely from the conception of spiritual being in general, which is altogether too hypothetical, but from an actual and universally conceded observation. Therefore I venture upon the indulgence of the reader and insert here an attempt at something of this kind which, although somewhat out of my way, and far enough removed from evidence, still seems to give occasion for not unpleasant surmises.

Among the forces which move the human heart, some of the most powerful seem to lie outside of it. They consequently are not mere means to selfishness and private interest, which would be an aim lying inside of man himself, but they incline our emotions to place the focus in which they combine, outside of us, in other rational beings. Thence arises a struggle between two forces, the proprium which refers everything to itself, and the public spirit by which the mind is driven or drawn towards others outside of itself.25 I do not dwell upon that instinct which causes us to depend so much and so universally upon the judgment of others, to consider outside approbation or applause requisite to a good opinion of ourselves. Sometimes a mistaken conception of honour comes up in this matter, but nevertheless there is even in the most unselfish and open natures a secret leaning to compare with the judgment of others what we have by ourselves recognized to be good and true, so as to make both concordant; on the other hand there is an inclination to stop, so to speak, each human soul on its way to knowledge, when it seems to go another path than that upon which we have entered. All this comes, perhaps, from our perception of the dependence of our own judgment upon the common sense of man, and it becomes a reason for ascribing to the whole of thinking beings a sort of unity of reason.

But I pass over this otherwise not unimportant consideration, and, for the present, take up another which, as far as our purpose is concerned, is more obvious and pertinent. When we consider our needs in relation to our environment, we cannot do it without experiencing a certain sensation of restraint and limitation which lets us know that a foreign will, as it were, is active in us, and that our own liking is subject to the condition of external consent. A secret power compels us to adapt our intentions to the welfare of others, or to this foreign will, although this is often done unwillingly, and conflicts strongly with our selfish inclination. The point to which the lines of direction of our impulses converge, is thus not only in ourselves, but there are besides powers moving us in the will of others outside of ourselves. Hence arise the moral impulses which often carry us away to the discomfiture of selfishness, the strong law of duty, and the weaker one of benevolence. Both of these wring from us many a sacrifice, and although selfish inclinations now and then preponderate over both, these still never fail to assert their reality in human nature. Thus we recognize that, in our most secret motives, we are dependent upon the *rule of the will of all*, and thence arises in the community of all thinking beings a moral unity, and a systematic constitution according to purely spiritual laws.26 If we want to call the fact that we feel forced to adapt our will to the will of all, *the sense of morality*, we thereby describe only a manifestation of that which actually takes place in us, without settling upon its causes. Thus Newton called the established law that all particles of matter have the tendency to approach each other, *gravitation*, because he did not want to have his mathematical demonstrations mixed up with possible philosophical disputes over the causes of gravitation. Nevertheless, he did not hesitate to treat gravitation as the true effect of a general interaction of matter, and therefore gave to it also the name of *attraction*.27 Should it not be possible to conceive the phenomenon of moral impulses in the mutual relations of thinking creatures as the consequence of an actual force, consisting in the fact that spiritual natures flow into each other? The sense of morality then would be the sensation of this dependence of the individual will upon the will of all, and would be a consequence of the natural and universal interaction whereby the immaterial world attains its unity, namely, by conforming itself to a system of spiritual perfection, according to the laws of this sense of morality, which would constitute its mode of cohesion. If we grant to these thoughts so much probability as to make it worth while to measure them by their consequences, we shall be drawn by their charm, perhaps unconsciously, into being partial to them. For in this case there seem to disappear most of the irregularities which otherwise, owing to the contradiction between the moral and physical relations of men here on earth, strike us as being so strange. The moral quality of our actions can, according to the order of nature, never be fully worked out in the bodily life of men, but it can be so worked out in the spirit-world, according to spiritual laws.28 The true purposes, the secret motives of many endeavours, fruitless by impotency, the victory over self, or the occasional hidden treachery in apparently good actions, are mostly lost as to their physical effect in the bodily state, but in the immaterial world they would have to be regarded as fruitful causes, and, consequently, according to spiritual laws and on account of the connection between the individual will and the will of all, they would mutually produce and receive effects appropriate to the moral quality of free will. For just because the morality of an action concerns the inner state of the spirit, it naturally can only in the immediate communion of spirits have, an effect adequate to its full morality. Thus it would happen that man's soul would already in this life have to take its place among the spiritual substances of the universe according to its moral state, just as, according to the laws of motion, the matter of the universe arranges itself into an order conformable to its material forces. When finally through death the communion of the soul with the body-world is abolished, life in the other world would be only a natural continuation of such connections as were formed with it already in this life, and all the consequences of the morality exercised here we would find there in the effects which a being standing in indissoluble communion with the whole spirit-world would have already achieved, according to spiritual laws.30 Present and future would be, as it were, out of one piece and constitute a continuous whole, even according to the order of nature. This latter circumstance is of especial importance. For in a speculation based merely upon reasoning there is a great difficulty if, in removing the inconvenience which follows from the incomplete harmony of morality and its consequences in this world, we have to resort to an extraordinary idea of the divine will. For, though our judgment of it might, according to our conceptions, be probable, a strong suspicion would remain that the weak conceptions of our understanding were applied to the Highest perhaps very erroneously. For it is incumbent upon man to judge of the divine will only from the harmony which he actually perceives in the world, or which, by the rule of analogy, according to the order of nature,31 he may suppose to be in it; he is not entitled to imagine new and arbitrary arrangements in the present or future world, according to some scheme of his own wisdom which he prescribes to the divine will.

We now turn our consideration again into the former path, and approach the aim which we have set before ourselves. If the facts of the spirit-world be such as we have stated, and the share of our soul in it be truly pictured in the sketch just made, then scarcely anything appears more strange than that communion with spirits is not quite a common and ordinary thing; and what is extraordinary about it is rather the scarcity of apparitions than their possibility. This difficulty is tolerably easy to remove and already has been partly removed. For the conception which the soul of man has of itself as of a spirit, which, moreover, it has obtained through contemplation of the immaterial, i.e., by observing itself in its relation to beings of similar nature, this conception is entirely different from that where its consciousness conceives itself as a man, by means of an image originated in the impression of corporeal organs and conceived of in relation to none but corporeal things. It is, therefore, indeed one subject, which is thus at the same time a member of the visible and of the invisible world, but not one and the same person; for, on account of their different quality, the conceptions of the one world are not ideas associated with those of the other world, thus, what I think as spirit, is not remembered by me as man, and, conversely, my state as man does not at all enter into the conception of myself as a spirit. Moreover, my ideas of the spirit-world may be ever so clear and perspicuous, still that would not suffice to make me, as a man, conscious of that world; and so, however clear an idea one may, by reasoning, derive of himself, i.e., of his soul, as a spirit, still, this idea is with no man an object of actual sight and experience.

This difference, however, in the nature of spiritual ideas and those belonging to the body-life of man must not be considered so great an obstacle as to remove all possibility of becoming, sometimes, conscious of the influences of the spirit-world even in this life. For spiritual ideas can pass over into the personal consciousness of man, indeed, not immediately, but still in such a way that, according to the law of the association of ideas, they stir up those pictures which are related to them and awake analogous ideas of our senses. These, it is true, would not be spiritual conceptions themselves, but yet their symbols.32 For, after all, it is one and the same substance which is a member both of this world and the other, and both kinds of ideas belong to the same subject and are connected with each other. How this is possible can be made intelligible by considering how our higher conceptions of reason, which approach the spiritual pretty closely, ordinarily assume, as it were, a bodily garment to make themselves clear.33 Thence it is that the moral qualities of deity are represented by the ideas of anger, jealousy, mercifulness, revenge,34 &c.; for the same reason poets personify the virtues, vices, and other qualities of human nature, though this is done in such a way that the true idea of the meaning shines through; in the same way the geometrician represents time by a line, although time and space have comformity only by relation and therefore agree, indeed, according to analogy, but never according to quality. This is the reason why the idea of divine eternity assumes even with philosophers the appearance of infinite time,35 be they never so careful not to mix them up; and one great cause why mathematicians are generally loath to admit the monads of Leibnitz may be that they cannot help but imagine these monads as little masses. Thus it is not improbable that spiritual sensations can pass over into consciousness if they act upon correlated ideas of the senses. In such a way ideas which are communicated by spiritual influx, would clothe themselves with the signs of that language which man uses for his other purposes. Thus the sensation of the presence of a spirit becomes converted into the picture of the human figure; the order and beauty of the immaterial world into fantasies which, under other circumstances, give pleasure to our senses in this life,36 &c.

Nevertheless this kind of apparition cannot be a common and ordinary thing but can occur only with persons whose organs have an unusual sensitiveness for intensifying, by harmonious motion, according to the inner state of the soul, the pictures of the imagination, to a higher degree than is usually the case, and should be the case, with healthy persons. Such abnormal persons would be confronted, in certain moments, with the appearance of many objects as if they were outside of themselves. They would think that spiritual natures present with them were affecting their bodily senses, while yet this is only a delusion of the imagination, occurring, however, in such a way that its cause is a true spiritual influence, not, indeed, perceivable immediately, but revealing itself to consciousness by correlated pictures of the imagination which assume the appearance of sensations.

Conceptions derived from education and all sorts of fancies that have crept into the mind would exercise their influence here, where delusion is mingled with truth, a real spiritual sensation being, indeed, the foundation, but converted into phantoms of sensuous things. It will further be admitted that the power to thus develop the impressions of the spirit-world into the clear perception of this world can hardly be of any use, because in such a process the spiritual sensation becomes necessarily so closely interwoven with the fancies of the imagination that it cannot be possible to distinguish the truth from the gross surrounding delusions. Such a state would likewise indicate a disease, because it presupposes an altered balance of the nerves, which are put into unnatural motion merely by the activity of purely spiritual sensations of the soul. Finally, it would not be at all strange to find the spirit-seer to be at the same time a dreamer, at least in regard to the mental pictures which he makes of his visions; because ideas, unknown to him by their very nature and incompatible with those of his bodily state, crowd in and drag into external sensation badly adjusted pictures, creating thereby wild chimeras and curiously distorted figures, which float in trailing garments before the senses, deceiving them in spite of the fact that such chimeras may be based upon a true spiritual influence.37

Now we need no longer be at a loss to give apparently rational causes for the stories about apparitions which so often cross the path of philosophers, as well as to account for all sorts of influences from spirits of which the rumour goes here and there.38 Departed souls and pure spirits can indeed never be present to our external senses, nor communicate with matter in any other way than by acting upon the spirit of man, who belongs with them to one great republic. The spirits must act in such a way that the ideas which they call up in man's mind clothe themselves in corresponding pictures according to the law of imagination, thus causing any objects which fit into the picture to appear as if they were outside of him. This deception can affect any one of the senses, and, however mixed it may be with incongruous fancies, it should not keep one from supposing spiritual influences in it. I should encroach upon the penetration of the reader if I should stop to apply this mode of explanation. For metaphysical hypotheses are possessed of such an immense flexibility that one must be very awkward not to be able to adapt this one to any story he hears even before investigating its truthfulness, which is in many cases impossible, and in still more is impolite to the narrator.

But if we balance against each other the advantages and disadvantages which might accrue to a person organized not only for the visible world, but also, to a certain degree, for the invisible (if ever there was such a person), such a gift would seem to be like that with which Juno honoured Teiresias, making him blind so that she might impart to him the gift of prophesying. For, judging from the propositions above made, the knowledge of the other world can be obtained here only by losing some of that intelligence which is necessary for this present world. I am not sure if even certain philosophers can be freed entirely from such a hard condition, when they turn their metaphysical telescopes upon such far-off regions and tell us of miraculous things. At least I do not grudge them their discoveries. But I am afraid that some man of sound sense but little polish might intimate to them what the coachman answered to Tycho Brahe, when, one night, the latter suggested to the man he might drive the shortest way by directing his course according to the stars: "My dear master, you may be an expert as to the sky, but here on earth you are a fool."39

THIRD CHAPTER.

ANTIKABALA. A FRAGMENT OF COMMON PHILOSOPHY AIMING TO ABOLISH COMMUNION WITH THE SPIRIT-WORLD.

Aristotle says, somewhere, "When we are awake, we have a common world, but when we dream, everybody is his own." It seems to me that it ought to be possible to reverse this latter proposition and say, if, among different human beings, every one has his own world, it may be supposed that they dream. With this understanding we will view the various imaginary worlds of these air-architects which each one inhabits quietly to the exclusion of others. Behold, for example, him who inhabits the Order of Things as it was framed by Wolf out of but little building material obtained from experience, but many conceptions gotten on the sly. Or we will view those who inhabit the world produced by Crusius out of nothing, by means of a few magical sayings about the thinkable and the unthinkable. And, as we find that their visions are contradictory, we will patiently wait until the gentlemen have finished dreaming. For if, at some time, by the will of God, they wake up, i.e., open their eyes to such a view as does not exclude conformity with other people's common sense, then none of them will see anything that does not appear evident and certain in the light of their proofs to others also, and the philosophers will then inhabit a common world, of the kind which mathematicians have already occupied for a long time. And this event cannot be delayed much longer, if certain signs and predictions, which for some time have appeared over the horizon of science, can be trusted.

Reason-dreamers have a certain relation with sensation-dreamers, among whom are usually counted those who occasionally deal with spirits. The reason is that they too, like the former, see something which no other healthy man sees, and have a communication of their own with beings which reveal themselves to nobody else, however keen the others' senses may be. If one supposes that the above-named apparitions rest upon mere fancies, the term "dreams" then becomes appropriate to them in so far as both are self-created pictures which nevertheless deceive the senses as if they were true objects. But if one imagines both kinds of deception to be so similar in their origin that the source of the one will be found sufficient for the other, he is greatly deceived. The man who, while awake, becomes so absorbed in the fancies and chimeras created by his ever active imagination as to pay little attention to the sensations of the senses with which he is mostly concerned at that moment, is justly called a waking dreamer. For the sensations of the senses need decrease only a little more in their intensity, and he will be asleep, and his chimeras will then be true dreams. The reason why they are no dreams while the dreamer pursues them awake, is, because he then perceives the dreams as in himself, but other objects as outside of himself; consequently he considers the dreams as effects of his own activity, but the perception of objects as part of .his received impressions from the outside. For in this situation everything depends upon the relation which man assumes the objects to have to himself as a man, and, consequently, also to his body. Thus, the same pictures can indeed occupy him very much in his waking state, but they cannot deceive him, however clear they may be. For although he has then, too, in his brain a fictitious impression of himself and his body, which he puts in relation to his fantastic pictures, nevertheless the real sensation of his body, by means of the external senses, establishes a contrast with those chimeras, or distinction from them, which goes to show the ones as self-created, the other as perceived.40 If he falls asleep, the idea of his body derived from impressions disappears, and only the fictitious idea remains. In relation to this latter idea, the other chimeras are now assumed to be outside of himself, and they are found to deceive the dreamer as long as he sleeps, because there is no sensation present which would furnish a basis for a comparison of the two whereby the original could be distinguished from the phantasm, i.e., the outside from the inside.

The spirit-seers, therefore, are entirely different from waking dreamers not only in degree, but in kind. For while they are waking, and often while they are experiencing other sensations with great vividness, the spirit-seers place some imagined things among the external objects which they really perceive. The only question is, how it is possible that they place the phantoms of their imagination outside of themselves, and even put them in relation to their body, which they sense through their external senses. The great clearness of the fantasy cannot be the cause, for the point at issue is, the place where an object is put; and, therefore, I demand that it be shown how the soul places such an image as it should perceive to be contained in itself, into an entirely different relation, namely, into a place outside of itself and among those objects which are offered to its real perception. I shall not be satisfied with the quotation of other cases which bear some resemblance with this deception, such as perhaps occur in the state of fever; for be the deceived well or sick, we do not want to know *if* such a thing happens also elsewhere, but *how* this deception is possible.

We find, however, in using our external senses, that besides the clearness with which the objects are seen, we perceive at the same time their location, perhaps not always with the same accuracy, still as a necessary condition of sensation, without which it would be impossible to perceive things as being outside of ourselves.41 Here it becomes quite probable that our soul locates the perceived object at that point where the different lines, indicating the direction of the impression, meet. That is why we see a radiating point at the meeting-place of those lines which we draw from the eye back in the direction of the rays. This point, which we call the point of vision, is, in its effect, the scattering point, but, in the way it is perceived, it is the point which collects the lines of direction determining the sensation (focus imaginarius). Thus we locate a visible object even with one eye alone; in the same way as, by means of a concave mirror, the image of an object is seen in the air just in that spot where the rays radiating from one point of the object meet before entering the eye.

The same theory, perhaps, can be applied to the impressions of sound, because its shocks, too, are transmitted in straight lines. Then we should say that the sensation of sound is accompanied by the perception of a focus imaginarius, and that this is placed in that point where the straight lines meet which are drawn to the outside from the vibrating nerve-structure inside of the brain. For the place and distance of a sounding object is perceived to some extent, even if the sound is low and comes from the back, and although the lines drawn from such a position do not strike the opening of the ear, but other places of the head. This makes one believe that the soul continues the lines of vibration externally in imagination, and places the sounding object in their meeting -point.42 The same can, in my opinion, be predicated of the other three senses, differing from sight and hearing in this respect that the object of sensation is in immediate contact with the organs of these other senses, and the lines indicating the place of the organic stimulus find in the organs themselves their meeting-point.

In applying this to the pictures of imagination, permit me to take as basis the hypothesis of Cartesius, approved of by most of the philosophers after him, that all representations of the imagination are accompanied by certain movements in the nerve-tissue or nerve-spirit of the brain, which movements are called "ideae materiales"; i.e., these representations are, perhaps, accompanied by the concussion or vibration of the fine element secreted by these nerve-tissues. This vibration is similar to the movements which the sense-impression might produce, and of which the nerve-vibration is a copy. But now I must ask that if it be granted that the principal difference between the nerve-movements in fantasies, and in sensations, consists in the fact that, with fantasies, the lines indicating the direction, of the movement meet inside of the brain, while in sensation they meet outside; then, since the focus imaginarius in which the objects are perceived in the clear sensations of the waking state is placed outside of myself, but the focus imaginarius of the fantasies entertained during the same state is placed inside of myself, I cannot fail, as long as I am awake, to distinguish from the sense-impressions these imaginations as fantasies.

If so much is admitted, it seems to me that I can adduce some reasonable cause for that kind of mind-disturbance called insanity, and, in its higher degree, trance. The peculiarity of this disease is that the confused individual places mere objects of his imagination outside of himself, and considers them to be real and present objects. Now I have stated that, according to the common order of things, the lines indicating the direction of the movement, and accompanying the fantasies in the brain as their material auxiliaries, must meet inside the brain, and that, consequently, the location of the picture in the subject's consciousness in the waking state must be placed inside of himself. If, therefore, I suppose that, by any accident or disease, certain organs of the brain are distorted or thrown out of their equilibrium in such a manner that the nerve movements, vibrating harmoniously with certain fantasies, occur according to such lines of direction as, continued, would meet outside of the brain, then the focus imaginarius would be placed outside of the thinking subject, and the image produced by mere imagination would be perceived as an object present to the external senses. Though such a phantom be only weak at the beginning, the consternation at the appearance of a thing which ought not to be there according to the natural order of things, will soon arouse attention, and will give to the phantom sensation such a vividness that the deluded person cannot doubt its reality. This delusion can affect any one of the external senses, for of each we have copied images in imagination, and the contortion of nerve-tissue can cause the focus imaginarius to be placed in that spot, whence the organic impression of a really existing bodily object would come. It is not astonishing, then, if the visionary believes to see or hear many a thing which nobody perceives besides him, or if these fancies appear to him and disappear suddenly, or if they beguile the sense of vision, for example, and can be apprehended by no other sense (if they cannot be felt, for instance), and thus seem to him intangible. The common ghost-stories depend so much on such indications as these that they easily justify the suspicion of hailing from such a source, In the same way the current conception of spiritual beings which we evolved out of common phraseology, is very much of the nature of this delusion, and does not belie its origin, since the quality of an intangible presence in space is said to constitute the essential characteristic of this conception.

It is further very probable that the idea of spectres, imbibed from education, furnishes the head of a diseased person with materials for deluding apparitions, and that a brain free from all such prejudices would not so soon hatch out phantasms of this kind, even though some aberration might befall it. Furthermore, as the disease of the visionary concerns not so much the reason, as a deception of the senses, it will be easily recognized that the unfortunate subject cannot remove the delusion by any reasoning; for a true or apparent impression of the senses precedes all the judgments of the reason, and carries with it immediate evidence, far excelling all other persuasion.43

The consequence resulting from all these considerations is in so far inconvenient, as it renders entirely superfluous the deep conjectures of the preceding chapter; and the reader, though he was ready to receive with some approval its idealistic notions, will nevertheless prefer that conception which allows of more comfort and brevity in judging, and which promises to find the more general approval. For, aside from the fact that it seems to conform more with a reasonable frame of mind to find the means of explanation in the material furnished by experience, than to lose one's self in the dizzy conceptions of a reason, partly inventing, partly jumping at conclusions, there is always found, in such speculations, occasion for scoffing, than which, whether justifiable or not, there is no stronger means of keeping back idle investigation. For it creates at once grave suspicion for one to attempt seriously to expound the fancies of a visionary, and the kind of philosophy which is found in such bad company is open to question. It is true, I have, in the preceding, not contested the insanity of such apparitions. Rather, while I have not made insanity to be the cause of an imagined communion with spirits, I have yet connected the two by considering insanity as the natural consequence of such communion. But what foolishness is there which could not be harmonized with a bottomless philosophy? Therefore, I do not at all blame the reader, if, instead of regarding the spirit-seers as half-dwellers in another world, he, without further ceremony, despatches them as candidates for the hospital, and thereby spares himself any further investigation. But, if everything then is to be treated on such a basis, the manner of handling such adepts of the spirit-world must be very different from that based upon the ideas given above; and if, formerly, it was found necessary at times to burn some of them, it now will suffice to give them a purgative. Indeed, from this point of view, there was no need of going so far back as to metaphysics, for hunting up secrets in the deluded brain of dreamers. The keen Hudibras could alone have solved for us the riddle, for he thinks that visions and holy inspirations are simply caused by a disordered stomach.

FOURTH CHAPTER.

THEORETICAL CONCLUSION FROM THE WHOLE OF THE CONSIDERATIONS OF THE FIRST PART.

The inaccuracy of scales used for commercial measurements, according to civil law, is discovered, if we let the merchandise and the weights exchange pans. So the partiality of the scales of reason is revealed by the same trick, without which, in philosophical judgments, no harmonious result can be obtained from the compared weighings. I have purified my soul from prejudices, I have destroyed any blind affection which ever crept in to procure in me an entrance for much fancied knowledge. I now have nothing at heart; nothing is venerable to me but what enters by the path of sincerity into a quiet mind open to all reasons — be thereby my former judgment confirmed or abolished, be I convinced or left in doubt. Wherever I meet with something instructive, I appropriate it. The judgment of him who refutes my reasons, is my judgment, after I first have weighed it against the scale of self-love, and, afterwards, in that scale against my presumed reasons, and have found it to have a higher intrinsic value. Formerly, I viewed human common sense only from the standpoint of my own; now I put myself into the position of a foreign reason outside of myself, and observe my judgments, together with their most secret causes, from the point of view of others. It is true, the comparison of both observations results in pronounced parallaxes, but it is the only means of preventing the optical delusion, and of putting conceptions in regard to the power of knowledge in human nature into their true places. You may say that this is very serious talk in connection with so trifling a problem as that under consideration, which deserves to be called a plaything rather than a serious occupation, and you are not exactly wrong in thus judging. But although one ought not to make a great ado about a small matter, yet one may perhaps be allowed to make use of such occasions; and unnecessary circumspection in small matters may furnish useful example in important matters. I find no attachment nor any other inclination to have crept in before examination, so as to deprive my mind of a readiness to be guided by any kind of reason *pro* or *con*, except one. The scale of reason after all is not quite impartial, and one of its arms, bearing the inscription, "Hope of the Future," has a constructive advantage, causing even those light reasons which fall into its scale to outweigh the speculations of greater weight on the other side. This is the only inaccuracy which I cannot easily remove, and. which, in fact, I never want to remove. I confess that all stories about apparitions of departed souls or about influences from spirits, and all theories about the presumptive nature of spirits and their connection with us, seem to have appreciable weight only in the scale of hope,44 while in the scale of speculation they seem to consist of nothing but air. If the answer to the problem in question were not in sympathy with a prior inclination, what reasonable man would be doubtful as to whether it were more plausible to assume the existence of a kind of beings which have no similarity whatever with anything taught him by his senses, or to attribute certain alleged experiences to a kind of self-deception and invention which, under certain circumstances, is by no means uncommon.

In fact this seems to be in general the main reason for crediting the ghost-stories so widely accepted. Even the first delusions about presumed apparitions of deceased people have probably arisen from the fond hope that we still exist in some way after death. And then, at the time of the shadows of night, this illusion has probably deluded the senses, and created out of doubtful forms phantoms corresponding to preconceived ideas. From these, finally, the philosophers have taken occasion to devise the rational idea of spirits, and to bring it into a system. You probably will recognise also in my own assumed doctrine of the communion of spirits this trend to which people commonly incline. For its propositions evidently unite only to give an idea how man's spirit leaves this world, i.e., of the state after death. But how it enters, i.e., of procreation and propagation, I make no mention. Nay, I do not even mention how it is present in this world, i.e., how an immaterial nature can be in an immaterial body and act by means of it.45 The very good reason for all this is that I do not understand a single thing about the whole matter, and, consequently, might as well have been content to remain just as ignorant as before in regard to the future state, had not the partiality of a pet notion recommended the reasons which offered themselves, however weak they were.

The same ignorance makes me so bold as to absolutely deny the truth of the various ghost stories, and yet with the common, although queer, reservation that while I doubt any one of them, still I have a certain faith in the whole of them taken together. The reader is free to judge as far as I am concerned. The scales are tipped far enough on the side containing the reasons of the second chapter to make me serious and undecided 'when listening to the many strange tales of this kind. But, as reasons to justify one's self are never lacking when the mind is prejudiced, I do not want to bother the reader with any further defence of such a way of thinking.

As I am now at the conclusion of the theory of spirits, I am bold enough to say that this study, if properly used by the reader, exhausts all philosophical knowledge about such beings, and that in future, perhaps, many things may be thought about it, but never more known. This assumption sounds rather vainglorious. For of such multifariousness are the problems offered by nature, in its smallest parts, to a reason so limited as the human, that there is certainly no object of nature known to the senses, be it only a drop of water or a grain of sand, which ever could be said to be exhausted by observation or reason. But the case is entirely different with the philosophical conception of spiritual beings. It may be complete, but in the negative sense, by fixing with assurance the limits of our knowledge, and convincing us that all that is granted to us is to know the diverse manifestations of life in nature and its laws; but that the principle of this life, i.e., the unknown and only assumed spiritual nature, can never be thought of in a positive way, because for this purpose no data can be found in the whole of our sensations; that therefore we have to resort to negations for the sake of thinking something so entirely different from everything sensuous; but that the possibility of such negations rests likewise neither upon experience nor upon conclusions, but upon invention, to which a reason deprived of all other expedients finally resorts. With this understanding pneumatology may be called a doctrinal conception of man's necessary ignorance in regard to a supposed kind of beings, and as such it can easily be adequate to its task.

And now I lay aside this whole matter of spirits, a remote part of metaphysics, since I have finished and am done with it.47 In future it does not concern me any more. By thus making the plan of my investigation more concentrated, and sparing myself some entirely useless inquiries, I hope to be able to apply to better advantage my small reasoning power upon other subjects. It is generally vain to try to extend the little strength one has over a wide range of undertakings. It is therefore a matter of policy, in this as other cases, to fit the pattern of one's plans to one's powers, and if one cannot obtain the great, to restrict one's self to the mediocre.

PART SECOND, WHICH IS HISTORICAL.

CHAPTER FIRST.
A STORY, THE TRUTH OF WHICH THE READER IS RECOMMENDED TO INVESTIGATE AS HE LIKES.

Sit mihi fas audita loqui. — Virgil.

Philosophy, which on account of its self-conceit exposes itself to all sorts of empty questions, finds itself often in awkward embarrassment in view of certain stories, parts of which it cannot *doubt* without suffering for it, nor *believe* without being laughed at. Both difficulties we find to a certain degree united in the current accounts of spirit visions, the first in listening to him who avouches their truth, the second in communicating them to others. In fact, there is no reproach more bitter to the philosopher than that of credulity, and of yielding to common fancies. And as those who know how to appear wise with little effort sneer at all those things which equalise, so to speak, the wise and the ignorant, in being incomprehensible to both of them, it is not astonishing that the apparitions, so frequently asserted, are finding wide acceptance, and yet, before the public, are either denied or hushed up. You may depend upon this much: an Academy of Sciences will never make this matter its prize question. Not that its members are entirely free from any belief in the opinion referred to, but because policy rightly shuts out questions raised either by presumption or vain curiosity. Thus stories of this kind will have at any time only secret believers, while publicly they are rejected by the prevalent fashion of disbelief.

Meanwhile, as this whole question seems to me to be neither important enough nor well enough studied out to be finally pronounced upon, I do not hesitate to relate here some information of the kind mentioned, and to submit it with absolute indifference to the kind or unkind judgment of the reader.

There lives at Stockholm a certain Mr. Swedenborg, a gentleman of comfortable means and independent position. His whole occupation for more than twenty years is, as he himself says, to be in closest intercourse with spirits and deceased souls; to receive news from the other world, and, in exchange, give those who are there tidings from the present; to write big volumes about his discoveries; and to travel at times to London to look after their publication. He is not especially reticent about his secrets, talks freely about them with everybody, seems to be entirely convinced of his pretensions, and all this without any apparent deceit or charlatanry. Just as he, if we may believe him, is the Arch-Spiritseer among all the spiritseers, he certainly is also the Arch-Dreamer among all the dreamers, whether we judge him by the description of those who know him, or by his works. But this will not hinder those who, otherwise, are favourable to influences from spirits, from supposing that there is some truth back of such phantasms. Still, as the credentials of all plenipotentiaries from the other world consist in the proofs48 which, by certain tests, they give of their calling in the present world, I must quote from what is spread abroad to authenticate the extraordinary capacities of the above-mentioned gentleman at least that which, with most people, still finds some credit.

Towards the end of the year 1761, Mr. Swedenborg was called to a princess, whose great intelligence and insight ought to render deception of such a nature impossible. The call was occasioned by the common report about the pretended visions of this man. After some questions which were intended to amuse her with his illusions, the princess dismissed him, after having charged him with a secret mission concerning his communication with spirits. Several days afterwards, Mr. Swedenborg appeared with an answer which was of such a nature as to create in the princess, according to her own confession, the liveliest astonishment, for the answer was true, and at the same time, could not have been given to him by any living human being. This story is drawn from the report sent by an ambassador at the court there, who was present at that time, to another foreign ambassador in Copenhagen; it exactly agreed also with all that special inquiry has been able to learn.

The following stories have no other proof than common report, which is rather doubtful evidence. Madame Marteville, the widow of a Dutch envoy at the Swedish court, was reminded by a goldsmith to pay some arrears due on a silver-service furnished her. The lady, knowing the economy of her deceased husband, was convinced that this debt must have been settled already in his lifetime, but she found no proof whatever among the papers he left. Woman is especially prone to credit the stories of soothsaying, interpretation of dreams, and similar wonderful things. The widow discovered therefore her trouble to Mr. Swedenborg, requesting him to procure from her husband in the other world information about the real facts of the claim — if it were true, as people said of him, that he had intercourse with deceased people. Mr. Swedenborg promised to do it, and, a few days afterwards, reported to the lady in her house, that he had obtained the desired information, and that the requisite receipts were in a hidden partition of a closet which he showed to her, and which, in her opinion, had been entirely emptied. A search was made at once, according to his description, and, together with the secret Dutch correspondence, the receipts were found, making void all claims.

The third story is of a kind of which it must be very easy to completely prove either the truth or the untruth. It was, if I am rightly informed, towards the end of the year 1759, when one afternoon Mr. Swedenborg, coming from England, landed in Gothenburg. The same evening he was invited to meet some company at the house of a resident merchant. After being present a short while he proclaimed, with evident consternation, the news that, just at that moment, a terrible fire was raging in Stockholm, in the Sudermalm. After the lapse of several hours, during which he had from time to time left the company, he reported to them that the fire was checked, and how far it had spread. This wonderful news was noised abroad the same evening, and the next morning was all over the town. Not until two days after did the first report from Stockholm arrive in Gothenburg. It agreed entirely, it is said, with Swedenborg's visions.49

It will probably be asked what on earth could have moved me to engage in such a contemptible business as that of circulating stories to which a rational man hesitates patiently to listen; nay, that I should even make them the subject of a philosophical investigation. But as the philosophy which we prefixed was equally a tale from the Utopia of metaphysics, I do not see anything unseemly in letting both appear together. Anyhow, why should it be more creditable to be deceived by blind confidence in the pretences of reason than by incautious belief in misleading stories?

The borders of folly and wisdom are marked so indistinctly that one can hardly walk long in the one region without making at times a little digression into the other. But so far as that sense of honour is concerned, which may sometimes be persuaded even against resisting reason, it seems to be a remnant of the old ancestral loyalty which, to be sure, does not exactly fit in with the present state of things, and therefore often becomes folly, yet, on that account, is not to be considered the natural heirloom of stupidity. I leave it, therefore, to the discretion of the reader to reduce the queer story with which I am meddling, — a doubtful mixture of reason and credulity, — into its components, and to make out what are the proportions of both ingredients in my mind. For, seeing that the main point in such a criticism is to preserve proper decorum, I am sufficiently guarded against ridicule by the fact that with this folly, if you want to call it by that name, I am in quite good and numerous company, and this, as Fontenelle believes, is alone sufficient at least to prevent one's being regarded as unwise. For it always has been, and, probably, always will be the case, that certain nonsensical things are accepted even by rational men, just because they are generally talked about. To that class belong sympathetic healings, the wand, forebodings, the effect of the imagination of pregnant women, the influences of the changing moon upon animals and plants, &c. Yea, a short time ago, the common peasantry made scholars pay them handsomely for so habitually ridiculing their credulity. For, by a good deal of hearsay from children and women, a great many intelligent men were finally persuaded to take a common wolf to be a hyena, although any rational man can easily see that an African beast would not disport itself in the woods of France. The weakness of man's reason, together with his curiosity, brings it about that, in the beginning, truth and deceit are snatched up promiscuously. But, gradually, the ideas are purified; a small part remains, the rest is thrown away as offal.

He to whom these ghost stories seem to be of importance, if he has money enough and nothing better to do, may, at any rate, make a journey for the sake of more accurate information, just as Artemidor travelled in Asia Minor to satisfy himself about the interpretation of dreams. Posterity of the same turn of mind will be very grateful to him for making it impossible for a second Philostratus to rise after many years, and make out of our Swedenborg a new Apollonius of Tyana, when the hearsay shall have matured to positive proof, and the inconvenient, though highly necessary, examination of eye-witnesses will have become impossible.

SECOND CHAPTER.

A DREAMER'S ECSTATIC JOURNEY THROUGH THE WORLD OF SPIRITS.

Somnia, terrores magicos, miracula, sagas,

Nocturnos lemures, portentaque Thessala.

Horace.

I cannot take it as in any way amiss in the cautious reader, if, during the development of this work, he should have grown doubtful about the manner of proceeding adopted by the author. For, as I treated the dogmatic part before the historic, and thus set reasons before experience, I gave cause for the suspicion of underhand-dealing, by having the whole thing before my mind from the start, and then feigning to know nothing but abstract considerations, so that I might finally surprise the reader who is expecting no such thing, by a pleasing confirmation from experience. In fact, this is a trick which philosophers have used at several times with very good success. To wit, all knowledge has two ends of which you can take hold, the one *a priori*, the other *a posteriori*. It is true, several modern scientists have pretended that one must, of necessity, begin at the latter. They think they can catch the eel of science at the tail, by first procuring enough knowledges from experience, and then ascending gradually to general and higher conceptions. But although this may not be unwise, it is not nearly learned enough, nor philosophical. For in this manner one soon arrives at a why which cannot be answered, and that is just as creditable for a philosopher as it is for a merchant to pleasantly ask one to come some other time when a bill of exchange is presented to him for payment. To avoid this inconvenience acute men have begun at the opposite farthest border, the outmost point of metaphysics. But a new difficulty is here incurred, of beginning I don't know where, and of coming I don't know whither; also that the reasoning, when continued, does not seem to fall in with experience; yea, it seems as if the atoms of Epicurus, after having fallen and fallen from eternity, might sooner meet by chance some time and form a world, than that common ideas will meet and exemplify these abstract principles. When the philosopher thus clearly saw that his reasons on the one hand and actual experience or report on the other might, like two parallel lines, run alongside each other into infinity without ever meeting, he agreed with others, as by mutual consent, that each should take the starting-point in his own way; each then should guide the reason not by the straight line of logic, but by giving to the lines of evidence an imperceptible twist, and so, by stealthily squinting in the direction of certain experiencies or testimonies, each one should bring the reason to the point of proving just what, unsuspected by the trustful pupil, he all the time had in mind as the experience to be rationally proved. Add to this that they call this road the road *a priori*, although they have imperceptibly directed it to the point *a posteriori*, by following a road already staked out. They do not tell you that, of course, because it is only fair for the initiated not to betray the tricks of the profession. With this ingenious method several men of merit have caught even secrets of religion by pure reasoning; just as a novelist makes the heroine flee into remote countries that there, by a lucky adventure, she haply may meet her lover; "et fugit ad salices, et se cupit ante videri." (Virgil). With such celebrated predecessors, I need not have been ashamed even if I really had made use of the same trick to help my work to a good ending. But I earnestly beg of the reader not to believe such a thing of me. Anyhow, of what use would it be to me now when I can deceive nobody any more, having given away the secret? Moreover, I undergo this misfortune, that the testimony which I have stumbled upon, and which resembles so uncommonly the philosophical creation of my own brain, looks desperately misshapen and foolish, so that I must rather expect the reader to consider my reasons as absurd on account of their relation to such confirmations, than that he will consider these latter reasonable on account of my reasons. I therefore declare without more ado that in regard to the alleged examples I mean no joke, and I declare once for all, that either one has to suppose more intelligence and truth to be in Swedenborg's works than a first glance will reveal, or that it is only chance when he coincides with my system; as poets sometimes, when they are raving, are believed to prophesy, or at least profess that they do, when, now and then, events bear them out.

I come to the point, the works of my hero. If many authors who are now forgotten, or, at least, in future will be without fame, deserve no small credit because, in the composition of big works, they took no heed of the expenditure of their reason, Mr. Swedenborg doubtless should carry highest honours among them all. For, surely, his bottle in the lunar world is quite full, and is inferior to none among all those which Ariosto has seen there, filled with the reason that was lost here, and which the owners one day will have to seek again; so utterly empty of the last drop of reason is his big work.50 Nevertheless, such a wonderful agreement we find there with what reason can obtain on the same subject by the most subtle investigations, that the reader will pardon me if I discover here that rare play of imagination which so many other collectors have found in the plays of nature, when, for example, in spotted marble they make out the Holy Family, or in stalactite formations they make out monks, baptismal fonts, and church organs, or even as the banterer Liscow discovered on the frosted window-pane the number of the beast and the triple crown, all of which nobody else sees but he whose head is filled with it beforehand.

The big work of this author comprises eight volumes quarto full of nonsense. He puts them before the world as a new revelation under the title of "Arcana Coelestia," and applies therein his visions mostly to the discovery of the hidden sense in the first books of Moses, and to a similiar mode of explanation of the whole of Scripture. All these fantastic interpretations do not concern me here, but, whoever desires it, may look up Dr. Ernesti's Theological Library, Volume first, for some information about them. Only the "audita and visa," i.e., what he professes to have seen with his own eyes and heard with his own ears, we will extract, principally from the appendices to his chapters, because they are the foundation of all the other fancies, and are also pretty well in the same line with the adventure which, in the foregoing, we have undertaken in the balloon of metaphysics. The author's style is plain. His stories and their arrangement seem really to be based upon fanatic observation, and afford little reason to suspect that fancies of a wrongly speculating reason have moved him to invent them, and use them for deception. In so far they are of some importance, and are really more deserving of being presented in a condensed form than many a plaything of brainless reasoners which swells our quarterlies. For a systematic delusion of the senses is a much more remarkable phenomenon than the deception of reason, the causes of which are well enough known, and which mostly could be prevented by an effort to guide the powers of mind, and to restrain somewhat an empty inquisitiveness. The delusion of the senses, on the other hand, concerns the first foundation of all judgments, against the perversion of which the rules of logic have little power. I distinguish, therefore, with our author, between delusions and the deductions thence, and pass over his incorrect reasonings, the consequences of his not stopping at his visions, — just as we often have to separate in a philosopher that which he observes from what he reasons, and just as even seeming experiences are, for the most part, more instructive than seeming reasons. While thus robbing the reader of some of the moments which otherwise he might have put to the study of the exhaustive discussion of the matter, without, however, being much more benefited, I have taken care, nevertheless, of his sensitive taste by leaving out many of the wild chimeras of the book, and reducing its quintessence to a few drops. I expect for that just as much gratefulness from the reader, as a certain patient believed he owed to his doctors because they made him eat only the bark of cinchona, while they might easily have compelled him to eat the whole tree.

Mr. Swedenborg divides his visions into three kinds. In the first kind he is liberated from the body, in a state mediate between sleeping and waking, in which he has seen, heard, even felt spirits. This he has experienced only three or four times. The second is being led away by the spirit, when he may be out walking on the street without losing himself, while at the same time his spirit is in entirely different regions and sees clearly elsewhere houses, men, forests, &c., and this perhaps for several hours, until he suddenly becomes aware again of his real place. That happened to him two or three times. The third kind of visions is what is usual with him, those which he has daily while wide awake; and from these visions his stories are taken.

All men, according to his testimony, are in equally close conjunction with the spirit-world; most men, however, do not perceive it, the difference between himself and others consisting only in the fact that *his interiors are opened,* a gift of which he always speaks with reverence (datum mihi est ex divina Domini misericordia). It may be seen from the context that this gift is supposed to consist in the faculty of becoming conscious of the obscure ideas which one's soul receives by its continual connection with the spirit-world. He distinguishes therefore in man the outer and the inner memory. The former he has as a person belonging to the visible world. On this fact also the distinction between the outer and inner man is founded; his own privilege consists in seeing himself already in this life as a person in the company of spirits, and in being recognised by them as man.51 In this inner memory everything is preserved which has disappeared out of the outer, — nothing of all the perceptions of a man is ever lost. After death the remembrance of everything that ever entered his soul, also of what was formerly hidden to himself, forms the complete book of his life.52

The presence of spirits, it is true, affects only his inner sense. But this makes them appear to him as being outside of himself, and in the form of the human figure. The language of spirits is an immediate communication of ideas, but it is always connected with the appearance of that language which the observer ordinarily speaks, and is represented as being outside of himself.53 A spirit reads in the memory of another spirit the ideas which are contained in the inner memory with clearness. Thus the spirits see in Swedenborg the perceptions which he has from this world, with such clearness, that they deceive themselves, and often imagine they perceive immediately those things which it is impossible for them to see;54 for no spirit has the least sensation from the corporeal world. Also, through communication with the souls of other living men, they can receive no idea of this world, because the interior of such men is not opened, and contains only ideas entirely obscure. For this reason Swedenborg is the very oracle of the spirits, who are just as curious to view in him the present state of the world, as he is curious to observe in their memory, as in a mirror, the wonders of the spirit-world. Although these spirits are also in the closest conjunction with the souls of all other men, operating upon them and being operated upon by them, they yet know this as little as men know it; so entirely obscure is that interior sense which belongs to the spiritual personality of men. The spirits therefore believe that those things which have been effected in them through the influence of the souls of men, have been thought by themselves alone; just as men in this life think no otherwise, than that all their thoughts and inclinations come from themselves, although, as a matter of fact, they often flow into them out of the other world.55 Each human soul has already in this life its place in the spiritworld, and belongs to a society, always in accordance with the inner state of good and truth, i.e., of will and understanding.29 But the places of spirits among themselves have nothing in common with space in the corporeal world. Thus the soul of a man in India can be next to the soul of another man in Europe, as far as their spiritual places are concerned, while those which, according to the body, live in one house, may be spiritually very far from one another. When man dies, the soul does not change its place, but only perceives itself to be in that place which, in relation to other spirits, it occupied already in this life. But although the relation of spirits among themselves is no real space, it has still with them the appearance of it,56 and their conjunctions are perceived under the accessory condition of nearness, their differences, on the other hand, as distances. In the same way spirits possess no extent, but yet present to each other the appearance of human figures. In this imaginary space there exists a universal community of spiritual natures. Swedenborg talks with departed souls at will, and reads in their memory (power of perception) that state which they observe in themselves, and sees it just as clearly as with bodily eyes. Moreover, the enormous distances which divide the rational inhabitants of the world are nothing in regard to the spiritual universe, and it is just as easy for one to talk with an inhabitant of Saturn, as with a deceased human soul. Everything depends on the condition of the interior state, and upon the conjunction in which spirits are according to the harmony of their states of good and truth. And the more remote spirits can easily enter into mutual communication through the intermediation of others. Thus man does not need to have actually dwelt in the other worlds for the sake of knowing them some day with all their wonders. His soul reads in the memory of the deceased citizens of other worlds the perceptions which they possess about their life and dwelling-place, and thereby sees objects as easily as by immediate observation.57

A principal conception in Swedenborg's phantasm is the following: — Corporeal beings have no substance of their own, but exist only through the spirit-world, not, however, that each body exists through one spirit, but through all taken together. For that reason the knowledge of material things has a double significance, an external meaning in regard to the inter-relations of matter, an internal meaning in so far as material effects indicate the powers of the spirit-world which cause them. Thus the parts in the body of man stand in relation to each other according to material laws. But in so far as the body is preserved by the spirit living in it, its various members and their functions are of value in indicating those powers of the soul by the operation of which they have their form, activity, and stability.58 This inner meaning is unknown to man, and it is that which Swedenborg, whose interiors are opened, wants to make known to the world. With all other things of the visible world the case is the same; they have, as I say, a signification as things, which amounts to little, and another as signs, which amounts to much.59 This also is the origin of all the new interpretations which he would make of the Scripture.60 For this inner meaning, the internal sense, i.e., the symbolic relation of all things told there to the spirit-world, is, as he fancies, the kernel of its value, the rest only the shell. Again, the important point in this symbolic conjunction of corporeal things, as images, with the interior spiritual state, is the following. All spirits present themselves to each other under the appearance of figures possessing extent; and the influences of all these spiritual beings among each other at the same time call forth the appearance of still other spiritual creatures possessing extent, thus, as it were, the appearance of a material world. The scenes of this world, however, are only symbols of its inner state; nevertheless they cause such a clear and enduring deception of the senses as to equal the real sensation of such objects. (A future interpreter will conclude from this that Swedenborg was an idealist, because he denies to this world its independent subsistence, and therefore held it to be only a systematic appearance, arising from the constitution of the spirit world.) Thus he talks about the gardens, vast countries, the dwelling-places, galleries, and arcades of the spirits, which he claims to see with his own eyes in the clearest light. And he assures us that, having spoken after their death with all his friends, he had nearly always found that those having died recently could persuade themselves with difficulty that they had died, because they beheld a similar world; also, that societies of spirits of the same inner state live in the same appearance in regard to the country and other things there, and that a change of state is accompanied by the appearance of a change of locality. The mass of wild and unspeakably absurd forms and figures which our dreamer believes to see quite clearly in his daily intercourse with spirits must be derived from the fact that, whenever spirits communicate their thoughts to the souls of men, these thoughts take the appearance of material things, which, however, present themselves to the subject only on the strength of their relation to an inner meaning, but, still, with all appearance of reality.

I have already stated that, according to our author, the many powers and qualities of the soul are in sympathy with those organs of the body which they govern. The whole outer man therefore corresponds to the whole inner man. If, then, a perceptible spiritual influx from the invisible world flows mainly into some one of the powers of the soul, he harmoniously feels its apparent presence also in the corresponding member of his outer man. Under this head he classifies a great variety of sensations in his body which he claims are always connected with spiritual contemplation. But their foolishness is too great for me to dare to quote even one of them.

From these data, if it be considered worth while, one may now form a conception of that most extravagant and queerest of fancies in which all his dreams culminate. Just as various powers and capacities form that unity which constitutes the soul or the inner man, in the same way also various spirits (whose principal traits have the same relation to each other as the many faculties of a single spirit have among themselves) form a society which has the appearance of a great man.17:36 In this image each spirit finds himself in that place and in that apparent member which is in accordance with his peculiar office in such a spiritual body. Again, all societies of spirits together, and the world of all these invisible beings, finally presents itself in the appearance of the *Grand Man, Maximus Homo*.61 A colossal and gigantic fancy, which, perhaps, has grown out of an old childish conception, just as in schools sometimes, as an aid to memory, a whole continent is pictured to the pupils under the image of a sitting virgin, &c. In this enormous man there is a universal, most intimate communion of one spirit with all others, and of all with one; and, whatever may be the positions or changes of living beings in regard to each other in this world, still each has his place in the Grand Man entirely distinct from his place here, a place which he never changes, which is in immeasurable space only according to appearance, but in reality signifies only a particular character of his relations and influences.

I am tired of copying the wild chimeras of this worst of all dreamers, and forbear continuing them to his descriptions of the state after death. I have still other scruples. For, although a collector of objects of natural history puts up in his press among the prepared objects of animal procreation not only such as are formed naturally but also abortions, he nevertheless has to be careful not to show them too plainly and not to everybody. For among the curious there might easily be some pregnant persons who might receive an injurious impression. And as among my readers some might be just as likely in an interesting condition in regard to spiritual conceptions, I should be sorry if they had received a detrimental shock by anything I have told. However, as I have warned them right at the start, I am responsible for nothing, and hope not to be burdened with the moon-calves which their fruitful imagination might bring forth on this occasion.

As it is, I have not substituted my own fancies for those of our author, but have offered his views in a faithful extract to the comfortable and economic reader who does not care to sacrifice seven pounds for a little curiosity. It is true, I have mostly avoided quoting the visions themselves, as such wild chimeras only disturb the sleep of the reader, and the confused meaning of his revelations has been brought now and then into somewhat intelligible language; but the main traits of the sketch have thereby not suffered in accuracy. Nevertheless, it is only in vain that one would hide the fact which, after all, is conspicuous to everybody, that all this labour finally comes to nothing. For, as the pretended private visions narrated in the book cannot prove themselves, the motive for bothering oneself with them could lie only in the supposition that the author might offer in substantiation happenings of the above-mentioned kind which could be confirmed by living witnesses. But nothing of the kind is found. And thus we retire with some confusion from a foolish attempt, making the rational though somewhat belated observation that it is often easy to think wisely, but unfortunately only after one has been for some time deceived.

I have treated an unfruitful subject which the inquiries and importunity of idle and inquisitive friends has forced upon me. By submitting my labours to their curiosity, I have still left their expectation unrewarded, and have satisfied neither the curious by novelties, nor the studious by reasons. If I had been animated in this work by no other intentions than those just stated, I should have wasted my time; for I have lost the confidence of the reader, whom, in his inquisitiveness and eagerness to know, I have led by a tiresome roundabout way to the same point of ignorance from which he started. But I really had an aim in view that seemed to me more important than the pretended one, and that, I believe, I have attained. Metaphysics, with which it is my fate to be in love, although only rarely can I boast of any favours from her, offers two advantages. The first is that it serves to solve the tasks which the questioning mind sets itself when by means of reason it inquires into the hidden qualities of things. But here the result only too often falls below expectation, and also this time the answer has evaded our too eager grasp.
Ter frustra comprensa manus, effugit imago,
Par levibus ventis volucrique simillima somno.
— Virgil.

The other advantage is more adapted to human reason, and consists in recognizing whether the task be within the limits of our knowledge and in stating its relation to the conceptions derived from experience, for these must always be the foundation of all our judgments. In so far metaphysics is the science of the boundaries of human reason. And as a small country always has many boundaries, and is generally more careful to intimately know and defend its possessions than blindly to set out upon conquests, it is this use of metaphysics, as setting boundaries, which is at the same time the least known and the most important, and which further is obtained only late and by long experience. In this case I indeed have not accurately defined the boundaries; but I have indicated them for the reader" so far that, after further consideration, he will find himself able to do without such vain investigations about a question the data of which he has to seek in a world different from that of which he is sensible. Thus I have wasted my time that I might gain it. I have deceived the reader so that I might be of use to him, and although I have offered him no new knowledge, I have nevertheless destroyed that vain belief and empty knowledge which inflates reason, and, in its narrow space, takes the place which might be occupied by the teachings of wisdom and of useful instruction.

The impatience of the reader, whom our considerations thus far have only wearied without giving instruction, may be appeased by the words with which Diogenes is said to have cheered his yawning listeners when he saw the last page of a tiresome book: "Courage, gentlemen, I see land!" Before, we walked, like Demokritus, in empty space, whither we had flown on the butterfly-wings of metaphysics, and there we conversed with spiritual beings. Now, since the sobering power of self-recognition has caused the silky wings to be folded, we find ourselves again on the ground of experience and common sense. Happy, if we look at it as the place allotted to us, which we never can leave with impunity, and which contains everything to satisfy us as long as we hold fast to the useful.

THIRD CHAPTER.
PRACTICAL CONCLUSION FROM THE WHOLE TREATISE.

It is the zeal of a sophist to inquire into any idle proposition and to set to the craving after knowledge no other limits than impossibility. But to select from among the innumerable tasks before us the one which humanity must solve, is the merit of the wise. After science has completed its course, it naturally arrives at a modest mistrust and, indignant with itself, it says: How many things there are which I do not understand! But reason, matured by experience so as to become wisdom, speaks through the mouth of Socrates when, among all the merchandise of a fair, he says serenely: "How many things there are which I do not need!" In this manner two endeavours of a dissimilar nature flow together into one, though in the beginning they set out in very different directions, the one being vain and discontented, the other staid and content. To be able to choose rationally, one must know first even the unnecessary, yea the impossible; then, at last, science arrives at the definition of the limits set to human reason by nature. All hollow schemes, perhaps not unworthy in themselves but lying outside of the sphere of men, will then flee to the limbus of vanity. Then even metaphysics will become that from which at present it is rather far off, and which would seem the last thing to be expected of her — the companion of wisdom. As long as people think it still possible to attain knowledge about things so far off, wise simplicity may call out in vain that such great endeavours are unnecessary. The pleasure accompanying the extension of knowledge will easily make it appear a duty, and will consider deliberate and intentional contentedness to be foolish simplicity, opposed to the improvement of our nature. The questions about the spiritual nature, about freedom and predestination, the future state, &c., at first animate all the powers of reason, and through their excellency draw man into the rivalry of a speculation which reasons and decides, teaches and refutes without discrimination, just according to the nature of the apparent knowledge in each case. But if this investigation develop into philosophy which judges its own proceedings, and which knows not only objects, but their relation to man's reason, then the lines of demarcation are drawn closer, and the boundary stones are laid which in future never allow investigation to wander beyond its proper district. We had to make use of a good deal of philosophy to know the difficulties surrounding a conception generally treated as being very convenient and common. Still more philosophy moves this phantom of knowledge yet further away, and convinces us that it is entirely beyond the horizon of man. For in the relations of cause and effect, of substance and action, philosophy at first serves to dissolve the complicated phenomena, and to reduce them to simpler conceptions. But when one has, finally, arrived at fundamental relations, philosophy has no business any more. Questions like "How something can be a cause, or possess power," can never be decided by reason; but these relations must be taken from experience alone. For the rules of our reason are applicable only to comparison in respect to identity or contrast. But in the case of a cause something is assumed to have come from something else; one can find therefore no connection in regard to identity. In the same way, if this effect is not already implied in what preceded, a contrast can never be made out; because it is not contradictory to merely assume one thing and abolish another. Thence the fundamental conceptions of causes, of forces, and of actions, if they are not taken from experience, are entirely arbitrary, and can be neither proved nor disproved.2:8:9 I know that will and understanding move my body, but I can never reduce by analysis this phenomenon, as a simple experience, to another experience, and can, therefore, indeed recognize it, but not understand it. That my will moves my arm is not more intelligible to me than if somebody said to me that he could stop the moon in his orbit. The difference is only that the one I experience, but that the latter has never occurred to me. I recognize in myself changes as of a living subject, namely, thoughts, power to choose, &c., &c., and, as these terms indicate things different in kind from any of those which, taken together, make up my body, I have good reason to conceive of an incorporeal and constant being. Whether such a being be able to think also without connection with a body, can never be concluded from this empirical conception of its nature. I am conjoined with beings kindred to myself by means of corporeal laws, but whether I am, or ever shall be, conjoined according to other laws which I will call spiritual, without the instrumentality of matter, I can in no way conclude from what is given to me. All such opinions, as those concerning the manner in which the soul moves my body, or is related to other beings, now, or in future, can never be anything more than fictions. And they are far from having even that value which fictions of science, called hypotheses, have. For with these no fundamental powers are invented; only those known already by experience are connected according to the phenomena; their possibility, therefore, must be provable at any moment. It is different in the former case, when even new fundamental relations of cause and effect are assumed, the possibility of which can never, nor in any way, be ascertained, and which thus are only invented by creative genius or by chimera, whichever you like to call it. That several true or pretended phenomena can be comprehended by means of such assumed fundamental ideas, cannot at all be quoted in their favour. For a reason may be given for everything, if one is entitled to invent at will actions and laws of operation. We must wait, therefore, until perhaps in the future world, by new experiences, we are informed about new conceptions concerning powers in our thinking selves which, as yet, are hidden to us. Thus the observations of later days, analysed by mathematics, have revealed to us the power of attraction in matter, concerning the possibility of which we shall never be able to learn anything further, because it seems to be a fundamental power. Those who would have invented such a quality without first having obtained the proof from experience, would rightly have deserved to be laughed at as fools. Because, in such cases, reasons are of no account whatever, neither for the sake of inventing, nor of confirming the possibility or impossibility of certain results: the right of decision must be left to experience alone. Just as I leave to time, which brings experience, the ascertainment of something about the famous healing-powers of the magnet in cases of toothache, when experience shall have produced as many observations to the effect that magnetic rods act upon flesh and bones, as we have already proving their effect on steel and iron. But, if certain pretended experiences cannot be classified under any law of sensation that is unanimously accepted by men: if, therefore, they would only go to prove irregularity in the testimony of the senses — which, indeed, is the case with rumoured ghost-stories — then it is advisable to simply ignore them. For the lack of unanimity and uniformity makes the historic knowledge about them valueless for the proof of anything, and renders them unfit to serve as basis for any law of experience within the domain of reason.

Just as, on the one hand, by somewhat deeper investigation, one will learn that convincing and philosophic knowledge is impossible in the case under consideration, one will have to confess, on the other hand, in a quiet and unprejudiced state of mind, that such knowledge is dispensable and unnecessary. The vanity of science likes to excuse its occupations by the pretext of importance; thus it is pretended in this case that a rational understanding of the spiritual nature of the soul is very necessary for the conviction of an existence after death; again, that this conviction is very necessary as a motive for a virtuous life. Idle curiosity adds that the fact of apparitions of departed souls even furnishes us with a proof from experience of the existence of such things. But true wisdom is the companion of simplicity, and as, with the latter, the heart rules the understanding, it generally renders unnecessary the great preparations of scholars, and its aims do not need such means as can never be at the command of all men. What? is it good to be virtuous only because there is another world, or will not actions be rewarded rather because they were good and virtuous in themselves? Does man's heart not contain immediate moral precepts, and is it absolutely necessary to fix our machinery to the other world for the sake of moving man here according to his destiny? Can he be called honest, can he be called virtuous, who would like to yield to his favourite vices if only he were not frightened by future punishment? Must we not rather say that indeed he shuns the doing of wicked things, but nurtures the vicious disposition in his soul; that he loves the advantages of actions similar to virtue, but hates virtue itself? In fact, experience teaches that very many who are instructed concerning the future world, and are convinced of it, nevertheless yield to vice and corruption, and only think upon means cunningly to escape the threatening consequences of the future.62 But there probably never was a righteous soul who could endure the thought that with death everything would end, and whose noble mind had not elevated itself to the hope of the future. Therefore it seems to be more in accordance with human nature and the purity of morals to base the expectation of a future world upon the sentiment of a good soul, than, conversely, to base the soul's good conduct upon the hope of another world. Of that nature is also that moral faith, the simplicity of which can do without many a subtlety of reasoning, and which alone is appropriate to man in any state, because, without deviations, it guides him to his true aims. Let us therefore leave to speculation and to the care of idle men all the noisy systems of doctrine concerning such remote subjects. They are really immaterial to us, and the reasons pro and con which, for the moment, prevail, may, perhaps, decide the applause of schools, but hardly anything about the future destiny of the righteous. Human reason was not given strong enough wings to part clouds so high above us, clouds which withhold from our eyes the secrets of the other world. The curious who inquire about it so anxiously may receive the simple but very natural reply, that it would be best for them to please have patience until they get there. But as our fate in the other world probably depends very much on the manner in which we have conducted our office in the present world, I conclude with the words with which Voltaire, after so many sophistries, lets his honest Candide conclude: "*Let us look after our happiness, go into the garden, and work.*"

Prolegomena to any Future Metaphysics

This book was first published in 1783, two years after the first edition of Kant's *Critique of Pure Reason*. One of Kant's shorter works, it contains a summary of the Critique's main conclusions, occasionally with arguments Kant had not used in the previous work. Kant characterizes his more accessible approach here as an "analytic" one, as opposed to the *Critique's* "synthetic" examination of successive faculties of the mind and their principles. The *Prolegomena* is also intended as a polemic, as Kant was disappointed by the poor reception of the *Critique of Pure Reason*, and so uses this text to repeatedly emphasize the importance of its critical project for the very existence of metaphysics as a science. The final appendix contains a detailed rebuttal to an unfavorable review of the Critique.

Kant proposed that his work be tested in small increments, beginning with the basic assertions. The *Prolegomena* can be used as a general outline to be compared to the Critique. He was not satisfied with certain parts of the Critique and suggested that the discussions in the *Prolegomena* be used to clarify those sections. The unsatisfactory parts were the deduction of the categories and the paralogisms of pure reason in the Critique. If the Critique and the Prolegomena are studied and revised by a united effort by thinking people, then metaphysics may finally become scientific. In this way, metaphysical knowledge can be distinguished from false knowledge. Theology will also be benefited because it will become independent of mysticism and dogmatic speculation.

Contents

INTRODUCTION

These Prolegomena are destined for the use, not of pupils, but of future teachers, and even the latter should not expect that they will be serviceable for the systematic exposition of a ready-made science, but merely for the discovery of the science itself.

There are scholarly men, to whom the history of philosophy (both ancient and modern) is philosophy itself; for these the present Prolegomena are not written. They must wait till those who endeavor to draw from the fountain of reason itself have completed their work; it will then be the historian's turn to inform the world of what has been done. Unfortunately, nothing can be said, which in their opinion has not been said before, and truly the same prophecy applies to all future time; for since the human reason has for many centuries speculated upon innumerable objects in various ways, it is hardly to be expected that we should not be able to discover analogies for every new idea among the old sayings of past ages.

My object is to persuade all those who think Metaphysics worth studying, that it is absolutely necessary to pause a moment, and, neglecting all that has been done, to propose first the preliminary question, 'Whether such a thing as metaphysics be at all possible?'

If it is a science, how comes it that it cannot, like other sciences, obtain universal and permanent recognition? If not, how can it maintain its pretensions, and keep the human mind in suspense with hopes, never ceasing, yet never fulfilled? Whether then we demonstrate our knowledge or our ignorance in this field, we must come once for all to a definite conclusion respecting the nature of this so-called science, which cannot possibly remain on its present footing.

It seems almost ridiculous, while every other science is continually advancing, that in this, which pretends to be Wisdom incarnate, for whose oracle every one inquires, we should constantly move round the same spot, without gaining a single step. And so its followers having melted away, we do not find men confident of their ability to shine in other sciences venturing their reputation here, where everybody, however ignorant in other matters, may deliver a final verdict, as in this domain there is as yet no standard weight and measure to distinguish sound knowledge from shallow talk. After all it is nothing extraordinary in the elaboration of a science, when men begin to wonder how far it has advanced, that the question should at last occur, whether and how such a science is possible?

Human reason so delights in constructions, that it has several times built up a tower, and then razed it to examine the nature of the foundation. It is never too late to become wise; but if the change comes late, there is always more difficulty in starting a reform. The question whether a science be possible, presupposes a doubt as to its actuality. But such a doubt offends the men whose whole possessions consist of this supposed jewel; hence he who raises the doubt must expect opposition from all sides.

Some, in the proud consciousness of their possessions, which are ancient, and therefore considered legitimate, will take their metaphysical compendia in their hands, and look down on him with contempt; others, who never see anything except it be identical with what they have seen before, will not understand him, and everything will remain for a time, as if nothing had happened to excite the concern, or the hope, for an impending change.

Nevertheless, I venture to predict that the independent reader of these Prolegomena will not only doubt his previous science, but ultimately be fully persuaded, that it cannot exist unless the demands here stated on which its possibility depends, be satisfied; and, as this has never been done, that there is, as yet, no such thing as Metaphysics. But as it can never cease to be in demand,[P] — since the interests of common sense are intimately interwoven with it, he must confess that a radical reform, or rather a new birth of the science after an original plan, are unavoidable, however men may struggle against it for a while.

Since the Essays of Locke and Leibniz, or rather since the origin of metaphysics so far as we know its history, nothing has ever happened which was more decisive to its fate than the attack made upon it by David Hume. He threw no light on this species of knowledge, but he certainly struck a spark from which light might have been obtained, had it caught some inflammable substance and had its smoldering fire been carefully nursed and developed.

Hume started from a single but important concept in Metaphysics, viz., that of Cause and Effect (including its derivatives force and action, etc.). He challenges reason, which pretends to have given birth to this idea from herself, to answer him by what right she thinks anything to be so constituted, that if that thing be posited, something else also must necessarily be posited; for this is the meaning of the concept of cause. He demonstrated irrefutably that it was perfectly impossible for reason to think a priori and by means of concepts a combination involving necessity. We cannot at all see why, in consequence of the existence of one thing, another must necessarily exist, or how the concept of such a combination can arise a priori. Hence he inferred, that reason was altogether deluded with reference to this concept, which she erroneously considered as one of her children, whereas in reality it was nothing but a bastard of imagination, impregnated by experience, which subsumed certain representations under the Law of Association, and mistook the subjective necessity of habit for an objective necessity arising from insight. Hence he inferred that reason had no power to think such, combinations, even generally, because her concepts would then be purely fictitious, and all her pretended a priori cognitions nothing but common experiences marked with a false stamp. In plain language there is not, and cannot be, any such thing as metaphysics at all.[P]

However hasty and mistaken Hume's conclusion may appear, it was at least founded upon investigation, and this investigation deserved the concentrated attention of the brighter spirits of his day as well as determined efforts on their part to discover, if possible, a happier solution of the problem in the sense proposed by him, all of which would have speedily resulted in a complete reform of the science.

But Hume suffered the usual misfortune of metaphysicians, of not being understood. It is positively painful to see how utterly his opponents, Reid, Oswald, Beattie, and lastly Priestley, missed the point of the problem; for while they were ever taking for granted that which he doubted, and demonstrating with zeal and often with impudence that which he never thought of doubting, they so misconstrued his valuable suggestion that everything remained in its old condition, as if nothing had happened. The question was not whether the concept of cause was right, useful, and even indispensable for our knowledge of nature, for this Hume had never doubted; but whether that concept could be thought by reason a priori, and consequently whether it possessed an inner truth, independent of all experience, implying a wider application than merely to the objects of experience. This was Hume's problem. It was a question concerning the concept's origin, not concerning the indispensable need of the concept. Were the former decided, the conditions of the use and the sphere of its valid application would have been determined as a matter of course.

But to satisfy the conditions of the problem, the opponents of the great thinker should have penetrated very deeply into the nature of reason, so far as it is concerned with pure thinking, — a task which did not suit them. They found a more convenient method of being defiant without any insight, viz., the appeal to common sense. It is indeed a great gift of God, to possess right, or (as they now call it) plain common sense. But this common sense must be shown practically, by well-considered and reasonable thoughts and words, not by appealing to it as an oracle, when no rational justification can be advanced. To appeal to common sense, when insight and science fail, and no sooner-this is one of the subtle discoveries of modern times, by means of which the most superficial ranter can safely enter the lists with the most thorough thinker, and hold his own. But as long as a particle of insight remains, no one would think of having recourse to this subterfuge. For what is it but an appeal to the opinion of the multitude, of whose applause the philosopher is ashamed, while the popular charlatan glories and confides in it? I should think that Hume might fairly have laid as much claim to common sense as Beattie, and in addition to a critical reason (such as the latter did not possess), which keeps common sense in check and prevents it from speculating, or, if speculations are under discussion restrains the desire to decide because it cannot satisfy itself concerning its own arguments. By this means alone can common sense remain sound. Chisels and hammers may suffice to work a piece of wood, but for steel-engraving we require an engraver's needle. Thus common sense and speculative understanding are each useful in their own way, the former in judgments which apply immediately to experience, the latter when we judge universally from mere concepts, as in metaphysics, where sound common sense, so called in spite of the inapplicability of the word, has no right to judge at all.

I openly confess, the suggestion of David Hume was the very thing, which many years ago first interrupted my dogmatic slumber, and gave my investigations in the field of speculative philosophy quite a new direction. I was far from following him in the conclusions at which he arrived by regarding, not the whole of his problem, but a part, which by itself can give us no information. If we start from a well-founded, but undeveloped, thought, which another has bequeathed to us, we may well hope by continued reflection to advance farther than the acute man, to whom we owe the first spark of light.

I therefore first tried whether Hume's objection could not be put into a general form, and soon found that the concept of the connection of cause and effect was by no means the only idea by which the understanding thinks the connection of things a priori, but rather that metaphysics consists altogether of such connections. I sought to ascertain their number, and when I had satisfactorily succeeded in this by starting from a single principle, I proceeded to the deduction of these concepts, which I was now certain were not deduced from experience, as Hume had apprehended, but sprang from the pure understanding. This deduction (which seemed impossible to my acute predecessor, which had never even occurred to any one else, though no one had hesitated to use the concepts without investigating the basis of their objective validity) was the most difficult task ever undertaken in the service of metaphysics; and the worst was that metaphysics, such as it then existed, could not assist me in the least, because this deduction alone can render metaphysics possible. But as soon as I had succeeded in solving Hume's problem not merely in a particular case, but with respect to the whole faculty of pure reason, I could proceed safely, though slowly, to determine the whole sphere of pure reason completely and from general principles, in its circumference as well as in its contents. This was required for metaphysics in order to construct its system according to a reliable plan.

But I fear that the execution of Hume's problem in its widest extent (viz., my Critique of the Pure Reason) will fare as the problem itself fared, when first proposed. It will be misjudged because it is misunderstood, and misunderstood because men choose to skim through the book, and not to think through it — a disagreeable task, because the work is dry, obscure, opposed to all ordinary notions, and moreover long-winded. I confess, however, I did not expect, to hear from philosophers complaints of want of popularity, entertainment, and facility, when the existence of a highly prized and indispensable cognition is at stake, which cannot be established otherwise, than by the strictest rules of methodic precision. Popularity may follow, but is inadmissible at the beginning. Yet as regards a certain obscurity, arising partly from the diffuseness of the plan, owing to which. the principal points of the investigation are easily lost sight of, the complaint is just, and I intend to remove it by the present Prolegomena.

The first-mentioned work, which discusses the pure faculty of reason in its whole compass and bounds, will remain the foundation, to which the Prolegomena, as a preliminary exercise, refer; for our critique must first be established as a complete and perfected science, before we can think of letting Metaphysics appear on the scene, or even have the most distant hope of attaining it.

We have been long accustomed to seeing antiquated knowledge produced as new by taking it out of its former context, and reducing it to system in a new suit of any fancy pattern under new titles. Most readers will set out by expecting nothing else from the Critique; these Prolegomena may persuade [a reader that metaphysics] is a perfectly new science, of which no one has ever even thought, the very idea of which was unknown, and for which nothing hitherto accomplished can be of the smallest use, except it be the suggestion of Hume's doubts. Yet even he did not suspect such a formal science, but ran his ship ashore, for safety's sake, landing on skepticism, there to let it lie and rot; whereas my object is rather to give it a pilot, who, by means of safe astronomical principles drawn from a knowledge of the globe, and provided with a complete chart and compass, may steer the ship safely, whither he goes.

If in a new science, which is wholly isolated and unique in its kind, we started with the prejudice that we can judge of things by means of our previously acquired knowledge, which., is precisely what has first to be called in question, we should only fancy we saw everywhere what we had already known, the expressions, having a similar sound, only that all would appear utterly metamorphosed, senseless and unintelligible, because we should have as a foundation out own notions, made by long habit a second nature, instead of the author's. However, the longwindedness of the work, so far as it depends on the subject, and not the exposition, its consequent unavoidable dryness and its scholastic precision are qualities which can only benefit the science, though they may discredit the book.

Few writers are gifted with the subtlety, and at the same time with the grace, of David Hume, or with the depth, as well as the elegance, of Moses Mendelssohn. Yet I flatter myself I might have made my own exposition popular, had my object been merely to sketch out a plan and leave its completion to others instead of having my heart in the welfare of the science, to which I had devoted myself so long; in truth, it required no little constancy, and even self-denial, to postpone the sweets of an immediate success to the prospect of a slower, but more lasting, reputation.

Making plans is often the occupation of an opulent and boastful mind, which thus obtains the reputation of a creative genius, by demanding what it cannot itself supply; by censuring, what it cannot improve; and by proposing, what it knows not where to find. And yet something more should belong to a sound plan of a general critique of pure reason than mere conjectures, if this plan is to be other than the usual declamations of pious aspirations. But pure reason is a sphere so separate and self-contained, that we cannot touch a part without affecting all the rest. We can therefore do nothing without first determining the position; of each part, and its relation to the rest; for, as our judgment cannot be corrected by anything without, the validity and use of every part depends upon the relation in which it stands to all the rest within the domain of reason. So in the structure of an organized body, the end of each member can only be deduced from the full conception of the whole. It may, then, be said of such a critique that it is never trustworthy except it be perfectly complete, down to the smallest elements of pure reason. In the sphere of this faculty you can determine either everything or nothing.

But although a mere sketch preceding the Critique of Pure Reason would be unintelligible, unreliable, and useless, it is all the more useful as a sequel. For so we arc ablc to grasp thc whole, to examine in detail the chief points of importance in the science, and to improve in many respects our exposition, as compared with the first execution of the work.

Having completed that work, I offer here such a plan which is sketched out after an analytical method, while the work itself [the Critique of Pure Reason] had to be executed in the synthetical style, in order that the science may present all its articulations, as the structure of a peculiar cognitive faculty, in their natural combination. But should any reader find this plan, which I publish as the Prolegomena to any future Metaphysics, still obscure, let him consider that not every one is bound to study Metaphysics, that many minds will succeed very well, in the exact and even in deep sciences, more closely allied to intuition [what can be sensed], while they cannot succeed in investigations dealing exclusively with abstract concepts. In such cases men should apply their talents to other subjects. But he who undertakes to judge, or still more, to construct a system of metaphysics, must satisfy the demands here made, either by adopting my solution, or by thoroughly refuting it, and substituting another. To evade it is impossible. In conclusion, let it be remembered that this much-abused obscurity (frequently serving as a mere pretext under which people hide their own indolence or dullness) has its uses, since all who in other sciences observe a judicious silence, speak authoritatively in metaphysics and make bold decisions, because their ignorance is not here contrasted with the knowledge of others. Yet it does contrast with sound critical principles, which we may therefore commend in the words of Virgil:

"Ignavum, fucos, pecus a praesepibus arcent."

["Bees defend their hives against drones, those indolent ones. "]

Section 1: Of the Sources of Metaphysics

If it becomes desirable to formulate any cognition as science, it will be necessary first to determine accurately those peculiar features which no other science has in common with it, constituting its characteristics; otherwise the boundaries of all sciences become confused, and none of them can be treated thoroughly according to its nature.

The unique characteristics of a science may consist of a simple difference of object, or of the sources of cognition, or of the kind of cognition, or perhaps of all three conjointly. On this, therefore, depends the idea of a possible science and its territory.

First, as concerns the sources of metaphysical cognition, its very concept implies that they cannot be empirical. Its principles (including not only its maxims but its basic notions) must never be derived from experience. It must not be physical but metaphysical knowledge, viz., knowledge lying beyond experience. It can therefore have for its basis neither external experience, which is the source of physics proper, nor internal, which is the basis of empirical psychology. It is therefore a priori knowledge, coming from pure Understanding and pure reason.

But so far Metaphysics would not be distinguishable from pure Mathematics; it must therefore be called pure philosophical cognition; and for the meaning of this term I refer to the Critique of the Pure Reason (II. "Methodology," Chap. I., Sec. 1), where the distinction between these two employments of the reason is sufficiently explained. So much concerning the sources of metaphysical cognition.

Section 2. Concerning the Kind of Cognition which can alone be called Metaphysical

Of the Distinction Between Analytical and Synthetical Judgments in General.

— The peculiarity of its sources demands that metaphysical cognition must consist of nothing but a priori judgments. But whatever be their origin, or their logical form, there is a distinction in judgments, as to their content, according to which they are either merely explicative, adding nothing to the content of the cognition, or expansive [ampliative], increasing the given cognition: the former may be called analytical, the latter synthetical, judgments.

Analytical judgments express nothing in the predicate but what has been already actually thought in the concept of the subject, though not so distinctly or with the same (full) consciousness. When I say: "All bodies are extended," I have not amplified in the least my concept of body, but have only analyzed it, as extension was really thought to belong to that concept before the judgment was made, though it was not expressed, this judgment is therefore analytical. On the other hand, this judgment, "All bodies have weight," contains in its predicate something not actually thought in the general concept of the body; it amplifies my knowledge by adding something to my concept, and must therefore be called synthetical.

The Common Principle of all Analytical Judgments is the Law of Contradiction.

— All analytical judgments depend wholly on the law of Contradiction, and are in their nature a priori cognitions, whether the concepts that supply them with matter be empirical or not. For the predicate of an affirmative analytical judgment is already contained in the concept of the subject, of which it cannot be denied without contradiction. In the same way its opposite is necessarily denied of the subject in an analytical, but negative, judgment, by the same law of contradiction. Such is the nature of the judgments: all bodies are extended, and no bodies are unextended (i.e., simple).

For this very reason all analytic judgments are a priori even when the concepts are empirical, as, for example, "Gold is a yellow metal," for to know this I require no experience beyond my concept of gold as a yellow metal. It is, in fact, the very concept, and I need only analyze it, without looking beyond it elsewhere.

Synthetical Judgments Require a Different Principle from the Law of Contradiction.

— There are synthetical a posteriori judgments of empirical origin; but there are also others which are proved to be certain a priori, and which spring from pure Understanding and Reason. Yet they both agree in this, that they cannot possibly spring from the principle of analysis, viz., the law of contradiction, alone; they require a quite different principle, though, from whatever they may be deduced, they must be subject to the law of contradiction, which must never be violated, even though everything cannot be deduced from it. I shall first classify synthetic judgments.

Judgments of experience [empirical judgments]

are always synthetical. For it would be absurd to base an analytical judgment on experience, as our concept suffices for the purpose without requiring any testimony from experience. That body is extended, is a judgment established a priori, and not an empirical judgment. For before appealing to experience, we already have all the conditions of the judgment in the concept, from which we have but to elicit the predicate according to the law of contradiction, and thereby to become conscious of the necessity of the judgment, which experience could not even teach us.

Mathematical judgments are all synthetical.

This fact seems hitherto to have altogether escaped the observation of those who have analyzed human reason; it even seems directly opposed to all their conjectures, though incontestably certain, and most important in its consequences. For as it was found that the conclusions of mathematicians all proceed according to the law of contradiction (as is demanded by all apodictic certainty), men persuaded themselves that the fundamental principles were known from the same law. This was a great mistake, for a synthetical proposition can indeed be comprehended according to the law of contradiction, but only by presupposing another synthetical proposition from which it follows, but never in and by itself.

First of all, we must observe that all proper mathematical judgments are a priori, and not empirical, because they carry with them necessity, which cannot be obtained from experience. But if this be not conceded to me, very good; I shall confine my assertion pure Mathematics, the very notion of which implies that it contains pure a priori and not empirical cognitions.

It might at first be thought that the proposition $7 + 5 = 12$ is a mere analytical judgment, following from the concept of the sum of seven and five, according to the law of contradiction. But on closer examination it appears that the concept of the sum of $7+5$ contains merely their union in a single number, without its being at all thought what the particular number is that unites them. The concept of twelve is by no means thought by merely thinking of the combination of seven and five; and analyze this possible sum as we may, we shall not discover twelve in the concept. We must go beyond these concepts, by calling to our aid some intuition [Anschauung], i.e., either our five fingers, or five points (as Segner has it in his Arithmetic), and we must add successively the units of the five, given in some intuition [Anschauung], to the concept of seven. Hence our concept is really amplified by the proposition $7 + 5 = 12$, and we add to the first a second, not thought in it. Arithmetical judgments are therefore synthetical, and the more plainly according as we take larger numbers; for in such cases it is clear that, however closely we analyze our concepts without calling images [Anschauung] to our aid, we can never find the sum by such mere dissection.

All principles of geometry are no less synthetical. That a straight line is the shortest path between two points is a synthetical proposition. For my concept of straight contains nothing of quantity, but only a quality. The concept of shortness is therefore altogether additional, and cannot be obtained by any analysis of the concept of straight. Here, too, intuition [Anschauung] must come to aid us. It alone makes the synthesis possible.

Some other principles, assumed by geometers, are indeed actually analytical, and depend on the law of contradiction; but they only serve, as identical propositions, as a method of concatenation, and not as principles, e. g., a=a, the whole is equal to itself, or $a + b > a$, the whole is greater than its part. And yet even these, though they are recognized as valid from mere concepts, are only admitted in mathematics, because they can be represented in some intuition [Anschauung].

What usually makes us believe that the predicate of such apodeictic [certain] judgments is already contained in our concept, and that the judgment is therefore analytical, is the duplicity of the expression, requesting us to think a certain predicate as of necessity implied in the thought of a given concept, which necessity attaches to the concept. But the question is not what we are requested to join in thought to the given concept, but what we actually think together with and in it, though obscurely; and so it appears that the predicate belongs to these concepts necessarily indeed, yet not directly but indirectly by an added visualization [Anschauung].

Section 3. A Remark on the General Division of judgments into Analytical and Synthetical

This division is indispensable, as concerns the Critique of human understanding, and therefore deserves to be called classical, though otherwise it is of little use, but this is the reason why dogmatic philosophers, who always seek the sources of metaphysical judgments in Metaphysics itself, and not apart from it, in the pure laws of reason generally, altogether neglected this apparently obvious distinction. Thus the celebrated Wolf, and his acute follower Baumgarten, came to seek the proof of the principle of Sufficient Reason, which is clearly synthetical, in the principle of Contradiction. In Locke's Essay, however, I find an indication of my division. For in the fourth book (chap. iii. Section 9, seq.), having discussed the various connections of representations in judgments, and their sources, one of which he makes "identity and contradiction" (analytical judgments), and another the coexistence of representations in a subject (synthetical judgments), he confesses (Section 10) that our a priori knowledge of the latter is very narrow, and almost nothing. But in his remarks on this species of cognition, there is so little of what is definite, and reduced to rules, that we cannot wonder if no one, not even Hume, was led to make investigations concerning this sort of judgments. For such general and yet definite principles are not easily learned from other men, who have had them obscurely in their minds. We must hit on them first by our own reflection, then we find them elsewhere, where we could not possibly have found them at first, because the authors themselves did not know that such an idea lay at the basis of their observations. Men who never think independently have nevertheless the acuteness to discover everything, after it has been once shown them, in what was said long since, though no one ever saw it there before.

Section 4. The General Question of the Prolegemena: Is Metaphysics at all Possible?

Were a metaphysics, which could maintain its place as a science, really in existence; could we say, here is metaphysics, learn it, and it will convince you irresistibly and irrevocably of its truth: this question would be useless, and there would only remain that other question (which would rather be a test of our acuteness, than a proof of the existence of the thing itself), "How is the science possible, and how does reason come to attain it?" But human reason has not been so fortunate in this case. There is no single book to which you can point as you do to Euclid, and say: This is Metaphysics; here you may find the noblest objects of this science, the knowledge of a highest Being, and of a future existence, proved from principles of pure reason. We can be shown indeed many judgments, demonstrably certain, and never questioned; but these are all analytical, and rather concern the materials and the scaffolding for Metaphysics, than the extension of knowledge, which is our proper object in studying it (Sect 2). Even supposing you produce synthetical judgments (such as the law of Sufficient Reason, which you have never proved, as you ought to, from pure reason a priori, though we gladly concede its truth), you lapse when they come to be employed for your principal object, into such doubtful assertions, that in all ages one Metaphysics has contradicted another, either in its assertions, or their proofs, and thus has itself destroyed its own claim to lasting assent. Nay, the very attempts to set up such a science are the main cause of the early appearance of skepticism, a mental attitude in which reason treats itself with such violence that it could never have arisen save from complete despair of ever satisfying our most important aspirations. For long before men began to inquire into nature methodically, they consulted abstract reason, which had to some extent been exercised by means of ordinary experience; for reason is ever present, while laws of nature must usually be discovered with labor. So Metaphysics floated to the surface, like foam, which dissolved the moment it was scooped off. But immediately there appeared a new supply on the surface, to be ever eagerly gathered up by some, while others, instead of seeking in the depths the cause of the phenomenon, thought they showed their wisdom by ridiculing the idle labor of their neighbors.

The essential and distinguishing feature of pure mathematical cognition among all other a priori cognitions is, that it cannot at all proceed from concepts, but only by means of the construction of concepts (see Critique, "Methodology," Chap. I., Section 1). As therefore in its judgments it must proceed beyond the concept to that which its corresponding visualization [Anschauung] contains, these judgments neither can, nor ought to, arise analytically, by dissecting the concept, but are all synthetical.

I cannot refrain from pointing out the disadvantage resulting to philosophy from the neglect of this easy and apparently insignificant observation. Hume being prompted (a task worthy of a philosopher) to cast his eye over the whole field of a priori cognitions in which human understanding claims such mighty possessions, heedlessly severed from it a whole, and indeed its most valuable, province, viz., pure mathematics; for he thought its nature, or, so to speak, the state-constitution of this empire, depended on totally different principles, namely, on the law of contradiction alone; and although he did not divide judgments in this manner formally and universally as I have done here, what he said was equivalent to this: that mathematics contains only analytical, but metaphysics synthetical, a priori judgments. In this, however, he was greatly mistaken, and the mistake had a decidedly injurious effect upon his whole conception. But for this, he would have extended his question concerning the origin of our synthetical judgments far beyond the metaphysical concept of causality, and included in it the possibility of mathematics a priori also, for this latter he must have assumed to be equally synthetical. And then he could not have based his metaphysical judgments on mere experience without subjecting the axioms of mathematics equally to experience, a thing which he was far too acute to do. The good company into which metaphysics would thus have been brought, would have saved it from the danger of a contemptuous ill-treatment, for the thrust intended for it must have reached mathematics, which was not and could not have been Hume's intention. Thus that acute man would have been led into considerations which must needs be similar to those that now occupy us, but which would have gained inestimably by his inimitably elegant style.

Metaphysical judgments, properly so called, are all synthetical. We must distinguish judgments pertaining to metaphysics from metaphysical judgments properly so called. Many of the former are analytical, but they only afford the means for metaphysical judgments, which are the whole end of the science, and which are always synthetical. For if there be concepts pertaining to metaphysics (as, for example, that of substance), the judgments springing from simple analysis of them also pertain to metaphysics, as, for example, substance is that which only exists as subject; and by means of several such analytical judgments, we seek to approach the definition of the concept. But as the analysis of a pure concept of the understanding pertaining to metaphysics, does not proceed in any different manner from the dissection of any other, even empirical, concepts, not pertaining to metaphysics (such as: air is an elastic fluid, the elasticity of which is not destroyed by any known degree of cold), it follows that the concept indeed, but not the analytical judgment, is properly metaphysical. This science has something peculiar in the production of its a priori cognitions, which must therefore be distinguished from the features it has in common with other rational knowledge. Thus the judgment, that all the substance in things is permanent, is a synthetical and properly metaphysical judgment.

If the a priori concepts, which constitute the materials of metaphysics, have first been collected according to fixed principles, then their analysis will be of great value. It might be taught as a particular part (as a philosophia definitiva), containing nothing but analytical judgments pertaining to metaphysics, and could be treated separately from the synthetical which constitute metaphysics proper. For indeed these analyses are not elsewhere of much value, except in metaphysics, i.e., as regards the synthetical judgments, which are to be generated by these previously analyzed concepts.

The conclusion drawn in this section then is, that metaphysics is properly concerned with synthetical propositions a priori, and these alone constitute its end, for which it indeed requires various dissections of its concepts, viz., of its analytical judgments, but wherein the procedure is not different from that in every other kind of knowledge, in which we merely seek to render our concepts distinct by analysis. But the generation of a priori cognition by concrete images as well as by concepts, in fine of synthetical propositions a priori in philosophical cognition, constitutes the essential subject of metaphysics.

Weary therefore of dogmatism, which teaches us nothing, and of skepticism, which does not even promise us anything, not even the quiet state of a contented ignorance; disquieted by the importance of knowledge so much needed; and lastly, rendered suspicious by long experience of all knowledge which we believe we possess, or which offers itself, under the title of pure reason: there remains but one critical question on the answer to which our future procedure depends, viz., is metaphysics at all possible? But this question must be answered not by skeptical objections to the asseverations of some actual system of metaphysics (for we do not as yet admit such a thing to exist), but from the conception, as yet only problematical, of a science of this sort.

In the Critique of Pure Reason I have treated this question synthetically, by making inquiries into pure reason itself, and endeavoring in this source to determine the elements as well as the laws of its pure use according to principles. The task is difficult, and requires a resolute reader to penetrate by degrees into a system, based on no data except reason itself, and which therefore seeks, without resting upon any fact, to unfold knowledge from its original germs. These Prolegomena, however, are designed for preparatory exercises; they are intended rather to point out what we have to do in order if possible to actualize a science, than to propound it. They must therefore rest upon something already known as trustworthy, from which we can set out with confidence, and ascend to sources as yet unknown, the discovery of which will not only explain to us what we knew, but exhibit a sphere of many cognitions which all spring from the same sources. The method of such Prolegomena, especially of those designed as a preparation for future metaphysics, is consequently analytical.

But it happens fortunately, that though we cannot assume metaphysics to be an actual science, we can say with confidence that certain pure a priori synthetical cognitions, pure Mathematics and pure Physics are actual and given; for both contain propositions, which are thoroughly recognized as apodictically certain, partly by mere reason, partly by general consent arising from experience, and yet as independent of experience. We have therefore some at least uncontested synthetical knowledge a priori, and need not ask whether it be possible, for it is actual, but how it is possible, in order that we may deduce from the principle which makes the given cognitions possible the possibility of all the rest.

Section 5. The General Problem: How is Cognition from Pure Reason Possible?

We have above learned the significant distinction between analytical and synthetical judgments. The possibility of analytical propositions was easily comprehended, being entirely founded on the law of Contradiction. The possibility of synthetical a posteriori judgments, of those which are gathered from experience, also requires no particular explanation; for experience is nothing but a continual synthesis of perceptions. There remain therefore only synthetical propositions a priori, of which the possibility must be sought or investigated, because they must depend upon other principles than the law of contradiction.

But here we need not first establish the possibility of such propositions so as to ask whether they are possible. For there are enough of them which indeed are of undoubted certainty, and as our present method is analytical, we shall start from the fact, that such synthetical but purely rational cognition actually exists; but we must now inquire into the reason of this possibility, and ask, how such cognition is possible, in order that we may from the principles of its possibility be enabled to determine the conditions of its use, its sphere and its limits. The proper problem upon which all depends, when expressed with scholastic precision, is therefore:

How are synthetic propositions a priori possible?

For the sake of popularity I have above expressed this problem somewhat differently, as an inquiry into purely rational cognition, which I could do for once without detriment to the desired comprehension, because, as we have only to do here with metaphysics and its sources, the reader will, I hope, after the foregoing remarks, keep in mind that when we speak of purely rational cognition, we do not mean analytical, but synthetical cognition.

Metaphysics stands or falls with the solution of this problem: its very existence depends upon it. Let any one make metaphysical assertions with ever so much plausibility, let him overwhelm us with conclusions, if he has not previously proved able to answer this question satisfactorily, I have a right to say this is all vain baseless philosophy and false wisdom. You speak through pure reason, and claim, as it were to create cognitions a priori. by not only dissecting given concepts, but also by asserting connections which do not rest upon the law of contradiction, and which you believe you conceive quite independently of all experience; how do you arrive at this, and how will you justify your pretensions? An appeal to the consent of the common sense of mankind cannot be allowed; for that is a witness whose authority depends merely upon rumor. Says Horace:

Quodcunque ostendis mihi sic, incredulus odi. ["All that which is proven to me thus, I hate and remain incredulous."]

The answer to this question, though indispensable, is difficult; and though the principal reason that it was not made long ago is, that the possibility of the question never occurred to anybody, there is yet another reason, which is this that a satisfactory answer to this one question requires a much more persistent, profound, and painstaking reflection, than the most diffuse work on metaphysics, which on its first appearance promised immortality to its author. And every intelligent reader, when he carefully reflects what this problem requires, must at first be struck with its difficulty, and would regard it as insoluble and even impossible, did there not actually exist pure synthetical cognitions a priori. This actually happened to David Hume, though he did not conceive the question in its entire universality as is done here, and as must be done, should the answer be decisive for all Metaphysics. For how is it possible, says that acute man, that when a concept is given me, I can go beyond it and connect with it another, which is not contained in it, in such a manner as if the latter necessarily belonged to the former? Nothing but experience can furnish us with such connections (thus he concluded from the difficulty which he took to be an impossibility), and all that vaunted necessity, or, what is the same thing, all cognition assumed to be a priori, is nothing but a long habit of accepting something as true, and hence of mistaking subjective necessity for objective.

Should my reader complain of the difficulty and the trouble which I occasion him in the solution of this problem, he is at liberty to solve it himself in an easier way. Perhaps he will then feel under obligation to the person who has undertaken for him a labor of so profound research, and will rather be surprised at the facility with which, considering the nature of the subject, the solution has been attained. Yet it has cost years of work to solve the problem in its whole universality (using the term in the mathematical sense, viz., for that which is sufficient for all cases), and finally to exhibit it in the analytical form, as the reader finds it here.

All metaphysicians are therefore solemnly and legally suspended from their occupations till they shall have answered in a satisfactory manner the question, How are synthetic cognitions a priori possible? For the answer contains the only credentials which they must show when they have anything to offer in the name of pure reason. But if they do not possess these credentials, they can expect nothing else of reasonable people, who have been deceived so often, than to be dismissed without further ado.

If they on the other hand desire to carry on their business, not as a science, but as an art of wholesome oratory suited to the common sense of man, they cannot in justice be prevented. They will then speak the modest language of a rational belief, they will grant that they are not allowed even to conjecture, far less to know, anything which lies beyond the bounds of all possible experience, but only to assume (not for speculative use, which they must abandon, but for practical purposes only) the existence of something that is possible and even indispensable for the guidance of the understanding and of the will in life. In this mariner alone can they be called useful and wise men, and the more so as they renounce the title of metaphysicians; for the latter profess to be speculative philosophers, and since, when judgments a priori are under discussion, poor probabilities cannot be admitted (for what is declared to be known a priori is thereby announced as necessary), such men cannot be permitted to play with conjectures, but their assertions must be either science, or are worth nothing at all.

It may be said, that the entire transcendental philosophy, which necessarily precedes all metaphysics, is nothing but the complete solution of the problem here propounded, in systematical order and completeness, and hitherto we have never had any transcendental philosophy. For what goes by its name is properly a part of metaphysics, whereas the former [transcendental] sciences has first to constitute the possibility of the latter, and must therefore precede all metaphysics. And it is not surprising that when a whole science, deprived of all help from other sciences, and consequently in itself quite new, is required to answer a single question satisfactorily, we should find the answer troublesome and difficult, nay even shrouded in obscurity.

As we now proceed to this solution according to the analytical method, in which we assume that such cognitions from pure reasons actually exist, we can only appeal to two sciences of theoretical cognition (which alone is under consideration here), namely, pure mathematics and pure natural science (physics). For these alone can exhibit to us objects in intuition (in der Anschauung), and consequently (if there should occur in them a cognition a priori) can show the truth or conformity of the cognition to the object in concreto, that is, its actuality, from which we could proceed to the reason of its possibility by the analytical method. This facilitates our work greatly for here universal considerations are not only applied to facts, but even start from them, while in a synthetic procedure they must strictly be derived in abstracto from concepts.

But, in order to rise from these actual and at the same time well-grounded pure cognitions a priori to such a possible cognition of the same as we are seeking, viz., to metaphysics as a science, we must comprehend that which occasions it, I mean the mere natural, though in spite of its truth not unsuspected, cognition a priori which lies at the bottom of that science, the elaboration of which without any critical investigation of its possibility is commonly called metaphysics. In a word, we must comprehend the natural conditions of such a science as a part of our inquiry, and thus the transcendental problem will be gradually answered by a division into four questions:

How is pure mathematics possible?

How is pure natural science possible?

How is metaphysics in general possible?

How is metaphysics as a science possible?

It may be seen that the solution of these problems, though chiefly designed to exhibit the essential matter of the Critique, has yet something peculiar, which for itself alone deserves attention. This is the search for the sources of given sciences in reason itself, so that its faculty of knowing something a priori may by its own deeds be investigated and measured. By this procedure these sciences gain, if not with regard to their contents, yet as to their proper use, and while they throw light on the higher question concerning their common origin, they give, at the same time, an occasion better to explain their own nature.

FIRST PART OF THE TRANSCENDENTAL PROBLEM: HOW IS PURE MATHEMATICS POSSIBLE?

Here is a great and established branch of knowledge, encompassing even now a wonderfully large domain and promising an unlimited extension in the future. Yet it carries with it thoroughly apodeictical certainty, i.e., absolute necessity, which therefore rests upon no empirical grounds. Consequently it is a pure product of reason, and moreover is thoroughly synthetical. [Here the question arises:] "How then is it possible for human reason to produce a cognition of this nature entirely a priori?" Does not this faculty [which produces mathematics], as it neither is nor can be based upon experience, presuppose some ground of cognition a priori, which lies deeply hidden, but which might reveal itself by these its effects, if their first beginnings were but diligently ferreted out?

Section 7.

But we find that all mathematical cognition has this peculiarity: it must first exhibit its concept in a visual intuition [Anschauung] and indeed a priori, therefore in an intuition which is not empirical, but pure. Without this mathematics cannot take a single step; hence its judgments are always visual, viz., intuitive; whereas philosophy must be satisfied with discursive judgments from mere concepts, and though it may illustrate its doctrines through a visual figure, can never derive them from it. This observation on the nature of mathematics gives us a clue to the first and highest condition of its possibility, which is, that some pure intuition [reine Anschauung] must form its basis, in which all its concepts can be exhibited or constructed, in concreto and yet a priori. If we can locate this pure intuition and its possibility, we may thence easily explain how synthetical propositions a priori are possible in pure mathematics, and consequently how this science itself is possible. Empirical intuition [viz., sense-perception] enables us without difficulty to enlarge the concept which we frame of an object of intuition [or sense-perception], by new predicates, which intuition [i.e., sense-perception] itself presents synthetically in experience. Pure intuition [viz., the visualization of forms in our imagination, from which every thing sensual, i.e., every thought of material qualities, is excluded] does so likewise, only with this difference, that in the latter case the synthetical judgment is a priori certain and apodeictical, in the former, only a posteriori and empirically certain; because this latter contains only that which occurs in contingent empirical intuition, but the former, that which must necessarily be discovered in pure intuition. Here intuition, being an intuition a priori, is before all experience, viz., before any perception of particular objects, inseparably conjoined with its concept.

Section 8.

But with this step our perplexity seems rather to increase than to lessen. For the question now is, "How is it possible to intuit [in a visual form] anything a priori?" An intuition [viz., a visual sense perception] is such a representation as immediately depends upon the presence of the object. Hence it seems impossible to intuit from the outset a priori, because intuition would in that event take place without either a former or a present object to refer to, and by consequence could not be intuition.

Concepts indeed are such, that we can easily form some of them a priori, viz., such as contain nothing but the thought of an object in general; and we need not find ourselves in an immediate relation to the object. Take, for instance, the concepts of Quantity, of Cause, etc. But even these require, in order to make them understood, a certain concrete use — that is, an application to some sense-experience [Anschauung], by which an object of them is given us. But how can the intuition of the object [its visualization] precede the object itself?

Section 9.

If our intuition [i.e., our sense-experience] were perforce of such a nature as to represent things as they are in themselves, there would not be any intuition a priori, but intuition would be always empirical. For I can only know what is contained in the object in itself when it is present and given to me. It is indeed even then incomprehensible how the intuition [Anschauung] of a present thing should make me know this thing as it is in itself, as its properties cannot migrate into my faculty of representation. But even granting this possibility, a visualizing of that sort would not take place a priori, that is, before the object were presented to me; for without this latter fact no reason of a relation between my representation and the object can be imagined, unless it depend upon a direct inspiration. Therefore in one way only can my intuition anticipate the actuality of the object, and be a cognition a priori, viz.: if my intuition contains nothing but the form of sensibility, antedating in my subjectivity all the actual impressions through which I am affected by objects. For that objects of sense can only be intuited according to this form of sensibility I can know a priori. Hence it follows: that propositions, which concern this form of sensuous intuition only, are possible and valid for objects of the senses; as also, conversely, that intuitions which are possible a priori can never concern any other things than objects of our senses.

Section 10.

Accordingly, it is only the form of sensuous intuition by which we can intuit things a priori, but by which we can know objects only as they appear to us (to our senses), not as they are in themselves; and this assumption is absolutely necessary if synthetical propositions a priori be granted as possible, or if, in case they actually occur, their possibility is to be comprehended and determined beforehand.

Now, the intuitions which pure mathematics lays at the foundation of all its cognitions and judgments which appear at once apodictic and necessary are Space and Time. For mathematics must first have all its concepts in intuition, and pure mathematics in pure intuition, that is, it must construct them. If it proceeded in any other way, it would be impossible to make any headway, for mathematics proceeds, not analytically by dissection of concepts, but synthetically, and if pure intuition be wanting, there is nothing in which the matter for synthetical judgments a priori can be given. Geometry is based upon the pure intuition of space. Arithmetic accomplishes its concept of number by the successive addition of units in time; and pure mechanics especially cannot attain its concepts of motion without employing the representation of time. Both representations, however, are only intuitions; for if we omit from the empirical intuitions of bodies and their alterations (motion) everything empirical, or belonging to sensation, space and time still remain, which are therefore pure intuitions that lie a priori at the basis of the empirical. Hence they can never be omitted, but at the same time, by their being pure intuitions a priori, they prove that they are mere forms of our sensibility, which must precede all empirical intuition, or perception of actual objects, and conformably to which objects can be known a priori, but only as they appear to us.

Section 11.

The problem of the present section is therefore solved. Pure mathematics, as synthetical cognition a priori, is only possible by referring to no other objects than those of the senses. At the basis of their empirical intuition lies a pure intuition (of space and of time) which is a priori. This is possible, because the latter intuition is nothing but the mere form of sensibility, which precedes the actual appearance of the objects, in that it, in fact, makes them possible. Yet this faculty of intuiting a priori affects not the matter of the phenomenon (that is, the sense-element in it, for this constitutes that which is empirical), but its form, viz., space and time. Should any man venture to doubt that these are determinations adhering not to things in themselves, but to their relation to our sensibility, I should be glad to know how it can be possible to know the constitution of things a priori, viz., before we have any acquaintance with them and before they are presented to us. Such, however, is the case with space and time. But this is quite comprehensible as soon as both count for nothing more than formal conditions of our sensibility, while the objects count merely as phenomena; for then the form of the phenomenon, i.e., pure intuition, can by all means be represented as proceeding from ourselves, that is, a priori.

Section 12.

In order to add something by way of illustration and confirmation, we need only watch the ordinary and necessary procedure of geometers. All proofs of the complete congruence of two given figures (where the one can in every respect be substituted for the other) come ultimately to this that they may be made to coincide; which is evidently nothing else than a synthetical proposition resting upon immediate intuition, and this intuition must be pure, or given a priori, otherwise the proposition could not rank as apodictically certain, but would have empirical certainty only. In that case, it could only be said that it is always found to be so, and holds good only as far as our perception reaches. That everywhere space (which (in its entirety] is itself no longer the boundary of another space) has three dimensions, and that space cannot in any way have more, is based on the proposition that not more than three lines can intersect at right angles in one point. But this proposition cannot by any means be shown from concepts, but rests immediately on intuition, and indeed on pure and a priori intuition, because it is apodictically certain. That we can require a line to be drawn to infinity (in indefinitum), or that a series of changes (for example, spaces traversed by motion) shall be infinitely continued, presupposes a representation of space and time, which can only attach to intuition, namely, so far as it in itself is bounded by nothing, for from concepts it could never be inferred. Consequently, the basis of mathematics actually are pure intuitions, which make its synthetical and apodictically valid propositions possible. Hence our transcendental [critical] deduction of the notions of space and of time explains at the same time the possibility of pure mathematics. Without some such deduction its truth may be granted, but its existence could by no means be understood, and we must assume "that everything which can be given to our senses (to the external senses in space, to the internal one in time) is intuited by us as it appears to us, not as it is in itself."

Section 13.

Those who cannot yet rid themselves of the notion that space and time are actual qualities inhering in things in themselves, may exercise their acumen on the following paradox. When they have in vain attempted its solution, and are free from prejudices at least for a few moments, they will suspect that the degradation of space and of time to mere forms of our sensuous intuition may perhaps be well founded.

If two things are quite equal in all respects as much as can be ascertained by all means possible, quantitatively and qualitatively, it must follow, that the one can in all cases and under all circumstances replace the other, and this substitution would not occasion the least perceptible difference. This in fact is true of plane figures in geometry; but some spherical figures exhibit, notwithstanding a complete internal agreement, such a contrast in their external relation, that the one figure cannot possibly be put in the place of the other. For instance, two spherical triangles on opposite hemispheres, which have an arc of the equator as their common base, may be quite equal, both as regards sides and angles, so that nothing is to be found in either, if it be described for itself alone and completed, that would not equally be applicable to both; and yet the one cannot be put in the place of the other (being situated upon the opposite hemisphere). Here then is an internal difference between the two triangles, which difference our understanding cannot describe as internal, and which only manifests itself by external relations in space. But I shall adduce examples, taken from common life, that are more obvious still.

What can be more similar in every respect and in every part more alike to my hand and to my ear, than their images in a mirror? And yet I cannot put such a hand as is seen in the glass in the place of its archetype; for if this is a right hand, that in the glass is a left one, and the image or reflection of the right ear is a left one which never can serve as a substitute for the other. There are in this case no internal differences which our understanding could determine by thinking alone. Yet the differences are internal as the senses teach, for, notwithstanding their complete equality and similarity, the left hand cannot be enclosed in the same bounds as the right one (they are not congruent); the glove of one hand cannot be used for the other. What is the solution? These objects are not representations of things as they are in themselves, and as the pure understanding would know them, but sensuous intuitions, that is, appearances, the possibility of which rests upon the relation of certain things unknown in themselves to something else, viz., to our sensibility. Space is the form of the external intuition of this sensibility, and the internal determination of every space is only possible by the determination of its external relation to the whole space, of which it is a part (in other words, by its relation to the external sense). That is to say, the part is only possible through the whole, which is never the case with things in themselves, as objects of the mere understanding, but with appearances only. Hence the difference between similar and equal things, which are yet not congruent (for instance, two symmetric helices), cannot be made intelligible by any concept, but only by the relation to the right and the left hands which immediately refers to intuition.

REMARK 1

Pure Mathematics, and especially pure geometry, can only have objective reality on condition that they refer to objects of sense. But in regard to the latter the principle holds good, that our sense representation is not a representation of things in themselves but of the way in which they appear to us. Hence it follows, that the propositions of geometry are not the results of a mere creation of our poetic imagination, and that therefore they cannot be referred with assurance to actual objects; but rather that they are necessarily valid of space, and consequently of all that may be found in space, because space is nothing else than the form of all external appearances, and it is this form alone in which objects of sense can be given.

Sensibility, the form of which is the basis of geometry, is that upon which the possibility of external appearance depends. Therefore these appearances can never contain anything but what geometry prescribes to them. It would be quite otherwise if the senses were so constituted as to represent objects as they are in themselves. For then it would not by any means follow from the conception of space, which with all its properties serves to the geometer as an a priori foundation, together with what is thence inferred, must be so in nature. The space of the geometer would be considered a mere fiction, and it would not be credited with objective validity, because we cannot see how things must of necessity agree with an image of them, which we make spontaneously and previous to our acquaintance with them. But if this image, or rather this formal intuition, is the essential property of our sensibility, by means of which alone objects are given to us, and if this sensibility represents not things in themselves, but their appearances: we shall easily comprehend, and at the same time indisputably prove, that all external objects of our world of sense must necessarily coincide in the most rigorous way with the propositions of geometry; because sensibility by means of its form of external intuition, viz., by space, the same with which the geometer is occupied, makes those objects at all possible as mere appearances.

It will always remain a remarkable phenomenon in the history of philosophy, that there was a time, when even mathematicians, who at the same time were philosophers, began to doubt, not of the accuracy of their geometrical propositions so far as they concerned space, but of their objective validity and the applicability of this concept itself, and of all its corollaries, to nature. They showed much concern whether a line in nature might not consist of physical points, and consequently that true space in the object might consist of simple [discrete] parts, while the space which the geometer has in his mind [being continuous] cannot be such. They did not recognize that this mental space renders possible the physical space, i.e., the extension of matter; that this pure space is not at all a quality of things in themselves, but a form of our sensuous faculty of representation; and that all objects in space are mere appearances, i.e., not things in themselves but representations of our sensuous intuition. But such is the case, for the space of the geometer is exactly the form of sensuous intuition which we find a priori in us, and contains the ground of the possibility of all external appearances (according to their form), and the latter must necessarily and most rigidly agree with the propositions of the geometer, which he draws not from any fictitious concept, but from the subjective basis of all external phenomena, which is sensibility itself. In this and no other way can geometry be made secure as to the undoubted objective reality of its propositions against all the intrigues of a shallow Metaphysics, which is surprised at them [the geometrical propositions], because it has not traced them to the sources of their concepts.

REMARK II.

Whatever is given us as object, must be given us in intuition. All our intuition however takes place by means of the senses only; the understanding intuits nothing, but only reflects. And as we have just shown that the senses never and in no manner enable us to know things in themselves, but only their appearances, which are mere representations of the sensibility, we conclude that "all bodies, together with the space in which they are, must be considered nothing but mere representations in us, and exist nowhere but in our thoughts." Now, is not this manifest idealism?

Idealism consists in the assertion, that there are none but thinking beings, all other things, which we think are perceived in intuition, being nothing but representations in the thinking beings, to which no object external to them corresponds in fact. Whereas I say, that things as objects of our senses existing outside us are given, but we know nothing of what they may be in themselves, knowing only their appearances, i. e., the representations which they cause in us by affecting our senses. Consequently I grant by all means that there are bodies without us, that is, things which, though quite unknown to us as to what they are in themselves, we yet know by the representations which their influence on our sensibility procures us, and which we call bodies, a term signifying merely the appearance of the thing which is unknown to us, but not therefore less actual. Can this be termed idealism? It is the very contrary.

Long before Locke's time, but assuredly since him, it has been generally assumed and granted without detriment to the actual existence of external things, that many of their predicates may be said to belong not to the things in themselves, but to their appearances, and to have no proper existence outside our representation. Heat, color, and taste, for instance, are of this kind. Now, if I go farther, and for weighty reasons rank as mere appearances the remaining qualities of bodies also, which are called primary, such as extension, place, and in general space, with all that which belongs to it (impenetrability or materiality, space, etc.) — no one in the least can adduce the reason of its being inadmissible. As little as the man who admits colors not to be properties of the object in itself, but only as modifications of the sense of sight, should on that account be called an idealist, so little can my system be named idealistic, merely because I find that more, nay, all the properties which constitute the intuition of a body belong merely to its appearance. The existence of the thing that appears is thereby not destroyed, as in genuine idealism, but it is only shown, that we cannot possibly know it by the senses as it is in itself.

I should be glad to know what my assertions must be in order to avoid all idealism. Undoubtedly, I should say, that the representation of space is not only perfectly conformable to the relation which our sensibility has to objects — that I have said — but that it is quite similar to the object, — an assertion in which I can find as little meaning as if I said that the sensation of red has a similarity to the property of vermilion, which excites this sensation in me.

REMARK III

Hence we may at once dismiss an easily foreseen but futile objection, "that by admitting the ideality of space and of time the whole sensible world would be turned into mere sham." At first all philosophical insight into the nature of sensuous cognition was spoiled, by making the sensibility merely a confused mode of representation, according to which we still know things as they are, but without being able to reduce everything in this our representation to a clear consciousness; whereas proof is offered by us that sensibility consists, not in this logical distinction of clearness and obscurity, but in the genetic one of the origin of cognition itself. For sensuous perception represents things not at all as they are, but only the mode in which they affect our senses, and consequently by sensuous perception appearances only and not things themselves are given to the understanding for reflection. After this necessary corrective, an objection rises from an unpardonable and almost intentional misconception, as if my doctrine turned all the things of the world of sense into mere illusion.

When an appearance is given us, we are still quite free as to how we should judge the matter. The appearance depends upon the senses, but the judgment upon the understanding, and the only question is, whether in the determination of the object there is truth or not. But the difference between truth and dreaming is not ascertained by the nature of the representations, which are referred to objects (for they are the same in both cases), but by their connection according to those rules, which determine the coherence of the representations in the concept of an object, and by ascertaining whether they can subsist together in experience or not. And it is not the fault of the appearances if our cognition takes illusion for truth, i.e., if the intuition, by which an object is given us, is considered a concept of the thing or of its existence also, which the understanding can only think The senses represent to us the paths of the planets as now progressive, now retrogressive, and herein is neither falsehood nor truth, because as long as we hold this path to be nothing but appearance, we do not judge of the objective nature of their motion. But as a false judgment may easily arise when the understanding is not on its guard against this subjective mode of representation being considered objective, we say they appear to move backward; it is not the senses however which must be charged with the illusion, but the understanding, whose province alone it is to give an objective judgment on appearances.

Thus, even if we did not at all reflect on the origin of our representations, whenever we connect our intuitions of sense (whatever they may contain), in space and in time, according to the rules of the coherence of all cognition in experience, illusion or truth will arise according as we are negligent or careful. It is merely a question of the use of sensuous representations in the understanding, and not of their origin. In the same way, if I consider all the representations of the senses, together with their form, space and time, to be nothing but appearances, and space and time to be a mere form of the sensibility, which is not to be met with in objects out of it, and if I make use of these representations in reference to possible experience only, there is nothing in my regarding them as appearances that can lead astray or cause illusion. For all that they can correctly cohere according to rules of truth in experience. Thus all the propositions of geometry hold good of space as well as of all the objects of the senses, consequently of all possible experience, whether I consider space as a mere form of the sensibility, or as something cleaving to the things themselves. In the former case however I comprehend how I can know a priori these propositions concerning all the objects of external intuition. Otherwise, everything else as regards all possible experience remains just as if I had not departed from the ordinary view.

But if I venture to go beyond all possible experience with my notions of space and time, which I cannot refrain from doing if I proclaim them qualities inherent in things in themselves (for what should prevent me from letting them hold good of the same things, even though my senses might be different, and unsuited to them?), then a grave error may arise due to illusion, for thus I would proclaim to be universally valid what is merely a subjective condition of the intuition of things and sure only for all objects of sense, viz., for all possible experience; I would refer this condition to things in themselves, and do not limit it to the conditions of experience

My doctrine of the ideality of space and of time, therefore, far from reducing the whole sensible world to mere illusion, is the only means of securing the application of one of the most important cognitions (that which mathematics propounds a priori) to actual objects, and of preventing its being regarded as mere illusion. For without this observation it would be quite impossible to make out whether the intuitions of space and time, which we borrow from no experience, and which yet lie in our representation a priori, are not mere phantasms of our brain, to which objects do not correspond, at least not adequately, and consequently, whether we have been able to show its unquestionable validity with regard to all the objects of the sensible world just because they are mere appearances.

Secondly, though these my principles make appearances of the representations of the senses, they are so far from turning the truth of experience into mere illusion, that they are rather the only means of preventing the transcendental illusion, by which metaphysics has hitherto been deceived, leading to the childish endeavor of catching at bubbles, because appearances, which are mere representations, were taken for things in themselves. Here originated the remarkable event of the antimony of Reason which I shall mention by and by, and which is destroyed by the single observation, that appearance, as long as it is employed in experience, produces truth, but the moment it transgresses the bounds of experience, and consequently becomes transcendent, produces nothing but illusion.

Inasmuch therefore, as I leave to things as we obtain them by the senses their actuality, and only limit our sensuous intuition of these things to this, that they represent in no respect, not even in the pure intuitions of space and of time, anything more than mere appearance of those things, but never their constitution in themselves, this is not a sweeping illusion invented for nature by me. My protestation too against all charges of idealism is so valid and clear as even to seem superfluous, were there not incompetent judges, who, while they would have an old name for every deviation from their perverse though common opinion, and never judge of the spirit of philosophic nomenclature, but cling to the letter only, are ready to put their own conceits in the place of well-defined notions, and thereby deform and distort them. I have myself given this my theory the name of transcendental idealism, but that cannot authorize any one to confound it either with the empirical idealism of Descartes, (indeed, his was only an insoluble problem, owing to which he thought every one at liberty to deny the existence of the corporeal world, because it could never be proved satisfactorily), or with the mystical and visionary idealism of Berkeley, against which and other similar phantasms our Critique contains the proper antidote. My idealism concerns not the existence of things (the doubting of which, however, constitutes idealism in the ordinary sense), since it never came into my head to doubt it, but it concerns the sensuous representation of things, to which space and time especially belong. Of these [viz., space and time], consequently of all appearances in general, I have only shown, that they are neither things (but mere modes of representation), nor determinations belonging to things in themselves. But the word "transcendental," which with me means a reference of our cognition, i.e., not to things, but only to the cognitive faculty, was meant to obviate this misconception. Yet rather than give further occasion to it by this word, I now retract it, and desire this idealism of mine to be called critical. But if it be really an objectionable idealism to convert actual things (not appearances) into mere representations, by what name shall we call him who conversely changes mere representations to things? It may, I think, be called dreaming idealism, in contradistinction to the former, which may be called visionary, both of which are to be refuted by my transcendental, or, better, critical idealism.

SECOND PART OF THE MAIN TRANSCENDENTAL PROBLEM: HOW IS THE SCIENCE OF NATURE POSSIBLE?

Section 14.

Nature is the existence of things, so far as it is determined according to universal laws. Should nature signify the existence of things in themselves, we could never know it either a priori or a posteriori. Not a priori, for how can we know what belongs to things in themselves, since this never can be done by the dissection of our concepts (in analytical judgments)? We do not want to know what is contained in our concept of a thing (for the [concept describes what] belongs to its logical being), but what is in the actuality of the thing superadded to our concept, and by what the thing itself is determined in its existence outside the concept. Our understanding, and the conditions on which alone it can connect the determinations of things in their existence, do not prescribe any rule to things themselves; these do not conform to our understanding, but it must conform itself to them; they must therefore be first given us in order to gather these determinations from them, wherefore they would not be known a priori.

A cognition of the nature of things in themselves a posteriori would be equally impossible. For, if experience is to teach us laws, to which the existence of things is subject, these laws, if they regard things in themselves, must belong to them of necessity even outside our experience. But experience teaches us what exists and how it exists, but never that it must necessarily exist so and not otherwise. Experience therefore can never teach us the nature of things in themselves.

Section 15.

We nevertheless actually possess a pure science of nature in which are propounded, a priori and with all the necessity requisite to apodeictical propositions, laws to which nature is subject. I need only call to witness that propaedeutic of natural science which, under the title of the universal Science of Nature, precedes all Physics (which is founded upon empirical principles). In it we have Mathematics applied to appearance, and also merely discursive principles (or those derived from concepts), which constitute the philosophical part of the pure cognition of nature. But there are

several things in it, which are not quite pure and independent of empirical sources:
such as the concept of motion, that of impenetrability (upon which the empirical
concept of matter rests), that of inertia, and many others, which prevent its being
called a perfectly pure science of nature. Besides, it only refers to objects of the
external sense and therefore does not give an example of a universal science of
nature, in the strict sense, for such a science must reduce nature in general, whether
it regards the object of the external or that of the internal sense (the object of Physics
as well as Psychology), to universal laws. But among the principles of this universal
physics there are a few which actually have the required universality; for instance, the
propositions that "substance is permanent, "and that "every event is determined by a
cause according to constant laws," etc. These are actually universal laws of nature,
which subsist completely a priori. There is then in fact a pure science of nature, and
the question arises, How is it possible?

Section 16.

The word nature assumes yet another meaning, which determines the object, whereas
in the former sense it only denotes the conformity to law of the determinations of the
existence of things generally. If we consider it materialiter (i.e., in the matter that
forms its objects), nature is the complex of all the objects of experience. And with
this only are we now concerned, for besides, things which can never be objects of
experience, if they must be known as to their nature, would oblige us to have recourse
to concepts whose meaning could never be given in concreto (by any example of
possible experience). Consequently we must form for ourselves a list of concepts of
their nature, the reality whereof (i.e., whether they actually refer to objects, or are
mere creations of thought) could never be determined. The cognition of what cannot
be an object of experience would be hyperphysical, and with things hyperphysical we
are here not concerned, but only with the cognition of nature, the actuality of which
can be confirmed by experience, though it [the cognition of nature] is possible a priori
and precedes all experience.

Section 17.

The formal aspect of nature in this narrower sense is therefore the conformity to law
of all the objects of experience, and so far as it is known a priori, their necessary
conformity. But it has just been shown that the laws of nature can never be known a
priori in objects so far as they are considered not in reference to possible experience,
but as things in themselves. And our inquiry here extends not to things in themselves
(the properties of which we pass by), but to things as objects of possible experience,
and the complex of these is what we properly call nature. And now I ask when the
possibility of a cognition of nature a priori is in question, whether it is better to arrange
the problem thus: How can we know a priori that things as objects of experience
necessarily conform to law? or thus: How is it possible to know a priori the necessary
conformity to law of experience itself as regards all its objects generally?

Closely considered, the solution of the problem, represented in either way, amounts,
with regard to the pure cognition of nature (which is the point of the question at issue),
entirely to the same thing. For the subjective laws, under which alone an empirical
cognition of things is possible, hold good of these things, as objects of possible

experience (not as things in themselves, which are not considered here). Either of the following statements means quite the same: "A judgment of observation can never rank as experience, without the law, that 'whenever an event is observed, it is always referred to some antecedent, which it follows according to a universal rule" or else "Everything, of which experience teaches that it happens, must have a cause."

It is, however, more convenient to choose the first formula. For we can a priori and previous to all given objects have a cognition of those conditions, on which alone experience is possible, but never of the laws to which things may in themselves be subject, without reference to possible experience. We cannot therefore study the nature of things a priori otherwise than by investigating the conditions and the universal (though subjective) laws, under which alone such a cognition as experience (as to mere form) is possible, and we determine accordingly the possibility of things, as objects of experience. For if I should choose the second formula, and seek the conditions a priori, on which nature as an object of experience is possible, I might easily fall into error, and fancy that I was speaking of nature as a thing in itself, and then move round in endless circles, in a vain search for laws concerning things of which nothing is given me.

Accordingly we shall here be concerned with experience only, and the universal conditions of its possibility which are given a priori. Thence we shall determine nature as the whole object of all possible experience. I think it will be understood that I here do not mean the rules of the observation of a nature that is already given, for these already presuppose experience. I do not mean how (through experience) we can study the laws of nature; for these would not then be laws a priori, and would yield us no pure science of nature; but [I mean to ask] how the conditions a priori of the possibility of experience are at the same time the sources from which all the universal laws of nature must be derived.

Section 18.

In the first place we must state that, while all judgments of experience [Erfahrungsurtheile] are empirical (i.e., have their ground in immediate sense perception), vice versa, all empirical judgments [empirische Urtheile] are not judgments of experience, but, besides the empirical, and in general besides what is given to the sensuous intuition, particular concepts must yet be superadded — concepts which have their origin quite a priori in the pure understanding, and under which every perception must be first of all subsumed and then by their means changed into experience.

Empirical judgments, so far as they have objective validity, are judgments of experience; but those which are only subjectively valid, I name mere judgments of perception. The latter require no pure concept of the understanding, but only the logical connection of perception in a thinking subject. But the former always require, besides the representation of the sensuous intuition, particular concepts originally begotten in the understanding, which produce the objective validity of the judgment of experience.

All our judgments are at first merely judgments of perception; they hold good only for us (i.e., for our subject), and we do not till afterwards give them a new reference (to an object), and desire that they shall always hold good for us and in the same way for everybody else; for when a judgment agrees with an object, all judgments concerning the same object must likewise agree among themselves, and thus the objective validity of the judgment of experience signifies nothing else than its necessary universality of application. And conversely when we have reason to consider a judgment necessarily universal (which never depends upon perception, but upon the pure concept of the understanding, under which the perception is subsumed), we must consider it objective also, that is, that it expresses not merely a reference of our perception to a subject, but a quality of the object. For there would be no reason for the judgments of other men necessarily agreeing with mine, if it were not the unity of the object to which they all refer, and with which they accord; hence they must all agree with one another.

Section 19.

Therefore objective validity and necessary universality (for everybody) are equivalent terms, and though we do not know the object in itself, yet when we consider a judgment as universal, and also necessary, we understand it to have objective validity. By this judgment we know the object (though it remains unknown as it is in itself) by the universal and necessary connection of the given perceptions. As this is the case with all objects of sense, judgments of experience take their objective validity not from the immediate cognition of the object (which is impossible), but from the condition of universal validity in empirical judgments, which, as already said, never rests upon empirical, or, in short, sensuous conditions, but upon a pure concept of the understanding. The object always remains unknown in itself; but when by the concept of the understanding the connection of the representations of the object, which are given to our sensibility, is determined as universally valid, the object is determined by this relation, and it is the judgment that is objective.

To illustrate the matter: When we say, "the room is warm, sugar sweet, and wormwood bitter," we have only subjectively valid judgments, I do not at all expect that I or any other person shall always find it as I now do; each of these sentences only expresses a relation of two sensations to the same subject, to myself, and that only in my present state of perception; consequently they are not valid of the object. Such are judgments of perception. Judgments of experience are of quite a different nature. What experience teaches me under certain circumstances, it must always teach me and everybody; and its validity is not limited to the subject nor to its state at a particular time. Hence I pronounce all such judgments as being objectively valid. For instance, when I say the air is elastic, this judgment is as yet a judgment of perception only — I do nothing but refer two of my sensations to one another. But, if I would have it called a judgment of experience, I require this connection to stand under a condition, which makes it universally valid. I desire therefore that I and everybody else should always connect necessarily the same perceptions under the same circumstances.

Section 20.

We must consequently analyze experience in order to see what is contained in this product of the senses and of the understanding, and how the judgment of experience itself is possible. The foundation is the intuition of which I become conscious, i.e., perception (perceptio), which pertains merely to the senses. But in the next place, there are acts of judging (which belong only to the understanding). But this judging may be twofold-first, I may merely compare perceptions and connect them in a particular state of my consciousness; or, secondly, I may connect them in consciousness generally. The former judgment is merely a judgment of perception, and of subjective validity only: it is merely a connection of perceptions in my mental state, without reference to the object. Hence it is not, as is commonly imagined, enough for experience to compare perceptions and to connect them in consciousness through judgment; there arises no universality and necessity, for which alone judgments can become objectively valid and be called experience.

Quite another judgment therefore is required before perception can become experience. The given intuition must be subsumed under a concept, which determines the form of judging in general relatively to the intuition, connects its empirical consciousness in consciousness generally, and thereby procures universal validity for empirical judgments. A concept of this nature is a pure a priori concept of the Understanding, which does nothing but determine for an intuition the general way in which it can be used for judgments. Let the concept be that of cause, then it determined the intuition which is subsumed under it, e.g., that of air, relative to judgments in general, viz., the concept of air serves with regard to its expansion in the relation of antecedent to consequent in a hypothetical judgment. The concept of cause accordingly is a pure concept of the understanding, which is totally disparate from all possible perception, and only serves to determine the representation subsumed under it, relatively to judgments in general, and so to make a universally valid judgment possible.

Before, therefore, a judgment of perception can become a judgment of experience, it is requisite that the perception should be subsumed under some such a concept of the understanding.; for instance, air ranks under the concept of causes, which determines our judgment about it in regard to its expansion as hypothetical. Thereby the expansion of the air is represented not as merely belonging to the perception of the air in my present state or in several states of mine, or in the state of perception of others, but as belonging to it necessarily. The judgment, "the air is elastic," becomes universally valid, and a judgment of experience, only by certain judgments preceding it, which subsume the intuition of air under the concept of cause and effect: and they thereby determine the perceptions not merely as regards one another in me, but relatively to the form of judging in general, which is here hypothetical, and in this way they render the empirical judgment universally valid.

If all our synthetical judgments are analyzed so far as they are objectively valid, it will be found that they never consist of mere intuitions connected only (as is commonly believed) by comparison into a judgment; but that they would be impossible were not a pure concept of the understanding superadded to the concepts abstracted from intuition, under which concept these latter are subsumed, and in this manner only combined into an objectively valid judgment. Even the judgments of pure mathematics in their simplest axioms are not exempt from this condition. The principle, "a straight line is the shortest between two points," presupposes that the line is subsumed under the concept of quantity, which certainly is no mere intuition, but has its seat in the understanding alone, and serves to determine the intuition (of the line) with regard to the judgments which may be made about it, relatively to their quantity, that is, to plurality (as judicia plurativa). For under them it is understood that in a given intuition there is contained a plurality of homogenous parts.

Section 21.

To prove, then, the possibility of experience so far as it rests upon pure concepts of the understanding a priori, we must first represent what belongs to judgments in general and the various functions of the understanding, in a complete table. For the pure concepts of the understanding must run parallel to these functions, as such concepts are nothing more than concepts of intuitions in general, so far as these are determined by one or other of these functions of judging, in themselves, that is, necessarily and universally. Hereby also the a priori principles of the possibility of all experience, as of an objectively valid empirical cognition, will be precisely determined. For they are nothing but propositions by which all perception is (under certain universal conditions of intuition) subsumed under those pure concepts of the understanding.

LOGICAL TABLE OF JUDGMENTS.

1. *As to Quantity.*	2. *As to Quality.*
Universal.	Affirmative.
Particular.	Negative.
Singular.	Infinite.
3. *As to Relation.*	4. *As to Modality.*
Categorical.	Problematical.
Hypothetical.	Assertorical.
Disjunctive.	Apodeictical.

TRANSCENDENTAL TABLE OF THE PURE CONCEPTS OF THE UNDERSTANDING.

1. *As to Quantity.*	2. *As to Quality.*
Unity (the Measure).	Reality.
Plurality (the Quantity).	Negation.
Totality (the Whole).	Limitation.
3. *As to Relation.*	4. *As to Modality.*
Substance.	Possibility.
Cause.	Existence.
Community.	Necessity.

PURE PHYSICAL TABLE OF THE UNIVERSAL PRINCIPLES OF THE SCIENCE OF NATURE.

1. Axioms of Intuition.	2. Anticipations of Perception.

3. Analogies of Experi- ence.	4. Postulates of Empirical Think- ing generally.

Section 21a.

In order to comprise the whole matter in one idea, it is first necessary to remind the reader that we are discussing not the origin of experience, but of that which lies in experience. The former pertains to empirical psychology, and would even then never be adequately explained without the latter, which belongs to the Critique of cognition, and particularly of the understanding.

Experience consists of intuitions, which belong to the sensibility, and of judgments, which are entirely a work of the understanding. But the judgments, which the understanding forms alone from sensuous intuitions, are far from being judgments of experience. For in the one case the judgment connects only the perceptions as they are given in the sensuous intuition, while in the other the judgments must express what experience in general, and not what the mere perception (which possesses only subjective validity) contains. The judgment of experience must therefore add to the sensuous intuition and its logical connection in a judgment (after it has been rendered universal by comparison) something that determines the synthetical judgment as necessary and therefore as universally valid. This can be nothing else than that concept which represents the intuition as determined in itself with regard to one form of judgment rather than another, viz., a concept of that synthetical unity of intuitions which can only be represented by a given logical function of judgments.

Section 22.

The sum of the matter is this: the business of the senses is to intuit — that of the understanding is to think. But thinking is uniting representations in one consciousness. This union originates either merely relative to the subject, and is accidental and subjective, or is absolute, and is necessary or objective. The union of representations in one consciousness is judgment. Thinking therefore is the same as judging, or referring representations to judgments in general. Hence judgments are either merely subjective, when representations are referred to a consciousness in one subject only, and united in it, or objective, when they are united in a consciousness generally, that is, necessarily. The logical functions of all judgments are but various modes of uniting representations in consciousness. But if they serve for concepts, they are concepts of their necessary union in a consciousness, and so principles of objectively valid judgments. This union in a consciousness is either analytical, by identity, or synthetical, by the combination and addition of various representations one to another. Experience consists in the synthetical connection of phenomena (perceptions) in consciousness, so far as this connection is necessary. Hence the pure concepts of the understanding are those under which all perceptions must be subsumed ere they can serve for judgments of experience, in which the synthetical unity of the perceptions is represented as necessary and universally valid.

Section 23.

Judgments, when considered merely as the condition of the union of given representations in a consciousness, are rules. These rules, so far as they represent the union as necessary, are rules a priori, and so far as they cannot be deduced from higher rules, are fundamental principles. But in regard to the possibility of all experience, merely in relation to the form of thinking in it, no conditions of judgments of experience are higher than those which bring the phenomena, according to the various form of their intuition, under pure concepts of the understanding, and render the empirical judgment objectively valid. These concepts are therefore the a priori principles of possible experience.

The principles of possible experience are then at the same time universal laws of nature, which can be known a priori. And thus the problem in our second question, "How is the pure Science of Nature possible?" is solved. For the system which is required for the form of a science is to be met with in perfection here, because, beyond the above-mentioned formal conditions of all judgments in general offered in logic, no others are possible, and these constitute a logical system. The concepts grounded thereupon, which contain the a priori conditions of all synthetical and necessary judgments, accordingly constitute a logical system. The concepts grounded thereupon, which contain the a priori conditions of all synthetical and necessary judgments, accordingly constitute a transcendental system. Finally the principles, by means of which all phenomena are subsumed under these concepts, constitute a physical system, that is, a system of nature, which precedes all empirical cognition of nature, makes it even possible, and hence may in strictness be called the universal and pure natural science.

Section 24.

The first one of the physiological principles [The Axioms of Intuition]] subsumes all phenomena, as intuitions in space and time, under the concept of quantity, and is so far a principle of the application of mathematics to experience. The second one [The Anticipations of Perception] subsumes the empirical element, viz., sensation, which denotes the real in intuitions, not indeed directly under the concept of quantity, because sensation is not an intuition that contains either space or time, though it places the respective object into both. But still there is between reality (sense-representation) and the zero, or total void of intuition in time, a difference which has a quantity. For between every given degree of light and of darkness, between every degree of beat and of absolute cold, between every degree of weight and of absolute lightness, between every degree of occupied space and of totally void space, diminishing degrees can be conceived, in the same manner as between consciousness and total unconsciousness (the darkness of a psychological blank) ever diminishing degrees obtain. Hence there is no perception that can prove an absolute absence of it; for instance, no psychological darkness that cannot be considered as a kind of consciousness, which is only out-balanced by a stronger consciousness. This occurs in all cases of sensation, and so the understanding can anticipate even sensations, which constitute the peculiar quality of empirical representations (appearances), by means of the principle: "that they all have (consequently that what is real in all phenomena has) a degree." Here is the second application of mathematics (mathesis intensortim) to the science of nature.

Section 25.

In the relation of appearances merely with a view to their existence, the determination is not mathematical but dynamical, and can never be objectively valid, consequently never fit for experience, if it does not come under a priori principles [The Analogies of Experience] by which the cognition of experience relative to appearances becomes even possible. Hence appearances must be subsumed under the concept of Substance, which is the foundation of all determination of existence, as a concept of the thing itself; or secondly so far as a succession is found among phenomena, that is, an event — under the concept of an effect with reference to cause; or lastly — so far as coexistence is to be known objectively, that is, by a judgment of experience — under the concept of community (action and reaction). Thus a priori principles form the basis of objectively valid, though empirical judgments, that is, of the possibility of experience so far as it must connect objects as existing in nature. These principles are the proper laws of nature, which may be termed dynamical.

Finally the cognition of the agreement and connection not only of appearances among themselves in experience [The Postulates of Empirical Thought], but of their relation to experience in general, belongs to the judgments of experience. This relation contains either their agreement with the formal conditions, which the understanding knows, or their coherence with the materials of the senses and of perception, or combines both into one concept. Consequently it contains Possibility, Actuality, and Necessity according to universal laws of nature; and this constitutes the physical doctrine of method, or the distinction of truth and of hypotheses, and the bounds of the certainty of the latter.

Section 26.

The third table of principles drawn from the nature of the understanding itself after the critical method, shows an inherent perfection, which raises it far above every other table which has hitherto though in vain been tried or may yet be tried by analyzing the objects themselves dogmatically. It exhibits all synthetical a priori principles completely and according to one principle, viz., the faculty of judging in general, constituting the essence of experience as regards the understanding, so that we can be certain that there are no more such principles, which affords a satisfaction such as can never be attained by the dogmatic method. Yet is this not all: there is a still greater merit in it.

We must carefully bear in mind the proof which shows the possibility of this cognition a priori, and at the same time limits all such principles to a condition which must never be lost sight of, if we desire it not to be misunderstood, and extended in use beyond the original sense which the understanding attaches to it. This limit is that they contain nothing but the conditions of possible experience in general so far as it is Subjected to laws a priori. Consequently I do not say, that things in themselves possess a quantity, that their actuality possesses a degree, their existence a connection of accidents in a substance, etc. This nobody can prove, because such a synthetical connection from mere concepts, without any reference to sensuous intuition on the one side, or connection of it in a possible experience on the other, is absolutely impossible. The essential limitation of the concepts in these principles then is: That all things stand necessarily a priori under the aforementioned conditions only as objects of experience.

Hence there follows secondly a specifically peculiar mode of proof of these principles:

they are not directly referred to appearances and to their relations, but to the possibility of experience, of which appearances constitute the matter only, not the form. Thus they are referred to objectively and universally valid synthetical propositions, in which we distinguish judgments of experience from those of perception. This takes place because appearances, as mere intuitions, occupying a part of space and time, come under the concept of quantity, which unites their multiplicity a priori according to rules synthetically. Again, so far as the perception contains, besides intuition, sensibility, and between the latter and nothing (i.e., the total disappearance of sensibility), there is an ever-decreasing transition, it is apparent that that which is in appearances must have a degree, so far as it (viz., the perception) does not itself occupy any part of space or of time.[P] Still the transition to actuality from empty time or empty space is only possible in time; consequently though sensibility, as the quality of empirical intuition, can never be known a priori, by its specific difference from other sensibilities, yet it can, in a possible experience in general, as a quantity of perception be intensely distinguished from every other similar perception. Hence the application of mathematics to nature, as regards the sensuous intuition by which nature is given to us, becomes possible and is thus determined.

Above all, the reader must pay attention to the mode of proof of the principles which occur under the title of Analogies of Experience. For these do not refer to the genesis of intuitions, as do the principles of applied mathematics, but to the connection of their existence in experience; and this can be nothing but the determination of their existence in time according to necessary laws, under which alone the connection is objectively valid, and thus becomes experience. The proof therefore does not turn on the synthetical unity in the connection of things in themselves, but merely of perceptions, and of these not in regard to their matter, but to the determination of time and of the relation of their existence in it, according to universal laws. If the empirical determination in relative time is indeed objectively valid (i.e., experience), these universal laws contain the necessary determination of existence in time generally (viz., according to a rule of the understanding a priori). In a Prolegomena I cannot further descant on the subject, but my reader (who has probably been long accustomed to consider experience a mere empirical synthesis of perceptions, and hence not considered that it goes much beyond them, as it imparts to empirical judgments universal validity, and for that purpose requires a pure and a priori unity of the understanding) is recommended to pay special attention to this distinction of experience from a mere aggregate of perceptions, and to judge the mode of proof from this point of view.

Section 27.

Now we are prepared to remove Hume's doubt. He justly maintains, that we cannot comprehend by reason the possibility of causality, that is, of the reference of the existence of one thing to the existence of another, which is necessitated by the former. I add, that we comprehend just as little the concept of Subsistence, that is, the necessity that at the foundation of the existence of things there lies a subject which cannot itself be a predicate of any other thing; nay, we cannot even form a notion of the possibility of such a thing (though we can point out examples of its use in experience). The very same incomprehensibility affects the Community of things, as we cannot comprehend how from the state of one thing an inference to the state of quite another thing beyond it, and vice versa, can be drawn, and how substances which have each their own separate existence should depend upon one another necessarily. But I am very far from holding these concepts to be derived merely from experience, and the necessity represented in them, to be imaginary and a mere illusion produced in us by long habit. On the contrary, I have amply shown, that they and the theorems derived from them are firmly established a priori, or before all experience, and have their undoubted objective value, though only with regard to experience.

Section 28.

Though I have no notion of such a connection of things in themselves, that they can either exist as substances, or act as causes, or stand in community with others (as parts of a real whole), and I can just as little conceive such properties in appearances as such (because those concepts contain nothing that lies in the appearances, but only what the understanding alone must think): we have yet a notion of such a connection of representations in our understanding, and in judgments generally; consisting in this that representations appear in one sort of judgments as subject in relation to predicates, in another as reason in relation to consequences, and in a third as parts, which constitute together a total possible cognition. Besides we know a priori that without considering the representation of an object as determined in some of these respects, we can have no valid cognition of the object, and, if we should occupy ourselves about the object in itself, there is no possible attribute, by which I could know that it is determined under any of these aspects, that is, under the concept either of substance, or of cause, or (in relation to other substances) of community, for I have no notion of the possibility of such a connection of existence. But the question is not how things in themselves, but how the empirical cognition of things is determined as regards the above aspects of judgments in general, that is, how things, as objects of experience, can and shall be subsumed under these concepts of the understanding. And then it is clear, that I completely comprehend not only the possibility, but also the necessity of subsuming all phenomena under these concepts, that is, of using them for principles of the possibility of experience.

Section 29.

When making an experiment with Hume's problematical concept (his crux metaphysicorum), the concept of cause, we have, in the first place, given a priori, by means of logic, the form of a conditional judgment in general, i.e., we have one given cognition as antecedent and another as consequence. But it is possible, that in perception we may meet with a rule of relation, which runs thus: that a certain phenomenon is constantly followed by another (though not conversely), and this is a case for me to use the hypothetical judgment, and, for instance, to say, if the sun shines long enough upon a body, it grows warm. Here there is indeed as yet no necessity of connection, or concept of cause. But I proceed and say, that if this proposition, which is merely a subjective connection of perceptions, is to be a judgment of experience, it must be considered as necessary and universally valid. Such a proposition would be, "the sun is by its light the cause of heat." The empirical rule is now considered as a law, and as valid not merely of appearances but valid of them for the purposes of a possible experience which requires universal and therefore necessarily valid rules. I therefore easily comprehend the concept of cause, as a concept necessarily belonging to the mere form of experience, and its possibility as a synthetical union of perceptions in consciousness generally; but I do not at all comprehend the possibility of a thing generally as a cause, because the concept of cause denotes a condition not at all belonging to things, but to experience. It is nothing in fact but an objectively valid cognition of appearances and of their succession, so far as the antecedent can be conjoined with the consequent according to the rule of hypothetical judgments.

Section 30.

Hence if the pure concepts of the understanding do not refer to objects of experience but to things in themselves (noumena), they have no signification whatever. They serve, as it were, only to decipher appearances, that we may be able to read them as experience. The principles which arise from their reference to the sensible world, only serve our understanding for empirical use. Beyond this they are arbitrary combinations, without objective reality, and we can neither know their possibility a priori, nor verify their reference to objects, let alone make it intelligible by any example; because examples can only be borrowed from some possible experience, consequently the objects of these concepts can be found nowhere but in a possible experience.

This complete (though to its originator unexpected) solution of Hume's problem rescues for the pure concepts of the understanding their a priori origin, and for the universal laws of nature their validity, as laws of the understanding, yet in such a way as to limit their use to experience, because their possibility depends solely on the reference of the understanding to experience, but with a completely reversed mode of connection which never occurred to Hume, not by deriving them from experience, but by deriving experience from them.

This is therefore the result of all our foregoing inquiries: "All synthetical principles a priori are nothing more than principles of possible experience," and can never be referred to things in themselves, but to appearances as objects of experience. And hence pure mathematics as well as a pure science of nature can never be referred to anything more than mere appearances, and can only represent either that which makes experience generally possible, or else that which, as it is derived from these principles, must always be capable of being represented in some possible experience.

Section 31.

And thus we have at last something definite, upon which to depend in all metaphysical enterprises, which have hitherto, boldly enough but always at random, attempted everything without discrimination. That the aim of their exertions should be so near, struck neither the dogmatical thinkers nor those who, confident in their supposed sound common sense, started with concepts and principles of pure reason (which were legitimate and natural, but destined for mere empirical use) in quest of fields of knowledge, to which they neither knew nor could know any determinate bounds, because they bad never reflected nor were able to reflect on the nature or even on the possibility of such a pure understanding.

Many a naturalist of pure reason (by which I mean the man who believes he can decide in matters of metaphysics without any science) may pretend, that lie long ago by the prophetic spirit of his sound sense, not only suspected, but knew and comprehended, what is here propounded with so much ado, or, if he likes, with prolix and pedantic pomp: "that with all our reason we can never reach beyond the field of experience." But when he is questioned about his rational principles individually, he must grant, that there are many of them which be has not taken from experience, and which are therefore independent of it and valid a priori. How then and on what grounds will he restrain both himself and the dogmatist, who makes use of these concepts and principles beyond all possible experience, because they are recognized to be independent of it? And even he, this adept in sound sense, in spite of all his assumed and cheaply acquired wisdom, is not exempt from wandering inadvertently beyond objects of experience into the field of chimeras. He is often deeply enough involved in them, though in announcing everything as mere probability, rational conjecture, or analogy, be gives by his popular language a color to his groundless pretensions.

Section 32.

Since the oldest days of philosophy inquirers into pure reason have conceived, besides the things of sense, or appearances (phenomena), which make up the sensible world, certain creations of the understanding, called noumena, which should constitute an intelligible world. And as appearance and illusion were by those men identified (a thing which we may well excuse in an undeveloped epoch), actuality was only conceded to the beings of thought.

And we indeed, rightly considering objects of sense as mere appearances, confess thereby that they are based upon a thing in itself, though we know not this thing as it is in itself, but only know its appearances, viz., the way in which our senses are affected by this unknown something. The understanding therefore, by assuming appearances, grants the existence of things in themselves also, and so far we may say, that the representation of such things as form the basis of phenomena, consequently of mere creations of the understanding, is not only admissible, but unavoidable.

Our critical deduction by no means excludes things of that sort (noumena), but rather limits the principles of the Aesthetic [the science of the sensibility] in such a way that they shall not extend to all things, as everything would then be turned into mere appearance, but that they shall only hold good of objects of possible experience. Hereby then objects of the understanding are granted, but with the inculcation of this rule which admits of no exception: that we neither know nor can know anything at all definite of these pure objects of the understanding, because our pure concepts of the understanding as well as our pure intuitions extend to nothing but objects of possible experience, consequently to mere things of sense, and as soon as we leave this sphere these concepts retain no meaning whatever.

Section 33.

There is indeed something seductive in our pure concepts of the understanding, which tempts us to a transcendent use, — a use which transcends all possible experience. Not only are our concepts of substance, of power, of action, of reality, and others, quite independent of experience, containing nothing of sense appearance, and so apparently applicable to things in themselves (noumena), but, what strengthens this conjecture, they contain a necessity of determination in themselves, which experience never attains. The concept of cause implies a rule, according to which one state follows another necessarily; but experience can only show us, that one state of things often, or at most, commonly, follows another, and therefore affords neither strict universality, nor necessity.

Hence the concepts of the understanding [categories] have a deeper meaning and import than can be exhausted by their empirical use, and so the understanding inadvertently adds for itself to the house of experience a much more extensive wing, which it fills with nothing but creatures of thought, without ever observing that it has transgressed with its otherwise lawful concepts the bounds of their use.

Section 34.

Two important, and even indispensable, though very dry, investigations had therefore become indispensable in the Critique of Pure Reason [viz., the two chapters "The Schematism of the Pure Concepts of the Understanding" and "The Ground of the Distinction of All Objects in General into Phenomena and Noumena]. In the former it is shown, that the senses furnish not the pure concepts of the understanding in concreto, but only the schedule for their use, and that the object conformable to it occurs only in experience (as the product of the understanding from materials of the sensibility). In the latter it is shown, that, although our pure concepts of the understanding and our principles are independent of experience, and despite of the apparently greater sphere of their use, still nothing whatever can be thought by them beyond the field of experience, because they can do nothing but merely determine the logical form of the judgment relatively to given intuitions. But as there is no intuition at all beyond the field of the sensibility, these pure concepts, as they cannot possibly be exhibited in concreto, are void of all meaning; consequently all these noumena, together with their complex, the intelligible world,[P] are nothing but representation of a problem, of which the object in itself is possible, but the solution, from the nature of our understanding, totally impossible. For our understanding is not a faculty of intuition, but of the connection of given intuitions in experience. Experience must therefore contain all the objects for our concepts; but beyond it no concepts have any significance, as there is no intuition that might be subsumed under them.

Section 35.

The imagination may perhaps be forgiven for occasional vagaries, and for not keeping carefully within the limits of experience, since it gains life and vigor by such flights, and since it is always easier to moderate its boldness, than to stimulate its languor. But the understanding which ought to think can never be forgiven for indulging in vagaries; for we depend upon it alone for assistance to set bounds, when necessary, to the vagaries of the imagination.

But the understanding begins its aberrations very innocently and modestly. It first elucidates the elementary cognitions, which inhere in it prior to all experience, but yet must always have their application in experience. It gradually drops these limits, and what is there to prevent it, as it has quite freely derived its principles from itself? And then it proceeds first to newly-imagined powers in nature, then to beings outside nature; in short to a world, for whose construction the materials cannot be wanting, because fertile fiction furnishes them abundantly, and though not confirmed, is never refuted, by experience. This is the reason that young thinkers arc so partial to metaphysics of the truly dogmatical kind, and often sacrifice to it their time and their talents, which might be otherwise better employed.

But there is no use in trying to moderate these fruitless endeavors of pure reason by all manner of cautions as to the difficulties of solving questions so occult, by complaints of the limits of our reason, and by degrading our assertions into mere conjectures. For if their impossibility is not distinctly shown, and reason's cognition of its own essence does not become a true science, in which the field of its right use is distinguished, so to say, with mathematical certainty from that of its worthless and idle use, these fruitless efforts will never be abandoned for good.

How is Nature itself possible?

Section 36.

This question — the highest point that transcendental philosophy can ever reach, and to which, as its boundary and completion, it must proceed-properly contains two questions.

First: How is nature at all possible in the material sense, by intuition, considered as the totality of appearances; how are space, time, and that which fills both — the object of sensation, in general possible? The answer is: By means of the constitution of our Sensibility, according to which it is specifically affected by objects, which are in themselves unknown to it, and totally distinct from those appearances. This answer is given in the Critique itself in the Transcendental Aesthetic, and in these Prolegomena by the solution of the first general problem.

Secondly: How is nature possible in the formal sense, as the totality of the rules, under which all phenomena must come, in order to be thought as connected in experience? The answer must be this: it is only possible by means of the constitution of our Understanding, according to which all the above representations of the sensibility are necessarily referred to a consciousness, and by which the peculiar way in which we think (viz., by rules), and hence experience also, are possible, but must be clearly distinguished from an insight into the objects in themselves. This answer is given in the Critique itself in the Transcendental Logic, and in these Prolegomena, in the course of the solution of the second main problem.

But how this peculiar property of our sensibility itself is possible, or that of our understanding and of the apperception which is necessarily its basis and that of all thinking, cannot be further analyzed or answered, because it is of them that we are in need for all our answers and for all our thinking about objects.

There are many laws of nature, which we can only know by means of experience; but conformity to law in the connection of appearances, i.e., in nature in general, we cannot discover by any experience, because experience itself requires laws which are a priori at the basis of its possibility.

The possibility of experience in general is therefore at the same time the universal law of nature, and the principles of the experience are the very laws of nature. For we do not know nature but as the totality of appearances, i.e., of representations in us, and hence we can only derive the laws of its connection from the principles of their connection in us, that is, from the conditions of their necessary union in consciousness, which constitutes the possibility of experience.

Even the main proposition expounded throughout this section — that universal laws of nature can be distinctly known a priori — leads naturally to the proposition: that the highest legislation of nature must lie in ourselves, i.e., in our understanding, and that we must not seek the universal laws of nature in nature by means of experience, but conversely must seek nature, as to its universal conformity to law, in the conditions of the possibility of experience, which lie in our sensibility and in our understanding. For how were it otherwise possible to know a priori these laws, as they are not rules of analytical cognition, but truly synthetical extensions of it? Such a necessary agreement of the principles of possible experience with the laws of the possibility of nature, can only proceed from one of two reasons: either these laws are drawn from nature by means of experience, or conversely nature is derived from the laws of the possibility of experience in general, and is quite the same as the mere universal conformity to law of the latter. The former is self-contradictory, for the universal laws of nature can and must be known a priori (that is, independent of all experience), and be the foundation of all empirical use of the understanding; the latter alternative therefore alone remains.[P]

But we must distinguish the empirical laws of nature, which always presuppose particular perceptions, from the pure or universal laws of nature, which, without being based on particular perceptions, contain merely the conditions of their necessary union in experience. In relation to the latter, nature and possible experience are quite the same, and as the conformity to law here depends upon the necessary connection of appearances in experience (without which we cannot know any object whatever in the sensible world), consequently upon the original laws of the understanding, it seems at first strange, but is not the less certain, to say: the understanding does not derive its laws (a priori) from, but prescribes them to, nature.

Section 37.

We shall illustrate this seemingly bold proposition by an example, which will show, that laws, which we discover in objects of sensuous intuition (especially when these laws are known as necessary), are commonly held by us to be such as have been placed there by the understanding, in spite of their being similar in all points to the laws of nature, which we ascribe to experience.

Section 38.

If we consider the properties of the circle, by which this figure combines so many arbitrary determinations of space in itself, at once in a universal rule, we cannot avoid attributing a nature to this geometrical thing. Two right lines, for example, which intersect one another and the circle, howsoever they may be drawn, are always divided so that the rectangle constructed with the segments of the one is equal to that constructed with the segments of the other. The question now is: Does this law lie in the circle or in the understanding, that is, Does this figure, independently of the understanding, contain in itself the ground of the law, or does the understanding, having constructed according to its concepts (according to the quality of the radii) the figure itself, introduce into it this law of the chords cutting one another in geometrical proportion? When we follow the proofs of this law, we soon perceive, that it can only be derived from the condition on which the understanding founds the construction of this figure, and which is that of the equality of the radii. But, if we enlarge this concept, to pursue further the unity of various properties of geometrical figures under common laws, and consider the circle as a conic section, which of course is subject to the same fundamental conditions of construction as other conic sections, we shall find that all the chords which intersect within the ellipse, parabola, and hyperbola, always intersect so that the rectangles of their segments are not indeed equal, but always bear a constant ratio to one another. If we proceed still farther, to the fundamental laws of physical astronomy, we find a physical law of reciprocal attraction diffused over all material nature, the rule of which is: "that it decreases inversely as the square of the distance from each attracting point, i.e., as the spherical surfaces increase, over which this force spreads," which law seems to be necessarily inherent in the very nature of things, and hence is usually propounded as knowable a priori. Simple as the sources of this law are, merely resting upon the relation of spherical surfaces of different radii, its consequences are so valuable with regard to the variety of their agreement and its regularity, that not only are all possible orbits of the celestial bodies conic sections, but such a relation of these orbits to each other results, that no other law of attraction, than that of the inverse square of the distance, can be imagined as fit for a cosmical system.

Here accordingly is a nature that rests upon laws which the understanding knows a priori, and chiefly from the universal principles of the determination of space. Now I ask: Do the laws of nature lie in space, and does the understanding learn them by merely endeavoring to find out the enormous wealth of meaning that lies in space; or do they inhere in the understanding and in the way in which it determines space according to the conditions of the synthetical unity in which its concepts are all centered? Space is something so uniform and as to all particular properties so indeterminate, that we should certainly not seek a store of laws of nature in it. Whereas that which determines space to assume the form of a circle or the figures of a cone and a sphere, is the understanding, so far as it contains the ground of the unity of their constructions. The mere universal form of intuition, called space, must therefore be the substratum of all intuitions determinable to particular objects, and in it of course the condition of the possibility and of the variety of these intuitions lies. But the unity of the objects is entirely determined by the understanding, and on conditions which lie in its own nature; and thus the understanding is the origin of the universal order of nature, in that it comprehends all appearances under its own laws, and thereby first constructs, a priori, experience (as to its form), by means of which whatever is to be known only by experience, is necessarily subjected to its laws. For we are not now concerned with the nature of things in themselves, which is independent of the conditions both of our sensibility and our understanding, but with nature, as an object of possible experience, and in this case the understanding, whilst it makes experience possible, thereby insists that the sensuous world is either not an object of experience at all, or else is nature.

APPENDIX TO THE PURE SCIENCE OF NATURE.

Section 39.

Of the System of the Categories. There can be nothing more desirable to a philosopher, than to be able to derive the scattered multiplicity of the concepts or the principles, which had occurred to him in concrete use, from a principle a priori, and to unite everything in this way in one cognition. He formerly only believed that those things, which remained after a certain abstraction, and seemed by comparison among one another to constitute a particular kind of cognitions, were completely collected; but this was only an aggregate. Now he knows, that just so many, neither more nor less, can constitute the mode of cognition, and perceives the necessity of his division, which constitutes comprehension; and now only he has attained a system.

To search in our daily cognition for the concepts, which do not rest upon particular experience, and yet occur in all cognition of experience, where they as it were constitute the mere form of connection, presupposes neither greater reflection nor deeper insight, than to detect in a language the rules of the actual use of words generally, and thus to collect elements for a grammar. In fact both researches are very nearly related, even though we are not able to give a reason why each language has just this and no other formal constitution, and still less why an exact number of such formal determinations in general are found in it.

Aristotle collected ten pure elementary concepts under the name of Categories. To these, which are also called predicaments, he found himself obliged afterwards to add five post-predicaments, some of which however (prius, simul, and motus) are contained in the former; but this random collection must be considered (and commended) as a mere hint for future inquirers, not as a regularly developed idea, and hence it has, in the present more advanced state of philosophy, been rejected as quite useless.

After long reflection on the pure elements of human knowledge (those which contain nothing empirical), I at last succeeded in distinguishing with certainty and in separating the pure elementary notions of the Sensibility (space and time) from those of the Understanding. Thus the 7th, 8th, and 8th Categories had to be excluded from the old list. And the others were of no service to me; because there was no principle [in them], on which the understanding could be investigated, measured in its completion, and all the functions, whence its pure concepts arise, determined exhaustively and with precision.

But in order to discover such a principle, I looked about for an act of the understanding which comprises all the rest, and is distinguished only by various modifications or phases, in reducing the multiplicity of representation to the unity of thinking in general: I found this act of the understanding to consist in judging. Here then the labors of the logicians were ready at hand, though not yet quite free from defects, and with this help I was enabled to exhibit a complete table of the pure functions of the understanding, which are however undetermined in regard to any object. I finally referred these functions of judging to objects in general, or rather to the condition of determining judgments as objectively valid, and so there arose the pure concepts of the understanding, concerning which I could make certain, that these, and this exact number only, constitute our whole cognition of things from pure understanding. I was justified in calling them by their old name, categories, while I reserved for myself the liberty of adding, under the title of predicables, a complete list of all the concepts deducible from them, by combinations whether among themselves, or with the pure form of the appearance, i.e., space or time, or with its matter, so far as it is not yet empirically determined (viz., the object of sensation in general), as soon as a system of transcendental philosophy should be completed with the construction of which I am engaged in the Critique of Pure Reason itself.

Now the essential point in this system of categories, which distinguishes it from the old rhapsodical collection without any principle, and for which alone it deserves to be considered as philosophy, consists in this: that by means of it the true significance of the pure concepts of the understanding and the condition of their use could be precisely determined. For here it became obvious that they are themselves nothing but logical functions, and as such do not produce the least concept of an object, but require some sensuous intuition as a basis. They therefore only serve to determine empirical judgments, which are otherwise undetermined and indifferent as regards all functions of judging, relatively to these functions, thereby procuring them universal validity, and by means of them making judgments of experience in general possible.

Such an insight into the nature of the categories, which limits them at the same time to the mere use of experience, never occurred either to their first author, or to any of his successors; but without this insight (which immediately depends upon their derivation or deduction), they are quite useless and only a miserable list of names, without explanation or rule for their use. Had the ancients ever conceived such a notion, doubtless the whole study of the pure rational knowledge, which under the name of metaphysics has for centuries spoiled many a sound mind, would have reached us in quite another shape, and would have enlightened the human understanding, instead of actually exhausting it in obscure and vain speculations, thereby rendering it unfit for true science.

This system of categories makes all treatment of every object of pure reason itself systematic, and affords a direction or clue how and through what points of inquiry every metaphysical consideration must proceed, in order to be complete; for it exhausts all the possible movements (momenta) of the understanding, among which every concept must be classed. In like manner the table of Principles has been formulated, the completeness of which we can only vouch for by the system of the categories. Even in the division of the concepts, which must go beyond the physical application of the understanding, it is always the very same clue, which, as it must always be determined a priori by the same fixed points of the human understanding, always forms a closed circle. There is no doubt that the object of a pure conception either of the understanding or of reason, so far as it is to be estimated philosophically and on a priori principles, can in this way be completely known. I could not therefore omit to make use of this clue with regard to one of the most abstract ontological divisions, viz., the various distinctions of "the notions of something and of nothing," and to construct accordingly (Critique, B402, B442-3) a regular and necessary table of their divisions (Critique, B348).

And this system, like every other true one founded on a universal principle, shows its inestimable value in this, that it excludes all foreign concepts, which might otherwise intrude among the pure concepts of the understanding, and determines the place of every cognition. Those concepts, which under the name of "concepts of reflection" have been likewise arranged in a table according to the clue of the categories, intrude, without having any privilege or title to be among the pure concepts of the understanding in Ontology. They are concepts of connection, and thereby of the objects themselves, whereas the former are only concepts of a mere comparison of concepts already given, hence of quite another nature and use. By my systematic division they are saved from this confusion. But the value of my special table of the categories will be still more obvious, when we separate the table of the transcendental concepts of Reason from the concepts of the understanding. The latter being of quite another nature and origin, they must have quite another form than the former. This so necessary separation has never yet been made in any system of metaphysics for, as a rule, these rational concepts all mixed up with the categories, like children of one family, which confusion was unavoidable in the absence of a definite system of categories.

THIRD PART OF THE MAIN TRANSCENDENTAL PROBLEM. HOW IS METAPHYSICS IN GENERAL POSSIBLE?

Section 40.

Pure mathematics and pure science of nature had no occasion for such a deduction, as we have made of both, for their own safety and certainty. For the former rests upon its own evidence; and the latter (though sprung from pure sources of the understanding) upon experience and its thorough confirmation. Physics cannot altogether refuse and dispense with the testimony of the latter; because with all its certainty, it can never, as philosophy, rival mathematics. Both sciences therefore stood in need of this inquiry, not for themselves, but for the sake of another science, metaphysics.

Metaphysics has to do not only with concepts of nature, which always find their application in experience, but also with pure rational concepts, which never can be given in any possible experience. Consequently the objective reality of these concepts (viz., that they are not mere chimeras), and the truth or falsity of metaphysical assertions, cannot be discovered or confirmed by any experience. This part of metaphysics however is precisely what constitutes its essential end, to which the rest is only a means, and thus this science is in need of such a deduction for its own sake. The third question now proposed relates therefore as it were to the root and essential difference of metaphysics, i.e., the occupation of Reason with itself, and the supposed knowledge of objects arising immediately from this incubation of its own concepts, without requiring, or indeed being able to reach that knowledge through, experience.

Without solving this problem reason never is justified. The empirical use to which reason limits the pure understanding, does not fully satisfy the proper destination of the latter. Every single experience is only a part of the whole sphere of its domain, but the absolute totality of all possible experience is itself not experience. Yet it is a necessary [concrete] problem for reason, the mere representation of which requires concepts quite different from the categories, whose use is only immanent, or refers to experience, so far as it can be given. Whereas the concepts of reason aim at the completeness, i.e., the collective unity of all possible experience, and thereby transcend every given experience. Thus they become transcendent.

As the understanding stands in need of categories for experience, reason contains in itself the source of ideas, by which I mean necessary concepts, whose object cannot be given in any experience. The latter are inherent in the nature of reason, as the former are in that of the understanding. While the former carry with them an illusion likely to mislead, the illusion of the latter is inevitable, though it certainly can be kept from misleading us.

Since all illusion consists in holding the subjective ground of our judgments to be objective, a self-knowledge of pure reason in its transcendent (exaggerated) use is the sole preservative from the aberrations into which reason falls when it mistakes its destination, and refers that to the object transcendently, which only regards its own subject and its guidance in all immanent use.

Section 41.

The distinction of ideas, that is, of pure concepts of reason, from categories, or pure concepts of the understanding, as cognitions of a quite distinct species, origin and use, is so important a point in founding a science which is to contain the system of all these a priori cognitions, that without this distinction metaphysics is absolutely impossible, or is at best a random, bungling attempt to build a castle in the air without a knowledge of the materials or of their fitness for any purpose. Had the Critique of Pure Reason done nothing but first point out this distinction, it had thereby contributed more to clear up our conception of, and to guide our inquiry in, the field of metaphysics, than all the vain efforts which have hitherto been made to satisfy the transcendent problems of pure reason, without ever surmising that we were in quite another field than that of the understanding, and hence classing concepts of the understanding and those of reason together, as if they were of the same kind.

Section 42.

All pure cognitions of the understanding have this feature, that their concepts present themselves in experience, and their principles can be confirmed by it; whereas the transcendent cognitions of reason cannot, either as ideas, appear in experience, or, as propositions, ever be confirmed or refuted by it. Hence whatever errors may slip in unawares, can only be discovered by pure reason itself — a discovery of much difficulty, because this very reason naturally becomes dialectical by means of its ideas, and this unavoidable illusion cannot be limited by any objective and dogmatical researches into things, but by a subjective investigation of reason itself as a source of ideas.

Section 43.

In the Critique of Pure Reason it was always my greatest care to endeavor not only carefully to distinguish the several species of cognition, but to derive concepts belonging to each one of them from their common source. I did this in order that by knowing whence they originated, I might determine their use with safety, and also have the unanticipated but invaluable advantage of knowing the completeness of my enumeration, classification and specification of concepts a priori, and therefore knowing it according to principles. Without this, metaphysics is mere rhapsody, in which no one knows whether he has enough, or whether and where something is still wanting. We can indeed have this advantage only in pure philosophy, but of this philosophy it constitutes the very essence.

As I had found the origin of the categories in the four logical functions of all the judgments of the understanding, it was quite natural to seek the origin of the ideas in the three functions of the syllogisms of reason. For as soon as these pure concepts of reason (the transcendental ideas) are given, they could hardly, except they be held innate, be found anywhere else, than in the same activity of reason, which, so far as it regards mere form, constitutes the logical element of the syllogisms of reason; but, so far as it represents judgments of the understanding with respect to the one or to the other form a priori, constitutes transcendental concepts of pure reason.

The formal distinction of syllogisms renders their division into categorical, hypothetical, and disjunctive necessary. The concepts of reason founded on them contained therefore, first, the idea of the complete subject (the substantial); secondly, the idea of the complete series of conditions; thirdly, the determination of all concepts in the idea of a complete complex of that which is possible. The first idea is psychological, the second cosmological, the third theological, and, as all three give occasion to Dialectics, yet each in its own way, the division of the whole Dialects of pure reason into its paralogism, its Antinomy, and its Ideal, was arranged accordingly. Through this deduction we may feel assured that all the claims of pure reason are completely represented, and that none can be wanting; because the faculty of reason itself, whence they all take their origin, is thereby completely surveyed.

Section 44.

In these general considerations it is also remarkable that the ideas of reason are unlike the categories, of no service to the use of our understanding in experience, but quite dispensable, and become even an impediment to the maxims of a rational cognition of nature. Yet in another aspect still to be determined they are necessary. Whether the soul is or is not a simple substance, is of no consequence to us in the explanation of its phenomena. For we cannot render the notion of a simple being intelligible by any possible experience that is sensuous or concrete. The notion is therefore quite void as regards all hoped-for insight into the cause of phenomena, and cannot at all serve as a principle of the explanation of that which internal or external experience supplies. So the cosmological ideas of the beginning of the world or of its eternity (a parte ante) cannot be of any greater service to us for the explanation of any event in the world itself. And finally we must, according to a right maxim of the philosophy of nature, refrain from all explanations of the design of nature, drawn from the will of a Supreme Being; because this would not be natural philosophy, but an acknowledgment that we have come to the end of it. The use of these ideas, therefore, is quite different from that of those categories by which (and by the principles built upon which) experience itself first becomes possible. But our laborious analytics of the understanding would be superfluous if we had nothing else in view than the mere cognition Of nature as it can be given in experience; for reason does its work, both in mathematics and in the science of nature, quite safely and well without any of this subtle deduction. Therefore our critique of the understanding combines with the ideas of pure reason for a purpose which lies beyond the empirical use of the understanding; but this we have above declared to be in this aspect totally inadmissible, and without any object or meaning. Yet there must be a harmony between that of the nature of reason and that of the understanding, and the former must contribute to the perfection of the latter, and cannot possibly upset it.

The solution of this question is as follows: Pure reason does not in its ideas point to particular objects, which lie beyond the field of experience, but only requires completeness of the use of the understanding in the system of experience. But this completeness can be a completeness of principles only, not of intuitions and of objects. In order however to represent the ideas definitely, reason conceives them after the fashion of the cognition of an object. The cognition is as far as these rules are concerned completely determined, but the object is only an idea invented for the purpose of bringing the cognition of the understanding as near as possible to the completeness represented by that idea.

Prefatory Remark to the Dialectics of Pure Reason

Section 45.

We have above shown in Section s 33 and 34 that the purity of the categories from all admixture of sensuous determinations may mislead reason into extending their use, quite beyond all experience, to things in themselves; though as these categories themselves find no intuition which can give them meaning or sense in concreto, they, as mere logical functions, can represent a thing in general, but not give by themselves alone a determinate concept of anything.

Such hyperbolical objects are distinguished by the appellation of noumena, or pure beings of the understanding (or better, beings of thought), such as, for example, "substance," but conceived without permanence in time, or "cause," but not acting in time, etc. Here predicates, that only serve to make the conformity-to-law of experience possible, are applied to these concepts, and yet they are deprived of all the conditions of intuition, on which alone experience is possible, and so these concepts lose all significance.

There is no danger, however, of the understanding spontaneously making an excursion so very wantonly beyond its own bounds into the field of the mere creatures of thought, without being impelled by foreign laws. But when reason, which cannot be fully satisfied with any empirical use of the rules of the understanding, as being always conditioned, requires a completion of this chain of conditions, then the understanding is forced out of its sphere. And then it partly represents objects of experience in a series so extended that no experience can grasp, partly even (with a view to complete the series) it seeks entirely beyond it noumena, to which it can attach that chain, and so, having at last escaped from the conditions of experience, make its attitude as it were final. These are then the transcendental ideas, which, though according to the true but hidden ends of the natural determination of our reason, they may aim not at extravagant concepts, but at an unbounded extension of their empirical use, yet seduce the understanding by an unavoidable illusion to a transcendent use, which, though deceitful, cannot be restrained within the bounds of experience by any resolution, but only by scientific instruction and with much difficulty.

The Psychological Idea

Section 46.

People have long since observed, that in all substances the proper subject, that which remains after all the accidents (as predicates) are abstracted, consequently that which forms the substance of things remains unknown, and various complaints have been made concerning these limits to our knowledge. But it will be well to consider that the human understanding is not to be blamed for its inability to know the substance of things, that is, to determine it by itself, but rather for requiring to know it which is a mere idea definitely as though it were a given object. Pure reason requires us to seek for every predicate of a thing its proper subject, and for this subject, which is itself necessarily nothing but a predicate, its subject, and so on indefinitely (or as far as we can reach). But hence it follows, that we must not hold anything, at which we can arrive, to be an ultimate subject, and that substance itself never can be thought by our understanding, however deep we may penetrate, even if all nature were unveiled to us. For the specific nature of our understanding consists in thinking everything discursively, that is, representing it by concepts, and so by mere predicates, to which therefore the absolute subject must always be wanting. Hence all the real properties, by which we know bodies, are mere accidents, not excepting impenetrability, which we can only represent to ourselves as the effect of a power of which the subject is unknown to us.

Now we appear to have this substance in the consciousness of ourselves (in the thinking subject), and indeed in an immediate intuition; for all the predicates of an internal sense refer to the ego, as a subject, and I cannot conceive myself as the predicate of any other subject. Hence completeness in the reference of the given concepts as predicates to a subject — not merely an idea, but an object — that is, the absolute subject itself, seems to be given in experience. But this expectation is disappointed. For the ego is not a concept, but only the indication of the object of the internal sense, so far as we know it by no further predicate. Consequently it cannot be in itself a predicate of any other thing; but just as little can it be a determinate concept of an absolute subject, but is, as in all other cases, only the reference of the internal phenomena to their unknown subject. Yet this idea (which serves very well, as a regulative principle, totally to destroy all materialistic explanations of the internal phenomena of the soul) occasions by a very natural misunderstanding a very specious argument, which, from this supposed cognition of the substance of our thinking being, infers its nature, so far as the knowledge of it falls quite without the complex of experience.

Section 47.

But though we may call this thinking self (the soul) substance, as being the ultimate subject of thinking which cannot be further represented as the predicate of another thing; it remains quite empty and without significance, if permanence — the quality which renders the concept of substances in experience fruitful — cannot be proved of it.

But permanence can never be proved of the concept of a substance, as a thing in itself, but for the purposes of experience only. This is sufficiently shown by the first Analogy of Experience [Critique, B224 ff.], and whoever will not yield to this proof may try for himself whether he can succeed in proving, from the concept of a subject which does not exist itself as the predicate of another thing, that its existence is thoroughly permanent, and that it cannot either in itself or by any natural cause original or be annihilated. These synthetical a priori propositions can never be proved in themselves, but only in reference to things as objects of possible experience.

Section 48.

If therefore from the concept of the soul as a substance, we would infer its permanence, this can hold good as regards possible experience only, not [of the soul] as a thing in itself and beyond all possible experience. But life is the subjective condition of all our possible experience, consequently we can only infer the permanence of the soul in life; for the death of man is the end of all experience which concerns the soul as an object of experience, except the contrary be proved, which is the very question in hand. The permanence of the soul can therefore only be proved (and no one cares for that) during the life of man, but not, as we desire to do, after death; and for this general reason, that the concept of substance, so far as it is to be considered necessarily combined with the concept of permanence, can be so combined only according to the principles of possible experience, and therefore for the purposes of experience only.

Section 49.

That there is something real without us which not only corresponds, but must correspond, to our external perceptions, can likewise be proved to be not a connection of things in themselves, but for the sake of experience. This means that there is something empirical, i.e., some phenomenon in space without us, that admits of a satisfactory proof, for we have nothing to do with other objects than those which belong to possible experience; because objects which cannot be given us in any experience, do not exist for us. Empirically without me is that which appears in space, and space, together with all the phenomena which it contains, belongs to the representations, whose connection according to laws of experience proves their objective truth, just as the connection of the phenomena of the internal sense proves the actuality of my soul (as an object of the internal sense). By means of external experience I am conscious of the actuality of bodies, as external phenomena in space, in the same manner as by means of the internal experience I am conscious of the existence of my soul in time, but this soul is only known as an object of the internal sense by phenomena that constitute an internal state, and of which the essence in itself, which forms the basis of these phenomena, is unknown. Cartesian idealism therefore does nothing but distinguish external experience from dreaming; and the conformity to law (as a criterion of its truth) of the former, from the irregularity and the false illusion of the latter. In both it presupposes space and time as conditions of the existence of objects, and it only inquires whether the objects of the external senses, which we when awake put in space, are as actually to be found in it, as the object of the internal sense, the soul, is in time; that is, whether experience carries with it sure criteria to distinguish it from imagination. This doubt, however, may easily be disposed of, and we always do so in common life by investigating the connection of phenomena in both space and time according to universal laws of experience, and we cannot doubt, when the representation of external things throughout agrees therewith, that they constitute truthful experience. Material idealism, in which phenomena are considered as such only according to their connection in experience, may accordingly be very easily refuted; and it is just as sure an experience, that bodies exist without us (in space), as that I myself exist according to the representation of the internal sense (in time): for the notion without us, only signifies existence in space. However as the Ego in the proposition, I am," means not only the object of internal intuition (in time), but the subject of consciousness, just as body means not only external intuition (in space), but the thing-in-itself, which is the basis of this phenomenon; [as this is the case] the question, whether bodies (as phenomena of the external sense) exist as bodies in nature apart from my thoughts, may without any hesitation be denied. But the question, whether I myself as a phenomenon of the internal sense (the soul according to empirical psychology) exist apart from my faculty of representation in time, is an exactly similar inquiry, and must likewise be answered in the negative. Arid in this manner everything, when it is reduced to its true meaning, is decided and certain. The formal (which I have also called transcendental) actually abolishes the material, or Cartesian, idealism. For if space be nothing but a form of my sensibility, it is as a representation in me just as actual as I myself am, and nothing but the empirical truth of the representations in it remains for consideration. But, if this is not the case, if space and the phenomena in it are something existing without us, then all the criteria of experience beyond our perception can never prove the actuality of these objects without us.

The Cosmological Idea

Section 50.

This product of pure reason in its transcendent use is its most remarkable curiosity. It serves as a very powerful agent to rouse philosophy from its dogmatic slumber, and to stimulate it to the arduous task of undertaking a critique of reason itself [Critique B432-595].

I term this idea cosmological, because it always takes its object only from the sensible world, and does not use any other than those whose object is given to sense, consequently it remains in this respect in its native home, it does not become transcendent, and is therefore so far not mere idea; whereas, to conceive the soul as a simple substance, already means to conceive such an object (the simple) as cannot be presented to the senses. Yet the cosmological idea extends the connection of the conditioned with its condition (whether the connection is mathematical or dynamical) so far, that experience never can keep up with it. It is therefore with regard to this point always an idea, whose object never can be adequately given in any experience.

Section 51.

In the first place, the use of a system of categories becomes here so obvious and unmistakable, that even if there were not several other proofs of it, this alone would sufficiently prove it indispensable in the system of pure reason. There are only four such transcendent ideas, as there are so many classes of categories; in each of which, however, they refer only to the absolute completeness of the series of the conditions for a given conditioned. In analogy to these cosmological ideas there are only four kinds of dialectical assertions of pure reason, which, as they are dialectical, thereby prove, that to each of them, all equally specious principles of pure reason, a contradictory assertion stands opposed. As all the metaphysical art of the most subtle distinction cannot prevent this opposition, it compels the philosopher to recur to the first sources of pure reason itself. This antinomy, not arbitrarily invented, but founded in the nature of human reason, and hence unavoidable and never ceasing, contains the following four theses together with their antitheses:

1

Thesis: The World has, as to, Time and Space, a Beginning (limit).

Antithesis: The World is, as to Time and Space, infinite.

2

Thesis: Everything in the World consists of [elements that are] simple.

Antithesis: There is nothing simple, but everything is composite.

3

Thesis: There are in the World Causes through Freedom.

Antithesis: There is no Liberty, but all is Nature.

4

Thesis: In the Series of the World-Causes there is some necessary Being.

Antithesis: There is Nothing necessary in the World, but in this Series All is incidental.

Section 52 a.

Here is the most singular phenomenon of human reason, no other instance of which can be shown in any other use. If we, as is commonly done, represent to ourselves the appearances of the sensible world as things in themselves, if we assume the principles of their combination as principles universally valid of things in themselves and not merely of experience, as is usually, nay without our Critique, unavoidably done, there arises an unexpected conflict, which never can be removed in the common dogmatical way; because the thesis, as well as the antithesis, can be shown by equally clear, evident, and irresistible proofs — for I pledge myself as to the correctness of all these proofs — and reason therefore perceives that it is divided with itself, a state at which the skeptic rejoices, but which must make the critical philosopher pause and feel ill at ease.

Section 52b.

We may blunder in various ways in metaphysics without any fear of being detected in falsehood. For we never can be refuted by experience if we but avoid self-contradiction, which in synthetical, though purely fictitious propositions, may be done whenever the concepts, which we connect, are mere ideas, that cannot be given (in their whole content) in experience. For how can we make out by experience, whether the world is from eternity or had a beginning, whether matter is infinitely divisible or consists of simple parts? Such concept cannot be given in any experience, be it ever so extensive, and consequently the falsehood either of the positive or the negative proposition cannot be discovered by this touchstone.

The only possible way in which reason could have revealed unintentionally its secret Dialectics, falsely announced as Dogmatics, would be when it were made to ground an assertion upon a universally admitted principle, and to deduce the exact contrary with the greatest accuracy of inference from another which is equally granted. This is actually here the case with regard to four natural ideas of reason, whence four assertions on the one side, and as many counter-assertions on the other arise, each consistently following from universally-acknowledged principles. Thus they reveal by the use of these principles the dialectical illusion of pure reason which would otherwise forever remain concealed.

This is therefore a decisive experiment, which must necessarily expose any error lying hidden in the assumptions of reason. Contradictory propositions cannot both be false, except the concept, which is the subject of both, is self-contradictory; for example, the propositions, "a square circle is round, and a square circle is not round," are both false. For, as to the former it is false, that the circle is round, because it is quadrangular; and it is likewise false, that it is not round, that is, angular, because it is a circle. For the logical criterion of the impossibility of a concept consists in this, that if we presuppose it, two contradictory propositions both become false; consequently, as no middle between them is conceivable, nothing at all is thought by that concept.

Section 52c.

The first two antinomies, which I call mathematical, because they are concerned with the addition or division of the homogeneous, are founded on such a self-contradictory concept; and hence I explain how it happens, that both the Thesis and Antithesis of the two are false.

When I speak of objects in time and in space, it is not of things in themselves, of which I know nothing, but of things in appearance, that is, of experience, as the particular way of cognizing objects which is afforded to man. I must not say of what I think in time or in space, that in itself, and independent of these my thoughts, it exists in space and in time; for in that case I should contradict myself; because space and time, together with the appearances in them, are nothing existing in themselves and outside of my representations, but are themselves only modes of representation, and it is palpably contradictory to say, that a mere mode of representation exists without our representation. Objects of the senses therefore exist only in experience; whereas to give them a self-subsisting existence apart from experience or before it, is merely to represent to ourselves that experience actually exists apart from experience or prior to it.

Now if I inquire after the magnitude of the world, as to space and time, it is equally impossible, as regards all my notions, to declare it infinite or to declare it finite. For neither assertion can be contained in experience, because experience either of an infinite space, or of an infinite time elapsed, or again, of the boundary of the world by a void space, or by an antecedent void time, is impossible; these are mere ideas. This quantity of the world, which is determined in either way, should therefore exist in the world itself apart from all experience. This contradicts the notion of a world of sense, which is merely a complex of the appearances whose existence and connection occur only in our representations, that is, in experience, since this latter is not an object in itself, but a mere mode of representation. Hence it follows, that as the concept of an absolutely existing world of sense is self-contradictory, the solution of the problem concerning its quantity, whether attempted affirmatively or negatively, is always false.

The same holds good of the second antinomy, which relates to the division of phenomena. For these are mere representations, and the parts exist merely in their representation, consequently in the division, or in a possible experience where they are given, and the division reaches only as far as this latter reaches. To assume that an appearance, e.g., that of body, contains in itself before all experience all the parts, which any possible experience can ever reach, is to impute to a mere appearance, which can exist only in experience, an existence previous to experience. In other words, it would mean that mere representations exist before they can be found in our faculty of representation. Such an assertion is self-contradictory, as also every solution of our misunderstood problem, whether we maintain, that bodies in themselves consist of an infinite number of parts, or of a finite number of simple parts.

Section 53.

In the first (the mathematical) class of antinomies the falsehood of the assumption consists in representing in one concept something self-contradictory as if it were compatible (i.e., an appearance as an object in itself). But, as to the second (the dynamical) class of antinomies, the falsehood of the representation consists in representing as contradictory what is compatible; so that, as in the former case, the opposed assertions are both false, in this case, on the other hand, where they are opposed to one another by mere misunderstanding, they may both be true.

Any mathematical connection necessarily presupposes homogeneity of what is connected (in the concept of magnitude), while the dynamical one by no means requires the same. When we have to deal with extended magnitudes, all the parts must be homogeneous with one another and with the whole; whereas, in the connection of cause and effect, homogeneity may indeed likewise be found, but is not necessary; for the concept of causality (by means of which something is posited through something else quite different from it), at all events, does not require it.

If the objects of the world of sense are taken for things in themselves, and the above laws of nature for the laws of things in themselves, the contradiction would be unavoidable. So also, if the subject of freedom were, like other objects, represented as mere appearance, the contradiction would be just as unavoidable, for the same predicate would at once be affirmed and denied of the same kind of object in the same sense. But if natural necessity is referred merely to appearances, and freedom merely to things in themselves, no contradiction arises, if we at once assume, or admit both kinds of causality, however difficult or impossible it may be to make the latter kind conceivable.

In appearance every effect is an event, or something that happens in time; it must, according to the universal law of nature, be preceded by a determination of the causality of its cause (a state of the cause), which the effect follows according to a constant law. But this determination of the cause as causality must likewise be something that takes place or happens; the cause must have begun to act, otherwise no succession between it and the effect could be conceived. Otherwise the effect, as well as the causality of the cause, would have always existed. Therefore the determination of the cause to act must also have originated among appearances, and must consequently, as well as its effect, be an event, which must again have its cause, and so on; hence natural necessity must be the condition, on which effective causes are determined. Whereas if freedom is to be a property of certain causes of appearances, it must, as regards these, which are events, be a faculty of starting them spontaneously, that is, without the causality of the cause itself, and hence without requiring any other ground to determine its start. But then the cause, as to its causality, must not rank under time-determinations of its state, that is, it cannot be an appearance, and must be considered a thing in itself, while its effects would be only appearances. If without contradiction we can think of the beings of understanding as exercising such an influence on appearances, then natural necessity will attach to all connections of cause and effect in the sensuous world, though on the other hand, freedom can be granted to such cause, as is itself not an appearance (but the foundation of appearance). Nature therefore and freedom can without contradiction be attributed to the very same thing, but in different relations — on one side as a phenomenon, on the other as a thing in itself.

We have in us a faculty, which not only stands in connection with its subjective determining grounds that are the natural causes of its actions, and is so far the faculty of a being that itself belongs to appearances, but is also referred to objective grounds, that are only ideas, so far as they can determine this faculty, a connection which is expressed by the word ought. This faculty is called reason, and, so far as we consider a being (man) entirely according to this objectively determinable reason, he cannot be considered as a being of sense, but this property is that of a thing in itself, of which we cannot comprehend the possibility — I mean how the ought (which however has never yet taken place) should determine its activity, and can become the cause of actions, whose effect is an appearance in the sensible world. Yet the causality of reason would be freedom with regard to the effects in the sensuous world, so far as we can consider objective grounds, which are themselves ideas, as their determinants. For its action in that case would not depend upon subjective conditions, consequently not upon those of time, and of course not upon the law of nature, which serves to determine them, because grounds of reason give to actions the rule universally, according to principles, without the influence of the circumstances of either time or place.

What I adduce here is merely meant as an example to make the thing intelligible, and does not necessarily belong to our problem, which must be decided from mere concepts, independently of the properties which we meet in the actual world.

Now I may say without contradiction: that all the actions of rational beings, so far as they are appearances (occurring in any experience), are subject to the necessity of nature; but the same actions, as regards merely the rational subject and its faculty of acting according to mere reason, are free. For what is required for the necessity of nature? Nothing more than the determinability of every event in the world of sense according to constant laws, that is, a reference to cause in the appearance; in this process the thing in itself at its foundation and its causality remain unknown. But I say, that the law of nature remains, whether the rational being is the cause of the effects in the sensuous world from reason, that is, through freedom, or whether it does not determine them on grounds of reason. For, if the former is the case, the action is performed according to maxims, the effect of which as appearance is always conformable to constant laws; if the latter is the case, and the action not performed on principles of reason, it is subjected to the empirical laws of the sensibility, and in both cases the effects are connected according to constant laws; more than this we do not require or know concerning natural necessity. But in the former case reason is the cause of these laws of nature, and therefore free; in the latter the effects follow according to mere natural laws of sensibility, because reason does not influence it; but reason itself is not determined on that account by the sensibility, and is therefore free in this case too. Freedom is therefore no hindrance to natural law in appearance, neither does this law abrogate the freedom of the practical use of reason, which is connected with things in themselves, as determining grounds.

Thus practical freedom, viz., the freedom in which reason possesses causality according to objectively determining grounds, is rescued and yet natural necessity is not in the least curtailed with regard to the very same effects, as appearances. The same remarks will serve to explain what we had to say concerning transcendental freedom and its compatibility with natural necessity (in the same subject, but not taken in the same reference). For, as to this, every beginning of the action of a being from objective causes regarded as determining grounds, is always a first start, though the same action is in the series of appearances only a subordinate start, which must be preceded by a state of the cause, which determines it, and is itself determined in the same manner by another immediately preceding. Thus we are able, in rational beings, or in beings generally, so far as their causality is determined in them as things in themselves, to imagine a faculty of beginning from itself a series of states, without falling into contradiction with the laws of nature. For the relation of the action to objective grounds of reason is not a time-relation; in this case that which determines the causality does not precede in time the action, because such determining grounds represent not a reference to objects of sense, e.g., to causes in the appearances, but to determining causes, as things in themselves, which do not rank under conditions of time. And in this way the action, with regard to the causality of reason, can be considered as a first start in respect to the series of appearances, and yet also as a merely subordinate beginning. We may therefore without contradiction consider it in the former aspect as free, but in the latter (in so far as it is merely appearance) as subject to natural necessity.

As to the fourth Antinomy, it is solved in the same way as the conflict of reason with itself in the third. For, provided the cause in the appearance is distinguished from the cause of the appearance (so far as it can be thought as a thing in itself), both propositions are perfectly reconcilable: the one, that there is nowhere in the sensuous world a cause (according to similar laws of causality), whose existence is absolutely necessary; the other, that this world is nevertheless connected with a Necessary Being as its cause (but of another kind and according to another law). The incompatibility of these propositions entirely rests upon the mistake of extending what is valid merely of appearances to things in themselves, and in general confusing both in one concept.

Section 54.

This then is the proposition and this the solution of the whole antinomy, in which reason finds itself involved in the application of its principles to the sensible world. The former alone (the mere proposition) would be a considerable service in the cause of our knowledge of human reason, even though the solution might fail to fully satisfy the reader, who has here to combat a natural illusion, which has been but recently exposed to him, and which he had hitherto always regarded as genuine. For one result at least is unavoidable. As it is quite impossible to prevent this conflict of reason with itself-so long as the objects of the sensible world are taken for things in themselves, and not for mere appearances, which they are in fact-the reader is thereby compelled to examine over again the deduction of all our a priori cognition and the proof which I have given of my deduction in order to come to a decision on the question. This is all I require at present; for when in this occupation he shall have thought himself deep enough into the nature of pure reason, those concepts by which alone the solution of the conflict of reason is possible, will become sufficiently familiar to him. Without this preparation I cannot expect an unreserved assent even from the most attentive reader.

The Theological Idea

Section 55.

The third transcendental idea, which affords matter for the most important, but, if pursued only speculatively, transcendent and thereby dialectical use of reason, is the ideal of pure reason. Reason in this case does not, as with the psychological and the cosmological Ideas, begin from experience, and err by exaggerating its grounds, in striving to attain, if possible, the absolute completeness of their series. It rather totally breaks with experience, and from mere concepts of what constitutes the absolute completeness of a thing in general, consequently by means of the idea of a most perfect primal Being, it proceeds to determine the possibility and therefore the actuality of all other things. And so the mere presupposition of a Being, who is conceived not in the series of experience, yet for the purposes of experience-for the sake of comprehending its connection, order, and unity — i.e., the idea [the notion of it], is more easily distinguished from the concept of the understanding here, than in the former cases. Hence we can easily expose the dialectical illusion which arises from our making the subjective conditions of our thinking objective conditions of objects themselves, and an hypothesis necessary for the satisfaction of our reason, a dogma. As the observations of the Critique on the pretensions of transcendental theology are intelligible, clear, and decisive [Critique, B595-670), I have nothing more to add on the subject.

General Remark on the Transcendental Ideas.

Section 56.

The objects, which are given us by experience, are in many respects incomprehensible, and many questions, to which the law of nature leads us, when carried beyond a certain point (though quite conformably to the laws of nature), admit of no answer; as for example the question: why substances attract one another? But if we entirely quit nature, or in pursuing its combinations, exceed all possible experience, and so enter the realm of mere ideas, we cannot then say that the object is incomprehensible, and that the nature of things proposes to us insoluble problems. For we are not then concerned with nature or in general with given objects, but with concepts, which have their origin merely in our reason, and with mere creations of thought; and all the problems that arise from our notions of them must be solved, because of course reason can and must give a full account of its own procedure. As the psychological, cosmological, and theological Ideas are nothing but pure concepts of reason, which cannot be given in any experience, the questions which reason asks us about them are put to us not by the objects, but by mere maxims of our reason for the sake of its own satisfaction. They must all be capable of satisfactory answers, which is done by showing that they are principles which bring our use of the understanding into thorough agreement, completeness, and synthetical unity, and that they so far hold good of experience only, but of experience as a whole. Although an absolute whole of experience is impossible, the idea of a whole of cognition according to principles must impart to our knowledge a peculiar kind of unity, that of a system, without which it is nothing but piecework, and cannot be used for proving the existence of a highest purpose (which can only be the general system of all purposes), I do not here refer only to the practical, but also to the highest purpose of the speculative use of reason.

The transcendental Ideas therefore express the peculiar application of reason as a principle of systematic unity in the use of the understanding. Yet if we assume this unity of the mode of cognition to be attached to the object of cognition, if we regard that which is merely regulative to be constitutive, and if we persuade ourselves that we can by means of these Ideas enlarge our cognition transcendently, or far beyond all possible experience, while it only serves to render experience within itself as nearly complete as possible, i.e., to limit its progress by nothing that cannot belong to experience: we suffer from a mere misunderstanding in our estimate of the proper application of our reason and of its principles, and from a Dialectic, which both confuses the empirical use of reason, and also sets reason at variance with itself.

CONCLUSION:

ON THE DETERMINATION OF THE BOUNDS OF PURE REASON

Section 57.

Having adduced the clearest arguments, it would be absurd for us to hope that we can know more of any object, than belongs to the possible experience of it, or lay claim to the least atom of knowledge about anything not assumed to be an object of possible experience, which would determine it according to the constitution it has in itself. For how could we determine anything in this way, since time, space, and the categories, and still more all the concepts formed by empirical experience or perception in the sensible world [Anschauung], have and can have no other use, than to make experience possible. And if this condition is omitted from the pure concepts of the understanding, they do not determine any object, and have no meaning whatever.

But it would be on the other hand a still greater absurdity if we conceded no things in themselves, or set up our experience for the only possible mode of knowing things, our mode of intuition of them in space and in time for the only possible way, and our discursive understanding for the archetype of every possible understanding; in fact if we wished to have the principles of the possibility of experience considered universal conditions of things in themselves.

Our principles, which limit the use of reason to possible experience, might in this way become transcendent, and the limits of our reason be set up as limits of the possibility of things in themselves (as Hume's Dialogues may illustrate), if a careful critique did not guard the bounds of our reason with respect to its empirical use, and set a limit to its pretensions. Skepticism originally arose from metaphysics and its licentious dialectics. At first it might, merely to favor the empirical use of reason, announce everything that transcends this use as worthless and deceitful; but by and by, when it was perceived that the very same principles that are used in experience, insensibly, and apparently with the same right, led still further than experience extends, then men began to doubt even the propositions of experience. But here there is no danger; for common sense will doubtless always assert its rights. A certain confusion, however, arose in science which cannot determine how far reason is to be trusted, and why only so far and no further, and this confusion can only be cleared up and all future relapses obviated by a formal determination, on principle, of the boundary of the use of our reason.

We cannot indeed, beyond all possible experience, form a definite notion of what things in themselves may be. Yet we are not at liberty to abstain entirely from inquiring into them; for experience never satisfies reason fully, but in answering questions, refers us further and further back, and leaves us dissatisfied with regard to their complete solution. This any one may gather from the Dialectics of pure reason, which therefore has its good subjective grounds. Having acquired, as regards the nature of our soul, a clear conception of the subject, and having come to the conviction, that its manifestations cannot be explained materialistically, who can refrain from asking what the soul really is, and, if no concept of experience suffices for the purpose, from accounting for it by a concept of reason (that of a simple immaterial being), though we cannot by any means prove its objective reality? Who can satisfy himself with mere empirical knowledge in all the cosmological questions of the duration and of the quantity of the world, of freedom or of natural necessity, since every answer given on principles of experience begets a fresh question, which likewise requires its answer and thereby clearly shows the insufficiency of all physical modes of explanation to satisfy reason? Finally, who does not see in the thoroughgoing contingency and dependence of all his thoughts and assumptions on mere principles of experience, the impossibility of stopping there? And who does not feel himself compelled, notwithstanding all interdictions against losing himself in transcendent ideas, to seek rest and contentment beyond all the concepts which he can vindicate by experience, in the concept of a Being, the possibility of which we cannot conceive, but at the same time cannot be refuted, because it relates to a mere being of the understanding, and without it reason must needs remain forever dissatisfied?

Bounds (in extended beings) always presuppose a space existing outside a certain definite place, and enclosing it; limits do not require this, but are mere negations, which affect a quantity, so far as it is not absolutely complete. But our reason, as it were, sees in its surroundings a space for the cognition of things in themselves, though we can never have definite notions of them, and are limited to appearances only.

As long as the cognition of reason is homogeneous, definite bounds to it are inconceivable. In mathematics and in natural philosophy human reason admits of limits but not of bounds, viz., that something indeed lies without it, at which it can never arrive, but not that it will at any point find completion in its internal progress. The enlarging of our views in mathematics, and the possibility of new discoveries, are infinite; and the same is the case with the discovery of new properties of nature, of new powers and laws, by continued experience and its rational combination. But limits cannot be mistaken here, for mathematics refers to appearances only, and what cannot be an object of sensuous contemplation, such as the concepts of metaphysics and of morals, lies entirely without its sphere, and it can never lead to them; neither does it require them. It is therefore not a continual progress and an approximation towards these sciences, and there is not, as it were, any point or line of contact. Natural science will never reveal to us the internal constitution of things, which though not appearance, yet can serve as the ultimate ground of explaining appearance. Nor does that science require this for its physical explanations. Nay even if such grounds should be offered from other sources (for instance, the influence of immaterial beings), they must be rejected and not used in the progress of its explanations. For these explanations must only be grounded upon that which as an object of sense can belong to experience, and be brought into connection with our actual perceptions and empirical laws.

But metaphysics leads us towards bounds in the dialectical attempts of pure reason (not undertaken arbitrarily or wantonly, but stimulated thereto by the nature of reason itself). And the transcendental Ideas, as they do not admit of evasion, and are never capable of realization, serve to point out to us actually not only the bounds of the pure use of reason, but also the way to determine them. Such is the end and the use of this natural predisposition of our reason, which has brought forth metaphysics as its favorite child, whose generation, like every other in the world, is not to be ascribed to blind chance, but to an original germ, wisely organized for great ends. For metaphysics, in its fundamental features, perhaps more than any other science, is placed in us by nature itself, and cannot be considered the production of an arbitrary choice or a casual enlargement in the progress of experience from which it is quite disparate.

Reason with all its concepts and laws of the understanding, which suffice for empirical use, i.e., within the sensible world, finds in itself no satisfaction because ever-recurring questions deprive us of all hope of their complete solution. The transcendental ideas, which have that completion in view, are such problems of reason. But it sees clearly, that the sensuous world cannot contain this completion, neither consequently can all the concepts, which serve merely for understanding the world of sense, such as space and time, and whatever we have adduced under the name of pure concepts of the understanding. The sensuous world is nothing but a chain of appearances connected according to universal laws; it has therefore no subsistence by itself; it is not the thing in itself, and consequently must point to that which contains the basis of this experience, to beings which cannot be known merely as phenomena, but as things in themselves. In the cognition of them alone reason can hope to satisfy its desire of completeness in proceeding from the conditioned to its conditions.

We have above (Section s 33, 34) indicated the limits of reason with regard to all cognition of mere creations of thought. Now, since the transcendental ideas have urged us to approach them, and thus have led us, as it were, to the spot where the occupied space (viz., experience) touches the void (that of which we can know nothing, viz., noumena), we can determine the bounds of pure reason. For in all bounds there is something positive (e.g., a surface is the boundary of corporeal space, and is therefore itself a space, a line is a space, which is the boundary of the surface, a point the boundary of the line, but yet always a place in space), whereas limits contain mere negations. The limits pointed out in those paragraphs are not enough after we have discovered that beyond them there still lies something (though we can never know what it is in itself). For the question now is, What is the attitude of our reason in this connection of what we know with what we do not, and never shall, know? This is an actual connection of a known thing with one quite unknown (and which will always remain so), and though what is unknown should not become the least more known-which we cannot even hope-yet the notion of this connection must be definite, and capable of being rendered distinct.

We must therefore accept an immaterial being, a world of understanding, and a Supreme Being (all merely noumena), because in them only, as things in themselves, reason finds that completion and satisfaction, which it can never hope for in the derivation of appearances from their homogeneous grounds, and because these actually have reference to something distinct from them (and totally heterogeneous), as appearances always presuppose an object in itself, and therefore suggest its existence whether we can know more of it or not.

But as we can never cognize these beings of understanding as they are in themselves, that is, definitely, yet must assume them as regards the sensible world, and connect them with it by reason, we are at least able to think this connection by means of such concepts as express their relation to the world of sense. Yet if we represent to ourselves a being of the understanding by nothing but pure concepts of the understanding, we then indeed represent nothing definite to ourselves, consequently our concept has no significance; but if we think it by properties borrowed from the sensuous world, it is no longer a being of understanding, but is conceived as an appearance, and belongs to the sensible world. Let us take an instance from the notion of the Supreme Being.

Our deistic conception is quite a pure concept of reason, but represents only a thing containing all realities, without being able to determine any one of them; because for that purpose an example must be taken from the world of sense, in which case we should have an object of sense only, not something quite heterogeneous, which can never be an object of sense. Suppose I attribute to the Supreme Being understanding, for instance; I have no concept of an understanding other than my own, one that must receive its intuitions by the senses, and which is occupied in bringing them under rules of the unity of consciousness. Then the elements of my concept would always lie in the appearance; I should however by the insufficiency of the appearance be necessitated to go beyond them to the concept of a being which neither depends upon appearance, nor is bound up with them as conditions of its determination. But if I separate understanding from sensibility to obtain a pure understanding, then nothing remains but the mere form of thinking without intuition, by which form alone I can know nothing definite, and consequently no object. For that purpose I should conceive another understanding, such as would directly perceive its objects, but of which I have not the least notion; because the human understanding is discursive, and can only cognize [indirectly] by means of general concepts. And the very same difficulties arise if I attribute a will to the Supreme Being; for I have this concept only by drawing it from my internal experience, and therefore from my dependence for satisfaction upon objects whose existence we require; and so the notion rests upon sensibility, which is absolutely incompatible with the pure concept of the Supreme Being.

Hume's objections to deism are weak, and affect only the proofs, and not the deistic assertion itself. But as regards theism, which depends on a stricter determination of the concept of the Supreme Being which in deism is merely transcendent, they are very strong, and as this concept is formed, in certain (in fact in all common) cases irrefutable. Hume always insists, that by the mere concept of an original being, to which we apply only ontological predicates (eternity, omnipresence, omnipotence), we think nothing definite, and that properties which can yield a concept in concreto must be superadded; that it is not enough to say, it is cause, but we must explain the nature of its causality, for example, that of an understanding and of a will. He then begins his attacks on the essential point itself, i.e., theism, as he; had previously directed his battery only against the proofs of deism, an attack which is not very dangerous to it in its consequences. All his dangerous arguments refer to anthropomorphism, which he holds to be inseparable from theism, and to make it absurd in itself; but if the former be abandoned, the latter must vanish with it, and nothing remain but deism, of which nothing can come, which is of no value, and which cannot serve as any foundation to religion or morals. If this anthropomorphism were really unavoidable, no proofs whatever of the existence of a Supreme Being, even were they all granted, could determine for us the concept of this Being without involving us in contradictions.

If we connect with the command to avoid all transcendent judgments of pure reason, the command (which apparently conflicts with it) to proceed to concepts that lie beyond the field of its immanent (empirical) use, we discover that both can subsist together, but only at the boundary of all lawful use of reason. For this boundary belongs as well to the field of experience, as to that of the creations of thought, and we are thereby taught, as well, bow these so remarkable ideas serve merely for marking the bounds of human reason. On the one hand they give warning not boundlessly to extend cognition of experience, as if nothing but world remained for us to cognize, and yet, on the other hand, not to transgress the bounds of experience, and to think of judging about things beyond them, as things in themselves.

But we stop at this boundary we limit our judgment merely to the relation which the world may have to a Being whose very concept lies beyond all the knowledge which we can attain within the world. For we then do not attribute to the Supreme Being any of the properties in themselves, by which we represent objects of experience, and thereby avoid dogmatic anthropomorphism; but we attribute them to his relation to the world, and allow ourselves a symbolic anthropomorphism, which in fact concerns language only, and not the object itself.

If I say that we are compelled to consider the world as if it were the work of a Supreme Understanding and Will, I really say nothing more, than that a watch, a ship, a regiment, bears the same relation to the watchmaker, the shipbuilder, the commanding officer, as the world of sense (or whatever constitutes the substratum of this complex of appearances) does to the unknown, which I do not hereby cognize as it is in itself, but as it is for me or in relation to the world, of which I am a part.

Section 58.

Such a cognition is one of analogy, and does not signify (as is commonly understood) an imperfect similarity of two things, but a perfect similarity of relations between two quite dissimilar things. By means of this analogy, however, there remains a concept of the Supreme Being sufficiently determined for us, though we have left out everything that could determine it absolutely and in itself; for we determine it as regards the world and as regards ourselves, and more do we not require. The attacks which Hume makes upon those who would determine this concept absolutely, by taking the materials for so doing from themselves and the world, do not affect us; and he cannot object to us, that we have nothing left if we give up the objective anthropomorphism of the concept of the Supreme Being.

For let us assume at the outset (as Hume in his Dialogues makes Philo grant Cleanthes), as a necessary hypothesis, the deistical concept of the First Being, in which this Being is thought by the mere ontological predicates of substance, of cause, etc. This must be done, because reason, actuated in the sensible world by mere conditions, which are themselves always conditional, cannot otherwise have any satisfaction, and it therefore can be done without falling into anthropomorphism (which transfers predicates from the world of sense to a Being quite distinct from the world), because those predicates are mere categories, which, though they do not give a determinate concept of God, yet give a concept not limited to any conditions of sensibility. Thus nothing can prevent our predicating of this Being a causality through reason with regard to the world, and thus passing to theism, without being obliged to attribute to God in himself this kind of reason, as a property inhering in him. For as to the former, the only possible way of prosecuting the use of reason (as regards all possible experience, in complete harmony with itself) in the world of sense to the highest point, is to assume a supreme reason as a cause of all the connections in the world. Such a principle must be quite advantageous to reason and can hurt it nowhere in its application to nature. As to the latter, reason is thereby not transferred as a property to the First Being in himself, but only to his relation to the world of sense, and so anthropomorphism is entirely avoided. For nothing is considered here but the cause of the form of reason which is perceived everywhere in the world, and reason is attributed to the Supreme Being, so far as it contains the ground of this form of reason in the world, but according to analogy only, that is, so far as this expression shows merely the relation, which the Supreme Cause unknown to us has to the world, in order to determine everything in it conformably to reason in the highest degree. We are thereby kept from using reason as an attribute for the purpose of conceiving God, but instead of conceiving the world in such a manner as is necessary to have the greatest possible use of reason according to principle. We thereby acknowledge that the Supreme Being is quite inscrutable and even unthinkable in any definite way as to what he is in himself. We are thereby kept, on the one band, from making a transcendent use of the concepts which we have of reason as an efficient cause (by means of the will), in order to determine the Divine Nature by properties, which are only borrowed from human nature, and from losing ourselves in gross and extravagant notions, and on the other hand from deluging the contemplation of the world with hyperphysical modes of explanation according to our notions of human reason, which we transfer to God, and so losing for this contemplation its proper application, according to which it should be a rational study of mere nature, and not a presumptuous derivation of its appearances from a Supreme Reason. The expression suited to our feeble notions is, that we conceive the world as if it came, as regarding its existence and internal plan, from a Supreme Reason. By this notion we both know the constitution, which belongs to the world itself, yet without pretending to determine the nature of its cause in itself, and on the other hand, we transfer the ground of this constitution (of the form of reason in the world) upon the relation of the Supreme Cause to the world, without finding thc world sufficient by itself for that purpose.

Thus the difficulties which seem to oppose theism disappear by combining with Hume's principle, "not to carry the use of reason dogmatically beyond the field of all possible experience," this other principle, which be quite overlooked: "not to consider the field of experience as one which bounds itself in the eye of our reason." The Critique of Pure Reason here points out the true mean between dogmatism, which Hume combats, and skepticism, which he would substitute for it — a mean which is not like other means that we find advisable to determine for ourselves as it were mechanically (by adopting something from one side and something from the other), and by which nobody is taught a better way, but such a one as can be accurately determined on principles.

Section 59.

At the beginning of this note I made use of the metaphor of a boundary, in order to establish the limits of reason in regard to its suitable use. The world of sense contains merely appearances, which are not things in themselves, but the understanding must assume these latter ones, viz., noumena, because it knows the objects of experience to be mere appearances. In our reason both are comprised together, and the question is, How does reason proceed to set boundaries to the understanding as regards both these fields? Experience, which contains all that belongs to the sensuous world, does not bound itself; it only proceeds in every case from the conditioned to some other equally conditioned object. Its boundary must lie quite without it, and this field is that of the pure beings of the understanding. But this field, so far as the determination of the nature of these beings is concerned, is an empty space for us; and if dogmatically determined concepts alone are in question, we cannot pass out of the field of possible experience. But as a boundary itself is something positive, which belongs as well to that which lies within, as to the space that lies without the given complex, it is still an actual positive cognition, which reason only acquires by enlarging itself to this boundary, yet without attempting to pass it; because it there finds itself in the presence of an empty space, in which it can conceive forms of things, but not things themselves. But the setting of a boundary to the field of the understanding by something, which is otherwise unknown to it, is still a cognition which belongs to reason even at this standpoint, and by which it is neither confined within the sensible, nor straying without it, but only refers, as befits the knowledge of a boundary, to the relation between that which lies without it, and that which is contained within it.

Natural theology is such a concept at the boundary of human reason, being constrained to look beyond this boundary to the Idea of a Supreme Being (and, for practical purposes to that of an intelligible world also), not in order to determine anything relatively to this pure creation of the understanding, which lies beyond the world of sense, but in order to guide the use of reason within it according to principles of the greatest possible (theoretical as well as practical) unity. For this purpose we make use of the reference of the world of sense to an independent reason, as the cause of all its connections. Thereby we do not purely invent a being, but, as beyond the sensible world there must be something that can only be thought by the pure understanding, we determine that something in this particular way, though only of course according to analogy.

And thus there remains our original proposition, which is the resume of the whole Critique: "that reason by all its a priori principles never teaches us anything more than objects of possible experience, and even of these nothing more than can be known in experience." But this limitation does not prevent reason leading us to the objective boundary of experience, viz., to the reference to something which is not itself an object of experience, but is the ground of all experience. Reason does not however teach us anything concerning the thing in itself: it only instructs us as regards its own complete and highest use in the field of possible experience. But this is all that can be reasonably desired in the present case, and with which we have cause to be satisfied.

Section 60.

Thus we have fully exhibited metaphysics as it is actually given in the natural predisposition of human reason, and in that which constitutes the essential end of its pursuit, according to its subjective possibility. Though we have found, that this merely natural use of such a predisposition of our reason, if no discipline arising only from a scientific critique bridles and sets limits to it, involves us in transcendent, either apparently or really conflicting, dialectical syllogisms; and this fallacious metaphysics is not only unnecessary as regards the promotion of our knowledge of nature, but even disadvantageous to it: there yet remains a problem worthy of solution, which is to find out the natural ends intended by this disposition to transcendent concepts in our reason, because everything that lies in nature must be originally intended for some useful purpose.

Such an inquiry is of a doubtful nature; and I acknowledge, that what I can say about it is conjecture only, like every speculation about the first ends of nature. The question does not concern the objective validity of metaphysical judgments, but our natural predisposition to them, and therefore does not belong to the system of metaphysics but to anthropology.

When I compare all the transcendental Ideas, the totality of which constitutes the particular problem of natural pure reason, compelling it to quit the mere contemplation of nature, to transcend all possible experience, and in this endeavor to produce the thing (be it knowledge or fiction) called metaphysics, I think I perceive that the aim of this natural tendency is, to free our notions from the fetters of experience and from the limits of the mere contemplation of nature so far as at least to open to us a field containing mere objects for the pure understanding, which no sensibility can reach, not indeed for the purpose of speculatively occupying ourselves with them (for there we can find no ground to stand on), but because practical principles, which, without finding some such scope for their necessary expectation and hope, could not expand to the universality which reason unavoidably requires from a moral point of view.

So I find that the psychological idea (however little it may reveal to me the nature of the human soul, which is higher than all concepts of experience), shows the insufficiency of these concepts plainly enough, and thereby deters me from materialism, the psychological notion of which is unfit for any explanation of nature, and besides confines reason in practical respects. The cosmological ideas, by the obvious insufficiency of all possible cognition of nature to satisfy reason in its lawful inquiry, serve in the same manner to keep us from naturalism, which asserts nature to be sufficient for itself. Finally, all natural necessity in the sensible world is conditional, as it always presupposes the dependence of things upon others, and unconditional necessity must be sought only in the unity of a cause different from the world of sense. But as the causality of this cause, in its turn, were it merely nature, could never render the existence of the contingent (as its consequent) comprehensible, reason frees itself by means of the Theological Idea from fatalism, (both as a blind natural necessity in the coherence of nature itself, without a first principle, and as a blind causality of this principle itself), and leads to the concept of a cause possessing freedom, or of a Supreme Intelligence. Thus the transcendental Ideas serve, if not to instruct us positively, at least to destroy the rash assertions of Materialism, of Naturalism, and of Fatalism, and thus to afford scope for the moral Ideas beyond the field of speculation. These considerations, I should think, explain in some measure the natural predisposition of which I spoke.

The practical value, which a merely speculative science may have, lies without the bounds of this science, and can therefore be considered as a scholium merely, and like all scholia does not form part of the science itself. This application however surely lies within the bounds of philosophy, especially of philosophy drawn from the pure sources of reason, where its speculative use in metaphysics must necessarily be at unity with its practical use in morals. Hence the unavoidable dialectics of pure reason, considered in metaphysics, as a natural tendency, deserves to be explained not as an illusion merely, which is to be removed, but also, if possible, as a natural provision as regards its end, though this duty, a work of supererogation, cannot justly be assigned to metaphysics proper.

The solutions of these questions which are treated in the Critique [in the chapter on the Regulative Use of the Ideas of Pure Reason] should be considered a second scholium which, however, has a greater affinity with the subject of metaphysics. For there certain rational principles are expounded which determine a priori the order of nature or rather of the understanding, which seeks nature's laws through experience. They seem to be constitutive and legislative with regard to experience, though they spring from pure reason, which cannot be considered, like the understanding, as a principle of possible experience. Now whether or not this harmony rests upon the fact, that just as nature does not inhere in appearances or in their source (the sensibility) itself, but only in so far as the latter is in relation to the understanding, as also a systematic unity in applying the understanding to bring about an entirety of all possible experience can only belong to the understanding when in relation to reason; and whether or not experience is in this way mediately subordinate to the legislation of reason: may be discussed by those who desire to trace the nature of reason even beyond its use in metaphysics, into the general principles of a history of nature. I have represented this task as important, but not attempted its solution, in the book itself.

And thus I conclude the analytical solution of the main question which I had proposed: "How is metaphysics in general possible?" by ascending from the data of its actual use in its consequences, to the grounds of its possibility.

SOLUTION OF THE GENERAL QUESTION OF THE PROLEGOMENA

HOW IS METAPHYSICS POSSIBLE AS A SCIENCE?

Metaphysics, as a natural disposition of reason, is actual, but if considered by itself alone (as the analytical solution of the third principal question showed), dialectical and illusory. If we think of taking principles from it, and in using them follow the natural, but on that account not less false, illusion, we can never produce science, but only a vain dialectical art, in which one school may outdo another, but none can ever acquire a just and lasting approbation.

In order that as a science metaphysics may be entitled to claim not mere fallacious plausibility, but insight and conviction, a Critique of Reason must itself exhibit the whole stock of a priori concepts, their division according to their various sources (Sensibility, Understanding, and Reason), together with a complete table of them, the analysis of all these concepts, with all their consequences, especially by means of the deduction of these concepts, the possibility of synthetical cognition a priori, the principles of its application and finally its bounds, all in a complete system. Critique, therefore, and critique alone, contains in itself the whole well-proved and well-tested plan, and even all the means required to accomplish metaphysics, as a science; by other ways and means it is impossible. The question here therefore is not so much how this performance is possible, as how to set it going, and induce men of clear heads to quit their hitherto perverted and fruitless cultivation for one that will not deceive, and how such a union for the common end may best be directed.

This much is certain, that whoever has once tasted critique will be ever after disgusted with all dogmatical twaddle which be formerly put up with, because his reason must have something, and could find nothing better for its support. Critique stands in the same relation to the common metaphysics of the schools, as chemistry does to alchemy, or as astronomy to the astrology of the fortune-teller. I pledge myself that nobody who has read through and through, and grasped the principles of critique, even in these Prolegomena only, will ever return to that old and sophistical pseudo-science; but will rather with a certain delight look forward to metaphysics which is now indeed in his power, requiring no more preparatory discoveries, and now at last affording permanent satisfaction to reason. For here is an advantage upon which, of all possible sciences, metaphysics alone can with certainty reckon: that it can be brought to such completion and fixity as to be incapable of further change, or of any augmentation by new discoveries; because here reason has the sources of its knowledge in itself, not in objects and their observation [Anschauung], by which latter its stock of knowledge cannot be further increased. When therefore it has exhibited the fundamental laws of its faculty completely and so definitely as to avoid all misunderstanding, there remains nothing for pure reason to know a priori, nay, there is even no ground to raise further questions. The sure prospect of knowledge so definite and so compact has a peculiar charm, even though we should set aside all its advantages, of which I shall hereafter speak.

All false art, all vain wisdom, lasts its time, but finally destroys itself, and its highest culture is also the epoch of its decay. That this time is come for metaphysics appears from the state into which it has fallen among all learned nations, despite of all the zeal with which other sciences of every kind are prosecuted. The old arrangement of our university studies still preserves its shadow; now and then an Academy of Science tempts men by offering prizes to write essays on it, but it is no longer numbered among thorough sciences; and let any one judge for himself how a man of genius, if he were called a great metaphysician, would receive the compliment, which may be well- meant, but is scarce envied by anybody.

Yet, though the period of the downfall of all dogmatical metaphysics has undoubtedly arrived, we are yet far from being able to say that the period of its regeneration is come by means of a thorough and complete Critique of Reason. All transitions from a tendency to its contrary pass through the stage of indifference, and this moment is the most dangerous for an author, but, in my opinion, the most favorable for the science. For, when party spirit has died out by a total dissolution of former connections, minds are in the best state to listen to several proposals for an organization according to a new plan.

When I say, that I hope these Prolegomena will excite investigation in the field of critique and afford a new and promising object to sustain the general spirit of philosophy, which seems on its speculative side to want sustenance, I can imagine beforehand, that every one, whom the thorny paths of my Critique have tired and put out of humor, will ask me, upon what I found this hope. My answer is: upon the irresistible law of necessity.

That the human mind will ever give up metaphysical researches is as little to be expected as that we should prefer to give up breathing altogether, to avoid inhaling impure air. There will therefore always be metaphysics in the world; nay, every one, especially every man of reflection, will have it, and for want of a recognized standard, will shape it for himself after his own pattern. What has hitherto been called metaphysics, cannot satisfy any critical mind, but to forego it entirely is impossible; therefore a critique of pure reason itself must now be attempted or, if one exists, investigated, and brought to the full test, because there is no other means of supplying this pressing want, which is something more than mere thirst for knowledge.

Ever since I have come to know critique, whenever I finish reading a book of metaphysical contents, which, by the preciseness of its notions, by variety, order, and an easy style, was not only entertaining but also helpful, I cannot help asking, "Has this author indeed advanced metaphysics a single step?" The learned men, whose works have been useful to me in other respects and always contributed to the culture of my mental powers, will, I hope, forgive me for saying, that I have never been able to find either their essays or my own less important ones (though self-love may recommend them to me) to have advanced the science of metaphysics in the least, and why? Here is the very obvious reason: metaphysics did not then exist as a science, nor can it be gathered piecemeal, but its germ must be fully preformed in the Critique. But in order to prevent all misconception, we must remember what has been already said, that by the analytical treatment of our concepts the understanding gains indeed a great deal, but the science (of metaphysics) is thereby not in the least advanced, because these dissections of concepts are nothing but the materials from which the intention is to carpenter our science. Let the concepts of substance and of accident be ever so well dissected and determined, all this is very well as a preparation for some future use. But if we cannot prove, that in all which exists the substance endures, and only the accidents vary, our science is not the least advanced by all our analyzes. Metaphysics has hitherto never been able to prove a priori either this proposition, or that of sufficient reason, still less any more complex theorem, such as belongs to psychology or cosmology, or indeed any synthetical proposition. By all its analyzing therefore nothing is affected, nothing obtained or forwarded and the science, after all this bustle and noise, still remains as it was in the days of Aristotle, though far better preparations were made for it than of old, if the clue to synthetical cognitions had only been discovered.

If any one thinks himself offended, he is at liberty to refute my charge by producing a single synthetical proposition belonging to metaphysics, which he would prove dogmatically a priori, for until he has actually performed this feat, I shall not grant that he has truly advanced the science; even should this proposition be sufficiently confirmed by common experience. No demand can be more moderate or more equitable, and in the (inevitably certain) event of its non-performance, no assertion more just, than that hitherto metaphysics has never existed as a science.

But there are two things which, in case the challenge be accepted, I must deprecate: first, trifling about probability and conjecture, which are suited as little to metaphysics, as to geometry; and secondly, a decision by means of the magic wand of common sense, which does not convince every one, but which accommodates itself to personal peculiarities.

For as to the former, nothing can be more absurd, than in metaphysics, a philosophy from pure reason to think of grounding our judgments upon probability and conjecture. Everything that is to be cognized a priori is thereby announced as apodeictically certain, and must therefore be proved in this way. We might as well think of grounding geometry or arithmetic upon conjectures. As to the doctrine of chances in the latter, it does not contain probable, but perfectly certain, judgments concerning the degree of the probability of certain cases, under given uniform conditions, which, in the sum of all possible cases, infallibly happen according to the rule, though it is not sufficiently determined in respect to every single chance. Conjectures (by means of induction and of analogy) can be suffered in an empirical science of nature only, yet even there the possibility at least of what we assume must be quite certain.

The appeal to common sense is even more absurd, when concept and principles are announced as valid, not in so far as they hold with regard to experience, but even beyond the conditions of experience. For what is common sense? It is normal good sense, so far it judges right. But what is normal good sense? It is the faculty of the knowledge and use of rules in concreto, as distinguished from the speculative understanding, which is a faculty of knowing rules in abstracto. Common sense can hardly understand the rule, that every event is determined by means of its cause, and can never comprehend it thus generally. It therefore demands an example from experience, and when it hears that this rule means nothing but what it always thought when a pane was broken or a kitchen-utensil missing, it then understands the principle and grants it. Common sense therefore is only of use so far as it can see its rules (though they actually are a priori) confirmed by experience; consequently to comprehend them a priori, or independently of experience, belongs to the speculative understanding, and lies quite beyond the horizon of common sense. But the province of metaphysics is entirely confined to the latter kind of knowledge, and it is certainly a bad index of common sense to appeal to it as a witness, for it cannot here form any opinion whatever, and men look down upon it with contempt until they are in trouble and can find in their speculation neither advice nor help.

It is a common subterfuge of those false friends of common sense (who occasionally prize it highly, but usually despise it) to say, that there must surely be at all events some propositions which are immediately certain, and of which there is no occasion to give any proof, or even any account at all, because we otherwise could never stop inquiring into the grounds of our judgments. But if we except the principle of contradiction, which is not sufficient to show the truth of synthetical judgments, they can never adduce, in proof of this privilege, anything else indubitable, which they can immediately ascribe to common sense, except mathematical propositions, such as twice two make four, between two points there is but one straight line, etc. But these judgments are radically different from those of metaphysics. For in mathematics I myself can, by thinking, construct whatever I represent to myself as possible by a concept: I add to the first two the other two, one by one, and myself make the number four, or I draw in thought from one point to another all manner of lines, equal as well as unequal; yet I can draw one only, which is like itself in all its parts. But I cannot, by all my power of thinking, extract from the concept of a thing the concept of something else, whose existence is necessarily connected with the former, but I must call in experience. And though my understanding furnishes me a priori (yet only in reference to possible experience) with the concept of such a connection (i.e., causation), I cannot exhibit it a priori in intuition, like the concepts of mathematics, and so show its possibility a priori. This concept, together with the principles of its application, always requires, if it is to hold a priori — as is requisite in metaphysics — a justification and deduction of its possibility, because we cannot otherwise know how far it holds good, and whether it can be used in experience only or beyond it also. Therefore in metaphysics, as a speculative science of pure reason, we can never appeal to common sense, but may do so only when we are forced to surrender it, and to renounce all purely speculative cognition, which must always be knowledge, and consequently when we forego metaphysics itself and its instruction, for the sake of adopting a rational faith which alone may be possible for us, and sufficient to our wants, perhaps even more salutary than knowledge itself. For in this case the attitude of the question is quite altered. Metaphysics must be science, not only as a whole, but in all its parts, otherwise it is nothing; because, as a speculation of pure reason, it finds a hold only on general opinions. Beyond its field, however, probability and common sense may be used with advantage and justly, but on quite special principles, of which the importance always depends on the reference to practical life.

This is what I hold myself justified in requiring for the possibility of metaphysics as a science.

APPENDIX: ON WHAT CAN BE DONE TO MAKE METAPHYSICS AS A SCIENCE ACTUAL

Since all the ways heretofore taken have failed to attain the goal, and since without a preceding critique of pure reason it is not likely ever to be attained, the present essay now before the public has a fair title to an accurate and careful investigation, except it be thought more advisable to give up all pretensions to metaphysics, to which, if men but would consistently adhere to their purpose, no objection can be made. If we take the course of things as it is, not as it ought to be, there are two sorts of judgments: (1) one a judgment which precedes investigation (in our case one in which the reader from his own metaphysics pronounces judgment on the Critique of Pure Reason which was intended to discuss the very possibility of metaphysics); (2) the other a judgment subsequent to investigation. In the latter the reader is enabled to waive for a while the consequences of the critical researches that may be repugnant to his formerly adopted metaphysics, and first examines the grounds whence those consequences are derived. If what common metaphysics propounds were demonstrably certain, as for instance the theorems of geometry, the former way of judging would bold good. For if the consequences of certain principles are repugnant to established truths, these principles are false and without further inquiry to be repudiated. But if metaphysics does not possess a stock of indisputably certain (synthetical) propositions, and should it even be the case that there are a number of them, which, though among the most specious, are by their consequences in mutual collision, and if no sure criterion of the truth of peculiarly metaphysical (synthetical) propositions is to be met with in it, then the former way of judging is not admissible, but the investigation of the principles of the Critique must precede all judgments as to its value.

APPENDIX: ON A SPECIMEN OF A JUDGMENT OF THE CRITIQUE PRIOR TO ITS EXAMINATION

A judgment is to be found in the Gottingischen gelehrten Anzeigen, in the supplement to the third division, of January 19, 1782, pages 40 et seq. [a review authored by Christian Garve]

When an author who is familiar with the subject of his work and endeavors to present his independent reflections in its elaboration, falls into the hands of a reviewer who in his turn, is keen enough to discern the points on which the worth or worthlessness of the book rests, who does not cling to words, but goes to the heart of the subject, sifting and testing more than the mere principles which the author takes as his point of departure, the severity of the judgment may indeed displease the latter, but the public does not care, because it gains thereby. And the author himself may be contented, as an opportunity of correcting or explaining his positions is afforded to him at an early date by the examination of a competent judge, in such a manner, that if he believes himself fundamentally right, he can remove in time any stone of offense that might hurt the success of his work.

I find myself, with my reviewer, in quite another position. He seems not to see at all the real matter of the investigation with which (successfully or unsuccessfully) I have been occupied. It is either impatience at thinking out a lengthy work, or vexation at a threatened reform of a science in which he believed he had brought everything to perfection long ago, or, what I am unwilling to imagine, real narrow-mindedness, that prevents him from ever carrying his thoughts beyond his school-metaphysics. In short, he passes impatiently in review a long series of propositions, by which, without knowing their premises, we can think nothing, intersperses here and there his censure, the reason of which the reader understands just as little as the propositions against which it is directed; and hence [his report] can neither serve the public nor damage me, in the judgment of experts. I should, for these reasons, have passed over this judgment altogether, were it not that it may afford me occasion for some explanations which may in some cases save the readers of these Prolegomena from a misconception.

In order to take a position from which my reviewer could most easily set the whole work in a most unfavorable light, without venturing to trouble himself with any special investigation, he begins and ends by saying: "This work is a system of transcendent (or, as he translates it, of higher) Idealism."

A glance at this line soon showed me the sort of criticism that I had to expect, much as though the reviewer were one who had never seen or heard of geometry, having found a Euclid, and coming upon various figures in turning over its leaves, were to say, on being asked his opinion of it: "The work is a text-book of drawing; the author introduces a peculiar terminology, in order to give dark, incomprehensible directions, which in the end teach nothing more than what every one can effect by a fair natural accuracy of eye, etc."

Let us see, in the meantime, what sort of an idealism it is that goes through my whole work, although it does not by a long way constitute the soul of the system.

The dictum of all genuine idealists from the Eleatic school to Bishop Berkeley, is contained in this formula: "All cognition through the senses and experience is nothing but sheer illusion, and only, in the ideas of the pure understanding and reason there is truth."

The principle that throughout dominates and determines my Idealism, is on the contrary: "All cognition of things merely from pure understanding or pure reason is nothing but sheer illusion, and only in experience is there truth."

But this is directly contrary to idealism proper. How came I then to use this expression for quite an opposite purpose, and how came my reviewer to see it everywhere?

The solution of this difficulty rests on something that could have been very easily understood from the general bearing of the work, if the reader had only desired to do so. Space and time, together with all that they contain, are not things nor qualities in themselves, but belong merely to the appearances of the latter: up to this point I am one in confession with the above idealists. But these, and amongst them more particularly Berkeley, regarded space as a mere empirical presentation that, like the phenomenon it contains, is only known to us by means of experience or perception, together with its determinations. I, on the contrary, prove in the first place, that space (and also time, which Berkeley did not consider) and all its determinations a priori, can be known by us, because, no less than time, it inheres in our sensibility as a pure form before all perception or experience and makes all intuition of the same, and therefore all its phenomena, possible. It follows from this, that as truth rests on universal and necessary laws as its criteria, experience, according to Berkeley, can have no criteria of truth, because its phenomena (according to him) have nothing a priori at their foundation; whence it follows, that they are nothing but sheer illusion; whereas with us, space and time (in conjunction with the pure conceptions of the understanding) prescribe their law to all possible experience a priori, and at the same time afford the certain criterion for distinguishing truth from illusion therein.

My so-called (properly critical) idealism is of quite a special character, in that it subverts the ordinary idealism, and that through it all cognition a priori, even that of geometry, first receives objective reality, which, without my demonstrated ideality of space and time, could not be maintained by the most zealous realists. This being the state of the case, I could have wished, in order to avoid all misunderstanding, to have named this conception of mine otherwise, but to alter it altogether was impossible. It may be permitted me however, in future, as has been above intimated, to term it "formal," or better still, "critical" idealism, to distinguish it from the dogmatic idealism of Berkeley, and from the skeptical idealism of Descartes.

Beyond this, I find nothing further remarkable in the judgment of my book. The reviewer criticizes here and there, makes sweeping criticisms, a mode prudently chosen, since it does not betray one's own knowledge or ignorance; a single thorough criticism in detail, had it touched the main question, as is only fair, would have exposed, it may be my error, or it may be my reviewer's measure of insight into this species of research. It was, moreover, not a badly conceived plan, in order at once to take from readers (who are accustomed to form their conceptions of books from newspaper reports) the desire to read the book itself, to pour out in one breath a number of passages in succession, torn from their connection, and their grounds of proof and explanations, and which must necessarily sound senseless, especially considering how antipathetic they are to all school-metaphysics; to exhaust the reader's patience ad nauseam, and then, after having made me acquainted with the sensible proposition that persistent illusion is truth, to conclude with the crude paternal moralization: to what end, then, the quarrel with accepted language, to what end, and whence, the idealistic distinction? A judgment which seeks all that is characteristic of my book, first supposed to be metaphysically heterodox, in a mere innovation of the nomenclature, proves clearly that my would-be judge has understood nothing of the subject, and in addition, has not understood himself.

My reviewer speaks like a man who is conscious of important and superior insight which he keeps hidden; for I am aware of nothing recent with respect to metaphysics that could justify his tone. But he should not withhold his discoveries from the world, for there are doubtless many who, like myself, have not been able to find in all the fine things that have for long past been written in this department, anything that has advanced the science by so much as a finger-breadth; we find indeed the giving a new point to definitions, the supplying of lame proofs with new crutches, the adding to the crazy-quilt of metaphysics fresh patches or changing its pattern; but all this is not what the world requires. The world is tired of metaphysical assertions; it wants the possibility of the science, the sources from which certainty therein can be derived, and certain criteria by which it may distinguish the dialectical illusion of pure reason from truth. To this the critic seems to possess a key, otherwise he would never have spoken out in such a high tone.

But I am inclined to suspect that no such requirement of the science has ever entered his thoughts, for in that case he would have directed his judgment to this point, and even a mistaken attempt in such an important matter, would have won his respect. If that be the case, we are once more good friends. He may penetrate as deeply as he likes into metaphysics, without any one hindering him; only as concerns that which lies outside metaphysics, its sources, which are to be found in reason, he cannot form a judgment. That my suspicion is not without foundation, is proved by the fact that he does not mention a word about the possibility of synthetic knowledge a priori, the special problem upon the solution of which the fate of metaphysics wholly rests, and upon which my Critique (as well as the present Prolegomena) entirely hinges. The Idealism he encountered, and which he hung upon,: was only taken up in the doctrine as the sole means of solving the above problem (although it received its confirmation on other grounds), and hence he must have shown either that the above problem does not possess the importance I attribute to it (even in these Prolegomena), or that by my conception of appearances, it is either not solved at all, or can be better solved in another way; but I do not find a word of this in the criticism. The reviewer, then, understands nothing of my work, and possibly also nothing of the spirit and essential nature of metaphysics itself; and it is not, what I would rather assume, the hurry of a man incensed at the labor of plodding through so many obstacles, that threw an unfavorable shadow over the work lying before him, and made its fundamental features unrecognizable.

There is a good deal to be done before a learned journal, it matters not with what care its writers may be selected, can maintain its otherwise well-merited reputation, in the field of metaphysics as elsewhere. Other sciences and branches of knowledge have their standard. Mathematics has it, in itself; history and theology, in profane or sacred books; natural science and the art of medicine, in mathematics and experience; jurisprudence, in law books; and even matters of taste in the examples of the ancients. But for the judgment of the thing called metaphysics, the standard has yet to be found. I have made an attempt to determine it, as well as its use. What is to be done, then, until it be found, when works of this kind have to be judged of? If they are of a dogmatic character, one may do what one likes; no one will play the master over others here for long, before some one else appears to deal with him in the same manner. If, however, they are critical in their character, not indeed with reference to other works, but to reason itself, so that the standard of judgment cannot be assumed but has first of all to be sought for, then, though objection and blame may indeed be permitted, yet a certain degree of leniency is indispensable, since the need is common to us all, and the lack of the necessary insight makes the high-handed attitude of judge unwarranted.

In order, however, to connect my defense with the interest of the philosophical commonwealth, I propose a test, which must be decisive as to the mode, whereby all metaphysical investigations may be directed to their common purpose. This is nothing more than what formerly mathematicians have done, in establishing the advantage of their methods by competition. I challenge my critic to demonstrate, as is only just, on a priori grounds, in his way, a single really metaphysical principle asserted by him. Being metaphysical it must be synthetic and cognized a priori from concepts, but it may also be any one of the most indispensable principles, as for instance, the principle of the persistence of substance, or of the necessary determination of events in the world by their causes. If he cannot do this (silence however is confession), he must admit, that as metaphysics without apodictic certainty of propositions of this kind is nothing at all, its possibility or impossibility must before all things be established in a critique of the pure reason. Thus he is bound either to confess that my principles in the Critique are correct, or he must prove their invalidity. But as I can already foresee, that, confidently as he has hitherto relied on the certainty of his principles, when it comes to a strict test he will not find a single one in the whole range of metaphysics he can bring forward, I will concede to him an advantageous condition, which can only be expected in such a competition, and will relieve him of the onus probandi by laying it on myself.

He finds in these Prolegomena and in my Critique [chapter on the theses and antitheses in "The Antinomy of Pure Reason"] eight propositions, of which two and two contradict one another, but each of which necessarily belongs to metaphysics, by which it must either be accepted or rejected (although there is not one that has not in this time been held by some philosopher). Now he has the liberty of selecting any one of these eight propositions at his pleasure, and accepting it without any proof, of which I shall make him a present, but only one (for waste of time will be just as little serviceable to him as to me), and then of attacking my proof of the opposite proposition. If I can save this one, and at the same time show, that according to principles which every dogmatic metaphysics must necessarily recognize, the opposite of the proposition adopted by him can be just as clearly proved, it is thereby established that metaphysics has an hereditary failing, not to be explained, much less set aside, until we ascend to its birth-place, pure reason itself, and thus my Critique must either be accepted or a better one take its place; it must at least be studied, which is the only thing I now require. If, on the other hand, I cannot save my demonstration, then a synthetic proposition a priori from dogmatic principles is to be reckoned to the score of my opponent, then also I will deem my impeachment of ordinary metaphysics as unjust, and pledge myself to recognize his stricture on my Critique as justified (although this would not be the consequence by a long way). To this end it would be necessary, it seems to me, that he should step out of his incognito. Otherwise I do not see how it could be avoided, that instead of dealing with one, I should be honored by several problems coming from anonymous and unqualified opponents.

APPENDIX: PROPOSALS AS TO AN INVESTIGATION OF THE CRITIQUE UPON WHICH A JUDGMENT MAY FOLLOW.

I feel obliged to the honored public even for the silence with which it for a long time favored my Critique, for this proves at least a postponement of judgment, and some supposition that in a work, leaving all beaten tracks and striking out on a new path, in which one cannot at once perhaps so easily find one's way, something may perchance lie, from which an important but at present dead branch of human knowledge may derive new life and productiveness. Hence may have originated a solicitude for the as yet tender shoot, lest it be destroyed by a hasty judgment. A specimen of a judgment, delayed for the above reasons, is now before my eye in the Gothaischen gelehrten Zeitung [24 August 1782], the thoroughness of which (without taking into consideration my praise, which might be suspicious) every reader will himself perceive, from the clear and unperverted presentation of a fragment of one of the first principles of my work.

Since an extensive structure cannot be judged of as a whole from a hurried glance, I propose to test it piece by piece from its foundations, so thereby the present Prolegomena may fitly be used as a general outline with which the work itself may occasionally be compared. This notion, if it were founded on nothing more than my conceit of importance, such as vanity commonly attributes to one's own productions, would be immodest and would deserve to be repudiated with disgust. But now, the interests of speculative philosophy have arrived at the point of total extinction, while human reason hangs upon them with inextinguishable affection, and only after having been ceaselessly deceived does it vainly attempt to change this into indifference.

In our thinking age it is not to be supposed but that many deserving men would use any good opportunity of working for the common interest of the more and more enlightened reason, if there were only some hope of attaining the goal. Mathematics, natural science, laws, arts, even morality, etc., do not completely fill the soul; there is always a space left over, reserved for pure and speculative reason, the vacuity of which prompts us to seek in vagaries, buffooneries, and mysticism for what seems to be employment and entertainment, but what actually is mere pastime; in order to deaden the troublesome voice of reason, which in accordance with its nature requires something that can satisfy it, and not merely subserve other ends or the interests of our inclinations. A consideration, therefore, which is concerned only with reason as it exists for it itself, has as I may reasonably suppose a great fascination for every one who has attempted thus to extend his conceptions, and I may even say a greater than any other theoretical branch of knowledge, for which he would not willingly exchange it, because here all other cognitions, and even purposes, must meet and unite themselves in a whole.

I offer, therefore, these Prolegomena as a sketch and text-book for this investigation, and not the work itself. Although I am even now perfectly satisfied with the latter as far as contents, order, and mode of presentation, and the care that I have expended in weighing and testing every sentence before writing it down, are concerned (for it has taken me years to satisfy myself fully, not only as regards the whole but in some cases even as to the sources of one particular proposition); yet I am not quite satisfied with my exposition in some sections of the doctrine of elements, as for instance in the deduction of the conceptions of the Understanding, or in that on the paralogisms of pure reason, because a certain diffuseness takes away from their clearness, and in place of them, what is here said in the Prolegomena respecting these sections, may be made the basis of the test.

It is the boast of the Germans that where steady and continuous industry are requisite, they can carry things farther than other nations. If this opinion be well founded, an opportunity, a business, presents itself, the successful issue of which we can scarcely doubt, and in which all thinking men can equally take part, though they have hitherto been unsuccessful in accomplishing it and in thus confirming the above good opinion. This is chiefly because the science in question is of so peculiar a kind, that it can be at once brought to completion and to that enduring state that it will never be able to be brought in the least degree farther or increased by later discoveries, or even changed (leaving here out of account adornment by greater clearness in some places, or additional uses), and this is an advantage no other science has or can have, because there is none so fully isolated and independent of others, and which is concerned with the faculty of cognition pure and simple. And the present moment seems, moreover, not to be unfavorable to my expectation, for just now, in Germany, no one seems to know wherewith to occupy himself, apart from the so-called useful sciences, so as to pursue not mere play, but a business possessing an enduring purpose.

To discover the means how the endeavors of the learned may be united in such a purpose, I must leave to others. In the meantime, it is my intention to persuade any one merely to follow my propositions, or even to flatter me with the hope that he will do so; but attacks, repetitions, limitations, or confirmation, completion, and extension, as the case may be, should be appended. If the matter be but investigated from its foundation, it cannot fail that a system, albeit not my own, shall be erected, that shall be a possession for future generations for which they may have reason to be grateful.

It would lead us too far here to show what kind of metaphysics may be expected, when only the principles of criticism have been perfected, and how, because the old false feathers have been pulled out, she need by no means appear poor and reduced to an insignificant figure, but may be in other respects richly and respectably adorned. But other and great uses which would result from such a reform, strike one immediately. The ordinary metaphysics had its uses, in that it sought out the elementary conceptions of the pure understanding in order to make them clear through analysis, and definite by explanation. In this way it was a training for reason, in whatever direction it might be turned. But this was all the good it did. This service was subsequently effaced when it favored conceit by venturesome assertions, sophistry by subtle dodges and adornment, and shallowness by the ease with which it decided the most difficult problems by means of a little school-wisdom, which is only the more seductive the more it has the choice, on the one hand, of taking something from the language of science, and on the other from that of popular discourse — thus being everything to everybody, but in reality nothing at all. By criticism, however, a standard is given to our judgment, whereby knowledge may be with certainty distinguished from pseudo-science, and firmly founded, being brought into full operation in metaphysics — a mode of thought extending by degrees its beneficial influence over every other use of reason, at once infusing into it the true philosophical spirit. But the service also that metaphysics performs for theology, by making it independent of the judgment of dogmatic speculation, thereby assuring it completely against the attacks of all such opponents, is certainly not to be valued lightly. For ordinary metaphysics, although it promised the latter much advantage, could not keep this promise, and moreover, by summoning speculative dogmatics to its assistance, did nothing but arm enemies against itself. Mysticism, which can prosper in a rationalistic age only when it hides itself behind a system of school-metaphysics, under the protection of which it may venture to rave with a semblance of rationality, is driven from this, its last hiding-place, by critical philosophy. Last, but not least, it cannot be otherwise than important to a teacher of metaphysics, to be able to say with universal assent, that what he expounds is science, and that thereby genuine services will be rendered to the commonweal.

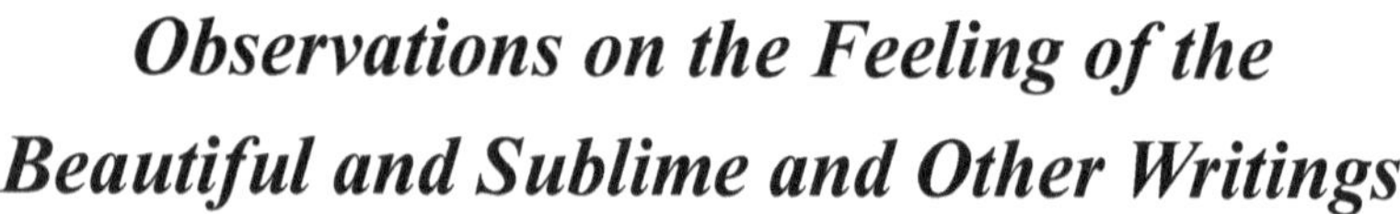

Observations on the Feeling of the Beautiful and Sublime and Other Writings

Contents

Thoughts on the Occasion of Mr. Johann Friedrich von Funk's Untimely Death

Highborn wife of the cavalry captain, Gracious Lady!

If people living amidst the turmoil of their practical affairs and diversions were occasionally to mix in serious moments of instructive contemplation, to which they are called by the daily display of the vanity of our intentions regarding the fate of their fellow citizens: thereby their pleasures would perhaps be less intoxicating, but their position would take up a calm serenity of the soul, by which accidents are no longer unexpected, and even the gentle melancholy, this tender feeling with which a noble heart swells up if it considers in solitary stillness the contemptibleness of that which, with us, commonly ranks as great and important, would contain more true happiness than the violent merriment of the flippant and the loud laughing of fools.

But thus the greatest crowd of human beings mixes very eagerly in the throng of those who, on the bridge that Providence has built over a piece of the abyss of eternity and that we call life, run after certain bubbles and do not trouble to take caution for the planks, who allow one after another to sink beside each other into the depths whose extent is infinity and by which they themselves, in the midst of their impetuous course, are eventually engulfed. In the portrayal of human life, a certain ancient poet brings forth a stirring breath by describing the newly born human being. The child, he says, at once fills the air with sad whimpers, as befits someone who must enter into a world where so many hardships await him. Only in the sequence of years does this human being connect with the art of making himself miserable the art of hiding it from himself with a blanket that he throws on the sad elements of life, and cultivate a flippant carelessness about the amount of ill that surrounds him and as it were inexorably finally drives him back to a much more painful feeling. Although he dreads death most of all ills, he still seems to pay very little attention to the example of it among his fellow citizens, unless closer ties particularly wake his heedfulness. At a time when a raging war opens the bolts of the dark abyss, so as to allow all affliction to break forth over the human race, one sees very well how the common sight of hardship and death instills a cold-natured indifference into those who have been threatened by both, so that they have little heed for the fate of their brothers. Only when in the quiet stillness of civic life, out of the circle of those who either closely concern us or whom we love, who had as many or more promising hopes as we have, and who have been attached to their intentions and plans with the same zeal as we are, only when these, I say, according to the decision of God, who omnipotently rules over all, are taken in the midst of the course of their endeavors; when death in peaceful stillness nears the sickbed of the infirm; when this giant, before which nature shudders, reaches the sickbed with slow steps, to embrace him in iron arms; only then is the feeling of those who otherwise dampen it with diversions truly awakened. A melancholy feeling speaks out of the interior of the heart that which in an assembly of Romans was once heard with so much applause because it is so in accordance with our common perception: I am a human being, and what befalls human beings can also happen to me. The friend or relative says to himself: I find myself in the turmoil of business and in the throng of life's duties, and my friend just recently also found himself in the same, I enjoy my life quietly and without worry, but who knows for how long? I amuse myself with my friends and seek him among these same friends,

Yet he is held fast in that cheerless place

By him who lets nothing remain [to us]

In eternity's powerful arms.

– Haller

These serious thoughts arise in me because of the early death of your dignified son, gracious woman, which you now so rightly mourn. As one of his former teachers, I feel this loss with grievous sympathy, although I can, surely, hardly express the extent of the sadness that must affect those who were linked with this hopeful young man through closer bonds. Your grace will allow me to add to these few lines, through which I strive to express the respect that I have entertained for my former pupil, some thoughts that arise in me in my current state of mind.

Every person forms his own plan of his destiny in this world. Skills that he wants to gain, honor and leisure in the future that he expects from them, lasting happiness in married life, and a long line of joys or of ventures constitute the images of the magic lantern that he ingeniously draws and plays in vivid succession in his imagination; death, which puts an end to this shadow play, appears only in the dark distance and is made obscure and unrecognizable by the light that is shed over the more pleasant places. During these reveries our true fate leads us along completely different ways. The lot that will really be granted to us seldom looks similar to what we promised ourselves, in every step that we take we find ourselves deceived in our anticipation; nevertheless the imagination goes about its business and does not tire of drawing up new plans, until death, which still seems to be far away, suddenly brings the whole game to an end. If the person is brought back by understanding from this world of fables, of which he is himself creator through imagination and in which he so gladly resides, to that which providence has truly designed for him, he is thereby put into confusion by a wondrous contradiction that he encounters there and which brings his plans entirely to naught, by presenting to his comprehension insoluble riddles. Budding merits of hopeful youth often fade prematurely under the weight of serious illnesses, and an unwelcome death strikes down the entire plan of hope on which one had counted. The man of skill, of merit, of wealth is not always the one to whom providence has set the farthest end to his life in order fully to enjoy the fruits of all of these. The friendships that are most fond, the marriages that promise the most happiness, are often mercilessly torn by premature death; meanwhile poverty and misery together pull a long thread on the dress of the Fates and many only appear to torment themselves or others by living so long. In this apparent contradiction, the supreme ruler nevertheless distributes his fortune to each with a wise hand. He conceals the end of our destiny in this world in inscrutable darkness, makes us busy with drives, consoled by hope, and, by the happy ignorance of the future, [keeps us] just as constantly thinking of aims and plans when they will soon all come to an end as if we stood at their beginning:

That each may fill the circle mark'd by Heav'n.

– Pope

Among these considerations the wise (although how seldom one such is found!) directs attention primarily to his great destiny beyond the grave. He does not lose sight of obligation, which is imposed by his position, which Providence has designed for him. Rational in his plans, but without obstinacy; confident of the fulfillment of his hope, but without impatience; modest in wishes, without dictating; trusting, without insisting; he is eager in the performance of his duties but ready in the midst of all these endeavors to follow the order of the Most High with a Christian resignation if it is pleasing to Him to call him away from the stage where he has been placed, in the middle of all these endeavors. We always find the ways of Providence wise and worthy of worship in those parts where we can understand it to some extent; should they not be more so, where we cannot understand? A premature death of those for whom we had much flattering hope gives us fright; but how often this can be, rather, the greatest grace of heaven! Wasn't the misfortune of many a person primarily in the delay of death, which was much too belated to make an end at the right time, after the most laudable performances of life?

The hopeful youth dies, and how much do we believe to be lost through such an early loss? Only in the book of destiny does it perhaps read differently. Seductions that have already arisen from afar in order to dash a not yet well-established virtue, afflictions and tribulations, which the future threatened, this blissfully happy one, whom an early death led away in a blessed hour, has escaped all of these; meanwhile friends and relatives, not knowing the future, mourn the loss of those years that they themselves imagine would have someday crowned the life of this family member with glory. Before I close these few lines, I want to draw a small sketch of the life and character of the blessedly deceased. That which I cite is known to me by the communication of his trusted tutor, who mourns him fondly, and from my own acquaintance with him. Yet how many are the good characteristics that are nobler the less they strive to fall openly on the eyes and that are known only to him who sees into the core of the heart!

Herr Johann Friedrich von Funk was born on the 4th of October, 1738 into a distinguished noble family in Kurland. From childhood, he never enjoyed full health. He was brought up with great care, showed much diligence in study, and had a heart that was created by nature to be formed to noble qualities. On the 15th of June, 1759, he came, with his younger brother, to this academy under the guidance of their private tutor. He submitted himself with all willingness to the exams of the then dean and brought honor to his diligence and the instruction of his tutor. He attended the lectures of the counselor of the consistory and Professor Teske, who is at the present time Rectoris Magnifici of the university, and likewise attended the lectures of Doctor of Jurisprudence Funck and my own, with an exemplary sedulousness. He lived withdrawn and quietly, through which he still also retained the little strength of his body, which was inclined to emaciation, until near the end of February of this year when he was gradually so weakened that neither the nursing and care that were given him nor the diligence of an adept doctor could any longer preserve him; so weakened that on the 4th of May this year, after he had prepared himself for an uplifting end with the fortitude and ardent devotion of a Christian, with the attendance of his trusted pastor he gently and blessedly passed away and was fittingly buried at the cathedral here.

He was of gentle and calm character, affable and modest toward everyone, kind and inclined toward universal benevolence, zealously solicitous in order to cultivate himself properly to the advantage of his house and his fatherland. He had never grieved anyone except through his death. He was eager to have unfeigned piety. He would have become an upright citizen of the world, except that the decree of the Most High willed that he should become one in heaven. His life is a fragment that leaves us much to have wished for, of which we have been deprived by early death. He would deserve to be represented as an exemplar to those who want to honorably leave behind the years of their upbringing and youth, if emulating a silent service appeals to those of fickle mind as much as the falsely shimmering qualities of those whose conceit pursues only an illusion of virtue without minding the essence of it. He is much mourned by those to whom he belonged, by his friends and everyone who knew him.

These, gracious lady, are the traits of the character of your formerly in life rightly so beloved son, which, so poorly they may be drawn, nevertheless renew the melancholy that you feel far too much over his loss. But these very bemourned qualities are those that bring no small solace; for only to those who carelessly place the most important of all intentions out of sight can it make no matter in which condition their family is consigned into eternity. I strain myself with the effort to set forth to your grace the extensive reasons for solace in this grief. The humble renunciation of our own wishes, when it pleases the wisest Providence to make a different decision, and the Christian longing for the one blessed goal which others before us have reached, are capable of calming of the heart more than all reasons of a dry and feeble eloquence.

I have the honor with the greatest respect to be,

Highborn Lady,

Gracious wife of the captain of cavalry,

Your Grace's

Königsberg,	Most obedient servant
The 6th of June, 1760.	I. Kant

Observations on the Feeling of the Beautiful and Sublime

First Section
On the distinct objects of the feeling for the sublime and the beautiful

The different sentiments of gratification or vexation rest not so much on the constitution of the external things that arouse them as on the feeling, intrinsic to every person, of being touched by them with pleasure or displeasure. Hence arise the joys for some people in what is disgusting to others, the passion of a lover that is often a mystery to everyone else, or even the lively repugnance that one person feels in that which is completely indifferent to another. The field for observations of these peculiarities of human nature is very extensive and still conceals a rich lode for discoveries that are as charming as they are instructive. For now I will cast my glance only on several places that seem especially to stand out in this region, and even on these more with the eye of an observer than of the philosopher.

Since a human being finds himself happy only insofar as he satisfies an inclination, the feeling that makes him capable of enjoying a great gratification without requiring exceptional talents is certainly no small matter. Stout persons, whose most inspired author is their cook, and whose works of fine taste are to be found in their cellar, get just as lively a joy from vulgarities and a crude joke as that of which persons of nobler sentiment are so proud. A comfortable man, who likes having books read aloud to him because that helps him fall asleep; the merchant to whom all gratifications seem ridiculous except for that which a clever man enjoys when he calculates his business profits; he who loves the opposite sex only insofar as he counts it among the things that are to be enjoyed; the lover of the hunt, whether he hunts fleas, like Domitian, or wild beasts, like A—: all of these have a feeling which makes them capable of enjoying gratification after their fashion, without their having to envy others or even being able to form any concept of others; but for now I do not direct any attention to this. There is still a feeling of a finer sort, thus named either because one can enjoy it longer without surfeit and exhaustion, or because it presupposes, so to speak, a susceptibility of the soul which at the same time makes it fit for virtuous impulses, or because it is a sign of talents and excellences of the intellect; while by contrast the former can occur in complete thoughtlessness. It is this feeling one aspect of which I will consider. Yet I exclude here the inclination which is attached to lofty intellectual insights, and the charm of which a Kepler was capable when, as Bayle reports, he would not have sold one of his discoveries for a princedom. This sentiment is altogether too fine to belong in the present project, which will touch only upon the sensuous feeling of which more common souls are also capable.

The finer feeling that we will now consider is preeminently of two kinds: the feeling of the sublime and of the beautiful. Being touched by either is agreeable, but in very different ways. The sight of a mountain whose snow-covered peaks arise above the clouds, the description of a raging storm, or the depiction of the kingdom of hell by Milton arouses satisfaction, but with dread; by contrast, the prospect of meadows strewn with flowers, of valleys with winding brooks, covered with grazing herds, the description of Elysium, or Homer's depiction of the girdle of Venus also occasion an agreeable sentiment, but one that is joyful and smiling. For the former to make its impression on us in its proper strength, we must have a feeling of the sublime, and in order properly to enjoy the latter we must have a feeling for the beautiful. Lofty oaks and lonely shadows in sacred groves are sublime, flowerbeds, low hedges, and trees trimmed into figures are beautiful. The night is sublime, the day is beautiful. Casts of mind that possess a feeling for the sublime are gradually drawn into lofty sentiments, of friendship, of contempt for the world, of eternity, by the quiet calm of a summer evening, when the flickering light of the stars breaks through the umber shadows of the night and the lonely moon rises into view. The brilliant day inspires busy fervor and a feeling of gaiety. The sublime touches, the beautiful charms. The mien of the human being who finds himself in the full feeling of the sublime is serious, sometimes even rigid and astonished. By contrast, the lively sentiment of the beautiful announces itself through shining cheerfulness in the eyes, through traces of a smile, and often through audible mirth. The sublime is in turn of different sorts. The feeling of it is sometimes accompanied with some dread or even melancholy, in some cases merely with quiet admiration and in yet others with a beauty spread over a sublime prospect. I will call the first the terrifying sublime, the second the noble, and the third the magnificent. Deep solitude is sublime, but in a terrifying way. For this reason great and extensive wastes, such as the immense deserts of Schamo in Tartary, have always   given us occasion to people them with fearsome shades, goblins, and ghosts.

The sublime must always be large, the beautiful can also be small. The sublime must be simple, the beautiful can be decorated and ornamented. A great height is just as sublime as a great depth, but the latter is accompanied with the sensation of shuddering, the former with that of admiration; hence the latter sentiment can be terrifyingly sublime and the former noble. The sight of an Egyptian pyramid is far more moving, as Hasselquist reports, than one can imagine from any description, but its construction is simple and noble. St. Peter's in Rome is magnificent. Since on its frame, which is grand and simple, beauty, e.g., gold, mosaics, etc., are spread in such a way that it is still the sentiment of the sublime which has the most effect, the object is called magnificent. An arsenal must be noble and simple, a residential castle magnificent, and a pleasure palace beautiful and decorated.

A long duration is sublime. If it is of time past, it is noble; if it is projected forth into an unforeseeable future, then there is something terrifying in it. An edifice from the most distant antiquity is worthy of honor. Haller's description of the future eternity inspires a mild horror, and of the past, a transfixed admiration.

Second Section
On the qualities of the sublime and the beautiful in human beings in general

Understanding is sublime, wit is beautiful. Boldness is sublime and grand, cunning is petty, but beautiful. Caution, said Cromwell, is a virtue for mayors. Truthfulness and honesty is simple and noble, jocularity and pleasing flattery is fine and beautiful. Civility is the beauty of virtue. An unselfish urge to serve is noble, refinement (politesse) and courtliness are beautiful. Sublime qualities inspire esteem, but beautiful ones inspire love. People whose feelings run primarily to the beautiful seek out their honest, steady, and serious friends only in case of need; for ordinary company, however, they choose jocular, clever, and courtly companions. One esteems many a person too highly to be able to love him. He inspires admiration, but he is too far above us for us to dare to come close to him with the familiarity of love.

Those in whom both feelings are united will find that they are more powerfully moved by the sublime than by the beautiful, but that without variation or accompaniment by the latter the former is tiring and cannot be enjoyed as long. The lofty sentiments to which conversation in a well-chosen company is sometimes elevated must intermittently dissolve into a cheerful joke, and laughing joys should make a beautiful contrast with moved, serious countenances, allowing for an unforced alternation between both sorts of sentiment. Friendship has primarily the character of the sublime, but sexual love that of the beautiful. Yet tenderness and deep esteem give the latter a certain dignity and sublimity, while flighty jocularity and intimacy elevate the coloration of the beautiful in this sentiment. In my opinion, tragedy is distinguished from comedy primarily in the fact that in the former it is the feeling for the sublime while in the latter it is the feeling for the beautiful that is touched. In the former there is displayed magnanimous sacrifice for the well-being of another, bold resolve in the face of danger, and proven fidelity. There love is melancholic, tender, and full of esteem; the misfortune of others stirs sympathetic sentiments in the bosom of the onlooker and allows his magnanimous heart to beat for the need of others. He is gently moved and feels the dignity of his own nature. Comedy, in contrast, represents intrigues, marvelous entanglements and clever people who know how to wriggle out of them, fools who let themselves be deceived, jests and ridiculous characters. Here love is not so grave, it is merry and intimate. Yet as in other cases, here too the noble can be united with the beautiful to a certain degree.

Even the vices and moral failings often carry with them some of the traits of the sublime or the beautiful, at least as they appear to our sensory feeling, without having been examined by reason. The wrath of someone fearsome is sublime, like the wrath of Achilles in the Iliad. In general, the hero of Homer is terrifyingly sublime, that of Virgil, by contrast, noble. Open, brazen revenge for a great offense has something grand in it, and however impermissible it might be, yet in the telling it nevertheless touches us with dread and satisfaction. When Shah Nadir was attacked at night in his tent by some conspirators, as Hanaway reports, after he had already received several wounds and was defending himself in despair, he yelled Mercy! I will pardon you all. One of the conspirators answered, as he raised his saber high: You have shown no mercy and deserve none. Resolute audacity in a rogue is extremely dangerous, yet it touches us in the telling, and even when he is dragged to a shameful death yet he enobles himself to a certain degree when he faces it spitefully and with contempt. On the other side, a cunningly conceived scheme, even when it amounts to a piece of knavery, has something about it that is fine and worth a laugh. A wanton inclination (*coquetterie*) in a refined sense, namely an effort to fascinate and to charm, is perhaps blameworthy in an otherwise decorous person, yet it is still beautiful and is commonly preferred to the honorable, serious demeanor.

The figure of persons who please through their outward appearance touches now upon one sort of feeling, now upon the other. A grand stature earns regard and respect, a small one more intimacy. Even brownish color and black eyes are more closely related to the sublime, blue eyes and blonde color to the beautiful. A somewhat greater age is associated more with the qualities of the sublime, youth, however, with those of the beautiful. It is similar with difference in station, and in all of those relations mentioned here even the costumes must match this distinction in feeling. Grand, sizable persons must observe simplicity or at most splendor in their dress, while small ones can be decorated and adorned. Darker colors and uniformity in costume are fitting for age, while youth radiates through brighter clothing with lively contrasts. Among the stations of similar fortune and rank, the cleric must display the greatest simplicity, the statesman the greatest splendor. The paramour can adorn himself as he pleases.

Even in external circumstances of fortune there is something that, at least in the folly of humankind, matches these sentiments. People commonly find themselves inclined to respect birth and title. Wealth, even without merit, is honored even by the disinterested, presumably because they associate with the representation of it projects for great actions that could be carried out by its means. This respect is even sometimes extended to many a rich scoundrel, who will never undertake such actions and has no conception of the noble feeling that can alone make riches estimable. What magnifies the evil of poverty is contempt, which cannot be entirely overcome even by merits, at least not before common eyes, unless rank and title deceive this coarse feeling and to some extent work to its advantage.

In human nature there are never to be found praiseworthy qualities that do not at the same time degenerate through endless gradations into the most extreme imperfection. The quality of the terrifying sublime,

if it becomes entirely unnatural, is adventurous. Unnatural things, in so far as the sublime is thereby intended, even if little or none of it is actually found, are grotesqueries. He who loves and believes the adventurous is a fantast, while the inclination to grotesqueries makes for a crank. On the other side, the feeling of the beautiful degenerates if the noble is entirely lacking from it, and one calls it ridiculous. A male with this quality, if he is young, is called a dandy, and if he is middle-aged, a fop. Since the sublime is most necessary for the greater age, an old fop is the most contemptible creature in nature, just as a young crank is the most repulsive and insufferable. Jokes and cheerfulness go with the feeling of the beautiful. Nevertheless a good deal of understanding can show through, and to this extent they can be more or less related to the sublime. He in whose cheerfulness this admixture cannot be noticed babbles. He who babbles constantly is silly. One readily notices that even clever people occasionally babble, and that it requires not a little intelligence to call the understanding away from its post for a brief time without anything thereby going awry. He whose speeches or actions neither entertain nor move is boring. The bore who nevertheless tries to do both is tasteless. The tasteless person, if he is conceited, is a fool.

I will make this curious catalog of human frailties somewhat more comprehensible through examples, for he who lacks Hogarth's burin must use description to make up for what the drawing lacks in expression. Boldly undertaking danger for our own rights, for those of the fatherland, or for those of our friends is sublime. The crusades and ancient knighthood were adventurous; duels, a miserable remnant of the latter out of a perverted conception of honor, are grotesqueries. Melancholy withdrawal from the tumult of the world out of a legitimate weariness is noble. The solitary devotion of the ancient hermits was adventurous. Cloisters and graves of that sort for the entombment of living saints are grotesqueries. Subduing one's passions by means of principles is sublime. Castigation, vows, and other such monkish virtues are grotesqueries. Holy bones, holy wood, and all that sort of rubbish, the holy stools of the Great Lama of Tibet not excluded, are grotesqueries. Among the works of wit and fine feeling, the epic poems of Virgil and Klopstock are among the noble, those of Homer and Milton among the adventurous. The *Metamorphoses* of Ovid are grotesqueries, the fairy tales of French lunacy are the most wretched grotesqueries that have ever been hatched. Anacreontic poems commonly come very close to the ridiculous.

The works of the understanding and acuity, to the extent that their objects also contain something for feeling, likewise take some part in the differences under consideration. The mathematical representation of the immeasurable magnitude of the universe, metaphysical considerations of eternity, of providence, of the immortality of our soul contain a certain sublimity and dignity. Yet philosophy is also distorted by many empty subtleties, and the semblance of thoroughness does not prevent the four syllogistic figures from deserving to be counted as scholastic grotesqueries.

Among moral qualities, true virtue alone is sublime. There are nevertheless good moral qualities that are lovable and beautiful and, to the extent that they harmonize with virtue, may also be regarded as noble, even though they cannot genuinely be counted as part of the virtuous disposition. Judgment about this is delicate and involved. One certainly cannot call that frame of mind virtuous that is a source of actions of the sort to which virtue would also lead but on grounds that only contingently agree with it, and which thus given its nature can also often conflict with the universal rules of virtue. A certain tenderheartedness that is easily led into a warm feeling of sympathy is beautiful and lovable, for it indicates a kindly participation in the fate of other people, to which principles of virtue likewise lead. But this kindly passion is nevertheless weak and is always blind. For suppose that this sentiment moves you to help someone in need with your expenditure, but you are indebted to someone else and by this means you make it impossible for yourself to fulfill the strict duty of justice; then obviously the action cannot arise from any virtuous resolution, for that could not possibly entice you into sacrificing a higher obligation to this blind enchantment. If, by contrast, general affection towards humankind has become your principle, to which you always subject your actions, then your love towards the one in need remains, but it is now, from a higher standpoint, placed in its proper relationship to your duty as a whole. The universal affection is a ground for participating in his ill-fortune, but at the same time it is also a ground of justice, in accordance with whose precept you must now forbear this action. Now as soon as this feeling is raised to its proper universality, it is sublime, but also colder. For it is not possible that our bosom should swell with tenderness on behalf of every human being and swim in melancholy for everyone else's need, otherwise the virtuous person, like Heraclitus constantly melting into sympathetic tears, with all this good-heartedness would nevertheless become nothing more than a tenderhearted idler.

The second sort of kindly feeling which is to be sure beautiful and lovable but still not the foundation of a genuine virtue is complaisance: an inclination to make ourselves agreeable to others through friendliness, through acquiescence to their demands, and through conformity of our conduct to their dispositions. This ground for a charming complaisance is beautiful, and the malleability of such a heart is kindly. Yet it is so far from being a virtue that unless higher principles set bounds for it and weaken it, all sorts of vices may spring from it. For without even considering that this complaisance towards those with whom we associate is often an injustice to those who find themselves outside of this little circle, such a man, if one takes this impulse alone, can have all sorts of vices, not because of immediate inclination but because he gladly lives to please. From affectionate complaisance he will be a liar, an idler, a drunkard, etc., for he does not act in accordance with the rules for good conduct in general, but rather in accordance with an inclination that is beautiful in itself but which in so far as it is without self-control and without principles becomes ridiculous.

Thus true virtue can only be grafted upon principles, and it will become the more sublime and noble the more general they are. These principles are not speculative rules, but the consciousness of a feeling that lives in every human breast and that extends much further than to the special grounds of sympathy and complaisance. I believe that I can bring all this together if I say that it is the feeling of the beauty and the dignity of human nature.28 The first is a ground of universal affection, the second of universal respect, and if this feeling had the greatest perfection in any human heart then this human being would certainly love and value even himself, but only in so far as he is one among all to whom his widespread and noble feeling extends itself. Only when one subordinates one's own particular inclination to such an enlarged one can our kindly drives be proportionately applied and bring about the noble attitude that is the beauty of virtue.

In recognition of the weakness of human nature and the little power that the universal moral feeling exercises over most hearts, providence has placed such helpful drives in us as supplements for virtue, which move some to beautiful actions even without principles while at the same time being able to give others, who are ruled by these principles, a greater impetus and a stronger impulse thereto. Sympathy and complaisance are grounds for beautiful actions that would perhaps all be suffocated by the preponderance of a cruder self-interest, but as we have seen they are not immediate grounds of virtue, although since they are ennobled by their kinship with it they also bear its name. Hence I can call them adopted virtues, but that which rest on principles genuine virtue.

The former are beautiful and charming, the latter alone is sublime and worthy of honor. One calls a mind in which the former sentiments rule a good heart and people of that sort good-hearted; but one rightly ascribes a noble heart to one who is virtuous from principles, calling him alone a righteous person. These adopted virtues nevertheless have a great similarity to the true virtues, since they contain the feeling of an immediate pleasure in kindly and benevolent actions. The good-hearted person will without any ulterior aim and from immediate complaisance conduct himself peaceably and courteously with you and feel sincere compassion for the need of another.

Yet since this moral sympathy is nevertheless not enough to drive indolent human nature to actions for the common weal, providence has further placed in us a certain feeling which is fine and moves us, or which can also balance cruder self-interest and vulgar sensuality. This is the feeling for honor and its consequence, shame. The opinion that others may have of our value and their judgment of our actions is a motivation of great weight, which can coax us into many sacrifices, and what a good part of humanity would have done neither out of an immediately arising emotion of good-heartedness nor out of principles happens often enough merely for the sake of outer appearance, out of a delusion that is very useful although in itself very facile, as if the judgment of others determined the worth of ourselves and our actions. What happens from this impulse is not in the least virtuous, for which reason everyone who wants to be taken for virtuous takes good care to conceal the motivation of lust for honor. This inclination is also not nearly so closely related as good-heartedness is to genuine virtue, since it is not moved immediately by the beauty of actions, but by their demeanor in the eyes of others. Since the feeling for honor is nevertheless still fine, I can call the similarity to virtue that is thereby occasioned the simulacrum of virtue.

If we compare the casts of mind of human beings in so far as one of these three species of feeling dominates in them and determines their moral character, we find that each of them stands in closer kinship with one of the temperaments as they are usually divided, yet in such a way that a greater lack of moral feeling would be the share of the phlegmatic. Not as if the chief criterion in the character of these different casts of mind came down to the features at issue; for in this treatise we are not considering the cruder feelings, e.g., that of self-interest, of vulgar sensuality, etc., at all, even though these sorts of inclinations are what are primarily considered in the customary division; but rather since the finer moral sentiments here mentioned are more compatible with one or the other of these temperaments and for the most part are actually so united.

An inward feeling for the beauty and dignity of human nature and a self-composure and strength of mind to relate all of one's actions to this as a general ground is serious and not readily associated with a fickle wantonness nor with the inconstancy of a frivolous person. It even approaches melancholy, a gentle and noble sentiment, to the extent that it is grounded in that dread which a restricted soul feels if, full of a great project, it sees the dangers that it has to withstand and has before its eyes the difficult but great triumph of self-overcoming. Genuine virtue from principles therefore has something about it that seems to agree most with the melancholic frame of mind in a moderate sense.

Good-heartedness, a beauty and fine susceptibility of the heart to be moved with sympathy or benevolence in individual cases as occasion demands, is very much subject to the change of circumstances; and since the movement of the soul does not rest upon a general principle, it readily takes on different shapes as the objects display one aspect or another. And since this inclination comes down to the beautiful, it appears to be most naturally united with that cast of mind that one calls sanguine, which is fickle and given to amusements. In this temperament we shall have to seek the well-loved qualities that we called adopted virtues.

The feeling for honor is usually already taken as a mark of the choleric complexion, and we can thereby take the occasion to seek out the moral consequences of this fine feeling, which for the most part are aimed only at show, for the depiction of such a character.

A person is never without all traces of finer sentiment, but a greater lack of the latter, which is comparatively called a lack of feeling, is found in the character of the phlegmatic, whom one also deprives even of the cruder incentives, such as lust for money, etc., which, however, together with other sister inclinations, we can even leave to him, because they do not belong in this plan at all.

Let us now more closely consider the sentiments of the sublime and the beautiful, especially in so far as they are moral, under the assumed division of the temperaments.

He whose feeling tends towards the melancholic is so called not because, robbed of the joys of life, he worries himself into blackest dejection, but because his sentiments, if they were to be increased above a certain degree or to take a false direction through some causes, would more readily result in that than in some other condition. He has above all a feeling for the sublime. Even beauty, for which he also has a sentiment, may not merely charm him, but must rather move him by at the same time inspiring him with admiration. The enjoyment of gratification is in his case more serious, but not on that account any lesser. All emotions of the sublime are more enchanting than the deceptive charms of the beautiful. His well-being will be contentment rather than jollity. He is steadfast. For that reason he subordinates his sentiments to principles. They are the less subject to inconstancy and alteration the more general is this principle to which they are subordinated, and thus the more extensive is the elevated feeling under which the lower ones are comprehended. All particular grounds of inclinations are subjected to many exceptions and alterations in so far as they are not derived from such a high ground. The cheerful and friendly Alceste says: I love and treasure my wife, because she is beautiful, flattering, and clever. But what if, when she becomes disfigured with illness, sullen with age, and, once the first enchantment has disappeared, no longer seems more clever than any other to you? If the ground is no longer there, what can become of the inclination? By contrast, take the benevolent and steady Adraste, who thinks to himself: I will treat this person lovingly and with respect, because she is my wife.

This disposition is noble and generous. However the contingent charms may change, she is nevertheless always still his wife. The noble ground endures and is not so subject to the inconstancy of external things. Such is the quality of principles in comparison to emotions, which well up only on particular occasions, and thus is the man of principles by contrast to one who is occasionally overcome by a good-hearted and lovable motivation. But what if the secret language of his heart speaks thus: I must come to the help of this human being, for he suffers; not that he is my friend or companion, or that I hold him capable of sometime repaying my beneficence with gratitude. There is now no time for ratiocination and stopping at questions: He is a human being, and whatever affects human beings also affects me. Then his conduct is based on the highest ground of benevolence in human nature and is extremely sublime, on account of its inalterability as well as the universality of its application.

I continue with my comments. The person of a melancholic frame of mind troubles himself little about how others judge, what they hold to be good or true, and in that regard he relies solely on his own insight. Since his motivations take on the nature of principles, he is not easily brought to other conceptions; his steadfastness thus sometimes degenerates into obstinacy. He looks on changes in fashion with indifference and on their luster with contempt. Friendship is sublime and hence he has a feeling for it. He can perhaps lose an inconstant friend, but the latter does not lose him equally quickly. Even the memory of an extinguished friendship is still worthy of honor for him. Talkativeness is beautiful, thoughtful taciturnity sublime. He is a good guardian of his own secrets and those of others. Truthfulness is sublime, and he hates lies or dissemblance. He has a lofty feeling for the dignity of human nature. He esteems himself and holds a human being to be a creature who deserves respect. He does not tolerate abject submissiveness and breathes freedom in a noble breast. All shackles, from the golden ones worn at court to the heavy irons of the galley-slave, are abominable to him. He is a strict judge of himself and others and is not seldom weary of himself as well as of the world.

In the degenerate form of this character, seriousness inclines to dejection, piety to zealotry, the fervor for freedom to enthusiasm. Insult and injustice kindle vengefulness in him. He is then very much to be feared. He defies danger and has contempt for death. In case of perversion of his feeling and lack of a cheerful reason he succumbs to the adventurous: inspirations, apparitions, temptations. If the understanding is even weaker, he hits upon grotesqueries: portentous dreams, presentiments, and wondrous omens. He is in danger of becoming a fantast or a crank.

The person of a sanguine frame of mind has a dominant feeling for the beautiful. His joys are therefore laughing and lively. When he is not jolly, he is discontent and he has little acquaintance with contented silence. Variety is beautiful, and he loves change. He seeks joy in himself and around himself, amuses others, and is good company. He has much moral sympathy. The joyfulness of others is gratifying to him, and their suffering makes him soft-hearted. His moral feeling is beautiful, yet without principles, and is always immediately dependent upon the impressions that objects make on him at the moment. He is a friend of all human beings, or, what is really the same, never really a friend, although he is certainly good-hearted and benevolent. He does not dissemble. Today he will entertain you with his friendliness and good sorts, tomorrow, when you are ill or misfortunate, he will feel genuine and unfeigned compassion, but he will quietly slip away until the circumstances have changed. He must never be a judge. The laws are commonly too strict for him, and he lets himself be bribed by tears. He is a bad saint, never entirely good and never entirely evil. He

is often dissolute and wicked, more from complaisance than from inclination. He is
liberal and generous, but a poor payer of his debts, since he has much sentiment for
goodness but little for justice. Nobody has as good an opinion of his own heart as he
does. If you do not esteem him, you must still love him. In the greater deterioration of
his character, he descends to the ridiculous, he is dawdling and childish. If age does
not diminish his liveliness or bring him more understanding, then he is in danger of
becoming an old fop.

He whom one means by the choleric constitution of mind has a dominant feeling for
that sort of the sublime which one can call the magnificent. It is really only the gloss
of sublimity and a strikingly contrasting coloration, which hides the inner content of
the thing or the person, who is perhaps only bad and common, and which deceives and
moves through its appearance. Just as an edifice makes just as noble an impression
by means of a stucco coating that represents carved stones, as if it were really made
from that, and tacked-on cornices and pilasters give the idea of solidity although they
have little bearing and support nothing, in the same way do alloyed virtues, tinsel of
wisdom, and painted merit also glisten.

The choleric person considers his own value and the value of his things and actions on
the basis of the propriety or the appearance with which it strikes the eye. With regard
to the inner quality and the motivations that the object itself contains, he is cold,
neither warmed by true benevolence nor moved by respect.ſ His conduct is artificial.
He must know how to adopt all sorts of standpoints in order to judge his propriety
from the various attitudes of the onlookers; for he asks little about what he is, but only
about what he seems. For this reason he must be well acquainted with the effect on
the general taste and the many impressions which his conduct will have outside of
him. Since in this sly attention he always needs cold blood and must not let himself
be blinded by love, compassion, and sympathy, he will also avoid many follies and
vexations to which a sanguine person succumbs, who is enchanted by his immediate
sentiment. For this reason he commonly appears to be more intelligent than he
actually is. His benevolence is politeness, his respect ceremony, his love is concocted
flattery. When he adopts the attitude of a lover or a friend he is always full of himself,
and is never either the one or the other. He seeks to shine through fashions, but since
everything with him is artificial and made up, he is stiff and awkward in them. He
acts in accordance with principles much more than the sanguine person does, who is
moved only by the impressions of the occasion; but these are not principles of virtue,
but of honor, and he has no feeling for the beauty or the value of actions, but only
for the judgment that the world might make about them. Since his conduct, as long
as one does not look to the source from which it stems, is otherwise almost as useful
as virtue itself, he earns the same esteem as the virtuous person in vulgar eyes, but
before more refined ones he carefully conceals himself, because he knows well that
the discovery of the secret incentive of lust for honor would cost him respect. He is
thus much given to dissemblance, hypocritical in religion, a flatterer in society, and
in matters of political party he is fickle as circumstances suggest. He is gladly a slave
of the great in order to be a tyrant over the lesser. *Naïveté*, this noble or beautiful
simplicity, which bears the seal of nature and not of art, is entirely alien to him. Hence
if his taste degenerates his luster becomes strident, i.e., it swaggers repulsively. Then
he belongs as much because of his style as because of his decoration to the galimatia,

(the exaggerated), a kind of grotesquerie, which in relation to the magnificent is the same as the adventurous or cranky is to the serious sublime. In cases of insults he falls back upon duels or lawsuits, and in civil relationships on ancestry, precedence, and title. As long as he is only vain, i.e., seeks honor and strives to be pleasing to the eye, then he can still be tolerated, but when he is conceited even in the complete absence of real merits and talents, then he is that which he would least gladly be taken for, namely a fool.

Since in the phlegmatic mixture there are ordinarily no ingredients of the sublime or the beautiful in any particularly noticeable degree, this quality of mind does not belong in the context of our considerations.

Of whichever sort these finer sentiments that we have thus far treated might be, whether sublime or beautiful, they have in common the fate of always seeming perverse and absurd in the judgment of those who have no feeling attuned to them. A person of calm and self-interested industry does not even have, so to speak, the organs to be sensitive to the noble feature in a poem or in an heroic virtue; he would rather read a Robinson than a Grandison[4] and holds Cato[42] to be an obstinate fool. Likewise, that seems ridiculous to persons of a somewhat more serious cast of mind which is charming to others, and the fluttering naïvete of a pastoral affair is to them tasteless and childish. And even if the mind is not entirely without a concordant finer feeling, yet the degrees of the susceptibility to the latter are very variable, and one sees that one person finds something noble and appropriate which comes across to another as grand, to be sure, but adventurous. The opportunities that present themselves in the case of nonmoral matters to detect something of the feeling of another can give us occasion also to infer with reasonable probability his sentiment with regard to the higher qualities of mind and even those of the heart. He who is bored with beautiful music arouses a strong suspicion that the beauties of a style of writing and the fine enchantments of love will have little power over him.

There is a certain spirit of trivialities (esprit des bagatelles), which indicates a sort of fine feeling, but which aims at precisely the opposite of the sublime: having a taste for something because it is very artificial and labored, verses that can be read forwards and backwards, riddles, watches in finger rings, flea chains, etc.; a taste for everything that is measured and painfully orderly, although without any utility, e.g., books that stand neatly arranged in long rows in the bookcase, and an empty head that looks upon them and rejoices, rooms that are adorned like optical cabinets and are everywhere washed clean combined with an inhospitable and morose host who occupies them; a taste for everything that is rare, however little intrinsic value it may otherwise have; the lamp of Epictetus, a glove of King Charles the Twelfth; in a certain way coin-collecting also belongs here. Such persons are very much under the suspicion that they will be grubs and cranks in the sciences, but in ethics will be without feeling for that which is beautiful or noble in a free way.

To be sure, we do one another an injustice when we dismiss one who does not see the value or the beauty of what moves or charms us by saying that he does not understand it. In this case it is not so much a matter of what the understanding sees but of what the feeling is sensitive to. Nevertheless the capacities of the soul have such a great interconnection that one can often infer from the appearance of the sentiment to the talents of the insight. For to him who has many excellences of understanding these talents would be apportioned in vain if he did not at the same time have a strong sentiment for the truly noble or beautiful, which must be the incentive for applying those gifts of mind well and regularly.

It is indeed customary to call useful only that which can satisfy our cruder sentiment, what can provide us with a surplus for eating and drinking, display in clothing and furniture, and lavishness in entertaining,

although I do not see why everything that is craved with my most lively feeling should not be reckoned among the useful things. Nevertheless, taking everything on this footing, he who is ruled by self-interest is a person with whom one must never argue concerning the finer taste. In this consideration a hen is better than a parrot, a cook pot more useful than a porcelain service, all the sharp heads in the world are not worth as much as a peasant, and the effort to discover the distance of the fixed stars can be left aside until people have agreed on the most advantageous way to drive the plow. But what folly it is to get involved in such a dispute, where it is impossible to arrive at concordant sentiments because the feeling is not at all concordant! Nevertheless, even a person of the crudest and most vulgar sentiment will be able to perceive that the charms and attractions of life which seem to be the most dispensable attract our greatest care, and that we would have few incentives left for such manifold efforts if they were to be excluded. At the same time, practically no one is so crude not to be sensitive that a moral action is all the more moving, at least to another, the further it is from self-interest and the more those nobler impulses stand out in it.

If I observe alternately the noble and the weak sides of human beings, I reprove myself that I am not able to adopt that standpoint from which these contrasts can nevertheless exhibit the great portrait of human nature in its entirety in a moving form. For I gladly grant that so far as it belongs to the project of great nature as a whole, these grotesque attitudes cannot lend it other than a noble expression, although one is far too short-sighted to see them in this connection. Nevertheless, to cast even a weak glance on this, I believe that I can note the following. There are very few people who conduct themselves in accordance with principles, which is on the whole good, since it is so easy to err with these principles, and then the ensuing disadvantage extends all the further, the more general the principle is and the more steadfast the person who has set it before himself is. Those who act out of good-hearted drives are far more numerous, which is most excellent, although it cannot be reckoned to individuals as a special personal merit; for these virtuous instincts are occasionally lacking, but on average they accomplish the great aim of nature just as well as the other instincts that so regularly move the animal world. Those always who have their dear self before them as the sole focal point of their efforts and who attempt to make everything turn on the great axis of selfinterest are the most common, and nothing can be more advantageous than this, for these are the most industrious, orderly, and prudent people; they give demeanor and solidity to the whole, for even without aiming at it they serve the common good, supply the necessary requisites, and provide the foundations over which finer souls can spread beauty and harmony. Finally, the love of honor is distributed among all human hearts, although in unequal measure, which must give the whole a beauty that charms to the point of admiration. For although the lust for honor is a foolish delusion if it becomes the rule to which one subordinates the other inclinations, yet as an accompanying drive it is most excellent. For while on the great stage each prosecutes his actions in accordance with his dominant inclinations, at the same time he is moved by a hidden incentive to adopt in his thoughts a standpoint outside himself in order to judge the propriety of his conduct, how it appears and strikes the eye of the observer. In this way the different groups unite themselves in a painting of magnificent expression, where in the midst of great variety unity shines forth, and the whole of moral nature displays beauty and dignity.

Third Section
On the difference between the sublime and the beautiful in the contrast between the two sexes

He who first conceived of woman under the name of the fair sex perhaps meant to say something flattering, but hit it better than he may himself have believed. For without taking into consideration that her figure is in general finer, her features more tender and gentle, her mien in the expression of friendliness, humor, and affability more meaningful and engaging than is the case with the male sex, and without forgetting as well what must be discounted as the secret power of enchantment by which she makes our passion inclined to a judgment that is favorable for her, above all there lies in the character of the mind of this sex features peculiar to it which clearly distinguish it from ours and which are chiefly responsible for her being characterized by the mark of the beautiful. On the other hand, we could lay claim to the designation of the noble sex, if it were not also required of a noble cast of mind to decline honorific titles and to bestow rather than receive them. Here it is not to be understood that woman is lacking noble qualities or that the male sex must entirely forego beauties; rather one expects that each sex will unite both, but in such a way that in a woman all other merits should only be united so as to emphasize the character of the beautiful, which is the proper point of reference, while by contrast among the male qualities the sublime should clearly stand out as the criterion of his kind. To this must refer all judgments of these two genders, those of praise as well as those of blame. All education and instruction must keep this before it, and likewise all effort to promote the ethical perfection of the one or the other, unless one would make unrecognizable the charming difference that nature sought to establish between the two human genders. For it is here not enough to represent that one has human beings before one: one must also not forget that these human beings are not all of the same sort.

Women have a stronger innate feeling for everything that is beautiful, decorative, and adorned. Even in childhood they are glad to be dressed up and are pleased when they are adorned. They are cleanly and very delicate with respect to everything that causes disgust. They love a joke and can be entertained with trivialities as long as they are cheerful and laughing. They have something demure about them very early, they know how to display a fine propriety and to be self-possessed; and this at an age when our well-brought-up male youth is still unruly, awkward, and embarrassed. They have many sympathetic sentiments, good-heartedness and compassion, they prefer the beautiful to the useful, and gladly transform excess in their support into parsimony in order to support expenditure on luster and adornment. They are very sensitive to the least offense, and are exceedingly quick to notice the least lack of attention and respect toward themselves. In short, they contain the chief ground for the contrast between the beautiful and the noble qualities in human nature, and even refine the male sex.

I hope I will be spared the enumeration of the male qualities to the extent that they are parallel with the former, and that it will be sufficient to consider both only in their contrast. The fair sex has just as much understanding as the male, only it is a beautiful understanding, while ours should be a deeper understanding, which is an expression that means the same thing as the sublime.

For the beauty of all actions it is requisite above all that they display facility and that they seem to be accomplished without painful effort; by contrast, efforts and difficulties that have been overcome arouse admiration and belong to the sublime. Deep reflection and a long drawn out consideration are noble, but are grave and not well suited for a person in whom the unconstrained charms should indicate nothing other than a beautiful nature. Laborious learning or painful grubbing, even if a woman could get very far with them, destroy the merits that are proper to her sex, and on account of their rarity may well make her into an object of a cold admiration, but at the same time they will weaken the charms by means of which she exercises her great power over the opposite sex. A woman who has a head full of Greek, like Mme. Dacier, or who conducts thorough disputations about mechanics, like the Marquise du Cha^telet, might as well also wear a beard; for that might perhaps better express the mien of depth for which they strive. The beautiful understanding chooses for its objects everything that is closely related to the finer feeling, and leaves abstract speculation or knowledge, which is useful but dry, to the industrious, thorough, and deep understanding. The woman will accordingly not learn geometry; she will know only so much about the principle of sufficient reason or the monads as is necessary in order to detect the salt in satirical poems which the insipid grubs of our sex have fabricated. The beauties can leave Descartes' vortices rotating forever without worrying about them, even if the suave Fontenelle wanted to join them under the planets, and the attraction of their charms loses nothing of its power even if they know nothing of what Algarotti has taken the trouble to lay out for their advantage about the attractive powers of crude matter according to Newton. In history they will not fill their heads with battles nor in geography with fortresses, for it suits them just as little to reek of gunpowder as it suits men to reek of musk.

It seems to be malicious cunning on the part of men that they have wanted to mislead the fair sex into this perverted taste. For well aware of their weakness with respect to the natural charms of the latter, and that a single sly glance can throw them into more confusion than the most difficult question in school, as soon as the woman has given way to this taste they see themselves in a decided superiority and are at an advantage, which it would otherwise be difficult for them to have, of helping the vanity of the weak with generous indulgence. The content of the great science of woman is rather the human being, and, among human beings, the man. Her philosophical wisdom is not reasoning but sentiment. In the opportunity that one would give them to educate their beautiful nature, one must always keep this relation before his eyes. One will seek to broaden her entire moral feeling and not her memory, and not, to be sure, through universal rules, but rather through individual judgment about the conduct that she sees about her. The examples that one borrows from other times in order to understand the influence that the fair sex has had in the affairs of the world, the various relationships in which it has stood to the male sex in other ages or foreign lands, the character of both so far as it can be illuminated by all this, and the variable taste in gratifications constitute her entire history and geography. It is a fine thing to make looking at a map that represents either the entire globe or the most important parts of the world agreeable to a woman. This is done by depicting it to her only with the aim of illustrating the different characters of the peoples that dwell there, the differences in their taste and ethical feeling, especially with regard to the effects that these have on the relationships between the sexes, together with some easy explanations from the differences in regions, their freedom or slavery. It matters little whether or not they know the particular divisions of these countries, their industries, power, and rulers. Likewise they do not need to know more of the cosmos than is necessary to make the view of the heavens on a beautiful evening moving for them, if they have somehow understood that there are to be found still more worlds and in them still more beautiful creatures. Feeling for paintings of expression and for music, not in so far as it expresses art but rather in so far as it expresses sentiment, all of this refines or elevates the taste of this sex and always has some connection with ethical emotions. Never a cold and speculative instruction, always sentiments and indeed those that remain as close as possible to the relationships of their sex. This education is so rare because it requires talents, experience, and a heart full of feeling, and a woman can do very well without anything else, as indeed she usually educates herself quite well on her own even without this.

The virtue of the woman is a beautiful virtue. That of the male sex ought to be a noble virtue. Women will avoid evil not because it is unjust but because it is ugly, and for them virtuous actions mean those that are ethically beautiful. Nothing of ought, nothing of must, nothing of obligation. To a woman anything by way of orders and sullen compulsion is insufferable. They do something only because they love to, and the art lies in making sure that they love only what is good. It is difficult

for me to believe that the fair sex is capable of principles, and I hope not to give offense by this, for these are also extremely rare among the male sex. In place of these, however, providence has implanted goodly and benevolent sentiments in their bosom, a fine feeling for propriety and a complaisant soul. But do not demand sacrifices and magnanimous self-compulsion. A man should never tell his wife if he risks part of his fortune for the sake of a friend. Why should he fetter her cheerful talkativeness by burdening her mind with an important secret that he alone is obliged to keep? Even many of her weaknesses are so to speak beautiful faults. Injury or misfortune move her tender soul to sadness. A man must never weep other than magnanimous tears. Any that he sheds in pain or over reversals of fortune make him contemptible. The vanity for which one so frequently reproaches the fair sex, if it is indeed a fault in her, is only a beautiful fault. For even leaving aside that the men who so gladly flatter woman would do badly if she were not inclined to take it well, she actually enlivens her charms by it. This inclination is an impulse to make herself agreeable and to show her good demeanor, to let her cheerful wit play, also to glisten with the changing inventions of her dress, and to elevate her beauty. In this there is nothing that is at all injurious to others, but rather, if it is done with good taste, there is so much refinement that it would be quite inappropriate to scold it with peevish criticism. A woman who is too inconstant and deceptive in this is called a silly woman; yet this expression does not have as harsh a sense as it does when applied with a change of the final syllable to a man, so that, indeed, if one understands the other, it can sometimes even indicate an intimate flattery. If vanity is a fault that in a woman is well deserving of forgiveness, nevertheless conceitedness in them is not only blameworthy, as in humans in general, but entirely disfigures the character of their sex. For this quality is exceedingly stupid and ugly and entirely opposed to engaging, modest charm. Such a person is then in a slippery position. She would let herself be judged sharply and without any indulgence; for whoever insists on haughtiness invites everyone around her to reproach her. Every discovery of even the least fault is a true joy to everyone, and the expression silly woman here loses its mitigated sense. One must always distinguish between vanity and conceitedness. The former seeks approbation and to a certain degree honors those on whose account the effort is made; the second already believes itself to be in complete possession of that approbation, and making no effort to acquire it, it also wins none.

If some ingredients of vanity do not at all disfigure a woman in the eyes of the male sex, still the more visible they are, the more they divide the fair sex from each other. They then judge each other quite sharply, because the charms of one seem to obscure those of the other, and those who still make strong pretensions to conquest are actually rarely friends with each other in the true sense.

Nothing is so opposed to the beautiful as the disgusting, just as nothing sinks more deeply beneath the sublime than the ridiculous. Thus a man can be sensitive to no insult more than that of being called a fool, and a woman to none more than being called disgusting. The English Spectator holds that no reproach can be more upsetting to a man than when he is held to be a liar, and none more bitter to a woman than being held to be unchaste. I will leave this for what it is worth in so far as it is judged with the strictness of morality. Only here the question is not what intrinsically deserves the greatest reproach, but rather what is actually felt as the harshest one. And here I ask every reader whether, if in thought he places himself in this position, he must not agree with my opinion. The maiden Ninon Lenclos made not the least claims to the honor of chastity, and nevertheless she would have been implacably offended if one of her lovers had gone so far in his judgment; and one knows the dreadful fate of Monaldeschi on account of such an expression in the case of a princess who hardly wanted to represent herself as a Lucretia. It is intolerable that one should not be able to commit evil even if one wants to, because then even its omission would always be only a very ambiguous virtue.

To distance oneself as far as possible from this sort of disgustingness takes purity, which is indeed becoming for every person, and which in the case of the fair sex is of the first rank among the virtues and can hardly be taken too far by it, although in the case of a man it can sometimes be exaggerated and then becomes ridiculous.

The sense of shame is a secrecy of nature aimed at setting bounds to a most intractable inclination, and which, in so far as it has the call of nature on its side, always seems compatible with good, moral qualities, even if it is excessive. It is accordingly most necessary as a supplement to principles; for there is no case in which inclination so readily becomes a sophist cooking up complaisant principles as here. At the same time, it also serves to draw a secretive curtain before even the most appropriate and necessary ends of nature, so that too familiar an acquaintance with them will not occasion disgust or at least indifference with respect to the final aims of a drive on to which the finest and liveliest inclinations of human nature are grafted. This quality is especially proper to the fair sex and very appropriate for it. It is also a coarse and contemptible rudeness to put the delicate modesty of the fair sex to embarrassment or annoyance by that sort of vulgar jokes that are called obscenities. However, since no matter how far one might try to go around this secret, the sexual inclination is still in the end the ground of all other charms, and a woman, as a woman, is always the agreeable object of a well-mannered entertainment, it can perhaps thus be explained why otherwise refined men occasionally allow themselves the liberty of letting some fine allusions shine through the little mischief in their jokes, which leads one to call them loose or waggish, and which, since they are neither accompanied by invasive glances nor intended to injure respect, makes them believe themselves to be justified in calling the person who receives them with an indignant or standoffish mien a stickler for honorableness. I mention this only because it commonly is regarded as a somewhat bold feature in refined society, and because in fact much wit has all along been squandered upon it; but as far as strict moral judgment is concerned, it does not belong here, since in the sentiment of the beautiful I have to observe and explain only the appearances.

The noble qualities of this sex, which nevertheless, as we have already noted, must never make the feeling of the beautiful unrecognizable, announce themselves by nothing more clearly and surely than by the modesty of a kind of noble simplicity and na¨ıvete in great excellences. From this shines forth a calm benevolence and respect toward others, combined at the same time with a certain noble trust in oneself and an appropriate self-esteem, which is always to be found in a sublime cast of mind. In so far as this fine mixture is both engaging in virtue of its charms and moving in virtue of respect, it secures all other shining qualities against the mischief of censure and mockery. Persons of this cast of mind also have a heart for friendship, which in a woman can never be valued enough, because it is so rare and at the same time must be so totally charming.

Since our aim is to judge of sentiments, it cannot be disagreeable to bring under concepts, so far as possible, the variety of the impression that the figure and facial features of the fair sex makes upon the masculine. This whole enchantment is at bottom spread over the sexual drive. Nature pursues its great aim, and all refinements that are associated with it, however remote from it they seem to be, are only veils, and in the end derive their charm from the very same source. A healthy and coarse taste that always remains close to this drive, is little troubled by the charms of demeanor, of the facial features, of the eyes, etc., in a woman, and as it is really concerned only with sex, often it sees the delicacy of others as empty flirtation.

If this taste is not exactly fine, still it is not on that account to be despised. For the greatest part of humanity follows by its means the great order of nature in a very simple and certain manner. By this means most marriages are brought about, and indeed among the most industrious part of humanity, and because the man does not have his head full of enchanting miens, languishing glances, noble demeanor, etc., and also understands nothing of these, he is thus all the more attentive to domestic virtues, thrift, etc., and to the dowry. As far as the somewhat finer taste is concerned, on account of which it might be necessary to make a distinction among the external charms of the woman, this is directed either to that which is moral in the figure and the expression of the face or to the immoral. With respect to the latter sort of agreeable qualities, a woman is called pretty: a well-proportioned build, regular features, a lovely contrast between the colors of eyes and face: all beauties that also please in a bouquet of flowers and earn a cold approbation. The face itself says nothing, although it may be pretty, and does not speak to the heart. As for the expression of the features, the eyes and the mien that are moral, this pertains either to the feeling of the sublime or of the beautiful. A woman in whom the agreeable qualities that become her sex are salient, especially the moral expression of the sublime, is called beautiful in the proper sense; one whose moral design, so far as it makes itself known in the mien or facial features, announces the qualities of the beautiful, is agreeable, and if she is that to a higher degree, charming. The former lets a glimmer of a beautiful understanding shine through modest glances beneath a mien of composure and a noble demeanor, and as in her face she portrays a tender feeling and a benevolent heart, she overpowers both the inclination and the esteem of a male heart. The latter displays cheer and wit in laughing eyes, a bit of fine mischief, coquetry in her jokes, and a roguish coyness. She charms, while the former moves, and the feeling of love of which she is capable and which she inspires in others is fickle but beautiful, while the sentiment of the former is tender, combined with respect, and constant. I will not get too involved with detailed dissections of this sort; for in such cases the author always seems to portray his own inclination. I will still mention, however, that the taste that many ladies have for a healthy but pale color can be understood here. For the latter commonly accompanies a cast of mind of more inward feeling and tender sentiment, which belongs to the quality of the sublime, while the red and blooming color indicates less of the former, yet more of the joyful and cheerful cast of mind; but it is more suitable to vanity to move and enchain than to charm and attract. By contrast, persons without any moral feeling and without an expression that indicates sentiments can be very pretty, yet they will neither move nor charm, unless it be that coarse taste that we have mentioned, which occasionally becomes somewhat more refined and then also chooses after its fashion. It is bad that pretty creatures of that sort easily succumb to the fault of conceitedness because of the awareness of the beautiful figure that the mirror shows them, and from a lack of finer sentiments; for they then make everyone cold to them, except for the flatterer, who is after ulterior motives and fashions intrigues.

Through these concepts one can perhaps understand something of the very different effect that the figure of one and the same woman has on the taste of men. I do not mention that which in this impression is too closely related to the sexual drive and which may agree with the particularly voluptuary illusion with which the sentiment of everyone is clothed, because it lies outside the sphere of finer taste; and it is perhaps correct, as M. de Buffon suspects, that that figure which makes the first impression at the time when this drive is still new and beginning to develop remains the archetype to which in future times all feminine forms must more or less conform, which can arouse the fantastic longing by means of which a somewhat crude inclination is made to choose among the different objects of a sex. As far as a somewhat finer taste is concerned, I maintain that the sort of beauty that we have called the pretty figure is judged fairly uniformly by all men, and that opinions about it are not so various as is commonly held. The Circassian and Georgian maidens have always been considered to be extremely pretty by all Europeans travelling through their lands. The Turks, the Arabs, and the Persians must be of very much the same taste, for they are very eager to beautify their populations with such fine blood, and one also notes that the Persian race has actually succeeded in this. The merchants of Hindustan likewise do not fail to extract great profit from a wicked trade in such beautiful creatures, by supplying them to the sweet-toothed rich men of their country, and one sees that as divergent as the caprice

of taste in these different regions of the world may be, that which is held to be especially pretty in one of them is also taken to be such in all the others. But where what is moral in the features is mixed into the judgment on the fine figure, there the taste of different men is always very different, in accordance with the difference in their ethical feeling itself as well as with the different significance that the expression of the face may have in every fancy. One finds that those forms that on first glance do not have a marked effect because they are not pretty in any decided way usually are far more engaging and seem to grow in beauty as soon as they begin to please on closer acquaintance, while in contrast the beautiful appearance that announces itself all at once is subsequently perceived more coldly, presumably because moral charms, when they become visible, are more arresting, also because they become effective only on the occasion of moral sentiments and as it were let themselves be discovered, each discovery of a new charm, however, giving rise to a suspicion of even more; whereas all the agreeable qualities that do not at all conceal themselves can do nothing more after they have exercised their entire effect all at the beginning than to cool off the enamored curiosity and gradually bring it to indifference.

Among these observations, the following remark naturally suggests itself. The entirely simple and crude feeling in the sexual inclinations leads, to be sure, quite directly to the great end of nature, and in satisfying its demands it is suited to make the person himself happy without detour; but because of its great generality, it readily degenerates into debauchery and dissoluteness. On the other side, an extremely refined taste certainly serves to remove the wildness from an impetuous inclination and, by limiting it to only a very few objects, to make it modest and decorous; but it commonly fails to attain the great final aim of nature, and since it demands or expects more than the latter commonly accomplishes, it very rarely makes the person of such delicate sentiment happy. The first cast of mind becomes uncouth, because it applies to all the members of a sex, the second brooding, because it really applies to none, but is rather occupied only with an object that the enamored inclination creates in thought and adorns with all the noble and beautiful qualities that nature rarely unites in one person and even more rarely offers to one who can treasure her and who would perhaps be worthy of such a possession. Hence arises the postponement and finally the complete renunciation of the marital bond, or, what is perhaps equally bad, a sullen regret of a choice that has already been made, which does not fulfill the great expectations that had been raised; for it is not uncommon for Aesop's cock to find a pearl when a common barley corn would have suited him better.

Here we can remark in general that, as charming as the impressions of tender feeling may be, nevertheless we have cause to be cautious in the refinement of it, unless we want to bring upon ourselves much discontent and a source of evils through excessive sensitivity. I would recommend to nobler souls that they refine their feeling as much as they can with regard to those qualities that pertain to themselves or those actions that they themselves perform, but that with regard to what they enjoy or expect from others they should preserve their taste in its simplicity: if only I understood how it is possible to bring this off. But if they were to succeed, then they would make others happy and also be happy themselves. It should never be lost sight of that, in whatever form it might be, one should not make very great claims on the happinesses of life and the perfection of human beings; for he who always expects only something average has the advantage that the outcome will seldom disappoint his hopes, although sometimes unsuspected perfections will also surprise him.

In the end, age, the great ravager of beauty, threatens all of these charms, and in the natural order of things the sublime and noble qualities must gradually take the place of the beautiful ones in order to make a person worthy of ever greater respect as she ceases to be attractive. In my opinion, the entire perfection of the fair sex in the bloom of years should consist in the beautiful simplicity that has been heightened by a refined feeling for everything that is charming and noble. Gradually, as the claims to charms diminish, the reading of books and the expansion in insight could, unnoticed, fill with Muses the place vacated by the Graces, and the husband should be the first teacher. Nevertheless, when finally the old age that is so terrible to all women arrives, she still belongs to the fair sex, and that sex disfigures itself if in a sort of despair over holding on to this character longer it gives way to a morose and sullen mood.

A person of years, who joins society with a modest and friendly essence, who is talkative in a cheerful and reasonable way, who favors with propriety the enjoyments of youth of which she no longer takes part, and who, with concern for everything, displays contentment and satisfaction in the joy that surrounds her, is always still a more refined person than a man of the same age and is perhaps even more lovable than a maiden, though in a different sense. To be sure, the platonic love asserted by an ancient philosopher when he said of the object of his inclination: The Graces reside in her wrinkles, and my soul seems to hover about my lips when I kiss her withered mouth, may be somewhat too mystical; yet such claims must then be relinquished. An old man who acts infatuated is a fop, and the similar pretensions of the other sex are then disgusting. It is never the fault of nature if we do not appear with a good demeanor, but is rather due to the fact that we would pervert her.

In order not to lose sight of my text, I will here add several considerations on the influence that one sex can have in beautifying or ennobling of the feeling of the other. The woman has a preeminent feeling for the beautiful, so far as it pertains to herself, but for the noble in so far as it is found in the male sex. The man, on the contrary, has a decided feeling for the noble that belongs to his qualities, but for the beautiful in so far as it is to be found in the woman. From this it must follow that the ends of nature are aimed more at ennobling the man and beautifying the woman by means of the sexual inclination. A woman is little embarrassed by the fact that she does not possess certain lofty insights, that she is fearful and not up to important business, etc.; she is beautiful and engaging, and that is enough. By contrast, she demands all of these qualities in the man, and the sublimity of her soul is revealed only by the fact that she knows how to treasure these noble qualities in so far as they are to be found in him. How else would it be possible for so many grotesque male faces, although they may have merits, to be able to acquire such polite and fine wives! The man, in contrast, is far more delicate with regard to the beautiful charms of the woman. By her fine figure, her cheerful naïvete and her charming friendliness he is more than adequately compensated for the lack of book-learning and for other lacks that he must make good by his own talents. Vanity and fashion may well give these natural drives a false direction, and make out of many a man a sweet gentleman, but out of the woman a pedant or an Amazon, yet nature still always seeks to return to its proper order. From this one can judge what powerful influences the sexual inclination could have in ennobling especially the masculine sex if, in place of many dry lessons, the moral feeling of woman were developed in good time to make her sensitive to what belongs to the dignity and the sublime qualities of the opposite sex, and thereby prepared to regard the ridiculous fops with contempt and to yield to no other qualities than to merits. It is also certain that the power of her charms would thereby gain overall; for it is apparent that their enchantment is often effective only on nobler souls, while the others are not fine enough to be sensitive to them. Thus when he was advised to let the Thessalians hear his beautiful songs, the poet Simonides said: These louts are too dumb to be beguiled by a man such as me. It has always been regarded as an effect of intercourse with the fair sex that male manners become gentler, their conduct more refined and polished, and their demeanor more elegant; but this is only an incidental advantage. What is most important is that the man become more perfect. This advantage is itself very much diminished by the observation that has been made that those men who have become involved too early and too frequently in those parties to which the woman has given the tone commonly become somewhat ridiculous, and are boring or even contemptible in male society, because they have lost the taste for an entertainment that is certainly cheerful, but must also have real content, that is humorous but must also be useful because of serious conversations.

as a man and the woman as a woman, i.e., that the incentives of the sexual inclination operate in accordance with nature to make the one more noble and to beautify the qualities of the other. If things come to the extreme, the man, confident of his merits, can say: Even if you do not love me I will force you to esteem me, and the woman, secure in the power of her charms, will answer: Even if you do not inwardly esteem us, we will still force you to love us. In the absence of such principles one sees men adopt feminine qualities, in order to please, and woman sometimes (although much more rarely) work up a masculine demeanor, in order to inspire esteem; but whatever one does contrary to the favor of nature one always does very badly.

In marital life the united pair should as it were constitute a single moral person, which is animated and ruled by the understanding of the man and the taste of the wife. For not only can one trust the former more for insight grounded in experience, but the latter more for freedom and correctness in sentiment; yet further, the more sublime a cast of mind is, the more inclined it also is to place the greatest goal of its efforts in the satisfaction of a beloved object, and on the other side the more beautiful it is, the more does it seek to respond to this effort with complaisance. In such a relationship a struggle for precedence is ridiculous, and where it does occur it is the most certain mark of a crude or unequally matched taste. If it comes down to talk of the right of the superior, then the thing is already extremely debased; for where the entire bond is really built only on inclination, there it is already half torn apart as soon as the ought begins to be heard. The presumption of the woman in this harsh tone is extremely ugly and that of the man in the highest degree ignoble and contemptible. However, the wise order of things brings it about that all these niceties and delicacies of sentiment have their full strength only in the beginning, but subsequently are gradually dulled by familiarity and domestic concerns and then degenerate into familiar love, where finally the great art consists in preserving sufficient remnants of the former so that indifference and surfeit do not defeat the entire value of the enjoyment on account of which and which alone it was worth having entered into such a bond.

Fourth Section
On national characters in so far as they rest upon the different feeling of the sublime and the beautiful

Among the peoples of our part of the world the Italians and the French are, in my opinion, those who most distinguish themselves in the feeling of the beautiful, but the Germans, the English, and the Spaniards those who are most distinguished from all others in the feeling of the sublime. Holland can be regarded as the land where this finer taste is fairly unnoticeable. The beautiful itself is either enchanting and touching, or laughing and charming. The former has something of the sublime in it, and in this feeling the mind is thoughtful and enraptured, while in the feeling of the second kind it is smiling and joyful. The first sort of beautiful feeling seems especially appropriate to the Italians, the second sort to the French. In the national character that has in it the expression of the sublime, this is either of the terrifying kind, which inclines a bit to the adventurous, or it is a feeling for the noble, or for the magnificent. I think I have grounds sufficient to attribute the first kind of feeling to the Spaniard, the second to the Englishman, and the third to the German.

The feeling for the magnificent is not by its nature original, like the other kinds of taste, and although a spirit of imitation can be associated with any other feeling, yet it is more characteristic of that for the glittering sublime, since this is really a mixed feeling out of that for the beautiful and that for the noble, where each, considered by itself, is colder, and hence the mind is free enough in the connection of them to attend to examples, and also has need for their incentive. The German will accordingly have less feeling in regard to the beautiful than the Frenchman, and less of that pertaining to the sublime than the Englishman, but his feeling will be more suited for the cases where both are to appear as combined, just as he will also luckily avoid the errors into which an excessive strength of either of these kinds of feeling alone could fall.

I touch only fleetingly the arts and the sciences the selection of which can confirm the taste of the nations that we have imputed to them. The Italian genius has distinguished itself especially in music, painting, sculpture, and architecture. There is an equally fine taste for all of these fine arts in France, although here their beauty is less touching. The taste with regard to poetic or rhetorical perfection runs more to the beautiful in France, in England more to the sublime. In France, fine jests, comedy, laughing satire, enamored dalliance, and the light and naturally flowing manner of writing are original; in England, by contrast, thoughts with deep content, tragedy, epic poetry, and in general the heavy gold of wit, which under the French hammer can be beaten into thin little leaves of great surface area. In Germany, wit still glimmers very much through a screen. Formerly it was strident; by means of examples and the understanding of the nation, however, it has become rather more charming and nobler, but the former with less naïvete and the latter with a less bold thrust than in the peoples mentioned. The taste of the Dutch nation for a painstaking order and decorousness that leads to worry and embarrassment also leaves little feeling for the unaffected and free movements of genius, the beauty of which would only be disfigured by the anxious avoidance of errors. Nothing can be more opposed to all the arts and sciences than an adventurous taste, since this distorts nature, which is the prototype of everything beautiful and noble. Thus the Spanish nation has also demonstrated little feeling for the fine arts and sciences.

The characters of mind of the peoples are most evident in that in them which is moral; for this reason we will next consider their different feeling in regard to the sublime and the beautiful from this point of view. The Spaniard is serious, taciturn, and truthful. There are few more honest merchants in the world than the Spanish. He has a proud soul and more feeling for great than for beautiful actions. Since in his mixture there is little to be found of generous and tender benevolence, he is often hard and also even cruel. The Auto da Fe endures not so much because of superstition as because of the adventurous inclination of the nation, which is moved by a venerable and terrifying rite, in which one sees San Benito, painted with figures of the devil, consigned to the flames that have been ignited by a raging piety. One cannot say that the Spaniard is haughtier or more amorous than anyone from another people, yet he is both in an adventurous way that is rare and unusual. To leave the plow standing and walk up and down the field with a long sword and cape until the stranger who is passing by has gone, or in a bullfight, where for once the beauties of the land are seen unveiled, to announce himself to his mistress with a special greeting and then in order to wage a dangerous fight with a wild animal to honor her, these are unusual and strange actions, which greatly diverge from what is natural.

The Italian seems to have a feeling which mixes that of a Spaniard and that of a Frenchman: more feeling for the beautiful than the former and more for the sublime than the latter. In this way, I think, the other features of his moral character can be explained.

The Frenchman has a dominant feeling for the morally beautiful.

He is refined, courteous, and complaisant. He becomes intimate very quickly, is humorous and free in conversation, and the expression of a man or a lady of good manners has a meaning that is comprehensible only to one who has acquired the refined feeling of a Frenchman. Even his sublime sentiments, of which he has not a few, are subordinated to the feeling of the beautiful and acquire their strength only through accord with the latter. He very much likes to be witty, and will without reservation sacrifice something of the truth for the sake of a witticism. By contrast, where he cannot be witty, he displays just as thorough an insight as someone from any other people, e.g., in mathematics and in the other dry or profound arts and sciences. A bon mot does not have the same fleeting value with him as elsewhere; it is eagerly spread about and preserved in books, as if it were the most important occurrence. He is a peaceful citizen and avenges himself against the oppressions of the tax collectors by satires or remonstrations to the courts, which, after they have in accordance with their intention given the fathers of the people a beautiful patriotic aspect, accomplish nothing further than being crowned with a glorious rebuke and praised in ingenious laudatory poems. The object to which the merits and national capabilities of this people are most devoted is woman. Not as if she were loved or esteemed here more than elsewhere, but rather because she provides the best opportunity for displaying in their best light the favorite talents of wit, cleverness, and good manners; incidentally a vain person of either sex always loves only himself or herself, while the other is only his or her plaything. Now since the French do not at all lack noble qualities, but these can only be animated through the sentiment of the beautiful, the fair sex could here be able to have a more powerful influence in awakening and arousing the noblest actions of the male sex than anywhere else in the world, if one were intent on favoring this direction of the national spirit a little. It is a pity that the lilies do not spin.

The fault which is closest to this national character is the ridiculous or, in a more polite expression, the lighthearted. Important things are treated like jokes, and trivialities serve for serious occupation. Even in advanced age the Frenchman still sings amorous songs, and is still as gallant as he can be towards the woman. In these remarks I have great authorities from this very same people on my side, and retreat behind a Montesquieu and d'Alembert in order to secure myself from any concerned indignation.

The Englishman is at the beginning of every acquaintance cold and indifferent toward a stranger. He has little inclination toward small niceties; by contrast, as soon as he is a friend he is ready to perform great services. In society, he makes little effort to be witty, or to display a refined demeanor, but he is understanding and resolute. He is a poor imitator, does not much ask how others judge, and simply follows his own taste. In relation to the woman he does not have the French refinement, but shows more respect to her and perhaps takes this too far, as in the marital state he commonly concedes an unrestricted authority to his wife. He is steadfast, sometimes to the point of being stiff-necked, bold, and resolute, often to the point of audacity, and acts according to principles, commonly to the point of being headstrong. He easily becomes an eccentric, not out of vanity, but because he troubles himself little about others and does not readily do violence to his own taste out of complaisance or imitation; for this reason he is rarely as much beloved as the Frenchman, but, once he is known, he is commonly more highly esteemed.

The German has a feeling that is a mixture of that of an Englishman and that of a Frenchman, but seems to come closer to the former, and the greater similarity with the latter is merely artificial and imitative. He has a happy mixture in the feeling of the sublime as well as the beautiful; and if he is not equal to an Englishman in the former or to the Frenchman in the latter, he surpasses them both in so far as he combines them. He displays more complaisance in intercourse than the former, and even if he does not bring quite as much agreeable liveliness and wit to society as the Frenchman, yet he displays there more moderation and understanding. In love, as in all other sorts of taste, he is also rather methodical, and since he combines the beautiful with the noble, he is in the sentiment of both sufficiently cool to occupy his head with considerations of demeanor, of splendor, and of appearance. Hence family, title, and rank are matters of great importance to him in civic relationships as well as in love. Far more than the previous ones he asks how people might judge him, and if there is something in his character that could arouse the wish for a major improvement, it is this weakness, in accordance with which he does not dare to be original, although he has all the talents for that, and that he is too concerned with the opinion of others, which deprives the moral qualities of all bearing, making them fickle and falsely contrived.

The Dutchman is of an orderly and industrious cast of mind, and since he looks only to what is useful, he has little feeling for what in a finer understanding is beautiful or sublime. For him a great man means the same as a rich man, by a friend he understands his business correspondents, and a visit that brings him no profit is very boring for him.

He makes a contrast to both the Frenchman and the Englishman and is to a certain extent a very phlegmatic German.

If we try to apply the sketch of these thoughts to a particular case, in order to assess, e.g., the feeling of honor, the following national differences are revealed. The sentiment for honor is in the Frenchman vanity, in the Spaniard haughtiness, in the Englishman pride, in the German pomp, and in the Dutchman conceitedness. At first glance these expressions seem to mean the same thing, but in the richness of our German language they mark very noticeable differences. Vanity strives for approval, is fickle and changeable, but its outward conduct is courteous. The haughty person is full of falsely imagined great merits and does not much seek the approval of others; his conduct is stiff and pompous. Pride is really only a greater consciousness of one's own value, which can often be quite correct (on account of which it is also sometimes called a noble pride; but I can never ascribe a noble haughtiness to someone, since the latter always indicates an incorrect and exaggerated self-appraisal); the conduct of the proud person toward others is indifferent and cold. The vainglorious person is a proud one who is at the same time vain. The approval, however, which he seeks from others, consists in testimonies of honor. Hence he likes to glitter with titles, ancestry, and pageantry. The German is particularly infected by this weakness. The words "gracious," "most gracious," "high-born," and "well-born" and more of that sort of bombast make his speech stiff and awkward and very much hinder the beautiful simplicity that other peoples can give to their style of writing. The conduct of a vainglorious person in social intercourse is ceremony.

The conceited person is a haughty person who expresses distinct marks of the contempt of others in his conduct. In behavior he is coarse. This miserable quality is the most distant from the finer taste, because it is obviously stupid; for challenging everyone around one to hatred and biting mockery through open contempt is certainly not the means for satisfying the feeling for honor.

In love the German and the English have a fairly good stomach, somewhat fine in sentiment, but more of a healthy and robust taste. In this point the Italian is brooding, the Spaniard fantastic, the Frenchman dainty.

The religion of our part of the world is not the matter of an arbitrary taste, but is of honorable origin. Hence only the excesses in it and that in it which properly belongs to human beings can yield signs of the different national qualities. I classify these excesses under the following headings: credulity, superstition, fanaticism, and indifferentism. The ignorant part of every nation is for the most part credulous, although it has no noticeable finer feeling. Persuasion depends simply upon hearsay and merely apparent authority, without any sort of finer feeling containing the incentive for it. One must seek the examples of whole peoples of this kind in the north. The credulous person, if he is of adventuresome taste, becomes superstitious. This taste is even in itself a ground for believing something more readily, and of two people, one of whom is infected by this feeling but the other of whom is of a cool and moderate cast of mind, the former, even if he actually has more understanding, is nevertheless more readily seduced by his dominant inclination into believing something unnatural than the latter, who is saved from this excess not by his insight but by his common and phlegmatic feeling. The person who is superstitious in religion gladly places between himself and the supreme object of veneration certain powerful and astonishing human beings, so to speak giants of holiness, whom nature obeys and whose imploring voices open or close the iron gates of Tartarus, who, while they touch the heavens with their heads, still have their feet on the earth beneath. In Spain, accordingly, the instruction of sound reason will have great obstacles to overcome, not because it must drive away ignorance there, but rather because it is opposed by an odd taste, to which what is natural is vulgar, and which never believes itself to have a sublime sentiment if its object is not adventurous. Fanaticism is so to speak a pious brazenness and is occasioned by a certain pride and an altogether too great confidence in oneself to come closer to the heavenly natures and to elevate itself by an astonishing flight above the usual and prescribed order. The fanatic talks only of immediate inspiration and of the contemplative life, while the superstitious person makes vows before pictures of great wonder-working saints and places his trust in the imaginary and inimitable merits of other persons of his own nature. Even the excesses, as we have noted above, bear signs of the national sentiment, and thus at least in earlier times fanaticism was mostly to be encountered in Germany and England and is as it were an unnatural outgrowth of the noble feeling that belongs to the character of these peoples, and it is in general nowhere near as harmful as the superstitious inclination, even though it is violent at the beginning, since the inflammation of a fanatical spirit gradually cools off and in accordance with its nature must finally attain to an orderly moderation, while superstition stealthily roots itself deeper into a quiet and passive quality of mind and entirely robs the shackled person of the confidence of ever freeing himself from a harmful delusion. Finally, a vain and frivolous person is always without stronger feeling for the sublime, and his religion is without emotion, for the most part only a matter of fashion, which he conducts with decorum and remains cold. This is practical indifferentism, to which the French national spirit seems to be most inclined, from which it is only a step to sacrilegious mockery and which fundamentally, when one looks to its inner worth, is little better than a complete denial.

If we now take a quick look through the other parts of the world, we find the Arab to be the noblest human being in the Orient, although with a feeling that very much degenerates into the adventurous. He is hospitable, generous, and truthful; but his tale and history and in general his sentiment always has something marvelous woven into it. His inflamed power of imagination presents things to him in unnatural and distorted images, and even the spread of his religion was a great adventure. If the Arabs are as it were the Spaniards of the Orient, then the Persians are the Frenchmen of Asia. They are good poets, courtly, and of rather fine taste. They are not such strict observers of Islam and allow their cast of mind, inclined to gaiety, a rather mild interpretation of the Koran. The Japanese can be regarded as it were as the Englishmen of this part of the world, although hardly in any other attribute than their steadfastness, which degenerates into the most extreme stiff-neckedness, their courage and their contempt of death. Otherwise they demonstrate few marks of a finer feeling. The Indians have a dominant taste for grotesqueries of the kind that comes down to the adventurous. Their religion consists of grotesqueries. Images of idols of enormous shape, the priceless tooth of the mighty ape Hanuman, the unnatural atonements of the Fakirs (heathen mendicant monks), etc., are in this taste. The voluntary sacrifice of the wives in the very same pyre that consumes the corpse of her husband is a repulsive adventure. What ridiculous grotesqueries do the verbose and studied compliments of the Chinese not contain: even their paintings are grotesque and represent marvelous and unnatural shapes, the likes of which are nowhere to be found in the world. They also have venerable grotesqueries, for the reason that they are of ancient usage, and no people in the world has more of them than this one.

The Negroes of Africa have by nature no feeling that rises above the ridiculous. Mr. Hume challenges anyone to adduce a single example where a Negro has demonstrated talents, and asserts that among the hundreds of thousands of blacks who have been transported elsewhere from their countries, although very many of them have been set free, nevertheless not a single one has ever been found who has accomplished something great in art or science or shown any other praiseworthy quality, while among the whites there are always those who rise up from the lowest rabble and through extraordinary gifts earn respect in the world.82 So essential is the difference between these two human kinds, and it seems to be just as great with regard to the capacities of mind as it is with respect to color. The religion of fetishes which is widespread among them is perhaps a sort of idolatry, which sinks so deeply into the ridiculous as ever seems to be possible for human nature. A bird's feather, a cow's horn, a shell, or any other common thing, as soon as it is consecrated with some words, is an object of veneration and of invocation in swearing oaths. The blacks are very vain, but in the Negro's way, and so talkative that they must be driven apart from each other by blows.

Among all the savages there is no people which demonstrates such a sublime character of mind as that of North America. They have a strong feeling for honor, and as in hunt of it they will seek wild adventures hundreds of miles away, they are also extremely careful to avoid the least injury to it where their ever so harsh enemy, after he has captured them, tries to force a cowardly sigh from them by dreadful tortures. The Canadian savage is moreover truthful and honest. The friendship he establishes is just as adventurous and enthusiastic as anything reported from the oldest and most fabulous times. He is extremely proud, sensitive to the complete worth of freedom, and even in education tolerates no encounter that would make him feel a lowly subjugation. Lycurgus probably gave laws to such savages, and if a law-giver were to arise among the six nations, one would see a Spartan republic arise in the new world; just as the undertaking of the Argonauts is little different from the military expeditions of these Indians, and Jason has nothing over Attakakullakulla except the honor of a Greek name. All of these savages have little feeling for the beautiful in the moral sense, and the

generous forgiveness of an insult, which is at the same time noble and beautiful, is as a virtue completely unknown among the savages, but is always looked upon with contempt as a miserable cowardice. Courage is the greatest merit of the savage and revenge his sweetest bliss. The other natives of this part of the world show few traces of a character of mind which would be disposed to finer sentiments, and an exceptional lack of feeling constitutes the mark of these kinds of human beings.

If we consider the relationship between the sexes in these parts of the world, we find that the European has alone found the secret of decorating the sensuous charm of a powerful inclination with so many flowers and interweaving it with so much that is moral that he has not merely very much elevated its agreeableness overall but has also made it very proper. The inhabitant of the Orient is of a very false taste in this point. Since he has no conception of the morally beautiful that can be combined with this drive, he also loses even the value of the sensuous gratification, and his harem is a constant source of unrest for him. He falls into all sorts of amorous grotesqueries, among which the imaginary jewel is one of the foremost, which he tries to secure above all others, whose entire value consists only in one's smashing it, and of which one in our part of the world generally raises much malicious doubt, and for the preservation of which he makes use of very improper and often disgusting means. Hence a woman there is always in prison, whether she be a maiden or have a barbaric, inept, and always suspicious husband. In the lands of the blacks can one expect anything better than what is generally found there, namely the female sex in the deepest slavery? A pusillanimous person is always a strict master over the weaker, just as with us that man is always a tyrant in the kitchen who outside of his house hardly dares to walk up to anyone. Indeed, Father Labat reports that a Negro carpenter, whom he reproached for haughty treatment of his wives, replied: You whites are real fools, for first you concede so much to your wives, and then you complain when they drive you crazy. There might be something here worth considering, except for the fact that this scoundrel was completely black from head to foot, a distinct proof that what he said was stupid. Among all the savages there are none among whom the female sex stands in greater real regard than those of Canada. In this perhaps they even surpass our civilized part of the world. Not as if they pay the women their humble respects; that would be mere compliments. No, they actually get to command. They meet and take council about the most important affairs of the nation, about war and peace. They send their delegates to the male council, and commonly it is their vote that decides. But they pay dearly enough for this preference. They have all the domestic concerns on their shoulders and share all of the hardships with the men.

If finally we cast a few glances at history, we see the taste of human beings, like a Proteus, constantly take on changeable shapes. The ancient times of the Greeks and Romans displayed clear marks of a genuine feeling for the beautiful as well as the sublime in poetry, sculpture, architecture, legislation, and even in morals. The regime of the Roman emperors altered the noble as well as the beautiful simplicity into the magnificent and then into the false brilliance of which what survives of their oratory, poetry, and even the history of their morals can still instruct us. Gradually even this remnant of the finer taste was extinguished with the complete decay of the state. The barbarians, after they had on their part established their power, introduced a certain perverted taste that is called the Gothic, and which ends up in grotesquerie. One saw grotesqueries not only in architecture, but also in the sciences and in the other practices. The degenerated feeling, once led on by false art, adopted any unnatural form other than the ancient simplicity of nature, and was either exaggerated or ridiculous. The highest flight that human genius took in order to ascend to the sublime consisted in adventures. One saw spiritual and worldly adventurers and often a repulsive and monstrous sort of bastard of both. Monks with the missal in one hand and the battle flag in the other, followed by whole armies of deceived victims in order to let their bones be buried under other regions of the sky and in a more sacred ground, consecrated warriors, sanctified by solemn oaths to violence and misdeeds, subsequently a strange sort of heroic fantasts, who called themselves knights and sought out adventures, tournaments, duels, and romantic actions. During this period religion together with the sciences and morals was distorted by wretched grotesqueries, and one notes that taste does not readily degenerate in one area without exhibiting distinct signs of its corruption in everything else that pertains to the finer feeling. The monastic vows made out of a great number of useful people numerous societies of industrious idlers, whose brooding way of life made them fit for concocting thousands of scholastic grotesqueries, which went thence out into the larger world and spread their kind about. Finally, after the human genius had happily lifted itself out of an almost complete destruction by a kind of palingenesis, we see in our own times the proper taste for the beautiful and noble blossom in the arts and sciences as well as with regard to the moral, and there is nothing more to be wished than that the false brilliance, which so readily deceives, should not distance us unnoticed from noble simplicity, but especially that the as yet undiscovered secret of education should be torn away from the ancient delusion in order early to raise the moral feeling in the breast of every young citizen of the world into an active sentiment, so that all delicacy should not merely amount to the fleeting and idle gratification of judging with more or less taste that which goes on outside of us.

Remarks in the Observations on the Feeling of the Beautiful and Sublime

[1] On the reverse of the cover, opposite 2:205

[Throughout, the subheadings are added by the translators, based on notations added in Marie Rischmuller's edition of the Remarks. These subheadings indicate where Kant's remarks were found relative to the copy of the Observations in which they were written. This first set of remarks, for instance, was written on the back of the cover of the Observations. The page numbers beginning with a volume number (such as "2:205") correspond to the page numbers in the Observations in the Academy Edition. Page numbers without a volume number (such as "opposite page one," below) refer to the page number in the first edition of the Observations.]

Men's art of appearing foolish and women's art of appearing clever

A human being can employ two kinds of beneficial emotions on another, respect and love, the former by means of the sublime, the latter by means of the beautiful. A woman unites both. This composite sentiment is the greatest impression that can ever befall the human heart. But only two faint sentiments can be equally strong. Should one of the two be strong, then the other must be weak. Now, let one ask oneself which of the two one may want to weaken. Principles are of the greatest sublimity. For example, self-esteem demands sacrifice. E.g. a man can be ugly, but not a witty woman.

The *Coquette* oversteps the feminine, the rough *Pedant* the masculine A *prude* is too masculine and a *petit maitre* too feminine.

It is ridiculous that a man wants to make a young woman fall in love through understanding and great merits.

The diversity of minds like that of faces. Characters Parallels between feeling and capacity

A more tender   A finer taste

more dull coarser

<Sympathy with the natural misfortune of others is not necessary, but [sympathy] with the injustice suffered by others is.>

The feeling I am dealing with is so constituted that I do not need to be taught (to ratiocinate) in order to feel it.

[R8] The finer feeling is that wherein the ideal, <not the chimerical,> contains <the noblest ground> of agreeableness.

Voltaire [has] known and I hope <Why women are embarrassed among each other>

Dolce piccante the pleasantly bitter

Bold <The audacious gulp Alexander took from the chalice was sublime though rash>

The splendor of the rainbow of the setting sun

Cato's death. Sacrifice <Our current constitution makes it so that women can also live without men, which spoils everything>

strange and peculiar

The powerful one is kind. *Jonathan Wild.*

The brave youth. Temple at *Ephesus*

Women are strong because they are weak <their courage> Menfolk will loosen up after vapeurs and hysterical coincidences.

Hat under the arms

Self-revenge is sublime. Certain vices are sublime. Assassination is cowardly and base. Many do not even have the courage for great vices.

Love and respect

Sexual love always presupposes lustful love, either in sensation or memory.

This lustful love is also either coarse or refined.

[R9] Affectionate love has a great mixture of respect, etc.

A woman does not reveal herself easily, which is why she does not drink. Since she is weak, she is clever.

In marriage unity not uniformity.

Affectionate love is also different from marital love4

Title page

[2] Obverse, upper margin

| – *Quod petis in te est nec te quasi-* | on moral rebirth |
| *veris extra Persius* | What satisfies a true or imagined need is useful *mihi bonum* |

Title page, under "Observations"

The first part of science is zetetic, the other dogmatic.

The desires that are necessary for a human being through his nature

are natural desires.

The human being who has no other desires, and none in a higher degree, than are necessary through the natural ones, is called the human being of nature and his capacity to be satisfied by little is the sufficiency of nature.

The amount of cognitions and other perfection[s] required for the satisfaction of nature is the simplicity of nature. The human being in [R10] whom one encounters the simplicity as well as the sufficiency of nature is the human being of nature.

One who has learned to desire more than what is necessary through nature is opulent.

Under "Beautiful and Sublime"

The needs of the human being of nature are the bare necessities make [breaks off]

One reason why the representations of death do not have the effect that they could is that, as industrious beings, by nature we properly should not think about it at all.

[3] Reverse of title page

Gaiety is wanton, annoying and disruptive, but the soul at peace is benevolent and kind.

Wit belongs to the dispensable things; a man who takes this to be the main thing in a woman is just like he who spends his fortune to buy monkeys and parrots.

One of the reasons why the dissipation of the female sex in unmarried circumstances is more reprehensible consists in the fact that if men in these circumstances have led a dissipated life, they have not simultaneously thereby prepared for unfaithfulness in marriage, for their concupiscence has indeed increased, yet their capacity has decreased. By contrast, in a woman the capacity is unlimited; if now concupiscence increases, then it can be held back by nothing. Therefore, it is presumed of unchaste women that they will be unfaithful wives, but not of men of the same kind.

Every purpose of science is either *eruditiv* (memory) or speculation (reason); both must result in making human beings more prudent (cleverer, wiser) in the world, which is generally suitable to human nature, and therefore more sufficient

[R] A tender love for women has the quality of developing other moral qualities, but a lustful one suppresses them.

<The taste that is moral makes one regard science that does not improve as base.>

The sensitive soul at peace is the greatest perfection in speech, in poetry, [and in] society, but it cannot always be so; rather, it is the ultimate goal, even in marriages. Young people indeed have much sentiment, but little taste; the enthusiastic or excited style ruins taste. Taste perverted through novels and gallant flirtations. The healthy, pampered, spoiled taste.

A reasonable but not clever man [is] not cunning, a clever but not wise man. higher manners

A woman has a fine taste in the choice of that which can affect the sentiments of men, and a man has a dull [taste]. Hence he pleases best when he thinks least of pleasing. In contrast, a woman has a dull healthy taste for that which is concerned with her own sentiments.

Sheet inserted after the title page

[4] Obverse

Bearded women, unbearded men. Valiant domestic.

The honor of a man consists in the valuation of his self, of a woman in the judgment of others. A man marries according to his judgment, a woman not against the judgment of the parents. A woman opposes injustice with tears, a man with anger.

Richardson goes so far at times puts a judgment of Seneca in a woman's mouth and adds to it "as my brother says." If she were married it would say "as my husband tells me."

Men become sweet towards women if the women become masculine. Insult to women in the habit of flattering them. [R2] Softness roots out virtue more than wantonness, the dignity of a housewife.

Vanity in women makes it so that they are only happy in the glitter outside the house.

The courage of a woman consists in the patient bearing of ill fortune for the sake of her honor or love. Of a man, in the eagerness to drive it away defiantly.

Omphale forced Hercules to spin.

Because so many foolish needs make us soft, the mere unrefined moral drive cannot give us enough powers; therefore, something fantastic must come in addition.

Whence the stoic says: My friend is sick, what does it matter to me? There is no human being who does not feel the heavy yoke of opinion, and no one does away with it.

What is chimerical in friendship in our state and fantastic in the ancient. *Aristotle Cervantes* would have done better if, instead of ridiculing the fantastic and romantic passion, he had directed it better. Novels make noble women fantastic and common ones foolish.

noble men also fantastic, common ones lazy

Rousseau's book serves to improve on the ancients

According to the simplicity of nature, a woman cannot do much good without the mediation of a man. In a state of inequality and wealth, she can immediately

Moral *luxury*. In sentiments that are without effect.

The inner distress about the inability to help or about the sacrifice in case one helps, as well as the cowardice that [R13] makes us believe that others suffer a lot even though they could easily endure it, brings about sympathy with others. Incidentally, this is a great antidote against selfishness. These drives are altogether very cold in the natural human being.

Natural elevations are degradations below one's rank, for example to raise oneself to the rank of a craftsman.

Relative evaluation is unnecessary, but in the state of inequality and injustice it is good to set oneself against the pompous magnates with a certain pride, or at least indifference, in order to be equal with respect to lower ones.

One must with a certain breadth

[5] Reverse, opposite page of the Observations, at 2:207

Although being tall does not make a man great, bodily size still coincides with the judgment about the moral

It is easier to educate a nobleman than a [common] human being. He is a despiser of the common rabble, for so he must in every case call the industrious and oppressed, in order for one to believe that he has been created to nourish them. The scholars in China let their nails grow on the left hand.

Among all ranks, none is more useless than [that of] the scholar as long as it is in the [state of] natural simplicity; and none more needed than the same in a condition of oppression through superstition or violence

Deliberations belong to small and beautiful casts of mind. A woman has affects as great as a man, but they are more thoughtful, specifically when it comes to respectability, the man is inconsiderate. The Chinese and

Indians have affects just as great as the Europeans, but they are calmer. woman is vengeful

The rising sun is just as splendid as the setting one, but the [R14] sight of the former touches on the beautiful, the latter on the tragic and sublime. That which a woman does in marriage leads much more to natural happiness than that which the man does, at least in our civilized state.

Because so many unnatural desires are found in the civilized condition, the occasion for virtue also sometimes arises, and since so much luxury is found in enjoyment and knowledge, science arises. In the natural state, one can be good without virtue and reasonable without science.

Whether a human being would have it better in a simple state is now difficult to see, because he has lost his feeling for simple pleasures.

2. because he commonly believes that the corruptions that exist in the

civilized state also exist in the state of simplicity.

[6] Page of the Observations, upper margin, at 2:207

Happiness without taste is based on simplicity and modesty of inclination, happiness with taste is based on the sensitive soul at peace; therefore one also must be able to be happy without society. Amusements, no needs. Rest after work is agreeable. One must not chase after gratification at all.

Lower margin

One must distinguish "he is in accordance with the taste of others" from "he has taste in the judgment about others." Women know very well how to evaluate in accordance with the taste of others, and therefore easily know the minds of others and have good taste to satisfy them, but they have a bad taste in other persons, which is good. For this reason, they also all marry the richest.

[R15]

[7] Page 2 of the Observations, marginal notes, next to lines 15–18, at 2:208

Tenderness and fondness of sensation

Taste chooses in trifles

Sheet inserted after page 2 of the Observations

[8] Obverse

Logical egoism <skillfulness in taking standpoints.> Common duties do not need the hope of another life as their motivation,

though greater sacrifice and self-denial surely have an inner beauty, but our feeling of pleasure about this can never be so strong in itself that it outweighs the annoyance of inconvenience unless the representation of a future state, in which moral beauty persists and happiness is increased by finding oneself even more capable of [moral] actions, comes to its assistance.

All pleasures are either bodily or ideal.

Concerning the latter [breaks off]

A woman is offended or oppressed <by crudeness> where no justification but only threat can help. She helps herself to her touching weapons of tears, melancholic reluctance and complaints, yet still endures the ill before she gives way to injustice. See here the courage of women. A man is indignant that one might be so bold as to insult him; he answers violence with violence, frightens, and makes the offender feel the consequences of injustice. See here the courage of a man. It is not necessary that a man be indignant at the ills of delusion; he can despise them in a masculine way. Yet he will be infuriated about these ills as true insults if they befall a woman.

[R6] A woman can use the most extreme weapons of her scorn – the scolding of counterreproaches – against a woman, but never against a man, except by means of the threats against another man.

When women squabble or fight, men laugh about it, but not vice versa.

Duels have – primarily for the sake of women – a ground in nature. In the current state, a man can use no other means against injustice than a woman, namely not according to the order of nature, but [according to] the civil society constitution by means of the authority.

Rousseau. Proceeds synthetically and starts from the natural human being, I proceed analytically and start from the civilized one.

The country life delights everyone, especially the shepherd's life, and yet boredom will consume the civilized one therein.

[9] Reverse, opposite page 3, at 2:208

The heart of the human being may be constituted as it will, the question here is only whether the state of nature or the moral civilized one develops more actual sin and readiness thereto. Moral ill can be so subdued that merely a lack of greater purity shows itself in actions, but never positive vice in a noticeable degree (whoever is not so saintly is for that reason not vicious); on the contrary, this can develop so far that it becomes detestable. The simple human being has little temptation to become vicious. Opulence alone accounts for the great temptation and the culture of moral sentiments and understanding will apparently never hold it back if the taste for opulence is already great.

Piety is the <means of> *complementi* [complements] of moral *Bonitaet* [goodness] towards holiness. In the relation of one human being to another that is not the question. We cannot naturally be holy and we lost this through original sin, although we certainly can be morally good.

Is it not enough for us that we a human being never lies, even though he has a secret inclination, which, were it brought under the conditions that develop it, would [make him] lie?

Do we ask whether a human being undertakes his actions of honesty, fidelity, etc. out of consideration for divine obligation, if he only does them, even though these actions are condemnable before God in so far as they do not arise thereby[?]

In order to prove that the human being is corrupt by nature one appeals to the civilized state. One should appeal to the natural one.

Actions of justice are those whose neglect will naturally make another hate us; actions of love those whose neglect will provide the reason others no reason for love towards us.

[10] Page 3 of the Observations

On the margin, next to lines 3 and 4, at 2:207

Utility, blooms

Lower margin

Because the basic talents basic qualities of women lead them to study man and to easily create a deception for his inclinations, they are made to govern and actually govern in all nations that have taste.

Sheet inserted after page 4 of the Observations [] Obverse, at 2:208

There is a most perfect (*moral*) world in accordance with the order of nature, and according to this we ask, in the same way, a supernatural [breaks off]

[R8] The virtuous one looks upon the rank of others with indifference, although if he refers it to himself, he looks at it with contempt.

One can either restrict one's opulent inclinations or, by keeping them, invent remedies against their insults. To the latter belong science and contempt for life on account of the imminence of death, and solace of the future [breaks off]

Boredom is a kind of longing for an ideal gratification.

The Holy Scripture has more effect on improvement if supernatural powers accompany it. Good moral education has more if everything should happen only in accordance with the order of nature.

I admit that through the latter we can produce no holiness, which is justifying, but we can produce a moral *Bonitaet coram foro humano* [Goodness before a human court], and this is even conducive to the former.

Just as little as one can say that nature has implanted in us an immediate inclination for acquisition (miserly greediness), so little can one say it has given us an immediate drive for honor. In general opulence, both develop and both just as are useful. But from this it can only be concluded that just as nature produces calluses during hard work, it also creates remedies for itself in its injuries.

The difference in rank implies that, as little as one puts oneself in the place of a work horse in order to imagine its wretched food, so little does one put oneself in the place of the miserable one in order to grasp misery.

[12] Reverse, opposite page 5, at 2:208

The precepts for the happy life can be twofold: 1. That one shall show how, after all the inclinations of honor [and] of opulence are already acquired, one acquires one's ends, and at the same time representations, which [R19] can prevent the sorrow that originates thereby, of the future life, of the nullity of this life, etc. 2. Or that one attempts to bring these inclinations themselves to moderation.

The Stoics' mistake [is] that through virtue they only searched for a counterweight to the pains of opulence. *Antisthenes's* school attempted to eradicate opulence itself.

The Stoics' doctrine of anger out of contempt for others. The current *moralists* presuppose much as ill and want to teach to overcome it, and presuppose much temptation to evil and prescribe motivations to overcome it. The *Rousseauian* method teaches to hold the former for no ill and, thus, the latter for no temptation.

There is no one more moderate in enjoyment than a miser. The miserly greediness arises from a desire for many enjoyments, to which there is no actual but a chimerical inclination in the miser, since he regards them to be great goods from hearsay, even though he himself is moderate. This is the boldest miserliness. The cowardly miserliness.

The threat of eternal punishment cannot be the immediate ground of morally good actions, although it may well be a strong counterweight to the temptations to evil so that the immediate sensation of morality is not outweighed.

There is no immediate inclination at all to <morally> evil actions, but certainly an immediate one to good actions.

[13] Page 5

Upper margin, at 2:208

This ideal feeling sees life in dead nature or imagines seeing it. Trees drink the neighboring brook. The zephyr whispers to the loved one. Clouds cry on a melancholic day. Cliffs threaten like giants. Solitude is yet inhabited by dreamy shadows and the deathly silence of graves.

[R20]

fantastic From there come the images and the spirit rich in imagery.

Right margin, next to lines 12 and 13

ideal ~~therefore beautiful~~

Next to lines 8–14

Philosophical eyes are microscopic. Their vision is exact but limited and is and its intention is truth. The sensual vision is bold and supports enthusiastic dissipation, which is stirring, yet only to be encountered in the imagination.

Lower margin

Beautiful and sublime are not the same. The latter swells the heart and makes the attention fixed and tense. Therefore, it exhausts. The former lets the soul melt in a soft sensation, and, in that it relaxes the nerves, it lets puts the feeling into a gentler emotion, which, however, where it goes too far, transforms into weariness, surfeit and disgust.

[14] Page 6

Marginal notes, next to line 3

bold

At the margin, next to lines 24–27

The majority of men are primarily effeminate or common and thus even worse to associate with than women.

Lower margin

Whence does it come that our parties without women are quite tasteless, since they were not so with the Greeks, nor with the [R21] Romans. At that time one spoke of virtue [and] of the fatherland; now this is an empty matter, into whose place, at best, false devotion can step. Among nothing but men, jokes have no proper life and also become uncivilized. We are soft and effeminate and must be among women.

Sheet inserted after page 6 [15] Obverse, at 2:209

The good-natured and the well-civilized human being are very much to be distinguished. The first does not need the representation of higher beings in order to control perverse drives, for they are natural and good.

If he thinks thereof he says that maybe he truly is in another life. One must be good and expect the rest. The second is 1. only civilized 2. well civilized. In the former case he has many fantastical joys that, in order to remain good, he must oppose with a representation which never can become intuiting. The second one is a civilized human being, who, if he is extended [in] his morality beyond the simplicity of nature, extends it to the object that he only wishes and believes.

This natural morality must also be the touchstone of all religion. For if it is uncertain whether people in the other religion can become blessed and whether the torments in this world cannot help them toward happiness in the future one, then it is certain that I would not have to persecute them. This latter would not however be the case if the natural sentiment were not sufficient for all execution of duty in this life.

When the Portuguese discovered Celebes the inhabitants understood the nullity of their religion, but sent to Malacca for Don Rug Perero as well as to Achin for the queen. [They] received two kinds of priests, etc.

Every coward lies, but not vice versa. That which makes weak produces lies. The ridiculous lust for honor and shame the most.

Shame and prudishness are to be distinguished. The former is a betrayal of a secret through the natural movement of the blood. The latter is a [R22] means of concealing a secret for the sake of vanity, the same in sexual arousal.

It is far more dangerous to be in war with free and profit-seeking people than with the subjects of a monarch. Utility that vanity has hereof.

I will speak of everything where there are only rarely exceptions. For according to the rule of prudence, that which happens so rarely that one thereof can regard it as a stroke of luck never happens, and in accordance with that is universal according to the rule of prudence where some cases of the contrary cannot be sought according to any rule. I speak of taste, I thus take my own judgments in accordance with the in such a way that they are (aesthetically) universally true according to the rule of taste, even though it properly logically – according to the rule of measured reason (logical) – holds only for some of them.

[16] Obverse, opposite page 7, at 2:209

A heart extended through sensibility prepares itself for longing and will finally be worn out [by] the sensations of all things of life; therefore it sighs for something which is outside its own circle, and as true as devotion is in itself it is just as fantastic with respect to most human beings, because they themselves are chimerical, and that they demonstrate their love [and] uprightness only with respect to God and are cold with respect to the former, yet dissemble with respect to the latter, comes from the fact that one can more easily deceive oneself concerning the former than the latter.

Because one can form a concept of higher moral qualities, sacrifice for the common best, everlasting devotion, fulfillment of marital intentions without lust, immediate inclination to science without honor, one imagines all these to be appropriate to the condition of a human being and finds the state one sees corrupted. But such desires are fantastical and arise from precisely the same sources as universal corruption. Exactly these flaws will no longer be regarded as blameworthy with respect to human beings once the remaining corruption is eliminated

[R23]

Whole nations can provide the example of a human being as such. One never finds great virtues where they are not also combined with great excesses, as with the English. Canadian savages. What is the cause. The French are more decent and all sublimity of virtue is also missing

The position of humanity within the order of created beings.

[17] Page 8

At the margin, next to line 7, at 2:210

Beautiful, cute

Sheet inserted after page 8

[18] Obverse, at 2:210

All devotion that is natural has a use only if it is the result of a good morality. The same goes for natural devotion that is related to a book. For this reason the spiritual teachers correctly say that it is good for nothing if it is not effected through the spirit of God, in which case it is an intuition, otherwise it is very prone to self-deception.

The reason why marriages are so cold-minded is this: because both members have such great external, chimerical connection to dignity [and] daintiness; and if each member so strongly depends on opinion, he becomes indifferent towards the opinion of the other. From this arises disdain, finally hate. In relation to this, romanic love is only the quality of a hero. *Coquette.*

Those who make a doctrine of piety out of the doctrine of virtue make a whole out of the part, for piety is only one kind of virtue.

It now often seems to us more and more that the human race has almost no value if it does not contain great artists and scholars; hence, the country people [and] farmers appear to be nothing to themselves and to be something only as the means for the support of the former. The injustice of this judgment [R24] already shows that it is false. For one feels that if one has extended one's inclinations – one may do whatever one wishes to do – life amounts to nothing and that the extension of these inclinations is therefore harmful.

There is a great difference between overcoming one's inclinations and eradicating them, that is, se bringing it about that one loses them; this is also different from restraining one's inclinations, that is, making it that someone never has them. The former is necessary for old people, the latter for young ones

There is a great difference between being a good human being and being a good rational being. Being perfect as the latter has no other limits except for finitude, being perfect as the former has many limits.

[9] Reverse, opposite page 9, at 2:210

It takes a very great art to prevent lying in children. For since they are far too wanton and far too weak to tolerate negative responses or punishments, they have very strong incitements to lie that older people never have. Especially since they can do nothing for themselves, as older people can, but everything depends on how they represent something according to the inclination that they notice in others. One must therefore only punish them for what they cannot deny, and not grant them something on the basis of excuses.

If one wants to approve form morality one must above all not introduce any motivations that would not render the action morally good,

e.g. punishments, rewards. Therefore, one must also depict the lie [as] immediately ugly, and, as it also is in fact, never subordinate it to any other rule of morality, for example duty towards others.

(One has no duties towards oneself, but one has absolute duties, that is, action is good in and for itself. It is also absurd that, in our morality, we should depend on ourselves.)

In medicine one says that the doctor is the servant of nature: just the same is valid in morality. Only hold off the external ill, [and] nature will take the best course.

[R25] If the doctor said that nature in itself is corrupted, by what means would he improve it. Likewise the moralist

The human being does not take part in the luck or misfortune of others before he himself feels content. Thus, bring it about that he is content with little, and you will make kind human beings. Otherwise, it is in vain.

The universal love of humankind has something high and noble in it, but in a human being it is chimerical. If one aims for it one gets used to deceiving oneself with longings and idle wishes. As long as one is so much dependent on things, one cannot participate in the happiness of others

[20] Page 9

At the margin, next to lines 16–19, at 2:211

Because dubious things are small, one calls a [breaks off]

Sheet inserted after page 10

[21] Obverse

The simple human being has very early a sentiment of what is right, but very late or never a concept thereof. That sentiment must be developed long before the concept. If one teaches him early to develop according to rules, he will never feel the sentiment

Once the inclinations are developed, it is difficult to represent the good or ill in other circumstances. Because I will now, without an everlasting enjoyment, waste away from boredom, I imagine this also to be the case with the Swiss who grazes his cows in the mountains. I <And the latter> cannot imagine how a human being who has had enough could still desire something more. One can hardly conceive how, in such a low state, this lowness does not fill him with pains. On the other hand, if the rest of

[R26] the human beings are infected with the ills of delusion, some cannot imagine how this delusion could be acquired by them. The noble man imagines that the ills of the disrespect caused by having one's glamor stolen can oppress a citizen, and the latter does not understand how the former could have become accustomed to count certain delightful things among his needs.

The sovereign who granted nobility wanted to give something that could serve certain persons in lieu of all other opulence. After all, they have the tidbit of nobility. Let the rest of the mob have the money

Can anything be more perverse than already to speak of the other world to children who have barely stepped into this one.

[22] Obverse, opposite page 11, at 2:211

Just as fruit, when it is ripe enough, breaks away from the tree and falls to the earth to let its own seeds take root, so the mature human being breaks away from his parents, transplants himself, and becomes the root of a new generation.

The man must depend on no one else, so that the woman depends entirely on him.

It must be asked how far inner moral grounds can bring a human being. It They will perhaps bring him so far, that, in a state of freedom without great temptations, he is good, but if the injustice of others or the force of delusion does violence to him, then this inner morality does not have enough power. He must have religion, and **encourage himself [R2   ] by means of the rewards of a future life; and human nature** is not capable of an immediate moral purity. But if, in a supernatural manner, purity were produced in him, then the future rewards would no longer have the quality of motivations

The difference between a false and a healthy morality is that the former seeks only antidotes for ills, while the latter takes care that the causes of this ill are not there at all

Reputation, if it indicates sublimity, is that which shimmers, if it indicates beauty, it is the pretty, or, also, the decorated of finery if it is contrived

Among all kinds of finery there is also the moral. The sublime with respect to rank consists in this, that it includes much dignity; the beautiful means [unreadable word] here the becoming

The reason why those of nobility commonly pay poorly

[23] Page

Upper margin, at 2:211

It is a great harm for the genius if the critique is prior to the art. If, in a nation, exemplars come in that blind it before it has developed its own talents.

Lower margin

Sublime disposition that overlooks trivialities and notices the good among deficiencies.

Tobacco

Sheet inserted after page 12 [24] Obverse, at 2:212

It is unnatural that a human being should spend the great part of his life in order to teach one child how it should live some day. Such tutors as *Jean Jacques* are therefore artificial. In the simple state only a few services are provided for a child; as soon as he has a bit of strength [R28] he carries out small, useful actions of the adult, as with the countryman or the craftsman, and gradually learns the rest.

It is therefore seemly that a human being spend his life teaching so many at once [how] to live that the sacrifice of his own life is by contrast not to be considered. Schools are therefore necessary. But in order for them

to be possible, one must raise *Emile*. One would wish that Rousseau

would show how schools can arise from this.

Preachers in the country could begin this with their own children and those of their neighbors. Taste is does not depend on our needs. The man must already be civilized if he is to choose a wife according to taste.

One shall not be very refined, for thereby only small traits are noticed; the big ones will only become apparent to the simple and coarse eye.

It is a burden for the understanding to have taste. I must read Rousseau for so long that the beauty of [his] expressions no longer disturbs [me], and only then can I finally examine him with reason.

That great people only glitter in the distance, that a sovereign is greatly diminished among his valets, stems from the fact that no human being is great

What constitutes a great hindrance to the doctrine of the happy eternity, and which lets one assume that the latter would be hardly adequate to our state, is that those who believe [in] it do not become less arduous about the happiness of this life, which yet would have to happen if our vocation would involve taking it as the great basis for our actions

[25] Obverse, opposite page 13, at **2:212**

If I now wanted to put myself into a great although not total independence from human beings, I would have to be able to be poor without [R29]

feeling it, and be able to be thought of as lowly without minding it. But if I were a rich man I would primarily add freedom from things and from human beings to my pleasures. I would not overload myself with things such as guests, horses, [and] underlings, about whose loss I would have to worry. I would have no jewels, because I can lose them, etc. I would neither my clothes adapt myself to the delusion of others, so that it would not really harm me, for example, reduce my acquaintance, but not so that it gives me comfort.

How freedom in the proper sense (the moral, not the metaphysical) would be the supreme principium of all virtue and also of all happiness

It is necessary to see how late art, daintiness and the civilized constitution are to be found, and how they never are found in some regions of the world (for example, where there are no domestic animals) so that one distinguishes that which is foreign and contingent to nature from that which is natural to it. If one considers the happiness of the savage it is not in order to return to the woods, but only in order to see what one has lost while gaining elsewhere; so that, among in the enjoyment and exercise of social opulence, one would not, with unhappy and unnatural inclinations, cling to the former, and would remain a civilized human being of nature. That consideration serves as the standard. For nature never makes a human being into a citizen, and his inclinations [and] endeavors are merely aimed at the simple state of life.

With most other creatures, it appears to be their main purpose that they live and that their species should live. If I presuppose this in the case of the human being, then I must not condemn the basest savage.

Sheet inserted after page 14 [27] Obverse

[R30] How, out of luxury, civil religion and also religious coercion (at least, with every new transformation) finally becomes necessary

The mere natural religion does not at all suit a state, rather skepticism would sooner do so

Anger is a very benign sentiment of weak human beings. An inclination to suppress it brings about irreconcilable hate. Women, clerics. One does not always hate the one at whom one is angry. Benignity of the human beings who are angry. Pretended mannerliness conceals anger and makes false friends.

For such a weak creature as the human being, the partly necessary, partly voluntary, ignorance of the future is very suitable

I can never convince another except by means of his own thoughts. I must, therefore, presuppose that the other has a good and correct understanding, otherwise it is futile to hope that he can be won over by my reasons. Likewise I can morally move no one except by means of his own sentiments; I must, therefore, presuppose that the other one has a certain *Bonitaet* of heart, for otherwise he will never feel abhorrence

<at> my portrayal of vice and never feel praise incentives in himself at my praise of virtue. But since it would be impossible that some *morally* correct sentiments would be in him, and that he could assume his sentiments to be in unison with those of the whole human race, if his evil were evil through and through, I must grant him partial goodness therein, and must depict the slippery resemblance of innocence and crime as deceptive.

[28] Obverse, opposite page 15, at 2:213

[R3] The supreme reason to create is because it is good. From this it must follow that since God, with his power and his great cognition, finds himself good, he also finds it good to *actualize* everything that is possible thereby. Second, that he has satisfaction in everything that is good for something, the most [satisfaction], however, in that which aims at the greatest good. The first is good as a consequence, the second as a ground.

B[ecause] Because revenge presupposes that human beings who hate each other remain close, if one could instead remove oneself as one wanted the reason for taking revenge would fall away; hence, revenge cannot be in nature, because the latter does not presuppose that human beings are confined next to each other. But it is very natural that anger is a very necessary quality and one very suited to a man; that is, if it is not a passion (which is to be distinguished from an *affect*)

One cannot imagine the agreeableness of something that one has not tasted, like the Carib detested salt, to which he had not gotten accustomed

Agesilaus and the Persian satrap despised each other; the former said, "I know the Persian voluptuousness, but mine is unknown to you"; he was wrong

The goods of soft opulence and of delusion; the latter come from the comparative estimation in sciences, in honor, etc.

Christianity says that one shall not devote one's heart to temporal things; by this it is now also understood that one shall early on prevent no one from acquiring such devotion. But to first nurture inclinations and then to expect supernatural assistance to rule them, that is to tempt God.

[R32]

[29] Page 16

At the margin, next to lines 8–12, at 2:214

The adventurous taste parodies.

Hudibras parodies grimaces cutely sublime. [unreadable word]

Sheet inserted after page 16 [30] Obverse

Graduated scale: freedom, equality, honor. (Delusion) Attention, henceforth he loses his entire life.

Two touchstones of the difference between the natural and the unnatural: 1. Whether it is proper to that which one cannot change, 2. Whether it can be common to all human beings or only to a few with the oppression of the rest

A certain great monarch in the North has, as one says, civilized his nation – would that God had wanted him to bring morals into it – this way, however, everything he did was political welfare and moral corruption

I can make no one better except by means of the remnant of good that is in him; I do not want to make any one more prudent except by means of the remnant of prudence that is in him

Vicious ones can be looked upon with affability, because vices come to them quite externally through our corrupted constitution

From the feeling of equality arises the idea of justice, both the idea of the suffer obliged as well as the idea of the obliging. The former is the obligation towards others, the latter is the felt obligation of others towards me.

In order for the latter to have a standard in the understanding, we are able to put ourselves in the place of others in thoughts, and, in order for there to be no lack of motivations for this, [R33] we will be moved through sympathy for the misfortune and distress of others just as through our own.

This obligation will be recognized as something whose lack in another would let me consider him my enemy, and would make me hate him. Never is anything more outrageous than injustice; all other ills that we endure are nothing in comparison. Obligation only concerns the necessary self-preservation and the in so far as it exists in accordance with the preservation of the species; all the rest are favors and goodwill. Still, I will hate everyone who sees me struggling in the ditch and coldheartedly passes by.

Kindnesses occur only due to inequality. For, by kindness, I understand a readiness to cause something good even in those cases where universal natural sympathy would be an insufficient ground for it. Now, it is simple-minded and natural to sacrifice as much leisureliness as I provide for another, because one human being counts as much as another. If I therefore should be willing, I must judge myself more harshly with respect to discomforts than another, [and] I must regard that, which I spare another, as a great ill and that, which I suffer myself, as a small one. A man would despise another if he showed such kindnesses towards him. The first inequality is of a man and a child, and of a man and a woman.

In a certain way, he considers it an obligation not to sacrifice anything to them, since he is strong, and they are weak.

[31] Reverse, opposite to page 17, at 2:214

All incorrect estimations of that which does not belong to the purposes of nature also destroys [sic] the beautiful harmony of nature. Because one [R34] holds the arts and sciences to be so very important, one decries those that do not have them, and brings us to injustices that we would not commit if we were to regard them as more equal to us.

If something is not ultimately suitable to the length of a lifetime, nor to its epochs, nor to the great part of all human beings, if it further is subject very much to chance, and is only possible with difficulty, it does not belong to the happiness and perfection of the human race. How many centuries have passed by before there were genuine sciences, and how many nations are there in the world that will never have them.

One must not say that nature calls us to the sciences, because it has given us capacities for them; for what concerns pleasure can be merely artificial. Since the availability of the sciences has been proven, one rather is to judge that we have a capacity of the understanding go that goes further than our vocation in this life; thus, there will be another life. If we seek to develop these here we will fill our post badly. A caterpillar that would feel that it ought to become a butterfly.

Scholars believe that everything is for their sake. Nobles as well. If one has traveled through barren France one can find comfort again at the Academy of sciences or at respectable societies, just as in Rome one can find delight to the point of drunkenness in the splendor of the churches and antiquities, if one has happily gotten away from all the beggars in the state of the Church

Precisely for the preceding reason, one should judge that those who want to know too much prematurely here will be, over there, castigated with imbecility as punishment. Just as a prematurely clever child either dies or withers and becomes dumb at an immature age.

A human being may become as artful as he wants, he still cannot force nature to follow other laws. He must either work for himself or [R35] others for him. And this work will rob others of as much of their happiness as he wants to increase his own beyond the average

If some want to enjoy without working then others will have to want to work without enjoying

Inserted sheet after page 20 [32] Obverse, 2:215

One can promote welfare either by allowing desires to expand and striving to satisfy them; one can promote rectitude if one allows the inclinations of delusion and opulence to grow and strives towards moral incentives to resist them. With both of these challenges, however, there is another solution, namely not allowing these inclinations to arise. Finally, one can also promote good conduct by setting aside all immediate moral goodness and merely taking the commands of a rewarding and punishing lord as a basis.

The ill for human beings inherent in science is above all that the greatest part of those who want to adorn themselves with it do not acquire any improvement of their understanding, but only a perversion of it, not to mention that for most of them it only serves as an instrument of vanity. The utility that the sciences have either consists in opulence, e.g., mathematics, or in the hindrance of those ills that they themselves have brought on, or also in a certain kind of modesty as a by-product.

The concepts of civil and of natural justice and the sentiment of obligation that arises from them are almost exactly opposite. If I beg from a rich man who has won his fortune through extortion from his peasants and give this to the very same poor, then in a civil sense I perform a very generous action, but in the natural sense only a common obligation.

In universal opulence, one complains about the divine government and about the government of the king. One does not consider that, concerning the [R36] latter, the very same ambition and immoderacy that controls the citizen can have no other form on the throne than what it has 2. that such citizens cannot be governed otherwise. The subject wants the master to overcome his inclination of vanity in order to promote the good of his lands and does not consider that, in the view of his inferiors, this demand could be made on him with the very same right. First of all, be wise, righteous, and moderate yourself, these virtues will soon rise to the throne and make the prince good as well. Look at the weak princes who, in such times, can show kindness and generosity; they hardly can exercise these without greater injustice towards others, because they put generosity into nothing other than the distribution of a bounty that one has stolen from others. The freedom that a prince accords to think and write in such a way as I am doing now is probably worth as much as many benefits [leading] to a greater opulence, because through that freedom all of this ill can yet be ameliorated.

[33] Reverse, opposite pages 21, at 2:216

The greatest concern of the human being is to know how properly to fulfill his station in creation, and to rightly understand what one must be in order to be a human being. But if he gets to know gratifications that are above or beneath him, or gets to know moral qualities that [are] yet his, which indeed flatter him but which but for which he is not organized, then and which oppose the (layout), the constitution that nature has suited to him, if he gets to know moral qualities that shimmer there, then he will disturb the beautiful order of nature, only to bring harm to himself and others, because he will have left his post, he knows [that he] cannot be content with that which is noble for, since he does not let himself be satisfied – to be that for which he is destined – since he steps out of the sphere of a human being, he is nothing, and the gap that he opens spreads his own ruin to the neighboring members.

Among the harms perpetrated by the flood of books in which our part of the world is annually drowned, not the least is that the actually useful ones that from time to time swim on the wide [R37] ocean of book-learning are overlooked, and under must share the fate of fugacity with the other chaff. The inclination to read a lot in order to say that one has read. The habit not to dwell long on a book and [breaks off]

Opulence brings human beings together into the city; Rousseau wants to bring them to the country

The ills related to the developing immoderateness of human beings quite replace themselves. The loss of freedom and the exclusive power of a ruler is a great misfortune, but it will just as much be an orderly system; indeed, there really is more order, though less happiness, than in free states. Softness in morals, idleness and vanity bring forth sciences. These give a new ornament to the whole, prevent much evil, and if they are raised to a certain level they ameliorate those ills that they themselves have perpetrated.

One of the greatest harms of science is that it takes away so much time that the youth are neglected in morals

Second, that it so accustoms the mind to the sweetness of specvlatiow that good actions are omitted

Page 21

[34] Upper margin

Moral beauty, simplicity, sublimity. Justice; righteousness is simplicity. The passion of the sublime is enthusiasm. In love, virtuous. Friendship. Beautiful ideal.

Sheet inserted after page 22 [35] Obverse

The first impression that an <understanding> reader <who does not only read out of vanity or in order to pass the time> acquires from the writings of Mr. *J. J. Rousseau* [R38] is that he has encountered an great uncommon acuity of the mind, a noble impetus of genius and a sensitive soul in such a high degree as has perhaps never before been possessed by a writer of any age or any people. The impression that follows next is bewilderment at strange and absurd opinions, which oppose what is generally held so much that one could easily form the suspicion that, by means of his extraordinary talents, the author only wanted to prove the power of a charming wit and through a magical power of eloquence and [2:44] play the strange man play the eccentric who stands out among all rivals in wit because of a disarming <invisible making> novelty. The third thought, to which one comes only with difficulty because it happens only rarely

One must teach youth to honor the common understanding for moral as well as logical reasons.

I myself am a researcher by inclination. I feel the entire thirst for cognition and the eager restlessness to proceed further in it, as well as the satisfaction at every acquisition. There was a time when I believed this alone could constitute the honor of humankind, and I despised the rabble who knows nothing. Rousseau has set me right. This blinding prejudice vanishes, I learn to honor human beings, and I would feel by far less useful than the common laborer if I did not believe that this consideration could impart a value to all others in order to establish the rights of humanity.

It is very ridiculous to say that you shall love other people, one rather must say that you have good reason to love your neighbor. This holds even for your enemy.

Virtue is strong; thus, what debilitates and makes one soft by pleasures, or makes one dependent upon delusion, is opposed to virtue. What makes life contemptible or even hateful to us does not lie in nature. What makes vice easy and virtue difficult does not lie in nature.

[R39] Universal vanity makes it so that one says only of those who never understand how to live (for themselves) that they know how to live It is not at all conducive to happiness to extend the inclinations to the level of opulence, for since there are many uncommonly many cases where circumstances are unfavorable for these inclinations [and] against a desired situation, they constitute a source of displeasure, grief and worry, of which the simple human being knows nothing

It also does not help here to preach noble endurance.

[36] Reverse, opposite page 23, at 2:217

If <there> is any science that the human being needs, it is that which teaches him properly to fulfill [and]

<hold> the position that has been assigned to him in creation, and from which he can learn what he one must be in order to be a human being. Suppose he had become familiar with deceptive temptations above or beneath him that, without being noticed, had brought him away from his <typical> position, then this instruction would lead him back again to the state of a human being; and, however small or imperfect he may then find himself, he still will be quite good for his assigned post, because he is <exactly> what he ought to be.

The mistake of saying "this is universal among us, [and] therefore universal in general" is easily avoided by intelligent people. But the following judgments seem more plausible: "Nature has given us the opportunity for pleasure, why do we not want to use it"; "we have the capacity for sciences, nature calls us to seek them"; we feel in us a moral voice that speaks to us that this is noble and righteous, or that this is a duty to do so"

Everything passes by us in a river, and the changeable taste and the different forms of human beings make the entire game [R40] uncertain and deceptive. Where do I find fixed points of nature that the human being can never disarrange, and that can give him signs as to which bank he must head for

That all magnitude is only relative and that there is no absolute magnitude is seen from the following. I measure in the sky by means of the diameter of the earth, the earth's diameter by means of miles, miles by means of feet, the latter by means of their relation to my body

[37] Page 23

At the margin, next to lines 11-12, at 2:217

Friendship, young people

At the margin, next to lines 16–18

Self-respect, equality

Inserted sheet after page 24 [38] Obverse, at 2:217

The question is which qualities which condition suits the human being, an inhabitant of the planet that orbits the sun at a distance of 200 diameters of the sun.

Just as little as I can ascend from here to the planet Jupiter, so little do I demand to have qualities that are proper only to that planet. He who is so wise with respect to another place in creation is a fool with respect to the one he inhabits

I do not at all have the ambition of wanting to be a seraph; my pride is only this, that I am a human being

The one sentence is difficult to sort out: that does not lie <or it lies> in nature, i.e., nature has given no drives for it, rather they are artificial; no such afflictions are innate, but they have grown accidentally[. T]he other sentence is easier: that does not conform with nature, i.e., that opposes whatever really lies in nature. [R4] Rousseau more often proceeds according to the former, and since human nature has now acquired such a desolate form, the natural foundations become dubious and unrecognizable

The moderate citizen can form no concept of what, then, the courtier, who, exiled to his estates can live as he pleases, can lack; meanwhile the latter grieves to death.

Many people have *theology* and no religion except perhaps in order to apologize for great acts of viciousness someday when they are threatened by the horrors of hell

On the value of this life in itself or and immediately and on the value of this life only as a means to another life

The life of those that only enjoy without consideration and morals appears to have no value <A sign of crude taste nowadays is that one requires so much pretty make-up; now, the finest taste is in simplicity.> With people and animals, a certain average size has the most strength

<In a civilized state, one becomes clever very late; indeed, one could say with Theophrastus that it is a shame that one then ceases to live when one hopes for success.>

Moral taste with respect to sexual inclination, since in that everyone wants to appear to be quite refined or even pure

Truth is not the main perfection of social life; beautiful illusion here, as in painting, drives it much further. On taste in marrying

[39] Reverse, opposite page 25, at 218

[R42] The certainty in [unreadable word] moral judgments by means of a comparison with the moral feeling is just as great as the [certainty] with logical sentiment; and through analysis I will make it as certain to a human being that lying is repulsive as that a thinking body is incoherent. Deception with respect to a moral judgment occurs in the same fashion as it does with respect to a logical one, but the latter is still more frequent

Concerning the metaphysical foundations of aesthetics, the different immoral feeling – concerning the foundations of moral world-wisdom

the different moral feeling – of human beings according to [their] difference in sex, age, education and government, race and climate is to be noted

On the religion of a woman – on bold facial expression. A certain timidity, suspicion, etc. suits them well. Their loquacity, use

Why difference in rank is mostly shown among women.

The woman is closer to nature. A man who knows how to live — what sort of woman will he marry

On Rousseau's attempt to move the best talents through love Women educate their men themselves; they can attribute it to themselves if they turn out badly.

The one who is foolishly accommodating becomes a grumpy husband On the empty longing through a disproportionate, and for human

beings poorly suited, feeling for the sublime. Novels.

Rousseau pulled his sweetheart to the village

[R43] A marriage of an overly refined <exquisite> man to a coquette.

One imagines two marriages, one of which is, so to say, of a respectable kind, and the other domestic.

Moral taste is inclined to imitation; moral principles rise above this. Where there are courts and great distinctions among human beings, everything is given over to taste; in republics it is otherwise. Therefore, taste in social gatherings is more refined in the former and cruder in the latter. One can be very virtuous and have little taste. If social life is to grow, taste must be extended, because the agreeableness of social gatherings must be easy; principles, though, are difficult. Among women, this taste is easiest. The moral taste easily agrees with illusion, the principle does not. Swiss, Dutch, French, imperial cities. Suicide in Switzerland

Taste for mere virtue is a bit crude; if it is refined, then it must be able to try it [virtue] mixed with folly

Sheet inserted after page 26 [40] Obverse, at 2:218

What the finer part of mankind calls life is a quaint weaving of trifling pleasures <diversions, boring distractions>, even more plagues — of vanity and a whole swarm of ludicrous diversions. The loss of the same, the loss of the same [sic] is regarded [as] death, commonly, though, even much worse than death, (a human being who knows how to live), who has lost the taste for it has become dead to [all] pleasure

Fine coarse feeling. Fine self-acting ideal, at times chimerical. One has reason not to refine his feeling very much, first in order not to open the gates to pain. Second, in order to be close to the useful

Sufficiency and simplicity demand a coarser feeling and make [one] happy

[R44] The beautiful is loved, the noble respected

The ugly with disgust, the ignoble despised

The courage of a woman to follow the man in misfortune and his affectionateness. The man feels himself in his wife, and communicates no pain to her; an affectionate, a braver man

Short people are supercilious and hot tempered, tall [ones] are calm

The natural human being is moderate, not on account of future health (for he foresees nothing), but on account of present well-being

One reason that ladies are haughty towards each other is that they are more similar to each other, because the basis of the noble class is in men. The reason that they are embarrassed and rivalrous around one another is that they the happiness of men does not arise as much from pleasure as from merits, whereby they make their happiness themselves, whereas the former [the ladies] are made happy by others. Their essential inclination to please is based on this

The reason why the excesses of lust are sensed so sharply is because they concern the grounds of propagatiow, that is, the preservation of the species; and because this is the only thing women are good for, therefore, it constitutes their highest perfection, whereas their own preservation depends on men

The capacity to create utility with fertility is limited for a woman and broadened for a man.

[41] Reverse, opposite page 27, at 2:218

Opulence causes one to draw a great distinction between one woman and another

One does not satisfy desires through loving, but through marrying; they are at the same time the purest

[R45] The mark of sociableness is not to prefer oneself to another every time. To prefer another to oneself every time is weak. The idea of equality *regulates* everything

In society and in *meetings*, simplicity and equality ease them and make them pleasant

Control delusion and be a man so that your wife esteems you highest among all human beings; thus, be yourself no servant of the opinions of others.

In order for your wife to honor you, she should not see in you a slave of the opinions of others. Be domestic; in your society, there shall not prevail opulence, but taste – comfort, and not exuberance – rather a choice of guests than of dishes

— It would be better for women if they really worked.

A good of delusion consists in the fact that only opinion is sought after, but the thing itself is either regarded with indifference or even hated. The first delusion is that of honor. The second of avarice. The latter only loves the opinion that he could have many goods of life with his money, though without ever wanting it in earnest as well

One who is not convinced by what is obviously certain is a blockhead.

One who is not moved by what is obviously a duty is a villain.

— A dull head and corrupt heart.

That the drive for honor comes from the desire for equality is to be seen from this. Would a savage search for another in order to show him his advantages? If he can be without him, he will enjoy his freedom. Only if he must be together with him, will he attempt to outdo him, therefore the desire for honor is mediate

The desire for honor is just as immediate as the miser's desire for money. Both originate in the same way

[42] Page 27

Lower margin, at 2:219

[R46] The Arcadian shepherd's life and our chivalrous life of the court are both of bad taste and unnatural, though alluring. For true pleasure can never take place where one makes it into one's occupation. The recreations of someone with an occupation, which are rare, short and without preparation, are alone lasting and of genuine taste. A woman, because she now has nothing to do but to seek distractions, irritates herself and gets a bad taste for men, who do not always know to satisfy this thwarted inclination

Sheet inserted after page 28 [43] Obverse, at 2:219

Others' love of honor is so highly valued because it indicates so much renunciation of other advantages

The question is whether, in order to move my affects or those of others, I shall take a position outside the world or in it. I answer that I find it [the position] in the state of nature, i.e., of freedom

Women have female virtues

Of compassion it is only to be noted that it must never rule, but must be subordinated to the capacity and reasonable desire to do good. He who cannot do without much or is lazy has an idle compassion.

The natural human being without religion is much to be preferred to the civilized ones with merely natural religion. For the latter's morality would have to have high degrees if it were to provide a counterweight to his corruption.

Meanwhile, a civilized human being without any religion is much more dangerous

For, in the natural state, no correct concept of [R47] God can arise at all and the false one that one makes himself is harmful. Consequently, the theory of natural religion can be true only where there is science; therefore, it cannot bind all human beings

Natural theology, natural religion. A supernatural theology can nevertheless be combined with a natural religion. Those who believe Christian theology nevertheless have only a natural religion in so far as the morality is natural. The Christian religion is supernatural with respect to the doctrine and also the powers to exercise it. How little do the usual Christians have cause to pause over the natural [one]

The cognition of God is either speculative, and this is uncertain and liable to dangerous errors, or moral through faith, and this conceives of no other qualities in God except those that aim at morality. This faith is either natural or supernatural; the former is [breaks off]

[44] Reverse

Opposite page 29, at 2:219

Providence is primarily to be praised in that it accords quite well with the present state of human beings, namely, that their foolish wishes do not conform to [its] direction, that they suffer for their follies, and nothing wants to harmonize with the human being who has stepped out of the order of nature. If we consider the needs of animals [and] plants, with these providence agrees. It would be quite inverted if the divine governance were to alter the order of things according to the delusion of human beings, just as it alters itself. It is just as natural that, as far as he has deviated from there, everything must seem to be inverted to him according to his degenerate inclinations.

Out of this delusion arises a kind of theology as a phantasm of opulence (for this is always fraught with soft and superstitious) and a certain shrewdness and cleverness to intertwine through subjugation the highest being into one's businesses and plans.

[R48] *Diagoras.*

Newton saw for the very first time order and regularity combined with great simplicity, where before him disorder and [a] poorly matched manifold was found; and since then comets run in geometrical courses.

Rousseau discovered for the very first time beneath the manifold of forms adopted by the human being the deeply hidden nature of the same and the hidden law, according to which providence is justified by his observations. Before that the objection of Alfonso and Manes still held.

After Newton and Rousseau, God is justified, and henceforth Pope's theorem is true

[46] Page 30

At the margin, next to lines 12–15, at 2:220

Agreeable melancholy

true virtue cries

Sheet inserted after page 32

[46] Obverse, at 2:221

The savage stays beneath the nature of a human being. The opulent one roams further outside of its limits and the morally contrived one goes above it.

On friendship in general

On the beautiful and noble of company and of hospitality; simplicity, magnificence

If something keeps a youth who has turned into a man from becoming a father, if something hinders one from enjoying life, even though it is short, and urges one to prepare for the future life in order to lose the present one, if something demands that we hate life, or find it unworthy or short, then it does not lie in nature

[R49] Male strength does not express itself in forcing oneself to accept the injustice of others when one can drive it back, but in bearing the heavy yoke of necessity, as well as abiding the deprivations as a sacrifice for freedom or for whatever else it is that I love. The acceptance of insolence is a monkish virtue

The *sanguine* accepts insults, because he fears the vast extent of avenging them

The foolishness of vaingloriousness consists in one who esteems others to be so important that he believes their opinion to give him such great value nevertheless despising them so much that he also views them to be nothing compared to himself

parallel to penuriousness

[47] Reverse, opposite page 33, at 2:221

The art of *appearing* agrees very well with the character of the beautiful. For since the beautiful does not aim at the useful, but at mere opinion – since, by the way, the thing itself that is beautiful becomes disgusting if it does not appear to be new – the art of giving an agreeable appearance with respect to things is very beautiful, since the simplicity of nature is always the same. The female sex possesses this art to a high degree, which also constitutes our entire happiness. Through this the deceived husband is happy, the lover or companion sees English virtues and much to conquer and believes himself to have triumphed over a strong enemy. Dissimulation is a perfection of ladies but a vice in men.

Frankness complies with the noble; it pleases even if it is clumsy but goodhearted to a woman

The choleric person is honored in his presence and criticized in his absence; he has few no friends at all. The melancholic, few and good, the sanguine, many and careless

[R50] The choleric person makes faces full of secrets

If one bears in mind that man and woman constitute a moral whole, then one must not ascribe the same qualities to them, but instead ascribe to one those qualities that the other is missing

<They do not have as much sentiment for the beautiful as the man does, but more vanity>

A woman endeavors to acquire still much more love than men. The latter content themselves with pleasing roughly one, but the former everyone. If this inclination is poorly understood, then there arises a person of universal devotion

[48] Page 33

Lower margin, at 2:222

All arousing delights are feverish, and deadly exhaustion and dull feeling follow upon ecstasies of joy. The heart is used up and sensation becomes coarse

Inserted sheet after page 34

[49] Obverse, at 2:222

<The melancholic is just and rancorous about injustice.>

Anger is a good-natured passion in the simplicity of nature, but it makes a fool in the silly vanities of society.

The melancholic who is choleric is terrible. Extinguished blue eyes filled the pale face of Brutus. (On humor, mood, hypochondria. The woman and a dreamer have moods.) The melancholic who is sanguine is cowardly, depressed, afraid of people, jealous. (The sanguineous person is *gallant*.) The melancholic loves more strongly and is less loved by women, because women are changeable. The choleric person is a schemer of state, mysterious, and important in trifles; the sanguineous one turns important things into jokes. The melancholic-sanguineous person is a hermit or penitent in religion; the melancholic-choleric [breaks off]

The sanguine-choleric is valiant as a choleric, vain as a sanguine person, driven to fame, and yet polite, loves change and is brave therein; for this reason he gives prestige to his pranks, him only greatly loves the coquette and his wife very much from the viewpoint of how she pleases others. The melancholic is domestic, the choleric person a courtier. The sanguine one thrusts himself into every jolly company. In misfortune, the melancholic-choleric person is bold and desperate; the sanguine one is in tears and disheartened; the choleric one is ashamed of being kept; the choleric-sanguine one distracts himself through amusement and is content, because he seems to be happy. In clothing, the melancholic-sanguineous person is tidy, but something is always missing. The choleric-sanguine one [is] of good choice with carelessness, the phlegmatic one is dirty, the melancholic-choleric one is pure and simple

[50] Reverse, opposite page 35, at 2:222

Before one asks about the virtue of women, one must first ask whether they need such a thing. In the state of simplicity, there is no virtue. With men, to protect strong inclinations and honesty; with women, loyal devotion and flattery.

In the opulent state, the man must have virtue, the woman honor. One can hardly put the movement of fine moral sentiments or decoration (moral yeomanry. Alongside the pomade tin, the [writings of] Gellert) in the place of domestic occupation, and one who weaves a gown for her husband always shames the gallant lady, who in place of this reads a tragedy.

Longings.

In conversation the melancholic is still and serious. The sanguine person [R52] talks a lot when one jokes and changes the subjects. The choleric one tries to set the tone and plays hard to get. The choleric one laughs forced by propriety; the sanguine one by habit and friendliness; the melancholic one still laughs when everything has stopped.

When both sexes degenerate, the degeneration of man is still far worse One who likes none but excessively raging expressions has a dull feeling; one who likes no one except very beautiful persons, only screaming colors [and] only great heroic virtues has a dull feeling. One who notices the gentle style of writing, the noble simplicity in morals [and] the hidden charm has a tender feeling. The feeling becomes more tender during one's middle age, but also gradually weaker. The tender feeling is not as strong as the coarse one

[51] Page 36

At the margin, next to line 18f., at 2:223

Valiant

Inserted sheet after page 36

[52] Obverse, at 2:222

Good consequences are to be sure marks of morality, but not always those the only ones, because they cannot always be recognized with certainty. How many good consequences some lies could have.

The ground of the *potestatis legislatoriae divinae* is not in kindness, for then the motivation would be gratitude (*subjective* moral ground, kind of feeling) and hence not strict duty. The ground of the *potestatis legislatoriae* presupposes inequality, and has the result that the a human being loses a degree of freedom with respect to another. This can only happen if he himself sacrifices his will to that of another; if he does this with respect to all his actions, he makes himself into a slave. A will that is subjected to that of another [is] imperfect and contradictory, for the human being has *spontaneitatem*; if he is subjected to the will of a human being [R53] (although he himself can choose) then he is ugly and contemptible; but if he is subjected to the will of God, then he is in accordance with nature. One must not perform actions out of obedience to a human being that one could perform out of inner motivations, and demanding obedience, where inner motivations would have done everything, produces slaves.

The body is mine for it is a part of my I and is moved by my faculty of choice. The entire animated or unanimated world that does not have its own faculty of choice is mine, in so far as I can compel it and move it according to my faculty of choice. The sun is not mine. The same holds for another human being, therefore nobody's property is a *Proprietat* or an exclusive property. But in so far as I want to appropriate something exclusively to myself, I will, at least, not presuppose the other's will or his action as being opposed to mine. I will therefore perform those actions that designate what is mine, cut down the tree, mill it, etc. The other human being tells me that this is his, for through the actions of his faculty of choice, it belongs to his own self, as it were.

[53] Reverse, opposite page 37, at 2:223

A will that is to be good must not cancel itself out if it is taken universally and reciprocally; for the sake of this, the other will not call his own what I have worked upon, since otherwise he would presuppose that his will moved my body

Thus, when a human being calls some things his own, he thereby tacitly promises in similar circumstances, through his will, not about something [breaks off]

The obedience of the child to the parents is not based 1. on gratitude 2. on the fact that they cannot sustain themselves, for that would be based on utility, but rather because they have no completed will of their own, and it is good to be directed by the will of others. But since so far they are an affair of the parents, because they only live through their [parents'] faculty of choice, thus it is morally good to be ruled by them. As soon as they can educate nourish themselves, obedience ends.

[R54] We belong to the divine affairs, as it were; we exist through Him and His will. There are some things that can be in accordance with God's will that would not be at all good from inner motivations, e.g., to slay one's son. The goodness of obedience now depends on this. My will is always subordinated to the will of God in its determinations; thus, it agrees with itself best when it agrees with the divine will; and it is impossible that for that, which is evil, to be in accordance with the divine will.

The woman seeks pleasure and expects necessities from others. The man seeks necessities and expects pleasure from the woman. If both seek necessities they probably are in agreement, but penurious; if both seek pleasure they are foolish

A man finds more pleasure in giving a woman amenities than a woman does, but the latter wants to appear to be giving rather than enjoying; because the former is surely her main purpose, in contrast, she admits to having received the necessities

[54] Page 38

Lower margin, at 2:224

*[Through signs related to inserted sheet after page 38]

One sees that this is true from the fact that a woman prefers herself, for she always wants to rule; a man, however, prefers his wife, for he wants to be ruled; he even makes for himself an honor thereof

Inserted sheet after page 38

[55] Obverse, at 2:223

I do not know what solace those who consider their imagined needs to be just and natural can find in a providence that denies them their fulfillment. I, of whom I certainly know that I suffer no ills but those which I bring upon myself, and that it only depends on me to become happy through the kindness of divine order, will never grumble about them

[R5] <Why must one speak French in order to be polite. *Dames Messieurs. Chapeaux Cornetten.*> [Ladies Gentlemen. Hats Cornets.] Now, if a woman marries a twenty-year-old man, she takes herself a fop. The reason for this, among others, is that he has not yet become acquainted with the deceptive art of women to appear better and more agreeable than they are. Therefore, he makes a poor husband, because he always believes that he probably could have chosen better, or also because he has really fallen for her and chosen poorly. But if with more age he knows the sex and sees the futile appearance, he returns to simplicity, where according to nature he already could have been at the beginning. Hence the path to a good marriage goes through wantonness –

an observation that is very unpleasant, especially because it is true

The time of maturity of a lord and of a farmer is never different. A woman is never mature without a man.

Men are much more in love than women, which also is natural. But if the latter grow in the art of appearing – an appearance which however ends in marriage – then from this must emerge a kind of deceived reluctance in marriage, which finds less agreeableness than it had expected. It is not good to make a future husband fall too much in love; one must save something for the future.

[The expression (the woman) is certainly polite and seems to prove that they were previously in a special room together with one another, as is still the case in England now.]

[56] Reverse, opposite page 39

The art of doing without, i.e., of not letting inclinations germinate in oneself, is the means to happiness; hence one can either seek to acquire honor, i.e., the high opinion of others, or strive to do without it entirely and be indifferent towards it.

That the choleric person is angry stems from his love of honor because he [R56] always believes [himself] to be insulted; the reasonable one desires nothing but equality and has little occasion to be angry.

In those lands where women are not beautiful they are treated tyrannically, as among savages, because the weak one must inspire inclination or else get oppressed

The main ground of lasting beauty is illusion. Make-up. A kind of untruth that is lovelier than truth. *Corregio* departed from nature

Women gladly love bold men – and these modest, decent men. Judgment of a woman by Bayle. *Hercules* endeared himself more to *Omphale* through his 72 girls than through his spinning.

As far as sex is concerned, women are more of a bawdy taste, men more of a fine one. They love civilities and court manners more in order to display their own vanity.

Whether the savage has had taste, the one whom the eating-houses pleased best [breaks off]

When the inclinations of women and men grow equally, they nevertheless must come into disproportion, namely, that the latter have less capacity in proportion to their inclination

Inserted sheet after page 44

[57] Obverse, at 2:224

In everything that pertains to beautiful or sublime sentiment, we do best if we let ourselves be led by the examples of the ancients. In sculpture, architecture, poetry, and oratory the ancient mores and the ancient political constitution. The ancients were closer to nature: we have much frivolous or opulent or servile corruption between ourselves and nature. Our age is the *seculum* of beautiful trivialities, bagatelles or sublime chimeras.

The sanguineous person goes where he is not invited; the choleric one does not go where he is not invited in accordance with propriety; the melancholic one prevents [himself from] not being invited at all. In society, the melancholic is still and pays attention; the sanguine one speaks what occurs to him; the choleric one makes comments and interpretations. Concerning domestic nature, the melancholic is <stingy> [and] penurious; the sanguineous one is a bad host. The choleric one is acquisitive, but magnificent. The generosity of the melancholic is magnanimity, of the choleric one is boasting, of the sanguine is thoughtlessness.

The melancholic person is jealous; the choleric one, power-hungry; the sanguine one, occupied with courting

The *coquette* is an excellent *maitresse*, but no wife at all, except for a Frenchman.

On providence. The fools that forsake the order of nature are astonished about providence, that it does not improve its terrible consequences; *Augustine* with his *crapula*.

Union is possible where one can be whole without the other, e.g., between two friends, and where neither is subordinated to the other. There can also be union in exchange or in contracts of a way of life. But unity depends on only two constituting a whole together in a natural way with respect to needs as well as what is agreeable. This exists with a man and a woman. Yet, here unity is tied to equality. The man cannot enjoy a single pleasure of life without the woman, and the latter can enjoy no necessities without the man. This also constitutes the difference between their characters. According to his inclination, the man will seek necessities solely in accordance with his judgment and pleasure in accordance with the pleasure of the woman, and further make the latter into necessities. The woman will seek pleasure according to her taste and leave the necessities to the man.

[58] Back side, opposite page 4, at 2:224

[R58] In countries where societies mostly consist of men, one values personal merit according to understanding, fidelity and the useful zeal of friendship or also of common utility. Where they are always intermingled with women, according to wit, suavity, jest, amusements, *Medisance* [malicious gossip].

In the case of the old Germans, before French mores corrupted us, women must have been in special rooms as in England.

A man who has a wife is complete, detaches himself from his parents, and is alone in the state of nature. He is so disinclined to associate himself with others, that he even fears the approach of others. Therefore, the state of war. *Hobbes*

The embarrassment and blushing that the ladies of fine manners do not need to have in themselves is very charming and particular to the sex, but where it still is encountered, there she is a good bulwark of chastity

Female grace. Femininities are laudable in a woman; if she has masculinities, then it is a reproach

In marrying, the infatuated blindness disappears so that the woman misses the unlimited reign over the heart of the man and the rank of goddess that she has had before the marriage. But the man does not feel himself ruled anymore as much as he was and wishes. The woman loses more in vanity, the man more in tenderness. The fantasy of infatuation had instilled even more exaggerated concepts in the man than in the woman

<The woman then wished to still rule as before, while the man wished to be ruled. The woman sees herself as being coerced to flatter, the man finds no other inclination in himself than kindness>

The man is stronger not only according to build, but also in principles and in the steadfastness to endure something; therefore, his clothes must be so, the woman's must be *delicate* and fettled

[R59] Taste in the choice of company. Taste for virtue, friendship. One turns more on taste than on bare necessities

Inserted sheet after page 42 [59] Obverse, at 2:225

Nature has equipped women to make affectionate and not to be affectionate

They are never equal to men in true tenderness, which can be seen in the fact that all women want to rule and the most reasonable men let themselves be dominated; now he who, in spite of being stronger himself, reluctantly surrenders his power must yet have more tenderness than she who is aware that it happens reluctantly, and yet prefers herself to the other

Women are more for lustful love, men are more for affectionate love. All widows marry, but not all widowers. No woman must marry a man who is vain

At best union can occur in the case of equality, but never unity; since there must be unity in marriage, everything must be ruled by one, the man or the woman. Now, it is inclination and not the understanding that rules here. Thus, the inclination of either the man or the woman can rule; the latter is the best

War can only bring about virtues if it is patriotic, i.e., if it does not serve to gain money and support, but to preserve oneself, and if the soldier again becomes a citizen

[60] Reverse, opposite page 43, at 2:225

Lustful love is the ground of sexual inclination. Hence, everything beautiful and sublime in this love is only a phantasm if this is not presupposed. The husband must be a man by night and day. This remark also serves to warn of affectionate and highly respectful love between the sexes, for the latter more often degenerates into the outbreak of lust.

[R60] The woman must be kept from being unfaithful through goodheartedness love and honor; if she the if man does not win her affection, then he can hardly count on her [sense of] duty. That is a reason why women must be met with kindness. For they have, by the way, a widely extended capacity.

The difference between he who requires little because he lacks little and he who requires little because he can do without a lot. *Socrates*. The enjoyment of a pleasure that is not a necessity; i.e., whatever one can spare is agreeableness. If, however, it is taken for a need, then it is concupiscence. The state of a human being who can do without is moderation, that of the one who counts what is very dispensable among his needs is opulence.

The contentment of a human being arises either from the fact that he satisfies many inclinations through many things that are agreeable, or from the fact that few he has not let many inclinations sprout, and therefore is content with a satisfied needs. The state of the one who is content because he does not know things that are agreeable is simple moderation, that of the one who knows them, but voluntarily dispenses with them because he fears the unrest that arises from them, is wise moderation. The former demands no self-constraint and privation, but the latter does; the former is easy to seduce, the latter has been seduced and is safer with respect to future [seduction]. The state of a human being without displeasures, therefore, because he does not know of greater pleasures being possible for <him>, and thus does not desire [them].

Virtue does not at all consist in prevailing over acquired inclinations under special circumstances, but in seeking to get rid of such inclinations and thus learning to do without them gladly. It does not consist in quarreling with natural inclinations, but in making it so that one has none but natural ones, for then one can always satisfy them

Inserted sheet after page 44 [61] Obverse, at 2:226

[R61] The characters of human nature are the degenerations of their vocation, in the same way the necessity of war, dominance and subservience of religions and of science

It is the question whether the noble and why it does not agree more6 with the useful than the beautiful [does]

Women will always prefer a man with masculine appeal who is wild, for they always believe that they will rule him. Most of the time they are right about this, and this excuses them if they fail. This is also the beautiful side of the female sex, that they can rule men

One will perhaps find more among men who deserve the gallows than women who get drunk

If one wants to maintain the fantastical [aspect] of love in the married state, then jealousies and adventures must take place; if one wants to maintain the courting, then the wife must be a *coquette*; if both should fall away, only the simplicity of nature remains

In countries that are rich and monarchical, where many have nothing to do with their private businesses of self-interest and with public businesses of the state, everything comes down to the skillfulness of society. From there arises politeness. In England there are rich people, but they have to do with the state; in Holland they are intertwined with self-interest On fashionable casts of mind

A woman is always ready to betray a lover who is highly respectful and to give herself in secret to him who, without much ado, is bold and enterprising. In the state of simplicity the man rules over the woman; in the state of opulence, the woman rules over the man. The finer taste of free association makes it necessary

[62] Reverse, opposite page 45, at 2:226

[R62] *Sensus subjecti bene vel male <affectio> afficiendi potestas leg-*

islatoria non nititur amore sed reverentia et facultate morali exterorquendi facultas logica leges ferendi (propter sapientiam) non est moralis ["The legislative power of affecting the subject's sense in a good way or in a bad way does not depend on love but on respect and on the moral power of necessitation; the logical faculty of making laws (in accordance with wisdom) is not moral."]

The still and peaceful serenity in the beautiful is turned inward with a man, outward with a woman

Pelisson and *Madame Sevigne*

Bold attitude and courting or disarming smile. <On the habit of women of adopting an earnest decency.>

Who himself is devoid of sentiments (that is, has feelings for judging but not for needs) can much more easily maintain them permanently in others. Therefore, the woman must be less affectionate

Because we have so much vain *Jalousie*, friends are also rivals. Therefore, friendship can only take place with needs

Light and warmth appear to differ from each other as sound and wind; light and color as sound and tone. Taut strings can must make *undulationes*. A coal fire in the hearth is a space empty of ether, which goes out through the chimney; since thereby ether is now being freed in all the surrounding bodies, they give warmth. Those who receive it in such a way are become warm those who give it are c [breaks off]

The question is whether, when bodies become warm, they let go of fire or take it in. It depends on whether bodies, in absolute coldness, are saturated with fire, for then are a warm body becomes cold if it absorbs fire, and it heats a body that it forces to let go of fire. Is a heated oven devoid of fire? Yes, it gradually absorbs the fire into itself, thereby releases the fire in others and makes them warm and becomes cold itself. In this way, the suns and also those are the spaces most empty of the fire element. The dispersion of light can thereby also be comprehended, for it is easier that the intrusion into [R63] an empty space should be followed endlessly by a thread of agitated matter than that an impact should.

29	29	29	
12	33	14	
58	87	116	
29	87	294	
	957	406	
	2	122	34
		36	
		4	8

Inserted sheet after page 46

[63] Obverse

In this way, light might perhaps be a movement towards the sun rather than one away from it

Sound, although air is squeezed out of the lungs, can perhaps be generated through the recession of air rather than through the driving away [of it]

Fire above a body (earth) makes it cold underneath; but only to a certain extent, for it releases the fire element from the closest one, the more remote one partly attracts so this already released fire element to itself; thus, many poles arise.

Let there be fire at a; the fire element is released before b, but it continuously becomes weaker than at y and x; the movement from b to a, which breaks into the empty space, is weaker than [the one that] is pulled from b in order to move towards c; thus bc becomes attractive and consequently cold; only by breaking in, does it accumulate in c, and this c although with delayed movement, so that c, indeed, is positively warm – i.e., lets fire go – but beyond c towards d [it gets] negative again.

[R64] The sun warms the earth, i.e., makes it so that the fire in it releases itself hence it must from the upper or rather that there is a space empty of fire on the earth; assume now a body being placed high in the air, the body is then in a space full of fire; thus, no fire comes out of itself

[or] into itself and it is because it does not let go of any such element

[64] Reverse, opposite page 47, at 2:227

The true concept of fire seems to consist in this, that in heating the fire [2:83] does not pass from the warm into the cold, but from the cold into the warm; in cooling, the body that is becoming cold is put in a state of absorbing, and fire passes into it. From this it follows that only the body that warms others becomes cold, and conversely the one that becomes cold warms others, for it cannot warm without releasing the fire in others, i.e., but the more it fills itself, the less it is in a state to release it in others. Yet, if a body becomes cold, it falls into a state of absorbing and thereby warms others. A body is cold with respect to others if it cools them, i.e., fills others with the fire element, and thus diminishes their state of absorbing by its becoming warm itself, i.e., by releasing fire. Comets are, among all heavenly bodies, those which are most full of the fire element. They come into the empty space of the ether, or rather their elemental fire, which rises behind them, is strongly released

<If there is a fire in the hearth, then the air in all [of its] expanse, and also the nearby bodies, will become warm. Because the fire is freed out of the air, remote [objects], however, attract it and become cold. Or so: the ether that is rushing by makes waves and is denser in some place than before, hence the body found there will suck rather than aspirate>

All the contrived rules for a wife exist in order to prevent others from not pleasing us more or making us lustful. Constrain your own concupiscence and your wife will be enough for you.

[R65] A valiant woman is something wholly different from a romanic beauty, the latter is best for a lover, the former for a husband. German women are valiant, French women *coquettes* who

A good housewife is honorable for the husband, how a gallant lady wants to earn this name

A man must show some contemptuousness with respect to his finery; it must be seen that he has worn the hat. His cuffs must not worry him

If I should choose a wife, I want to take one who does not have much wit, but feels it.

The corruption of our time can be boiled down to this, that no one demands to be content with himself, or also good, but instead to appear so

One complains that marriages are not as good as the unmarried state. The reason for this is above. One never enjoys oneself.

Inserted sheet after page 48 [63] Obverse

Poena est vel politica vel moralis. Prior ut causa impulsiua est ratio omissionis posterior causatum commissionis. Moralis est proprie afflictiva vel vindicativa sed habet etiam rationem medii ad correctionem vel peccatoris respectu antecedentium vel futurorum demeritorum.

The cause of all moral punishment is this. All evil action would never happen if it were sensed through moral feeling with as much aversion as it deserves. But if it is carried out, then it is a proof that physical stimulation [unreadable word] has sweetened it and the action has seemed good; but now it is nonsensical and ugly that what is morally evil should yet be good on the whole; consequently, in the outcome, a physical evil must make good for the absence of aversion that was missing in the action.

<To a certain extent, it is fortunate that marriages become difficult, because if [R66] they became frequent, the masters would multiply and injustice would become still more common>

Women are far cleverer in judging male merits and their weaknesses of which one can make use, than men are among each other. Men, by contrast, more easily see the value of a woman than a woman sees that of another, but they do not as easily see the shortcomings as a woman sees those of another. Thus, women rule over men and deceive them more easily than the other way around. It is easy to deceive a man, but not the other way around. Traitor. You don't love me anymore, you believe more in what you see, etc.; no man can say such a thing to a wife.

she even sees what he does not see himself and sees correctly

They rightly carry out such intrigues in retaliation for the injustice we show them, in that we want them chaste and have been unchaste ourselves

<The reason why there are so many cuckolds is because the time of the debaucheries of men has ended and that of women has begun.>

[66] Reverse, opposite page 49, at 2:228

It is very good that the woman is chosen; she herself cannot choose Why aging seems so terrible to a woman, [but] not to men, for the sublime applies to the latter

Youth is a great perfection for a woman in marriage; one still loves her afterwards in old age for the sake of the memory of her youth. That elderly women marry comes about because of our injustice.

Women are all avaricious except where vanity is stronger; they are all devout and acquiescent to the clerics. The honor of a man resides in his judgment of himself, that of a woman in the judgment of others

[R66] If a man were found by whom I was hated, it would worry me. Not as if I were afraid of him, but because I would find it hideous to have something in oneself that could become a reason for hate in others, for

I would suspect that another could not have developed a dislike without any apparent reason at all. Therefore, I would seek him out, I would make myself better known to him, and after I the disadvantages would have seen some benevolence toward me having developed in him, I would let it <myself> be satisfied with this without ever wanting to take advantage of it. But if I saw it as inevitable that common and raffish prejudices, a wretched envy or an even more contemptuous [and] jealous vanity make it impossible to entirely avoid all hatred, well then I would say to myself, it is better that I be hated than that I be despised. Hatred This motto is based on an entirely different ground than that which self-interest concocts for us, [namely that] I want to be envied rather than pitied. The hatred of my fellow citizens does not nullify their concept of equality, but contempt makes me small in the eyes of others and always causes a very annoying delusion of inequality. Yet, it is much more harmful to be despised than to be hated.

[67] Page 50

At the margin, 2:229

They laugh easily and gladly, and it increases their charms

Inserted sheet after page 50 [68] Obverse, at 2:229

Female pride. Male pride

The corrupted woman was *Arria Margaretha* Maultasch

It is not appropriate that a woman makes the man happier by something other than her person. With her money a woman buys herself a jester or a tyrant

The greatest perfection is domesticity

[R68] <Women are incomparably able to control their countenance, [they] have more accent, [they are] eloquent>

The human being has his own inclinations, and they in virtue of his power of choice he has a hint from nature to arrange his actions in accordance with these. Now, there can be nothing more horrendous than that the action of a human being shall stand under the will of another. Hence no antipathy can be more natural than that which a human being has towards slavery. For this reason a child cries and becomes bitter if it has to do what others want without one having bothered to make it attractive to him. And it only wishes to be a man soon and to operate according to its will. What new servitude toward things must it impose in order to introduce the latter[?]

Already in her build, a woman is equipped so that she will be sought after, i.e., that she will know how to provoke advances and be clever at yielding or also at refusing.

Hence she would have to know how to win over but also how to conceal desires in order to prevent disdain.

Therefore, she can adopt a decent and cool nature more easily than a man, can pretend excellently, and is equipped with all qualities for always appearing as what she should be. She is therefore soberly eloquent, never imprudent, etc.

Shamefulness is never a ground of chastity, but something that in place of the latter, by means of the incentive of propriety, generates the very same effects

A woman wants men to be enterprising in matters of love

[69] Reverse, opposite page 51 at 2:229

The sweetness that we find in respecting beneficence towards human beings is an effect of the feeling of the universal well-being that would occur in the state of freedom

The refinement of times is an adeptness at deceiving and our academies furnish a great multitude of swindlers.

[R69] Drunkenness is the failing of a man Roughness

Anger

The law-giving power of God with respect to the first human being is based on property. The human being was freshly placed in the world, all trees belonged to God and he forbade him one of them.

This idea ended. The law-giving power of God over the Jewish people is grounded in the social contract. God wanted to lead them out of Egypt and give them another country if they obeyed him; <At that time, he was not a God of human beings, but of the Jews> when they subsequently had kings, God still reserved supremacy for himself, and the kings were only satraps or vassals. In the New Testament, this ground comes to an end. The universal ground of the law-giving power of God is presupposed, but the bindingness is grounded only in a kindness, which does not want to make use of any severity. Thus, in genuine Christianity, this is wholly annihilated with respect to the law-giver, and the Father is introduced

Paul judges that the law only produces reluctance, because it makes it so that one unwillingly does what has been commanded, and indeed this is how things are. For this reason he sees the law as abolished by Christ and only [sees] grace, namely a ground to love God quite from one's heart, which is not possible according to nature, and by means of which actions will be brought to morality and not to theocratic politics.

[71] Page 51

At the margin, next to lines 22-25, at 2:230

Is generally unclean as Magliabechi; she is disguised by a loose mouth. As my brother says [breaks off]

Lower margin

One can hate him who is right, but one is forced to respect him highly. Selfishness fights against common utility. The latter acquires love from inclination

[72] Page 52

At the margin, at 2:230

Yet men may always devote troublesome and sleepless nights to their research if the woman only knows how she is supposed to rule them.

Inserted sheet after page 52

[72] Obverse

<On the mutterings against providence>

On freedom

In whatever state he finds himself, the human being is dependent on many <external> things. He always depends on some things because of his needs, on others because of his concupiscence, and since he <surely> is the administrator of nature but not its master, he must <rather> accommodate himself to its coercion, because he does not find that it will always accommodate itself to his wishes. But what is much harder <and more unnatural> than this yoke of necessity is the dependence subjection of one human being under the will of another human being. There is no misfortune more terrible to him who is would be accustomed to freedom – [who] <would have enjoyed the good of freedom> – than to see himself delivered under to a creature of his own kind, who could force him to do what he wants. There is also no doubt that [breaks off]

It also <requires> a very long habituation to have made when make <the> the horrible terrible thoughts of subservience tolerable, because everyone must feel it in himself that even though there are many adversities that one may not always want to cast off at the risk of one's life, still in the choice between slavery and the risk of death there would [R71] be no reservation about preferring the latter.

[73] Obverse, opposite page 53 at 2:230

The cause of this is also very clear and rightful. All other ills of nature are still subject to certain laws that one gets to know in order subsequently to choose how far one wants to give into them or be subjected to them. The heat of the burning sun, the harsh winds, the motions of the water still allow the human being to devise something that will protect him against them or at least [breaks off]

But the will of every human being is upon the effect of his own drives [and] inclinations, and agrees only with his own true or imagined welfare. But if I was free before, nothing can present a more dreadful prospect of sorrow and despair to me than that in the future my state shall not reside in my own will, but in the will of another. Today it is extremely cold, I can go out or stay at home, whichever I prefer; but the will of another does not determine what is most agreeable to me on this occasion, but what is most agreeable <to him>. I want to sleep so he wakes me. I want to rest or play, and he forces me to work. The wind that rages outside may well force me to flee to a cave, but here or elsewhere it finally leaves me in peace, but my master seeks me out, and since the cause of my misfortune has reason, he is far more skillful at tormenting me than all elements. Even if I presume that he is good, who guarantees me that he will not change his mind. The motions of matter hold to a certain determinate rule, but the obstinacy of the human being is without any rule

[74] Page 53

At the margin, at 2:230

Those who regard the marital excesses as trifles that would deserve no contumely or punishment revenge make the strongest satires of marriage, because then it the state of marriage itself is not different [R72] from gallantry, from that of the most indifferent sort.

Lower margin

The woman takes a satire of her sex as a joke, because she knows well that the mockery of the little shortcomings of her sex actually applies to the men themselves, who only love her all the more for the sake of them; but a satire of marriage insults them all, because this seems to be more serious, and because they also feel there is some truth in this reproach. But if such a principle got the upper hand, her sex would be degraded to men's power of choice.

Inserted sheet after page 53 [74] Obverse, at 2:230<

On the rightful expression "gentlemen" [meiwe Herrew]>32

In subjection there is also someth not only something externally dangerous but something also a certain ugliness and a contradiction that at

the same time indicates its unlawfulness. An animal is not yet a complete being because it is not conscious of itself; and its drives and inclinations may be opposed by another or not, it surely feels its ill, but it [the ill] disappears for it in a moment, and it does not know of its own existence. But that the human being himself should, as it were, need no soul and should have no will of his own, and that another soul should move my limbs is absurd and perverse: Also in our constitutions every human being who is subordinated to a great degree is contemptible to us—[breaks off]

Livery

<Instead of freedom appearing to elevate me above the cattle, it places [R73] me even beneath them, since I can more easily be coerced>

Someone like that is, as it were, by himself, nothing but the houseware of another. I could just as well indicate my respect to the boots of the master as to his lackey. In short, the human being who is dependent in this way is no longer a human being; he has lost this rank, he is nothing except another human being's belonging.

Subjection and freedom often are commonly admixed to a certain degree, and one depends on the other. But even the small degree of dependence is much too great an ill not naturally to terrify. This feeling is very natural but one can also greatly weaken it. The power to withstand other ills can become so small that slavery seems a lesser ill than adversity. Nevertheless, it is certain that in human nature it stands above [breaks off]

Indeed, the cattle are coerced by the human beings, but the human being by the delusion of the human being

The momentary violence of an attack is much less than servitude

[76] Reverse, opposite page 55, at 2:231

There may quite well be stimulations that the human being prefers to freedom for a moment, but he certainly must feel sorry right after that. Society makes it so that one evaluates oneself only comparatively. If others are not better than me, I am good; if all are worse, I am perfect.

Comparative evaluation is still distinguished from honor.

Chastity cannot be a lack of amorous passion, [R74] since then it really is a flaw, namely if this passion is too small for the whole purpose; but it is good in so far as it is appropriate to age <and> estate, but this *Bowitaet* [goodness] is not moral.

To preserve chastity is either an immediate shamefulness (a concern to make one's sexual character contemptible) or a mediate one – a consequence of the general concept of honor. The latter is either merely a concern to bring no dishonor upon oneself – and this is a means of preserving virtue against which much ado could be made – or a tender irritability of an inner self-reproach in so far as it is connected with sincerity and not able to conceal itself, that is, shows itself in blushing; this quality is the best means of preservation.

We have all sorts of drives that should serve us as means to serve and more often immediately rule others. First, comparing ourselves with

others in order for us to be able to evaluate ourselves; from this arises the falsity of evaluating one's worth comparatively, [i.e.,] arrogance, and of evaluating one's happiness in just the same way, [i.e.,] jealousy. Second, putting ourselves in the place of another in order for us to know what he feels and judges. From this arises blind pity, which also brings justice into disorder. Third, the investigating the judgments of others because this can correct the truth of ours morally as well as logically. From this arises the desire for glory. Fourth, acquiring and saving oneself all sorts of things for enjoyment; from this arises greed, which is miserly. One says that ambition is the final weakness of the wise. I believe that in so far as the wisdom is not of the kind that presupposes old age the love of women is the final weakness.

[77] Page 56

Marginal notes next to lines 9–14, at 2:231

That a woman possesses femininities is no ill, but that they be encountered in a man surely is one. Likewise, it is a biting mockery rather than a word of praise that a woman possesses masculinity

Next to lines 18-22

[R75] A woman restricts the heart of a man; and one usually loses a friend when he marries

Lower margin

Thus the man is a dandy in the marital state

Inserted sheet after page 56

[78] Obverse, at 2:231

The naming of *dames* and *chapeaux*, although it is a fashionable trifle in the social interaction among Germans, indicates quite well the foolishness in taste that creeps in among us, and that makes us into a mimic of the most ridiculous customs of a *nation* that is lively and clownish in its own character. The everlasting social interaction of the French with women is in accordance with their character, yet this is not so with the Germans. Our women also do not have by far the lively *coquetterie* of the French. Therefore, this manner of association must always be somewhat vulgar. They are still proud here

Since women are weak, they are much less capable of virtue; but they have that which can make it dispensable

Virtue becomes ever more necessary, but also ever more impossible in our present constitution

Since virtue shows strength, it must be suitable for warlike states, more for *Rome* than *Carthage*.

Unity in society is not possible among many

If we count the labors of another among [our] needs, why not also his wife

Men only evaluate their worth in relation to one another if they are in society: women [evaluate theirs] only in relation to men, because now every charming quality discovered or pretention to win over questions every other's [R76] courting claim; thus, they strongly disparage each other

Every well-mannered woman seeks to charm the entire sex, even though she does not mean to profit thereby. This is because, since they should be sought after, they must possess a general inclination to please; for if this were restricted, she might fall for him who does not want her.

In marriages, this inclination steps beyond its restrictions

[79] Reverse, opposite page 57 at 2:232

<On the amenities that one makes into a need and vice versa. Ideal pleasures. Chimerical ones that deceive in [their] fulfillment>

On need and amenities. Rest, change, boredom

On opulence and sufficiency. Preparation, foresight

On ambition.

<On courage and cowardice, health and sickness>

On the goods of delusion. Stinginess

On sexual inclination. On science

On fine and crude sentiments

On foresight

On the human being of simplicity

On the natural human being in comparison with the civilized one; <on the extent of the welfare of both>

On the value of human nature

[R77] One who is free values himself more than one who is slavish Dependence on violence is not as disreputable as the [dependence] on

delusion

<On industriousness and laziness>

On the opulence of civilized human beings.

On the sciences, on healthy and fine understanding

On enjoyment and delusion, *prevoiance* [foresight] <On the capacity of enjoyment and of delusion>

On welfare and misery

<moral>

On generosity and guiltiness

On the drive for acquisition or for defense. War On truth and lies. On propriety and righteousness

On friendship. On the perfection of human nature

On sexual inclination

Virtue, religion. On the natural and artificial state, education

The officer who became embarrassed – or who pretended to become so – by the gaze of Lovis XIV. expressed the sentiment of a slave. The embarrassment of a man with respect to a woman does no harm to his noble qualities; his boldness is here crude indifference. A woman must not be embarrassed in consideration of male virtue, *conscia decoris Venus* [Venus is conscious of her propriety]. Her noble propriety is calm and gentle, not bold. I revere the beautiful girl in a noble or princely person.

[R78] If he already talks of virtue all the time, he is corrupt; if he constantly talks of religion, he is [corrupt] to the most extreme degree

The clergymen in the country could hold large schools for the education of children

[88] Page 57

Upper margin, at 2:232

Beauty is commanding. Merit [unreadable word] peaceful and yielding. The wife sustains the affectionateness of the man through jealousy

At the margin, next to lines 2–19

The man from whom escapes a tear that has been held back with difficulty. Therefore, his pain, which he compresses in his chest, chokes him if tender wistfulness moves him and the effort to bear it unwaveringly shines forth in his behavior. A woman can let her grief out in lamentations with propriety and relieves herself [of] her sentiment. She also passes easily from pain to joy, even if the former has been serious, which is good for a beautiful sex as well. The man loves more affectionately, the woman more steadily.

Inserted sheet after page 58 [81] Obverse, at 2:232

On inequality

Once this has begun, the ill of oppression is not nearly so great as that the minds of the oppressed become abject and value themselves lowly. A peasant is a much viler human being and has cruder vices than a savage who lacks everything, and just the same [holds for] a common worker.

If I went into the workshop of a craftsman, I would not wish that he could read my thoughts. I dread this comparison; he would realize the great inequality in which I stand to him. I recognize that I cannot live a single day without his industriousness, that his children are brought up to be useful people.

On the defensive passions.

[R79] Although the human being hates no other human being by nature, he does indeed fear him. Hence he is on his guard, and the equality that he thinks he is losing every moment brings him to arms.

The state of war soon begins. But since it is based on a noble ground, it surely brings forth great ills but no ignominy. It is less likely to dishonor human nature than a slavish peace∗

[Our present war aims only at the acquisition of money and luxury. That of the Ancients [aimed] at equality and the predominance, not of wealth, but of power; with the latter virtue can still subsist]

Virtue that depends on strength also can last long only in warlike states. The English still have the most virtue among all European nations. Their *luxury* is acquired through hard work and is wasted with savagery

[82] Reverse, opposite page 59, at 2:233

Everything that unnerves kills virtue at its sources.

The female sex is closer to nature than the male. For the present age is the age of propriety, of beauty, of good behavior. But those are her specific inclinations

The male sex has come to an end, and the noble qualities no longer endure after everything has degenerated into ornamentation

The state of virtue is a violent one; thus, it can only be encountered in a violent state of the commonwealth.

To a certain degree, the opulent life increases [the number of] human beings. Women cease to work, they have more children. There are enough prostitutes who want to suckle children or poor women who neglect their own and raise the children of the noble, etc. Opulence of an even greater degree makes for a stagnation in growth and finally a dimunition. From this arises poverty. But before this begins, or when it emerges, the greatest vices occur

[R80] On *religion* in the natural state.

One must not regard savages without religion as people who are to be subordinated to our [people] with religion. For one who does what God wills him to do – by means of the incentives God put in his heart – is obedient to Him without knowing of His existence. One who recognizes God, but who is brought to such actions only through the naturally good morality, has theology, or if he honors God for the sake of his morality, then this is only a morality whose object has been broadened. If their faith is not alive Christians can become blessed just as little as those who have no revelation at all; but with the former something more has happened than what naturally takes place.

Inserted sheet after page 60 [83] Obverse, at 2:233

If Diogenes had cultivated the field instead of rolling his barrel, he would have been great.

One must not ban any books now; that is the only way the harm that they destroy themselves. We have now come to the point of return. If one lets them flood, rivers form their own banks. The dam that we set against them serves only to make their destructions unending. For the authors of useless things have as their excuse the injustice of others.

In states where industriousness concerning things of necessity no honor is not honored and highly esteemed, where the people who engage in such trades do not value themselves, there a man without honor is the worst good-for-nothing, dissolute, deceptive, insidious, and thieving. But where the simplicity of nature rules, honor can very well be done without. See there, honor wreaks much ill, and then it also serves as a means to prevent the greatest excesses of the very same [ill]. The sciences wreak much ill, and then they also serve as a means to better their own evil. War creates more evils than it takes away [R81], but to a certain extent it brings about the state of equality and noble courage. In such a way corruption as well as virtue cannot endlessly rise in human

nature

[84] Reverse, opposite page 61, at 2:234

He who is not proud himself watches the game of vanity among noble ladies with no small pleasure

Shamefulness, frailty. Embarrassment.

Satire never improves; thus, even if I had the talents for it, I would not make use of them. The vanity of a woman is either that of her sex or that of her status.

The pride of sex or of status

Because nobility and the honor based upon it merely depend on the arbitrary choice of princes, pride in them is very foolish. <He who is angry and strong does not hate>

That the drive for honor only arises from the idea of equality can be seen from this: 1. because as far as another is stronger, yet only appears not to make any comparison, we surely fear him from which esteem arises), but we do not hate him 2. that the inclination to show one's worth to superiors is noble, but to equals or inferiors is <worthy of hate>; and that a human being who does not value himself is despised.

The highest peak of fashionable taste is <when young men [become] refined early,> acquire vulgar boldness, but the young woman soon casts aside reserved modesty and has learned early how to play the game of *coquetterie* with liveliness. For this is necessarily the most charming manner, which catches the eye the most; in such a society, a reasonable man looks like a dolt or a pedant, a modest and decent woman like a common landlady, and the finer part of society plays the role of courtiers. Thus, those of common taste soon withdraw [R82], and reason and domestic virtue are old, rusted memorials of taste, that kept for remembrance. But as with all ills that one can never bring to the highest point without the scale turning to the other side, here again stagnation and return is found. For gradually the women who have practiced the female art long before marriage will exercise this freedom with great ease in a state where they can do it with security. Men, warned by such examples, instructed by the very seduction that they themselves have instigated, and in anticipation of a wild vanity that will never let them rest, love the marriages of others but complicate their own. Contempt for the beautiful sex follows the adoration [of it] and, what is most terrible for it, the male sex is prudent so as to no longer be deceived by them. The greatest obstacle to the male sex's ability to return to happy simplicity is the female sex.

[85] Page 61

Upper margin, at 2:234

I plant human beings. Propriety. A helpful instinct of chastity.

Marginal notes at lines 1–4

Men are exceedingly easy to deceive, women are not.

Lower margin

Old-fashioned seclusion also has its troubles. Social interaction becomes speechless, full of stiff *ceremony*, [and of] rustic and sodden prudery.

The vanity and the juggler's game of gallant social interaction serve, to an extent, to put passion under to sleep through the shifting games of distraction and to divert [it] with the finery of fashion and empty vanity, instead of solitude introducing there that which society had forbidden.

Inserted sheet after page 62 [86] Obverse, at 2:234

[R83] Blushing is a beautiful quality of women, and it is not impudence that makes destroys blushing; rather, she who does not easily blush easily becomes impudent and wanton

There are by far more men who have reason to praise the generosity of (those) women who do not use the legal privilege that nature gives them

to fulfill the fair demand on their husband, if need be, through other men than there are men who can complain [about it]. With so many enervated persons men, a foolish or chimerical honor-project is arises, in which they want to turn marriage into friendship and demand great virtues of the wife for a self-overcoming of those impulses that are quite fair and that the former cannot satisfy

A woman is able to make men virtuous, but is not also virtuous [herself]. Strange as it is, they are even the greatest means of chastity in men, for nothing makes an otherwise flighty man more chaste than love toward a girl.

A woman has a quick concept of everything concerning *sentiments* but she does not feel them. For instance, take a heroic virtue: the man will consider when he is supposed to practice it himself, the woman, however, when it is done toward her or done by her husband. Imagine a Speak of great discretion and she will think of such a lover. Thus, some virtues that have no noticeable tendency toward her sex will not be respected by them (for instance, the simplicity of nature)

This is excellent, for the woman is the whetstone of virtue, *frangere vix cotis* [the whetstone breaks with difficulty], etc., and male virtue would also have toward no object of use if the woman were so herself, for then she would be able to do without

Perhaps this is a secret cause, on account of which we always attach ourselves to women in such a way, whether we want to or not

[87] Reverse, opposite page 63, at 2:235

[R84] Absolute cold is where a body is saturated with fire, absolute warmth where it has let go of all fire, which is possible, i.e., since the *attraction* is exactly equal to the *expansive force* of the same

Whether I can impute *anteactum* [prior deed] to a morally changed human being

If a body draws fire from others it warms them, if it lets it go it cools them.

If the warmth is in a, then a is put into the absorbing state through the loss of its fire element. Thus, there must be coldness in b as more fire element is there to be encountered and is attracted by the parts themselves; because the fire element will be accumulated in b, it must spread itself out and yield an empty space in c, which will be warm, and so forth. On the ethereal waves in warmth, on those in light. Yet this distinction can only last for a short time.

If water is above fire, then there is an empty space underneath; hence, if the water has let go all the fire – i.e., boils – then, if one removes it, [the fire] must absorb [at the bottom] – i.e., heat – and at the top leave at the bottom and absorb at the top because the movement was once given to the element; thus, it is hot at the top and cool at the bottom. In boiling, bubbles, which ascend, must develop at the bottom; the fire element, which releases itself, is not able to pass through copper as quickly as through water and gathers in bubbles; in these, vapors emerge and soar while constituting an elastic medium.

All bodies vitrify and are comparatively empty of fire element; therefore, while light produces warmth in others, at its innermost it here yields only light, that is, not so much a discharge of ether as an adjustment of it.

Inserted sheet after page 64

[88] Obverse

[R85] The magnitude of punishment is either to be evaluated *practically*, namely, that it be great enough to prevent the action, and then no greater punishment is allowed;

but a punishment as great as is physically necessary is not always morally possible.

Or its magnitude is evaluated in moral *proportion*: e.g., of the man who kills another in order to take his money, it will be judged that, because he has valued another's life as less than his own money, one must also value his life less than the amount of money settled for anyone else's life

Few care about deceiving their prince, which is a sign that they feel the injustice of the government

<*timor indolis ingenvi est filialis altera servilis*> [The fear of a noble character is either that of a child or that of a servant]

Indoles est <respectu motivorum> vel ingenua vel abiecta haec vel tanquam mercenarii vel tanquam mancipii [Character <with regard to motives> is either noble or servile abject, the latter is that of a mercenary or that of a slave.]

On the method of morality: since one regards all the qualities that are now common to all human beings from birth on as natural (not originating from sin) and extracts from that the rules as to how they can be good in [this] state, [one] does not err even if the *supposition* could be false. In this way, I can say that the human being of nature, who does not know of God, is not evil

Because God was a political law-giver in the Old Testament, he also gave political reasons for rewards and punishments, but not moral ones, except in later times. <A prince cannot put a reward on all of his laws because he himself has nothing>

Indoles ingenua est vel amoris vel reverentiae dominatur prior in evangelio posterior in lege. Amor non poterat in veteri testamento locum habere ideo tum reverentia. In novo testamento amor non potest nisi divinitus oriri [The noble character is either that of love or that of reverence; the first dominates in the Gospels, the second in the Law. Love could not have had a place in the Old Testament, thus there was reverence. In the New Testament love cannot exist unless it comes from God.]

[89] Reverse, opposite page 65, at 2:235

[R86] On the *Republic* of *Geneva*; on *Rousseau's* peculiar way of life. Love is either lustful <corporeal> or moral <spiritual>

Toward women something of the first is always intermingled, it can also be toward the elderly, or else they will only be valued as men. Fathers spoil daughters, and mothers spoil sons

All follies have this in common with each other, that the images that they allure float in the air and have no support or stability. You marry a woman without wit, without manners, without birth and family, what a decline of your taste. Oh, that is not the rule of my taste, you may answer. But what will the people say, consider how the world will judge you. Before I get involved with this important difficulty, I ask you first what one understands by such people and the world whose opinion is decisive for my happiness. Those are, one answers me, a multitude of persons in which each is just as distressed [by] what people want to say, and I belong among the number of these so-called people whose judgment is so important. Oh, I answer, we people altogether do not at all want to bother each other about the opinion of another any longer because it robs us of enjoyment; for now we understand each other, or I, at least, understand all of you; I am no *comedian* who is paid by applause.

Conceit and stingy greed are never to be healed.

Women are never generous; this is also entirely proper, for since they are not actually the ones who acquire, but the ones who save, it would be wrong because if they gave away for nothing because that is an affair of gentlemen. But they are only subordinated gentlemen; and although they never want to be, nature still retains its rights. Yet they invest in finery because this does not appear to them to be given away and they rightfully *use* that which belongs to men collectively

Inserted sheet after page 66 [99] Obverse, at 2:236

[R87] Error is never more useful than truth, all things considered, but ignorance often is

The understanding of children is the one that only judges that which is currently useful to it. The masculine understanding judges about future

use; the aged understanding judges about despises current use and has an imagined use as purpose, which will never exist in the future. With respect to the understanding, women are indeed children and, with respect to the future, they are given to stinginess in spite of all foresight. With respect to the future, the valiant man acquires <his> own powers and sacrifices his concerns to others rather than being distressed by external circumstances. In the household, an admirable unity arises out of this.

If one merely depends on things then one does not require much reason but only understanding

Arrogance for the sake of religion is the most ridiculous, for the thought that others do not become blessed should make me sympathetic and helpful rather than arrogant. Arrogance for the sake of money is common and coarse because it is based on that which easily passes from one to another; thus, it is crude. That for the sake of freedom is noble and proud. That for the sake of birth is finer because it is permanent, and that for the sake of office is the most admissible.

[91] Reverse, opposite page 67, at 2:236

The Jews, Turks, and Spaniards have arrogance of religion; they are also either treacherous if they are cowardly or tyrannical if they are powerful. The Dutch [are arrogant] for the sake of money, the English for the sake of freedom and power. The conceit of nations because of their great monarch causes vanity, and vanity also brings about [a] monarchical constitution. A

and money-grubbing. Spanish arrogance will show a spirit of persecution in all religions, and so also with the Turks.

[R88] Where there are many nobles and many obedient [to them], there is partly flattery and otherwise arrogance, as with the Poles.

A woman only cares for delight but not for the necessity of life. Therefore, they let the man take care of the needs, while they take care of taste. And in religion they let others determine what is true, while they are intent on imitating it fashionably with good form.

I want to note one more thing (but this is said just among us men): through their behavior, they can make [others] more chaste than they themselves are and console themselves over the loss of an inclination through the satisfaction of vanity by having instilled great respect. Women like to see a strong man so that they seem to be coerced in a good way

The woman makes of men what she wants; she has formerly made heroes and now makes monkeys. Whether she makes reasonable men is to be doubted; the latter cannot be formed by others at all, but must become so by themselves

On taste for society in distinction from that in society

Sheet inserted after page 68

[92] Obverse, at 2:237

The capacity for pleasure and displeasure is feeling in general. Lack of feeling [breaks off]

The capacity for pleasure and displeasure in things that do not belong to needs [is] taste. The latter is coarse taste in so far as it in is close to needs; the refined one is the true taste in that which is remote from needs.

[R89] In so far as the powers of the soul must not be merely passive but active and creative, taste is called spiritual and ideal (when the noblest feeling is not moved by external sensation but by that which one creates for it)

With regard to morality, feeling either merely belongs remains with the needs, i.e., obligation, or it goes further; in the latter case it is sentiment. The beautiful and the sublime in the highest degree are closely related.

If they are to be felt, both presuppose the soul at peace. Thus Yet they are so different that if busyness, is increasing cheerfulness, and liveliness are increasing the beautiful shines forth; if they end and peaceful contentment

shows through, the sublime stands out. In the early morning, the former; in the evening, the latter.

In its lesser forms, the beautiful is related to the change out of varying novelty. The sublime, with constancy, oneness, and inalterability. With beauty, manifoldness; with the noble, unity

[93] Reverse, opposite page 69, at 2:237

Only the dispensable is beautiful, but the noble can be combined with the useful. Yet in moral matters, the noble must not be considered from the viewpoint of usefulness. Blossoms are beautiful, fruit is useful.

[<Spring is beautiful and girls are beautiful; autumn and wives are useful.

<The usefulness of girls [consists in] that they are sterile>>]

In these refined sentiments it is presupposed that the human being does not depend on things through bare necessity, otherwise the refined taste are is foolish. <Enchanted by beauty, astonished by sublimity>

The beautiful in a lesser degree is agreeable and pretty, if great not sublimity disappears, [it is] cute. If the beautiful is imitated, it is decorated, like golden hens. The sublime is in a lesser [breaks off]

[R9] With the feeling of the sublime, the powers of a human being seem to become stretched, as it were; with the beautiful, they contract.

The taste that extends itself with respect to the immediate sexual inclination is the lustful one and is a sign of corruption with respect to [breaks off]

There are moral and nonmoral necessities (obligations), which one presupposes before there is talk of beauties. Sciences inside the head are for some human beings as useless as hair powder on top of the same. And as it would be quite foolish to have flour on [one's] curls and none in one's soup, so it is incongruous to know dispensable arts and to misconceive those that constitute the welfare of life.

Before we think of civilities, we must first be truthful and honest. It is peculiar that the lover bothers himself over a free woman before he knows whether she is also faithful. Before we ask for generosity

Inserted sheet after page 70

[94] Obverse

we must remind ourselves [of] obligation. Stop, brazen ones – shouted the merchant.

Good manners with inner improbity, the suavity of women without domesticity is like many ribbons and a dirty shirt.

The common opinion that previous times were better comes from the ill that one feels and the presupposition that otherwise everything would be good.

[R91] Clothes are only signs of comfort and excess with respect to life. They must not be made so that they draw attention exclusively to themselves. (Garish colors are repugnant to the eye, which gets attacked too much.) Likewise with rank and title. Those who have little worth themselves are doomed to golden frames.

In marriage, mere love without respect is already enough to attach the man to the woman, and mere respect without love is enough to attach the woman to the man. Thus, although understanding and merits have little effect on the woman outside of marriage, the most harmonious marriage is still the one where the man instills respect through understanding, even if the ages are different. *Wolmar*

I would like to be the happy Saint-Preux rather than the one who courts a wife

[95] Reverse, opposite page 71, at 2:238

The correct cognition of the construction of the world according to Newton is perhaps the most beautiful product of inquisitive human reason; meanwhile, Hume notes that the philosopher can easily get distracted in this delightful rumination by a little brunette maiden, and that rulers are not moved to despise their conquests because of the smallness of the earth in comparison to the universe. The cause is that it is indeed beautiful but unnatural to lose oneself outside of the circle that heaven has fixed for us. It is the same with the sublime contemplations of the heaven of the blessed.

If light had a streaming movement, then its strength when striking a slanted surface not and the warming would not behave like the square of the sine of the inclination, but like its *cube*.

That the poles do exert attraction at all is clear from the experiment of *Bougeurs* who put a magnetic needle on a piece of copper

Inserted sheet after page 72 [96] Obverse

[R92] The Spectator says that the fool and the clever one are different in that the former thinks aloud, etc. This is a very correct remark typical of our present kind of prudence. Now, because both sexes progress *proportionately* in this and the female one generally surpasses the male

one in the art of appearance, woman must now be much more perfect in this and dominate.

That the anticipation of death is not natural is to be seen from the fact that the consideration of death accomplishes nothing at all against the inclination to make preparations as if one were to live long, and from this and the human being makes arrangements at the end of his life as seriously as if he would not live at all. From this, vanity and the thirst for glory after death may originate because the natural human being flees shame and knows nothing of death. Hence the natural drive extends beyond death, which surprises it

In morals as in the art of medicine, that doctor is best who teaches me how I can be above diseases and remedies. This art is easy and simple. But the one that allows all corruption and removes it afterwards is artificial and complicated.

The *odium theologorum* has its ground in that it is held to be contrary to the propriety of the clergy to express the fast and vigorous movements of anger, and since this is suppressed it degenerates into secret bitterness. Parallel with women and Indians.

[97] Reverse, opposite page 73, at 2:239

Gigantism is a disease; one could ask whether it is not also so with respect to intellectual qualities; at any rate it seldom makes [one] happy. *Cato, Brutus*. Gigantic plans without power and insistence are like children whose heads are too big. Premature prudence. *Margarethe Maultasch*.

[R93] I praise mediocrity. Good, content citizen.

Difficult relationship between rank and *talents*. *Alexander* had large weapons left behind, not in order to form the opinion of the Indians about of the gigantic size of his army, but rather in order to confirm it.

Tender taste is wounded (screaming) by the very strong prominence of gaiety, of affectation, [and] of loquacity and loves peaceful and gentle beauty.

Coarse taste (is very different from lack of feeling) requires stronger stimulation, vivaciously brought out, and shows its wear and tear. Old, exhausted lover. <Whether the youth that loves tragedies would not have a coarse taste.>

ugly and nasty.

The ideal of beauty may very well be preserved in hope but not in possession. <Wantons become very skeptical with respect to the chastity of women and make others so as well>

I do not know whether it is true what they say about the very extended loyalty of married women in the most civilized nations and let those judge who know it from experience. This much I do know, that if all sentiments grow beyond their boundaries, the female capacity, which is not so restricted, will go much further than the male.

Nothing can replace the loss of female grace, not even the noblest propriety.

Outside of marriage, debauchery is most dangerous for the female sex to conceal by all arts; for the male one it is so within marriage. Hence one can already suspect prior to any experience that the female sex will be reserved before marriage and excessive in marriage, vice versa, though, with the male sex.

[R94]

Page 74

At the margin, next to lines 14–21, at 2:239

The woman seems to lose more than the man because with the former the beautiful qualities end, yet with the man the noble ones remain. The old woman seems to be no longer good for anything.

Inserted sheet after page 74

[99] Obverse, at 2:239

All pleasures that are connected to the fulfillment of needs are called coarse. Drinking, sleeping, eating, and cohabitation. The last is considered so crude that *Tiresias* had to endure an unpleasant encounter with *Juno* because he attributed it primarily to the female sex.

Thus, taste always attaches to that which actually is no bare necessity. From this it follows that if resemblance to nature is the requirement in painting – e.g., *landscapes, portraits* – then this nature must be captured; for the rest, ideal pleasures constitute the noblest. Nature is not good enough for our pleasure. In addition to this, softness and tenderness of our organs, indeed our imagination. Hence painting can very well depart from nature, like poetry and theatrical action.

Truth is more of an obligation than beauty. Thus, one must conceal obligation in order to be beautiful.

The tenderness of the nerves is one of the governing determinations of taste, for the degree of *contrast* or of *affect* – the hardness of sensations – will thereby be restricted, etc.

Harmony arises from the agreement of the manifold, in *music* just as in *poetry* and painting. These are points of rest for some nerves

Unity is in accordance with comfort in so far as it is connected with *activity*, which desires manifoldness.

[R95]

[100] Reverse, opposite page 75, at 2:240

On refinement and the extent of these sentiments The sense of the eye provides long and tender albeit very ideal pleasures; displeasure is small except in sex. Horror [is] great.

The sense of hearing effects enduring pleasures. But only through change is [breaks off] less ideal but very lively, the displeasures are small and short-lived. The sense of smell gives a bit of ideal pleasure; they are short in pleasure and strong and short. Strong in displeasure, for disgust requires change.

The sense of taste is not at all ideal; it is great in pleasure but short and broken off – [it] requires change (without bare necessity). Displeasure is far more sensitive and [so is] disgust.

The sense of feeling is short and exhaustive in lust, short and sensitive in warmth [and] in titillation; in pain it can last long and be great. [It] can easily be outweighed by the understanding (except for the sexual inclination).

The sense of vision reveals most moral things, but then also the sense of hearing

That in marriages the chastity of women is harder to preserve than that of men stems from the fact that their capacity to give is greater than that of men; hence the fantastical desires can go further in their case.

Inserted sheet after page 76 [101] Obverse

On the old physiognomic characters in comparison with the moral ones Beautiful and gallant actions primarily consist in those [R96] to which

one has no obligation. Obligation is a kind of moral need; whatever relates itself more closely to it is simple.

All affects that elicit tenderness and moral sentiment must be taken from the determinations of a human being; therefore [breaks off]

Because if one already presupposes beauty as necessary it becomes a kind of need, thus simplicity is also possible with the beautiful and the sublime

Because after all such sentiments for the beautiful, which sometimes are stronger than needs, it requires a great art to achieve the simplicity of nature, even though it is superfluous – since one only does not want to depart from it – yet still great, therefore [this simplicity] is a special kind of the sublime

A pampered feeling, which is not strong enough for simplicity, is female. Nature at peace is the greatest beauty (yet trickling brooks) because they lull the human to sleep), grazing herds of cattle. Hence the evening [is] even more moving than the morning

Gaiety is not beautiful [and] also does not last. On the agreement of beautiful faces and beautiful bodies with the soul

[102] Reverse, opposite page 77, at 2:241

The free enjoyment of lustful inclination and the unconcealed discovery of its object nullifies everything ideal that can be spread through inclination; therefore, it is so difficult to preserve the ideal pleasures in marriages. Unless one concedes dominance to the wife.

Some persons please more if one is away from them, others if one is more present; the former are better suited for the ideal pleasures of marriage

When fantastical love pairs well with knightly virtue.

[R97] Novels end with marriages <and the history begins>; however, they still can be prolonged beyond them through jealousy, for instance, a wife who is a *coquette* of her husband and of others

All female beauty is spread by the sexual drive, for suppose you exp realize that a woman has a certain ambiguity of her sex, all your infatuations will cease, although this does nothing to the pleasant qualities, which you believe to enchant you alone.

A pregnant woman is obviously useful but not so beautiful. Maidenhood is useless but agreeable

Sheet inserted after page 78 [103] Obverse, at 2:241

It is quite bad that we do not at all want to allow women to be ugly, even when they are old.

Because needs are common, the domesticity of a woman is considered a thing to be dismissed among *gallant* men.

If the main work arises from the pleasures then the latter become flat. I love the French as such but not the Germans when they imitate them. Some women misuse the permission that women have to be ignorant In proportion to their power to do evil, princes are by far less corrupt than the common man.

Inner honor. Self-esteem. External honor as a means to insure oneself of the former. Therefore, a man of honor. *honestas* External honor as a means is true, as the end a delusion. The former concerns advantage either for self-preservation, equality, or preservation of the species. The [R98] desire for honor (immediate) either concerns the opinion of important perfections (patriotism) and is called ambition, or concerns trifles and is called vanity. The consciousness of one's honor, which one believes oneself to be in possession of, and that without measuring oneself against others, is called pride. Dignity. *Gallantry* is either of pride or of vanity; the former of a *petitmaitre*, the latter of a fop. The proud one who

despises others is arrogant. The vain one if he wants to show that through pomp [it is] presumptuous. The arrogant one who shows his disdain is pompous

[104] Reverse, opposite page 79, at 2:242

The honor of a man with respect to a woman is courage, and that of a woman chastity. These points are peculiar. When the age becomes soft then the honor of the former is sweetness, and that of the latter understanding and boldness; the former makes the romanic, the latter the affected and courtly or fashionable

Because philosophy is not a thing of bare necessity but of agreeableness, hence it is strange that one wants to restrict it through painstaking laws

Because the man in courtship chooses the woman as his ruler, he poeticizes her [as being] very admirable, since one will hardly submit to a wretched idol; conversely, the woman wants to dominate. Spectator, black monkey. *Applies* to the hidden secret of all tender inclination toward the sex

The strongest preferences pleasures become flat first

What it means to be domestic; to make a need out of society. Boredom. The housewife is honorable. The beautiful propriety of her domestic care, intermixed with cleanliness and ornament; [she] must not appear to prefer being out of the house rather than at home

The man is the one who solicits, the woman the one who chooses; that is the point of making [R99] oneself scarce. Shall she choose the romanic dreamer, the fool in his finery, or the selfish and phlegmatic – unfeeling – one.

Saint-Evremond wanted to choose a wife and chose a *coquette*. That happened because he was from a country where every woman is a *coquette*, though not toward her husband.

The man who does not make his amusements into his business but into recreation, who knows how to live – i.e. who does not make acquisition but its enjoyment his aim – who likes the peaceful pleasure of company and friendship, he is a man

All pleasures become insipid if they are not recreations but occupations. The wife and the husband who have something to do will not become tired of another

The wife possesses the skill of always being a woman much more than the husband [that of being a man], but will she not prefer to employ this skill elsewhere than with her husband, who is insipid to her

[105] Page 79

Marginal note at lines 3–4, at 2:242

The standard of happiness is the household

Marginal notes at line 10 – lower margin

I walk out from a blooming field and the Arcadian valleys to barren fields

The novel ends and the history begins. Henceforth the magical haze, <through> which the enamored madness had seen its idol, gradually disperses. The marriage-bed receives a human [R100] girl, and she, otherwise worshiped as a goddess, as a wife stifles the protest of her slave the next morning. The lover, previously intoxicated by his imaginations, wakes from a beautiful reverie and [breaks off]

The sight of blossoms.   A *gallant* person always blossoms

[106] Page 80

Upper margin, at 2:242

Love is a unity   Solomon never loved. The

Inserted sheet after page 88

[107] Obverse, at 2:242

Beauty is without utility because the latter is a pressing of a thing to other purposes, thus it indicates no perfection complete in itself. Hence the more useful things are, the more corners they show, so to speak, as means to adapt themselves to other connections; the curve of a sphere is perfect in itself

Gallantry: a new kind of beauty of manners.   *Politesse.*

The former is a certain sweetness in pleasing behavior, the latter a certain good-natured cautiousness

The former is affected, the latter peaceful and composed. Not every woman is beautiful in the physical or intellectual sense, but gallantry meets them all with that subjection that is shown by him who, through his inclination, is ruled by a weaker one

The sentiment for the beauty of young boys constituted the origin of Greek love – the disgraceful most disgraceful passion that ever has been and in the nature that has ever perverse stained <human> nature, and that [passion] no doubt deserved that the its criminals be turned over to the revenge and scolding of women, who etc.

[R101] The permitted illusion is a kind of untruth that is not then a lie; it is an inducement for ideal pleasures whose object is not in things

Illusion in a large gathering, as if all these were cleverer than one

He who thought himself the president in the marriage-bed wanted to contrive something that could make him strong against the befuddling magical power of illusion

Illusion is so compatible with the beautiful – but not with the noble – that even if one becomes aware of it, it still pleases. To appear as clever, pious, hearty, honest

[108] Reverse, opposite page 8, at 2:243

Benevolence is a calm inclination to regard the happiness of others as an object of one's joy and also as a motive of one's actions. Compassion is an affect of benevolence toward the needy, according to which we imagine that we would do what is in our power to help them; it is thus for the

most part a chimera, because it is neither always in our power nor in our will. The citizen is compassionate toward others who are oppressed by the prince. The nobleman is compassionate toward another nobleman, but himself hard on the peasants.

With opulence the fantasy of the love of humanity cvltivates itself and the capacity and appetite reduces itself. The simple human being attends to no other except to him he can help

The understanding brings about no increase of the moral feeling; in this sense, he who ratiocinates only has rather cooled-off affects and is more cool-minded, consequently less evil and less good. The morally good rather makes [one] reasonable

One has long tried to explain the feeling of pleasure in the ridiculous.

In nature nothing is ridiculous

[R102] One demands illusion with respect to clerics and women; the former shall appear to take no part in frivolous pleasures, the latter [shall appear to have] no inclination for lustful intimacy at all. Thereby one makes them deceitful

[The] illusion of religion as it is finally taken for the thing itself. Then [it] is a delusion.

One must pay respect to clerics for the sacrifice of so many freedoms and pleasures. (They are within boundaries almost as narrow as those a woman is in)

One must deal attentively with both because both do not have on their side either the capacity or the propriety in order to boldly resist an insult

Inserted sheet after page 82 [109] Obverse, at 2:243

The formal aspect of all perfection consists in manifoldness (in addition duration and strength) and unity; it can also give pleasure by itself.

Sensitive.

Insensitive.

The will is perfect in so far as in accordance with the laws of freedom it is the greatest ground of the good in general. The moral feeling is the feeling of the perfection of the will.

Whether God is the originator of all morality, i.e., whether we can distinguish good from evil only through the recognized will of God

Sulzer says that what facilitates and promotes the natural efficacy of the soul touches me with pleasure. This says only that it promotes the natural striving after pleasure

Unius corruptio est alterius generatio. [The corruption of one is the generation of another.] Through smell, nature has wanted to warn us of rottenness as the greatest ground of the dissolution and the ferment of the destruction of animals.

[R103] The man is stronger than the woman in all capacities; yet he is weaker with respect to inclination, which he cannot tame as well, and also with respect to the excitability of his tenderness and confidence. The woman is weaker with respect to power but also more cool-headed and therefore more capable

Among all [inclinations], sexual inclination adopts the most ideal embellishment

One reason why women soon show off their great understanding is that one accommodates them in the choice of subjects; thus they finally believe that there are no others.

Women have a very swift but no systematic conception; they quickly grasp something as much as is necessary to talk about it and believe that there is nothing better

[110] Reverse, opposite page 83, at 2:244

On the means to measure the dryness and humidity of the air

With women, my generosity makes me into a slave; with men, my cowardice

The very great respect for human beings is based on chimerical merits that we ascribe to others

That author who said that when he observes a grave man in his serious or sublime appearance, he moderates his blind reverence through the representation of his familiarity with women or with the common necessity. He would not have needed this representation. However, this appears to be why the Roman church has forbidden clerics from having wives

The free will (of someone with needs) is good for itself if it wants everything that contributes to its perfection (pleasure), and good for the whole if at the [R104] same time it desires the perfection of all. However destitute the human being who has this will may be, the will is still good. Other things may be useful; other human beings may do a lot of good in a certain action through a lot of power and a small degree of will; yet the ground of willing the good is still uniquely and solely moral.

The mathematician and the philosopher: they differ in that the former requires data from others while the latter examines them himself. Hence the former can prove <from> any revealed religion.

The fable of the swallow that wanted to catch birds there

Inserted sheet after page 84 [111] Obverse, at 2:244

The French only love laughing beauty, the *Italians* only stirring beauty.

A selfish (lustful) human being needs a person whom he can love; a generous (affectionate) one needs a person who loves him, i.e., whom he can make happy through his compliant behavior

With respect to her unhappiness in marriage, no woman will readily admit that the long fasting in her marital gratification offends her, for the woman always wants to appear to only give and not to need; if they appear to be in need of this an inequality will arise out of it because otherwise they are already in need of the man with respect to all other things.

Her refusal is a kind of beautiful untruth

All things, if they are only recognized as they are, have little that is agreeable in them; they elevate the sentiment only by appearing [to be] what they are not; all ideal pleasures are promoted through the art of appearing. If a woman could always appear as she liked, [R104] this skill would be very loveable; now the ill lies in that the thing comes and the illusion disappears

[111] Reverse, opposite page 84, at 2:244

He who does more than he owes is called kind; in so far as he has no obligation at all to the other, who him nevertheless has nothing but obligations to him, he is merciful

A natural human being can be merciful toward no one, for he has obligations toward everyone. However, he can be merciful toward a captured enemy

In our condition, when general injustice is established, the natural rights of the lowly cease; thus, the latter are only debtors; the nobles owe them nothing. Therefore, these nobles are called merciful lords. He who requires nothing from them but justice and can hold them to their obligations does not need this subjection

A woman's modest (civil) behavior, if she is equal, is an obligation; female grace is kindness and must be asked for, not demanded. Therefore, noble ladies can certainly be called merciful women, but their husbands not merciful lords. If she is defiant and pompous, then she commits an offense against her obligation; if she is indifferent then she is treated as equal.

On common and rustic faces

What maintains the delusion2 of the inequality of classes is, among other things, that the lowly themselves imagine this [inequality to exist], on account of which a bourgeois woman feels the lowliness in herself, hates it and shows her disquiet, which the pride of the noble [breaks off]

<A merciful lord who has no money is an absurdity, but a merciful lady without money can certainly exist>

[R106] On the "He," "Her," and "She" On even and uneven numbers

On the feeling of youth

On the reasons why he who pays is thanked although he does not do give more than he gets. Only money makes it this way. (Pope's joke: if there were no money.) For he who has money is richer than the one who has goods because he has the choice. He who sells dispensable things (*gallantry*-grocer, *caffetier*) and lives on this must be more polite than his customer, but not he who sells necessary things, especially if he always finds a customer

Sheet inserted after page 86

[113] Obverse, at 2:245

A married man acquires and deserves more esteem than a single man or an old bachelor.

A wife [is] more than a girl. A widow [is] also more than a girl. The reason is because the vocation is then completed and also the other persons appear to be in need, i.e., a girl wants to have a husband (without difficulties), but a wife never wants to be a girl. Moreover, an encounter

<with> a wife is looked upon equivocally, and it is the same, only the other way around, with the husband

He who is supposed to teach others how to be wise with little knowledge must know a lot. It is very much to wish for that this art become further *cultivated*. Dumb and wise ignorance [breaks off]

The habit of representing the deity on the model of princes has brought forth many false concepts of *religion*, for example, insults. The honor of God [breaks off]

If I presuppose that everything in the relations between the sexes goes amiss then there are two possibilities: 1. that the girl is abstinent and debauched as a wife, 2. that the girl is debauched and abstinent as a wife. The second is more in accordance with nature, the first with the age [R107] of propriety, for the wife if the wife gives birth it will seem every time as if her husband is the father.

Among friends, each can talk about himself, because the other attends to it as if it concerns himself; among people and friends of *fashion*, one must never talk about oneself (also not in books); unless one wants to say something of oneself that can be laughed about.

In fashionable society I must regard each as exclusively self-loving; therefore I must praise no one who is present nor anyone absent, and thus must either joke or slander in order for it to be *interesting*. <*Slander* is based in part on the drive for equality. Ostracism. Aristides >

[114] Reverse, opposite page 87, at 2:245

The capacity to recognize something as a perfection in others does not yet bring about the consequence that we ourselves feel pleasure in it.

But if we have a feeling for finding pleasure in this, then we will also be moved to desire it and to apply our powers to it. Thus, it is to be asked whether we feel pleasure immediately in the well-being of others or whether the immediate appetite actually lies in the possible exercise of our power to promote it. Both are possible, but which is real[?] Experience teaches that a human being in the simple state regards the happiness of others with indifference, but if he has promoted it, it pleases him infinitely more. The ill of others is commonly just as indifferent, but if I have caused it, it displeases just as if it has been done by another. And concerning the affectionate instincts of compassion and sympathy, we have reason to believe that they are merely great strivings to mitigate the ills of others, taken from the self-approval of the soul, which bring about these sentiments.

We take pleasure in certain perfections of ours, but much more if we ourselves are the cause. Most of all if we are the freely acting cause.

To subordinate everything to the free faculty of choice is the greatest perfection. And the perfection of the free [R8] faculty of choice as a cause of possibility is far greater than all other causes of the good even if they would bring about the actuality [of the good]

[115] Page 88

Upper margin, at 2:246

With the French, the thought is sooner ready than the <does not mature by means of> reasons, indeed it does not await their development and examination. The German seeks reasons for all thoughts and improves; [he] is patient

Under line 17

The French demand almost as much leniency as women. *Maupertuis*

Inserted sheet after page 88

[116] Obverse

<*Habitu*>

actionis ex voluntate singulari est solipsismus Moralis —communi – justicia

[<Habit> The attitude of an action from a single will is moral solipsism; [the attitude of an action from the] common [will is moral] justice]

The feeling of pleasure and displeasure concerns either that with respect to which we are passive or else ourselves as an active *principium* [principle] of good and evil through freedom. The latter is moral feeling. Past physical evil offends delights us, but [past] moral evil grieves us, and the kind of joy we take in the good that befalls us is entirely different from that we take in what we do.

We have little feeling for whether the condition of another is evil or good except in so far as we feel capable of alleviating the former [or] promoting the latter. Sympathy is an instinct that works only on rare and very important occasions; its other effects are artificial.

[R109] Since the greatest inner perfection and the perfection that arises from it consist in the subordination of all of the capacities and *receptiuities* to the free faculty of choice, the feeling for the *Bonitat* of the free faculty of choice must be immediately much different from and also greater than all of the good consequences that thereby can be *brought about*.

This faculty of choice contains either the merely individual will as well as the general will, or the human being considers himself at the same time in *consensu* with the general will.

That which is necessary through the general will is an obligation, what [breaks off]

[117] Reverse, opposite page 89

Since the human being of nature needs little – and the more he needs (*egenus*) the more miserable he is – the human being is perfect in so far as he can do without; but in so far as he still has a lot of power left to promote the needs and happiness of others he has a feeling for a will that is beneficent beyond itself. Since the faculty of choice, in so far as it is also useful to the acting subject, is physically necessary with regard to bare necessity, it has no immediate goodness. Hence the moral goodness of action is unselfish.

In the state of nature, one cannot be selfish, but also not for the common good; friendships however are possible in the same [state]

Male adolescence is more open to friendship because it is more unselfish, more affectionate, more <benevolent>, and more honest than the later [age]

On happiness in all human ages. Youthful flightiness prevents and restlessness prevent much pleasure. The old one has fewer lively inclinations, but he satisfies the calm ones. Yet we must not interchange the positions of life

[R110] One already has biased attitudes towards a nation that has the same language. Prussian, Livonians. Likewise the total diversity of languages causes *national* hatred. But, if the speech of the mob in one language comes close to the speech of the rulers in the other then it causes contempt. But all of this at a distance.

Inserted sheet after page 90 [118] Obverse, at 2:247

Sensus internus voluptatis et taedii est prior appetitione et aversatione quia receptivitas gaudendi aut aversandi subjecto inest quanquam adhuc objecti hujus sensus ignarus sit ut ignoti nulla est cupido. Appetitio vel est primitiua vel deriuatiua prior est uaria etiam qua qualitatem. Sensus internus si allegatur ut principium probandi logicum legis moralis est qualitas occulta si ut facultas animae cuius ratio ignoratur est phaenomenon

[The inner sense of pleasure and displeasure precedes desire and aversion, since the receptivity to the enjoyment and aversion lies in the subject, even if it, the subject, does not have any knowledge of the object of this sense, as there cannot be a desire for something unknown. Desire is either original or derived; the former also varies with respect to quality. The inner sense, if it is held to be a logical principle for the judgment of the moral law, is an occult quality; if it is a faculty of the soul whose ground is unknown, then it is a phenomenon.]

A *pactum* is not possible between a *domino* and a *mancipio*. God entered into an alliance with humans because they do not have a sufficient practical concept of his *domino*, and so that they are led by the *analogy* with the *pacto* of men, and not to abhor the authoritative strictness.

A virtuous action is at all times a morally good action that occurs or at least has occurred reluctantly

Omnis bonitas conditionalis actionis est vel sub conditione possibili (uti problemata) uel actuali (uti regulae prudentiae quilibet vult sanus esse) sed in bonitate mediata vel conditionali ro velle absolute non est bonum nisi adsint uires et circumstantiae temporis loci. Et in tantum quatenus uoluntas est efficiens est bonum sed poterit haec bonitas etiam qua uoluntatem solam spectari. si desint uires tamen est laudanda uoluntas in magnis uoluisse sat est et perfectio haec absoluta quatenus utrum aliquid inde actuatur nec ne est indeterminatum dicitur moralis

[All conditional goodness of an action depends on either a possible condition (as in problems) or on an actual one (as in the rules of prudence, [e.g.] everyone wants to be reasonable), but in mediate or conditional goodness the absolute will is not good if the powers and circumstances of time and place are lacking. And insofar as the will is effective it is good, but one can also consider this goodness with respect to the will alone; even if the powers should be lacking, the will is still praiseworthy. With regard to great deeds, it suffices to have willed them. And this absolute perfection, whether something is effected by it or not, is called moral.]

[119] Reverse, opposite page 9

<The woman can abstain much more with regard to pleasures [and] needs, but not with regard to vanity>

[R111] The equilibrium of sentiments is the soul at peace. This smooth surface is only disturbed through passions. It is a main ground of happiness not only to feel agreeable, but also to be conscious of this in one's entire condition, which is hindered <by> strong sentiment

The natural human being is spared this disquiet through lack of feeling

*Contentment with respect to needs is called simplicity. In so far as agreeable things themselves are counted among necessities it is partly beautiful and partly noble simplicity.

Where dispensability appears with respect to necessities, combined with the effort to produce things that are agreeable, that is contrived; with respect to the beautiful [it is] ornamented [and] decorated; with respect to the sublime [it is] magnificent [and]

grandiose.

Taste, indeed, does not concern needs, but it must not prevent them, as in the case of luxuriousness.

Regularity accords with simplicity, for if the one the rule did not determine the kind of connections, it would be so contingent and indeterminate that it would also contradict the needs. For example, symmetry. Following in pairs. Thus, among that which is interconnected, it serves to assign to each thing its purpose.

<What is agreeable can greatly oppose necessities, but when they agree with them, then there is beautiful simplicity. The needs of human beings are closely related to the ease of thinking and representing something. From this comes the agreeableness of order. Symmetry.>

Inserted sheet after page 92 [120] Obverse, at 2:248

<in Deo simul est subjectiua>

[In God it is at the same time subjective.]

Bonitas actionis liberae objectiua vel quod idem est necessitas objectiua est [R112] vel conditionalis vel categorica prior est bonitas actionis tanquam medii posterior tanquam finis illa igitur mediata haec immediata illa continet necessitatem practicam problematicam haec pp

[The goodness of a free action is objective, or what is the same, the objective necessity is either conditional or categorical. The former is goodness of an action as means, the latter as an end; hence the former is mediated, the latter is unmediated; the former contains a practical, problematic necessity, the latter, etc.]

Actio libera conditionalis bona non est ideo categorie necessaria. e.g. liberalitas mea aliis egenis est utilis ergo oportet esse liberalem Minime. Sed si quis uult esse aliis utilis esto liberalis. Si autem actio utili liberalitatis ingenuae non solum aliis sed et in se bona sit tum est obligatio.

[A free action that is conditionally good is not for that reason a categorical necessity, e.g., my liberality to another person who is destitute is useful, and therefore one ought to be liberal. By no means [does this follow]. But if someone wants to be useful to another, he will have to be liberal. If, however, an action of genuine liberality is not only good for another but good in itself, then it is an obligation.]

De sensu morali et possibilitate oppositi

[On the moral sense and the possibility of its opposite.]

Adstrinxit quidem prouidentia sensum moralem publicae ut uniuersali utilitati ut et priuato commodo ita tantum ut arbitrii bonitas non judicetur tantum valere quantum valet

[Indeed providence has so connected moral sense to public and universal utility as well as to private advantage that the goodness of the free will is not esteemed as highly as it is actually worth.]

When I say that this action will bring me more honor than the other, I mean to say that I appeal to the universal judgment that the judgment I pass on my own action is grounded.

Controversies in world-wisdom have the benefit that they promote the freedom of understanding and arouse mistrust towards the doctrine itself, which was supposed to be constructed upon the ruins of another. In refuting, one is still so happy [breaks off]

In most languages simplicity and stupidity mean almost the same. That is because a human being of simplicity is easily betrayed by a human being of artifice whom he considers to be as honest as himself

[121] Reverse, opposite page 93, at 2:248

There is always so much talk about virtue. But one must eliminate injustice before one can be virtuous. One must suppress leisureliness, opulence, and everything that oppresses others while elevating me, so that I am not one of all those who oppress their own kind. All virtue is impossible without this decision.

All virtue is grounded on ideal feeling. Hence, in the state of opulence, no virtue is found in a human being who has merely corporeal feeling; in the state of nature, however, simplicity in straightforward sentiments and simplicity in mores subsist together quite well

[R113] Where the lengths of days <throughout the year> are more [equal, is more orderly; thus in France and England more than in Petersburg. For, since here, on a bright day in summer, one at best can wake up late, one does so also in winter.

It is funny that opulence now makes the [upper] ranks poor, especially the princes

The misery of human beings is not to be bewailed, but to be laughed at: *Democritus*

Swift's linen weaver, etc.

Among all vanities the most common is that one wants to appear to be happy; hence one admit pretends that one does not want to do something good (for example, marrying, serving the commonwealth) rather than that one cannot do it; because he who does without that something or refrains from it is merely happy according to his own will in so far as he has sufficient capacity to satisfy his desires

Inserted sheet after page 94 [122] Obverse, at 2:249

We can see other worlds in the distance, but gravity forces us to remain on the earth; we still can see other perfections of the spirits above us, but our nature forces us to remain human beings.

Because in society all mine and thine depends on *pacta*, yet these [depend] on keeping one's word, love of truth is the *foundation* of all social virtue, and lying is the main vice against others next to robbery, murder and *stuproviolatio* [rape]

If human beings subordinate *morality* to religion (which is also only possible and necessary in the case of the oppressed rabble) they thereby become hostile, hypocritical, [and] slanderous; but if they subordinate religion to morality, then they are kind, benevolent, and just

[R114] <All choice must concern future taste>

True marriage in its perfection, poeticized marriage in its perfection.

Perfect happiness, peace

The human being in his perfection is not in the state of simplicity, in sufficiency, nor in the state of opulence, but in the return from the latter state to the former. Remarkable character of human nature. This most perfect state rests on the tip of a hair; the state of nature can simple and original nature does not last long; the state of renewed nature is more lasting, but never as innocent.

very social women do not blush anymore, and if they are untrue [they blush] even less than men; the *etourdi* [scatterbrain] who does not blush

A great proof of opulence is that now entire states are becoming constantly poorer. National debt. Standing armies

All amusements intoxicate, i.e., prevent one from not feeling the entire sum of happiness

[123] Reverse, opposite 95

It is to be asked whether all of morality could not be deduced through the soul at peace – [which is] indeed to be understood with respect to the natural human being. Delightful things and excesses are opposed to peace. The sexual inclination finds its peace only in marriage. To offend others unsettles oneself. Affects in general unsettle. It is horrible that through this morality no other human being benefits

[<Except that this is already a great virtue[:] to do no evil.>]

Religion determines the way of life of the Jews. For since they are always concerned about being forced to [adapt to] another, they detest every way of life in which they would not have enough freedom to avoid it. Therefore, they do not cultivate the field

In the case of this soul at peace, friendship is no *enthusiasm*, sympathy [is] no soft-heartedness, gentleness not *ceremony*. Desire, no longing. The feeling soul at peace is therefore not inactive according to the body or the understanding, but only according to desires and pleasures

[R115] In flourishing countries, the innkeepers and workers are polite and try to serve, but the customers and guests are commanding, and there is, so to speak, more industry than money, i.e., the money itself has an inner *principium* of its increase. In poor countries, there is still more money than industry.

In rich countries, the merchants (*en detail*) are cold-minded and it is the customer is fair without haggling, because there are just as many wares as money; in poor [countries], there are more wares than money, and the merchants are groveling.

[124] Page 95 Lower margin

In all nations, the habit of drinking among men has ceased as soon as social gatherings were adorned with women. The Greeks drank; the old Germans [and] Prussians. The English still drink because the women are more separated. It would still be good in the case of special women. Our way of life is nowadays *Arcadian*, as it were; one always socializes, and love and play entertain them. But black sorrow, discord, and tedium rule at home

Inserted sheet after page 96 [125] Obverse, at 2:250

Why an old woman is an object of disgust for both sexes except when she is very cleanly and not a *coquette*.

Necessitas actionum <objectiva (bonitatis)> vel est conditionalis (sub conditione alicujus boni appetiti) vel categorica prior est problematica et si appetiones quae spectantur tanquam conditiones necessariae actionis non solum ut possibiles sed ut actuales spectantur est necessitas prudentiae. Ad [R6] eam cognoscendam necesse erit omnes dignoscere animi humani appetiones et instinctus ut fieri possit. computatio quid sit pro inclinatione subjecti melius. et hoc quidem non solum pro praesenti sed et futuro statu. Necessitas categorica actionis tanti non constat sed poscit solum applicationem facti ad sensum moralem

[The necessity of actions <their objective (goodness)> is either conditional (under the condition of some desired good) or categorical. The former is problematic and, if the desires that are seen as necessary conditions of actions are seen as not only possible but actual, this is a necessity of prudence. In order to know this, it will be necessary to know all of the drives and instincts of the human soul so that a calculation may be made about what is better for the inclination of the subject. And this indeed not only for the present, but also for the future state. The categorical necessity of an action does not depend on so much; rather, it requires only the application of the facts to moral feeling.]

Poterit equidem in quibusdam uitae conditionibus mendacium esse admodum utile ideoque per regulam prudentiae mentiendum sed ad hoc requiritur uasta astutia et sagacitas consectaria si moraliter consideratur per simplicitatem moralem illico cognoscitur quod factu opus si

[In certain situations in life a lie can be exceedingly useful, and thus lying will be in accordance with the rule of prudence, but for this, extensive astuteness and the shrewdness that follows from it is required. If one considers it morally, on the basis of moral simplicity, it will be immediately known what one should do.]

Quantumuis modo falsiloquium aliis aliquando admodum sit utile tamen erit mendacium nisi ad illud incumbat obligation stricta hinc uidere est falsi ueracitatem non a Philantropia sed a sensu juris quo fas ac nefas distinguimus pendere. Hic sensus autem originem ducit a mentis humanae natura per quam quo se bonum quid sit bonum categorice (no utile) judicat non ex priuato commodo <nec ex alieno> sed eandem actionem ponendo in aliis si oritur contradictio oppositio et contrarietas displicet si harmonia et consensus placet. Hinc facultas stationum moralium ut medium heuristicum. Sumus enim a natura sociabiles et quod improbamus in aliis in nobis probare sincera mentenon possumus. Est enim sensus communis ueri et falsi non nisi ratio humana generatim tanquam criterium ueri et falsi et sensus boni uel mali communis criterium illius. Capita sibi opposita certitudinem logicam corda moralem tollerent.

]As much as false testimony might sometimes be useful to others, it is still a lie if no strict obligation necessitates it. From this, one can see truthfulness does not depend on philanthropy, but on the sense of justice, through which we learn to distinguish what is permitted from what is forbidden. This sense, however, has its origin in the nature of the human mind, through which one judges what is in itself good categorically good (not useful), not according to private benefit or benefit to others, but through supposing the same action in others; if a contradiction and contrast then arises, it displeases; if harmony and unison arise, they please. Hence the ability to put oneself in the place of others [functions] as a heuristic means. Indeed we are by nature social and could not sincerely approve in ourselves of what we criticize in others. The common sense of true and false is indeed nothing other than human reason taken generally as the criterion of true and false, and the common sense of good and evil is the criterion of the latter. Opposing minds would eliminate logical certainty, opposing hearts, moral certainty.]

Bonitas uoluntatis ab effectibus et earum immediata uoluptate repetita est vel priuatae vel publicae utilitatis et prior rationem habet in indigentia posterior in potentia boni prior propriae utilitatis posterior communis utilitatis instinctus ambo simplicitati naturali conformes. Sed uoluntatis tanquam principii liberi bonitas non quatenus proficiscuntur illae utilitates inde sed quatenus in se sunt possibiles cognoscitur. Et non aliorum felicitas pro ratione [breaks off]

[The goodness of the will [unreadable word] is derived from the effects of private or public use and from the immediate pleasure in them, and the former has its basis in need, the latter in the power for the good; the former is related to one's own utility, the latter to general utility; both feelings conform to natural simplicity. But the goodness of the will as a free principle is recognized not insofar as such forms of utility arise from it, but insofar as they are possible in themselves. And not the happiness of others for the reason.]

[126] Reverse, opposite page 97

Obligation <the natural one towards human beings> has a certain measure; the duty of love has none. The former consists in this that nothing happens anymore other than what I myself have let another want, and that I give him only what is his; [R117] consequently, everything, after such an action, is equal. (Sympathy is excepted from this.)

If I promise him something, then I rob him of something, for I have created a hope that I do not fulfill. If he is in hunger and I do not help him, then I have violated no obligation. But if I gladly desired to receive from others in case that I should be hungry myself – even on the condition of paying it back – then it would be an obligation to satisfy [them]. I A robber certainly wishes that he may be pardoned, but knows well that he would not pardon if he were the judge. The judge punishes, although he knows that if he were the *delinquent* he would not want to be punished, but hinder with punishment it is different. The deprivation of life does not happen through the judge, but through the criminal, because of his misdeed. No one, if he is in need, can imagine that if he were a rich man, he would help every needy person

In primo hominis statu <obedientia> ipsius erat tanquam mancipii deinde tanquam subditi post tanquam filii et facultas legislatoria tanquam domini, principis, patris

[In the first state of the human being, his obligation obedience was that of a slave, then that of a subject, hereafter that of a son; the law-giving power was that of a master, of a prince, of a father.]

Obligans tanquam dominus <despota> mancipium causas impulsiuas non nisi poenas statuit obligans princeps subditum (legitimum) praemia et poenas obligans pater tanquam filium non nisi amorem et praemia. Ratio obligandi prior est seruitium naturale et debitum secunda rationes morales pacti continet tertium omnia priora ac internam simul moralitatem complectitur

[Whoever put slaves under obligation to himself as a master (despot), set only punishments as incentives; the prince who put his (legitimate) subject under obligation set rewards and punishments [as incentives]; the father who put his son under obligation set only love and rewards [as incentives]. The ground of obligation is natural servitude and debt in the first case; the second contains the moral grounds of a contract; the third contains all of the previous and, at the same time, an inner morality.]

Christ sought to bring human beings to simple sufficiency through *religion*, [that is], in that he presented to them the glory of heaven; his speeches could only produce perverse concepts among the Jews, because the latter for no other price all along founded their religion only on empty concepts, and constructed the latter [their religion] on no other *condition* than the reestablishment of their kingdom

All truthfulness presupposes an idea of equality; hence the Jews, who

in their opinion have no duty at all towards others, lie and deceive without having any pangs of conscience. *haereticis non est fides* [In heretics there is no faith.]

[R118]

[127] Page 98

Upper margin

Honor cannot be a basic drive; otherwise, one who engages in drinking and fighting (*dueling*), while they are in fashion, would be justified, because he concerns himself with the opinion of others

Inserted sheet after page 98 [128] Obverse

Women are by nature much more domestic than men because they have children to nurse. Our gallant women who do not have any [children] and our maidens who know that they will never nurse are not domestic because

it is not necessary. Their beautiful disposition for tidy housekeeping and for the care of a sick person, and likewise for the thrifty use of acquisitions [breaks off]

Male dignity and female grace get lost in society. *Madame Montagu*

Authors seem to be thorough if they dispense with all wit, just as coarse people seem to be honest

Just as one deceives oneself through the appearance of wealth, so a woman at last believes herself actually to have those virtues to the appearance of which she has devoted herself at the beginning.

It takes more to be good as a common human being than to be a good prince. If he is just not exceptionally evil, then he is already good for that purpose.

No matter how much understanding he has, the young man full of sentiment will easily be persuaded by the female illusion and wants to be deceived; he is, in all seriousness, submissive and meek. The wan experienced and smart wanton has long ago understood the mirage of illusion; he therefore is bold, unabashed, and because he relieves the other sex from the coercion of being careful about decency he is agreeable to it.

[R119] *Duels* have their true origin in the time of gallantry from the inclinations of women, for when it comes to general courtship, the beauty chooses the most hearty one and triumphs over her rivals through this, that her lover is horrible to theirs. When it comes to insults that befall her, he cannot sustain himself in her reckoning other than through strong-heartedness.

Who would want to take away propriety from women

Epicurus seems to me to be different from *Zeno* in that the former conceived of the virtuous soul at peace to be victorious after having overcome moral hindrances, while the latter [conceived of the soul to be victorious] in fighting and in practice. *Antisthenes* did not have such a high idea; he wanted that one should only reflect on vain ostentation and false happiness and choose to be a simple man rather than a great one

[129] Reverse, opposite page 95, at 2:251

Quatenus meae voluntati res modificabilis paret mea est sed possum meam voluntatem alteri veluti devincire

[An object is mine insofar as it is subject to be modified according to my will, but I can, so to speak, transfer my will to another.]

Obligation is communal selfishness *in aequilibrio*

officium est vel beveplaciti discretionary vel debiti actiones priores svwt moraliter spontaneae posteriores moraliter coactae. (haec differt a coactione politica) voluntas est vel propria hominis vel communis hominum. [Duty is either chosen discretionary or imposed. The former actions are morally spontaneous, the latter are morally coerced. (This differs from political coercion.) The will is either the particular will of a human being or the general will of humankind.]

(necessarium aliquod est ex uoluntate bona hominis propria uel communi)

["(Anything necessary arises from the specific good will of a human being or from the general [will].)"

<*fas nefas*>

[Right [and] wrong.]

Uoluntas Actio spectata secundum uoluntatem hominum communem est si sibimet ipsi contradicat est externe moraliter impossibilis (illibitum) fac me alterius domin frumentum occupatum ire tam si spetco hominem neminem sub ea conditione ut sibi ipsi eripiatur quod acquisit acquirere velle quod alterius est idem secundum privatum volo et secundum publicum aversor.

[An action that contradicts itself, when considered from the perspective of the general will of human beings, is externally morally impossible (forbidden). Suppose I were about to take the fruits of another. If I then see that, under the condition that what one acquires will soon be snatched away, nobody wants to acquire anything, then I will desire another's goods from the private point of view while rejecting them from the public one.]

Quatenus enim aliquid a uoluntate alicujus plenarie pendet eatenus impossibile est ut sibi ipsi contradicat (objectiue). Contradiceret autem uoluntas diuina sibimet ipsi si uellet homines esse quorum uoluntas opposita esset uoluntati ipsius. Contradiceret hominum uoluntas sibimet ipsi si uellent quod ex uoluntate communi abhorrerent.

[In so far as something depends entirely on the will of a subject, it is impossible that it [the will of a subject] contradicts itself (objectively). The divine will, however, would contradict itself if it willed there to be human beings whose will was opposed to its own will. The will of human beings would contradict itself if they willed something that they would abhor according to their general will.]

Es autem uoluntas communis is statu collisionis praegnantior propria

[In the case of a collision, however, the universal will is weightier than the individual one.]

Actionis <hypothetica> necessitas <conditionalis> ut medii ad finem possibilem est problematica ad finem actualem est necessitas <categorica> prudentiae necessitas categorica es moralis.

[The <hypothetical> <conditional> necessity of an action as a means to a possible end is problematic, [as a means] to an actual end it is the <categorical> necessity of prudence, the categorical necessity is moral.]

It belongs to morality to make *stationes*; first, in the judgment of others about the deed (from this, if it becomes an instinct, ambition arises and goes further than the means for determining legitimacy); secondly, in judgment the sentiment of others, so that one feels their distress or their happiness (hence moral sympathy arises as an instinct)

The origin of the love of honor regarding the beauty of actions thus lies in a badly understood medio of *directing* one's own morality, which falsely becomes an end

The origin of the love of honor regarding the judgment of physical qualities lies in the means to freedom, preservation of oneself and [one's own] kind.

[130] Page 99, lower margin

To compare oneself to others is a means, yet to make comparative greatness or worth into one's intention is perverse and the origin of envy

[R121] Bravery is only a means; the savage values it as an end.

Eventually, one happily can place honor in drinking and in vices

[131] Page 100, upper margin

Man and woman do not have the same *sentiment* and also should not have it, but just from this arises the unity, not of the *identity*, but of the *subordination* of inclinations, since each feels that the other is necessary to him for the greatest perfection. Friendship presupposes *sentiments* that agree

Inserted sheet, after page 100

[132] Obverse

In the case of a great corruption of mores, maidens keep themselves chaste and women live in excess, because the latter then only act against obligation, while the former act against propriety

<It is already an honor not to be despised.>

I need things or also human beings. Honor is either mediate or immediate. In the first case, it is a drive of enjoyment; in the second, of delusion. In the first case, the needs are either true or imaginary, to which honor is a means, and the first [is] either in the natural or the degenerate state. Needs for things in the natural state <to procure them for oneself> do not require honor (because everyone can procure them for himself); but in order to preserve them and oneself, they demand that others have an opinion of our equality, so that our freedom does not suffer, since we can seek our needs as we please. Man's natural need of acquisition is a woman. For this, he needs the opinion not of superiority over but of equality with other men, and he also easily acquires this. In both cases, however, the human being will raise the drive of real honor above equality, partly [so] that freedom [should] be more secure, partly because he begins to prefer one woman over another, so that she will also prefer him. Finally, in the state of <inequality>, the [R22] drive of honor will either be that of true needs or of artificial ones.

In Sparta, it was true one because by means of it one remained free, but in an opulent country, where freedom is lost, it becomes all the more necessary. At the same time, the honor of delusion arises primarily with respect to sex, to which, in the end, the honor that is a means of enjoyment gets sacrificed

[133] Reverse, opposite page 101, at 2:252

Slavery is either that of force or that of blindness. The latter is based either on the dependence on things (opulence) or on the delusion of other human beings (vanity). The latter is more incongruous and also harder than the former because things are much more in my own power than the opinions of others, and it is also more despicable

The loss of freedom is grounded either on dependence or on subservience. In the first case, one is ruled by means of one's inclination (either to things or to human beings, as in love and friendship, [and] parental love) or contrary to one's inclinations. The former is a consequence of weak opulence, the latter, however, of fearful cowardice and is a consequence of the first

The drive of honor with respect to [one's] sex also becomes pure delusion in the end. And honor, which is supposed to promote self-preservation, promotes this pure delusion, and vanity is a cause of the lack of marriage.

With a woman, the drive of honor is directed solely at sexual union, and by means of the same at needs, because she must be sought; since this is not necessary with men, she will only be attracted by business, and thus can sooner resolve to lack honor

That which very much proves the *fantastic nature* of love is that one loves the beloved object more in its absence than in its presence; with friendship, it is different.

[R123]

[134] Page 102 Upper margin

The drive of honor is grounded on the drive for equality and the drive for unity. Two powers that move the animal world, as it were. The instinct for unity is either unity in judgments and thoughts or also in inclinations. The former brings about logical perfection, the latter moral one.

Left margin

The only naturally necessary good of a human being in relation to the will of others is equality (freedom) and, with respect to the whole, unity. Analogy: Repulsion, through which the body fills its own space just as everyone [fills] his own. Attraction, through which all parts combine into one.

The truth of a perfection consists in the magnitude of the pleasure that is not exclusive with regard to itself and with regard to other greater ones. If falsity could be durable and more pleasurable than truth, then the pleasure from this deception would be a true pleasure, though a false cognition

Lower margin

The natural instincts of active benevolence towards others consist in love towards the [other] sex and towards children. That towards other human beings merely concerns equality and unity

There is unity in the *sovereign* state but not equality; if the latter is combined with unity, then it constitutes the perfect *republic*

Inserted sheet at page 102

[135] Obverse

[R124] The drive to evaluate oneself merely comparatively, with respect to one's worth as well as with respect to one's welfare, is far more widespread than the drive for honor, and contains the latter within itself. It does not lie in nature and is an indirect result of the use of the means to know one's own state better through the comparison with others. Ambition, which is a spur of science, arises from the comparison of our judgment with the judgment of others; thus as a means [ambition] presupposes esteem for the judgment of others

The Indians are remarkably calm and not violent

The South Americans---indifferent and phlegmatic

The Negroes---very careless and vain

The Europeans--lively and hot-tempered

The *affects* of the Indians are nevertheless still stronger than [those] of the Europeans

A reason why Montesquieu was able to say so many excellent things is that he presupposed that those who introduced customs or gave laws would have had a reasonable ground in each case

The main intention of Rousseau is that education be free and also make a free human being

We must honor common understanding and common taste

A woman does not like to give away, in contrast, she takes. No one knows contentment; everyone asserts delightfulness in its place. <Golden rain in the lap of Danae. Jupiter a bull. In *Amphitryon*, Alcmene was honest>

How education helps public regulation is to be seen from the fact that the former makes many goods, e.g., silk [and] gold, etc., entirely dispensable, whereas the latter prohibits in vain because it only offends thereby

[R125] A woman loves less affectionately than a man or otherwise she would not claim dominance over him and demand obviously prefer herself to him. She is also aware that she tolerates more affection; if the man does not have this refined sentiment, he is called clumsy and hard by her

Marriage gives no other ideal pleasure than mere sympathy. Illusion is sometimes better than truth, for the pleasure from the former

is a true pleasure. Make-up; if one knows it [the illusion], then it is no longer a deception.

[136] Reverse, page 103, at 2:253

Living long and little or living short and much; living much in enjoyment or in action. Both in the greatest ratio is the best.

That the capacity for life decreases from the 6th year on

It is to be noted that we do not value the *Bonitat* of an action because it is useful to another, or otherwise we would not value it more highly than the utility it creates.

The moral feeling applied to one's own actions is conscience Providence probably gave us this feeling for the sake of universal

perfection, yet in such a way that the latter is not thought of in its greatness, just as we have the sexual drive for reproduction without *intending* it.

De stationibus	Physicis	the moon is inhabited
[on stations]	*Logicis*	in absence, *egoism*
	Moralibus	in absence, *solipsisimvs moralis*

statio moralis vel per instinctum. Sympathia vel misericordia vel per intellectum

[Moral position, either through instinct. Sympathy or pity. Or through intellect.]

[R26] Magnetic force is probably based on the heterogeneity (*diversa gravitas specifica*) of ethereal matter, of which iron is full (the earth is full of iron), [and] whereby the heavier [thing] sinks downward

Hence the magnetic quality reveals itself more in length – e.g., more if a clump of iron is long and vertical instead of thick and short – precisely because the *quantity* of ether must here provide greater difference in density. One can assume that the little clumps that have their *negative* and positive pole are small.

Inserted sheet after page 104

[137] Obverse, at 2:253

Electricity consists of particles that have been rubbed off; the magnetic [force] does not. Hence the latter is penetrating and works in proportion to mass; the former does not.

The two poles of the same sign repel each other because two elastic ether-spheres of similar density push themselves, but [in the case of those poles that are] not of the same sign one [pole] will be engulfed by the others – because it is of a lighter kind (already according to its elements, not merely *ob rarefactionem*) – and the magnet will be pulled

The needle's heavy end sinks into the universal magnetic atmosphere and the other end rises

The sensitive soul at peace, in faces, in societies, in eloquence

Poetry in marriages and the sexual drive

The difference of the sexes

Blessedness and cheerfulness

Perhaps that the moon, by affecting the electrical (refringing) matter that extends much higher, brings about the great causes of the winds and of the ebb and flow

Perhaps that it is itself the compressed heavenly air; from the *centro gravitates coeli* to the *centro* of the earth.

[R127] <Paris, the seat of science and of the ridiculous, also contains

petit Maitressen>

Etourderie (tasteless brazenness) rises above the effort at appearance and expresses only a certain boisterous reliability with respect to that which can please. The petitmaitre is an *etourdi* who is gallant, but he must appear to be well known in the great world. He has good luck with women. The Germans travel to France to become *etourdi*, but they achieve only the appearance of a brazen jester. The *coquette* expresses the awareness of her rule over the hearts of men and makes their caresses into her toys. The petitmaitre and the coqeettes are never in love, but both pretend to be so. A dandy is actually a fool for fancy clothing and is very different from the petitmaitre who even affects free carelessness.

[138] Reverse, opposite page 105, at 2:254

Were the I suppose magnetic matter to be a sphere of heterogeneous ether, which however in each expanse contains all species one beneath the other, although the denser parts [are] closer to the center of the earth, the lighter ones above. If this ether-sphere shared a *centrum* with the earth, then no *direction* toward the poles would take place; were its centrum on the axis, then no *declination* would take place. For, since because the intersection of the horizons of two spheres is a circle – upon which the needle must stand perpendicularly if it shall sink as deep as possible into the magnetic circle326 – yet all these circles run parallel with the *equator*, then the needles will hold the *meridian*.

If this *centrum* is not in the axis, then there is only *linea expers variationis* where the meridian of the earth coincides with the *meridiano magnetico*. Now, because the axis magnetic axis lies in such a way on a plane with the earth's axis that the meridian that goes through the earth's poles also goes through the magnetic ones, the *linea expers variationis* would be a meridian at all times. Now, should it not be a meridian, then the magnetic horizon must be spheroid or else irregular; in that case, however, the magnetic attractions must not point to the *centro* of the magnetic spheroid, but instead also diverge from it. Suppose that this oblateness comes from the centrifugal force of the earth; then in such the size of the divergence from the magnetic *centro* will be to the divergence from the *cewtro* of the earth as the [force of] gravity329 is to the conducting magnetic force. Therefore, the magnetic horizon can be bent in very different ways, and not only the *inclination*, but also the *declination* can be very diverse.

Inserted sheet after page 106

[139] Obverse

Moral delusion consists in one's really taking opinion about a possible moral perfection to be real.

We have selfish and altruistic sentiments. The former are older than the latter, and the latter are first generated in the sexual inclination. A human being is needy, but also has power over needs. He [who is] in the state of nature is more capable of altruistic and active sentiments; he [who is] in a state of opulence has imaginary needs and is selfish. One sympathizes more with the ill – particularly the injustice – that others suffer than with their welfare. The sympathetic sentiment is true if it is equal to the altruistic powers, otherwise it is chimerical. It is universal in an indeterminate way in so far as it is directed to one among all those whom I can help, or in a determinate way, towards helping everyone who suffers; the latter is chimerical. Good-heartedness arises through the *culture* of moral but inactive sentiments and is a moral delusion. On the private good-heartedness to do no evil and to fulfill one's obligation towards justice

The morality that wants nothing but unselfishness is chimerical, as is the one that is sympathetic to imagined needs. The morality that affirms selfishness alone is crude

The *officia beneplaciti* can never entail that one robs oneself of one's own needs, but the *officia debiti* surely can, for these are moral needs

[R29] Virtue carries along with it a natural wage, although not in goods of opulence, but [in goods] of sufficiency

It is possible to conceive of a most perfect human being of nature, but not of artifice

The former takes care not to impose some obligations on himself. And also the latter

[140] Reverse, opposite page 107, at 2:255

The sweetness of current need is chimerical Friendship of agreeableness or of needs. They must be equal, otherwise it is not called friendship, but enjoyment

Friendship is always reciprocal, hence not between father and child, and since the wife never desires the man's well-being as much as the latter desires hers, marriage is only closely related to the most perfect friendship.

In the state of opulence, marriages must cease to become friendships. The friendship of delusion that consists in reciprocal good wishes without effect is foolish but beautiful, that of sociable friendliness and concordant sentiments is the most common, but such [a person] is a socializer, perhaps open-hearted and discreet, but no friend.

The education of Rousseau is the only means to help civil society flourish again. For since opulence constantly increases – from which arise need, oppression and contempt of the classes – laws can accomplish nothing against this, as in Sweden. Thereby all governments also become more orderly and wars more infrequent. *Censors* should be instituted; but where will the first ones come from[?] Switzerland [is] the only country.

Russia.

[R130] The doubt that I assume is not dogmatic, but a doubt of postponement. Zetetics searchers. I will raise the reasons from both sides. It is amazing that one worries about danger from that. Speculation is not a matter of bare necessity. Knowledge with respect to the latter is secure. The method of doubt is useful because it *preserves* the mind, not to act according to speculation, but according to common sense and *sentiment*. I seek the honor of *Fabius Cunctator*.

Truth has no value in itself, it is all the same whether an opinion about the inhabitation of many worlds is true or false. One must not confuse truth with truthfulness. Only the manner in which one arrives at truth has a determinate value, because that which leads to error can also do so in practical matters

If the pleasure from the sciences is supposed to be the motive, then it is all the same whether it is true or false. In this, the ignorant and precocious have an advantage over the reasonable and cautious. The final end is to find the human being's vocation

[141] Page 107

Lower margin, at 2:255

The opinion of inequality also makes human beings unequal. Only the doctrine of Mr. *Rousseau* can bring it about that even the most learned philosopher, with his knowledge, earnestly regards himself, without help from religion, as no better than the common man.

Inserted sheet after page 108

[142] Obverse

What a miserable condition it is when oppression is so universal and common that an industrious and honest human being cannot merely demand justice, but instead must beg for mercy. The more we misconceive of our obligations, when we are not yet entirely corrupted, the more favors remain for us; we especially neglect obligations toward some and give favors to others.

[R131] In order for the weakness of women in the active qualities to be counterbalanced by something, nature has made men weak in so far as they very much surrender themselves to illusion and let themselves be easily deceived. The man is inclined to form great conceptions of a beloved object and to feel himself unworthy, as it were, with respect to her. Yet the woman commonly imagines herself worthy of courtship and forms no fantastical ideas of the man's superiority. They soon believe that they are able to take command over the man's heart. The man is inclined to value his wife or his lover higher than himself, the woman never. If one merely considers the sex's intention, then the woman obviously rules and is more clever. The generous one believes more easily than the selfish and weak one.

The *Gallantry* (of men) is the art of appearing to be in love. Women's *coquetterie* is the art of giving the appearance of the inclination to conquer. Both are ridiculous in marriages. \The art of appearing virtuous is propriety, and especially that of appearing chaste; modesty, refined and selective in taste, prudery, appearing affable, politesse, refinement. The persons who understand the arts best make the worst marriages

If appearance is employed for the purpose of marriage, then it is still good; if it lasts after marriage, then it is very ridiculous. Yet men demand such women, who, as they say, do them credit, who are sought after, who one would gladly like to take from them.

[143] Reverse, opposite page 109

est obligatio stricta erga dominumex obseqvio <reverentia> erga benefactorem ex amore iw novo foedere licet deum amare in veteri revereri

[There is a strict duty toward the Lord out of obedience <reverence>, toward the benefactor out of love; in the new covenant, one can love God, in the old covenant, one can revere Him.]

Bodies are either positive, transparent, or *negative* (*reflecting*), or zero
(black). All bodies on the surfaces are both at the same time, especially small lamellae.

The small lamellae of iron magnets have this quality and pull themselves in whole clumps with their opposite poles. Electrical bodies only have it on the surface

[R32] <In the case of women, book-reading occurs in order to appear learned>

<The marriage that has no illusion, likewise honorableness >

jus cum sit complexus regularum obligationum debiti habitus Actionum cum jure ex rationibus juris determinandarum est justicia quae uel uel est obligantis (actiua) vel obligati (passiua). Prior exigit actiones aliorum conformiter robore quantenus <ad quas quales> per rationes juris necessitantur Posterior est habitus se ad actiones determinandi quae per rationes juris sunt ab aliis necessitantur: Si actionum habitus sit justitiae adaequatus prior erit justicia severa posterior [breaks off]

[While the law is the sum of the obligations related to that which is owed, the disposition of actions that should be determined by reasons of law constitutes justice, which is either that of the one who obligates (active) or that of the one who is obligated (passive). The former requires actions of others <insofar as they are> necessitated by reasons of law. The latter is the disposition to determine oneself to actions that are necessitated by others for reasons of law: . . . If the disposition of actions corresponds to justice, then the former will be strict justice, the latter.]

Habitum officiorum limites justiciae actiuae excedentium Aequitas, justiciae passivae itidem

[The state of actions of duties that exceeds the limits of active justice [is] equity; it is the same [regarding those duties] of passive justice.]

Indoles

["predisposition" or "character."]

<The illusion of friendship. *Aristotle* –;if we wake, we have *mundum commenem* [a common world]>

De sententia respectu juris civilis summum jus summa injuria. respectu ciuis vera non respectu judicis

[Regarding the sentence in civil law, 'the greatest right, the greatest wrong': It is true with respect to the citizen, but not with respect to the judge.]

<A young husband is not good because he has not yet considered the falsity of appearance>

Hume believes that the clergy very much practice the art of appearing. Truth is only suitable in a nightdress; in the suit of the parade appearance [is suitable]. To appear to be all sorts of things in clothes. Make-up.

Alexander v. Antipater; purple interior

Envy ceases when I can wipe away the deceiving appearance of others' happiness and perfection

[R33] On the means of imagining a president or a dignified man with his wife

[144] Page 110

Upper margin, at 2:256

The most perfect woman. Understanding and brave, reasonable, if she is voluntarily excused from ratiocination. <Clever, wise – witty, refined> The exemption from domestic affairs makes foolish women <*gallant.*> Foolish women.

He who knows how to satisfy his desire is clever; he who knows how to master it is wise. World-wisdom

Left margin, next to lines 21–28

Costs and expenses. These are expenses if one loses the pleasures

that one can get for money or work and thus also [loses] the latter. The miser has the greatest expenses; he who knows how to live so, with the expenditure of all money, [has] the greatest profit. Also avaricious. To use it every time for one's contentment (not delightfulness).

Lower margin, between the text and the closing vignette

Just as the size of a human being cannot grow above the mean without his becoming weaker, and also cannot remain below the mean without his being too weak, so it is with ethical and delicate qualities

Lower margin, under the vignette

Greek Roman face. Characters of *nations* in social interaction: the Spanish, French, Germans, [and] English

That our youths and men are still so childish is because they did not have enough permission to be children earlier. Thus, the trees whose blossoms were not allowed to burst forth properly in the spring bloom in [R134] the fall

[145] Inside of the back cover

Simplicity is either ignorant or reasonable and wise simplicity

In all moral *definitions*, the expression *mediocritas* [the mean] is very wretched and indefinite – e.g., *in parsimonia* – for it only indicates that there is a degree that is not good on account of its size, without saying how large the good would have to be.

This *mediocritas aurea* [the golden mean] is a *qualitas occulta* [occult quality]

Difference between: he knows how to appear or he knows how to live.

One could say that metaphysics is a science of the limits of human reason

The doubts of the same do not remove useful certainty, but useless certainty

Metaphysics is useful in that it removes the appearance that can be harmful

In metaphysics, it is partiality not to also think from the opposite side, and it [is] also a lie not to say it; in actions it is different

One only falls in love with illusion, but one loves truth. If one should reveal the illusion of most human beings, then they would seem like that bride of whom one says that [when] she had taken off her beautiful silken eyebrows, a pair of ivory teeth, excellent ringlets and a few handkerchiefs that had supported her bosom, and had wiped off her make-up, her astonished lover [breaks off]

Illusion demands refinement and art, truth demands simplicity and peace. According to Swift, everything in the world is clothes

The most ridiculous is this: that one creates illusion toward others for so long that one oneself imagines it to be true; this is what children do with *religion*. Illusion, when the one who intends it takes it for the thing itself, is delusion.

The illusion that the woman *intends* as a means to the attainment of marital love is no delusion, but [it] surely is aside from this condition. On the art of making the easy difficult

Loose Sheets to the Observations on the Feeling of the Beautiful and Sublime

The inclination of women toward novels perhaps comes about because they wish that love were the sole inclination by which men are ruled.

Just as the greatest excess that arises from free government ultimately amounts to throwing everything into slavery and finally poverty, so the unnatural freedom of the female sex and the agreeableness that they thereby enjoy and impart must at last amount to making them completely despicable and finally to making them into slaves.

Mr. Hume believes that a woman who has no knowledge of the history of her fatherland or of Greece and Rome cannot ever keep company with people of understanding. Yet he does not consider that they are not there to serve men as support for cogitation but as support for the recuperation from it. History is of no use without a degree of philosophy, even if it were just moral philosophy. In this, however, the woman only needs the part of history that concerns that morality which relates to her sex.

The woman, because she always wants to rule, takes herself a fool without reservation.

The valiant wife wants to be honored through her husband; the vain wife does not ask for this honor but wants to catch the [public] eye herself. The *coquette* has the intention of inspiring inclinations, even though she has none herself; it is a mere game of vanity.

All inclinations are either exclusive or sympathetic. The former are selfish, the latter are altruistic. However, self-love and self-esteem are not exclusive according to their nature; but egoism and self-conceit are. The love of women is exclusive with respect to other men in accordance with the law of nature. The purely lustful drive or the amorous rage can even be exclusive with respect to the object of love, hence rape, Herod, etc. The immediate drive for honor is exclusive with respect to honor. The quality of the mind to desire in objects everything exclusively, where this drive is not justified by nature, is called envy. Envy is a kind of balefulness. But emulation – a sadness about inequality – can probably only concern an imagined inequality; in any case, it is then only a perverse application of a good law of nature. The drives that are sympathetic are the best: only in the case of sexual drives must sympathy concern only the object of the amorous inclination.

Women's refusals are to them an irresistible drive to create illusion; those men who have not yet become extremely wanton have the quality that they are very easily deceived by this illusion; this relation holds the strength of the reciprocal inclination within bounds.

The moral state, when the taste for a great amount of artificial pleasures and charms is missing, is simplicity; the [moral state] in which this taste is acquired is virtue; heroic virtue however even aims at the overcoming of needs. Thus, one can be good without virtue. Correct judgment, which is acquired through experience that depends on needs, is understanding; if taste extends to many things and the manifoldness of the issue is magnified, then reason – indeed, even fine reason – is necessary. But healthy reason is that fine reason, which returns to that which is necessary to judge and know. One can be very understanding without great fineness of reason.

Simple taste easily gets out of hand and moral simplicity is easily deceived due to a lack of knowledge of seductive temptation; hence the greatest perfection is [breaks off]

The woman who has acquired no particular taste for all those distractions, gallantries and vanities can be good without virtue and understanding without brooding. If she is pulled from the midst and from the seat of these fine pleasures, then thousands of enticements affect her and she needs virtue in order to be a good woman.

In domestic life, in company that is spirited, good-hearted and calm, no witticism, no books and courtly manners and ratiocination is needed, but if so much refined taste, concupiscence, and fashion is acquired, then reason is required in order to prevent one from becoming a foolish woman. The most perfect woman would be the one who knows the various fine delights of life, manners [and] gallantry in their beautiful charms, and has taste, but, through reasonable insight into their uselessness, voluntarily readies herself for domesticity and simplicity, and knows how to constrain herself through virtue.

A woman needs even more virtue in marriage than a man, especially if the necessity of modest appearance has gone completely out of fashion

and gallant freedom, as innocent as it may sound, emerges. For she has a safer game, as one can easily guess, and will be more solicited.

One can presuppose in accordance with the rule of prudence that one never encounters that which is extremely rare and, where it is encountered, hard to recognize; for this reason it is not at all in accordance with prudence to let oneself be guided by this deceitful pleasantness of women Elderly persons very much love jokes and that which arouses laughter; youth falls in love with the moving tragic that arouses strong sentiments. What is the cause[?]

I find this mistake [to be] almost universal: that one does not ponder the shortness of human life enough. It is surely perverse to have it in mind in order to despise human life and in order to look only toward the future one. But [one should have it in mind] so that one may live right at his position and not postpone it [life] too far through a foolish fantasy about the plan of our actions. The epitaphs of various ancients lend themselves to the encouragement of lustful and opulent enjoyment and of avaricious greediness for pleasure. But if well understood, it [the epitaph] only serves to liberate the mind through sufficiency from the rule of such drives that entangle us in preparations whose enjoyment is not in proportion with the efforts due to the brevity of life. The consideration of the nearness of death is agreeable in itself and a corrective for bringing human beings toward simplicity and for helping them towards the sensitive peace of the soul, which begins as soon as the blind ardor, with which one previously chased after the imagined objects of one's wishes, ceases.

The woman who is constantly busy with taking care of choice finery must be kept in this practice in marriage. For, since she has maintained no inclination for cleanliness and agreeableness except to please others, she will become foul and swinish if she lives alone with her husband.

In society, the man is more preoccupied with the contemplation of that which pleases him in a woman, while the woman [focuses] more on that which pleases men in herself.

All pleasures of life have their great charm while one hunts after them; [their] possession is cold and the enchanting spirit has evaporated. So, the acquisitive merchant has thousands of pleasures while he earns money. If he considers enjoying it after earning it thousands of worries will torment him. The young lover is extremely happy [when] in hope, and the day on which his happiness rises to its highest also brings it to a decline again.

A certain calm self-confidence combined with the marks of respect and modesty secures trust and goodwill; in contrast, a boldness that appears to give little respect to others brings about hate and reluctance

In *disputes*, a calm attitude of the mind combined with kindness and leniency toward the opponent is a sign that one is in possession of the power through which the understanding is certain of its victory. Just as Rome sold the fields on which Hannibal stood.

When facing the eyes of a large crowd, few human beings will endure their mockery and contempt with a calm mind, even if they know that those [in the crowd] are all ignorant fools. The great crowd always creates awe, indeed, even the audience shivers with fright at the false step of him who compromises himself in their presence, although each individual, if he were alone with the speaker, would find little disparaging in his disapproval. But if the great crowd is absent, a composed man can very well regard their judgment with complete indifference.

With regard to a beautiful object, an intense passion, an embarrassment and a languishing longing adorns the man very well; in the case of a woman, though, calm affectionateness. It is not good that the woman offers herself to the man or anticipates his declarations of love. For he who alone has the power must necessarily be dependent upon her who has nothing but charms, and the latter must be conscious of the value of her charms, otherwise there would be no equality but slavery

The mechanical in laughter is the vibration of the diaphragm and the lungs, as well as the contorted face, since the mouth is pulled from elsewhere, etc. Women and fat people like to laugh. One laughs most violently when one is supposed to behave seriously. One laughs most strongly about him who looks serious. Strong laughter is tiring [and] breaks into tears, as sadness does. Laughter that is aroused by tickling is at the same time very exhausting, but that [which is aroused] through imagination amuses, though it can lead to *convulsions*. [One] about whom I laugh myself, then if I suffer damages from him, I can no longer be mad. The recollection of the ridiculous gives much pleasure and also does

not wear off as easily as other agreeable stories. The Abbe´ *Terrasson* with the cap on his head.

The ground of laughter seems to consist in the trembling of quickly pinched nerves, which propagates through the entire system; other pleasures come from uniform movements of the fluid of the nerves. Thus, if I hear something that has an appearance of a prudent purposeful relation, but which entirely cancels itself out in trifles, then the nerve that is bent towards one side becomes repelled and trembling, as it were. Indeed, I would not want to wager, yet I will attest it any time.

Pelisson who should have been painted instead of the devil.

Sexual inclination is either amorous need or amorous concupiscence. In the state of simplicity, the former rules and thus [there is] no taste yet. In the state of artifice the amorous concupiscence becomes either one of the enjoyment of all or one of ideal taste. The latter constitutes lustful immoderateness. In all of this two things are to be noted. The female sex is either mingled with the male sex in free company or excluded.

If the latter is the case then no moral taste occurs, but at the most, simplicity (lending the Spartans' wives), or it is a lustful delusion, as it were, an amorous greed to possess much for enjoyment without being able to really enjoy any of it; Salomon. In the state of simplicity, mutual need ruled. Here is need on one side and lack on the other. There was fidelity without temptation; here guards of chastity, which is not possible in itself. In the free interaction of both sexes, which is a new invention, concupiscence grows, but so does moral taste. One of the qualities of this drive is that it probably underlies the ideal charms but must always be carried on as a kind of secret; from this arises a kind of modest propriety even with respect to strong desires, without which the latter would be common and, in the end, liable to tedium. Second, that the female sex takes on the illusion as if it were not a need in her case; this is necessary if the amorous inclination is supposed to remain combined with ideal pleasures and moral taste in the state of artifice. In lustful passion this illusion is not necessary at all. Hence female acquiescence merely appears to be either forced or a sign of favor

A young man who expresses no amorous inclination at all will be indifferent in the eyes of the woman.

Whether [or not] there really can be a use for religion that immediately pertains to future blessedness, still the most natural first [use of religion] is that it arranges mores in such a way that they are good for fulfilling one's station in the present world, so that one thereby becomes worthy of the future one. For things that concern fasting, ceremony, and chastening, those have no use for the present world. But if this internal use is to be achieved, morality must be refined before religion.

Montesquieu says that it would be entirely unnatural for a woman to rule a house but that it could very well happen that she should rule a country.

If mores are entirely simple and all luxury is banned, then the man rules; if public affairs are in the hands of a few and the majority of men become idle, then women leave their solitude and have great influence over men. If women *inspire* virtue and romanic esteem in men, then they rule the man hereafter in the household through kindness; if they do not win him through coquetterie before they have seduced him and turned him into a fool, then they will rule him imperiously and willfully. In a good marriage both have only one will and that is the will of the wife; likewise in a bad marriage, but with the distinction that the husband agrees with the will of the wife in the first case, [while] in the second case he opposes her, yet is outweighed.

This is the age of the rule of women, but with little honor because they degrade the man in his worth. They first make him vain, yielding, and foolish, and after they have deprived him of the dignity of male honor, they have no obstacle. In all marriages, women rule, but also over men of worth.

There are two paths in the Christian religion, in so far as it is supposed to improve morality: 1. beginning with the revelation of mysteries, in that one expects a sanctification of the heart from a divine supernatural influence; 2. beginning from the improvement of morality according to the order of nature and, after the greatest possible effort spent on this, expecting supernatural assistance according to the divine order of his decrees expressed in revelation.

For it is not possible by beginning with revelation, to expect moral improvement from this instruction as a result according to the order of nature.

The *refined* view into the future, if it is carried out to the end, namely [to] the goal of imminent death, brings its own *remedium* with it. For why should one torment oneself with many concerned preparations given that death will soon interrupt them

A man easily develops high esteem toward a woman who captures him, while the woman for her part has more inclination than respect. Hence it comes about that the man expresses a kind of generosity in overcoming his own lustful inclination, without which many women would be seduced. A tempted wanton is a dangerous man among women.

It is good that, although the sensitive heart at peace is always beautiful, the affect of love nevertheless suits the man very well before marriage, while quiet submissiveness suits the woman: so that the man can appear to be in love without the least bit of bad manners, yet the woman only appears to love.

It is strange that women have so much attentiveness and memory in things pertaining to ornament, propriety, and politesse, while men have so little.

One is not compassionate with respect to the grief and distress of another but with respect to those in so far as their causes are natural and not imagined. Therefore a craftsman has no compassion for a bankrupt merchant who is degraded to the position of a broker or a servant because he does not see that the merchant lacks anything other than imagined necessities. A merchant has no compassion for a courtier who has fallen from grace and must live on his own estates after the loss of his posts. Yet if both are regarded as benefactors of humanity, then one does not consider the ills according to one's own sentiment, but according to the sentiment of the other. But the merchant has compassion for the downfall of another who is otherwise honest if he obtains no advantage from it because he has just the same imagined need as the other. At the most, one also has compassion in the case of an otherwise gentle woman for her grief about imagined misfortune, because one despises a man for his weakness in such a case, but not a woman. But everyone has compassion for the ill that is opposed to true needs. From this it follows that the good-heartedness of a human being of much opulence will contain a very extensive compassion, while that of the human being of simplicity will contain a very restricted one. One has unlimited compassion for one's children

The more extensive the compassion is, when the powers remain the same, the more idle it is; the more the imagined needs also grow here, the greater is the obstacle of the remaining capacity to do good. Hence the goodwill of the opulent state becomes a mere delusion

There is no sweeter idea than idleness and no activity [sweeter] than that which is aimed at pleasure. This is also the object that one has before one's eyes if one wants to sit down in peace, but all of this is a phantasm. He who does not work dies of boredom and is, at the most, numbed by delightful things and exhausted, but never refreshed and satisfied

The drive for honor with respect to those qualities whose higher value can make the judgment of others resolute and universal is ambition; the drive for honor with respect to the less significant qualities, about which the judgment of others [is] frivolous and changeable, is vanity.

Self-esteem, humility. The scornful laughter that is worthy of being laughed at [should] be hated rather than despised.

Self-esteem pertains to equality, and the latter leads to respect if it is badly understood.

Why incapacity is regarded as even more ignominious than an evil will, namely in such cases where incapacity also cancels out the good consequences at the same time

That the desire for honor is partly based on the condition of equality can be seen from the fact that nobles greatly despise the judgment of the lower ones. One sees that it is based on the sexual drive because the contempt of a woman is very offensive

Essay on the Maladies of the Head

The simplicity and frugality of nature demands and forms only common concepts and a clumsy sincerity in human beings; artificial constraint and the luxury of a civil constitution hatches punsters and subtle reasoners, occasionally, however, also fools and swindlers, and gives birth to the wise or decent semblance by means of which one can dispense with understanding as well as integrity, if only the beautiful veil which decency spreads over the secret frailties of the head or the heart is woven close enough. Proportionately as art advances, reason and virtue will finally become the universal watchword, yet in such a way that the eagerness to speak of both can well dispense instructed and polite persons from bothering with their possession. The universal esteem which both praised properties are accorded nevertheless shows this noticeable difference that everyone is far more jealous of the advantages of the understanding than of the good properties of the will, and that in the comparison between stupidity and roguery no one would hesitate a moment to declare his preference for the latter; which is certainly well thought out because, if everything in general depends on art, fine cleverness cannot be dispensed with, but sincerity, which in such relations is only obstructive, can well be done without. I live among wise and well-mannered citizens, that is to say, among those who are skilled at appearing so, and I flatter myself that one would be so fair as to credit me with as much finesse that even if I were presently in possession of the most proven remedies for dislodging the maladies of the head and the heart, I would still hesitate to lay this old-fashioned rubbish in the path of public business, well aware that the beloved fashionable cure for the understanding and the heart has already made desirable progress and that particularly the doctors of the understanding, who call themselves logicians, satisfy the general demand very well since they made the important discovery: that the human head is actually a drum which only sounds because it is empty. Accordingly, I see nothing better for me than to imitate the method of the physicians, who believe they have been very helpful to their patient when they give his malady a name, and will sketch a small onomastic of the frailties of the head, from its paralysis in *imbecility* to its raptures in *madness*; but in order to recognize these loathsome maladies in their gradual origination, I find it first necessary to elucidate their milder degrees from idiocy to *foolishness*, because these properties are more widespread in civil relations and lead nonetheless to the former ones.

The *dull* head lacks wit; the *idiot* lacks understanding. The agility in grasping something and remembering it, likewise the facility in expressing it properly, very much depend on wit; for that reason he who is not stupid can nevertheless be very dull, in so far as hardly anything gets into his head, even though afterward he may be able to understand it with a greater maturity of judgment; and the difficulty of being able to express oneself proves nothing less than the capacity of the understanding, it only proves that wit is not performing enough assistance in dressing up the thought with all kinds of signs of which several fit it most aptly. The celebrated Jesuit *Clavius* was run out of school as incapable (because according to the testing procedure of the understanding employed by tyrannical schoolmasters, a boy is useful for nothing at all if he can write neither verses nor essays). Later he came upon mathematics, the tables turned, and his previous teachers were idiots compared to him. The practical judgment concerning matters, such as the farmer, the artist, or the seafarer, etc., need it, is very different from judgment one possesses about the techniques with which human beings deal with one another. The latter is not so much understanding as craftiness, and the lovable lack of this highly praised capacity is called simplicity. If the cause of this is to be sought in the weakness of the power of judgment, then such a human being is called a *ninny, simpleton*, etc. Since intrigue and false

devices have gradually become customary maxims in civil society and have very much complicated the play of human actions, it is no wonder when an otherwise sensible and sincere man for whom all this cunning is either too contemptible to occupy himself with it or who cannot move his honest and benevolent heart to make himself such a hated concept of human nature were to get caught everywhere by swindlers and give them much to laugh about – so that in the end the expression "a good man" designates a simpleton no longer in a figurative manner but directly, and occasionally even designates a cuckold. For in the language of rogues no one is a sensible man but the one who holds everyone else for no better than what he himself is, namely a swindler.

The drives of human nature, which are called passions when they are of a high degree, are the moving forces of the will; the understanding only comes in to assess both the entire result of the satisfaction of all inclinations taken together from the end represented and to find the means to this end. If, e.g., a passion is especially powerful, the capacity of the understanding is of little help against it; for the enchanted human being sees very well indeed the reasons against his favorite inclination, but he feels powerless to give them active emphasis. If this inclination is good in itself and the person is otherwise reasonable, except for the overweighing penchant obstructing the view of the bad consequences, then this state of fettered reason is folly. A foolish *person* can have a good deal of understanding even in the judgment concerning those actions in which he is foolish; he must even possess a good deal of understanding and a good heart before being entitled to this milder appellation for his excesses. The foolish *person* can even be an excellent adviser for others, although his advice has no effect on himself. He will become shrewd only through damage or through age, which however only displaces one folly to make room for another one. The amorous passion or a great degree of ambition have always made foolish persons of many reasonable people. A young girl compels the formidable Alcides to pull the thread on the distaff, and Athen's idle citizens send *Alexander* with their silly praise to the end of the world. There are also inclinations of lesser vehemence and generality which nevertheless do not lack in generating folly: the building demon, the inclination to collect pictures, book mania. The degenerate human being has left his natural place and is attracted by everything and supported by everything. To the foolish person there is opposed the shrewd *man*; but he who is without folly is a wise *man*. This wise *man* can perhaps be sought for on the moon; possibly there one is without passion and has infinitely much reason. The insensitive person is safe from folly through his stupidity; to ordinary eyes, however, he has the mien of a wise person. *Pyrrho* saw a pig eating calmly from his trough on a ship in a storm while everyone was anxiously concerned and said pointing to it: "Such ought to be the calm of a wise person." The insensitive one is *Pyrrho*'s wise person.

If the predominant passion is odious in itself and at the same time insipid enough to take for the satisfaction of the passion precisely that which is contrary to the natural intention of the passion, then this state of reversed reason is *foolishness*. The foolish person understands the true intention of his passion very well, even if he grants it a strength that is able of fettering reason. The fool, however, is at the same time rendered so stupid by his passion that he believes only then to be in possession of the thing desired when he actually deprives himself of it. *Pyrrhus* knew very well that bravery and power earn universal admiration; he followed the drive for ambition and was nothing more than for what *Kineas* held him, namely a foolish person. However, when *Nero* exposes himself to public mockery by reciting wretched verses to obtain the poet's prize and still says at the end of his life: *qvantus artifex morior*!, [What an artist dies with me!] then I see in this feared and scorned ruler of Rome nothing better than a fool. I hold that every offensive folly is properly grafted on to two passions, arrogance and greediness. Both inclinations are unjust and are therefore hated, both are insipid in their nature, and their end destroys itself. The arrogant person expresses an unconcealed presumption of his advantage over others by a clear disdain for them. He believes that he is honored when he is hissed at, because there is nothing clearer than that his disrespect for others stirs up their vanity against the presumptuous person. The greedy person believes that he needs a great deal and cannot possibly do without the least of his goods; however, he actually does without all of them by sequestering them through parsimony. The delusion of arrogance makes in part *silly*, in part *inflated* fools, according to whether silly inconstancy or rigid stupidity has taken possession of the empty head. Stingy avarice has from time immemorial given occasion for many ridiculous stories which could hardly be more strangely concocted than they actually occured. The foolish person is not wise; the fool is not clever. The mockery that the foolish person draws on himself is amusing and sparing, the fool earns the sharpest scourge of the satirist, yet he still does not feel it. One may not fully despair that a foolish person could still be made shrewd. But he who thinks of making a fool clever is washing a Moor. The reason is that in the former a true and natural inclination reigns which at most fetters reason, but in the latter a silly phantom reigns that reverses reason's principles. I will leave it to others to decide whether one has actual cause to be troubled about Holberg's strange prediction, namely that the daily increase in fools is a matter of concern and gives rise to fears that they could eventually get it into their heads to found the fifth monarchy.[2] Supposing, however, that they were up to this, they might nevertheless not get too excited at that because one could easily whisper in the other's ear what the wellknown jester of a neighboring court yelled to the students who ran after him as he rode through a Polish town in fool's attire: "You gentlemen, be industrious, learn something, because if we are too many, then we all can no longer have bread."

I come now from the frailties of the head which are despised and scoffed at to those which one generally looks upon with pity, or from those which do not suspend civil community to those in which official care provision takes an interest and for whom it makes arrangements. I divide these maladies in two, into those of impotency and into those of reversal. The first come under the general appellation of imbecility, the second under the name of the *disturbed mind*. The imbecile finds himself in a great impotency of memory, reason, and generally even of sensations. This ill is for the most part incurable, for if it is difficult to remove the wild disorders of the disturbed brain, then it must be almost impossible to pour new life into its expired organs. The appearances of this weakness, which never allow the unfortunate person to leave the state of childhood, are too well known for it to be necessary to dwell long on this.

The frailties of the disturbed head can be brought under as many different main genera as there are mental capacities that are afflicted by it. I believe to be able to organize them all together under the following three divisions: first, the reversal of the concepts of experience in *derangement*, second, the power of judgment brought into disorder by this experience in *dementia*, third, reason that has become reversed with respect to more universal judgments in *insanity*. All remaining appearances of the sick brain can be viewed, it seems to me, either as different degrees of the cases mentioned or as an unfortunate coalition of these ills among one another, or, finally, as the engrafting of these ills on powerful passions, and can be subordinated under the classes cited.

With respect to the first ill, namely derangement, I explain its appearances in the following way. The soul of every human being is occupied even in the healthiest state with painting all kinds of images of things that are not present, or with completing some imperfect resemblance in the representation of present things through one or another chimerical trait which the creative poetic capacity draws into the sensation. One has no cause at all to believe that in the state of being awake our mind follows other laws than in sleep. Rather it is to be conjectured that in the former case the lively sensible impressions only obscure and render unrecognizable the more fragile chimerical images, while they possess their whole strength in sleep, in which the access to the soul is closed to all outer impressions. It is therefore no wonder that dreams are held for truthful experiences of actual things, as long as they last. Since they are then the strongest representations in the soul, they are in this state exactly what the sensations are in being awake. Now let us suppose that certain chimeras, no matter from which cause, had damaged, as it were, one or other organ of the brain such that the impression on that organ had become just as deep and at the same time just as correct as a sensation could make it, then, given good sound reason, this phantom would nevertheless have to be taken for an actual experience even in being awake. For it would be in vain to set rational arguments against a sensation or that representation which resembles the latter in strength, since the senses provide a far greater conviction regarding actual things than an inference of reason.

At least someone bewitched by these chimeras can never be brought by reasoning to doubting the actuality of his presumed sensation. One also finds that persons who show enough mature reason in other cases nevertheless firmly insist upon having seen with full attention who knows what ghostly shapes and distorted faces, and that they are even refined enough to place their imagined experience in connection with many a subtle judgment of reason. This property of the disturbed person, due to which, while being awake and without a particularly noticeable degree of a vehement malady, he is used to representing certain things as clearly sensed of which nevertheless nothing is present, is *derangement*. The deranged person is thus a dreamer in waking. If the usual illusion of his senses is only in part a chimera, but for the most part an actual sensation, then he who is in a higher degree predisposed to such reversal is a *fantast*. When after waking up we lie in an idle and gentle distraction, our imagination draws the irregular figures such as those of the bedroom curtains or of certain spots on a near wall, into human shapes, and this with a seeming correctness that entertains us in a not unpleasant manner but the illusion of which we dispel the moment we want to. We dream then only iw part and have the chimera in our power. If something similar happens in a higher degree without the attention of the waking person being able to detach the illusion in the misleading imagination, then this reversal lets us conjecture a fantast. Incidentally, this self-deception in sensations is very common, and as long as it is only moderate it will be spared with such an appellation, although, if a passion is added to it, this same mental weakness can degenerate into actual fantastic mania. Otherwise human beings do not see through an ordinary delusion to what is there but rather what their inclination depicts for them: the natural history collector sees cities in florentine stone, the devout person the passion story in the speckled marble, some lady sees the shadow of two lovers on the moon in a telescope, but her pastor two church steeples. Fear turns the rays of the northern light into spears and swords and in the twilight a sign post into a giant ghost.

The fantastic mental condition is nowhere more common than in hypochondria. The chimeras which this malady hatches do not properly deceive the outer senses but only provide the hypochondriac with an illusory sensation of his own state, either of the body or of the soul, which is, for the most part, an empty whim. The hypochondriac has an ill which, regardless which place it may have as its main seat, nevertheless in all likelihood migrates incessantly through the nerve tissue to all parts of the body. It draws above all a melancholic haze around the seat of the soul such that the patient feels in himself the illusion of almost all maladies of which he as much as hears. Therefore he talks of nothing more gladly than of his indisposition, he likes to read medical books, he recognizes everywhere his own misfortunes; in society he may even suddenly find himself in a good mood, and then he laughs a lot, dines well and generally has the look of a healthy human being. As regards his inner fantastic mania, the images in his brain often receive a strength and duration that is burdensome for him. If there is a ridiculous figure in his head (even if he himself recognizes it as only an image of fantasy) and if this whim coaxes an unbecoming laugh out of him in the presence of others without him indicating the cause of it, or if all kinds of obscure representations excite a forceful drive in him to start something evil, the eruption of which he himself is anxiously apprehensive about, and which nevertheless never comes to pass: then his state bears a strong resemblance to that of the deranged person, except that it is not that serious. The ill is not deeply rooted and lifts itself, in so far as the mind is concerned, usually either by itself or through some medication. One and the same representation affects the sensation in quite different degrees according to the different mental state of human beings. Therefore there is a kind of fantastic mania that is attributed to someone only because the degree of the feeling through which he is affected by certain objects is judged to be excessive for the moderate, healthy head. In this regard, the *melancholic* is a fantast with respect to life's ills. Love has quite a number of fantastic raptures, and the fine artifice of the ancient governments consisted in making the citizens into fantasts regarding the sense of public well-being. If someone is more excited by a moral sensation than by a principle, and this to a larger extent than others could imagine according to their own insipid and often ignoble feeling, then he is a fantast in their opinion. Let us place Aristides among usurers, *Epictetus* among courtiers and *Jean-Jacques Rousseau* among the doctors of the Sorbonne. I think I hear loud derision and a hundred voices shout: *What fantasts*!

This two-sided appearance of fantasy in moral sensations that are in themselves good is *enthusiasm*, and nothing great has ever been accomplished in the world without it. Things stand quite differently with the *fanatic* (*visionary, enthusiast*). The latter is properly a deranged person with presumed immediate inspiration and a great familiarity with the powers of the heavens. Human nature knows no more dangerous illusion. If its outbreak is new, if the deceived human being has talents and the masses are prepared to diligently accept this leaven, then even the state occasionally suffers raptures. Enthusiasm leads the exalted person to extremes, *Muhammad* to the prince's throne and *John of Leyden* to the scaffold. To a certain extent, I can also count the disturbed *faculty of recollection* among the reversedness of the head, in so far as it concerns the concepts of experience. For it deceives the miserable person who is afflicted by it through chimerical representations of who knows what a previous state, which actually never existed. Someone who speaks of the goods that he alleges to have possessed formerly or of the kingdom that he had, and who otherwise does not noticeably deceive himself with regard to his present state, is a deranged person with regard to recollection. The aged grumbler, who strongly believes that the world was more orderly and the human beings were better in his youth, is a fantast with regard to recollection.

Up to this point the power of the understanding is not actually attacked in the disturbed head, at least it is not necessary that it be; for the mistake actually resides only in the concepts. Provided one accepts the reversed sensation as true, the judgments themselves can be quite correct, even extraordinarily reasonable. A disturbance of the understanding on the contrary consists in judging in a completely reversed manner from otherwise correct experience; and from this malady the first degree is dementia, which acts contrary to the common rules of the understanding in the immediate judgments from experience. The *demented person* sees or remembers objects as correctly as every healthy person, only he ordinarily explains the behavior of other human beings through an absurd delusion as referring to himself and believes that he is able to read out of it who knows what suspicious intentions, which they never have in mind. Hearing him, one would believe that the whole town is occupied with him. The market people who deal with one another and by chance glance at him are plotting against him, the night watchman calls out to play pranks at him, in short, he sees nothing but a universal conspiracy against himself. The melancholic is a gloomy person who is demented with respect to his sad or offensive conjectures. But there are also all kinds of amusing dementia, and the amorous passion flatters itself or is tormented with many strange interpretations that resemble dementia. An arrogant person is to a certain measure a demented person who concludes from the conduct of others staring at him in scorn that they admire him. The second degree of the head that is disturbed with respect to the higher power of cognition is properly reason brought into disorder, in so far as it errs in a nonsensical manner in imagined more subtle judgments concerning universal concepts, and can be called *insanity*. In the higher degree of this disturbance all kinds of presumed excessively subtle insights swarm through the burned-out brain: the contrived length of the ocean, the interpretation of prophecies, or who knows what hotchpotch of imprudent brain teasing. If the unfortunate person at the same time overlooks the judgments of experience, then he is called crazy. But there is the case where there are many underlying correct judgments of experience, except that, due the novelty and number of consequences presented to him by his wit, his sensation is so intoxicated that he no longer pays attention to the correctness of the connection of these judgments. In that case often a very glittering semblance of dementia arises that can exist along with great *genius* to the extent that slow reason is no longer able to accompany the excited wit. The state of the disturbed head that makes it unreceptive to outer sensations is *amentia*; in so far as rage rules in the latter it is called *raving*. Despair is a temporary dementedness in someone who is hopeless. The raging vehemence of a disturbed person is generally called *frenzy*. The frantic, in so far as he is demented, is mad.

The human being in the state of nature can only be subject to a few follies and hardly any foolishness. His needs always keep him close to experience and provide his sound understanding with such easy occupation that he hardly notices that he needs understanding for his actions. Indolence moderates his coarse and common desires, leaving enough power to the small amount of the power of judgment which he needs to rule over those desires to his greatest advantage. From where should he draw the material for foolishness, since, unconcerned about another's judgment as he is, he can be neither vain nor inflated? Since he has no idea at all of the worth of goods he has not enjoyed, he is safe from the absurdity of stingy avarice, and because not much wit finds entrance to his head, he is just as well secured against every craziness. In like manner the disturbance of the mind can occur only seldom in this state of simplicity. Had the brain of the savage sustained some shock, I do not know where the fantastic mania should come from to displace the ordinary sensations that alone occupy him incessantly. Which dementia can well befall him since he never has cause to venture far in his judgment? Insanity, however, is surely wholly and entirely beyond his capacity. If he is ill in the head, he will be either idiotic or mad, and this, too, should happen most rarely, since he is for the most part healthy because he is free and in motion. The means of leavening for all of these corruptions can properly be found in the civil constitution, which, even if it does not produce them, nevertheless serves to entertain and aggravate them. The understanding, in so far as it is sufficient for the necessities and the simple pleasures of life, is a *sound understanding*, however, in so far as it is required for artificial exuberance, be it in enjoyment or in the sciences, is the refined *understanding*. Thus the sound understanding of the citizen would already be a very refined understanding for the natural human being, and the concepts which are presupposed by a refined understanding in certain estates are no longer suited for those who are closer to the simplicity of nature, at least in terms of their insights, and those concepts usually make fools out of them when they take them over. Abbot *Terrasson* differentiates somewhere the ones of a disturbed mind into those who infer correctly from false representations and those who infer wrongly from correct representations. This division seems to be in agreement with the propositions advanced earlier. In those of the first type, the fantasts or deranged persons, it is not the understanding that properly suffers but only the faculty that awakens the concepts in the soul of which the power of judgment afterward makes use by comparing them. These sick people can be well opposed by judgments of reason, if not to put an end to their ill, at least still to ease it. However, since in those of the second kind, the demented and insane persons, the understanding itself is attacked, it is not only foolish to reason with them (because they would not be demented if they could grasp these rational arguments), but it is also extremely detrimental. For one thus gives their reversed head only new material for concocting absurdities; contradiction does not better them, rather it excites them, and it is entirely necessary in dealing with them to assume an indifferent and kind demeanor, as though one did not notice at all that their understanding was lacking something.

I have designated the frailties of the power of cognition *maladies of the head*, just as one calls the corruption of the will a *malady of the heart*. I have also only paid attention to their appearances in the mind without wanting to scout out their roots, which may well lie in the body and indeed may have their main seat more in the intestines than in the brain, as the popular weekly journal that is generally well known under the name of The Physician, plausibly sets forth in its 150th, 151st, and 152nd issues. I can not even in any way convince myself that the disturbance of the mind originates from pride, love, too much reflection, and who knows what misuse of the powers of the soul, as is generally believed. This judgment, which makes of his misfortune a reason for scornful reproaches to the diseased person, is very unkind and is occasioned by a common mistake according to which one tends to confuse cause and effect. When one pays attention only a little to the examples, one sees that first the body suffers, that in the beginning, when the germ of the malady develops unnoticed, an ambiguous reversedness is felt which does not yet give suspicion of a disturbance of the mind, and which expresses itself in strange amorous whims or an inflated demeanor or in vain melancholic brooding. With time the malady breaks out and gives occasion to locate its ground in the immediately preceding state of the mind. But one should rather say that the human being became arrogant because he was already disturbed to some degree, than that he was disturbed because he was so arrogant. These sad ills still permit hope of a fortunate recovery, if only they are not hereditary, and it is the physician whose assistance one chiefly has to seek in this. Yet, for honor's sake, I would rather not exclude the philosopher, who could prescribe the diet of the mind – but on the condition that, as also for most of his other occupations, he requires no payment for this one. In recognition, the physician would also not refuse his assistance to the philosopher, if the latter attempted now and then the great, but always futile cure of foolishness. He would, e.g., in the case of the frenzy of a *learned crier* consider whether cathartic means taken in strengthened dosage should not be successful against it. If, according to the observations of *Swift*, a bad poem is merely a purification of the brain through which many detrimental moistures are withdrawn for the relief of the sick poet, why should not a miserable brooding piece of writing be the same as well? In this case, however, it would be advisable to assign nature another path to purification so that he would be thoroughly and quietly purged of the ill without disturbing the common wealth through this.

Inquiry Concerning the Distinctness of the Principles of Natural Theology and Morality

Being an answer to the question proposed for consideration by the Berlin Royal Academy of Sciences for the year 1763

Verum animo satis haec vestigia parva sagaci

Sunt, per quae possis cognoscere caetera tute

[But to a wise spirit these small clues will be sufficient:

by their means you can safely come to know the rest.]

Introduction

The question proposed for consideration is such that, if it is appropriately answered, higher philosophy must as a result acquire a determine form. If the method for attaining the highest possible degree of certainty in this type of cognition has been established, and if the nature of this kind of conviction has been properly understood, then the following effect will be produced: the endless instability of opinions and scholarly sects will be replaced by an immutable rule which will govern didactic method and unite reflective minds in a single effort. It was in this way that, in natural science, Newton's method transformed the chaos of physical hypotheses into a secure procedure based on experience and geometry. But what method is this treatise itself to adopt, granted that it is a treatise in which metaphysics is to be shown the true degree of certainty to which it may aspire, as well as the path by which the certainty may be attained? If what is presented in this treatise is itself metaphysics, then the judgment of the treatise will be no more certain than has been that science which hopes to benefit from our inquiry by acquiring some permanence and stability; and then all our efforts will have been in vain. I shall, therefore, ensure that my treatise contains nothing but empirical propositions which are certain, and the inferences which are drawn immediately from them. I shall rely neither on the doctrines of the philosophers, the uncertainty of which is the very occasion of this present inquiry, nor on definitions, which so often lead to error. The method I shall employ will be simple and cautious. Some of the things I shall have to say may be found to be lacking in certainty; but such things will only have an elucidatory function and will not be employed for purposes of proof.

First Reflection: General comparison of the manner in which certainty is attained in mathematical cognition with the manner in which certainty is attained in philosophical cognition

§ I Mathematics arrives at all its definitions synthetically, whereas philosophy arrives at its definitions analytically

There are two ways in which one can arrive at a general concept: either by the *arbitrary combination* of concepts, or by *separating out* that cognition which has been rendered distinct by means of analysis. Mathematics only ever draws up its definitions in the first way. For example, think arbitrarily of four straight lines bounding a plane surface so that the opposite sides are not parallel to each other. Let this figure be called a *trapezium*. The concept which I am defining is not given prior to the definition itself; on the contrary, it only comes into existence as a result of that definition. Whatever the concept of a cone may ordinarily signify, in mathematics the concept is the product of the arbitrary representation of a right-angled triangle which is rotated on one of its sides. In this and in all other cases the definition obviously comes into being as a result of *synthesis.*

The situation is entirely different in the case of philosophical definitions. In philosophy, the concept of a thing is always given, albeit confusedly or in an insufficiently determinate fashion. The concept has to be analyzed; the characteristic marks which have been separated out and the concept which has been given have to be compared with each other in all kinds of contexts; and this abstract thought must be rendered complete and determinate. For example, everyone has a concept of time.

But suppose that that concept has to be defined. The idea of time has to be examined in all kinds of relation if its characteristic marks are to be discovered by means of analysis: different characteristic marks which have been abstracted have to be combined together to see whether they yield an adequate concept; they have to be collated with each other to see whether one characteristic mark does not partly include another within itself. If, in this case, I had tried to arrive at a definition of time synthetically, it would have had to have been a happy coincidence indeed if the concept, thus reached synthetically, had been exactly the same as that which completely expresses the idea of time which is given to us.

Nonetheless, it will be said, philosophers sometimes offer synthetic definitions as well, and mathematicians on occasion offer definitions which are analytic. A case in point would be that of a philosopher arbitrarily thinking of a substance endowed with the faculty of reason and calling it a spirit. My reply, however, is this: such determinations of the meaning of a word are never philosophical definitions. If they are to be called definitions at all, then they are merely grammatical definitions. For no philosophy is needed to say what name is to be attached to an arbitrary concept. Leibwiz imagined a simple substance which had nothing but obscure representations, and he called it a *slumbering monad*. But, in doing so, he did not define the monad. He merely invented it, for the concept of a monad was not given to him but created by him. Mathematicians, on the other hand, it must be admitted, sometimes have offered analytic definitions. But it must also be said that for them to do so is always a mistake. It was in this way that Wolff considered similarity in geometry: he looked at it with a philosophical eye, with a view to subsuming the geometrical concept of similarity under the general concept. But he could have spared himself the trouble. If I think of figures, in which the angles enclosed by the lines of the perimeter are equal to each other, and in which the sides enclosing those angles stand in identical relations to each other – such a figure could always be regarded as the definition of similarity between figures, and likewise with the other similarities between spaces. The general definition of similarity is of no concern whatever to the geometer. It is fortunate for mathematics that, even though the geometer from time to time gets involved in the business of furnishing analytic definitions as a result of a false conception of his task, in the end nothing is actually inferred from such definitions, or, at any rate, the immediate inferences which he draws ultimately constitute the mathematical definition itself. Otherwise this science would be liable to exactly the same wretched discord as philosophy itself.

The mathematician deals with concepts which can often be given a philosophical definition as well. An example is the concept of space in general. But he accepts such a concept *given* in accordance with his clear and ordinary representation. It sometimes happens that philosophical definitions are given to him from other sciences; this happens especially in applied mathematics. The definition of fluidity is a case in point. But, in a case like that, the definition does not arise within mathematics itself, it is merely employed there. It is the business of philosophy to analyze concepts which are given in a confused fashion, and to render them complete and determinate.

The business of mathematics, however, is that of combining and comparing given concepts of magnitudes, which are clear and certain, with a view to establishing what can be inferred from them.

§ 2 Mathematics, in its analyses, proofs, and inferences examines the universal under signs in concreto; philosophy examines the universal by means of signs in abstracto

Since we are here treating our propositions only as conclusions derived immediately from our experiences, I *first of all* appeal, with regard to the present matter, to arithmetic, both the general arithmetic of indeterminate magnitudes and the arithmetic of numbers, where the relation of magnitude to unity is determinate. In both kinds of arithmetic, there are posited first of all not things themselves but their signs, together with the special designations of their increase or decrease, their relations etc. Thereafter, one operates with these signs according to easy and certain rules, by means of substitution, combination, subtraction, and many kinds of transformation, so that the things signified are themselves completely forgotten in the process, until eventually, when the conclusion is drawn, the meaning of the symbolic conclusion is deciphered. *Secondly*, I would draw attention to the fact that in geometry, in order, for example, to discover the properties of all circles, one circle is drawn; and in this one circle, instead of drawing all the possible lines which could intersect each other within it, two lines only are drawn. The relations which hold between these two lines are proved; and the universal rule, which governs the relations holding between intersecting lines in all circles whatever, is considered in these two lines *in concreto*.

If the procedure of philosophy is compared with that of geometry it becomes apparent that they are completely different. The signs employed in philosophical reflection are never anything other than words. And words can neither show in their composition the constituent concepts of which the whole idea, indicated by the word, consists; nor are they capable of indicating in their combinations the relations of the philosophical [2:29] thoughts to each other. Hence, in reflection in this kind of cognition, one has to focus one's attention on the thing itself: one is constrained to represent the universal *in abstracto* without being able to avail oneself of that important device which facilitates thought and which consists in handling individual signs rather than the universal concepts of the things themselves. Suppose, for example, that the geometer wishes to demonstrate that space is infinitely divisible. He will take, for example, a straight line standing vertically between two parallel lines; from a point on one of these parallel lines he will draw lines to intersect the other two lines. By means of this symbol he recognizes with the greatest certainty that the division can be carried on *ad infinitum*. By contrast, if the philosopher wishes to demonstrate, say, that all bodies consist of simple substances, he will first of all assure himself that bodies in general are wholes composed of substances, and that, as far as these substances are concerned, composition is an accidental state, without which they could exist just as well; he will then infer, therefore, that all composition in a body could be suspended in imagination, but in such a way that the substances, of which the body consists, would continue to exist; and since that which remains of a compound when all composition whatever has been canceled is simple, he will conclude that bodies must consist of simple substances. In this case, neither figures nor visible signs are capable of expressing either the thoughts or the relations which hold between them.

Nor can abstract reflection be replaced by the transposition of signs in accordance with rules, the representation of the things themselves being replaced in this procedure by the clearer and the easier representation of the signs. The universal must rather be considered *in abstracto*.

§3 In mathematics, unanalyzable concepts and indemonstrable propositions are few in number, whereas in philosophy they are innumerable

The concepts of magnitude in general, of unity, of plurality, of space, and so on, are, at least in mathematics, unanalyzable. That is to say, their analysis and definition do not belong to this science at all. I am well aware of the fact that geometers often confuse the boundaries between the different sciences, and on occasion wish to engage in philosophical speculation in mathematics. Thus, they seek to define concepts such as those just mentioned, although the definition in such a case has no mathematical consequences at all. But this much is certain: any concept is unanalyzable with respect to a given discipline if, irrespective of whether or not it be definable elsewhere, it need not be defined, not, at any rate, in this discipline. And I have said that concepts are rare in mathematics. I shall go still further and deny that, strictly speaking, any such concepts at all can occur in mathematics; by which I mean that their definition by means of conceptual analysis does not belong to mathematical cognition – assuming, that is, that it is actually possible elsewhere. For mathematics never defines a given concept by means of analysis; it rather defines an object by means of arbitrary combination; and the thought of that object first becomes possible in virtue of that arbitrary combination.

If one compares philosophy with this, what a difference becomes apparent. In all its disciplines, and particularly in metaphysics, every analysis which can occur is actually necessary, for both the distinctness of the cognition and the possibility of valid inferences depend upon such analysis. But it is obvious from the start that the analysis will inevitably lead to concepts which are unanalyzable. These unanalyzable concepts will be unanalyzable either in and for themselves or relatively to us. It is further evident that there will be uncommonly many such unanalyzable concepts, for it is impossible that universal cognition of such great complexity should be constructed from only a few fundamental concepts.

For this reason, there are many concepts which are scarcely capable of analysis at all, for example, the concept of a *representation*, the *concepts* of *being next* to each other and *being* after each other. Other concepts can only be partially analyzed, for example, the concepts of space, time, and the many *different feelings* of the human soul, such as the feeling of the *sublime*, the beautiful, the *disgusting*, and so forth. Without exact knowledge and analysis of these concepts, the springs of our nature will not be sufficiently understood; and yet, in the case of these concepts, a careful observer will notice that the analyses are far from satisfactory. I admit that the definitions of *pleasure* and *displeasure*, of desire and *aversion*, and of numberless other such concepts, have never been furnished by means of adequate analyses. Nor am I surprised by this *unanalyzability*. For concepts which are as diverse in character as this must presumably be based upon different elementary concepts. The error, committed by some, of treating all such cognitions as if they could be completely analyzed into a few simple concepts is like the error into which the early physicists fell. They were guilty, namely, of the mistake of supposing that all the matter of which nature is constituted consists of the so-called four elements – a view which has been discredited by more careful observation.

Furthermore, there are only a few fundamental *indemonstrable propositions* in mathematics. And even if they admit of proof elsewhere, they are   [2 : 2 8] nonetheless regarded as immediately certain in this science. Examples of such propositions are: the whole is *equal* to all its parts *takes* together; there can *only* be owe straight *line between* two *points*, and so forth. Mathematicians are accustomed to setting up such principles at the beginning of their inquiries so that it is clear that these are the only obvious propositions which are immediately presupposed as true, and that all other propositions are subject to strict proof.

If a comparison were to be made between this and philosophy, and, in particular between this and metaphysics, I should like to see drawn up a table of the indemonstrable propositions which lie at the foundation of these sciences throughout their whole extent. Such a table would constitute a scheme of immeasurable scope. But the most important business of higher philosophy consists in seeking out these indemonstrable fundamental truths; and the discovery of such truths will never cease as long as cognition of such a kind as this continues to grow. For, no matter what the object may be, those characteristic marks, which the understanding initially and immediately perceives in the object, constitute the data for exactly the same number of indemonstrable propositions, which then form the foundation on the basis of which definitions can then be drawn up. Before I set about the task of defining what space is, I clearly see that, since this concept is given to me, I must first of all, by analyzing it, seek out those characteristic marks which are initially and immediately thought in that concept. Adopting this approach, I notice that there is a manifold in space of which the parts are external to each other; I notice that this manifold is not constituted by substances, for the cognition I wish to acquire relates not to things in space but to space itself; and I notice that space can only have three dimensions etc. Propositions such as these can well be explained if they are *examined in concreto* so that they come to be cognized intuitively; but they can never be proved. For on what basis could such a proof be constructed, granted that these propositions constitute the first and the simplest thoughts I can have of my object, when I first call it to mind? In mathematics, the definitions are the first thought which I can entertain of the thing defined, for my concept of the object only comes into existence as a result of the definition. It is, therefore, absolutely absurd to regard the definitions as capable of proof. In philosophy, where the concept of the thing to be defined is given to me, that which is initially and immediately perceived in it must serve as an indemonstrable fundamental judgment, for since I do not yet possess a complete and distinct concept of the thing, but am only now beginning to look for such a concept, it follows that the fundamental judgment cannot be proved by reference to this concept. On the contrary, such a judgment serves to generate this distinct cognition and to produce the definition sought. Thus, I shall have to be in possession of these primary fundamental judgments prior to any philosophical definition of the things under examination. And here the only error which can occur beforehand is that of mistaking a derivative characteristic mark for one which is primary and fundamental. The following reflection will contain some considerations which will put this claim beyond doubt.

§ 4 The object of mathematics is easy and simple, whereas that of philosophy is difficult and involved

The object of mathematics is magnitude. And, in considering magnitude, mathematics is only concerned with how many times something is posited. This being the case, it is obvious that this science must be based upon a few, very clear fundamental principles of the general theory of magnitudes (which, strictly speaking, is general arithmetic). There, too, one sees the increase and decrease of magnitudes, their reduction to equal factors in the theory of roots – all of them originating from a few simple fundamental concepts. And a few fundamental concepts of space effect the application of this general cognition of magnitudes to geometry. In order to convince oneself of the truth of what I am saying here all one needs to do is contrast, for example, the ease one has in understanding an arithmetical object which contains an immense multiplicity, with the much greater difficulty one experiences in attempting to grasp a philosophical idea, in which one is trying to understand only a little. The relation of a trillion to unity is understood with complete distinctness, whereas even today the philosophers have not yet succeeded in explaining the concept of freedom in terms of its elements, that is to say, in terms of the simple and familiar concepts of which it is composed. In other words, there are infinitely many qualities which constitute the real object of philosophy, and distinguishing them from each other is an extremely strenuous business. Likewise, it is far more difficult to disentangle complex and involved cognition by means of analysis than it is to combine simple given cognitions by means of synthesis and thus to establish conclusions. I know that there are many people who find philosophy a great deal easier than higher mathematics. But what such people understand by philosophy is simply what they find in books which bear the title. The outcome of the two inquiries shows the difference between them. Claims to philosophical cognition generally enjoy the fate of opinions and are like the meteors,

the brilliance of which is no guarantee of their endurance. Claims to philosophical cognition vanish, but mathematics endures. Metaphysics is without doubt the most difficult of all the things into which man has insight. But so far no metaphysics has ever been written. The question posed for consideration by the Royal Academy of Sciences in Berlin shows that there is good reason to ask about the path in which one proposes to search for metaphysical understanding in the first place.

Second Reflection: The only method for attaining the highest possible degree of certainty in metaphysics

Metaphysics is nothing other than the philosophy of the fundamental principles of our cognition. Accordingly, what was established in the preceding reflection about mathematical cognition in comparison with philosophy will also apply to metaphysics. We have seen that the differences which are to be found between cognition in mathematics and cognition in philosophy are substantial and essential. And in this connection, one can say with Bishop *Warburton* that nothing has been more damaging to philosophy than mathematics, and in particular the *imitation* of its method in contexts where it cannot possibly be employed. The *application* of the mathematical method in those parts of philosophy involving cognition of magnitudes is something quite different, and its utility is immeasurable.

In mathematics I begin with the definition of my object, for example, of a triangle, or a circle, or whatever. In metaphysics I may never begin with a definition. Far from being the first thing I know about the object, the definition is nearly always the last thing I come to know. In mathematics, namely, I have no concept of my object at all until it is furnished by the definition. In metaphysics I have a concept which is already given to me, although it is a confused one. My task is to search for the distinct, complete, and determinate concept. How then am I to begin? *Augustine* said: "I know perfectly well what time is, but if someone asks me what it is I do not know." In such a case as this, many operations have to be performed in unfolding obscure ideas, in comparing them with each other, in subordinating them to each other and in limiting them by each other. And I would go as far as to say that, although much that is true and much that is penetrating has been said about time, nonetheless no real definition has ever been given of time. For, as far as the nominal definition is concerned, it is of little or no use to us, for even without the nominal definition the word is understood well enough not to be misused. If we had as many correct definitions of time as there are definitions to be found in the books devoted to the subject, with what certainty could inferences be made and conclusions drawn. But experience teaches us the opposite.

In philosophy and in particular in metaphysics, one can often come to know a great deal about an object with distinctness and certainty, and even establish reliable conclusions on that basis prior to having a definition of that object, and even, indeed, when one had no intention of furnishing one. In the case of any particular thing, I can be immediately certain about a number of different predicates, even though I am not acquainted with a sufficiently large number of them to be able to furnish a completely determinate *concept* of the *thing*, in other words, a definition. Even if I had never defined what an appetite was, I should still be able to say with certainty that every appetite presupposed the representation of the object of the appetite; that this representation was an anticipation of what was to come in the future; that the feeling of pleasure was connected with it; and so forth. Everyone is constantly aware of all this in the immediate consciousness of appetite. One might perhaps eventually be able to arrive at a definition of appetite on the basis of such remarks as these, once they had been compared with each other. But as long as it is possible to establish what one is seeking by inference from a few immediately certain characteristic marks of the thing in question, and to do so without a definition, there is no need to venture on an undertaking which is so precarious. In mathematics, as is known, the situation is completely different.

In mathematics, the significance of the signs employed is certain, for it is not difficult to know what the significance was which one wished to attribute to those signs. In philosophy generally and in metaphysics in particular, words acquire their meaning as a result of linguistic usage, unless, that is, the meaning has been more precisely determined by means of logical limitation. But it frequently happens that the same words are employed for concepts which, while very similar, nonetheless conceal within themselves considerable differences. For this reason, whenever such a concept is applied, even though one's terminology may seem to be fully sanctioned by linguistic usage, one must still pay careful attention to whether it is really the same concept which is connected here with the same sign. We say that a person distinguishes gold from brass if, for example, he recognizes that the density to be found in the one metal is not to be found in the other. We also say that an animal distinguishes one kind of provender from another if it eats the one and leaves the other untouched. Here, the word "distinguishes" is being used in both cases even though, in the first case, it means "recognize the difference," which is something which can never occur without *judging*, whereas in the second case it merely signifies that *different actions* are performed when different representations are present, and in this case it is not necessary that a judgment should occur. All that we perceive in the case of the animal is that it is impelled to perform different actions by different sensations; and that is something which is perfectly possible without its in the least needing to make a judgment about similarity or difference.

From all this there flow quite naturally the rules which govern the method by which alone the highest possible degree of metaphysical certainty can be attained. These rules are quite different from those which have hitherto been followed. They promise, if they are adopted, to produce a happier outcome than could ever have been expected on a different path. The first and the most important *rule* is this: one ought not to start with definitions, unless that is, one is merely seeking a nominal definition, such as, for example, the definition: that of which the opposite is impossible is necessary. But even then there are only a few cases where one can confidently establish a distinctly determinate concept right at the very beginning. One ought, rather, to begin by carefully searching out what is immediately certain in one's object, even before one has its definition. Having established what is immediately certain in the object of one's inquiry, one then proceeds to draw conclusions from it. One's chief concern will be to arrive only at judgments about the object which are true and completely certain. And in doing this, one will not make an elaborate parade of one's hope of arriving at a definition. Indeed, one will never venture to offer such a definition, until one has to concede the definition, once it has presented itself on the basis of the most certain of judgments. The *second rule* is this: one ought particularly to distinguish those judgments which have been immediately made about the object and relate to what one initially encountered in that object with certainty. Having established for certain that none of these judgments is contained in another, these judgments are to be placed at the beginning of one's inquiry, as the foundation of all one's inferences, like the axioms of geometry. It follows from this that, when one is engaged in metaphysical reflection, one ought always particularly to distinguish what is known for certain, even if that knowledge does not amount to a great deal. Nonetheless, one may experiment with cognitions which are not certain to see whether they may not put us on the track of certain cognition; but care must be taken to ensure that the two sorts of cognition are not confused. I shall not mention the other rules of procedure which this method has in common with every other rational method. I shall merely proceed to render these rules distinct by means of examples.

The true method of metaphysics is basically the same as that introduced by *Newton* into natural science and which has been of such benefit to it. *Newton's* method maintains that one ought, on the basis of certain experience and, if need be, with the help of geometry, to seek out the rules in accordance with which certain phenomena of nature occur. Even if one does not discover the fundamental principle of these occurrences in the bodies themselves, it is nonetheless certain that they operate in accordance with this law. Complex natural events are explained once it has been clearly shown how they are governed by these well-established rules. Likewise in metaphysics: by means of certain inner experience, that is to say, by means of an immediate and self-evident inner consciousness, seek out those characteristic marks which are certainly to be found in the concept of any general property. And even if you are not acquainted with the complete essence of the thing, you can still safely employ those characteristic marks to infer a great deal from them about the thing in question.

Example of the only certain method for metaphysics illustrated by reference to our cognition of the nature of bodies

For the sake of brevity, I refer the reader to the proof which is briefly given at the end of Section 2 of the First Reflection. I do so with a view to first establishing here as my foundation the proposition: all bodies must consist of simple substances. Without determining what a body is, I nonetheless know for certain that it consists of parts which would exist even if they were not combined together. And if the concept of a substance is an abstracted concept, it is without doubt one which has been arrived at by a process of abstraction from the corporeal things which exist in the world. But it is not even necessary to call them substances. It is enough that one can, with the greatest certainty, infer from them that bodies consist of simple parts. The self-evident analysis of this proposition could easily be offered, but it would be too lengthy to present here. Now, employing infallible proofs of geometry, I can demonstrate that space does not consist of simple parts; the arguments involved are sufficiently well known. It follows that there is a determinate number of parts in each body, and that they are all simple, and that there is an equal number of parts of space occupied by the body, and they are all compound. It follows from this that each simple part of the body (each element) occupies a space.

Suppose that I now ask: What does "occupying a space" mean? Without troubling myself about the essence of space, I realize that, if space can be penetrated by anything without there being anything there to offer resistance, then one may, if need be, say that there was something in this space but never that the space was being occupied by it. By this means I cognize that a space is occupied by something if there is something there which offers resistance to a moving body attempting to penetrate that same space. But this resistance is impenetrability. Accordingly, bodies occupy space by means of impenetrability, But impenetrability is a force, for it expresses a resistance, that is to say, it expresses an action which is opposed to an external force. And the force which belongs to a body must also belong to the simple parts of which it is constituted. Accordingly, the elements of every body fill their space by means of the force of impenetrability. However, I proceed to ask whether the primary elements are not themselves extended since each element in the body fills a space? At this juncture, I can for once introduce a definition which is immediately certain. It is the definition, namely, that a thing is *extended* if, when it is posited in itself (*absolute*), it fills a space, just as each individual body, even if I imagine that nothing existed apart from it, would fill a space. However, if I consider an absolutely simple element, then, if it is posited on its own (with no connection with anything else), it is impossible that there should exist within it a multiplicity of parts existing externally to each other, and impossible that it should occupy a space *absolute*. It cannot, therefore, be extended. However, the cause of the element occupying a space is the force of impenetrability which it directs against numerous external things. I therefore realize that whereas the multiplicity of its external action flows from that fact, multiplicity in respect of inner parts does not. Hence, the fact that it occupies a space in the body (*in nexu aliis*) [in connection with other bodies] is not the reason for its being extended.

I shall just add a few words in order to reveal the shallowness of the proofs offered by the metaphysicians when, in accordance with their custom, they confidently establish their conclusions on the basis of definitions which have been laid down once and for all as the foundation of their argument. The conclusions instantly collapse if the definitions are defective. It is well known that most *Newtonians* go further than *Newton* himself and maintain that bodies, even at a distance, attract each other immediately (or, as they put it, through empty space). I do not propose to challenge the correctness of this proposition, which certainly has much to be said for it. What, however, I do wish to say is that metaphysics has not in the least refuted it. First of all, bodies are at a *distance* from each other if they are *not touching* each other. That is the exact meaning of the expression. Now, suppose that I ask what I mean by "touching". Without troubling about the definition, I realize that whenever I judge that I am touching a body I do so by reference to the resistance which the impenetrability of that body offers. For I find that this concept originates ultimately from the sense of touch. The judgment of the eye only produces the surmise that one body will touch another; it is only when one notices the resistance offered by impenetrability that the surmise is converted into certain knowledge. Thus, if I say that one body acts upon another immediately at a *distance* then this means that it acts on it immediately, but not by means of impenetrability. But it is by no means clear here why this should be impossible, unless, that is, someone shows either that impenetrability is the only force possessed by a body, or at least that a body cannot act on any other body immediately, without at the same time doing so by means of impenetrability. But this has never yet been proved, nor does it seem very likely that it ever will be. Accordingly, metaphysics, at least, has no sound reason to object to the idea of immediate attraction at a distance. However, let the arguments of the metaphysicians make their appearance. To start with, there appears the definition: The immediate and reciprocal presence of two bodies is touch. From this it follows that if two bodies act upon each other immediately, then they are touching each other. Things which are touching each other are not at a distance from each other. Therefore, two bodies never act immediately upon each other at a distance etc. The definition is surreptitious. Not every immediate presence is a touching, but only the immediate presence which is mediated by impenetrability. The rest is without foundation.

I shall now proceed with my treatise. It is clear from the example I have adduced that both in metaphysics and in other sciences there is a great

deal which can be said about an object with certainty, before it has been defined. In the present case, neither body nor space has been defined, and yet there are things which can be reliably said of both. What I am chiefly concerned to establish is this: in metaphysics one must proceed analytically throughout, for the business of metaphysics is actually the analysis of confused cognitions. If this procedure is compared with the procedure which is adopted by philosophers and which is currently in vogue in all schools of philosophy, one will be struck by how mistaken the practice of philosophers is. With them, the most abstracted concepts, at which the understanding naturally arrives last of all, constitute their starting point, and the reason is that the method of the mathematicians, which they wish to imitate throughout, is firmly fixed in their minds. This is why there is a strange difference to be found between metaphysics and all other sciences. In geometry and in the other branches of mathematics, one starts with what is easier and then one slowly advances to the more difficult operations. In metaphysics, one starts with what is the most difficult: one starts with possibility, with existence in general, with necessity and contingency, and so on – all of them concepts which demand great abstraction and close attention. And the reason for this is to be sought chiefly in the fact that the signs for these concepts undergo numerous and imperceptible modifications in use; and the differences between them must not be overlooked. One is told that one ought to proceed synthetically throughout. Definitions are thus set up right at the beginning, and conclusions are confidently drawn from them. Those who practice philosophy in this vein congratulate each other for having learnt the secret of thorough thought from the geometer. What they do not notice at all is the fact that geometers acquire their concepts by means of *synthesis*, whereas philosophers can only acquire their concepts by means of *analysis* – and that completely changes the method of thought.

If philosophers, having entered the natural path of sound reason, first seek out what they know for certain about the abstracted concept of an object (for example, space or time); and if they refrain from claiming to offer definitions; and if they base their conclusions on these certain data alone, making sure that, even though the sign for the concept in question has remained unchanged, the concept itself has not undergone modification whenever its application has changed – if philosophers adopt this approach then, although they may not, perhaps, have quite so many opinions to hawk around, the views they do have to offer will be of sound value. I should like to adduce one more example of this latter procedure. Most philosophers adduce as examples of obscure concepts those which we have in deep sleep. *Obscure* representations are representations of which we are not conscious. Now, some experiences show that we also have representations in deep sleep, and since we are not conscious of them it follows that they were obscure. In the case before us here, the term "*consciousness*" is ambiguous. Either one is not conscious that one has a representation, or one is not conscious that one has had a representation. The former signifies the obscurity of the representation as it occurs in the soul, while the latter signifies nothing more than that one does not remember the representation. Now, all that the example adduced shows is that there can be representations which one does not remember when one is awake; but from this it by no means follows that they may not have been clearly present in consciousness while one was sleeping. A case in point would be the example, adduced by Savvage, of the person suffering from catalepsy, or the ordinary actions of sleepwalkers. People have a tendency to jump too readily to conclusions, without paying attention to differing cases and investing the relevant concept with a significance appropriate to each respective instance. This may explain why, in the present case, no attention has been paid to what is probably a great mystery of nature: the fact, namely, that it is perhaps during sleep that the soul exercises its greatest facility in rational thought. The only objection which could be raised against this supposition is the fact that we have no recollection of such rational activity when we have woken up; but that proves nothing.

Metaphysics has a long way to go yet before it can proceed synthetically. It will only be when analysis has helped us towards concepts which are understood distinctly and in detail that it will be possible for synthesis to subsume compound cognitions under the simplest cognition, as happens in mathematics.

Third Reflection: On the nature of metaphysical certainty

§ I Philosophical certainty is altogether different in nature from mathematical certainty

One is certain if one knows that it is impossible that a cognition should be false. The degree of this certainty, taken objectively, depends upon the sufficiency in the characteristic marks of the necessity of a truth. But taken subjectively, the degree of certainty increases with the degree of intuition to be found in the cognition of this necessity. In both respects, mathematical certainty is of a different kind to philosophical certainty. I shall demonstrate this with the greatest possible clarity.

The human understanding, like any other force of nature, is governed by certain rules. Mistakes are made, not because the understanding combines concepts without rule, but because the characteristic mark which is not perceived in a thing is actually denied of it. One judges that that of which one is *not conscious* in a thing does *not exist*. Now, *firstly*, mathematics arrives at its concepts synthetically; it can say with certainty that what it did not intend to represent in the object by means of the definition is not contained in that object. For the concept of what has been defined only comes into existence by means of the definition; the concept has no other significance at all apart from that which is given to it by the definition. Compared with this, philosophy and particularly metaphysics are a great deal more uncertain in their definitions, should they venture to offer any. For the concept of that which is to be defined is given. Now, if one should fail to notice some characteristic mark or other, which nonetheless belongs to the adequate distinguishing of the concept in question, and if one judges that no such characteristic mark belongs to the complete concept, then the definition will be wrong and misleading. Numberless examples of such errors could be adduced, and for that very reason I refer only to the above example of touching. *Secondly*, mathematics, in its inferences and proofs, regards its universal knowledge under signs *in concreto*, whereas philosophy always regards its universal knowledge *in abstracto*, as existing alongside signs. And this constitutes a substantial difference in the way in which the two inquiries attain to certainty. For since signs in mathematics are sensible means to cognition, it follows that one can know that no concept has been overlooked, and that each particular comparison has been drawn in accordance with easily observed rules etc. And these things can be known with the degree of assurance characteristic of seeing something with one's own eyes. And in this, the attention is considerably facilitated by the fact that it does not have to think things in their universal representation; it has rather to think the signs as they occur in their particular cognition which, in this case, is sensible in character. By contrast, the only help which words, construed as the signs of philosophical cognition, afford is that of reminding us of the universal concepts which they signify. It is at all times necessary to be immediately aware of their significance. The pure understanding must be maintained in a state of constant attention; how easy it is for the characteristic mark of an abstracted concept to escape our attention without our noticing, for there is nothing sensible which can reveal to us the fact that the characteristic mark has been overlooked. And when that happens, different things are taken to be the same thing, and the result is error.

What we have established here is this: the grounds for supposing that one could not have erred in a philosophical cognition which was certain can never be as strong as those which present themselves in mathematics. But apart from this, the intuition involved in this cognition is, as far as its exactitude is concerned, greater in mathematics than it is in philosophy. And the reason for this is the fact that, in mathematics, the object is considered under sensible signs *in concreto*, whereas in philosophy the object is only ever considered in universal abstracted concepts; and the clarity of the impression made by such abstracted concepts can never be as great as that made by signs which are sensible in character. Furthermore, in geometry the signs are similar to the things signified, so that the certainty of geometry is even greater, though the certainty of algebra is no less reliable.

§ 2 Metaphysics is capable of a certainty which is sufficient to produce conviction

Certainty in metaphysics is of exactly the same kind as that in any other philosophical cognition, for the latter can only be certain if it is in accordance with the universal principles furnished by the former. We know from experience that, even outside mathematics, there are many cases where, in virtue of rational principles, we can be completely certain, and certain to the degree of conviction. Metaphysics is nothing but philosophy applied to insights of reason which are more general, and it cannot possibly differ from philosophy in this respect.

Errors do not arise simply because we do not know certain things. We make mistakes because we venture to make judgments, even though we do not know everything which is necessary for doing so. A large number of errors, indeed almost all of them, are due to this latter kind of overhastiness. You have certain knowledge of some of the predicates of a thing. Very well! Base your conclusions on this certain knowledge and you will not go wrong. But you insist on having a definition at all costs. And yet you are not sure that you know everything which is necessary to drawing up such a definition; nonetheless, you venture on such an undertaking and thus you fall into error. It is therefore possible to avoid errors, provided that one seeks out cognitions which are certain and distinct, and provided that one does not so lightly lay claim to be able to furnish definitions. Furthermore, you could also establish a substantial part of an indubitable conclusion, and do so with certainty; but do not, on any account, permit yourself to draw the whole conclusion, no matter how slight the difference may appear to be. I admit that the proof we have in our possession for establishing that the soul is not matter is a good one. But take care that you do not infer from this that the soul is not of a material nature. For this latter claim is universally taken to mean not merely that the soul is not matter, but also that it is not a simple substance of the kind which could be an element of matter. But this requires a separate proof – the proof, namely, that this thinking being does not exist in space in the way in which a corporeal element exists in space, that is to say, in virtue of impenetrability; it also requires proof that this thinking being could not, when combined with other thinking beings, constitute something extended, a conglomerate. But no proof has actually been given yet of these things. Such a proof, were it to be discovered, would indicate the incomprehensibility of the way in which a spirit is present in space.

§ The certainty of the first fundamental truths of metaphysics is not of a kind different from that of any other rational cognition, apart from mathematics

The philosophy of *Crusius* has recently claimed to give metaphysical cognition quite a different form. It has done so by refusing to concede to the law of contradiction the preeminent right to be regarded as the supreme and universal principle of all cognition. *Crusius* introduced a large number of other principles which were immediately certain and indemonstrable, and he maintained that the correctness of these principles could be established by appeal to the nature of our understanding, employing the rule that what I cannot think as other than true is true. Such principles include: what I cannot think as existing has never existed;

all things must be somewhere and somewhen, etc. I shall briefly indicate the true character of the first fundamental truths of metaphysics; at the same time, I shall offer a brief account of the true content of *Crusius'* method, which is not as different from that of the philosophy contained in this treatise as may, perhaps, be thought. On this basis, it will also be possible to establish in general the degree of possible certainty to which metaphysics can aspire.

All true propositions must be either affirmative or negative. The form of every *affirmation* consists in something being represented as a characteristic mark of a thing, that is to say, as identical with the characteristic mark of a thing. Thus, every affirmative judgment is true if the predicate is *identical* with the subject. And since the form of every *negation* consists in something being represented as in conflict with a thing, it follows that a negative judgment is true if the predicate *contradicts* the subject. The proposition, therefore, which expresses the essence of every affirmation and which accordingly contains the supreme formula of all affirmative judgments, runs as follows: to every subject there belongs a predicate which is identical with it. This is the law of *identity*. The proposition which expresses the essence of all negation is this: to no subject does there belong a predicate which contradicts it. This proposition is the law of *contradiction*, which is thus the fundamental formula of all negative judgments. These two principles together constitute the supreme universal principles, in the formal sense of the term, of human reason in its entirety. Most people have made the mistake of supposing that the law of contradiction is the principle of all truths whatever, whereas in fact it is only the principle of negative truths. Any proposition, however, is indemonstrable if it is immediately thought under one of these two supreme principles and if it cannot be thought in any other way. In other words, any proposition is indemonstrable if either the identity or the contradiction is to be found immediately in the concepts, and if the identity and the contradiction cannot or may not be understood through analysis by means of intermediate characteristic marks. All other propositions are capable of proof. The proposition, a body is divisible, is demonstrable, for the predicate and the subject can be shown by analysis and therefore indirectly: a body is *compound*, but what is compound is divisible, so a body is divisible. The intermediate characteristic mark here is *being* compound. Now, in philosophy there are, as we have said above, many indemonstrable propositions. All these indemonstrable propositions are subsumed under the formal first principles, albeit immediately. However, in so far as they also contain the grounds of other cognitions, they are also the first material principles of human reason. For example: a body is compound is an indemonstrable proposition, for the predicate can only be thought as an immediate and primary characteristic mark in the concept of a body. Such material principles constitute, as *Crusius* rightly says, the foundation of human reason and the guarantor of its stability. For, as we have mentioned above, they provide the stuff of definitions and, even when one is not in possession of a definition, the data from which conclusions can be reliably drawn.

And *Crusius* is also right to criticize other schools of philosophy for ignoring these material principles and adhering merely to formal principles. For on their basis alone it really is not possible to prove anything at all. Propositions are needed which contain the intermediate concept by means of which the logical relation of the other concepts to each other can be known in a syllogism. And among these propositions there must be some which are the first. But it is not possible to invest some propositions with the status of supreme material principles unless they are obvious to every human understanding. It is my conviction, however, that a number of the principles adduced by *Crusius* are open to doubt, and, indeed, to serious doubt.

This celebrated man proposes setting up a supreme rule to govern all cognition and therefore metaphysical cognition as well. The supreme rule is this: What *cannot* be *thought* as other thaw *true* is *true*, etc. However, it can easily be seen that this proposition can never be a ground of the truth of any cognition. For, if one concedes that there is no other ground of truth which can be given, apart from the impossibility of thinking it other than true, then one is in effect saying that it is impossible to give any further ground of truth, and that this cognition is indemonstrable. Now, of course, there are many indemonstrable cognitions. But the feeling of conviction which we have with respect to these cognitions is merely an avowal, not an argument establishing that they are true.

Accordingly, metaphysics has no formal or material grounds of certainty which are different in kind from those of geometry. In both metaphysics and geometry, the formal element of the judgments exists in virtue of the laws of agreement and contradiction. In both sciences, indemonstrable propositions constitute the foundation on the basis of which conclusions are drawn. But whereas in mathematics the definitions are the first indemonstrable concepts of the things defined, in metaphysics, the place of these definitions is taken by a number of indemonstrable propositions which provide the primary data. Their certainty may be just as great as that of the definitions of geometry. They are responsible for furnishing either the stuff, from which the definitions are formed, or the foundation, on the basis of which reliable conclusions are drawn. Metaphysics is as much capable of the certainty which is necessary to produce conviction as mathematics. The only difference is that mathematics is easier and more intuitive in character.

Fourth Reflection: Concerning the distinctness and certainty of which the fundamental principles of natural theology and morality are capable

§ I The fundamental principles of natural theology are capable of the greatest philosophical certainty

Firstly, distinguishing one thing from another is easiest and most distinct if the thing in question is the only possible thing of its kind. The object of natural religion is the unique first cause; its determinations are such that they cannot easily be confused with those of other things. But the greatest conviction is possible when it is absolutely necessary that these and no other predicates belong to a thing. For in the case of contingent determinations it is generally difficult to discover the variable conditions of its predicates. Hence, the absolutely necessary being is an object such that, as soon as one is on the right track of its concept, it seems to promise even more certainty than most other philosophical cognition. In this part of my undertaking, all that I can do is consider the possible philosophical cognition of God in general; for if we were to examine the philosophical theories relating to this object which are actually current, we should be taken too far afield. The chief concept which here offers itself to the metaphysician is that of the absolutely necessary existence of a being. In order to arrive at this concept, the metaphysician could first of all ask the question: Is it possible that *absolutely nothing* at all *should* exist? Now, if he realizes that, were absolutely nothing at all to exist, then no *existence* would be given and there would be *nothing* to *think* and there would be no possibility – once that is realized, all that needs to be investigated is the concept of the existence of that which must constitute the ground of all possibility. He will develop this idea and establish the determinate concept of the absolutely necessary being. I do not wish to become involved in a detailed investigation of this project, but I shall say this much: as soon as the existence of the unique, most perfect and necessary Being is established, then the concepts of that Being's other determinations will be established with much greater precision, for these determinations will always be the greatest and most perfect of their kind; they will also be established with much greater certainty, for the only determinations which will be admitted will be those which are necessary. Suppose, for example, that I am to determine the concept of the divine *omnipresence*. I have no difficulty in recognizing the following fact. The Being, upon which everything else depends – for it is itself independent – determines through its presence the place of everything else in the world; it does not, however, determine for itself a place among those things, for if it did it would belong to the world as well. Therefore, strictly speaking, God does not exist in any place, although He is present to all things in all the places *in which things* exist. Likewise, I realize that, whereas the things in the world which follow upon one another are in His power, nonetheless He does not in virtue of that fact determine for Himself a moment of time in this series; as a consequence, nothing is past or future in relation to God. If, therefore, I say that God foresees the future, this does not mean that God sees that which relative to Him is future. It rather means that God sees that which, relative to certain things in the world, is future, that is to say, that which follows upon a state of those certain things in the world. From this it can be seen that cognitions of the future, the past and the present are not, relative to the action of the divine understanding, different from each other; God rather cognizes them all as actual things in the universe. This foreknowledge can be imagined much more determinately and with much greater distinctness in God than in a thing which belongs to the totality of the world.

Metaphysical cognition of God is thus capable of a high degree of certainty in all those areas where no analogon of contingency is to be encountered. But when it comes to forming a judgment about His free actions, about providence, or about the way in which He exercises justice and goodness, there can only be, in this science, an approximation to certainty, or a certainty which is moral. For there is still a great deal of obscurity surrounding the concepts which we have of these determinations, even when they occur in ourselves.

§ 2 The fundamental principles of morality in their present state are not capable of all the certainty necessary to produce conviction

In order to make this claim clear I shall merely show how little even the fundamental concept of obligation is yet known, and how far practical philosophy must still be from furnishing the distinctness and the certainty of the fundamental concepts and the fundamental principles which are necessary for certainty in these matters. The formula by means of which every obligation is expressed is this: one *ought* to do this or that and abstain from doing the other. Now, every *ought* expresses a necessity of the action and is capable of two meanings. To be specific: either I ought to do something (as a *means*) if I want something else (as an *end*), or I *ought* immediately to do something else (as an *end*) and make it actual. The former may be called the necessity of the means (*necessitas problematica*), and the latter the necessity of the ends (*necessitas legalis*). The first kind of necessity does not indicate any obligation at all. It merely specifies a prescription as the solution to the problem concerning the means I must employ if I am to attain a certain end. If one person tells another what actions he must perform or what actions he must abstain from performing if he wishes to advance his happiness, he might perhaps be able, I suppose, to subsume all the teachings of morality under his prescription. They are not, however, obligations any longer except in the sense, say, in which it would be my obligation to draw two intersecting arcs if I wanted to bisect a straight line into two equal parts. In other words, they would not be obligations at all; they would simply be recommendations to adopt a suitable procedure, if one wished to attain a given end. Now since no other necessity attaches to the employment of means than that which belongs to the end, all the actions which are prescribed by morality under the condition of certain ends are contingent. They cannot be called obligations as long as they are not subordinated to an end which is necessary in itself. Take the following examples: I ought to advance the total greatest perfection; or: I ought to act in accordance with the will of God. To whichever of these two principles the whole practical philosophy is to be subordinated, the principle chosen must, if it is to be a rule and ground of obligation, command the action as being immediately necessary and not conditional upon some end. And here we find that such an immediate supreme rule of all obligation must be absolutely indemonstrable. For it is impossible, by contemplating a thing or a concept of any kind whatever, to recognize or infer what one ought to do, if that which is presupposed is not an end, and if the action is a means. But this cannot be the case; if it were, our principle would not be a formula of obligation; it would be a formula of problematic skill.

Having convinced myself after long reflection on this matter, I can now briefly show the following. The rule: perform the most perfect action in your power, is the first formal *ground* of all obligation to act. Likewise, the proposition: abstain from doing that which will hinder the realization of the greatest possible perfection, is the first formal *ground* of the duty to *abstain* from *acting*. And just as, in the absence of any material first principles, nothing flowed from the first formal principles of our judgments of the truth, so here no specifically determinate obligation flows from these two rules of the good, unless they are combined with indemonstrable material principles of practical cognition.

It is only recently, namely, that people have come to realize that the faculty of representing the *true* is *cognition*, while the faculty of experiencing the good is *feeling*, and that the two faculties are, on no account, to be confused with each other. Now, just as there are unanalyzable concepts of the true, that is to say, unanalyzable concepts of that which is encountered in the objects of cognition, regarded in itself, so too there is an unanalyzable feeling of the good (which is never encountered in a thing absolutely but only relatively to a being endowed with sensibility). One of the tasks of the understanding is to analyze and render distinct the compound and confused concept of the good by showing how it arises from simpler feelings of the good. But if the good is simple, then the judgment: "This is good," will be completely indemonstrable. This judgment will be an immediate effect of the consciousness of the feeling of pleasure combined with the representation of the object. And since there are quite certainly many simple feelings of the good to be found in us, it follows that there are many such unanalyzable representations. Accordingly, if an action is immediately represented as good, and if it does not contain concealed within itself a certain other good, which could be discovered by analysis and on account of which it is called perfect, then the necessity of this action is an indemonstrable material principle of obligation. Take for example the principle: love him who loves you. This is a practical principle which is, it is true, subsumed, albeit immediately, under the supreme formal and affirmative rule of obligation. For since it cannot be further shown by analysis why a special perfection is to be found in mutual love, it follows that this rule has not been proved practically. In other words, the rule has not been proved by tracing it back to the necessity of another perfect action. It is rather subsumed immediately under the universal rule of good actions. It is perhaps possible that the example I have adduced does not present the matter with sufficient distinctness and persuasiveness. However, the limits of a treatise such as the present one – limits which, perhaps, I have already overstepped – do not permit me the completeness I would wish. An immediate ugliness is to be found in the actions, which conflicts with the will of Him, from Whom all goodness comes and to Whom we owe our existence. This ugliness is clearly apparent, provided that we do not straightaway focus our attention on the disadvantages, which may, as consequences, accompany such behavior. Hence, the proposition: do what is in accordance with the will of God, is a material principle of morality. Nonetheless, it is formally though immediately subsumed under the supreme universal formula, of which mention has already been made. In both practical and in theoretical philosophy one must avoid lightly taking for indemonstrable that which in fact is capable of proof. Notwithstanding, those principles, which as postulates contain the foundations of all the other practical principles, are indispensable. *Hutcheson* and others have, under the name of moral feeling, provided us with a starting point from which to develop some excellent observations.

It is clear from what has been said that, although it must be possible to attain the highest degree of philosophical certainty in the fundamental principles of morality, nonetheless the ultimate fundamental concepts of obligation need first of all to be determined more reliably. And in this respect, practical philosophy is even more defective than speculative philosophy, for it has yet to be determined whether it is merely the faculty of cognition, or whether it is feeling (the first inner ground of the faculty of desire) which decides its first principles.

Postscript

Such are the thoughts I surrender to the judgment of the Royal Academy of Sciences. I venture to hope that the reasons presented here will be of some value in clarifying the subject, which was what was requested. In what concerns the care, precision and elegance of the execution: I have preferred to leave something to be desired in that respect, rather than to allow such matters to prevent my presenting this inquiry for examination at the proper time, particularly since this defect is one which could easily be remedied should my inquiry meet with a favorable reception.

M. Immanuel Kant's Announcement of the Program of his Lectures for the Winter Semester 1765–1766

There is always a certain difficulty involved in the instruction of young people, and it is this: the knowledge one imparts to them is such that one finds oneself constrained to outstrip their years. Without waiting for their understanding to mature, one is obliged to impart knowledge to them, which, in the natural order of things, can only be understood by minds which are more practiced and experienced. It is this which is the source of the endless prejudices of the schools – prejudices which are more intractable and frequently more absurd than ordinary prejudices. And it is this, too, which is the source of that precocious prating of young thinkers, which is blinder than any other self-conceit and more incurable than ignorance. This difficulty, however, is one which cannot be entirely avoided, and the reason is this. In an epoch which is characterized by an elaborately complex social organization, a knowledge of higher things is regarded as a means to advancement and comes to be thought of as a necessity of life. Such knowledge ought by nature, however, really to be regarded merely as one of life's adornments – one of life's inessential beauties, so to speak. Nonetheless, even in this branch of instruction, it is possible to make public education more adapted to nature, even though it will not be possible to bring it into perfect harmony with it. The natural progress of human knowledge is as follows: first of all, the understanding develops by using experience to arrive at intuitive judgments, and by their means to attain to concepts. After that, and employing reason, these concepts come to be known in relation to their grounds and consequences. Finally, by means of science, these concepts come to be known as parts of a well-ordered whole. This being the case, teaching must follow exactly the same path. The teacher is, therefore, expected to develop in his pupil firstly the man of *understanding*, then the man of *reason*, and finally the man of *learning*. Such a procedure has this advantage: even if, as usually happens, the pupil should never reach the final phase, he will still have benefited from his instruction. He will have grown more experienced and become more clever, if not for school then at least for life.

If this method is reversed, then the pupil picks up a kind of reason, even before his understanding has developed. His science is a borrowed science which he wears, not as something which has, so to speak, grown within him, but as something which has been hung upon him. Intellectual aptitude is as unfruitful as it ever was. But at the same time it has been corrupted to a much greater degree by the delusion of wisdom. It is for this reason that one not infrequently comes across men of learning (strictly speaking, people who have pursued courses of study) who display little understanding. It is for this reason, too, that the academies send more people out into the world with their heads full of inanities than any other public institution.

The rule for proceeding is, therefore, as follows. Firstly, the understanding must be brought to maturity and its growth expedited by exercising it in empirical judgments and focusing its attention on what it can learn by comparing the impressions which are furnished by the senses. It ought not to venture any bold ascent from these judgments and concepts to higher and more remote judgments and concepts. It ought rather to make its way towards them by means of the natural and well-trodden pathway of the lower concepts, for this path will gradually take it further than any bold ascents ever could. But all this should be done, not in accordance with that capacity for understanding which the teacher perceives, or thinks he perceives in himself, and which he mistakenly presupposes in his pupils, but rather in accordance with that capacity for understanding which must of necessity be generated in that faculty by the practice which has just been described. In short, it is not *thoughts* but *thinking* which the understanding ought to learn. It ought to be led, if you wish, but not carried, so that in the future it will be capable of *walking* on its own, and doing so without stumbling.

The peculiar nature of philosophy itself demands such a method of teaching. But since philosophy is strictly speaking an occupation only for those who have attained the age of maturity, it is no wonder that difficulties arise when the attempt is made to adapt it to the less practiced capacity of youth. The youth who has completed his school instruction has been accustomed to *learn*. He now thinks that he is going to *learn* philosophy. But that is impossible, for he ought now to learn to philosophize. Let me explain myself more distinctly. All the sciences which can be learned in the strict sense of the term can be reduced to two kinds: the historical and the mathematical. To the first there belong, in addition to history proper, natural history, philology, positive law, etc. In everything historical, it is one's own experience or the testimony of other people which constitute what is actually given and which is therefore available for use, and which may, so to speak, simply be assimilated. In everything mathematical, on the other hand, these things are constituted by the self-evidence of the

concepts and the infallibility of the demonstration. It is thus possible in both types of knowledge to learn. That is to say, it is possible to impress either on the memory or on the understanding that which can be presented to us as an already complete discipline. In order, therefore, to be able to learn philosophy as well there must already be a philosophy which actually exists in the first place. It must be possible to produce a book and say: "Look, here is wisdom, here is knowledge on which you can rely. If you learn to understand and grasp it, if you take it as your foundation and build on it from now on, you will be philosophers." Until I am shown such a book of philosophy, a book to which I can appeal, say, as I can appeal to *Polybius* in order to elucidate some circumstance of history, or to *Euclid* in order to explain a proposition of mathematics – until I am shown such a book, I shall allow myself to make the following remark. One would be betraying the trust placed in one by the public if, instead of extending the capacity for understanding of the young people entrusted to one's care and educating them to the point where they will be able in the future to acquire a more mature insight of their *own* – one would be betraying the trust placed in one by the public, if, instead of that, one were to deceive them with a philosophy which was alleged to be already complete and to have been excogitated by others for their benefit. Such a claim would create the illusion of science. That illusion is only accepted as legal tender in certain places and among certain people. Everywhere else, however, it is rejected as counterfeit currency. The method of instruction, peculiar to philosophy, is zetetic, as some of the philosophers of antiquity expressed it (from Sητετν). In other words, the method of philosophy is the method of *enquiry*. It is only when reason has already grown more practised and only in certain areas, that this method becomes dogmatic, that is to say, decisive. The philosophical writer, for example, upon whom one bases one's instruction, is not to be regarded as the paradigm of judgment. He ought rather to be taken as the occasion for forming one's own judgment about him, and even, indeed, for passing judgment against him. What the pupil is really looking for is proficiency in the method of reflecting and drawing inferences for himself. And it is that proficiency alone which can be of use to him. As for the positive knowledge which he may also perhaps come to acquire at the same time – that must be regarded as an incidental consequence. To reap a superabundant harvest of such knowledge, he needs only to plant within himself the fruitful roots of this method.

If one compares the above method with the procedure which is commonly adopted and which differs so much from it, one will understand a number of things which would otherwise strike one as surprising. For example: why is there no other kind of specialized knowledge which exemplifies so many masters as does philosophy? Many of those who have learned history, jurisprudence, mathematics, and so forth, nonetheless modestly disclaim that they have learned enough to be able to teach the subject themselves. But why, on the other hand, is it rare to find someone who does not in all seriousness imagine that, in addition to his usual occupation, he is perfectly able to lecture on, say, logic, and moral philosophy, and other subjects of the kind, should he wish to dabble in such trivial matters? The reason for this divergence is the fact that, whereas in the former science there is a common standard, in the latter science each person has his own standard. It will likewise be clearly seen that it is contrary to the nature of philosophy to be practiced as a means to earning one's daily bread – the essential nature of philosophy is such that it cannot consistently accommodate itself to the craze of demand or adapt itself to the law of fashion – and that it is only pressing need, which still exercises its power over philosophy, which can constrain it to assume a form which wins it public applause.

In the course of the present semester which has just begun, I propose to hold private lectures on the following science, which I intend to handle in an exhaustive fashion.

Metaphysics. I have sought to show in a short and hastily composed work that this science has, in spite of the great efforts of scholars, remained imperfect and uncertain because the method peculiar to it has been misunderstood. Its method is not *synthetic*, as is that of mathematics, but *analytic*. As a result, that which is simple and the most universal in mathematics is also what is easiest, whereas in the queen of the sciences it is what is most difficult. In mathematics, what is simple and universal must in the nature of things come first, while in metaphysics it must come at the end. In mathematics one begins the doctrine with the definitions; in metaphysics one ends the doctrine with them; and so on in other respects. For some considerable time now I have worked in accordance with this scheme. Every step which I have taken along this path has revealed to me both the source of the errors which have been committed, and the criterion of judgment by reference to which alone those errors can be avoided, if they can be avoided at all. For this reason, I hope that I shall be able in the near future to present a complete account of what may serve as the foundation of my lectures in the aforementioned science. Until that time, however, I can easily, by applying gentle pressure, induce A. G. Baumgarten, the author of the textbook on which this course will be based – and that book has been chosen chiefly for the richness of its contents and the precision of its method – to follow the same path. Accordingly, after a brief introduction, I shall begin with empirical psychology, which is really the metaphysical science of the *human being* based on experience. For in what concerns the term "soul," it is not yet permitted in this section to assert that he has a soul. The second part of the course will discuss corporeal *nature* in general. This part is drawn from the chapters of the Cosmology which treat of matter and which I shall supplement with a number of written additions in order to complete the treatment. In the first of these sciences (to which, on account of the analogy, there is added empirical zoology, that is to say, the consideration of animals) we shall examine all the organic phenomena which present themselves to our senses. In the second of these sciences we shall consider everything which is *inorganic* in general. Since everything in the world can be subsumed under these two classes, I shall then proceed to ontology, the science, namely, which is concerned with the more general properties of all things. The conclusion of this enquiry will contain the distinction between *mental* and material beings, as also the connection or separation of the two, and therefore *rational* psychology. The advantage of this procedure is this: it is the already experienced student who is introduced to the most difficult of all philosophical investigations. But there is another advantage as well: in every reflection, the abstract is considered in the form of a concrete instance, furnished by the preceding disciplines, so that everything is presented with the greatest distinctness. I shall not have to anticipate my own argument; in other words, I shall not have to introduce anything by way of elucidation which ought only to be adduced at a later stage – an error which is both common and unavoidable in the synthetic method of presenting things. At the end there will be a reflection on the cause of all things, in other words the science which is concerned with God and the world. There is one other advantage which I cannot but mention. Although it is a product of accidental causes, it is not, however, to be lightly esteemed. It is an advantage which I hope will accrue from the employment of this method. Everyone knows with what eagerness the spirited and volatile youth attend the start of a course, and how subsequently the lecture theatres grow gradually increasingly empty. Now, I am assuming that what ought not to happen will, in spite of all reminders, continue to happen in the future. Nonetheless, the aforementioned method of teaching has a utility of its own. The student, whose enthusiasm has already evaporated even before he has got to the end of empirical psychology (though this is scarcely to be expected if such a procedure as the one I have described is adopted) will, nonetheless, have benefited this much: he will have heard something which he can understand, on account of its easiness; and he will have heard something which he can enjoy, in virtue of its interest; and he will have heard something which he can use, because of the frequency with which it can be given an application in life. On the other hand, if he should be deterred from proceeding further by ontology, which is difficult to understand, that which he might perhaps have grasped if he had continued could not have been of any further use to him at all.

2. Logic. Of this science there are really two kinds. The first kind is a critique and canon of *sound understanding*. In one direction, it borders on crude concepts and ignorance, and, in the other, it borders on science and learning. It is with this type of logic that all philosophy, at the start of academic instruction, ought to be prefaced. It is, so to speak, a quarantine (if the expression be permitted) which must be observed by the apprentice who wishes to migrate from the land of prejudice and error, and enter the realm of a more enlightened reason and the science. The second kind of logic is the critique and canon of real *learning*. The only way in which it can be treated is from the point of view of the sciences of which it is supposed to be the organon. The purpose of such a treatment is to make the procedure employed by the science concerned more consonant with the rules, and to render the nature of the discipline itself, as well as

the means for improving it, accessible to the understanding. In this way, I shall add at the end of the metaphysics a reflection on the method which is peculiar to it, and which can serve as an organon of this science. This reflection would have been out of place at the beginning, for it is impossible to make the rules clear, unless there are some examples to hand by means of which the rules can be elucidated *in concreto*. The teacher must, of course, be in possession of the organon, before he presents his account of the science in question, so that he can be guided by it; but he must never present the organon to his audience except at the end of his presentation. The critique and the canon of the whole of philosophy in its entirety, this complete logic, can therefore only have its place in instruction at the end of the whole of philosophy. The reason is this. It is the knowledge of philosophy, which we have come to acquire, and the history of human opinions which alone make it possible for us to reflect on the origin both of its insights and of its errors. And it is this alone which enables us to draw up a precise ground plan, on the basis of which an edifice of reason, which is permanent in duration and regular in structure, can be erected.

I shall be lecturing on logic of the first type. To be more specific, I shall base my lectures on Meier's handbook, for he has, I think, kept his eye focused on the limits of the intentions which we have just now mentioned. And he also stimulates us to an understanding, not only of the cultivation of reason in its more refined and learned form, but also of the development of the ordinary understanding, which is nonetheless active and sound. The former serves the life of contemplation, while the latter serves the life of action and society. And in this, the very close relationship of the materials under examination leads us at the same time, in the *critique* of *reason*, to pay some attention to the *critique* of taste, that is to say, aesthetics. The rules of the one at all times serve to elucidate the rules of the other. Defining the limits of the two is a means to a better understanding of them both.

3. Ethics. Moral philosophy has this special fate: that it takes on the semblance of being a science and enjoys some reputation for being thoroughly grounded, and it does so with even greater ease than metaphysics, and that in spite of the fact that it is neither a science nor thoroughly grounded. The reason why it presents this appearance and enjoys this reputation is as follows. The distinction between good and evil in actions, and the judgment of moral rightness, can be known, easily and accurately, by the human heart through what is called sentiment, and that without the elaborate necessity of proofs. In ethics, a question is often settled in advance of any reasons which have been adduced – and that is something which does not happen in metaphysics. It will not, therefore, come as a surprise that no one raises any special difficulties about admitting grounds, which only have some semblance of validity. For this reason, there is nothing more common than the title of a moral philosopher, and nothing more rare than the entitlement to such a name.

For the time being, I shall lecture on *universal practical philosophy* and the *doctrine of virtue*, basing both of them on *Baumgarten*. The attempts of *Shaftesbury, Hutcheson* and *Hume*, although incomplete and defective, have nonetheless penetrated furthest in the search for the fundamental principles of all morality. Their efforts will be given the precision and the completeness which they lack. In the doctrine of virtue I shall always begin by considering historically and philosophically what *happens* before specifying what *ought to happen*. In so doing, I shall make clear what method ought to be adopted in the study of the human being. And by human *being* here I do not only mean the *human being* as he is distorted by the mutable form which is conferred upon him by the contingencies of his condition, and who, as such, has nearly always been misunderstood even by philosophers. I rather mean the unchanging *nature* of human beings, and his distinctive position within the creation. My purpose will be to establish which perfection is appropriate to him in the state of primitive innocence and which perfection is appropriate to him in the state of wise innocence. It is also my purpose to establish what, by contrast, the rule of human behavior is when, transcending the two types of limit, he strives to attain the highest level of physical or moral excellence, though falling short of that attainment to a greater or lesser degree. This method of moral enquiry is an admirable discovery of our times, which, when viewed in the full extent of its program, was entirely unknown to the ancients.

4. Physical geography. Right at the beginning of my academic career, I realized that students were being seriously neglected, particularly in this respect: early on they learned the art of subtle argumentation but they lacked any adequate knowledge of historical matters which could make good their lack of *experience*. Accordingly, I conceived the project of making the history of the present state of the earth, in other words, geography in the widest sense of the term, into an entertaining and easy compendium of the things which might prepare them and serve them for the exercise of practical reason, and which might arouse within them the desire to extend even further the knowledge which they had begun to acquire in their study of the subject. The name which I gave to the discipline, constituted by that part of the subject on which my chief attention was at the time focused, was that of physical geography. Since then I have gradually extended the scheme, and I now propose, by condensing that part of the subject which is concerned with the physical features of the earth, to gain the time necessary for extending my course of lectures to include the other parts of the subject, which are of even greater general utility. This discipline will therefore be a physical, moral, and political geography. It will contain, first of all, a specification of the remarkable features of *nature* in its three realms. The specification will, however, be limited to those features, among the numberlessly many which could be chosen, which particularly satisfy the general desire for knowledge, either because of the fascination which they exercise in virtue of their rarity, or because of the effect which they can exercise on states by means of trade and industry. This part of the subject, which also contains a treatment of the natural relationship which holds between all the countries and seas in the world, and the reason for their connection, is the real foundation of all history. Without this foundation, history is scarcely distinguishable from fairy stories. The *second* part of the subject considers the *human being*, throughout the world, from the point of view of the variety of his natural properties and the differences in that feature of the human being which is moral in character. The consideration of these things is at once very important and also highly stimulating as well. Unless these matters are considered, general judgments about the human being would scarcely be possible. The comparison of human beings with each other, and the comparison of the human being today with the moral state of the human being in earlier times, furnishes us with a comprehensive map of the human species. *Finally,* there will be a consideration of what can be regarded as a product of the

reciprocal interaction of the two previously mentioned forces, namely, the condition of the states and nations throughout the world. The subject will not be considered so much from the point of view of the way in which the condition of states depends on accidental causes, such as the deeds and fates of individuals, for example, the sequence of governments, conquests, and intrigues between states. The condition of states will rather be considered in relation to what is more constant and which contains the more remote ground of those accidental causes, namely, the situation of their countries, the nature of their products, customs, industry, trade, and population. Even the reduction, if I may use the term, of a science of such extensive prospects to a smaller scale has its great utility. For it is only by this means that it is possible to attain that unity without which all our knowledge is nothing but a fragmentary patchwork. In a sociable century, such as our own, am I not to be permitted to regard the stock which a multiplicity of entertaining, instructive, and easily understood knowledge offers for the maintenance of social intercourse as one of the benefits which it is not demeaning for science to have before its eyes? At least it cannot be pleasant for a man of learning frequently to find himself in the embarrassing situation in which Isocrates, the orator, found himself: urged on one occasion when he was in company to say something, he was obliged to reply: What I *know* is *not suitable* to the *occasion*; *and* that which is *suitable* to the *occasion* I do *not know*.

This is a brief indication of the subjects on which I shall be lecturing in

the university in the course of the coming semester which has just started. I thought it necessary to say something in this connection in order to explain my method, where I have now found it opportune to make some alterations. *Mihi sic est usus*: *Tibi ut opus facto est, face*. (Terewce). [For my part, such is my practice; you, for your part, do what you deem fitting.]

Herder's Notes from Kant's Lectures on Ethics

... Do I have, not merely a self-interested feeling, but also a disinterested feeling of concern for others? Yes – the weal and woe of another touches us directly: the mere happiness of another pleases us in the telling: even that of fictional persons whose tale we know of, or in distant ages – this common concern is so great that it collides with the self-interested feeling. The sense of it is indeed a noble feeling, nobler than the self-interested one. Nobody despises it: everyone wishes for it, though not all have it in the same degree; in some it is great, and the greater it is, the more it is felt as a perfection. It is universal, though seldom so great that it inspires active exertions – in misers, for example, with whom self-interest has become very strong. As needy beings the creator gave us self-interest in our own perfection. As beings who have the power to be of service to our fellows, He gave us a disinterested concern for the perfection of others. The concern for others ranks high, since even the concern for self can be subordinated to it, but not vice versa. The more self-interested, the poorer (at least in thought), and hence the more to be despised. The disinterested feeling for the welfare, etc., of another has our own perfection, not as an end, but as a means.

Hobbes followed the plan of Lucretius and Epicurus, whose principles were of less nobility, by far, than those of the Stoics. And likewise the majority of Germans relate everything to self-interest, since it is fine to derive everything from a single *principium*, however little they may do this in metaphysics, etc. It was argued (1) that here we put ourselves in the other's shoes, and the deception of fancy creates this pleasure, which arises, not directly, but indirectly, from the other's pleasure. This false ordering of the matter comes about because, in the disinterested feeling, we always envisage the other's joy, and such joy as we may have in his person. But if we had no disinterested feelings, this would not occur, because we do not *convince* ourselves that we are in his person – imagine yourself, too, in the shoes of a wealthy idler; you will not take any pleasure in him. This putting of oneself in the other's shoes is thus necessary, indeed, but is merely a means to vivacity, which presupposes the disinterested feeling. I have no pity for Damien's misfortune, though I do for that of Julius Caesar, since Brutus, his friend, murdered him. (2) It is said that the pleasure we have in [the welfare of others] is merely our own end, and a more refined self-interest. *Responsio*: the pleasure itself presupposes (1) a power of having it; (2) I cannot explain pleasure by means of pleasure. I will pleasure means, merely: I have pleasure in pleasure, and thus already presupposes a certain feeling. So there are merely lower grades of it. This feeling also constitutes a great beauty of our nature. A self-interested feeling presupposes our own imperfections, which can be acquired (so are not God-given), and imply neediness. A disinterested feeling presupposes our own perfections: the grounds for it may lie in the acquisition of other perfections, and it presupposes perfection. The disinterested feeling is like a force of attraction, and the self-interested feeling like a force of repulsion. The two of them, *in conflictu*, constitute the world.

Free actions are good (1) in virtue of the consequences, and (to that

extent) physically good; (2) in virtue of the intention, and (to that extent) morally good. The measuring-rod is very different in the two. Small will and great capacity is less morally good even in great benefactions. Great will and small capacity is morally better, even in benefactions that are small. We also esteem moral acts, not by their physical effects, but for their own sake, even when they are self-interested, and not always when disinterested (as Hutcheson mistakenly believes). Morally good actions must be directed to a physical good, but not measured by this. Physically good actions are always indifferent; they may be free effects, or necessary ones, for the good lies in the effect, and is measured by the consequences; the good is no greater than the effect. But morally free actions have a goodness which is assessed, not by the effect, but by the (free) intent; otherwise, the morally good would be less than the physically good. But this contradicts feeling and emotion. Free actions may be immediately good (give pleasure), not as means to consequences, so that their value is not to be measured by the results, and they are not equivalent to the physical causes that produce the same effect.

Pleasure in free actions directly is called moral feeling. We have a moral feeling, which is (1) universal (2) unequivocal. At neglect of another I feel displeasure, hatred; not because he has to starve, but because of the neglect, for at privation through sickness I feel pity. A great disproportion, which enhances self-interested feeling till the other feeling is outweighed, does not abolish the latter; for when we hear morally good things of another, we are touched with pleasure. A direct pleasure at the other's misfortune is devilish, and not to be thought of among us (though there can certainly be an indirect pleasure, and displeasure, and likewise direct displeasure). The moral feeling is unanalyzable, basic, the ground of conscience . . .

The feeling inspired by morality (without profit) is beautiful or sublime; my joy at the perfected in myself (feeling of self-esteem, of one's own worth) is noble; my joy at satisfaction (feeling of goodwill) is beautiful. Here the division of all actions according to these classes is completely reconstituted.

Sources of morality:

Morality as such. Moral beauty (not obligation, right and wrong) – In morality perfection is never the transcendental; not what belongs merely to the essence, for the essence might be better still.

Solely from the fact that it is in accordance with *our* nature, it is not perfection merely, for I can have a better nature, e.g. angel; thus death is good. Hence the supreme law of morality is: act according to your moral nature. My reason can err; my moral feeling, only when I uphold custom before natural feeling; but in that case it is merely implicit reason; and my final yardstick still remains moral feeling, not true and false; just as the capacity for true and false is the final yardstick of the understanding, and both are universal.

In order not to err in logical matters, I must seek out the 1*st propositio* of the true.

In order not to err in moral matters, I must seek out the 1*st propositio* of the good.

The natural feeling is here opposed to the artificial; the feeling of modesty, for example, is almost artificial; Spartan children went naked up to 4 years old; Indian women never cover up the breasts, in Jamaica they go stark naked – and yet the feeling is very strong; Caesar, Livia, when dying would not uncover themselves.

Spartan women thrown naked on the street, worse than capital punishment.

Yet artificial, as with showing the fingers among the Chinese.

Thus marriage with a sister is artificially abhorred; but sacred with the Egyptians. To distinguish the artificial from the natural, we must therefore push back to the origin, as we do to distinguish prejudices (maxims) from certainty. One would have to investigate the feeling of the *natural* man, and this is far better than our artificial feeling; Rousseau has looked into it . . .

71. Can we, even without presupposing God's existence and His *arbitrium*, derive all obligations from within? *Responsio*: not merely in the affirmative, for this, rather, is *ex natura rei* [from the nature of the case], and we conclude from this to God's choice.

From the *arbitrium divinum* [divine choice] I cannot myself obtain the relevant concepts of the good, unless the concept of the morally good be assumed beforehand; apart from that, the sheer *arbitrium* of God is good merely in a physical sense. In short, the judgment as to the perfection of God's *arbitrium* presupposes the investigation of moral perfection.

Supposing the *arbitrium* of God to be known to me, where is the necessity that I should do it, if I have not already derived the obligation from the nature of the case? God wills it – why should I? He will punish me; in that case it is injurious, but not in itself wicked; that is how we obey a despot; in that case the act is no sin, in the strict sense, but politically imprudent; and why does God will it? Why does He punish it? Because I am obligated to do it, not because He has the power to punish. The very application of the *arbitrium divinum* to the *factum*, as a ground, presupposes the concept of obligation; and since this constitutes natural religion, the latter is a part, but not the basic principle, of morality. It is probable that, since God by His *arbitrium*, is the ground of all things, this is also the case here; He is indeed the ground of it, but not per *arbitrium*, for since He is the ground of possibility, He is also the material ground (since in Him all things are given) of geometrical truths and morality. In Him there is already morality, therefore, and so His choice is not the ground.

The quarrel between reformers and Lutherans over *arbitrium divinum* and *decretus absolutus* is based on the fact that even in God, morality must exist; and every conception of the divine *arbitrium* itself vanishes, if morality is not presupposed; this cannot, however, be demonstrated from the world (where it is merely possible), since the good things of the world may merely be physical consequences. How dreadful, though, is a God without morality. The jus *naturae divinum*, and even *positivum*, vanishes, if there be no morality as ground of the relation and conformity of my *arbitrium* and that of God. Without the prior assumption of obligation, punishments come to nothing; what God displays is merely ill-will; the physical consequences I can avoid, and thus the action is no longer a transgression. Morality is more general than the *arbitrium divinum*.

For one who has not wholly fulfilled his obligation, morality is incomplete, if all grounds of obligation are not included, and in that case, the *arbitrium divinum* is a ground of external obligation for our morality. So the *arbitrium divinum* should never be left out, as an external obligating ground; thus our moral perfection becomes incomplete, if it arises solely from inner morality, and is considered without reference to God's *arbitrium*. In the absence of the latter, my action is already still moral, indeed, but not so completely good, morally, as when it conforms to all grounds.

Those who attend solely to the *arbitrium* Dei are considering merely their liability to the jus *naturae divinum*; but we should attend also to the inner morality, and consider obligation as well. *Ethica rationalis*: the one without the other is not universal morality, and indeed far less than this; we are virtuous already from the nature of the case, pious only in having regard to the *arbitrium divinum*. To disregard the one is wicked; to disregard the other, godless; the former are moral errors, the latter, sins; the former concern the moral teacher, the latter, the preacher; the one wishes to have people morally good, the other wants their moral goodness to be complete. In education, we have first to awaken the moral feeling, and then must apply it to God's *arbitrium*; without that, religion is a prejudice, and hypocrisy. He who has a notion of the external obligation, without the inner, sees the motivating grounds as tasks, which do not make him moral at all, but merely politically crafty. If an immediate divine inspiration and influence are added to this, then (in that case only) the *arbitrium* Dei is sufficient. Thus cultivation of the moral feeling takes precedence over the cultivation of obedience.

Can an atheist be tolerated in society? There is the atheist *in sensu privationis*, ignorant in the knowledge of God, who never thinks about the matter; and the atheist *in sensu contradictorie* [in the privative/the contradictory sense], who errs in the knowledge of God, though well acquainted with the subject. The former are to be tolerated, because obligation remains – apart from the new motivating ground that is derived from God's *arbitrium*, and morality is still present. Such are many nations, who are, in a fashion, civilized folk; for example, the Hottentots, now informed by the Dutch that God is called a great commander – they possess moral feeling, nonetheless; their Hottentot ditties of ungrateful Holland are evidence of this. The atheist may be one who denies God from wantonness and lack of respect for the better conviction; or one who does so, not from wantonness, but because he thinks himself incapable of a better conviction. The former has a moral ground for his atheism, and is very dangerous to society. The latter has a logical ground for it, and is not so dangerous. Should the former have received the idea of the divine as a mere premise of his education, it is at least worthy already of respect and consideration. Since he has now been able to overcome this strong and weighty feeling, he may be presumed to have great moral wickedness in his principles. The majority of *wanton* atheists are in Rome, Paris, etc., where there is also the greatest hypocrisy; on them, too, theism has been imprinted, but because of certain errors, totally rejected – because of trifles, a feeling so worthy of veneration, and venerable even as a delusion, has been mocked; what wickedness, and what will that come to in regard to obligation towards other, lesser beings? Atheism may first occur with misgivings – without any show of proof, merely by imitation; but at once the misgivings are repressed, and people acquire an actual readiness to be atheists, for they think that others may have proved it, or could if they thought more about it. Atheists by reasoned conviction are dangerous simply because of the consequences, since others, from a desire to imitate, may follow their example. Because of their careful investigation, it is presumed that their morality is good. Hence they are not to be punished, and need, rather, to be persuaded, or their example removed, as with Spinoza, for example. He is not to be execrated, but deplored. He was honorable, with a very high degree of morality, but extremely speculative, and supposed that with the new Cartesian philosophy he might perhaps find out something altogether new; and as Descartes had destroyed everything, so he, Spinoza, also destroyed the concept of God, and thought he had demonstrated this . . .

§1. Ethics, the science of inner duties, is ranked under general practical philosophy, and alongside law, the science of outer duties.

The *jus naturae* and ethics are thus quite different, since the one demands liabilities, the other, obligations.

The topic of observation is in each case society, and for us, society in the state of *nature*, in so far as mankind does not impose on it the combination with others, and still less politics and economic laws.

Moral perfection is moral as end, and not as means; by that very fact it touches and satisfies us, not by relation to the effect, but immediately in itself. Nor is the action measured by the quality of the effect, but by the intention; for example, the death of a man, as effect, is of very small account, in regard to contingency and the whole; but the killing of a man is in itself of much importance, and is avenged.

Since the distinction between liability and obligation is very subtle, let us state it more clearly:

Ethics: the science of actions that are validly imputable before no other *forum* save the *internal* one. For example, even cases that partly belong before the *forum externum* (*jus*), fall into ethics, in so far as they belong before the *forum internum*. The principles of all that pertains to the *forum externum* are presented in natural law. The principles of all that pertains to the *forum* iwterwvm are presented in ethics.

Ethica est scientia imputabilitatis actionum liberarum coram foro interno. [Ethics is the science of the imputability of free actions before the inner tribunal.] We shall therefore not require to cast even a glance at any possible *forum externum.*

Ethics explained by a doctrine of virtue is good in as much as virtue belongs solely before the inner tribunal; but since virtue entails, not just morally good actions, but at the same time a great possibility of the opposite, and thus incorporates an inner struggle, this is therefore too narrow a concept, since we can also ascribe ethics, but not virtue (properly speaking) to the angels and to God; for in them there is assuredly holiness but not virtue.

§2. Philosophical ethics is ethics in so far as it is known philosophically, and thus not from the testimony of others, such as sages, for example, but on the basis of the matter itself.

§3. Utility, and *perfection* are in themselves clear.

§4. Morality is *laxa* or *rigida*, depending on whether it contains *pauca or multa motiva ad pauca or multa moleste apparentia;* [few or many motives to few or many irksome tasks] for example, if it impels men merely to kindness, sobriety, and moderation, it is too feeble; if it impels them also to self-sacrifice, to greater goods, it is serious; for the one coddles men, and presents them with easy duties, while the other represses the deceptive joys of the lower faculties of desire. The greater the moral perfection of the action is to be, the greater must be the obstacles, and the struggle, and hence the more needful, in that case, is the strict ethic. The other never constitutes true virtue, though

it often produces moral goods as well; but the satisfaction of the strict ethic is serious, and is a *noble* morality.

§5. The ethic of our author is *blandiens* [coaxing], since he always wrongly presupposes the broad concept of obligation, to which he attributes motivating grounds of utility, merely, in an improper sense of the term "ethics." For only he performs a morally good action, who does it from principles, not as a means, but as an end. By *sensitive jucunda* [pleasing/displeasing to the senses] I can certainly motivate, as by practical means, but cannot oblige, as by moral motivating grounds. Likewise by *sensitive molesta*; and so if it is to be *philosophia ethica*, it has to be moral, and the ethical motivating grounds should always be moral and not merely practical as physical means; even though the latter may become mediately motivating grounds, they would properly be a part of politics, which should, moreover, have been written down. All these subjectively motivating grounds are very good, and often preparatory to ethics, and hence, too, we have appended them; but they must always be distinguished from *ethical* grounds, since the latter must be drawn solely from noble, virtuous, and free choice. The tender-hearted ethic makes for a beautiful morality; the strict and serious ethic for a sublime one. Thus the charities of a rich man, *qua* consequence of kindliness, are morally beautiful; but as a consequence of principles and a sense of obligation, they are *sublime*.

Everyone, to be sure, has need, in part, of *sensitive jucunda*, and in part of *sensitive molesta*, even for moral actions. For our moral feelings are so buried away under the sensuous, and the sensory motivating grounds thus make it easier for the soul subsequently to make its decisions on principle. By those principles which outweigh the sensory motives, we are brought nearer, as it were, to the domain of morality. This extends, not merely to the teaching of ethics, but also to education and religion . . .

§8. Should the Christian ethic be given priority over philosophical ethics, or vice versa? One must certainly be explained from the other, as theoretical physics is explained from experimental physics; but the *natural* ethic must rightly be given priority, (1) since the other is related to it; (2) since the natural ethic contains also a ground of the other's truth; (3) since the natural ethic shows us many obligations which are impossible *secundum quid* [by derivation], and thus leads to the Christian ethic; the former creates the contradiction in man, that he *imputes* to himself something [2:6] which he cannot omit; it creates the collision between impotence and the moral ordinance, which the Christian ethic reconciles. (4) The revealed ethic, if it is to be practical, must ground itself upon the motives of the *natur*al ethic. Like any revelation, it presupposes natural powers, e.g. capacities of the soul that are fit for the purpose. Otherwise, it would be at most a miraculously transforming book; but in fact it is a book that lays *obligations* upon us, and presupposes instruments and receptivity in the face of revealed religion.

§10. *Perfice te ut finem* [perfect yourself as to the end/as to the means], and *ut medium*, are the two major rules of our author.

By this perfection is meant either moral perfection, and in that case the latter is already presupposed, so that this rule is not a basic one, for it presupposes a ground; or else by this perfection is meant something undetermined, e.g. health, etc., and again it is not a basic rule, on account of its instability. If I am to seek perfection as a rule, this amounts to saying: Desire all perfections, a proposition quite certain, indeed, subjectively speaking, whereby we always act; but objectively speaking an empty proposition, since it is wholly identical. The sole moral rule, therefore, is this: Act according to *your moral feeling!* In *philosophia practica prima* this feeling is defined merely negatively, viz., that it is not the physical, as means to an end; so merely as a relationship. This distinction is bungled by Baumgarten throughout his entire book, which is otherwise the richest *in context*, and perhaps his best book; though everything he says may make for great practical perfection, it does not constitute moral perfection. The latter he omits to define, according to the taste of the philosophy of Wolf, which continually based perfection on the relation between cause and effect, and thus treated it as a means to ends grounded in desire and aversion. With us, both moral and physical feeling are always combined. For God, in His goodness, has for the most part laid down the same rules for practical and moral perfections. So let us set forth, not only the difference, but also the consensus, between the two . . . morally good actions are thus, in their highest stages, religious acts; but this is not the first stage from which we begin. On the contrary, moral beauty (weak morality) is made prior to the moral nobility of actions in terms of what is right, and this new and higher morality is only brought in afterwards. It contains a relationship to the greatest supreme rule, which is the ground of everything, and thus constitutes the greatest harmony. Meanwhile, I must first abstract my actions from the divine will, in order even to recognize the goodness of that will. But once I have perceived it with sufficient abundance, exactitude and vividness, it becomes the supreme basis, (1) because the knowledge is then noble, and (2) because it provides the highest degree of vividness. But if my knowledge of God does not yet have life enough, I must concern myself with other beings; otherwise, all this knowledge of God would remain merely dead, and fail of its purpose. We begin, then, with moral beauty, and with moral liability – these are grounds of morality that are sensuous and vivid. When a man then rises to the highest level, that shows him as God's supreme instrument; but if he begins at that point, there arises from it a hypocritical religion; our author's method is therefore incorrect, since it begins from religion, whereas it ought to have started from a morality, which would then be increasingly purified.

Obligation towards God (religion) is not merely a practical necessity of making use of God, as of a means to certain ends. Our author, however, puts the use of God as a means before His immediate goodness. Yet *obligatio* should merely have explained morally good actions in direct relation to God as an end; if I follow God's will, because he has coupled my best interests with those of others, then this is a borrowed God, and it is merely the practical attitude of a self-interested agent. The highest degree of connection with God as a means is when we utilize the divine will as a means to the betterment of our own morality. Julie says, for example: Our good actions are noticed by witnesses: – she uses God's will to better her morality; but to use it merely as a means to happiness is ignoble, and no religion . . .

§14–22. The man who acts from motives of *welfare* is thereby subtly self-interested, and is not acting from religion, since he does not act from morality, and the sole motivating grounds of religion are those of *blessedness*; to entice us to our duties, as physical goods, from *happiness*, and thus derive all motivating grounds from pleasure, but yet make blessedness the motive to morality, and happiness the motive to welfare. That is mere *misbinding*, but since *happiness* and *blessedness* require one way, they do not actually conflict, on the whole, though they have to be distinguished. Even self-interest prepares us for religion, though without constituting it.

§19. Perhaps the image of God consisted in the immediately clear sensation of the divine presence – not symbolic, but intuitive; not from inference but from sensation; and in that case, how vivid the effect upon morality and the ground of blessedness. With us, perhaps, the broadest and vaguest concept thereof still resides, even now, in conscience. If we directly improve our moral feeling, we approach the divine presence in sensation; so maybe such people again develop the image, although their spiritual utterances sound fanatical; and religion elevates us to the highest degree of such sensation.

§22. This is true morality; a part of it already precedes all religion, but a part is greatly enhanced by religion, and since religion enhances the whole *summa* of morality, this is a *truly* binding ground of motivation . . .

§44. All enthusiasm is hard to prevent, lest we fall at once into the opposite vice of coldness. But in drawing conclusions from speculation it must be avoided, since passions do not confute or confirm opinions, but in regard to the truth are always blind; though in regard to the practically good they may be useful.

§45. When pietists make the idea of religion dominant in all conversation and discourse, and it has to be inferred from their constant behavior that this idea has lost the light of novelty, then they are mere twaddlers. But were this state of mind *ours* in this world, it would be the most blessed of all.

§46. Try especially to always couple the idea of God with your morality; first with your *natur*al moral feeling, so that your immediate liking for the good becomes, in the light of God, religion. Try also to make the idea of God *dominant* in the *depths* of the soul. This is difficult, but if it always predominates in clear ideas, then it will also pass over into the obscure ones . . .

§72. Thou shalt love this or that, is not said apodeictically, since it is no more of a duty than to *hold* something to be *true*; for it is not a *voluntary* action, but a mere arousal of feeling. So the command is merely: Do everything that can be a means to this. Nevertheless, though I perceive the appropriateness of love, it cannot always be in my power, any more than it often is when I would like to be rid of it. But when I perceive myself in the *defective* state of *cold-heartedness*, whether towards God, or my benefactor, or my brother who loves me, then I try to impress on myself the moral qualities that arouse one to love. For example, consider especially that God loves you (the very remark already inspires love), and that men may be moved at receiving your love; so love them as objects of one of the gentlest of impulses.

§73. To feel the *concursus divinus* [divine reinforcement], suppose yourself in possibly worse circumstances, and you will then feel your own to be that much the better.

§75. In so far as we regard all acts of God as the best means, to the best end, of happiness, we may be completely at ease. The great mutability of things, and the storms of my passions, can best be comforted by the thought that I am placed in the world, and placed there by supreme goodness, not for my own benefit; and however uncertain the order of nature may be, it is nevertheless under the supreme being; and in this way, then, *religion* alone may be completely reassuring. For even a naturally good and moral man must always tremble before *blind* fate.

§7. Since all God's acts (1) cannot be self-interested, and (2) are aimed at happiness, and thus are real *benefactions*, they arouse, by that very fact, *thankfulness*; and anyone insusceptible to any disinterested beneficence, will also be insusceptible to gratitude, and vice versa; for if he does not feel the *nobility* of well-doing in his own actions, how will he do so in the case of another? And nobody will feel gratitude even for God's benefactions, who does not himself feel the *beauty* of well-doing; for example, the magnificence of a summer's evening will itself have an effect upon the benevolent.

That love is [not] tender, which seeks to please the object of love; the latter is in fact *amorous* love. Amor is, in fact, *tener, quo quis amatum laedere, admodum reformidat* [Love is tender when it shuns entirely anything harmful to the beloved]; amorousness does not presuppose esteem, but tenderness does. That which does not merely wish to make the other into an object of desire, as amorousness does, but presupposes, rather, something *noble* in the way of thinking, does not offend, of itself, by a want of love, since it merely takes away something *beautiful*. But he who regards tenderness as a *duty* incumbent on him, and so fears to withdraw it, gives offence. Amorousness occurs also among the foolish, and is often very *pleasing*, but there is a want of esteem in it; the *tender* lover shows respect, and desires to preserve his own esteem, and is therefore not so laughing, not merely pleasing.

In love towards God, the amorous, and even the *tender* elements must disappear, since both are very anthropomorphic, and always presuppose a secret grace and favor. These are, however, simply the greatest of duties, and thus the highest degree of tender love, albeit without the name. Resignation to the divine will is necessary, in that we must trust God to have the utmost wisdom and benevolence. Thus Socrates told the praying Alcibiades: Cast your eyes down, and say, Give me, O God, what is best, whether I ask for it or not.

Love for the *creature* is always good, in so far as it is considered to be a creature; and idolatrous creature-love is merely the excessive degree of it.

If we walk upright in our inmost soul, then we shall not, perhaps, find love, but the esteem and reverence that arise from greatness, and bring fear rather than love as their consequence. The moral beauty of God, and His benevolence, are far less vivid in us, () because we are accustomed, as grumblers, to attribute our ills to God; and (2) because we have a dim idea that God's benefactions may perhaps have cost Him very little love – for we take our *own virtue*, which always has obstacles to overcome, as a measure; and since that is not so with God, we also perhaps concede him little benevolence. The world cost Him but a word, etc., etc., and since the return of love always presupposes love, our *natur*al love towards God is therefore so labored and small; nevertheless, through the agreeable feeling that, without our earning it, so much bounty streams upon us, we are seized by something akin to love. Only revealed religion discloses to us a love, on God's part, that cost Him an effort, and so, properly understood, can arouse love in return.

Mistrust in God: If I had no other evidences of God's benevolence beyond the course of nature, the judgment to that effect would inspire little confidence, since in human life I perceive a constant entanglement, and the opposite of good. It is not, therefore, from *individual* cases that I seek to determine the *general* concept of *benevolence* as *such*; for in that case I merely regard each action, in isolation, as a touchstone of benevolence, but cannot therefore conclude to the total happiness of my existence as a whole. And it is likewise possible to be without *mistrust* of God, if I do not attribute to Him the fulfillment of individual wishes. Despite my honesty, I can, for example, perhaps be unlucky for a long time. *Trust in* God is felt, therefore, merely in regard to the whole of our life, but not with respect to the *externals* of particular specific cases; otherwise, it can become a *tempting* of God. As the most benevolent of beings, God will, in total, at the end of it all, make everything good; without specifying the cases in which He is to evince benevolence, precisely in accordance with our own presumptions. In short, I shall one day be able to regard my whole existence with confidence; that is trust in God.

It is extravagant if, in individual cases, I rely upon God's goodness, as determined by my own intent; and it is for this reason a tempting of God, that I think myself able, by my own wish, to determine precisely the case where God's goodness is to display itself. A marriage with an uncertain outcome cannot be settled by trusting to God, for He might be no less wise and benevolent, were He even to let me starve. I see this in such a case, because if my wish proves false, I could not stupidly declare that His goodness has been ... [unfinished]

Awe presupposes reverence, and the latter, the feeling for the sublime in moral perfections, just as love presupposes the iwtvitvs8 of morally beautiful perfections. The sublime is a perfection that is distinguished from the beautiful, and in both, the perfections may move us either morally or *nonmorally*. To be moved by a morally perfect sublimity is reverence; it does not always presuppose love, for the grounds of the two are very different, and reverence, indeed, can actually suppress love, if the moral sublimity of the other seems greatly to collide with our own qualities, and we have not credited him with suitable goodwill in regard to ourselves. Thus a grave clergyman, who evokes our reverence, often arrives very inopportunely in a gathering where the beautiful predominates. Love wishes for closer union; sublimity frightens us away. Thus for the most part we have the greatest love for those we revere less, for example, the female sex, whose very weaknesses we forgive for the sake of their beauty, and are even delighted to win. So also there can be reverence for God, without loving Him, just as a miscreant may perhaps have great respect for his *upright* judge, but never loves him. Awe is a higher form of reverence, and thus in itself not mingled with love; but since reverence is commonly coupled with an anxiety not to offend its object, there arises from this the true concept of awe, which is also quite wholly distinct from fear, since we are guarding, not against the evil that he might visit upon us, but against that which we do ourselves. The fear of God is thus quite different from *fearfulness* towards God, the latter being a servile fear, which by no means increases reverence, but in fact diminishes love; for as soon as we see somebody against us, a degree of love is eliminated; who loves anyone, in so far as he punishes us? The fear of God (i.e. awe) is childlike, and that can coexist with love, because it is much on guard against the other's displeasure; and the childlike fear of God is thus an awe *coupled* with love. We guard against God's displeasure because of His beautiful and sublime qualities; but not, to that extent, from fear; it is ourselves we are in fear of, for we would in contrast be hateful in our own eyes.

§89. Deficiency, here, may thus be either want of *fearfulness* towards God, or a lack of the fear of God; the two are very different and have to be separated. The former is much the worse; the servile fear recoils from actions because of punishment, and I would fear someone in servile fashion, were I to shun him because of an evil to be apprehended. This destroys love, and is to be guarded against, therefore, in tender minds, since the frightful always engraves itself far more deeply, and even afterwards is not wholly softened in the presence of *beautiful* qualities. *Human* fear is again either fearfulness towards mew, or of them; the one fears the evil of men more than that of God, the other holds men more greatly in awe than God. For example, to prefer the displeasure of God to that of an awe-inspiring ruler, is the latter kind of human fear; and a reprobate who, as La Mettrie tells us, is frightened only of torture and authority, evinces *fearfulness* towards mew. The latter is no moral defect, but a political one; just as the opposite fearfulness [towards God] presupposes, not morality, but mere calculation. The former kind of fear is moral, however, just as is the awe at moral qualities.

§90. Not everyone, who fulfills a command, *obeys* it on that account, if he does not fulfill it *just because* it has been commanded. Thus men fulfill many divine commands from their own impulses – through their own moral feeling – and yet with the *false luster* of one who obeys. Indeed, often the judgment concerning the divine command is superfluously added in this way, being entertained, *per subreptum* [surreptitiously], even prior to the true ground. Universal obedience seems to be impossible for us, so long as the knowledge of God is not the dominant idea in us; and in a future state, perhaps it will be like that, since everything else will then be very easily subordinated thereto . . .

Wisdom and *prudence* are different. A man of much prudence may choose ends, for which he selects his means in the best way possible, without in fact being wise, i.e., having chosen a good end. Wisdom chooses ends, and the want of it makes men dolts; *prudence* chooses means, and without it, on the contrary, they are fools. Womenfolk have little wisdom, but much prudence, and more than men; for keeping their own secrets, finding out those of others, and conducting embassies, women would be better. But men (if they have not, by laxity, become womanish) are able to choose better ends, and avoid doltishness. But feelings often make dolts of us, even though we may display the utmost prudence in the process. Passions, for the most part, run counter to wisdom, since they choose silly ends. *To seek honour* is not doltish; but to seek it overmuch is silly, because this end, though natural in itself, bulks too large in comparison with others. *The puffed-up person*, on the other hand, is a fool, because in this he has no proper end, though he may well choose good means for it. Any intention which, in regard to itself, is nothing, makes a man a dolt. An intention that is relatively of no importance makes him silly. An intention unattainable by any means makes him a fool.

So, too, in religion. A man shows himself a dolt, if he does not sufficiently subordinate the lesser intentions to the main one; for example, an old man, who instead of regulating his passions, wishes to provide for his children. *Prudence* is evinced in religion, if I select the appropriate means; he who errs in his ends, errs the more grossly; for a good end at least makes the morality good. The error of a dolt is morally the greater; that of a fool, logically the greater. The one is immediate, the other mediate, since the means are not well chosen. The nature of the end determines the morality . . .

Self-abasement is the opposite of self-esteem. He who so grovels that he lowers himself, does not feel his own worth, though the other is distinguished only by an empty title, which depends merely on illusion.

Humility presupposes a correct estimation of self, and keeps it in bounds. We have more reason to observe imperfections than perfections, since they are more numerous, and the contemplation of perfections can very easily do harm. *Humility* is therefore not a *monkish virtue*, as Hume believes, but already needful even in natural morality. A vain science, such as geography or stargazing, can give us less distinction than moral worth. The latter will balance off imperfection with perfection; it is by rules of morality, not well-being, that I must be humble. Such humility will not be mingled with hypocrisy, but will be felt in that I perceive that I am not higher than others; and in fact, all men are not so far apart in that respect. The educator should implant self-esteem and humility, so that respect is evoked by achievements only, and not by illusion. The spoiling of the upper class is attributable to the middle class, and subjugation, luxury and pomp are the result. Here I also begin to reform myself, and then Rousseau's ideas become attractive. If I compare myself with others, and form a lesser opinion of them, this should not arise from self-esteem. The latter compares itself with itself. In humility we compare ourselves with others to our disadvantage; otherwise the imperfections of others would give me occasion for rejoicing, and this is morally evil. To despise others is also in this respect a bad method, that it evokes hatred instead. To be sure, I may compare my imperfections with the better circumstances of others, if I perceive the possibility of a greater perfection; but I should not always be taking notice of this. I should not take note of relative imperfection – that doesn't matter; whether I am *inferior* to the other – the comparison is harmful, as it is in ranking perfection and imperfection; just so long as I go on, in addition, to frame my self-estimate as a whole, and also feel my imperfections, but not imperfection as calculated against the other. His worth remains the same, whether it be above mine or below it. From this comes hypocritical humility, which extenuates itself; and even an upright man despises such a person, not because of his imperfection, but because he declares it. That he feels it, is good for himself; but that he declares it – what is the good of that? It is useless. Humility is that honest self-esteem which is also aware of one's perfections, and must be sharply distinguished from self-abasement, which merely inspires contempt . . .

§171. Pride is an inclination to think highly of oneself *in comparison* with others. It asks, not what one is worth, but how much more one is worth than another. It cannot well be *mistaken*, if it merely finds its own worth in the fact that others are imperfect. Thus this imperfection of theirs is the reason for its own joy, and that makes it a moral defect. It may be outwardly evinced, and is then called self-conceit.

The *vain man* seeks merely the *opinion* of others; he is wholly turned outward from himself, and does not judge by his own feeling: Frenchmen.

The *proud man* already believes in his own worth, but esteems it solely by the lesser stature of other people, and is thus at fault: Spaniards.

The *self-assured man* does not compare himself at all, and is inwardly good; but outwardly he must then be of sober mien.

The *man of pride*, who allows it to be very conspicuous, is also externally at fault, and is said to be *puffed-up*; disdain (Dutchmen).

Haughtiness is pride in display (since there is pride in the whole demeanor). Germans are vain and haughty.

Self-estimation is either *absolute* or relative; the latter is *inadequate*, since the other person may be very wicked, and so this does not determine that my own state is a good one; it is also evil, because it presupposes an inclination to take pleasure in the moral imperfection of another.

And thus humility, too, is strictly *absolute*, though the relative form can certainly help out the absolute one; it must never become ignoble, however, in that I become vexed at the virtues of others. Thus even the signs of humility are *absolute*, in that I should display them modestly, on the whole, and not relatively to others, since by the moral rules they are weedless, and could be evil, in that they may make us self-abasing, and other people proud. As against this, the civil order demands outward marks of precedence, which emphasize relative merit; but this is absurd, since by such boasting absolute esteem is diminished. This relative worth is plainly false, since it changes with the circumstances. How does a prince figure among peasants? And how before his king? A man who dwells merely on that is *indoles abjecta*. I esteem a person of note hypocritically, on account of his rank; truly, on account of his inner worth, when he has risen (on his merits) into the middle class; and the more highly, because he has had so many obstacles to overcome . . .

Conscience is *logica*, in that I am aware of some property; and *moralis*, in that I couple this with my moral feeling. Defects are therefore logical, in the want of consciousness concerning one's actions, as with frivolous people, or young folk; and moral, in the want of moral feeling concerning one's actions, as with old scoundrels, who have been prevaricating for so long, that in time that feeling is stifled, and a sham version takes over; for example, a shopkeeper's catechism.

The falsified conscience adultera is () *erronea*, when it is logically falsified; (2) *prave*, when it is morally so. The one goes astray, by intellectual error (*errores*); the other feels wrongly, by emotional defect (*depravitates*).

To distinguish the natural from the acquired conscience is often difficult. Much that is acquired is taken to be *natur*al. The parental curse that we might incur through a marriage that we do not seek to contract in the proper way, is an acquired conscience. Since, by natural law, the father would retain parental control only until such time as the son is able to govern himself, all duty of obedience (other than gratitude) would have lapsed, and does so here, since it has been acquired only through custom. But when Voltaire holds all conscience to be *acquired*, and demonstrates it by various examples drawn from different nations, he goes too far; the Eskimos, who kill their parents as a loving service to them, are to some degree justified, since they foresee a more ignominious death for them in the hunting that is *necessary* for survival.

To what degree our conscientious feelings are acquired, in *particular* cases, is hard to say. Our relationships with friends are perhaps acquired – the feelings are too greatly enhanced; as they also are in moral concepts.

Of bad actions, conscience judges far more strongly and correctly after the deed than before, and *beforehand*, more strongly than in course of the act. This is exemplified in the *pangs of conscience* that are bound to result after a lustful act. The reason: any passion draws attention to the gracious side, and clouds the other – and once the passion is there no longer, then the cloud also falls away.

If we men here in the world are not always in a state of passion, we are nevertheless the prey of impulse; in a state of mind such that passion has to judge of things; and thus throughout life, our judgment is never wholly impartial. It is itself the judge in its own case. Debarred from passion after death, we are then impartial judges upon ourselves, and on our morality; the judgment upon our life will then be far more vivid and truthful, and we shall perceive the abhorrent aspects more clearly still. So long as passion remains, however, the judgment becomes even more partisan. The fiercer the passions, the more clouded the moral feeling, and even the physical one, so that physical evil is also left over. If *conscience* is silent before the deed, or if it *grumbles* ineffectually, it is a bad conscience, and in the latter case a pedant that fails to restrain, and yet plagues us. Yet there is one hope for a more lively impression: the conscience that speaks *long beforehand* is stronger than the one that immediately precedes, since the former, from a long perspective, presupposes a greater impression. Otherwise, however, the conscience that immediately precedes is the stronger. Hence one who is caught with dagger in hand is not punished with death. The *conscientia consequens* is thus the strongest, but bad when the *conscientia antecedens* does not precede it; to be sorry afterwards is no reparation.

Since our life is a whole in its existence, one part of it cannot be sacrificed to another; the pleasure of the one must also be the pleasure of the other, and happiness a whole. Foresight, a daughter of affluence, is the source of unhappiness; enjoyment of the present, with attention to our morality, is our happiness. We have to enjoy these things in this world, and the all-too-abundant talk of eternity must not tear us away from time; eternity should serve merely to diminish the evil of this world, but not to lessen its joy. Man engineers downright robberies of himself; robbing himself of youth, in order to secure enjoyment of old age, of which he then deprives himself, through getting set in his habits. A part of life should not be sacrificed to the whole.

I can employ the higher powers of mind for utility's sake, and that is good; or for the sake of appearances, and that is bad. The motive for enhancing my powers is largely the good *opinion* of other people. But this is either an actual lie, or if truthful, is nevertheless (if it serves no useful purpose) chimerical when regarded immediately in itself, since it does not promote the best in me. Apart from that, since all show is far easier than substance, honor is wholly false; and therefore is harmful to the human race. The philosopher throws a veil over his own weaknesses, just as the Chinese were unwilling to accept the calendar, so as not to run into mistakes. The teacher, who perceives the falsity of his views, is still happy to let himself be honored, and does not admit his errors. Should not Crusius, over so many years, have recognized the untruth of his insistent utterances? But he does not say so. The pursuit of honor is more harmful to morality than any other passion; all others have something real about them, but this one is a phantom of the brain. I depart entirely from my inner state of moral goodness, and try to improve it with something external; and what harm the sciences do then. The pursuit of honor will perhaps be totally suspended in beings somewhat higher than ourselves; with us, it is still useful as a counter to great immorality, and to stiffen our resolve against extreme laziness, and thus it is needed for the lesser morality of mankind. Self-esteem, however, is rooted in morality; not in calculating on the opinion of other people. Thus people seldom marry on their own account; always with a view to others.

Suspension of judgment can occur from moral motives or logical ones.

Prudential planning decides, up to a point, with certainty, yet indicates the uncertainties, the want of assurance, the uncompleted matters that are merely set aside. In social matters, the suspension of judgment is very necessary, and a sign of humility, that should be achieved still more in practical affairs than in writing. Of all people, however, the scholar is the most covetous of honor, and thinks of nothing else; works for it, apportions it himself, and is the trumpet of fame. Knowledge as such is splendid, and without the highest insight, the highest of beings would not be the most perfect; but man must learn to recognize his limitations, not merely in logic, but in morals as well. In themselves, mathematics or numismatics are well worth knowing; but not, perhaps, for us; such eagerness for knowledge can eventually throw us entirely out of our orbit. All these attractions cause us, thereafter, to become stuck in the mud, so to speak; the child hastens, in prospect, ahead of the man; the earth-dweller has his eyes on eternity; and thus he is unfit for either state.

Learn to shun the impulses that diminish morality; pursue the moral use of your powers of cognition. They may also be greatly cultivated in other things, but prematurely so; between the sublimest human spirit and the lowest man there is no true difference of merit, save in regard to morality.

At present, mere scientific acumen must serve to compensate the defects of the sciences; otherwise there would be no need of them, for the *analogon rationis* [analogue of reason] is a surer guide in morality than reason is, and the good man's feeling more reliable than the reason that makes palpable errors in its inferences. Since the *analogon rationis* is actually given for our guidance, reason, equipped as it is with many needless adornments, must certainly not acquire many privileges. Confined by the law of necessity, and by human folly, we must therefore not be puffed up; to despise the useful guide, yet take the long way round to get home, is self-destroying.

A readiness in all circumstances to posit good ends for oneself, or to choose the best means, is *presence of mind*. Womenfolk are able to select good means, but not good ends. By long reflection we must accustom ourselves to presence of mind *in ancipiti*. Young people should first accept counsel, therefore.

That man alone is blessedly happy, who has the highest enjoyment of pleasure that he is capable of in the circumstances. So this life is to be distinguished from that to come. Blessed happiness consists:

1. of happiness; nonmoral good; physical well-being. Since this depends on external factors, it can be very defective, and very changeable.

2. of blessedness: the morally good.

The longing for mere well-being must therefore, by the law of mutability, already make for unhappiness, since all physical things relate to the whole, and cannot always affect us favorably. The morally good, in which we are the ground, is thus immutable, and fruitful in physical goodness, so that everything which comes about *through* me must come from moral goodness. If I am to make myself indifferent towards evil, am I also so towards the good?

If I am to make myself receptive to the good, am I also so towards evil? Responsiveness to physical good often becomes a ground of aversion, and one must therefore try to make oneself impervious to certain things. This costs us deprivations, indeed; though they are not painful, since the feeling about them simultaneously *diminishes*, and a much finer moral feeling awakens for them instead. The savage, moreover, is in a state of *indifference* about many things. Virtue calls for maxims and principles, which are very different from instincts, and even from morality; and thus there can be forms of conduct that are abhorrent, without being vices, because they actually presuppose maxims, and are only *figuratively* called vices – just as actions from good instincts are only figuratively called *virtues*.

The motivating ground for acting according to principles is the constancy that remains ever the same, whereas good *instincts* depend on impression and variable circumstances. These latter, in fact, are provided by human society. Maxims, on the other hand, are actually universal *principles*, under which particular cases can be subsumed, plus the skill of subsuming such cases. Moreover, there are indeed maxims that are *analogous* to virtue, for example, maxims of honor; and how many have acquired great luster from these alone.

Self-conquest: No victory gives more evidence of personal activity than this, and hence it is the most satisfying . . .

Of the sexual impulse we must judge, not merely in accordance with our civilized state, but according to the natural condition of man. And then, this impulse was very powerful, in order to sustain the species. Those who hold God's end to be always the principal one should consider here, whether the natural man has the providential intention to sustain the human race, or merely an inclination to immediate pleasure. The former is indeed the main end, but not the only one, and the remainder must certainly not conflict with it, but they can nevertheless be noninjurious to it; and it is thus altogether too scrupulous to forbid married couples those intimacies which are not immediately connected with propagation. The sexual impulse would not have developed so early, but only once the powers of the body had matured, for it would not have been accelerated by instruction. The impulse satisfied itself merely by immediate pleasure, and there would probably not have been a permanent bond. But since, no doubt, the man will have felt that the impulse would recur, he would allow the woman to follow him into the forest; she became his companion, and both would have cared for the children. He would have had to help her while she was suckling them, and thus arose monogamy, since there are as [2:49] many women as men. The impulse would not have been so rampant then,

since the fantasied pleasures of the civilized were lacking. Moreover, this impulse is covered with the veil of shame, which is also found among the majority of savages, and is quite unlike any other form of shame, and restrains the impulse. There is much truth in the objections of the cynic: we should be ashamed only of what is dishonorable; but for all that, there is a genuine shame-instinct, which has indeed no rational cause, and is strange, but whose aims are (1) to restrain the untamed sexual impulse; and (2) to maintain the attraction of it by secrecy. The male sex, which has more principles, possesses this shame in a lesser degree; for want of principles, the woman has a great deal of it, and it dominates her; and where this shame has already been uprooted in women, all virtue and respectability have lost their authority, and they go further in shamelessness than the most dissolute of men. Such shame, moreover, has an *awalogon* with an act that is intrinsically dishonorable, and this has produced the stupid *shame of monkishwess*. It is not, however, in itself the mark of an unpermitted act, but the veil of an honorable one, which propagates mankind. In addition to the sexual impulse, the female sex has many other qualities, which all focus on beauty, and are therefore charms and allurements. The male sex has friendship and devotion; the female, roguishness, kindness, etc.

The man has an acute judgment of beauty; coarse male kisses and matrimony are not so disgusting to womenfolk, and this is the wisest arrangement. This impulse is nowadays the source of so many vices, and plunged into such indecencies – so how, then, is it possible, amid such general corruption, where so many inhuman vices have sprung up, to effect an improvement? The Spartans let girls up to 9, and boys up to 3, go naked in the years before puberty. Our artificial virtues are chimeras, and become vices, if the hidden is regarded as vicious. As soon as chastity of speech, clothing, and demeanor increases, true chastity is thrust aside. Where one side of a thing is shown, the other side tempts us from out of the chimerical land of fantasy. Perhaps Rousseau has hit upon the best method. The precocious sexual urge must be confined, lest it hamper our growth and development, and enervate normal bonding, to our subsequent regret; yet this is to be accomplished, not by hiding the impulse, but by holding up to the young man an image of the beauty that he is one day to make happy, and which will wish to have him pure. In that case, he will not throw himself away, but will travel with this image, and save it up for his happiness. The quite total removal of the concept never achieves this effect; it is rather by the following principles: As I summarize the duties of the man in the words: Be a man, so there is also a plan for womanly duties: Be a woman, etc. Unity and union are altogether different; the friendship between two men, from the concept of the sublime, can have unity, as can the friendship between women, from the concept of the beautiful. But in matrimony there must be not mere unity, but union, for a *single* purpose, the perfection of the marriage. Now to this end nature has endowed the pair with different gifts, whereby one has dominance over the other. The woman allures, the man arouses; the woman admires, the man loves; and so each prevails over the other, and there is union without tyranny on the husband's part, or servitude on that of the wife, but by way, rather, of mutual dominance. Thus the ultimate goal of the bond between the two sexes is marriage. But if the *husband* becomes *womanish*, or the *wife mannish*, the marriage is inverted and not perfect. Imagine a learned lady, bold and robust: she is then a competitor to my worth; I cannot prevail over her, and the marriage will not be perfect. Imagine a bejewelled man, a feeble, dressy fellow: he is then a competitor to the woman's beauty: she cannot prevail over him, and again the marriage is imperfect. On the contrary, she will be more pleased with a man of natural dignity and self-confidence, with a plain, unaffected style of dress. The two sexes should not be mixed up; *womanliness* is no reproach to a woman, but manliness is, and in our country, owing to their lesser education, the womenfolk are closer to nature than those amazons in France, for example. Thanks to their delicacy of feeling, they are still able to make the difference quite clear . . .

Endeavoring to please others: The motivating ground of utility is nonmoral; the inclination to please is moral – it does more to bring men together.

Complaisance is a species of it, and the opposite of self-will, since I adjust myself to the will of another. It is a slippery quality – may be praiseworthy, but soon invites censure and contempt, since it shows that a man has no will of his own, and is without moral worth. It is a quality of weak souls. The noble prefer self-will, and the faults that result from it are not so grave as those due to complaisance, which in many people is often a cause of idleness. The young must still try to please, since as yet they have few principles. In trifles (and human life is so full of them that it almost seems to be a trifle itself, compared with the whole of what exists) self-will tends to separate us, etc.; but in morality it is worthy of praise.

Honorableness: Rousseau's conception of honor is purely internal, and such, also, is honorableness; a *true* self-esteem for one's inner worth. The judgment of others is merely an *accessorium*. It takes *personal* fortitude to overcome the constraints of conventional morality.

Egoismus moralis has two forms: that which breaches the limits in *selfesteem*, or in love of benevolence; since I am constantly promoting my own interest.

Self-abasement may be to oneself, or to others. The latter makes others puffed-up, and oneself into a worm. It proceeds from the former, and often makes our perfection useless, as when I do nothing for myself out of honor, but do it instead out of contempt.

Love towards others already indicates a lesser need in oneself for other things; self-love must take precedence, since the love for others simply rests upon it. That he, who thus loves others, enlarges his own happiness, is a property of dependents, and hence of created beings. He who enlarges the system of his love, also enlarges the well-being of his fellow men. How love is extended, is a practical question; I cannot say, as an absolute injunction, Thou shalt love! This love is that of wishing well, or of pleasing well. The latter is also nonmoral, but wishing well presupposes a morality of beauty: the idea of the *beautiful* in the action is the means thereto.

Affability is a sign of our love, and is not a real and efficient quality, i.e., readiness to be of service is symbolic, since we show the inclination to it, e.g. in our demeanor. Rules are very difficult – affable friendliness requires greater equality.

Indifference, as a moral quality, is the opposite of human love; but even by this cold-bloodedness I may understand a very good trait, if it holds the love inspired by sympathy in check, and gives it due measure. If the sympathetic inclinations are blind and serve no purpose, the stoic must say: If you cannot be of help to others, then what business is it of yours, pray?

Friendship is very complex; it already presupposes the *alter ego*, and does not always exist where I love another and he loves me; for () I shall not, on that account, simply disclose my secrets to him; and (2) I am not convinced, either, that he will sacrifice something for my sake. We have to be able to assume that his efforts on his own behalf will be made also for us, and ours for his; but that is a great deal to expect, and so friends are few. If I multiply friends, I diminish friendship, and hence it is already much, to have but one true friend. Between different persons there can certainly be sincere human love, though not in the degree of friendship; for the latter is the highest form of that love, and presupposes an identity of personality. Yet some people come reasonably close to this, and are also said to be friends. Friendship proper is in part impossible (owing to the number of our own requirements), and in part needless (since my security is already manifestly looked after by many others) . . .

Compassion. The ability to put ourselves in the position of another, is not moral only, but also logical, since I can project myself into the standpoint of another, e.g. of a follower of Crusius. So too in moral matters, when I project myself into another's feelings, to ask what he will be thinking about it. If I put myself, by a fiction, into another's shoes, this is a *heuristic* step, in order the better to get at certain things. It can be quite skillfully done, yet not moral, since I am not actually in his position; except in the case of true sympathy, where we really feel ourselves to be in his place. The *feeling of pity* would not be sufficient for morality. In the savage state, instincts are enough; everyone looks after himself; few are in need, and in that case pity is adequate. In civil society, where the needy have multiplied, it would often – however widespread – be futile to be merely sorry for them, and hence the feeling is much weakened, and evinced only to those in the direst necessity. In the common man, however, whose needs are fewer, and who can thus be the readier to share, the nearer he is to simplicity, these compassionate instincts will be greater. The civilized man is much constrained by self-serving artificial desires, so that pity is here replaced by the concept of what is right, what is seemly. This can never be futile, because I shall not be bound to the impossible; here virtue becomes calm and rational, and no longer remains a mere animal instinct, though such instincts certainly operate pretty regularly in the state of nature. In general, however, civil motives are insufficient . . .

Lying is simply too restricted, as an injury to the other; as untruth, it already has an immediately abhorrent quality, for (a) this most *trenchantly* separates human society, of which truth is the bond; *truth* is simply lost, and with it, all the happiness of mankind; everything puts on a mask, and every indication of civility becomes a deceit; we make use of other men to *our own* best advantage. The lie is thus a higher degree of untruth. (b) So soon as the lust for honor becomes a prevailing principle, it already sets no bounds to the lie. Self-interest cannot be so strong a reason, for lying is not an *enduring* means of advantage, since others shun the liar. The greediest shopkeepers of all are the most *honorable* in their dealings, simply from self-interest, and this is thus often a reason for truthfulness, etc. The lust for honor makes *lying* easier, since here the inner content is not so apparent; religion and well-being, for example, can easily be simulated, and not so readily exposed. (c) The longing for imaginary perfections, that perhaps were not thought suitable before; for example, a disinterested zeal to serve, is a *fantasy* too high for us. But since we can indeed be of service to a person in certain matters, there is the wish, in fantasy, to sacrifice ourselves; and since this cannot actually *be*, there is the wish, at least, for it to *seem so*. Second example: The fantasied desire for infinite knowledge, that is impossible to us, creates the *semblance* of this knowledge. In the indulgence in knowledge and enjoyment, do we therefore find the lie that is most abhorrent of all to the *natural man*?

Valve of the love of truth: It is the basis of all virtue; the first law of nature, Be truthful!, is a ground (1) of virtue towards others, for if all are truthful, a man's untruth would be exposed as a *disgrace*; (2) of virtue to oneself, for a man cannot hide from himself, nor is he able to contain his abhorrence.

The *feeling of shame* (which is later made subject to delusion, and envelops even the best actions), seems to be a natural means (*pudor*, not merely *pudicitium* in the pursuit of pleasure) of promoting truthfulness and betraying falsehood. If we wanted to use such shame, simply to betray the lie, it is very *practicable*. Providence would certainly not have furnished it to delude us, for it is the greatest of tortures; it is given, rather for betrayal – *involuntary* betrayal. It has never been there to cause us anxiety, but rather to betray *something* which nature did not want to hide. To thus make use of this shameful feeling as an antidote against lying, we must not employ it for any other purpose, e.g. to show up a child. Here I use merely the means for imitation; if he has behaved or spoken stupidly, I simply persuade, and as a *child* there is much that becomes him, which is not becoming to the *man*. But supposing that, regardless of his love of truth, he has *but once* told a lie, from self-interest, because the love of truth is not so lively as physical feeling; in that case I do not talk to him of *obedience* (of which no child has the *concept*, nor is of an age to do so), but simply of *untruth*. In the end he acquires as much abhorrence for it as he has for a spider. *Incest* with a sister is abhorrent, not because God has forbidden it, but because the wrongness of it has been imprinted since childhood. Such is the power of ideas of dreadfulness; and if a son were to see his father's abhorrence of lying, he would by moral sympathy perceive the same himself. Suppose him now grown up, then everything would go better. I would openly declare my intention, for example, that I am working, not for the benefit of science, but from self-interest; I would yearn only for an official position that I am capable of filling. Nowadays, however, there is *untruth*, not merely in the world, but also before God, in solitude, since we cannot stand even before Him without pretence. To be truthful, we would now have to forfeit a great deal, and so each of us shies away from the truth, and most of all in a nightshirt. Untruth may end by deceiving itself, and so self-examination becomes equally slippery; the good side of kindheartedness, for example, is put before its reprehensible aspect, and men eventually become deceivers even towards God: for example, Job's comforters. Certain untruths are not called lies, because the latter are strictly *untruth*s that are contrary to *duty*; not, however, as our author thinks, merely to the duty to myself, but also to that towards others. The importance of the love of truth is so great that one can almost never make an exception to it.

Untruth, to the great *advantage* of *another*, still has something *sublime* in it, that is near allied to virtue. Yet to speak *truth*, to the dis*advantage* of *oneself*, is sublimer still, and to speak untruth to one's *own advantage* is doubtless always immoral. But since the highest morality is not on a par with the moral level of man, this is not, indeed, quite settled. Yet because the bounds of a man's strength and obligation are hard to determine, this *human* ethic of untruth will be as confused as the *logica probabilism* [logic of the probable]. Every coward is a liar; Jews, for example, not only in business, but also in common life. It is hardest of all to judge Jews; they are cowards. Children, for example, that are brought up cowards, tell lies, since they are weak in conquering themselves, etc. But not every liar is a coward, for there are inveterate scoundrels as well.

With us, in many cases, a small untruth does not seem untoward, for weak persons; the case is often complicated; if another asks him something, a man cannot remain silent, for that would be to assent, etc., etc. In short, we should investigate the degree of morality that is suited to men. As with all fine inclinations, we can also enlarge the desire for holiness; but not all can be moral men, when they are weak or needy, since in few cases are we able to attain to holiness. If our untruth is in keeping with our main intent, then it is bad; but if I can avert a truly great evil only by this means, then ... etc. Here goodness of heart takes the place of sincerity. To obtain a great good by untruthfulness is far less excusable than to ward off a great evil by that means; for (1) our inclination to our happiness is often fanciful, and morality should not be sacrificed on that account; (2) the taking away of what I have is a greater denial than a withdrawal of what I might have. A white lie is often a *contradictio in adjecto*; like pretended tipsiness, it is *untruth* that breaches no *obligation*, and is thus properly no lie. *Joking* lies, if they are not taken to be true, are not immoral. But if it be that the other is ever meant to believe it, then, even though no harm is done, it is a lie, since at least there is always deception. If untruth presupposes cleverness and skill, we get *artful* lying and repute; courtiers and politicians, for example, have to achieve their aims by lying, and everyone should flee any position in which *untruth* is indispensable to him.

The inclinations of men in nature are to be distinguished from those that evolve from artificial motives; a primary piece of self-knowledge. An ethic for man, *determined* in his nature, by his knowledge, powers, and capacities, has yet to be written. For by reason we can also discern rational perfections that are suitable, indeed, for a higher being, but not for him. We here have to investigate his limitations; and to become acquainted with the *natural man*, let us adopt this as our rule, that we take those parts that are unalterable by any art; and what is contrary to them will be artificial. Such regular inclinations of nature are: (1) *self-preservation*, and (2) the inclination to preserve the species; these may be increased or diminished by reflection, but reflection does not produce the urge. We must also, reflection notwithstanding, eat and cover ourselves; the sexual impulse is purely a lustful thing. The *arrangements* of nature are ancient, original, irresistible *reflection.*

Freedom is also an urge, because anyone wishes to follow his *own* will, and against physical hindrances he knows of means for this; but not against the will of another. This he considers to be the greatest misfortune, and so it is, since in part it is far more vexatious, and in part irremediable.

Hence all animals are *equally* free. From freedom there arises the desire for *equality*, especially in strength (or else by cunning), since this is the ... [unfinished]

From the urge to equality there arises the urge to *honor*; if the other would take power over me, he must be made to think that I am equal to him. That is *honor*, and it takes two forms:

1. to preserve myself; to have *strength*, and to show it, in order not to become a serf.

2. to preserve one's kind; the man, being stronger, covets the trust of the woman, so that he may preserve and defend her. He will choose a wife, and must ensure that he is *pleasing to her*; and since she is weak, she sets store by valor. This second urge to honor is more effective than the first. Hence Rousseau extols the sexual impulse. The first he can defy, but this one is strong in its effect.

The *urge* to *know* does not lie in *nature*; to us, indeed, it is now indispensable, but simply through long practice. The reason for it, in ourselves, is merely *tedium*. The scientific urge for purposes of self-preservation depends merely on the contingency of our condition; immediate *honor* is never the source, but always the end.

A thing cannot lie in nature, if (1) it can never be satisfied, and (2) it is out of proportion to the shortness of life, and to great desire.

In general, a thing is *unnatural* if it is contrary to the urges of nature; the scientific impulse is not merely somewhat at variance with the urge to self-preservation; it is particularly adverse to the sexual urge.

However, I am simply to know the *natural man*, not in the present connection, to be owe. My heart may not yearn for that, indeed, but I must *nevertheless* adapt myself to it. So let ambition be no passion; since I despise it, it plagues me not; but I still need it as a goal, in order to be effective. Science, and the like, must not therefore be a blind thirst (so I must not be bored without it; not unsociable; not contemptuous of the unlearned, but gladly cherishing them); yet I still need it *externally*, as a goal. One can never attain to inner virtue in any other way. For the moralist or cleric already (1) presupposes comforts, honor, etc., though that is unnatural; (2) extends duties contrary to nature, e.g. by deriving marriage, not from the sexual impulse, but from the command of God.

People also fabricate false virtues; those that are appropriate to the *natural* man are too elevated and hyperbolical for the artificial one. The happy man is he who is good without virtue (by feeling, without concepts; the *man* does, the philosopher *knows* it). The happy man is he who is knowledgeable without science. Both of those things are mere glitter, etc. Plan of judgments of the common judgment. Examination of nature and art; thence to judge projects. One should look first to the median;

otherwise the height is never reached, since our life is commonly too short, and the project too fanciful.

§348. Relationship of men; towards a concept of the system of human love: the love of *well-wishing* (of the other's greater welfare) is either active or wishful. The merely *yearning* or *wishful* love comes either from the degree of weakness, or from the disposition, in that it is merely fanciful. For a degree of love that is all-too-elevated for my practical capacity is just as ineffectual as a *want* of love. *Excessiveness* in the way of life also creates such wishes and yearnings, and is not good, since it is (1) *useless*;

(2) deceptive, in that it squanders time and actually impedes practical love; for the love that is too little practical has the love that is all-too-greatly *fanciful* as its cause. So to enquire into them both, let us note () that a person does not actively love another *until he is himself in a state of wellbeing*; since he is the *principium* of the other's good, let him first better himself. He should be at ease with himself, and thus the more there is of excess, the less there is of practical human love. For by excess we multiply in fancy our own needs, and thus make practical love *difficult*, i.e., *eo ipso rare*. To make itself practical, it puts itself at ease with itself, making do with little; and from this comes practical love, etc. All other motives produce fanciful urges, and hence in a condition of simplicity there will be much practical love, and in a state of luxury, little; but more of the fanciful kind, and since this cannot be satisfied, for in that case the entire human race would be before me, *I merely wish*, and have simply thought up the fancy for myself, because practical love is wanting in me.

Transfer a man of nature (not a man of the woods, who is perhaps a chimera, but a simple man) into the midst of artificial society; a man whose heart is not set on anything. The man whose love is *real*, loves *in a more limited way*, and his love cannot be extended to *everyone*, without his *forgetting*, for his own part, to take note of his *own position*. Thus a natural man has a care for himself, without informing himself much about the well-being of others. Our professions of sympathy, as compliments, seem foolish to him. Nevertheless, his love will be practical, e.g. for one who is suddenly in danger. Here this instinct cannot be eradicated by wickedness; it unites the whole human race, and is powerful, since it often does not wait upon reason. Yet this truly practical instinct is directed, not so much to the increase of good, as to the *prevention of great and sudden harms*; and as soon as they are too much for his powers, wishings and pityings strike him as too foolish; he would have to divert his attention from himself, and so he is perfectly ready to turn his thoughts elsewhere. In present-day civil society, since the needs multiply, the objects of pity mount up; the capacity of men itself declines, since in part really, and in part through illusion, they are weak and thus miserable; for the evils of illusion, which make me *in imagination*, and a thousand others in reality similar, are on the increase. What must *human* love be here? A topsoil, an imagined human love, a yearning of the fancy, is the natural consequence. So it now spreads abroad, and corrupts the heart. Since, through morality, the fanciful love of humanity is so widely diffused in people by instruction, it remains a matter of speculation everywhere in life, a topic of romances, such as Fielding's, etc., that has no effect, since (2) it is too exalted, and (2) does not get rid of the obstacles.

True love is (2) rectitude: It is the love we have by nature, the fundamental love, for it is founded upon a living feeling of *equality*; otherwise, favor, etc., will come of it, but here, *rectitude*; that I owe nothing. Equality means that the natural man is equal to all others, and they to him, and since moral sympathy is imprinted on all, he has to put himself in the other's place; and from this there follows *living rectitude*. From it there arises the obligation to alleviate the woes of others, which is equivalent to rectitude. Take, for example, one who fails to give me warning of a ditch; you would require this of others, so you must do it yourself. Without love of humanity this rectitude would be merely a semblance. Man in the civil state is called on to have love of *rectitude* only towards a few; yet truly the whole *human* race has an obligation to it for every single person; not, however, each individual, because his possibilities are lessened. From love of *humanity*, favor will arise, since it selects people, without special compulsion or desert. The love due to favor, if it is not to be artificial, too extreme, too overpowering, has to be built upon love of humanity. Here we must examine how far the duties of society can be grafted on to love of *humanity* and the obligation towards it; on to *rectitude*– such is the indispensable goal of moral theory, and *rectitude* is based on the exalted *feeling* of *equality*. There exists in man a moral sympathy, to put oneself in the other's place; it is the basis of *righteous* love, and holds it to be an *obligation*, etc., and the opposite hateful. *Righteous* love differs from *kindly* love, in that absence of the former is hateful, while absence of kindly love means that one is not to be praised in a higher degree. Actions to which I am bound by the rule of rectitude are *obligations*. The boundaries between the two cases, where someone must hate the other, and simply does not love him, are very distinct, but hard to discriminate. Anyone who puts something before an obligation to himself, would find himself hateful. Nature has not framed us to be *generous*, but to be selfsustaining; sympathetic, indeed, to the woes of others, yet in such a way that the sum shall not be zero; that I not sacrifice as much as I redeem, but preserve myself and my kind.

In the state of nature, obligations are few, and the sense of them is great.

In the civil state, there are more obligations, and the sense of them is small.

In the one, men have little to do with one another, but the helpful actions they do encounter, have a bearing on their natural state: natural evils, and not the fabricated ills of delusion.

In the other, the commercium is greater. Many helpful actions are needed, even on account of the numerous invented evils, and hence there are many grounds for giving aid, but more obligations upon oneself. Many people live unjustly at the expense of others, and therefore incur so many debts that no room is left for kindness. They are a major reason for acts of violence towards others; and to such people their ill-fortune is not indifferent to them, as in the state of nature; rather, they have brought it on themselves. Hence there are many obligations; and here we have the first axiom: *All men are equal to one another*. To the savage, it is a principle; but to us, who have strayed so far from it, it is a thing to be proved, and the basis of *ethics*. Every *man* has an equal right to the soil. Thus *obligations* multiply, but the *sense* of them diminishes. For, (1) the sense of *equality* declines; I feel my superiority, though others yet rank above me, and I think myself willing to take after God. Yet I still am under *obligation*, for (2) there is a decline of *moral sympathy*; a cause of the harshness of superior folk, and of the misfortune of the poor. Their oppressions continue, since the others do not even claim responsibility for them.

Acts of goodness. Man fancifully exaggerates his moral capacity, and sets before himself the most perfect goodness; the outcome is nonsense; but what is required of us? The Stoic's answer: I shall raise myself *above myself*, will become a *savage*, rise superior to my own afflictions and needs, and with all my might be good, be the *image of godhood*. But how so, for godhood has no obligations, yet you certainly do; anyone has a right upon me, on my work and help. Now the god departs, and we are left with *man*, a poor creature, loaded with obligations. *Seneca* was an impostor, *Epictetus* strange and fanciful. All *goodness* is not, in itself, *obligation*; from this it follows that our education, and mutual education, must be such that our sympathies do not become *fanciful*, but remain confined to the practical. I must be *upright*, and attend to my obligations; but the exalted pretension of wanting to love the whole of mankind is a fraud. He who loves the Tartar, loves not his neighbor. Loving all, we love *none*, and our love is therefore less. In place of rendering assistance to everyone, there should be simple *courtesy*, which is () not hatred, and (2) a mere calm willingness to assist in emergencies, according to *our* powers. Out of *rectitude* (but not *ardent* desire) there may be sacrifice; to that I am not obligated, though I am to courtesy, which has beauty because it springs from *equal*ity, and goes with self-esteem. To inferiors we owe, not favor merely, but a courteous attitude; to superiors, not hatred, but courtesies; for they are simply *equals*. All favor is offensive; here I shall neither cringe nor despise; with no lofty ideas of *virtue*, I shall be *honorable*, without wishing to be a great *saint* ...

§368. The doctrine of *tolerance* is generally well known, and much invoked by the persecuted; its limits, however, are still very indefinite. It is (1) *moral tolerance*, as a duty that one person bears to another, without constituting them members of a state. Since all true religion is internal, and lies in the relationship of the human heart towards God, a man may judge of the signs thereof in another, but not of the religion itself. The external practice of religion can be imitated, without anything within. In Rome, the majority are atheists, including even popes. Now since the signs are so ambiguous, it is a *duty* not to deny somebody a religion, because in signs he differs from myself; for I *cannot* have insight into an inner religion. It is thus (1) possible with difficulty only, and (2) also unnecessary, according to the concerns of nature; because the judgment upon others, the presumptions of doing this, calls for great authority, if it is not to be an offense. Now in the state of nature there is no such authority, since religion is a relationship to God; to myself it can only represent a form of conduct, which religion admittedly elevates, but which can be sufficient for me even without religion. For example, the Talapoins of Pegu; if they receive me, I *ought* not to trouble myself at all, for my own part, about their religion. I have a concern for what may be conformable to my welfare, but religion plays no part in that. Why should I not have a concern for it, out of a *general love of mankiwd*? *Responsio*: It is certainly worthy of note, but afterwards. In short, a moral code can exist without religion. But now if I detect in it a religion that may be very injurious to my own interests, for example, the vindictiveness that springs from religion, then it does concern me. A *persecuting* religion can be an object of suspicion, even in a state of nature, that I may guard myself against it, and keep out of its way.

(2) *Civil Tolerance*. In the state of nature there is less occasion for religion, than there is for it as a means to civic well-being. Religion is for our eternal well-being, and for this and other reasons it is a major motivating ground to many human duties. But how if there be no religion? Is it always equally necessary, with regard to our welfare in the present? *Responsio*: No, and it is the less necessary in a state of nature, because there are fewer occasions for those departures from human duties, to which religion is held

to be an antidote. Peoples that possess no other religion than some ancient traditional fancies, have much that is good among them, and little that is bad; warfare excepted, and that, too, is just a customary habit.

So since here there is little occasion for it, the other's religion is likewise of little concern to me. But as soon as the *interest* grows, and perfections have ascended to the fanciful level, moral feeling is no longer so sure a guide. In the end, that feeling becomes too weak to resist fervor; the love of humanity cools off; here the moral grounds of motivation are too feeble to provide defense against everything; higher grounds are called for, and thus religion becomes ever more needful (in the civil state; it can never be so in the natural one), and finally we get superstitious religion, in the degree to which extravagances increase. For things that I can do without, I shall not lie, and still less perjure myself; but, attracted by many things, to which I cleave, I have to be bound by oath against such major sources of temptation. There is an ever greater need for fantastical ceremonies, which in fact mean nothing, but are able to conquer rampant immorality. Here, religion is a police-force; morally, its boundaries are defined, but in civil society they become vague, because already we are at a loss to provide means sufficient to preserve us from ruin.

In regard to civil tolerance, religion is a matter of indifference to the natural man; there is already morality in his heart, before he has religion; so long as, in the state of simplicity, there are forces that impel him to be good, and no incentives are required for the avoidance of evil, he does not need religion. But when many of his comforts turn into necessities, his impulses gain the upper hand, so that morality becomes too weak, and the religion of nature does not suffice. For this, more understanding and philosophical reflection are required, than can be expected of the whole human race. So it has to be complemented by a revelation, either pretended or true.

The Pulserro bridge of the Persians produces many noble deeds, so Chardin tells us. Pure morality asks for no rewards, etc., but this pure morality is nowadays not present in the human heart; nor can the religion of nature provide aid to morality. Without basing itself on reason, a revelation at least offers a pretence of doing so. All civilized nations have a revelation of their own, and the barbarous ones a myth. India has one of the most ancient. The dispute as to which is the true revelation, cannot be decided here. In religion of this kind, to be suitable to the most considerable portion of men, much must be symbolic, to make the duties of nature venerable by many solemnities; certain ceremonies must make the matter worthy of respect. A custom once adopted must not be impeached, for till now it has been the foundation of the state, and if it is changed (though only fractionally) and for the better, we finally come to think that, since something has been altered, it could all of it be false. Hence republics are at their strictest concerning the old religion.

Can a government protect a multiplicity of religions? *Responsio*: Yes; in so far as any one of them is already established, it is far better to protect it, instead of wishing to improve it; because eventually an indifference to all religion would result. The multiplicity of religions creates an attachment to your own, and the civic utility is very much the same; for, as experience shows, Holland, for example, is a well-governed state. To be sure, were the principles, if pursued, to be adverse to the state, as with the Jews, for example, who are permitted by the Talmud to practice deceit, then the natural feeling rectifies this false article of religion. Such evil freedoms are not followed; the principles of the Catholics, for example, would in practice be adverse to the state, but this does not actually occur. The improvements of religion relate, therefore, merely to the political, for example, monastic orders. If a customary traditional religion, that is not based on rational demonstration, is generally accepted, anybody ought to be prohibited, on the state's account, from impugning it, even when errors are perceived therein. Nor can anybody deprive me of my ability to think for myself, and that should not be permitted. But since I take the greatest of pleasure in imparting my opinion to my fellow citizens, is it not injustice to forbid me from doing this? Yes indeed; however, the general welfare is not possible without these simple injustices, where luxury is concerned. In a state of perfect tolerance, a particular moral beauty must prevail; if everyone states his opinion, then every part will be put in a special light, and *truth* will be suppressed by coercion. Nor is any given error ever a moral transgression, even though it be an offense against the state. A universal tolerance is possible, but only if we again return to the first state of things; in that case, we are also morally good without God. Why should I not state my opinion of religion? In regard to this world, the decision concerning tolerance is solely a matter for authority; not for anyone else, and not for any clergyman. The latter is interested only in truth or falsity, not in what is useful or harmful; and the truth he is unable to decide. The cleric and his adversary are both citizens, about whom only authority has anything to say. But what degree of freedom do they have? To give no freedom at all is just as injurious as to give too much. Precisely because of a total lack of freedom, clever men become indifferentists. For this tolerance, the most subtle question is, whether there are errors worthy of respect.

So let us have moral tolerance, for it is in no way a form of doubt. Yet many religions foster a real hatred among men, when they set up their opponents as devils rather than men. Moral tolerance is called for in everything. Let us look upon the other with love; he errs, yet I do not hate him on that account, but have pity for him, that through error he should go astray. No individual who is morally intolerant is guilty of a crime, for the state has no concern with him. With luxury, religion proliferates in ceremonies; with profusion it declines; and one day complete tolerance may be possible.

Should authority, too, be concerned with the cure of souls? *Responsio*: This question must extend to all nations. Can the authority that is convinced of its religion forbid all others? *Responsio*: No, for if every nation, which also believes itself persuaded of its own religion, likewise totally denies entry to arguments from the other side, then all access to the truth would be closed off. Each thinks it has the truth, and if this belief is a reason for prohibition, then all nations possess such a right. Thus authority can certainly practice intolerance for political reasons, but not for the sake of salvation hereafter. However righteous a religion may be, and however great the conviction of it, there follows from this no right to deny entry to other opinions, for salvation's sake; for it is hard to distinguish between true and false conviction. Can an authority proselytize for a religion? *Responsio*: Yes, the propagation of a truth by argument is morally always useful (though it may often be politically harmful, since it frequently promotes zealotry as well); but it is also man's prerogative to require arguments. This method is reasonable, and the compulsion to declare something true, that one did not hold before, is very unjust and offensive, extremely damaging and never useful, save perhaps to do away with certain other injustices.

Arguments for coercion. As soon as I regard a religion as the sole means of blessedness, then it is plainly a matter of humanity to snatch men from perdition, and here, assuredly, all means are good, for even small evils in this life are nothing to those that are eternal. So means of compulsion are not unjust if they are means; but physical coercion never produces conviction, as with the Saxons under Charlemagne. *Objectio*: But much consideration needs also to be given to the descendants, who, even if their ancestors were merely made hypocrites by coercion, will perhaps have good and true conviction, through a better education.

All this seems plausible; but in brief, () no means that is adverse to the supreme prerogatives of mankind, is a good one. Now men are all equal, and should mere inequality, coercion, be the means of eternal happiness, it is a means of injustice, which already presupposes force. (2) The whole of mankind rises up against *having* to maintain something. From all this it follows that, in regard to the hereafter, authority must avail itself merely of the prerogatives of mankind: the arguments, in which every man has a share.

The common man, who never uses or misuses reason, must admittedly be guided, and this, therefore, for the most part, in an historical way. The less noble portion, which uses and misuses arguments, should not be taught merely by authority, but supported by grounds of reason. If education has been rightly conducted, there is no injustice required in securing tolerance.

1. The subject will be brought up tolerant, with error distinguished from crime.

2. It will not be harmful to him, since he is being educated by means of reason.

To coerce other into *opinions*, or into *silence*, is in this way harmful as a moral intolerance, that one can thereupon never guard against the evil consequences of abhorrence:

1. Every man wants to have his own opinion as the general one; the *causes* of which are:

2. that he supposes all morality to be based on religion, and thus hates the other, for he sees in him wickedness rather than error. It is the clergyman's duty to expel this intolerance from the heart. Education should be made into the seedbed of moral tolerance.

3. a man's intolerance is often *founded upon great ignorance*. Since he cannot answer by reason, he thinks of it as an enemy that will expose his nakedness. He who has no arguments to offer is hostile to counterarguments. A clergyman, who has examined himself (we may suppose), will have no hatred, even for the ignorant theologian.

Moral intolerance, to be sure, is in itself already an absurdity, and if a proper education were to be universal, then political tolerance could be universal too. At present, however, authority must be vigilant *everywhere* ...

Selected Notes and Fragments from the 1760s

Notes on anthropology prior to 1770

618. 1769? (1764–68?)

The strikingly natural or naïve (later addition: in the use of the under-standing, if nature appears as art, is called naivety), the unexpectedly natural.

Poetic art is an artificial play of thoughts.

We play with thoughts if we do not labor with them, that is, are [not] necessitated by an end. One merely seeks to entertain oneself with thoughts.

For this it is necessary that all the powers of mind are set into an harmonious play. Thus they must not be a hindrance to themselves and to reason, although they must also not promote it. The play of images, of ideas, of affects and inclinations, finally of mere impressions in the division of time, of rhythm (versification) and unison (rhyme). The play of the senses is for verse [breaks off]

(Later addition: Composition. 1. Poetry. 2. Oratory: harmony of thoughts and of the imagination. B. 1. Painting and music: harmony of intuitions and sentiments, both through relation to thoughts.)

It is no labor, thus also no servitude, yet is still the knowledge of poesy. It must be counted as a merit of the poet that one learns nothing through him; he must not himself make labor out of play. Poesy is the most beautiful of all play, for it involves all of our powers of mind. It has rhythm from music. Without the measure of syllables and rhymes it is no regular play, no dance.

The sensible play of thoughts consists in the play of speech (versification) and of words (rhyme). It goes well with music. It awakens the mind.

Poets are not liars, except in panegyrics. But they have abolished the doctrine of the gods through their fables.

The play of impressions is music.

The play of sentiments: the novel, theater.

The play of thoughts, sensations (images or forms (theater)) and impressions: poesy. The impressions are only through the language, since they are to accompany the thoughts.

Poesy has neither sensations nor intuitions nor insights as its end, but rather setting all the powers and springs in the mind into play; its images should not contribute more to the comprehensibility of the object, but should give lively motion to the imagination. It must have a content, because without understanding there is no order and its play arouses the greatest satisfaction.

Every action is either business (which has an end) or play which (later additiow: serves for entertainment) certainly has a point, but not an end. In the latter the action has no end, but is itself the motivating ground.

In all products of nature there is something that is related merely to the end, and something that concerns merely the correspondence of the appearance with the state of mind, i.e., the manner, the vestiment. The latter, even if one does not understand any end, often counts for everything. E.g., figure and color in flowers, tone and harmony in music. Symmetry in buildings.

(*Addition: Suaviter in modo, fortiter in re.*) [Agreeable in manner, strong in substance.]

619. 1769

The primary elements of our cognitions are sensations. This is what one calls those representations in which the mind is regarded as merely passive, acted upon by the presence of an object. They comprise the matter, as it were, of all our cognition. For the form is given subsequently by the soul's own activity. This sensation, in so far as it signifies merely the state of the subject, is called feeling; but if it pertains (is in relation to) an outer object, then it is called appearance. From this we see that all of our representations are accompanied with a feeling, for they are affections of the state of the soul.

620. 1769. M 219, at the beginning of M § 606

The first faculty of the human soul and the condition of the rest is sensibility, by means of which the soul receives representations as effects of the presence of the object and does not produce them itself. As something belonging to the state of the subject, the representation of sensibility is called sensation; but as something that is related to an object, appearance. There are sensations without noticeable appearance, and appearances without noticeable sensation; yet both are always present.

621. 1769? (1764–68?)

All art is either that of instruction and precept or of genius; the former

has its a priori rules and can be taught. Fine art is not grounded on any science and is an art of genius.

(Later addition: Even an inference contains beauty: as a cognition it is related to the object, as a modification of the mind that is sensed, to the subject.)

622. 1769? (1764–68?)

The rational cognition of the beautiful is only criticism and not science; it explains the *phaenomenon*, but its proof is a posteriori.

(Later addition: Science and art; the latter, of imitation or of genius.) (Later addition: All appearance is of succession or simultaneity; the former is ——,the latter the image.)

Good taste occurs only in the period of healthy but not merely subtle reason.

(Later addition: Taste for a thing (inclination) is not always taste for the same thing, e.g., music.)

(Later addition: The judgment of the amateur, of the connoisseur (the latter must know the rules), of the master.)

In the case of sensation I always judge only subjectively, hence my judgment is not also valid for others; in the case of experience, objectively.

Whether beauty and perfection, hence their causes as well as the rules for judging of them, do not stand in a secret connection. E.g., a beautiful person often has a good soul.

Tender sensitivity belongs to a judgment concerning that which can be agreeable etc. to everyone; receptivity to one's own state; the former pertains to the man, the latter to the woman. The power of choice must rule over this, and a limitation of it to the minimum is moderation, *apathia*.

(Later addition: Beauty in and for itself, if it is not accompanied, say, with vanity, arouses no desire, except only through charm.)

623. 1769? (1764–68?)

One has no a priori grounds for justifying a taste, but only the general consensus in an age of rational judging.

(Later addition: One's own or personal sentiments must be distinguished from substituted ones; the latter can be a disagreeable imitation, but still be personally agreeable. (The good is always agreeable in substituted sentiment.))

624. 1769? (1764–68?)

(Later addition: Sensible cognition is the most perfect among all those who intuit; confusion is only contingently attached to it.)

In the case of taste the representation must be sensible, i.e., synthetic and not through reason; second: intuitive; third: concerning the proportions of the sensations, immediate. Thus the judgment of taste is not objective, but subjective; not through reason, but a posteriori through pleasure and displeasure; further, it is not a mere sensation, but rather that which arises from sensations that are compared. It does not judge of the useful and the good, but of the contingently agreeable, bagatelles (later addition: so far as their appearance is consonant with the laws of the faculty of sensation.)

625. 1769? (64–68?)

In everything that is to be approved in accordance with taste there must be something that facilitates the differentiation of the manifold (singling out); something that promotes comprehensibility (relations, proportions); something that makes grasping it together possible (unity); and finally, something that promotes its distinction from everything that is possible (precision).

Beauty has a subjective *principium*, namely the conformity with the laws of intuitive cognition; but this is not an obstacle to the universal validity of their judgments for human beings, if the cognitions are identical.

(Later addition: In objects of love one readily confuses charm with beauty.)

One cannot very well convince someone who has a false taste; one can convince others that he has a false taste, but can only bring him to abandon his opinion by examples.

626. 1769? (1766–68?)

(Later addition: An idea is the basis of the intuition. Beautiful things, cognitions.)

What pleases in appearance, but without charm, is pretty, seemly, proper (harmonious, symmetrical). If the charm springs from the immediate sensation, then the beauty is sensible; but if it has sprung from associated thoughts, then it is called ideal. Almost all of the charm of beauty rests on associated thoughts.

That the grounds of the distinction of beauty are merely subjective can be seen from the fact that one cannot possibly conceive of a more beautiful shape for a rational being than the human shape.

All cognition of a product is either criticism (judging) or discipline (later addition: doctrine) (instruction) or science. If the relations that constitute the form of the beautiful are mathematical, i.e., those where the same unit is always the basis, then the first principle of the cognition of the beautiful is experience and its criticism; second, a discipline is necessary that yields rules that are sufficiently determinate for practice (as in the case of the mathematics of probability), and this comes down to a science the principles of which are, however, empirical.

If the relations that constitute the ground of beauty are relations of quality (e.g., identity and difference, contrast, likeliness, etc.): then no discipline is possible, and even less science, but merely criticism. Architecture (in the general sense) (the art of horticulture, etc.) is a discipline, likewise music. For in the former it is a matter of pleasing relations in the division of space, in the latter with regard to time. Hence the scholastic term "aesthetics" must be avoided, because the object permits no scholastic instruction; one could just as well demonstrate amorous charms by a term of art.

There are immediate sentiments of the senses or hypothetical (and substituted) sentiments. The former arise from everything that pertains to our state and when we ourselves are the object of our consideration. The latter: when we as it were transform ourselves into an alien person and invent for ourselves a sensitivity that we approve or desire. The sensitivity always concerns our own state and its charm or disagreeableness. One can have such substituted sentiments with regard to such states or actions toward which one has no personal sentiment of one's own. E.g., an imagined normal life after an illness; magnanimity were one to win the big jackpot. Voltaire has the most excellent sentiments in the name of the Romans and of everyone in the tragedy. Such substituted sentiments make [us] neither happy nor unhappy except when they are connected *indirecte* with our state. They are only *fictiones aestheticae* and are always agreeable.

627. 1769?

Taste is the selection of that which is universally pleasing in accordance with rules of sensibility. It pertains preeminently to sensible form; for with respect to this there are rules that are valid for all.

628. 1769

The inner perfection of a thing has a natural relation to beauty, for the subordination of the manifold under an end requires a coordination of it in accordance with common laws. Hence the same property through which an edifice is beautiful is also compatible with its goodness, and a face would have to have no other shape for its end than for its beauty. Of many things in nature we cognize beauty, but not ends; it is to be believed that the satisfaction in their appearances is not the aim but the consequence of their aim.

630. 1769

In everything beautiful, that the form of the object facilitates the actions of the understanding belongs to the gratification and is subjective; but it is objective that this form is universally valid.

638. 1769

The question is whether the play of sensations or the form and shape of intuitions is immediately agreeable or pleases only through providing the understanding with comprehensibility and facility in grasping a large manifold and at the same time with distinctness in the entire representation.

To shape there belongs not merely the form of the object in accordance with spatial relations in appearance, but also the matter, i.e., sensation (color).

639. 1769

The sensible form (or the form of sensibility) of a cognition pleases either as a play of sensation or as a form of intuition (immediately) or as a means to the concept of the good. The former is charm, the second the sensibly beautiful, the third self-sufficient beauty. The charm is either immediate, as Rameau believes that it is in music, or mediate, as in laughing and crying; the latter is ideal charm. Through neither of these does the object please in the intuition. The object pleases immediately in the intuition if its form fits with the law of coordination among appearances and facilitates sensible clarity and magnitude. Like symmetry in buildings and harmony in music. The object pleases in the intuitive concept if its relation to the good can be expressed through a concept that pleases in sensible form.

(conventional or natural taste.)

640. 1769

Through feeling I do not judge about the object at all and hence do not judge objectively. Hence I do not believe myself to have erred if I choose other objects of sentiment and also not if I have a dispute with others. A poor building, a ridiculous book gratifies, but it does not please on that account, and the most beautiful building gives him who regards it a poor substitute for a missed meal unless through novelty and rarity, etc. By means of taste I judge of the object, whether my state is much or little affected by it. If I call it beautiful, I do not thereby declare merely my own satisfaction, but also that it should please others. We are ashamed when our taste does not correspond to that of others. In matters of taste one must distinguish charm from beauty; the former is often lost in this or that, but the beauty remains. The decorated room always remains beautiful, but it has lost its charm with the death of the beloved, and the lover chooses other objects. This concept of beauty, says Winckelmann, is sensual, i.e., one does not distinguish the charm from the beauty; for in fact they were just as much connected (although not confused) among the ancients as among the moderns, although perhaps they were distinguished in the concepts of the artist who wanted to express them.

The beautiful person pleases through her figure and charms through her sex. If you whisper into someone's ear that this admired beauty is a castrato, then the charm disappears in an instant, but the beauty remains. It is difficult to separate this charm from the beauty; but we need only to leave aside all our particular needs and private relations, in which we distinguish ourselves from others, and then the cool-headed judgment of taste remains. In the judgment of the connoisseur, who cannot view it without abhorrence, the debtor's prison nevertheless remains a beautiful building; but this judgment is without any charm; it pleases in taste, but displeases in sentiment.

641. 1769

Just as judgments of taste are mixed up with sentiments, judgings of good and evil are likewise never completely pure, but have a strong supplement of other representations of beauty or charm mixed in. Benevolence receives strong recommendations from honor, from the love of others, through the flattering reckoning of the happiness of others to one's own account. If generosity is directed toward a woman who is young and beautiful then all these charms are elevated by the interest in sex.

646. 1769–1770

A representation is sensible if the form of space and time is in it; it is even more sensible if sensation is connected with it (color). It is maximally sensible if it is ascribed to the observer, and indeed as observed by others. Beautiful objects are those whose internal order pleases in accordance with the laws of *intuitus*. Beautiful appearances of objects, e.g., pictures.

647. 1769–70. M 230

Taste is really [crossed out the capacity] the faculty for choosing that which sensibly pleases in unison with others. Now since unanimity is not so necessary in sensations as in appearance, taste pertains more to appearance than to sensation. If we blame someone for a lack of taste, we do not say that it does not have taste for him but that it does not have taste for others. A perverted taste, moreover, is that which applies to what is evil or injurious.

648. 1769–17

Taste in appearance is grounded on the relations of space and time that are comprehensible to everyone, and on the rules of reflection.

Just because in taste it comes down to whether something also pleases others, it takes place only in society, that is, only in society does it have a charm.

650. 1769–70

All of our representations, when they are considered with regard to that which they represent, belong to two main species: sensibility and reason. The former consist in the relation of objects to the capacity of our nature to be stimulated or in a certain way altered by them. The latter, however, applies to all objects as such, in so far as they are considered apart from all relation to the sensitivity of the subject.

Sensible representations are sensations and require sense, or appearances and are grounded on the faculty of intuition; the former [*crossed out* consist] are represented alterations of the state of the subject through the presence of the object; the latter are representations of the object itself in so far as it is exposed to the senses.

There are two sorts of cognitions of reason: through reflection9 (rational) and through concepts of reason. Geometry contains rational reflection on objects, but only through sensible concepts. Rational reflection is common to all cognition.

653. 1769–70

That which pleases in taste is not actually the facilitation of one's own intuitions, but rather the universally valid in the appearance, thus that the universal intuition or the universal rules of feeling are accommodated by the merely private feeling. For in the relation of sensations there is also something that is universally valid, although each sensation may have only a private validity of agreeableness.

The facility of sensations makes for gratification, but not the faculty of cognition, except in so far as that which we cognize has a relation to our state. Hence in solitude the proportions of sensibility cannot provide any gratification, but those of what belongs to us can do so in society, for others thereby have something to thank us for.

654. 1769–70

In the beautiful there is something that relates merely to others, namely the symmetry, and something that relates to the possessor, namely the comfortableness and usefulness; the latter is still to be distinguished from the immediate charm.

655. 1769–70

The play of shapes and sensations is also present in fireworks. For in the appearance there is either an object, which is always placed in space, or merely a sensation, but in accordance with relations of time; the former is called the shape, the latter the play, both are often found together. One is sensitive either to one's state in action or in passivity, in so far as one feels oneself to be dependent or to be a ground of one's state. Hence sensation is either active or passive. The sensation is active in the case of the form of appearances on account of the comparison that one makes. The active sensation is in itself always agreeable as well as all passive ones that promote the active one. But it is not a sensation of the object, but is immanent. All sensation of personality, namely of oneself as an active principle, is active; but the sensation of oneself as an object of other forces is passive; and the more it is merely passive, the more disagreeable is it. The passive gratifications seem to be forceful only by means of the active springs that they set into motion.

659. 1769–70

Pleasure: A; indifference: *non* A; displeasure: −A. There is no indifference of sensation, except only relative to this or that sense; for with regard to all the senses together, i.e., one's state, something is always either agreeable or disagreeable. Likewise in the case of the beautiful or the good. But there is a counterbalance: $A - A = o$. One says: Satisfaction, indifference, dissatisfaction. Gratification, indifference, abhorrence. Beautiful, ordinary, ugly. Good, worthless, evil. Respect, disdain, contempt. Hatred, coldness, love. For just as all simple sensations are agreeable and become disagreeable only through conflict, so all simple relations of sensibility or reason that are positive are good and become evil only through conflict.

670. 1769–70

With regard to the beautiful or to taste there is in addition to art criticism, observation, and comparison of objects with taste through analysis. The science of the beautiful, however, is an attempt to explain the *phaenomena* of taste.

671. 1769–70

Taste is the basis of [crossed *out* criticism and] judging, genius however of execution. Criticism is judging in accordance with universal rules. But since these rules must be grounded on taste, a man of taste is better than a learned critic. But there is also a doctrine of judgings that rest on universal principles of reason, such as logic, metaphysics, and mathematics.

He can always be well satisfied with himself whose judging does not demand for perfection more than he is capable of doing. Taste without genius brings dissatisfaction with oneself; sharp criticism of oneself (it is peculiar that this is so difficult) with inadequate capacities makes one write not at all or with much anxiety; in contrast, much genius and little taste brings forth crude yet valuable products.

672. 1769–70

We have dealt with that which pleases in so far as it belongs to our state or affects that and concerns our well-being. Now we speak of that which pleases in itself, whether our state is altered by it or not, thus with what pleases in so far as it is cognized rather than sensed. Since every object of sensibility has a relation to our state, even that which belongs to cognition and not to sensation, namely in the comparison of the manifold and the form (for this comparison itself affects our state, costing us effort or being easy, enlivening our entire cognitive activity or hemming it in): thus there is something in every cognition that belongs to agreeableness; but thus far the approval does not concern the object, and beauty is not something that can be cognized, but only sensed. That which pleases in the object and which we regard as a property of it must consist in that which is valid for everyone. Now the relations of space and time are valid for everyone, whatever sensations they may have. Thus in all appearances the form is universally valid; this form is also cognized in accordance with common rules of coordination; thus what fits the rules of coordination in space and time necessarily pleases everyone and is beautiful. That which is agreeable in the intuition of the beautiful comes down to the comprehensibility of a whole, but the beauty comes down to the universal validity of this fitting relation.

The good must please without relation to the condition of appearance.

673. 1769–70

A clock is agreeable in so far as it measures time for someone; it is beautiful in so far as it pleases everyone in intuition; in so far as it may be connected with a possible willing in general, whether it is connected with agreeableness or not, and thus can serve everyone for the measurement of time, it is good, and thus without relation to the state of the person who is thereby to be affected with charm.

Freedom is necessarily agreeable to everyone, therefore good; likewise understanding.

To love one's own freedom comes from agreeableness; but to love freedom in general is because it is good. But this love itself is good; for whoever loves freedom in general, whoever loves well-being in general, demands it for everyone, thus his will also pleases everyone.

676. 1769–70

The perfection of a cognition with regard to the object is logical, with regard to the subject aesthetic. The latter, since it magnifies the consciousness of one's state through the relation in which one's senses are placed toward the object and through appropriation, magnifies the consciousness of life and is therefore called lively. Abstract representation practically cancels the consciousness of life.

683. 1769–70

In order for sensibility to have a determinate form in our representation it is necessary that it have an order and not just be grasped together. This order is a connection of coordination, and not subordination of the sort that reason institutes. The basis of all coordination, hence the form of sensibility, is space and time. The representation of an object in accordance with the relations of space is shape, and the imitation of this is the image. The form of appearance without representation of an object consists merely in the order of sensations in accordance with temporal relation, and the appearance is called a sequence (or series or play). All objects can be sensibly or intuitively cognized only under a shape. Other appearances do not represent objects at all, but only alterations. Pantomime is an intuitive form of a series of human shapes, while dance is one of a succession of movements in accordance with time; both together are mimetic dance. Dance is to the eye what music is to the ear, only in the case of the latter there are finer divisions of time in more exact proportion. The arts are either formative or imitative._The latter are painting and sculpture. They concern either merely the form or also the material. That which concerns merely form is landscape design; that which also concerns the material is architecture (even the art of furnishing); even tactics and maneuvers are a kind of the beautiful arrangement. To the formative arts there belongs in general the art of producing any beautiful form, such as the art of beautiful vessels, of the goldsmith, the jeweler, the furnisher, even the finery of a woman, just as much as architecture. Likewise all work of gallantry.

Dance loses its charm if one will no longer please the other sex. For that reason the inclination to the dance does not last long among married men; but among women it lasts until they are old because they continue to want to please.

Appearance is a representation of the senses so far as it pertains to an object; sensation, if it pertains merely to the subject. The reflected appearance is the shape, the reflected sensation [breaks off]

685. 1769–70

The play of shapes and sensations requires, first, equal divisions of time (uniformity in the measure of time) or beat, 2. a comprehensible proportion that can be drawn from the relation of the alterations of the parts.

The charm in dance is either corporeal and rests on the seemly motion of the limbs, that in music on the proportionate movement of the vessels of the body through harmonious tones. Ideal charm rests on the relation that the alterable shapes have on the affects or that which the tones that accompany one another have on the human voice and the expression of sentiment.

686. 1769–70

The contemplation of the beautiful is a judging and not an enjoyment. This appearance makes for some gratification, but nowhere near as much as in relation to the judgment of satisfaction in beauty; rather this consists merely in the judgment concerning the universality of the satisfaction in the object. From this it can be seen that, since this universal validity is useless as soon as society is lacking, then all the charm of beauty must also be lost; just as little would even any inclination to beauty arise *in statu solitario*.

696. 1769–70

All perfection seems to consist in the agreement of a thing with freedom, hence in purposiveness, general usefulness, etc. Since all things in an empirical sense are properly only that which they are taken to be in relation to the law of sensibility, the perfection of objects of experience is a correspondence with the law of the senses, and this, as appearance, is called beauty; it is so to speak the outer side of perfection, and the object pleases merely in being contemplated. Satisfaction through taste and through *sentiment* have in common that the object is approved without regard to the influence that it may have on the feeling of the subject through intuition or use. Only taste approves of something so far as it merely affects the senses; *sentiment* in so far as it is judged by reason. What is most fit for the entire play of the senses thereby indicates correspondence with the sensibility of the human being and through that perfection, since in the end this comes down to consensus with happiness.

697. 1769–70

There are three sorts of pleasure in an object through feeling: . Immediate pleasure through sensation. 2. Pleasure in our state concerning the possession of this object. 3. Pleasure in our person. If the first pleasure obtains without the second then it serves for judging.

698. 1769–70

In the beautiful it is not so much the thing as its appearance that pleases. In so far as we compose its representation from parts that are seen in themselves the human body yields a concept that contains nothing beautiful.

There is a beauty in the cognitions of reason. Even usefulness can be a sum of appearances.

Notes on moral philosophy prior to 1770

6560. 1762–63?

The weakness of human nature consists in the weakness of the moral feeling relative to other inclinations. Hence providence has strengthened it with supporting drives as *analogis instinctorum moralium* [analogues of moral instincts], e.g., honor, *storge*, pity, sympathy, or also with rewards and punishments. When these are among the motives, then morality is not pure. The morality that excludes all these *motiva auxiliaria* is chimerical.

6581. 1764–68

Of the *sensu morali*. The rules of prudence presuppose no special inclination and feeling, but only a special relation of the understanding to them. The rules of morality proceed from a special, eponymous feeling, upon which the understanding is guided as in the former case.

According to the Stoics, active love has its maximum when it is equal to one's powers. There is no internal measure in space, but only arbitrary ones; but a circle is an absolute measure.

The doctrine of the mean is really that a greatest good [breaks off]

6586. 1764–68

There are different grades of the determination of our power of choice:

1. In accordance with universal laws of the power of choice in general, right.

2. In accordance with universal rules of the good in general, goodness.

3. In accordance with universal rules of private good, rational self-love.

4. In accordance with particular rules of a private inclination, sensuous drive.

The *motiva moralia* are of different grades: [9:9]

The right of another.

My own right.

The need of another.

My own need.

Utility to myself is not the ground of a right.

Utility for many does not give them a right against one. Right is not grounded on motives of goodness.

In moral matters, we see very sharply but not clearly through *sentiment*; e.g., a braggart is held in contempt for a *criminis publici*, since one will not entirely sacrifice private duties for public ones. One takes pity on a miscreant.

6589. 1764–68

Something is good in so far as it is in agreement with the will; agreeable, in so far as it agrees with sensation; now I can think of a will while abstracting from the charm of the person who wills or of the subject to whom this charm is a response, thus I can think of something good without regard to charm. Yet without all charm nothing is good; but goodness consists in the relation to the will, until finally absolute goodness consists in the correspondence of happiness with the will.

6590. 1764–68

Whatever contributes to the happiness of human beings does not thereby belong to their perfection. If the righteous man is unhappy and the vicious man is happy, then not human beings but the order of nature is imperfect.

In duties toward oneself the worth of a person and not of the condition must comprise the motive. Soul and body and their perfection belong to one's person. Perfection does not consist in accidental goods, e.g. knowledge, elegance, etc., but in the essential. The perfection of one's body must be given preference over all pleasures. Only in view of great obligation to comply with the right of another, e.g. to preserve one's virginity, is the body no longer attributed to the person; accordingly death itself, although not voluntary death, is bound up with the worth of one's person.

6583. 1764–68

The order of reflection on human beings is as follows:

1. The natural indeterminacy in the type and proportion of his capacities and inclinations and his nature, which is capable of all sorts of configurations.

2. The determination of the human being. The actual state of human beings; whether it consists in simplicity or in the highest cultivation of his capacities and the greatest enjoyment of his desires. Whether a natural final end is illuminated by the degree of ability would be very worthwhile to investigate. Whether the sciences belong to this necessarily.

(4. The wild or the raw human being [*crossed out* of nature]. Whether this condition would be a state of right and of satisfaction. Difference between the personal perfection of the raw human being and that which he has in the view of another. Whether the human being can remain in this condition.)

3. The human being of nature should be considered merely according to his personal properties without looking at his condition. Here the question is merely: what is natural and what is from external and contingent causes? The state of nature is an ideal of outer relationships of the merely natural, that is, of the raw human being. The social condition can also consist of persons of merely natural properties.

Emile or the ethical human being. Art or cultivation of powers and inclinations which harmonize the most with nature. Through this the natural perfection is improved.

5. In the outer condition. The social contract (civil union) or the ideal of the right of a state (according to the rule of equality) considered *in abstracto*, without looking at the special nature of human beings.

6. Leviathan: the condition of society, which is in accordance with the nature of human beings. According to the rules of security. I can be either in a state of equality and have freedom to be unjust myself and suffer, or in a state of subjection without this freedom.

7. The union of nations: the ideal of the right of nations as the completion of society in view of outer relationships.

The social contract, or public right as a ground of the [*crossed out* public] supreme power. Leviathan or the supreme power as a ground of public right.

6596. 1764–68

All right action is a *maximum* of the free power of choice when it is taken reciprocally.

The human being is disposed to see the extreme in every quantity, the *maximum* and *minimum*, in part because he does not stop in addition and subtraction without this *terminum*, in part because he needs a measure: The greatest is thought either [as] undetermined, in so far as one thinks the mere extending, as (number) space, time (everything); or [as] determined: if the greatest depends on determined relations. The greatest of all beings can be thought to be determined in many ways according to relations which the many realities of things can have towards one another, in order to diminish or increase the quantity.

This greatest is itself given either through certain determinations of a thing, which are in changing relations towards one another, or it consists merely in arbitrary increase. The latter is an ideal of fiction, the first is an ideal of reason, which is differentiated into the merely mathematical and the philosophical ideal. The smallest (of what is movable) can be called a moment.

There are no real *maximum* and *minimum* in an absolute sense in quantitative *continuis*, but there are in *discretis*.

6598. 1769–70

The means are only the form of intention, or the method of execution, the end is the matter. Actions are rational with regard to the means or to the end; in the first case reason determines the form, in the second case reason also determines the matter of the intention.

The understanding is only mediately good, as a means to another good or to happiness. The immediate good can be found only in freedom. For, because freedom is a capacity for action, even if it does not please us, freedom is not dependent upon the condition of a private feeling; however, it always refers only to that which pleases, so it has a relation to feeling and can have a universally valid relation to feeling in general. Hence nothing has an absolute worth but persons, and this consists in the goodness of their free power of choice. Just as freedom contains the first ground of everything that begins, so is it also that which alone contains self-sufficient goodness.

The moral feeling is not an original feeling. It rests on a necessary inner law to consider and to sense oneself from an external standpoint. Likewise in the personality of reason: there one feels oneself in the universal and considers one's *individuum* as a contingent subject like an *accidens* of the universal.

6601. 1769–70

Of the ethical ideal of the ancients, the highest good. It is either negative or positive, that is, the absence of vice and pain, innocence and modesty, or virtue and happiness. These last are either so subordinated that happiness is a necessary consequence of virtue or virtue is a necessary form of the means to happiness. The first is Stoicism, the second is Epicureanism. Finally, the ground of the highest good is either in nature or in community with the highest being. The former *principium* is natural, the second mystic. This latter is the Platonic theory.

We highly respect everything that is good in itself; we love that which is good respective to us. Both are sentiments. The former is preeminent in the idea of approval, the latter is more a ground of inclination. Whatever we find worthy of the highest respect we really respect highly; whatever we find worthy of love we do not always love, namely if it is not especially connected to us.

Both sentiments are somewhat opposed to one another. Partiality towards us makes us love, but not highly respect, the one who is partial to us.

We have a greater drive to be respected than to be loved – but a greater drive to love others than to respect them. Because in love towards another one senses his own superiority, in respect for another he limits this superiority.

All real moving causes of action are either pathological (or subjective) and are called impulses or they are . . . (objective) and are called *motiva*.

The latter are pragmatic or moral. The universal pragmatic *imperativi* are also categorical; however, they are more like such sentences which say what everyone wills rather than what he should will.

6603. 1769–70

Whatever pleases only under the condition of a certain inclination or feeling is agreeable; whatever pleases under the condition of a certain nature of the power of cognition, through which all objects of feeling must be known, is beautiful; whatever has a universal and necessary relation to happiness in general without relation to a special feeling or a special cognitive ability, is good. E.g., nonexistence necessarily displeases, although this displeasure is outweighed by special aversions; illness, mutilation of a person require no special feeling in order to displease. Everything right has a general relation to happiness, in so far as each produces happiness through himself, but in such a way that the rules of private intention do not contradict one another according to universal laws. All duties of love consist in the desire to further universal happiness (not merely one's own) through one's own actions.

An arbitrarily fabricated intention without motivating grounds [breaks off?]

6605. 1769–70

There is a free power of choice which does not have its own happiness as an aim but rather presupposes it. The essential perfection of a freely acting being depends on whether this freedom [crossed ovt of the power of choice] is not subject to inclination or in general would not be subject to any foreign cause at all. The chief rule of externally good actions is not that they conform with the happiness of others, but with their power of choice, and in the same way the perfection of a subject does not depend on whether he is happy but on whether his condition is subordinated to freedom: so also the universally valid perfection, that the actions must stand under universal laws of freedom.

6607. 1769–70

The ancients did not coordinate happiness and morality but subordinated them; because both amount to two different things whose means are distinct, they are often in conflict. The Stoic doctrine is the most genuine doctrine of true morals but the least suited to human nature. It is also the easiest to examine. The Epicurean is less true but [*crossed out* more] perfectly suited to the inclinations of humans. The Cynic is most in accord with human nature in idea but least natural in execution and is the ideal of the most artificial education as well as of civil society.

The Stoic ideal is the most correct pure ideal of morals, however incorrect [applied] *in concreto* to human nature; it is correct that one should so act but false that one will ever so act. The ideal of Epicurus is false according to the pure rule of morals and thus false in the theory of moral *principii*, although correct in moral doctrine; only it conforms most often with human volition. The Cynic ideal concerns only the mean and is correct in theory but very difficult in *praxi*, although the *worma*. The former ideals were merely theories of moral philosophy, the Cynic ideal merely a doctrine of the mean.

6610. 1769–670

Morality is an objective [*crossed out* dependence] subordination of the will under the motivating grounds of reason. Sensibility (practice) is a *subordinatio* of the will under inclination.

Inclinations, united through reason, agree with happiness, i.e., with well-being from the enduring satisfaction of all our inclinations. Single inclinations, if they hinder attention to the satisfaction of the remaining ones, contradict happiness. [*Crossed out* Affects] Passions thus naturally contradict not just morality but also happiness. Happiness, however, only contingently agrees with morality (*actualiter sive subjective*) [actually or subjectively]; but objective it agrees with morality necessarily, i.e., the worthiness to be happy.

6611. 1769–70

(Later addition: Concept, idea, ideal. The concept is a universal ground of differentiation (mark). Only the a priori concept has true universality and is the *principium* of rules. Concerning virtue, only a judging in accordance with concepts, hence *a priori*, is possible. Empirical judging, in accordance with representations in pictures or in accordance with experience, gives no laws but only examples, which an a priori concept requires for judging. Many are not capable of deriving their principles from concepts.

An idea is the a priori cognition of the [*crossed out* pure] understanding, through which the object becomes possible. It refers to the objectively practical as a *priwcipium*. It contains the greatest perfection for a certain purpose. A plant is possible only in accordance with an idea. That exists only in the understanding and, for humans, in concepts. The sensible is only the image, e.g., in the case of a house the idea contains all the ends. The sketch is only the sensible in conformity with the idea. All morality rests on ideas, and its image in the human being is always imperfect. In the divine understanding there are intuitions of itself, hence archetypes. An ideal is the representation of an object of sense in conformity with an idea and the intellectual perfection in it. Ideals pertain only to objects of the understanding and occur only in human beings and are *fictiones* to them. It is a fiction used to posit an idea in intuition *in concreto*.

The three ideals of morality from concepts. The mystical ideal of Plato's intellectual intuition. Holiness is an ideal of supersensible influence.

Concept of plants, but not idea.)

The ideal of innocence. Of prudence. Of [*crossed out* wisdom. virtue] Of wisdom and of holiness. (*Later addition*: ideals, etc. etc. The Cynic ideal was negative.)

In the 1st, simplicity in morals and moderation in well-being.

2. Morality is seen as the necessary consequence of the prudent aim at happiness, therefore well-being in amusements and virtue in the active cognition of the means.

3. Wisdom has as its sole end the good, perfection; and well-being depends not on things and sensations, but instead the wise person is happy in his virtue. To the Epicureans special laws of morality were dispensable, to the Stoics special laws of prudence were dispensable.

4. Holiness sees well-being as blessedness. Results from community with God.

(*Later addition*: Platonism: with God through nature; Christianity: through supernatural means. Philosophy or fantasy. Enthusiastic, fantastic, mystical.)

The Epicurean ideal consisted in the satisfaction of the whole union of inclinations, the Stoic ideal in power and dominion over all inclinations. That of holiness, in moral peace with all inclinations, i.e., their harmony, or also release from them, the Cynic ideal in the extermination of all inclinations.

(Later addition: The Cyrenaic philosophy. De la Mettrie makes morality into mere adroitness in satisfying our desires. Helvetius.)

(Later addition: 1. The natural human being (not the raw and animal but the wise human being who is regulated according to the intentions of nature). 2. The man of the world. 3. The wise man. 4. The Christian and Platonist.)

(Later addition: The highest good. The grounds of the highest good lie either in nature, and the precepts are only negative, like moderation and innocence, namely not to corrupt nature, or in art, applied to happiness (prudence), or in morality (virtue, wisdom), or in a being above nature: holiness and blessedness.)

(Later addition: Morality, worthiness to be happy, lies in conduct. All worthiness lies in the use of freedom.)

6619. 1769–70

Epicurus takes the subjective ground of execution, which moves us to action, for the objective ground of adjudication. Zeno reverses this. That Epicurus reduces it all to bodily stimuli appears to be more an opinion, used to explain the decisions of human beings, than a prescription. The greatest spiritual joys find the ground of their own approbation in the intellectual concept, to be sure, but their *elateres* in the sensible.

It is noteworthy that the representations of utility and of honor are not able to produce any strong resolution to emulate virtue, unlike the pure picture of virtue in itself; and even if one is driven in secret by a view to honor, one does it not for the sake of this honor alone but only in so far as we can imagine that the principles of virtue have produced it through a hidden conviction. We must hide the mechanism of our self-interested impulses from our own eyes.

The most powerful means to impel human beings toward the morally good is thus the representation of pure virtue, in order to esteem it highly and to see clearly that one can esteem oneself only in so far as one is in conformity with virtue, but also to show that this is the only means to become valued and loved by others, followed by the greatest security and ease; one does not do the good for the sake of these, but they accompany the good. One must excite the inclinations that most closely agree with morality: love of honor, sociability, freedom.

The *praxis* of morality thus consists in that formation of the inclinations and of taste which makes us capable of uniting the actions that lead to our enjoyment with moral principles. This is the virtuous person, consequently the one who knows to conform his inclinations to moral principles.

(Later addition: The presently anticipated uses can also impel us, even without any morality, to the same action that ethics would command. Only from mere motives of self-love no one would ever undertake such actions universally and in accordance with a universal rule without any moral motive or conviction thereof.)

6621. 1769–70

The doctrine of virtue does not so much restrict the gratifications of sensibility as teach how to chose among the various types of them those that have greatest agreement with the rules of universal approbation, which in turn is always the best universal rule of prudence. Because to rely upon one's directing oneself in every case not with a rule but according to the greatest gain is too anxiety-producing and always leaves the mind in unrest. (Moreover the conduct that one universally prescribes must also be assumed as if its intention were known and approved universally.) There are, however, various sources of satisfaction from which we can choose. If by following universally approved means I cannot acquire riches, still I will have the confidence of my friends; I will be restricted, but can live without worry over responsibility, or freely. (Later addition: Science, skill, prudence, wisdom, knowledge, skill, etc., etc. Because knowledge can exist without skill.)

In general, nature seems to us to have in the end subordinated sensible needs for the sake of all our actions. Only it was necessary that our understanding at the same time projected universal rules, in accordance with which we had to order, restrict, and make coherent the efforts at our happiness, so that our blind impulses will not push us now here, now there, just by chance. Since the latter commonly conflict with one another, a judgment was necessary, which with regard to all of these impulses projects rules impartially, and thus in abstraction from all inclination, through for all human beings, would produce the greatest harmony of a human being with himself and with others. One must place in these rules the essential conditions under which one can give one's drives a hearing, and posit these rules as if their observation in itself could be an object of our volitions, and we must prosecute even with the sacrifice of our happiness, although to be sure they are only the constant and reliable form [thereof].

Epicurus placed the ends of all virtuous as well as vicious actions merely in the relationship of the objects to sensibility, i.e., to the satisfaction of inclinations, and he distinguished virtue only through the form of reason with regard to the means.

Zeno posited all ends of virtuous actions merely in the intellectual and the conquest of the whole of sensibility.

According to him, self-approval was the whole of true happiness. Yet the contingencies of conditions were not a person's own. The merely inner worth of the person.

6624. 1769–70

The theories of the ancients appear to be aimed at bringing together the two elements or essential conditions of the highest good, happiness and morality. Diogenes brought happiness down to something negative, namely simplicity of nature. Epicurus brought morality down to selfproduced happiness. Zeno brought happiness down to self-sufficient morality. The systems of the moderns try to find the *principium* of moral judgment. Besides those that derive it from empirical sources (custom or authority), they divide themselves into the moral theorists of pure reason and those of moral sentiment. Among the former, takes the rule of truth to be the guiding rule of morality, Wolff assumes it to be the concept of perfection. But the general concept of perfection is not comprehensible through itself, and from it no practical judgments can be supplied; rather it is itself more a derived concept in which that which occurs in particular cases is given the general name "perfect." From this concept (from which one would certainly not judge what pain or pleasure is) all practical precepts are derived (although only tautological rules, namely that one should do the good), with regard to morality as well as to happiness, and this difference is not shown.

6625. 1769–70

All systems derive morality either from reason or from feeling (from the coercion of authorities and from custom).

Those from reason: either from truth or from perfection (the middle road of inclination: Aristotle). Wolff turns the general name of "perfection" into a ground for determining morality and does not name the conditions under which actions and ends are good and deserve the name "perfection."

6626. 1769–70

The doctrine of moral feeling is more a hypothesis to explain the *phaenomenon* of approbation that we give to certain actions than anything that should firmly establish maxims and first principles that are objectively valid concerning how one should approve or reject something, act or refrain from acting.

6627. 1769–70

The conditions without which the approval of an action cannot be universal (not stand under a universal principle of reason) are moral. The moral conditions of actions make the actions that agree with them permitted and restrict the pathological actions. The approbation of an action cannot be universal if it does not contain grounds of approbation that are without relation to the sensible impulses of the agent. Universal approbation accordingly pertains to the objective end of the matter or of a capacity, (e.g.,) of the freedom of speech, and this restricts all subjective ends. Hence the ends that the human being has from inclination are to be distinguished from the end for which the human being has for this or that quality, limb, or inclination. The latter is the primordial or original end, the former the properly subordinate end.

6628. 1769–70

The first investigation is: Which are the *principia prima dijudicationis moralis* (Later addition: theoretical rules of *dijudication*), i.e., which are the highest maxims of morality and which is its highest law.

2. Which is the rule of application (later addition: for practical application of adjudicative rules) to an object of adjudication (sympathy for others and an impartial spectator).

3. Through what do the moral conditions become *motiva*, i.e. on what rests their *vis movens* and thus their application to the subject? The latter are first the *motivum* essentially bound up with morality, namely the worthiness to be happy.

6629. 1769–70

If it were certain that all good actions met with no advantage and that good fortune were merely a prize for cunning or a gift of blind accident, then

a well-thinking person would still follow the moral rule from sentiment, as long as it did not bring about his own greatest injury, on account of its greater beauty. If happiness could thereby be immediately attained, then the moral beauty would be entirely entwined with self-interest and would never earn the honor of merit. Now being virtuous brings a natural advantage in accordance with universal laws, although in exceptional cases vice can also be a means to gratification; but now since virtue does not carry with it a certain advantage; thus one must unite the motivating grounds with the utility that they produce.

6633. 1769–70

The supreme principles *dijudicationis moralis* are to be sure rational, but only *principia formalia*. They do not determine any end, but only the moral form of every end; hence *in concreto* the *principia prima materialia* [first-order, material principles of actions; concrete maxims falling under the general formal principle of moral judgment] are presented in accordance with this form.

6634. 1769–70

Hutcheson's principle is unphilosophical, because it introduces a new feeling as a ground of explanation, and second because it sees objective grounds in the laws of sensibility.

Wolff's principle is unphilosophical, because it makes empty propositions into principles and offers the *abstractum* in all *quaesitis* as if were the ground of cognition for the *quaesitii*, just as if one were to seek the ground of hunger in the desire for happiness.

The ideal of the Christians has the peculiarity that it makes the idea of moral purity not only into the [*crossed out* ground] principio of *dijudication*, but also into the unremitting guideline by which he should be judged. The incapacity that we would like to plead is not clear, and hence the greatest anxiety arises from the ideal of holiness. The Christian lifts this anxiety by saying that God would make good this lack of holiness, thereby doing away with the inner incapacity for following rules. Whoever believes that one must make himself worthy and capable of this supplementation through all natural efforts is the practical Christian. But whoever believes that one must merely be passive in regard to all those actions in order to produce them through the labor of his heart and to produce his dispositions, and that in place of these certain religious efforts can move the divinity to pour holiness into them [breaks off]

6639. 1769–70

The categorical (objective) *necessitas* of free actions is necessity in accordance with laws of the pure will, the [*crossed out* hypothetical] conditional: in accordance with laws of the will affected (through inclinations).

6648. 1769–70

An action that is good in and of itself must necessarily be good for everyone, thus not related to feeling.

6659. 1769

Lex moralis est vel absoluta (unconditional) *vel hypothetica*. (Later addition: The former obligates without any condition, the latter is restricted through conditions of its necessity.)

6674. 1769

The moral laws are grounds of the divine will. The latter is a ground of our will by means of its goodness and justice, in accordance with which God connects happiness with good behavior.

If there were no God, then all our duties would vanish, because there would be an absurdity in the whole in which well-being would not agree with good behavior, and this absurdity would excuse the other.

I should be just toward others; but who protects my right for me?

Religion Within the Bounds of Bare Reason

Contents

FIRST PART of THE PHILOSOPHICAL THEORY OF RELIGION.

OF THE INDWELLING OF THE BAD PRINCIPLE ALONG WITH THE GOOD; OR, ON THE RADICAL EVIL IN HUMAN NATURE.

THAT the world lieth in wickedness is a complaint as old as history, even as what is still older, poetry; indeed, as old as the oldest of all poems, sacerdotal religion. All alike, nevertheless, make the world begin from good; with the golden age, with life in paradise, or one still more happy in communion with heavenly beings. But they represent this happy state as soon vanishing like a dream, and then they fall into badness (moral badness, which is always accompanied by physical), as hastening to worse and worse with accelerated steps; so that we are now living (this now being however as old as history) in the last times, the last day and the destruction of the world are at the door; and in some parts of Hindostan the judge and destroyer of the world, Rudra (otherwise called Siva), is already worshipped as the God that is at present in power; the preserver of the world, namely, Vishnu, having centuries ago laid down his office, of which he was weary, and which he had received from the creator of the world, Brahma.

Later, but much less general, is the opposite heroic opinion, which has perhaps obtained currency only amongst philosophers, and in our times chiefly amongst instructors of youth; that the world is constantly advancing in precisely the reverse direction, namely, from worse to better (though almost insensibly): at least, that the capacity for such advance exists in human nature. This opinion, however, is certainly not founded on experience, if what is meant is moral good or evil (not civilization), for the history of all times speaks too powerfully against it, but it is probably a good-natured hypothesis of moralists from Seneca to Rousseau, so as to urge man to the unwearied cultivation of the germ of good that perhaps lies in us, if one can reckon on such a natural foundation in man. There is also the consideration that as we must assume that man is by nature (that is, as he is usually born) sound in body, there is thought to be no reason why we should not assume that he is also by nature sound in soul, so that nature itself helps us to develop this moral capacity for good within us. "Sanabilibus ægrotamus malis, nosque in rectum genitos natura, si sanari velimus, adjuvat," says Seneca.

But since it may well be that there is error in the supposed experience on both sides, the question is, whether a mean is not at least possible, namely, that man as a species may be neither good nor bad, or at all events that he is as much one as the other, partly good, partly bad? We call a man bad, however, not because he performs actions that are bad (violating law), but because these are of such a kind that we may infer from them bad maxims in him. Now although we can in experience observe that actions violate laws, and even (at least in ourselves) that they do so consciously; yet we cannot observe the maxims themselves, not even always in ourselves: consequently, the judgment that the doer of them is a bad man cannot with certainty be founded on experience. In order then to call a man bad, it should be possible to argue à priori from some actions, or from a single consciously bad action, to a bad maxim as its foundation, and from this to a general source in the actor of all particular morally bad maxims, this source again being itself a maxim.

Lest any difficulty should be found in the expression nature, which, if it meant (as usual) the opposite of the source of actions from freedom, would be directly contradictory to the predicates morally good or evil, it is to be observed, that by the nature of man we mean here only the subjective ground of the use of his freedom in general (under objective moral laws) which precedes every act that falls under the senses, wherever this ground lies. This subjective ground, however, must itself again be always an act of freedom (else the use or abuse of man's elective will in respect of the moral law could not be imputed to him nor the good or bad in him be called moral). Consequently, the source of the bad cannot lie in any object that determines the elective will through inclination, or in any natural impulse, but only in a rule that the elective will makes for itself for the use of its freedom, that is, in a maxim. Now we cannot go on to ask concerning this, What is the subjective ground why it is adopted, and not the opposite maxim? For if this ground were ultimately not now a maxim but a mere natural impulse, then the use of freedom would be reduced to determination by natural causes, which is contradictory to its conception. When we say then, man is by nature good, or, he is by nature bad, this only means that he contains a primary source (to us inscrutable) of the adoption of good or of the adoption of bad (law violating) maxims: and this generally as man, and consequently so that by this he expresses the character of his species.

We shall say then of one of these characters (which distinguishes man from other possible rational beings, it is innate, and yet we must always remember that Nature is not to bear the blame of it (if it is bad), or the credit (if it is good), but that the man himself is the author of it. But since the primary source of the adoption of our maxims, which itself must again always lie in the free elective will, cannot be a fact of experience, hence the good or bad in man (as the subjective primary source of the adoption of this or that maxim in respect of the moral law) is innate merely in this sense, that it is in force before any use of freedom is experienced (in the earliest childhood back to birth) so that it is conceived as being present in man at birth, not that birth is the cause of it.

REMARK.

The conflict between the two above-mentioned hypotheses rests on a disjunctive proposition; man is (by nature) either morally good or morally bad. But it readily occurs to every one to ask whether this disjunction is correct, and whether one might not affirm that man is by nature neither, or another that he is both at once, namely, in some parts good, in others bad. Experience seems even to confirm this mean between the two extremes.

It is in general, however, important for Ethics to admit, as far as possible, no intermediates, either in actions (adiaphora) or in human characters; since with such ambiguity all maxims would run the risk of losing all definiteness and firmness. Those who are attached to this strict view are commonly called rigourists (a name that is meant as a reproach, but which is really praise): and their antipodes may be called latitudinarians. The latter are either latitudinarians of neutrality, who may be called indifferentists, or of compromise, who may be called syncretists.

The answer given to the above question by the rigourists is founded on the important consideration: That freedom of elective will has the peculiar characteristic that it cannot be determined to action by any spring except only so far as the man has taken it up into his maxim (has made it the universal rule of his conduct); only in his way can a spring, whatever it may be, co-exist with the absolute spontaneity of the elective will (freedom). Only the moral law is of itself in the judgment of reason a spring, and whoever makes it his maxim is morally good. Now if the law does not determine a man's elective will in respect of an action which has reference to it, an opposite spring must have influence on his elective will; and since by hypothesis this can only occur by the man taking it (and consequently deviation from the moral law) into his maxim (in which case he is a bad man), it follows that his disposition in respect of the moral law is never indifferent (is always one of the two, good or bad.)

Nor can he be partly good and partly bad at the same time. For if he is in part good, he has taken the moral law into his maxim; if then he were at the same time in another part bad, then, since the moral law of obedience to duty is one and universal, the maxim referring to it would be universal, and at the same time only particular, which is a contradiction.

When it is said that a man has the one or the other disposition as an innate natural quality, it is not meant that it is not acquired by him, that is, that he is not the author of it, but only that it is not acquired in time (that from youth up he has been always the one or the other). The disposition, that is, the primary subjective source of the adoption of maxims can be but one, and applies generally to the whole use of freedom. But it must have been itself adopted by free elective will, for otherwise it could not be imputed. Now the subjective ground or cause of its adoption cannot be further known (although we cannot help asking for it); since otherwise another maxim would have to be adduced, into which this disposition has been adopted, and this again must have its reason. Since, then, we cannot deduce this disposition, or rather its ultimate source, from any first act of the elective will in time, we call it a characteristic of the elective will, attaching to it by nature (although in fact it is founded in freedom). Now that when we say of a man that he is by nature good or bad, we are justified in applying this not to the individual (in which case one might be assumed to be by nature good, another bad), but to the whole race, this can only be proved when it has been shown in the anthropological inquiry that the reasons which justify us in ascribing one of the two characters to a man as innate are such that there is no reason to except any man from them, and that therefore it holds of the race.

I.: OF THE ORIGINAL INCAPACITY FOR GOOD IN HUMAN NATURE.

We may conveniently regard this capacity [Anlage] under three heads divided in reference to their end, as elements in the purpose for which man exists: —

1. The capacities belonging to the animal nature of man as a living being.

2. To his humanity as a living and at the same time rational being.

3. To his personality as a rational and at the same time responsible being [capable of imputation].

1. The capacities belonging to the Animal Nature of man may be brought under the general title of physical and merely mechanical self-love, that is, such as does not require reason. It is threefold: — first, for the maintenance of himself; secondly, for the propagation of his kind, and the maintenance of his offspring; thirdly, for communion with other men, that is, the impulse to society. All sorts of vices may be grafted on it, but they do not proceed from that capacity itself as a root. They may be called vices of coarseness of nature, and in their extreme deviation from the end of nature become brutal vices: intemperance, sensuality, and wild lawlessness (in relation to other men).

2. The capacities belonging to his Humanity may be brought under the general title of comparative, though physical, self-love (which requires reason), namely, estimating one's self as happy or unhappy only in comparison with others. From this is derived the inclination to obtain a worth in the opinion of others, and primarily only that of equality: to allow no one a superiority over one's self, joined with a constant apprehension that others might strive to attain it, and from this there ultimately arises an unjust desire to gain superiority for ourselves over others. On this, namely, jealousy and rivalry, the greatest vices may be grafted, secret and open hostilities against all whom we look upon as not belonging to us. These, however, do not properly spring of themselves from nature as their root, but apprehending that others endeavour to gain a hated superiority over us, these are inclinations to secure this superiority for ourselves as a defensive measure, whereas Nature would use the idea of such competition (which in itself does not exclude mutual love) only as a motive to culture. The vices that are grafted on this inclination may therefore be called vices of culture, and in their highest degree of malignancy (in which they are merely the idea of a maximum of badness surpassing humanity), ex. gr. in envy, in ingratitude, malice, &c., are called devilish vices.

3. The capacity belonging to Personality is the capability of respect for the moral law as a spring of the elective will adequate in itself. The capability of mere respect for the moral law in us would be moral feeling, which does not of itself constitute an end of the natural capacity, but only so far as it is a spring of the elective will. Now as this is only possible by free will adopting it into its maxim, hence the character of such an elective will is the good character, which, like every character of free elective will, is something that can only be acquired, the possibility of which, however, requires the presence of a capacity in our nature on which absolutely nothing bad can be grafted. The idea of the moral law alone, with the respect inseparable from it, cannot properly

be called a capacity belonging to personality; it is personality itself (the idea of humanity considered altogether intellectually). But that we adopt this respect into our maxims as a spring, this seems to have a subjective ground additional to personality, and so this ground seems therefore to deserve the name of a capacity belonging to personality.

If we consider these three capacities according to the conditions of their possibility, we find that the first requires no reason; the second is based on reason which, though practical, is at the service of other motives; the third has as its root reason, which is practical of itself, that is, unconditionally legislative: all these capacities in man are not only (negatively) good (not resisting the moral law), but are also capacities for good (promoting obedience to it). They are original, for they appertain to the possibility of human nature. Man can use the two former contrary to their end, but cannot destory them. By the capacities of a being, we understand both its constituent elements and also the forms of their combination which make it such and such a being. They are original if they are essentially necessary to the possibility of such a being; contingent if the being would be in itself possible without them. It is further to be observed that we are speaking here only of those capacities which have immediate reference to the faculty of desire and to the use of the elective will.

II.: OF THE PROPENSITY TO EVIL IN HUMAN NATURE.

By propensity (propensio) I understand the subjective source of possibility of an inclination (habitual desire, concupiscentia) so far as this latter is, as regards man generally, contingent. It is distinguished from a capacity by this, that although it may be innate, it need not be conceived as such, but may be regarded as acquired (when it is good), or (when it is bad) as drawn by the person on himself. Here, however, we are speaking only of the propensity to what is properly, i.e. morally bad, which, as it is possible only as a determination of free elective will, and this can be adjudged to be good or bad only by its maxims, must consist in the subjective ground of the possibility of a deviation of the maxims from the moral law, and if this propensity may be assumed as belonging to man universally (and therefore to the characteristics of his race) will be called a natural propensity of man to evil. We may add further that the capability or incapability of the elective will to adopt the moral law into its maxims or not, arising from natural propensity, is called a good or bad heart.

We may conceive three distinct degrees of this: — first, it is the weakness of the human heart in following adopted maxims generally, or the frailty of human nature; secondly, the propensity to mingle non-moral motives with the moral (even when it is done with a good purpose and under maxims of good), that is impurity; thirdly, the propensity to adopt bad maxims, that is the depravity of human nature or of the human heart.

First, the frailty (fragilitas) of human nature is expressed even in the complaint of an apostle: "To will is present with me, but how to perform I find not;" that is, I adopt the good (the law) into the maxim of my elective will; but this, which, objectively in its ideal conception (in thesi) is an irresistible spring, is subjectively (in hypothesi), when the maxim is to be carried out, weaker than inclination.

Secondly, the impurity (impuritas, improbitas) of the human heart consists in this, that although the maxim is good in its object (the intended obedience to the law), and perhaps also powerful enough for practice, yet it is not purely moral, that is, does not, as ought to be the case, involve the law alone as its sufficient spring, but frequently (perhaps always) has need of other springs beside it, to determine the elective will to what duty demands. In other words, that dutiful actions are not done purely from duty.

Thirdly, the depravity (vitiositas, pravitas), or if it is preferred, the corruption (corruptio), of the human heart, is the propensity of the elective will to maxims which prefer other (not moral) springs to that which arises from the moral law. It may also be called the perversity (perversitas) of the human heart, because it reverses the moral order in respect of the springs of a free elective will; and although legally good actions may be consistent with this, the moral disposition is thereby corrupted in its root, and the man is therefore designated bad.

It will be remarked that the propensity to evil in man is here ascribed even to the best (best in action), which must be the case if it is to be proved that the propensity to evil amongst men is universal, or what here signifies the same thing, that it is interwoven with human nature.

However, a man of good morals (bene moratus) and a morally good man (moraliter bonus) do not differ (or at least ought not to differ) as regards the agreement of their actions with the law; only that in the one these actions have not always the law for their sole and supreme spring; in the other it is invariably so. We may say of the former that he obeys the law in the letter (that is, as far as the act is concerned which the law commands), but of the latter, that he observes it in the spirit (the spirit of the moral law consists in this, that it is alone an adequate spring). Whatever is not done from this faith is sin (in the disposition of mind). For if other springs beside the law itself are necessary to determine the elective will to actions conforming to the law (ex. gr. desire of esteem, self-love in general, or even good-natured instinct, such as compassion), then it is a mere accident that they agree with the law, for they might just as well urge to its transgression. The maxim, then, the goodness of which is the measure of all moral worth in the person, is in this case opposed to the law, and while the man's acts are all good, he is nevertheless bad.

The following explanation is necessary in order to define the conception of this propensity. Every propensity is either physical, that is, it appertains to man's will as a physical being; or it is moral, that is, appertaining to his elective will as a moral being. In the first sense, there is no propensity to moral evil, for this must spring from freedom; and a physical propensity (founded on sensible impulses) to any particular use of freedom, whether for good or evil, is a contradiction. A propensity to evil, then, can only attach to the elective will as a moral faculty. Now, nothing is morally bad (that is, capable of being imputed) but what is our own act. On the other hand, by the notion of a propensity we understand a subjective ground of determination of the elective will antecedent to any act, and which is consequently not itself an act. Hence there would be a contradiction in the notion of a mere propensity to evil, unless indeed this word "act" could be taken in two distinct senses, both reconcilable with the notion of freedom. Now the term "act" in general applies to that use of freedom by which the supreme maxim is adopted into one's elective will (conformably or contrary to the law), as well as to that in which actions themselves (as to their matter, that is, the objects of the elective will) are performed in accordance with that maxim. The propensity to evil is an act in the former sense (peccatum originarium), and is at the same time the formal source of every act in the second sense, which in its matter violates the law and is called vice (peccatum derivativum); and the first fault remains, even though the second may be often avoided (from motives other than the law itself). The former is an intelligible act only cognizable by reason, apart from any condition of time; the latter sensible, empirical, given in time (factum phœnomenon). The former is especially called, in comparison with the second, a mere propensity; and innate, because it cannot be extirpated (since this would require that the supreme maxim should be good, whereas by virtue of that propensity itself it is supposed to be bad); and especially because, although the corruption of our supreme maxim is our own act, we cannot assign any further cause for it, any more than for any fundamental attribute of our nature. What has just been said will show the reason why we have, at the beginning of this section, sought the three sources of moral evil simply in that which by laws of freedom affects the ultimate ground of our adopting or obeying this or that maxim, not in what affects the sensibility (as receptivity).

III.: MAN IS BY NATURE BAD.

"Vitiis nemo sine nascitur."

— *Horat.*

According to what has been said above, the proposition: Man is bad can only mean: He is conscious of the moral law, and yet has adopted into his maxim (occasional) deviation therefrom. He is by nature bad is equivalent to saying: This holds of him considered as a species; not as if such a quality could be inferred from the specific conception of man (that of man in general) (for then it would be necessary); but by what is known of him through experience he cannot be otherwise judged, or it may be presupposed as subjectively necessary in every man, even the best.

Now this propensity itself must be considered as morally bad, and consequently not as a natural property, but as something that can be imputed to the man, and consequently must consist in maxims of the elective will which are opposed to the law; but on account of freedom these must be looked upon as in themselves contingent, which is inconsistent with the universality of this badness, unless the ultimate subjective ground of all maxims is, by whatever means, interwoven with humanity, and, as it were, rooted in it; hence we call this a natural propensity to evil; and as the man must, nevertheless, always incur the blame of it, it may be called even a radical badness in human nature, innate (but not the less drawn upon us by ourselves).

Now that there must be such a corrupt propensity rooted in men need not be formally proved in the face of the multitude of crying examples which experience sets before one's eyes in the acts of man. If examples are desired from that state in which many philosophers hoped to find pre-eminently the natural goodness of human nature, namely, the so-called state of nature, we need only look at the instances of unprovoked cruelty in the scenes of murder in Tofoa, New Zealand, the Navigator Islands, and the never-ceasing instances in the wide wastes of North-West America (mentioned by Captain Hearne), where no one has even the least advantage from it; and comparing these with that hypothesis, we have vices of savage life more than enough to make us abandon that opinion. On the other hand, if one is disposed to think that human nature can be better known in a civilized condition (in which its characteristic properties can be more perfectly developed), then one must listen to a long melancholy litany of complaints of humanity; of secret falsehood, even in the most intimate friendship, so that it is reckoned a general maxim of prudence that even the best friends should restrain their confidence in their mutual intercourse; of a propensity to hate the man to whom one is under an obligation, for which a benefactor must always be prepared; of a hearty good-will, which nevertheless admits the remark that "in the misfortunes of our best friends there is something which is not altogether displeasing to us"; and of many other vices concealed under the appearance of virtue, not to mention the vices of those who do not conceal them, because we are satisfied to call a man good who is a bad man of the average class. This will give one enough of the vices of culture and civilization (the most mortifying of all) to make him turn away his eye from the conduct of men, lest he should fall into another vice, namely, misanthropy. If he is not yet satisfied, however, he need only take into consideration a condition strangely compounded of both, namely, the external condition of nations — for the relation of civilized nations to one another is that of a rude state of nature (a state of perpetual preparation for war), and they are also firmly resolved never to abandon it — and he will become aware of principles adopted by the great societies called States, which directly contradict the public profession, and yet are never to be laid aside, principles which no philsopher has yet been able to bring into agreement with morals, nor (sad to say) can they propose any better which would be reconcilable with human nature; so that the philosophical millennium, which hopes for a state of perpetual peace founded on a union of nations as a republic of the world, is generally ridiculed as visionary, just as much as the theological, which looks for the complete moral improvement of the whole human race.

Now the source of this badness (1) cannot, as is usually done, be placed in the sensibility of man and the natural inclinations springing therefrom. For not only have these no direct reference to badness (on the contrary, they afford the occasion for the moral character to show its power, occasion for virtue), but further we are not responsible for their existence (we cannot be, for being implanted in us they have not us for their authors), whereas we are accountable for the propensity to evil; for as this concerns the morality of the subject, and is consequently found in him as a freely acting being, it must be imputed to him as his own fault, notwithstanding its being so deeply rooted in the elective will that it must be said to be found in man by nature. The source of this evil (2) cannot be placed in a corruption of Reason which gives the moral law , as if Reason could abolish the authority of the law in itself and disown its obligation; for this is absolutely impossible. To conceive one's self as a freely acting being, and yet released from the law which is appropriate to such a being (the moral law), would be the same as to conceive a cause operating without any law (for determination by natural laws is excluded by freedom), and this would be a contradiction. For the purpose then of assigning a source of the moral evil in man, sensibility contains too little, for in taking away the motives which arise from freedom it makes him a mere animal being; on the other hand, a Reason releasing from the moral law, a malignant reason, as it were (a simply bad Rational Will, ["Wille"] involves too much, for by this antagonism to the law would itself be made a spring of action (for the elective will cannot be determined without some spring), so that the subject would be made a devilish being. Neither of these views, however, is applicable to man.

Now although the existence of this propensity to evil in human nature can be shown by experience, from the actual antagonism in time between human will and the law, yet this proof does not teach us its proper nature and the source of this antagonism. This propensity concerns a relation of the free elective will (an elective will, therefore, the conception of which is not empirical) to the moral law as a spring (the conception of which is likewise purely intellectual); its nature then must be cognized à priori from the concept of the Bad, so far as the laws of freedom (obligation and accountability) bear upon it. The following is the development of the concept: —

Man (even the worst) does not in any maxim, as it were, rebelliously abandon the moral law (and renounce obedience to it). On the contrary, this forces itself upon him irresistibly by virtue of his moral nature, and if no other spring opposed it he would also adopt it into his ultimate maxim as the adequate determining principle of his elective will, that is, he would be morally good. But by reason of his physical nature, which is likewise blameless, he also depends on sensible springs of action, and adopts them also into his maxim (by the subjective principle of self-love). If, however, he adopted them into his maxim as adequate of themselves alone to determine his will without regarding the moral law (which he has within), then he would be morally bad. Now as he naturally adopts both into his maxim, and as he would find each, if it were alone, sufficient to determine his will, it follows that if the distinction of the maxims depended merely on the distinction of the springs (the matter of the maxims), namely, according as they were furnished by the law or by an impulse of sense, he would be morally good and bad at once, which (as we saw in the Introduction) is a contradiction. Hence the distinction whether the man is good or bad must lie, not in the distinction of the springs that he adopts into his maxim, but in the subordination, i. e. which of the two he makes the condition of the other (that is, not in the matter of the maxim but in its form). Consequently a man (even the best) is bad only by this, that he reverses the moral order of the springs in adopting them into his maxims; he adopts, indeed, the moral law along with that of self-love; but perceiving that they cannot subsist together on equal terms, but that one must be subordinate to the other as its supreme condition, he makes the spring of self-love and its inclinations the condition of obedience to the moral law; whereas, on the contrary, the latter ought to be adopted into the general maxims of the elective will as the sole spring, being the supreme condition of the satisfaction of the former.

The springs being thus reversed by his maxim, contrary to the moral order, his actions may, nevertheless, conform to the law just as though they had sprung from genuine principles: provided reason employs the unity of maxims in general, which is proper to the moral law, merely for the purpose of introducing into the springs of inclination a unity that does not belong to them, under the name of happiness (ex. gr. that truthfulness, if adopted as a principle, relieves us of the anxiety to maintain consistency in our lies and to escape being entangled in their serpent coils). In which case the empirical character is good, but the intelligible character bad.

Now if there is in human nature a propensity to this, then there is in man a natural propensity to evil; and since this propensity itself must ultimately be sought in a free elective will, and therefore can be imputed, it is morally bad. This badness is radical, because it corrupts the source of all maxims; and at the same time being a natural propensity, it cannot be destroyed by human powers, since this could only be done by good maxims; and when by hypothesis the ultimate subjective source of all maxims is corrupt, these cannot exist; nevertheless, it must be possible to overcome it, since it is found in man as a freely acting being.

The depravity of human nature, then, is not so much to be called badness, if this word is taken in its strict sense, namely, as a disposition (subjective principle of maxims) to adopt the bad, as bad, into one's maxims as a spring (for that is devilish); but rather perversity of heart, which, on account of the result, is also called a bad heart. This may co-exist with a Will ["Wille"] good in general, and arises from the frailty of human nature, which is not strong enough to follow its adopted principles, combined with its impurity in not distinguishing the springs (even of well-intentioned actions) from one another by moral rule. So that ultimately it looks at best only to the conformity of its actions with the law, not to their derivation from it, that is, to the law itself as the only spring. Now although this does not always give rise to wrong actions and a propensity thereto, that is, to vice, yet the habit of regarding the absence of vice as a conformity of the mind to the law of duty (as virtue) must itself be designated a radical perversity of the human heart (since in this case the spring in the maxims is not regarded at all, but only the obedience to the letter of the law).

This is called innate guilt (reatus), because it can be perceived as soon as ever the use of freedom manifests itself in man, and nevertheless must have arisen from freedom, and therefore may be imputed. It may in its two first degrees (of frailty and impurity) be viewed as unintentional guilt (culpa), but in the third as intentional (dolus), and it is characterized by a certain malignancy of the human heart (dolus malus), deceiving itself as to its own good or bad dispositions, and provided only its actions have not the bad result which by their maxims they might well have, then not disquieting itself about its dispositions, but, on the contrary, holding itself to be justified before the law. Hence comes the peace of conscience of so many (in their own opinion conscientious) men, when amidst actions in which the law was not taken into counsel, or at least was not the most important consideration, they have merely had the good fortune to escape bad consequences. Perhaps they even imagine they have merit, not feeling themselves guilty of any of the transgressions in which they see others involved; without inquiring whether fortune is not to be thanked for this, and whether the disposition which, if they would, they could discover within, would not have led them to the practice of the like vices, had they not been kept away from them by want of power, by temperament, education, circumstances of time and place which lead into temptation (all things that cannot be imputed to us). This dishonesty in imposing on ourselves, which hinders the establishment of genuine moral principle in us, extends itself then outwardly also to falsehood and deception of others which, if it is not to be called badness, at least deserves to be called worthlessness, and has its root in the radical badness of human nature, which (inasmuch as it perverts the moral judgment in respect of the estimation to be formed of a man, and renders imputation quite uncertain both internally and externally) constitutes the corrupt spot in our nature, which, as long as we do not extirpate it, hinders the source of good from developing itself as it otherwise would.

A member of the English Parliament uttered in the heat of debate the declaration, "Every man has his price." If this is true (which every one may decide for himself) — if there is no virtue for which a degree of temptation cannot be found which is capable of overthrowing it — if the question whether the good or the bad spirit shall gain us to its side only depends on which bids highest and offers most prompt payment — then what the Apostle says might well be true of men universally: "There is no difference, they are altogether sinners; there is none that doeth good (according to the spirit of the law), no not one."

IV.: ON THE ORIGIN OF THE EVIL IN HUMAN NATURE.

Origin (primary) is the derivation of an effect from its primary cause, that is, one which is not in its turn an effect of another cause of the same kind. It may be considered either as a rational or a temporal origin. In the former signification, it is only the existence of the effect that is considered; in the latter, its occurrence, so that it is referred as an event to its cause in time. When the effect is referred to a cause which is connected with it by laws of freedom, as is the case with moral evil, then the determination of the elective will to the production of it is not regarded as connected with its determining principle in time, but merely in the conception of the reason, and cannot be deduced as from any antecedent state, which on the other hand must be done when the bad action, considered as an event in the world, is referred to its physical cause. It is a contradiction then to seek for the time-origin of free actions as such (as we do with physical effects); or of the moral character of man, so far as it is regarded as contingent, because this is the principle of the use of freedom, and this (as well as the determining principle of free will generally) must be sought for simply in conceptions of reason.

But whatever may be the origin of the moral evil in man, the most unsuitable of all views that can be taken of its spread and continuance through all the members of our race and in all generations is, to represent it as coming to us by inheritance from our first parents; for we can say of moral evil what the poet says of good:

. . . Genus et proavos, et quæ non fecimus ipsi, Vix ea nostro puto. . . .

It is to be observed, further, that when we inquire into the origin of evil, we do not at first take into account the propensity to it (as peccatum in potentia), but only consider the actual evil of given actions, in its inner possibility, and in what must concur to determine the will to the doing of them.

Every bad action, when we inquire into its rational origin, must be viewed as if the man had fallen into it directly from the state of innocence. For whatever may have been his previous conduct, and of whatever kind the natural causes influencing him may be, whether moreover they are internal or external, his action is still free, and not determined by any causes, and therefore it both can and must be always judged as an original exercise of his elective will. He ought to have left it undone, in whatever circumstances he may have been; for by no cause in the world can he cease to be a freely acting being. It is said indeed, and justly, that the man is accountable for the consequences, of his previous free but wrong actions; but by this is only meant, that one need not have recourse to the subterfuge of deciding whether the later actions are free or not, because there is sufficient ground for the accountability in the admittedly free action which was their cause. But if a man had been never so bad up to the very moment of an impending free action (even so that custom had become second nature), yet not only has it been his duty to be better, but it is now still his duty to improve himself; he must then be also able to do so, and if he does not, he is just as accountable at the moment of acting as if, endowed with the natural capacity for good (which is inseparable from freedom), he had stepped into evil from the state of innocence. We must not inquire then what is the origin in time of this act, but what is its origin in reason, in order to define thereby the propensity, that is to say, the general subjective principle by which a transgression is adopted into our maxim, if there is such a propensity, and if possible to explain it.

With this agrees very well the mode of representation which the Scriptures employ in depicting the origin of evil as a beginning of it in the human race, inasmuch as they exhibit it in a history in which that which must be conceived as first in the nature of the thing (without regard to the condition of time) appears as first in time. According to the Scriptures, evil does not begin from a fundamental propensity to it — otherwise its beginning would not spring from freedom — but from sin (by which is understood the transgression of the moral law as a divine command); while the state of man before all propensity to evil is called the state of innocence. The moral law preceded as a prohibition, as must be the case with man as a being not pure, but tempted by inclinations (Gen. ii. 16, 17). Instead now of following this law directly as an adequate spring (one which alone is unconditionally good, and in respect of which no scruple can occur), the man looked about for other springs (iii. 6), which could only be conditionally good (namely, so far as the law is not prejudiced thereby), and made it his maxim — if we conceive the action as consciously arising from freedom — to obey the law of duty not from duty, but from regard to other considerations. Hence he began with questioning the strictness of the law, which excludes the influence of every other spring; then he reasoned down obedience to it to the mere conditional conformity to means (subject to the principle of self-love), whence, finally, the predominance of sensible motives above the spring of the law was adopted into the maxim of action, and so sin was committed (iii. 6). Mutato nomine, de te fabula narratur. That we all do just the same, consequently "have all sinned in Adam, " and still sin, is clear from what has preceded; only that in us an innate propensity to sin is presupposed in time, but in the first man, on the contrary, innocence, so that in him the transgression is called a fall; whereas in us it is conceived as following from the innate depravity of our nature. What is meant, however, by this propensity is no more than this, that if we wish to apply ourselves to the explanation of evil as to its beginning in time, we must in the case of every intentional transgression pursue its causes in a previous period of our life, going backwards till we reach a time when the use of reason was not yet developed: in other words, we must trace the source of evil to a propensity towards it (as a foundation in nature) which, on this account, is called innate. In the case of the first man, who is represented as already possessing the full power of using his reason, this is not necessary, nor indeed possible; since otherwise that natural foundation (the evil propensity) must have been created in him; therefore his sin is represented as produced directly from a state of innocence. But we must not seek for an origin in time of a moral character for which we are to be accountable, however inevitable this is when we try to explain its contingent existence (hence Scripture may have so represented it to us in accommodation to this our weakness).

The rational origin, however, of this perversion of our elective will in respect of the way in which it adopts subordinate springs into its maxims as supreme, i. e. the origin of this propensity to evil, remains inscrutable to us; for it must itself be imputed to us, and consequently that ultimate ground of all maxims would again require the assumption of a bad maxim. What is bad could only have sprung from what is morally bad (not the mere limits of our nature); and yet the original constitution is adapted to good (nor could it be corrupted by any other than man himself, if he is to be accountable for this corruption); there is not then any source conceivable to us from which moral evil could have first come into us. Scripture, in its historical narrative, expresses this inconceivability, at the same time that it defines the depravity of our race more precisely by representing evil as pre-existing at the beginning of the world, not however in man, but in a spirit originally destined for a lofty condition. The first beginning of all evil in general is thus represented as inconceivable to us (for whence came the evil in that spirit?), and man as having fallen into evil only by seduction, and therefore as not fundamentally corrupt (i. e. even in his primary capacity for good), but as still capable of an improvement; in contrast to a seducing spirit, that is, a being in whom the temptation of the flesh cannot be reckoned as alleviating his guilt; so that the former, who, notwithstanding his corrupt heart, continues to have a good Rational Will ["Wille"], has still left the hope of a return to the good from which he has gone astray,

GENERAL REMARK. ON THE RESTORATION OF THE ORIGINAL CAPACITY FOR GOOD TO ITS FULL POWER.

What man is or ought to be in a moral sense he must make or must have made himself. Both must be the effect of his free elective will, otherwise it could not be imputed to him, and, consequently, he would be morally neither good nor bad. When it is said he is created good, that can only mean that he is created for good, and the original constitution in man is good; but this does not yet make the man himself good, but according as he does or does not adopt into his maxim the springs which this constitution contains (which must be left altogether to his own free choice), he makes himself become good or bad. Supposing that a supernatural co-operation is also necessary to make a man good or better, whether this consists only in the diminution of the obstacles or in a positive assistance, the man must previously make himself worthy to receive it and to accept this aid (which is no small thing), that is, to adopt into his maxim the positive increase of power, in which way alone it is possible that the good should be imputed to him, and that he should be recognised as a good man.

Now how it is possible that a man naturally bad should make himself a good man transcends all our conceptions; for how can a bad tree bring forth good fruit? But since it is already admitted that a tree originally good (as to its capacities) has brought forth bad fruit, and the fall from good to bad (when it is considered that it arises from freedom) is not more conceivable than a rising again from bad to good, the possibility of the latter cannot be disputed. For notwithstanding that fall, the command "we ought to become better men," resounds with undiminished force in our soul; consequently, we must be able to do so, even though what we ourselves can do should be insufficient of itself, and though we should thereby only make ourselves susceptible of an inscrutable higher assistance. It must, however, be presupposed that a germ of good has remained in its complete purity, which could not be destroyed or corrupted — a germ that certainly cannot be self-love, which, when taken as the principle of all our maxims, is in fact the source of all evil.

The restoration of the original capacity for good in us is then not the acquisition of a lost spring towards good; for this, which consists in respect for the moral law, we could never lose, and, were it possible to do so, we could never recover it. It is then only the restoration of its purity, as the supreme principle of all our maxims, by which it is adopted into these not merely in combination with other springs or as subordinate to these (the inclinations) as conditions, but in its entire purity as a spring sufficient of itself to determine the elective will. The original good is holiness of maxims in following one's duty, by which the man who adopts this purity into his maxims, although he is not himself as yet on that account holy (for there is still a long interval between maxim and act), nevertheless is on the way to approximate to holiness by an endless progress. Firmness of purpose in following duty, when it has become a habit, is called also virtue, as far as legality is concerned, which is its empirical character (virtus phenomenon). It has then the steady maxim of conformity of actions to the law, whatever may be the source of the spring required for this. Hence virtue in this sense is gradually acquired, and is described by some as a long practice (in observing the law) by which a man has passed from the propensity to vice, by gradual reform of his conduct and strengthening of his maxims, into an opposite propensity. This does not require any change of heart, but only a change of morals. A man regards himself as virtuous when he feels himself confirmed in the maxims of observance of duty, although this be not from the supreme principle of all maxims; but the intemperate man, for instance, returns to temperance for the sake of health; the liar to truth for the sake of reputation; the unjust man to common fairness for the sake of peace or of gain, &c., all on the much-lauded principle of happiness. But that a man should become not merely a legally but a morally good (Godpleasing) man, that is, virtuous in his intelligible character (virtus noumenon), a man who, when he recognises a thing as his duty, needs no other spring than this conception of duty itself; this is not to be effected by gradual reform, as long as the principle of his maxims remains impure, but requires a revolution in the mind (a transition to the maxim of holiness of mind), and he can only become a new man by a kind of new birth, as it were by a new creation (Gospel of John, iii. 5, compared with Gen. i. 2) and a change of heart.

But if a man is corrupt in the very foundation of his maxims, how is it possible that he should effect this revolution by his own power and become a good man of himself? And yet duty commands it, and duty commands nothing that is not practicable for us. The only way this difficulty can be got over is, that a revolution is necessary for the mental disposition, but a gradual reform for the sensible temperament, which opposes obstacles to the former; and being necessary, must therefore be possible; that is, when a man reverses the ultimate principle of his maxims by which he is a bad man by a single immutable resolution (and in so doing puts on a new man); then so far he is in principle and disposition a subject susceptible of good; but it is only in continued effort and growth that he is a good man, that is, he may hope with such purity of the principle that he has taken as the supreme maxim of his elective will, and by its stability, that he is on the good (though narrow) road of a constant progress from bad to better. In the eyes of one who penetrates the intelligible principle of the heart (of all maxims of elective will), and to whom therefore this endless progress is a unity, that is, in the eyes of God, this comes to the same as being actually a good man (pleasing to Him), and in so far this change may be considered as a revolution; but in the judgment of men, who can estimate themselves and the strength of their maxims only by the superiority which they gain over sensibility in time, it is only to be viewed as an ever continuing struggle for improvement; in other words, as a gradual reform of the perverse disposition, the propensity to evil.

Hence it follows that the moral culture of man must begin, not with improvement in morals, but with a transformation of the mind and the foundation of a character, although men usually proceed otherwise, and contend against vices singly, leaving the general root of them untouched. Now even a man of the most limited intellect is capable of the impression of an increased respect for an action conformable to duty, in proportion as he withdraws from it in thought all other springs which could have influenced the maxim of the action by means of self-love; and even children are capable of finding out even the least trace of a mixture of spurious springs of action, in which case the action instantly loses all moral worth in their eyes. This capacity for good is admirably cultivated by adducing the example of even good men (good as regards their conformity to law), and allowing one's moral pupils to estimate the impurity of many maxims from the actual springs of their actions; and it gradually passes over into the character, so that duty simply of itself commences to acquire considerable weight in their hearts. But to teach them to admire virtuous actions, however great the sacrifice they may cost, is not the right way to maintain the feeling of the pupil for moral good. For however virtuous anyone may be, all the good he can ever do is only duty; and to do his duty is no more than to do what is in the common moral order, and therefore does not deserve to be admired. On the contrary, this admiration is a lowering of our feeling for duty, as if obedience to it were something extraordinary and meritorious.

There is, however, one thing in our soul which, when we take a right view of it, we cannot cease to regard with the highest astonishment, and in regard to which admiration is right or even elevating, and that is the original moral capacity in us generally. What is that in us (we may ask ourselves) by which we, who are constantly dependent on nature by so many wants, are yet raised so far above it in the idea of an original capacity (in us) that we regard them all as nothing, and ourselves as unworthy of existence, if we were to indulge in their satisfaction in opposition to a law which our reason authoritatively prescribes; although it is this enjoyment alone that can make life desirable, while reason neither promises anything nor threatens. The importance of this question must be deeply felt by every man of the most ordinary ability, who has been previously instructed as to the holiness that lies in the idea of duty, but who has not yet ascended to the investigation of the notion of freedom, which first arises from this law; and even the incomprehensibility of this capacity, a capacity which proclaims a Divine origin, must rouse his spirit to enthusiasm, and strengthen it for any sacrifices which respect for this duty may impose on him. The frequent excitement of this feeling of the sublimity of a man's moral constitution is especially to be recommended as a means of awaking moral sentiments, since it operates in direct opposition to the innate propensity to pervert the springs in the maxims of our elective will, and tends to make unconditional respect for the law the ultimate condition of the admission of all maxims, and so restores the original moral subordination of the springs of action, and the capacity for good in the human heart in its primitive purity.

But is not this restoration by one's own strength directly opposed to the thesis of the innate corruption of man for everything good? Undoubtedly, as far as conceivability is concerned, that is to say, our discernment of its possibility, just as with everything which has to be regarded as an event in time (change), and as such necessarily determined by laws of nature, whilst its opposite must yet be regarded as possible by freedom in accordance with moral laws; but it is not opposed to the possibility of this restoration itself. For if the moral law commands that we shall now be better men, it follows inevitably that we also can be better. The thesis of innate evil has no application in dogmatic morality; for its precepts contain the very same duties, and continue in the same force, whether there is in us an innate propensity to transgression or not. In the culture of morality this thesis has more significance, but still it means no more than this, that in the moral cultivation of the moral capacity for good created in us, we cannot begin from a natural state of innocence, but must start from the supposition of a depravity of the elective will in assuming maxims that are contrary to the original moral capacity, and, since the propensity thereto is ineradicable, with an unceasing effort against it. Now, as this only leads to a progress in infinitum from bad to better, it follows that the transformation of the disposition of a bad into that of a good man is to be placed in the change of the supreme inner principle of all his maxims, in accordance with the moral law, provided that this new principle (the new heart) be itself immutable. A man cannot, however, naturally attain the conviction [that it is immutable], either by immediate consciousness, or by the proof derived from the course of life he has hitherto pursued, for the bottom of his heart (the subjective first principle of his maxims) is inscrutable to himself; but unto the path that leads to it, and which is pointed out to him by a fundamentally improved disposition, he must be able to hope to arrive by his own efforts, since he ought to become a good man and can only be esteemed morally good by virtue of that which can be imputed to him as done by himself.

Now reason, which is naturally disinclined to moral effort, opposes to this expectation of self-improvement all sorts of corrupt ideas of religion, under the pretext of natural impotence (among which is to be reckoned, attributing to God Himself the adoption of the principle of happiness as the supreme condition of His commands). Now we may divide all religions into two classes — favour-seeking religion (mere worship), and moral religion, that is, the religion of a good life. By the former a man either flatters himself that God can make him eternally happy (by remission of his demerits), without his having any need to become a better man, or if this does not seem possible to him, that God can make him a better man, without his having to do anything in the matter himself except to ask for it; which, as before an all-seeing being asking is no more than wishing, would in fact be doing nothing; for if the mere wish were sufficient, every man would be good. But in the moral religion (and amongst all the public religions that have ever existed the Christian alone is moral) it is a fundamental principle that everyone must do as much as lies in his power to become a better man, and that it is only when he has not buried his innate talent (Luke xix. 12-16), when he has used the original capacity for good so as to become a better man, that he can hope that what is not in his power will be supplied by a higher co-operation. But it is not absolutely necessary that man should know in what this co-operation consists; perhaps it is even inevitable that if the way in which it happens had been revealed at a certain time, different men at another time should form different conceptions of it, and that with all honesty. But then the principle holds good: "it is not essential, and therefore not necessary for everyone to know what God does or has done for his salvation," but it is essential to know what he himself has to do in order to be worthy of this assistance.

APPENDIX.

In the work called France, for the year 1797, Part VI. No. 1, on Political Reactions, by Benjamin Constant, the following passage occurs: —

"The moral principle that it is one's duty to speak the truth, if it were taken singly and unconditionally, would make all society impossible. We have the proof of this in the very direct consequences which have been drawn from this principle by a German philosopher, who goes so far as to affirm that to tell a falsehood to a murderer who asked us whether our friend, of whom he was in pursuit, had not taken refuge in our house, would be a crime."

The French philosopher opposes this principle in the following manner:— "It is a duty to tell the truth. The notion of duty is inseparable from the notion of right. A duty is what in one being corresponds to the right of another. Where there are no rights there are no duties. To tell the truth then is a duty, but only towards him who has a right to the truth. But no man has a right to a truth that injures others." The πρῶτον ψεῦδος here lies in the statement that "To tell the truth is a duty, but only towards him who has a right to the truth."

It is to be remarked, first, that the expression "to have a right to the truth" is unmeaning. We should rather say, a man has a right to his own truthfulness (veracitas), that is, to subjective truth in his own person. For to have a right objectively to truth would mean that, as in meum and tuum generally, it depends on his will whether a given statement shall be true or false, which would produce a singular logic.

Now, the first question is whether a man — in cases where he cannot avoid answering Yes or No — has the right to be untruthful. The second question is whether, in order to prevent a misdeed that threatens him or some one else, he is not actually bound to be untruthful in a certain statement to which an unjust compulsion forces him.

Truth in utterances that cannot be avoided is the formal duty of a man to everyone, however great the disadvantage that may arise from it to him or any other; and although by making a false statement I do no wrong to him who unjustly compels me to speak, yet I do wrong to men in general in the most essential point of duty, so that it may be called a lie (though not in the jurist's sense), that is, so far as in me lies I cause that declarations in general find no credit, and hence that all rights founded on contract should lose their force; and this is a wrong which is done to mankind.

If, then, we define a lie merely as an intentionally false declaration towards another man, we need not add that it must injure another; as the jurists think proper to put in their definition (mendacium est falsiloquium in præjudicium alterius). For it always injures another; if not another individual, yet mankind generally, since it vitiates the source of justice. This benevolent lie may, however, by accident (casus) become punishable even by civil laws; and that which escapes liability to punishment only by accident may be condemned as a wrong even by external laws. For instance, if you have by a lie hindered a man who is even now planning a murder, you are legally responsible for all the consequences. But if you have strictly adhered to the truth, public justice can find no fault with you, be the unforeseen consequence what it may. It is possible that whilst you have honestly answered Yes to the murderer's question, whether his intended victim is in the house, the latter may have gone out unobserved, and so not have come in the way of the murderer, and the deed therefore have not been done; whereas, if you lied and said he was not in the house, and he had really gone out (though unknown to you) so that the murderer met him as he went, and executed his purpose on him, then you might with justice be accused as the cause of his death. For, if you had spoken the truth as well as you knew it, perhaps the murderer while seeking for his enemy in the house might have been caught by neighbours coming up and the deed been prevented. Whoever then tells a lie, however good his intentions may be, must answer for the consequences of it, even before the civil tribunal, and must pay the penalty for them, however unforeseen they may have been; because truthfulness is a duty that must be regarded as the basis of all duties founded on contract, the laws of which would be rendered uncertain and useless if even the least exception to them were admitted.

To be truthful (honest) in all declarations is therefore a sacred unconditional command of reason, and not to be limited by any expediency.

M. Constant makes a thoughtful and sound remark on the decrying of such strict principles, which it is alleged lose themselves in impracticable ideas, and are therefore to be rejected ():— "In every case in which a principle proved to be true seems to be inapplicable, it is because we do not know the middle principle which contains the medium of its application." He adduces () the doctrine of equality as the first link forming the social chain (); "namely, that no man can be bound by any laws except those to the formation of which he has contributed. In a very contracted society this principle may be directly applied and become the ordinary rule without requiring any middle principle. But in a very numerous society we must add a new principle to that which we here state. This middle principle is, that the individuals may contribute to the formation of the laws either in their own person or by representatives. Whoever would try to apply the first principle to a numerous society without taking in the middle principle would infallibly bring about its destruction. But this circumstance, which would only show the ignorance or incompetence of the lawgiver, would prove nothing against the principle itself." IIc concludes () thus: "A principle recognised as truth must, therefore, never be abandoned, however obviously danger may seem to be involved in it." (And yet the good man himself abandoned the unconditional principle of veracity on account of the danger to society, because he could not discover any middle principle would serve to prevent this danger; and, in fact, no such principle is to be interpolated here.)

Retaining the names of the persons as they have been here brought forward, "the French philosopher" confounds the action by which one does harm (nocet) to another by telling the truth, the admission of which he cannot avoid, with the action by which he does him wrong (lædit). It was merely an accident (casus) that the truth of the statement did harm to the inhabitant of the house; it was not a free deed (in the juridicial sense). For to admit his right to require another to tell a lie for his benefit would be to admit a claim opposed to all law. Every man has not only a right, but the strictest duty to truthfulness in statements which he cannot avoid, whether they do harm to himself or others. He himself, properly speaking, does not do harm to him who suffers thereby; but this harm is caused by accident. For the man is not free to choose, since (if he must speak at all) veracity is an unconditional duty. The "German philosopher" will therefore not adopt as his principle the proposition (): "It is a duty to speak the truth, but only to him who has a right to the truth," first on account of the obscurity of the expression, for truth is not a possession, the right to which can be granted to one, and refused to another; and next and chiefly, because the duty of veracity (of which alone we are speaking here) makes no distinction between persons towards whom we have this duty, and towards whom we may be free from it; but is an unconditional duty which holds in all circumstances.

Now, in order to proceed from a metaphysic of Right (which abstracts from all conditions of experience) to a principle of politics (which implies these notions to cases of experience), and by means of this to the solution of a problem of the latter in accordance with the general principle of right, the philosopher will enunciate: — 1. An Axiom, that is, an apodictically certain proposition, which follows directly from the definition of external right (harmony of the freedom of each with the freedom of all by a universal law). 2. A Postulate of external public law as the united will of all on the principle of equality, without which there could not exist the freedom of all. 3. A problem; how it is to be arranged that harmony may be maintained in a society, however large, on principles of freedom and equality (namely by means of a representative system); and this will then become a principle of the political system, the establishment and arrangement of which will contain enactments which, drawn from practical knowledge of men, have in view only the mechanism of administration of justice, and how this is to be suitably carried out. Justice must never be accommodated to the political system, but always the political system to justice.

"A principle recognised as true (I add, recognised à priori, and therefore apodictic) must never be abandoned, however obviously danger may seem to be involved in it," says the author. Only here we must not understand the danger of doing harm (accidentally), but of doing wrong; and this would happen if the duty of veracity, which is quite unconditional, and constitutes the supreme condition of justice in utterances, were made conditional and subordinate to other considerations; and, although by a certain lie I in fact do no wrong to any person, yet I infringe the principle of justice in regard to all indispensably necessary statements generally (I do wrong formally, though not materially; and this is much worse than to commit an injustice to any individual, because such a deed does not presuppose any principle leading to it in the subject. The man who, when asked whether in the statement he is about to make he intends to speak truth or not, does not receive the question with indignation at the suspicion thus expressed towards him that he might be a liar, but who asks permission first to consider possible exceptions, is already a liar (in potentia), since he shows that he does not recognize veracity as a duty in itself, but reserves exceptions from a rule which in its nature does not admit of exceptions, since to do so would be self-contradictory.

All practical principles of justice must contain strict truths, and the principles here called middle principles can only contain the closer definition of their application to actual cases (according to the rules of politics), and never exceptions from them, since exceptions destroy the universality, an account of which alone they bear the name of principles.

II.: — ON THE SAYING "NECESSITY HAS NO LAW".

There is no casus necessitatis except in the case where an unconditional duty conflicts with a duty which, though perhaps great, is yet conditional; e. g. if the question is about preserving the State from disaster by betraying a person who stands towards another in a relation such as, for example, that of father and son. To save the State from harm is an unconditional duty; to save an individual is only a conditional duty, namely, provided he has not been guilty of a crime against the State. The information given to the authorities may be given with the greatest reluctance, but it is given under pressure, namely, moral necessity. But if a shipwrecked man thrusts another from his plank in order to save his own life, and it is said that he had the right of necessity (i. e. physical necessity) to do so, this is wholly false. For to maintain my own life is only a conditional duty (viz. if it can be done without crime), but it is an unconditional duty not to take the life of another who does not injure me, nay, does not even bring me into peril of losing it. However, the teachers of general civil right proceed quite consistently in admitting this right of necessity. For the sovereign power could not connect any punishment with the prohibition; for this punishment would necessarily be death, but it would be an absurd law that would threaten death to a man if when in danger he did not voluntarily submit to death. — From "Das mag in der Theorie richtig seyn, u. s. w." (Rosenkr., vii., .)

Universal Natural History and Theory of Heaven

This early treatise was written in 1755 and is based on a 1750 work by the English astronomer Thomas Wright, the first scientist to describe the shape of the Milky Way and speculate that faint nebulae were distant galaxies. *Universal Natural History and Theory of Heaven* proposes that the Solar System is merely a smaller version of the fixed star systems, such as the Milky Way and other galaxies. The cosmogony Kant proposes in this book is closer to today's accepted ideas than that of some of his contemporary thinkers. Kant's ideas are strongly influenced by atomist theory, in addition to the thoughts of the Roman Lucretius.

The book concludes with an almost mystical expression of appreciation for nature: "In the universal silence of nature and in the calm of the senses the immortal spirit's hidden faculty of knowledge speaks an ineffable language and gives undeveloped concepts, which are indeed felt, but do not let themselves be described."

Contents

TRANSLATOR'S NOTE

Immanuel Kant (1724-1804) published *The Universal Natural History and Theory of Heaven* in 1755. This English text is based on Georg Reimer's edition of the complete works of Immanuel Kant (1905). The translation was first completed and posted on the web in 1998. It has been considerably revised for this September 2008 version, mainly to improve the accuracy and fluency of the translation.

In the translated text, the Table of Contents has been altered to include the Dedication and the Preface and moved to the front before these sections. The endnotes (indicated with a numerical superscript link) come from Kant's original text except for those which are provided by the translator. The latter are prefaced in the endnote by the comment *[Translator's note],* and the former by the phrase *[Kant's note].*

In the English translation I have used the original lines from the works of Alexander Pope and Joseph Addison in those places where Kant quotes the often quite loose German versions of these English poets. The translations of the von Haller quotations are my own.

There are also occasional references to two earlier English versions of Kant's text: those by Stanley L. Jaki (Scottish Academic Press, 1981) and by William Hastie (first published in 1900, reprinted by University of Michigan Press, 1969). The translator of the present text would like to acknowledge the great help he has received from these two earlier translations. Anyone seeking a detailed contextual examination of Kant's scientific ideas in this essay should consult the Jaki edition, which is outstanding in this respect.

Ian Johnston

Liberal Studies Department

Vancouver Island University

September 2008

DEDICATION

To the most serene, the mightiest king and master

Frederick

King of Prussia

Margrave of Brandenburg

Lord Chamberlain and Elector of the Holy Roman Empire

Sovereign and Highest Lord of Silesia, etc. etc.

My most all-honoured King and Master,

Most serene and mighty king,

Most All-honoured King and Master,

The feeling of my own lack of worth and the radiance from the throne cannot make my foolishness so timid, when the honour which the most gracious monarch dispenses with equal magnanimity among all his subjects gives me grounds for hope that the boldness which I undertake will not be looked upon with ungracious eyes. In most submissive respect I here lay at the feet of your eternal kingly majesty one of the most trifling samples of that eager spirit with which your highness's schools, through the encouragement and the protection of their illustrious sovereign, strive to emulate other nations in the sciences. How happy I would be if the present endeavour could succeed in making the efforts with which the humblest and most respectful subject constantly tries to make himself in some way of service to the Fatherland win the highest possible feeling of goodwill of his king. With the utmost devotion until my dying day,

Your eternal majesty's most humble servant

The author

Königsberg

14 March, 1755

PREFACE

I have selected a subject which, both in view of its inherent difficulty and also with respect to religion, can right at the very start elicit an unfavourable judgment from a large section of readers. To discover the systematic arrangement linking large parts of creation in its entire infinite extent and to bring out by means of mechanical principles the development of the cosmic bodies themselves and the cause of their movements from the first state of nature, such insights seem to overstep by a long way the powers of human reason. From another perspective, religion threatens with a solemn accusation about the presumption that one is allowed to be so bold as to attribute to nature left to itself such consequences in which we rightly become aware of the immediate hand of the Highest Being and worries about encountering in the inquiry into such views a defence of the atheist. I do perceive all these difficulties, and yet I do not become fainthearted. I feel all the power of the obstacles ranged against me, and nevertheless I am not despondent. On the basis of a slight assumption I have undertaken a dangerous journey, and I already see the promontories of new lands. Those people who have the resolution to set forth on the undertaking will set foot on these lands and have the pleasure of designating them with their very own names.

I made no commitment to this endeavour until I considered myself secure from the point of view of religious duties. My enthusiasm has doubled as I witnessed at every step the dispersal of the clouds which behind their obscurity seemed to hide monsters and which, after they scattered, revealed the majesty of the Highest Being with the most vital radiance. Since I know that these efforts are free of all reproach, I will faithfully introduce what well-meaning or even weak-minded people could find shocking in my proposal and am candidly ready to submit it to the strict inspection of a council of true believers, which is the mark of an honest disposition. The champion of the faith, therefore, may be allowed to let his reasons be heard first.

If the planetary structure, with all its order and beauty, is only an effect of the universal laws of motion in matter left to itself, if the blind mechanism of natural forces knows how to develop itself out of chaos in such a marvellous way and to reach such perfection on its own, then the proof of the primordial Divine Author which we derive from a glance at the beauty of the cosmic structure is wholly discredited, nature is self-sufficient, the divine rule is unnecessary, Epicurus lives once again in the midst of Christendom, and an unholy philosophy treads underfoot the faith which proffers a bright light to illuminate it.

If I found this criticism had a firm basis, then the conviction which I have of the infallibility of divine truths is for me so empowering, that I would consider everything which contradicts it sufficiently refuted by that fact and would reject it. But the very agreement which I encounter between my system and religion raises my confidence in the face of all difficulties to an unshakable composure.

I recognize all the value of those proofs which people derive from the beauty and perfect organization of the cosmic structure to confirm the most eminently wise Author. If we do not obstinately deny all conviction, then we must agree with such incontrovertible reasons. But I maintain that the people who defend religion in this way, by using these reasons badly, perpetuate the conflict with the naturalists, because they present an unnecessarily weak case.

People are accustomed to take note of and to point out the harmonies, beauty, purposes, and a perfect interplay of means and ends in nature. But while they, on the one hand, extol nature, on the other hand, they seek to diminish it again. This fine arrangement, they say, is foreign to nature. Left alone to its universal laws, it would bring forth nothing but disorder. The harmonies demonstrate a foreign hand, which knew how to force material left without any regularity into a wise design. But I answer that if the universal efficient material laws were established equally as a result of the highest design, then they could presumably have no purposes except to strive to act on their own to fulfil the plan which the Highest Wisdom has set out for Itself or, if this is not the case, should we not be drawn into the temptation of believing that at least matter and its general laws were independent and that the most eminently wise power, which knew how to make use of them so splendidly, may indeed be great, but not infinite, certainly powerful, but not totally self-sufficient?

The defender of religion fears that the harmony which can be explained by a natural tendency of matter would demonstrate the independence of nature from divine providence. He clearly confesses that if people can discover natural reasons for all the order in the cosmic structure, reasons which can bring this into existence from the most universal and essential characteristics of matter, then it may be unnecessary to invoke a highest Ruling Power. According to the natural scientist's calculations, he finds nothing to quarrel with in this claim. He acquires examples which establish the fertility of general natural laws for perfectly beautiful consequences and brings true believers into danger through reasons, which in their hands could become invincible weapons. I wish to cite examples. People have already often proposed, as one of the clearest proofs of a benevolent providence solicitous of human welfare, that in the hottest parts of the earth the sea winds, right at the very time when the heated soil most requires their cooling, spread over the land and refresh it, as if they had been summoned. For example, in the island of Jamaica, as soon as the sun has climbed sufficiently high to heat the soil most strongly, just after 9 in the morning, a wind begins to rise from the sea and blows from all sides over the land. Its strength increases proportionally with the elevation of the sun. Around 1 in the afternoon, when it naturally is the hottest, the wind is at its strongest. It gradually decreases again with the setting of the sun, so that in the evening the very same stillness reigns as at the start. Without this welcome arrangement, the island would be uninhabitable. All coastal lands lying in the hot places on the Earth enjoy this same benefit. Moreover, it is most essential for them, because, since they are the lowest places on dry land, they also suffer the greatest heat. For the higher regions in the country, which this sea wind does not reach, are also in less need of it, because their higher location places them in a region of cooler air. Is not all this beautiful? Are there not clear purposes which have been realized by judiciously applied means? However, by way of a counterargument the natural scientist must find the natural causes of this in the most general characteristics of air, with no need to assume any special arrangements for the phenomenon. He observes correctly that these sea winds have to go through such periodic movements, even if no human beings lived on the island, thanks to no property other than the elasticity of air and gravity, without having any purposeful intention in the matter, even if it is indispensably necessary merely for the growth of plants. The sun's heat upsets the air's equilibrium by thinning out the air over the land, thus allowing the cooler sea air to rise from its position and take its place.

What benefits generally advantageous to our planet Earth do the winds not possess? And what uses does the keen intelligence of human beings not make of them? However, no other arrangements were necessary to create them except these same general properties of air and heat, which also had to occur on the Earth without reference to these purposes.

At this point the freethinker says: if you concede the point that when people can derive useful and purposeful arrangements from the most general and simplest natural laws, then we have no need for the special rule of a Highest Wisdom and thus you see here proofs which will catch you by your own admission. All nature, especially inorganic nature, is full of such proofs, which permit us to recognize that matter, which organizes itself through the mechanical operation of its own forces, has a certain correctness in its effects and without compulsion satisfactorily acts by rules of what is appropriate. When, in order to come to the rescue of the worthy cause of religion, a well-meaning person wishes to contest this capacity of general natural laws, then he will embarrass himself and by a poor defence give atheism a chance to triumph.

However, let us see how these reasons, which we fear in the hands of our opponents as injurious, are, by contrast, strong weapons to use in the fight against them. Matter, which organizes itself according to its most general laws, produces through its natural behaviour or, if we prefer, through a blind mechanical process, good consequences, which appear to be the design of a supremely High Wisdom. When we observe air, water, and heat left to themselves, they produce wind and clouds, rain, streams which moisten the lands, and all the useful consequences without which nature would have had to remain sad, empty, and barren. However, they produce these results not through mere chance or accident, which could just as readily have resulted in something detrimental. But we see that these consequences are limited by its natural laws so as to work only in this way. What should we then think of this harmony? How would it really be possible that things with different natures should strive to work in cooperation with one another for such perfect coordination and beauty, even with purposes in such matters which are to a certain extent beyond the range of lifeless material stuff, namely, for the benefit of human beings and animals, unless they recognized a common origin, that is, an Infinite Understanding, in which all things were designed with reference to their essential properties? If their natures were necessarily isolated and independent, what an astonishing contingency that would be, or rather, how impossible it would be that with their natural efforts they should mesh so exactly together, as if an overriding wise selection had united them.

Now, I confidently apply this concept to my present enterprise. I summon up the material stuff of all worlds in a universal confusion and create out of this a perfect chaos. According to the established laws of attraction, I see matter developing and modifying its motion through repulsion. Without the assistance of arbitrary fictions, I enjoy the pleasure of seeing a well-ordered totality emerge under the influence of the established laws of motion, something which looks so similar to the same planetary system which we see in front of us, that I cannot prevent myself from believing that it is the same. This unanticipated unfolding of the order of nature on a grand scale I find at first suspicious, because it establishes such a well-coordinated and correct system on such a meagre and simple foundation. Finally, on the basis of the previously outlined observation, I advise myself that such a natural development is not something unheard of in nature but that its fundamental striving necessarily brings such things with it and that this is the most marvellous evidence of its dependence on that Primordial Essence which has within Itself the source of being and the first laws by which nature operates. This insight doubles my trust in the proposal I have made. The confidence increases with each step I take as I continue on, and my timidity disappears completely.

But the defence of your system, it will be said, is at the same time a defence of the opinions of Epicurus, to which it has the closest similarity.[1*] I will not completely deny all agreement with him. Many people have become atheists through the apparent truth of such reasons which, with a more scrupulous consideration, could have convinced them as forcibly as possible of the certain existence of the Highest Being. The consequences which a perverse understanding infers from innocent basic principles are often very blameworthy. Although his theory was what one would expect from the keen intelligence of a great spirit, Epicurus' conclusions were also of this kind.

I will also not deny that the theory of Lucretius or of his predecessors (Epicurus, Leucippus, and Democritus) has much similarity to mine.[2*] Like those philosophers, I set out the first condition of nature as that state of the world consisting of a universal scattering of the primordial materials of all planetary bodies, or atoms, as they were called by these writers. Epicurus proposes a principle of heaviness which drives these elementary particles downwards, and this appears not very different from Newton's power of attraction, which I assume. He also assigned to these particles a certain deviation from the straight linear movement of their descent, although at the same time he had an absurd picture of the cause and consequences of this deviation. This deviation comes about to some extent with the alteration in the straight linear descent, a change which we derive from the force of repulsion of the particles. Finally, came the eddies, which arose from the confused movement of the atoms, a major part of the theories of Leucippus and Democritus. We will meet them also in our theory. But such a close affinity with a theory which was the true theory of atheism in ancient times does not lead mine to be grouped in the company of their errors. Even with the most foolish opinions which can win popular applause, sometimes there is some truth to remark upon. A false basic assumption or a pair of unexamined coordinating principles lead people from the footpath of truth through unnoticed misdirections right into the abyss. Nonetheless, there remains, in spite of the above-mentioned similarity, a fundamental difference between the ancient cosmogony and the present one, so that one can derive from the latter totally opposite consequences.

The previously mentioned teachers of the mechanical development of the cosmic structure derived all order which can be observed in it from chance accident, which allowed the atoms to come together in such a fortunate way that they created a well-ordered totality. Epicurus was even so unconscionable that he demanded that the atoms swerved from their direct linear movement without any cause, so that they could run into each other. Collectively these writers pushed this absurdity so far, that they even attributed the origin of all living creatures to this blind collision and, in effect, derived reason from irrationality. In my theory, by contrast, I find matter bound to certain necessary laws. I see a beautiful and orderly totality developing quite naturally in its complete dissolution and scattering. This does not happen through accident or chance. By contrast, we see that natural characteristics necessarily bring this condition with them. Hence, will we not be moved to inquire why matter had have just such laws which aim at order and propriety? Was it really possible that many things, each of which has its own nature independent of the others, should on their own constitute themselves in such a way that a well-ordered totality thereby arises? And if they do this, is there not an undeniable proof of the commonality of their first primordial origin, which must be a self-sufficient Highest Reason, in which the natures of things were designed for harmonious purposes?

The material which is the primordial stuff for all things is thus bound to certain laws. Freely left subject to these laws, it must necessarily bring forth beautiful combinations. It has no freedom to deviate from this plan of perfection. Since it also finds itself subject to the loftiest wise purpose, it must of necessity be set in such harmonious relationships through a First Cause which rules over it. *There is a God for just this reason, that nature, even in a chaotic state, can develop only in an orderly and rule-governed manner.*

I have such a high opinion of the honest minds of those people who confer upon this proposal the honour of testing it, that I remain confident that, where the basic principles mentioned above will still not be able to get rid of all worries about the deleterious consequences of my system, nevertheless at least they place the sincerity of my intentions beyond doubt. If, in spite of this, there are malicious zealots who consider it a duty worthy of their holy calling to attach shameful explanations to the most innocent opinions, then I am sure that their judgment will have precisely the opposite effect among reasonable people. Besides, people will not deprive me of the right which Descartes enjoyed in his time among disinterested critics when he ventured to explain the development of world bodies from merely mechanical laws.[3*] I wish therefore to quote from the author of Universal World History:[4*] "Thus we can do nothing other than believe that the attempt of this philosopher, who endeavoured to explain the development of the world in a certain time from confused matter simply through the continuation of a movement once impressed on it using a few easy and universal laws of motion, or of others *who since then have, with more approval, attempted the same thing through the primordial properties of matter, with which it was created, is far from being worthy of punishment or demeaning to God, as many have imagined, since in this way a higher idea of His infinite wisdom is far more likely to be brought about.*"

I have sought to clear away the difficulties which seem, from a religious point of view, to threaten my propositions. There are some no less significant difficulties with respect to the subject matter itself. Even if it is true, people will say, that God has set in the forces of nature a hidden art of developing a perfect world order out of chaos on their own, will human understanding, which is so stupid in the commonest circumstances, be capable of investigating hidden properties in such a massive enterprise? Such an undertaking amounts to much the same thing as when people say: Give me only the material, and I will create a world out of it for you. Can the weakness of your insights, which are shamed by the most insignificant things, which come into your mind daily and close by, not teach you that it is vain to discover the infinite and what was happening in nature even before there was a world? I demolish this difficulty, for I clearly show that of all the attempts which could be devised to learn about nature, this very endeavour may be the one in which we can most easily and surely go right to the origin. Just as among all problems of research into nature, none will be resolved more correctly and certainly than the true constitution of the planetary structure on a large scale, the laws of motions, and the inner workings which drive all planetary orbits, in which Newtonian philosophy can provide such insights that we find nothing like them in any other part of philosophy, in the same way I maintain that among all the natural phenomena whose first cause we are investigating, the origin of the planetary system and the production of the heavenly bodies, together with the causes of their movements, is the one which we may hope to consider reliably from first principles. The reason for this is easy to perceive. The heavenly bodies are round masses with the simplest development which a body whose origin we are exploring can ever have. Their movements are equally clear. They are nothing other than a free continuation of an impetus impressed upon them once, a motion which, combined with the force of attraction of the body at the mid-point, becomes circular. Moreover, the space in which they move is empty, the intermediate distances, which separate them from each other, are exceptionally large, and thus everything is laid out for undisturbed motion as well as for clear observation of them in as manifest a way as possible. In my view, we could say here with certain understanding and without presumption: Give me the material, and I will build a world out of it! That is, give me the material, and I will show you how a world is to come into being out of it. For if there is material present which is endowed with an inherent power of attraction, then it is not difficult to establish those causes which could have led to the arrangement of the planetary system, considered on a large scale. We know what is involved for a body to acquire a spherical shape. We grasp what is required for freely suspended spheres to take on a circular movement around the middle point towards which they are attracted. The position of the orbits relative to each other, the agreement in the direction, the eccentricity, everything can arise from the simplest mechanical causes, and we may hope with confidence to discover them, because they can be established with the easiest and clearest reasons. However, can we boast of such advantages for the smallest plants or insects? Are we in a position to say, give me the material, and I will show you how a caterpillar could have developed? Do we not remain here on the bottom rung because of our ignorance of the true inner constitution of the object and of the development inherent in its multiple elements? Thus, people must not let themselves be disconcerted when I venture to say that we will be able to understand the development of all the cosmic bodies, the causes of their movements, in short, the origin of the entire present arrangement of the planetary system, before we completely and clearly understand the development of a single plant or caterpillar on mechanical principles.

These are the reasons on which I base my confidence that the physical part of natural philosophy gives us hope that in future it will indeed have the same perfection to which Newton raised the mathematical part of the subject. Next to the laws according to which the arrangement of the cosmic structure stands in its present state perhaps there are no others in the entire study of nature so capable of such mathematical accuracy as those laws by which it has developed, and without doubt the hand of an experienced surveyor would find work in these fields unproductive.

Now that I have allowed myself to promote a favourable reception for what I am proposing in my examination, I will be permitted briefly to explain the way I have dealt with it. The first part is concerned with a new system for the structure of the cosmos on a large scale. Mr. Wright from Durham, whose essay I learned about in the *Freie Urteile* from Hamburg for the year 1751, first gave me the occasion to consider the fixed stars, not as a scattered teeming mass without perceptible order, but as one system with the closest similarity to a planetary system.[5] Thus, just as in the latter the planets are located very near to a common plane, the fixed stars in their positions are also related as closely as possible to a certain plane which must be imagined drawn through the entire heavens, and because of their densest accumulation toward this same plane they project that band of light called the Milky Way. I have become convinced that, since this zone illuminated by countless suns is very precisely structured in the orientation of an extremely large circle, our sun must similarly be located very near this large interconnecting plane. While I was exploring the causes of this structure, I have found it very probable that the so-called fixed or firm stars could really be slowly moving, wandering stars of a higher order. To endorse what will be found about this concept later in its own section, I wish only to cite here a passage from a text by Mr. Bradley concerning the movement of the fixed stars:[6] "If we wish to judge the result of a comparison between our best contemporary observations and earlier ones with tolerable accuracy, then it seems clear that some fixed stars really have changed position with respect to each other and, indeed, in such a way, that we see this is not the result of some movement in our planetary system, but can be ascribed only to a movement of the stars themselves. Arcturus readily provides strong proof of this point. For when we compare the present declination of Arcturus with its location as determined by Tycho as well as by Flamsteed, we will find that the difference is greater than we can assume to have arisen from the inaccuracy of their observations.[7] We have reason to suppose that other examples of a similar phenomenon must occur among the large number of visible stars, because their positions relative to each other could have altered for various reasons. For if we imagine that our own solar system changes its position in celestial space, then after a certain time has gone by, this will give rise to a perceptible change in the angular distance of the fixed stars. And because in such a case this would have a greater effect on the positions of the nearest stars than on the positions of the ones far distant, then their positions would appear to change, although the stars themselves really remain immovable. And if, by contrast, our own planetary system stands still and some stars do, in fact, move, these will similarly change their apparent position, and the apparent movement will be greater the closer the stars are to us or the more the direction of their motion is arranged so that we can perceive it. Now, since the positions of the stars could thus be altered by so many different causes, when we consider the astonishing distances at which some of them are indubitably located, it will take the observations of several human lifetimes to determine the laws for the perceptible alterations of even a single star. Thus, it must be even more difficult to establish laws for all the most remarkable stars."

I cannot precisely determine the boundaries between Mr. Wright's system and my own, nor in what parts I have merely copied his design or developed it further. However, I had very good reasons to expand one aspect of the design considerably. I took into account the species of nebulous stars, which M. de Maupertuis considers in his treatment of the shape of the stars and which display more or less open elliptical shapes, and I easily convinced myself that they could only be an accumulation of many fixed stars.[8] The fact that these shapes, when measured, were always round taught me that here there must be arranged an unimaginably numerous host of stars and, further, that they are around a common mid-point, because, if that were not the case, their free positioning in relation to each other would display wholly irregular shapes, not measurable figures. I also perceived that in the system in which they are brought together they must be for the most part limited to a single plane, because they are not circular but elliptical in shape, and that because of their pale light they are located incredibly far away from us. What I have concluded from these analogies the discussion will itself present for the unprejudiced reader's evaluation.

In the second part, which contains the proposal most germane to this treatise, I endeavour to develop the arrangement of the cosmic structure from the simplest condition of nature merely by mechanical laws. If, for those who are shocked at the daring of this undertaking, I may venture to propose a certain order in the manner with which they honour my ideas by testing them, I would request that they first read through the eighth section, which, I hope, will prepare their judgment for a correct insight. Meanwhile, when I invite the well-disposed reader to examine my opinions, I am justly concerned that, since hypotheses of this sort commonly are considered no better than philosophical dreams, it is a sour pleasure for a reader to resolve to undertake a careful investigation on his own into the histories of nature and patiently to follow the author through all the turns by which he moves around the difficulties which he runs into, so that at the end the reader perhaps laughs at his own credulity, like those who look at the London Market Crier.[9] However, I dare to promise that, if the reader will, as I hope, be convinced by the preparatory chapter placed at the start to undertake such a physical adventure based on such plausible assumptions, he will not meet, as he continues on his way, as many crooked diversions and impassable obstacles as he is perhaps worried about at the beginning.

In fact, I have rejected with the greatest care all arbitrary fictions. After I place the world in the simplest chaos, I have applied to it no forces other than the powers of attraction and repulsion, so as to develop the great order of nature. These two forces are both equally certain, equally simple, and at the same time equally primal and universal. Both are taken from Newtonian philosophy. The first is now an incontestably established law of nature. The second, which Newtonian science perhaps cannot establish with as much clarity as the first, I here assume only in the sense which no one disputes, that is, in connection with the smallest distributed particles of matter, as, for example, in vapours. From such simple grounds as these, I have produced the system which follows in a natural manner, without imagining any consequences other than those which the reader's attentiveness must observe entirely on its own.

Finally, may I be permitted to provide a short explanation concerning the validity and the alleged value of those propositions which will appear in the following theory and according to which I hope to be assessed by reasonable judges. We evaluate an author fairly by the same stamp which he impresses on his own work. Thus, I hope people will demand from the different parts of this treatise no stronger validity for my opinions that what I myself establish for them in the scale of values. Generally, the greatest geometrical precision and mathematical certainty can never be demanded from a treatise of this sort. If the system is based upon analogies and harmonies in accordance with the rules of credibility and a correct way of thinking, then it has met every demand raised by its object. I believe I have reached this level of quality in some parts of this essay, as in the theory of the system of fixed stars, in the hypothesis about the composition of the nebulous stars, in the general design for the mechanical development of the cosmic structure, in the theory of Saturn's ring, and in some others. In some particular parts the treatment will be somewhat less persuasive, as, for example, the determination of the relationships of the eccentricity, the comparison of the masses of the planets, the various deviations of comets, and some others.

Therefore, when in the seventh section I pursue the consequences of this theory as far as possible, attracted by the fecundity of the system and the pleasing nature of the greatest and most awesome subject imaginable, always guided by analogy and a reasonable credibility, although with a certain boldness, and when I propose to the power of imagination the infinite nature of the entire creation, the development of new worlds and the destruction of old ones, and the unlimited space of chaos, I hope that people will be sufficiently indulgent to the attractive charm of the subject and the pleasure which one has in witnessing the harmony in one's theory pushed to its furthest limit not to judge it according to the strictest geometrical precision, which, in any case, does not occur in a theory of this sort. I await exactly the same fairness with respect to the third part. There people will constantly come across something more than merely arbitrary, although always something less than certain.

PART ONE

OUTLINE OF A SYSTEMATIC ARRANGEMENT OF THE FIXED STARS AND OF THE VAST NUMBER OF SUCH SYSTEMS OF FIXED STARS

Is the great chain, that draws all to agree,

And drawn supports, upheld by God, or thee?

(Pope)[10*]

SHORT OUTLINE OF THE NECESSARY FUNDAMENTAL PRINCIPLES OF NEWTONIAN PHILOSOPHY REQUIRED FOR AN UNDERSTANDING OF THE FOLLOWING THEORY[11*]

Six planets, including three with accompanying satellites, Mercury, Venus, Earth with its moon, Mars, Jupiter with four satellites, and Saturn with five, describe orbits around the sun as the mid-point and, together with the comets, which do the same thing from all sides in very long orbits, make up a system which we call the Solar System or the planetary world structure. The fact that the movement of all these bodies takes the form of a circle and returns back on itself presupposes two forces which are equally necessary for any sort of theory, namely, a projectile force, by which at every point of their curved linear movement the bodies would continue on a straight line and disappear into the infinite distance, unless another force, whatever it may be, constantly required them to leave this path and move on a curved track around the mid-point of the sun. This second force, as geometry itself has established with certainty, always aims at the sun and is therefore called the sinking force, the centripetal force, or gravity.

If the orbits of the celestial bodies were exact circles, then the very simplest breakdown of the compounded curved movements would reveal that a continuous impulse towards the central point would be required for the arrangement. However, although the movements of all planets and comets are ellipses in which the sun is located at a common focal point, higher geometry with the help of Kepler's model (according to which the *radius vector* or the line drawn from the planet to the sun always cuts out on its elliptical path areas proportional to the times) similarly establishes with unequivocal certainty that a force must constantly draw the planet throughout its entire orbital path towards the midpoint of the sun.[12*] This sinking force, which governs throughout the whole space of the planetary system and directs itself to the sun, is thus an accepted natural phenomenon. Equally clearly demonstrated is the law according to which this force extends from the mid-point of the sun into the far distances. It always decreases inversely as the square roots of the distances from the centre increase. This rule is derived in an equally infallible way from the time which the planets need at different distances to complete their orbits. These times are always in a ratio to the square root of the cubes of their average distance from the sun. From this we deduce that the force which pulls these cosmic bodies to the mid-point of their orbits must decrease inversely as the square of the distance.

This very same law which governs among the planets in their movements around the sun occurs also in connection with small systems, namely, with those which are made up of moons moving about their main planet. Their orbital times are in exactly the same way proportional to the distances and establish a relationship of the force which causes sinking towards the planet, which is exactly the same as the one by which the planet is pulled towards the sun. All this, derived from the most infallible geometry and uncontested observations, has been placed forever beyond contradiction. From this arises now the idea that this sinking force may be exactly the same impetus which is called heaviness on the surface of the planet and which gradually diminishes with the distances from the surface according to the above-mentioned law. We see this from the comparison of the quantity of heaviness on the surface of the earth with the force which pulls the moon to the mid-point of its orbit. These stand in relation to each other just as the force of attraction in the entire planetary system, namely, in inverse proportion to the square of the distances. Hence people also call this frequently reported central force gravity.

Moreover, because there is the highest degree of probability that if an effect occurs only in the presence of and in proportion to the distance to a certain body and if the direction of this effect is related as precisely as possible to this body, then it is credible that this body is the cause of the effect, however it occurs. Therefore, we have sufficient reason to think that this universal downward movement of the planets towards the sun can be attributed to the power of attraction of the sun and to ascribe the capacity for the power of attraction in general to all the celestial bodies.

Hence, if a body is left free to the influence of this impulse which drives it to sink toward the sun or some other planet, then it will fall towards it with a constantly accelerating motion and soon will be united with that same mass. However, if it gets a push directing it to the side, then, if that push is not powerful enough to achieve an exact equilibrium with the sinking force, the body will sink down to the central mass with a curved movement. And if, before the sinking body touches the outer surface of the central mass, the impulse impressed on it has grown at least strong enough to shift it from the vertical line about half the thickness of the body at the mid-point, then it will not touch this surface but, after it has swung closely around it, will, thanks to the velocity achieved in its fall, be raised up high again just as far as it fell, so as to continue its path in a constant circular movement.

Thus, the difference between the orbital paths of the comets and the planets consists in the sideways deviation in opposition to the force which drives them to fall. The more these two forces approach an equilibrium, the more the orbit will become circular in shape; the more unequal they are, the weaker the projectile force in relation to the force pulling to the centre, then the longer the orbit, or, as we say, the more eccentric the orbit is, because the celestial body in one part of its path comes far closer to the sun than in another.

Because nothing in all nature is exactly balanced, no planet has an entirely circular motion. However, the comets deviate the most from a circular orbit, because at their first distance from the sun the impetus which was impressed on them towards the side was the least proportional to the force pulling them to the centre.

In this treatise I will very often use the expression a systematic arrangement of the cosmic structure. So that people will have no difficulty clearly imagining what this term is to mean, I will explain it briefly. Strictly speaking, all the planets and comets which belong to our cosmic structure already form a system by the fact that they rotate around a common central body. However, I take this term in an even narrower sense, because I consider the more precise relationships which have united them with each other in a regular and uniform way. The orbits of the planets are, in relation to each other, as nearly as possible on a common plane, namely, on the extended equatorial plane of the sun. The deviations from this rule occur only in connection with the outermost borders of the system, where all movements gradually cease. When therefore a certain number of cosmic bodies, ordered around a common mid-point and moving around it are at the same time restricted to a certain plane, so that they have minimal freedom to deviate on both sides of this plane, and when the deviation occurs gradually only with those which are furthest distant from the mid-point and participate less in the interconnections than the others, then I say that these bodies are bound together in a systematic arrangement.

ON THE SYSTEMATIC ARRANGEMENT OF THE FIXED STARS

The theory of the general arrangement of the cosmic structure has not achieved any remarkable progress since the time of Huygens.[13*] At this point we still know no more than we already knew then, namely, that six planets with ten companions, all of which have the circle of their orbit set almost on a single plane, and the eternal spheres of the comets, which run riot on all sides, make up a single system, whose mid-point is the sun, towards which everything sinks, around which their movements run, and from which they all are illuminated, warmed, and kept alive, and finally that the fixed stars are just so many suns, the mid-points of similar systems, in which everything may be set up in just as large and orderly a way as in our system and that infinite space teems with cosmic systems, whose number and excellence have a relationship to the infinite nature of their Creator.

The systematic arrangement which took place in the union of the planets which move around the sun disappeared in the crowd of fixed stars, and it seemed as if the rule-governed relationship encountered in miniature does not hold sway on a large scale among the links of all the worlds. The fixed stars were subject to no law, by which their positions were confined relative to each other, and we saw all heaven and the heaven of all heavens filled without order and without design. Since human curiosity limited itself in this way, we did nothing further, other than to infer from this state the immensity of the One who had revealed Himself in such inconceivably huge works and to admire Him.

It was reserved for Mr. Wright, an Englishman from Durham, to take a happy step to an observation which he himself does not seem to have developed into anything insightful and whose useful application he did not sufficiently note. He looked at the fixed stars not as a disorganized and scattered swarm without purpose but found a systematic arrangement in their totality and a general relationship of these stars with respect to a major plane of the space which they occupy.

We wish to improve the idea which he presented and to redirect it, so that it can generate important consequences. The complete confirmation of these is something we leave for future ages.

Anyone who gazes at the starry heavens on a clear night will notice that bright band which presents a steady light through the crowd of stars which have accumulated there more than elsewhere and which perceptibly lose themselves in the huge expanse. People have called this band the Milky Way. Because of the structure of this recognizably distinct area in the sky, it is remarkable that observers of the heavens were not long ago prompted to derive from it strange conclusions about the locations of the fixed stars. For we see that the band has an immense circular orientation and, indeed, in a continuous arrangement taking up the entire heavens. These two factors possess such a precise determination and characteristics so recognizably different from uncertain approximations that from them keen astronomers should long ago naturally have been motivated attentively to investigate the explanation for such a phenomenon.

The stars are not placed on the apparently hollow sphere of the heavens, but from our point of view stand at some distance from each other, some further than others, disappearing into the depths of the heavens. From this phenomenon it follows that, at those distances where they are located one behind the other in relation to us, they do not occur in an equal scattering in every direction, but must be arranged in particular relation to a certain plane which goes through our viewpoint and to which their locations are fixed as closely as possible.

This relationship is such an unambiguous phenomenon that even the remaining stars, which are not included in the white band of the Milky Way, are themselves observed to be that much closer together and more dense, the nearer they are located to the circle of the Milky Way, so that of the 2000 stars which the naked eye perceives in the sky, we find the largest number in a relatively narrow area, the middle of which is taken up by the Milky Way.

Now, if we imagine a plane drawn through the starry heavens and extending an unlimited distance and assume that all the fixed stars and all the solar systems have a common spatial relationship to this plane, so that they are closer to it than to any other areas, then the eye which is located on this common plane, as it looks out into this field of stars, into the hollow spherical surface of the firmament, will see the thickest accumulation of stars in the direction of the drawn plane, in the form of an area illuminated with more lights. This band of light will sweep out in the direction of a huge circle, because the onlooker's viewpoint is on the plane itself. This area will be swarming with stars. Because of the undifferentiated smallness of bright points, a single one of which escapes the eye, and because of the apparent density of a uniform white gleam, it will look, in a word, like a Milky Way. The rest of the heavenly host, whose relationship with the drawn plane becomes less and less apparent or which are also located closer to the observer's position, will be seen as more scattered, although their accumulation will be related to this same plane. From this, finally, it follows that, because from our solar system we see this arrangement of fixed stars in the orientation of a very large circle, our solar system is located in precisely the same large plane and makes one system with the others.

In order that much better to penetrate the composition of the common interrelationship governing this cosmic structure, we wish to try to discover the cause which has arranged the locations of the fixed stars, relating them to a single common plane.

The Sun does not limit the extent of its powers of attraction to the narrow region of the planetary system. According to all appearance, this power extends an infinite distance. The comets which go very far above Saturn's orbit are forced by the sun's powers of attraction to turn back again and to move in orbits. Whether it is more likely for the nature of a force apparently incorporated into the essence of matter to act without limits and whether, in addition, it will be really recognized as such by those who assume Newton's principles, we wish only to have it conceded that this power of attraction of the sun extends approximately to the nearest fixed star and that the fixed stars act on each other as just so many suns to the same extent. Thus, it follows that the entire host of fixed stars strives to come closer together through this power of attraction, so that all the world systems are in a situation where sooner or later they fall into one clump, through this reciprocal moving closer together, which is continuous and unhindered, unless these systems are saved from this disaster by forces which pull away from the central point, as with the spheres in our planetary system. These forces bend the heavenly bodies away from falling in a straight line and, working together with the forces of attraction, bring about the timeless orbits. Thus the structure of creation is preserved from collapse and has been skilfully created to last eternally.

Hence, all the suns in the firmament have orbiting motions, either around one common central point or around many. But with them, we can everywhere apply the analogy of what we observe about the orbital paths of our solar system, namely, that just as that very cause which has imparted to the planets a force moving them away from the centre, through which they maintain their orbits, has directed their orbital paths so that they are all related to a single plane, so also the cause, whatever it might be, which has given the suns of the higher world as well as so many wandering stars of the higher world structure the force of their orbit has at the same time brought their orbits as much as possible into one plane and has worked to limit deviation from this plane.

According to this conception, we can picture the system of fixed stars to a certain extent by means of the planetary system, if we magnify the latter infinitely. For if instead of six planets with their ten satellites we assume many thousands of similar bodies, and instead of the twenty-eight or thirty comets which we have observed, we assume a hundred or a thousand times more of them, and if we think of these particular bodies as generating their own light, then to the eye of the observer who looks out at them from the Earth there would appear exactly the same light as appears from the fixed stars of the Milky Way. For the planets we have imagined, because of their close relationship to the same common plane in which we find ourselves with our Earth, would display a densely lit area made up of countless stars, whose direction went in a very large circle. This band of light would have a sufficient number of stars everywhere, although, according to this hypothesis, as moving stars, they are not fixed to a single spot. For, because of their movement, there would always be enough stars on anyone side, even though other stars had moved from that location.

The width of this illuminated zone, which projects a sort of zodiac, will be set by the different levels of deviation of designated erratic stars from their reference plane and by the inclination of their orbits in relation to this same plane. Since most of them are near this plane, their number will appear more scattered in relation to the extent they are distant from it. However, the comets, which occupy all regions without distinction, will cover the field of the heavens on both sides.

The shape of the heaven of fixed stars thus has no cause other than the same systematic arrangement on a grand scale as the cosmic structure of the planetary system on a small scale, since all the suns make up one system, whose common interconnecting plane is the Milky Way. Those which are the least related to this plane will be seen to the side; for that very reason, however, they are less dense, more widely scattered, and less frequent. They are, so to speak, comets among the suns.

This new theory, however, attributes a forward motion to the suns, and yet everyone acknowledges that they are motionless and that they have been fixed in their positions from the start. The name which the fixed stars have acquired from this seems confirmed and unambiguous because of all the centuries of observation. This difficulty, if soundly based, would destroy the proposed theory. But this lack of movement, according to all appearances, is only something apparent. It is either merely an exceeding slowness, caused by the enormous distance of their orbits from the common mid-point or the impossibility of perceiving them brought about by the distant location of the observer. Let us estimate the plausibility of this notion by calculating the movement which one of the fixed stars located close to our sun would have, assuming that our sun is the mid-point of its orbit. If, following Huygens, we assume that the distance of this star is more than 21000 times greater than the distance of the sun from the Earth, it then follows from the established law of the time of orbiting bodies, which is proportional to the square root of the cube of the distances from the mid-point, that the time which this star must take to complete its circle once around the sun would be more than one and a half million years and that in 4000 years this would have established a shift in its position of only about one degree. Now, because perhaps only a very few fixed stars are as close to the sun as Huygens assumed for Sirius, and because the distance of the rest of the heavenly host perhaps exceeds by far the distance of Sirius, therefore they would require a far longer time for such periodic orbits. Moreover, it is also more probable that the motion of the suns in the celestial stars goes around a common mid-point whose distance away is extraordinarily far, and the forward motion of the stars can hence be exceedingly slow. Consequently, we can probably assume from this that all the time since human beings have been keeping records of celestial observations has perhaps still not been sufficient for them to notice the change which has taken place in these stellar positions. We must meanwhile not yet give up hope that we will discover this change in time. To achieve that will require subtle and careful observers, together with a comparison of observations far distant from each other. We must direct these observations especially at the stars of the Milky Way, the main plane of all movement.[14] Mr. Bradley has observed the almost imperceptible movement of the stars. The ancients marked stars in particular places in the sky, and we see new ones in other places. Who knows that these are not the latter which have merely changed position? The excellence of the instruments and the perfecting of our knowledge of the stars give us ground to hope for the discovery of such remarkable and important observations.[15] The plausibility of the matter itself, based on nature and analogy, supports this hope so well, that it can stimulate the attentive work of scientists to bring it to completion.

The Milky Way is, so to speak, also the zodiac of new stars, alternately appearing and disappearing in this region in a way hardly matched in any other celestial region. If this alteration in their visibility proceeds from their periodic moving further away and closer to us, it seems clear from the proposed systematic arrangement of the stars that such a phenomenon must mainly be seen only in the region of the Milky Way. For there are stars in that location moving in very elongated orbits around other fixed stars, as satellites move around their main planets. Thus, the analogy with our planetary system, in which only heavenly bodies near the common plane of movement have a companion moving around them, requires that only the stars in the Milky Way will have suns orbiting around them.

I am coming to that part of the proposed theory which makes it most particularly attractive because of the sublime picture it presents of creation's plan. The series of ideas which has led me to it is short and natural. It consists of the following. If a system of fixed stars, all spatially related to a common plane, just as we have sketched out the Milky Way, is so far distant from us that all perception of individual stars making up the system is no longer possible, even with a telescope, if the distance of this system has exactly the same relationship to the distance of the stars in the Milky Way as the latter have to the distance of the sun from us, in short, if such a world of fixed stars is seen at such an immeasurable distance from the eye of the observer located outside this world, then this world will appear in a small angle as a tiny and weakly lit area, with a circular shape if its plane is oriented directly in the line of sight and elliptical if it is viewed from the side. The weakness of the light, the shape, and the recognizable extent of its diameter will clearly distinguish such a phenomenon, when present, from all the stars which are seen individually.

We do not need to search a long time for this phenomenon among the observations of the astronomers. It has been clearly confirmed by different observers. People have wondered about its strangeness, have made assumptions, and have subscribed sometimes to odd imaginary images and sometimes to plausible ideas, which, however, just like the former, had no basis. We are talking about the nebulous stars or, rather, a type of them, which M. de Maupertuis wrote about as follows:[16] "There are small places whose light is somewhat more than the darkness of empty celestial space, which all are alike in the fact that they display more or less open ellipses, but their light is much weaker than any other that we are aware of in the heavens." The author of the *Astrotheology* imagined that these were openings in the firmament through which he believed he saw heavenly fire.[17] A philosopher of illuminating insights, the above-mentioned M. de Maupertuis, in thinking about the shape and the recognizable diameter of these stars, considers that they are astonishingly large celestial bodies which display an elliptical shape because of the large flattening caused by the impetus of their rotation, when viewed from the side.

It is easy to be convinced that this last explanation also cannot hold. Because this kind of nebulous stars must undoubtedly be at least as far away from us as the other fixed stars, not only would their size be astonishing (for in this respect they would have to exceed by a factor of many thousands even the largest stars), but the strangest point of all would be that with this extraordinary size, made up of self-illuminating bodies and suns, these stars should display the dimmest and weakest light.

Much more natural and comprehensible is the idea that there are no such individual huge stars but systems of many stars, whose distance makes them appear in such a narrow space, that the light, which cannot be seen for each individual star, because of the countless crowd of them, comes out in a uniform pale glow. The analogy with the system of stars in which we find ourselves, their shape, which is exactly as it must be according to our theory, the weakness of the light, which this previously mentioned infinite distance requires, all these endorse perfectly the idea that these elliptical figures should be taken as exactly the same world systems and, so to speak, as Milky Ways, whose structure we have just gone through. And if suppositions in which analogy and observation are in full agreement and support each other have precisely the same value as formal proofs, then we must take the certainty of this system as demonstrated.

Now the attentiveness of those who observe the heavens has sufficient motivation to concern itself with this undertaking. The fixed stars, as we know, are all connected to a common plane and thus create a coordinated totality, a world of worlds. We see that in the immeasurable distances there are more such star systems and that creation in the entirely of its infinite extent is everywhere systematic and mutually interconnected.

We could further suppose that these particular higher world orders are not unconnected to each other and through this mutual relationship establish once again an even more immeasurably great system. In fact, we see that the elliptical shapes of these sorts of nebulous stars, which M. de Maupertuis mentions, have a very close relationship to the plane of the Milky Way. Here a wide field stands open to discoveries, for which observation must provide the key. The properly named nebulous stars and those about which there is a dispute whether we should call them nebulous must be investigated and tested according to the guidelines of this theory. If we view the parts of nature according to a design and a plan we have discovered, then certain characteristics reveal themselves which are otherwise overlooked and remain hidden, when observation squanders its time on all objects without any guidance.

The theory which we have proposed opens up for us a view of the infinite field of creation and offers an idea of the work of God appropriate to the infinite nature of the Great Master Builder. If the size of a planetary system in which the Earth is hardly seen as a grain of sand fills the understanding with astonishment, how delightfully astounded we will be when we examine the infinite crowd of worlds and systems which fill the totality of the Milky Way. But how much greater this wonder when we know that all these immeasurable arrangements of stars once again create a numbered unity, whose end we do not know and which is perhaps, like the previous one, inconceivably large and yet, once again, only a unit in a new numbered system. We see the first links of a progressive relationship of worlds and systems, and the first part of this unending progression already allows us to recognize what we are to assume about the totality. Here there is no end, but an abyss of a true infinity, in which all capacity of human thought sinks, even when it is uplifted with the help of mathematics. The wisdom, goodness, and power which has revealed itself is limitless and, to exactly the same extent, fruitful and busy. The plan of its revelation must, therefore, be, just like it, infinite and without borders.

However, there are important discoveries to be made, and not just in large things, which serve to expand the idea we can formulate about the magnitude of creation. In smaller things there is no less undiscovered, and we see even in our solar system the links of a system which stand immeasurably far from one another and between which we have not yet found the intermediate parts. Saturn is the outermost of the wandering stars which we know about. Are there to be no more planets between Saturn and the least eccentric comet which comes down to us from a distance perhaps ten or more times removed, no planet whose orbit could approach more closely a comet's orbit than Saturn does? And should not other planets be gradually changing into comets by means of a series of intermediate types approximating the composition of comets and linking together the family of planets with the family of comets?

The law according to which the eccentricity of the planetary orbits is directly related to their distance from the sun supports this assumption.[18*] The eccentricity in the movements of the planets increases with the distance of the planet from the sun, and the furthest planets, therefore, come closer to the condition of comets. We can thus assume that there are still other planets beyond Saturn which are even more eccentric and hence even more closely akin to comets, thanks to a continual gradation which finally turns planets into comets. The eccentricity of Venus is 1/126th of the semi-axis of its elliptical orbit; in the case of Earth, the eccentricity is 1/58th; in the case of Jupiter, it is 1/20th, and in the case of Saturn 1/17th. Thus, the eccentricity evidently increases with the distances. It is true that Mercury and Mars are exceptions to this law, because their eccentricity is much greater than the measurement of their distance from the sun permits. But we will learn in what follows that the very same cause which gave some planets in their development a small mass also deprived them of the impulse required for a circular path, with the result that they were pulled into an eccentric movement, thus leaving them incomplete in two respects.

Is it not a probable consequence that the increase in the eccentricity of the cosmic bodies located immediately beyond Saturn will be approximately proportional to the ones beneath, and that the planets are related to the family of comets through a less abrupt gap?[19*] For it is certain that this very eccentricity is the fundamental difference between the comets and the planets. The comet's tail and its misty spheres are only consequences of eccentricity. Similarly, the particular cause, whatever it may be, which has given the celestial bodies their orbital paths, because of the greater distances not only was weaker in making the circular impulse equal to the downward force, thereby allowing eccentric movements, but also for this very reason was less capable of bringing the orbits of these spheres into the common plane on which the lower bodies move. Thus was produced the deviation of the comets to all regions.

According to this hypothesis, we would still perhaps hope for the discovery of new planets beyond Saturn, which would be more eccentric than Saturn and thus closer to the characteristic of comets. But for this very reason we would be able to see them only for a short time, that is, when they approach the sun. This factor, together with the smaller extent of their approach and the weakness of their light, has hindered their discovery up to now and must make that difficult in future. If we wanted, we could call the last planet and the first comet the one whose eccentricity was so large that in its approach to the sun it intersected the orbit of the nearest planet to it, and perhaps Saturn's, as well.

PART TWO. SECTION ONE

Concerning the first condition of Nature, the development of the celestial bodies, the causes of their movement and their systematic interrelationship both with the structure of planets in particular and also with the entire creation.

See plastic Nature working to this end,

The single atoms each to other tend,

Attract, attracted to, the next in place

Form'd and impell'd, its neighbour to embrace.

See Matter next, with various life endu'd

Press to one centre still, the gen'ral Good.

(Pope)[20]

Concerning the Origin of the Planetary World Structure in General and the Causes of Its Movements

So far as concerns the reciprocal relationships which the parts of the cosmic structure have among themselves and through which they reveal the cause which brought them about, observation of this arrangement displays two aspects, both of which are equally probable and worthy of consideration. On the one hand, if we think of the fact that six planets with ten companions describe orbits around the sun at their mid-point, that all move in one direction, in fact, the same direction as the axial rotational of the sun itself, which governs all their orbits though the power of attraction, that their orbits do not deviate far from a common plane, namely, the extrapolated equatorial plane of the sun, that among the furthest celestial bodies belonging to the solar system, in the region where the common cause of movement was, according to the hypothesis, not so strong as in the region close to the mid-point, deviations from the precision of these conditions occur, which are sufficiently related to the lack of impressed motion, if, I say, we consider all this interconnection, then we will come to believe that one cause, whatever it may be, had a pervasive influence throughout the entire extent of the system and that the conformity in the direction and position of the planetary orbits is a consequence of the coordinated agreement which they must have had with that material cause through which they were set in motion.

On the other hand, if we consider the space in which the planets of our system orbit, then we find it is completely empty and deprived of all material stuff which could have subjected these celestial bodies to a common set of influences and brought with it coordination among their movements.[21] This fact has been established with more perfect certainty and its probability is, where possible, greater than the probability of the previous claim. Swayed by this reason, Newton could not point to any material cause which should maintain by its extension into the space of the planetary system the commonality of movements. He maintained that the immediate hand of God had set up this order without the use of natural forces.

Considering the matter impartially, we see that the reasons here on both sides are equally strong. And they have an equal value as completely certain. However, it is also just as clear that there must be a concept which could and should unite these two apparently conflicting reasons and that in this concept we are to seek the true system. We wish briefly to announce that concept. In the present arrangement of space, in which the spheres of all the planetary worlds move around, there is no material cause present which could impress itself on or direct their movements. This space is completely empty, or at least as good as empty. Thus, it must have in earlier times been differently constituted and full of matter sufficiently capable of conferring movement on all the celestial bodies located there and of bringing them into harmony with its motion and, as a consequence, into harmony with each other. When the power of attraction unified the above-mentioned space and collected all the scattered matter in particular clusters, the planets must have from then on freely and unchangingly continued the orbital movement, once impressed upon them, in an unresisting space. The reasons for the first-mentioned probability absolutely require this notion. And since there is no third possibility between the two, we look upon this idea with approval as an excellent one, an approval which raises it above the plausibility of a hypothesis. If we wished to be long winded, we could, with a series of successive inferences in the manner of a mathematical demonstration, with all the display which this involves and with an even greater plausibility than its introduction in physical subjects customarily elicits, finally arrive at the proposal itself, which I will set down, concerning the origin of the cosmic structure. But I would rather present my opinions in the form of a hypothesis and leave it to the reader's insight to put its value to the test, than render its validity suspect because of the appearance of a devious demonstration, something which might thus captivate the ignorant but lose the approval of those who understand.

I assume that all the matter making up the spheres belonging to our solar system, all the planets and comets, at the origin of all things was broken down into its elementary basic material and filled the entire space of the cosmic structure in which these developed bodies now move around. If we consider this state of nature in and of itself, without reference to a system, it seems to be merely the simplest which can follow upon nothingness. At that time nothing had yet developed. The incorporation of heavenly bodies located separate from one another, their distance from each other controlled according to the powers of attraction, and their shape, arising from the equilibrium of the collected materials, are a later condition. Nature, on the immediate edge of creation, was as raw and undeveloped as possible. Only in the fundamental properties of the elements which make up the chaos can we perceive the sign of that perfection which nature has from its origin, since its being is a consequence arising from the eternal idea of the Divine Understanding. The simplest, most universal characteristics, apparently designed without purpose, the material, which seems merely passive and in need of forms and structures, has in its simplest condition a tendency to build itself up by a natural development to a more perfect arrangement. The difference in the types of elements by itself was the most important factor contributing to the movement of nature and to the development of chaos, so that the tranquillity which would have ruled in a state of universal equality among the scattered elements would be lifted, and the chaos begin to develop itself at points where the particles have a stronger power of attraction. The types of this basic material are undoubtedly infinitely different, to match the immensity which nature displays in every respect. Given the equal distribution in planetary space, the materials with the greatest specific density and power of attraction, which in and of themselves take up less room and are also rarer, therefore become more scattered than the lighter varieties of material. Elements with a specific heaviness one thousand times greater are a thousand, perhaps a million, times more scattered than those which are lighter in this proportion. And since these differences must be imagined as infinite as possible, then, just as there can be one sort of physical component which exceeds another in its measured density, as a sphere drawn with the radius of the planetary system exceeds another sphere with the diameter of the thousandth part of a line, so the heavier type of scattered elements are separated from each other by a much greater distance than the lighter kinds.

The universal tranquillity in space replete in this way lasts only for an instant. The elements have essential forces which set each other in motion and are, indeed, themselves an origin of life. The material is under an immediate impulse to develop. The denser type of scattered materials, thanks to the power of attraction, collect from a spherical area around them all the material with a lesser specific weight. But they themselves, together with the material which they have united with them, converge in the points where the small pieces of an even denser type are located, and these again to even denser points, and so on. When we think about this idea of a self-developing nature throughout the entire extent of chaos, we will easily see that all the consequences of this process will finally consist of the assembling of different clusters, which, after the completion of their development, would be calm and eternally motionless because of the equality in the force of attraction.

But nature has still other forces in store, which manifest themselves especially when the material is dispersed in fine particles, so that these particles repel each other and by their conflict with the power of attraction induce that movement, which is, as it were, an enduring life of nature. Because of this force of repulsion, which reveals itself in the elastic nature of fumes, in the diffusion from strong-smelling bodies, and the spreading of all gaseous materials and which is an uncontested phenomenon of nature, the elements sinking towards their points of attraction will shift each other sideways from their vertical movement, and the straight linear descent will end up in orbital movements which surround the mid-point towards which they were sinking at the centre. In order clearly to grasp the development of the cosmic structure, we want to limit our observation of the infinite essence of nature to a particular system, like the one to which our sun belongs. Once we have explored the development of this system, then we will be able to proceed in a similar way to the origin of the higher world structures and bring together into one theory the infinite nature of the entire creation.

Thus, if a point is found in a very large space where the power of attraction of the elements located there exerts a stronger influence than at any other points around it, then the basic material stuff of elementary particles spread out in all the surrounding area will sink toward this point. The first effect of this general sinking is the development of a body at this mid-point of the attraction which, so to speak, proceeds to grow from an infinitely small seed in rapid stages. But as this mass increases, it will, in exactly the same proportion, with its more powerful force move the surrounding particles to unite with it. When the mass of this central body has grown so extensive that the velocity with which it draws the small particles to itself from great distances is diverted sideways by the weak level of the force of repulsion with which these particles interfere with one another, it produces lateral movements, which, thanks to the centrifugal force *[Centerfliehkraft]*, are such that they can move in a circle around the central body. Thus, large vortexes of small particles develop, each of which, because of the combination of the force of attraction and the force leading to a sideways rotation describes its own curving path. These sorts of circles all intersect each other, something which their large scattering in this space leaves room for. Meanwhile, these movements, in various ways in conflict with each other, strive naturally to bring one another into equilibrium, that is, into a single state where the movement of one hinders the movement of another as little as possible. This occurs, first, because the particles restrict the movement of other particles for as long as it takes until they all are moving forward in one direction; and second, because the particles restrict their vertical movement, thanks to which they approach the centre of the attraction, until the time when they are all moving horizontally, that is, in circles running parallel around the sun at their mid-point, no longer intersecting with one another, and, thanks to the equilibrium between the centrifugal force *[Schwungskraft]* and the force drawing them downwards, maintaining constant free circular orbits at the heights where they are suspended, so that finally only those particles remain suspended in the volume of space which have attained through their fall a velocity and through the resistance of other particles a direction by means of which they can continue a free circular movement. In this condition, where all the particles run around the central body in one direction and in circles arranged in parallel, namely, in free circular movements by means of the required centrifugal force, the conflict and the collision of the elements disappear, and everything is in the condition of the smallest reciprocal interaction. This result always occurs naturally with materials subject to conflicting movements. It is thus clear that from the scattered mass of particles a large number must, on account of the resistance through which they seek to bring each other to this state, succeed in attaining such an exact arrangement, although a much greater number do not reach this condition and serve only to increase the cluster of the central body, into which they sink, since they cannot hold their position freely at the height where they are suspended, but intersect the circles of the lower particles and eventually, because of the resistance, lose all their movement. This body at the middle point of the force of attraction, which, on account of of the large amount of its assembled material, has accordingly become the main piece of the planetary structure, is the sun, although at this time it does not yet immediately have that flaming glow, which breaks out on its surface when its development is fully complete.

We must still note that while all the elements of self-developing nature, as demonstrated, thus move in one direction around the sun as the mid-point, in the case of such orbits which are set up in a single direction and which occur, so to speak, around a common axis, the rotation of fine material cannot remain in this way, because, according to the laws of central motion, all orbital movements must intersect the mid-point of the force of attraction with the plane of their rotation. Among all these orbits moving in one direction around a common axis, however, there is only one which intersects the mid-point of the sun. Therefore, all the material from both sides of this imagined axis moves quickly to that circle which goes directly through the axis of rotation right at the central point of the common downward movement. This circle is the plane which establishes a relationship for all the elements hovering around; as much as possible they accumulate around it and, by contrast, leave the regions far away from this plane empty. For those elements which cannot approach so closely to this plane towards which everything is drawn will not be able to maintain themselves indefinitely in those places where they are suspended, but, as they collide with the elements floating around, will bring about their own final fall toward the sun.

Thus, if we consider this fundamental material of the planets hovering around in a state where it develops itself through the power of attraction and the mechanical consequence of the general law of repulsion, then we see a region which is contained between two planes standing not far from each other. In the middle of these two is located the common interconnecting plane, extending from the mid-point of the sun out to an unknown distance. All the particles we can think of carry out mathematically precise circular movements in free orbits on this common plane, each proportional to the extent of its distance and to the force of attraction which governs there. Because in such an arrangement they interfere with each other as little as possible, they would remain in this form for ever, if the force of attraction of these particles of basic matter did not then start to exercise its effect and in this way to cause new developments, the seeds of planets which are to arise. For since the elements moving around the sun in parallel circles and positioned where the distance from the sun is not very different, because of the equality in the parallel movements, are almost calm relative to each other, then the force of attraction of elements located there with an excessive specific attraction initiates at once a significant effect, collecting the nearest particles to start the development of a body. In proportion to the growth of its cluster, the power of attraction of this body expands, and elements from a wide area move to combine with it.[22*]

In this system, the development of the planets has this advantage over any other theoretical possibility: the cause of the masses provides simultaneously the cause of the motions and the position of the orbits. Indeed, even the deviations from the greatest precision in this arrangement, as well as the harmonies themselves, arc illuminated in an instant. The planets are developed out of particles, which, at the heights where they are suspended, have precise movements in circular orbits. Thus, the masses formed by their combination will continue exactly the same movements at precisely the same level and in exactly the same direction. This is sufficient to understand why the movement of the planets is approximately circular and why their orbits are on a single plane. Moreover, they would be exactly circular if the distance from which they gather the elements for their development were very small and thus if the difference in their movements were very insignificant.[23*] But because the development of a thick planetary cluster involves a wider surrounding area, throughout which the fine basic stuff is scattered so much in celestial space, the difference in the distances of these elements from the sun and thus also the difference in their velocities are no longer insignificant. As a result, given this difference in the movements, it would be necessary, in order to maintain on the planet an equilibrium between the central forces and the circular velocity, for the particles which collide with the planet from different distances and with different motions to offset each other's aberrations exactly. Although this, in fact, occurs fairly accurately, nonetheless, this compensation falls somewhat short of perfection and brings the deviations from circular movement and eccentricity with it.[24*] It is just as easy to shed light on the fact that although the orbits of all planets should properly be in one plane, nevertheless in this part we also come across a small deviation, because, as already discussed, the elementary particles which find themselves as close as possible to the general plane of their movements nevertheless take up some space on either side of it. It would be only too fortunate a coincidence if all the planets were to begin to develop exactly in the middle between these two sides on the plane connecting them, something which would already cause some inclination of their orbits towards each other, although the impulse of the particles from both sides would restrict this deviation as much as possible, allowing it only within narrow limits. Thus, we must not be surprised about the fact that here, too, we rarely come across the most precise accuracy in the arrangements, as is the case with all things in nature, because generally the multiplicity of circumstances involved in every natural condition does not permit an exact regularity.

PART TWO. SECTION TWO

Concerning the Different Densities of the Planets and the Relationship of Their Masses

We have shown that the particles of the elementary basic material, distributed equally by themselves in cosmic space, through their sinking downward towards the sun remain suspended in the places where the velocity which they attained in their descent reaches a precise equilibrium in relation to the force of attraction and that their direction would be altered so as to be perpendicular to the radius of the circle, as should be the case with circular movements. However, if we now think of the particles of different specific density at the same distance from the sun, then the ones with a greater specific heaviness drive more deeply through the resistance of the other particles toward the sun and will not be diverted from their path as soon as the lighter ones. Thus, their movement will form a circular orbit only at a closer distance to the sun. On the other hand, the elements of the lighter type are diverted from a straight vertical fall earlier and take on circular movements before they are driven so deep toward the centre. Thus, they remain suspended at greater distances away. Moreover, they are not able to drive so deeply downward through the space filled with the elements, without the resistance of these elements decreasing their motion, and they will not be able to attain the high level of velocity required for a circular movement closer to the mid-point. Hence, according to the required equilibrium in the movements, the specifically lighter particles will orbit at distances further from the sun; the heavier ones occur, however, at closer distances. The planets which are built out of these elements will therefore be of a denser variety when they are nearer the sun than when they are formed from the combination of these atoms further away from the sun.

Thus, there is a sort of statistical law which establishes for the material of cosmic space an inverse relationship between its distance from the centre and its density. Nonetheless, it is just easy to grasp that it is not essential that each distance contain only particles of the same specific density. Of the particles of a certain specific type, some remain hovering at greater distances from the sun and attain the permanent circular motion appropriate to their fall at a greater distance. These have moved down toward the sun from further away. On the other hand, those whose original location in the universal distribution of the materials in chaos was nearer the sun, regardless of the fact that their density is no greater than the former group, will attain a circular orbit closer to the sun. Since the locations of the materials in relation to the mid-point of their descent is determined not only by the specific heaviness of the material but also by its original place in the first calm state of nature, it is therefore easy to see that very different types of material will combine at every distance from the sun, so as to remain suspended there and that, nevertheless, generally we will find the denser material more frequently closer to the mid-point than further away and thus that, notwithstanding the fact that the planets will be a mixture of very different materials, nonetheless, in general, their masses must be denser in proportion to their closeness to the sun and less dense when their distances away are greater.

In the matter of this law governing planetary densities, our system manifests an advantageous comprehensiveness in comparison with all those ideas which people have come up with or even could come up with about its cause. Newton, who established the density of some planets by calculation, thought that the cause of this relationship set according to the distance was to be found in the appropriateness of God's choice and in the fundamental motives of His final purpose, since the planets closer to the sun must endure more solar heat and those further away are to manage with a lower level of heat, something which would not seem to be possible, unless the planets near the sun were composed of a denser kind of material and those further away of a lighter material. But to perceive the inadequacy of such an explanation does not really require much reflection. A planet, for example, our Earth, is composed of types of material very different from each other. Of these, it was necessary only that the lighter varieties, which will be more deeply penetrated and affected by the same solar working and whose composition has a relationship to the heat through which the sun's rays work, be spread out on the planet's outer surface. But the fact that the mixture of the remaining material in the total cluster must have this relationship sheds light on nothing at all, because the sun has no effect on the inside of the planets. Newton was afraid that if the Earth had been in a lower position in the proximity of Mercury, then in the sun's rays it would have to burn up like a comet, and the Earth's materials would have insufficient protection against fire not to become scattered by this heat. But, by contrast, it is the sun's own material stuff, which is four times lighter than the material making up the Earth, which would have to be destroyed by this blazing heat. Or why is the Moon twice as dense as the Earth, yet still suspended at the very same distance away from the sun as the Earth? Thus, we cannot attribute the proportional densities to the relationship with the sun's heat, without entangling ourselves in the greatest contradictions. Instead we recognize that a cause which allocates the locations of the planets according to the density of their clusters must have had a relationship to the inner material and not to the material on the surface. This cause would have to determine this relationship with the density only according to the total composition, still permitting a differentiation in the materials in one and the same celestial body, without regard to the consequences which it established. Whether some statistical law other than the one which is presented in our theory can achieve this satisfactorily I leave to the insight of the reader to judge.

The relationship of the planetary densities brings with it one more circumstance which corroborates the validity of our theory by completely endorsing the previously proposed explanation. The celestial body standing at the mid-point of other spheres orbiting around it is commonly of a lighter sort than the bodies orbiting most closely around it. The Earth with respect to the Moon and the Sun with respect to the Earth manifest such a relationship vis-à-vis their densities. According to the proposal which we have laid out, such a relationship is necessary. For the lower planets were built up mainly from the excess elementary material which, thanks to the advantage of its density, could have driven with the required degree of velocity right to an area close by the mid-point. By contrast, the body at the very mid-point was put together out of the material of all varieties present, without distinction, which did not attain the velocity required by the law. Since among these, the lighter materials make up the greatest portion, it is easy to see that, because the celestial body orbiting closest to the mid-point or the ones nearest to it has within it, as it were, a selection of the denser forms of material, but the central body has a mixture of all types, without differentiation, then the former will be a substance of a denser sort than the latter. In fact, the moon has twice the density of the Earth, and the Earth is four times denser than the sun, which, according to all assumptions, will be exceeded by the planets even closer to the sun, Venus and Mercury, with an even higher degree of density.

We now turn our attention to the relationship which, according to our theory, the masses of the celestial bodies should have in comparison to their distances from the sun, in order to test the results of our system against Newton's infallible calculations. It does not require many words to make people understand that the central body must always be the major part of its system and that, consequently, the sun must be preponderantly greater than the planets collectively, just as the same point will hold for Jupiter and Saturn in relation to their nearby planets. The central body is developed from the downward sinking from the entire extent of the sphere of its power of attraction of all particles incapable of attaining the most precisely established circular movement and a close relationship to the common plane. The number of these must undoubtedly be extraordinarily greater than the number of those which attain orbital movement. To apply this observation in particular to the sun: if we wish to estimate the spatial extent in which particles with a circular orbit which have served as basic material for the planets have deviated furthest from the common plane, then we can assume that it is, as an approximation, somewhat larger than the width of the greatest deviation of the planetary orbits from each other. Now, while they deviate from the common plane on both sides, their greatest angular difference with respect to each other is hardly 7.5 degrees. Thus, we can picture all the material out of which the planets were developed as having been distributed in that space which we imagine between two planes extending out from the mid-point of the sun and enclosing an angle of 7.5 degrees. However, a zone 7.5 degrees wide extending in the direction of the largest circle is a bit more than the seventeenth part of the spherical surface. Thus, the physical space between the two planes, which cut out a part of planetary space in the width of the above mentioned angle, is somewhat more than a 17th part of the physical contents of the entire sphere. Hence, according to this hypothesis, all material used for planetary development would comprise approximately the seventeenth part of the material which the sun assembled for its composition on both sides out as far as the furthermost planet is located. But this cluster of the central body has a preponderance over the combined content of all the planets which is not 17 to 1 but 650 to 1, as Newton's calculations have established. However, it is easy to see that in the higher regions beyond Saturn, where planetary development either ceases or is rare, where only a few comet bodies have arisen, and especially where the movements of the basic material, because in that location it is not rapid enough to attain the equilibrium with the centripetal force as required by law, as happens in the regions close to the centre, ended up in an almost universal sinking toward the mid-point and increased the size of the sun with all the material from such a vast expanse of space, it is easy, I say, to see that for these reasons the sun would have to acquire such a preponderantly large mass.

However, in order to compare the planets with each other with respect to their masses, we first observe that, in accordance with the method of development I have indicated, the quantity of material which combines in the composition of a planet depends particularly on the extent of its distance from the sun, for the following reasons: (1) Because of its power of attraction, the sun limits the sphere of the planet's power of attraction; however, in the same circumstances, it does not restrict the more distant planets so narrowly as the close ones. (2) The circle from which all the particles have come together to make a more distant planet will be described with a larger radius and thus contain more basic material than the smaller circles. (3) For the very reasons just mentioned, the width between the two planes of the greatest deviation at a constant angle is greater at a greater distance than at a small distance. On the other hand, this advantage for the more distant planets over the ones lower down will be limited by the fact that the particles nearer the sun will be of a denser type and, everything considered, will also be less scattered than at a greater distance away. But we can easily estimate that for the development of large masses the first advantage far exceeds the limitation just mentioned and that, in general, the planets which develop far distant from the sun would have to acquire larger masses than the ones close to the sun. This happens insofar as we imagine a planet's development with only the sun present. But if we admit the development of several planets at different distances, then one planet will restrict the extent of the power of attraction of another planet through the sphere of its own force of attraction. This brings about an exception to the previous principle. For the planet which is near another one of exception mass will lose a very great deal from the sphere of its development and thus will become unusually smaller than the relationship of its solar distance by itself requires. On the whole, the planets have a greater mass as they are further from the sun, just as Saturn and Jupiter, in general, the two main parts of our system, are thus the biggest because they are furthest from the sun. However, deviations from this analogy do occur. But in them the mark of their common development is always manifest: the principle which we maintain concerning the heavenly bodies, namely, that a planet of exceptional size takes away from the nearest ones on both sides the mass appropriate to them, given their distance from the sun. For it attracts to itself a portion of the material which should go into the development of both of them. In fact, because of its location, Mars should be bigger than the Earth. But Mars has a diminished mass because of the force of attraction from Jupiter, which is so large and close by. And although Saturn itself has an immediate advantage over Mars because of its distance from the sun, nevertheless Saturn has not been entirely free from suffering a considerable loss thanks to Jupiter's power of attraction. And it seems to me that Mercury owes its exceptionally small mass not only to the force of attraction of the powerful sun, which is so close to it, but also to the fact that Venus is a neighbouring planet. If we compare the presumed density of Venus with its size, Venus must be a planet of considerable mass.

Everything agrees as splendidly as we might wish in order to confirm the adequacy of a mechanical theory for the origin of the cosmic structure and the celestial bodies. Now, as we estimate the space in which the material stuff of the planets was distributed before their development, we wish to consider how diffuse the material was which filled this middle space at that time and how free or unrestricted the particles suspended all around were to establish their rule-governed motions in it. If the space holding in itself all the planetary material was contained in that part of the sphere of Saturn which was between two imaginary planes subtended at an angle of about 7 degrees to each other from the mid-point of the sun out into the full reaches of space (and which therefore comprised one seventeenth of the entire sphere which we can describe with a radius equal to the distance of Saturn), then in order to calculate the diffusion of the basic planetary material filling this space, we wish to set the distance of Saturn at 100,000 Earth diameters. Thus, the entire sphere of Saturn's orbit will exceed the volume of Earth's globe by a factor of 1000 billion.[25*] If we take instead of the seventeenth part only the twentieth part of the space in which the elementary basic stuff was suspended, this still must exceed the volume of Earth's sphere by a factor of 50 billion. Now, if, following Newton, we set the mass of all the planets along with their satellites at only 1/650 of the mass of the cluster of the sun, then the Earth, which is only 1/169282 of this mass, will be related to the collective mass of all the planetary material in the ratio of 1 to 276.5. And if we then made all this material the same specific density as the Earth, we would produce a body which would take up a space 276.5 times greater than the Earth.[26*] Assuming that the density of the entire cluster of the Earth is not much greater than the density of the firm material which we encounter under Earth's outermost layer, as is required by the characteristics of the shape of the Earth, and assuming that this outer material is about 4 or 5 times denser than water and that water is 1000 time heavier than air, then, if all the planetary material were expanded to the density of air, it would take up a space almost 1,400,000 times larger than Earth's sphere. Comparing this space with the space in which, according to our theory, all planetary material was spread out, it is 30 million times smaller. Thus, the scattering of the planetary material in this space is much more thinly distributed than the particles of our atmosphere. In fact, the thin density of this scattered distribution, as inconceivable as it may appear, was nonetheless neither unnecessary nor unnatural. It had to be as thin as possible, in order to permit the suspended particles all freedom of movement, almost as in an empty space, and infinitely to reduce the resistance which they could have created for each other. They could, however, have assumed such a thinly distributed state on their own. We cannot doubt this point if we know a little about the diffusion which matter undergoes when it is transformed into vapour or when, to stay on the subject of the heavens, we consider the thinning out of the material in the tail of a comet, whose diameter, of an unheard of thickness, exceeds the diameter of the earth by a factor of well over a hundred and yet it is so transparent that the small stars can be seen through it, something which our air, when it is illuminated by the sun at a height many thousand times smaller, does not allow.

I conclude this section by bringing out an analogy which in and of itself can raise the present theory of the mechanical development of the celestial bodies above the probability of a hypothesis to a formal certainty. If the sun is composed of particles of the same basic material from which the planets have developed and if the difference between them consists only in the fact that in the sun undifferentiated material of all sorts accumulated, while in the planets the density of their types was distributed according to the different distances, then if we consider the material of all the planets as a collective unity, from their complete intermixing the result would have to be a density almost equal to the density of the sun. Now, this necessary consequence of our system finds happy confirmation in the comparison which M. de Buffon, that justly celebrated philosopher, set out between the densities of the total aggregate of planetary material and the material of the sun.[27*] He found a similarity between the two in the ratio of 640 to 650. When unbiased and necessary consequences of a theoretical conception encounter such happy confirmations in true natural relationships, can we really then believe that mere contingency has brought about this agreement between theory and observation?

PART TWO. SECTION THREE

Concerning the Eccentricity of the Planetary Orbits and the Origin of Comets

We cannot make the comets a special class of celestial bodies entirely different from the family of planets. Here, as elsewhere, nature works by imperceptible stages, and while going through all the series of changes, links together distant qualities with ones close at hand, thanks to a chain of intermediate rungs. The eccentricity in the case of the planets is the result of a lack of that impetus by which nature strives to make planetary movement precisely circular, something which, however, she can never perfectly attain because of the intervening influence of various causes. However, the deviation from circular motion is greater at the larger distances from the sun than close by.

This condition goes through a constant scale with all possible levels of eccentricity from the planets right up finally to the comets. True, this interconnection seems to be severed in the case of Saturn because of a large gap which completely separates the family of comets from the planets. But in the first part we have remarked that there may well be still other planets beyond Saturn which are more like comets because of a greater deviation from circularity in their orbital path and that it is only through a lack of observations (or also the difficulty involved in such observations) that this affinity was not long ago revealed as clearly to eye as to the understanding.

In the first section of this part we have already referred to a cause which can render eccentric the orbit of a cosmic body developing out of the basic material suspended all around, if we also assume that this body in all its locations has carefully balanced forces moving it directly in a circular motion. Because the planet collects materials from places at a considerable distance from each other, where the orbital velocities are different, the materials collectively reach the planet with different degrees of inherent orbital velocity. These deviate from the velocity appropriate to the distance of the planet from the sun and thus induce an eccentricity for the planet insofar as these different impressions of the particles fail to offset each other's deviation completely.

If the eccentricity had no other cause, it would be moderate everywhere. Also it would be less significant with the small planets far from the sun than with the closer and larger planets, that is, if we assumed that previously the particles of the basic material really did have a precise circular movement. Now, these estimates do not agree with observation, since, as has already been mentioned, the eccentricity increases with the distance from the sun, and the small size of the masses appears instead to create an exception to an increase in eccentricity, as we see with Mars. Thus, we are forced to limit the hypothesis about the precise circular movement of the particulate basic materials, so that, while they very nearly attain the determined precision in the regions near the sun, they nevertheless admit wider deviations from that precision the further the elementary particles hovered from the sun. Such an adjustment of the basic principle of the free circular movement of the basic material is more naturally appropriate. For regardless of the spatial diffusion, which seems to leave them free to limit each other at the point of completely balanced equilibrium of the central forces, no less considerable are the causes which hinder the attainment of this natural goal. The further the dispersed parts of the original material are from the sun, the weaker the force which induces them to sink down. The resistance of the particles below, which should bend their fall sideways and force them to assume a direction perpendicular to the radius of the circle, is proportionally diminished as these particles sink downward under it either to be incorporated into the sun or to assume an orbit in a region closer to the sun. The fact that this more distant material has a predominant specific lightness does not permit it to acquire the downward movement, which is the basis for everything, with the force necessary to move the resisting particles aside, and perhaps these distant particles still restrict each other in order finally to attain this uniformity after a long time. Thus, among these distant particles already small masses have developed as the starting point of so many celestial bodies, which, because they are assembled from weakly moving material, have only an eccentric movement with which they sink toward the sun and on the way are increasingly diverted from a perpendicular fall by taking on more quickly moving pieces. Finally, however, they remain comets if those spaces in which they have developed have, through the sinking down toward the sun or through the assembling in particular clusters, become cleansed and empty. This is the reason why the eccentricity of the planets and those celestial bodies called comets increases with the distance from the sun. Comets have their name for the very reason that in this characteristic they far exceed the planets.[28] There are, it is true, two exceptions which violate the law concerning the increase in eccentricity with the increasing distance from the sun. We see them in the two smallest planets of our system, Mars and Mercury. But with the first the cause is presumably the vicinity of a planet as large as Jupiter, which through its power of attraction on its side of Mars deprives it of particles for its development and thus only allows Mars a special area in the direction of the sun in which to extend itself. This brings with it an excessive central force and eccentricity. So far as Mercury, the lowest but also the most eccentric of the planets, is concerned, it is easy to believe that, because the sun's axial rotation does not yet by a long way equal Mercury's velocity, not only does the resistance which the sun presents to the material in the space surrounding it deprive the nearest particles of their central movement but also this resistance could easily extend right out to Mercury, and its orbital velocity would on this account have been considerably diminished.

Eccentricity is the most notable mark differentiating the comets. Their atmosphere and tail, which expand through the heat of their close approach to the sun, are only consequences of the eccentricity, although they have always served in times of ignorance as uncommon images of horror, announcing to the common folk imaginary destinies. Astronomers, who pay more attention to the laws of motion than to the strangeness in the shape, notice a second characteristic distinguishing the family of comets from planets, namely, unlike planets, comets do not confine themselves to the zone of the zodiac, but establish their orbits in all celestial regions without restriction. This peculiarity has exactly the same cause as the eccentricity. The planets have confined their orbits to the narrow region of the zodiac because the elementary material in the vicinity of the sun acquires circular movements which in each revolution try to intersect the interrelated plane and do not allow a body, once developed, to deviate from this surface towards which all the material from both sides presses. Thus, basic material from the spaces far from the mid-point, which, weakly moved by the force of attraction, cannot attain free orbital movement for the very reason which produces eccentricity, is not capable of accumulating at this height on the plane interconnecting all planetary movement so as to maintain the bodies developed there primarily on this track. Since it is not limited to a particular region, as is the case with the lower planets, the scattered basic material will instead develop on its own into celestial bodies equally easily on both sides, far from the interconnecting plane just as often as it will near to it. Therefore, comets will be fully free to descend toward us from all regions. However, those which first developed in a place not far above the planetary orbits will manifest less deviation from the limitations of their paths as well as less eccentricity. With the increasing distances from the mid-point of the system, this lawless freedom of the comets in relation to their deviations increases and loses itself in the depths of the heavens in a total lack of orbital movement. This leaves the bodies developing in the outer regions free to fall toward the sun and establishes the last frontiers of the systematic arrangement.

In this outline of the comet's movements, I assume that, so far as their direction is concerned, for the most part they have one in common with the planets. It seems to me that in the case of the comets close by this is undoubtedly true. Also this similarity of form cannot get lost in the depths of the heavens before the point where the elementary basic stuff in the least energetic state of motion establishes the rotation which arises in all directions from the downward sinking. For, because of the commonality of the movements lower down, the time required to align them in a common direction is, on account of the large distance, too long for them to be able to extend themselves far enough for the natural development in the lower region to take place. Hence, there will perhaps be comets which will establish their orbits in the opposite direction, namely, from east to west, although I might equally well almost persuade myself, for reasons which I am reluctant to cite here, that of the nineteen comets in which we have observed this peculiarity, in some of them an optical illusion may have given rise to this observation.

I must still note something about the masses of the comets and about the density of their material. For the reasons mentioned in the previous section, according to the rules the development of these celestial bodies in the upper regions should proceed always according to the principle that, as the distance increases, their masses get larger. And we can believe that a few comets are larger than Saturn and Jupiter. But it is just not credible that this quantity of the masses always increases in this manner. The scattering of the basic materials and the specific lightness of their particles make the development in the furthest region of cosmic space slow. The uncertain diffusion of this material in the entire infinite expanse of this space without any tendency to accumulate in the direction of a certain plane permits several smaller developments in place of a single considerable one. And the lack of central force draws the largest portion of the particles down to the sun, without their having assembled themselves into masses.

The specific density of the stuff out of which the comets develop is more worthy of attention than the size of their masses. Presumably, since they develop in the uppermost reaches of the cosmic structure, the particles which compose them are of the lightest sort. We cannot doubt that this is the major cause of the vapour sphere and the tail, which distinguish them from the other celestial bodies. We cannot attribute this dispersal of the comet's material in a vapour mainly to the effect of solar heat. A few comets in their approach to the sun hardly reach the depth of the Earth's orbit. Many remain between the orbits of Earth and Venus and then turn back. If such a moderate level of heat dissolves and thins out the material on the surface of these bodies to this extent, then they would have to consist of the lightest material which undergoes, under the influence of heat, more thinning out than any material whatsoever in all nature.

Moreover, it is not possible to attribute the vapours which arise so frequently from the comet to the heat which its body has left over from the earlier approaches to the sun. For indeed we may suppose that at the time of its development a comet has gone through quite a few orbits with greater eccentricity and that these were reduced only gradually. But the other planets, for which we could assume the very same, do not manifest this phenomenon. However, they would inherently display it, if the varieties of the lightest material included in the composition of the planets were present just as much as they are with the comets.

The Earth has something in itself which we can compare with the dispersal of the comet's vapours and their tails.[29] The finest particles which the effect of the sun draws from Earth's outer surface pile up around one of the poles, when the sun directs the semi-circle of its orbit into the opposite hemisphere. The finest and most energetic particles, which arise in the hot equatorial regions, having attained a certain atmospheric altitude, are compelled by the effect of the sun's rays to move away to and accumulate in those regions which at that period are directed away from the sun and buried in a long night. These particles compensate the inhabitants of the icy regions for the absence of the great light, which even at this distance sends them the effects of its heat. Just this same power of the sun's rays, which creates the Northern Lights, would bring out a vapour circle with a tail, if the finest and volatile particles on the Earth were encountered just as frequently on the Earth as on the comets.

PART TWO. SECTION FOUR

Concerning the Origin of Moons and the Axial Rotation of the Planets

The attempt of a planet to develop from the range of basic materials is at the same time the cause of its axial rotation and produces the moons which are to orbit around it. What the sun with its planets is on a large scale a planet with a sphere of attraction extending far out is on a small scale, namely, the major part of a system whose pieces have been set in motion through the force of attraction of the central body. Since the developing planet activates for its development the particles of the basic material from the total sphere of its power of attraction, it will produce from all these sinking motions, thanks to their reciprocally interacting effects, circular movements, and will, in fact, finally produce movements which settle upon a single common direction. Some of these motions will get moderated appropriately for free circular movement and in this limited area will be located close to a common plane. In this space, as with the main planets around the sun, the moons also will develop around the planets, when the extent of the power of attraction of such cosmic bodies offers favourable conditions for their production. Incidentally, what was said in connection with the origin of the solar system can be applied equally well to the system of Jupiter and of Saturn. The moons will have arranged their orbital circles in one direction almost in a single plane and this, in fact, for the same reasons as those in the large-scale analogy. But why do these satellites in their common orientation move far more in the direction in which the planets move than in any other? The moons' orbits are not produced through the circular movements of the planet. They acknowledge as cause only the power of attraction of the main planet, and, so far as this force is concerned, all directions are equally good. Mere contingency will select the direction out of all possible directions, according to which the sinking movement of the material changes into circles. In fact, the circular path of the main planet does nothing at all to impress orbital motion around the planet upon the material out of which the moons are to develop. All the particles surrounding the planet move with it in the same motion around the sun and are thus, in relation to the planet, respectively at rest. The power of attraction of the planet achieves everything by itself. But since, as far as direction is concerned, this power is in and of itself indifferent to them all, the orbital movement which is to arise out of that requires only a small external stimulus to deflect it more to one side than to the others. This small degree of steering the orbital movement acquires from the forward movement of the elementary particles which run simultaneously around the sun but at a higher velocity and reach the sphere of the planet's power of attraction. For this requires the particles closer to the sun, which orbit at a faster momentum, to abandon the direction of their path when they are already at a considerable distance and to move up over the planet in an extended curve. Because these particles have a higher degree of velocity than the planet itself has, when they are drawn down by the planet's power of attraction, they produce in their perpendicular descent and also in the descent of the other particles a curved deviation from west to east. It requires only this slight steering to see to it that the orbital movement in which the descent, initiated by the power of attraction, finishes up takes on this direction rather than any other. For this reason, all the moons will coordinate their direction with the direction of the orbit of the main planets. However, the plane of their path also cannot deviate far from the plane of the planetary orbits, because the material out of which they develop, for the very reason which we have referred to concerning orbital direction in general, is also guided according to this most precise arrangement, namely, coordinating itself with the plane of the principal orbits.

From all this we clearly see what the circumstances are in which a planet may be able to acquire satellites. The power of attraction of the planet must be large and, as a result, the extent of the sphere in which this power is effective must extend far out, so that not only are the particles which move to the planet through a long descent, without regard to the effects of resistance, at length able to attain the velocity for a free orbital momentum, but also there must be present sufficient material for the development of moons in this region, something which cannot occur with a slight power of attraction. Thus, only planets with large masses and at a great distance from the sun are endowed with satellites. Jupiter and Saturn, the two largest and also most distant of the planets have the most moons. The Earth, much smaller than those planets, is assigned only one. And Mars, which on account of its distance might have merited some share of this advantage, goes without because its mass is so small.

We observe with pleasure how the same force of attraction of the planet which brought the material for building moons and at the same time determined its movement extends to the very body of the planet itself, in giving it an axial rotation, by means of exactly the same action through which the planet develops, in the common direction from west to east. The particles of the descending basic material, which, as mentioned, acquire a common rotational movement from west to east, fall for the most part onto the surface of the planet and are mixed into its cluster, because they do not have the appropriate velocity to maintain themselves in freely suspended orbital motion. Since they now come into the composition of the planet, they must, as parts of it, continue just the same rotational movement and in exactly the same direction which they had before they were united with the planet. And because, in general, we can see from the foregoing that the number of particles which the lack of necessary movement drives down to the central body must be very much greater than the number of those others capable of attaining the appropriate degree of velocity, then we can easily grasp why this central body will in its axial rotation be a long way from possessing the velocity to achieve an equilibrium between the gravity on its surface and the centrifugal force. Nevertheless, the axial rotation of planets with a larger mass and at a considerable distance from the sun will be much faster than with the small ones close to the sun. In fact, Jupiter has the fastest axial rotation that we are aware of, and I do not know what system would enable us to reconcile this fact with a body whose cluster exceeds all the others, unless we could see that its movements are themselves the effect of that power of attraction which this celestial body exerts in accordance with the mass of this very cluster. If the axial rotation were an effect of an external cause, then Mars would have to have a more rapid axial rotation than Jupiter, for the very same power of movement affects a smaller body more than a larger one. We would quite correctly be surprised at this, since all the orbital movements diminish with distance from the mid-point, but the speeds of the rotations increase with the distance. With Jupiter the rotational movement could be even three and a half times faster than its annual motion around the sun.

Thus, we must recognize in the daily rotations of the planets the very same cause which is, in general, the common origin of movement in nature, namely, the force of attraction. This style of explanation, therefore, will successfully prove its truth through the natural quality of its basic concept and the natural consequences of that.

But if the development of a body itself produces the axial rotation, then it is reasonable that all the spheres of the cosmic structure must have it. Why, then, does the moon not have it? It does seem, although the idea is false, to have reached a kind of rotation, because it always has the same side turned towards the earth, but this comes far more from a kind of overbalancing of one hemisphere than from a true rotating momentum. Must the moon really have rotated on its axis at an earlier period more quickly and through some unknown cause or other have gradually reduced this movement until it was brought to this slight and measured remainder? We need to resolve this question only in connection with one of the planets. Then the application to all planets will follow of itself. I am postponing this solution to another occasion, because it has a necessary connection to the assignment which the Royal Academy of Sciences in Berlin has established for the prize in the year 1754.

The theory which is to explain the cause of the axial rotations must also be able to produce from exactly the same causes the orientation of the planetary axes in relation to their orbital plane. We have reason to be surprised why the equator of the daily rotation is not in the same plane as the one in which the moons orbit as they move around the same planets. For this same movement which directs the orbit of a satellite, through its extension to the body of the planet, produced its axial rotation, and it should give it exactly the same determinate direction and orientation. Celestial bodies which have no planets orbiting closely around them, nevertheless, because of exactly the same movement of the particles which served them as material and the same law which limited each one to the plane of its periodic orbit, settle into an axial rotation which, for the same reasons, had to coincide with the direction of their orbital plane. As a result of this cause, it is reasonable that the axes of all celestial bodies would have had to be oriented perpendicular to the common interconnecting plane of the planetary system, which does not deviate far from the ecliptic.[30] But the axes are perpendicular only with the two most important parts of this cosmic structure, with Jupiter and the sun. With the others whose rotation we know, the axes are at an angle in relation to the plane of their orbits, Saturn more than the others, but the Earth more than Mars, whose axis is also almost perpendicular to the ecliptic. The equator of Saturn (insofar as we are able to ascertain it from the direction of its ring) is inclined at an angle of 31 degrees to the plane of its orbit. However, the Earth is inclined towards its plane at an angle of only 23.5 degrees. We can perhaps attribute the cause of this deviation to the inequality in the movements of the material which came together to build the planet. The preponderant movement of the particles was around the planet's mid-point in the direction of the plane of its orbit. And there the interconnecting plane was in place around which the elementary particles accumulated to make the movement there circular, where possible, and to pile up material for the development of the satellites, which for this reason never deviate far from the plane of the planet's orbit. If the planet developed for the most part only out of these particles, then its axial rotation in its first growth would be as little offset from that plane as the satellites which orbit around it. But the planet develops, as the theory has established, more from particles which sank down on both sides and whose number or velocity appears not to have been totally balanced, so that one hemisphere would be able to acquire a small excess of movement with respect to the other and thus cause some displacement of the axis.

Setting these reasons aside, I consider this explanation only as a supposition which I do not have the confidence to establish. My true view is as follows. The axial rotation of the planets in the original state of their first development was quite accurately aligned with the plane of their annual rotation, and causes were present which pushed these axes out of their first position. A celestial body which is moving out of its first volatile condition into a firm condition undergoes, when it develops completely in this way, a large change in the regularity of its outer surface. This surface becomes firm and hardens while the deeper material has not yet sufficiently sunk down according to the measure of its specific gravity. The lighter types of material intermixed in its cluster, after separating out from the rest, finally move under the outermost crust, which has become firm, and create large holes. The largest and widest of these holes, for reasons which would take too long to discuss here, occur under or near the equator. The above mentioned crust finally sinks down into these depressions and produces various inequalities, mountains and rifts. Now, since in something like this manner, as must apparently have happened with the Earth, the Moon, and Venus, the outer crust became uneven, the planet could not achieve an equilibrium any more on all sides in the circle of its axial rotation. A few prominent sections of considerable mass, which had nothing equal to them on the opposite side, which could act as an effective counterweight to the momentum, must have then shifted the axial rotation and sought to place it in a position around which the material was equally poised. Thus, exactly the same cause as in the complete development of the celestial body changes its outer crust from a horizontal state into broken up inequalities. This general cause has made it necessary to change somewhat the original orientation of the planet's axis. We perceive this to be the case with all the celestial bodies which the telescope can reveal sufficiently clearly. But this change has its limits, so that the deviation is not excessive. The inequalities, as already mentioned, show up more near the equator of an orbiting celestial body than at a distance from it. In the region of the poles they disappear almost entirely. The discussion of the causes of this I am reserving for another time. Thus, the most prominent masses rising above the even surface will be found near the equatorial circle. Since the masses strive to bring themselves close to this circle because of the major influence of their momentum, they will be able to raise the axis of the celestial body at the most only a few degrees out of its perpendicular orientation with its orbital plane. As a consequence, a celestial body which has not yet fully developed will still have this orientation of its axis perpendicular to its orbital path. The angle will perhaps be altered only with the long succession of centuries. Jupiter appears to be still in this condition. The preponderance of its mass and size and the lightness of its material meant that it had to assume a firm and calm condition a few centuries later than other celestial bodies. Perhaps the inside of its cluster is still in motion, as the parts composing it sink toward the centre according to the determination of their heaviness, and through the separation of the thinner varieties from the heavy ones it is developing a firm state. According to such an account, Jupiter cannot yet appear calm on its outer surface. Collapses and ruin govern there. The telescope itself has confirmed that for us. The shape of this planet is constantly changing, while the Moon, Venus, and the Earth remain unaltered. Indeed, we can also with justice estimate that the completion of the developmental period is several centuries later in the case of a celestial body which exceeds our Earth in size by a factor of more than twenty thousand and which has a smaller density by a factor of four. When its outer surface reaches a tranquil composition, then undoubtedly much larger inequalities, like the ones which cover the surface of the Earth, combined with the velocity of its rotational impulse, will in a relatively short period give its axial rotation the constant orientation which the equilibrium of its forces will require.

Saturn, which is three times smaller than Jupiter, because of its greater distance from the sun can perhaps have the advantage of a faster development than Jupiter. At least Saturn's much quicker axial rotation and the large ratio of its centrifugal force to the gravity on its outer surface (which is to be presented in the following section) see to it that the inequalities which have thus presumably developed there have very quickly given it a shift toward the side of the excess weight through a displacement of the axis. I freely concede that this part of my system concerning the position of the planetary axes is still incomplete and quite far from being subject to geometrical calculation. I preferred to reveal this candidly rather than through all sorts of devious but apparently competent reasons damage the rest of the theory and give it a weak part. The section which follows can provide confirmation of the credibility of the entire hypothesis. There we wish to explain the movements of the cosmic structure.

PART TWO. SECTION FIVE

Concerning the Origin of Saturn's Ring and the Calculation of the Daily Rotation of the Planet from the Relationships to this Ring

Thanks to the systematic arrangement in the cosmic structure, its parts are linked together by a ladder of alterations in their characteristics, and we can assume that a planet located in the remotest region of the world will have approximately the same characteristics which the nearest comet would take on, if through a diminution of its eccentricity, it were raised into the family of planets. With this in mind, we wish to examine Saturn as if it had gone through several orbits with a greater eccentricity, in a manner similar to the motion of a comet, and had been gradually brought into a path more similar to a circle.[31*] The heat which the planet incorporated in its approach to the sun raised the light material from its outer surface. As we know from previous sections, this material, in the case of the most distant celestial bodies, is excessively thinly distributed and with low levels of heat undergoes diffusion. Meanwhile, after the planet was brought in several orbits to the distance where it is now suspended, in such a moderate climate it gradually lost the heat it had absorbed, and the vapours, which still constantly spread around it from its outer layer, gradually stopped moving up into tails. New materials did not move upward any longer with the same frequency to supplement the old ones. In short, the vapours already going around Saturn remained, for reasons which we will refer to presently, suspended in a permanent ring around the planet and kept the reminder of its previous comet-like nature, while Saturn's body exuded the heat and finally became a calm and cleansed planet. Now we wish to point out the secret which in this celestial body could have held the vapours which had come up from it in free suspension, indeed, which changed these vapours from an atmosphere spread out around the planet into the form of a ring standing completely apart from it everywhere. I assume that Saturn had an axial rotation. Nothing more than this is necessary to reveal the entire secret. No mechanism other than this single one produced for the planet the phenomenon mentioned above, as an immediate mechanical result. I am sufficiently confident to assert that in all of nature only a few things can be brought to such a comprehensible origin as this special feature of the heavens can be derived from the raw state of the planet's first development.

The vapours rising up from Saturn had their own inherent movement and established themselves freely at the altitude to which they rose. This motion they acquired as parts of the planet from its axial rotation. The particles which moved up from close to the equator of the planet must have had the fastest motions, and those further away right up to the poles that much slower motions, according to the higher latitude of the place from which they arose. The relationship to the specific heaviness established the different altitudes to which the particles rose. But the only particles which could maintain their locations at their distance away in a constant free circular momentum were the ones set at those distances which demanded a central force similar to the velocity which these particles had made their own thanks to the axial rotation. The remaining particles, to the extent that the interaction with the others could not bring them this precise velocity, must either through their excess motion leave the planetary sphere or through their lack of motion necessarily sink back onto the planet. The particles scattered throughout the total extent of the vapour sphere, thanks to the very same central law, in the motion of their curved momentum, would strive to intersect the extended equatorial plane of the planet from both sides. And in coming together on this plane from both hemispheres, they would stop each other and accumulate there. Since I assume that the above-mentioned vapours are the very ones which the planet in its cooling last sent back up, all the scattered vapour material will collect close to this plane in a space not particularly wide and leave the space on both sides empty. In this new and changed orientation, however, the materials will nonetheless continue exactly the same movement which they maintained while suspended in free concentric circular orbits. In such a manner, the circle of vapour now alters its shape, which was a full sphere, into the form of an extended surface coinciding precisely with Saturn's equator. But this surface must also, for exactly the same mechanical reasons, finally assume the form of a ring, whose outer edge will be determined by the effect of the sun's rays, which, by means of their force, scatter and disperse those particles which have distanced themselves a certain way from the mid-point of the planet, as they do with comets, and in this way designate the outer limit of their circle of vapours. The inner edge of this emerging ring will be determined by the relationship to the velocity of the planet under its equator. For that distance away from its mid-point where this velocity attains an equilibrium with the power of attraction for that location is the closest approach to the planet where the particles which have arisen from its body are able to describe circular orbits thanks to their own movement acquired from the planet's axial rotation. Because the particles closer than that require a higher velocity for such an orbit, which they cannot have because the movement even on the equator of the planet is not faster, they will maintain eccentric orbits which intersect each other, weaken each other's motions, and finally will all fall back down onto the planet from which they arose. Now, there we see an amazingly strange phenomenon, the sight of which since its discovery has always astonished astronomers and whose cause we could not ever entertain even a probable hope of discovering, come about in an easy mechanical way, free of all hypotheses. What happened to Saturn, as can easily be seen from this, would happen just as regularly to any comet with a sufficient axial rotation, if it were set at a constant height in which its body could gradually cool down. Nature, left to its own forces, is fertile in excellent results, even in chaos, and the development following from this produces such wonderful relationships and harmonies for a creature's common needs that it even enables us to recognize with unanimous certainty in the eternal and unchanging laws of their fundamental characteristics that Great Being in whom they are all united, thanks to their common dependency in a collective harmony. Saturn derives important advantages from its ring. It lengthens its day and under so many moons illuminates its night to such an extent, that the absence of the sun is easily forgotten. But must we then, on that account, deny that the common development of material through mechanical laws, without the need for anything other than their universal regulations, could have produced relationships which create advantages for reasoning creatures? All beings have a common dependency on a single cause: the Divine Understanding. They can therefore produce no other consequences after them except those which bring with them an image of the perfection of exactly the same Divine Idea.

Now we wish to calculate the time of the axial rotation of this celestial body from the relationships of its ring, according to the hypothesis of its development mentioned above. Because all the movement of the ring's particles is a motion absorbed from the axial rotation of Saturn, on whose outer surface they were located, the fastest movement which these particles possess among themselves will be the same as the fastest rotation which occurs on Saturn's outer surface. In other words, the velocity at which the particles of the ring orbit on its inner edge is equal to the velocity of the planet at its equator. But we can easily find that when we look for it in the velocity of one of Saturn's satellites, for we assume that it is proportional to the square root of the distances from the mid-point of the planet. From the velocity we have discovered, the time of Saturn's axial rotation is immediately given: it is six hours, twenty-three minutes, and fifty-three seconds. This mathematical calculation of an unknown movement for a celestial body, which is perhaps the only prediction of its kind in the real theory of nature, awaits confirmation from the observations of future ages. The telescopes known up to this time do not enlarge Saturn sufficiently, so that we can discover the spots (which we can assume are on its outer surface) in order to be able to perceive its axial rotation through their forward displacement. But the telescopes have perhaps not yet reached that perfection which we can hope from them and which the hard work and skill of the craftsmen seem to promise us. If we once succeed in providing visible confirmation of our conjectures, how certain the theory of Saturn would be and what an overwhelming credibility the entire system which is built upon the same principles would derive from that. The time of Saturn's daily rotation establishes the relationship of the centrifugal force away from the mid-point at its equator to the force of gravity on its outer layer. The former is to the latter as 20 is to 32. Thus, the force of gravity is only around 3/5 greater than the centrifugal force. Such a large proportion as this brings about necessarily a very observable difference in the diameters of this planet. And we could anticipate that this difference must have developed to such an extent that the observation of this planet, although it is only enlarged a little by the telescopes, would have to make it all too clearly visible. But in truth this does not happen, and the theory could thus suffer a disadvantageous blow. A thorough proof completely removes this difficulty. According to Huygens' hypothesis, which assumes that the gravitational force inside a planet is the same throughout, the difference in the diameters is proportional to the diameter at the equator in a ratio twice as small as the proportion of the centrifugal force to the gravitational force at the poles.[32*] For example, in the case of the Earth, the force moving away from the mid-point at the equator is 1/289 of the gravitational force at the poles. Thus, in Huygens' hypothesis, the diameter of the equatorial plane is 1/578th greater than the earth's axis. The cause is as follows: the gravitational force, according to what has been assumed, inside the Earth's cluster in all regions close to the mid-point is as great as it is on the outer surface, but the centrifugal force diminishes as one moves close to the mid-point. Thus, the centrifugal force is not always 1/289th of the gravitational force. For these reasons, the entire loss in weight of a liquid column on the plane of the equator amounts, not to 1/289th but to half of that, i.e., to 1/578th. On the other hand, according to Newton's hypothesis, the centrifugal force, which initiated the axial rotation, has the same relationship to the gravitational force at a specific location on the entire equatorial plane right to the mid-point, because the gravitational force inside the planet, assuming the planet has the same density throughout, decreases with the distance from the mid-point in the same proportion as the centrifugal force decreases, so that the latter is always 1/289th of the former. This creates a lightening of the liquid column at the equatorial plane and also a rise in it of 1/289. This difference of the diameters in this theory is increased even more by the fact that the shortening of the axis involves bringing the parts closer to the mid-point, and with that an increase in the gravitational force; but the increase in length of the equatorial diameter involves moving parts further from the very same mid-point and thus lessening the gravitational force. For this reason, the flattening of the Newtonian spheroid increases to the point where the difference in the diameters increases from 1/289 to 1/230.

According to these reasons, the diameters of Saturn would have to be in an even larger ratio to each other than 20 to 32. They would have to reach a proportion almost equal to 1 to 2, a difference which is so large that the slightest attentiveness would not miss it, no matter how small Saturn might appear through the telescopes. But from this one can only conclude that the assumption of the uniform density, which seems to be quite correctly applied to the case of the Earth's body, in the case of Saturn deviates far too widely from the reality. This is already inherently probable in the case of a planet whose cluster consists, for the greatest part of its content, of the lightest materials and which leaves the heavier sorts of materials much freer to settle down toward the mid-point, according to their gravitational make up, than do those celestial bodies whose much denser stuff delays the settling down of the material and allows it to harden before this settling can occur. When we also assume in the case of Saturn that the density of its material in the interior increases as one moves closer to the centre, then the gravitational force no longer declines in this ratio, but the growing density compensates for the deficiency in those parts which are set at heights above the point located in the planet and which contribute nothing by their power of attraction to the planet's gravitational power there.[33*] When this preponderant density of the deepest material is very large, thanks to the laws of attraction, the density changes the gravitational force which in the interior declines toward the centre into something almost uniform and establishes the ratio of the diameters close to Huygens' proportion, which is always half the ratio between the centrifugal force and the gravitational force. Thus, since with respect to each other, these were as 2 is to 3, then the difference in the diameters of Saturn will not be 1/3, but 1/6 of the equatorial diameter. Finally, this difference will still be concealed because Saturn, whose axis makes a constant angle of 31 degrees with its orbital plane, never orients the position of its axis perpendicular to its equator, as happens with Jupiter, something which diminishes the appearance of the previous difference by almost one third. Under such circumstances, and especially considering Saturn's great distance away, we can easily believe that the flattened shape of its body will not be as readily visible as we would think. However, astronomy, whose progress depends particularly on the perfecting of the instruments, with their help will perhaps be in a position to discover such a remarkable characteristic, if I do not flatter myself excessively.

What I say about the shape of Saturn can, to some extent, serve as a general remark about the natural theory of the heavens. According to an exact calculation, Jupiter has a ratio of the gravitational force to the centrifugal force at its equator of at least 9.25 to 1. If its cluster were of uniform density throughout, in accordance with Newton's theories, this planet should show a difference between its axis and the equatorial diameter even greater than 1/9. But Cassini found it to be only 1/16, Pound 1/12 and sometimes 1/14.[34*] At least all these different observations, which in their difference confirm the difficulty of this measurement, agree in that they establish the difference as much smaller than it should be in Newton's system, or rather, according to his hypothesis of uniform density. And if we therefore change the assumption about the uniform density, which permits such a wide discrepancy between theory and observation, into the much more probably assumption that the density of the planetary cluster is arranged so that it increases towards the centre of the planet, then we will validate the observations not only of Jupiter but also of Saturn, a planet much harder to measure, so as to be able to understand clearly the cause of the smaller flattening of its spherical body.

From the development of Saturn's ring, we have taken the opportunity to venture on the bold step of determining through calculation the time of its axial rotation, something which the telescopes are not capable of discovering. Let us add to this attempt at a physical prediction yet another concerning the very same planet, a claim whose validity we can expect to be witnessed by more perfect instruments of future ages.

According to our assumption that Saturn's ring is an accumulation of particles which, after they arose as vapours from the outer surface of this celestial body, thanks to the momentum which they receive and continue from the planet's axial rotation, maintain themselves at the altitude of their distance away in free circular movement, these particles do not have the same periodic orbital times at all their distances from the mid-point. The times are, by contrast, determined according to the square root of the cube of their distance from the planet, if the particles are to keep themselves suspended according to the laws of the central forces. Now, the time in which, according to this hypothesis, the particles of the inner edge complete their orbit is about ten hours, and the orbital time for the particles on the outer edge is, according to the appropriate calculations, fifteen hours. Thus, when the lowest parts of the ring have completed three orbits, the furthest parts have completed only two. Even if we estimate that the interference which the particles create for each other in the plane of the ring through their great dispersal is as insignificant as we like, it is nevertheless probable that the slower movement of the particles further away in each of their orbits gradually delays and retards the more quickly moving lower parts. On the other hand, the lower parts would have to impart to the upper parts some of their motion, so as to create a more rapid rotation. If this reciprocal interaction were not finally interrupted, this process would last until such a time as all the particles in the ring, both the low ones and those further away, were brought to rotate in the same time, in which state they would be at rest relative to each other and would have no effect in displacing one another. But such a condition, if the movement of the ring ended up like this, would destroy it completely. For if we take the middle of the plane of the ring and establish that the movement there remain what it was before and what it must be to be capable of achieving free orbital movement, the lower particles would not hold themselves suspended at their altitude, because they would be held back considerably, but would intersect each other in oblique and eccentric motions. The more distant particles, however, through the impulse of a motion greater than it should be for the central force at their distance from the planet, would move away from Saturn further than the outer boundary of the ring set by the effect of the sun and would, of necessity, be scattered behind the planet by the sun's effect and carried away.

But we need not fear all this disorder. The mechanism of the developing motion of the ring involves an arrangement which, thanks to the very causes which should destroy it, establish it in a secure state by means of which it is divided up into several concentric circular bands which, because of the intervening gaps which separate them, have no more common interaction with each other. For while the particles orbiting on the inner edge of the ring with their faster motion push forward the particles above somewhat and accelerate their orbit, the higher level in velocity provides these particles with an excess of centrifugal force and moves them further away from the place where they were suspended. But if we assume that while these particles strive to separate themselves from the lower ones, they have to overcome a certain interconnection which, whether it is because they are scattered vapours, nevertheless appears to be not entirely insignificant for them, then this increased level of momentum seeks to overcome the interrelationship mentioned above, but will not do so by itself, so long as the excess in the centrifugal force causing them to move around in the same orbital time as the lowest particles does not exceed the central force of their position and their interconnectedness. And for this reason the interconnectedness must remain in a stripe of a certain breadth of this ring, although because its parts perform their orbits in the same time, the upper particles must make an effort to pull themselves away from the lower ones, but not in a larger width, because, while the velocity of these particles orbiting in equal times increases with the distances more than it should according to the central laws, when it has gone beyond the level which can sustain the interconnection of the vapour particles, they must tear themselves away from it and take up a distance away from the planet appropriate to the excess momentum of the orbital forces over the centripetal force at that location. In this way, the intervening space will be set up, which keeps the first band of the ring away from the rest. And in the same way, the accelerated motion of the particles above, through the rapid rotation of those below, and their interconnection with them, which seeks to hinder the separation, will make a second concentric ring, from which the third arises around a moderate intervening gap. We could calculate the number of these circular bands and the width of the intervals between them, if we knew the extent of the interconnection linking the particles to each other. But we can be satisfied that we have, in general, found out with a good degree of probability the composition of Saturn's ring, which prevents its destruction and keeps it suspended through free movements.

The conjecture gives me no little satisfaction thanks to the hope of seeing it confirmed some day through effective observations. A few years ago there was a report from London that when people observed Saturn with a new Newtonian telescope, an improved model by Mr. Bradley, its ring seemed to be essentially a combination of many concentric rings, separated by intervening spaces. This report has not been taken further since that time.[35*] The observational instruments have opened up for our understanding the knowledge of the most distant boundaries of the cosmic structure. If now it is particularly up to them to undertake new steps in this business, from the attentiveness of our time to all those things which can expand human ideas we really can have probable grounds for hoping that they will turn particularly in a direction which presents them with the greatest expectation of important discoveries.

However, if Saturn has been so fortunate as to make a ring for itself, why then has no other planet shared this advantage? The reason is clear. The ring is to arise from the ascending vapours of a planet, which it gives off in its raw condition, and the planet's axial rotation must give these vapours their impetus which they only have to continue when they have reached the altitude where they can attain an exact equilibrium between the planet's gravitational power and the motion imparted to them. Thus, we can easily determine by calculation the altitude to which the vapours from a planet must rise, if they are to maintain themselves in a free circular movement by means of the motions which they had at the planet's equator, provided we know the diameter of the planet, the period of its axial rotation, and the gravitational force on its outer surface. According to the law of central movement, the distance of a body which can go freely in circles around a planet at a velocity equal to the planet's axial rotation is in exactly the same ratio to the semi-diameter of the planet as the centrifugal force away from the centre at the equator is to the gravitational force. Given these reasons, the distance of the inner edge of Saturn's ring is equal to 8, when we assume that the half-diameter of the planet is 5. These two numbers are in the same ratio as 32 to 20, which, as we have previously noted, expresses the ratio of the gravitational force to the centrifugal force at the equator. For the same reasons, if we establish that Jupiter is to have a ring developed in this way, its smallest half-diameter would exceed the half-diameter of Jupiter by a factor of 10. That would exactly match the distance where its most remote satellite orbits around it. For these reasons and also because the vapours rising up from a planet cannot expand so far out from it, it is impossible for Jupiter to develop a ring. If we wanted to know why the Earth has acquired no ring, we will find the answer in the size of the half diameter, which the inner edge of the ring alone would have to have had. This would have to have been 289 Earth semi-diameters. With the slower moving planets the possibility for the development of a ring gets even more remote. Thus, there is no example left where a planet could have acquired a ring in the manner which we have explained, other than the example of the planet which really has one. This is not an insignificant confirmation of the plausibility of our manner of explanation.

But what makes me almost certain that the ring going around Saturn has not come about in the common way and was not built up through the universal laws of development governing throughout the entire system of planets, which also produced Saturn's satellites, and certain, I say, that no external material provided the material for this ring, but that it is a creation of the planet itself, which moved its most volatile parts upward up by heat and gave them a rotational momentum from its own axial rotation, is this fact: unlike the other satellites of this planet and, in general, all orbiting bodies which accompany a main planet, the ring is not oriented on the common interrelated plane of planetary motions, but deviates from it considerably. This is a certain proof that it did not develop from the common basic material and acquire its motion from the sinking down of this material, but arose from the planet long after its complete development and, through the orbital force implanted in it, as the planet's separated part, acquired from the planet's axial rotation a related motion and direction.

The pleasure of having grasped one of the strangest peculiarities of the heavens in the full extent of its nature and development has involved us in an extensive discussion. With the permission of our indulgent readers, let us keep going wherever we like, all the way to excess, so that after we have permitted ourselves a pleasant sort of arbitrary opinion with a kind of freedom from restraint, we will turn back to the truth once more with that much more caution and care.

Could we not imagine that the Earth, exactly like Saturn, once had a ring? It might have arisen from its outer layer precisely as Saturn's did and have maintained itself a long time, since the Earth had gone from a much faster rotation than the present one to the existing rate, for who knows what reasons. Or we could attribute the building of it to the common basic material sinking down according to the rules which we explained above, which we must not take so strictly if we want to indulge in our liking for the unusual. But what a supply of beautiful explanations and consequences such an idea offers us! A ring around the Earth! How beautiful the sight for those who were made to live on Earth as a paradise. How much comfort for those whom nature was to greet with a smile on all sides! But this is still nothing in comparison to the confirmation which such a hypothesis can derive from the ancient lore of the creation story, no small recommendation for approval among those people who believe they are not dishonouring revelation but endorsing it when they use it to ennoble the excess displays of their wit. The waters of the firmament, which the Mosaic account talks of, have already caused interpreters no small problem. Would it not be possible for us to use this ring to assist ourselves out of this difficulty? This ring undoubtedly consisted of vapours rich in water. And in addition to the advantage which it could provide for the first inhabitants on the earth, we have the fact that it was, when necessary, capable of breaking apart in order to punish the world, which had made itself unworthy of such beauty, with deluges. Either a comet, whose power of attraction brought the rule-bound movements of ring's parts into total confusion, or the cooling in the region where it was positioned united its scattered vapour particles and hurled them down upon the ground in the most horrifying of all inundations. We understand readily what the consequences of this were. The whole world went under water and absorbed, in addition to the foreign and volatile vapours of this unnatural rain, that slow poison which brought all creatures closer to death and destruction. From now on the shape of a pale light bow vanished from the horizon, and the new world, which could never remember what this looked like without experiencing terror before this fearful instrument of the divine revenge, saw perhaps with no less dismay in the first rainfall that coloured bow which seems to develop its shape like the first one, but which through the covenant of a forgiving heaven was to be a sign of grace and a memorial to the lasting establishment of the now changed surface of the Earth. The similarity in the form of this memorial sign to the event I have described could make such a hypothesis appealing for those people who follow the prevailing inclination to bring the wonders of revelation into one system with the orderly laws of nature. I find it more advisable completely to sacrifice the transitory approval which such agreement can arouse for the true pleasure which comes from the perception of regular interconnections when physical analogies reinforce each other in the designation of physical truths.

PART TWO. SECTION SIX

Concerning the Lights of the Zodiac

The sun is surrounded by a subtle and vaporous essence, going around it at the level of its equatorial plane up to a great altitude, with only a small extension on both sides. So far as this is concerned, we cannot be certain whether, as M. de Mairan pictures it, it touches the outer surface of the sun in the shape of an uneven polished lens (*figura lenticulari*) or, like Saturn's ring, is always located at a distance away.[36*] It may be either of these. But sufficient similarity remains to establish a comparison of this phenomenon with Saturn's ring and to infer a common origin. If this spread out material is something flowing out from the sun, and it is most probable to consider it in that manner, then we cannot miss the cause which has brought it to the common plane of the sun's equator. The lightest and most volatile material, which the sun's fire raises and has for a long time already raised from its outer surface will through the same process expand far over it and remain suspended at a distance, according to how light it is, where the forward driving effect of its rays comes into an equilibrium with the gravitational power of these vapour particles, or they will be reinforced by the stream of newer particles which continuously come up to them from below. Now, because the sun, as it rotates on its axis, imparts to these vapours torn away from its outer surface their regular motion, the latter maintain a certain orbital momentum by which, in accordance with the central laws, they are driven from both sides in their circular motion to intersect the sun's extrapolated equatorial plane. And thus, because they are driven down to this in equal quantities from both hemi-spheres, they pile up there with equal forces and form an extended flat surface on the designated solar equatorial plane.

But regardless of this similarity with Saturn's ring, there remains a fundamental difference, which causes the phenomenon of the zodiac light to differ considerably from Saturn's ring. The particles of Saturn's ring maintain themselves in freely suspended circular orbits through the implanted rotating motion; but the particles of the zodiacal light are kept at their altitude by the power of the sun's rays, without which their inherent motion from the axial rotation of the sun would be far from sufficient to hold them in free orbits and to prevent their falling down. For since the centrifugal force of the axial rotation on the surface of the sun is not even 1/40000 of the power of attraction, these vapours which have moved upward would have to be 40000 semi-solar diameters away from it in order to find at such a distance a power of gravitation which could for the first time achieve an equilibrium with their allotted motion. Thus, we are certain that this solar phenomenon is not given to it in the same way as Saturn's ring.

Nevertheless, there remains a not insignificant probability that this solar necklace perhaps acknowledges the same cause which nature collectively acknowledges, namely, the development out of the universal basic material, whose parts, since they were suspended all around the highest regions of the solar world, first moved down to the sun in a late descent only after the full and complete development of the entire system, with weaker curved motion, but still from west to east, and, thanks to this type of orbital path, intersected the extrapolated solar equatorial plane. By their accumulation there on both sides, once this motion stopped, they occupied a plane stretching out in this location, where they now maintain themselves always at the same altitude, in part through the power of repulsion of the sun's rays, in part through the real orbital motion they have attained. The present explanation has no value other than what one gives to an assumption and makes no demand other than for an arbitrary acceptance. The judgment of the reader may direct itself to that option which seems to him most worthy of adopting.

PART TWO. SECTION SEVEN

Concerning Creation in the Total Extent of its Infinity both in Space and Time

With its immeasurable size and its infinite multiplicity and beauty radiating out in all directions around it, the cosmic structure presents a silent wonder. If the picture of all this perfection now stirs the imaginative power, from a different perspective the understanding derives another type of delight, when it observes how so much splendour, such an enormous greatness, flows out from one single universal rule in an eternal and justified order. The planetary structure in which the sun at the centre makes the spheres found in its system orbit in eternal circles by means of its powerful force of attraction is entirely developed, as we have seen, from the originally distributed basic stuff of all planetary material. All the fixed stars which the eye discovers in the high recesses of the heavens and which appear to display a kind of extravagance are suns and central points of similar systems. The analogy permits us here no doubt that these were built and developed in the same manner as the one in which we find ourselves, from the smallest particles of elementary materials which filled empty space, this infinite extension of the Divine Presence.

Now, if all planets and planetary systems acknowledge the same sort of origin, if the power of attraction is unlimited and universal, if the power of repulsion of the elements is similarly continuously at work, and if, in comparison with the Infinite, the large and the small are both small, should not the cosmic structures have acquired in a like manner an interconnecting relationship and a systematic coordination among themselves, as the celestial bodies of our solar system have on a small scale, like Saturn, Jupiter, and the Earth, which are special systems on their own and yet are linked together amongst themselves as parts in an even greater system? If we take one point in the infinite space in which all the suns of the Milky Way were developed, a point around which, for some unknown reason, the first development of nature out of chaos began, then at that location the largest mass and a body of the most exceptional power of attraction will have arisen, which thus would have become capable of forcing everything in a huge sphere around it in the process of developing systems to move down towards it as their central point and to build around it on a large scale a system like the one which the same elementary basic material which developed the planets created around the sun on a small scale. Observation makes this supposition almost indubitable. The army of stars, through its orientation in relation to a common plane, makes up a system just as much as the planets of our solar system do around the sun. The Milky Way is the zodiac of these higher world orders, which deviate from its zone as little as possible. Its band is always illuminated by their lights, just as the zodiac of planets is illuminated here and there by the shining of these spheres, although only in a very few points. Each one of these suns, along with its orbiting planets, makes up a particular system of its own, but this does not prevent them from being parts of an even greater system, just as Jupiter or Saturn, in spite of their own satellites, are confined in the systematic arrangement of an even greater cosmic structure. Can we not acknowledge with such a precise harmony in the arrangement the same cause and manner of production?

Now, if the fixed stars make up a system whose extent is determined by the sphere of attraction of the body located at the centre, will not more solar systems and, so to speak, more Milky Ways have arisen, which were produced in the limitless field of space? With astonishment we have seen figures in the heavens which are nothing other than such systems of fixed stars restricted to a common plane, such Milky Ways, if I may express myself in this way, which present themselves to our eyes in different positions with a weakly glimmering elliptical shape appropriate to their infinite distance away. They are systems, so to speak, of infinitely more infinite diameter than the diameter of our solar system, but without doubt they arose in the same way, are organized and arranged by the same causes, and maintain themselves by the same dynamics as our system in its arrangement.

If we see these systems of stars once more as links on collective nature's great chain, we have just as many reasons as before to think of them in a mutual relationship and in combinations which, thanks to the laws governing throughout all nature, constitute the first development of a new and even greater system, controlled by the force of attraction of a body with incomparably more forceful attractive power than were all former systems, from the centre of their rule-bound positions. The force of attraction, the cause of the systematic arrangement among the fixed stars of the Milky Way, still works even at the distance of these very cosmic structures to bring them out of their positions and to bury the world in an unavoidable impending chaos, if the allotted rule-bound forces of motion did not develop a counterweight to the force of attraction and produce from the combination of the two of them that relationship which is the basis of the systematic arrangement. The force of attraction is without doubt a characteristic of matter as widely extensive as the coexistence which creates space, because it unites substances through a mutual dependency, or, to speak more precisely, the power of attraction is just this common relationship which unites the parts of nature in space. Thus, it expands through the total extent of space right into all its infinite distances. If the light from these remote systems, which is only an impressed movement, reaches us, must not the power of attraction, this primordial origin of motion, which antedates all motion, which requires no foreign cause and cannot be halted by any barrier, because it works in the innermost core of matter in the universal calm of nature without any external impulse, must not the force of attraction, I say, have set in motion these systems of fixed stars with their material in an undeveloped scattering in the first movements of nature, regardless of their immeasurable distances away, a motion which, as we have seen on a small scale, is the very origin of the systematic union and the enduring permanence of its links, the factor which keeps them secure from collapse?

But then what will finally be the end of the systematic arrangements? Where will creation itself cease? We well note that to think of creation in relation to the power of the Infinite Being means it must have no boundaries at all. We come no nearer to the infinity of the creative power of God if we enclose the space of its revelation in a sphere described with the radius of the Milky Way than if we enclose it in a ball with a diameter an inch long. Everything finite which has its limits and a determined relationship to unity is equally far away way from infinity. Now, it would be absurd to set the Divine into effective action with an infinitely small part of His creative capacity and to imagine His infinite power, the treasure house of a true infinity of natures and worlds, incapacitated and locked into an eternal deficiency in practice. Is it not much more appropriate or, to express the matter better, is it not necessary to present the embodiment of creation as something which cannot be measured by any standard, which is how it must be, in order to bear witness to that power? For this reason the field of the revelation of divine properties is just as infinite as these properties themselves.[37] Eternity is not sufficient to bear witness to the Highest Essence where it is not united with spatial infinity. It is true that attraction, shape, beauty, and perfection are relationships of the basic elements and of substance making up the material of the cosmic structure. And we notice it in the arrangement which the wisdom of God still effects at all times. It is also most appropriate to the wisdom of God that these develop themselves as an unforced consequence out of the universal laws implanted in them. And therefore we can with good reason establish that the order and arrangement of the cosmic structure take place gradually from the supply of created natural matter in a temporal succession. But the basic material itself, whose properties and forces form the basis for all changes, is an immediate result of the Diving Being and itself must be simultaneously so rich and so perfect that the development of its compositions could in the flow of eternity extend over a plan enclosing in itself everything which can be, a plan which has no dimensions, which is, in short, infinite.

Now, if creation is spatially infinite or at least was really already that from the beginning as far as its material is concerned or according to its form or development is prepared to become so, cosmic space will become active with worlds without number and without end. Will that systematic union, which we have previously mentioned in particular among all the particles, now extend to the totality and the universe collectively, the All of nature, be tied together in a single system through the union of the power of attraction and the centrifugal force? I say yes. If nothing but separate cosmic structures without having among themselves any unifying relationship to a totality were the only things present, then, if we were to assume this chain of links as truly endless, we could imagine that a precise equality in the power of attraction in its parts on all sides could keep this system secure from destruction which the inner reciprocal force of attraction threatens them with. But this condition needs to be determined with such precise measurement of the distances carefully weighed against the power of attraction that the slightest displacement would bring destruction to the universe and would deliver it over to collapse. The time would be long, but finally it would have to come to an end. A cosmic arrangement which did not keep itself going in the absence of a miracle does not have the mark of permanence which is the sign of God's choice. Thus, we find it much more appropriate if we make of creation collectively a single system creating all worlds and world structures, which fill all infinite space and which are made with reference to a single central point. A scattered confusion of cosmic structures, which might be separated from each other by distances as great as you like, would have an unhindered tendency to rush to dissolution and destruction, unless there were in place a certain arrangement in relation to a common mid-point, the centre of the power of attraction in the universe and, because of systematic movements, the foundation point of all nature.

Around this universal central point of downward movement in all nature, both developed and raw, at which is undoubtedly located the cluster with the most extensive power of attraction, encompassing in its sphere of attraction all worlds and ordered systems which time has produced and eternity will produce, we can probably assume that nature initiated its development and also that there the systems have accumulated in the greatest density but that further away from that mid-point, the systems are lost in ever increasing stages of disorder in the infinity of space. We could assume this principle from the analogy to our solar system, and this arrangement can, in any case, serve to show that at great distances not only the common central body but also all the systems moving in close proximity to it collectively combine their power of attraction and, so to speak, out of a single cluster exercise their effect on systems even further away. This will then help us to grasp all nature in the entire infinity of its extent in one single system.

Now, in order to trace the foundation of this universal system of nature from the mechanical laws of matter striving to develop, in the endless space of the dispersed elementary basic material some point or other of this matter must have accumulated with the greatest density, so as to have assembled through the development going on there more than anywhere else a mass which serves as the foundation point. It is indeed the case that in an infinite space no point can really justifiably be called the centre. But thanks to a certain relationship based upon the inherent levels of density of the primordial stuff, according to which at the time of creation this material had accumulated more densely particularly at one certain location and its density had grown increasingly scattered with the distance away from this point, such a place can have the privilege of being called the centre. And it truly does become that through the development of the central mass because of the strongest power of attraction in it. It becomes the point to which all the remaining basic material incorporated in particular developments moves down, and thus, no matter how far unfolding nature may extend, it creates out of the entire totality only a single system in the infinite sphere of creation.

However, what is important and what, provided that it wins approval, is worthy of the greatest attention is the fact that, as a consequence of the ordering of nature in this system of ours, creation or, rather, the development of nature, first begins with this central point and with constantly progressive steps extends itself gradually out into all the further distances, in order to fill limitless space with worlds and order in the progress of eternity. Let us contemplate this picture with quiet pleasure for a moment. I find nothing which can elevate the human spirit to a more noble astonishment than this part of the theory concerning the successive completion of creation, as it opens up for humanity a glimpse into the unending field of the Almighty. If people grant me that the matter which is the building stuff of all worlds is not homogeneous in the entire infinite space of the Divine Presence but was distributed in accordance with a certain law which perhaps concerned itself with the density of the particles and according to which with the increasing distance from a certain point, like the location of the densest accumulation, the scattering in this primordial material increases, then in the original movement of nature the development will have started in the region next to this centre and then, in a progressive temporal sequence, the more remote space will have gradually developed worlds and planetary structures in a systematic arrangement linked to this centre. Any one finite period, whose duration is connected to the magnitude of the completed work, will, in its development, always produce a sphere only a finite distance from this central point. The remaining infinite part will meanwhile still be combating confusion and chaos and will be that much further from a condition of complete development, the further away it is located from the sphere of already developed nature. As a consequence of this, although from the place where we reside we have a view into, as it seems, a fully completed world and, so to speak, into an infinite host of planetary structures which are systematically united, nevertheless we find ourselves in reality only in proximity to the mid-point of all nature, where it has already developed out of chaos and attained its appropriate completion. If we could step over to a certain sphere, we would there witness chaos and the scattering of the elements, which, in proportion to their proximity to the central point partly leave their raw condition and are closer to the completion of their development. But with the degrees of distance away they gradually are lost in a total scattering. We would see how the limitless space of the Divine Presence, in which we find the store of all possible natural developments, buried in a quiet night, full of matter to serve as the stuff of worlds to be produced in the future and full of the initiating energies to bring it into motion. With a weak stimulus these begin those movements with which immeasurable nature of this barren space is still to be activated in the future. Perhaps a succession of millions of years and centuries is to flow by before the sphere of developed nature in which we find ourselves grows to the perfection now inherent in it. And perhaps an even longer period will elapse before nature will take such a wide step into chaos. But the sphere of developed nature is ceaselessly occupied with expanding itself. Creation is not the work of a moment. After creation made a beginning by producing infinite substances and materials, it is efficacious with constantly increasing degrees of fecundity throughout the total succession of eternity. Millions and whole mountains of millions of centuries will pass, during which new worlds and new world systems will constantly develop and reach completion, one after the other, in the expanses far from the central point of nature. Regardless of the systematic arrangement among their parts, they will have a common relationship to the central point, which became the first point of development and the centre of creation through the capacity of the power of attraction of its preponderant mass. The infinity of the future temporal succession, for which eternity is inexhaustible, will thoroughly activate all the spaces of God's presence and gradually set it into rule-bound regularity, appropriate to the excellence of its design. And if, in a daring picture, we could, so to speak, sum up all eternity in a single idea, then we would be able to see the entire infinite space filled with world systems and a completed creation. However, because, in fact, in the temporal sequence of eternity the part to come is always infinite and the part gone by is finite, the sphere of developed nature is always only an infinitely small part of that being which has in it the seeds of future worlds and strives to develop itself out of the raw condition of chaos in long or short periods of time. Creation is never complete. True, it once began, but it will never cease. It is always busy bringing forth new natural phenomena, new things, and new worlds. The work which it brings into being has a relationship to the time nature expends on it. It needs no less than an eternity to bring the entire limitless extent of infinite spaces alive with numberless worlds without end. We can say about creation what the noblest of the German poets writes about eternity.

Eternity! Who knows you?

For you worlds are days and humans moments.

Perhaps the thousandth sun is now turning

And thousands still remain behind.

Like a clock animated by a weight,

A sun rushes by, moved by the power of God.

Its impulse comes to an end, and another throbs.

But you remain and do not count them.

(von Haller)[38*]

There is no small pleasure in letting one's imagination roam over the limits of completed creation into the space of chaos and to see half raw nature in the vicinity of the sphere of the developed world losing itself gradually through all the stages and shades of incompleteness in the whole of undeveloped space. But is that not a culpable daring, people will say, to throw down a hypothesis and to praise it as a design for the delight of the understanding, a plan which is perhaps merely too arbitrary when we claim that nature is only developed to an infinitely small extent and limitless spaces are still at strife with chaos, so that they will display in the succession of future times entire hosts of worlds and world systems in all appropriate order and beauty? I am not so devoted to the consequences which my theory offers that I should not acknowledge how the conjecture about the successive expansion of creation through endless spaces containing material for that purpose cannot fully counter the objection that it is beyond proof. Meanwhile, however, I hope from those who are in a position to appreciate levels of probability, that such a map of infinity, although it touches on a plan that seems destined to be concealed forever from human understanding, will not for that reason immediately be seen as a fantasy, especially when we take the analogy as an aid which must always show us the way in such cases where the understanding lacks the guiding threads of indubitable proofs.

However, we can still support the analogy with reasons worthy of consideration. The insight of the reader who, I may flatter myself, will approve will perhaps be able to multiply these reasons with even more important ones. For when we consider that creation does not bring with it a characteristic stability, insofar as it does not establish for the common striving of the power of attraction, which works through all its parts, such a precise universal modification which can sufficiently withstand the tendency of this power to bring destruction and disorder, unless creation allotted the orbital forces which, in combination with the central tendency, fixes in place a systematic arrangement, then we will be required to assume a common central point for the entire totality of worlds, a point which holds all the parts of this totality together in a united relationship and makes only one system out of the entire essence of nature. If, in addition to this, we pursue the idea of the development of world bodies out of scattered elementary matter, as we have outlined the subject previously, but do not limit the idea here to one particular system, and instead extend it to all nature, then we will have to imagine such a distribution of the basic matter in the space of primordial chaos which naturally involves a central point of all creation, so that in the latter the effective mass which encompasses all nature collectively in its sphere of attraction brings the material together and makes the general relationship work, so that all worlds make up only one single structure. However, in limitless space a sort of distribution of the primordial basic material can hardly be imagined which is to establish a true central point towards which collective nature is to sink down, other than one in which the distribution is arranged according to a law of increasing disorder from this point out into all the far distances. This law, however, at the same time establishes a difference in the time which a system requires in the different regions of limitless space to come to its mature development. This period is shorter, the closer the location of the development of a world system is to the centre of creation, because in the closer region the elements of matter have accumulated more thickly; by contrast, the further the distance away from this centre, the longer the time required, because the particles there are more scattered and are later in coming together in order to develop.

If people consider the entire hypothesis that I have drawn up to the full extent of what I have said, as well as what I will still actually present, they will at least not think that the boldness of its claims cannot be excused. We can estimate the inevitable tendency which each world system brought to completion has to move gradually towards its destruction among the reasons which can establish that the universe, in contrast to that destruction, will be fertile with worlds in other regions, to make up for the deficiency which it has suffered in one location. Although the entire part of nature that we know about is only equivalent to an atom in comparison with what remains hidden above or below our horizons, it nevertheless confirms this fertility of nature, which is without limit, because it is nothing other than the working out of the Divine Omnipotence itself. Numberless animals and plants are destroyed every day and are a sacrifice to mortality. But nature, with its inexhaustible productive capacity, creates just as many over again in other places and fills up the emptiness. Considerable parts of the earth's surface which we inhabit are being buried once again in the sea out of which they were pulled at a favourable time. But in other places, nature makes up for the loss and produces other areas which were hidden deep under water, in order to extend over these areas new riches from her fertile store. In the same way, worlds and world systems go under and are swallowed up in the abyss of eternity. But, on the other hand, creation is always busy organizing new developments in other regions of the heavens and making up for the loss with advantage.

We should not be amazed to admit mortality even in the greatness of God's works. Everything finite, with a starting point and a cause, has within itself the mark of its limited nature. It must die and have an end. On account of the excellence of its arrangements, the duration of a world system has a inherent permanence which, according to our ideas, comes close to a limitless time span. Perhaps a thousand, perhaps millions of centuries will not destroy it. But because vanity, which adheres to finite natures, works continuously for their destruction, so eternity will hold in itself all possible periods, in order finally to bring about through a gradual decay the moment of its collapse. Newton, this great admirer of the attributes of God in the perfection of His works, the one who with the deepest insight into the excellence of nature combined the greatest devotion for the revelation of Divine Omnipotence, saw himself compelled to predict the decay of nature through the natural tendency which the mechanics of movement had to bring it about. If a systematic arrangement comes close to a state of confusion as the essential result of its fallibility over a long period of time, even in the very smallest part that we can imagine, then in the endless current of eternity there must be a moment in time when this gradual diminution exhausts all movement.

However, we must not lament the destruction of a cosmic structure as a real loss for nature. It demonstrates its richness with a kind of dissipation which, while a few parts pay tribute to mortality, maintains it undamaged in the full extent of nature's perfection with numberless new productions. What a countless number of flowers and insects a single cold day destroys. But how little we miss them, regardless of the fact that they are beautifully natural works of art and proofs of Divine Omnipotence! In another place, this death will be made up once again with excess. Humanity, which appears to be the masterpiece of creation, is itself no exception to this law. Nature shows that it is just as rich and just as inexhaustible in the production of the most excellent of creatures as it is of the most insignificant and that even their destruction is a necessary shadow amid the multiplicity of its suns, because producing humanity cost nature nothing. The harmful effects of infected air, earthquakes, and inundations wipe out entire peoples from the surface of the earth, but it does not appear that nature has suffered any damage because of this. In the same way, entire worlds and systems leave the stage when they have played out their roles. The infinite nature of creation is large enough that it looks upon a world or a Milky Way of worlds in comparison with it as we look upon a flower or an insect in comparison with the Earth. In the meantime, while nature beautifies eternity with changing scenes, God remains busy with a ceaseless creation, forming material for the development of even greater worlds.

Who sees with equal eye, as God of all,

A hero perish, or a sparrow fall,

Atoms or systems into ruin hurl'd,

And now a bubble burst, and now a world.

(Pope)[39*]

Let us therefore get our eyes used to these terrifying collapses as the customary methods of providence and look at them with even a kind of pleasure. In fact, nothing is more appropriate to the richness of nature than this. For when a world system in the long sequence of its duration exhausts all the multiplicity which its organization can contain, when it has now become an expendable link in the chain of being, then nothing is more fitting than that it play the last role in the drama of the passing changes of the universe, which is part of every finite thing, namely, it gives up what it owes to mortality. Nature demonstrates, as mentioned, even in the small parts of its being this rule of its processes, which eternal fate has prescribed for it on a large scale. And I repeat that the magnitude of what is to pass away is in this matter not the slightest obstacle, for everything large becomes small. Yes, it becomes, so to speak, just a point, if we compare it with the infinity which creation will present throughout the succession of eternity in limitless space.

It appears that for worlds, as for all natural things, this fatal ending is subject to a certain law whose consideration gives the theory a new appropriate feature. According to this principle, the fatal ending originates among those celestial bodies located closest to the central point of the universe, just as the production and development first began close to this mid-point. From there the decay and destruction gradually work their way outward into the further distances, in order to bury all the world which has gone through its time, by means of a gradual decline in its motions, finally in a single chaos. On the other hand, nature is ceaselessly busy on the borders opposite to the developed world producing worlds from the raw material of the scattered elements, and while nature on one side close to the mid-point is aging, so on the other side it is young and fertile in new generations. The developed world, according to this, finds itself in a limited space in the middle, between the ruins of what has been destroyed and the chaos of undeveloped nature. And if we imagine, as is probable, that a world already growing to completion could last a longer time than it required to become developed, then the extent of the universe will in general increase, regardless of all the destruction which mortality ceaselessly brings about.

However, if we are still willing to allow an idea which is just as probable as the arrangement of the divine works is appropriate, then the satisfaction aroused by such a description of nature's changes will be raised to the highest level of delight. Can we not believe that nature, which was capable of setting itself up out of chaos into a rule-bound order and a finely tuned system, is equally in a position just as easily to organize itself once more out of the new chaos, into which the diminution of its motions has lowered it, and to renew the first unity? Might the springs which brought the scattered material stuff into motion and order not be able once more to be made effective by extended forces after the motionlessness of the machine has rendered them inert and, through the very same universal principles, be harmoniously restricted in the way in which the original development was produced? We will not examine the matter very long before conceding this, if we consider that, after the final exhaustion of the orbital motions in the cosmic structure has thrown the planets and comets together down onto the sun, the sun's fire must increase immeasurably through the mixing of so many large bodies, especially since the distant spheres of the solar system, as a consequence of the theory we have previously established, contain the lightest and most effective fuel in all nature. This fire, given the highest intensity by the new fuel and the most volatile materials, will without doubt not only break down everything into the smallest elements once more but will also in this way spread them out with an expansive force appropriate to the heat and at a velocity which is not weakened by any resistance in the middle region. It will scatter and spread them out once again in the same wide space which they occupied before the first development of nature, so that, after the intensity of the central fire is damped down by the almost total destruction of the sun's mass, through the combination of the forces of attraction and repulsion the old generations, together with their systematically interrelated movements, will be repeated with no less regularity and will present a new cosmic structure. Thus, when a particular planetary system suffers destruction in this way and has been re-established by the fundamental forces, when indeed this play repeats itself again as before, then finally the period approaches when, in the same manner, the large system of which the fixed stars are links will collectively experience chaos through the lessening of it motions. We will have even fewer doubts here that the uniting of such an endless number of rich fiery storehouses as these burning suns, together with their attendant planets, will scatter the material making up their masses, which has been dissolved by the indescribable inferno, in the old space of the sphere in which they developed, and there the materials will provide for new developments through the same mechanical laws. As a result of this, the barren space can become active with worlds and systems once more. When we follow this phoenix of nature, which is only burned up in order to live again, renewed once more from its ashes, through all infinity of times and spaces, when we see how it progresses, even in the region where it decays and grows old, inexhaustible in new phenomena and, on another border of creation, in the space of undeveloped raw matter, with constant strides to unfold the plans of the divine revelation in order to fill eternity as well as all spaces with its wonders, then the spirit thinking about all this is lost in deep astonishment. But still dissatisfied with such great events as these, whose mortality cannot adequately satisfy the soul, he wishes to learn at close hand about that Being whose understanding and whose greatness are the fountain of that light which extends itself over all nature, as it were, from a central point. With what kind of awe must the soul not contemplate its very own essence, when it observes that it is to survive even all these changes. It can say to itself what the philosophical poet says concerning eternity:

When then a second night will bury this world,

When from everything nothing remains but the place,

When still many other heavens bright with other stars

Will have completed their course,

You will be as young as now, just as far from death

As eternally alive as now.

(von Haller)

O how happy the soul, when among the tumult of the elements and the ruins of nature, it is at any time set on a height from which it can see rushing past, as it were, below its feet the devastation which the frailty of worldly things brings about! A blessedness which the understanding is never permitted to dare to expect teaches us to hope with conviction for the revelation. For when the bindings which keep us tied to the vanity of living creatures fall away in the moment established for the transformation of our being, then the immortal soul, freed from its dependency on finite things, will find in the companionship with the infinite essence the enjoyment of true blessedness. All nature, which has a universal harmonious relationship to the pleasure of the Deity, can fill that reasoning creature with nothing but eternal satisfaction, which finds itself united with this original fountain of all perfection. Nature seen from this central point will show on all side nothing but security, nothing but propriety. The changing natural scenes are not able to upset the calm bliss of a soul which has once been lifted up to such a height. While it already tastes in advance this condition with a sweet hope, it can set its mouth to work on those hymns of praise with which in future all eternity will resound.

When Nature fails, and day and night

Divide thy works no more,

My ever grateful heart, O Lord,

Thy mercy shall adore.
Through all Eternity to Thee
A joyful song I'll raise;
For, oh! Eternity's too short
To utter all Thy praise.
(Addison)[40*]

PART TWO. SUPPLEMENT TO SECTION SEVEN

Universal Theory and History of the Sun in General

There is still a major question the answer to which is essential in the natural theory of the heavens and in a complete cosmogony, namely, why will the middle point of every system consist of a burning body? Our planetary system has the sun as the central body, and the fixed stars visible to us are, all things considered, mid-points of similar systems.

In order to grasp why in the development of a planetary structure the body serving as the mid-point of the power of attraction must have a fiery body, while the other circular structures in the sphere of its power of attraction remain dark and cold world bodies, we need only remember the way in which a planetary system is produced, something we have outlined in detail in the previous parts. In the greatly expanded space in which the spread out elementary basic material prepares developments and systematic movements, the planets and comets are built up only out of those parts of the elementary basic matter moving downward towards the central point of the force of attraction which, through their fall and the reciprocal interaction of the particles collectively, were precisely adjusted for the velocity and direction required for orbital motion. This portion is, as has been established above, the smallest part of the total amount of matter moving downward and, in fact, is only what is left over of the denser varieties, which have been able to attain the degree of precision from the resistance of the other parts. In this mixture there are particularly light types of matter floating around, which, hindered by the resistance of space, do not in their descent push on through to the velocity appropriate to periodic orbits and which therefore, given the weakness of their orbital impetus, will all collectively fall down to the central body. Now, because these lighter and volatile parts are also the most effective at maintaining a fire, we see that, with their addition the body at the central point of the system has the distinction of becoming a flaming sphere, in a word, a sun. By contrast, the heavier and inert materials and those particles which are poor fuel for a fire will make planets which are robbed of these properties merely cold and dead clusters.

This addition of such light materials is also the reason why the sun ends up with a smaller specific density, so that it is even four times less dense than our Earth, the third planet away from the sun, although it is natural to think that in this central point of the planetary structure, as its lowest point, the heaviest and densest sorts of material are to be found and that without the addition of such a large amount of the lightest matter its density would exceed that of all planets.

The intermixing of the denser and heavier types of elements with these lightest and most volatile ones serves also to make the central body suitable for the most intense blaze which is to burn and maintain itself on its outer surface. For we know that the fire in whose nourishing fuel dense materials are found mixed in with volatile matter has the advantage of a greater intensity than those flames which are sustained only by the light varieties of matter. However, this mixture of some heavier sorts among the lighter types is a necessary consequence of our theory about the development of world bodies. It even benefits from the fact that the force of the heat does not immediately scatter the burning material on the outer surface and that the fire will be gradually and constantly fed by the fuel supply within the planet.

Now that we have resolved the question why the central body of a large system of stars is a flaming sphere, that is, a sun, it appears not irrelevant to concern ourselves with this subject some more and to investigate the state of such a celestial body in a careful examination, especially since the assumptions can here be derived from more effective reasons than are commonly used where investigations into the composition of distant celestial bodies are concerned.

To begin with, I firmly maintain that we can have no doubt that the sun is truly a flaming body and not a mass of smouldering and glowing material heated to the highest degree, as a few people have wished to infer from certain difficulties they claim to find in connection with the former view. For when we consider that a flaming fire has this fundamental distinction over and above every other form of heat, that it, so to speak, works on its own, instead of being diminished or exhausting itself by sharing its heat and that through this it rather acquires even more strength and intensity and thus requires only material and fuel to maintain itself so as to keep going continuously, whereas, by contrast, the glow of a mass heated to the highest degree is in a merely passive condition, which by the common interaction with the material in contact with it constantly diminishes and has no forces of its own to expand from a small beginning or to revive itself again should it diminish, when we consider this, I say, (and I am not mentioning the other reasons) then we will already be sufficiently capable of seeing that that property must, in all probability, be attributed to the sun, the fountain of light and heat in every planetary system.

Now, if the sun, or rather suns in general, are flaming spheres, then the first requirement of their outer surfaces, which we can deduce from this point, is that air must be found on them, because without air no fire burns. This condition gives rise to remarkable consequences. For, first of all, if we first establish the atmosphere of the sun and its weight in relationship to the sun's cluster, how compressed will this air be and how capable will it become on account of this very compression to maintain the most intense level of fire through its elasticity *[Federkraft]*? According to all assumptions, in this atmosphere, the clouds of smoke from the materials broken up by the flames (which, we cannot doubt, have a mixture of coarse and lighter particles in them), once they have risen up to an altitude which keeps the air cooler for them, fall down with heavy rains of pitch and sulphur and provide new fuel for the flames. This very atmosphere is also, for the same reasons as on our Earth, not free from the motions of the winds, which, however, according to this view, must far exceed in intensity everything that the power of the imagination can merely picture. When some region or other on the surface of the sun, either through the suffocating force of the vapours pouring out or because of the limited supply of combustible material, sees the eruption of flames diminish, then the air above cools to some extent, and since it is contracting, makes room for the air in the immediate vicinity to rush into its space with a force proportional to its expansion and to re-ignite the extinguished flames.

However, all flames always consume a great deal of air, and there is no doubt that the elasticity of the volatile elements of the air which encircle the sun must, in this way, over time suffer not insignificant damage. If we apply here on a large scale what Mr. Hales has, through careful research, proven in this matter with respect to the effect of flames in our atmosphere, then we can see the ceaseless striving of the particles of smoke coming out of the flames to destroy the elasticity *[Elasticität]* of the sun's atmosphere as a serious problem, the solution to which is associated with difficulties.[41*] Because the flames which burn over the entire surface of the sun themselves consume the air essential for their combustion, the sun is in danger of going out entirely when the largest portion of its atmosphere has been consumed. True, from the dissolution of certain materials fire also produces air. But the experiments demonstrate that more is always consumed than produced. In fact, when a part of the sun's fire under the suffocating vapours is deprived of the air which serves to maintain it, then, as we have already noted, violent storms destroy the vapours and work to carry them away. But on a large scale we will be able to make the replacement of this necessary element understandable in the following manner, if we bear in mind that in the case of a flaming fire the heat acts almost exclusively above it and only a little underneath it. When it has suffocated for reasons we have cited, its intensity turns to the inside of the sun's body and forces the deep hollow places to let the air enclosed in their depths break out and renew the fire once more. If, using that freedom permitted in dealing with such unknown circumstances, we assume there are in these depths special materials which, like saltpetre, are inexhaustibly rich with elastic air, then the sun's fire will not be able to suffer easily from a deficiency for an extremely long period, because the supply of air is constantly renewed.

However, we do see the clear marks of mortality also in this inestimably valuable fire which nature sets up as the world's torch. There comes a time when it will be extinguished. The dispersal of the most volatile and finest materials, which, scattered by the intensity of the heat, never turn back again, and add to the stuff of the zodiacal light, the accumulation of incombustible and burned out materials, for example the ashes on the surface, and finally the lack of air will establish an end point when the sun's flames at some point in the future go out and eternal darkness will take over in its place, now the central point of light and life of the entire planetary structure. The alternating impulse of its fires by which it opens new caverns to become vital again and through which it renews itself perhaps several times before being overcome could provide an explanation for the disappearance and renewed illumination of a few fixed stars. There would be suns which are close to being extinguished and which still strive a number of times to live on from their debris. This explanation may win approval or not, but we will certainly let this idea serve for us to recognize that since, in one way or another, an unavoidable decay threatens the perfection of all planetary systems, we will find no difficulty with the laws referred to previously concerning their collapse through the tendency of the mechanical arrangement, which will, nonetheless, be particularly worthy of acceptance, since it brings with it the seeds of a renewal in the interaction with chaos.

Finally, let us use the power of our imaginations to picture such an amazingly strange object as a burning sun, as it were, at close hand. We see at a glance wide seas of fire, raising their flames towards the heavens, frantic storms, whose fury doubles the intensity of the burning seas, while they themselves make the fiery seas overflow their banks, sometimes covering the higher regions of this world body, sometimes allowing them to sink back down within their borders. Burned out rocks extend their frightening peaks up above the flaming chasms, whose inundation or exposure by the seething fiery element causes the alternating appearance and disappearance of the sun spots. Thick vapours which suffocate the fire, lifted up by the power of the winds, make dark clouds, which in fiery downpours crash back down again and as burning streams flow from the heights of firm land of the sun into the flaming valleys, the cracking of the elements, the debris of burned up material and nature wrestling with destruction — these bring about, along with the most awful condition of their disorder, the beauty of the world and the benefits for its creatures.[42*]

If, then, the mid-points of all large planetary systems are burning bodies, then we can assume that this is most particularly the case with the central body of that immeasurable system which comprises the fixed stars. Now, if this body, whose mass must be proportional to the magnitude of its system, were a self-illuminating body or a sun, will it not be visible with a exceptional illumination and size? However, we do not see anything like such a predominantly different fixed star shining out among the host in the heavens. In fact, we must not think it strange if such a thing does not occur. If the mass of such a sun was equivalent to a mass 10000 times greater than our sun, nevertheless, if we assume its distance away was 100 times greater than the distance of Sirius, it could appear no larger or brighter than Sirius.

However, perhaps it is reserved for future ages to discover at some later date at least the region where the central point of the system of fixed stars to which our sun belongs is located or perhaps really to determine where we must place the central body of the universe towards which all its parts aim with a common downward motion.[43*] As for what the composition of this fundamental part of the entire creation may be and what may be found on it, we wish to leave it to Mr. Wright from Durham to determine. With a fantastic enthusiasm, in this happy place he elevates, so to speak, on a throne of nature collectively a powerful being of the divine variety, with spiritual forces of attraction and repulsion, which, effective in an infinite sphere around it, draws all virtue to it but pushes back all vice. We do not wish to allow the daring of our conjectures, which we have permitted perhaps too much, to slip the reins into arbitrary poetical fictions. The Godhead is equally present in the infinity of the entire cosmic space everywhere. Wherever there are natures capable of rising above creature dependency into the company of the Highest Essence, that Essence will be immediately close at hand. The entire creation is permeated by His forces, but only that person who knows how to liberate himself from the living creature, the person who is noble enough to appreciate that only in the enjoyment of this original fountain of perfection is the highest level of blessedness to be sought alone and by himself, only that person is capable of finding himself closer to this true point interconnecting all excellence than to any other place in all nature. Meanwhile, if I, without sharing the Englishman's enthusiastic picture, am to offer my conjectures about the different levels of the spiritual world from the physical relationship of their dwelling places in relation to the mid-point of creation, then I would seek with more probability the most perfect classes of reasoning beings further from this mid-point rather than close to it. The perfection of creatures endowed with reason, insofar as they are dependent on material composition, in connection with which they are limited, depends a very great deal on the fineness of the material stuff whose influence determines these creatures in their perception of the world and in their response to it. The inertia and resistance in matter excessively restrict the freedom of the spiritual beings in their work and in the clarity of their sensations of external things. It dulls the edge of their capabilities, since they cannot obey their movements with appropriate facility. For when we assume, as is likely, that the densest and heaviest sorts of materials are close to the mid-point of nature and, by contrast, that the increasing degrees of fineness and lightness are at the greater distances in the same proportion as in the analogy which governs our planetary structure, then the result is understandable. The reasoning beings whose place for development and habitation is located closer to the mid-point of creation are sunk in a stiff and immobile matter, which keeps their powers enclosed in an invincible inertia and is equally incapable of transmitting and reporting on the impressions of the universe with the necessary clarity and ease. Thus, we will have to count these thinking beings in the low group. By contrast, with the distances away from the common centre, this perfection in the spiritual world, which rests on the reciprocal dependency of it on matter, will grow as if on a constant scale. At the lowest depths toward the sinking point, therefore, we have to place the poorest and least perfect groups of thinking creatures and below this is the place where in all shades of diminution the excellence of beings finally loses itself in the utter lack of thought and reflection. In fact, if we consider that the central point of nature marks simultaneously the start of its development out of raw matter and its frontier with chaos, if we establish in addition that the perfection of spiritual beings, which really have an outermost border marking their beginning, where their capabilities jostle back and forth with unreason, but which have no limit to going forward over which they cannot be raised and instead discover in that direction a complete infinity in front of them, then, if indeed there is to be a law according to which dwelling places are distributed for reasoning creatures in accordance with the order of their relationship to the common mid-point, we will have to put the lowest and least perfect types, which, as it were, make up the beginning of the family of the spiritual world, in that place designated the start of the entire universe, in order at the same time as this to fill in the same forward movement all infinity of time and space with endlessly growing levels of perfection of the thinking capacity and, as it were, gradually to come closer to the goal of the highest excellence, namely, to the Godhead, but without ever being able to attain that.

PART TWO. SECTION EIGHT

General Proof of the Correctness of a Mechanical Theory, of the General Arrangement of the Planetary Structure, in particular of the Correctness of the Present Theory

We cannot look at the planetary structure without recognizing the supremely excellent order in its arrangement and the sure marks of God's hand in the perfection of its interrelationships. After reason has considered and wondered at so much beauty and excellence, it rightly grows indignant at the daring foolishness which permits itself to ascribe all this to chance and a happy contingency. There must have been a Highest Wisdom to make the design, and an Infinite Power must have produced it. Otherwise it would be impossible to encounter in the planetary structure so many purposes cooperating in a single intention. It comes down only to deciding whether the plan for the structure of the universe is already set in the fundamental composition of eternal natures by the Highest Understanding and implanted in the eternal laws of motion, so that they develop themselves freely from them in a manner appropriate to the most perfect order or whether the general characteristics of the component parts of the world are completely incapable of harmony and have not the slightest united relationship and it must have absolutely required an alien hand to produce that restriction and coordination which permit us to see the perfection and beauty in it. An almost universal judgment has made most philosophers oppose the capability of nature to produce something ordered through its universal laws, just as if it meant that we were challenging God's rule over the world, when we seek the primordial developments in the forces of nature, as if these forces were a principle independent of the Godhead and were an eternally blind fate.

However, if we consider that nature and the eternal laws prescribed for substances in their reciprocal relationships are not a self-sufficient, necessary principle with no connection to God, and, for that very reason, we see that because nature demonstrates so much harmony and order in what it produces by universal laws, the essential natures of all things must have their common origin in one particular Original Essence, and that for this reason nature must reveal nothing but mutual interrelationships and harmony, because its properties originate in one single Highest Intelligence, whose wise idea has planned it with universal interconnections and has planted in it that capability, whereby, left alone in its own state to do its work, it brings forth nothing but beauty, nothing but order; when we, I say, consider this, then nature will seem more worthy to us than it commonly appears, and we will expect nothing from natural developments but harmony, nothing but order. If we, by contrast, permit an ungrounded judgment that the universal natural laws in and of themselves produce nothing but disorder, and that all the coordination for useful purposes shining forth in relation to natural arrangements reveals the immediate hand of God, then we will be forced to transform all nature into miracles. We will have to account for the beautifully coloured bow appearing amid the rain drops, when it separates the colours of the sun's light, on the basis of its beauty, the rain on the basis of its benefits, the winds on the basis of the indispensable advantages which they bring in countless ways in answer to human needs, in short, we must not explain all the changes of the world which bring delight and order with them on the basis of implanted natural forces of matter. The natural scientist who begins by surrendering to such a philosophy will have to make a solemn apology before the judgment seat of religion. In fact, there will then be no more nature. There will be only a God in the machine who produces the world's changes. But what then will this curious method of demonstrating the certain existence of a Highest Being out of the fundamental incapacity of nature prove by way of an effectively counter to Epicurus? If the natures of things bring forth by the eternal laws of their being nothing but disorder and absurdity, then they will show in that very manner the nature of their independence from God. What sort of an idea will we be able to create for ourselves of a divinity whom the universal natural laws obey only through some sort of compulsion and in and of themselves act against the wisest designs of the Divinity? Will the enemy of providence not win just as many victories from these false basic principles, when he can point to harmonies which the universally effective natural laws produce without any special limitations? And is it possible that he would really lack examples of such things? By contrast, let us with greater propriety and correctness conclude the following: nature left to its general properties is fertile in nothing but beautiful and perfect fruits, which not only display in themselves harmony and excellence, but also are in harmony to the total extent of their being with benefits for humanity and with the glorification of the properties of God. From this it follows that its fundamental characteristics can have no independent necessity but that they must have their origin in a Single Intelligence, the basis and the fountain of all being, in which they are designed according to common interrelationships. All things connected together in a reciprocal harmony must be united among themselves in a single being on which they collectively depend. Thus, there is present a Being of all beings, an Infinite Intelligence and Self-sufficient Wisdom, from which nature, even in its potentiality, draws its origin according to the whole embodiment of its purposes. From now on we must not deny the capacity of nature, claiming it is disadvantageous to the existence of a Highest Being. The more perfect nature is in its developments, the better its universal laws lead to order and harmony, then the more certain the proof of the Godhead from which nature derives these relationships. Its productions are no longer effects of contingency and results of accidents. Everything flows from it according to unchanging laws which thus must display nothing other than nature's skill, because they are exclusively features of the wisest of all designs from which disorder is prohibited. The chance collisions of the atoms of Lucretius did not develop the world. Implanted forces and laws which have their source in the Wisest Intelligence were an unchanging origin of that order inevitably flowing out from nature, not by chance, but by necessity.

If we can thus dispense with an old and ungrounded judgment and the shoddy philosophy which seeks to hide under a pious appearance an indolent lack of wisdom, then I hope to base a sure conviction on incontrovertible reasons *that the world gives evidence of a mechanical development from the general natural laws as the origin of its arrangement and, secondly, that the manner of the mechanical development which we have presented is the true one.* If we wish to render judgment whether nature is sufficiently capable of bringing into existence the ordering of the planetary structure through a mechanical sequence of its laws of motion, then we must first consider how simple the movements are which the celestial bodies observe: they have nothing inherently in them which requires a more precise determination than what the universal rules of natural forces bring with them. The orbital movements arise from the combination of the force moving downward, which is a certain consequence of the properties of matter, and the projectile movement, which can be seen as the effect of the first, as a velocity attained through the fall downward in which only a certain cause was necessary to deflect the vertical fall sideways. After once attaining the required determination of these movements, nothing else is necessary to maintain the orbital motions permanently. They arise in empty space through the combination of the projectile force, once impressed, with the power of attraction flowing from fundamental natural forces, and from that point on they suffer no change. The analogies in the harmony of this movement themselves demonstrate the reality of a mechanical origin so clearly that we can entertain no doubts about it, for the following reasons:

1. These movements have a continuous shared direction: of the six main planets and the ten satellites, not a single one moves, either in its forward motion or in its axial rotation, in any other direction than from west to east. Moreover, these directions are so precisely coordinated that they deviate only a little from a common plane, and this plane, to which everything is related, is the equatorial plane of the body which rotates on its axis at the central point of the entire system in exactly the same direction and which has become, through its predominant power of attraction, the reference point for all motions and thus necessarily participates in them as precisely as possible. This is proof that the collective movements arose and were determined in a mechanical way in accordance with general natural laws, that the cause which either impressed or guided the sideways movements governed all the space of the planetary structure and there obeyed the laws which materials located and moving in a common space observe, and that all the different movements finally assume a single direction to align themselves as precisely as possible with a single plane.

2. The velocities are constituted as they must be in a space where the force of movement is at the central point, namely, they decrease in steady degrees with the distances from this point and are lost in the remotest distances with a total exhaustion of movement, which displaces the vertical fall to the side only very slightly. Beyond Mercury, which has the greatest orbital force, we see these velocities diminish in stages and in the outermost comets they are as insignificant as they can be without falling straight down toward the sun. We cannot object that the rules of the central movements in circular orbits require that the closer to the mid-point of the general downward motion, the faster the orbital velocity must be. For why must the particular celestial bodies near to this centre have circular orbits? Why are the closest ones not very eccentric and the ones further away not orbiting in circles? Or rather, since they all deviate from this measured geometric precision, why does this deviation increase with the distances? Do these relationships not indicate a point to which all movement originally was directed and, according to the measure of its proximity to this point, attained a greater level of precision, before other determining factors changed its directions into what they are now?

If, however, we now wish to exclude the planetary structure and the origin of movements from the general natural laws in order to ascribe them to the immediate hand of God, then we immediately realize that the analogies referred to openly contradict such an idea. For, firstly, with reference to the general harmony in direction, it is clear that here there is no reason why the celestial bodies must organize their orbits precisely in one single direction, unless the mechanics of their development had determined the matter. For the space in which they move provides an infinitely small resistance and limits their movements as little in one direction as in another. Thus, God's choice would not have the slightest motive for tying them to one single arrangement, but would reveal itself with a greater freedom in all sorts of deviations and difference. There is still more. Why are the planetary orbits so exactly related to a common plane, namely, to the equatorial plane of that large body which rules their orbits in the mid-point of all motion? This analogy of the immediate hand of God, instead of showing a reason for its inherent propriety, is rather the cause of a certain confusion, which would be removed through a free deviation in the planetary orbits. For the forces of attraction of the planets now disturb to a certain extent the similarity in the form of their movements, and they would not obstruct one another at all, if they were not so precisely moved to a common plane.

Even more than all these analogies, the clearest mark of the hand of nature is revealed in the lack of the most precise determination in those relationships which it has striven to attain. If it were for the best that the planetary orbits were oriented almost on a common plane, why are they not oriented with extreme precision? And why has a portion of that deviation remained in place, when it should be avoided? If, therefore, the orbits of planets near the sun have received a large enough orbital momentum to maintain an equilibrium with the force of attraction, why is there still something lacking for a complete equilibrium? And why are their orbits not perfectly circular, if only the Wisest Intention, reinforced with the greatest capability, worked to produce this arrangement? Is it not clear to see that the cause which set up the orbital paths of the celestial bodies, while striving on its own to bring them to a common plane, could not achieve that completely and that, in the same way, the force which governed celestial space when all matter, now developed into spheres, received its orbital velocities, really worked to bring the spheres near the mid-point into an equilibrium with the force pulling downward, but was unable to achieve complete precision. Can we not here recognize the general method of nature, which, because of the interference of the different interactions, is always made to deviate from exactly determined measurements? And will we really find the reasons for this way of constructing things only in the end purposes of such an immediately commanding Highest Will? We cannot, without demonstrating stubbornness, deny that the estimable way of explaining the characteristics of nature through a recitation of their benefits does not in this instance contain the hoped for proof to demonstrate a basis for it. Certainly, with respect to benefits for the world, it was entirely irrelevant whether the planetary orbits were fully circular or a little eccentric, or whether they fully coincided with the common interrelating plane or should still deviate somewhat from it. Rather, if it was indeed necessary to be restricted with this sort of harmony, then it would be best for them to have it completely in themselves. If what the philosopher said is true, that God constantly practices geometry, and if this is reflected in the methods of the general natural laws, then certainly this principle of the immediate work of the Omnipotent Will would be perfectly traceable and the latter would reveal in itself all the perfection of geometrical precision. The comets belong among these natural deficiencies. We cannot deny that, with respect to their paths and the changes they thereby undergo, we should see them as imperfect links in creation, which can neither serve to provide comfortable dwelling places for reasoning beings nor to become useful for the greatest good of the entire system, in that they, as has been conjectured, could at some point have served the sun as nourishment. For it is certain that most comets would not achieve this purpose before the collapse of the entire planetary system had been reached. In the theory of the immediate highest organizing of the world without a natural development from universal natural laws such an observation would be objectionable, although at the same time it is certain. But in a mechanical form of explanation, the beauty of the world and the revelation of omnipotence of the Almighty are glorified by this in no small way. Since nature contains in itself all possible stages of heterogeneous variety, it extends its circumference over all types from perfection to nothingness, and even the deficiencies are a sign of the excess for which its essence is inexhaustible.

We can believe that the analogies cited could well prevail over prejudice to make the mechanical origin of the planetary system worthy of adopting, if certain reasons derived from the very nature of the subject did not still seem to contradict this theory completely. Celestial space, as has already been mentioned several times, is empty, or at least filled with infinitely sparse material, which, as a result, can provide no means of impressing the common motions on celestial bodies. This difficulty is so significant and valid that Newton, who had reason to trust the insights of his philosophy as much as any other mortal, saw himself compelled here to abandon the hope of resolving through natural law and material forces the transmission of the orbital forces present in the planets, in spite of all the harmony which pointed to a mechanical origin.[44*] It is a troubling decision for a philosopher to give up the effort of an investigation in the case of a compound phenomenon which is still remote from the simple basic laws and to be satisfied with the reference to the immediate hand of God. Nevertheless, Newton acknowledged here the dividing line separating nature and the finger of God from each other, the pattern of set laws of the former and the nod of the latter. After the doubt of such a great philosopher, it may appear presumptuous still to hope for some fortunate progress in a matter of such difficulty.

But this very difficulty which deprived Newton of the hope of understanding on the basis of natural forces the orbital forces allotted to the heavenly bodies, whose direction and arrangements make up the system of the planetary structure, was the origin of the theory which we have presented in the previous sections. It sets up a mechanical theory, but one which is far from the one which Newton found unsatisfactory and on account of which he rejected all basic causes, because, if I may be so bold as to say it, he made a mistake in maintaining that his doctrine was the only possible one of its kind. It is quite easy and natural, with the help of Newton's difficulty, from a short and basic conclusion to reach certainty about the mechanical style of explanation which we have set down in this treatise. If we presuppose (and we cannot do otherwise than acknowledge the fact) that the previous analogies establish with the greatest certainty that the harmonious and well-ordered interrelated movements and orbits of the celestial bodies point to a natural cause as their origin, then this cause cannot be the same material which now fills celestial space. Thus, the material which earlier filled these expanses and whose movement was the reason for the present orbiting of the heavenly bodies, after it had collected on these spheres and thus cleaned out the spaces which we now see as empty, or, what flows directly from this, the materials themselves out of which the planets, the comets, even the sun are made up, must at the start have been spread out in the space of the planetary system and, in this condition, have set themselves in the motions which they maintained when they united in particular clusters and developed the celestial bodies, which contain in themselves all the previously scattered matter making up the worlds. We have little difficulty seeing in this idea the mechanical impulse which might have set in motion this material of self-developing nature. The very impulse which brought about the union of the masses, the force of attraction, which is inherently present in matter and which thus, with the first stirring of nature, is really suitable to consider the first cause of motion, was the source of that mechanical impulse. The direction which, through the effects of this force, always aims right at the mid-point, here creates no problems. For it is certain that the fine material of the scattered elements in its vertical motion downward must have developed motion in different directions both through the heterogeneity of the points of attraction and through the obstacles which their vectors create by intersecting with each other. Among these motions the certain natural law which causes all materials restricting each other through reciprocal interaction finally to be brought to a condition where they induce change in each other as little as possible produces both the uniformity in the direction and the appropriate levels of velocity, which are carefully balanced at each distance according to the centripetal force. Through the combination of these, the elements do not strive to deviate either above or below, for all the elements thus have been made to run, not just in one direction, but also in almost parallel free circles around the common point of downward motion in the sparse celestial space. These movements of the particles must have kept going from this time on, once the planetary spheres had developed out of them, and remain in place now, through the combination of the sideways momentum implanted once and the centripetal force, for an unrestricted future period. On this basic principle, so easy to grasp, rest the uniformity in the directions of the planetary orbits, the precise relationship to a common plane, the amount of the projectile impetus appropriate to the power of attraction at a location, the decreasing precision of these analogies over distance, and the free deviation of the outermost celestial bodies on both sides as well as in the opposite direction. If these indications of the reciprocal dependency in the requirements for development point with more obvious certainty to a material in motion originally distributed through all space, then the total lack of all materials in this now empty celestial space, except for what the bodies of the planets, the sun, and the comets are composed of, proves that this very material would have had to have been at the start in a condition of being spread out. The ease and correctness with which all the phenomena of the planetary structure have been derived from the assumption of this basic principle in the previous sections is the completion of such a conjecture and gives it a value which is no longer arbitrary.

The certainty of a mechanical theory for the origin of the planetary structure, particularly of ours, will be elevated to the highest peak of conviction, if we consider the development of the celestial bodies themselves, the importance and size of their masses, according to the relationship which they have with respect to their distance from the central point of gravitation. For in the first place, the density of their material, when we consider them as a total cluster, decreases in constant stages with distances from the sun, a fixed condition which points so clearly to the mechanical arrangements of the initial development that we can demand no more. They are put together out of materials in such a way that those of the heavier sort have reached a deeper position in relation to the common point of downward motion and, by contrast, the lighter sort a distance further away. This condition is necessary in all sorts of natural development. But with an arrangement issuing from the immediate Divine Will, there is not the slightest reason to encounter the relationships mentioned above. For although it might immediately seem that spheres further away must consist of lighter materials so that they could not notice the necessary effect of the diminished force of the sun's rays, this purpose pertains only to the composition of the material located on the outer surface and not to the deeper varieties on the inside of its cluster. The heat of the sun never has any effect on these inner materials, which serve only to make effective the planet's power of attraction, which is to make the bodies moving around it sink down towards it. Therefore, they cannot have the slightest relationship to the strength or weakness of the sun's rays. If we then ask why the densities of the Earth, Jupiter, and Saturn, as determined by the correct calculations of Newton, stand in relation to each other as 400 to 94.5 to 64, then it would be absurd to attribute the cause to God's intention, which adjusted the densities according to the degrees of solar heat, for then our Earth can serve as a counterexample. In the case of the Earth, the sun only affects such a small part under the outer layer with its rays, that the part of the Earth's cluster which must have some relationship with these rays does not by a long way make up the millionth part of the total planet. And the remaining part is entirely indifferent in this matter. Thus, if the material of which the celestial bodies consist has a well-ordered relationship in mutual harmony with the distances and if the planets cannot now restrict each other, separated as they are from each other in empty space, then their matter must have previously been in a condition where they were able to bring about a common effect on one another in order to limit them to locations proportional to their specific gravity. This could have happened only if their parts before development had been spread out in the entire space of the system and if they took up locations appropriate to their densities, in accordance with the general laws of motion.

The relationship among the sizes of the planetary masses, which increases with distances, is the second reason by which the mechanical development of the celestial bodies, and especially our theory of that, is clearly demonstrated. Why do the masses of the celestial bodies approximately increase with the distances? If we subscribe to a theory which assigns everything to God's choice, then no purpose can be imagined why the further planets have to have larger masses other than the fact that because of the preponderant strength within their sphere of attraction they would be able to hold onto one or several moons, which are to serve the inhabitants destined for the planets by making their stay comfortable. But this purpose could have been achieved just as well by a preponderant density in the interior of their clusters. And why then would the lightness in the material flowing from special grounds, something which goes against this relationship, have had to remain and be so overwhelmed by the preponderance of the volume that the mass of the higher planets became more significant than the mass of the lower ones? When we do not take into account the manner of the natural development of these bodies, then we have difficulty being able to provide a reason for this relationship. But in the light of mechanical theory nothing is easier to grasp than this arrangement. When the material of all planetary bodies was still spread out in the space of the planetary system, the power of attraction developed spheres out of these particles. Undoubtedly the spheres must have been bigger the further the location of their developing globe was away from that common central body, which from the mid-point of the entire space limited and hindered this combining as much as it could by means of its powerful force of attraction.

We will notice with satisfaction the features of this development of the celestial bodies from basic material spread out at the start in the width of the intervening spaces separating their orbits from each other. These, according to this concept, must be deemed empty compartments from which the planets have appropriated the materials for their development. We perceive how these intervening spaces between the orbits have a relationship to the size of the masses which developed out of them. The width between the orbits of Jupiter and Mars is so large that the space enclosed in it exceeds the area of all the lower planetary orbits taken together. But it is worthy of the largest of all the planets, the one which has more mass than all the others collectively. We cannot attribute this distance of Jupiter from Mars to the intention that their powers of attraction were to interfere with each other as little as possible. For according to such a reason, the planet between two orbits would always find itself closest to the planet whose power of attraction combined with its own could disturb their dual orbits around the sun as little as possible; as a result, the planet would be closer to the one with the smallest mass. Now, according to the correct calculations of Newton, the force with which Jupiter can affect the orbit of Mars is related to the force which it exercises on Saturn through their combined forces of attraction is as 1/12512 to 1/200. So we can easily calculate by how much Jupiter would have had to be closer to the orbit of Mars than to that of Saturn, if their distance away had been determined with their external relationship in mind and not through the mechanism of their development. However, this phenomenon is quite different. For in relation to the two orbits above and below it, a planetary orbit often stands further away from the one in which a smaller planet runs than from the path of the larger mass of the two. However, the extent of the space around the orbit of each planet always has a correct relationship to its mass. Thus, it is clear that the manner of their development must have established these relationships and that, because these arrangements seem to be bound up with this development, as their causes and effects, we will in reality estimate it most correctly if we consider the space included between the orbits as the container of that material out of which the planets were built. From this it immediately follows that the size of these spaces must be proportional to masses of the planets. However, this relationship will be augmented with the further planets because of the greater scattering of the basic material in their first state in these regions. Therefore, of two planets which are almost equal to each other in mass, the one further away must have a larger space in which to develop, that is, a greater distance to the two nearest orbits, both because the material there was inherently of a specifically lighter variety and because it was more widely scattered than in the case of the planet which developed closer to the sun. Thus, although the Earth together with the moon still does not appear to be equal to Venus in its physical contents, nevertheless, it required for itself a greater room for development, because it had to be built out of a more scattered material than this lower planet. For these reasons, we can assume, so far as Saturn is concerned, that its sphere of development stretched much further on the distant side than on the side of the central point (as this holds true for almost all planets). Consequently, the intervening space between Saturn's orbit and the path of the higher celestial body next to Saturn, which we can assume is above it, will be much wider than the space between Saturn and Jupiter.

Thus, everything in the planetary structure proceeds in stages out into all limitless distances with accurate relationships to the first force of development, which was more effective near the central point than far away. The diminution of the impressed projectile motion, the deviation from the most precise agreement in the direction and the orientation of the orbits, the densities of the celestial bodies, the scarcity of nature in relation to the space where they developed, everything diminishes stage by stage from the centre into the far distances. Everything shows that the first cause was bound up with the mechanical rules of movement and did not take place through a free choice.

But what illustrates as clearly as anything else the natural development of the celestial bodies out of the basic material originally spread out in the now empty celestial space is the agreement, which I take from M. de Buffon (which, however, in his theory does not by a long way have the benefit it does in ours). For, according to his observation, if we add up together the planets whose masses we can determine by calculation, namely, Saturn, Jupiter, Earth, and the Moon, they give a cluster whose density stands in relation to the density of the body of the sun as 640 to 650. In this comparison, since these are the major parts of the planetary system, the remaining planets (Mars, Venus, and Mercury) hardly merit counting. Thus, we will with good reason be astonished at the remarkable equality which governs between the materials of the planetary structure collectively, if we consider it as a single united cluster, and the mass of the sun. It would be an irresponsible foolishness to ascribe this analogy to chance, that materials, among a variety so infinitely different that there are a few encountered even on our Earth which are fifteen thousand times more dense than others, nevertheless comes so near a ratio of 1 to 1 in the total. And we must concede that, if we consider the sun as a mixture of all types of matter, which in the structure of the planets are separated from each other, all of them together seem to have developed in one space, originally full of material uniformly spread out. These materials were collected on the central body without distinction. For the development of the planets, however, they were divided up in proportion to the altitudes. I leave it to those who cannot subscribe to the mechanical development of the celestial bodies to explain from the motives of God's choice such a remarkable arrangement as this, if they can. I will finally stop establishing more proofs for a matter of such convincing clarity as the development of the planetary structure out of the forces of nature. If people are in a position to remain unmoved in the midst of so many convincing details, then they must either lie far too deep in the bonds of prejudice or be entirely incapable of rising above the jumble of received opinions to the observation of the purest truth of all. Meanwhile, we can believe that nobody except the very foolish, on whose approval we may not count, can deny the correctness of this theory, if the harmonies which the planetary structure has in all its links to the benefits of reasoning creatures did not appear to have something more than general natural laws as its basis. We believe correctly that skilful arrangements which point to a worthy purpose must have as their originator a Wise Intelligence, and we will become completely satisfied when we consider that, since the natures of things acknowledge no other original source than just this, their fundamental and universal arrangements must have a natural inclination to proper and really mutual harmonious consequences. We will thus not allow ourselves to feel strange if we become aware of the arrangements of the planetary structure rich in mutual advantages for creatures and attribute these to a natural consequence arising out of the general laws of nature. For what issues from these is not the effect of blind accident or of unreasoning necessity. It is, in the last analysis, based upon the Highest Wisdom from which the universal arrangements derive their harmony. One conclusion is entirely correct: If, in the arrangement of the world, order and beauty shine forth, then a God exists. But another is no less well established: If this order could have emerged from the general natural laws, then all of nature is necessarily the effect of the Highest Wisdom.

If people nevertheless let themselves at their own discretion acknowledge the immediate application of the Divine Wisdom in all the ordering of nature, which includes in itself harmony and beneficial purposes, while they do not credit the development out of general laws of motion with any harmonious consequences, then I would like to advise them in their contemplation of the planetary structure to direct their eyes not to a single celestial body but to the totality, in order to tear themselves for once away from this delusion. If the steep inclination of the Earth's axis in relation to the plane of its annual orbit is to be a proof of the immediate hand of God because of the well loved changes in the seasons, then people should insist on this relationship in connection with the other celestial bodies. Then they will become aware that it is different in each one and that in this difference there are even some planets that do not have this feature at all, as, for example, Jupiter, whose axis is perpendicular to the plane of its orbit, and Mars, whose axis is almost perpendicular. Both of these enjoy no difference in the seasons and are, nonetheless, as much works of the Highest Wisdom as the others are. The moon satellites of Saturn, Jupiter, and the Earth would seem to be special configurations of the Highest Being, if the free departure from this purpose throughout the entire planetary system did not illustrate that nature produced these arrangements without being disturbed by an extraordinary constraint in its free actions. Jupiter has four moons, Saturn five, the Earth one, and the other planets none at all, although it immediately seems that the other planets were in greater need of moons than the former group because of their longer nights. If we admire the proportional equilibrium of the projectile force impressed on the planets with the centripetal force at their distance as the reason why they run almost in circles around the sun and are adapted to be residences for reasoning creatures because of the uniformity in the heat distributed in this way and look upon that as the immediate finger of the Almighty, then we will be led back at once to the general laws of nature, when we consider that this planetary arrangement loses itself gradually with all grades of diminution in the depths of the heavens and that even the Highest Wisdom, which derived satisfaction from the regularity of planetary motion, did not exclude the deficiency with which the system ends, since it runs out in complete irregularity and disorder. Regardless of the fact that it is essentially established for perfection and order, nature includes in itself in the range of its multiplicity all possible changes, even deficiency and deviation. Just this unlimited fecundity of nature has produced the inhabited celestial globes, as well as the comets, the useful mountains and the harmful cliffs, the habitable landscapes and barren deserts, the virtues and vices.

PART THREE

Which contains in it an attempt, based on natural analogies, to establish a comparison between the inhabitants of different planets.

He, who through vast immensity can pierce,

See worlds on worlds compose one universe,

Observe how system into system runs,

What other planets circle other suns,

What varied Being peoples every star,

May tell why Heaven has made us as we are.

(Pope)[45*]

APPENDIX

In my view it is a disgrace to the nature of philosophy when we use it to maintain with a kind of flippancy free-wheeling witty displays having some apparent truth, unless we are immediately willing to explain that we are doing this only as an amusement.[46*] Thus, in the present essay I will not introduce any propositions except those which can really expand our understanding and which are at the same time so plausibly established that we can scarcely deny their validity.

It may appear that in this sort of project the freedom to be poetical has no real limits, that in judging the make-up of those who live in distant worlds we could allow unbridled fantasy much more free rein than a painter in an illustration of the flora and fauna of undiscovered lands, and that these very ideas could not be proved right or wrong. Nevertheless, we must admit that the distances of the celestial bodies from the sun involve certain relationships which bring with them a vital influence on the different characteristics of the thinking natures found on these very bodies. Their way of working and suffering is associated with the composition of the material to which they are bound and depends upon the quantity of impressions which the world arouses in them, according to the relationship of their living environment with the centre of the power of attraction and heat.

I am of the opinion that it is not particularly necessary to assert that all planets must be inhabited. However, at the same time it would be absurd to deny this claim with respect to all or even to most of them. Given the richness of nature, where worlds and systems are only sunny dust specks compared to the totality of creation, there could, in fact, also be deserted and uninhabited regions without the slightest function in nature's purpose, namely, the contemplation by sensible beings. It would be conceded, even if one wished to consider things on the basis of God's wisdom, that sandy and uninhabited deserts make up large stretches of the earth's surface and that there are in the earth's oceans abandoned islands where no human being is found. Meanwhile, a planet is far less in relation to the totality of creation than is a desert or an island in relation to the earth's surface.

Perhaps all the celestial bodies have not yet completely developed. Hundreds and maybe thousands of years are necessary for a large celestial body to reach a stable material condition. Jupiter still appears to be in this state of disharmony. The remarkable changes in its form at different times have already led astronomers for a long time to assume that the planet must be experiencing large upheavals and is a long way from having a calm outer surface, a condition which must pertain for a planet to be inhabited. If Jupiter is uninhabited and even if it is never to have any inhabitants, would that not be an infinitely small natural expenditure compared to the immeasurable size of the total creation? And if nature were carefully to display all her richness in every point of space, would that not be much more a sign of nature's poverty than of her abundance?

But it is more satisfying for us still to assume that if Jupiter is uninhabited right now, nonetheless the planet will be inhabited in the future, when it has had time to develop completely. Our Earth perhaps existed for a thousand years or more before it was in a condition to be able to support human beings, animals, and plants. The fact that a planet reaches this complete state only after a few thousand years does nothing to detract from the reason for its existence. For this very reason the planet will be around for a longer time in the future in its state of complete development, once it has attained it. For there is a certain natural principle that everything which has a beginning gets steadily closer to its dissolution and that much closer to destruction the further it is from its origin.

One can only approve of the satirical portrayal by that witty person from the Hague who, after quoting the general news from the scientific world, could humorously present the imaginary picture of the necessary habitation of all planets. "Those creatures who live in the forests of a beggar's head," he says, "had for a long time thought of their dwelling place as an immeasurably large ball and themselves as the masterworks of creation. Then one of them, whom Heaven had endowed with a more refined soul, a small Fontenelle of his species, unexpectedly learned about a nobleman's head. Immediately he called all the witty creatures of his district together and told them with delight: 'We are not the only living beings in all nature. Look here at this new land. More lice live here.'"47 If the final part of this conclusion provokes laughter, that happens not because it is far removed from the way human beings judge things, but because that very same mistake, which among human beings has basically a similar cause, seems more excusable in our case.

Let us judge in an unprejudiced manner. This insect, which in its way of living as well as in its lack of worth expresses very well the condition of most human beings, can be used for such a comparison with good results. Since, according to the louse's imagination, nature is endlessly well suited to its existence, it considers irrelevant all the rest of creation which does not have a precise goal related to its species as the central point of nature's purposes. The human being, who similarly stands infinitely far from the highest stages of being, is sufficiently bold to flatter himself with the same imaginative picture of his existence as essential. The limitlessness of creation contains within itself, with equal necessity, all natures which its superbly fecund richness produces. From the most refined classes of thinking beings right down to the most despicable insect, no link is irrelevant to nature. And not a single one can fail to appear without in the process fracturing the beauty of the whole, which consists in the interrelatedness. Meanwhile, everything is determined by universal laws which nature effects through the combination of forces originally planted in it. Because nature's process produces only what is appropriate and ordered, no particular purpose is permitted to disturb and break her results. In its initial development a planet's creation was only an infinitely small consequence of nature's fertility, and it would now be somewhat absurd that nature's well-grounded laws should defer to the specific purposes of this atom. If the composition of a celestial body establishes natural barriers against its becoming inhabited, then it will not have inhabitants, even though in and of itself the planet would be more beautiful if it had its own population. The excellence of creation loses nothing in such a case, for among all large quantities the infinite is the one which is not diminished by the subtraction of a finite part. It would be as if one wished to complain that the space between Jupiter and Mars is unnecessarily empty and that there are comets which are not populated. In fact, however, that insect may appear as unworthy to us as we wish, but to nature it is certainly more appropriate to maintaining its entire class than a small number of more excellent creatures, of which there would nevertheless be infinitely many, even if one region or locale should lack them. Because nature is endlessly fertile in producing both species, in their preservation and their destruction we really see both equally abandoned disinterestedly to the universal laws. Indeed, has the possessor of those inhabited forests on the beggar's head ever created greater disasters among the races of this colony than the son of Philip brought about among the race of his fellow citizens, when his wicked genius gave him the idea that the world was created only for his sake?[48*]

However, most of the planets are certainly inhabited, and those that are not will be in the future. Now, what sort of interconnections will be brought about among the different types of these inhabitants through the relationship between their place in the cosmic structure and the central point from which the warmth which gives life to everything extends outwards? For it is certain that, with the materials of these celestial bodies this heat will bring with it certain relationships in their compositions proportional to the distance from the centre. In this comparison, the human being, who is, among all sensible beings, the one we know most clearly, although at the same time his inner composition is still an unexplored problem, must serve as the foundation and common reference point. We do not wish here to comment on his moral characteristics or even on the physical arrangement of his structure. We want only to explore how the capacity to think sensibly and the movement of his body, which obeys that, suffer restrictions because of the material composition to which he is linked, proportional to the distance from the sun. Regardless of the infinite distance encountered between the power of thought and the movement of matter, between the reasoning spirit and the body, it is nevertheless certain that a human being, who receives all his ideas and conceptions from impressions which the universe awakens in his soul by means of the body, both with respect to their clarity and to the skill of combining and comparing them, which we call the capacity for thought, is totally dependent on the composition of this material stuff to which the Creator has bound him.

The human being is created to take in the impressions and emotions which the world is to arouse in him through that very body, which is the perceptible part of his being.

The body's material serves not only to impress on the imperceptible spirit which lives inside him the first ideas of the external world but also is indispensable in its inner working for repeating these impressions and linking them together, in short, for thinking.[49*] As a person's body grows, his intellectual capabilities also proportionally attain the appropriate stage of full development and first acquire a staid and soberly mature capacity when the fibres of his corporeal machine have gained the strength and endurance which mark the completion of their development. Those capabilities develop early enough within him, thanks to which he can cope sufficiently with the necessities of life to which he is bound by dependence on external things. Some people's development remains at this level. The ability to combine abstract ideas and, through a free use of one's understanding, to gain control over passionate tendencies comes late. Some never reach this state during their entire lives. However, in all people this ability is weak; it serves the more primitive forces which it should nonetheless govern. In the control of these lower forces consists the good quality of a person's nature. When we consider the life of most people, it seems that this creature has been created to absorb liquids, like a plant, to grow, to propagate the species, and finally to grow old and die. Among all living things, human beings are the poorest at realizing the purpose of their existence, because they exhaust their excellent capabilities in those pursuits which other creatures, with far less capability, nonetheless attain more confidently and conveniently. The human being would even be the creature most worthy of contempt among all of them, at least from the point of view of true wisdom, if the hope for the future did not elevate him and if the time for a full development of the powers closed up inside him did not lie in store.

When we look for the cause of the obstacles which keep human nature so debased, we find it in the coarseness of the material stuff in which his spiritual component is buried, in the stiffness of the fibres and the sluggishness and immobility of the fluids which should obey the movements of his spirit. The cerebral nerves and fluids provide him only crude and unclear ideas, and because he cannot offset the provocation of sensory stimulations in the inner workings of his thought process by means of sufficiently powerful ideas, he is taken over by his passions and dulled and disturbed by the turmoil of elements which maintain his machine. The attempts of reason to stand up against this and to drive away the confusion with light from the power of judgment are like moments of sunshine when thick clouds constantly interrupt and darken their serenity.

This coarseness in the stuff and fabric of the constitution of human nature is the cause of that lethargy which keeps the soul's capabilities continually weak and powerless. Coping with reflections and ideas clarified by reason is an exhausting condition. The soul cannot be placed in it without resistance. And because of a natural tendency the physical machine soon falls out of that state back into a condition of suffering, since sensory stimulations have a determining influence on and govern all its behaviour.

This lethargy in his power to think, a consequence of the dependence on a crude and awkward material, is the source not only of vice but also of error. The soul is held back because of the difficulty involved in the effort to scatter the clouds of confused notions and to distinguish universal knowledge, which arises from comparing ideas, from sense impressions, and prefers to bestow a quick approval on and is content with the possession of an opinion which the sluggishness of its nature and the resistance of the material scarcely allow it to see in perspective.

In this dependency, the spiritual capabilities disappear at the same time as the vitality of the body. When, on account of the weakened circulation of the fluids, extreme old age keeps warm in the body only thick juices, when the flexibility of the fibres and the agility in all movements decrease, then the powers of the spirit congeal in a similar fatigue. Rapidity of thought, clarity of ideas, liveliness of wit, and the capacity of memory grow feeble and cold. The ideas which, through long experience, have become ingrained still compensate to some extent for the departure of these powers, and the understanding would betray its incapacity even more clearly, if the intensity of passions, which require its rein, did not decline at the same time and even earlier.

From all this it is clear that the powers of the human soul are limited and hemmed in by the obstacles of a coarse material stuff to which they are most intimately tied. But there is still something all the more worth remarking: the fact that this specific composition of the stuff has an essential relationship to the degree of influence with which the sun enlivens it and makes carrying out the animal functions efficient, an influence proportional to its distance away. This necessary connection with the fire which spreads out from the mid-point of the planetary system so as to maintain the required motion in the material stuff is the basis for an analogy which will be firmly established here between the different inhabitants of the planets. Thanks to this relationship, every single class of these inhabitants is bound by the necessity of its nature to the place which has been allocated to it in the universe.

The inhabitants of Earth and Venus would not be able to exchange their living environments without the mutual destruction of both. The material out of which the inhabitants of Earth are made is proportional to the degree of heat for their distance from the sun. Thus, it is too light and volatile for an even greater heat, and in a hotter sphere it would suffer from violent movements and a breakdown of its nature, arising from the scattering and drying up of the fluids and a violent tension in its elastic fibres. The inhabitants of Venus, whose cruder structure and sluggishness in the elements of their formation require a stronger solar influence, would in a cooler celestial region freeze and die from a lack of vitality. In the same way, the body of an inhabitant of Jupiter would have to consist of far lighter and more volatile material, so that the very small motion which the sun can induce at this distance away could move these machines just as powerfully as it does in the lower regions. I summarize all this in one general idea: *the material stuff out of which the inhabitants of different planets, including even the animals and plants, are made must, in general, be of a lighter and finer type, and the elasticity of the fibres as well as the advantageous construction of their design must be more perfect in proportion to their distance away from the sun.*

This relationship is so natural and well grounded that not only do the fundamental motives of higher purpose, which in the study of nature are normally considered merely weak reasons, lead to it, but also at the same time the proportions of the specific composition of the materials making up the planets confirm it. These are derived from Newton's calculations as well as from the basic principles of cosmogony, which endorse the same principle according to which the material stuff out of which the celestial bodies are built is always of a lighter type in the more distant ones than in those closer to the sun. This point must necessarily bring with it a similar relationship for the creatures which develop and maintain themselves on them.

We have established a comparison between the material composition which sensible creatures on the planets essentially have in common. Thus, following the introduction of this concept, it is easy to consider that these relationships will also lead to a result which, so far as their spiritual capacities are concerned, has a necessary dependence on the material of the machine which they inhabit. Thus, we can conclude with more than probable assurance that the excellence of thinking natures, the speed of their imaginations, the clarity and vivacity of their ideas, which come to them from external stimuli, together with the ability to combine ideas, and finally, too, the rapidity in actual performance, in short, the entire extent of their perfection, is governed by a particular rule according to which these characteristics will always be more excellent and more complete in proportion to the distance of their dwelling places from the sun.

Since this relationship is so plausible that it is almost a demonstrated certainty, we have an open field for pleasant speculations arising from the comparison of the characteristics of these different inhabitants. Human nature, which in the scale of being holds, as it were, the middle rung, is located between the two absolute outer limits of perfection, equidistant from both. If the idea of the most sublime classes of sensible creatures living on Jupiter or Saturn provokes the jealousy of human beings and discourages them with the knowledge of their own humble position, a glance at the lower stages brings content and calms them again. The beings on the planets Venus and Mercury are reduced far below the perfection of human nature. What a view worthy of our astonishment! On one side we saw thinking creatures among whom a Greenlander or a Hottentot would be a Newton; on the other side we saw people who would admire Newton as if he were an ape.

Superior beings, when of late they saw

A moral Man unfold all Nature's law,

Admir'd such wisdom in an earthly shape,

And shew'd a NEWTON as we shew an Ape.

(Pope)[50*]

What an advance in knowledge will the insight of those blissful beings of the highest celestial spheres not attain! What beautiful results will this illumination of knowledge not have for their moral constitution! When intellectual insights have the appropriate level of perfection and clarity, they have in themselves far more vital charms than the attractions of sense and are able to govern these successfully and tread them underfoot. How beautifully will the very Godhead, who pictures Himself in all creatures, present His own portrait in these thinking beings; like a sea unmoved by storms of passion, they will calmly receive and shine back His image! We will not extrapolate these assumptions beyond the limits prescribed for a physical treatise; only we do once again take note of the above mentioned analogy *that the perfection of the spiritual as well as the material worlds in the planets from Mercury right up to Saturn, or perhaps beyond Saturn (insofar as there are still other planets), grows and advances in an appropriate sequence of stages proportional to their distance from the sun.*

Since this principle flows, in part, naturally from the consequences of the physical interrelationship between the dwelling places and the centre of the system, it is, to that extent, appropriately acceptable. On the other hand, a real look at the most excellent habitations prepared for the superb perfection of these natures in the higher regions confirms this rule so clearly that it should almost demand complete assent. The active speed associated with the merits of a lofty nature is better fitted to the rapidly changing time periods of the higher spheres than the slowness of lethargic and more imperfect creatures.

Telescopes teach us that the changes in day and night on Jupiter occur in ten hours. What would an inhabitant of Earth really do with this division of time, if he were placed on this planet? The ten hours would scarcely be sufficient for the rest this crude machine requires to recuperate in sleep. What would the preparation for going through waking up, getting dressed, and the time taken up with eating demand as a share of the available time? And how would a creature whose activities occur so slowly not be rendered confused and incapable of anything effective when his five hours of business would be suddenly interrupted by an intervening period of darkness of exactly the same duration? However, if Jupiter is inhabited by more perfect beings who combine more elastic forces and a greater agility in practice with a more refined development, then we can believe that these five hours are for them exactly equivalent to and more than the twelve hours of the day for the humble class of human beings. We know temporal demands are somewhat relative. This cannot be known and understood except from a comparison of the size of the task which is to be performed and the quickness with which it is carried out. Thus, the very same time which for one type of creature is, as it were, merely an instant can for another creature be a long period in which a large sequence of changes develops because of its speed and efficiency. According to plausible calculation of the axial rotation of Saturn, which we have dealt with above, the planet has a very much shorter division of day and night. It therefore allows us to assume even more advantageous capabilities in the nature of its inhabitants.

Finally, everything comes together to confirm the proposed principle. Nature has visibly distributed her goods as richly as possible to the far regions of the world. The moons, which compensate the active beings of these blissful regions for the loss of daylight with a sufficient substitute, are placed in that area in the greatest number, and nature appears to have taken care to make them effective with its full assistance, so that there is be scarcely any time when the moons are prevented from using it. So far as moons are concerned, Jupiter has an obvious advantage over all the lower planets, and Saturn once again has the advantage over Jupiter. The arrangement whereby Saturn has the beautiful and useful ring going around it probably creates even greater advantages for its composition. By contrast, the lower planets, for whom this advantageous feature would be a useless waste and whose class approaches much more closely the borders of irrationality, either do not share such an advantage at all or only very little.

However (and here I anticipate an objection which could destroy all the harmony I have mentioned) we cannot consider the greater distance from the sun, this source of light and life, as nothing but a drawback for which the spaciousness of the dwelling places in the further planets would serve as only a partially useful remedy, making the objection that in fact the higher planets have a less advantageous situation in the cosmic structure, a position which would be injurious to the perfection of those abodes, because they receive a weaker influence from the sun. For we know that the effects of light and heat are determined, not by their absolute intensity, but by the capacity of the material stuff which absorbs them and, to a greater or lesser extent, resists their impetus and that, therefore, the very same distance at which we could designate a moderate climate for a coarser type of material would destroy more subtle liquids and would be a damaging intensity for them. Thus, only a more refined material stuff composed of more mobile elements is appropriate to make the distances of Jupiter or Saturn from the sun a fortunate location.

Finally, because of a physical connection, the excellence of the natures in these higher regions of the heavens seems to be connected with an ability to last which is appropriate to it. Decay and death can afflict these excellent beings less than they do our low natures. Exactly the same torpor in the material and coarseness of the stuff, the specific principle in the degradation in the lower echelons, are the cause of the tendency which they have to decay. When the juices which nourish the animal or human being and make it grow, as they are assimilated among the small fibres and increase its bulk, can no longer expand the spatial dimensions of their vessels and canals, when growth is already complete, then these nourishing liquids which add to the body's mass must, through the mechanical impulse which is used to feed the animal, constrict and block up the hollow sections of their vessels and destroy the structure of the entire machine with a gradually increasing paralysis. We can believe that, although mortality also eats away at the most perfect beings, nevertheless there is an advantage in the refined quality of the material stuff, in the elasticity of the vessels, and in the lightness and efficacy of the fluids which make up those more perfect entities living in the distant planets. This benefit checks for a much longer time the frailty which results from the inertia of a coarse material and gives these creatures a durability whose length is proportional to their perfection. Thus, the fragility of human life is appropriately linked to human baseness.

I cannot leave these observations without anticipating a doubt about it, which could naturally arise from a comparison of these opinions with our previous principles. In dealing with the dwelling places in the planetary structure, we have acknowledged the wisdom of God in the number of satellites which illuminate the planets with the most distant orbits, in the velocity of their axial rotation, and in the composition of their material stuff, which is proportional to the effects of the sun. This Divine Wisdom has organized everything so beneficially for the advantage of sensible beings who inhabit the planets. But how would we now reconcile the concept of intentionality with a mechanical theory, so that what the Highest Wisdom itself devised is assigned to raw material stuff and the rule of providence is turned over to nature left to act on its own? Is the first not rather a confession that the organizing of the cosmic structure is not developed through the general laws of the latter?

We will soon dispose of this doubt if we only think back to what was cited previously in a similar case. Must not the mechanism of all natural movements have an essential tendency towards only such consequences as those which really coincide with the project of the Highest Reason in the full context of interrelationships? How can they have erratic inclinations and an independent scattering originally, when all their characteristics, from which these consequences develop, are themselves regulated by the eternal idea of the Divine Understanding, in which all things must necessarily interconnect with each other and fit together? When we think correctly, how can we justify the kind of judgment where we see nature as a rebellious subject, which can be kept on a regular track and in communal harmony only through some kind of compulsion which sets limits to her free conduct, unless we maintain something to the effect that nature is a self-sufficient principle, whose characteristics acknowledge no cause and which God seeks to force according to His purposeful plan, to the extent that this is possible? The closer we come to getting to know nature, the more we will realize that the universal ways in which things are made are not strange and separate from each other. We will be sufficiently convinced that they have essential connections, through which they are coordinated, to support each other in providing a more perfect state, in the reciprocal effects of the elements on the beauty of material things and at the same time for the benefit of the spiritual realm and that, in general, the single natures of things in the field of universal truths already make up amongst themselves, so to speak, a system, in which one is related to another. We will also immediately realize that the connection between them in their common origin is unique to them and that from this they, as a totality, have created their fundamental properties.

And now to apply this repeated observation to the proposed goal: the very same universal laws of motion which have allocated to the highest planets a location far from the mid-point of the power of attraction and inertia in the planetary system, have at the same time in this way set them in the most advantageous condition to develop themselves as far as possible from the point where they are connected to the coarse material and, indeed, with greater freedom. However, these laws have also simultaneously set the distant planets in a rule-bound relationship to the influence of the heat which, in accordance with the same law, extends out from this mid-point. Now, it is these very requirements which have removed obstructions from the development of the cosmic bodies in these distant regions and made the production of movements, which is dependent upon this development, faster and, in brief, created a more properly established system. Since finally the spiritual beings necessarily depend upon the material stuff to which they are personally bound, it is no wonder that the perfection of nature is shaped by both points into a single coordinated system of causes and on the same foundations. In a more precise view, this harmony is also not something sudden or unanticipated. Because through a similar principle the latter beings have been infused into the universal constitution of matter, the spiritual world is more perfect in the distant spheres for exactly the same reasons that the physical world is.

Thus, everything in the total extent of nature holds together in an uninterrupted series of stages through the eternal harmony which makes all the steps related to each other. The perfections of God have clearly revealed themselves at our levels and are no less beautiful in the lowest classes than in the more lofty ones.

Vast Chain of Being! Which from God began,

Natures ethereal, human, angel, man,

Beast, bird, fish, insect, what no eye can see,

No glass can reach! From Infinite to thee,

From thee to nothing.

(Pope)[51*]

We have continued the earlier conjectures, being faithful to the main idea of physical relationships. This has kept them on the path of a reasonable credibility. Should we permit ourselves one more digression from this track into the field of fantasy? Who indicates to us the border where grounded probability stops and arbitrary fictions begin? Who is so bold as to dare an answer to the question whether sin exercises its sway also in the other spheres of the cosmic structure or whether virtue alone has established her control there?

The stars perhaps enthrone the exalted soul

As here vice rules, there virtue has control.

(von Haller)

Does not a certain middle position between wisdom and irrationality belong to the unfortunate capacity to sin? Who knows whether the inhabitants of those distant celestial bodies are not too refined and too wise to allow themselves to fall into the foolishness inherent in sin; whereas, the others who live in the lower planets adhere too firmly to material stuff and are provided with far too little spiritual capacity to have to drag the responsibility for their actions before the judgment seat of justice? With this in mind, would the Earth and perhaps even Mars (so that the painful consolation of having fellow sufferers in misfortune would not be taken from us) be alone in the dangerous middle path, where the experience of sensual charms has a powerful ability to divert from the ruling mastery of the spirit. The spirit, however, cannot deny its ability to resist, unless its inertia prefers instead to allow itself to be carried away by these charms. Thus, here is the dangerous transition point between weakness and the capacity to resist, for the very same advantages which raise the spirit above the lower classes, set it up at a height from which it can again sink down infinitely deeper under them. In fact, both planets, Earth and Mars, are the most central rungs of the planetary system, and for their inhabitants we can assume perhaps with some probability a physical condition as well as a moral constitution half way between the two end points. But I prefer to leave this thought to those who find in themselves more reassurance in dealing with unprovable knowledge and more motivation to set down an answer.

CONCLUSION

We do not really know what the human being truly is today, although our awareness and understanding should instruct us in this matter. How much less would we be able to guess what a human being is to become in future! However, the curiosity of the human soul grasps with great eagerness for this far distant subject and strives to put some light on such unilluminated knowledge.

Is the everlasting soul for the full eternity of its future existence, which the grave itself does not destroy but only changes, always to remain fixed at this point of the cosmos, on our Earth? Is it never to share a closer look at the rest of creation's miracles? Who knows whether it is not determined that in future the soul will get to know at close quarters those distant spheres of the cosmic structure and the excellence of their dwelling places, which already attract its curiosity from far away? Perhaps that is why some spheres of the planetary system are already developing, in order to prepare for us in other heavens new places to live after the completion of the time prescribed for our stay here on Earth. Who knows whether those satellites do not circle around Jupiter so as to provide light for us in the future?

It is permissible and appropriate to entertain ourselves with ideas of this kind. But no one will ground future hope on such uncertain imaginary pictures. When vanity has demanded its share of human nature, then the immortal spirit will, with a swift leap, raise itself up above everything finite and further develop its existence in a new relationship with the totality of nature, which arises out of closer ties with the Highest Being. From then on, this lofty nature, which in itself contains the source of blissful happiness, will no longer be scattered among external objects in order to seek out a calming effect among them. The collective essence of creatures, which has a necessary harmony with the pleasure of the Highest Original Being, must also have this harmony for its own pleasure and will light upon it only in perpetual contentment.

In fact, when we have completely filled our dispositions with such observations and with what has been brought out previously, then the sight of a starry heaven on a clear night gives a kind of pleasure which only noble souls experience. In the universal stillness of nature and the tranquillity of the mind, the immortal soul's hidden capacity to know speaks an unnamable language and provides inchoate ideas which are certainly felt but are incapable of being described. If among thinking creatures of this planet there are malicious beings who, regardless of all incitements which such a great subject can offer, are nevertheless in the condition of being stuck firmly in the service of vanity, how unfortunate this sphere is that it could produce such miserable creatures! But, on the other hand, how fortunate this sphere is that a way lies open, under conditions which are the worthiest of all to accept, to reach a blissful happiness and nobility, something infinitely far above the advantages which the most beneficial of all nature's arrangements in all planetary bodies can attain!

The Form and Principles of the Sensible and the Intelligible World

Contents

SECTION I
ON THE IDEA OF A WORLD IN GENERAL

Paragraph *1*

As the analysis of a substantial composite terminates only in a part which is not a whole, that is, in a *simple part*, so synthesis terminates only in a whole which is not a part, that is, the *world*.

In this exposition of the underlying concept I have had regard not only to the marks pertaining to the distinct cognition of the object, but somewhat also to the *two-fold* genesis of the concept from the nature of the mind, which, being serviceable to a method of deeper metaphysical insight, by way of example appears to me not a little commendable. For it is one thing, the parts being given, to conceive the *composition* of the whole by an abstract notion of the intellect, and another thing to *follow out* this general *notion* considered as a problem of the reason by the cognitive sensuous faculty, that is, to represent it to one's self in the concrete by a distinct intuition. The former is done through the class concept by *composition*, as several things are contained either under it or mutually, and hence by intellectual and universal ideas. The latter rests on the *conditions* of time, inasmuch as the concept of a composite is possible genetically, that is by *synthesis*, by the successive union of part to part, and falls under the laws of *intuition*. Similarly, a substantial composite being given, we easily attain to the idea of the simple parts by the general removal of the intellectual notion of *composition;* for what remains after the removal of conjunction are the simple parts. But according to the laws of intuitive cognition this is not done, that is, all composition is not removed, except by a regress from the given whole to *any possible parts* whatsoever — in other words, by an analysis again resting on the condition of time. But since in order to a composite a *multiplicity*, in order to a whole, the *allness*, of parts is required, neither the analysis nor the synthesis will be complete; hence neither by the former will the concept of the *simple* part emerge, nor by the latter the concept of the *whole*, unless either can be gone through within a time that is finite and assignable.

But since in a *continuous quantity* the *regress* from the whole to assignable parts, and in an *infinite quantity* the *progress* from the parts to the given whole *are endless*, complete analysis in the one and complete synthesis in the other direction are impossible; hence neither the whole in the first case as to *composition*, nor the composite in the latter case as to *totality* can be thought completely in accordance with the laws of intuition. *Unthinkable* and *impossible* being vulgarly deemed to have the same meaning, it is plain why the concepts of the *continuous* as well as that of the *infinite* are rejected by most men as concepts whose representation *according to the laws of intuitive cognition* is impossible. Although I do not here champion these notions, especially not the first, which are considered exploded by many schools, still the following reminder is of the greatest moment. Those who use so perverse an argumentation have fallen into a grave error. For whatever is repugnant to the laws of the intellect and reason is of course impossible, but that which being the object of pure reason does merely *not fall under* the laws of intuitive cognition is not so. For here the disagreement between the *sensuous* and the *intellectual* faculties, whose natures

I shall presently explain, indicates nothing except *that the abstract ideas which the mind has received from the intellect can often not be followed out in the concrete and converted into intuitions*. This *subjective* difficulty generally feigns some objective repugnance and easily deceives the incautious, the limits by which the human mind is circumscribed being taken for those by which the essence of things themselves is contained.

Furthermore, as the argument from intellectual reasonings easily shows that substantial composites being given, whether by the testimony of the senses or otherwise, the simple parts and the world are also given, so does our definition point out causes contained in the nature of the subject why the notion of a world should not seem merely arbitrary and made up, as in mathematics, only for the sake of the deducible consequences. The mind intent upon resolving as well as compounding the concept of a composite demands and presumes boundaries in which it may acquiesce in the former as well as in the latter direction.

Paragraph *2*

In defining the World the following points require attention:

Matter (in the transcendental sense), that is, the *parts* which are here assumed to be *substances*. We might plainly be regardless of coincidence between our definition and the meaning of the common word, the question being, so to speak, of a problem arising in accordance with the laws of reasoning, namely, how several substances may coalesce into one, and on what condition rests this one's being no part of another. But the force of the word World, as commonly used, of itself falls in with us. For no one will attribute *accidents* to the *World* as *parts*, but as *determinations, states;* hence the so-called world of the *ego*, unrestrained by the single substance and its accidents, is not very appositely called a World, unless, perhaps, an imaginary one. For the same reason it is not permissible to refer the successive series — namely, of states — as a part to the mundane whole; for modifications are *not parts*, but *consequences* of the subject. Finally, as to the nature of the substances constituting the world, I have not here called into debate whether they be *contingent* or necessary, nor do I hide such a determination unproved in the definition in order subsequently, as is sometimes done, to draw it thence by some specious argumentation. But I shall show further on that their contingency can be amply concluded from the conditions here posited.

Form, which consists in the *co-ordination* of the substances, not in their subordination. For *co-ordinates* are to be regarded as mutual complements to a whole, *subordinates* as effect and cause, or generally, as principle and consequence. The former relation is reciprocal and *homonymous*, any correlate in respect to any other being considered as at once determining and determined. The latter is *heteronymous;* on the one hand dependence only, causality on the other. This co-ordination is conceived as real and objective, not as ideal, and resting in the mere pleasure of a subject making up a whole by the summation of any multiplicity whatever. For the grasping of several things can by no contrivance be made a *whole of representation*, nor, for that reason, *a representation of the whole*. Therefore, if there be any totals of substances connected by no bond, a grasping of them together, the mind forcing the multiplicity into ideal oneness, will be called nothing more than a plurality of worlds comprehended in a single thought. But the connection constituting the *essential* form of a world is looked upon as the principle of the *possible influences* of the substances composing that world. For an actual influence pertains not to essence but to state, and the transitive forces, the causes of the influences, suppose some principle by which it is possible that the states of several things in other respects existing independently of each other are mutually related as consequences, which principle being abandoned, the possibility of transitive force in a world is an illicit assumption. And, furthermore, this *form essential* to the world is on that account *immutable*, and exposed to no vicissitude whatever. It is so in the first place for a logical reason, since any change supposes the identity of the subject with determinations succeeding one another in turn. Hence the world, remaining the same world through all the states succeeding one another, preserves the same fundamental form. For it does not suffice to the identity of the whole that all the *parts* be identical, the identity of characteristic *composition* is required also. But it follows especially from a *real cause*. For the nature of the world, which is the primary inner principle of whatever variable determinations may pertain to its state, never by any possibility being opposite to itself, is naturally, that is, by itself, immutable; hence there is given in any world whatever some form ascribable to its nature, constant and invariable, as the perennial principle of any contingent and transitory form pertaining to the state of the world. They who hold this disquisition superfluous are confuted by the concepts of space and time, conditions, as it were, given by their very own selves and primitive, by whose aid, that is to say, without any other principle, it is not only possible but necessary for several actual things to be regarded as reciprocally parts constituting a whole. But I shall show presently that these are plainly not *rational* notions, nor the bonds which they form objective *ideas*, but phenomena; and that though they witness, to be sure, some principle which is the common universal bond, it is not set forth by them.

Universality, which is the *absolute* allness of the appertaining parts. For, *regard* being had to any given composite, though it may be besides a part of another, still there always obtains a certain comparative allness, namely, that of the parts belonging to it as a particular quantity. But in this case whatsoever things are regarded as mutually parts of *whatsoever* whole, are understood to be conjointly posited. This absolute *totality*, apparently an everyday and perfectly obvious concept, especially when, as happens in the definition, it is enunciated negatively, when canvassed thoroughly becomes the crucial test of the philosopher. For it is scarce conceivable how the *inexhaustible series* of the states of the universe succeeding one another *eternally* be reducible to a *whole* comprehending all changes whatsoever. Since it is necessary to very infinitude to be without *end*, and hence no successive series is given but what is the part of another, completeness or *absolute totality* is by parity of reasoning plainly excluded. For although the notion of a part can be taken in a universal sense, and although everything contained under this notion, if regarded as posited in the same series, constitutes unity, yet the concept of the *whole* appears to exact their all being *taken simultaneously*, which in the case given is impossible. For, although to the whole series nothing succeeds, there is given in the succession no posited series to which nothing succeeds, unless it be the last. There will, then, in eternity be something which is last, which is absurd. Perhaps some may think that the difficulty which besets a successive infinite is absent from a *simultaneous infinite*, for the reason that apparently *simultaneity* plainly professes to embrace *all at the same time*. But, if the simultaneous infinite be admitted, the successive infinite also will have to be conceded, and the negation of the latter cancels the former. For the simultaneous infinite offers matters everlastingly inexhaustible to a successive progress in infinitum through its innumerable parts, which numberless series actually being given in the simultaneous infinite, a series though inexhaustible by successive addition could be given as a *whole*. In solution of the perplexing problem note; that both the successive and the simultaneous co-ordination of several things, since they rest upon the concept of time, do not pertain to the *intellectual* concept of a whole, but only to the conditions of *sensuous intuition;* hence though not sensuously conceivable, they do not on that score cease being intellectual concepts. For in order to the latter it suffices that co-ordinates be given, no matter how, and that they be thought of as all pertaining to a unit.

SECTION II
ON THE DISTINCTION BETWEEN THE SENSIBLE AND THE INTELLIGIBLE GENERALLY

Paragraph *3*

Sensibility is the *receptivity* of a subject by which it is possible for its representative state to be affected in a certain way by the presence of some object. *Intelligence*, rationality, is the *faculty* of a subject by which it is able to represent to itself what by its quality cannot enter the senses. The object of sensibility is sensuous; what contains nothing but what is knowable by the intellect is intelligible. In the older schools the former was called *phenomenon*, the latter *noumenon*. To the extent to which knowledge is subject to the laws of sensuousness it is sensuous; to the extent to which it is subject to the laws of intelligence it is *intellectual* or rational.

Paragraph *4*

Since whatever is in sensuous knowledge depends upon the subject's peculiar nature, as the latter is capable of receiving some modification or other from the presence of objects which on account of subjective variety may be different in different subjects, whilst whatever knowledge is exempt from such subjective condition regards the object only, it is plain that what is sensuously thought is the representation of things *as they appear*, while the intellectual presentations are the representations of things *as they are*. Now there is in sense representation something which may be called the *matter*, namely, the *sensation*, and in addition to this something which may be called the *form*, namely, the *appearance* of the sensible things, showing forth to what extent a natural law of the mind co-ordinates the variety of sensuous affections. Furthermore, as the sensation constituting the *matter* of sensuous representations argues, to be sure, the presence of something sensible, but depends as to quality on the nature of the subject, as the latter is modifiable by the object; exactly so does the *form* of that representation witness certainly some reference or relation among the sensuous percepts, but itself is not, as it were, the shadowing forth or outlining of the object, but only a certain law inherent in the mind for co-ordinating among themselves sensuous percepts arising from the presence of the object. For by form or appearance the objects do not strike the sense, hence in order that various sense-affecting objects may coalesce into some whole of representation, there is need of an inner principle of the mind by which, in accordance with stable and innate laws, that variety shall take on some *appearance*.

Paragraph *5*

To sensual cognition then pertains both the matter which is sensation and by which the knowledge is said to be *sensual*, and the form by which, even though we find it without any sensation, the representations are called *sensuous*. On the other hand, as to *intellectual* concepts, it is above all to be well noted that the use of the intellect, or of the superior faculty of the soul, is two-fold. By the first use are *given* the very concepts both of things and relations. This is the *real use*. By the second use they, whencesoever given, are merely by common marks *subordinated* to one another, the lower to the higher, and compared among themselves according to the principle of contradiction. This is called the *logical* use. The logical use of the intellect is common to all the sciences; the real use is not. For a cognition given in any wise is regarded either as contained under or as opposed to a mark common to several cognitions, and this either by immediate apposition, as in *judgments* in order to distinct cognition, or mediately, as in *reasoning*, in order to adequate cognition. Thus sensuous knowledge being given, sensuous percepts are by the logical use of the intellect subordinated to other sensuous percepts, as to common concepts, and phenomena to the more general laws of phenomena. In this connection it is of the greatest moment to note that cognitions must continue to be regarded as sensuous, no matter how great may have been the logical use of the intellect upon them. For they are called sensuous *on account of their origin*, not of their *collation* by identity and opposition. Hence, empirical laws, though of the greatest generality, are, nevertheless, sensual, and the principles of sensuous form in geometry, the relations in determinate space, however much the intellect arguing according to logical rules from what is sensuously given, by pure intuition, be employed upon them, do not for that matter pass beyond the class of sense-percepts. That in sense-percepts and phenomena which precedes the logical use of the intellect is called *appearance*, while the reflex knowledge originating from several appearances compared by the intellect is called *experience*. Thus there is no way from appearance to experience except by reflection according to the logical use of the intellect. The common concepts of experience are termed *empirical*, its objects *phenomena*, and the laws as well of experience as of all sensuous cognition generally are called the laws of phenomena. Empirical concepts, then, are not by a reduction to greater universality rendered intellectual in the *real sense* and do not transcend the species of sensuous cognition, but, however high abstraction may carry them, remain indefinitely sensuous.

Paragraph *6*

Now as to *strictly intellectual concepts* in which the *use* of the *intellect* is *real*. Such concepts both of objects and relations are given by the very nature of the intellect, are not abstracted from any use of the senses, and do not contain any form of sensuous knowledge as such. It is needful here to take note of the extreme ambiguity of the word *abstract*, which, in order not to confuse our disquisition on intellectual concepts, must be removed to begin with, for properly we should say *abstract from some things*, not *abstract something*. The former denotes that in a concept we give no attention to other matters in whatsoever way they may be connected with it; but the latter, that it is not given but in the concrete and so as to be separated from what it is conjoined with. Hence an intellectual concept *abstracts* from everything sensuous, it is *not abstracted* from sensuous things, and perhaps would be more correctly called *abstracting* than *abstract*. Intellectual concepts it is more cautious, therefore, to call *pure ideas*, and concepts given only empirically, *abstract* ideas.

Paragraph *7*

From the foregoing it will be seen that it is badly to expound the sensuous to call it the *more confusedly* known, and the intellectual the *distinctly* known. For these are only logical distinctions and plainly do *not touch* the *data* underlying all logical comparison. The sensuous may be exceedingly distinct, while intellectual concepts are extremely confused. The former we observe in the prototype of sensuous knowledge, *geometry;* the latter, in the organon of all intellectual concepts, *metaphysics.* It is evident how much toil the latter is expending to dispel the fogs of confusion darkening the common intellect, though not always with the happy success of the former science. Nevertheless, any cognition retains the marks of its origin, the former, however distinct, being called by genesis sensuous; the latter, no matter how confused, remaining intellectual, as for instance, the *moral* concepts, which are known not experientially but by the pure intellect itself. The writer fears that Wolf by the distinction between the sensuous and the intellectual, which to him is only logical, checked, perhaps wholly, and to the great detriment of philosophy, that noble enterprise of antiquity of discussing the nature of phenomena and noumena, turning us from the investigation of these to what are frequently but logical trifles.

Paragraph *8*

The *primary* philosophy containing the *principles* of the use of *pure intellect* is *metaphysics.* But there is a science *propaedeutical* to it, showing the distinction of sensuous cognition from intellectual, a specimen of which we present in this dissertation. Empirical principles not being found in metaphysics, the concepts to be met with in it are not then to be sought for in the senses, but in the very nature of pure intellect; not as *connate* notions, but as abstracted from laws whose seat is in the mind, by attending to the actions of the mind on the occasion of experience, and hence as *acquired.* Of this species are possibility, existence, necessity, substance, cause, etc., with their opposites and correlates, which, never entering as parts into any sensual representation, can by no means have been abstracted thence.

Paragraph *9*

The purpose of intellectual concepts is mainly twofold; in the first place *refutative,* by which they are of negative use, when, shutting off sensuous concepts from noumena, though not advancing science a hair's breadth, they maintain however its immunity from the contagion of error. In the second place *dogmatic,* following which the general principles of pure intellect, such as are set forth in ontology or rational psychology, go forth into an exemplar inconceivable except by pure intellect, and the common measure of all other things considered as realities, namely, *noumenal perfection.* The latter is such either in the theoretical or in the practical sense. In the former it is the highest being, *God.* In the latter sense, it is *moral perfection. Moral philosophy,* then, inasmuch as supplying the first *principles of judgment,* is not cognized except by pure intellect, and itself belongs to pure philosophy, and Epicurus reducing its criteria to deduction from the sense of pleasure or pain is rightly reprehended, together with some moderns following him a certain distance from afar, as Shaftesbury and his adherents. In any class of things having variable quantity the *maximum* is the common measure and the principle of cognition. Now the *maximum of perfection* is called *ideal,* by Plato, Idea — for instance, his Idea of a Republic — and is the principle of all that is contained under the general notion of any perfection, inasmuch as the lesser grades are not thought determinable but by limiting the maximum. But God, the Ideal of perfection, and hence the principle of cognition, is also, as existing really, the principle of the creation of all perfection.

Paragraph *10*

To man, no *intuition* of intellectual concepts is given, only *symbolical cognition*, and intellection is granted us only by universal concepts in the abstract, not by the concrete singular. For all intuition is restricted by some principle of form under which alone anything can be *discerned* by the mind immediately or as *singular*, and not merely conceived discursively by general concepts. This formal principle of our intuition — space and time — is the condition under which something can be an object of our senses, and hence as a condition of sensuous knowledge is not a medium for intellectual intuition. Besides, all the material of our cognition is given only by the senses, but the noumenon, as such, is not conceivable by representations drawn from sensations; hence the intellectual concept, as such, is destitute of all *data* of human intuition. For the intuition of our mind is always *passive*, and therefore possible only to the extent to which something can affect our senses. But the divine intuition, the cause — not the consequence, of objects, being independent, is the archetype, and hence perfectly intellectual.

Paragraph *11*

But although phenomena are properly the appearances of things, but not ideas, or express the inner and absolute quality of objects, their cognition is nevertheless of the truest. For in the first place, being apprehended sensual concepts, they, being consequences, witness the presence of the object, contrary to Idealism; and as regards judgments concerning that which is sensuously known, since truth in judging consists in the agreement of the predicate with the given subject, and since the concept of the subject as a phenomenon is given only by relation to the sensuous cognitive faculty, the sensuously observable predicates being given according to the same, it is plain that the representations of subject and predicate are made according to common laws, and hence give occasion for perfectly true cognition.

Paragraph *12*

All sense-objects are phenomena, but that which, not touching our senses, contains the form only of sensuality, belongs to pure intuition, that is, an intuition devoid of sensations, but not on that account, intellectual. Phenomena of the external sense are examined and set forth in *physics;* those of the internal sense in empirical psychology. But pure human intuition is not a universal or logical concept *under which*, but a singular in which all sensible objects are thought, and hence contains concepts of space and time, which, since they determine nothing concerning sensible objects as to *quality*, are not the objects of science except as to *quantity*. Hence *pure mathematics* considers *space* in *geometry* and *time* in *pure mechanics*. To these is to be added a certain concept, intellectual to be sure in itself, but whose becoming actual in the concrete requires the auxiliary notions of time and space in the successive addition and simultaneous juxtaposition of separate units, which is the concept of *number* treated in *arithmetic*. Pure mathematics, then, expounding the form of our entire sensuous cognition, is the organon of all intuitive and distinct knowledge, and since its objects are not only the formal principles of all intuition, but themselves original intuitions, it confers cognition both perfectly true, and the model of the highest degree of clearness to others. There is *given, therefore, a science of sensual things*, though being phenomena there is not given a real intellection, but a logical one only; hence it is plain in what sense those borrowing from the Eleatic school are to be thought to have denied a science of phenomena.

SECTION III
ON THE PRINCIPLES OF THE FORM OF THE SENSIBLE WORLD

Paragraph *13*

The principle of the form of a universe is that which contains the cause of the universal tie by means of which all substances and their states pertain to one which is called a *world*. The principle of the form of the *sensible world* is that which contains the cause of the universal tie of all things regarded as *phenomena*. The form of the *intelligible world* acknowledges an objective principle, that is, some cause by which it is the colligation of what exists in it. But the world regarded as phenomenon, that is, in respect to the sensibility of the human mind, acknowledges no principle of form but a subjective one, that is, a certain mental law by which it is necessary that all things qualified for being objects of the senses would seem to pertain *necessarily* to the same whole. Whatever be, therefore, the principle of the form of the sensible world, it will comprise only *actual* things in as far as thought of as possibly falling under *sense-perception;* hence neither immaterial substances, which as such are excluded by definition from the external senses altogether, nor the cause of the world, which, since by it the mind exists and has the power of sense-perception, cannot be the object of the senses. These formal principles of the *phenomenal universe* which are absolutely primary, universal, and, so to speak, the outlines and conditions of anything else whatsoever in human sensuous cognition, I shall now show to be two: time and space.

Paragraph 14 OF TIME

The idea of time does not originate in, but is presupposed by the senses. Whether things falling under sense-perception be simultaneous or in line of succession cannot be represented but by the idea of time; nor does succession beget the concept of time; it appeals to it. Hence the notion of time, though acquired by experience, is badly defined by a series of actual things existing one *after* another, for what the word *after* means I understand only by the previous concept of time. For those things are *after* one another which exist at *different times*, as those are *simultaneous* which exist at the *same time*.

The idea of time is singular, not general. For any time whatever is thought only as a part of one and the same unmeasured time. If you think two years you cannot represent them to yourself but in a mutually determinate position, and if they do not immediately follow one the other, you cannot think of them except as connected by some intermediate time. Which of different times is *first* and which *later* can be defined in no way by any marks conceivable by the intellect, unless you are willing to run into a circle, and the mind discerns it by no more than one intuition. Besides, we conceive of all actual things as posited *in* time, not as contained as common marks *under* a general notion of time.

The idea of time, therefore, *is an intuition*, and being conceived before all sensation as the condition of the relations occurring in sensible things, it is not a sensual but *pure intuition*.

Time is a continuous quantity and the principle of the laws of continuity in the changes of the universe. For a *continuous* quantity is one which does not consist of simple parts. But since by time are only thought relations without any mutually related data, there is in time — as a quantity — composition, which being conceived wholly removed leaves nothing over. But a composite of which, composition being removed, nothing is left, does not consist of simple parts. Therefore, etc. Any part of time, then, is time; and the simple things in time, namely, the *moments*, are not parts of it, but termini between which time intervenes. For two moments being given, time is not given, except as in them actualities succeed each other; hence, beside the given moment it is necessary that time be given in the latter part of which there is another moment.

The metaphysical law of *continuity* is this: *All changes are continuous* or flowing, that is, opposite states succeed each other only by an intermediate series of different states. For since two opposite states are in different moments of time, and some time is always intercepted between two moments, in which infinite series of moments the substance is neither in one assignable state nor the other, nor yet in none, it will be in different states, and so on infinitely.

The celebrated Kästner, calling in question this Leibnitzian law, calls on its defenders to demonstrate that the *continuous motion of a point around the sides of a triangle is impossible*, it being necessary to prove this if the law of continuity be granted. Here is the demonstration required. Let the letters *a b c* denote the three angular points of a rectilineal triangle. If the point did move continuously over the lines *ab, bc, ca,* that is, over the perimeter of the figure, it would be necessary for it to move at the point *b* in the direction *ab*, and also at the same point *b* in the direction *bc*. These motions being diverse, they cannot be *simultaneous*. Therefore, the moment of presence of the movable point at vertex *b*, considered as moving in the direction *ab*, is different from the moment of presence of the movable point at the same vertex *b*, considered as moving in the same direction *bc*. But between two moments there is time; therefore, the movable point is present at point *b* for some time, that is, it *rests*. Therefore it does not move continuously, which is contrary to the assumption. The same demonstration is valid for motion over any right lines including an assignable angle. Hence a body does not change its direction in continuous motion except by following a line no part of which is straight, that is, a curve, as Leibnitz maintained.

Time is not something objective and real, neither a substance, nor an accident, nor a relation. It is the subjective condition necessary by the nature of the human mind for coordinating any sensible objects among themselves by a certain law; time is a *pure intuition*. Substances as well as accidents we co-ordinate whether according to simultaneity or succession by the concept only of time; hence the notion of time as the principle of form outranks the concepts of the former. Any relations so far as occurring in sense-perception, whether simultaneous or successive, involve nothing but the determination of positions in time, to wit, either in the same point or in different points of the latter.

Those who assert the objective reality of time either conceive of it as a continuous flow in what exists, without, however, any existing thing, as is done especially by the English philosophers, an absurd fiction, or as something real abstracted from the succession of inner states, as it has been put by Leibnitz and his followers. The falsity of the latter opinion, besides obviously exposing it to the vicious circle in the definition of time, and, moreover, plainly neglecting *simultaneity*, the most important consequence of time, disturbs all sound reason, because it demands instead of the determining of the laws of motion by the measure of time, that time itself, as to its nature, be determined by what is observed in motion or some series of inner changes, whereby plainly all certitude of rules is abolished. That we can estimate the *quantity* of time only in the concrete, namely, either by *motion* or by a *series of thoughts*, arises from the concept of time resting only on an inherent mental law, it not being a connate intuition; whence the act of the mind co-ordinating the impressions is elicited only by the aid of the senses. So far from its being possible to deduce and explain the concept of time from some other source by force of reason, it is presupposed by the very principle of contradiction, it underlies it by way of condition. For *a* and *not-a* are not repugnant unless thought of the *same thing simultaneously*, that is, at the same time; they may *belong* to the same thing *after* each other, at different times. Hence the possibility of changes is not thinkable except in time. Time is not thinkable by changes, but reversely.

But although *time* posited in itself and absolutely be an imaginary thing, yet as appertaining to the immutable law of sensible things as such, it is a perfectly true concept, and the patent condition of intuitive representation throughout all the infinite range of possible sense-objects. For since simultaneous things as such cannot be placed before the senses but by the aid of time, and since changes are unthinkable except by time, it is obvious that this concept contains the universal form of phenomena, and that, indeed, all events observable in the world, all motions, all internal changes, agree necessarily with the temporal axioms of cognition which we have partly expounded, *since only under these conditions can they become sense-objects and be co-ordinated*. It is, therefore, absurd to excite reason against the primary postulates of pure time, as, for example, continuity, etc., since they follow from laws prior and superior to which nothing is found, and since reason herself in the use of the principle of contradiction cannot dispense with the support of this concept, so primitive and original is it.

Time, then, is the absolutely first *formal principle of the sensible world*. For all sensible things of whatsoever description are unthinkable except as posited either simultaneously or one after another, and, indeed, as if involved and mutually related by determinate position in the tract of unique time, so that by this primary concept of everything sensuous originates necessarily that formal whole which is not a part of another, that is, the *phenomenal World*.

Paragraph 15 OF SPACE

The concept of space is not abstracted from external sensations. For I am unable to conceive of anything posited without me unless by representing it as in a place different from that in which I am, and of things as mutually outside of each other unless by locating them in different places in space. Therefore the possibility of external perceptions, as such, *presupposes* and does not *create* the concept of space, so that, although what is in space affects the senses, space cannot itself be derived from the senses.

The concept of space is a singular representation comprehending all things *in itself*, not an abstract and common notion containing them *under* itself. What are called *several spaces* are only parts of the same immense space mutually related by certain positions, nor can you conceive of a cubic foot except as being bounded in all directions by surrounding space.

The concept of space, therefore, is a pure intuition, being a singular concept, not made up by sensations, but itself the fundamental form of all external sensation. This pure intuition is in fact easily perceived in geometrical axioms, and any mental construction of postulates or even problems. That in space there are no more than three dimensions, that between two points there is but one straight line, that in a plane surface from a given point with a given right line a circle is describable, are not conclusions from some universal notion of space, but only *discernible* in space as in the concrete. Which things in a given space lie toward one side and which are turned toward the other can by no acuteness of reasoning be described discursively or reduced to intellectual marks. There being in perfectly similar and equal but incongruous solids, such as the right and the left hand, conceived of solely as to extent, or spherical triangles in opposite hemispheres, a difference rendering impossible the coincidence of their limits of extension, although for all that can be stated in marks intelligible to the mind by speech they are interchangeable, it is patent that only by pure intuition can the difference, namely, incongruity, be noticed. Geometry, therefore, uses principles not only undoubted and discursive but falling under the mental view, and the *obviousness* of its demonstrations — which means the clearness of certain cognition in as far as assimilated to sensual knowledge — is not only greatest, but the only one which is given in the pure sciences, and the *exemplar* and medium of all *obviousness* in the others. For, since geometry considers the *relations of space*, the concept of which contains the very form of all sensual intuition, nothing that is perceived by the external sense can be clear and perspicuous unless by means of that intuition which it is the business of geometry to contemplate. Besides, this science does not demonstrate its universal propositions by thinking the object through the universal concept, as is done in intellectual disquisition, but by submitting it to the eyes in a single intuition, as is done in matters of sense.

Space is not something objective and real, neither substance, nor accident, nor relation; but *subjective* and ideal, arising by fixed law from the nature of the mind like an outline for the mutual co-ordination of all external sensations whatsoever. Those who defend the reality of space either conceive of it as an *absolute* and immense *receptacle* of possible things, an opinion which, besides the English, pleases most geometricians, or they contend for its being the relation of existing things *itself*, which clearly vanishes in the removal of things and is thinkable only in actual things, as besides Leibnitz, is maintained by most of our countrymen. The first inane fiction of the reason, imagining true infinite relation without any mutually related things, pertains to the world of fable. But the adherents of the second opinion fall into a much worse error. Whilst the former only cast an obstacle in the way of some rational or noumenal concepts, otherwise most recondite, such as questions concerning the spiritual world, omnipresence, etc., the latter place themselves in fiat opposition to the very phenomena, and to the most faithful interpreter of all phenomena, to geometry. For, not to enlarge upon the obvious circle in which they become involved in defining space, they cast forth geometry, thrown down from the pinnacle of certitude, into the number of those sciences whose principles are empirical. If we have obtained all the properties of space by experience from external relations only, geometrical axioms have only comparative universality, such as is acquired by induction. They have universality evident as far as observed, but neither necessity, except as far as the laws of nature may be established, nor precision, except what is arbitrarily made. There is hope, as in empirical sciences, that a space may some time be discovered endowed with other primary properties, perchance even a rectilinear figure of two lines.

Though the *concept of space* as an objective and real thing or quality is imaginary, it is nevertheless *in respect to all sensible things* not only *perfectly true*, it is the foundation of truth in external sensibility. Things cannot appear to the senses under any form but by means of a power of the soul co-ordinating all sensations in accordance with a fixed law implanted in its nature. Since, therefore, nothing at all can be given the senses except conformably to the primary axioms of space and their consequences which are taught by geometry, though their principle be but subjective, yet the soul will necessarily agree with them, since to this extent it agrees with itself; and the laws of sensuality will be the laws of nature *so far as it can be perceived by our senses*. Nature, therefore, is subject with absolute precision to all the precepts of geometry as to all the properties of space there demonstrated, this being the subjective condition, not hypothetically but intuitively given, of every phenomenon in which nature can ever be revealed to the senses. Surely, unless the concept of space were originally given by the nature of the mind, so as to cause him to toil in vain who should labor to fashion mentally any relations other than those prescribed by it, since in the fiction he would be compelled to employ the aid of this very same concept, geometry could not be used very safely in natural philosophy, For it might be doubted whether this same notion drawn from experience would agree sufficiently with nature, the determinations from which it was abstracted being, perchance, denied, a suspicion of which has entered some minds already. *Space*, then, is the absolutely first *formal principle of the sensible world*, not only because by its concept the objects of the universe can be phenomena, but especially for the reason that it is. essentially but one, comprising all externally sensible things whatsoever; and hence constitutes the principle of the *universe*, that is, of that whole which cannot be the part of another.

COROLLARY

Here, then, are *two principles of sensuous cognition*, not, as in intellectual knowledge, general concepts, but *single and nevertheless pure intuition*, in which the parts, and especially the simple parts, do not, as the laws of reason prescribe, contain the possibility of the composite, but, according to the pattern of sensuous intuition, the *infinite* contains the reason of the part, and finally of its thinkable simple part or rather limit. For unless infinite space as well as infinite time be given, no definite space and time is assignable *by limitation*, and a point as well as a moment is unthinkable by itself and only conceived in a space and time already given as the limits. All primitive properties of these concepts are then beyond the purview of reason, and hence cannot intellectually be explained in any way. Nevertheless, they are *what underlies the intellect* when from intuitive primary data it derives consequences according to logical laws with the greatest possible certainty. *One* of these concepts properly concerns the intuition of the *object;* the other the *state,* especially the *representative* state. Hence space is employed as the type even of the concept of *time* itself, representing it by a line, and its limits — moments — by points. Time, on the other hand, *approaches* more to a *universal* and *rational concept,* comprising under its relations all things whatsoever, to wit, space itself, and besides, those accidents which are not comprehended in the relations of space, such as the thoughts of the soul. Again, time, besides this, though it certainly does not dictate the laws of reason, yet *constitutes* the principal *conditions under* favor of *which the mind compares its notions according to the laws of reason.* Thus, I cannot judge what is impossible except by predicating *a* and *not-a* of the same subject *at the same time.* And especially, considering experience, though the reference of cause to effect in external objects were to lack the relations of space, still in all things, external or internal, the mind could by the auxiliary relation of time alone be informed which is the first and which latter or caused. And even the *quantity* of space itself cannot be rendered intelligible unless, referring it to measure as to a unity, we set it forth in number, which itself is but multiplicity distinctly cognized by numeration, that is, by the successive addition of one to one in a given time.

Lastly, the question will arise in any one as if spontaneously, whether either *concept* be *connate* or *acquired.* The latter by what has been shown seems refuted already, but the former, smoothing the way for *lazy philosophy,* declaring vain by the citing of a first cause any further quest, is not to be admitted thus rashly. But beyond doubt *either concept is acquired,* not, it is true, abstracted from the sense of objects, for sensation gives the matter not the form of human cognition, but from the very action of the mind co-ordinating its sense-percepts in accordance with perpetual laws, as though an immutable type, and hence to be known intuitively. For sensations excite this act of the mind but do not influence intuition, neither is there anything connate here except the law of the soul in accordance with which it conjoins in a certain way its sensations derived from the presence of an object.

SECTION IV

ON THE PRINCIPLE OF THE FORM OF THE INTELLIGIBLE WORLD

Paragraph *16*

Those who deem space and time to be something real and the absolute bond, so to speak, of all possible substances in space, hold nothing else to be required in order to conceive how an original relation can belong to several existing things as the primitive condition of possible influence and the principle of the essential form of the universe. For since whatever exists is, according to their opinion, necessarily somewhere, it seems to them quite superfluous to inquire why things are present to one another in a certain manner, since this is of itself determined by the universality of all-comprehending space. But this concept, besides relating as has been shown rather to the sensuous laws of the subject than to the conditions of the objects themselves, even granting it the greatest reality, still denotes nothing but the intuitively given possibility of universal co-ordination, leaving undealt with the question solvable only by the intellect: *In what principle does this very relation of all substances rest, which intuitively regarded is called space?* The question of the *principle of the form of the intelligible world* turns, therefore, upon making apparent in what manner it is possible *for several substances to be in mutual commerce*, and for this reason to pertain to the same whole, which is called world. We do not here consider the world, let it be understood, as to matter, that is, as to the nature of the substances of which it consists, whether they be material or immaterial, but as to form, that is to say, how among several things taken separately a connection, and among them all, totality can have place.

Paragraph *17*

Several substances being given, the *principle* of their possible *intercommunication is not apparent from their existence solely*, but something else is required besides from which their mutual relations may be understood. For on account of mere existence they are not necessarily related to anything, unless it be to their cause; but the relation of an effect to the cause is not intercommunication, but dependence. Therefore, if any commerce intervenes among them, there is need of an exactly determining specific reason.

The sham cause in *physical influence* consists in rashly assuming that the commerce of substance and transitive forces is sufficiently knowable from their mere existence. Hence it is not so much a system as rather the neglect of all philosophical system as a superfluity in the argument. Freeing the concept from this defect, we shall have a species of commerce alone deserving to be called real, and from which the whole constituting the world merits being called real, and not ideal or imaginary.

Paragraph *18*

A whole from necessary substances is impossible. For, since the existence of each stands for itself without dependence on any other, a dependence which in necessary substances clearly cannot befall, it is plain that not only does the intercommunication of substances (that is, the reciprocal dependence of their states) not follow from their existence, but as necessary substances cannot belong to them at all.

Paragraph *19*

The whole, therefore, of substances is a whole of contingent things, and the *world consists essentially of only contingent things*. Besides, no necessary substance is in connection with the world except as a cause with the effect, and, therefore, not as a part with its complements making up a whole, since the bond connecting parts is mutual dependence, which in a necessary being cannot occur. The cause, therefore, of the world is an extramundane being, and so is not the soul of the world, nor is its presence in the world local, but virtual.

Paragraph *20*

The mundane substances are beings from, another being; not from several, but *all from one*. For, suppose them to be caused by several necessary beings. In intercommunication there are not effects from causes alien to all mutual relation. Hence, the *unity* in the *conjunction of the substances of the universe is the consequence of the dependence of all on one*. Therefore, the form of the universe witnesses the cause of matter, and only the *sole cause of all things is the cause of the universe*, nor is there an *architect* of the world not at the same time its *creator*.

Paragraph *21*

If there were several primary and necessary causes together with their effects, their works would be *worlds*, not a *world*, since they would in no wise be connected into one whole. And vice versa, if there be several actual worlds without one another, several primary and necessary causes are given, so, however, as to give intercommunication neither to one world with another, nor to the cause of one with the world caused by another.

Several actual worlds without one another *are not*, therefore, *impossible by the very concept*, as Wolf hastily concluded from the notion of a complex or multiplicity which he deemed sufficient to a whole, as such, but only on condition *that there exist but one necessary cause of all things*. If several are admitted, *several worlds without one another will be possible* in the strictest metaphysical sense.

Paragraph *22*

If, as we validly conclude from a given world to a single cause of all its parts, we may similarly argue reversely from the given cause common to all to their interconnection, and hence to the form of the world — though I confess this conclusion does not seem as plain to me — then the primary connection of substances will not be contingent but *by the sustentation* of all *by the common principle*, necessary, and hence the harmony proceeding from their very subsistence founded in a common cause would proceed according to the usual rules. Such a *harmony* I term *established generally;* as that which does not take place except as far as any individual states of a substance are adapted to the condition of another is *harmony established particularly;* the communion by the former being real and *physical*, by the latter ideal and *sympathetic*.

All communion, then, of the substance of the universe is *eternally established* by the common cause of all, and either established generally by physical influence — as amended; see paragraph 17 — or adapted particularly to their states; and the latter either rests *originally* in the primary constitution of every substance or is impressed on the *occasion* of any change whatever; the first being called *pre-established harmony*, the latter *occasionalism*. If, then, on account of the sustentation of all substances by one, the *conjunction* of all constituting them a unit be *necessary*, the universal commerce of substances will be by *physical influence*, and the world a real whole; if not, the commerce will be sympathetic, that is a harmony without true commerce, and the world only an ideal whole. To me the former, though not demonstrated, appears abundantly proved by other reasons.

SCHOLIUM

If it were right to overstep a little the limits of apodictic certainty befitting metaphysics, it would seem worth while to trace out some things pertaining not merely to the laws but even to the causes of sensuous intuition, which are only *intellectually* knowable. Of course the human mind is not affected by external things, and the world does not lie open to its insight infinitely, except *as far as itself together with all other things is sustained by the same infinite power of one*. Hence it does not perceive external things but by the presence of the same common sustaining cause; and hence space, which is the universal and necessary condition of the joint presence of everything known sensuously, may be called the *phenomenal omnipresence*, for the cause of the universe is not present to all things and everything, as being in their places, but their places, that is the relations of the substances, are possible, because it is intimately present to all. Furthermore, since the possibility of the changes and successions of all things whose principle as far as sensuously known resides in the concept of time, supposes the continuous existence of the subject whose opposite states succeed; that whose states are in flux, lasting not, however, unless sustained by another; the concept of time as one infinite and immutable in which all things are and last, is the *phenomenal eternity* of the general *cause*. But it seems more cautious to hug the shore of the cognitions granted to us by the mediocrity of our intellect than to be carried out upon the high seas of such mystic investigations, like Malebranche, whose opinion that *we see all things in God* is pretty nearly what has here been expounded.

SECTION V
ON THE METHOD RESPECTING THE SENSUOUS AND THE INTELLECTUAL IN METAPHYSICS

Paragraph *23*

In all sciences whose principles are given intuitively, whether by sensual intuition, that is, experience, or by an intuition sensuous, to be sure, but pure — the concepts of space, time, and number — that is to say, in the natural and in the mathematical sciences, *use gives method*, and by trying and finding after the science has been carried to some degree of copiousness and consonancy it appears by what method and in what direction we must proceed in order to finish and to purify it by removing the defects of error as well as of confused thoughts; exactly as grammar after the more copious use of speech, and style after the appearance of choice examples in poetry and oratory, furnished vantage-ground to rules and to discipline. But the *use of the intellect* in the sciences whose primitive concepts as well as axioms are given by sensuous intuition is only *logical*, that is, by it we only subordinate cognitions to one another according to their relative universality conformably to the principle of contradiction, phenomena to more general phenomena, and consequences of pure intuition to intuitive axioms. But in pure philosophy, such as metaphysics, in which the *use of the intellect* in respect to principles is *real*, that is to say, where the primary concept of things and relations and the very axioms are given originally by the pure intellect itself, and not being intuitions do not enjoy immunity from error, *the method precedes the whole science*, and whatever is attempted before its precepts are thoroughly discussed and firmly established is looked upon as rashly conceived and to be rejected among vain instances of mental playfulness. For, since here the right use of the reason constitutes the very principles and the objects as well, what axioms are to be thought of concerning them become primarily known solely by its own nature, the exposition of the laws of pure reason is the very origin of the science, and their distinction from spurious laws the criterion of truth. The method of the science not being practiced much nowadays, except what logic prescribes to all sciences generally, that fitted for the peculiar nature of metaphysics being simply ignored, it is no wonder that those who everlastingly turn the Sisyphean stone of this inquiry do not seem so far to have made much progress. Though here I neither can nor will expatiate upon so important and extensive a subject, I shall briefly shadow forth what constitutes no despicable part of this method, namely, the *infection between sensuous and intellectual cognition*, not only as creeping in on those incautious in the application of principles, but even producing spurious principles under the appearance of axioms.

Paragraph *24*

In substance the whole method of metaphysics as to the sensuous and the intellectual amounts to this precept; to take care *not to allow the principles at home in sensuous cognition to outstray their limits and affect the intellectual concepts*. For, since the *predicate* in any judgment enounced intellectually *is a condition* in the absence of which the subject is asserted to be unthinkable, the predicate hence being the principle of cognition, it will, if a sensuous concept, be only the condition of a possible sensuous cognition — and hence will square well enough with the subject of a judgment whose concept is also sensuous. But if it be applied to an intellectual concept, the judgment will be valid only according to subjective laws, and hence must not be affirmed objectively and predicated of the intellectual notion itself, but *only as a condition in the absence of which the sensuous cognition of the given concept does not take place.*

Now, since the tricks of the intellect by the subordination of sensuous concepts as though intellectual marks may be called, analogously to the accepted meaning, *a fallacy of subreption*, the exchanging of intellectual and sensual concepts will be a *metaphysical fallacy of subreption*, the *intellectualized phenomenon*, if the barbarous expression be permissible, and hence I call such a *hybrid* axiom as palms off the sensuous as necessarily adhering to the intellectual concept, a *surreptitious axiom*. From these spurious axioms have gone forth, and are rife throughout metaphysics, principles deceiving the intellect. In order that we may have, however, a readily and clearly knowable criterion of those judgments, a touchstone, so to speak, by which to distinguish them from genuine judgments, and at the same time if, perhaps, they seem to cling tenaciously to the intellect, an assaying art by which we can justly estimate how much belongs to the sensuous and how much to the intellectual sphere, I think it necessary to go into the question more deeply.

Paragraph *25*

Here, then, is the *principle of reduction* for any spurious axiom: *If concerning any intellectual concept something pertaining to time and space relations be predicated generally, it is not to be enounced objectively, but denotes only the condition without which the given concept is not knowable sensuously.* That such an axiom is spurious, and, if not false, at least a rash and question-begging assertion, appears thus: the subject of the judgment being intellectually conceived pertains to the object, whilst the predicate, since it contains the determinations of space and time, pertains only to the conditions of human sensuous cognition, which, not adhering of necessity to any cognition whatsoever of the object, cannot be enounced concerning the given intellectual concept universally. The intellect's being so readily subject to this fallacy of subreption comes of its being deceived under the plea of another and perfectly true rule. For we rightly suppose that *that which can be cognized by no intuition whatever is utterly unthinkable* and hence impossible. But since we cannot attain by any mental striving, even fictitiously, to any other intuition but that according to the form of space and time, it happens that we deem all intuition whatever impossible which is not bound by these laws, passing by the pure intellectual intuition exempt from the laws of the senses, such as the divine, by Plato called the Idea, and hence subject all possible given things to the sensual axioms of space and time.

Paragraph *26*

All sleights of substitution of sensuous cognition under guise of intellectual concepts, from which spurious axioms originate, can be reduced to three species, whose general formulae are the following:

The sensual condition under which alone the *intuition* of an object is possible, is the condition of its *possibility.*

The sensual condition under which alone *data can be compared in order to form the intellectual concept of the object*, is the condition of the very possibility of the object.

The sensual condition under which alone the subsumption *of an* object under a given intellectual concept is possible, is the condition of the possibility of the object.

Paragraph *27*

A spurious axiom of the *first class* is: *Whatever is, is somewhere and sometime.* Now by this spurious principle all beings, even though they be intellectually cognized, are restricted in existence by the conditions of space and time. Hence people discuss all sorts of inane questions, such as concerning the places of immaterial substances — of which, for that very reason, there is no sensuous intuition, nor, under that form, any representation — in the corporeal universe, or the seat of the soul; and as they improperly mix sensual things with intellectual concepts, like square figures with round, it oftens happens that of the disputants one appears as milking a he-goat, and the other as holding the sieve under. The presence of immaterial substances in the corporeal world is virtual, not local, though thus improperly talked about. Space does not contain the conditions of possible mutual activities, except those of matter. What may constitute the external relations of forces in immaterial substances, as well among themselves as toward bodies, altogether escapes the human intellect, as was acutely noted, for instance, in a letter to a German prince by the clear-sighted Euler, otherwise a great investigator and judge of phenomena. But when people have arrived at the concept of a highest and extra-mundane being, they are fooled by these shadows flitting before the intellect to a degree beyond the force of language to express. The presence of God they figure to themselves as a *local* one, involving God in the world as if also comprised in infinite space, compensating Him for this limitation by a locality, so to speak, *eminently* conceived, that is, infinite. But it is absolutely impossible to be at the same time in several places, since different places are mutually without each other, and hence what is in several places is outside of itself, which implies being present to itself externally. But as to time, having not only exempted it from the laws of sensual knowledge, but transferred it beyond the limits of the world to the extra-mundane Being Himself as a condition of His existence, they involve themselves in an inextricable labyrinth. Hence they cudgel their brains with absurd questions, such as, for instance, why God did not make the world many centuries earlier. They persuade themselves that it is easy to conceive, to be sure, how God may discern what is present, that is, what is actual in the *time in which he is*, but how He may foresee what is future, that is, what is actual in the *time in which He is not yet*, they deem an intellectual difficulty; as if the existence of the Necessary Being descended through all the moments of an imaginary time, and, having already exhausted a part of His duration, saw before Him the eternity He was yet to live simultaneously with the present events of the world. All these difficulties upon proper insight into the notion of time vanish like smoke.

Paragraph *28*

The prejudices of the second species, since they impose upon the intellect by the sensual conditions restricting the mind if it wishes in certain cases to attain to what is intellectual, lurk more deeply. One of them is that which affects knowledge of quantity, the other that affecting knowledge of qualities generally. The former is: *every actual multiplicity can be given numerically*, and hence, every infinite quantity; the latter, *whatever is impossible contradicts itself.* In either of them the concept of time, it is true, does not enter into the very notion of the predicate, nor is it attributed as a qualification to the subject. But yet it serves as a means for forming an idea of the predicate, and thus, being a condition, affects the intellectual concept of the subject to the extent that the latter is only attained by its aid.

As to the *first*, as every quantity and any series whatever are distinctly known only by successive co-ordination, the intellectual concept of amount and multiplicity arises only by the aid of this concept of time, and never attains to completeness unless the synthesis can be gone through with in finite time. It is hence that the *infinite series* of co-ordinate things cannot be comprehended distinctly according to the limits of our intellect; it hence by the fallacy of subreption seems impossible. According to the laws of pure intellect any series of effects has its *principle*, that is, there is not given in a series of effects a regress without a limit; whilst according to sensual laws any series of co-ordinate things has its assignable *beginning*. These propositions, the latter of which involves the *mensurability* of the series, the former the dependence of the whole, are taken hastily for identical. In the same way, to the *argument of the intellect*, proving that a substantial composite being given so are the elements of composition, that is, the simple things, there is adjoined a *supposititious* one suborned from sensual knowledge, namely, that in such a composite there is not given an infinite regress in the composition of the parts, that is to say, that in any composite there is given a definite number of parts, a sense certainly not germane to the former, and hence substituted rashly for it. For that the quantity of the world is limited, not the maximum, that it owns a principle, that bodies consist of simple parts, can certainly be cognized rationally. But that the universe as to its mass is mathematically finite, that its age as elapsed can be given by measure, that the number of simple parts constituting any body whatever is a definite number, are propositions openly proclaiming their origin from the nature of sensual knowledge; however true they may be held to be, they bear the undoubted stigma of their origin.

As for the *latter spurious axiom*, it originates from a rash conversion of the principle of contradiction. For to this primitive judgment the concept of time adheres to the extent that contradictorily opposed data being given *at the same time* in the same thing, the impossibility is plain, which is enounced thus: *whatever simultaneously is and is not, is impossible*. Here, as the intellect predicates something in a case given according to sensual laws, the judgment is perfectly true and obvious. On the contrary, converting this axiom, saying: *whatever is impossible is and is not at the same time*, or involves a contradiction, we predicate through sensual knowledge something concerning the object of reason generally, thus subjecting the intellectual conception of the possible and the impossible to the conditions of sensual knowledge, namely, to the relations of time; which certainly is true enough of the laws restricting and limiting the human intellect, but cannot be conceded objectively and generally by any means. Of course, our intellect *perceives no impossibility* except where it can note the simultaneous enunciation of opposites concerning the same thing, that is, only where contradiction occurs. Wherever, therefore, this contradiction does not occur, there is no room for the judgment of impossibility by the human intellect. But that on this account it should be open to no intellect whatever, and hence that *what does not involve contradiction is therefore possible*, is concluded rashly by taking the subjective conditions of judgment for objective ones. It is for this reason that a host of fictitious *forces*, gotten up *ad libitum*, bursts, in the absence of self-contradiction, from any constructive, or, if you prefer, from every chimerical mind. For as a *force* is nothing but a *relation* of a substance *a* to *something else b*, an accident, as of a reason to the consequence, the possibility of any force does *not rest in the identity* of the cause and the effect, or the substance and the accident, and hence even the impossibility of forces made up falsely does *not depend solely on contradiction*. Therefore it is not permissible to assume as possible any *original force* unless the force be *given by experience*. Neither can the possibility be conceived *a priori* by any perspicacity of the intellect.

Paragraph *29*

The spurious axioms of the *third* kind from conditions proper to the *subject* whence they are transferred rashly to the *object* are plentiful, not, as in those of the Second Class, because the only way to the intellectual concept lies *through the sensuous data*, but because only by aid of the latter can the concept *be applied* to that which is *given* by experience, that is, can we know whether something is contained under a certain intellectual concept or not. To this class belongs the threadbare one of the schools: *whatever exists contingently does at some time not exist*. This spurious principle springs from the poverty of the intellect, having insight frequently into the *nominal*, rarely into the *real*, marks of contingency or necessity. Hence, whether the opposite of any substance be possible, an insight hardly obtained from *a priori* marks, is not otherwise known than by its being evident *that at some time that substance was not;* and changes rather witness contingency than contingency mutability, so that were nothing fleeting and transitory to occur in the world, a notion of contingence would hardly be possible in us. Therefore, though the direct proposition is perfectly true: *whatever at some time was not is contingent*, its converse indicates nothing but the conditions under which we can alone distinguish whether something exists necessarily or contingently. Hence if enunciated as a subjective law, which indeed it is, it should be enounced thus: *Sufficient marks of contingency of that of which it is not evident that at some time it was not, are not, by common intelligence, given*. This, however, tacitly deviates into an objective condition, as though in its absence there were no room for contingence; which being done, a counterfeit and erroneous axiom arises. For this world though existing contingently *is sempiternal*, that is, simultaneous with all time. It is a rash assertion that there was a time when it did not exist.

Paragraph *30*

To these spurious principles must be added some others of great affinity with them, not imparting to the given intellectual concept any blemish of sensuous cognition, but deceiving the intellect so as to take them for arguments drawn from the object, though they are commended to us only by the peculiar nature. of the intellect *for the convenience* of its free and ample use. Therefore, these as well as those enumerated above, rest in *subjective* reasons, although not in the laws of sensuous, but in those of intellectual cognition itself, namely, in the conditions under which it appears easy and quick to the mind to make use of its insight. I shall beg leave to throw in here, by way of conclusion, some mention of these principles, not as yet, as far as I know, set forth distinctly. I call, then, *principles of convenience* rules of judging to which we freely submit, and to which we adhere as if they were axioms, for the only reason that, *were we to depart from them, scarcely any judgment concerning a given object would be permissible to our intellect.* In this list belong the following: *First*, that by which we assume that *everything in the universe is done according to the order of nature*, which principle by Epicurus was proclaimed without any restriction, and by all other philosophers unanimously with extremely rare exceptions, not to be admitted but from supreme necessity. Still we thus affirm, not on account of possessing so ample a knowledge of the events of the world according to the common laws of nature, or because the impossibility or smaller hypothetical possibility of supernatural things is plain to us, but because departing from the order of nature there would be no use for the intellect, the rash citation of the supernatural being the couch of lazy understandings. For the same reason we take care to shut out from the exposition of phenomena *comparative miracles*, namely, the influence of spirits, since, as we do not know their nature, the intellect, to its great detriment, would be turned aside from the light of experience, by which alone it is able to provide for itself laws of judging, into the night of species and causes unknown to us. The *second is the partiality for unity* proper to the philosophical mind, whence this wide-spread canon has flown forth: *principles are not to be multiplied beyond supreme necessity*, to which we give in our adhesion, not because we have insight into causal unity in the world either by reason or experience, but as seeking it by an impulse of the intellect which seems to itself to have by thus much advanced in the explication of phenomena, by as much as it is granted to it to descend from the same principle to a greater number of consequences, The *third* of this kind of principles is: *matter neither originates nor perishes;* all the changes in the world concern *form* only; a postulate which on the recommendation of common sense has spread through all philosophical schools, not because it is to be taken as having been found so, or as having been demonstrated by arguments *a priori*, but because if we were to admit that matter itself is fleeting and transitory, nothing at all that is stable and lasting would be left any longer to serve for the explication of phenomena according to universal and perpetual laws, and hence nothing at all would be left for the exercise of the intellect.

This method, especially in respect to the distinction between sensual and intellectual knowledge, which, when reduced by more careful investigation to exactness, will occupy the position of a propaedeutical science, will certainly be of unlimited benefit to all intending to penetrate into the very recesses of metaphysics.

Note. — As in this last section the tracing out of the method occupies all the space at disposal, and the rules prescribing the true form of arguing concerning sensuous things shine by their own light and do not borrow it from the illustrative examples, I have thrown in but a cursory mention of the latter. For this reason it is not strange if some things should seem to have been asserted with more audacity than truth, they certainly calling, when a broader treatment shall be possible, for greater force of arguments. Thus, what is alleged in paragraph 27 on the locality of immaterial substances lacks an explication which, if the reader please, may be found in Euler in the place cited, Vol. II, p, 52. For the soul is not in communion with the body as being detained in a certain place in the latter, but a determined place in the universe is attributed to it, for the reason that it is in mutual commerce with some body, which commerce being dissolved all its position in space is removed. Its *locality*, therefore, is *derivative* and contingently applied to it, *not primitive* and a necessary condition of its existence, because whatever things cannot by themselves be objects of external senses such as man's, that is, *immaterial* substances, are exempt altogether from the universal condition of *externally sensible things*, namely, space. Hence absolute and immediate locality may be denied to the soul, while yet hypothetical and mediate locality may be attributed to it.